Variety that's music to your ears

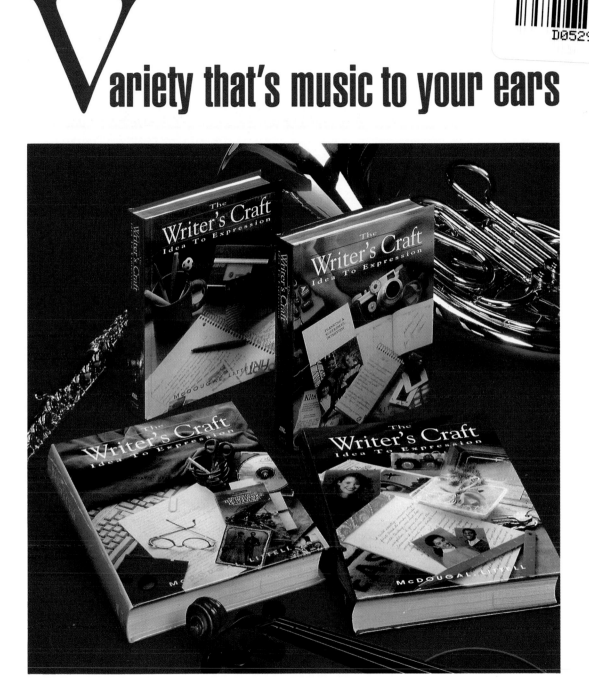

McDougal, Littell

The Writer's Craft

A complete English course for grades 9-12

Literature and writing capture the rhythm of real life!

Three-part harmony!

The Writer's Craft creates the perfect harmony: literature, writing, and grammar. But the real beauty lies in its flexible approach to teaching. You can begin with writing, begin with grammar and usage, or begin with any specific writing skills you choose. This flexibility results from a unique three-part arrangement.

1) The Writer's Workshops

Classic literature and contemporary professional writing serve as models for the wide variety of writing assignments.

For focusing on specific skills, cross-references in the Workshops direct you and your students to:

2) The Writing Handbook

where you'll find mini-lessons on the writing process, writing style, and academic skills;

and 3) The Grammar and Usage Handbook

where you'll find grammar instruction and practice provided within the context of drafting, revision, proofreading, and literature.

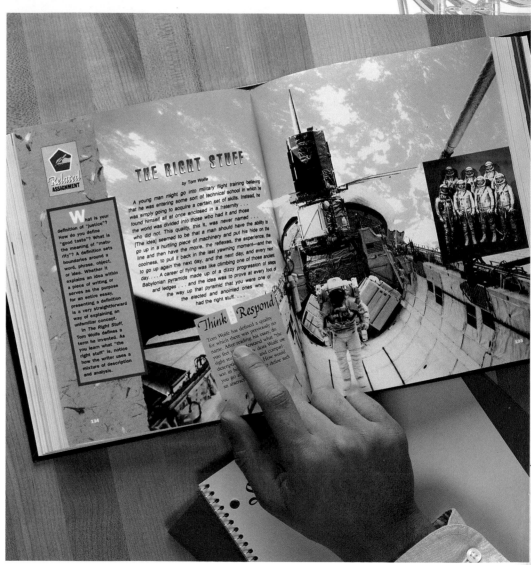

All pages from Grade 10

The Writer's Craft motivates students with literature that ranges from traditional and contemporary classics, to newspaper and magazine articles, to storyboards for a television commercial. Once literature sets the stage for writing, students enjoy working on everything from a persuasive essay to copy for an advertisement. *And that's just within a single writing mode!*

The many ways to perform persuasive writing:

Grade 9
- Supporting Opinions
- Letter to the Editor
- Critical Review

Grade 10
- Controversial Issue
- Persuasive Speech
- Editorial

Grade 11
- Persuasive Essay
- Satire
- Ad Copy

Grade 12
- Argument Analysis
- Establishing Conflict
- Debate

A specific writing mode or skill is explored through three literature-based assignments in the Writer's Workshops. ▶

WRITER'S **8** WORKSHOP

Writing About Literature

Related Assignment
INTERPRETING ART

Guided Assignment
INTERPRETIVE ESSAY

Related Assignment
DIRECTOR'S NOTES

Guided ASSIGNMENT
Interpretive Essay

A FIRE TRUCK

Related ASSIGNMENT

Interpreting Art

ainters, writers,

Related ASSIGNMENT
Director's Notes

Notes for
MATEWAN   *by John Sayles*

One of the most important people in the production of any drama is the director. He or she is responsible for creating an interpretation of the work and communicating that vision to the actors.

Directors often write notes explaining their ideas. John Sayles wrote these notes while preparing to direct *Matewan*, a movie about a strike at an Appalachian coal mine in the 1920's. The character Hickey works for the company that is trying to end the strike. The information in Sayles's notes was used by the actor who played Hickey in the film.

As you read, imagine that you will be acting the role of Hickey and think about how these notes might help you portray the character.

This is a character sheet, a [few thoughts] that I'd either mail to the actors in advance or give to them when they got to West Virginia. Since we didn't have time for rehearsal before shooting, these were meant to help the actors think about their characters and to be the basis for further discussions we might have.

Hickey
A few thoughts on the character of Hickey. Hickey is someone who volunteered for service in [World War I], probably out of boredom, and was older than most of the cannon-fodder he found around him in the trenches. He was in some heavy, grisly hand-to-hand combat . . . and his mind has not returned from the place where it's kill-or-be-killed. Hickey feeds on violence, or at least the atmosphere of violence, and everything he does is to control and shape that atmosphere. When he meets someone new he immedi-

ately starts to push to see if they'll push back and how much—he's constantly filing information for future conflict. He wants people to be afraid of him, realizing that intimidation is often more effective than actual violence. He realizes he is a foreigner in a guerrilla conflict—anyone, man, woman or child, could shoot him in the back at any time. . . . Hickey has a dog-eat-dog world view and wants to be the big dog. Violence is a sickness with him. . . .

Think & Respond

What was John Sayles's purpose for writing these notes? Would these notes help you if you were preparing to play the role of Hickey? What else might you like to know about Hickey? If you were directing a production of a play, what might you say to help the actors play their parts? What would you say in program notes for the theater audience?

The Writer's Workshops put writing center stage!

Each Writer's Workshop explores a writing mode or skill through three literature-based assignments.

The Guided Assignment provides specific suggestions, strategies, and choices for each stage of the writing process.

The Related Assignments build on and extend the skills presented in the Guided Assignments.

▼

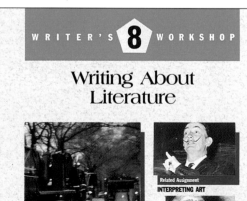

WRITER'S **8** WORKSHOP

Writing About Literature

Guided Assignment
INTERPRETIVE ESSAY

Related Assignment
INTERPRETING ART

Related Assignment
DIRECTOR'S NOTES

Y ou've had a great deal of experience at interpretation. All your life, you've interpreted people's actions and words in order to find what they meant for you—love, hate, anger, fear, hope. Interpreting literary texts is a more specialized form of this same process. You read a poem or story, you watch a movie or play; then you explore the experience. You sort out your feelings and test your understanding in order to gain a deeper appreciation. In the next three assignments, you will practice rereading and interpreting literary texts. You'll write an interpretive essay on a literary work of your choice, then go on to interpret works of visual and dramatic art.

237

Cross-references to the Handbooks offer additional help. ▶

Critical thinking is developed through problem-solving strategies at each stage of the writing process.

The Writer's Workshops give your students an *immediate invitation to write* with writing models and assignments that guide them from prelude to polished piece. But instead of following a lockstep approach, students can improvise with the composing process to fit their needs for each assignment. Students can also reflect on and learn from the process.

DRAFT AND DISCOVER

HANDBOOKS
FOR HELP & PRACTICE
Introductions, pp. 352–355
Elaboration, pp. 364–369

PROBLEM
S O L V I N G
What techniques can I use to explore the items I am comparing?

1. Experiment with openers. Look over your prewriting notes and consider how you want to begin. For example, simply setting down a few plain sentences to identify your items may help you get started. You may find one or more of these strategies helpful.

Strategies

- **Definition** As a way to get your bearings, give a full definition of your items and the features that make them similar or set them apart.
- **Description** Describe each item in terms of one or more of the five senses.
- **Analogy** Think of a more familiar pair of items that are related to each other in the same way as the pair you are discussing. Compare your items to these more familiar ones.
- **Classification** Sort the features of your items into different categories and discuss each category.

Dresses, oil painting by Lisa Milroy, 1985. Saatchi Collection, London

2. Think about the organization of your draft. There are two basic patterns for organizing comparisons. One is the **subject-by-subject** pattern, in which you discuss all the features of one subject and then discuss all the features of the other. The second pattern is the **feature-by-feature** pattern, in which you address each feature in turn, and show how the subjects are similar or different in terms of that feature. The following chart shows the two patterns.

Subject by Subject	Feature by Feature
Introduction	Introduction
Subject A	Feature 1
Feature 1	Subject A
Feature 2	Subject B
Subject B	Feature 2
Feature 1	Subject A
Feature 2	Subject B
Conclusion	Conclusion

COMPUTER
—TIP—
Move paragraphs back and forth as a rough, quick way to decide which method of organization seems more effective for your topic.

After discussing his ideas with two other student writers, Josh began his draft by briefly describing the basis for his comparison. Then he went on to examine specific similarities and differences, quoting lines from the poems to illustrate his points. Here is the beginning of his unrevised draft.

ONE STUDENT'S PROCESS

"Ex-Basketball Player" by John Updike and "To an Athlete Dying Young" by A. E. Housman are two poems about athletes who have made their mark in particular sports: basketball and track. Both poems focus on what happens to the athletes after their moment of glory. They are both sad poems, and both express very similar themes—they both mourn the fleeting nature of success and fame.

Updike's basketball player and Housman's runner have both enjoyed applause. Housman's track star won a big race for his home town. Updike's Flick Webb was the best basketball player in the county.

▲

Models of student writing promote a feeling of belonging to a community of writers.

A variety of tips offer useful and timely advice.

Language instruction is targeted to the point of use in the writing process.
▼

REVIEW YOUR WRITING

Questions for Yourself
- Did I say what I wanted to say, or did I get sidetracked into pursuing some other goal?
- Did I meet the opposition's objections, or did I simply state my own case and pretend there was no other side?
- If this were someone else's paper, would I be convinced?

Questions for Your Peer Readers
- Which of my arguments did you find most convincing? Which did you find least convincing?
- Can you think of additional arguments to support my point of view?
- Are there arguments against my point of view that I haven't considered?

---

3. Proofread your work. Make a clean copy, incorporate your changes, correct errors in grammar, usage, punctuation, or spelling.

Grammar
—TIP—
When you include a lengthy quotation (8 type lines or longer) in an essay, set it off from the rest of the paragraph, indent it from the left, and do *not* enclose it in quotation marks.

LINKING
GRAMMAR AND WRITING

Quoting Literary Texts

Make sure all quotations from literary texts are exact and set off with quotation marks. When quoting more than one line of poetry, put a slash between lines of the poem.

PROBLEM: He admires "its phoenix-red simplicity" enshrined in that not extinguished fire.

REVISED: He admires its "phoenix-red simplicity, enshrined/ In that not extinguished fire."

See Grammar Handbook 41, pages 825–826, for more help with this problem.

The Phoenix is a legendary bird that renews itself by fire every hundred years.

▲

Peer response activities specific to the assignment give students a sense of audience and purpose.

Handbooks are the perfect accompaniment to the workshops!

HANDBOOKS
FOR HELP & PRACTICE

**Introductions,
pp. 352–355**

**Elaboration,
pp. 364–369**

Page references in the workshops ▲
direct students to the handbooks for
more detailed explanations of skills
and concepts.

TYPES OF ELABORATION

What types of details should you use to develop your main ideas? The answer depends on the type of idea you wish to develop. To support an opinion, you may wish to use facts and statistics, or you may decide to quote an authority. To present a great many specific facts in a brief space, you might use a chart, a table, or some other kind of graphic aid. To describe a person, place, or thing, you would want to use sensory details. To illustrate a point, you can describe an incident. To clarify a point, you can provide examples.

Facts and Statistics A fact is a statement that can be proved either by the use of reference materials or by first-hand observation. **Statistics** are facts expressed in numbers. Notice in the following article how the writer used facts and statistics to develop the main idea.

COMPUTER TIP

A computer data bank can be a good source for facts and statistics.

▼

According to Earth's first complete wilderness inventory, a third of the planet's land mass remains unchanged by humans. That's approximately 18 million square miles, but only a fifth of it is legally protected. The bulk of the world's wilderness—41 percent—lies in the barren polar regions. Some of it extends into northern Canada, Alaska, and the Soviet Union. A much smaller tract snakes through Tibet, Afghanistan, Saudi Arabia, and Africa. North America is the wildest of the settled continents, with over 37 percent wilderness. Europe is the tamest, with less than three percent of its land left untouched.

AMBIO, "How Wild Is the World?"

PROFESSIONAL
M O D E L

Among the Sierra Nevada Mountains, California, 1868, by Albert Bierstadt

Elaboration **365**

Strategies and skills common to all
◄ types of writing can be quickly located
in the Writing Handbook.

Thematic exercises in the Grammar and Usage Handbook can serve as a stimulus for writing. ▶

Grammar and usage practice occurs in the context of the writing process. ▶

Two handbooks act in concert with the workshops to give you flexibility in playing to your students' needs. The **Writing Handbook** features mini-lessons on the writing process, style, and academic skills. The **Grammar and Usage Handbook** provides instruction and practice in the context of writing, revision, and literature. Suggestions in the Pupil's Edition and Teacher's Edition help both you and your students decide when and how to use these lessons.

▲ **Students can experiment in different formats while applying new skills.**

Grammar practice in the Handbooks is reinforced with literature models in the Workshops.
▼

Page 588 (Grammar Handbook):

Writing Theme
Ecosystems

Practice Your Skills

A. CONCEPT CHECK

Adjective and Adverb Phrases. List the prepositional phrases in the following passage. Tell whether the phrase is used as an *Adjective* or *Adverb*. Notice how the writer uses prepositional phrases to add clarity and interest to the nouns and verbs in the passage.

(1) The inhabitants of the wall were a mixed lot, and they were divided into day and night workers, the hunters and the hunted. (2) At night the hunters were the toads that lived among the brambles, and the geckos, pale, translucent, with bulging eyes, that lived in the cracks higher up the wall. (3) Their prey was the population of stupid, absent-minded crane-flies that zoomed and barged their way among the leaves; moths of all sizes and shapes . . . fluttered in soft clouds. . . .
Gerald Durrell, "The World in a Wall"

B. REVISION SKILL

Sentence Expansion and Combination Use prepositional phrases to make your writing smoother. Revise the following sentences by changing the information in parentheses into an adjective or adverb phrase. Add or delete words as necessary.

(1) Many mammals have adapted to a harsh way of life. (They live in the desert.) (2) To survive, desert animals store food and get water. (Plants provide water.) (3) The heat of the day is intense.) Some mammals use water very slowly. (4) Other desert mammals have characteristics that help them hide. (They avoid predators.) (5) Others have adaptations that help them move quickly. (They cross the hot desert sand.) (6) The light color of some animals blends. (It blends with the sand.) (7) Others have fringed toes. (These toes are for quick movement.) (8) Most desert animals are active during the cooler hours, when there is dew. (The dew is on the ground.) (9) Jackrabbits, prairie dogs, and predators live there. (The desert environment is fragile.) (10) A drama unfolds daily between hunters and hunted. (Their environment is stark.)

C. APPLICATION IN WRITING

A Scientific Report One answer to the world's hunger problems may lie in farming the sea. Sea farming, or aquaculture, is the controlled production of fish, shellfish, and marine plants. Imagine that you are a staff member of the first sea farm. Use a variety of prepositional phrases in a paragraph describing your first harvest.

588 Grammar Handbook

Page 589:

"Now! ... *That* should clear up a few things around here!"

APPOSITIVES AND APPOSITIVE PHRASES

An **appositive** is a noun or pronoun that usually follows another noun or pronoun and identifies or explains it.

Balloonist *Julian Nott* is planning an around-the-world flight. (The appositive *Julian Nott* identifies *balloonist*.)

An **appositive phrase** consists of an appositive and its modifiers.

Nott's balloon, *a new model with a pressurized gondola*, can ascend seven miles. (The appositive *model* explains the subject *balloon*. The adjective *new* and the adjective phrase *with a pressurized gondola* modify *model*.)

Sometimes the appositive phrase precedes the word it explains.

A noted pilot of her era, Anne Morrow Lindbergh was also a writer of exceptional ability. (The appositive *pilot* explains the subject *Anne Morrow Lindbergh*.)

An appositive may be compound.

Antoine de Saint-Exupéry, a *writer* and an *artist*, began his career in aviation as a mail pilot.

Using Phrases and Clauses   **589**

Sentence COMPOSING

Using Present Participial Phrases

Effective writers often use present participial phrases as modifiers. These phrases begin with a present participle, a verb form ending in *-ing*. They may also contain other words or even whole clauses (see model 3), related to the participle. These phrases, which will be the focus of the next three lessons, usually occur at the end of a sentence, describing in greater detail a noun mentioned earlier. Note that a comma precedes each phrase here.

MODELS
1. (Short)   She held the quilts securely in her arms, <u>stroking them.</u> **Alice Walker, "Everyday Use"**
2. (Medium)   Just before supper Miguel came into the kitchen, <u>stamping the bits of dirty snow from his overshoes.</u> **Durango Mendoza, "The Passing"**
3. (Long)   First there was the local apple crop, <u>threatening to rot because the harvesters had all gone into the army or war factories.</u> **John Knowles, *A Separate Peace***

A. Combining Sentences Combine each sentence pair to form one sentence that ends with a present participial phrase. To do this, first find the present participial phrase in the second sentence. Then use a comma to join the phrase to the end of the first sentence.

Example   She had just returned from a week by the sea. She was recuperating from the strain of nursing so many nights.

Result   She had just returned from a week by the sea, recuperating from the strain of nursing so many nights.
Algernon Blackwood, "The Tradition"

1. Away she darted. She was stretching close to the ground.
Francis Parkman, *The Oregon Trail*

2. Bea bustled about. Bea was managing to keep up with both the

Everything you need to orchestrate your classroom!

Teacher's Edition
You'll find the *Teacher's Edition* instrumental for orchestrating comprehensive and exciting lessons!

Teaching Preview Pages offer:
- **Workshop Overviews**
- **Preparation Guides** with overviews of support materials
- **Management Guidelines**
- **Linking Literature, Writing, and Grammar** teaching options

Point-of-Use Teaching Strategies include
suggestions for:
- **Preteaching** Handbook mini-lessons
- **Modeling** writing techniques
- **Individualizing Instruction** for varying ability levels and for students with special needs
- **Collaborative Opportunities** for building a community of writers
- **Spot Checks** to help keep students on target
- **Avoiding Stumbling Blocks** common to writers
- **Personal Touch** for teachers as co-writers
- **Managing the Paper Load**
- **Speaking and Listening** opportunities
- **Linking Grammar and Writing**
- **Guidelines for Evaluation**
- **Reteaching**
- **Extension and Enrichment**
- **Helping students learn from their writing processes** by questioning and reflecting
- **Summary and Closure** for reviewing key points

Plus ... cross-curricular connections, activities for motivating, and more!

Teacher's Resource File
You'll applaud our vast repertoire of creative approaches to writing and practical teaching support!

Transparencies to teach writing
- Thinking Skills Transparencies and Worksheets
- Fine Art Transparencies and Writing Prompts
- Student Revision Model Transparencies

Additional Writing Resources
- Ideas for Writing
- Peer Response Guides
- Elaboration, Revision, and Proofreading Worksheets
- Writing Resource Book
- Writing About Literature

Language Resources
- Grammar and Usage Practice Book
- Vocabulary Development
- Oral Communications Booklet

Management and Assessment Resources
- Lesson Plans
- Tests and Assessments Booklet
- Standardized Test Practice
- Guidelines for Evaluating Writing

Software available!
- Writer's DataBank
- Grammar Test Generator
- Electronic English Handbook

The Writer's Craft series includes:
- Grade 9
- Grade 10
- Grade 11
- Grade 12

 McDougal, Littell

Publishing for a new school of thought

P.O. Box 1667 Evanston, IL 60204

AR, OK, TX, NM *Call 800-346-3570*

AL, FL, GA
LA, MS, NC
SC, TN, VA
WV *Call 800-258-9006*

AK, AZ, ID
NV, OR
UT, WA *Call 800-424-3077*

California *Call 800-845-6444*

All other states & international **800-323-5435**

#0249P

Contents of the Teacher's Edition

The Writer's Workshops

The authors of *The Writer's Craft* believe that writing is an exciting journey of discovery where students explore ideas, examine options, problem-solve, and share what they have done with others. Every assignment in each Writer's Workshop builds upon these ideas.

Cause and Effect

Guided ASSIGNMENT

FROM
THE WATER IS WIDE
BY PAT CONROY

When something important happens in life, we usually want to know why. By analyzing causes and effects, we can understand the world better, learn from mistakes, and even make improvements.

In the following excerpt, Pat Conroy analyzes what went wrong to destroy life on the island of Yamacraw, off the coast of South Carolina. As you read, notice how one primary cause sets off a chain of effects that leads to the end of a way of life.

[Yamacraw] is not a large island, nor an important one, but it represents an era and a segment of history that is rapidly dying in America. The people of the island have changed very little since the Emancipation Proclamation. Indeed, many of them have never heard of this proclamation. They love their island with genuine affection but have watched the young people move to the city, to the lands far away and far removed from Yamacraw. The island is dying, and the people know it.

In the parable of Yamacraw there was a time when the black people supported themselves well. . . . Each morning the strong young men would take to their bateaux and search the shores and inlets for the large clusters of oysters, which the women and old men in the factory shucked into large jars. Yamacraw oysters were world famous . . . and the oyster factories operating on the island provided a substantial living for all the people. Everyone worked and everyone made money. Then a villain appeared. It was an industrial factory situated on a knoll above the Savannah River many miles away from Yamacraw. The villain spewed its excrement into the river, infected the creeks, and as silently as the pull of the tides, the filth crept to the shores of Yamacraw. As every good health inspector knows, the unfortunate consumer who lets an infected oyster slide down his throat is flirting with hepatitis. . . . Soon after this, little white signs were placed by the oyster banks forbidding anyone to gather the oysters. Ten thousand oysters were now as worthless as grains of sand. . . .

Since a factory is soulless and faceless, it could not be moved to understand the destruction its coming had wrought. When the oysters became contaminated, the island's only industry folded almost immediately. The great migration began. A steady flow of people faced with starvation moved toward the cities. They left in search of jobs. . . . Over 300 people left the island. They left reluctantly, but left permanently and returned only on sporadic visits to pay homage to the relatives too old or too stubborn to leave. As the oysters died, so did the people.

Think and *Respond*

What does Pat Conroy say caused the waters around Yamacraw to become polluted? According to Conroy's analysis, what effects did the pollution have on the island's way of life? What do you think was Conroy's goal in analyzing the chain of events on Yamacraw? How could you use a cause-and-effect analysis to explore a problem or situation?

148

Starting from Literature

Each Guided and Related Assignment begins with a model that focuses on a specific writing type or strategy.

• **The introduction** presents the writing type to be covered, previews the model, and sets a purpose for reading.

• **Models** cover a wide range of writing types, from traditional and contemporary literature, to newspaper and magazine articles, to TV story boards. Students gain a sense of how writing functions in the real world.

• **Think and Respond** questions allow students to respond to what they have read and prepare them to begin writing a piece of their own.

Responding to Media

Related ASSIGNMENT

Oil potential spawns fears in Alaska tribe

Every day you are bombarded with information from radio, television, magazines, newspapers, movies, billboards, and books. To make sense of all these messages, which sometimes are confusing and contradictory, you must learn to respond to them personally and critically. As you read the newspaper article on this page, think carefully about the information you are being given. Are both sides of the issue being presented fairly?

From USA TODAY

Trimble Gilbert's people have lived in Arctic Village, Alaska, in the barren prairie of the Arctic Circle, for 1,000 years. From the world beyond, they want only privacy.

But Gilbert, and about 300 Gwich'in Indians holding a tribal meeting in Arctic Village this week, now find themselves caught up in an environmental drama that stretches to the Persian Gulf 6,000 miles away.

Arctic Village lies in the shadow of the ghostly, frozen Arctic National Wildlife Refuge, home to a 1.5-million-acre coastal plain some think could be a mother lode of oil.

"North America's Saudi Arabia," is what some have called the ANWR; others report the smell of oil in the snow.

Congressional interest in exploring the ANWR—opposed by the Gwich'in who fear it would disrupt the caribou they depend on for subsistence and culture—was put on hold after [recent] . . . oil spills.

But [tension in the Middle East] has scrambled the picture. Some Congress members are now eyeing the ANWR, as well as offshore sites in Florida, California and the Northwest.

"We're proud to be in the United States, to be American Indians. But we can see the future," says Gilbert, the chief, spokesman and pastor for the Gwich'in—pronounced *GWI-chin*—of Arctic Village. "If we lose the caribou, we don't know how we're going to live here."

To environmentalists, renewed interest in ANWR—as well as calls to lift [the] . . . ban on drilling in coastal areas in the Lower 48—is both an overreaction and a symptom of a nonexistent national energy policy. . . .

286

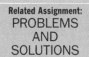

Related Assignment: PROBLEMS AND SOLUTIONS

Starting from Literature

Objective
To respond to a literary excerpt as a springboard to writing.

Teaching Strategies

Motivate
Ask students to think about problems they may have had in the past or those that face them now. Suggest that all people have problems and that those who are successful in life work out solutions. Discuss with students people they know or have read about who have solved problems in their lives.

Tap Prior Knowledge
Have students recall their favorite characters from literature and discuss how they dealt with the problems that faced them. Did they solve their problems alone or did they seek help? Encourage students to suggest alternate courses of action that the characters might have followed.

Set a Purpose
Discuss the side-column notes, and ask students to restate Harry's problem. Then call attention to the purpose-setting statement at the end of the side column, and have students read the excerpt.

Problems and Solutions

from "THE TORN INVITATION"
by Norman Katkov

Harry Wojick feels he has one problem his sophomore classmates don't have—his mother. He finds nearly everything about her embarrassing, including her appearance, her speech, her mannerisms. He has not even given her an invitation to his school open house. But his close friend Frankie feels very differently about Harry's mother.

As you read this story excerpt, think about how Frankie tries to solve a problem between two people he loves.

When he came into the kitchen, Theresa Wojick turned from the stove, smiling at her son, rubbing her hands on her apron as she walked to meet him. She held him at the elbows, examining him carefully, her face warm and her eyes gentle, welcoming him as though he had returned from a long and perilous journey. . . .

Harry went to the sink to wash and, turning, saw the table set for three.

"For Frankie Thomas," his mother whispered, looking at her son. "His mother is gone again till half the night, and leaves cold cuts. Boy like Frankie to eat cold cuts," she whispered. "You call him, Harry."

"Why can't she learn to speak English?" he asked himself savagely, turning away. "She's been here long enough!"

Harry walked through the short hall and under the arch which led into the living room. He saw the frail, black-haired boy with whom he had grown up, sitting in the chair under the lamp. "Hey, Frankie," Harry said. "Come on and eat." Harry whistled shrilly and came back into the kitchen.

He pulled the chair out and held it suspended off the clean, bare floor, his fingers tightening on the wood. There, next to his plate, was the white, square envelope, and atop it, covered by a transparent sheet of thin paper, was the embossed invitation.

Harry looked at his mother, who had her back to him, busy at the stove. He heard Frankie coming through the house and knew [that Frankie had put the invitation there], knew it. He moved the chair at last and sat down and, without touching it, his hands holding his knees, he read the invitation from the faculty of Hamilton High School to an open house in honor of all the students' mothers.

It was tomorrow.

Harry knew that all right. Had known it for ten days and had kept it a secret. . . .

Think & Respond

Harry saw his mother as a problem. Do you think Harry had other problems that he didn't see? Was Frankie helpful in solving Harry's problems? Have you ever, like Harry, had a painful problem with another person? Or, like Frankie, have you seen a friend in a difficult situation and wanted to help? What solutions did you try? How successful were you?

Think and Respond

Elicit Personal Responses
Discuss responses to the excerpt, focusing on students' reactions to Frankie's solution. Ask students to suggest other solutions Frankie might have tried and to consider the possible effects of each.

Explore the Author's Techniques
You might call on volunteers to read the story aloud, paragraph by paragraph. Pause for discussion after each section, focusing on the elements Katkov introduces. For example, he introduces Theresa, presenting her as a caring and loving person. (Page 198, paragraph 1: She held . . . journey.) He then reveals one of the problems and Harry's feelings about it. (Page 198, paragraph 3: "For . . . son. "His . . . cuts. Boy . . . whispered. Page 199, paragraph 1: "Why . . . away.) Finally, Katkov reveals the major conflict and Frankie's attempt to solve it. (Page 199, paragraph 3: There . . . invitation. Paragraph 4: He heard . . . it. Paragraph 6: Had known . . . secret.) Ask students to speculate on the reasons Frankie might have had for his actions. What outcome did Frankie hope for or expect?

Link Literature to Writing
Point out that the excerpt provided an example of a personal problem and an attempt to resolve it. Suggest that as students approach the assignment that follows, they think about problems that they, other people, or fictional characters like Harry have experienced. How might those problems be solved?

Literature Connection

Author Note Norman Katkov was born in Russia in 1918. His knowledge of the experiences of immigrants may well be reflected in this excerpt. A versatile writer, Katkov has authored several books, scripts for television shows and a film, as well as a variety of material for newspapers and magazines.

Storyboard

Although we usually think of narratives as stories that are written down or told orally, they can also be presented visually. Film, for example, is a familiar medium for visual narratives. Cartoons, dramatic scenes, and commercials are all narratives.

A storyboard serves as a drafting device for a visual narrative. The storyboard shown in the model is from a television advertisement for an automobile financing company. Notice that each sequence of the three-frame storyboard can be read like a separate paragraph; notes above the drawing establish the setting and dialogue below carries the action.

Sequence No.: 1
Camera Treatment: Opening long shot: Empty bank lobby with teller window; no customers
Time to: seconds
Transition to next sequence: Zoom in on customer

Video Teller: Hello, I'm Leona, your automatic teller. Can I help you with a student loan?
Customer: No, an auto loan, Leona. (Customer pushes fast forward button on remote control unit. Teller bounces around screen, then stops at:)
Teller: A home improvement loan?
Customer: Ugh!

Teaching Strategies

Teacher's notes provide you with all the help you need:

• Prereading suggestions to help motivate and focus your students

• Follow-up ideas to help students respond to the reading and to tie the literature to the writing assignment that follows.

Suggestions on the Teaching Preview page (see T12) provide other ideas for springing into writing from literature.

Moving to Writing

After discussing the model, your students are invited to write on their own. The detailed Guided Assignments lead students through each stage of the writing process, where they are presented with different strategies and encouraged to experiment, problem solve, and collaborate with others.

INVITATION TO Write

Russell Baker provided comical instructions for carving a turkey. Now write your own description of a process—one that shows how to do something, tells how something works, or explains how an event takes place.

Does everyone know how to play Monopoly, or how Joe Montana scored a touchdown with just seconds to go? Of course not. That's why process explanations are so useful. They help people learn from each other about how to do something, how something works, or how an event happened. To help others learn about processes you understand, you need to analyze what goes into the process—what steps are involved and sometimes what skills and materials are needed. In the assignment that follows, you will analyze a process and share information by explaining the process to others.

▶ PREWRITE AND EXPLORE

HANDBOOKS
FOR HELP & PRACTICE
Sharing Techniques, pp. 323–325
Appropriate Details, p. 355
Solving Problems, pp. 456–458
Sources of Information, pp. 476–478
Interviewing Skills, pp. 481–482

1. Look for ideas. You complete, observe, or are part of different processes every day. Think about which of these processes most interest you, or try one or more of the following activities to help you identify a process you would like to explain.

Exploratory Activities

- **Observing** Watch favorite performers or athletes in motion and make notes or sketches of the steps they use to complete an action. You may also want to study photos or videotapes.
- **Brainstorming about science and history** Complete the sentence "I wonder how . . ." in as many ways as possible. Perhaps you've always wondered how volcanoes erupt, how a microwave oven works, or how the Statue of Liberty was designed and installed. Let your mind roam free to think of ideas that intrigue you.

- **Inventing** Think of games or machines you might like to invent and how they might work. You might enjoy brainstorming ideas with a partner and trying them out together.
- **Interviewing** Think of something you wish you knew how to do, such as the Heimlich maneuver, and interview someone in your community who is familiar with the process.
- **Reading literature** Think of fictional works you've read, such as Jack London's "To Build a Fire," in which an explanation of a process adds reality to a scene. Consider a process you might explain as part of a realistic narrative of your own.

One student, Danny, decided to observe his favorite athletes—professional baseball players. He videotaped a baseball game and observed the tape in slow motion, making sketches and notes about pitching and batting. His sketches and notes about pitching follow.

PROBLEM SOLVING
How can I find a process that is interesting or important to me?

ONE STUDENT'S PROCESS

1. stands on mound, leaning toward home plate
2. watches catcher for a sign
3. shifts his weight to his back leg and goes into a windup
4. brings his front leg up waist high, rotates his body away from home plate
5. reaches pitching hand back toward second, swings his raised leg, and pushes off his back leg
6. brings pitching arm around, elbow first, and releases the ball about a foot in front of his head

---

- **The Invitation to Write** refers back to the literary model and describes the assignment students are to complete.

- Creative **Exploratory Activities** help students find topics they can care about.

- Throughout the lesson, cross-references to the **Handbooks** provide you with ideas for mini-lessons and show your students where they can look for additional help.

- **One Student's Process** follows a student writer through every stage of the assignment.

Also consider whether there is any background information your readers will need before you begin explaining the process. If you are explaining something that readers can do themselves, are there any materials they need to gather or skills they must have before they can do the process? Plan to give this information at the beginning of your explanation, as Russell Baker did.

DRAFT AND DISCOVER

1. Begin your draft. Begin your draft by explaining why the process is important, useful, or worth understanding. Then, with your writing goals in mind, try to describe the process in a lively way that will engage the reader's interest. One of the best ways to accomplish this is to concentrate on telling or showing why this process is important or interesting to you. If you have trouble making your writing lively, try one or more of the following techniques.

Strategies

- **Description** Provide enough details so that readers can understand the process exactly or, if appropriate, repeat the steps themselves. Use precise, vivid words to describe the process. In "Slice of Life," for example, Russell Baker used the words *torso, posterior, thigh, drumstick,* and *gristle* to identify parts of a turkey. He used the vivid words *skewered, sawing,* and *sever* to describe the carver's motions.
- **Definition** To keep your readers from becoming confused, define any special terms they might not understand.
- **Illustrations** Look for places where illustrations might help your readers understand the process you are explaining. Often a simple diagram can show an action that is difficult to explain in words. A flowchart can help readers understand at a glance how all the steps in a process are related. See the Related Assignment on page 168 for help in creating a flow chart.
- **Ways to begin** Use your introduction to establish clearly for your readers what you will be explaining. Think of ways to make your readers recognize why

HANDBOOKS

Writing Introductions, pp. 341–342 Using Diagrams, pp. 357–358

PROBLEM
S O L V I N G

How can I make my writing lively?

Informative Writing **153**

- **Drafting Strategies** demonstrate how modes and purposes can be woven together.
- **Problem-Solving notes** show students that writing is a series of questions and decisions.

- **Writer's Choice** options remind students that there is no one right way to complete any piece of writing.
- **Review questions** for both the writer and the peer reader make revision a rich, interactive process.
- **The Standards for Evaluation** feature shares assessment secrets with the students.
- **Revisions in progress** show peer response at work.
- **Writing Tips, Computer Tips, and Grammar Tips** provide helpful advice where students need it.

COMPUTER
TIP

Invite another writer to type in comments and questions in a different font. Answer them, and then erase the reader's comments.

HANDBOOKS

FOR HELP & PRACTICE

Peer Response, pp. 378–382
Grammatical Voice, pp. 417–418
Evaluating Ideas, pp. 452–453
Faulty Reasoning, pp. 453–455

 Writer's Choice Do you want to maintain your original position or reevaluate it in light of your responses?

5. Take a break. Give your draft a rest. Then return to it by asking yourself—and your peer readers—challenging questions such as the following.

REVIEW YOUR WRITING

Questions for Yourself
- Does my paper help me understand the issue more completely?
- Do I clearly state the nature of the issue and my position on it?
- Do I recognize possible objections to my views? Do I answer them?
- Have I included facts and details to support my position?
- Have I included a strong conclusion?

Questions for Your Peer Readers
- Is my paper interesting to read?
- Does the opening make the issue clear?
- Where do you think my position is strongest? Where do you think my position is weakest?
- Does my paper sound as if I respect you as a reader? Does my paper sound as if I respect those who disagree with me?
- Can you think of other points to support my view? To oppose it?

REVISE YOUR WRITING

1. Evaluate your responses. Think about your own and your readers' reactions to your paper. Which ones have hit on points that you ought to change? Also keep in mind these guidelines for evaluating persuasive writing.

Standards for Evaluation

Effective persuasive writing . . .

- states the topic clearly in an effective introduction.
- supports a clearly stated opinion with facts or reasons, and elaborates on each reason.
- maintains a reasonable tone.
- takes opposing views into account and answers them.
- uses language effectively and avoids faulty logic.
- includes a conclusion that sums up reasons or provides a call to action.

2. Problem-solve. Rework your draft to fix the problems you have identified. Helen made the changes below after a peer reader wrote suggestions on her first draft.

ONE STUDENT'S PROCESS

Most of us go through our entire lives without ever seeing an animal dying in a laboratory cage. Its easy for us not to think about the suffering thats involved, because we don't see it.

More than 100 million animals die each year in the or labatories of the world.

For a moment, however, try to imagine an island populated by 100 million sick, injured, and dying animals—mice lumpy with tumors, cats writhing in pain after surgery, rabbits blinded by irritating chemicals, pregnant baboons injured in staged automobile accidents, dogs with stomaches weighed down by lethal doses of shoe polish or floor wax.

According to veterinarian and animal-rights advocate Dr. Michael W. Fox,

I agree that it's a terrible situation. Perhaps more details could make it seem more real.

The figure 100 million is impressive. Where did you get it?

Writing
TIP

To give your writing a lively, personal tone, imagine that your reader is sitting across the table from you.

216 Workshop 7

Persuasion **217**

T5

- **An annotated student model** shows how a completed piece of writing meets the standards presented in the lesson. ▶

- **Linking Grammar and Writing** provides a springboard to language instruction.
- **Creative publishing ideas** make sure students have a real audience for their writing. ▶

- **Learning from Your Writing Process** encourages students to reflect on what they've learned.
- **Writer to Writer** lets students know that professional writers face the same concerns they do. ▼

ONE STUDENT'S PROCESS

Product Testing on Animals Is Wrong!

Helen Tanaka

Most of us go through our entire lives without ever seeing an animal dying in a laboratory cage. It's easy for us not to think about the suffering that's involved, because we don't see it. For a moment, however, try to imagine an island populated by 100 million sick, injured, and dying animals—mice lumpy with tumors, cats writhing in pain after surgery, rabbits blinded by irritating chemicals, pregnant baboons injured in staged

Appeals to audience in an appropriate voice

States the topic clearly in an effective introduction

Supports opinion with detailed reasons

Cites facts to support opinions

Persuasion   **219**

---

3. Proofread your work. Make a clean copy of your paper and then check it for errors in grammar, usage, and mechanics. If you've used statistics to support your argument, make sure they're accurate.

LINKING
GRAMMAR AND WRITING

Active Versus Passive Voice

Good persuasive writing usually uses the active voice to make readers feel involved.

PROBLEM: The same reactions are not always shared by people and animals.

CORRECTED: People and other animals don't always share the same reactions.

See Grammar Handbook 33, pages 590–592, for additional help with this problem.

HANDBOOKS
FOR HELP & PRACTICE
Publishing Your Work,
pp. 402–403
Discussion Skills,
pp. 479–480

PUBLISH AND PRESENT

- **Create a leaflet or brochure out of your persuasive paper.** Illustrate it and distribute copies.
- **Give an oral report based on your paper.** Instead of just reading your report aloud, adapt it for a more informal presentation. You might give a brief introduction to your report and then hold a question-and-answer session to involve your classmates.

- **Form a readers' circle.** Get together with peers who have written on the same topic or related topics. Use your discussion as a launching pad for exploration of related topics.
- **Keep your paper in your writing portfolio.** Refer to it whenever you write another persuasive piece.

7

LEARNING FROM YOUR WRITING PROCESS

WRITER TO WRITER

It is a great mistake to regard a dictionary definition as "telling us all about" a word.

S. I. Hayakawa, U.S. Senator and author

1. Reflect on your writing. Now that you have completed your composition that defines and have read several others, think about the process you followed. Ask yourself the questions below and record your answers in your writing log or attach the page you record your answers on to your definition.

- What did you learn from writing this composition that you might use in the future? In particular, what ways of defining ideas can you use in other pieces of writing?
- Of all the definitions you've read (Didion's, the student's, any of your classmates', and your own), which ones did you like the most? Why did you like them? What made these good definitions? What do you think made them good pieces of writing?

2. Apply your skills. Try your hand at one or more of the following activities.

- **Cross curricular** Choose a key term from a math or science book. Write a brief definition of the term. Then do some thinking and reading about the subject in preparation for writing a longer, extended definition.
- **Literature** Read a poem that defines an abstract term, such as "Spring is like a perhaps hand" by e.e. cummings. Then try writing your own poem. Choose an abstract term like *beauty, justice, friendship,* or *love.* Write a series of vivid, concrete images—thing you can see, touch, taste, hear, or smell—that define the term for you.
- **Related assignments** Follow the suggestions on pages 134–142 to write an extended metaphor or a comparison and contrast composition.

The streamlined **Related Assignments** provide general guidelines for students but allow them the freedom to problem-solve within motivating, less-traditional formats.

Oral Histories	Flow Charts	Learning Logs
Advertisements	Tall Tales	Advice Columns
Song Lyrics	Editorials	Family Histories

The Writing Handbook

When do you want to teach your students about transitional devices? When they write a story? Before they explain a process? Perhaps you want to review the concept with each lesson. With the unique Writing Handbook, *you* decide what your students need to learn and when they need to learn it.

The Writing Handbook is divided into three sections, each with a wealth of mini-lessons:

- Writing Process
- Style
- Academic Skills

Use the cross-references in the Writer's Workshops to decide when to present lessons, or teach them whenever *you* see the need. You can also encourage your students to use the lessons independently.

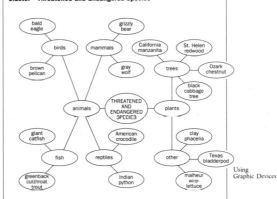

Using Graphic Devices

At various points during the writing process you may find it difficult to sort out your ideas because you cannot clearly "see" what you are thinking. Using graphic devices—making pictures of what's on your mind—is a good way to help organize your ideas and generate new ones. Some of the graphic devices shown in this lesson can help you find ideas. Others will be more helpful in later stages of the writing process, when you begin elaborating and organizing your ideas, or when you are drafting and revising.

USING DIAGRAMS

Clustering is a way of showing the relationships among ideas. It is a particularly good way to generate ideas because it allows related ideas to "grow" freely from one another. In a **cluster,** a number of related ideas are grouped together using circles and lines. Two similar ways to show related ideas are **idea trees** and **spider maps**. In an idea tree, the main ideas are shown as "branches" and related ideas as "twigs" on the branches. In a spider map, related ideas are connected like the legs on a spider. Study the examples below.

Cluster—Threatened and Endangered Species

Writing
TIP
Graphic devices can be helpful in both generating and developing ideas.

Using Graphic Devices **357**

- **Each mini-lesson** focuses on a key concept or skill.

- **Literary, professional, and student models** provide examples of different techniques and strategies.

- **Abundant practice** enables students to practice their new skills or hone abilities they already have.

- **Teaching suggestions** in the Teacher's Edition show how mini-lessons can be used for reference, preteaching or reteaching.

USING TOPIC SENTENCES

A paragraph is often built on a **topic sentence,** a sentence that states the main idea, or topic, of the paragraph. Sometimes the topic sentence establishes what will be said in the paragraph. Other times the topic sentence summarizes what has been said. A topic sentence can be found anywhere in a paragraph—at the beginning, at the end, or in the middle.

Beginning with the Topic Sentence As you read the following paragraph, notice how the main idea is stated in its first sentence. All the other sentences illustrate or "prove" the main idea with specific details. This is one of the most common ways to develop a paragraph.

> The town was dead. Its beds were empty and cold. The only sound was the power hum of electric lines and dynamos, still alive, all by themselves. Water ran in forgotten bathtubs, poured out into living rooms, onto porches, and down through little garden plots to feed neglected flowers. In dark theaters, gum under the many seats began to harden with tooth impressions still in it.
>
> **Ray Bradbury, *The Martian Chronicles***

LITERARY MODEL

Moon Rise, Hernandez, New Mexico, 1941. Photograph by Ansel Adams

Grammar and Usage Handbook

Research has shown that grammar and usage lessons, taught in isolation, do not improve student writing. Indeed, they can sometimes have a negative effect. *The Writer's Craft* solves this problem with its innovative Grammar and Usage Handbook. Every lesson provides instruction and practice in the context of writing, revision, and literature. Students learn not only the *what*, but also the *why* and *how* of language skills.

MISPLACED AND DANGLING MODIFIERS

Place a verbal or verbal phrase as close as possible to the word it modifies.

I saw an alligator at the other side of that pond looking through my binoculars.

Did you find the sentence above unclear or perhaps humorous? If a verbal or verbal phrase is misplaced, it may appear to modify the wrong word and can confuse the reader. In addition, poorly placed modifiers distract the reader from what is actually being said. A word that modifies the wrong word or group of words is called a **misplaced modifier.**

Unclear The three Simpson children attempted to wash the family dog, *giggling wildly.* (Is the dog *giggling wildly?*)

You can easily correct this sentence by bringing the participial phrase and the word it modifies closer together.

Clear *Giggling wildly*, the three Simpson children attempted to wash the family dog. (The participial phrase *Giggling wildly* now clearly modifies *children.*)

Another kind of error is the **dangling modifier.** This error occurs when the word that the verbal phrase should logically relate to is not in the sentence.

Unclear *To mow the lawn,* the grass must be dry. (Who will mow the lawn? The grass?)

One way to correct a dangling modifier is to add the word that ___ relates to. Sometimes additional rewording is ___ sentence clear.

___ *lawn,* you should make sure the grass is dry. ___ w the wording of this sentence has been ___ he phrase *To mow the lawn* now modifies *you.*)

Using Verbals and Appositives **691**

INDEFINITE PRONOUNS

Indefinite pronouns do not refer to a definite person or thing. An indefinite pronoun usually does not have an antecedent.

Several of the cars were over ten years old.

Occasionally an indefinite pronoun has an antecedent.

The chess players began the game. *Both* were concentrating.

Some indefinite pronouns are singular, and some are plural. Others can be singular or plural, depending on the context.

		Indefinite Pronouns		
Singular	another	each	everything	one
	anybody	either	neither	somebody
	anyone	everybody	nobody	someone
	anything	everyone	no one	something
Plural	both	few	many	others
	several			
Singular or Plural	all	any	most	none
	some			

Practice Your Skills

A. CONCEPT CHECK

Indefinite Pronouns Write the indefinite pronouns in each sentence. Identify each pronoun as *Singular* or *Plural.*

1. No one knows exactly how many people live in the United States, but the Bureau of the Census does its best to find out.
2. The census begins with a list of all of the households in the country.
3. Many people are hired, and some go from door-to-door.
4. Each of the apartments in a building is a separate entry.
5. Then the Bureau sends a form to everyone on the list.
6. Most of the households receive a short form to fill out.
7. Others receive a form with very detailed questions.
8. A difficulty arises when someone does not have a permanent home.
9. Special personnel try to contact anyone without a home.
10. If the census is to succeed, everybody must cooperate.

Writing Theme
The Census

Using Pronouns **561**

• Each lesson begins with a thorough introduction to the concept. Numerous charts and examples clarify the explanation.

• **Thematic exercises** center around a subject that can be used as a springboard to writing.

- **A variety of exercises** provide meaningful application of each concept.

    Concept Checks review the basic idea of the lesson in a simple format.

Drafting and Revision Skills exercises put the concept to work through such activities as sentence combining and elaboration.

Application in Writing allows students to experiment with different formats while applying new skills.

Application in Literature activities show the concept at work in professional writing.

Proofreading activities provide opportunities to sharpen editing skills.
▼

Practice Your Skills

A. CONCEPT CHECK

Adverbs Write the adverbs in this paragraph and the word each modifies. Also tell that word's part of speech.

(1) At dawn the wind fell away, and the ship cruised slowly in the deceptively calm sea. (2) The crew had just finished its morning chores. (3) Suddenly the rain came down in torrents. (4) It soon filled the empty water drums. (5) Then the clouds lifted and the sun broke through. (6) Steam rose from the soaked decks and gradually drifted away. (7) By dark, however, the boat was pitching wildly. (8) Finally, the captain headed the ship south, and it eventually sailed beyond the squall.

Writing Theme
Sailing

B. DRAFTING SKILL

Choosing Adverbs The novelist Henry James once wrote to a friend, "I'm glad you like adverbs—I adore them; they are the only qualifications I really much respect." Write the following passage twice, each time using different adverbs to fill each blank.

(1) Cheryl walked _____ down the block. (2) In the east, the sun had _____ risen. (3) She looked around _____ . (4) As she reached the end of the dock, a board creaked _____ under her foot. (5) The sound was _____ audible. (6) Cheryl breathed _____ . (7) Then she leaned _____ against a piling. (8) Above her, a bird called out _____ , exactly mirroring her own feelings. (9) The sound of voices talking _____ came to her from one of the boats. (10) She turned and walked _____ toward the source of the sounds.

C. APPLICATION IN WRITING

Describing a scene. Adverbs help a writer describe action precisely. Imagine that you want to describe the scene below in a story. Use adverbs to recreate the in...

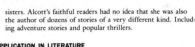

sisters. Alcott's faithful readers had no idea that she was also the author of dozens of stories of a very different kind. Including adventure stories and popular thrillers.

C. APPLICATION IN LITERATURE

Using Fragments Effectively As you have learned, professional writers sometimes use fragments for special purposes. Find the fragments in the following passage. Write them on your paper and then add words to make them complete sentences. Compare the two versions and suggest why Saroyan used the fragments in his writing.

(1) [Homer McCauley] got out of bed and brought out his body-building course from New York and began reading the instructions for the day. (2) His brother Ulysses watched, as he always did . . . . (3) After some ordinary preliminary exercises, including deep breathing, Homer lay flat on his back and lifted his legs stiffly from the floor.
(4) "What's that?" Ulysses said.
(5) "Exercises."
(6) "What for?"
(7) "Muscle."
(8) "Going to be the strongest man in the world?"
(9) "Naah."
(10) "What then?"
(11) "You go back to sleep," Homer said.
(12) Ulysses got back in bed but sat up, watching.
(13) At last Homer began to get dressed.
(14) "Where you going?"
(15) "School."

William Saroyan, _The Human Comedy_

C. PROOFREADING SKILL

Correcting Errors with Modifiers Proofread the following paragraphs. Then rewrite them, correcting all of the errors, including errors in spelling, punctuation, and grammar. Pay special attention to the use of adjectives and adverbs.

Scientists divide whales into two main groups according to there methods of feeding. The largest group is call toothed whales. These kind of whales do not feed on nothing smaller than fish. Among these toothed whales are dolphins porpoises, and killer whales.

The second group, called baleen whales, is more larger in size than toothed whales, baleen whales feed on tiny shrimplike animales known as plankton. The blue whale, part of this second group, is larger than any animal. Oddly, the group of larger whales' eat the more smaller-sized food.

Scrimshaw on a whale tooth shows whalers towing a dead whale to their ship.

Complete Sentences **527**

Review and Assessment

How can you check your students' progress? The Pupil's Edition and Resource File for *The Writer's Craft* offer a wide variety of assessment tools.

Writing Assessments

• **Writing Prompts** Based on state assessments used by many states and colleges, these prompts allow you to check student writing progress.

• **Guides to Analytic and Holistic Scoring** Guidelines help you check achievement on any writing assignment.

• **Portfolio Assessment Suggestions** in the Pupil Book and guidelines in this Teacher's Edition (see T-28) will help you use this effective evaluative technique.

Grammar and Usage Assessment

• **Checkpoints**
These provide a mixed review after every two or three sections.

• **Section Reviews**
Application and Review Sets allow you to evaluate student progress after every main Handbook section.

• **Skills Assessment**
Structured like many state and college assessments, these items allow a mixed review of dozens of language concepts.

• **Pretests and Mastery Tests**
The standardized format of these tests provide you with a quick way to evaluate student understanding.

Writing Prompts: Persuasion

A. In many cities and towns across the country, street performers have made a comeback. They play instruments, juggle, or even tell jokes, hoping to earn money for their efforts. Some people feel that these performers enliven a town; others are annoyed by the noise and crowds they attract. *What do you think your community's policy toward these people should be? Write an article to be submitted to your local government defending your point of view.*

B. Jan, who exercises regularly, claims that her workouts relax her and increase her energy. Marc, a fan of spectator rather than participant sports, believes that physical activity for its own sake can become compulsive, leading to injury and to a distorted sense of values. *Write an article for a youth fitness newsletter supporting your opinions on this issue.*

C. Some people would argue that working students are in a good position today. These people might point out that part-time employment opportunities enable students to earn money while still in school and that minimum wage laws ensure that they are paid reasonably for their work. Others might argue that working distracts students from their studies. *Write a letter to the editor of your local newspaper explaining your views on student employment and offering suggestions for action.*

D. *Write a movie review that you will present to the members of your school Teen Screen Club. Choose a movie you have seen recently and be sure to support your recommendation with details about specific aspects of the film, such as plot, characterization, and action.*

E. Experimentation using animals is a major source of scientific knowledge. Many people oppose animal experimentation, however, on the grounds that animal life is as important as human life and that laboratory procedures cause animals unnecessary pain and suffering. On the other hand, proponents may say that laboratory animals are treated with respect and that experiments provide knowledge that will benefit all living things. *In a letter to the editor of your local newspaper, present and support your stand on animal experimentation.*

CHECK POINT
PAGES 663–669

Writing Theme
Overcoming Difficulties

A. Write the conjunctions and interjections in the following sentences. Identify each as a *Coordinating Conjunction, Correlative Conjunction, Subordinating Conjunction, Conjunctive Adverb,* or *Interjection.*

1. Elvis Presley was born on January 8, 1935, in a shack in Tupelo, Mississippi, but he rose to wealth and fame unrivaled in the history of rock music.
2. Oh, how his father Vernon worked to provide for his wife and son.
3. At about ten years of age, Elvis asked his parents if he could have a bicycle.
4. They had neither the money nor any way of obtaining it.

APPLICATION AND REVIEW

A. Application in Literature Write the italicized words or phrases in the following passage. Tell whether each verbal is a *Gerund, Participle,* or *Infinitive.*

(1) The dragon Smaug approached the village. . . . *Roaring,* he swept back over the town. (2) A hail of dark arrows leaped up and snapped and rattled on his scales and jewels; and their shafts fell back, *kindled by his breath* burning and hissing into the lake. No fireworks you ever imagined equalled the sights that night. (3) At the *twanging of the bows* and the *shrilling of the trumpets,* the dragon's wrath blazed to its height, till he was blind and mad with it. (4) No one had dared *to give battle to him* for many an age; nor would they have dared now, if it had not been for the grim-voiced man (Bard was his name), wh[...] and urging the M[...] arrow.

(5) Fire leape[...] while high in the [...] trees by the shore [...] *leaping* shadows [...] swooped, straight [...] taking no heed *to* [...] seeking only to se[...]

GRAMMAR
HANDBOOK
37

Writing Theme
Myth and Legend

To[...]
B[...]

B. Sentence Combining
ing the instruction in [...]
and make any other nec[...]

1. The dragon appears [...]
   It is a mythical beas[...]
   an appositive.)
2. In the Orient, drago[...]
   supernatural wisdom [...]
   luck. (Use two partic[...]

670

Skills
ASSESSMENT

TEST 1 *Grammar Handbooks 29–32*

Directions One or more of the underlined sections in the following sentences may contain errors of grammar, usage, punctuation, spelling, or capitalization. Write the letter of each incorrect item, then rewrite the item correctly. If there is no error in an item, write E.

Example Edith Hamiltons' book *Mythology* makes it clear. That
                    A   **B**
Zeus' power was not unlimited. No error
                        C   **D**   **E**
Answer A—Edith Hamilton's; B—clear that

1. Although it is commonly accepted by astronomers and other scientists that the Universe

Special Features

Throughout the pupil's editions, special features provide opportunities for students to enjoy themselves as they learn.

- **Sketchbooks**
Sometimes funny, sometimes thought-provoking, the Sketchbooks let students experiment with "no-risk writing."

- **Sentence Composing**
By imitating the sentences of professional writers, students develop their own more sophisticated style.

- **On the Lightside**
Your students will learn that language study can be fun.

Sketchbook

It was at ten o'clock to-day that the first of all Time Machines began its career. I gave it a last tap, tried all the screws again, put one more drop of oil on the quartz rod, and sat myself in the saddle. . . .

H. G. Wells
THE TIME MACHINE

What if a time machine took you to another era? What age would you like to have lived in? How would your life have been different then? How would it have been the same? What could you learn from the people living in that time period? What could you teach them?

Additional Sketches
How do they do that? How does it work?

Write a recipe. It could be directions for cooking something, but it doesn't have to be. It could be a recipe for success, for happiness, or for anything else you can think of.

146

Sentence COMPOSING

Delayed Modifiers

Experienced writers sometimes place adjectives after (rather than before) the person, place, or thing they describe to add interest, variety, and style to their sentences. Notice how the author, instead of writing "The <u>somber and dull</u> forests," adds power to the model sentence by delaying the adjectives that describe the forest.

> **MODEL**
> The forests, <u>somber and dull</u>, stood motionless and silent on each side of the broad stream.
> **Joseph Conrad, "The Lagoon"**

A. Combining Sentences Combine the two sentences by placing the adjectives from the second sentence in the place indicated by a caret (∧).

Example The forests,∧, stood motionless and silent on each side of the broad stream. The forests were somber and dull.

Combined Sentence The forests, <u>somber and dull</u>, stood motionless and silent on each side of the broad stream.

1. A bird somewhere, ∧ , called for its friends. The bird was lonely and lost.
   Robert Lipsyte, The Contender

2. The red fearless eyes still looked at him, ∧ . The eyes were imperson~~~ unafraid and detached.
   John Steinbeck, Th~~~

3. The old house was the same, ∧ , but as we stared down the stree~~~ thought we saw an inside shutter move. The house was droopy ar~~~
   Harper Lee, To Kill a Moc~~~

4. The screen glowed silver, and soon life began to unfold, ∧ . Life ~~~ beautiful and passionate and sad.
   William Faulkner, "Dry Sep~~~

5. The diggers gathered about the rim of the pit, ∧ . The diggers wer~~~ staring.
   Edmund Ware, "An Underground E~~~

6. A sigh, ∧ , marked an almost imperceptible pause, and then his wor~~~ flowed on, without a stir, without a gesture. The sigh was short and~~~
   Joseph Conrad, Tales of ~~~

Sentence ~~~

On the Lightside

SPEAKING CAJUN

Perhaps you have tasted gumbo, or jambalaya, or creole, or other Cajun dishes. These complex recipes are reflections of the culture of the Cajuns, who have lived for more than two hundred years in the bayous of southern Louisiana. During this time, however, the Cajuns have contributed more than food; they have also created a rich and hearty language called the Cajun dialect. Like their food, the Cajun language is a spicy mixture. It is basi~~~ ~~~ French,

Canada. When the British captured the colony, they forced out everyone who would not swear allegiance to the British. Many of the Acadians moved to Louisiana. There they established their own communities and maintained a separate culture. Their French language did not have the words to describe some of the things they encountered in this frontier land, so they borrowed words from the English settlers, Native Americans, and slaves they encountered in this new homeland. Over time, they even changed ~~~ name to

Using The Teacher's Edition

The Teacher's Edition of *The Writer's Craft* provides you with all the help you will need to prepare comprehensive, exciting lessons.

WORKSHOP 7   Persuasion

Teaching Preview

Workshop Overview

Persuasion is writing that attempts to convince the reader to adopt the writer's position on an issue or to take action. Students will apply the skills of definition, classification, analysis, and synthesis that they developed in previous Workshops as they write to persuade a targeted audience. Workshop 7 includes the following Guided and Related Assignments:

1. **Guided: Supporting Opinions** builds on the skills of definition, analysis, classification, and synthesis developed in preceding Workshops by inviting students to identify issues they already care strongly about and to write persuasively in support of their positions
2. **Related: Letter to the Editor** develops skills introduced in the Guided Assignment by asking students to express opinions in a familiar format
3. **Related: Literary Evaluation** builds on the skills of evaluating and expressing opinions introduced in the Guided Assignment by encouraging students to view real-world entertainment experiences in critical terms

Preparation Guide

1. Use the Overview and the Teacher's Choice descriptions on page 307 as a basis for deciding which assignment(s) to teach.
2. Preview the assignment and the teacher's notes. The teaching suggestions and your knowledge of your class's abilities should allow you to identify quickly the concepts that may require preteaching or extra support. The Handbook mini-lessons suggested in the Preteaching notes within the lesson can also provide guidance in this area.
3. Preview the adjacent chart for support materials in the Teacher's Resource File that may be used with this Workshop. Resources are for use with the Guided Assignment unless otherwise noted.

Workshop Support Materials

Resources	For Use With
Data Sheet 7	Exploratory Activities, p. 210
Ideas for Writing—Persuasive	Identify an Issue, p. 210
Thinking Skills Transparency and Worksheet: Drawing Conclusions	Explore the Issue, p. 212
Elaboration Worksheet 7	Begin Your Draft, p. 213
Peer Response Worksheet 7	Test Your Arguments, p. 215
Guidelines for Evaluating Writing 7	Standards for Evaluation, p. 217
Student Revision Model Transparency 7	Problem-solve, p. 217
Revision and Proofreading Worksheet 7	Proofread Your Work, p 218
Writing Prompt for Assessment Persuasive	

Professional Resources and Media

Books and Journals	Films and Videos
Lampert, Kathleen W., "Using Dialogues to Teach Argumentation," *Exercise Exchange*, Vol. 30 (Spring 1985), pp. 6–10.	*The Persuasive Paper*, Dallas Community College District, Mesquite, TX (1976). (30 min.)
	Computer Software
	Persuasive Essay, Jr., Intellectual Software (Division of Queue, Inc.) Bridgeport, CT. Apple II, II+, IIe, IIc; IBM PC.

206a Workshop 7

Linking Literature, Writing, and Grammar

The following options may be used to provide students with an integrated language experience. Begin by assigning and discussing any of the recommended pieces of literature, which can be found in most classroom anthologies. Use the suggested strategy to provide a link to the Guided Assignment.

Linking Literature and Writing

Option 1
Starting Point: "Non-Jocks Deserve a Chance" by Susan Swartz on pages 208–209 of *The Writer's Craft*
Strategy: Use the teaching suggestions on pages 208–209 to lead students into the Guided Assignment.

Option 2
Starting Point: "The Secret Life of Walter Mitty" by James Thurber
Strategy: As students read and discuss this short story, have them imagine that they are someone close to Mitty—perhaps his wife, doctor, friend, or co-worker. Invite them to speak persuasively to Mitty in an attempt to bring him out of his fantasy world. After students decide which attempt at persuasion was most effective, lead them into the Guided Assignment.

Option 3
Starting Point: "Fire and Ice" by Robert Frost
Strategy: As students read and discuss the poem, have them choose which kind of ending for the world they would prefer—in fire or in ice. Have them give persuasive reasons for their choice. Also discuss which approach Robert Frost favors and his reasons. Remind students that identifying and evaluating reasons or arguments that support a piece of persuasive writing are important for readers and writers. Then lead them into the Guided Assignment.

Workshop Management Guidelines

The adjacent chart indicates the number of days recommended for each phase of the Guided and Related Assignments. Stars indicate portions of the assignment that may be completed outside the classroom if time is limited or if teachers wish the activity to be completed by students independently.

Linking Writing and Grammar

Before the drafting or revision stages of this assignment, tell students that effective persuasion demands writing that moves the reader. One of the most reliable methods of strengthening your position is to express the reasons for your thinking in appropriate phrases and clauses. Ask students to find examples of the effective use of phrases and clauses in their own writing as you write the following examples on the board:

WEAK: I support the school building program. New construction is expensive. Teachers need space to teach effectively.

STRONG: Although new construction is expensive, I support the school building program because teachers need space to teach effectively.

Go over pages 721–734 of the Grammar and Usage Handbook. If problems still appear in student papers, assign the exercises on those pages for reteaching. Additional practice can be found in the Grammar and Usage Resource Book on pages 230–231.

Supporting Opinions	Writing—1 day*
Starting from Literature—1 day	Reviewing—1 day*
Prewrite—3–4 days*	Publish—1–2 days
Draft—2–3 days*	
Revise—1–2 days*	**Literary Evaluation**
Publish—1–2 days	Starting from Literature—1 day
Learning—1 day*	Thinking Through—1–2 days*
Reteaching—open	Writing—1 day*
Extension and Enrichment—open*	Reviewing—1 day*
Sentence Composing—1 day*	Publish—1–2 days

Letter to the Editor	
Starting from Literature—1 day	
Examining the Issue—1–2 days*	

Workshop 7 **206b**

Teaching Preview Pages

These pages appear before every Writer's Workshop and contain the following information:

• Workshop Overview
Introduces the focus of the workshop and explains the relationships among the Guided and Related Assignments.

• Preparation Guide
Guides your planning decisions and provides a chart of available support materials in the Teacher's Resource File.

• Linking Literature, Writing, and Grammar
Presents three options for basing each writing assignment on literature. Shows how to link any option with a grammar and usage mini-lesson.

• Workshop Management Guidelines
Indicates recommended number of days for each assignment, with suggestions for independent study.

Workshop Introduction

In the Pupil's Edition, this page allows both students and teachers to see — at a glance — the focus of the workshop and the writing types they will be exploring.

- **Workshop Objectives**

Lists general objectives for the Workshop as a whole.

- **Teacher's Choice**

Helps the teachers choose assignments by describing each one, suggesting which students might benefit most, and recommending when it might best be taught.

Lesson Notes

The Teacher's Edition continues to help the teacher throughout the lesson. In addition to the literature notes shown on page T3, each lesson contains the following material:

- **Objectives**

Specific goals for each part of the lesson.

- **Preteaching Suggestions**

Ideas for using mini-lessons from the Writing Handbook.

- **Teaching Strategies**

Point-of-Use notes that truly make this one book for all students. Included are suggestions for

Modeling
Speaking and Listening Opportunities
Teaching Tips
Individualizing Instruction Tips for teaching LEP, LD, cultural diversity, and different ability levels
Collaborative Opportunities
Spot Checks
Stumbling Blocks Potential problems and tips to avoid them
Personal Touch Suggestions for making yourself into a co-writer in the classroom
Managing the Paper Load Ideas for cutting down on grading and review

---

Informative Exposition: Classification

Related Assignment
EXTENDED METAPHOR

Writer's Workshop 4:
Informative Exposition: Classification

Objectives

Guided Assignment:
DEFINITION
To recognize examples of extended definition and to plan, draft, revise, proofread, and share an extended definition

Related Assignment:
EXTENDED METAPHOR
To identify the characteristics of extended metaphor and to write, review, and share an extended metaphor

Related Assignment:
COMPARISON AND CONTRAST
To identify the characteristics of comparison and to write, review, and share a comparison of two people or things

Teacher's Choice

Guided Assignment
Definition This assignment is appropriate for most students because it can accommodate a wide range of topics and skill levels, and it draws on students' particular interests. The assignment also reinforces students' ability to classify and analyze information—prerequisites to the process of synthesis, which students will explore in Workshop 5. This assignment may be most useful after students have had experience with writing descriptions.

Related Assignments
Extended Metaphor This assignment is especially appropriate for advanced students and those keenly interested in literature. Visual learners may find photographs or other works of art useful springboards to writing.
Comparison and Contrast This assignment may be useful with students who are interested in the natural and social sciences. Ties to literature are also evident.

Workshop 4 **117**

Prewrite and Explore

Objectives

1. To use prewriting activities to generate ideas for a description of a process
2. To select a topic and explore goals and audience for a process description
3. To gather and organize information for a process description

Preteaching

Preview the Prewrite and Explore section. If there are skills or concepts that your students may need help with, present them at this point. The following mini-lesson references may help you in your selection and instruction. The cross-references in the pupil text will give students access to the same lessons for independent study.

Handbook Mini-Lessons
- Sharing Techniques, pp. 323–325
- Appropriate Details, p. 335
- Solving Problems, pp. 456–458
- Sources of Information, pp. 476–478
- Interviewing Skills, pp. 481–482

Teaching Strategies

Modeling

Show a videotape of a professional football or basketball player in action. If possible, show the action in slow motion. Encourage students to identify the steps followed and list them on the board. If videotapes are unavailable, you might have a student athlete pantomime the steps used to complete an action and list them on the board.

◆ *Individualizing Instruction*

LEP Students Encourage students to identify processes with which they are familiar and to dramatize or sketch the steps for a peer who can help supply English words.

150 Workshop 5

INVITATION *to* Write

Russell Baker provided comical instructions for carving a turkey. Now write your own description of a process—one that shows how to do something, tells how something works, or explains how an event takes place.

Does everyone know how to play Monopoly, or how Joe Montana scored a touchdown with just seconds to go? Of course not. That's why process explanations are so useful. They help people learn from each other about how to do something, how something works, or how an event happened. To help others learn about processes you understand, you need to analyze what goes into the process—what steps are involved and sometimes what skills and materials are needed. In the assignment that follows, you will analyze a process and share information by explaining the process to others.

PREWRITE AND EXPLORE

1. Look for ideas. You complete, observe, or are part of different processes every day. Think about which of these processes most interest you, or try one or more of the following activities to help you identify a process you would like to explore.

Exploratory Activities

- **Observing** Watch favorite performers or athletes in motion and make notes or sketches of the steps they use to complete an action. You may also want to study photos or videotapes.
- **Brainstorming about science and history** Complete the sentence "I wonder how . . ." in as many ways as possible. Perhaps you've always wondered how volcanoes erupt, how a microwave oven works, or how the Statue of Liberty was designed and installed. Let your mind roam free to think of ideas that intrigue you.

HANDBOOK
FOR HELP & PRACTICE
Sharing Techniques, pp. 323–325
Appropriate Details, p. 355
Solving Problems, pp. 456–458
Sources of Information, pp. 476–478
Interviewing Skills, pp. 481–482

150 Workshop 5

Springboard

Present as a warmup exercise a rapid association of ideas. Begin by mentioning a person, place, thing, or idea. Students should then supply as many "how to" topics as they can that are related to that idea. For example, the first word mentioned might be school. Students may suggest topics, such as how to use the computers in the computer lab or how to study for a test. Continue supplying topics until all ideas have been exhausted. Then have a student offer another word or phrase that will suggest other how-to topics.

- **Brainstorming** Write the heading "If I Ruled the World" at the top of a sheet of paper. With two or three classmates, make a list of issues that are important to you and what you would do about them.
- **Reading literature** Think about the conflicts in works you've read. For example, the barber in "Lather and Nothing Else" by Hernando Tellez had to decide whether or not to kill his enemy. If you had to choose sides in such a conflict, which side would you be on?

2. Share promising ideas. Look over the ideas you've generated, and narrow your choices down to the most promising issues. Then share them with classmates, listening for their responses to your ideas and also listening for issues mentioned by other students that you might like to pursue.

3. Select and define an issue. Select the issue that seems most promising to you and freewrite for ten minutes presenting your view of it. Don't hesitate to present arguments against your position; you will want to consider and perhaps deal with opposing positions as you write. If you have trouble defining your issue, try listing the basic ideas or positions involved. Here is the list one student, Helen, made of the positions on the issue of product-testing on animals.

Writing —TIP—
Look for issues that have a personal meaning to you.

ONE STUDENT'S PROCESS

animals are subjected to testing for consumer products

some manufacturers conduct cruel experiments that ignore animal rights

some animal rights advocates want tests on animals stopped even when helpful to humans

some scientists feel other testing methods can be used

I Stand Here—I love animals, think unnecessary testing should be stopped

---

◆ *Individualizing Instruction*

Learning Styles Help visual learners choose an issue by bringing in current news magazines and allowing students to browse through the photographs. Visual and auditory learners might also watch or listen to a news analysis program on television or radio for ideas on current or controversial issues.

Spot Check

As students work through the exploratory activities to select a topic, make sure they are looking at controversial issues and not just matters of personal preference.

Stumbling Block

As students identify and explore their topics for persuasive writing, encourage them to analyze their feelings about the issue carefully. If after defining the issue they are still unsure about how they feel about it, encourage them to look for another topic. (You might refer students to the Data Sheets and the Ideas for Writing Booklet as other sources of ideas for topics.) Emphasize that it is very difficult to persuade someone else about something you are not sure of yourself.

T13

Teacher's Edition *continued*

- **Guidelines for Evaluation** Rubrics for evaluating final student papers.

- **Reteaching** Suggestions for providing additional instruction in areas where students were not successful.

- **Extension and Enrichment Ideas** Moves students beyond the assignment.

- **Learning from Your Writing Process** Helps students learn from each assignment and build writing portfolios.

- **Summary and Closure** Reviews the key points of the lesson.

- **Other Features**

  Connections
  Links to Literature, Science, Social Studies, and the Fine Arts

  Springboards
  Motivating quotes and activities

  Off the Record
  Humor for you—just because you need it sometimes!

Linking Grammar and Writing

As students revise their drafts, suggest that they pay attention to the use of adjectives and adverbs and other modifiers such as the prepositional and participial phrase. You might use or direct students to Handbook 34, Using the Correct Modifier, pages 628–629; Handbook 35, Prepositional Phrases as Modifiers, pages 657–658; and Handbook 37, The Participial Phrase, page 684.

Guidelines for Evaluation

The following guidelines may be used for a close evaluation of a personal narrative. See the Guidelines for Evaluating Writing in the Teacher's Resource File for additional help with holistic or analytic scoring.

Ideas and Content
- relates a meaningful experience
- includes details that fully develop character, setting, and plot
- includes descriptive details and effective dialogue
- demonstrates the importance of the event to the writer
- reflects an awareness of audience in word choice and detail

Structure and Plot
- consistently uses the first-person point of view
- includes a beginning, middle, and end
- uses transition words and phrases
- uses chronological order effectively
- groups related ideas into paragraphs
- uses clear, varied sentences

Grammar, Usage, and Mechanics
- uses standard grammar and usage
- uses correct spelling, punctuation, and capitalization

Managing the Paper Load

Remember that you need not grade all of the points listed above. For grammar and mechanics in particular, limit your focus when grading. Before students finish revising, explain the criteria that you will use for evaluation.

I like your beginning, but can you do more to set the scene?

I can't picture what's happening. How about using dialogue here?

I'm confused about when this is happening.

2. Problem solve. Rework your draft, taking into consideration your own review of your narrative and the responses of your peer readers. Think about the comments your peer readers have made, but don't feel bound by them. As you revise, keep in mind your own goals for your writing.

Charles made these changes to the beginning of his draft as he responded to the suggestions of a peer reader.

ONE STUDENT'S PROCESS

"I have an announcement to make," Dad said. We were just beginning dinner. My mother looked up while I continued to eat. I was in a hurry. The guys were waiting. Dad asked, "May I have your attention too, Chuck?" I was surprised at his question. Dad knew I always ate dinner quickly so I could play basketball. Then Dad told us that things hadn't been going very well at the factory. Well last week he heard from Jack who moved to Florida and found a job there. Jack said his plant is looking for more people. My dad decides he's going to try it.

3. Proofread your work. Make a clean copy that includes all your changes. Then check for errors in grammar, usage, and mechanics because these kinds of errors can distract a reader. Remember that verb tense and the punctuation of dialogue are particularly important in narrative writing.

96   Workshop 3

96   Workshop 3

Social Studies Connection

Autobiographies Point out that well-known leaders often write their memoirs or autobiographies in personal narrative form. Suggest that students find and read the memoirs or autobiographies of figures they admire such as Winston Churchill or Gandhi. Tell students to look for the characteristics of an effective personal narrative as they read.

Then something happened. On my way out the door to basketball one afternoon, I yelled, "Mom, I won't be home for dinner." She didn't answer, so I went to look for her. She had her back to me, kneeling beside a carton and carefully wrapping the family photographs she had taken off the wall. When I said, "Mom," she didn't turn around. I walked around the box and said, "Mom, I won't be. . . ." I broke off my words in mid-sentence. My mother was crying.

"I guess you caught me," she said, trying to smile. "But, why . . .?"

"Oh, I guess I was just feeling sentimental—you know, old pictures and everything." Then she looked at me, and the smile disappeared. "No, Chuck, it's really more than that."

"You mean you don't want to move either! That's great! When Dad realizes how we both feel, he'll agree to stay here." I was on a roll again, already planning what I was going to tell the guys.

My mother looked at me a little sadly. "I wish it were that simple, Chuck. You're right. I don't want to move, but then neither does your father. We've lived in this city all our lives."

"Then, let's stay!" I could hardly believe that maybe things would go my way after all.

"Chuck, think about it. What will happen if we stay? I don't have a job. You know your father's plant is in danger of closing. How can we afford a place to live, food to eat, or even basketball shoes for you if we don't have jobs?" The smile returned for a moment as she mentioned the shoes.

I went back to my room and tentatively fingered one of the empty cartons. "How was I to know?" I protested, half to myself and half to the cartons. For once in my life, I didn't have a quick answer. I needed time to digest what Mom had said. Basketball would have to wait today.

Middle of narrative is well-developed. Descriptive details help reader picture the scene between mother and son.

Narrative is told in chronological order.

Ending shows the significance of the narrative.

Personal Narrative   99

Reteaching

Assess the needs of students who were not successful in developing an effective personal narrative and identify two or three areas in which additional practice is needed. Assign the appropriate Handbook Mini-Lessons, along with the support materials listed for each lesson. A concept commonly requiring reteaching for this assignment is

Chronological Order: Handbook 4

The following suggestions and resources may also be useful.

1. Dialogue Remind students that a successful narrative contains natural-sounding dialogue. To help students achieve better dialogue, suggest that pairs of students act out scenes from their narratives in which two or more characters interact. Have students develop and record dialogue for the scenes. Students can then use this dialogue to replace some of the narration in their drafts.

2. Characterization To help students develop their characters, suggest that they select one or more characters from their narratives and do five minutes of focused freewriting about each character. Tell students to include as many descriptive details as possible. Circulate and help students as they weave some of these details into their personal narrative.

3. Grammar and Usage: Shifts in Tense In a small group, review with students rules of verb tense. Ask students to find examples of sentences with errors of this type in their drafts. As a group revise the sentences.

Extension and Enrichment

- Suggest that students use the techniques of dialogue and description in their diaries or journals.
- Some students might enjoy using their personal narratives to develop a play. Suggest that students work in small groups to select a narrative, identify one or more scenes, develop a script with dialogue and stage directions, and create props.

LEARNING FROM YOUR WRITING PROCESS

WRITER TO WRITER

There is only one trait that marks the writer. He is always watching. It's a kind of trick of mind and he is born with it.
Morley Callaghan, Canadian novelist and short-story writer

...your writing. Ask yourself the following questions, ...y useful thoughts or ideas in your own writing log:
...hniques did I find helpful in writing my process ...on?
...s most difficult about writing this piece?
...cessful was I in analyzing all the steps in the

...skills. Try one or more writing activities in the fol-

...ricular Visit a science class and observe an experi-
...rogress. Ask questions about the experiment and
...n it. Then submit an explanation of the process to
...n you observed and ask how well you explained the

...Read a biographical or autobiographical selection,
...Christmas Memory," "These Were the Sioux," or "I
...y the Caged Bird Sings." Describe a process that
...on in the time and place described in the selection
...usual in your own time and place.

...Call a representative of a local organization, such
...ling group, the police department, the fire depart-
...your local Red Cross. Ask if there are any health- or
...ed processes you can help the organization to edu-
...ublic about. Prepare pamphlets or posters about the
...d distribute or display them at your local shopping

...ssignments Follow the suggestions on pages 162–
...rite a cause-effect analysis or create a flowchart.

Informative Writing   161

Learning from Your Writing Process

Objective

To analyze and reflect upon what has been learned about the writing process and the writing of a description of a process

Teaching Strategies

Reflecting on the Process

Encourage students to share their thoughts as well as to suggest any other questions that might be useful in thinking about the writing experience. Suggest that students think about and try to recognize the things that went especially well, not just those that were not successful.

Writing Portfolio

Suggest that students save their evaluations with their final process descriptions in their writing portfolios. Encourage students to review their self-evaluations from the Guided Assignment in Workshop 4, in which they explored another kind of informative writing. How do their assessments differ? Do they see any common strengths or weaknesses?

Summary and Closure

Before proceeding to the next lesson, be sure students have internalized the following key ideas:
1. A process description explains how to do something, how something works, or how an event happened.
2. An effective process description includes a clear explanation of the steps, logical order, and appropriate transitions.
3. Many informational books are based entirely on descriptions of process. However, this type of writing is also found in short stories and novels.

Give students time to summarize what they have learned by describing the characteristics of an effective description of a process and by explaining how the skill of writing effective process descriptions can help them in other school subjects, particularly science and social studies.

Informative Writing   161

Off the Record
"Writing is so difficult that I often feel that writers, having had their hell on earth, will escape all punishment hereafter."
Jessamyn West
To See the Dream

Teacher's Resource File

M otivation, reinforcement, creative approaches to writing, and practical teaching support are the hallmarks of the Teacher's Resource File.

Ideas for Writing
Data sheets for each Guided Assignment and a wealth of writing prompts ensure that no student will be without a writing idea.

Fine Art Transparencies and Writing Prompts
Both classic and contemporary art reproductions provide springboards to writing.

▼

You can't believe it! During your first week as local news editor for the *Newburg Daily News*, the storm of the century has hit. Every *News* reporter is out covering the storm, trying to keep track of downed power lines, slippery roads, blocked streets, car accidents, power outages, fires, floods, school cancellations, and other effects of the extreme rain and violent wind. You, on the other hand, sit in the news office, guiltily warm and comfortable, sorting out the information fed to you by the reporters. You have to organize the facts so that coherent articles about the storm can be written. How do you make sense of all the details? What causes the power outages, for example?

To help "see" the situation, summarize some causes and effects of the storm on the cause-and-effect chart.

Thinking Skills   *Cause-and-Effect Chart*
                             Graphic Organizer

violent storm

1. floods

Details:
Gutters blocked by leaves blown from trees, causing rainwater to back up into streets

2. roadblocks

Details:
Flooding causes washed-out roadbeds, which are then blockaded by police

3 downed power lines

Details:
Old trees, pushed over by wind, fall on power lines and pull them down

Conclusion, or Statement of Significance
Great expense will result from the damage caused by the storm.

For use with Cause-and-Effect Worksheet 1   Thinking Skills Transparencies   14

Cause-and-Effect Chart Transparency

Worksheet

Transparency

Mixed Activities 1

The Persistence of Memory (Persistance de la Mémoire), Salvador Dali

Activity A
Narration   Dali's work is a prime example of surrealism, a style in which images seem unrelated to reason or convention. In the real world clocks do not turn limp nor do they become food for insects. What you see in a surrealistic painting cannot happen in real life. Or can it? Freewrite a surrealistic narrative in which seemingly unrelated characters are brought together in a series of unusual situations. Include in your story an explanation of how they cope with the unusual events. Try to maintain a thread of symbolic meaning through your narration.

Activity B
Persuasion   Dali's surrealistic style always brings out strong reactions. While some observers consider surrealism an important development that has expanded the limits of art, others criticize it as undisciplined and wild. Choose some style to which you react strongly. This may be a style of art, music, fashion, or film. Write a persuasive

Starting Points for Writing   *Mixed Activities 1*

Thinking Skills Transparencies and Worksheets
These graphic organizers can be used to help students find or develop ideas. Practice activities are included.

Guidelines for Evaluating Writing
Includes evaluation guidelines and models of strong, average, and weak student responses.

Writing About Literature
Extra advice to help students respond to and write about literature.

The Persistence of Memory (Persistance de la Mémoire), Salvador Dali, 1931

The Persistence of Memory, a chilling surrealist dream image, is one of the most famous paintings by Salvador Dali (1904–). Here Dali takes

Teacher's Resource File *continued*

Revising and Proofreading

Use the following checklist to focus your attention when you are revising persuasive writing.

Questions for Revising
1. Do I clearly state the nature of the issue and my position on it?
2. Do I recognize and answer possible objections to my views?
3. Do I support my argument with pertinent facts and compelling reasons?
4. Do I avoid illogical arguments based on faulty reasoning?

Elaboration

Persuasion: Supporting Opinions

The paragraph below is from a persuasive essay about the destruction of coral reefs in the Pennekamp Coral Reef State Park off Key Largo, Florida. Use the **Suggestions for Elaboration** to further develop the ideas in the paragraph, both by adding information to existing sentences and by creating new sentences. Pertinent details, quotations, and other information can be found in the **Prewriting Notes**. Write your new paragraph on a separate sheet of paper.

(1) The problem at Pennekamp is people. (2) Each year, large numbers of swimmers, boaters, and divers visit the park. (3) They often damage the fragile coral and litter the water and park grounds. (4) Pennekamp Coral Reef State Park is slowly being destroyed by the very people for whom it was created.

Prewriting Notes

• boats spew petroleum into the water • 2 million visitors each year (1 million swimmers, divers, boaters) • writer & photographer Fred Ward: "the cummulative devastation is enormous." • boats crash into fragile reefs • 6,000 people on a warm weekend • some coral pieces may have taken centuries to grow • litter from visitors includes foam cups, glass, plastic bags, aluminum cans, tangled fishing line • tired swimmers often stand on/damage coral • illegal fish spearing/specimen collecting continue • concession operator Randy Pegram: "We're 'maxed out' every other weekend. Pennekamp has to close the gates because there's no more room for cars."

Suggestions for Elaboration

• Rewrite sentence 1 to create a more effective topic sentence.

• Elaborate on the main idea of sentence 2 by citing statistics and quoting a knowledgeable source.

• Include examples and other pertinent information to support sentence 3.

• Elaborate on sentence 4, including a quotation to strengthen the impact of the writer's opinion.

Workshop 8   Persuasion   **69**

◀ **Elaboration, Revision, and Proofreading Worksheets**
Practice activities give students extra experience with three key writing skills.

Peer Response Guides
Students are given prompts to guide them through peer response sessions for each Guided Assignment.

Writing Resource Book
Provides practice and reteaching exercises for each section of the Writing Handbook.

▼

Point of View 1

At some stage of their writing process, writers must decide on a point of view, or "angle," from which to present their information. They can choose **first-person, third-person,** or **second-person point of view,** depending on their writing purpose.

When using first-person point of view, a writer tells a story as experienced by only one character, the narrator. Use of the pronoun *I* often signals this point of view, although the narrator does not necessarily stand for the writer.

When using the third-person point of view, signaled by the pronouns *he* and *she,* a writer tells a story as observed by a narrator who does not take part in the action. Such a narrator seems to be all-knowing, commenting on what the characters think and feel as well as what they do.

Second-person point of view is signaled by the pronoun *you,* (which can be either stated or understood) and is used only in special circumstances, such as giving orders or directions or explaining a process.

A. Identifying Point of View

Read each short narrative below. Identify each as **first-person** or **third-person** narrative. Underline the words that help you arrive at your answer.

1. The door was stuck. Sandy pulled and pushed, but the heavy obstacle would not move. He went to the desk to find something sharp to stick into the lock. As he neared the desk, the phone rang, they stopped abruptly, as if the wire had been cut. His mind raced, and he wondered who had been on the line. _____

2. "Hello," I said, half whispering, as I picked up the phone. The only sound on the other end was the hollow echo you get when no one is there. I kept on speaking, however, as if by wishing and speaking I could make someone be there. _____

B. Writing from a Different Point of View

Read the narrative that follows. Rewrite it as a first-person narrative. Where the blank spaces appear, add sentences or phrases that describe the narrator's thoughts.

Crash! Roar! The thunder made every part of the small, tired old boat tremble as it would fall apart. They were all shaking that night as they made their way to the new land. So many things ran through his mind. _____ He tried to make his way across the slippery deck toward his mother, but the deck lurched up and he had to grab the railing or plunge into the black, swirling water. He wondered if _____.

_____
_____
_____
_____
_____
_____
_____
_____

Writer Handbook   **21**

▶ **Student Revision Models**

Analysis 2

Helping Potential   Become Graduates
~~Facing the Problem of Dropouts~~

1   Too many students are leaving high school before graduation. In our

2   city the current dropout rate is ~~11%;~~ *eleven percent,* and our own school is coming

3   dangerously close to that rate. *so many students from leaving school? How* What can we do to stop that? What can

4   we do to stop this *alter* horrible pattern of *wasted potential that leads many of* *ing their are* *Three approaches that might help students avoid*

5   our peers into dead-end lives? I suggest the following steps: (1) an

6   intensive tutoring program, ~~(2)~~ a stepped-up counseling program, and

Student Revision Model Transparencies
Ideal for modeling purposes, these transparencies provide practice in analyzing and responding to the writing of others.

Grammar and Usage Practice Book ▶

Over 300 pages of practice and reteaching exercises reinforce concepts taught in every Grammar Handbook section.

Vocabulary Development

Thirty-six lessons improve student vocabulary through a variety of activities and word lists based on SAT and ACT examinations.

Tests and Assessment Booklet

This complete testing and assessment portfolio offers Pretests, Skills Assessment, and Mastery Tests for all grammar, usage, and mechanics concepts. Writing Prompts for Assessment are provided for each Guided Assignment in the text to help prepare students for evaluation stituations.

▼

Part 1
Verb Phrases

A. Using Verbs and Verb Phrases

Write sentences on the lines below by adding a predicate to each subject. The predicate should contain a verb phrase—a main verb used with one or more helping verbs.

1. Telephones with special features _____

2. Long-forgotten memories _____

3. Our natural environment _____

4. Photography _____

5. Recent inventions _____

B. Using Verb Phrases in Writing

Imagine that you have been awarded a scholarship to a summer course that offers college credits. It is a fiction writers' workshop. Your classmates are friendly, imaginative, and witty. You will be sending the scholarship committee a summary of your experience. On the lines below, rewrite your rough notes as a paragraph of five sentences for your report. Include some verb phrases.

an unusual type of class . . . the instructor's enthusiasm . . . a typical student . . . interest in the workshop . . .criticism of one's work . . . professional writers . . . talent and humor . . .

_____
_____
_____
_____
_____
_____
_____
_____

Workshop 8 Persuasion   **1**

Name _____   Date _____   Score _____
Handbook 33
Pretest

Using Verbs

A. Identifying Action and Linking Verbs

Choose the answer that identifies the boldfaced verb in each sentence. (4 points each)

1. We must have **watched** at least ten boring commercials during that program.
   ○ A. action verb   ○ B. linking verb

2. Ulysses S. Grant **became** President after serving as the commanding general of the Union armies in the Civil War.
   ○ A. action verb   ○ B. linking verb

3. The air **didn't seem** as humid after the afternoon thundershower.
   ○ A. action verb   ○ B. linking verb

4. In 1987, stockbrokers **worried** about another crash of the stock market like the one in 1929.
   ○ A. action verb   ○ B. linking verb

B. Identifying Transitive and Intransitive Verbs

Choose the answer that identifies the boldfaced verb in each sentence. (4 points each)

5. Before Pedro left for first period, he **closed** his locker securely.
   ○ A. transitive verb   ○ B. intransitive verb

6. In order to observe signs of spring, we **walked** to the park.
   ○ A. transitive verb   ○ B. intransitive verb

7. For twenty-six years, Jane Goodall **studied** the behavior of wild chimpanzees in Africa.
   ○ A. transitive verb   ○ B. intransitive verb

8. The drum and bugle corps **practiced** every morning and evening for weeks before the national competition.
   ○ A. transitive verb   ○ B. intransitive verb

C. Identifying Active and Passive Voice

Choose the voice of the boldfaced verb in each sentence. (4 points each)

9. Edgar Allan Poe **wrote** beautiful poems as well as horror stories.
   ○ A. active voice   ○ B. passive voice

10. Poe's works **are read** by lovers of good literature in many countries.
    ○ A. active voice   ○ B. passive voice

11. Janice **analyzed** the symbols in Poe's poetry.
    ○ A. active voice   ○ B. passive voice

12. Poe's stories **were used** as models by later writers.
    ○ A. active voice   ○ B. passive voice

Go on to the next page   98

Lesson Plans

Suggestions for preparing lessons that follow the Lesson Cycle on page T37.

Computer Software

Provides a data base and useful strategies that can be used during the writing process. A Grammar Test Generator includes all concepts from the program.

Standardized Test Practice

Teaches students strategies for different standardized test question formats.

▼

Analogies

Analogies are pairs of words that are related to each other. In many analogy questions, you are given two words that are related to each other in some way. Your job is to find two other words that are related to each other in the same way. A typical analogy question on a standardized test looks like this:

> BUTTON : SNAP ::   (A) zipper : jacket   (C) fork : utensil
> ● pencil : pen   (D) crayon : draw   (E) book : read

To answer analogy questions, use the following strategies:

1. First, think about the many different relationships that can be expressed in analogies, for example, cause and effect, size, shape or time.

2. Second, determine the relationship between the first pair of words given. Then, create a sentence that contains both words and that shows the relationship between them. The first pair of words in the above example can be used as follows:

Is there a better way to teach writing?

Philosophy and Rationale

Authors:
Peter Elbow, Professor of English, University of Massachusetts at Amherst
Sheridan Blau, Senior Lecturer in English and Education, University of California at Santa Barbara

Teachers are constantly bombarded with confident pronouncements from experts and textbooks about the teaching of writing. But tidy theories don't usually hold up in the complex realities of the high school classroom. This book, therefore, is based on the classroom experience of many teachers teaching in many different circumstances: experiences of success and of frustration and of puzzlement.

The truth is, writing is not a body of theoretical knowledge or precepts. Writing, rather, is a body of practices and strategies and activities—above all, a *craft*. Therefore if we truly want to teach writing, we must engage students in the activities of craftspersons. We must ask them to be writers and see themselves as writers. The premise of the book, then, is that we can and should treat our students as writers—putting strong faith in them yet also making strong demands on them.

The best way to explain what this book is about is to list some of the important things we know about writers:

Writers are not all alike. Therefore, there is no single "writing process" or lock-step set of procedures that works for all writers or is appropriate for all students. Indeed, even the same person needs different processes on different occasions and for different kinds of writing. *The Writer's Craft* is based on the premise that students are no more like each other than other writers are, and that it is counterproductive to try to impose one alleged "writing process" on all students for all writing.

Writers make choices. Since writers are *not* alike, it follows, then, that they encounter different problems as they work and employ different strategies. Therefore this book is not organized in a linear fashion where every student follows the same path. Rather, it assumes that students will blaze their own trails. As each assignment is presented in the book, students are given numerous important but necessary decisions to make. (For example, "Do you want to start out by making an outline before you have done any writing, or wait until you've explored your ideas on paper or written a discovery draft? Good writers proceed in both ways.") Some assignments offer a great deal of guidance to the student and others offer very little. In short, the assignments as a whole follow a coherent path, yet there are many opportunities for choice.

Writers learn to write by writing. This book, therefore, does not require a lot of reading *about* writing. Instead it constantly invites the student to write: to write often, in many different forms and contexts, and for different audiences.

Writers learn by reflecting. Writers think about what they do. They observe themselves, learn from practice, think about the choices they make. They talk to others who are engaged in the same business, sharing problems and successes, and comparing the writing choices each of them made. So this book asks students to look not only at *what* they write but at *how* they write, to reflect for themselves on the complicated vagaries of their own writing processes, and to talk with other students and with teachers about how things went.

Writers learn by reading. Thus the book puts a big emphasis on reading the writing of others: the writing of fellow students in the class, the writing of well-known published writers, and some writing by students in other parts of the country (which is included in the book). The readings by published writers in the wider world are not just literary pieces: they also represent a wide range of other types of writing—from magazine articles to scripts to workaday on-the-job writing. The book reprints these writings as chances for students to see what other writers have done: not as pieces to revere—to put under glass like paintings in a museum—but rather as opportunities for students to come at them as fellow writers and questioners. Always, throughout the book, the question is, "Let's see: what choices was the writer making here?"

There is a community of writers. A few writers may squirrel themselves away from others and write entirely on their own, but, as the last two points above illustrate, most writers have important connections with other writers and with a larger community. The teachers behind this book have consciously emphasized this connected model of the writer. The book asks students to work with the smaller community of other writers in the class: to talk about writing and compare notes and drafts and discuss the writing process and give responses to each other. And it also asks students to work with and see themselves as part of the larger community of writers and readers in the world.

Writers must care about what they write. If they just do exercises, if they just find ideas and transmit them *like telegraph operators,* they will have no personal investment in what they write. This book shows students how to find writing ideas that matter to them. It encourages them to take responsibility for what they write, take ownership, take pride.

Writers have a lot to say. Because students are young and inexperienced—because they sometimes even tell us, "I

have nothing to write about"—it is tempting to think of them as empty vessels that must be filled. But the teachers behind this book have found that their best teaching comes when they emphasize not what students *don't* know and can't do, but what they *do* know and can do. When we build on the considerable knowledge and language skills that students already have, they learn new things much faster. Experienced writers trust their own thinking, and students, too, must be given some confidence in themselves to function at their best.

Good writers explore and discover as they write. The book helps students to learn how to start from what they *don't* know as well as from what they do know—and then write their way to understanding. In short, writing is thinking, not just recording what is already worked out in some book or in one's mind. To write is to observe, to analyze, to solve problems, to make decisions. This book gives students continual practice in various forms of thinking.

Writers should experiment. The teachers behind this book made a conscious choice to push for a variety of writing experi-

ences. Students should write in diverse modes. They should push at the edges of their experience and develop skills that come from trying various kinds of writing—from learning logs to narratives to essays to visual "story boards." And not all writing need be earnest and heavy. Writers and students need low-stakes writing, too, in order to learn to take some of the risks and have some of the fun that is necessary if a writer is to develop. So while the book asks that most major assignments go through multiple drafts and be carefully revised, it also asks students in the "sketchbook" and journal sections to make quick sketches and learn to play with writing.

Teachers have a unique opportunity with this program. The perspective that writing is a craft, and that students learn most from writing, provides teachers with an exciting role. Instead of feeling compelled to lecture or provide ready-made advice that fits all students and all situations, a teacher can instead be a coach, guide, responder, and nudger—one who will encourage those students who are too timid or fearful, and yes, push those who need a push.

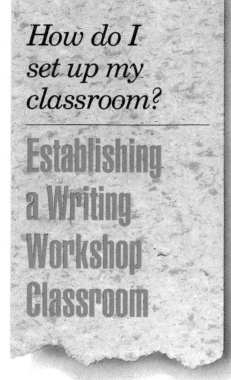

How do I set up my classroom?

Establishing a Writing Workshop Classroom

Author:
Linda Lewis, Writing Specialist, Ft. Worth Independent School District

How can a teacher organize a classroom for effective writing instruction? Perhaps predictably, there is no one best way. Outstanding writing classrooms take many different forms, each reflecting the preferences and personalities of the teacher and students who form that particular writing community. All effective classrooms, however, provide a caring, supportive environment that encourages even the most reluctant students to grow as writers. This environment is based on certain expectations:

• Everyone writes
• Everyone shares
• Everyone responds

If these expectations are met, a fourth goal is achieved:

• Everyone succeeds

Creating a Favorable Atmosphere

An effective writing classroom is actually a social place — an interactive community of writers. In such a classroom, the students are responsible for their own learning and committed to their own growth as writers; however, they are equally responsible for the learning and development of others.

Establishing Expectations. The teacher's approach to writing can have a tremendous impact on the classroom. Therefore, the following attitudes should be evident in every day's activities.

• **Writing is a meaningful activity**
To help students realize that writing has purpose, they should be encouraged to read as much as possible and to become aware of the power of the written word. Magazine excerpts, speeches, business proposals, and newspaper articles are all excellent vehicles for making this point. To reinforce this understanding, the students' own writing must be done for real purposes and real audiences. *The Writer's Craft* can be used to give students opportunities to apply their skills in activities as diverse as oral histories and storyboards.

• **Everyone can write** The basic assumption that underlies an effective writing classroom is that everyone has both something to say and the basic tools with which to say it. Even reluctant writers should be engaged in producing whole texts, not just sentences or paragraphs. The teacher can reinforce this expectation by emphasizing and evaluating not only the student's final writing product, but also his or her individual process and progress.

• **Writing involves sharing and responding** The purpose of almost all writing is communication. Therefore, students should be encouraged to share

their writing at every stage of the writing process and to solicit the types of responses that they need from their peers. See pages T24 – T27 for more information on peer response and collaborative learning.

Setting Up the Classroom. The arrangement and content of the classroom itself can dynamically reinforce and enhance the feeling of a writing community.

• **The furniture** Student desks or tables can be arranged in many different configurations to facilitate various aspects of the writing activity. For example, some teachers prefer to have the class carry out individual and large-group activities with desks in traditional rows, rearranging them in clusters for collaborative work or peer-response sessions and in a large circle for sharing finished work. Others designate specific areas of the room for various writing activities, perhaps providing an editing corner, a conference table, tables for group response activities, and an area with student desks for private writing.

• **Displays of illustrative materials**
Writing — by the students, the teacher, and professional writers — should be profusely displayed in the classroom, and changed as the teacher or students discover exciting new models. Several drafts of a given piece of writing, quotations by published authors about their writing process and products, and favorite writing samples can be included in these displays. A special motivational display, for example, could include brief autobiographical blurbs and pictures that students compile for their hypothetical future books.

• **Reference sources** In addition to providing an appropriate arrangement of furniture and motivational displays, an effective writing classroom should include a reference area stocked with various dictionaries, thesauruses, handbooks, and other reference books.

Some teachers also provide files of writing done by students in previous classes.

Roles of Teacher and Students

To promote the individual and collaborative goals of effective writing instruction, both the teacher and the students must be aware of the different roles they can play in the classroom.

The teacher's roles. There is no one writing process that will work for all students in all writing situations. Therefore, an effective writing teacher is a co-writer, collaborator, coach, and facilitator, rather than a lecturer.

• **The teacher as co-writer and collaborator** Probably one of the best ways for a teacher to advance the expectations of a writing classroom is to become a writer along with the students. In sharing not only finished writing products, but also work in progress, the teacher can instruct students through direct involvement and interaction.

• **The teacher as coach and facilitator** In addition to writing with students, the teacher can facilitate their learning in many ways. For example, during exploratory activities the teacher can help students find topics in which they can become invested; during drafting, support and problem-solve with individual students as needed; and during revision, provide guidance and individual or small-group instruction.

Monitoring writing groups is another way the teacher can help writers to grow.

The students' roles. Like the teacher, the students in an interactive writing classroom play many different roles.

• **The student as writer** It is important that students view themselves as writers with ideas to communicate to others, not as students completing an assignment for the teacher. The kinds of "real world" writing assignments included in *The Writer's Craft* can help create this attitude in the classroom. So can the use of peer response groups and an emphasis on other actual audiences. Probably the most important way to make students feel like writers, however, is to *treat* them as writers, to respect their ability as craftpersons and encourage them to analyze writing problems, explore options, and experiment with techniques.

• **The student as collaborator** In a writing workshop classroom, students are encouraged to share work in progress, help each other problem solve, and contribute ideas to the work of peers, if asked. Students who are not used to such an arrangement may at first have difficulty with this more open approach to writing, and should be allowed to work independently. However, teachers can encourage interaction by having writers work with single partners initially, and then combine to form groups as they become conversant and comfortable with sharing.

• **The student as responder** Student writing improves dramatically when students share their writing with each other. (See Peer Sharing and Peer Response on page T24.) There are several specific ways that teachers can help students become effective peer responders: (1) have students evaluate "training papers" by students from other classes before addressing the writing of classmates, (2) have them role-play successful and unsuccessful response groups and critique the interactions, (3) model appropriate comments using transparencies such as those available in the Teacher's Resource File.

Ensuring Success

The success of a writing classroom depends largely on three factors: (1) clarity of goals, (2) commitment to working toward them, and (3) criteria for assessing progress and achievement. The teacher who is able to establish a favorable atmosphere for writing and clear goals for writers as described above, is well on the way to success. Developing concrete standards of evaluation and making students aware of them is another important factor.

Standards of evaluation Students are more apt to become successful writers if they understand the specific criteria by which their writing will be judged before they undertake an assignment. The Standards for Evaluation in the Guided Assignments, as well as the Guidelines for Evaluating Writing in the Teacher's Resource File, can help students become familiar with and learn to identify the qualities of good writing and develop strategies for effecting them as they write.

In addition, students should be encouraged to reflect on their writing process as they complete each piece. They should also examine their writing portfolios from time to time and note their consistent strengths and weaknesses as well as specific aspects of their development as writers.

A writing workshop classroom can be a lively and stimulating place. And when it is successful, the teacher's expectations and those of the students become reality: everyone writes, everyone shares, everyone responds, and everyone succeeds.

How can I combine literature, writing, and grammar?

Integrating the Language Arts

Authors:

Arthur N. Applebee, Professor of Education, State University of New York at Albany

Judith A. Langer, Professor of Education, State University of New York at Albany

The English language arts curriculum has always been compartmentalized into a variety of special topics, including literature, writing, and grammar. Thought of as separate subjects, they have competed for time and attention in the classroom and in instructional materials. In this view, if we give more time to writing, then we must give less time to literature or grammar. This compartmentalization reflects a "building block" approach to student learning, implying that the various aspects of the language arts can be taught separately and yet can still be put together by the student into some meaningful whole. This approach lends itself well to neatly organized segments of curriculum planning, presented in elaborate scope and sequence charts meant to coordinate the teaching of particular skills within each particular segment of the English curriculum.

Yet this building block approach does not fit very well with the ways in which human beings learn and use language. Rather than learning skills in isolation, we learn them best in the context of experiences. Young children learn to talk because they want to communicate their needs and share their interests with those around them. Older students similarly learn to read and write most effectively when they are reading, writing, and talking about things that interest and matter to them — and when they have a purpose for reading and writing about these things. An integrated approach to the language arts is much more effective in promoting "higher literacy" in students than the building block approach.

The workshops in *The Writer's Craft* reflect the importance of an integrated approach to student language learning, and offer a variety of ways in which teachers can foster the integration of writing with literature and grammar. Some general suggestions follow.

Integrating Writing with Literature

The primary emphasis in many English classrooms is on the teaching of literature. The following suggestions provide ideas for integrating literature with the kinds of writing activities suggested in *The Writer's Craft*:

1. Let students think through writing. Use the students' responses to the literature — their developing understandings and interpretations — as the prompt for a writing activity. As students discuss and debate their responses, the motivation and opportunity to work out their ideas in writing can develop naturally out of their discussions. This is particularly true with the selections in McDougal, Littell's *Responding to Literature* series, which places a similar emphasis on a process-oriented approach to the teaching of English language arts.

2. Use literary selections as springboards. The literature students read may suggest similar situations they want to explore, or concepts they want to analyze, or it may prompt them to create their own contribution to a particular genre.

3. Use selections as examples of how other writers have gone about the craft of writing. Students can profitably spend some time discussing their responses to the selections, sorting out their differing evaluations and interpretations, before examining the ways in which the selections have been shaped and crafted.

4. Let students explore their understandings of and reactions to other students' writing. Examples of student work can be discussed in the same ways that you discuss published selections. If drafts are available, student work may be particularly useful in highlighting the choices a writer makes, and the effects those choices have on readers.

Integrating Grammar Instruction

Students gain effective control of the conventions of written English when they are given many opportunities to use them in the context of their own writing. Isolated exercises in punctuating dialogue, for example, are likely to mean very little to students; learning how to punctuate dialogue because they want to incorporate it into a narrative of their own is much more likely to lead to long-term learning. Similarly, practice in the use of conjunctions in subordinate clauses will be little more than game playing; addressing subordination in the context of developing a complex argument is much more likely to lead to a real mastery of the thinking strategies that underlie such grammatical devices.

To integrate grammar with writing and literature:

1. Encourage students to examine unusual features of the literature they read. Discuss how those features influence students' reactions. For example, students may become aware of the effect of Hemingway's short, simple sentences or of James Joyce's complex syntactical arrangements.

2. Emphasize specific writing conventions that may help while students are drafting or revising particular types of writing. Information about how to punctuate dialogue is likely to be particularly relevant when writing a story or reporting on an interview, for example. Information about formal versus informal usage is likely to be most relevant in writing to unknown or distant audiences.

3. Use opportunities for publication to provide instruction in grammar and usage tailored to individual students. Problems with the conventions of written English are usually highly individualized. In any given class, one student may have trouble with pronoun referents, another with managing the subjunctive, and still another with semicolons. Instruction to deal with such problems will be most effective as each student is revising a work to share with others. At that point, they will usually have a fairly clear idea of what they want to say, and are likely to be ready for help in saying it as clearly and effectively as they can. The Mini-lessons in the Grammar and Usage Handbook are particularly useful in this context.

4. Let students teach one another. Some of the most effective instruction in grammar can come from peer responses to student writing. Because different students have different strengths, they can provide very effective help in "polishing" one another's drafts for publication — and the process of explaining the suggestions they make will strengthen each student's understanding of effective grammar and usage. For example, student pairs can help by reading each others' work and marking a "check" on any portion of the paper that doesn't "sound right" to them. The "check" can highlight questions about spelling, mechanics, grammar, or word choice and can signal useful places the writer can rethink when polishing the piece.

Each of the workshops in *The Writer's Craft* highlights one or another aspect of grammar and usage in the context of the particular types of writing that students are being asked to do. Rather than isolated skill and drill, this grammar content is designed to highlight the relationship between knowledge of the conventions of language and the craft of writing. Each workshop encourages students to experiment with language to make their own writing more effective.

The Language Arts Trio: Literature, Writing, and Grammar

Approached in these ways as interrelated segments of larger activities, the language arts "building blocks" can be taught just as systematically as the old scope-and-sequence charts implied — but much more effectively. When teachers integrate literature, writing, and grammar in their instructional program, the language arts will build upon and support each other. Instead of completing isolated lessons that assume the students will later be able to transfer the separate language arts skills to real literacy situations, students will learn language skills in complete and meaning-laden contexts in the first place. Thus, students' reading, writing, and language skills will develop in concert, in ways both students and their teachers recognize as meaningful, purposeful, and useful.

Is there a way to get students more involved?

Peer Sharing and Peer Response

Author:
Peter Elbow, Professor of English, University of Massachusetts at Amherst

Paul Goodman once said, "If we learned to speak the way we learn to write, there'd be lots more people who can't speak." Why? Because in many classrooms the context for writing is inexorable: the student writes, the teacher grades, and the teacher is the only audience. Imagine what speaking would be like if we spoke only to one person, and if every time we ever spoke, we were evaluated. Is this really the best way for students to learn to write? Does this diet of nothing but teacher grades and "corrected" papers really provide students with the nourishment they need to be better writers? *And* do tall stacks of papers only for teachers' eyes make for sane writing teachers?

There is another alternative: peers as audience and peers as responders. Peers are not a substitute for teachers as audience and responders, but a supplement or addition. Classmates are not asked to evaluate or correct each others' papers but rather to do what they are best at: to function as an audience, and provide an honest account of how they understand the text, how they reacted, and what was going on in their minds as they read. More and more teachers are finding peer responding a crucially helpful strand in their teaching.

Why Use Peer Response?

The use of peer response groups helps teachers to create a powerful change in their classrooms. Why is peer response so effective?

Students need audiences. One of the greatest weaknesses in student writing is a lack of awareness and connection with audience. When students write only for the teacher (which usually means for a grade), they often fall into certain bad habits — treating writing as an empty school exercise, and attempting simply to just "get it right" or "give teachers what they want." Yet surprisingly, students often care less about what they turn in to

teachers than they do about what they read to or share with each other. They often hand writing to teachers that they don't really believe in.

When students write for their peers, however, they become very concerned about what they say and how they say it. In fact, the most powerful thing about the regular use of peer sharing and response groups is that students naturally and easily begin to learn that writing is not so much a matter of "figuring out what the teacher wants" but rather of discovering what they themselves have to say and then seeing whether they have gotten it across effectively to readers.

Just as this textbook tries to teach students that not everyone writes in the same way, so too does it teach students that not everyone reads in the same way. Peer response introduces students to the complex but ultimately empowering truth that the same text often produces different responses in different readers. The writer is then left in the position of having to evaluate those different responses and make writerly decisions about how to revise.

Teachers need relief. Another powerful reason teachers are making more and more use of peer response groups is brutally practical: the paper load for teachers. Students don't learn to write well unless they write a great deal — which means writing more papers than teachers have time to read carefully and comment on. Peer sharing and response groups provide a way to increase the amount of writing that students do while assuring them of a response. For even though students may not be skilled at providing evaluation and advice, they are excellent at providing the one thing that writers need most — *an audience*.

Types of Response

Most students have never written words that they didn't turn in to a teacher for evaluation and criticism. Yet limiting feedback to this kind of response can cripple students' writing. Student writing almost always takes a big turn for the better when this traditional audience-relation is balanced by use of the other relationships described below. Indeed, this variety of types is crucial, for it provides the ideal "balanced audience diet" that students need — a balance among different relations to readers.

Private writing. Students need opportunities to write privately — to do some writing that they don't show to anyone. This provides a crucial foundation of safety and comfort in writing and an arena for risk-taking.

Pure sharing. Students need opportunities to share their writing with readers — but sometimes just for the sake of sharing with no response at all. This increases the risk ("going public"), and yet still provides a strong degree of safety since there is no feedback. The emphasis is placed on *communicating* rather than *feedback*. Sharing heightens the social dimension of writing, and there is also an enormous amount of extremely efficient learning that goes on, especially when the sharing is oral. Nothing teaches us so much about writing as the feel of our own sentences in our mouths and the sound of them in our ears. The process also gives students experience in working in groups before having to learn feedback techniques.

Limited feedback. Students sometimes need opportunities to share writing and get responses — but not get criticism. By holding off the question of "how good is the writing?" students discover what is probably the most useful kind of feedback — learning how readers *understand* their words. Limited feedback, therefore, involves more risk, more feedback, and more learning. But because there is no criticism or advice, students find it a rewarding way to share, and can listen nondefensively to responses from readers.

Full feedback. By working in peer groups in the two ways previously described, students heighten their reading and responding skills. Now they are ready to give and receive responses to the more demanding writerly questions like these: "What worked well and not so well? What suggestions do you have?"

This textbook provides a rich range of specific suggestions, prompts, and examples to enable students to learn how to become good peer responders to each other. By taking advantage of these techniques, students will find an audience, their teacher will gain time to teach, and writing will remain the exciting exchange of ideas and opinions it should always be.

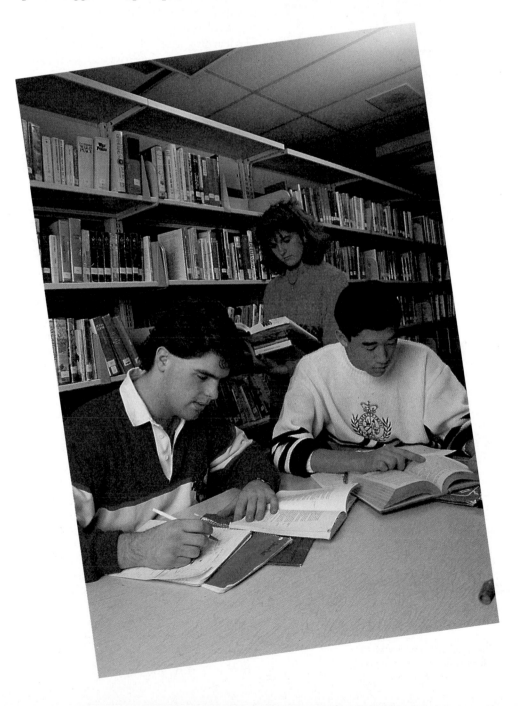

Is there a way to get students more involved?

Collaborative and Cooperative Learning

Author:
David Wallace, Researcher with the Center for the Study of Writing at Carnegie-Mellon University

Learning to use one's knowledge in collaboration with others is essential for success in and out of school. Consequently, group learning is becoming central to classrooms across the curriculum.

Collaborative learning is defined as any group activity that asks students to work together on a task. Advocates of collaborative learning assert that it motivates students to learn, improves social skills, and promotes self-esteem in students of all abilities. The students work together, and the teacher focuses on the different groups, carefully listening, watching, suggesting, and being prepared to work through any problems that naturally arise in the context of group work.

In **cooperative learning,** a more structured type of collaborative work, the success of one individual is linked to that of others. Each group member is responsible for helping other members to learn and for contributing a piece to a whole. Cooperative learning might be used, for example, if students were directed to stage a play, create an advertising campaign, complete a complex report, or produce a book of oral histories. Each student is held accountable for his or her own contributions and each student's mastery is assessed.

The following is a list of strategies for using collaborative and cooperative learning with your students.

Getting Started

Divide the class into groups. Group students of differing abilities or talents together; assure students that creativity, problem-solving abilities, listening skills, empathy, and writing skills share equal importance in group work. Also, remind students that while they are responsible for their own learning, they are also responsible for helping others in the group to learn. Students should work together in an atmosphere of care, acceptance, trust, and support. Competi-

tion has no role in collaborative learning. The size of groups depends on the purpose of the collaborative effort. Small groups of two or three students each are most appropriate when students are sharing personal writing and will benefit most from the individual attention one or two peers can offer. Larger groups of no more than six members can be effective too, particularly if the assignment is large or complex.

Specify objectives and purpose. Set clear, specific goals and objectives for each collaborative learning session. Also make sure students understand on what criteria they will be assessed.

Provide a structure. Assign specific responsibilities to students working in groups, or have the students do so themselves. For example, students working in a discussion group can take on specific roles, such as facilitator or discussion leader, recorder, reporter, and materials manager. If students are working cooperatively on a larger project, such as a research report, the assignment itself may be divided into parts and assigned; each student is responsible for completing his or her share of the work and for helping to join the pieces into a cohesive whole.

Monitor progress and achievement. The teacher's role during cooperative learning is that of facilitator or consultant. As group members work together, the teacher should circulate among them, mentally noting behavior and participation for future performance assessment. If necessary, the teacher should enter a group to clear up any misunderstandings or to ask questions that will direct students' thinking. If more than one group is having difficulty, the teacher may interrupt to reteach or clarify a point with the entire class.

Address assessment. Certain informal collaborative situations, such as peer response, require no evaluation procedure. Some situations, however, require assessment and grading to keep students account-

able for successful group process, for their own learning, and for that of other group members. Options for using grades to reward students for group learning include:
• averaging individual scores within each group;
• giving a single score to all group members who have worked cooperatively on a single product;
• giving all group members the lowest score;
• choosing at random one group member's paper or exam to grade;
• giving individual scores plus bonus points for successful group performance and the development of social skills

Students should share in the assessment process by evaluating their own performance and that of their group. Students may judge that they've been successful if they have met the designated goals of the collaborative learning session. In evaluating group process, they might consider such questions as, "Did I feel supported? challenged? confronted? Were feelings hurt or were ideas shared and feedback given in an encouraging, supportive way? How might we improve the process next time?" Teachers and students should discuss what works and what doesn't work in group process and brainstorm together on ways of improving collaborative learning skills.

Ideas for Collaborative Learning

The Writer's Craft encourages students to work together in groups to explore concepts and ideas, problem-solve, brainstorm, and collaborate during all phases of the writing process. The collaborative learning activities that follow can be effectively adapted for use in the English classroom.

Collaborative planning. While students working alone during the planning stage rarely go beyond deciding what information to include in their texts, students planning in pairs or small groups consider the full range of writing variables and keep them in mind throughout the writing process. Developed at the Center for the Study of Writing at Berkeley and Carnegie-Mellon University under co-director Linda Flower, collaborative planning helps students become more aware of their writing process; students learn to evaluate and think critically about their writing options, and through dialogue with teachers and peers, they learn to monitor their own learning about writing.

Before students begin to draft a writing assignment, divide the class into pairs or groups of three; have them take turns in the roles of writer and partner, talking through their writing ideas. While the writer talks about his or her plan, partners help the writer by acting as a sounding board, listening carefully, asking for clarification or elaboration, and suggesting alternatives. For collaborative planning to be successful, writers should be prepared to discuss their ideas about content, audience, purpose, and form; partners should be prepared to support the writer, help elaborate writing plans, and explore new possibilities.

Jigsaw projects. Students may choose to work collaboratively on any large or complex project, dividing the assignment into "pieces" and assigning each student to a piece. Students creating a video, for example, could divide the project into such "pieces" as research, scriptwriting, direction, and production. Students would then work together to meld the pieces into a coherent whole.

Learning partners. After presenting new information on a topic or giving an assignment to the entire class, have students review the material out loud with a peer, using their notes as necessary to summarize or explain. For example, students could meet in small groups after grammar instruction. They could take turns paraphrasing the new rules out loud, presenting examples of the concept at work, or finding examples in their reading. The whole group can then complete or review the answers to the practice activities together, make necessary corrections, and submit a single set of answers for grading.

Research groups. Students may conduct research on a topic and pool information into a written or oral report. Students will need to divide the work load equally, with each person responsible for researching a particular aspect of their outline. Students will join the pieces of information into a cohesive whole; one grade can be assigned to the entire group.

Problem solving. Have small groups of students work together to address a problem of mutual concern in the school or community. Students should first brainstorm a list of ideas and issues, select and narrow a single topic, develop and then execute a plan of action, such as a letter-writing campaign, petition drives, community interviews, editorial writing, and so on. Groups should periodically report the status of their efforts to the entire class.

Are tests the only way to check progress?

Assessment and Response to Student Writing

Authors:
Arthur N. Applebee, Professor of Education, State University of New York at Albany
Judith A. Langer, Professor of Education, State University of New York at Albany

Traditionally, much of the work in the teaching of writing has occurred in the process of responding to and assessing what students write. Teachers have given students topics to write about, and then have spent a great deal of time marking the papers that result — giving grades, making suggestions for ways the writing could have been improved, and correcting errors.

Such an approach is exhausting for teachers — the paperload quickly becomes overwhelming — and discouraging for students — whose papers "bleed" with the teachers' red penciling. Such an approach also works against what we know about the writing process. When students write about topics that have substance and depth, we can expect their work to be characterized by growth and change over time. They will try out and abandon ideas. They will reorganize sections. Beginnings and endings will drift out of alignment with the rest of the text and need to be redrafted. This is the "normal" state of affairs among the best of writers, and characterizes the *process* of crafting a text.

For students to engage in the kinds of thoughtful exploration described above, evaluation — judgments about how well the work has been done — needs to be separated from response — reactions to the paper and ideas for further development that come from an interested reader. This is because evaluation, although well-intentioned, can become too much a focus of ongoing instruction, and therefore inhibiting to students; it teaches them not to take risks, not to try new forms, not to draft and redraft, but to concentrate on letter-perfect work that says little and goes nowhere.

Response is the critical feature in writing instruction; it helps students know what works, what doesn't, and how to go about improving what they have written. The ideal writing environment invites students to engage in exploratory writing and offers response to work-in-process.

Evaluation and grades are postponed until later.

Providing Effective Response

Teachers can use a number of strategies to ensure that students receive sufficient and helpful response to their work. The most powerful is the use of peer readers and peer response groups (see pages T24–T25). The following suggestions should also be kept in mind:

1) Limit the amount of writing to which you, the teacher, respond.

Writers need frequent responses from interested readers, but that does not mean that the teacher needs to read everything that is written. Instead students may be asked to share with each other initial brainstorming about a topic, to reflect upon one another's notes and journals, and to respond to early drafts.

These early drafts and explorations have served their purpose once they have been discussed with an interested reader, or mined for the nuggets that will become part of later drafts. Therefore, there is no reason for the teacher to read them, too: indeed, the teacher can become a bottleneck and may inadvertently turn students back toward thoughts already abandoned.

2) Respond to work in progress as a collaborator rather than an evaluator.

Teachers can, of course, be very helpful while students are working on their drafts. They can show new ways to solve writing problems, suggest other issues to consider, and offer their own responses as readers about what parts are clear, what parts are interesting, and what parts fail to convince. These kinds of responses are instructional in the best sense: the teacher's suggestions about work in progress can become part of the developing writer's repertoire of strategies and models, available for use in other contexts.

Exploring Assessment

Reader response is certainly the most productive way to respond to student writing, but evaluation is, of course, necessary. Report cards demand grades, and students want to know how they are doing. But there are a number of ways in which evaluation can be managed so it supports rather than subverts the processes of teaching and learning.

Choose criteria carefully. Since writing should be considered a process for exploring ideas and sharing them with others, it follows that conventions of writing should be treated as part of this process rather than as the focus of instruction. It is easy, however, for both writers and teacher to get bogged down in usage and mechanics.

Therefore, to prevent both writers and evaluators from losing track of the key issues of writing, it is important to have clear, consistent standards about what "writing well" will mean in your class. If "writing well" is to mean exploring ideas and experimenting with ways to share them effectively, then students who try to do this should be rewarded with higher grades — even if their experiments lead them to make mistakes. A new and difficult task, completed with some uncertainty, may reflect much more growth in writing achievement than a simple task completed with little thought and no "error."

Use a variety of evaluation methods.
In recent years, teachers have developed a number of different ways to formalize their evaluations of student writing. Most of these have been used in the context of large-group assessment, where the concern is with how well students are doing *relative to* one another or to some external criterion. Using such procedures (for example, general impression [or holistic] scoring, analytic scoring, or primary trait scoring) is generally inappropriate within a classroom when used in a formal sense, but can be extremely helpful when used informally to guide teachers' and students' mutual understandings of the goals of the writing task. These methods, however, should be used sparingly and combined with more flexible techniques such as peer response and

portfolio assessment.

For those occasions when holistic or analytic evaluations are desired, the Writing Workshops in *The Writer's Craft* include specific criteria for evaluation of various types of writing, as does the booklet *Evaluating Student Writing* in the Teacher's Resource File. Underlying these criteria are a few, broad questions that can be used in assessing how well the writing succeeds:
• Is the writer's purpose clear? Has it caught my interest?
• Is there enough detail for me to accept or reject what the writer has said?
• Does the writing carry me through clearly from beginning to end, or are there places where I get lost or miss the point?
• Do the drafts indicate the student is learning to use the responses of readers effectively, or are successive drafts little more than neater versions of the same text?
• Has the writer taken care in the final draft to avoid distracting, careless errors in presentation?

Using Portfolios

Writers vary in how well they write from topic to topic and day to day. Again, this is normal and natural, but we often forget about it when judging how well a writer writes. To offer a well-grounded evaluation of a student's writing skills, we need to examine a broad sample of that student's work.

Portfolios of student work offer one of the best vehicles for classroom-based assessment, for two reasons: 1) They typically contain a variety of different samples of student work; and 2) they make it easy to separate evaluation from the process of instruction. Evaluation can be based on the diverse samples of work in the portfolio rather than on the day-to-day progress of an individual piece of classroom work.

Portfolios take almost as many forms as there are teachers, and can be tailored to virtually any classroom situation. The major options involve the form that portfolios take, what is included in them, and how they are evaluated. *continued*

Portfolio Options

Form. Portfolios are a cumulative collection of the work students have done. The most popular forms include

- a traditional "writing folder" in which students keep their work
- a bound notebook with separate sections kept for work in progress and final drafts
- a looseleaf notebook in which students keep their drafts and revisions
- a published collection of carefully selected and hand-bound work.

Content. Portfolios provide an ideal way to illustrate how a student's work has developed over time, and will give students, parents, administrators, and other teachers a much stronger sense of what students can do. Portfolios may contain

- everything a student writes for a particular class
- a selection of "best work" representing the diverse kinds of writing that a student has done
- selections chosen to represent each of the types of writing a student has done during a grading period
- a diverse collection of a student's performance including drawings and illustrations, tape recordings or videotapes of group work, and readings or dramatic presentations of the student's writing
- drafts and revisions
- a selection of finished work, chosen by the student, the teacher, or the student and teacher working together

Students can also be encouraged to reflect further upon their own progress as writers, providing an introductory essay summarizing their work as they see it in the portfolio. Like the reflective activities included at the end of each workshop in this textbook, such reflection can help students become aware of and take control over their own growth as writers.

Evaluating Content. Just as teachers vary in the form and content of the portfolios they ask their students to build, they also vary in how they use portfolios to determine students' grades.

An approach that many teachers have found to be particularly effective is to base grade a selection of work from the portfolio — chosen to reflect the range of types of writing that students have done during the grading period. Students can be asked to select the pieces to be graded, making the choice themselves or in conjunction with the teacher. With this approach, they should be given guidelines for what to choose: a narrative, a synthesis, and a persuasive essay, perhaps, plus an additional piece of their own choosing. The particular guidelines should reflect the goals and assignments in the writing program during the grading period.

The ability to choose works to be graded — rather than being graded on everything — can be a powerful motivational device as well. Many teachers give their students the opportunity to work further on the selections they want to have graded. Returning to these writings at a later point, students often recognize for themselves ways to make their writing more effective, and may reshape them substantially before offering them for evaluation.

Weaning students from excessive evaluation. Many teachers who are new to such a workshop approach, postponing evaluation rather than interjecting it into the writing process, worry that students want quicker grades. If they aren't graded, will they do the work? One transitional device that works well in many classrooms is to give points when students have completed each separate part of the work. Everyone who completes a first draft, for example, might get a point, with another for doing a revision. These points can be totaled across the marking period to become part of the final grade.

If evaluation is separated from instruction, if criteria for evaluation are kept consistent with those stressed during instruction, and if response becomes a responsibility shared with students as well as the teacher, assessment can become an effective complement to the process of learning to write.

How do I meet the needs of different students?

Teaching Writing to Language Minority Students

Authors:
Marguerite Calderone, Associate Professor of Education in Psychology, University of Texas, El Paso
Sheridan Blau, Senior Lecturer in English and Education, University of California, Santa Barbara

Increases in the immigrant population during the past two decades have dramatically transformed the cultural makeup of many American classrooms. Not since the great wave of immigrations around the turn of the last century have English teachers in American schools been so challenged to meet the special language needs of their students.

Few veteran English teachers are likely to feel professionally prepared to operate successfully in a multi-cultural, multi-lingual classroom. What follows here are some strategies for teaching writing to language-minority students — strategies that research has shown are especially effective with non-English speaking students but which are equally applicable to all students.

Developing Prior Knowledge

The more experience a writer has with the concepts and terms associated with a topic for writing, the easier it will be to write about that topic. Similarly, the more knowledge a teacher has of the culture and background of minority students, the easier it will be to adapt teaching strategies and writing assignments to meet their needs.

Hold class discussions. Clarify cultural references and provide general information to the entire class. Encourage language minority students to comment on similarities to and differences from their own cultures.

Explore teaching alternatives. The use of visual aids and hands-on experiences are effective strategies for building prior knowledge and student confidence.

Encourage students to write about their native customs, holidays, geography, and foods. Such topics will be more comfortable for language-minority students. Additionally, the felt-pride from sharing their native culture will act as strong motivation for writing.

Provide opportunities for reading popular American magazines and newspapers. These activities will familiarize language-minority students with American people, places, and events. Television, movies, theater, and similar cultural activities will have the same impact.

Developing Vocabulary and Genre Knowledge

Mastering English vocabulary and patterns of discourse is essential to building writing proficiency among language-minority students. Students who are asked to write about a school or government election, for example, must be familiar with the terms and concepts of the subject, such as *parties, platform, campaign, run-off, running mate,* and so on. Ideally, preteaching vocabulary would become a regular part of each assignment. *continued*

Similarly, students who are asked to write a mock political campaign speech will feel entirely unable to do so unless they know what one looks and sounds like. All students should be given the opportunity to read a number of models of whatever type of writing they are being asked to produce.

Peer Interaction

Through group discussion, students with limited English proficiency can build a repertoire of concepts, phrases, and rhetorical strategies by trial-and-error, questioning, and modeling. Whenever possible, divide the class into small discussion groups. Each group should include at least one language-minority student. Establish a protocol that requires all students to speak within the group. In this way language-minority students will be exposed to vocabulary and rhetorical strategies they can model and be encouraged to try out their developing English proficiency.

Writing in the Primary Language

There is strong research evidence showing that limited-English proficiency students in American schools can make significant progress toward literacy in English by reading and writing for some time in their primary language, making the transition to writing exclusively in English as they acquire English fluency. Allowing students to write in their primary language during the early stages of English acquisition offers the following advantages:

• It establishes a firm basis for acquiring universal reading and writing skills that are easily transferred from one language to another.

• It promotes success, enhances self-esteem, and builds students' confidence in their abilities as readers and writers.

• It enables students to function at the highest levels of their cognitive abilities,

unhampered by their limited English proficiency.

How can writing in languages other than English become a realistic instructional strategy in classes where teachers don't speak the primary language or languages of their non-English speaking students? Following are some strategies for implementing this instructional strategy:

• Encourage students to write in their primary language whenever they encounter a particularly demanding or complex writing assignment. This will enable them to clarify their thinking about the topic even if no one else can read what they've written.

• Have students write in their primary language only during the prewriting stage. Allowing them to focus their topic, generate ideas, and organize their material in a familiar language will lead to enhanced comprehension and increased motivation.

• Seek out individuals fluent in the student's primary language to act as responders. Such individuals might be teacher aides, parents, or classmates who speak the student's primary language but who are also fluent in English. Of course, if there are several students who share the same primary language, they can act as peer reviewers for one another.

• Invite students to translate their own primary language essays. Such translations should not be treated as final drafts, however, but as rough draft translations produced for the benefit of the teacher. Teachers who receive these translations can respond to the ideas contained in the translated essay rather than on problems in English language usage.

Additional Strategies

Following are some additional strategies for working with language minority students.

• Preview the assignment to spot potential areas of difficulty — with cul-

tural concepts, language requirements, research needs, and so on. Provide preteaching as necessary.

• Read aloud difficult parts of the assignment or lesson, allowing time for questions and clarification.

• Precede writing activities with similar oral activities to allow students to separate the task of clarifying ideas from that of translating them into written form.

• Provide guided practice, especially with prewriting and revising techniques.

• Increased, individualized feedback and monitoring will enhance student comprehension and offer support — both of which lead to more successful writing experiences.

References

California State Department of Education (1981). *Schooling and Language Minority Students: A Theoretical Framework.* California State University, Los Angeles, EDAC.

Cummins, J. (1986). *Empowering Minority Students.* Sacramento, CA: California Association for Bi-Lingual Education.

Damon, W. (1984). "Peer Education: The Untapped Potential." *Journal of Applied Developmental Psychology*: 5, 331-343.

Stevens, R. J.; Madden, N. A.; Slavin, R. E.; & Farnish, A. M. (1987). Cooperative Integrated Reading and Composition (CIRC). Baltimore, MD: Center for Research on Elementary and Middle Schools, Johns Hopkins University.

Calderone, M.; Tinajero, J.; & Hertz-Lazarowitz, R. (1990). "Effective Transition into English Reading Through CIRC." Baltimore, MD: Center for Research on Effective Education for Disadvantaged Students, Johns Hopkins University.

How do I meet the needs of different students?

Addressing Different Learning Styles

People of all ages perceive and process information in different ways. A familiarity with learning styles can help educators develop teaching strategies to meet the needs of all students in the classroom.

The Types of Learners

Research on left and right brain functions has led to a variety of theories about preferred learning styles. The left brain is thought to be the center for analytical, logical, verbal, sequential, and convergent thinking, while the right brain is thought to be the center for emotion and visual, spatial, creative, experiential, and divergent cognitive styles. Left-brain students, who have traditionally been rewarded by the educational system, tend to excel in such school subjects as reading, mathematics, and computer programming. Right-brain dominant students tend to excel in art, dance, music, and geometry.

In addition to left/right brain classification, students are often categorized according to three learning styles: visual, auditory, and kinesthetic.

Visual learners best comprehend and retain information presented in the form of graphs, charts, diagrams, and other visual images, such as fine art and photographs. Often, they benefit from a multimedia approach to learning.

Auditory learners, like visual learners, often benefit from a multi-media approach to learning. They need not only to read it and see it, but to hear it and discuss it.

Kinesthetic learners process information through tactile sensations, learning from activities that enable them to work with their hands or create meaning through movement and physical expression.

Harvard psychologist Howard Gardner has taken the analysis of learning styles and left and right brain dominance to yet another level in his theory of multiple intelligences.

The Seven Types of Intelligence

Linguistic	Verbal excellence, reading and writing skills
Logical-Mathematical	Conceptual, logical, abstract thinking
Spatial	Interest in visual images and pictures; designing, building, and inventing
Musical	Sensitivity to rhythm, singing, moving to and playing music
Bodily-Kinesthetic	Communicating with body language; processing information through bodily sensations
Interpersonal	Organizing, communicating, socializing, understanding others
Intrapersonal	Preferring to work alone and being independent, private, and self-motivated

Everyone has multiple intelligences and different styles of learning. However teachers, who tend to be left-brain oriented and strong in linguistic and logical-mathematical intelligences, often teach primarily in the modes most com-

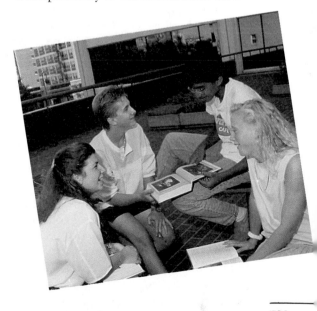

fortable for them. They may therefore be unconsciously leaving a number of students out of the learning process. Yet how can any teacher adequately address the bewildering array of learning styles that may be present in any one classroom?

With its integrated approach to the development of writing, *The Writer's Craft* helps solve this problem by providing students with opportunities to work in a variety of learning modes. Teachers need only encourage students to take advantage of various learning strategies to maximize their intellectual and creative potential.

Applications in *The Writer's Craft*

Teacher's notes throughout the text point out the following learning opportunities:

Fine Art and Illustrations The art program throughout *The Writer's Craft* provides visual or spatial learners with an engaging and entertaining way into the material. Invite students to consider how the art enhances and reflects concepts in the text, and use the illustrations as springboards to creative writing.

Workshops and Related Assignments At each grade level, Workshops and Related Assignments include a broad range of activities, not all of which are writing based. Visual and spatial learners, for example, will particularly enjoy creating story boards, pictorial essays, flow charts and organizational charts, and interpreting art. Auditory and musical learners will especially like creating videos, writing choral poems and song lyrics, and making oral presentations and rebuttals.

Exploratory Activities Workshops begin with a wide range of Exploratory Activities, providing students with options for entering writing assignments comfortably and naturally. The teacher can encourage students to experiment with the options until they find those that work best.

Graphic Organizers Graphic devices

such as spider maps, tree diagrams, flow charts, and pie graphs can be a tremendous boon to visual and kinesthetic students who learn from the physical act of writing ideas, organizing them spatially, and seeing and making the connections between them. Left-brain dominant students can organize their information with time lines, charts, and analysis frames.

Publishing Options The wide variety of publishing options offered throughout the Workshops allows students to tailor their work to their own learning styles. In different assignments, for example, students may be encouraged to include photographs or drawings, build models, incorporate music, or use videotapes, recordings, slides, or photos in a multimedia presentation.

Collaborative and Independent Learning Auditory and interpersonal learners may enjoy working collaboratively to brainstorm solutions to problems, discuss ideas, and share their writing. (See pages T26 to T27.) Peer response sessions are also ideal for these kinds of learners. However, each lesson is so complete that the intrapersonal, or solitary, learner can succeed with little help from others.

Special Help with Learning Disabilities

Learning disabled students typically have average or above-average potential; however, specific areas of deficiency (which vary from student to student) make the processing of information and the acquisition of skills more difficult. Students with learning disabilities often display some or all of the following characteristics.

- Low reading level
- Low motivation
- Difficulty organizing work or ideas
- Poor memory
- Difficulty sequencing and processing information
- Difficulty following directions and

completing assignments

- Difficulty thinking, reasoning, and generalizing
- Hyperactivity and distractability
- Poor fine-motor coordination and handwriting

It is essential to remember that learning disabilities are often physiologically based and beyond the student's control. What can appear to be inattentiveness or an uncooperative attitude may, in fact, reflect an inability to learn through conventional channels.

Whenever possible, teachers should provide opportunities for LD students to process information in their own preferred learning style. This approach will allow them to maximize their intellectual and creative potential in school. The following general strategies, along with any of the alternative strategies described in the section on Learning Styles, will help students get the most from classroom experiences.

- Seat students toward the front of the classroom where there are no obstructions to seeing or hearing.

- Present essential directions or material from the text both orally and in writing.

- Supply visual aids whenever possible to reinforce material from the text.

- To help students compensate for poor short- and long-term memory, repeat important ideas frequently and begin each lesson with a summary of material covered the previous day.

- When giving an assignment, model sample problems on the board, breaking the process down into clearly ordered steps.

- Encourage collaborative learning. Carefully monitor sessions to make sure they take place in an atmosphere of care, empathy, and support.

- Occasionally pair students according to ability for special peer-review sessions. For example, pair an LD student who has difficulties with sequencing and ordering events with a student who is particularly strong in those areas.

I've got a computer... Now what?

Teaching English in The Electronic Age

Author:
Dawn Rodrigues, Associate Professor of English, Colorado State University

New technology brings exciting changes to the curriculum. In the English classroom, the most visible of these changes has been the arrival of the computer, with all of its attendant software. The sheer volume of available material has proven to be occasionally intimidating, but teachers *can* take control of the technology by selectively integrating computer programs and strategies into their teaching.

Benefits of the Computer

Although research on the use of the computer in English classrooms is still somewhat limited, many studies have revealed some significant benefits of using a word processor:

• Students enjoy composing on a computer, tending to write more and work harder at their writing.

• Students do not resist revision, since changes can be more easily executed.

• Collaboration among students increases.

Computers have also proven to be especially helpful with low-ability students or those with handicaps and learning disabilities. First, the actual *physical* act of writing becomes easier, and the process as a whole becomes less intimidating — when words on a screen can be instantly deleted, writing anxiety diminishes. Second, the process of using the computer forces special needs students to focus more directly on their task. Finally, the clean, printed text eliminates some students' embarrassment over poor handwriting — for the first time in their lives, they can be proud of their writing.

In another important benefit, students using computers start to *understand* more about the writing process. As they watch words appear and disappear, as they see chunks of text move from one section of their essay to another, they see the process of thinking and writing in action.

New Strategies for Writing Instruction

With the increasing availability of computers, teachers can recommend that students use composing and collaborative strategies that were not possible before. Many of these strategies, such as invisible writing, listmaking, and the development of a writer's file, can be found in *The Writer's Craft* in the feature labeled Computer Tip. Some other strategies follow:

• Students can leave gaps in their paper where they need to add material or where they want to invite response from others. Notes such as the following, to themselves or their peer readers, can provide the cues: CAN YOU HELP ME THINK OF A BETTER EXAMPLE HERE? or MAYBE THIS WOULD WORK AS THE INTRO — TRY LATER.

• Students can work on portions of the draft that they are most comfortable with, and then electronically paste the pieces together as their ideas take shape.

• Teachers and peer readers can read drafts on screen and leave notes to the writer at the appropriate points.

Making It Work

Making students comfortable with computers does not require that the entire class meet regularly in a lab. At many schools, a teacher can reserve a computer lab on occasion for the entire class. On those days, the teacher can introduce valuable computer-writing techniques, such as the use of an "alternate screen" to store outlines or notes while composing in the other window. Spell-checkers, on-line thesauruses, and specialized software programs can also be introduced. If a lab is not available, the teacher can occasionally bring a computer into the classroom to demonstrate various techniques, run through software programs, or allow students to demonstrate favorite word-processing strategies.

No matter how the computer is used, however, it is important to remember that not all students adapt to word processing in the same way. Therefore, the teacher must be prepared to provide plenty of individual instruction. For example, freed from the restrictions of pen and paper, some students may overwrite. These individuals must be shown how to evaluate content and delete unnecessary material. Other students may have trouble adapting pen-and-paper planning or revision to the screen. These writers could be encouraged to use print-outs in combination with composing on screen until they become more comfortable with the computer.

Conclusion

Computers, when used creatively, can be a powerful addition to a writing class. The computer has the amazing ability to transform itself into whatever the teacher or writer wants it to be — a magic slate for writing, an electronic window to an audience, or an endless resource for ideas and strategies. It allows teachers to create an almost unlimited set of instructional techniques, and a chance to re-envision writing instruction.

What do I do each day?

Planning the Curriculum

The Writer's Craft provides teachers with a unique resource for developing an English program that can be tailored to individual classrooms, teaching styles, and curriculum needs. The flexible Workshop/Handbook format of the books is ideally suited to the demands of the modern classroom, where state, district, and school requirements must all be met even as teachers work to address the specific needs of their students.

Targeting Objectives

State and District Objectives The assignments and lessons in *The Writer's Craft* cover all of the concepts most commonly listed in state and district guidelines. By referring to the objectives listed with every Writer's Workshop and Handbook mini-lesson, teachers can choose those assignments that best allow them to meet the requirements of their own states and districts.

Classroom Objectives Specific classroom needs can be identified through the use of diagnostic materials provided in the Teacher's Resource File. Grammar Pretests and Writing Assessment Prompts allow teachers to pinpoint areas where students need extra help. Writing Assignments and Mini-lessons can then be chosen accordingly.

Literature-Based Objectives English teachers increasingly are being asked to formally integrate the language arts: literature, writing, and grammar. A feature called Linking Literature, Grammar, and Writing, which appears on the Teaching Preview Pages of this Teacher's Edition, provides guidance in linking writing and grammar logically to a piece of literature.

Planning the Lesson

The Writer's Craft provides teachers with a clear, detailed resource for planning lessons.

Teaching Preview Pages The Teaching Preview pages that precede each Writer's Workshop include the following:

- An overview of the Workshop
- A chart of useful support materials from the Teacher's Resource File
- Suggestions for linking literature, grammar, and writing
- Workshop Management Guidelines, detailing the number of days needed for each writing assignment and noting which steps can be completed outside the classroom as independent study

Lesson Plans The Teacher's Resource File includes a booklet of Lesson Plans that help teachers structure each lesson according to the suggested Lesson Cycle on the following page. Included on the Lesson Plans are a review of Objectives and Resources, and suggestions for breaking a long-term writing assignment over several days.

Teacher's Notes Each lesson in *The Writer's Craft* is accompanied by detailed notes that provide helpful advice and teaching strategies. Used during the Teaching Preview, they can help teachers choose approaches and select appropriate support materials from the Teacher's Resource File.

Addressing Different Ability Levels

One of the key problems teachers face centers around the necessity of preparing multiple lesson plans for students of different ability levels. Often, time does not allow such meticulous preparation, or the diversity of student abilities requires a prohibitive number of alternatives. Additionally, pigeonholing students into "ability levels" often ignores the fact that weaker students may excel with some kinds of assignments, while stronger students may flounder on others. The result of this apparently unmanageable situation is often guilt for the teacher and frustration for students.

The Writer's Craft has solved this problem through the structure of its lessons. Built-in options throughout each assignment allow students to choose approaches that best suit their abilities or learning styles. The Writing Handbook and Grammar and Usage Handbook allow students — of any ability level or background — who are having problems to find additional help. Each student, therefore, can proceed as quickly or methodically as he or she likes, without disturbing the rest of the class.

So that students receive the full benefit of these options, the teacher may want to preview the following options within the writing assignments and be prepared to point them out to students during the lesson:

Writer's Choice
Exploratory Activities
Strategies
Publishing Options
Handbook Mini-lessons (cross-references)

The article Addressing Different Learning Styles on pages T33–T34 provides additional useful information.

What do I do each day?

Suggested Lesson Cycle

The lesson cycle presented at right has been proven to be an effective teaching strategy. *Writer's Craft* resources appropriate to each phase of the lesson are listed on the right. The lesson cycle may be applied in two basic ways:

1. As the structure of complete, self-contained daily lessons
2. As the overall structure of a multi-day assignment with the central section (in squares) repeated as often as necessary.

- Pupil Text
- Teacher's Edition
- Resource File

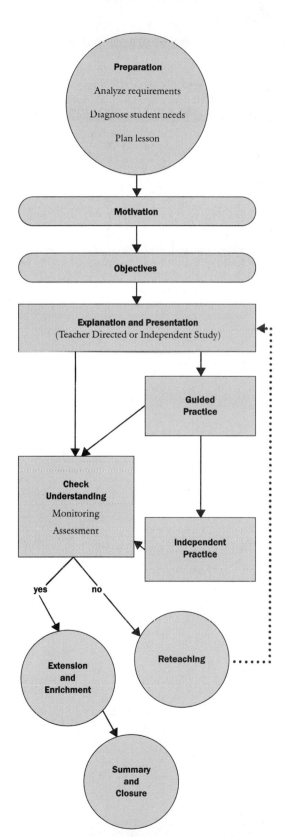

The Writer's Craft

Preparation
State and District Curricula
- Writing Resource Book
- Grammar and Usage Practice Book
- Grammar Pretests
- *The Writer's Craft* Lesson Plans
- Teaching Preview
- Teacher's Choice

Motivation
- Starting from Literature
- Motivate
- Think and Respond
- Springboard

Objectives
- Assignment Rationale
- Objectives
- Set a Purpose

Explanation and Presentation
- Preteaching
- Writer's Workshops
- Handbook Mini-Lessons
- Teaching Strategies
  Teaching Tips
  Individualizing Instruction
  Collaborative Opportunities

Guided and Independent Practice
- Teaching Strategies
- Guided and Related Assignments
- Mini-Lesson Activities and Exercises
- Teacher's Resource File
  Ideas for Writing
  Thinking Skills Transparencies
  Fine Art Transparencies
  Student Revision Model Transparencies
  Peer Response Guides

Check Understanding
- Spot Check
- Teacher's Resource File
  Writing Assessment Prompts
  Guidelines for Evaluating Writing
  Grammar Post-Tests
- Writing Portfolio
- Managing the Paper Load

Reteaching
- Reteaching Notes
- Handbook Mini-Lessons
- Teacher's Resource File
  Writing Resource Book
  Grammar and Usage Practice Book
  Elaboration, Revision, and
    Proofreading Worksheets

Extension and Enrichment
- On the Lightside
- Sketchbooks
- Connections
- Extension and Enrichment

Summary and Closure
- Learning from Your Writing Process
- Summary and Closure

Assignment Chart

Concept Development in *The Writer's Craft*

The Writer's Craft grows in sophistication as your students do, providing a rich variety of writing assignments that become more challenging in every grade. **Guided Assignments** are listed in bold, followed by Related Assignments, in each strand below.

Writing Strands	Grade 9	Grade 10	Grade 11	Grade 12
Personal and Expressive Writing	**Journal Writing to Public Writing** Personal Letter Learning Log	**Autobiographical Incident** Family History Tall Tale	**Memoir** College Application Song Lyric	**Reflective Essay** Autobiographical Incident Monologue
Observation and Description	**Focused Description** Field Notes Haiku	**Observing Situations and Settings** Interview Character Sketch	**Interview Profile** Eyewitness Report Oral History	**Journalistic Narrative** Personality Profile Video
Narrative and Literary Writing	**Personal Narrative** Oral History Storyboard	**Poetry** Story Monologue	**The Short Story** Dramatic Scene Narrative Poem	**Dramatic Writing** Story Choral Poem
Informative Exposition: Classification	**Definition** Extended Metaphor Comparison and Contrast	**Comparison and Contrast** Definition Analogy	**Classification** Comparison and Contrast Organizational Chart	**Explaining Concepts and Ideas** Science Report Collaborative Writing
Informative Exposition: Analysis	**Describing a Process** Cause-and-Effect Analysis Flowchart	**Cause and Effect** Myth Hypothesis	**Examining Changes** Science Fiction Pictorial Essay	**Subject Analysis** Graphic Aid Project Evaluation
Informative Exposition: Synthesis	**Essay of Advice** Consumer Report Problems and Solutions	**Problem and Solution** Advice Essay Group Discussion	**Drawing Conclusions** Lab Report Opinion Poll	**Making Proposals** Rebuttal Oral Presentation
Persuasion	**Supporting Opinions** Letter to the Editor Critical Review	**Controversial Issue** Persuasive Speech Editorial	**Persuasive Essay** Satire Ad Copy	**Argument Analysis** Establishing Conflict Debate
Writing about Literature	**Personal Response to Literature** Point of View Responding to Media	**Interpretative Essay** Interpreting Art Director's Notes	**Critical Analysis** Personal Response Parody	**Literary Analysis** Exploring a Proverb Critical Review
Reports	**The Short Research Paper** I-Search Paper	**Research Report** Saturation Report	**Research Report** Genealogical Research	**Research Paper** Career Search
Writing for Assessment	**Responding to Essay Questions** Responding to a Writing Prompt	**Essays in Other Subjects**	**Written Exams**	**Responding to Readings**

The
Writer's Craft

The
Writer's Craft
Idea To Expression

SENIOR AUTHOR
SHERIDAN BLAU
University of California at Santa Barbara

CONSULTING AUTHOR
PETER ELBOW
University of Massachusetts at Amherst

SPECIAL CONTRIBUTING AUTHOR
DON KILLGALLON
Baltimore County Public Schools

SENIOR CONSULTANTS
Arthur Applebee
State University of New York at Albany

Judith Langer
State University of New York at Albany

 McDougal, Littell & Company
Evanston, Illinois
New York · Dallas · Sacramento · Columbia, SC

SENIOR AUTHOR

Sheridan Blau, Senior Lecturer in English and Education and former Director of Composition, University of California at Santa Barbara; Director, South Coast Writing Project; Director, Literature Institute for Teachers

The Senior Author, in collaboration with the Consulting Author, helped establish the theoretical framework of the program and the pedagogical design of the Workshop prototypes. In addition, he guided the development of the spiral of writing assignments, served as author of the Literary Workshops, and directed the Contributing Authors in the completion of Guided Assignments.

CONSULTING AUTHOR

Peter Elbow, Professor of English, University of Massachusetts at Amherst; Fellow, Bard Center for Writing and Thinking

The Consulting Author, in collaboration with the Senior Author, helped establish the theoretical framework for the series and the pedagogical design of the Writer's Workshops. He also provided material for use in the Writer's Handbooks and reviewed selected units for consistency with current research and the philosophy of the series.

SENIOR CONSULTANTS

These consultants reviewed lesson prototypes to ensure consistency with current research. In addition, they reviewed and provided editorial advice on the completed Writer's Workshops.

Arthur N. Applebee, Professor of Education, State University of New York at Albany; Director, Center for the Learning and Teaching of Literature; Senior Fellow, Center for Writing and Literacy

Judith A. Langer, Professor of Education, State University of New York at Albany; Co-director, Center for the Learning and Teaching of Literature; Senior Fellow, Center for Writing and Literacy

SPECIAL CONTRIBUTING AUTHOR

Don Killgallon, English Chairman, Educational Consultant, Baltimore County Public Schools. Mr. Killgallon conceptualized, designed, and wrote all of the features on sentence composing.

ACADEMIC CONSULTANTS

In collaboration with the Consulting Author and Senior Author, the Academic Consultants helped shape the design of the Workshops. They also reviewed selected Workshops and mini-lessons to ensure appropriateness for the writing classroom.

Linda Lewis, Writing Specialist, Fort Worth Independent School District

John Parker, Professor of English, Vancouver Community College

CONTRIBUTING AUTHORS

C. Beth Burch, Visiting Assistant Professor in English Education, Purdue University, Indiana, formerly English Teacher with Lafayette High School

Sandra Robertson, English Teacher, Santa Barbara Junior High School in California; Fellow and teacher-consultant of the South Coast Writing Project and the Literature Institute for Teachers, both at the University of California, Santa Barbara

Linda Smoucha, formerly English Teacher, Mother Theodore Guerin High School, River Grove, IL

Carol Toomer Boysen, English Teacher, Williams School, Oxnard, California; Fellow and teacher-consultant of the South Coast Writing Project and the Literature Institute for Teachers

Richard Barth-Johnson, English Teacher, Scattergood Friends School, West Branch, Iowa; National Writing Project Fellow

John Phreaner, formerly Chairman of the English Department at San Marcos High School, Santa Barbara; Co-director of the South Coast Writing Project and the Literature Institute for Teachers

Wayne Swanson, Educational Materials Specialist, Chicago, IL

Joan Worley, Assistant Professor of English and Director of the Writing Center at the University of Alaska, Fairbanks; National Writing Project Fellow

Cherryl Armstrong, Assistant Professor of English at California State University, Sacramento; National Writing Project Fellow

Valerie Hobbs, Co-director of the Program in Intensive English, University of California, Santa Barbara; Fellow of the South Coast Writing Project and the Literature Institute for Teachers

STUDENT CONTRIBUTORS

Brandy Barton, Cedar Rapids, IA; Ryan Fiel, San Marcos, CA; Jason Moneymaker, DeSoto, TX; Andy Ness, Seattle, WA; Kathy O'Brill, Northfield, IL; Victoria Reilly, Bethpage, NY; Adam Shoughnessy, Watertown, MA.

TEACHER REVIEWERS

Joanne Bergman, English Teacher, Countryside High School, Clearwater, FL

Regina Dalicandro, English Department Chairperson, Mather High School, Chicago, IL

Sister Sheila Holly, S.S.J., M.A., English Department Chairperson, Saint Maria Goretti High School, Philadelphia, PA

Dr. William J. Hunter, Assistant Principal, English Department, John Jay High School, Brooklyn, NY

Margaret N. Miller, Language Arts Consultant (6-12); Library Coordinator (K-12), Birdville I.S.D., Fort Worth, TX

Janet Rodriguez, English Teacher, Clayton Valley High School, Concord, CA

Mark Rougeux, English and Journalism Teacher; Newspaper Advisor, Glenville High School, Cleveland, OH

Bennie Malroy Sheppard, English Teacher, High School for Law Enforcement and Criminal Justice, Houston, TX

Sue Wilson, English Department Chairperson, Wade Hampton High School, Greenville, SC

ISBN 0-8123-7008-2   TE ISBN 0-8123-7009-0
Copyright © 1992 by McDougal, Littell & Company
Box 1667, Evanston, Illinois 60204
All rights reserved. Printed in the United States of America.

91 91 93 94 95 – VJM – 10 9 8 7 6 5 4 3 2

Contents Overview

Writer's Workshops

WRITER'S WORKSHOP

Guided Assignments

Related Assignments

Writing Handbook

WRITING HANDBOOK

Mini-lessons in
- Writing Process
- Style
- Academic Skills

Grammar and Usage Handbook

GRAMMAR HANDBOOK

Mini-lessons in
- Grammar
- Usage
- Mechanics

Y ou are an individual. You think and act in ways that are uniquely your own. This book recognizes that individuality. On every page you will be encouraged to discover techniques best suited to your own personal writing style. Just as important, you will learn to think your way through every writing task.

In each of the Writer's Workshops, you will experiment with ideas and approaches as you are guided through a complete piece of writing. Cross-references to the Handbooks will allow you to find additional help when you need it. Then, as you write, you will discover what you think about yourself—and about the world around you.

Table of Contents

Starting Points

Writer to Writer introduces students to the philosophy of *The Writer's Craft* and to the idea of a community of writers.

Discovering Your Writing Process demonstrates the recursive nature of writing by following one student through a writing assignment.

For more in-depth treatment of each stage of the writing process, see the Writing Handbook, pages 324–360.

Writer's Workshops

In the *Writer's Workshops*, students learn to write by writing—not by reading about writing.

Each *Writer's Workshop* explores a particular writing type through three writing assignments.

Guided Assignments provide basic information about the writing type and detailed suggestions for each stage of the writing process.

Related Assignments provide varied contexts in which students can apply skills learned in the *Guided Assignments*. A streamlined format challenges students to make their own writing decisions.

Each assignment begins with literature or other professional writing—both traditional and contemporary.

The assignment follows one student through the entire writing process and presents the completed piece of writing as an annotated *Student Model*.

Learning experiences such as the *Video* assignment accommodate individual learning styles.

Narrative and Literary Writing

Sketchbooks offer creative stimuli that encourage students to experiment with writing in no risk activities.

A wide variety of exploratory prewriting activities enable students to find personally meaningful topics and a wealth of background information.

Multiple drafting and revising strategies encourage students to develop a unique writing process that fits their own topics and writing styles.

Informative Exposition: Classification

Questions for both the writer and the peer reader foster self-assessment and peer response.

Standards for Evaluation provides a checklist that enables students to assess how effectively their writing meets the general criteria for a specific writing type.

The *Sentence Composing* features allow students to analyze and imitate the sentences of professional writers, adding variety and sophistication to their own writing styles.

Informative Exposition: Analysis

The *Linking Grammar and Writing* features demonstrate the vital connections between effective writing and standard grammar, usage, and mechanics.

Creative options for publishing and presenting encourage students to share their writing.

Collaborative planning activities in which students help one another develop their writing skills foster an atmosphere of mutual cooperation and support.

Learning from Your Writing Process helps students focus on their composing strengths and weaknesses and grow as writers through learning log activities and and new writing applications.

Preparing an oral presentation provides an alternative format for expression of ideas and develops vital speaking and listening skills.

Informative Exposition: Synthesis

Persuasion

All key modes and purposes are covered in both traditional and non-traditional formats.

Students learn to anticipate audience response by examining underlying assumptions—an important aspect of successful persuasion.

Problem-solving activities and questions lead students to discover and work through issues of primary importance at each stage of the writing process.

Writing activities centered on key literary concepts foster understanding and appreciation of literature.

Writing About Literature

Students combine responses to literature with expression in writing.

On the Lightside enlivens the text with humorous, offbeat, and informative reflections on the fascinating and sometimes contrary nature of our language.

Developing criteria and making judgments are skills that aid students in effectively forming and expressing opinions.

Reports

The research paper affords practice in gathering, organizing, synthesizing, and correctly documenting information.

The practical context of a career search offers an alternative application of research strategies.

Writing for Assessment

Students gain experience and confidence in writing for assessment—an increasingly important task both across the curriculum and in the business world.

GUIDED ASSIGNMENT
Responding to Readings

Writing Handbook Mini-lessons

WRITING PROCESS

Prewriting

Students can use the *Writing Handbook* independently as a reference source, guided by cross-references in the *Writer's Workshops;* teachers can use it as the basis for focused mini-lessons.

Literary, professional, and student models enhance the teaching in the *Writing Handbook.*

Handbook 4 presents graphic devices as invaluable tools for writing, especially for visual learners.

Handbook 2 helps students find writing ideas by examining the worlds within and beyond themselves.

The practical suggestions for collaborative planning in Handbook 6 foster cooperation within the community of writers.

Drafting

Revising and Publishing

Specific, practical approaches to peer response in Handbook 12 enable students to be helpful collaborators in the writing process.

The key topic of elaboration is covered comprehensively in Handbook 9.

The *Style* section—Handbooks 15–21—helps students refine and increase the sophistication of their writing.

The *Academic Skills* section covers topics necessary for success in any classroom.

The suggestions in Handbook 16 are particularly helpful to expressive, descriptive, and narrative writing.

In Handbook 22 comprehensive lists of Greek and Latin roots aid students in vocabulary growth and preparation for standardized tests.

Handbooks 17 and 18 highlight aspects of the language that promote an appreciation of literature and enhance descriptive and literary writing.

Handbook 23 emphasizes the connection between clear thinking and clear writing.

Handbooks 24 and 25 provide an overview of research skills and reference works that enables students to locate and efficiently use the resources best suited to a given task.

Handbooks 27 through 30 prepare students for the world beyond the classroom—college and career.

The importance of the media and of careful application of critical thinking skills is addressed in Handbook 30 and throughout the book.

Grammar and Usage Handbook Mini-lessons

The *Grammar and Usage* mini-lessons present grammar in the context of writing.

Skills Assessment pages—including a pretest, a post-test, and four proficiency tests—provide teachers with the instruments to gauge learning and provide students with practice at taking standardized tests.

Thematic exercises offer usage practice as well as cross-curricular knowledge.

Lessons include a wide variety of exercises: Concept Checks, Drafting and Revision activities, Applications in Literature, Applications in Writing, and Proofreading activities.

Checkpoints occur periodically throughout the *Grammar Handbook* to assess student comprehension of grammatical principles.

Application and Review can be used for review, for extra practice, or as a check of student mastery of a topic.

The *Appendix* provides resources commonly used by writers including a detailed glossary of terms related to composition and literature.

Writer to Writer

DISCOVERING YOUR WRITING PURPOSE

Writing is an extraordinary application of ordinary skills. It offers you both power and knowledge in dealing with and understanding yourself and your world.

Writing as Power

▼

Writing can give you power, for we live in a complicated technological society, and those people who can collect information, order it into significant meaning, and then communicate it to others will influence the course of events within the town or nation, school or university, company or corporation.

Donald Murray, writer and educator

Writers, from the authors of the Magna Carta to the compilers of the NFL rule book, have shaped the world. Your writing, too, can give you power. If you have problems with a friend, school administrator, or car insurance company, you can write an explanation and effect a solution. When you enter the business world, your

As the school year begins, one of a teacher's greatest challenges is to convince students of the relevance of the subject they are about to study. This section is designed to help teachers meet that challenge. The material in this section has two important functions. First, it provides students with a reason to care about writing. Through numerous examples, and using quotes from actual students, it helps answer the critical question "Why write?"

Equally important, the material familiarizes students with the unique three-part organization of this book. It introduces them to the concept of "learning to write by writing" and describes the ten Writer's Workshops that make up the core of the book. It also explains how students can participate in their own writing instruction by showing them how to refer to the Writing Handbook and the Grammar and Usage Handbook as they complete each writing assignment. At the beginning of the year, the teacher should guide students through this section, referring them to appropriate examples of various features as each one is introduced. Notes in the side column throughout this chapter suggest appropriate pages for reference. These page numbers refer students to the progression of a hypothetical Writer's Workshop assignment.

Writer's Workshops

As an example of the kinds of writing covered in the **Writer's Workshops,** have students turn to page 207, which provides an introduction to the key writing assignments developed in Writer's Workshop 7.

Guided Assignments

Suggest that students turn to the **Guided Assignment** on Argument beginning on page 208 to review the kinds of suggestions for writing that are provided in this feature of the book. Here students will find suggestions for starting from literature, prewriting and exploring, drafting and discovering, revising and proofreading, and publishing and presenting their work.

Related Assignments

To show students an example of the kinds of **Related Assignments** offered in the text, have them turn to page 228 for additional applications of the persuasive writing skills introduced in the Guided Assignment. These Related Assignments provide students with tips for starting from literature, prewriting, writing, reviewing, and publishing and presenting their work.

ideas for improvements (as well as your request for a raise) will be met with the suggestion that you "put it in writing." The more effectively you can communicate through writing, the more effective you will be in accomplishing your goals.

The Community of Writers Writing is a craft, and writers must practice it often to learn to do it well. Your progress as a writer, like the writing process itself, will be recursive rather than linear: that is, you will not always move smoothly and continuously forward in a step-by-step progression. Rather, you will sometimes jump forward, sometimes turn back to previous steps, as your writing skills evolve and you find a process that works best for you. As you establish and refine your writing process, you will receive help from your teacher, who functions as an editor and fellow writer, and from your classmates, who serve as peer planners and reviewers. In this way your classroom becomes a community of writers.

As you grow older, you begin to take your place within a larger community of writers as well. You may write an announcement for a company newsletter or an acceptance speech for an annual awards ceremony. You may write a fundraising appeal for your service group, to be mailed to business leaders within your town; you may write to an elected representative, voicing your concern and urging action. You may contribute an article to a nationally distributed periodical. Your writing reaches beyond you, broadening your sphere of communication and influence.

Collaborative Writing One of the benefits of being part of a community of writers is the opportunity to participate in **collaborative writing.** In your classroom, as your teacher directs, you may collaborate with classmates by brainstorming together, by sharing writing tasks on a project, or by working together to revise. Within the larger writing community, for example, you may collaborate with fellow members of an advisory committee to write a proposal for action. Such collaboration exposes you to a wealth of ideas and viewpoints, as well as providing you with helpful support as you write. In the business and academic worlds, in fact, much writing is produced by teams and committees.

This textbook itself is the product of a community of writers. One person could not have written it alone, nor could a group of people working individually. What you see is the result of many people functioning sometimes separately and sometimes collaboratively in a complex community. The skills you learn in this book will enable you to become a fully contributing member of that community.

Writing as Knowledge

> We do not write in order to be understood; we write in order to understand.
>
> **C. Day Lewis, essayist**

In addition to giving you power to affect the outside world, writing can give you insights into that world and, perhaps more important, into yourself as well. Many writers, both professionals and students, have observed that it isn't until they write about a topic that they discover what they think about it. Writing thoughts down is slower than simply thinking them, but writing also extends the range of complexities that the mind can deal with. For example, without writing, you could easily think up something to do on a Saturday, but you could not so easily clarify the links between Flannery O'Connor's life and the themes of her fiction. You would probably need to list events and trace connections in writing to formulate a causal analysis.

Learning logs, journals, and writing portfolios offer excellent opportunities to write for understanding. Recording what you are learning, both in and out of school, in a **learning log** enables you to clarify and reflect on what you have learned. As the number of entries in your log increases, you can watch your reflections broaden and deepen. You also will begin to see connections that enable you to integrate and use your knowledge most effectively.

In **journals,** you have a place to write whatever you like without necessarily showing it to anyone. You can explore your thoughts, clear your mind of problems by writing them out, or experiment creatively with the sounds and rhythms of language. (Some writers also keep a writer's file or sourcebook in their journals, assembling clippings, photos, bits of conversation, and interesting work by other authors.) In a **writing portfolio,** you can collect your finished pieces of writing. By reviewing the materials in your portfolio, you can track your progress as a writer, noting the development of your writing process and of your writing voice.

Have students turn to page 206 for an example of one of the **Sketchbooks** presented in the text. This page provides students with opportunities for ungraded writing that may be useful in the assignments that follow.

Handbooks

As an example of how students can use the **Writing Handbook** to help them during the writing of a Guided Assignment, have them turn to page 472 ("Refining Critical Thinking and Writing Skills") and look at the discussion of arguments and logical fallacies on pages 474–478 of this section. Then have students turn to page 729 ("Using Comparisons Correctly") as an example of how they can refer to the **Grammar and Usage Handbook** to solve problems in grammar, usage, and mechanics as they proofread assignments in the Writer's Workshops or any other work in progress.

USING THIS BOOK

One thing that is always with the writer—no matter how long he has written or how good he is—is the continuing process of learning how to write.   **Flannery O'Connor, novelist**

Professional writers and educators agree that the only way to learn to write is the way you learn any other skill—by doing it. In using this book, you will begin writing immediately, following the specific guidelines presented in the Writer's Workshops. While you write, you will be directed to the **Writing Handbook** and the **Grammar and Usage Handbook** for additional help as you need it.

Writer's Workshops

The **Writer's Workshops** are rich forums for writing. Each workshop focuses on a specific writing strategy or type and allows you to explore it in three different settings—a guided assignment and two related assignments.

Guided Assignments The guided assignments introduce the basic strategy or type and provide specific suggestions for completing the piece of writing. If you need additional explanation or practice as you write, you can consult the handbooks at the back of the book. These assignments encourage you to explore your own approaches.

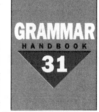

Related Assignments Two related writing applications accompany each guided assignment. The related assignments allow you to extend the skills presented in the guided assignments with more opportunity to structure your own writing process.

Additional Writing Opportunities The book also offers many occasions to play with ideas and practice your style. The **Sketchbooks** give you the opportunity to do short, quick writings that you may or may not share or develop into a finished piece of writing. The **Sentence Composing** features provide numerous sentences from professional writers that you can use as models to improve and vary your own writing style and technique.

Handbooks

Everyone learns by different means and needs different help in the process. This text addresses individual differences by providing detailed information related to writing in handbooks that you can consult at any point in your writing process and in any way you need—for quick reference or for thorough practice of a skill. The **Writing Handbook** covers aspects of the writing process, style, and academic skills; the **Grammar and Usage Handbook** covers grammar, usage, and mechanics.

Adapting the Book to Your Needs

Use this book in any way that works well for you as you complete a specific piece of writing. You will not necessarily use it the same way for every writing activity or the same way your classmates use it. That's appropriate, since every writing situation and every writer is different. This book provides you with the direction, background information, and flexibility you need to write well in any situation and to keep growing personally as a writer.

Sentence Composing feature beginning on page 233 can be used to illustrate the professional models and accompanying sentence-combining exercises that students can use to improve their writing technique and style as they work through assignments in each Writer's Workshop.

Objectives

- To become familiar with the stages of the writing process
- To understand the flexible and recursive nature of the writing process
- To view writing as a process of exploration and discovery

Teaching Strategies

You may want to use this section before beginning the Writer's Workshops if any of the following situations is true:

1. Students are not familiar with the idea of a writing process.

2. Students need to review the terms or techniques associated with the writing process.

3. Students are not used to viewing the writing process as a flexible, recursive activity that can be shaped to fit different writing tasks and individual writing styles.

The belief that "writing is thinking made visible" is central to the instructional approach of this textbook. In every activity, students are shown that writing is a process of examining options, making choices and decisions, and solving problems. It is essential, therefore, that students not view the writing process as a lockstep procedure with one right approach.

To help teachers communicate this idea, this section follows one student through the completion of a writing assignment. The student makes various decisions and choices and uses a number of different techniques. As you discuss the material with your students be sure to ask them what decision they might have made on the same assignment, and emphasize that their decisions are equally valid.

Discovering Your Writing Process

Whenever you write anything—a letter, a poem, an essay, or a postcard—you discover more about yourself and the world. Writing extends and enhances the familiar processes of thinking and speaking and helps you to discover new strategies for creating, communicating, and understanding ideas.

THE STAGES OF THE WRITING PROCESS

There are as many writing styles as there are writers, so your writing is bound to be highly personal—a unique expression of you and your experiences. Nonetheless, most writers work through four basic stages as they write:

- **prewriting**—getting your creative juices flowing by exploring ideas and collecting materials
- **drafting and discovery**—trying out your ideas on paper to see how they sound, how well they fit together, and where they lead
- **revising and proofreading**—reviewing your writing to evaluate how well you have achieved your goals
- **publishing and presenting**—sharing your completed writing with others

Many writers do not work through these four stages in chronological order. Some writers feel more comfortable bypassing the prewriting stage and beginning their first drafts immediately. Others revise one paragraph before writing another. Whatever process they choose, however, all writers share the same goal—to express their ideas and feelings as precisely and as eloquently as they can. So the writing process you should use is the one that works best for you and enables you to achieve that goal.

The diagram at the left illustrates the flexible, dynamic nature of the writing process.

ANALYZING ONE STUDENT'S PROCESS

To understand the writing process in action, consider how one student, Steve, created a piece of writing for publication in a detective magazine. Notice the various writing techniques he used and how he adapted the writing process to suit his personal style.

Prewriting

At this stage of his development as a writer, Steve felt that he was ready to try to get published professionally and decided to write a piece for his favorite mystery magazine. First, he would have to choose a topic. At some point he also would have to establish a general purpose as well as his specific personal goals for writing. In addition, he needed to identify his audience, choose a form for his piece, and gather and develop information. As you analyze Steve's writing process, consider how you might approach the same activity.

Choosing a Topic Recently, Steve had watched a television program commemorating the one hundredth anniversary of Sir Arthur Conan Doyle's first story about the famous sleuth, Sherlock Holmes. The show reminded Steve of a movie adaptation of the Sherlock Holmes tale *Adventure of the Speckled Band,* which had fascinated him. Steve thought he might like to write about Doyle and his fictional detective. He began by doing some freewriting to help him recall his impressions of the Sherlock Holmes character.

ONE STUDENT'S PROCESS

Holmes is a great example of competence in action. Funny, but his pipe never seems to go out, and that cape gives him an aura of mystery and intrigue. I think it would be incredibly exciting to lead the life of an independent, respected detective. And he's always right! Always! He seems cool and distant, yet people are captivated by him. I wonder if Doyle modeled Holmes after himself or someone else he knew. If nothing else, Doyle must have shared Holmes's quick, deductive mind.

Stages of the Writing Process

As students read about the four basic stages of the writing process, ask them if these stages sound familiar from their own writing experiences. Then explain that this section presents the stages of the writing process in detail, and that they should keep their own writing in mind as they go through this section.

Prewriting: Choosing a Topic

Have students compare the interests Steve touches upon in his freewriting—Holmes's personality and its possible sources—with the topic he finally decides to focus on: the various film and video adaptations of the Sherlock Holmes stories. Ask students what points in his freewriting they might have followed up, and what topics they might have consequently settled upon. Use the discussion to emphasize the idea that choosing a topic is a process in itself. Success in this stage depends on keeping an open mind and following a train of associations wherever they might lead, staying alert to possibilities as one explores the information one turns up.

Prewriting: Purpose and Personal Goals

Discuss the difference between a purpose for writing and a personal goal. Help students recognize that the term "purpose" is being used here to identify the effect the writing is intended to have on or for the audience. The personal goal is what the writer hopes to get out of the process of writing the particular piece. Have students identify Steve's personal goal and his purpose. They may, for example, note that Steve's purpose is to present an analysis that will help his audience better understand an interesting literary and social phenomenon. His personal goal, however, is to satisfy his own curiosity about what has made Holmes so popular over the years, a question that may intrigue him because he himself finds the great detective so charming: in solving the riddle of Holmes's popularity he will be finding out something about himself. Emphasize that writers need both a purpose to keep their writing focused and a personal goal—to keep themselves motivated.

Steve then began searching for some facts about Holmes's creator. He found a biography of Sir Arthur Conan Doyle in the city library that explained how Doyle had actually modeled Sherlock Holmes after one of his medical school professors. Because Steve was very interested in movies, he also went to a local video store, where he found fourteen Sherlock Holmes titles. These included a 1939 version of *The Hound of the Baskervilles* and a 1985 adventure tale called *Young Sherlock Holmes*. As he watched these movies, Steve realized that he wanted to know why so many had been made and that he was actually more interested in the video adaptations of the Holmes literature than in Doyle himself. Steve thus decided to focus his writing on these adaptations.

Establishing a Purpose The most common purposes for writing are to **express yourself, to analyze, to inform, to entertain,** and **to persuade.** Sometimes your writing will combine several purposes. For example, if you wrote a humorous story about a bumbling detective, your primary purpose probably would be to entertain your audience. If you discussed your fondness for detective stories, you might have two purposes: to express your feelings and to persuade your audience to read and develop an appreciation for detective stories.

Writers not only establish a general purpose for writing, but they also determine specific, **personal goals** they want to accomplish. For example, you might want to analyze the appeal of an author's works, learn more about a literary character, or understand the historical context of a novel or play. Many writers determine their purpose and goals for writing by asking themselves questions such as the following:

- What do I want my writing to accomplish?
- How do I want my audience to respond to my writing?

As Steve considered these questions, he was able to bring the purpose and goals of his writing into sharper focus.

ONE STUDENT'S PROCESS

Almost everyone knows who Sherlock Holmes is, but most people probably have never thought about why so many movies are made about him. I'd like to explain why movies about Holmes are so popular. Since many of my readers might have seen Young Sherlock Holmes or maybe a TV version of a Sherlock Holmes story, I could start by discussing modern adaptations. Then I could describe some earlier films for comparison. This will give me a chance to talk about how filmmakers convey the drama and suspense created by good writers.

Identifying Your Audience Knowing your audience—the people who will read what you write—will enable you to determine not only what type of information you need to include, but also the best way to present that information. Sometimes your audience will be predetermined. For example, if you are writing a movie review for your school's film club, your audience is the club members. Other times you can choose who your audience will be or decide whether you even want to share your work with others.

Some writers choose to write for their own satisfaction and identify an appropriate audience later. Usually, however, you will want to identify your audience at some point during your writing process. Keeping an audience in mind will help you communicate effectively by tailoring your writing to meet your readers' needs. To help you understand your audience, ask yourself questions such as the following.

- What do my readers already know about the topic? What do they need to know to understand it?
- What aspects of my subject will my readers likely find most interesting?
- What approach and language will make my presentation most effective?

Because Steve planned all along to submit his work to the mystery magazine, he knew his audience would be readers of the magazine. He jotted down some notes about those readers to give him a clearer picture of their needs and expectations.

Discovering Your
Writing Process   **9**

Prewriting: Identifying an Audience

Have students discuss the implications of the fact that Steve knows exactly who his audience will be. Ask them what they might add to Steve's evaluation of what he should present and what he can leave out for this audience. Then ask students to consider how Steve's task would change if he were writing for an audience of science-fiction fans instead of mystery fans. Use this twist to help students recognize the relationship between audience and purpose. If Steve were writing for science-fiction fans, he would not only have to provide more background information, but he would have to try to persuade his audience that mystery fiction is interesting and worth reading about.

Prewriting: Choosing a Form

Have students discuss how the form of a piece of writing depends on the writer's purpose and audience. Ask them to identify some other purposes Steve might try to achieve and what form these purposes would dictate. Then have them go through the same process for different possible audiences. Finally, have students decide if they would have chosen the same form as Steve, given his purpose and audience. Use variations in students' responses to underline the fact that while purpose, audience, and form are related, and writers are somewhat hemmed in by these considerations, they nonetheless have choice and can pursue a variety of different options, depending on their personal interests.

ONE STUDENT'S PROCESS

I can assume that my audience already knows many of Holmes's personality traits and his deductive method of solving crimes. But they will want to know how movies about him capture his personality so well—which actors played him best—and which directors succeeded in conveying Doyle's tone and mood.

Choosing a Form   Form is the type of writing in which you express your ideas. Stories, plays, essays, poems, articles, reports, speeches, letters, and journal entries are different forms for communicating ideas, feelings, opinions, and information. The best form for your writing might not be clear initially, but it may emerge as you focus your topic, consider your purpose and personal goals, and identify your audience. Since Steve already knew where he wanted to submit his piece of writing, he first considered the standards for submitting manuscripts set by the mystery magazine. These guidelines, which were listed in the magazine itself, were very broad, stating only that the material must be original work. Therefore, Steve was free to choose a form for his writing.

Suppose Steve had decided that his purpose was to entertain his readers by showing the humorous side of Sherlock Holmes. In that case, he might have written a comic play full of ridiculous clues for his hero to follow. On the other hand, if Steve had decided to write something for the community film society, he might have written a report explaining the techniques filmmakers used to showcase the mystery and suspense in Sherlock Holmes movies.

Steve had already decided that his general purpose was to analyze the screen popularity of Sherlock Holmes and his specific goal was to help his readers appreciate Holmes's character. He also knew that his audience consisted of readers of the magazine. After considering his purpose and audience, Steve decided that an article would be the most suitable form for his writing.

Gathering and Developing Information   Steve knew that to write a truly informative article, he had to do some research on his subject. He began by watching several videotapes of Sherlock Holmes movies and television presentations. He also consulted several books that included still photographs from Holmes movies. In addition, he read reviews of filmmakers' adaptations of Doyle's stories. Then he read several of the stories themselves.

The librarian who helped Steve find many of his source materials suggested that Steve interview the president of the Deerstalkers, a local club for Sherlock Holmes enthusiasts. Steve developed a list of questions and took notes during the interview. He used quotation marks to indicate the president's exact words.

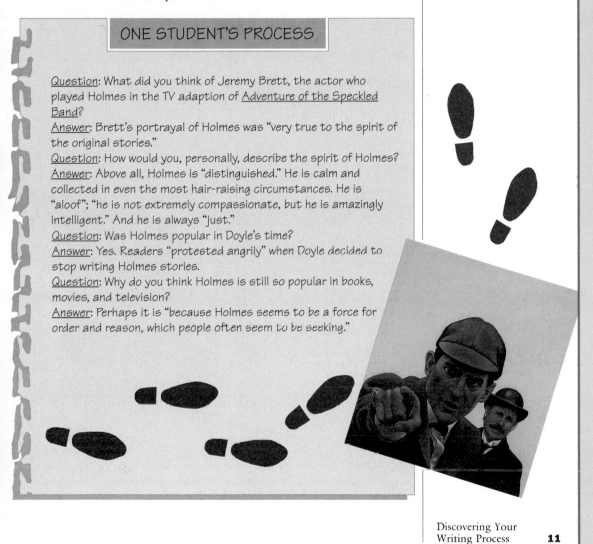

ONE STUDENT'S PROCESS

<u>Question</u>: What did you think of Jeremy Brett, the actor who played Holmes in the TV adaption of <u>Adventure of the Speckled Band</u>?
<u>Answer</u>: Brett's portrayal of Holmes was "very true to the spirit of the original stories."
<u>Question</u>: How would you, personally, describe the spirit of Holmes?
<u>Answer</u>: Above all, Holmes is "distinguished." He is calm and collected in even the most hair-raising circumstances. He is "aloof"; "he is not extremely compassionate, but he is amazingly intelligent." And he is always "just."
<u>Question</u>: Was Holmes popular in Doyle's time?
<u>Answer</u>: Yes. Readers "protested angrily" when Doyle decided to stop writing Holmes stories.
<u>Question</u>: Why do you think Holmes is still so popular in books, movies, and television?
<u>Answer</u>: Perhaps it is "because Holmes seems to be a force for order and reason, which people often seem to be seeking."

Discovering Your
Writing Process **11**

Prewriting: Gathering and Developing Information

As students read how Steve gathered and organized information, have them think about alternatives they might have pursued. What other sources of information might they have explored? What questions would they have added to the ones Steve asked of the president of the club? Discuss the idea that the questions one asks affect the information one gathers. Ask students how the information Steve has gathered from the president might affect the piece he writes.

Drafting

As students read how Steve began his draft, point out that a writer need not identify a clear line between exploratory note-jotting and drafting. If, that is, while he is turning his notes into paragraphs, Steve's thoughts take flight, he does not have to put his notes aside and begin at the beginning of his piece. He can just keep writing, see where his thoughts and notes take him, and then come back and work on an actual, usable introduction later.

Drafting and Discovery

Drafting is the discovery stage of writing—the time when you begin to create and organize your own meaning from the facts and ideas you have gathered. As you draft, follow your thoughts wherever they lead. This is the time to experiment with form and content, to change your opinions or your examples, or even to start over again with a new focus for your writing.

As Steve began drafting his article, he realized that he needed to discuss the character of Holmes in order to explain Holmes's popularity. He looked through his notes and found the following information, which he used to draft a paragraph about Holmes's personality.

ONE STUDENT'S PROCESS

o Holmes is an encyclopedia of knowledge on every subject.
o Holmes is an intellectual, not just another brawny superhero.
o Holmes is always cool and rational, even in the most terrifying situations.
o Everyone daydreams about being as brilliant, self-assured, and invincible as Holmes.

As he drafted, Steve also discovered that his notes contained some information about famous actors who have portrayed Sherlock Holmes. He decided to include a few paragraphs in his article about these actors because he felt they had helped make Sherlock Holmes a popular character. As he looked over the information in his notes, Steve realized he would need more details and anecdotes about the actors.

Like Steve, you can use the drafting stage to expand, alter, or refocus your topic. You may find that you want to backtrack, change your purpose, or broaden your personal goals for writing. Feel free to experiment as you draft. Don't worry about making mistakes in grammar, usage, or the mechanics of writing. You will have the opportunity to correct errors, consider effective word choice, and check your logic later in the writing process.

Because drafting is a discovery process, it usually involves some amount of revision. Some writers continually rework and reshape their writing as they draft. Others write first and revise later. You may find that your first draft needs very little revision; or you may need to write several drafts. You might want to reconsider your audience and purpose for writing. You may need to experiment with form, conduct additional research, or even rethink your topic. No matter how much you revise as you draft, pay attention to the direction your writing is taking, and keep the following questions in mind:

- **Content** Are you developing your initial ideas or focusing on just one or two details? Is a new idea emerging as the real focus of your work? If your writing is taking a new direction, do you want to pursue that or return to your original ideas? What questions might your readers ask?
- **Structure** What are the relationships among the ideas you are expressing—spatial, temporal, causal, comparative? How can you organize your ideas so that they will clearly express these relationships? If your ideas have changed since you began drafting, how should you restructure your writing?

Peer Response

One way to help solve a problem in your life, clarify an idea, or find a new way of doing something is to talk things over with friends. The same strategy can also work when you're writing. Discussion with your peers can help you at any stage of the writing process—to find new ideas, see your subject from a different perspective, or identify problems in logic, mechanics, or usage. Peer responses enable you to see your own writing more clearly and objectively.

Drafting: "Peer Response"

Have students look at the excerpt from Steve's piece in light of the questions he wants answered. Ask them to formulate a few responses to his questions orally and have the class discuss the best ways to express these responses. Point out that writers can hear and absorb responses to their work best if they first receive some positive feedback—what did they do right?

Revising and Proofreading

Have students look at the changes and corrections on Steve's draft. First have them evaluate the choices he made: Did he improve the work? Did he meet the objections of his peer readers? Would students have made the same changes and corrections? Why or why not? Then have students consider the way Steve marked his corrections onto his paper. Discuss the need to mark changes and corrections in a way that is legible and clear; point out that when readers can't follow what they have done easily enough to read their own work aloud smoothly, they may have a hard time knowing if their piece is flowing properly and sounding coherent.

After finishing his first draft, Steve set it aside for a few days. When he reread it, he wanted to change it but wasn't sure how. He had some friends read his draft and respond to these questions:

- What did you like best about my article? least?
- Were there any parts that seemed confusing or dull?
- What message am I trying to get across?
- What did you want to know more about?
- Was the beginning interesting?
- What did you think about the ending?

Here are some of the responses Steve received from his friends.

Your introduction really captured my interest.

How? What did he look like?

Who? How did their portrayals differ from Rathbone's?

"Elementary, my dear Watson." With those four words, Sherlock Holmes dismisses the most complex deductive processes as child's play. Playing that superhuman character, however, could hardly have been easy for the actors who portrayed Holmes. The actor most identified with Sherlock Holmes was Basil Rathbone. Rathbone looked the part. Movie audiences must have agreed, since Rathbone played Holmes many times. The first Rathbone film was Hound of the Baskervilles. This film is highly regarded. Later films, set in wartime London, are less popular. Many other notable actors besides Rathbone have portrayed Sherlock Holmes.

Revising

After rereading his draft and considering his friends' responses, Steve reevaluated his writing and was ready to revise his article.

Like Steve, you should set your draft aside for a few hours—or even days—before revising. When you reread what you have written, you will better be able to evaluate whether you have achieved your general purpose and your personal goals.

As you revise, consider your peer readers' comments carefully. However, make only those changes that you believe will improve your piece. If you do decide to make a change, determine what kind of revision it requires:

- Rethinking content
- Reworking structure
- Refining mechanics and usage

Content Your peer readers' comments, new information or perspective, or knowledge that you have reached a dead end in your writing may lead you to revise its content. You may find that you can improve your draft by reworking it; or you might want to try some different prewriting activities or perhaps even to change the subject of your writing.

When you consider the content of your writing, ask yourself whether you have expressed your main ideas clearly. Also make sure you have developed your ideas fully. The "Checklist for Rethinking Content" on page 392 includes additional questions to consider.

Structure When you are satisfied that your content is clear and fully developed, consider whether your writing is organized as effectively as possible. Look over your peer readers' comments to see if any of them had trouble following your ideas. If you decide to rework the structure of your writing, examine its overall organization. Make sure you have included all the necessary information and arranged it logically. Examine your transitions to make sure they effectively connect your ideas and show the relationships between them. Finally, eliminate any details that blur the focus of your writing. Refer to the "Checklist for Reworking Structure" on page 394 for additional suggestions.

Mechanics After you have revised your content and structure, you can refine and polish your writing by editing, or proofreading, your work. Review your work carefully to make your sentences clear and concise and to correct errors in punctuation, spelling, grammar, and usage. See the "Checklist for Refining Mechanics" and the standard revising and proofreading marks on pages 394–395.

Steve used these marks when he revised his first draft. Notice that he incorporated many of the changes suggested by his peer readers. He also corrected errors he found in the structure and mechanics of his writing.

Discovering Your
Writing Process   **15**

Ask students to look back at the excerpt from Steve's article in terms of the purpose he stated at the outset. How close is he coming to achieving his purpose—explaining why movies about Holmes have been so enduringly popular? Ask students to suggest some revisions of content, some revisions of structure, and some revisions of mechanics that would help bring his piece closer to achieving its purpose. Discuss the differences among these three kinds of changes, and why each, in its own way, is a crucial category of revision.

Have students compare the various listed publishing formats as ways for Steve to publish his piece. Ask them to discuss writings that they have experienced in more than one format. For example, have students ever read a book and then seen a movie version of it? How were the two formats different? What were the advantages and disadvantages of each?

These two sentences will read more smoothly if I combine them.

This sentence has nothing to do with Rathbone.

"Elementary, my dear Watson." With those four words, Sherlock Holmes dismisses the most complex deductive processes as child's play. Playing that superhuman character, however, could hardly have been easy for the actors who portrayed Holmes. The actor most~~best~~ identified with Sherlock Holmes was Basil Rathbone. Rathbone looked the part, —tall, slender, aloof, with arched eyebrows. Movie audiences must have agreed, since Rathbone played Holmes the famous detective many times. The first Rathbone film was Hound of the Baskervilles. Neville Crick, a British film critic, called Rathbone's performance "perfect." ~~This film is highly regarded.~~ ~~Later films, set in wartime London, are less popular.~~ Many other notable actors besides Rathbone have portrayed Sherlock Holmes, including John Barrymore, Raymond Massey, and Peter Cushing; however, the critics' and audiences' favorite was clearly Basil Rathbone.

Publishing and Presenting

For most writers, sharing their finished work is the final stage of the writing process. You may choose not to share journal writing or writing that you feel is incomplete or very personal. You may also continue revising your work even after sharing it. However you choose to handle the publishing and presenting process, you can find many exciting avenues for sharing your work.

Reader's circles Form a reader's circle with at least three other students. Take turns reading your writing to the group and discussing the ideas it conveys and the feelings it evokes.

Writing exchange groups As a class, share your writings with students from another class or school.

Collected works Publish an anthology of student work. The anthology might focus on a particular form or on writings about a particular subject.

Print media Submit your writing to your school or community newspaper or to a magazine.

Performances Dramatize your work and produce it for your class, school, or community.

Videos and multimedia presentations Create a video or multimedia expression of your work. Enhance your writing by using music, slides, pantomime, acting, dance, or a combination of these art forms to accompany it.

Portfolios Collect your work in a file and reread it occasionally. Choose the pieces you like best and mount them in a portfolio of your writing. Use the portfolio as a sample of your work or as a measure of your progress from month to month.

EXTENDING YOUR WRITING PROCESS

You can learn and grow as much from how you write as from what you write. Whenever you finish a piece of writing, reflect on your writing experience as well as your finished product. Ask yourself questions such as the following to help you better understand your process.

- Did I become involved in my topic and learn something important about it?
- Which stages of the writing process were easiest for me? Which were most difficult?
- What part of my writing process is getting easier?
- What was the biggest problem I encountered during my writing process? What solution did I find? How can I use this experience to improve my writing process next time?
- When I compare this piece of writing with others in my portfolio, do I see any changes in my writing style?
- What features of my peers' or professional writers' work would I like to experiment with in my own writing?
- How can I apply the skills I have learned?

Write the answers to these questions and attach them to your finished work before placing it in your portfolio. This record of your writing process will help you become more aware of your progress and goals as a writer and help you attain them.

Swinging, by Vasily Kandinsky, 1925

Humanities Connection

Art Note *Swinging* (1925) is by the Russian painter and theorist Wassily Kandinsky (1866–1944). Kandinsky is generally regarded as the founder of abstract painting. He dispensed with subject matter—landscapes, people, objects—and painted compositions of pure color and form. Ask: Why do you think Kandinsky named his works as if they were musical compositions?

Writer's Workshops

Personal and Expressive Writing

Workshop Overview

Personal and expressive writing is writing that grows out of the writer's responses to events in his or her own life. Such writing offers individuals a way to reflect on the value and impact of their experiences. Most students find it among the most accessible and inviting forms of writing because, in preparation for it, they need little more than their memories and their powers of reflection. This kind of writing is recommended for early in the year for several reasons. Because it is comfortable and familiar, it allows students to develop skills within a nonthreatening context. In addition, it shows students the value of becoming invested in their own writing, an important notion that will serve them well in all other writing they do. The Workshop includes the following Guided and Related Assignments:

1. **Guided: Reflective Essay** helps students develop techniques and strategies for exploring the significance of experiences and for narrating those experiences
2. **Related: Autobiographical Incident** develops reflective and narrative skills introduced in the reflective essay by having students explore and recount a specific incident from their own lives and explain its deeper meaning
3. **Related: Monologue** provides an objective approach to expressive writing by having students examine the inner workings of characters' minds

Preparation Guide

1. Use the Overview above and the Teacher's Choice descriptions on page 21 as a basis for deciding which assignment(s) to teach.

2. Preview the assignment and the teacher's notes. The teaching suggestions and your knowledge of your class's abilities should allow you to identify quickly the concepts that may require preteaching or extra support. The Handbook mini-lessons suggested in the Preteaching notes within the lesson can also provide guidance in this area.

3. Preview the adjacent chart for support materials in the Teacher's Resource File that may be used with this Workshop. Resources are for use with the Guided Assignment unless otherwise noted.

Workshop Support Materials

Resources	For Use With
Ideas for Writing: Data Sheets, p. 1; Additional Ideas, p. 18	Look for ideas, p. 24
Thinking Skills Transparencies: Cause/Effect Chart; *Worksheets*, p. 11	Explore your idea, p. 26
Elaboration/Proofreading, p. 1	Strategies, p. 29
Peer Response Guides, p. 7	Review Your Writing, p. 31
Evaluating Writing, pp. 8, 19–22	Standards for Evaluation, p. 31
Student Revision Trans., pp. 5–8	Problem-solve, p. 32
Elaboration/Proofreading, p. 2	Proofread your essay, p. 32
Tests and Assessment: Prompts, p. 1	

Professional Resources and Media

Books and Journals

Rhea, Philip L. "Writing for Natural Purposes." *English Journal.* Volume 75.2 (February 1985): pp. 43–50. (writing letters, biographies, pamphlets)

Films and Videos

Narration and Description. Films Incorporated Education. (30 min.)

"Narrative and Descriptive." *The Write Course Series.* Dallas Community College District, Mesquite, Texas. 1984. (30 min.)

Computer Software

Finding a Writing Style, Write On: Secondary Collection, Humanities Software, San Francisco, California. Apple II, II+, IIe, IIc. (sentence structure, point of view, writing, editing)

Linking Literature, Writing, and Grammar

The following options may be used to provide students with an integrated language experience. Begin by assigning and discussing any of the recommended pieces of literature, which can be found in most classroom anthologies. Use the suggested strategy to provide a link to the Guided Assignment.

Linking Literature and Writing

Option 1
Starting Point: excerpt from *Hunger of Memory* by Richard Rodriguez on pages 22–23 of *The Writer's Craft*
Strategy: Use the teaching suggestions on pages 22–23 to lead students into the Guided Assignment.

Option 2
Starting Point: "Lines Composed a Few Miles Above Tintern Abbey" by William Wordsworth
Strategy: Point out that Wordsworth wrote this reflective poem while revisiting the ruins of Tintern Abbey after an absence of five years. As students respond to the poem, help them recognize that the scene—as well as the time that had passed since he had last seen it—made the speaker in the poem aware of a sense of loss as well as a sense of new maturity and insight that increasing years brought. Encourage students to think of places or objects that might trigger important reflections and insights for them on which they might base a reflective essay.

Option 3
Starting Point: "The Marx Brothers" by J. B. Priestley
Strategy: As students respond to this essay, ask them to evaluate its structure. What made Priestley think about the Marx Brothers? Where in his essay does he narrate events? Where in his essay does he reflect on his experiences? What conclusions does his draw about the Marx Brothers from his personal experience? Encourage students to consider ways in which they might apply the kind of structure Priestley has used as they write their own essays.

Linking Writing and Grammar

Before the drafting or revision stage of this assignment, caution students to watch carefully the way they use verb tenses. Remind students that if they describe experiences from the past and then discuss their current reflections about them, they should keep verb tenses consistent: past tense to describe past events and present tense to describe current feelings. Ask students to check their work for consistent use of verb tenses as you write the following examples on the board:

PAST TENSE: A huge wave *welled* up and *seemed* about to engulf me. I *screamed* in terror.

PRESENT TENSE: When I *look* back and *think* about that wave, I still *feel* that same terror.

Go over the rules about the consistent use of verb tenses on pages 641–653 of the Grammar and Usage Handbook. If problems with verb tense usage still appear in student papers, assign the exercises on those pages for reteaching. Additional practice can be found in the Grammar and Usage Practice Book on page 41.

Workshop Management Guidelines

The adjacent chart indicates the number of days recommended for each phase of the Guided and Related Assignments. Stars indicate portions of the assignment that may be completed outside the classroom if time is limited or if teachers wish the activity to be completed by students independently.

Reflective Essay
Starting from Literature—1 day
Prewrite—1–2 days*
Draft—1–2 days*
Revise—1–2 days
Publish—open
Learning—1 day*
Reteaching—open
Extension/Enrichment—open
Sentence Composing—1 day*

Autobiographical Incident
Starting from Literature—1 day
Exploring—1–2 days*
Drafting—1–2 days*
Reviewing—1–2 days
Publishing—open
Reteaching—open
Extension/Enrichment—open

Monologue
Starting from Literature—1 day
Preparing—1–2 days*
Creating—1–2 days*
Reviewing—1–2 days
Publishing—open
Reteaching—open
Extension/Enrichment—open

Sketchbook

Objective

To understand the purpose of the sketchbooks

To use a map of an imaginary life and an invitation to create a similar map as springboards to generating ideas for life maps

Using the Prompt

The writing activities suggested in the Sketchbook are designed to be informal in order to allow risk-taking and discovery and should not be graded.

The humorous Bobland map contains elements from Robert Atwan's fantasies but also suggests his many interests. Encourage students to suggest how they might shape maps of their own to reflect their interests. Also invite them to suggest the kinds of symbols and names they might include to reflect important events from their lives. Urge students to use a variety of topological elements, such as mountains, rivers, lakes, cities, and towns, to reflect different elements from their lives, shaping and naming them to reflect different ideas. If a student has a particular interest in tennis, for example, he or she might include a racquet-shaped town named Raquettown on the map.

Use the ideas in the Additional Sketches section with those students who need a different starting point for generating ideas about their lives.

Encourage students to keep their writing in their Writing Portfolios for possible use in the workshop that follows.

Sketchbook

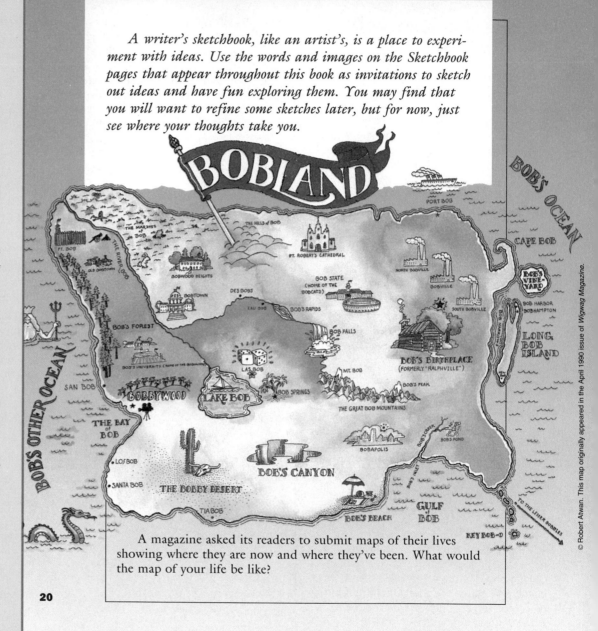

A writer's sketchbook, like an artist's, is a place to experiment with ideas. Use the words and images on the Sketchbook pages that appear throughout this book as invitations to sketch out ideas and have fun exploring them. You may find that you will want to refine some sketches later, but for now, just see where your thoughts take you.

A magazine asked its readers to submit maps of their lives showing where they are now and where they've been. What would the map of your life be like?

Personal and Expressive Writing

Related Assignment

AUTOBIOGRAPHICAL INCIDENT

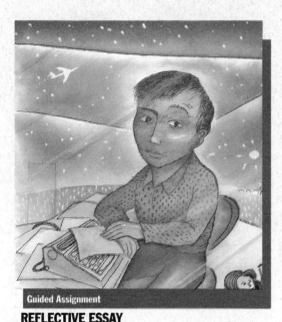

Guided Assignment

REFLECTIVE ESSAY

Related Assignment

MONOLOGUE

All your life you've been learning lessons from the world's best teacher—experience. This teacher has taught you how to manage in your daily life—how to be the best person you can be, how to cope with adversity, how to help yourself and others, how to share joy and sorrow. Much writing that illustrates basic truths about human nature draws on lessons taught by experience.

In the following guided assignment, you will consider some important personal experience and explain what it taught you about life. In the related assignments, you will investigate your past for help in writing an autobiographical narrative and a monologue.

21

Objectives

Guided Assignment:
REFLECTIVE ESSAY
To identify the distinguishing characteristics of a reflective essay; use prewriting activities to choose a topic for a reflective essay; draft, revise, proofread, and share a reflective essay

Related Assignment:
AUTOBIOGRAPHICAL INCIDENT
To identify the basic characteristics of an autobiographical incident; to write an autobiographical incident

Related Assignment:
MONOLOGUE
To recognize the elements of a fictional monologue; to write a fictional monologue

Teacher's Choice

Guided Assignment
Reflective Essay The reflective essay draws exclusively on personal experience, and presents techniques and methods for one of the most familiar and easily executed of the writing modes. Therefore, it may be ideal as a first assignment.

Related Assignments
Autobiographical Incident This Related Assignment calls on students to use narrative skills and visual impressions and should be used after students have completed the guided assignment.
Monologue This assignment is especially useful for those interested in literature, who may base their writing on favorite characters.

Guided Assignment: REFLECTIVE ESSAY

Assignment Rationale

Students will benefit from writing a reflective essay because it alerts them to the connection between life experience and powerful writing and because it calls on them to go through two important thought processes. The writer must *reconstruct and narrate* an experience as well as *recognize and explain* the significance of that experience. The reflective essay has been positioned as the first guided assignment because students will benefit from recognizing early in the year the importance of becoming personally invested in their writing. It is also a good first assignment because students will be familiar with the narrative and feel comfortable as they develop skills.

Starting from Literature

To respond to a professional model of a reflective essay as a springboard for writing

Teaching Strategies

Motivate

Ask students to think of a memory that has become important to them and to examine the kind of thinking they do when they recall the memory. Discuss the way in which recalling and examining significant memories can help clarify them and make them more valuable and meaningful.

Tap Prior Knowledge

Ask students to recall a time when they were alone, working on something that was important to them. Have students share how they felt after they had been working for a long time. Explain that, in the excerpt they will read, Richard Rodriguez describes working on his autobiography.

Reflective Essay

Reflective writing employs memories of a past event to make a statement about human experience. As a small boy Richard Rodriguez came to the United States from Mexico with his family. In this excerpt from his autobiography *Hunger of Memory*, Rodriguez uses his mother's reactions to his first published essay to reflect on the life and obligation of a writer.

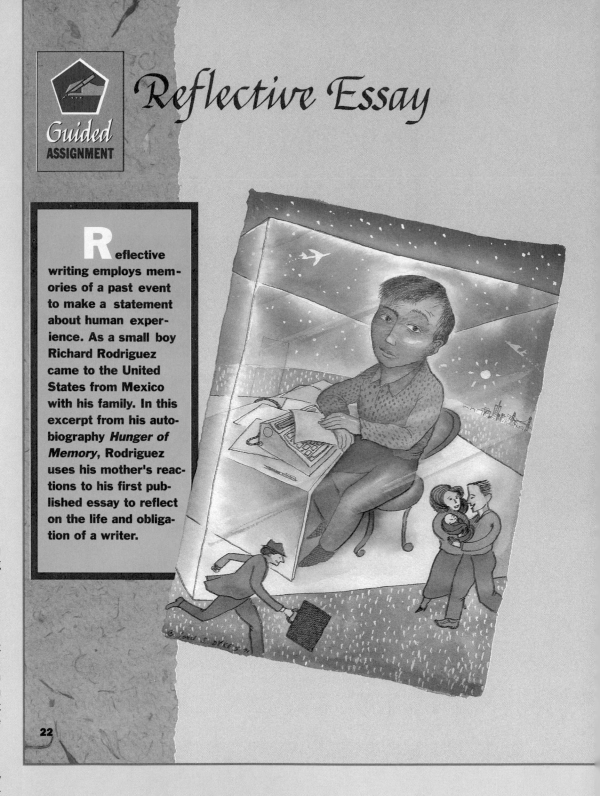

22

by Richard Rodriguez I am writing about those very things my mother has asked me not to reveal. Shortly after I published my first autobiographical essay seven years ago, my mother wrote me a letter pleading with me never again to write about our family life. "Write about something else in the future. Our family life is private." And besides: "Why do you need to tell the *gringos* about how 'divided' you feel from the family?"

I sit at my desk now, surrounded by versions of paragraphs and pages of this book, considering that question.

Hunger *of* Memory

When I decided to compose this intellectual autobiography, a New York editor told me that I would embark on a lonely journey. Over the noise of voices and dishes in an East Side restaurant, he said, "There will be times when you will think the entire world has forgotten you. Some mornings you will yearn for a phone call or a letter to assure you that you still are connected to the world." There *have* been mornings when I've dreaded the isolation this writing requires. Mornings spent listless in silence and in fear of confronting the blank sheet of paper. There have been times I've rushed away from my papers to answer the phone; gladly gotten up from my chair, hearing the mailman outside. Times I have been frustrated by the slowness of words, the way even a single paragraph never seemed done.

I had known a writer's loneliness before, working on my dissertation in the British Museum. But that experience did not prepare me for the task of writing these pages where my own life is the subject. Many days I feared I had stopped living by committing myself to remember the past. I feared that my absorption with events in my past amounted to an immature refusal to live in the present. Adulthood seemed consumed by memory. I would tell myself otherwise. I would tell myself that the act of remembering is an act of the present. (In writing this autobiography, I am actually describing the man I have become—the man in the present.)

Times when the money ran out, I left writing for temporary jobs. Once I had a job for over six months. I resumed something like a conventional social life. But then I have

turned away, come back to my San Francisco apartment to closet myself in the silence I both need and fear.

I stay away from late-night parties. (To be clearheaded in the morning.) I disconnect my phone for much of the day. I must avoid complex relationships—a troublesome lover or a troubled friend. The person who knows me best scolds me for escaping from life. (*Am* I evading adulthood?) People I know get promotions at jobs. Friends move away. Friends get married. Friends divorce. One friend tells me she is pregnant. Then she has a baby. Then the baby has the formed face of a child. Can walk. Talk. And still I sit at this desk laying my words like jigsaw pieces, a fellow with ladies in housecoats and old men in slippers who watch TV. Neighbors in my apartment house rush off to work about nine. I hear their steps on the stairs. (They will be back at six o'clock.) Somewhere planes are flying. The door slams behind them.

"Why?" My mother's question hangs in the still air of memory.

The loneliness I have felt many mornings, however, has not made me forget that I am engaged in highly public activity. I sit here in silence writing this small volume of words, and it seems to me the most public thing I have ever done. My mother's letter has served to remind me: I am making my personal life public. Probably I will never try to explain my motives to my mother and father. My mother's question will go unanswered to her face. Like everything else on these pages, my reasons for writing will be revealed instead to public readers I expect never to meet.

Richard Rodriguez uses this es say to reveal important truths about life as a writer. What kinds of details does he use to create a strong portrait of a writer's life? How does he vary his sentences to strengthen the impact of his essay? What incidents from your own life revealed important truths to you?

Literature Connection

Author Note   Richard Rodriguez was born in 1944 and grew up in San Francisco. He was educated at Stanford, Columbia, the University of California, Berkeley, and the Warburg Institute, London. His autobiography *Hunger of Memory* describes his alienation from his own culture.

Prewrite and Explore

Objectives

1. To use prewriting techniques to choose a personal experience on which to base a reflective essay
2. To uncover the deeper significance of the experience
3. To recognize narrative techniques that can be used in a reflective essay
4. To identify goals and audience for the reflective essay

Preteaching

Preview the Prewrite and Explore section. If there are skills or concepts students may need help with before prewriting, present them at this time. The mini-lesson references below may help you in your selection and instruction. The cross references in the pupil text give students access to the same lessons for independent study.

Handbook Mini-Lessons
- Writing Variables, p. 329
- Reflecting, p. 331
- Hypothesis Testing, pp. 472–473

You may also find the Data Sheet for this assignment useful during the Prewrite and Explore phase. Other materials that may be useful are the Thinking Skills Transparencies; the Thinking Skills Worksheets; the Fine Art Transparencies: Starting Points for Writing; the Writing Prompts for Fine Arts Transparencies; and *Ideas for Writing*.

INVITATION TO Write

Writing *Hunger of Memory* taught Richard Rodriguez important lessons about life as a writer. Now write your own reflective essay based on an experience that taught you a lesson about life.

When you write a reflective essay, you do not simply narrate an important personal experience. You take that experience one step farther by showing its larger significance—how it reflected or underscored some important truth about life. Reflective writing enables you to share a part of your life with your readers and also prompts them to think about similar experiences in their own lives. Autobiographies, letters, and memoirs frequently contain reflective writing.

PREWRITE AND EXPLORE

HANDBOOKS
FOR HELP & PRACTICE

Writing Variables, p. 329
Reflecting, pp. 331–332
Hypothesis Testing, p. 472

1. Look for ideas. Try some of the following activities to help you remember experiences in your life that have taught you important lessons about the world and your place in it.

Exploratory Activities

- **Experience inventory** Freewrite about some "first experiences" and some "most experiences." Use the following suggestions to get started, but feel free to add any others you wish: the first time I was left on my own, the first time an adult really listened to me, the first time I fell in love, the first time I knew I was grown up, the most foolhardy thing I ever did, the most embarrassing thing that ever happened to me, the most courageous moment of my life.
- **Photoplay** Look through an album of family photographs. Do the photos remind you of any special experiences from your past? Freewrite in your journal about any remembrances of people and places suggested by these photographs.

• **Heroes and heroines**   A reflective essay can also be based on an incident from the life of someone you admire. Make a list of people who inspire you. What have these people done to earn your admiration? Jot down some notes about an incident from each person's life that best illustrates his or her heroic qualities.

Teacher Gloria de Souza developed a unique approach to education that has made her an important force for change and improvement in India's schools.

• **Reading literature**   A line from a story, play, or poem can often spark memories of past experiences. What personal experiences do the following quotes from literature suggest to you? Add any of your favorite literary quotes to this list and respond to them as well.

"It was the best of times, it was the worst of times."
Charles Dickens

"I have always depended on the kindness of strangers."
Tennessee Williams

"He feared most of all the choices, that cried to be taken."
Gwendolyn Brooks

"Fame is fickle food . . ."
Emily Dickinson

2. Choose an idea.   The prewriting activities you've engaged in should have yielded a long list of remembrances—both personal experiences and the experiences of others. If you are still searching for ideas, check your journal, look at the writing you did for the Sketchbook on page 20, or try the suggestions in "Apply Your Skills" on page 37. Then decide which of the experiences you've come up with would make the best subject for a reflective essay. To make an effective choice, keep in mind the purpose of reflective writing—to relate an incident from your past or from the life of another person and show how it illustrates some basic truth about human nature or experience.

Look through your list for experiences that will enable you to fulfill this purpose. You might want to talk over some possible choices with classmates. Which experience interests them most? Why? Which experience do they feel teaches an important lesson? Do any of their experiences remind you of incidents in your own life?

PROBLEM
S O L V I N G

What experiences have had special meaning to me?

Teaching Tip: Exploratory Activities

Before having students do the first Exploratory Activity, be sure they recognize that they will be sharing their work with peer reviewers and may be asked to publish their essays. Caution them against choosing a topic that is too personal or that may cause them embarrassment.

Stumbling Block

Students who are having difficulty coming up with an essay idea may find the Data Sheet for this assignment particularly helpful. You may also want to use the Fine Arts Transparencies or refer students to *Ideas for Writing*.

  Individualizing Instruction

Cultural Differences   As students select their topics, be aware that some cultures and some families do not approve of sharing personal experiences. Steer students for whom such sharing may not be acceptable in the direction of selecting heroes or heroines to write about.

   Auditory Learners   After making their initial lists of ideas, auditory learners may benefit from brainstorming ideas aloud in small groups, letting one idea trigger another.

Social Studies Connection

   Political and military leaders as well as figures in social movements often use their autobiographies to explore important times in their lives during which they made fateful choices. Encourage students to read autobiographies of leaders in fields that interest them to see how the leaders' experiences influenced their views and actions.

Stumbling Block

Some students may find it difficult to dig into the deeper significance of their experiences. Encourage these students to dig as far as they can, but point out that the deeper significance of their experience may become apparent only as they actually begin writing their essays. To help them delve deeper, encourage them to ask themselves such questions as: "Why do I remember this experience more clearly than others?" "What was most important to me during this experience—my own behavior or the behavior of others?" "What different emotions did I go through during the experience? Why did my emotions change?"

Collaborative Opportunity

Students may benefit from working in small groups as they explore the meaning of their experiences. Group members may be able to provide insights that are not obvious to the individuals who actually had the different experiences.

3. Explore your idea. Reflecting on a subject means giving it complete and thoughtful consideration. As you reflect on the meaning of the experience you've chosen, don't settle for its most obvious significance. Your essay will be more meaningful if you dig a little deeper. In fact, *digging* is a good way to explore the significance of your experience.

Imagine you're an archaeologist exploring the remains of some ancient village. As you uncover one layer of artifacts—pottery fragments, tools, bits of jewelry —you learn something about the people who inhabited this village. If you stop at the first level, however, your information will be incomplete. So you uncover a second layer, and then a third, and so on until a complete picture of the village begins to emerge.

You can apply the same process to your idea. Write down the most obvious lesson you learned from your experience. That's the first level of meaning. Then think about what you've written. What else did your experience teach you? Write two sentences or phrases that extend the lesson you want to communicate. Now you have a second level of meaning. Continue in this manner until you've thoroughly considered your subject. Then use your reflections to write a sentence or two that state the true significance of your experience—the deepest level of meaning.

Shawn decided to write about a sports injury that helped him see his life from a different perspective. Throughout this guided assignment, you will follow Shawn's process as he completes his essay. Here's how he reflected on the significance of his experience. Notice how that significance evolved as he dug deeper and uncovered new levels of meaning.

26   Workshop 1

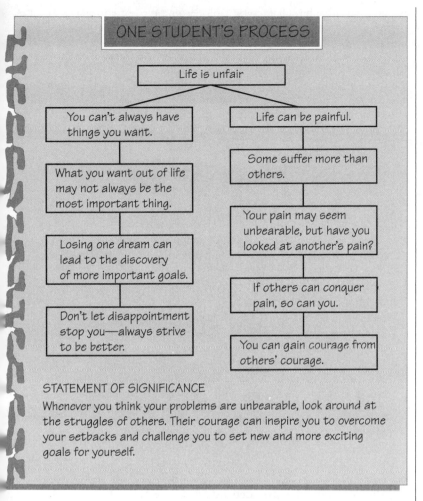

ONE STUDENT'S PROCESS

Life is unfair

You can't always have things you want.

Life can be painful.

What you want out of life may not always be the most important thing.

Some suffer more than others.

Losing one dream can lead to the discovery of more important goals.

Your pain may seem unbearable, but have you looked at another's pain?

Don't let disappointment stop you—always strive to be better.

If others can conquer pain, so can you.

You can gain courage from others' courage.

STATEMENT OF SIGNIFICANCE

Whenever you think your problems are unbearable, look around at the struggles of others. Their courage can inspire you to overcome your setbacks and challenge you to set new and more exciting goals for yourself.

4. Identify narrative elements. A reflective essay relates a personal experience. Sometimes that experience is mentioned only briefly, however, and the writer focuses the major part of the essay on his or her reflections about the experience. In his essay, for example, Richard Rodriguez included some narration of what life was like for him as he wrote his autobiography. Rodriguez, however, spent most of his time thinking about how the experience affected him.

PROBLEM

S O L V I N G

How will I convey my experience and its impact?

Reflective Essay   **27**

Elaborate on the idea of personal goals for a reflective essay by discussing the goals Richard Rodriguez probably had in mind—to help readers understand the life of a writer and to elicit the reader's sympathy—and the goals Shawn probably has in mind—to share an important lesson and to give others hope when they face difficult situations.

Draft and Discover

Objectives

1. To draft a reflective essay, using various narrative techniques to describe an experience and its significance
2. To respond to one's own writing and that of a peer

You may also wish to use the Elaboration Worksheet and the Peer Response Guide during the Draft and Discover phase.

Preteaching

Look through the content of the Draft and Discover section for skills or strategies with which students may need special help. The mini-lessons listed below may help you in your selection and instruction.

> #### Handbook Mini-Lessons
> * Organizing Your Work, pp. 349–357
> * Drafting Styles, pp. 361–362
> * Elaborative Details, p. 376
> * Figurative Language, pp. 435–437

A good narrative has characters, a plot, some type of conflict, and a theme. It also creates a feeling of tension or suspense about the outcome. Think about the story that will be part of your essay. As you do, list the elements that will make it an effective narrative. Identify the characters. Write a brief plot summary. State the conflict. Explain what will create the tension. Describe the theme. The theme is likely to be the statement of significance you wrote after you reflected on your experience. Notice how Shawn planned the narrative section of his essay.

ONE STUDENT'S PROCESS

o <u>Characters</u>—me and Darren, my physical therapist
o <u>Plot</u>—I am injured in a baseball game. After surgery, I learn I won't be able to play baseball anymore. I enter rehabilitation with a bad attitude. Darren shows me the burn unit at the institute. I learn to look at life differently.
o <u>Conflict</u>—I feel if I can't play baseball, my life is just about over. I don't want to do well in rehabilitation—I fight it.
o <u>Tension</u>—Will I give up rehabilitation? Will I change my attitude? Can Darren help me to care?
o <u>Theme</u>—When your problems seem unbearable, look at the struggles of others who are less fortunate. Their courage can inspire you to set new and exciting goals for yourself.

 Writer's Choice   Your essay can be primarily narrative or mainly reflective, depending on the type of experience you have to relate.

PROBLEM
S O L V I N G

What do I want my readers to come away with?

5. Try collaborative planning.   Discuss your plans for your reflective essay with a partner. Cover the following issues:

* Your goals—what your readers will learn, think, or feel
* Your audience—who your readers are likely to be and how difficult it may be for them to understand your point of view

Springboard

To help students delve further into their experiences, write a series of color words, weather words (for example, *calm, stormy, breezy, tornado-like*), taste words, and/or smell words on index cards. Show the cards to the group one at a time, and ask students to jot down words that reflect the tone or feeling of all or part of their experience. Be sure students recognize that the words are not meant to reflect *literally* on their experience; students are to use them to help generate the appropriate emotional tenor in their writing.

DRAFT AND DISCOVER

1. Begin drafting. If you are writing your essay as a narrative, use your plot summary as a skeleton outline for your draft. Conflict should be apparent but does not need to be stated directly. If you focus on reflections about an incident, look for examples, anecdotes, and analogies you can use to clarify your reactions and make the significance of your experience clear to your readers.

2. Organize your essay. The following strategies can help you express your ideas clearly.

Strategies

- **Chronological order** The most common way to arrange narrative events is in the order in which they occurred.
- **Flashback** A flashback takes the reader to an event that happened prior to the present. Consider using a flashback to explain some past event that clarifies the actions in the present. Richard Rodriguez, for example, writes in the present but uses flashbacks to recall events from the past.
- **In medias res** This Latin phrase means "into the midst of things." A writer might begin a mystery story with a murder and then circle back to the events that led up to the murder. Consider beginning your essay in the middle or even at the end to emphasize the significance of an experience.

3. Elaborate on ideas. Precise, vivid words and images will enhance your narration and help you convey the significance of your reactions. Here are some descriptive strategies to try.

- **Simile** A **simile** is a comparison using *like, as,* or *resembles.* Rodriguez used a simile to suggest the difficulty of writing: "I sit at this desk laying my words like jigsaw pieces."
- **Metaphor** A **metaphor** is a comparison between two unlike things that doesn't use such words as *like, as,* or *resembles.* Instead, a metaphor is *implied.* Rodriguez made an implied comparison between still air and memory when he wrote "My mother's question hangs in the still air of memory."
- **Personification** Humans and inanimate objects may be compared through the use of **personification**—endowing the objects with human qualities.

 The ancient DeSoto's engine **protested, coughed,** and **died.**

HANDBOOKS
FOR HELP & PRACTICE

Organizing
Your Work,
pp. 349–357
Drafting Styles,
pp. 361–362
Elaborative Details,
pp. 376–378
Figurative Language,
pp. 435–436

PROBLEM
SOLVING

What are effective ways to present my ideas?

Teaching Strategies

 Individualizing Instruction

Basic Students Basic students may find it useful to organize their ideas on index cards, using separate sets to identify and describe characters, setting, and elements of plot.

 ESL Students Students for whom English is a second language may feel more comfortable drafting their reflective essays in their native languages. Encourage students to write as much as they can in English but to move freely into their native language when they begin to encounter difficulties. Non-English sections of the essays can be translated at a later time after students have gotten all of their ideas down on paper.

Speaking and Listening

Encourage students to experiment with figures of speech like simile and metaphor by brainstorming ways of completing sentences such as the following:

- The sun was shining bright as . . .
- Her hair covered her shoulders like . . .
- A clock is . . .
- The road was a . . .

Collaborative Opportunity

Have students form small groups and discuss stories they have recently read. Ask them to group the stories by the strategies they use—chronological order, flashback, or *in medias res.* Have students share the results of their discussion with the class.

Literature Connection

 Stories to Read Encourage students to find and share examples of figurative language in the following stories: "A Child's Christmas in Wales" by Dylan Thomas and "The Secret Sharer" by Joseph Conrad.

Critical Thinking

Evaluating Ask students to read the beginning of Shawn's essay with a view toward seeing how effectively he is applying the techniques suggested on the previous page. How effective is his use of flashback? Could he use description anywhere to improve the paragraph? What has Shawn done well? What could he do to improve the opening? Encourage students to incorporate into their own writing any insights they gain.

Managing the Paper Load

During the drafting process, encourage students who are experiencing difficulties to confer with you. Trouble-shooting at this point should reduce the number of problems you will see in later drafts.

Writing
═TIP═

Be judicious in your use of figurative language. Overuse can make your writing sound stilted and forced.

• **Analogy** An **analogy** is also a comparison, one that stresses how two different things are alike.

> Kelly approaches her schoolwork the same way a worker bee lives out its life—it's all work and no play day after day.

Shawn began his draft by using precise, vivid language to narrate the incident during which he was injured. Then he described in chronological order what happened during his recuperation and what happened to change his viewpoint about his experience. He concluded by explaining the significance of the experience to him. The following is the beginning of Shawn's unrevised first draft.

ONE STUDENT'S PROCESS

Three years ago this spring, I thought my life had come to an end. On a warm, breezy afternoon in May, I stood on first base during the final inning of a varsity baseball game between my team, the Summervale Panthers, and the team from Roosevelt High. As Roosevelt's pitcher leaned in for the sign, I took a long lead off first base, intending to break toward second with the pitch. As the ball sailed toward the plate, I took off. I slid into second, headfirst, my right arm reaching for the bag. Then the shortstop hurried over to take the throw from the catcher. He stumbled and fell. His knee landed hard on the elbow of my outstretched arm. I heard a loud crack and felt a sharp stab of pain. Then I passed out.

4. Set your essay aside. After you complete the first draft of your essay, take a break. Then go back to the essay, rereading it and sharing it with several peer readers. Use questions such as the following to help you recognize the strengths and weaknesses in what you have written.

Music Connection

Composers sometimes reflect on life in their music. One famous musical reflection is Tchaikovsky's Pathétique Symphony. Its movements reflect on passion, love, disillusionment, and reconciliation. Play one movement for students and ask them to share what it suggests to them.

REVIEW YOUR WRITING

Questions for Yourself

- Are the events in my essay presented in an orderly way?
- Have I used description effectively?
- Is the significance of my experience clear?
- Have I related my experience clearly to the lesson I believe I learned?

Questions for Your Peer Readers

- Did I make it clear why my experience holds such significance for me?
- Did my essay hold your interest? Where, if anywhere, did you feel your interest lagging?
- Is any part confusing? What makes that part unclear?
- When you finished reading my essay, what did you think, feel, or want to do?
- Do my reflections hold true in your life as well? How?

REVISE YOUR WRITING

1. Evaluate your responses. Think about your own responses to your essay and the responses of your peer readers. Consider which ideas would improve the essay. Also consider that an effective reflective essay usually displays certain basic characteristics.

Standards for Evaluation

An effective reflective essay . . .

- is written from the first-person point of view.
- tells about an important experience in the writer's life or in the life of someone the writer admires.
- uses the writer's experience to make a general observation about life.
- encourages readers to think about the significance of the writer's experience in light of their own lives.
- uses precise, vivid descriptive language and images.

HANDBOOKS
FOR HELP & PRACTICE

Unity and Coherence, pp. 382–391
Peer Response, pp. 397–400
Dialogue in Nonfiction, p. 455

Reflective Essay   **31**

Teaching Strategies

Peer Response

As students respond to each other's work, be sure that they recognize that the writers alone make the final decision about which suggestions to incorporate into their work. Writers may wish to have peers respond only to particular questions from the list or to particular questions of their own. You may want to use the Peer Response Guide for this assignment as students provide feedback on each other's work.

Revise Your Writing

Objectives

1. To evaluate the responses to the first draft of a reflective essay
2. To revise the draft based on the writer's assessment of the responses
3. To proofread for errors in spelling, grammar, usage, and mechanics

Preteaching

Preview the Revise Your Writing section. Based on your preview and using your knowledge of your students' first drafts, decide which skills and strategies to review. You may wish to preteach revision by using the Student Revision Model Transparency or the Revision Worksheet for this assignment. The Proofreading Worksheet and mini-lessons listed below may also be useful during preteaching.

Handbook Mini-Lessons
- Unity/Coherence, pp. 382–391
- Peer Response, pp. 397–400
- Dialogue in Nonfiction, p. 455

Guidelines for Evaluation

The following guidelines may be used for a close evaluation of a reflective essay. See the Guidelines for Evaluating Writing in the Teacher's Resource File for additional help with holistic or analytic scoring.

Ideas and Content
- relates an important experience in the writer's life or in the life of someone the writer admires
- describes the experience clearly
- explains the significance of the experience
- includes images as appropriate to convey ideas
- uses precise and vivid language

Structure and Form
- demonstrates a sound organizational strategy, showing relationships among features
- uses first-person point of view
- uses transitional words and phrases to achieve clarity and flow
- draws logical conclusions based on the writer's experience

Grammar, Usage, and Mechanics
- uses standard grammar and usage
- uses correct punctuation
- uses correct spelling

Managing the Paper Load

Keep in mind that you do not need to grade all of the points listed above. You may find it helpful to use the Writing Evaluation Guidelines and Sample Papers for this assignment as you do your evaluations. Students may find the Sample Papers, which contain examples of strong, average, and weak reflective essays, useful in helping them recognize what goes into a strong reflective essay.

Teaching Tip: Revising

Use the Student Revision Model Transparency for this assignment to help students recognize the kinds of revisions that can improve a reflective essay.

Grammar TIP

You are writing your reflective essay in the first person. Be careful to consistently use the first-person pronoun *I*.

Exciting but also confusing. You skip too fast to what happens after the operation.

I like the way tension builds here.

I could use more information. What's a compound fracture? Why can't you play baseball anymore?

32   Workshop 1

2. Problem-solve. Carefully consider your draft in light of your own responses, your peer reader's comments, and the Standards for Evaluation. Think about which suggested revisions are in keeping with your goals and audience. Decide which changes you will make. Then rework your draft. Shawn made the following changes to one section of his reflective essay. Look at the suggestions of one peer reader and notice how Shawn responded to these suggestions.

ONE STUDENT'S PROCESS

After a worried, whispered consultation, the doctors called in a specialist to perform emergency reconstructive surgery.

I was rushed to the hospital emergency room. As I lay in bed following the operation, my arm encased in plaster, the surgeon delivered her verdict. The surgery, she said, had gone well. The bones in my arm would knit together again, and there would be almost no scarring, however, I had suffered no simple broken arm. I *The bones around the elbow joint had shattered, and* had a compound fracture of my elbow and forearm. I was going to need quite a bit of physical therapy to regain the normal use of my arm.

"And I'm afraid," she said, "that your baseball playing *Your elbow will never withstand the stress of throwing a ball with any velocity.* days are over." She said some other things, too, but I was too stunned to listen.

3. Proofread your essay. After you've revised your essay, prepare a clean copy. Read this copy carefully, looking especially for errors in grammar, usage, punctuation, and spelling. Since it is often difficult to see your own mistakes, you might also want to have a friend read your essay to look for any mistakes you might have missed. Neatly correct any errors you find.

LINKING
GRAMMAR AND WRITING

Quotation Marks

If your essay is narrative, you may be including dialogue. Review the following rules for using quotation marks.

1. Periods and commas appear inside the quotation marks.

   "Put these on," he said.

2. Question marks or exclamation points appear inside the quotation marks when they are part of the quoted material and outside when they are not.

   Bob wheeled around and shouted, "I don't believe it!"
   Did he really say, "I've never been more bored"?

3. When a quotation is divided, both parts appear in quotation marks. The first word of the second part of the quotation is capitalized only if it begins a new sentence.

   "I want to know," she said, "when the play begins."

4. Begin a new paragraph each time the speaker changes.

See Grammar Handbook 41 for additional help.

PUBLISH AND PRESENT

- **Publish a book.** With your classmates, turn your essays into a book. Decide on a way to organize the essays—in alphabetical order by author, for example, or by general topic. Create a table of contents. Then copy and bind the essays into book form.
- **Present the essay orally.** Form a small group with classmates and read your essays aloud. Share positive comments about one another's work, and talk about ways the essays reflect experiences that are universal.
- **Create a personal essay collection.** Begin collecting your writing about your experiences. Such a collection can help you probe your feelings and give other readers insights into who you are.
- **Save your reflective essay in your writing portfolio.**

HANDBOOKS
FOR HELP & PRACTICE

**Preparing
Manuscript,
pp. 414–415**

Reflective Essay   **33**

As you confer with students or as you circulate around the room, note the use of the passive voice in students' writing. Have students review the active and passive voice as appropriate, using Grammar and Usage Handbook 34, and encourage students to rewrite passive-voice sentences.

Publish and Present

Objective

To publish and present a reflective essay

> **Handbook Mini-Lesson**
> - Preparing Manuscript, pp. 414–415

Teaching Strategies

Cooperative Learning

Creating a book of reflective essays provides an excellent opportunity for cooperative learning. Students can contribute their special talents to putting the book together. Encourage students to form groups to focus on organizing the book and writing its table of contents, selecting paper and cover materials, designing the cover, creating the illustrations, and developing page layouts.

Personal Touch

If you have written a reflective essay and your students will be sharing their essays in a public way, include your essay along with theirs. For example, you could include your essay in the class book of reflective essays or take part in a group oral reading.

Using the Model

Ask students to identify the elements and strategies in Shawn's work that they think work well. Students will probably agree with the annotations; encourage them to find additional elements that they like. Then ask which of Shawn's ideas or techniques they might like to try in their own writing.

ONE STUDENT'S PROCESS

Out at Second

Shawn O'Malley

Narrative begins with a strong description

Three years ago this spring, I thought my life had come to an end. On a breezy afternoon in May, I stood on first base during the final inning of a varsity baseball game between my team, the Summervale Panthers, and our rivals from Roosevelt high. As Roosevelt's pitcher leaned in for the sign, I took a long lead off first base, intending to break toward second with the pitch. As the ball sailed toward the plate, I took off, digging my spikes into the infield dirt. I slid into second, headfirst, my right arm reaching for the bag. As the shortstop hurried over to take the throw from the catcher, he stumbled and fell. His knee landed hard on the elbow of my outstretched arm. I heard a loud crack and felt a sharp stab of pain. Then I passed out.

I was rushed to the hospital emergency room. After a worried, whispered consultation, the doctors called in a specialist to perform emergency reconstructive surgery. As I lay in bed following the operation, my arm en-

cased in plaster, the surgeon delivered her verdict. The surgery, she said, had gone well. The bones in my arm would knit together again, and there would be almost no scarring. However, I had suffered no simple broken arm. I had a compound fracture of my elbow and forearm. The bones around the elbow joint had shattered, and I was going to need quite a bit of physical therapy to regain the normal use of my arm.

"And I'm afraid," she said, "that your baseball-playing days are over. Your elbow will never withstand the stress of throwing a ball with any velocity." She said some other things, too, but I was too stunned to listen.

More than my elbow was shattered that afternoon. I had been playing baseball since I was able to walk— T-ball, Little League, junior varsity, varsity. I was counting on a baseball scholarship to pay my college expenses. My best friends—my only friends—were the guys on the team. Now it seemed as if everything had been taken away from me.

Suggests the conflict of the narrative

Six weeks later, the cast came off and physical therapy began. During those six weeks, I grew nearly impossible. I spoke to almost no one, and when I did I either lashed out in anger or whined in complaint. My family and friends stopped trying to deal with my mood swings. They left me alone, and I sulked.

Includes good transition to show chronology

My first week of therapy was a similar story. Darren, my therapist, would explain the exercises that would restore mobility to my arm, and I would complain that they were too hard, or hurt too much, and that I really didn't care. By the end of the week, I had become openly hostile with Darren. That's when he took matters into his hands.

When I showed up for my hour-long session on Monday, there was a note from Darren taped to the door. It said to meet him at the entrance to the Culver Wing. When I asked a passing nurse where the Culver Wing was located, he look puzzled. "It's on 3 South," he said. "It's the burn trauma ward."

I stepped off the elevator on 3 South to find Darren waiting for me near the nurse's station. "Put these on," he said, handing me a gown, surgical mask and cap, latex gloves, and slip-on shoe covers.

"What's this for?" I asked.

"Put them on, follow me, and keep quiet," he said.

Use of dialogue adds drama to narrative

We passed through two swinging doors and into another world. I will never forget what I saw and heard as we passed from room to room in that trauma unit.

There was a six-year-old girl whose legs had been burned in a car accident and who was learning to walk again. Darren explained to me that grafted skin doesn't grow or stretch like normal skin, so every step the girl tried to take was agony. She screamed and cried as she

Reflective Essay   **35**

Reteaching

Assess the needs of students who were not successful in developing an effective reflective essay and identify two or three areas in which additional practice is needed. Assign the appropriate Handbook Mini-Lessons, along with the support materials listed for each lesson. Concepts commonly requiring reteaching for this assignment are:

Unity/Coherence: Handbook 10.
Creating Mood: Handbook 16.

The following suggestions and resources may also be useful:

1. Poor Organizing Have students tell the main events from a simple story. As they tell the story, write each event on a separate index card. Show students the different ways you would arrange the cards if you were using each of the three strategies discussed in the assignment—chronological order, flashback, and *in media res*— and discuss the advantages of each method of organization. Conclude by discussing with students which of the techniques would be most effective with their reflective essays.

2. Faulty Pronoun Agreement Select examples of improper use of pronouns and antecedents and copy them onto overhead transparencies or the chalkboard. Discuss with students how the problems should be corrected.

Extension and Enrichment

• Have students recall some of the famous lessons taught through proverbs and fables. (Examples: A stitch in time saves nine; Don't swap horses in the middle of the stream; The grass is always greener on the other side of the fence.) Encourage students to select a lesson they find particularly true and write their own fable or story to illustrate it.

• Have students write about an important experience they have had from the third-person point of view. Encourage them to try to imagine themselves as someone else might see them as they undergo the experience.

Description adds impact to narrative

worked her way along two parallel bars. Somehow, she made it to the end.

In another room, a man about my father's age was lying on a draped gurney. Darren said he had suffered chemical burns when a tank at the chemical plant where he worked exploded. Doctors were stripping off the lifeless, burned skin from his chest, a process called "debridement." A nurse encouraged him to scream to distract him from the excruciating pain.

For the next half hour, as we moved quietly through the trauma unit, I saw and heard much more of the same. Finally, I told Darren I was feeling sick. We left the Culver Wing and walked out into the institute's rooftop solarium. I sat down and dropped my head between my knees as Darren started talking.

"You might not believe it, Shawn," he said, "but just about all those people we saw today will walk out of here. They may never forget their pain, but they'll make it. It seems the worse they're hurt, the harder they try to recover. Sometimes I wonder if I would have that kind of courage."

He paused and then went on. "Think about what you saw today, Shawn. Tomorrow, either be ready to work—and work hard—or don't bother coming back to therapy. Those people we saw today need me. I don't have time to waste on someone with your bad attitude." When I looked up, he was gone.

Significance is made clear in closing paragraph

I went back the next day, and every day for four weeks after that. I continued to work on my arm at home and in the weight room at school. Today, my arm looks normal and is almost as strong as it once was. I still can't put stress on it—baseball and other sports are out except for cross-country. And I know when it's going to rain long before the forecasters do—the elbow stiffens up and aches. But whenever I start feeling sorry for myself, I think about that afternoon in the Culver Wing three years ago. I think about the courage I saw there, the incredible will to survive and go on. That's enough to remind me that my limitations aren't really limitations at all, and I'm grateful that I'm able to tackle whatever challenges life has in store for me.

LEARNING FROM YOUR WRITING PROCESS

WRITER TO WRITER

I write of one life only. My own. If my story is true, I trust it will resonate with significance for other lives.

Richard Rodriguez, Essayist

1. Reflect on your writing. Write a note that you can attach to your reflective essay as an introduction or place in your writing portfolio, reflecting on your writing process in producing your essay. As you reflect on your essay, consider the following questions:

- How has writing this essay influenced your thinking about the experience you tell about? Do you have a different or new sense of its significance?
- What has writing this essay taught you about yourself or about your past?
- What parts of your essay or stages in writing it did you find most difficult? How did you get through the difficulties?
- What have you learned, as a result of writing this essay, about yourself as a writer?

2. Apply your skills. Use what you have learned in this workshop about reflective writing to complete one or more of the following activities.

- **Cross-curricular** Make a list of four or five significant historical or scientific discoveries. Choose the one that interests you the most or about which you know the most. After thoughtful reflection, write a brief essay explaining how that event changed some aspect of the world.
- **Literature** Select a favorite poem. Write a brief essay reflecting on how the theme of the poem relates to your life and to life in general.
- **Related assignments** Follow the suggestions on pages 40–48 for writing an autobiographical incident and a monologue.

Off the Record

I'M SORRY DAD, BUT GROWING UP IS A FULL TIME JOB AND I JUST CAN'T FIT HOMEWORK INTO MY SCHEDULE.

Objective

To analyze and reflect upon what students have learned about the writing process and about the writing of a reflective essay

Teaching Strategies

Reflecting on the Process

The answers to the first two questions may be very personal, and students may want to keep their responses to themselves. However, students may find support for their growth as writers by sharing their responses to the last two questions, which deal with what they can learn as writers from their experiences with the reflective essay.

Writing Portfolio

Ask students to respond to the last two questions in writing, to attach their responses to their finished reflective essays, and to put all the materials in their Writing Portfolio. Point out that as they progress as writers they may look back at their responses to see how their ideas grow and change.

Summary and Closure

Before proceeding to the next lesson, be sure students have internalized the following concepts:

1. A reflective essay includes a description of events and reflection on the significance of these events.

2. A reflective essay includes narration and a theme and may include character, plot, conflict, and tension.

3. An effective reflective essay uses a personal experience to convey an important lesson about life.

Give students time to summarize what they learned by describing the characteristics of effective reflective essays and by explaining why knowing how to write a reflective essay might help them in other school subjects.

Starting from Literature

Objective

To respond to a professional model of an autobiographical incident as a springboard to expressive writing

Teaching Strategies

Motivate

Begin by sharing with students a "minor" event from your past that left you with major insights. Ask students to recall events, perhaps from their childhoods, that have affected them and that they would feel comfortable telling others about. Let them recount some of the events and describe the events' effects on them.

Tap Prior Knowledge

Ask students to describe times when they have felt like strangers or outsiders. Have them discuss how these experiences changed their ways of seeing themselves.

Set a Purpose

Focus on the side-column notes. Tell students that Colón's thoughts often appear as questions. Suggest that, as they read, they pay special attention to these questions and to the feelings and values they reveal. (Author pronunciation: Jesús Colón—hā sōōs′ kō lōń)

Related ASSIGNMENT

Autobiographical Incident

LITTLE THINGS ARE **BIG**

BY JESÚS COLÓN

How often do you find yourself in the center of a group of friends, telling a story about something that happened to you? Your friends listen intently because the story reminds them of a similar experience of their own.

A good autobiographical anecdote touches the emotions or the common experience of listeners and readers. As you read Jesús Colón's account of an experience on a subway platform, notice how he conveys the thoughts that ran through his mind as he tried to decide what he should do.

It was very late at night on the eve of Memorial Day. She came into the subway at the 34th Street Pennsylvania Station. I am still trying to remember how she managed to push herself in with a baby on her right arm, a valise in her left hand and two children, a boy and girl about three and five years old, trailing after her. She was a nice looking white lady in her early twenties.

At Nevins Street, Brooklyn, we saw her preparing to get off at the next station—Atlantic Avenue—which happened to be the place where I had to get off. Just as it was a problem for her to get on, it was going to be a problem for her to get off the subway with two small children to be taken care of, a baby on her right arm and a medium sized valise in her left hand.

And there I was, also preparing to get off at Atlantic Avenue, with no bundles to take care of—not even the customary book under my arm without which I feel that I am not completely dressed.

As the train was entering the Atlantic Avenue station, some white man stood up from his seat and helped her out, placing the children on the long, deserted platform. There were only two adult persons on the long platform some time after midnight on the eve of last Memorial Day.

I could perceive the steep, long concrete stairs going down to the Long Island Railroad or into the street. Should I offer my help as the American white man did at the subway car? Should I take care of the girl and the boy, take them by their hands until they reached the end of the steep, long concrete stairs of the Atlantic Avenue station.

Courtesy is a characteristic of the Puerto Rican. And here I was—a Puerto Rican—hours past midnight, a valise, two white children and a white lady with a baby on her arm palpably needing somebody to help her at least until she descended the long concrete stairs.

But how could I, a Negro and a Puerto Rican, approach this white lady who very likely might have preconceived prejudices against Negroes and everybody with foreign accents, in a deserted

38

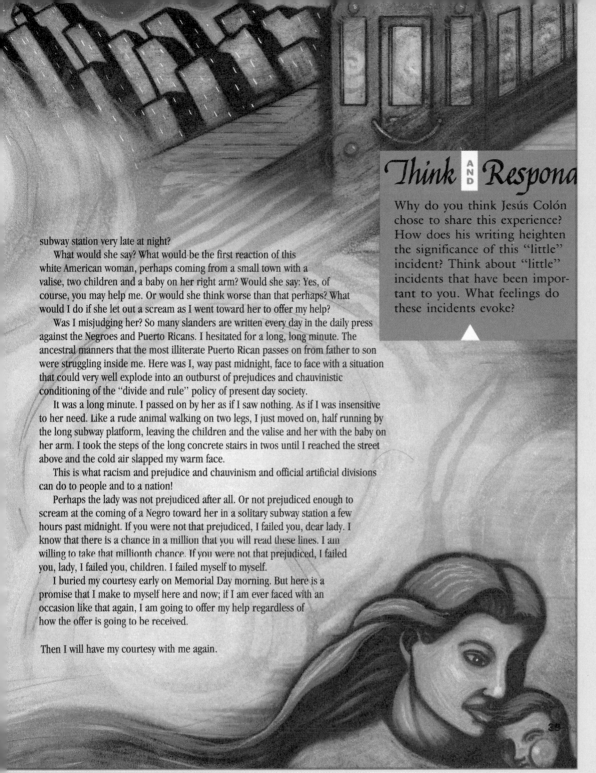

subway station very late at night?

What would she say? What would be the first reaction of this white American woman, perhaps coming from a small town with a valise, two children and a baby on her right arm? Would she say: Yes, of course, you may help me. Or would she think worse than that perhaps? What would I do if she let out a scream as I went toward her to offer my help?

Was I misjudging her? So many slanders are written every day in the daily press against the Negroes and Puerto Ricans. I hesitated for a long, long minute. The ancestral manners that the most illiterate Puerto Rican passes on from father to son were struggling inside me. Here was I, way past midnight, face to face with a situation that could very well explode into an outburst of prejudices and chauvinistic conditioning of the "divide and rule" policy of present day society.

It was a long minute. I passed on by her as if I saw nothing. As if I was insensitive to her need. Like a rude animal walking on two legs, I just moved on, half running by the long subway platform, leaving the children and the valise and her with the baby on her arm. I took the steps of the long concrete stairs in twos until I reached the street above and the cold air slapped my warm face.

This is what racism and prejudice and chauvinism and official artificial divisions can do to people and to a nation!

Perhaps the lady was not prejudiced after all. Or not prejudiced enough to scream at the coming of a Negro toward her in a solitary subway station a few hours past midnight. If you were not that prejudiced, I failed you, dear lady. I know that there is a chance in a million that you will read these lines. I am willing to take that millionth chance. If you were not that prejudiced, I failed you, lady, I failed you, children. I failed myself to myself.

I buried my courtesy early on Memorial Day morning. But here is a promise that I make to myself here and now; if I am ever faced with an occasion like that again, I am going to offer my help regardless of how the offer is going to be received.

Then I will have my courtesy with me again.

Think AND Respond

Why do you think Jesús Colón chose to share this experience? How does his writing heighten the significance of this "little" incident? Think about "little" incidents that have been important to you. What feelings do these incidents evoke?

Guiding Your Writers

Objectives

1. To choose a topic for an autobiographical incident
2. To write an autobiographical incident whose tone suits its purpose
3. To publish and present an autobiographical incident

Preteaching

Preview the content of the lesson. If there are skills or concepts students may need help with, present them at this time. The mini-lesson references below may help you in your selection and instruction.

> **Handbook Mini-Lessons**
> - Reflecting, p. 331
> - Informal Sharing, p. 412
> - Tone, pp. 424–425
> - Dialogue in Nonfiction, p. 455

Teaching Strategies

Personal Touch

As students begin exploring, share with them an incident from your high-school or elementary-school years that had a strong effect on you and that still affects you today. If appropriate, explain why the incident has remained meaningful to you.

INVITATION TO Write

Jesús Colón's article demonstrates how a writer can use a simple story to reveal values that are important to him. Use the guidelines below to write about an incident in your life that had special significance for you.

Many events and experiences in your life have had a lasting impact on you. In at least some small way, they have changed you, your beliefs, or your entire outlook. By exploring such an incident in writing, you can more thoroughly examine its impact on you and the meaning that you drew from it. In this assignment you can explore and evaluate an important event in your past.

E X P L O R I N G   Y O U R   P A S T

1. Choose an event. What should you write about? The best ideas are frequently the ones you tend to overlook, the ones that are closest to you. You might spend some private time rummaging through your grade-school and high-school keepsakes, boxes of favorite childhood games, autograph books, and photo albums. Is there a picture, a souvenir from a summer at camp, or a ticket stub from a game or a concert that strikes an emotional chord or triggers powerful memories? Also, do not overlook the present. What has happened during the past few days—at home, with friends, or at work—that has affected you in some way?

As you list ideas, mark those that evoke the strongest personal response from you. When you are finished listing, freewrite on one or two of the most powerful memories, remembering the details of each experience and examining their significance to you.

2. Evaluate your ideas. Choose a subject that is more than just an interesting incident. Which event contained special meaning for you or had a special impact? Which event taught you something that would be meaningful to other readers?

HANDBOOKS
FOR HELP & PRACTICE

Reflecting,
pp. 331–332
Informal Sharing,
p. 412
Tone, pp. 424–425
Dialogue in
Nonfiction,
p. 455

40   Workshop 1

Literature Connection

Author Note Jesús Colón (1901—) was born in Puerto Rico. His *A Puerto Rican in New York* collects his reminiscences of his years in the Puerto Rican community of New York City. His varied career has included work as a physical laborer, a journalist, and a labor organizer.

3. Identify your goals. Once you have selected your topic, it is time to determine your specific goals. What do you want to accomplish by telling this autobiographical incident? Do you want to entertain, to teach a lesson, or to elicit a strong emotional response? For example, Colón wanted to encourage people to live up to what they really believe in. What will your narrative do? What kind of response do you want to elicit from your audience?

4. Choose a tone. Writing can be serious, humorous, formal, or informal. In his account, Colón used a simple, straightforward, almost reporter-like tone to convey the situation and his own dilemma. Decide what tone would be suitable for your narrative and your goals, as well as for your audience. Are you writing for adults? Are you entertaining a younger audience? Know your audience before you begin to draft your anecdote so that you can gauge your tone and style effectively.

DRAFTING YOUR NARRATIVE

1. Begin your narrative. Try freewriting for a while, playing with your story. Be relaxed about style, grammar rules, and punctuation. There will be time later to perfect your mechanics. At this point it is the story that is important.

2. Use dialogue to dramatize your story. Since Colón never approaches the woman, he cannot appropriately use dialogue. However, he does speculate about what the woman might say, thus giving us a more complete picture of her. Try to use dialogue to re-create a scene, to breathe life into your characters, or to change the pace of your narrative.

3. Vary your writing techniques. As you think about your story, consider some of the ways you can make your writing more vivid. For example, using descriptive details can enliven your narrative. Try to include graphic details that appeal to the five senses: sight, hearing, taste, touch, and smell. Describe the setting for the anecdote as concretely and colorfully as you can. Do not hesitate to describe your own feelings at various points as you unfold the incident. Colón clearly portrays his feelings when he says "like a rude animal walking on two legs, I just moved on. . . ."

Writing **TIP**

Spend some time reading the Sunday newspaper. Look especially for human-interest stories that trigger a strong emotional response. Would you like to model your narrative on one of these stories?

Autobiographical Incident **41**

Teaching Tip: Personal Goals

Remind students that the power and appeal of these anecdotes depend partly on the degree of meaning they have for the writer. Suggest that each student choose an event that seems significant to him or her, even if the student is not sure why it seems so. Explain that, as the student works with the episode, its significance will become clearer, and the excitement of the writer's discovery will communicate itself to readers as well.

Individualizing Instruction

Basic Students Remind students that the narrative portions of their autobiographical incidents should contain transitions that make the sequence of events clear to the reader.

Advanced Students Suggest that students consider experimenting with flashback and flash forward as they narrate their incidents.

Peer Response

Let students form small groups to read one another's drafts. They should briefly tell what they liked best about each, and explain why they responded as they did. This short, positive experience with peer response will help students to see which elements make autobiographical incidents effective. It will also allow them to begin identifying their own writing strengths. Join one of the groups and participate in the response process, being careful not to dominate it. Emphasize that each writer is in charge of deciding how best to use the group's comments.

Springboard

Students have seen how selective repetition functions in a nonfiction passage; now let them explore the uses of selective repetition in poetry. Read or play a recording of a ballad (perhaps one of the medieval ballads in their literature text) and point out the repetition in its refrain. Discuss the effects of the repetition. Suggest that students use repetition in composing their own ballads, perhaps focusing on a recent event. Remind them that ballads can be either serious or humorous.

Guidelines for Evaluation

A good autobiographical incident
- focuses on one central event
- shows the meaning the event had for the writer
- uses a clear temporal organization
- is made vivid by pertinent sensory words
- reveals a tone that underscores the meaning of the incident
- displays standard grammar and correct usage and mechanics

Reteaching

Assess the needs of students who were not successful in developing an effective autobiographical incident and identify two or three areas in which additional practice is needed. Assign the appropriate Handbook Mini-Lessons, along with the support materials listed for each lesson. Concepts commonly requiring reteaching for this assignment are

Elaboration: Handbook 9
Unity: Handbook 10

The following suggestions and resources may also be useful.

1. Unclear organization Remind students that an autobiographical incident is a narrative and needs chronological organization. Direct them to Handbooks 8 (Narrative Introductions) and 10 (Coherence). Have students focus on the use of transitions such as *first, next, beforehand, afterwards* to clarify the sequence of events.

2. Uneven Tone Explain that *tone* refers to the writer's attitude toward the subject of the writing. Have students sum up their attitudes toward their subjects in a sentence, then in one or two words. Then suggest that they brainstorm ways to change their wording so that it reveals their tone more clearly.

 Writer's Choice The elements of surprise and irony often work well in an autobiographical anecdote. Try to use these elements to appeal to your readers' interest and sense of humor, if they are appropriate to your story.

REVIEWING YOUR WRITING

1. Reread your narrative. Many writers find it helpful to let a piece of writing rest awhile before doing the final shaping. If you have time, put your work away for a while. After a few days, reread your narrative. You will probably gain a fresh perspective on your writing. Does it achieve the goals you set? Is the significance of the incident clear? If, in answering these questions, you discover any lapses in your narrative, now is the time to repair them.

2. Think about the story. An autobiographical incident is, in effect, a brief story. It should therefore contain similar elements. Are your characters well defined? Does the narrative flow smoothly? Have you focused on only those events that contribute to the incident? Ask a peer reader to respond to these questions, and to other points you want to check.

3. Rework material. If necessary, revise your material. Remember that your details should not only re-create the incident, they should also show the significance of what happened to you. Polish the dialogue and word choice so that each sentence conveys your message exactly.

PUBLISHING AND PRESENTING

- **Read your narrative to a small group.** Watch their reactions. Did your anecdote trigger the emotion you desired? Invite comments from your audience.
- **Take to the airwaves.** If your school has a radio station, consider establishing a weekly radio spot such as the kind popularized by Garrison Keillor, who wrote *Lake Wobegon Days.* Open the spot to anyone who has a story to share.
- **Become a columnist.** A weekly column in the school newspaper might be an alternative to a radio broadcast.
- **Seek a broader audience.** Submit your narrative to a local newspaper or to a teen or young adult magazine. Many publications are looking for fresh young talent.

42   Workshop 1

Literature Connection

Poetry Students may enjoy seeing how poets have used autobiographical incidents. Show them such diverse examples as Wordsworth's ''Composed Upon Westminster Bridge,'' Matthew Arnold's ''Dover Beach,'' D.H. Lawrence's ''Snake,'' Dylan Thomas's ''Fern Hill,'' and Ted Hughes's ''Hawk Roosting.''

Springboard

Many writers have created fictional ''autobiographies'' of others (DeFoe's *Robinson Crusoe* and John Gardner's *Grendel,* for example). Students might write an ''autobiographical'' incident in the voice of someone else, perhaps of a famous person or a literary figure.

On the Lightside

WORD SEPARATION

Imagine trying to read this book if there were no paragraphs, no spaces between words, no capitalization, and no punctuation. It is not a totally ridiculous notion. In fact, that is how books were written before the Middle Ages.

In antiquity, people generally read aloud, so the sound of a word was more important than how it looked on a page. When texts were transcribed, the scribes merely wrote the letters one after another, leaving it up to the readers to separate the words. Medieval readers, however, began to sense that texts were being corrupted. They felt their scribes sometimes made mistakes, particularly with proper names, by mixing together letters. As a result, the concept of dividing the unbroken script into distinct words came into use. But it was not until the eighth and ninth centuries that capital letters came to be used, and it wasn't until the eleventh century that paragraphs and other grammatical marks started finding their way into texts. Often, these marks were added by readers after books were transcribed. Even after printing came

Fifteenth century
painting of a scribe

into use, monks went through the books in their libraries word-for-word, adding punctuation, accents, and hyphens the printers did not provide.

If today's rules of grammar and mechanics at times seem overwhelming, imaginewhatitwouldbe likeiftherewerenorulesatall.

43

On the Lightside

Have students find, display, and compare facsimiles of early manuscripts. Discuss differences students notice in letter formation, word separation, paragraphing, and page decoration.

You might want to introduce students to the ligature. Ask a volunteer to look up the word *ligature* in a dictionary and read its definitions to the class. Bring out that the basic meaning is "something that is used to bind," as in surgery. In language it means "a written or printed character consisting of two or more letters that are united." A glance at a page of Old English reveals frequent use of the ligature æ, as in *fæder* (father) and *gæs* (grass). This Old English ligature spelled the vowel sound you hear in *bat*. Today, most typefaces include ligatures for certain letter combinations such as *œ*.

You might ask students to devise a ligature of their own, providing an original rationale for its use. For example, students might merge silent *e* with the letter that precedes it to signal that *e* is silent, as in *home, take,* and *complete.*

Starting from Literature

Objective

To respond to a professional model of a written monologue as a springboard to reflective writing

Teaching Strategies

Motivate

Ask students to describe their methods for making difficult decisions. If necessary, prompt them by suggesting techniques like talking with a friend, listing pros and cons, or taking a long walk to put things in perspective. Tell them that the monologue they will now read brings to life a character who discusses his decisions with an inanimate object.

Tap Prior Knowledge

Ask students if they have seen the stage musical or movie version of *Camelot* and encourage them to share their memories of their viewing experiences. You may wish to mention that *Camelot* is based on a novel by T. H. White called *The Once and Future King,* which in turn was inspired by early tales of the legend of King Arthur and the Knights of the Round Table. Elicit from students what they know about the setting, character, and plot elements of the story of Arthur's kingdom of Camelot.

Set a Purpose

As students read the side-column notes, remind them—if not previously touched on in class discussion—that in *Camelot* King Arthur and Sir Lancelot (Lance) are best friends. Queen Guinevere (Jenny) loves Arthur deeply, but she and Lancelot have also fallen in love, and Arthur realizes it. Excalibur is Arthur's sword. Because the side column poses several questions, suggest that, as students read, they jot down notes about Arthur's dilemma and about his personality and values.

Monologue

Have you ever mentally replayed a disagreement with a classmate or imagined different ways to handle a conflict with a parent? Sometimes arguing with ourselves helps us resolve a troubling situation.

Playwrights often use internal arguments to reveal the personal struggles of characters. Through monologue, or solo conversations, characters tell us aloud of their inner conflicts. As you read this monologue from the musical *Camelot,* try to define the dilemma that King Arthur faces. What personal values and beliefs help him decide what to do?

✣ FROM CAMELOT ✣

PROPOSITION ✣ *If I could choose, from every woman who breathes on this earth, the face I would most love, the smile, the touch, the voice, the heart, the laugh, the soul itself, every detail and feature to the smallest strand of hair they would all be Jenny's.*

PROPOSITION ✣ *If I could choose from every man who breathes on this earth a man for my brother and a man for my son, a man for my friend, they would all be Lance.* (His bitterness mounts.) *Yes, I love them. I love them, and they answer me with pain and torment. Be it sin or not sin, they betray me in their hearts, and that's far sin enough. I see it in their eyes and feel it when they speak, and they must pay for it and be punished. I shan't be wounded and not return it in kind. I'm done with feeble hoping. I demand a man's vengeance!* (He moves violently, then tries to control himself.)

44

✦ BY ALAN JAY LERNER ✦

PROPOSITION ✦ *I'm a king, not a man. And a civilized king. Could it possibly be civilized to destroy what I love? Could it possibly be civilized to love myself above all? What of their pain and their torment? Did they ask for this calamity? Can passion be selected?* (His voice rising.) *Is there any doubt of their devotion . . . to me, or to our Table?* (He raises high the sword in his hand.) *By God, Excalibur, I shall be a King! This is the time of King Arthur, and we reach for the stars! This is the time of King Arthur, and violence is not strength and compassion is not weakness. We are civilized!*

RESOLVED ✦ *We shall live through this together, Excalibur: They, you and I! And God have mercy on us all.* (The decision made, he becomes almost relaxed, almost at peace.) *They're waiting for us at the table.* (He starts to walk off.) *Let's not delay the celebration.*

Think AND Respond

What conflict does King Arthur face? How does he decide to resolve it? What do you learn about Arthur from this monologue? How did the writer convey these impressions to you? What kind of character or conflict can you imagine presenting in a monologue?

Literature Connection

Apostrophe Explain that a monologue addressing one other person or thing, as Arthur addresses Excalibur, is called an *apostrophe*. Students may enjoy such powerful examples of apostrophe as John Donne's "Death Be Not Proud," Ben Jonson's "On My First Son," Andrew Marvell's "To His Coy Mistress," and John Keats's "Ode on a Grecian Urn."

Think and Respond

Elicit Personal Responses

Encourage students to share some of the words they wrote describing Arthur's character and personality. As students begin discussing the Think and Respond questions, be sure they understand that Arthur is trying to decide how to deal with the realization that his wife and his best friend are in love. Ask students if, on the basis of this monologue, they expect that Arthur will confront Lance and Jenny. If so, what will he say or do? If not, what will he do instead? Have students identify the parts of the monologue that allow them to make these predictions.

Explore the Author's Techniques

To help students use the model, point out that the author has carefully chosen Arthur's diction, as well as his actions, to bring him to life. Arthur's speech contains a great deal of selective repetition, both of key words and of sentence structures (parallel structure), giving it a distinctive rhythm and intensity. Suggest that students use selective repetition, parallel structure, or other devices (repeated use of metaphor or hyperbole, for example) to create distinctive diction in their own monologues.

Link Literature to Writing

Point out that a monologue is a particularly intense kind of reflective writing. Explain that, in this assignment, students will have a chance to write monologues of their own. Encourage them to craft their monologues, as Alan Jay Lerner does, to reveal the speaker's personality and values.

Guiding Your Writers

Objectives

1. To choose a conflict and a point of view for a monologue
2. To write a monologue in which diction develops character and point of view is consistent
3. To publish and present a monologue

Preteaching

Preview the content of the lesson. If there are skills or concepts students may need help with, present them at this time. The mini-lesson references below may help you in your selection and instruction. The cross references in the pupil text give students access to the same lessons for independent practice.

Handbook Mini-Lessons

- Choosing Different Voices, pp. 419–420
- Emphasis/Tone/Mood, pp. 423–428
- Varieties of Language, pp. 429–434
- Poetic Language, pp. 434–438
- Point of View, pp. 446–451

Teaching Strategies

 Individualizing Instruction

Basic Students For students who are struggling to come up with a topic, suggest imagining what might have gone on in the mind of a famous figure from history, sports, politics, or the entertainment world as he or she prepared for the event that was to make him or her famous.

INVITATION TO Write

The monologue from *Camelot* helps the audience understand King Arthur's internal struggle. Now use the guidelines below to write a monologue of your own, presenting a conflict from a fictional character's point of view.

Like all reflective writing, a monologue involves the working out of ideas and inner struggles. However, a monologue, unlike a reflective essay, presents a fictional situation, not a real one. A monologue gives the audience a chance to see the inner workings of a character's mind.

PREPARING A MONOLOGUE

HANDBOOKS
FOR HELP & PRACTICE

Choosing Different Voice, pp. 419–422

Emphasis/Tone/Mood, pp. 423–428

Varieties of Language, pp. 429–434

Poetic Language, pp. 435–438

Point of View, pp. 446–449

1. Select a situation. You may want to choose a conflict inspired by a piece of literature you have read. For example, the clashing of wills between Eliza Doolittle and Henry Higgins in George Bernard Shaw's *Pygmalion* might inspire a monologue by either character. Alternatively, you may want to create a situation from your own imagination: competition between classmates, temptation to cheat on an examination, or conflicts involving loyalty to a friend are possible situations from which a monologue might arise.

2. Choose a point of view. Once you have chosen a situation, you must decide from whose point of view the conflict will be argued. Presumably Jenny or Lance in *Camelot* would have engaged in a much different monologue from Arthur's even though they would have been reacting to the same situation. You may want to experiment by talking into a tape recorder, recording the thoughts and ideas of various characters about the same conflict. Speak always in the first person as though you were actually acting the part of the character. As you listen to your tape, decide which point of view you are most comfortable with. Also, begin to think which ideas can shape the monologue.

Springboard

Point out the use of parallel structure in Arthur's monologue, and explain that parallel structure can add power and emphasis to speech and writing. Help alert students to writers' frequent use of parallel structure by having teams compete against each other to find examples of parallel structure in written materials in the classroom and to explain the effects created by the parallelism. Set a time limit of fifteen minutes. The team with the most examples wins.

CREATING A REALISTIC MONOLOGUE

1. Reveal character through word choice. The way a character speaks reveals a great deal about his or her personality. For example, Arthur uses formal and elegant language, suiting his position as a king as well as the nobility of his character. He also prefaces his thoughts with "Proposition" and "Resolved." These words, used in formal logic, help us to see that Arthur is a very rational person. Yet the beautiful images and tender phrases he uses to describe his wife and his friend reveal a romantic and poetic soul as well. What would very informal speech or violent language reveal about a character? How might you indicate through word choice that a character is highly emotional?

2. Show, don't tell about, a character. You can learn much about Arthur's character from the questions he asks himself. From these questions, you come to realize that Arthur values civilized behavior and compassion above vengeance. Because you see him struggle and doubt, you are more convinced of his values than you would be if he just declared them. Think of ways you can show your character's values other than just stating them.

 Writer's Choice Introducing your monologue with a few sentences of background information will save you from the awkwardness of having to include the needed information in the monologue itself.

3. Experiment with narrative techniques. Not all characters speak as coherently or logically as Arthur. Some might jump from one idea to another, in a stream of consciousness, because the author wants to communicate an insecure or agitated state of mind. For example, in Shakespeare's *Macbeth,* the agonized king argues with himself as he stands alone on stage. Then the tolling of a bell reminds Macbeth of a death knell and then his desire to kill King Duncan takes over. You may want to experiment with stream of consciousness in your monologue.

Writing
—TIP—
You may want to organize your monologue in a problem-situation pattern. First, the conflict will be presented and debated. Then, some type of resolution will emerge.

Tette de Femme,
Pablo Picasso

47

Managing the Paper Load

As students draft, provide a checklist of your evaluation guidelines for monologues. Have students revise in class, and allow each student a two-minute impromptu editorial conference with you when the student feels that the monologue is finished. Go down the checklist together to the first "no" answer. Praise the mastery of criteria prior to the "no," and assign the task of changing this "no" to a "yes." (If all answers are "yes," the student may turn in the work to be checked off or graded.)

Linking Grammar and Writing

Arthur's monologue, like many speeches, contains sentence fragments. Explain that fragments can be effective when used appropriately; here, they show emotion or confusion in the speaker. Students may want to use fragments for a similar purpose in their monologues. Unintentional fragments, however, cause the writer to lose credibility. Grammar Handbook 32 shows students how to recognize and correct unintentional fragments.

Collaborative Opportunity

Let students work in groups of five to scan their work for grammar and mechanics problems and correct them before turning in final drafts. One person in each group can check for spelling, one for punctuation, one for sentence completeness, one for agreement, and one for dangling or misplaced modifiers and tense shifts.

Humanities Connection

Art Note *Head of Woman* (1957) is a study for a monument by the Spanish artist Pablo Picasso (1881–1973), who may be the most important figure in 20th-century art. Picasso experimented with and mastered many different media and styles. He was astonishingly original and prolific; estimates of his creative output range from eight to ten thousand works. This construction is an example of his inventive later career. Ask: How is an artist's "study" for a larger piece like a writer's rough draft?

Guidelines for Evaluation

The following guidelines may be used for a close evaluation of a monologue.
A good monologue
- focuses on a single conflict
- provides enough details to make both the conflict and the speaker's personality clear
- has a consistent point of view
- reveals character through diction
- uses correct grammar and mechanics

Reteaching

Assess the needs of students who were not successful at developing an effective monologue. Assign the appropriate Handbook Mini-Lessons. Concepts commonly requiring reteaching for this assignment are:

> Different Voices: Handbook 15
> Point of View: Handbook 20

The following suggestions and resources may also be useful.

1. Unclear Focus An unclear focus indicates that the student does not have a specific idea of the central conflict. Define *conflict* as "a problem or challenge, internal or external, that a character must deal with." Instruct students to have the character directly state what the conflict is and how it affects him or her. Tell them to bring the rest of the monologue into line with that controlling statement, then delete the controlling statement.

2. Weak Characterization If the character's diction lacks individuality, circle several of the commonplace nouns, verbs, modifiers, and phrases used. Call them "character potential" and direct students to change the wording to fulfill the potential. They can find ideas either by listening to the speech of real-life characters similar to theirs or by consulting a thesaurus.

4. Consider adding stage directions. In Arthur's monologue, the stage directions serve as hints to the actor for appropriate movements, gestures, and tones of voice. As you draft your monologue, consider what your character should do as he or she speaks. If you want your character to perform movements such as pacing to and fro or wringing hands, add the necessary directions to your script.

REVIEWING YOUR WRITING

1. Perform your monologue for a small audience. As you read, check the monologue for clarity. Have you provided enough information for your listeners to understand the situation? Is the point of view clear and consistent throughout the monologue?

2. Check word choice and speech patterns. Remember that your goal is to reveal character through speech. Make sure that the vocabulary you chose and the sentence structures you created are appropriate for your character.

The Far Side Cartoons by Gary Larson are reprinted by permission of Chronicle Features, San Francisco, CA.

PUBLISHING AND PRESENTING

- **Conduct mock tryouts for actors.** Use your own monologue and those of your classmates as material for tryouts for an imaginary play. You will need a director who will decide who reads the part best, as well as a group of potential actors eager to land a part in the "play."
- **Present a staged reading of your monologue.** Complete your staging with costumes, stage props, lighting, and music.

Humanities Connection

Let students work in small groups to explore some of the many manifestations of the Arthur legend. One member of each group can research historical roots of the legend, one can review Malory's *Le Morte D'Arthur,* one Tennyson's *Idylls of the King,* one T.H. White's tetralogy *The Once and Future King* (on which *Camelot* is based), and one *Camelot.* After students have reported their findings to their groups, each group can collaborate further on a paragraph summarizing the historical development of the character of Arthur.

Sentence

Analyzing Sentence Structures

In these Sentence Composing lessons, you will analyze and imitate the sentence structures used by professional writers. Then you will use those structures to add emphasis, clarity, and detail to your own writing.

Notice the differences in structure in the three sentences below.

MODELS

1. Along the roads around Goderville, the peasants and their wives were coming toward the little town, for it was market day.
2. The men walked with plodding steps, their bodies bent forward at each thrust of their long bowed legs.
3. They were deformed by hard work, by the pull of the heavy plow which raises the left shoulder and twists the torso, by the reaping of the wheat which forces the knees apart to get a firm stand, by all the slow and strenuous labors of life on the farm.

Guy de Maupassant, "The Piece of String"

A. Identifying Imitations Identify the sentence that imitates the structure of the model.

Model: Along the roads around Goderville, the peasants and their wives were coming toward the little town, for it was market day.

1 a. When the computer beeped, Maria suddenly realized that the data was inaccurate, a fault of the information she had been given.
   b. Near the end zone by the flagpole, Coach Royden and his team were trotting toward the field, for it was time for the second half.

Model: The men walked with plodding steps, their bodies bent forward at each thrust of their long bowed legs.

2 a. Our car stalled at every intersection, its carburetor clogged with all manner of accumulated engine sludge.
   b. He stood ironing the shirt, and he felt his thoughts sweeping back and forth with the iron.

Sentence Composing: Analyzing Sentence Structures

Objectives

1. To analyze the structure of sentences
2. To compose sentences that imitate the structures of others
3. To create variety in a paragraph through the use of specific sentence structures

Preteaching

These exercises focus on the variety that can be created through the use of different sentence structures. Before completing the activities, some students may need review of basic sentence parts and structure as well as the use of phrases and clauses. Refer to the following sections of the Grammar Handbook for preteaching content:

Phrases and Clauses
   Prepositional Phrases, pages 591–592
   Using Phrases Correctly, page 602
   Clauses, pages 605–606
   The Structure of a Sentence, pages 616–617

ANSWER KEY

12-1 Analyzing Sentence Structures

A. Identifying Imitations
   1. b
   2. a
   3. b

B. Unscrambling Sentences

1. Near the exit to the stadium, the cars and trucks were coming to a grinding halt, because there was road work.

2. The drivers sat with forced patience, their faces peering out through the windshields with angry, tired expressions.

3. They were upset by the delay, by the length of the twisting detour that slowed commuter traffic and wrecked schedules, by the noise of the jackhammer that broke the pavement up to expose the yellow topsoil, by all the unexpected but inevitable problems of travel on highways.

Model: They were deformed by hard work, by the pull of the heavy plow which raises the left shoulder and twists the torso, by the reaping of the wheat which forces the knees apart to get a firm stand, by all the slow and strenuous labors of life on the farm.

3 a. Since no one had believed Corky's wild story, she had retired to her room to sulk and brood over the incident, to write angry notes to all of us, and to fume about the injustices in her life.

   b. We felt proud of our school, of its standing in a competitive league that challenges the best teams and destroys the worst, of its reputation in a district that urges the teachers always to demand high academic performance, of its longstanding and thorough commitment to the best interests of the students.

B. Unscrambling Sentences Unscramble each group of sentence parts below to create a sentence that matches the model.

Model: Along the roads around Goderville, the peasants and their wives were coming toward the little town, for it was market day.

1 a. because there was road work
  b. near the exit to the stadium
  c. the cars and trucks were coming to a grinding halt

Model: The men walked with plodding steps, their bodies bent forward at each thrust of their long bowed legs.

2 a. their faces peering out
  b. through the windshields with angry, tired expressions
  c. the drivers sat with forced patience

Model: They were deformed by hard work, by the pull of the heavy plow which raises the left shoulder and twists the torso, by the reaping of the wheat which forces the knees apart to get a firm stand, by all the slow and strenuous labors of life on the farm.

3 a. by the length of the twisting detour
  b. by all the unexpected but inevitable problems of travel on highways
  c. that slowed commuter traffic and wrecked schedules
  d. they were upset by the delay
  e. by the noise of the jackhammer
  f. that broke the pavement up to expose the yellow topsoil

C. Imitating Sentences
Answers will vary.
Application
Answers will vary.

C. Imitating Sentences Now you will apply your skills to new sentences. Write a sentence that imitates the structure of each model sentence below. Major parts of each model are separated by slash marks (/). Punctuate your sentences as the models are punctuated.

>**Model** Sometimes in the night / the ranch people, / safe in their beds, / heard a roar of hoofs go by. **John Steinbeck, *The Red Pony***

>**Student Sentence** Often in the spring / the school children, / curious about the tulips, / saw a bunch of buds open up.

1. Time,/ as we know it, / is a very recent invention.
Aldous Huxley, "Time and the Machine"

2. Next morning I woke up / at my usual hour, / fizzling like a bottle of champagne. **Frank O'Connor, "My Oedipus Complex"**

3. Hooking the window back, / he noticed that a little tree / in the Square Gardens / had come out in blossom, / and that the thermometer stood at sixty. **John Galsworthy, "The Flowering Quince"**

4. He closed his eyes and swung wildly, / and Angel, / laughing, / belted the side of his headguard. **Robert Lipsyte, *The Contender***

5. One day a big locust whirred drily past her head, / and she jumped up with a cry, / scattering her sewing things.
Nadine Gordimer, "The Soft Voice of the Serpent"

6. The twins, / smeary in the face, / eating steadily from untidy paper sacks of sweets, / followed them in a detached way.
Katherine Anne Porter, *Ship of Fools*

Application Write a paragraph describing a group activity (for example, a barbecue, a concert, or a sports event). In your paragraph, include imitations of at least two of the model sentences in this lesson.

Grammar Refresher In order to analyze a sentence, you must be able to identify its subject and predicate. For information on identifying subject and predicate, see Handbook 32.

Workshop Overview

Writing based on observation and description expresses a writer's perceptions of the people and places that make up his or her world. Such writing requires the writer to note concrete, sensory details to enable readers to picture people and things as they actually appear and to present these details in ways that allow readers to experience things as the writer has experienced them. This type of writing is often integrated into other forms: novels, short stories, poems, letters, and different kinds of journalistic writing. For that reason, observation and description should be taught fairly early in the year. Workshop 2 includes the following Guided and Related Assignments:

1. **Guided: Journalistic Narrative** shows students how to gather details, facts, and reactions first-hand and helps students find a unique angle to convey such factual information using techniques often associated with fiction
2. **Related: Personality Profile** suggests how students can apply the observation and research skills as they profile someone they admire
3. **Related: Video** introduces the video camera as an electronic aid to observation and description

Preparation Guide

1. Use the Overview above and the Teacher's Choice descriptions on page 53 as a basis for deciding which assignment(s) to teach.

2. Preview the assignment and the teacher's notes. The teaching suggestions and your knowledge of your class's abilities should allow you to identify quickly the concepts that may require preteaching or extra support. The Handbook mini-lessons suggested in the Preteaching notes within the lesson can also provide guidance in this area.

3. Preview the adjacent chart for support materials in the Teacher's Resource File that may be used with this Workshop. Resources are for use with the Guided Assignment unless otherwise noted.

Workshop Support Materials

Resources	For Use With
Ideas for Writing: Data Sheets, p. 3; Additional Ideas, p. 18	Look for ideas, p. 56
	Choose a subject, p. 57
Thinking Skills Transparencies: Observation Chart; *Worksheets,* p. 1	Begin reporting, p. 57
Elaboration/Proofreading, p. 3	Elaborate on ideas, p. 60
Peer Response Guides, p. 9	Review Your Writing, p. 61
Evaluating Writing, pp. 9, 23–26	Standards for Evaluation, p. 61
Student Revision Trans., pp. 9–10	Problem-solve, p. 61
Elaboration/Proofreading, p. 4	Proofread your work, p. 62
Tests and Assessment: Prompts, p. 2	

Professional Resources and Media

Films and Videos

Descriptive Writing—Figurative and Literal. Capricorn Film Prod., San Mateo, California (18 min.)

Narration and Description. Films Incorporated Education (30 min.) "Narrative and Descriptive." *The Write Course Series.* Dallas Community College District, Mesquite, Texas, 1984. (30 min.)

Teaching Writing in the Classroom. International Telecommunication Services, Reston, Virginia. 1990. (4 films, 15 min. each) (programs for teachers/staff development)

Computer Software

Electronic English Handbook, Technology Training Associates. McDougal, Littell & Company, P.O. Box 1667, Evanston, IL.

Linking Literature, Writing, and Grammar

The following options may be used to provide students with an integrated language experience. Begin by assigning and discussing any of the recommended pieces of literature, which can be found in most classroom anthologies. Use the suggested strategy to provide a link to the Guided Assignment.

Linking Literature and Writing

Option 1

Starting Point: excerpt from *Small Victories* by Samuel G. Freedman on pages 54–55 of *The Writer's Craft*

Strategy: Use the teaching suggestions on pages 54–55 to lead students into the Guided Assignment.

Option 2

Starting Point: passage from *A Journal of the Plague Year* by Daniel Defoe in which Defoe describes the great pit in the churchyard of Aldgate Parish

Strategy: Before students begin reading this piece of fiction, be sure they recognize that Defoe was attempting to make this work seem as realistic and plausible as possible, as if it were a journalistic account. As you discuss the selection, encourage students to note the kinds of details Defoe uses and how Defoe employs fictional techniques, such as narration and dialogue, in what was intended to be read as a work of nonfiction.

Option 3

Starting Point: "The Secret Sharer" by Joseph Conrad

Strategy: Point out that modern journalists often describe real events using the elements of fiction to make their writing livelier and more inviting. As they respond to the story, ask students to identify some of Conrad's closely observed details and to discuss ways in which his narration and use of dialogue move the story along and lend it an air of realism. Tell students that they will be able to apply many of the fictional techniques Conrad uses so successfully to write about true events.

Linking Writing and Grammar

Before the drafting or revision stage of this assignment, point out that in journalistic writing, as in most other writing, it is critical that the readers know at all times exactly who or what is being referred to. The writer must make sure that all pronouns have clear antecedents. Often a noun must be used in place of a pronoun to clarify references within a sentence. Ask students to find examples of pronouns used with clear antecedents in their own work as you write the following examples on the board:

UNCLEAR: The woman and her friend disappeared into her house. (Whose house did the woman and her friend go into?)

CLEAR: The woman and her friend disappeared into the woman's house.

UNCLEAR: The five boys tossed the notes into the trash. Then he casually walked off. (Whom does the sentence mean by *he*?)

CLEAR: The five boys tossed the notes into the trash. Then the tallest boy casually walked off.

Go over the rules for pronouns and antecedents on pages 710–715 of the Grammar and Usage Handbook. If problems with vague or indefinite pronoun references persist in student papers, assign the exercises on those pages for reteaching. Additional practice can be found in the Grammar and Usage Practice Book on pages 66 and 67.

Workshop Management Guidelines

The adjacent chart indicates the number of days recommended for each phase of the Guided and Related Assignments. Stars indicate portions of the assignment that may be completed outside the classroom if time is limited or if teachers wish the activity to be completed by students independently.

Journalistic Narrative

Starting from Literature—1 day
Prewrite—1–2 days*
Draft—1–2 days*
Revise—1–2 days*
Publish—open
Learning—1 day*
Reteaching—open
Extension/Enrichment—open
Sentence Composing—1 day*

Personality Profile

Starting from Literature—1 day
Preparing—3–5 days*
Writing—1–2 days*
Reviewing—1–2 days
Publishing—open
Reteaching—open
Extension/Enrichment—open

Video

Starting from Literature—1 day
Planning—2–4 days*
Taping—3–5 days*
Reviewing—2–4 days*
Publishing—open
Reteaching—open
Extension/Enrichment—open

Sketchbook

Objective

To use a photograph as a springboard to informal writing

Using the Prompt

The purpose of this activity is to allow students the freedom to experiment with ideas and writing forms. Since this activity is meant to be informal, it should not be graded.

As a warm-up activity, show students several interesting objects, such as a seashell or embroidered handkerchief. Allow students to study the objects for several minutes. Then remove the objects from view; have students list as many details about the objects as they can. After students are satisfied with their lists, show them the objects again so that they can check their descriptions for accuracy.

Have students discuss the photograph and the question that follows. Remind students that the details they notice about people and activities may be unique to them and that there is no one right way to view a person or event.

Some students might prefer to work with the suggestions in the Additional Sketches. Encourage them to respond to the idea that holds the most appeal.

Have students save their sketches in their Writing Portfolios for possible use in the assignment that follows.

Sketchbook

Bank Langmore, the Texas photographer who captured this shot of cowboys bathing, noticed that "the last things they take off are their hats, . . . even when they are taking a bath or crawling into their bedrolls."

What do you notice about the people and activities around you?

Additional Sketches

If you could meet any person in the world, whom would you choose? What would you talk about?

Watch someone doing a common, everyday task. See if you can write a description of the person's actions that includes details you've never noticed before.

52

WRITER'S **2** WORKSHOP

Observation and Description

Guided Assignment
JOURNALISTIC NARRATIVE

Related Assignment
PERSONALITY PROFILE

Related Assignment
VIDEO

How accurately could you describe everything you saw today? What was the weather like? With whom did you talk? What make was the car that screeched around the corner? In the routine of our lives, we look at many things without really seeing them. Yet when we concentrate, we can see an extraordinary amount of detail.

In this workshop, you will focus your powers of observation and description. In the guided assignment, you will write a narrative based on your close observation of an experience or event. In the related assignments, you will use your descriptive powers to write a profile of a person and to create a video that captures a scene.

53

Objectives

Guided Assignment:
JOURNALISTIC NARRATIVE
To recognize the characteristics of a journalistic narrative; to prewrite, draft, revise, proofread, and share a journalistic narrative

Related Assignment:
PERSONALITY PROFILE
To research or interview a subject for a personality profile; to write a personality profile that creates a unified impression

Related Assignment:
VIDEO
To recognize the interplay between the audio and visual images in a videotape; to create a video

Teacher's Choice

The following information may help you choose the assignments that best fit the needs and interests of your students.

Guided Assignment

Journalistic Narrative This Guided Assignment is suitable for presentation early in the year, preferably after students have tried their hand at personal narrative writing. Students' narrative skills will be broadened by the addition of various observational techniques.

Related Assignments

Personality Profile This assignment should appeal to students who like doing research; the option to interview is especially suited to auditory learners.

Video Students interested in the broadcast media should enjoy learning to create their own video. This activity is suitable for all learning styles because of its integration of auditory, visual, and kinesthetic modes.

JOURNALISTIC NARRATIVE

Assignment Rationale

This workshop will help students appreciate an increasingly common form of journalistic writing that tells a true story using techniques commonly found in fiction. At the same time, the assignment represents a natural progression from the previous workshop. In this workshop, students narrate events about people other than themselves. They also develop analytical skills that they can apply to other forms of nonfiction writing.

Starting from Literature

Objective

To respond to a professional model of a journalistic narrative as a springboard to writing

Teaching Strategies

Motivate

Ask students to recall journalistic pieces that have made them feel as if they were in the midst of events. How did the pieces do this? How involved were the writers in the action? How did the pieces differ from journalistic pieces that left them feeling less involved?

Tap Prior Knowledge

Ask students whether they have ever had a particularly inspiring and compassionate teacher. Tell students that journalist Samuel G. Freedman has written about such a teacher, introducing her in a scene that shows much about her students and their families.

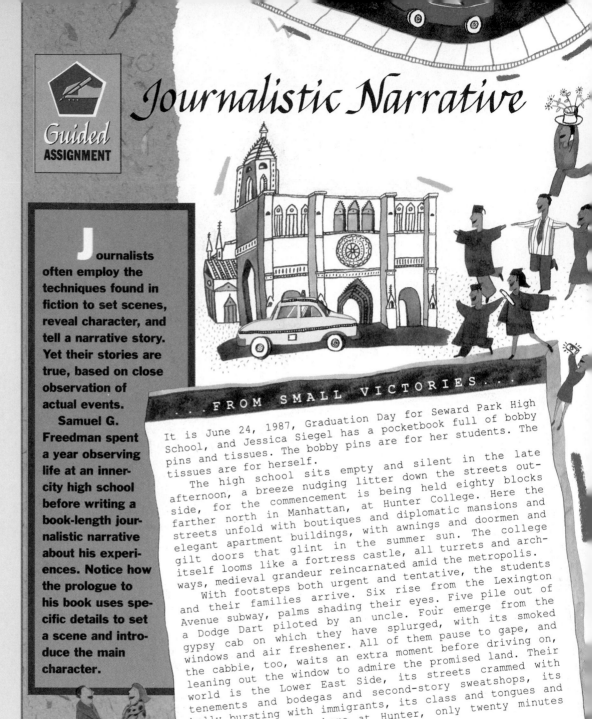

Guided ASSIGNMENT

Journalistic Narrative

Journalists often employ the techniques found in fiction to set scenes, reveal character, and tell a narrative story. Yet their stories are true, based on close observation of actual events.

Samuel G. Freedman spent a year observing life at an inner-city high school before writing a book-length journalistic narrative about his experiences. Notice how the prologue to his book uses specific details to set a scene and introduce the main character.

...FROM SMALL VICTORIES...

It is June 24, 1987, Graduation Day for Seward Park High School, and Jessica Siegel has a pocketbook full of bobby pins and tissues. The bobby pins are for her students. The tissues are for herself.

The high school sits empty and silent in the late afternoon, a breeze nudging litter down the streets outside, for the commencement is being held eighty blocks farther north in Manhattan, at Hunter College. Here the streets unfold with boutiques and diplomatic mansions and elegant apartment buildings, with awnings and doormen and gilt doors that glint in the summer sun. The college itself looms like a fortress castle, all turrets and archways, medieval grandeur reincarnated amid the metropolis.

With footsteps both urgent and tentative, the students and their families arrive. Six rise from the Lexington Avenue subway, palms shading their eyes. Five pile out of a Dodge Dart piloted by an uncle. Four emerge from the gypsy cab on which they have splurged, with its smoked windows and air freshener. All of them pause to gape, and the cabbie, too, waits an extra moment before driving on, leaning out the window to admire the promised land. Their world is the Lower East Side, its streets crammed with tenements and bodegas and second-story sweatshops, its belly bursting with immigrants, its class and tongues and customs so foreign here at Hunter, only twenty minutes from home.

BY SAMUEL G. FREEDMAN

And so they wait and fidget a bit—seniors in their graduation gowns, sisters with cameras, mothers with the afternoon off from the factory. Some don the blue formality of Sunday church, others the heels and sequins of a merengue club. A little brother wiggles in a tuxedo, and an older boyfriend prances in a sweatshirt marked "Slick." A girl cradles a Polaroid snapshot in both her hands as if it were an heirloom locket. A workman maneuvers through the mob and into the auditorium with a floral arrangement balanced on his head. A hot dog vendor works the crowd, scented steam rising from his aluminum cart. It is all confusing, and not a little daunting, and so the air fills with Chinese and Spanish, the languages in which most of the families find solace and take refuge.

These seniors have traveled to a border, to a frontier. Some will never cross it. They will take their diplomas and shrink back southward, back to the comforting, familiar thing, back to the many menaces. But others will wield their diplomas as passports and will step into the new, the strange, the almost inconceivable. A few of them will even attend college here at Hunter, descendants of a sort to the immigrant daughters of Crown Heights and Morrisania and East Harlem and indeed the Lower East Side and Seward Park High School, who a half-century ago entered this edifice just as exhilarated and just as intimidated.

From down the block Jessica Siegel watches, identifying students outlined by the western sun. She has had perhaps 325 of the 450 graduates in her English and journalism classes. She has been teacher, advisor, mentor, and mother. Now, as she has every June for the past nine years, she must say goodbye and farewell. There is no mistaking her, even from a distance. You can see that mop of dirty-blond curls bouncing in cadence with her step. You can see that multicolored smock from Mexico, the one with two birds flanking a fruit bowl. And as she moves into the mob of seniors, you can hear her shout, "Anybody need bobby pins?"

Think AND Respond

How would *you* describe the atmosphere at the graduation ceremony Freedman describes? How does Freedman use descriptive details to set the scene? What ideas does this journalistic narrative give you for eyewitness accounts you could write?

Literature Connection

Author Note Samuel G. Freedman is a former reporter for *The New York Times;* he has won numerous awards for investigative reporting and feature writing. His book *Small Victories* follows teacher Jessica Siegel through the 1987–88 school year at an inner-city New York City school where 92% of the students go on to higher education.

Set a Purpose

Before students read the excerpt, discuss the side-column notes, elaborating on how this writer takes an everyday event and retells it in story form. Explain that the excerpt they will now read is an example of a journalistic narrative. Then have students read the excerpt seeking to identify the specific details the author uses to make the people, places, and event come alive.

Think and Respond

Elicit Personal Responses

Have students write their responses in their journals or reading logs before opening the discussion to the class. Encourage students to give examples of descriptive details that made them feel that they were observers at the scene.

Explore the Author's Techniques

To help students use the excerpt as a model for their own writing, work through the selection with students, calling attention to the author's techniques; for example, Freedman's use of description to set the scene and reveal character (Page 54, paragraph 2: "Here the streets unfold. . . . reincarnated amid the metropolis"); his introduction of Jessica Siegel (Page 54, all of paragraph 1); and his reintroduction of her (Page 55, all of paragraph 2). Suggest that students may want to emulate some of these descriptive techniques as they write their journalistic narrative.

Link Literature to Writing

Remind students that in his journalistic narrative, Samuel G. Freedman makes readers feel that they are onlookers at the graduation and makes readers care about the people and the event being described. Tell students that in the following assignment, they will have an opportunity to create their own journalistic narrative. Suggest that as students think about a topic for their journalistic narrative, they concentrate on people or events that are important to them and on how they can make their readers "see" the people and event and make their readers care.

Prewrite and Explore

Objectives

1. To use prewriting techniques to select a topic for a journalistic narrative
2. To choose appropriate sources to gather information about the subject
3. To determine purpose, goals, and audience for a journalistic narrative

Preteaching

Preview the Prewrite and Explore section. If there are skills or concepts students may need help with before prewriting, present them at this time. The mini-lesson references below may help you in your selection and instruction. The cross references in the pupil text give students access to the same lessons for independent study.

> #### Handbook Mini-Lessons
> - Observing, p. 332
> - Interview, p. 378

You may also wish to use the Thinking Skills Transparencies; Thinking Skills Worksheets; Fine Art Transparencies: Starting Points for Writing; Writing Prompts for Fine Art Transparencies; and the Data Sheet for this assignment along with *Ideas for Writing* as resources during the Prewrite and Explore phase.

Teaching Strategies

 Individualizing Instruction

Cultural Differences As an alternate Exploratory Activity, have students share some of the culture associated with their families' backgrounds. Suggest that students consider choosing as a topic a cultural or sports event that is indigenous to their culture.

INVITATION TO Write

Samuel G. Freedman's book was the result of his close observation of his subject over a period of time. Now it is your turn to write a journalistic narrative about an event or experience you can witness.

Journalistic narratives combine the techniques of nonfiction and fiction. The main purpose of journalism is to inform—to present factual information about a subject. By closely observing a subject and asking incisive questions, a journalist can gather the material needed to develop a rich, accurate portrait. Then, by presenting the information as a narrative, the journalist can also tell a story. The journalistic narratives in magazines, newspaper feature sections, and nonfiction books employ such elements as character, setting, mood, and plot to tell compelling stories that often read like good fiction.

HANDBOOKS
FOR HELP & PRACTICE

Observing,
p. 332
Interviewing,
p. 378

PREWRITE AND EXPLORE

1. Look for ideas. What have you always wanted to do? Where have you wanted to go? Is there someone or something you are curious about? Writing a journalistic narrative is a way to investigate firsthand subjects that intrigue you. Try one or more of the following activities to look for subjects to explore.

Exploratory Activities

- **Listing** What are your special interests? List them and then freewrite about aspects of them that you could explore through an eyewitness account.
- **Events** With a group of classmates, brainstorm for ideas about events—everything from sports to concerts to public meetings—that you could witness and describe.
- **Places** What places hold special meaning to you? What places would you like to know more about? List interesting and unusual places you could visit and describe.

Springboard

To help students think of appropriate topics for a journalistic narrative, you might bring in a "calendar" section from a local newspaper that lists coming events in your area. Ask students to share any experiences they had at these or similar events in the past. Have students brainstorm possible writing topics connected to each event.

Many events, such as this exciting rescue, make good subjects for journalistic narratives.

- **A day in the life** If you could be a fly on the wall, observing everything that happens around you for a day, where would you want to be?
- **Reading literature** Find examples of dramatic journalistic narratives, such as those written by Tom Wolfe, Norman Mailer, or Joan Didion, and examine the techniques that the writers used. What ideas do these narratives give you for ones you could write?

2. Choose a subject. Look over your ideas, and freewrite about the ones you find most promising. Keep in mind that you will need to gather firsthand information about your subject, so choose one you will be able to research effectively. If you have trouble finding a subject, thumb through your journal, check your writing for the Sketchbook on page 52, and consider the suggestions under "Apply Your Skills" on page 65.

3. Gather background information. First, acquaint yourself generally with the subject. Newspapers are a valuable resource, both for facts about subjects and for ideas on people to talk to. Check your library's newspaper indexes, magazine indexes, and books.

4. Identify your sources. Your sources are people you can talk to, written information you can gather, and physical evidence—both objects and places—you can observe and describe. Brainstorm by yourself or with classmates to find ideas on what types of evidence you can gather and how you can go about your reporting.

5. Begin reporting. Your main tools in reporting are your powers of observation and your ability to ask questions.

- **Observation** Just noticing what goes on around you will provide some of your most important reporting. Record your observations of everything you see.

Writing
—TIP—

Pick a subject you really like and want to learn more about.

 Individualizing Instruction

Advanced Students You might focus the attention of advanced students on the way Tom Wolfe goes so far as to invent words and phrases in such works as *The Electric Kool-Aid Acid Test* and "Mau-Mauing the Flak Catchers." Wolfe does this to give his writing a special flair as well as to convey a deeper sense of his subject. Advanced students might be interested in inventing their own words and phrases in their journalistic narratives.

Spot Check

Circulate around the classroom to check that each student's choice of topic is appropriate for a journalistic narrative; that is, a student should be able to observe events that will be described or interview people connected to the topic. If you find students who are having difficulty thinking of an appropriate topic, you might refer them to the Data Sheet for this assignment or to *Ideas for Writing*. You might also use the Fine Arts Transparencies.

 Individualizing Instruction

Learning Styles Visual and kinesthetic learners might want to take photographs, sketch out a scene, or make a videotape; auditory learners may wish to use a cassette player to record their observations.

Teaching Tip: Interviewing

Remind students that when they interview, they should record some of the actual words and phrases of the person being interviewed. Being able to supply examples of the interviewee's speech pattern and word choice adds authenticity to an article.

Critical Thinking

Judging Have students evaluate the notes that Fred took, concentrating on techniques that they themselves might try. For example, Fred uses chronological order but also records a physical description of the setting and of McLean; he tells the reactions of others, quotes McLean, and uses understandable abbreviations.

Teaching Tip: Audience

Since this essay is a journalistic narrative, have students identify who their ideal audience would be and then write for that audience. For example, students might write for an audience of a daily newspaper, a science journal, an entertainment weekly, or a sports magazine. Discuss how their identification of an audience would affect their presentation.

COMPUTER TIP

If you, the school, or your library have access to an on-line database or index, it can be an excellent source of information.

• **Interviews** Talk to the people involved in your subject. Come prepared with a list of questions you want answered, but keep yourself open to new information. As you talk to people, you may find your story moving in directions you hadn't anticipated. Also, ask the people you interview to suggest other people you should consult.

6. Record your information. Accurate reporting of information is essential in journalistic writing. As you explore your subject, take notes recording facts, details, your own reactions, and questions you want to follow up.

Fred had been intrigued by a gem mine in the mountains near his hometown ever since he and his friends had stumbled on it during a camping trip. He decided to contact the mine owners and ask if he could write a feature story on the mine for his local newspaper. Here are some of the notes he took on his tour of the mine.

ONE STUDENT'S PROCESS

Coming up to the mine. Day is foggy, drizzly. Bumpy road snakes around through the hills, ends abruptly. Oak trees all around. Simple whitewashed frame at steep slope. John McLean, foreman: sandy hair, full bushy beard.

Tim digs in soupy pocket, pulls out quartz, small tourmaline. Everyone oohs and ahs but McLean. McL: "There are no gems here. Those are too small to bother with."

Using ropes to pull us through zigzag passageways. Air smells. McL: "It's nitro from blasting yesterday."

MINE SITE

7. Share your notes. Go over your notes with a small group of writers. Look for ideas about what central idea, angle, or theme seems to be emerging from your notes. What details do you and your writing group feel are still missing? Try freewriting for ten minutes for ideas on how you might shape your narrative.

 Writer's Choice Do you want to make yourself a part of your narrative and tell it from the first-person point of view, or do you want to report what you see using the third-person point of view?

8. Determine your purpose and goals. In journalistic writing, your overall purpose is to inform. However, you may also have some personal goals. They may be as simple as satisfying your curiosity; or you may wish to learn more about a subject, share your enthusiasm for it, or draw attention to a problem.

9. Identify your audience. Keep in mind how much or little your readers know about your subject. You may need to define key terms or provide background information so they can easily follow your narrative.

DRAFT AND DISCOVER

1. Look for an angle. When journalists approach a story, they don't just gather facts and report them. They analyze their subject in order to find a dominant impression, or angle, that captures its significance.

As Fred thought about the gem mine, he first considered focusing on how it operates or on its history. However, as he reviewed his notes, what struck him most was the excitement of searching for gems. That would be his angle.

2. Organize your draft. Many journalistic narratives are presented chronologically, from start to finish. Some start in the middle, describing some attention-grabbing incident, and then use a flash-back to fill in the reader about events that led up to it. Freedman uses the graduation-day scene to introduce the characters and issues he would discuss; then later he returns to the beginning of the school year and tells his story in chronological order. Another alternative is to present a series of loosely related scenes, each one revealing important points about your subject.

PROBLEM
SOLVING

How can I decide what direction my writing should take?

HANDBOOKS

FOR HELP & PRACTICE

Narrative Introductions, pp. 371–374

Elaborative Details, pp. 376–378

Mood, pp. 426–427

Point of View, pp. 446–447

Mastering Dialogue, pp. 452–455

Journalistic Narrative **59**

Draft and Discover

Objectives

1. To draft a journalistic narrative, using description, narration, and dialogue to convey a unified description of the subject
2. To respond to one's own writing and to that of one's peers

Preteaching

Preview the Draft and Discover section. If there are skills or concepts students may need help with before drafting, present them at this time. The mini-lesson references below may help you in your selection and instruction.

> ### Handbook Mini-Lessons
> - Narrative Introductions, pp. 371–374
> - Elaborative Details, pp. 376–378
> - Mood, pp. 426–427
> - Point of View, pp. 446–447
> - Mastering Dialogue, pp. 452–455

You may also wish to use the Elaboration Worksheet and the Peer Response Guide during the Draft and Discover phase.

Teaching Strategies

 Individualizing Instruction

Visual Learners To organize their drafts, these students might like to use a time line, outline, cluster, or tree diagram so that they can visualize the relationships among ideas. You may wish to use Thinking Skills Transparencies or Thinking Skills Worksheets with these students.

Springboard

Have students discuss Gabriel Garcia Marquez's words about drafting: "One of the most difficult things is the first paragraph. I have spent many months on a first paragraph and once I get it, the rest just comes out very easily. In the first paragraph you solve most of the problems. . . ." Since students don't have months to write the first paragraph, discuss the strategies they use to begin their drafts and move beyond the opening. Share strategies you have found helpful in your own writing, and mention the possibility of putting off the introductory paragraph until the rest of the narrative is written.

Self-Evaluation

Suggest that students also survey the Questions for Your Peer Readers and try to predict how a reader will respond to their paper. Use of the Peer Response Guide may be helpful in clarifying ideas.

Managing the Paper Load

During drafting, circulate around the classroom, noting those students who seem to be struggling with their material. Engage these students in short question-and-answer sessions aimed at uncovering problems. Discovering and helping resolve problems at this stage will reduce your paper load later.

PROBLEM

S O L V I N G

How can I make my experience real for my readers?

---

3. Elaborate on ideas. The following strategies can be helpful in revealing the essential qualities of your subject.

Strategies

• **Description** Look for the telling details that will make your subject real for the reader. For instance, Freedman described a girl who "cradles a Polaroid snapshot in both her hands as if it were an heirloom locket."
• **Narration** Think about ways of using narration to build suspense or create a mood. You can enhance your narrative by using techniques associated with fiction, such as creating a vivid character, setting a scene, and developing a plot.
• **Dialogue** Using direct quotations can reveal the character of the people you write about and convey the atmosphere of the event you are describing.

Fred decided to begin his narrative with a description of his group approaching the gem mine.

ONE STUDENT'S PROCESS

On a foggy, drizzly day not long ago, a small expedition made its way up the dirt road through the hills not too far from Lake Henshaw. The road ended halfway up a steep slope covered with oak trees. This spot was the entrance to the Himalaya Mine. It's not very impressive to look at, but in the past century a fortune in gems has come from this mine.

 Writer's Choice Some journalistic narratives are written in the present tense to heighten the "you are there" quality. You can choose to use present or past tense, depending on the impression you want to make.

4. Reread and react. Once you have completed your draft, set it aside for a time. Then review it, and ask your peer readers to respond to it.

Social Studies Connection

Historical Fiction Suggest that students read portions of a historical novel, such as *The Rise of David Levinsky* by Abraham Cahan, and an encyclopedia entry on the same topic, such as immigration in the late 1800's or Ellis Island. Encourage students to compare the two accounts, noting whether either or both use the techniques of a journalistic narrative.

REVIEW YOUR WRITING

Questions for Yourself
- Have I found a strong angle, or is my journalistic narrative a collection of random pieces of information?
- Have I used descriptive details to vividly re-create people, places, and events?
- Have I made clear why my subject is important to me?

Questions for Your Peer Readers
- What dominant impression did you get from my essay?
- What sentences or passages stand out as particularly vivid or memorable?
- Is anything unclear, irrelevant, or unnecessary?
- Is there anything I wrote about that you would like to know more or less about?

REVISE YOUR WRITING

1. Evaluate your responses. Look over the responses you have received and see what changes you want to make. Also keep in mind these guidelines for evaluating journalistic narratives.

Standards For Evaluation

An effective journalistic narrative . . .

- presents a dominant impression or angle on its subject.
- accurately presents information about the subject.
- uses facts and descriptive details to present a vivid picture of the subject.
- tells an engaging, easy-to-follow story.
- demonstrates a clear sense of audience.

2. Problem-solve. The draft on the next page shows changes that Fred made in response to suggestions from his peer readers. Rework your own draft, incorporating all the revisions you have decided to make.

HANDBOOKS
FOR HELP & PRACTICE

Unity/Coherence, pp. 382–391
Peer Response, pp. 397–400
Varieties of Language, pp. 429–433
Using Source Materials, pp. 482–489

Revise Your Writing

Objectives
1. To evaluate the responses to the first draft of a journalistic narrative
2. To revise the draft
3. To proofread for errors

Preteaching

Preview the Revise Your Writing section. Based on this preview and on problems you may have noted in students' drafts, identify skills you want to review. The mini-lessons listed below may proved helpful.

Handbook Mini-Lessons
- Unity/Coherence, pp. 382–391
- Peer Response, pp. 397–401
- Varieties of Language, pp. 429–433
- Using Source Material, pp. 482–488

You may also wish to use the Student Revision Model Transparencies, the Revision and Proofreading Worksheets, and the Guidelines for Evaluating Writing for this assignment as resources.

Guidelines for Evaluation

The following guidelines may be used for a close evaluation of a journalistic narrative. See the Guidelines for Evaluating Writing in the Teacher's Resource File for additional help with holistic or analytic scoring.

Ideas and Content
- presents a dominant impression
- imparts accurate information
- uses vivid facts and description
- incorporates language appropriate to audience
- uses vivid and precise words

Structure and Form
- uses narration to develop a story about the subject
- organizes the material in an easy-to-follow manner

Grammar, Usage, and Mechanics
- uses standard grammar and correct usage, punctuation, and spelling

Publish and Present

Objective

To publish and present a journalistic narrative

Handbook Mini-Lessons
- Publishing Your Writing,
  pp. 413–415

Teaching Strategies

Modeling

For students who choose the option of submitting their articles to a newspaper or magazine, model the kind of cover letter you might write to accompany such a submission.

Listening and Speaking

Suggest to students who choose the option of making a video version of their journalistic narratives that they review the tips for making a videotape. Encourage students to rehearse before they make their video.

ONE STUDENT'S PROCESS

> More precise word choice would help.

> Nice description! I feel like I'm there.

> Why wasn't he impressed?

One of the novices knelt and put [thrust] his hand into the hole [pocket] which was wet [soupy] with water that had come [seeped] in during the night. Soon he pulled out a few chunks of quarts [quartz] and a few pale pink crystals [tourmalines] that fit in the palm of his hand. Then a few larger crystals of a deeper pink. Each discovery was greeted with wild enthusiasm by the others, who were clamoring impatiently for a chance to dig in the hole; but our foreman McLean was not impressed. "There are no gems here," he said. "Those are too small to bother with."

Grammar TIP

Be sure to check that you have spelled proper names and other proper nouns correctly.

HANDBOOKS
FOR HELP & PRACTICE

Publishing
Your Writing,
pp. 413–415

---

3. Proofread your work. Make a clean copy that incorporates all your changes, and look for errors in grammar and mechanics.

LINKING
GRAMMAR AND WRITING
Precise Nouns and Verbs

Using precise nouns and verbs will enhance your descriptions. For example, Samuel G. Freedman could have written, "Five [people] get out of a car driven by an uncle." Instead, he wrote, "Five *pile* out of a *Dodge Dart piloted* by an uncle."

4. Publish and present. Collect all the journalistic narratives written by classmates and publish them, with each article laid out with appropriate photographs or illustrations.

- **Submit your article to a newspaper.** Contact the editor of your school or community newspaper about printing your article.
- **Save your work in your writing portfolio.**

Literature Connection

Selection to Read Students might enjoy reading the nonfiction narrative "Shooting an Elephant" by George Orwell. Suggest that students think about the characteristics of a journalistic narrative and determine whether this selection can be classified as such.

The Search for Buried Treasure

Fred Dobbs

On a foggy, drizzly day not long ago, a small expedition made its way up the rutted dirt road that snaked through the hills not too far from Lake Henshaw. The road ended halfway up a steep slope covered with oak trees. There in front of us was only a simple, white-washed frame around an opening in a hill. This drab spot marked the entrance to the Himalaya Mine. It's not very impressive to look at, but in the past century a fortune in gems has come from within.

The Himalaya is a tourmaline mine. Tourmaline, a pencil-shaped crystal that comes in a variety of translucent colors, is gaining popularity among jewelry designers, gem carvers, and mineral specimen collectors. On this day, our small expedition of novice miners would have a chance to search for this rare gem.

Mine foreman John McLean, a sandy-haired man who looks the part of a miner with his full, bushy beard, outfitted us with hard hats and miners' lamps, and then led us into the cool, dank darkness of the mine. McLean directed us down a sloping tunnel toward a crater, about ten feet in diameter, that was the beginning of a new shaft. The previous day, he said, a pocket (a clay-filled opening in the stone) had

Uses descriptive details to set the scene

Narrates the story of the exploration of the mine

Journalistic Narrative **63**

Using the Model

Have students refer to the standards for evaluation list on page 61 and find passages in the student model that correspond to each item. Students should also use those standards and the side column notes or Fred Dobbs' essay to evaluate their own narratives.

Teaching Tip: Assessment Prompts

Now that students have completed their journalistic narratives, you may want to use the Writing Prompts for Assessment for this assignment to give students experience in taking tests calling for journalistic narratives. You may also want to use the *Writing About Literature Booklet* to give students practice in writing about journalistic narratives.

Reteaching

Assess the needs of students who were not successful developing an effective journalistic narrative and identify two or three areas in which additional practice is needed. Assign the appropriate Handbook Mini-Lessons, along with the support materials listed for each lesson. Concepts commonly requiring reteaching for this assignment are:

Elaborative Details: Handbook 9
Interviewing: Handbook 9

The following suggestions and resources may also be useful.

1. Poor Organization Suggest that students go back and make an "after the fact" outline. In other words, have students outline their finished essays so that they can see gaps or inconsistencies in their organization. You might also pair students, directing them to outline each other's paper.

2. Imprecise Words   Remind students that vivid descriptions depend on precise words. Have students work in small groups to identify dull and imprecise words in one another's essays. Using a thesaurus or dictionary, students should try to replace these words with words that will make their descriptions come alive.

Extension and Enrichment

• Students can compare and contrast the techniques used in feature stories from various sections of the newspaper. For example, students might compare the amount of dialogue and descriptive language in a sports feature and in a human interest story.

• Suggest that students use descriptive detail to write a short poem based on some aspect of the topic they used for their journalistic narrative.

Presents a dominant impression, or angle—the excitement of a group searching for gems

Uses dialogue to present information

Uses precise, vivid words to describe the action

Reinforces the dominant impression in the conclusion

been discovered that might contain tourmaline.

One of the novices knelt and thrust his hand into the pocket, which was soupy with water that had seeped in during the night. Soon he pulled out a few chunks of quartz and a few pale pink tourmalines that fit in the palm of his hand, then a few larger crystals of a deeper pink. Each discovery was greeted with wild enthusiasm by the others, who were clamoring impatiently for a chance to dig in the hole; but our foreman, McLean, was not impressed.

"There are no gems here," he said. "Those are too small to bother with."

Then another novice miner reached down and pulled out a giant specimen—a pointed crystal four inches tall and three inches in diameter, half pink and half green.

McLean was finally impressed. "If it looks as good outside in the daylight as it does here, it's probably a $3,000 piece," he said.

McLean next led us up a zigzag passageway to another shaft. The acrid smell of nitroglycerin from the previous day's blasting lingered in the air as we hoisted ourselves up the ropes that guided us. Again we dug for buried treasure. Here the clay was soft and gooey, but mixed in were shards of quartz and other materials that could easily slice open unsuspecting fingers. Two novice miners had to give up early when they opened deep gashes in their hands.

Meanwhile, McLean methodically cleaned out a pocket, hardly stopping to examine the crystals he found. "You get jaded," he said. To him, a fine crystal is a commodity that will buy another case of dynamite so he can continue his job. Still, he appreciates the wonderment of what the earth can create. He guided me to a pocket and coached me as I groped through the muck. Finally, I felt the outline of a crystal—a rich, pink, finger-sized shaft of tourmaline.

As the crystal was released from the clay, McLean said approvingly, "You're the first to touch this in eighty million years."

64   Workshop 2

WRITER TO WRITER

Hating to ask questions and never trusting the answers has defined the type of reporting I do. What I do is hang around. Become part of the furniture. An end table in someone's life. It is the art of the scavenger: set a scene, establish a mood, get the speech patterns right.

John Gregory Dunne, journalist, novelist, and screenwriter

1. Reflect on your writing. As an end note for your journalistic narrative, write a brief narrative describing your experiences writing it. Tell how you reported your piece, explaining any difficulties you encountered and how you might avoid them in the future. Describe how you gathered details. Did you find enough to write rich descriptions? Consider what you would do differently if you were to write another journalistic narrative.

2. Apply your skills. Try completing one or more of the following activities.

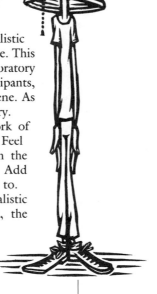

- **Cross-curricular** Using the techniques of a journalistic narrative, re-create a moment in the history of science. This might be a moment of discovery or a visit to the laboratory of a famous scientist. Feel free to interview participants, create quotes, or even make yourself part of the scene. As an alternative, re-create an important event in history.
- **Literature** Select a scene from a well-known work of literature and re-create it in a journalistic narrative. Feel free to interview characters, quoting directly from the work and making up quotations of your own. Add yourself to the scene as a new character, if you want to.
- **General** Attend a sports event and write a journalistic narrative describing the occasion—the spectators, the setting, and the experience as a whole.
- **Related assignments** Follow the suggestions on pages 68–74 to create a personality profile or a video.

Journalistic Narrative **65**

Learning from Your Writing Process

Objective

To analyze and reflect on what has been learned about the writing process and about the writing of a journalistic narrative

Teaching Strategies

Reflecting on the Process

As students write the brief narrative, encourage them to focus on one or two of the suggested ideas, rather than trying to respond to all of them. Remind students that the response to what they would do differently is often the most valuable of all.

Writing Portfolio

Have students attach their brief narrative to their essay and place it in their Writing Portfolio. Encourage them to compare their personal narrative with their journalistic narrative, noting areas of improvement.

Summary and Closure

Before proceeding to the next lesson, be sure that students have internalized the following key points:

1. Journalistic narrative and personal narrative techniques are similar, but a journalistic narrative requires research.

2. Narration, description, dialogue, and facts are important elements in a journalistic narrative.

3. An effective journalistic narrative focuses on a single impression in language appropriate to the audience.

Allow students time to summarize what they learned by describing the elements of an effective journalistic narrative and by telling why knowing how to write one might help them in other circumstances, both in and out of school.

Related Assignment:
PERSONALITY PROFILE

Starting from Literature

Objective

To respond to a professional model as a springboard for writing

Teaching Strategies

Motivate

Ask students to name the people in the world today who interest them most—anyone from sports and entertainment figures to world leaders. Ask students how they know about these people. A great deal of their information probably comes from personality profiles presented in the news media. Articles, interviews, and feature stories expand our knowledge of people's backgrounds and personal lives, teaching us more than we would learn from their actions alone.

Tap Prior Knowledge

Ask students what they already know about Michael Jordan. For students who don't follow basketball, have a basketball fan in the class explain who Jordan is and what makes him special. Then invite the class to read the excerpt and discover or rediscover one of contemporary America's most visible and admirable personalities.

Set a Purpose

Have students look for the various elements Donnelly uses to make her article a vivid character sketch. Strong word choices (''his perfectly proportioned frame . . . soars up''), choices of details (the ''Jordan for President'' sign), and bits of information (the ''love of the game'' clause in his contract) work together to make us feel we are getting to know Michael Jordan as a real person.

Personality Profile

Related ASSIGNMENT

Basketball player Michael Jordan—already a legend in the sports world! Obviously writer Sally Donnelly thinks so, as you will discover when you read this excerpt from a personality profile she wrote for *Time* a few years back.

While you are reading, notice how Donnelly interweaves descriptions of Jordan's physical characteristics and actions with his personality traits to convey her enthusiasm and admiration for Jordan, not only as an outstanding athlete but also as an exceptional human being.

66

Election night, 1988. In a darkened Madison Square Garden, a murmur of anticipation ripples through the standing-room-only crowd. On the floor below, the guest of honor stands, head bent, a bit overwhelmed and maybe a bit embarrassed by the spectacle. "Ladies and gentleman," booms a voice as the spotlight rakes the now cheering audience, "No. 23, Miiichaaael Jooordaaan!" As one, the 19,591 men, women, and children rise to pay thunderous tribute. . . .

So what's all the fuss about? Simply that this is the first time during the 1988-89 season that the world's most exciting basketball player is visiting New York. A JORDAN FOR PRESIDENT sign even appears in the stands, a semiserious calling to a higher order.

For now, Michael Jeffrey Jordan is high enough, thank you. . . . He is the hottest player in America's hottest sport. Only 25, Jordan has already won every major individual award the NBA has to offer. . . . Small wonder some sportscasters call Jordan "Superman in Shorts."

Such high-flying praise is all the more astounding given Jordan's size. At 6 ft. 6 in., he is a full inch shorter than the average NBA player, but he transcends his handicap by spending most of his time above the others. His perfectly proportioned frame. . . soars up, around and over the mere mortals he opposes. Most guards . . .prefer the quiet of the perimeter to the violent collisions of leviathans under the hoop. But Jordan is most dangerous around the basket, with his arsenal of double-clutch lay-ups and

GREAT **LEAPIN' LIZARDS**

hyperspace dunks over men very nearly a foot taller. . . .

For Jordan, the world of basketball is a world without bounds. He gyrates, levitates and often dominates. Certainly he fascinates. In arenas around the country, food and drink go unsold because fans refuse to leave their seats for fear of missing a spectacular Jordan move to tell their grandchildren about. . . .

Jordan is one of only a handful of NBA players who truly seem to enjoy themselves. [He] plays as if what he calls "the best job in the world" might be gone tomorrow. He even has a "love of the game" clause written into his contract, which allows him to play basketball anytime, and anywhere, the urge strikes, especially on the playgrounds back home in North Carolina. But Jordan's delight in the sport is not the main reason he plays basketball. Competition drives Michael Jordan. Incessantly.

Think AND Respond

Sally Donnelly's goal in writing this profile was to stamp a vivid impression of the whole Michael Jordan, athlete and human being, on readers' minds. In your opinion, did she succeed? Why? Whose personality or achievement would you like to profile?

67

Think and Respond

Elicit Personal Reponses

Have students jot down their informal responses first using the Think and Response questions as a guide. Then discuss the questions aloud. Begin by discussing Michael Jordan himself, but shift the focus quickly to the Donnelly article as a piece of writing.

Explore the Author's Techniques

Point out how Donnelly interweaves general information with specific scenes, quotations, and details. This technique is used in almost all personality profiles. Information alone would be boring; details and descriptions alone would not tell us much about the subject. Working together, the two aspects entertain and inform at the same time.

Link Literature to Writing

All of us at times have described people orally or in writing. A friend wants to know, "What is Joe like?" and we describe him. Or we write a letter from summer camp describing a counselor's quirks. A formal personality profile is a more highly elaborated, carefully planned version of the same process—as illustrated in Donnelly's piece. Tell students that the following assignment will help them turn this universal pastime into a conscious technique.

Literature Connection

Ask students to scan the biographical notes in their literature textbook about authors whose work they have liked. These can be excellent sources of subjects and preliminary information for personality profiles.

Physical Education Connection

Invite a coach or basketball player from your school to give your class a talk on what makes Michael Jordan not merely a very good player but a great one. Focus on how Jordan's approach can help people striving in any endeavor.

Guiding Your Writers

Objectives

1. To choose a subject for a personality profile
2. To gather information
3. To choose a form and draft a personality profile
4. To publish and present a personality profile

Preteaching

Preview the remainder of the assignment. If there are skills or concepts your students may need help with at the outset, present them now. The mini-lesson references below may help you in your selection and instruction. The cross references in the pupil text give students access to the same lessons for independent practice.

Handbook Mini-Lessons

- Interview, p. 378
- Unity/Coherence, pp. 382–391
- Varieties of Language, pp. 429–433
- Problem Solving, pp. 473–474
- Research Skills, pp. 479–490

Teaching Strategies

Individualizing Instruction

LD Students There have been many famous, successful people who have overcome learning disabilities, (e.g., Albert Einstein and Nelson Rockefeller). Students may want to select a contemporary figure who has prevailed against a disability, concentrating on the characteristics that ensured the subject's success.

Learning Styles Some students may prefer to do most of their research in the library, others in the field through interviews. Lead them to design their topics with these preferences in mind.

INVITATION TO Write

Sally Donnelly's piece on Michael Jordan has given you a feel for Jordan as an individual. Now try your hand at writing a profile of a special individual of your choice.

The personality profile is a popular feature in most newspapers and magazines. Therefore, when you are writing your personality profile, you will use some of the same skills and techniques you employed in writing a newspaper story. You will need to make observations, do research, and conduct interviews to gather information on your subject.

▶ PREPARING YOUR PROFILE

1. Choose a subject. The person you decide to profile should be someone you admire. He or she doesn't have to be a contemporary celebrity such as Michael Jordan, or a historical figure such as Eleanor Roosevelt. You may prefer to write about a subject closer to home—a favorite relative, a neighbor, or a local government or business leader. Choose someone, though, whose story or particular qualities you consider special.

2. Research or interview to gather information. You can start researching a historical figure in encyclopedias or in the library card catalog. Sunday newspaper supplements and the *Readers' Guide to Periodical Literature* are useful sources of information about contemporary celebrities. If you decide to profile a lesser-known person, interviewing is the best method for getting information. Also think about interviewing other people who know your subject well. They may give you information that is not available anywhere else.

3. Set your goal for writing. To help decide on your goal, ask yourself questions like these: What makes this person special to me? What impression of him or her do I want to leave in the minds of my readers?

HANDBOOKS

FOR HELP & PRACTICE

Interviewing,
p. 378
Unity/Coherence,
pp. 382–390
Varieties of
Language,
pp. 429–434
Problem Solving,
pp. 472–473
Research Skills,
pp. 479–489

Springboard

Create a grab-bag of topics by having each student write down the names of three people worth profiling. Each name should be on a separate piece of paper, folded and placed in a box or bag. You might open and read all the names at once, or let students in search of topics investigate the grab-bag independently.

WRITING YOUR PROFILE

1. Choose a form. Your profile may take any of several forms. One possibility is a narrative describing a day in your subject's life; another is analysis that elaborates on certain characteristics, actions, and traits of your subject, one at a time. Choose one of these or any other form that works well for you.

2. Be selective. Review the information you've gathered, and select only those facts that will help you reach your writing goal. Notice how Sally Donnelly's profile emphasizes two main things about Michael Jordan: his physical traits as an athlete and his personal values.

3. Try out your ideas in a draft. Capture your readers' attention at once with a title and opening paragraph that make your subject come alive: you might begin with an interesting quotation from your subject, or show the person in action. Then develop your profile by presenting other special traits of your subject.

REVIEWING YOUR WRITING

1. Invite constructive criticism. Ask peer readers to go over your draft. Does it achieve your goal? Does it make readers feel they now know your subject?

2. Check for precise words and significant details. Have you used exact nouns, lively modifiers, and action-oriented verbs? Does each descriptive detail suggest something of the subject's traits and values?

PUBLISHING AND PRESENTING

- **Enter an oral reading lottery.** Have someone draw names of at least ten students who will read their profiles aloud. Discuss each one.
- **Collect the class's profiles in an "Unforgettable Individuals" booklet.** Include photographs of the subjects, if possible. Distribute copies to the school and local library and to senior citizen centers in your community.

Writing TIP

You can set your profile in a special place that will itself reveal interesting information about your subject. Actors, for instance, are often interviewed in their dressing rooms between scenes.

Guidelines for Evaluation

The following guidelines can be used for close evaluation of a personality profile. See the Guidelines for Evaluating Writing in the Teacher's Resource File for additional help with holistic or analytical scoring.

A good personality profile . . .

- deals with a person the writer and reader care about
- uses reliable information about the subject
- creates a unified tone and impression
- captures the reader's attention at the beginning
- describes the subject as a whole person, not a one-dimensional figure
- uses vivid language to make the subject come alive
- uses standard grammar and correct usage, capitalization, punctuation, and spelling

Reteaching

Assess the needs of students who were not successful developing an effective personality profile. Assign the appropriate Handbook Mini-Lessons. Concepts commonly requiring reteaching for this assignment are

Interview: Handbook 9
Research Skills: Handbook 24

The following suggestions and resources may also be useful.

1. Modifers Some profiles fail because students use too many adjectives to describe their subjects. Have students underline the modifiers in their profiles to determine whether they convey a unified impression of the person in question.

2. Interest If a profile fails to make its subject come alive, discuss with the writer why he or she chose that particular person to write about. Perhaps the writer chose the subject out of a sense of obligation rather than any particular enthusiasm. Encourage students to rethink their profiles, selecting a person about whom they have a strong opinion.

Social Studies Connection

Ask volunteers to research articles or books in which historical figures were profiled by their contemporaries or near-contemporaries. Plutarch's *Lives of the Noble Romans* is the classic example in ancient history; examples in American history include John Adams' diaries, Emerson's *Representative Men*, William Hearndon's memoir of Lincoln, and Arthur Schlesinger's *A Thousand Days* about John F. Kennedy. Have students compare contemporaneous views with our own and discuss how reading contemporaneous memoirs enlarged their views of historical figures.

Related Assignment:
VIDEO

Starting from the Model

Objectives

1. To recognize the conventions and impact of journalistic videotaping
2. To use the skills of observation, description, and narration to create a journalistic videotape

Teaching Strategies

Motivate

Ask students to name current local events or controversies that they see as significant. Prompt them, if necessary, by naming some of importance to you. Ask where they gained their awareness of these issues; guide them in seeing that the media provides this awareness. Then ask which type of media coverage has the most impact on them (print, radio, or TV).

Tap Prior Knowledge

Ask students to think about the structure of TV news programs: which portion, audio or video, usually carries the bulk of the story? What is the role of the other portion? (The audio carries the bulk of the story, while the video highlights significant details and provides illustration.) Next, ask students to recall recent television coverage of major issues. Which roles did audio and video play? Might they, as reporters, have used the two elements differently?

Set a Purpose

Elicit examples of televised news stories students can recall. Have them consider the impact of memorable visual images. Discuss how words and pictures come together to tell a complete story.

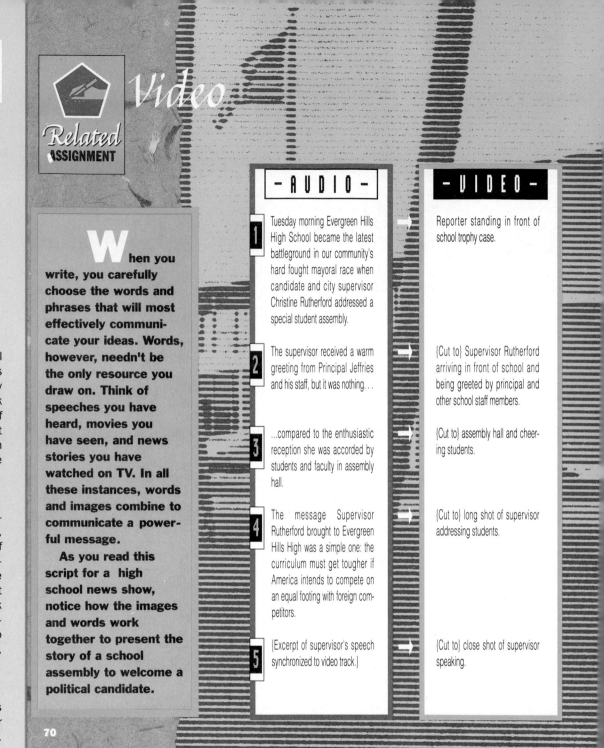

Related ASSIGNMENT

Video

When you write, you carefully choose the words and phrases that will most effectively communicate your ideas. Words, however, needn't be the only resource you draw on. Think of speeches you have heard, movies you have seen, and news stories you have watched on TV. In all these instances, words and images combine to communicate a powerful message.

As you read this script for a high school news show, notice how the images and words work together to present the story of a school assembly to welcome a political candidate.

— AUDIO —

1. Tuesday morning Evergreen Hills High School became the latest battleground in our community's hard fought mayoral race when candidate and city supervisor Christine Rutherford addressed a special student assembly.

2. The supervisor received a warm greeting from Principal Jeffries and his staff, but it was nothing...

3. ...compared to the enthusiastic reception she was accorded by students and faculty in assembly hall.

4. The message Supervisor Rutherford brought to Evergreen Hills High was a simple one: the curriculum must get tougher if America intends to compete on an equal footing with foreign competitors.

5. {Excerpt of supervisor's speech synchronized to video track.}

— VIDEO —

Reporter standing in front of school trophy case.

{Cut to} Supervisor Rutherford arriving in front of school and being greeted by principal and other school staff members.

{Cut to} assembly hall and cheering students.

{Cut to} long shot of supervisor addressing students.

{Cut to} close shot of supervisor speaking.

70

- AUDIO -

6 Supervisor Rutherford's remarks put her squarely at odds with her opponent, State's Attorney Larry O'Brien, who favors retaining the present curriculum while putting the Evergreen Hills school system on on a twelve-month schedule.

7 Supervisor Rutherford acknowledged she didn't expect to find many votes here yesterday—after all, only a small percentage of Evergreen Hills High students are eligible to vote. But she did view this campaign stop as a good opportunity to drive home her theme of curriculum reform in front of an audience that views her opponent's position—the twelve-month school year— with alarm.

8 This is Ricardo Juarez reporting for "The Morning Show," Evergreen Hills High.

- VIDEO -

(As audio track continues) two reaction shots: student in audience; Principal Jeffries. When audio of supervisor's speech ends, cut from principal to shot of supervisor shaking students' hands as students applaud and she leaves the auditorium.

(Cut to) reporter in front of trophy case.

Think AND *Respond*

Why do you suppose the reporter chose to begin and end his report in front of the trophy case? Does the reporter always describe the image being shown on the tape? Why? How did the reporter organize his report? What type of event would you like to capture on videotape and narrate?

Think and Respond

Elicit Personal Responses

Ask students which portion of the video seemed most effective to them. Then let them volunteer the answers to the six journalism questions regarding the content of the report.

Explore the Producer's Techniques

As you go over the Think and Respond questions with students, be sure they understand that each part of the video portion provides details describing or illustrating a fact in the audio portion.

Link Literature to Writing

Point out to students that the producers of the news report use the visual portion to illustrate only the more significant details from the audio portion. Suggest that students use a similar technique in their own videos, letting one portion add emphasis to the parts of the other portion that they want to underscore or that might be important to the audience.

Explain that, as students film their videotapes, they may find that the equipment gives them less control over the audio than the video. In that case, the video portion would establish chronology and provide the main facts, and the audio portion would be used to support it and add emphasis.

Social Studies Connection

Assign students to watch at least half an hour of TV news daily for a week, taking notes on how the audio portions and the video portions of the reports relate to one another. Ask them to list three examples of especially effective reports and to decide which elements made them effective. In addition, ask students to note examples of selective editing betraying bias.

Guiding Your Writers

Objectives

1. To plan a video to appeal to a specific audience
2. To film and present a video

Preteaching

Preview the content of the lesson. If there are skills or concepts students may need help with, present them now. The mini-lesson references below may help you in your selection and instruction. The cross references in the pupil text give students access to the same lessons for independent practice.

Show students the video cameras they will use and explain how they work. If no video cameras are available, tell students that they will write up plans for the audio and video portions of a projected videotape of a local event.

Handbook Mini-Lessons

- Observing, pp. 331–332
- Planning Your Work, p. 348
- Collaborative Planning, pp. 358–360
- Introductions/Conclusions, pp. 365–375
- Vantage Point, pp. 450–451

INVITATION TO Write

News excerpts like the one you just read may appear for only one minute, but they can convey a great deal of information. Now plan a one-to-three-minute videotape of an event that you think will have an impact on your audience or community.

The skills of observation you employed to write your journalistic narrative become even more important when you take up a video camera. When your audience views your videotape, they will literally see the event through your eyes. As you prepare to tape, think of yourself as a member of your audience. Ask yourself what they would like to see and at what points they want to look more closely. Don't be intimidated by the video equipment—it's easy to use. All those hours of television watching have already taught you what makes a good video.

GETTING READY TO TAPE

HANDBOOKS

FOR HELP & PRACTICE

Reflecting/
Observing,
pp. 331–332
Planning Your Work,
p. 348
Collaborative
Planning,
pp. 358–360
Introductions/
Conclusions,
pp. 365–375
Vantage Point,
pp. 450–451

1. Decide what you want to tape. Your goal is to choose an event that can be covered within a one-to-three-minute period. Consider where you must go to tape your event. An individual sports competition, a public meeting, or a rally on a controversial topic might provide you with good footage. Perhaps you prefer to tape in a particular classroom, the school's lunchroom, on a street corner, or at a public park.

2. Think about your story line. If possible, decide on the story you want to tell, or the message or point you want to convey. Of course, these may not become completely clear until after you have taped quite a few scenes and details.

3. Practice camera shots and moves. Become familiar with some of the events available to you. In a **long shot,** you can portray a large canvas with many small details. Following such a shot, you might

---

Humanities Connection

Ask students to decide what they would include on a ten-minute videotape to be included aboard a spacecraft aimed at the far edge of our galaxy. Which images and sounds might give other intelligences an idea of human culture and values and of the variety of life on earth? Let students work in groups to plan their tapes; then let each group share its ideas with the rest of the class.

(Students may be interested in the fact that a CD of Earth sounds, with a device to play it, actually was included on a space probe launched in the 1980's. It included, among other things, a Bach fugue, the songs of humpback whales, and a newborn baby's cry.)

zoom in closer to your subject. You can also **pan,** moving the camera horizontally; **tilt,** moving the camera vertically; or **track,** moving at right angles to or parallel with your subject. Experiment with these different camera movements until you are familiar with the effects they achieve.

4. Select a focus for your tape. A camera is like the voice that tells a story on a page. Decide if you want your camera to be an impartial witness to events—an omniscient third-person narrator like the television news camera—or if you prefer to take a subjective viewpoint in order to make a more personal statement.

TAPING YOUR STORY

1. Establish a background for your story. Begin with a long shot that shows where you are and gives your audience a clear context for your story.

2. Balance long shots with detailed close-ups. Every single shot should tell part of your story, and few shots should last longer than about six to ten seconds. You can cut away between shots by pressing the PAUSE button and then releasing it when you find your next shot.

Teaching Tip: Audience

Suggest to students that, before they begin, they jot down a description of the audience their video will be aimed toward. Explain that the audience may be the general public, or it may be members of a certain age group (children, teenagers, seniors) or a certain interest group (environmentalists, sports fans, hobbyists), or even workers in a given field. The audience descriptions should specify age, interests, and other relevant details, and students should keep these audiences in mind as they plan and film their videos.

Humanities

Have students use dictionaries to look up the derivations of the verbs *zoom, pan, tilt,* and *track* as they apply to filmmaking. (*Zoom* is imitative; *pan* a clip from *panorama,* with Greek roots; *tilt* has links to Old Scandinavian; and *track* has links to Germanic.) Point out that the variety of these derivations illustrates the complex history of the English language. Suggest that students explore derivations of other terms related to TV and film-making and report on their findings.

Guidelines for Evaluation

The following guidelines may be used for a close evaluation of a videotape.

A good videotape
- covers a single event
- has a clear story line or point
- conveys a consistent point of view
- is structured to appeal to its intended audience
- effectively relates audio portions to video portions
- uses an appropriate variety of camera shots and moves

Reteaching

Assess the needs of students who were not successful developing an effective videotape. Assign the appropriate Handbook Mini-Lessons. Concepts commonly requiring reteaching for this assignment are

Planning Your Work: Handbook 5
Vantage Point: Handbook 20

The following suggestions and resources may also be useful.

1. Unclear Sequence If students' videos fail to establish a clear sequence of events, point out several places in which the confusion is most apparent. Direct students to clear up the confusion by listing each shot and the audio that accompanies it, then rearranging the list to establish chronological order. They can then retape, following the new sequence.

2. Unrelated Audio Because most home video equipment provides little control over audio pickup, students may have confusing or inappropriate audio that distracts from the impact of their productions. Suggest that they erase the entire audio and substitute a cassette tape containing narration and/or background music synchronized to the video.

Writing
—TIP—

A storyboard may help you clarify your video in your own mind before you do any actual cutting.

Writer's Choice Sometimes you may need to take shots that last longer than ten seconds. If you have to focus on one shot for so long, keep your audience's interest by zooming, panning, or otherwise moving your camera.

3. End your story. Make sure your tape comes to a natural conclusion. You may want to end with a long shot or by slowly moving your camera away from the subject and fading out.

4. Edit your tape. If the equipment is available, cut and splice different portions of your tape to tighten your story or allow your focus to come through more clearly.

5. Add narration or music. If your tape has no sound, you will need to add some narration or music to clarify the focus of your story.

R EVIEWING YOUR VIDEO

1. View your tape by yourself or with an eyewitness to the event. Decide whether your tape tells the story you intended to tell. Did your focus come through clearly? Did the narration or background music you added contribute effectively to your story?

2. Make another tape. The wonderful thing about videotaping is that you can always tape over your mistakes. Now that you know more about how to create the effects you want, tape your story again, or follow the same steps to tape a different story.

P UBLISHING AND PRESENTING

- **Contact a local station.** If your tape shows an event of local importance, send it to your local or cable television station.
- **Compare tapes.** Compare your tape with that of a friend who taped the same event. How does your point of view differ from your friend's?
- **Consider a video yearbook.** Explore the idea of a video yearbook, a concept many schools are using. A production team can decide the best arrangement for the tapes, and a design group can add graphics or narration between each tape. Decide whether you need an anchorperson or reporters to introduce the various segments.

74 Workshop 2

Humanities Connection

Encourage students to apply their videotaping skills to literature and other arts. Some may wish to tape a succession of visual images to complement a poem or a short literary passage recited on the audio portion. Others may enjoy choosing a piece of instrumental music and "illustrating" it.

Sentence
COMPOSING

Imitating Sentence Structures

Effective writers often use phrases and clauses to elaborate on the main idea of a sentence. In the sentence below, notice the three present participles (verb forms ending in -ing and used as modifiers). Each begins a phrase, and the three participial phrases parallel each other, which gives the sentence detail and a rhythm that catches the reader's interest.

Model: Sometimes a gaggle of them came to the store, filling the room, chasing out the air, and changing the well-known scents.

A. Identifying Imitations   Identify the sentences that imitate the model.

1. After lunch Lee returned to his research, pieces of which were spread all over the desk in the workroom above the garage, and picked up the slide that had so intrigued him.

2. Sometimes a pack of hunting dogs roamed through the field, circling the abandoned barn, sniffing constantly for the trail, and never stopping their frantic pursuit.

3. Often a horde of job applicants arrived at the office, completing the long application, sitting tensely in the waiting room, and repeatedly rearranging their nervous legs.

4. When the alarm clock went off, it sent a jolt through him, as if someone had opened up his head, located his brain, and flicked a finger against it.

5. Soon a more relaxed version of the young woman appeared in the room, commanding the attention of everyone, speaking confidently to the audience, and never losing her quiet poise.

B. Unscrambling Sentences   Decide which sets of sentence parts can be made into sentences whose structure matches the model. Then, for the ones that match the model, unscramble the parts and write the sentences.

1 a. and occasionally calling to a passing friend
  b. watching the people go by
  c. often a group of us stood on the corner
  d. shifting from one foot to another

2 a. we always felt uneasy
  b. not knowing whether to worry about our pets
  c. whenever a coyote howled at night
  d. and wishing they were safe at home

Sentence Composing   **75**

Objectives

1. To identify and analyze sentences that contain series of participial phrases
2. To combine sentences through the use of new participial phrases
3. To compose sentences that contain a series of participial phrases

Preteaching

These exercises focus on the use of participial phrases. Some students may need review of basic sentence parts and structure as well as the use of participial phrases. Refer to the following sections of the Grammar Handbook for preteaching content:

Phrases and Clauses
  Verbals and Verbal Phrases, pages 594–596
  Using Phrases Correctly, page 602

ANSWER KEY

12-2 Duplicating Sentence Structures

A. Identifying Imitations
  2, 3, 5

B. Unscrambling Sentences
  1. Often a group of us stood on the corner, shifting from one foot to another, watching the people go by, and occasionally calling to a passing friend.
  2. no

3. Every Monday morning the class of seniors sat at their desks, chatting with each other, comparing notes about their weekends, and sometimes sharing whispered secrets.

4. no

5. no

6. Nervously Ken rummaged around for the assignment, fumbling around in his notebook, dropping everything with a crash onto the floor, and calling attention to what should have been unnoticed.

C. Combining Sentences

1. Always a crowd of spectators filled the stands, spreading their nervous excitement, hooting their cheers, and even trying to outshout the fans of the opposing team.

2. Frequently a gathering of senior citizens sat in the park, enjoying the balmy weather, playing cards and checkers, and sometimes telling their all-time favorite stories.

---

3 a. chatting with each other
 b. every Monday morning the class of seniors sat at their desks
 c. comparing notes about their weekends
 d. and sometimes sharing whispered secrets

4 a. but Bea did it without hesitation
 b. on the bulletin board in the math room
 c. no one had yet solved the problem
 d. and without even thinking hard

5 a. Beowulf dove into the murky depths
 b. with the warning still ringing in his ears
 c. and found the lair of the monster's hideous mother
 d. until his lungs were strained to bursting

6 a. fumbling around in his notebook
 b. dropping everything with a crash onto the floor
 c. nervously Ken rummaged around for the assignment
 d. and calling attention to what should have been unnoticed

C. Combining Sentences   Use the first sentence in each set as a foundation. Whenever necessary, change the verbs in the sentences following the foundation into present participles. Then insert the participial phrases into the foundation, forming a sentence that matches the model it follows.

> **Example**   He hit his stride then. He *gripped the baton in his right hand.* He *watched the other runners fall away.* He *floated down the track as if he could fly.*

> **Combined**   He hit his stride then, gripping the baton in his right hand, watching the other runners fall away, floating down the track as if he could fly.

Model: Sometimes a gaggle of them came into the store, filling the room, chasing out the air, and changing the well-known scents.

1. Always a crowd of spectators filled the stands. They spread their nervous excitement. They hooted their cheers. They even tried to outshout the fans of the opposing team.

2. Frequently a gathering of senior citizens sat in the park. They enjoyed the balmy weather and played cards and checkers. They sometimes told their all-time favorite stories.

Model: That winter my mother and father came and we set up house-keeping, buying furniture on the installment plan, being cheated, and yet knowing no way to avoid it.

Richard Wright, *Black Boy*

3. That morning we brought out the arrowhead, and Renee examined it. She was eyeing it in a curious way. She was growing interested. And yet she was showing no sign of recognizing it.

4. Friday evening the breeze picked up, and a deep blush spread over the sky. It was changing the clouds to the color of ripe peaches. It was deepening to red. And then it was vanishing as quickly as it had come.

D. Expanding Sentences   Both model sentences above end in a series of three participial phrases. Expand each sentence below by adding a similar series of participial phrases.

> *Example*   At least once a week, the computer went crazy.
>
> *Student Sentence*   At least once a week, the computer went crazy, throwing strange patterns on the screen, refusing to do what the keystroke asked it to do, acting like a stubborn electronic donkey that wouldn't budge.

1. Sometimes the class made the teacher proud to be a teacher.

2. Too often the car would suddenly break down.

3. Unexpectedly the music would make her forget all her troubles.

4. Suddenly the weather changed dramatically and drastically.

5. Now a group of ninth-grade students invaded the cafeteria.

E. Imitating Sentences   Now that you are familiar with the arrangement of sentence parts in the models, write three sentences that imitate the structure of the models.

Application   Write a short paragraph that includes one of the imitations you wrote for Exercise E.

Grammar Refresher   The sentences in this lesson contain present participial phrases. For more about phrases, see Handbook 33. For more about present participles and present participial phrases, see Handbook 33.

3. That morning we brought out the arrowhead and Renee examined it, eyeing it in a curious way, growing interested, and yet showing no sign of recognizing it.

4. Friday evening the breeze picked up and a deep blush spread over the sky, changing the clouds to the color of ripe peaches, deepening to red, and then vanishing as quickly as it had come.

D. Expanding Sentences
Answers will vary.

E. Imitating Sentences
Answers will vary.
Application
Answers will vary.

Narrative and Literary Writing

Workshop Overview

Narrative and literary writing draws on personal experiences and beliefs as a starting point for travels into realms of the imagination. Such writing includes short stories, novels, poetry, and drama. By exploring narrative and literary writing, students will develop skills in plotting action, creating well-rounded characters, developing and describing conflict, writing effective dialogue, and using other literary techniques, including the techniques of expressive and descriptive writing presented in Workshops 1 and 2. Workshop 3 includes the following Guided and Related Assignments:

1. **Guided: Dramatic Writing** shows students ways of developing character, setting, plot, conflict, and mood for a dramatic scene; also helps students build a scene using only dialogue and stage and set directions

2. **Related: Story** offers students an opportunity to apply what they have learned about dramatic dialogue as well as other narrative techniques as they write a short story

3. **Related: Choral Poem** helps students further develop their skills in creating dramatic literature by transforming a poem they have written or chosen into a script for oral presentation

Preparation Guide

1. Use the Overview above and the Teacher's Choice descriptions on page 79 as a basis for deciding which assignment(s) to teach.

2. Preview the assignment and the teacher's notes. The teaching suggestions and your knowledge of your class's abilities should allow you to identify quickly the concepts that may require preteaching or extra support. The Handbook mini-lessons suggested in the Preteaching notes within the lesson can also provide guidance in this area.

3. Preview the adjacent chart for support materials in the Teacher's Resource File that may be used with this Workshop. Resources are for use with the Guided Assignment unless otherwise noted.

Workshop Support Materials

Resources	For Use With
Ideas for Writing: Data Sheets, p. 5; Additional Ideas, p. 20	Look for ideas, p. 82
	Choose an idea, p. 83
Thinking Skills Transparencies: Interaction Graphic; *Worksheets,* p. 13	Explore your idea, p. 85
Elaboration/Proofreading, p. 5	Organize the draft, p. 86
Peer Response Guides, p. 11	Review Your Writing, p. 88
Evaluating Writing, pp. 10, 27–28	Standards for Evaluation, p. 89
Student Revision Trans., pp. 11–14	Problem-solve, p. 89
Elaboration/Proofreading, p. 6	Proofread your work, p. 91
Tests and Assessment: Prompts, p. 3	

Professional Resources and Media

Books and Journals

Otten, Nick and Marjorie Stelmach. "Telling Stories." *English Journal,* Vol. 76.6, October 1987, pp. 87–88. (analysis of a story)

Films and Videos

Celebrate the Word. Nebraska Educational Communication Corporation, Lincoln, Nebraska. 1976. (30 min.) (rhythm of words through poetry, responsive readings, dialogue)

Linking Literature, Writing, and Grammar

The following options may be used to provide students with an integrated language experience. Begin by assigning and discussing any of the recommended pieces of literature, which can be found in most classroom anthologies. Use the suggested strategy to provide a link to the Guided Assignment.

Linking Literature and Writing

Option 1

Starting Point: scene from *The Elephant Man* by Bernard Pomerance on pages 80–81 of *The Writer's Craft*
Strategy: Use the teaching suggestions on pages 80–81 to lead students into the Guided Assignment.

Option 2

Starting Point: "A Worn Path" by Eudora Welty
Strategy: Have students focus on particular ways in which Welty uses dialogue to convey background information and elements of plot and character. What do we learn about Phoenix through what she and the other characters say? How does Welty rely on dialogue to convey why Phoenix is visiting the clinic? Why does Welty have Phoenix speak in non-standard English? Encourage students to discuss ways in which they might convert scenes from this or another short story into a dramatic scene.

Option 3

Starting Point: Act I from *The Importance of Being Earnest* by Oscar Wilde
Strategy: Have students focus on ways in which Wilde uses dialogue to develop characters as well as convey actions and conflicts. What do we learn about Jack, Algernon, and Gwendolen, for example, from what they say? What are their attitudes and situation? What techniques does Wilde use to convey this information? Explain that students will be relying almost exclusively on dialogue as they develop their own dramatic scenes and encourage them to note techniques used by Wilde that they might want to apply to their own scenes.

Linking Writing and Grammar

Before the drafting or revision stage of this assignment, stress the importance of recognizing and correcting sentence fragments. Occasionally students may want to use sentence fragments to make their characters speak in everyday ways (for example: HORACE: And then . . .) However, unintended sentence fragments make dialogue difficult to follow. Have students review their drafts for sentence fragments as you write the following examples on the board:

WRONG: SERGEANT: After the curtains were drawn. One shot was heard. Then the telephone rang.

CORRECTED: SERGEANT: After the curtains were drawn, one shot was heard. Then the telephone rang.

Go over the guidelines for recognizing and correcting sentence fragments on pages 579–582 and 621–624 of the Grammar and Usage Handbook. If problems with sentence fragments continue in students' work, assign the exercises on those pages for reteaching. Additional practice can be found in the Grammar and Usage Practice Book on pages 16 and 17.

Workshop Management Guidelines

The adjacent chart indicates the number of days recommended for each phase of the Guided and Related Assignments. Stars indicate portions of the assignment that may be completed outside the classroom if time is limited or if teachers wish the activity to be completed by students independently.

Dramatic Writing

Starting from Literature—1 day
Prewrite—1–2 days*
Draft—1–2 days*
Revise—1–2 days
Publish—open
Learning—1 day*
Reteaching—open
Extension/Enrichment—open
Sentence Combining—1 day*

Story

Starting from Literature—1 day
Finding Your Story—1–2 days*
Writing—1–2 days*
Reviewing—1–2 days
Publishing—open
Reteaching—open
Extension/Enrichment—open

Choral Poem

Starting from Literature—1 day
Choosing and Analyzing—1–2 days*
Preparing—1–2 days*
Practicing and Performing—2–3 days*
Reteaching—open
Extension/Enrichment—open

Sketchbook

Objective

To use a poem as a springboard to informal writing

Using the Prompt

Before beginning the activity, make sure students recognize that Sketchbook activities are ungraded and are meant to give them an opportunity to experiment with writing technique. Then talk with students about the mood the poem generates as well as the picture it creates in their minds. Focus attention on specific elements the poet uses, such as the repetition of the opening words in each stanza; the repetition of the last line in each stanza; or the use of plain, unadorned language. Have students brainstorm phrases they might use to open successive stanzas or paragraphs in poems or poemlike pieces of writing, and then encourage them to write on their own, using the Frost poem as a model.

Use the ideas from the Additional Sketches section as an alternative for students who prefer a different starting point. Encourage students to get all their ideas down quickly, looking for colorful ways to give the scene or episode energy and life.

Have students keep their writing in their writing portfolios. Point out that there may be ideas in their Sketchbook writing that they will want to use in this or later workshops.

Sketchbook

"The Pasture"

I'm going out to clean the pasture spring;
I'll only stop to rake the leaves away
(And wait to watch the water clear, I may):
I sha'n't be gone long.—You come too.

I'm going out to fetch the little calf
That's standing by the mother. It's so young
It totters when she licks it with her tongue.
I sha'n't be gone long.—You come too.

Robert Frost

Write a poem or something somewhat poemlike that uses some of the elements Frost uses. For example, you may want to start each stanza with a phrase like "I'm going . . . ," then tell where you're going, and end each stanza with a recurring line or phrase.

Additional Sketches

Alone on stage, blinded by the spotlight, you say . . .

Set a scene from your latest blockbuster movie, or narrate an episode from a movie that you've seen and remember vividly.

78

Narrative and Literary Writing

Guided Assignment
DRAMATIC WRITING

Related Assignment
STORY

Related Assignment
CHORAL POEM

I n 1938, many thousands of people jumped into their automobiles to flee an invasion from Mars. They had been listening to a radio version of *The War of the Worlds*. The medium of radio demonstrated the extraordinary power of dramatic narrative to move the hearts and minds of audiences.

Film and video plays today are just the most recent manifestations of an ancient art form—the drama. In this workshop, you will explore ways you can combine dialogue and staging in a dramatic scene to convey situations and ideas. You will then use the techniques of the drama to create a story and a choral poem.

79

Objectives

Guided Assignment:
DRAMATIC WRITING
To recognize the characteristics of dramatic writing and to draft, revise, proofread, and share a dramatic scene

Related Assignment:
STORY
To generate ideas for a story and to draft, revise, proofread, and share a story

Related Assignment:
CHORAL POEM
To choose or write a poem for oral presentation and to perform a dramatic reading of a poem

Teacher's Choice

Guided Assignment
Dramatic Writing In writing drama, students will use narrative elements that have been discussed in Workshops 1 and 2. For this reason, the workshop will probably be most successful if presented after Workshops 1 and 2 have been completed. The workshop should enrich students' appreciation of dramatic works they may currently be reading.

Related Assignments
Story This assignment should interest all kinds of learners since it calls on students to write about any kind of experience. In addition, narration is a natural form of writing so reluctant learners will not feel threatened by the assignment.
Choral Poem Because this Related Assignment calls on students to dramatize a poem orally, it should be especially effective with auditory learners.

Assignment Rationale

Because corporations are using it more and more in professional training, continuing education, public relations, and advertising, students will find dramatic writing a useful skill to master. In addition, individual students may aspire to write for the entertainment industry. This assignment will challenge students to convey their message almost exclusively through dramatic dialogue and stage and set directions.

Starting from Literature

Objective

To respond to a professional model of dramatic writing as a springboard to writing

Teaching Strategies

Motivate

Ask students to explore their own feelings about physical appearance. If everyone realizes that "beauty is only skin deep," why is physical beauty considered so important and valuable?

Tap Prior Knowledge

Discuss with students how they respond when they see someone who is disfigured. Ask students to explore why they react in this way and how their reaction may make the other person feel. Explain that in the scene they will read, Bernard Pomerance describes what happens when a nurse is faced with a man disfigured by a rare disorder.

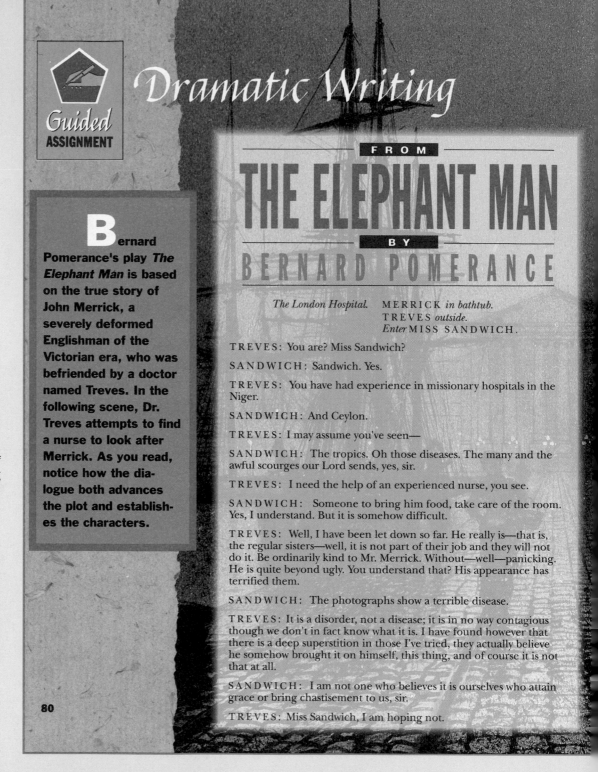

Guided ASSIGNMENT

Dramatic Writing

FROM
THE ELEPHANT MAN
BY
BERNARD POMERANCE

Bernard Pomerance's play *The Elephant Man* is based on the true story of John Merrick, a severely deformed Englishman of the Victorian era, who was befriended by a doctor named Treves. In the following scene, Dr. Treves attempts to find a nurse to look after Merrick. As you read, notice how the dialogue both advances the plot and establishes the characters.

The London Hospital. MERRICK *in bathtub.* TREVES *outside.* Enter MISS SANDWICH.

TREVES: You are? Miss Sandwich?

SANDWICH: Sandwich. Yes.

TREVES: You have had experience in missionary hospitals in the Niger.

SANDWICH: And Ceylon.

TREVES: I may assume you've seen—

SANDWICH: The tropics. Oh those diseases. The many and the awful scourges our Lord sends, yes, sir.

TREVES: I need the help of an experienced nurse, you see.

SANDWICH: Someone to bring him food, take care of the room. Yes, I understand. But it is somehow difficult.

TREVES: Well, I have been let down so far. He really is—that is, the regular sisters—well, it is not part of their job and they will not do it. Be ordinarily kind to Mr. Merrick. Without—well—panicking. He is quite beyond ugly. You understand that? His appearance has terrified them.

SANDWICH: The photographs show a terrible disease.

TREVES: It is a disorder, not a disease; it is in no way contagious though we don't in fact know what it is. I have found however that there is a deep superstition in those I've tried, they actually believe he somehow brought it on himself, this thing, and of course it is not that at all.

SANDWICH: I am not one who believes it is ourselves who attain grace or bring chastisement to us, sir.

TREVES: Miss Sandwich, I am hoping not.

80

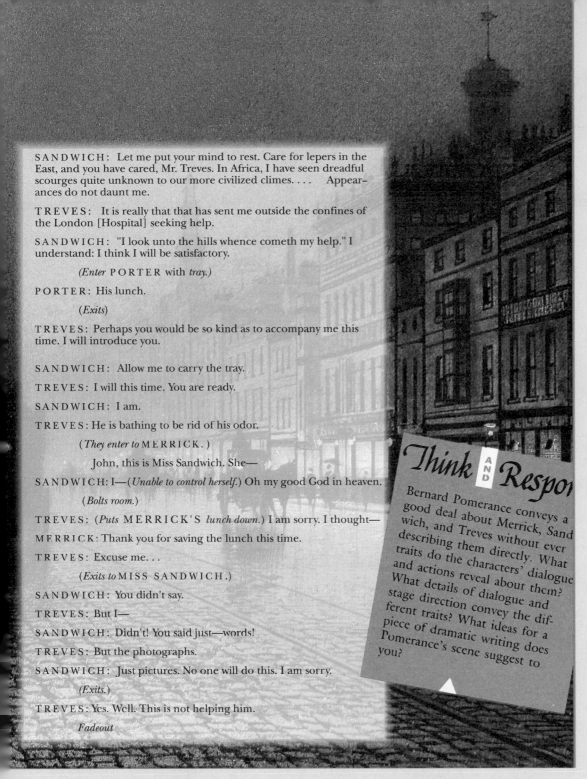

SANDWICH: Let me put your mind to rest. Care for lepers in the East, and you have cared, Mr. Treves. In Africa, I have seen dreadful scourges quite unknown to our more civilized climes. . . .   Appear-ances do not daunt me.

TREVES: It is really that that has sent me outside the confines of the London [Hospital] seeking help.

SANDWICH: "I look unto the hills whence cometh my help." I understand: I think I will be satisfactory.

> (*Enter* PORTER *with* tray.)

PORTER: His lunch.

> (*Exits*)

TREVES: Perhaps you would be so kind as to accompany me this time. I will introduce you.

SANDWICH: Allow me to carry the tray.

TREVES: I will this time. You are ready.

SANDWICH: I am.

TREVES: He is bathing to be rid of his odor.

> (*They enter to* MERRICK.)
>
>   John, this is Miss Sandwich. She—

SANDWICH: I—(*Unable to control herself.*) Oh my good God in heaven.

> (*Bolts room.*)

TREVES: (*Puts* MERRICK'S lunch down.) I am sorry. I thought—

MERRICK: Thank you for saving the lunch this time.

TREVES: Excuse me. . .

> (*Exits to* MISS SANDWICH.)

SANDWICH: You didn't say.

TREVES: But I—

SANDWICH: Didn't! You said just—words!

TREVES: But the photographs.

SANDWICH: Just pictures. No one will do this. I am sorry.

> (*Exits.*)

TREVES: Yes. Well. This is not helping him.

> *Fadeout*

Think AND Respond

Bernard Pomerance conveys a good deal about Merrick, Sand-wich, and Treves without ever describing them directly. What traits do the characters' dialogue and actions reveal about them? What details of dialogue and stage direction convey the dif-ferent traits? What ideas for a piece of dramatic writing does Pomerance's scene suggest to you?

Set a Purpose

Before students begin reading, focus on the side-column notes. Explain that the se-lection is a scene from a full-length play that won numerous awards when it was performed in New York in 1979. Remind students to note what the characters are like and how this information is conveyed through what the characters say and do.

Think and Respond

Elicit Personal Responses

Encourage students to discuss how they feel toward the characters. Which do they like and which do they dislike? What is it about the characters that evokes these re-sponses? Focus on how the playwright arouses interest in Mr. Merrick without having the character say a word in the scene.

Explore the Author's Techniques

To give students insights into the craft of dramatic writing, go through the scene with them, exploring the author's techniques. Help students recognize how Pomerance uses Sandwich's words ("The tropics. Oh those diseases. The many and the awful scourges our Lord sends, yes, sir", etc.) to convey her self-satisfaction and superfici-ality while using Treves's words ("Be ordi-narily kind to Mr. Merrick. Without—well—panicking. He is quite beyond ugly", etc.) to suggest his deep compassion. Help stu-dents see, too, how actions—Sandwich's bolting from the room, for example—are also used to convey plot and character.

Link Literature to Writing

Point out that in choosing his topic for *The Elephant Man,* Bernard Pomerance drew on history, basing his drama on a true story. Students should recognize that real events—events from history as well as from today's newspaper—are one excel-lent source for dramatic ideas. Explain that the Guided Assignment that follows will help them generate ideas as well as de-velop them into effective dramatic scenes.

Prewrite and Explore

Objectives

1. To use prewriting techniques to generate ideas for a dramatic scene
2. To explore characters, setting, plot, conflict, and mood for the dramatic scene
3. To identify the audience and goals for the dramatic scene
4. To explore the dramatic scene through outlining, writing a synopsis, or play-acting

Preteaching

Preview the Prewrite and Explore section. If there are skills or concepts students may need help with before prewriting, present them at this time. The mini-lesson references below may help you in your selection and instruction. The cross references in the pupil text will give students access to the same lessons for independent study.

Handbook Mini-Lessons

- Reflecting, pp. 331–332
- Observation Charts, p. 341
- Plot Diagrams, p. 346
- Collaborative Planning, pp. 358–360
- Elaborative Details, pp. 376–378

INVITATION TO Write

Bernard Pomerance used his dramatic scene to convey what key characters in his play are like and to underscore his play's conflict. Now it is your turn to write a dramatic scene for stage, screen, or radio.

Some of the most popular stories nowadays are not stories that people read. They are stories dramatized and presented on stage, screen, television, or radio. Dramas have the same elements as stories: **plot, character,** and **setting.** Also, like stories, they revolve around a central conflict. This conflict may take place within a character's mind or between a character and some external force.

Dramas are meant to be acted out, using speech and movements. As a result, dramas differ from stories in important ways. Information about characters, plot, and conflict must be conveyed almost entirely through **dialogue,** or what the characters say. Additional information about setting, how characters move and speak, and sound effects, can be conveyed through stage or set directions.

Writing a full-fledged play your first time out is a large task. You should master the basics before trying an entire drama. In this assignment, you will write just one scene. You might introduce the characters, the setting, and a central conflict, or you might develop one key moment.

HANDBOOKS

FOR HELP & PRACTICE

Reflecting, pp. 331–332

Observation Charts, p. 341

Plot Diagrams, p. 346

Collaborative Planning, pp. 358–360

Elaborative Details, pp. 376–378

▶ PREWRITE AND EXPLORE

1. Look for ideas. Drama and conflict are all around you. Try some of the following activities to look for dramatic ideas.

Exploratory Activities

- **Browsing** Many writers for stage, screen, and radio get their ideas from news headlines. Sometimes they actually buy the rights to true stories. At other times, they use a headline as a

---

Springboard

You might use what playwright Edward Albee says about his writing process as the basis for student discussion: "The process goes like this: I discover that I have gotten an idea somewhere. I never *get* an idea—I discover that I *have* one. Then over the next six months or a year or two years, it gradually, slowly develops—I think about it occasionally. The characters are forming . . . (W)hen the idea seems both vague enough and clear enough . . . and the characters seem three-dimensional enough to carry the burden of work by themselves, then I go to the typewriter. So the actual writing time is very short . . . a month to three months. But the prewriting process . . . takes a good deal of time."

springboard for their own imaginations from which they develop completely different characters and settings. Look through newspapers and magazines, and you will probably find a great many ideas.

- **Recalling and freewriting**   Think of a time in your own life when you felt a really strong emotion—whether positive or negative. Freewrite about this time and this emotion and see if you can come up with an idea for a character who is embroiled in a similarly emotion-producing situation.
- **Charting**   Create a character with interesting traits and skills. Think of conflicts, internal and external, in which this character might be involved. List these in a chart with such headings as *Internal Conflicts, Conflicts with People, Conflicts with Institutions, Conflicts with Things in the Natural World,* and *Conflicts with Social or Political Forces.*
- **Asking "what if" questions**   Ask yourself off-the-wall "what if" questions about ordinary things in your experience. For example, the makers of the movie *Who Framed Roger Rabbit?* probably asked themselves, "What if cartoon characters were real and treated like second-class citizens?" Ask yourself about the conflict potential of each situation you dream up.
- **Reading literature**   A common source of dramatic ideas is material that already exists in another form. Dramas have been based on legends, biographies, comic books, comic strips, historical events, and events from the Bible. Bernard Pomerance based *The Elephant Man* on memoirs about John Merrick written by Sir Frederick Treves. Consider taking a real historical character and creating a dramatic version of a portion of that character's life or taking an existing story, such as a myth or fable, and retelling it in dramatic form.

2. Choose an idea.   Look through your ideas. Choose one or more that look promising and freewrite about them, seeing which ones have the most potential. Share your freewriting with a small group of classmates. If you are having trouble finding an idea, you might also glance through your journal, look at the writing you did for the Sketchbook on page 78, or check the "Apply Your Skills" section on page 97.

Dale asked himself a series of "what if" questions. Then he did some freewriting and chose the idea that seemed most workable. Throughout this workshop, you will follow Dale's process as he develops his ideas into a dramatic scene.

PROBLEM
SOLVING

How will I find ideas for a scene with a strong conflict, riveting characters, or an intriguing setting?

Dramatic Writing   **83**

Modeling

Model for students how you might use the first Exploratory Activity. Look through a recent newspaper with students, talking about which stories would and would not work as the basis for an effective drama. Then invite volunteers to look through another newspaper and think out loud for the class.

Teaching Tip: Charting

Use the Basic Category Chart in the Thinking Skills Transparencies to help students with the "Charting" activity.

 ## Individualizing Instruction

Visual Learners   Encourage visual learners to use such graphic organizers as cluster diagrams, spider maps, analysis frames, or sequence chains to help them generate and organize their ideas. You will find examples of these graphic organizers among the Thinking Skills Transparencies. Also refer students to Writer's Handbook 4, Applying Graphic Devices.

Cultural Differences   Encourage students to draw on legends or heroes from their own cultures or to use experiences unique to their cultures as a basis for their dramatic scenes.

Teaching Tip: More Sources

Use the Data Sheet for this assignment with those students who are having difficulty coming up with a dramatic idea. You might also want to use the *Ideas for Writing Booklet* or the Fine Art Worksheets with these students.

Critical Thinking

Judging Encourage students to judge which of Dale's ideas are most workable and why. Then ask them to add other workable ideas to Dale's list. Students still in need of an idea may choose to work with one of these.

ONE STUDENT'S PROCESS

What if . . .

dolphins were tired of the way people were experimenting with them and decided to capture people to experiment with?

* human minds were like computer files and one could make copies of them, erase them, copy one program on top of another, and so on?

a group of people traveled back in time and were able to change the Constitution in some way?

a scientist developed a new strain of rice that grew without moisture but didn't realize the rice would have some disastrous effect twenty years later?

What if someone is going to be erased and doesn't want to be?

3. Explore your idea. Before you begin drafting, you will want to make decisions about your drama's basic elements—character, setting, plot, and conflict. You may wish to freewrite about each element, or use charts, clusters, or sketches to gather details.

- **Character** Identify your main characters and describe their physical characteristics and important attitudes and beliefs. Then flesh out these characters by writing minibiographies or résumés listing their education, work experience, and interests. You may also want to draw sketches of your characters and establish unique identities for them by giving them special habits, such as habitual turns of phrase or gestures.
- **Setting** Decide where and when your drama takes place. Establish both its physical setting and its time period. You may want to draw sketches of your settings and set designs and create floor plans. You can use these sketches to plan how your characters will move.
- **Plot** Make a rough plan of what will happen in the beginning, middle, and end of your drama. In many dramas, the beginning introduces the characters and establishes the conflict. The middle develops the conflict, adding complications and sometimes showing attempts at a resolution. The end resolves the conflict and presents the final outcome. You may want to make a time line of your plot, divided into appropriate units, such as minutes, hours, or days.
- **Conflict** Decide what the central conflict will be. You may wish to experiment by freewriting about a turning point or showdown that reveals the conflict that must be resolved.

 Writer's Choice Once you have looked over the notes you have developed, you can decide what type of scene you feel most comfortable writing. You can write an introductory scene, one that develops a key character, one that develops the central conflict, or any other scene.

4. Create a mood. Once you have established the basic elements of your drama, consider the general emotional quality, or atmosphere, you want to convey. All elements of a drama contribute to the mood, and a skillful writer manipulates elements consciously to change the mood as appropriate throughout the drama.

5. Use collaborative planning. With a partner discuss your potential audience by considering such questions as these: Are you writing for children? Do you want your work to be viewed primarily by teenagers? By parents? By adults in general?

Who will my characters be? What will happen in my drama? Where will my drama take place?

One way to create realistic characters is to base them on people you know. This can help you give your characters natural-sounding speech.

Dramatic Writing **85**

Ask students to recall the definitions of the terms *character, setting, plot,* and *conflict.* Definitions should include the following:

character: a person, animal, or thing in a literary work
setting: the time and place of a literary work and the work's emotional underpinning
plot: the series of related events that make up the story. The plot includes an introduction, complications, a climax, and a resolution.
conflict: a struggle or clash between opposing characters or opposing forces. A conflict can be external—a character faces an outside force—or internal—a character faces a conflict within his or her own mind.

Individualizing Instruction

Learning Styles Visual learners will find it useful to create the charts, clusters, sketches, or time lines suggested in the "Explore your idea" section. Auditory learners may feel more comfortable discussing ideas with partners. Kinesthetic learners may benefit from acting out characters, plot, and conflicts with partners and then listing the characteristics and ideas that surface. They might also profit from using simple props that they make or gather to work out their settings.

Teaching Tip: Mood

Help students explore how sound effects (including music), dialogue, and lighting could be used to convey atmosphere in different situations. Have students suggest possible atmospheres and situations or use the following:
- an eerie atmosphere in a house
- a happy atmosphere at a graduation
- an atmosphere of hope and anticipation at a welcome home party
- an atmosphere of fear on a battlefield

Music Connection

Music and Mood Help students explore how background music can convey mood. Have them listen to and discuss the moods created by works from different cultures as well as works in different styles, such as jazz and rock. Students might also explore the moods created by such classical pieces as Debussy's *La Mer,* Elgar's *Pomp and Circumstance,* Dvořák's *Slavonic Dances,* and Moussorgsky's *St. John's Night on the Bare Mountain.*

Draft and Discover

Objectives

1. To draft a dramatic scene, using dialogue and stage and set directions to develop characters and plot
2. To respond to one's own writing and that of a peer

Preteaching

Look through the content of the Draft and Discover section for skills or strategies students may need special help with. The mini-lessons listed below may be used in providing this instruction.

> ### Handbook Mini-Lessons
> - Drafting Styles, pp. 361–362
> - Emphasis/Tone/Mood, pp. 423–428
> - Varieties of Language, pp. 429–434
> - Dialogue in Drama, pp. 452–453

Teaching Strategies

Speaking and Listening

You may want to have students work on writing dialogue in pairs. Students can write dialogue for a few minutes and then read it aloud to each other, checking that it sounds natural or that an accent or special way of speaking has been successfully captured.

 Individualizing Instruction

Auditory Learners Auditory learners might benefit from dictating their dialogue into a tape recorder and then playing it back to see how natural it sounds and how effectively it conveys what they intended. They can transcribe, or write down, the tape-recorded dialogue if they are satisfied with what they hear.

Once you have decided what audience to appeal to, establish what you want to accomplish. Will you be introducing your characters? Will you be presenting your central conflict or developing it? Will you be dramatizing the climax? Also keep in mind the overall goal of your drama, which could include teaching a lesson or getting the audience to see something in an entirely new light.

6. Explore your scene. Before you begin writing your scene, develop a rough plan. You might write an outline or a synopsis. You might also take the roles of the characters in your scene and play the parts of each one, having them talk to each other. Your scene will grow out of what the characters say.

7. Playact. With your rough plan in place, explore your scene further with a partner. Take different parts and perform them. See how the characters interact and speak. Experiment with ways of moving your plot forward through dialogue and actions.

HANDBOOKS
FOR HELP & PRACTICE

Drafting Styles,
pp. 361–362
Emphasis/Tone/
Mood,
pp. 423–428
Varieties of
Language,
pp. 429–434
Dialogue in Drama,
pp. 452–453

PROBLEM
SOLVING

**How can I *show*
rather than *tell*
in my scene?**

DRAFT AND DISCOVER

1. Begin your draft. If you have trouble starting, simply place your characters in a situation and have them start talking to one another. The scene will grow out of what they say. If you feel more comfortable with one part of your scene than you do with others, start with that part and build around it.

2. Organize the draft. You will want to organize your dialogue and stage and set directions in ways that *show* rather than *tell* your audience what is happening. Think of your scene as a series of moments, like the moments caught in photographs, being presented to the eyes of the audience. Here are some strategies you can use.

Strategies

- **Dialogue** Use your dialogue to move your story along. Do the characters see some danger? Advance the plot by having them describe the danger, express their reactions to it, and pursue an escape from it. Use your dialogue to show your characters' personalities as well. Bernard Pomerance used Treves's dialogue to portray him as a dedicated and devoted doctor. Try to create real people with natural-sounding voices and try to make each voice distinct. Experiment with different speech patterns and levels of language.

86   Workshop 3

- **Stage and set directions** Use your stage and set directions to establish setting; describe costumes; tell characters when, where, and how to move; describe the use of props; and detail sound effects. Directions for a screen or television play should also specify the point of view from which a shot should be seen and whether the shot is long, close, or panning.

You will need to put your dialogue and stage and set directions in a format that will make them easy to use for actors and directors. If you are writing for the stage or radio, use the format of the scene from *The Elephant Man* (page 80). If you are writing for the movies or television, follow that of *Replacement Parts* (page 92).

 Writer's Choice A narrator can move a drama forward by providing background information or raising important issues. Would a narrator be useful in your scene?

Dale decided to write his scene as a television play. He also decided to use a narrator and to develop an introductory scene in which he would present his setting and characters and establish his central conflict. Here is how he used dialogue and stage and set directions in the unrevised first draft of his scene.

ONE STUDENT'S PROCESS

INTERIOR. BREAKFAST TABLE AT BED AND BREAKFAST CLOSE-UP. CENTER TOP OF TABLE WITH FOOD.

NARRATOR (Voice over). It isn't often that a mother and daughter get to take a vacation together, to linger over coffee and Danish just to shoot the breeze.

MOTHER (v.o.). Just try a bite. Like this. (SOUND OF MOTHER EATING)
DAUGHTER (v.o.). I'm not putting that in my mouth.

PULL BACK TO REVEAL *MOTHER* AND *DAUGHTER* FROM ABOVE. EACH HAS A SHAVEN BALD HEAD AND WEARS A TOGALIKE GARMENT.

COMPUTER TIP

Your word-processing program may be able to help you automatically format your dialogue and stage directions. In addition, computer programs are available for formatting screenplays.

Spot Check

Circulate among students as they begin their drafts to see how effectively they are integrating dialogue and stage directions. Check to see that students are actively aware of the resources—stage directions, sound effects, and a narrator as well as dialogue—they can use to move their plots forward.

Stumbling Block

Caution students against becoming bogged down in the format of their plays as they draft. Be sure they recognize that they will be able to work out details of format at a later stage and that now it is most important simply to get their ideas down.

Teaching Tip: Script Terminology

Be sure students understand the following special terms used by Dale in his writing and commonly used in screenplays and teleplays:
interior: shot should take place indoors (often written as *int.*)
close-up: camera focuses on people or items that are described in text that follows the direction
voice over or *v.o.:* words spoken by an unseen narrator or character
pull back: camera moves back to reveal more of a scene

Critical Thinking

Analysis Ask students to analyze Dale's opening. Have them consider the following questions: Is the setting clear enough? If you were directing this scene, would you have enough information to proceed? Is the opening intriguing enough to make you want to continue? What suggestions would you make to Dale for improving this opening?

Peer Response

Be sure students recognize that the choice of peer-response technique is up to them. They may read their scenes aloud to a partner to hear how they sound without asking for comments; select specific questions from this page they want their peer readers to answer; come up with other questions of their own to ask their peer readers; or ask for general, free-form responses. Stress that writers should listen closely to their peer readers, but that the final decisions about what changes to make are up to them. The Peer Response Worksheet for this assignment may help students clarify their feedback on each other's drafts.

3. Reread and react. Reread your draft aloud to make sure your dialogue sounds natural and believable. You may also want to share your draft with one or more peer readers by assigning the various roles and reading the scene aloud. Make sure your stage and set directions give information that will help actors and directors convey your meaning. The following are questions you can ask yourself and the readers or listeners who review your draft as you look for the strengths and weaknesses in your work.

R E V I E W   Y O U R   W R I T I N G

Questions for Yourself

- Is the conflict introduced, developed, or resolved in a powerful and interesting way? Is the part of the plot presented in my scene clearly understandable?

- Do I have a vivid sense of who my characters are? Of what they look and sound like? Do they have their own distinct habits, emotional states, or mannerisms?

- Is my setting clear? What details can I add to make it more vivid? Have I put to good use the appropriate methods for developing setting, including set pieces, costumes, sound effects, and characters' comments?

- Are there places where I can do more to *show* instead of *tell*?

Questions for Your Peer Readers

- Does the scene capture your attention from the very beginning? If not, how can I change the opening so that it really involves you?

- Do my characters seem like real people to you? Is their dialogue convincing and natural?

- Does this scene take place in a recognizable locale? Can you picture the time and place in your mind? Which details of my setting are most and least effective?

- How do my characters, conflict, and setting make you feel? How do your feelings change or develop as the scene progresses?

- Is there any part of the scene that is not clear to you? If so, what part?

Music Connection

Musicals   Musicals use all the elements of dramatic writing but add the element of music. Encourage students to watch such popular musicals as *Grease, The Sound of Music, Annie, The Music Man,* and *My Fair Lady* to see how music works with dialogue and staging to develop plot and character. These musicals are available on videotape.

R EVISE YOUR WRITING

1. Evaluate your response. Consider your own responses and those of your peers. Then, based on these responses, revise your draft. As you revise, also keep in mind that effective dramatic writing generally displays certain basic characteristics.

Standards for Evaluation

Effective dramatic writing . . .

- deals with an interesting conflict that is clearly conveyed by the plot.
- sustains the interest of the audience.
- uses the elements of character and setting to create a convincing world of its own.
- uses language appropriate to its characters.
- shows rather than tells what is occurring.
- includes complete stage directions as necessary.
- uses appropriate format for dramatic writing.

2. Problem-solve. Revise your draft, making changes based on your own review and the reviews of peer readers or listeners. Dale made changes in his draft in response to the comments of one peer listener. They are shown on the next page.

HANDBOOKS

FOR HELP & PRACTICE

Introductions/ Conclusions, pp. 365–375

Elaborative Details, pp. 376–378

Unity/Coherence, p. 388

Revising Effectively, pp. 392–396

Varieties of Language, pp. 429–433

Dramatic Writing   **89**

Revise Your Writing

Objectives

1. To evaluate the responses to the first draft of a dramatic scene
2. To revise the draft based on the writer's assessment of the responses
3. To proofread for errors in spelling, grammar, usage, and mechanics

Preteaching

Based on problems you may have noted in students' drafts or on a preview of the revising section, identify the skills you want to review. The mini-lessons listed below may be useful to you for instructional purposes. You may also want to use the Student Revision Model Transparencies and the Revision Worksheets.

> ### Handbook Mini-Lessons
> - Introductions/Conclusions, pp. 365–375
> - Elaborative Details, pp. 376–378
> - Unity/Coherence, p. 388
> - Varieties of Language, pp. 429–433

Teaching Strategies

 Individualizing Instruction

LD Students You might ask an aide to word process the drafts of students with writing disabilities so that they can evaluate and revise their work more efficiently.

Critical Thinking

Analyzing Ask students whether they agree or disagree with the comments of Dale's peer reader. Then ask students for additional suggestions they might make to improve this section of Dale's scene.

Guidelines for Evaluation

The following guidelines may be used for a close evaluation of a dramatic scene. See the Guidelines for Evaluating Writing in the Teacher's Resource File for additional help with holistic or analytic scoring.

Ideas and Content
- establishes a definite conflict
- includes interesting, engaging characters
- uses character, setting, and plot in combination to create a well-defined world
- shows rather than tells what is happening and what characters are like
- uses language appropriate for its audience

Structure and Form
- uses a logical organization to convey clearly what is happening
- sustains audience interest through pacing
- uses the written form appropriate to the medium in which it is meant to be presented

Grammar, Usage, and Mechanics
- uses standard grammar and usage unless trying to establish character through nonstandard language patterns
- punctuates sentences correctly
- uses correct spelling

Managing the Paper Load

You do not need to grade all the elements listed in the Guidelines for Evaluation. Select those that have received the greatest attention in your classroom and tell students in advance what criteria you will be using in your evaluation. Various methods of evaluation are discussed on pages T28–T29.

ONE STUDENT'S PROCESS

I love this weird stuff—could you add details to make it even stranger?

Gets better and better, but you could make this grabbier by cutting to the operating room and showing someone undergoing the operation.

REPORTER. Technicains at Brigham and Women's Rejuvenation center in the North American state of Boston are still trying to sort out how the three erasures could have occurred. Normally, before people go through rejuvenation, technicians copy the contents of their minds ˄ into a nanotech storage unit, or NSU. (HOLDS UP PRISM-SHAPED INSTRUMENT LIKE THAT SEEN STICKING FROM *MOTHER'S* HEAD.) During the copying process, backups are made and shipped to separate storage locations. , so that if anything goes wrong at one location, there will be a good, clean copy of the person on file elsewhere.

, including all stored memories, habitual processing routines, and so on,

INT. BRIGHAM AND WOMEN'S REJUVENATION CENTER LABORATORY — MEDIUM CLOSE SHOT OF *TECHNICIAN* WITH INSET OF *REPORTER'S* TALKING HEAD. *REPORTER'S HEAD SWIVELS 120° TO SPEAK DIRECTLY TO TECHNICIAN. TECHNICIAN LOOKS AT HEAD AS THOUGH SPEAKING TO A PHYSICALLY PRESENT PERSON.*

REPORTER. So how could this tragedy have happened?

TECHNICIAN. We just don't know. When time came for these three rejuvs, we did standard grafts of the recently backed up NSUs. However, in these ˄ cases, after operations, there are *no readings for mental functions.*

three

were

INT. OPERATING THEATER. A TEENAGER ON A STRETCHER IS BEING FITTED WITH A PRISM BY SURGEONS. TECHNICIAN (Cont., v. o.)

3. Proofread your work. Once you are finished with your revisions, make a final copy and proofread it carefully for errors in grammar, usage, spelling, and mechanics.

LINKING
GRAMMAR **AND** WRITING
Formats for Dramatic Writing

The basic formats and the use of capitalization, punctuation, and abbreviations in dialogue and stage directions vary among the different forms of dramatic writing. For information on specific formats, see sources such as the following:

Cole, Hillis R., and Judith Haag. *The Complete Guide to Standard Script Formats.* Hollywood: CMC Publishing, 1980.

Field, Sid. *The Screenwriter's Workbook.* New York: Dell, 1988.

Goldman, William. *Adventures in the Screen Trade.* New York: Warner Books, 1983.

Hilliard, Robert L. *Writing for Television and Radio.* New York: Hastings House, 1976.

PUBLISH AND PRESENT

- **Present your scene as reader's theater.** In reader's theater, a play is read by actors who present the dialogue and the stage directions, either standing in position or sitting in chairs. To present your scene as reader's theater, assign the different parts to different readers. Choose a narrator to read the stage directions. Place someone in charge of sound effects.
- **Produce your scene.** Choose several scenes from your class to produce and present to other classes. Select students to direct the scenes; to play the parts; and to plan simple sets, costumes, and props. If possible, videotape your scenes.
- **Complete your play and have the drama teacher review it.** Develop additional scenes to complete your whole play. Ask your school's drama teacher to give you some suggestions for improving your work.
- **Save your work in your writing portfolio.**

HANDBOOKS
FOR HELP & PRACTICE

Preparing Manuscript, pp. 414–415

Publish and Present
Objective
To publish and present a dramatic scene

> ### Handbook Mini-Lesson
> - Preparing Manuscript, pp. 414–415

Teaching Strategies
Cooperative Learning

Producing several of the scenes will provide an excellent opportunity for cooperative learning. Divide the class into groups, making sure each group has students with strengths in the different areas needed—directing, art, music and sound effects, and acting. Assign or have each group choose a leader to make sure the scene production moves as smoothly as possible.

Science Connection

If students are producing their scenes, encourage them to think about what they are learning in chemistry, physics, and computer science and how they might apply ideas from the various sciences to create sound effects or other special effects.

Teaching Tip: Rehearsals

If students are presenting their scenes, either as reader's theater or in full productions, find spaces for them to rehearse and store their props and other equipment. Encourage actors to practice their parts by standing in front of mirrors and watching themselves as they speak or by recording their lines on tape so that they can monitor their diction, tone, and speed of delivery. Encourage students who are creating background sound effects to tape some of them. Students creating costumes may benefit from the advice of an interested parent or school sewing teacher.

Uses screenplay format, including abbreviations for set directions such as INT for "interior," SFX for "special effects," and v.o. for "voice over"

Uses dialogue to present believable, engaging characters

Set directions provide descriptions for understanding characters.

ONE STUDENT'S PROCESS

Replacement Parts

Dale Berger

ACT ONE

INT. BREAKFAST TABLE AT BED AND BREAKFAST

CLOSE-UP

CENTER TOP OF BREAKFAST TABLE WITH A PLATE OF CROISSANTS AND DANISH, A PITCHER OF ORANGE JUICE, ANOTHER OF COFFEE.

SFX: BIRDS TWITTER

NARRATOR (v.o.) It isn't often that a mother and daughter get a chance to talk—really to talk. That's why it's such a good idea to take a short vacation together, to linger over coffee and Danish just to shoot the breeze.

HANDS OF *MOTHER* AND *DAUGHTER* REACH INTO SHOT, GRABBING DANISH, POURING JUICE, ETC.

MOTHER (v.o.) Just try a bite. Like this. (SOUND OF MOTHER EATING)
DAUGHTER (v.o.) I'm not putting that in my mouth. It's too weird.

PULL BACK TO REVEAL *MOTHER* AND *DAUGHTER* FROM ABOVE. EACH HAS A SHAVEN BALD HEAD AND WEARS A TOGALIKE GARMENT. THE *DAUGHTER* HAS A TRIANGULAR PATCH ON THE TOP REAR CROWN OF HER HEAD. EMBEDDED IN THE SAME POSITION ON THE *MOTHER'S* HEAD IS A PRISM-SHAPED MECHANICAL DEVICE, TRIANGULAR AT ITS BASE AND RAISED TWO TO THREE INCHES FROM THE *MOTHER'S* SKULL. *MOTHER* AND *DAUGHTER* ARE REMARKABLY SIMILAR IN APPEARANCE.

92   Workshop 3

MOTHER (TO *DAUGHTER*) You know that I'm spending a great many credits on this vacation. The least you can do is to try and have the whole experience. Come on now. Just a nibble.

DAUGHTER It's *too* weird. I can't believe people actually used to nourish themselves this way.

MOTHER OK . . . I tell you what. Take a few bites while I watch the news, and then we'll go out to the feelioport.

DAUGHTER Great. Now you're talking.

ANGLE ON *MOTHER*, WHO SWIVELS IN CHAIR.

POINT OF VIEW SHOT—MOTHER'S VIEW OF A PASTORAL SCENE THROUGH WINDOW BY THE TABLE

MOTHER (v.o.) News on.

Develops characters to
make them part of
their own distinct world

Springboard

You might use the following theatrical anecdote to teach students that it is not necessary that everyone like their play:

One of the most beloved plays of the American stage is Thornton Wilder's *Our Town*. How did the audience and critics first respond to it? Not with overwhelming enthusiasm. Eleanor Roosevelt commented, "Yes, *Our Town* was original and interesting. No, it was not an enjoyable evening in the theatre." *Variety* thought that "as theater, it is not only disappointing but hopelessly slow. . . . (It is) the season's most extravagant waste of fine talent."

Now that students have completed their dramatic scenes, you may want to use the Writing Prompts for Assessment for this assignment to give students practice in responding to assessment prompts that call for dramatic writing. You may also want to use the *Writing About Literature Booklet* to give students practice in writing about drama.

Uses language and situations appropriate for its intended audience—young adults and adults

TIGHT SHOT—PASTORAL SCENE THROUGH WINDOW. IRIS OPEN SLOWLY TO WALL-SIZED COMPUTER SCREEN. LOGO FOR "CONNECT PNN," A NEWS NETWORK, WITH INSET TALKING HEAD OF *PERSONAL NEWS ANNOUNCER*.

PERSONAL NEWS ANNOUNCER Connect PNN, your Personal News Network. Good morning, Sarah 42. Today is Tuesday, August 14. Are you enjoying your vacation?

MOTHER (v.o.) Yes. Very much.

PERSONAL NEWS ANNOUNCER I'm glad to hear it. You have no appointments scheduled. There is a priority news bulletin from the office of Reproductive and Rejuvenatory Affairs. Do you wish to see it?

ANGLE ON *MOTHER*

MOTHER Sure. (ASIDE TO *DAUGHTER*) These things are getting chattier and chattier.

INT. DAY, UNITED NATIONS. INSET HEAD OF *REPORTER*.

REPORTER Officials here at the United Nations are stunned by reports from the North American Sector that three citizens have, to use an ancient word, *died*. Yes, died.

EXT. DAY, ENTRANCE TO FUTURISTIC HOSPITAL WITH SIGN READING "BRIGHAM AND WOMEN'S REJUVENATION CENTER." INSET TALKING HEAD OF *REPORTER*.

REPORTER Technicians at Brigham and Women's Rejuvenation Center in the North American state of Boston are still trying to sort out how the three erasures could have occurred. Normally, before people go through rejuvenation, technicians copy the contents of their minds, including all stored memories, habitual processing routines, and so on, into a nanotech storage unit, or NSU. (HOLDS UP PRISM-SHAPED INSTRUMENT LIKE THAT SEEN STICKING FROM *MOTHER'S* HEAD.) During the copying process, backups are made and shipped to separate storage locations, so that if anything goes wrong at one location, there will be a good, clean copy of the person on file elsewhere.

INT. REJUVENATION CENTER LABORATORY—MEDIUM CLOSE SHOT OF *TECHNICIAN* WITH INSET OF *REPORTER'S* HEAD. *REPORTER'S* HEAD SWIVELS 120° TO SPEAK DIRECTLY TO *TECHNICIAN*. *TECHNICIAN* LOOKS AT HEAD AS THOUGH SPEAKING TO A PHYSICALLY PRESENT PERSON.

REPORTER So how could this tragedy have happened?
TECHNICIAN We just don't know. When time came for these three rejuvs, we did standard grafts of the recently backed up NSUs.

INT. OPERATING THEATER. A TEENAGER ON A STRETCHER IS BEING FITTED WITH A PRISM BY SURGEONS.

TECHNICIAN (cont., v.o.) However, in these three cases, after the operations, there were *no readings for mental functions*. Three NSUs failed, and we don't know why. This would not be a tragedy, except that *all the backup NSUs for these citizens also failed*.

INT. REJUVENATION CENTER, DATA PROCESSING LABORATORY. *TECHNICIAN* AND INSET OF *REPORTER'S* HEAD.

REPORTER So these three citizens are . . . dead. Is that a fair assessment?
TECHNICIAN (STRICKEN) Well, it appears that . . . yes . . . I guess you could say that they . . . that they no longer exist . . . that's correct.
REPORTER Thank you. That was technician Amahl 47 of Boston Rejuv.

INT. FAMILY AT BREAKFAST TABLE

MOTHER News hold.
DAUGHTER What does the telly mean, that these people have "died"?
MOTHER Well, back before the rejuv was invented, people didn't live forever. Then, in the twenty-first century scientists figured out how to grow perfect copies of people from genetically altered somatic, or body, cells—to make *clones*. However, try as they might, scientists could never figure out how to stop people from growing old and dying.

Dialogue moves plot along.

To sensitize students to the power of sound effects and music, encourage them to listen to a television drama blindfolded and to try to identify all the sounds other than dialogue that they hear. Encourage them to ask themselves these questions: How much of the drama is conveyed exclusively through sound effects and music? What different information do these sounds provide? What different emotions do they evoke?

Reteaching

Assess the needs of students who are not successful in developing an effective dramatic scene and identify two or three areas in which additional practice is needed. Assign the appropriate Handbook Mini-lessons, along with the support materials listed for each lesson. Concepts commonly requiring reteaching for this assignment are

Plot Diagrams, Handbook 4
Emphasis/Tone/Mood, Handbook 16

The following suggestions and resources may also be useful.

1. Poor Organizing Remind students that a successful scene must move the action of the play forward toward a resolution. Have students use a plot diagram such as the one below to outline their scene. Make sure they identify the conflict and the climax of the scene.

← climax

conflict

← resolution

2. Poor Character Development Select a scene from *Hamlet* or another play you are studying and read through the stage directions. Point out words and phrases the playwright uses that indicate tone of voice, gesture, or posture. Discuss how students can use similar techniques to establish character.

Shows rather than tells what is occurring by describing character's actions

Uses narration to reveal the conflict

DAUGHTER What do you mean, "growing old"?

MOTHER Well, people used to wear out. Like disposable automobiles. That's when we hit on the idea of creating clone children, like you, and then doing a mind swap once the children became teen-agers.

DAUGHTER Sure, I understand that. You'll have your mind inserted in me, and then a new clone will be made and raised to be a teen-ager, and then the minds will be swapped again, and so on forever and forever. But what is this death? I don't understand that part.

MOTHER Let's see. (THINKS FOR A MOMENT) You know, of course, that when we do the rejuv, and my mind goes into your body, your mind will be erased because it's just a temporary.

DAUGHTER (NOT AN ASSENT, BUT WITH THE MEANING, "YES, GO ON TO THE IMPORTANT PART.") OK.

MOTHER Well, death is like being erased. Only it happens to immortals, like me.

DAUGHTER How very odd. You mean *erase an immortal*?

MOTHER Well, it *never* happens. At least not often, thank goodness.

DAUGHTER (AFTER A PAUSE) How weird!

MOTHER Are you OK?

DAUGHTER Oh, yeah. Sure. If you don't mind, though, I'd like to stay around the hotel for a bit. Why don't you just go on to the feelioport, and I'll catch up later.

MOTHER OK, but don't be long.

INT. *DAUGHTER'S* ROOM IN BED AND BREAKFAST. SHE LOOKS INTO A MIRROR AND TOUCHES THE PATCH ON THE BACK OF HER HEAD.

MUSIC. PULL BACK

NARRATOR (v.o.) Sarah 43, daughter of the immortal Sarah 42 of Boston State in the North American Sector of Planet Earth, year A.D. 2385. Genetically engineered to be, for her mother, a replacement part. It is a utopian world in which death does not exist and perfection has at last been attained. Or has it? This is the question that Sarah 43 is beginning to ask herself—in contradiction to her own biological programming.

96   Workshop 3

LEARNING FROM YOUR WRITING PROCESS

WRITER TO WRITER

[T]he rule of dramatic structure [is this]: **Every story, every plot, every subplot has to have a beginning, a middle, and an end.** This is a classic dramatic structure and is what makes a story a story. As simple as it seems, the lack of a complete story is one of the most common mistakes that writers make.

Carl Sautter, screenwriter

1. Reflect on your writing. Write an introduction to your dramatic scene in which you share with the audience for your play some of the background on how this play came to be written and what it means to you. Tell about where you got your ideas for your characters or plot, what other plays or TV shows or fiction influenced your work, and what you hope your audience will understand or appreciate in your drama. Attach your introduction to your dramatic scene when you submit it to your teacher and when you place it in your portfolio.

2. Apply your skills. The following are some additional writing activities involving skills practiced in this workshop.

- **Cross-curricular** Imagine that you have been hired to write a 30-second public-service radio commercial for a cause related to public health, such as ending drug abuse or cigarette smoking or raising money for cancer research. Write the commercial, using the dramatic skills that you have acquired in this workshop.
- **Literature** Choose a short story by a classic American writer such as Nathaniel Hawthorne or Edgar Allan Poe. Write a dramatic adaptation of the story to be presented as reader's theater, as a film, or as a conventional play. Remember that you may have to add dialogue or even whole scenes to make an effective dramatization.
- **Related assignments** Follow the suggestions on pages 100–107 to write a story and present a choral poem.

Learning from Your Writing Process

Objective

To analyze and reflect upon what has been learned about the writing process and the writing of a dramatic scene

Teaching Strategies

Reflecting on the Process

You may want to have volunteers share their introductions with the class. Encourage listeners to discuss how their own experiences compare with those of the volunteers.

Writing Portfolio

When students are ready to place their scenes and introductions in their Writing Portfolios, encourage them to review what they have learned from previous writing assignments and to assess how writing the dramatic scene has added to their skills and confidence.

Summary and Closure

Before proceeding to the next lesson, be sure students have internalized the following concepts:

1. Character, plot, setting, and conflict are the basic elements of dramatic writing just as they are the basic elements of narrative writing.

2. In dramatic writing, character, plot, setting, and conflict are conveyed through dialogue and stage and set directions.

3. An effective piece of dramatic writing engages its audience with its characters and situations.

Allow students to summarize what they learned by describing the characteristics of effective dramatic writing and by telling why knowing how to write a dramatic scene might help them later in life.

Starting from Literature

Objective

To use a professional model as a spring-board to writing a story

Teaching Strategies

Motivate

You might introduce the lesson—without providing any introduction—by starting to tell a fictional story of your own. Then stop and ask, "What have I been doing?" After students respond, guide them to name the distinguishing characteristics of a story—including narrative voice, characters, setting, and plot.

Tap Prior Knowledge

Discuss students' favorite stories from the literature they have studied, fiction they have read outside of class, TV, movies, and real life. Ask if any students have relatives or friends who are especially good at telling stories. Discuss what qualities a good story contains, such as suspense, humor, and sympathetic characters.

Set a Purpose

Ask students whether, in their experience, the most interesting stories are always about major events such as disasters and wars or about simple things that happen to real people. Opinions may differ; both kinds of subject matter are valid. Point out that Gwendolyn Brooks, like many story writers, writes about an occurrence that might happen on an ordinary day to an ordinary person, but she makes it seem momentous. Urge students to look for similar moments in their own lives and those of people they know.

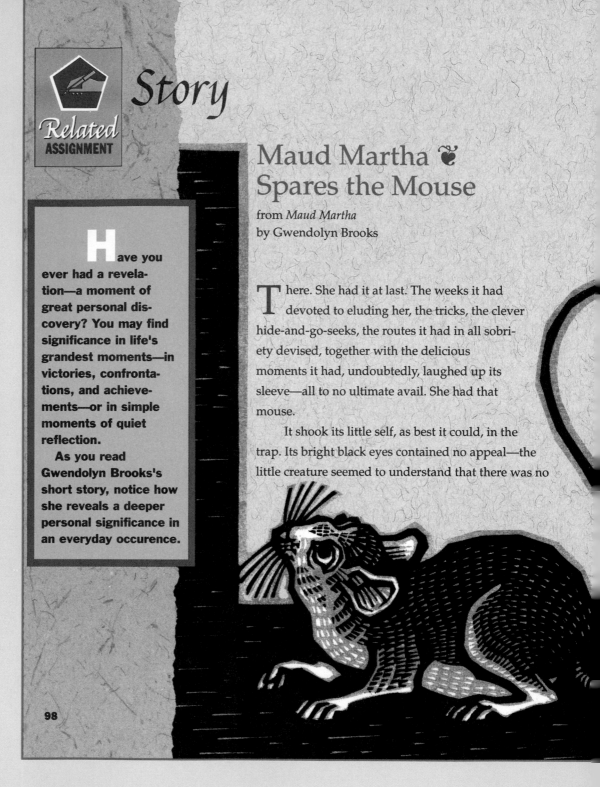

Related ASSIGNMENT

Story

Have you ever had a revelation—a moment of great personal discovery? You may find significance in life's grandest moments—in victories, confrontations, and achievements—or in simple moments of quiet reflection.

As you read Gwendolyn Brooks's short story, notice how she reveals a deeper personal significance in an everyday occurence.

Maud Martha 🍒 Spares the Mouse

from *Maud Martha*
by Gwendolyn Brooks

There. She had it at last. The weeks it had devoted to eluding her, the tricks, the clever hide-and-go-seeks, the routes it had in all sobriety devised, together with the delicious moments it had, undoubtedly, laughed up its sleeve—all to no ultimate avail. She had that mouse.

It shook its little self, as best it could, in the trap. Its bright black eyes contained no appeal—the little creature seemed to understand that there was no hope of mercy from the eternal enemy, no hope of reprieve or postponement—but a fine small dignity. It waited. It looked at Maud Martha.

She wondered what else it was thinking. Perhaps that there was not enough food in its larder. Perhaps that little Betty, a puny child from the start, would not, now, be getting fed. Perhaps that, now, the family's seasonal house-cleaning, for lack of expert direction, would be left undone. It might be regretting that young Bobby's education was now at an end. It might be nursing personal regrets. No more the mysterious shadows of the kitchenette, the uncharted twists, the unguessed halls. No more the sweet delights of the chase, the charms of being unsuccessfully hounded, thrown at.

Maud Martha could not bear the little look.

"Go home to your children," she urged. "To your wife or husband." She opened the trap. The mouse vanished.

Suddenly, she was conscious of a new cleanness in her. A wide air walked in her. A life had blundered its way into her power, and it had been hers to preserve or destroy. She had not destroyed. In the center of that simple restraint was—creation. She had created a piece of life. It was wonderful.

"Why" she thought, as her height doubled, "why, I'm good! I am *good*."

She ironed her aprons. Her back was straight. Her eyes were mild, and soft with a godlike loving-kindness. 🌰

Think AND Respond

What conflict does Maud Martha face, and how does she resolve it? How does the narrator reveal the meaning of the incident for Maud Martha? What point do you think Gwendolyn Brooks was trying to make? What incidents have you experienced that could be the starting points for stories?

Literature Connection

Author Note One of the most well-known African-American poets, Gwendolyn Brooks was born in Topeka, Kansas, in 1917 but has spent most of her life in Chicago. She won the Pulitzer Prize in 1950 for her book *Annie Allen*. In 1963 she was named Poet Laureate of Illinois, succeeding Carl Sandburg. In 1985–86 she served as Poetry Consultant to the Library of Congress, the nearest equivalent to a national poet laureate. Students may also enjoy her poetry, collected in such volumes as *The Bean Eaters*.

Guiding Your Writers

Objectives

1. To generate story ideas
2. To draft and revise a story
3. To publish and present a story

Preteaching

Preview the remainder of the lesson at this time, and present any skills or concepts you feel your students will need help with. The mini-lesson references below may help you in your selection and instruction. The cross references in the pupil book will give students access to the same lessons for independent practice.

Handbook Mini-Lessons
- Reflecting, p. 331
- Gathering Information, p. 332
- Narrative Introductions/Conclusions, pp. 371–374
- Elaborative Details, pp. 376–381
- Unity/Coherence, pp. 382–391
- Dialogue in Fiction, pp. 452–453

Teaching Strategies

Stumbling Block

Thinking of ideas is one of the biggest sticking points for those young writers who lack confidence in their imaginations. One solution is to supply students with a title as a starting point. George Garrett's classic anthology, *The Girl in the Black Raincoat*, is a collection of stories, all with the same title, written by his creative writing students. You might suggest such titles as "Up on a Tightrope," "The Mask," "The Shape of Things to Come," or "Into the Woods" for students to use.

INVITATION TO Write

Gwendolyn Brooks built an engaging story around a simple incident. Now write your own story, relating an experience that happened to you, retelling a tale you have heard before, or creating a completely new story.

Stories are all around you. Your everyday activities, the daily news, and your private thoughts can all be sources of ideas you can turn into stories. Your stories might be mostly true or entirely made up. You are limited only by your own imagination. Yet no matter what you write, from a simple anecdote to a complex drama, you will rely on the same basic elements: characters, setting, plot, and a conflict, or struggle, that must be resolved.

FINDING YOUR STORY

HANDBOOKS
FOR HELP & PRACTICE

Reflecting,
p. 331
Gathering
Information,
p. 332
Narrative
Intros/Conclusions,
pp. 371–375
Elaborative Details,
pp. 376–381
Unity/Coherence,
pp. 382–391
Dialogue in Fiction,
pp. 452–453

1. Generate story ideas. Personal experiences are often the best starting points for stories. Think about things you have experienced, scenes you have witnessed, or unusual people you have observed. What ideas for stories do these experiences and observations suggest? Also consider stories that you could "borrow" from happenings in the news, or set your mind free to consider the imaginary and the improbable. As a short story writer, you are free to go wherever your story takes you.

2. Explore the elements of your story. Consider elements of stories—characters, setting, plot, and conflict. Who will appear in your story? Where will your story take place? What happens in your story? What conflict must be resolved? Freewrite about each of these elements, or use charts, clusters, or time lines to gather the details you can use to develop your story. Pay particular attention to developing a meaningful conflict. For example, the conflict in "Maud Martha Spares the Mouse" is seemingly simple, but the way that Gwendolyn Brooks resolves the story's conflict reveals a deeper significance.

100   Workshop 3

Literature Connection

Ask a volunteer to define the term *realism*, and discuss what students know about literary realism from previous courses. Discuss alternatives to realism, such as fantasy and science fiction. Ask students to point to aspects of realism in "Maud Martha Spares the Mouse." Emphasize, that students may use realistic or non-realistic approaches in their own stories.

3. Set goals for your story. You may want your readers to sympathize with a particular character, or to understand why a character acted as he or she did. Similarly, your goal may be to strike fear into your audience or to make a point or deliver a message. In any case, all the elements of your story should contribute to your specific goal or goals.

4. Choose a narrator. Who will tell your story? You can choose a first person narrator who participates in the story and relates his or her own experiences, or a third person narrator who stands outside the story and describes the action. You can even make a third person narrator omniscient—able to understand the thoughts and motivations of characters as well as their actions—like the narrator in "Maud Martha Spares the Mouse." Notice how the narrator reveals Maud Martha's reasons for sparing the mouse and the effect her action has on her mood.

 Writer's Choice Regardless of whether you use a first or third person narrator, you can choose to make your narrator an active participant in your story or someone who tells about the actions happening to others.

Story **101**

ESL Students ESL students may be able to imagine more sophisticated stories than they can write in English. You might suggest that they write their first drafts in their native languages and then translate their drafts into English.

    Basic Students At the beginning of the drafting process, reluctant writers may need to be reassured that mechanical flaws in their work are not signs of lack of talent.

 Individualizing Instruction

Learning Styles Just as students vary in their learning styles, story writers vary in their methods of approaching their work. Some plan stories in their entirety before setting down a word; others improvise from scratch; most combine planning and improvisation. Some writers think consciously about technical matters such as point of view and theme; others rely on intuition. Encourage your students to discover and trust their own patterns.

Teaching Tip: Point of View

Reassure students that there is no scientific formula for the "right" point of view in a story. The best point of view is the one that feels best to the writer and, later, the reader. Students who are unsure whether to use the first or third person can be encouraged to try both, in separate sample openings.

Teaching Tip: Dialogue

Good written dialogue sounds believable when read aloud. Students may want to read their characters' dialogue aloud to peers or to themselves. It is a plus—though not within the grasp of most student writers—if each character has a distinct way of speaking.

 ## Individualizing Instruction

Gifted and Talented The most talented student writers may have challenging, personal artistic visions that happen not to strike responsive chords in their classmates—or their teachers. Be sensitive to this possibility. Confer with students and their peer readers, focusing on the writers' intentions and whether those intentions were successfully realized on the page.

Teaching Tip: Revision

Before students begin their second draft, make sure that each writer has a good idea of what needs to be fixed in his or her work—for instance, "The character of Sam needs to be fleshed out, and there are too many long sentences."

WRITING YOUR STORY

1. Begin drafting. By now, you should have a good idea about what you want to happen in your story, but keep yourself open to new ideas as you write. Start with any part of your story, and see where it takes you. You can rearrange the sections later.

2. Create a vivid world. Careful description can put your readers in the middle of the action and help them understand why events are taking place. Add details of sight, sound, touch, taste, and scent to draw your readers into the setting and mood of your tale.

3. Develop your characters. Rather than simply telling about your characters, show them in action. Put them in a situation and show how they think, act, and talk. Using dialogue to have characters speak in their own voices is an effective way to reveal what they are really like.

4. Organize your story. Many writers tell their stories in chronological order, starting with the first incident. Others begin in the middle or even at the end, using an attention-grabbing incident to capture their readers' attention. Then they use flashbacks to fill the readers in on the events that led up to the incident. Remember that whatever order you use, your story should show the development and eventual resolution of a conflict.

Math Connection

Even math can be made into a story. To quell your students' doubts, bring in a library copy of Edwin Abbott's geometrical novel *Flatland*.

REVIEWING YOUR WRITING

1. Reread your story. Does your tale have a strong beginning that attracts the attention of readers? Do you establish a conflict and explore the conflict in the middle of the story? Does the ending resolve the conflict or reveal the outcome? Is the setting vividly described with sensory details? Do the characters ring true to life? Have you developed your characters by showing them in action, rather than by merely telling about them? Have you met the goals that you set for yourself?

2. Proofread your story. Check your writing for errors in spelling, punctuation, and grammar. If your story takes place in the past, have you been consistent in the tense of your verbs?

3. Ask a friend to read your story. After you have worked on a story for a long time, you probably can't be objective about it. For a fresh response, ask a friend or classmate to read your story and tell you which parts were confusing and which worked well.

4. Rewrite your story. Most authors write several drafts of their stories, improving them each time. Taking your reader's comments into consideration, redraft your story. Look for ways that you can make the story clearer, more suspenseful, or more compelling.

PUBLISHING AND PRESENTING

- **Tell your story aloud.** Decide whether you will use different voices for different characters and whether you want to mime the actions of the story. Don't forget to make eye contact with everyone in your audience.
- **Present your story as reader's theater.** If your story is largely dialogue, have members of your class act it out in a readers' theater. Take the role of the narrator, and assign your classmates to play the different characters of your story.
- **Submit your story for publication.** Send your story to a magazine that publishes young authors.
- **Enter your story in writing contests.** Your school or local library may sponsor competitions for young writers.
- **Hold a program for parents.** Present a selection of your class's stories in an evening program. Use several methods for presenting the stories.

Writing
TIP

As you redraft, use a synonym dictionary to find the precise word you want and to keep from repeating the same words. Also avoid using the passive voice, substituting active verbs wherever possible.

Guidelines for Evaluation

The following guidelines may be used for close evaluation of a story. See the Guidelines for Evaluating Writing in the Teacher's Resource File for additional help with holistic or analytic scoring. A good story . . .

- compels reader interest
- establishes and explores a single central conflict
- develops credible characters the reader cares about
- has a clearly defined setting
- resolves the central conflict at the end

Reteaching

Assess the needs of students who were not successful developing an effective story. Assign the appropriate Handbook Mini-Lessons. Concepts commonly requiring reteaching for this assignment are

Narrative Conclusions: Handbook 8
Dialogue in Fiction: Handbook 21

The following suggestions and resources may also be useful.

1. Lack of Coherence One of the common failings of student-written stories is that they do not hang together. Point out that a story must focus on a central conflict; there should be no unrelated incidents. In order to reinforce the point, suggest that students summarize their stories in a paragraph, stating each significant event in a sentence. Reading over their paragraphs will help them see whether their stories hold together convincingly and whether unnecessary events have been included.

2. Inappropriate Slang and Colloquialisms Examine students' papers to make sure that slang and colloquialisms, when used, are appropriate reflections of characters' or narrators' voices, rather than authorial mistakes. Display unlabeled examples of slang and colloquialisms on an overhead transparency, and invite students to distinguish those used appropriately from those used inappropriately.

Humanities Connection

Ask students—perhaps with the help of a librarian or music teacher—to look up pieces of music that "tell" stories. Examples include Mussorgsky's *A Night on Bald Mountain* and Tchaikovsky's *1812 Overture*. You might play the pieces for the class and discuss how the music describes the scenes.

Starting from Literature

Objectives

1. To recognize how choral poems combine elements of poetry and drama
2. To script and present a choral poem

Teaching Strategies

Motivate

Ask students why they think people still choose to attend live presentations like circuses, plays, musicals, or concerts, when they can see the same things much more easily on television or in movie theaters. Guide their responses toward an appreciation of the power of live performance.

Tap Prior Knowledge

Ask students to describe their associations with the word *circus*. Prompt students by offering some of your own ideas or memories, if necessary. Elicit a wide variety of associations, meanings, and images, and write them all on the board.

Set a Purpose

Let students form groups of five. Explain that members of each group should choose one narrator and four speakers. They will first read the choral poem silently, then practice reading it aloud. After the practice, merge the groups and have them read to one another.

Point out that the choral poem has two components—the poet's words, and the scriptwriter's directions to readers—but that the two are so tightly interwoven that they seem all of one piece. Suggest that, as they work, students decide which of the scriptwriter's ideas are most effective and which are least effective.

Related **ASSIGNMENT**

Choral Poem

The End of the World

based on a poem by Archibald MacLeish

Long before poems were written down, ballads and verse narratives were recited aloud and passed from generation to generation. When you hear a choral, or group, presentation of a poem, you may feel a bit like those ancient listeners to poetry—as though you are seeing a very condensed and exciting play.

With your classmates, choose parts, rehearse, and read aloud this choral version of "The End of the World" by Archibald MacLeish. How does the script help you to interpret the poem for an audience?

104

[The sound of circus music, a calliope, perhaps, is heard very faintly in the background as the first speaker begins. The calliope music disappears after the first stanza. The first stanza is read excitedly, and there is in the background a general hubbub—crowd noise, clapping, random voices. For the first stanza, which evokes a circus scene, you may prefer to use small groups of speakers rather than individual speakers. The speakers should communicate an almost breathless excitement.]

SPEAKER 1:   Quite unexpectedly
SPEAKER 2:   (Interrupting)   as Vasserot
               The armless ambidextrian was lighting
               A match between his great and second toe
SPEAKER 3:   (Continuing without pause)
               And Ralph the lion was engaged in biting
               The neck of Madame Sossman while the drum
               Pointed,

[Here you hear a slight drum roll.]

SPEAKER 4:   (Again, without pause)
                        and Teeny was about to cough
               In waltz-time swinging Jocko by the thumb—
SPEAKER 1:   (As if finally being allowed to finish his or her original sentence)
               Quite unexpectedly (pause) the top blew off:

[At this point we hear a loud explosion-like noise, then the sound of wind whistling faintly in the background. This second stanza should be much quieter than the first one. Fewer speakers should read it, to give the audience a sense of the desolation and emptiness of the end of the world.]

SPEAKER 2:   And there,
SPEAKER 3:   (Forceful)
                        there overhead,

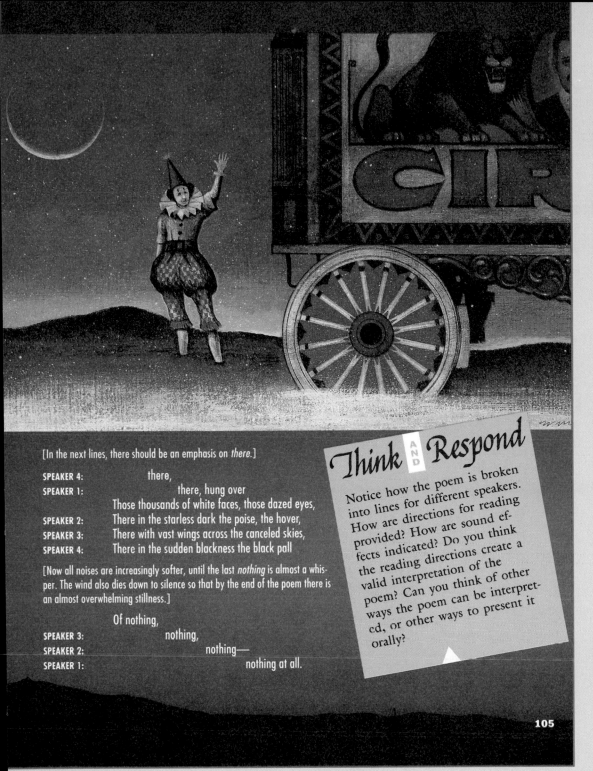

[In the next lines, there should be an emphasis on *there*.]

SPEAKER 4:   there,
SPEAKER 1:   there, hung over
                 Those thousands of white faces, those dazed eyes,
SPEAKER 2:   There in the starless dark the poise, the hover,
SPEAKER 3:   There with vast wings across the canceled skies,
SPEAKER 4:   There in the sudden blackness the black pall

[Now all noises are increasingly softer, until the last *nothing* is almost a whisper. The wind also dies down to silence so that by the end of the poem there is an almost overwhelming stillness.]

                 Of nothing,
SPEAKER 3:   nothing,
SPEAKER 2:   nothing—
SPEAKER 1:   nothing at all.

Think AND Respond

Notice how the poem is broken into lines for different speakers. How are directions for reading provided? How are sound effects indicated? Do you think the reading directions create a valid interpretation of the poem? Can you think of other ways the poem can be interpreted, or other ways to present it orally?

105

Elicit Personal Responses

Ask students, now that they have performed and heard the MacLeish poem, which of the scriptwriter's ideas seemed most effective to them and which seemed least effective. Encourage them to explain why they feel as they do and to offer alternative ideas for presenting the poem. Help them to clarify the point of the poem and to see that effective scripting highlights the point. As the class discusses the Think and Respond questions, be sure students have noticed the conventions for indicating sound effects (bracketed text between lines of poetry) and for giving directions to readers (instructions in parentheses, accompanying the lines of poetry).

Explore the Author's Techniques

Ask students for words and phrases that describe the overall mood of the poem. Then ask for ideas about how the images, rhyme, and meter of the poem help to create the mood. Guide students in connecting these ideas with the ways the scriptwriter has brought out the elements of the poem; for example, the use of louder and then quieter voices, interruptions, background sounds, emphasis on specific words.

Link Literature to Writing

Explain that students may use Mac-Leish's techniques to write their own poems, or they may choose poems from their literature texts or from other sources to arrange for choral reading. In their arrangements, urge them to employ the techniques and conventions used by the writer who scripted the MacLeish poem. Point out that a knowledge of how choral poems can be arranged will be an interesting influence on the students' choice of poetic elements if they decide to write their own poems.

Literature Connection

Poetry   Read aloud Robert Frost's "Fire and Ice" and at least the conclusion of T. S. Eliot's *The Hollow Men* ("This is the way the world ends . . ."). After each, ask students to find ways that the poem is both similar to and different from the MacLeish poem. Elicit suggestions about how each might be scripted for choral reading. How could the mood of each poem be brought out? How could the rhyme and meter be handled? This group practice in planning a script will help students in their individual work later. Some students may also choose either of these two poems for scripting on their own.

Guiding Your Writers

Objectives

1. To choose or write a poem for choral reading
2. To script and present a choral poem

Preteaching

Preview the content of the lesson. If there are skills or concepts students may need help with, present them at this time. The mini-lesson references below may help you in your selection and instruction. The cross references in the pupil text give students access to the same lessons for independent practice.

> **Handbook Mini-Lessons**
> - Peer Response, pp. 400–401
> - Emphasis/Tone/Mood, pp. 423–428
> - Using Poetic Language, pp. 434–438
> - Using Dialogue in Poetry, p. 454

Teaching Strategies

 Individualizing Instruction

ESL Students Suggest that students whose first language is not English choose poems in their native languages. If you do not speak the language and no published translations exist, encourage students to try their hands at translating the poems. Translation into a second language is not easy, but it is an extremely effective way to improve fluency.

INVITATION TO Write

You have just read or performed a choral interpretation of "The End of the World." Now write a poem on a subject you care about or choose a published one. Then prepare the text for a choral presentation.

When you listen to a choral reading of a poem, you experience drama; the speakers act out or dramatize the words of the poem. A choral interpretation also draws on the inherent qualities of poetry —rhythm, meter, and rhyme. Pay special attention to these elements in the poem you write or choose because they provide the music of the poem and make listening to it a rich experience.

HANDBOOKS
FOR HELP & PRACTICE

Peer Response, pp. 400–401
Emphasis/Tone/ Mood, pp. 423–428
Using Poetic Language, pp. 435–438
Using Dialogue in Poetry, p. 454

CHOOSING A POEM

1. Find a poem to interpret. Choose a poem that appeals to you or intrigues you, or write about a topic that is important to you. Look also for a poem (or write one) with interesting rhymes or rhythms that you can exploit in an oral reading. A ballad with a refrain or a poem with more than one speaker works well. Narrative poems, like the old Scottish ballad "Sir Patrick Spens" are good choices, as are many of the expansive poems of Walt Whitman and Carl Sandburg.

2. Choose a form. There are many ways to prepare a poem for a choral presentation. You may, for example, choose to have one primary speaker who tells a story or presents a situation, and a chorus or group of speakers who respond in unison. Other scripts may call for several speakers, small groups, or combinations of individuals and groups. The public library may have recordings of choral poetry that will give you ideas for preparing your poem.

Writer's Choice You may want to explore the possibility of presenting some of the choral poems or odes from ancient Greek tragedies, such as Sophocles' *Antigone* or *Oedipus Rex*.

106 Workshop 3

Humanities Connection

Explain that *surrealism* ("beyond realism") was a literary and artistic movement in the earlier part of this century that involved the juxtaposition of unrelated, even random images in an attempt to evoke a higher level of meaning. The circus images in "The End of the World," oddly juxtaposed and almost grotesque, are surrealistic.

Literature Connection

Oxymoron In the third line of "The End of the World," Archibald MacLeish refers to an "armless ambidextrian." Point out that this is an example of an *oxymoron*, "an apparently contradictory or paradoxical phrase that makes its own kind of sense." Another example is Milton's classic description of Hell from *Paradise Lost*. "No light, but rather darkness visible . . ."

3. Analyze the poem. As you prepare to assign parts to speakers, look for places where the poem naturally divides. These natural breaks occur between stanzas, before refrains, at punctuation marks, or preceding the introduction of a new speaker. Parenthetical material—text between a set of parentheses, dashes, or commas—can often be read by another voice. Sets of quotation marks also suggest spots to introduce a new speaker.

PREPARING THE POEM

1. Create a script. After you arrange the poem into several parts, transform it into a script. Begin by writing the names of the speakers in the left margin, beside their parts.

2. Consider the dynamics. How can the dynamics—the speed, volume, and intensity with which lines are spoken—add to your interpretation? Add directions for delivery in parentheses, as in the script for "The End of the World." Some lines may need to be whispered; others may need to be shouted. Your readers may sing or chant some lines slowly or spew out others rapidly. They can sound hesitant, joyful, fearful, arrogant, or sad.

3. Add sound effects. In between the individual speaking parts, note sound effects that you think may be effective.

PERFORMING A CHORAL POEM

1. Rehearse and revise. Practice until your performance is smooth and polished. As you practice, you may discover that you want to alter certain parts of the script to make the reading even more effective. If you can tape your rehearsals, do so. Sometimes it is easier to be objective about your work when you listen to it on tape.

2. Prepare an introduction. Before you perform, prepare an introduction so that one of your group can introduce the poem and the readers to the audience.

3. Perform the poem. For the public performance of your poem, choose an appropriate location such as the stage in a drama classroom. Be sure the lighting is appropriate and coordinate your sound effects and any props that may be required for the choral reading. After the performance, have a group member invite the audience to share their reactions and interpretations.

Writing
TIP

You can always tape the sounds and play the tape rather than creating the sound effects during the live reading.

Guidelines for Evaluation
The following guidelines may be used for a close evaluation of a choral poem.

A good choral poem
- creates a vivid and clear impression of the poem's mood
- uses scripting appropriate to the elements of the poem
- includes specific directions to performers
- specifies sound effects

Reteaching

Assess the needs of students who were not successful developing an effective choral poem. Assign the appropriate Handbook Mini-Lessons. Concepts commonly requiring reteaching for this assignment are

Using Poetic Language: Handbook 18
Using Dialogue in Poetry: Handbook 21

The following suggestions and resources may also be useful.

1. Indistinct Mood For the students whose scripts do not clearly and strongly underscore a poem's mood, define mood as "the emotional atmosphere of a poem" or "the feelings a poem creates in the reader." Have students sum up the mood of the poem in one or two words. Then direct them to find the parts of the poem that contribute strongly to the mood and to highlight those parts in their scripts.

2. Misinterpreted Syntax and Diction Students who have chosen complex poems may create unclear scripts because they have misunderstood the poem's syntax or diction. Have them rewrite the poem as a series of clear sentences in their own words. They can then use their paraphrase to monitor their scripting and check it for clarity and faithfulness to the original.

Springboard

Let students form teams and compete at creating humorous or unusual scripting for limericks or other very brief, light poems. Write out appropriate poems, of approximately equal length, on slips of paper, and distribute them to teams at random. Set a time limit for preparation; then allow a practice session before each team presents its "oeuvre" to the rest of the class.

Humanities Connection

Tell students that some composers have created tone poems, the musical equivalent of verbal poems. Play Smetana's "The Moldau," Debussy's "La Mer," or one of Sibelius's tone poems. Suggest that, as students listen, they freewrite, recording images the music creates in their minds. Afterwards, encourage them to craft their writing into poems of their own.

On the Lightside

You might want to run a Bulwer Lytton contest in your own classroom. First, have volunteers read aloud the sample entries on this page, and have the class discuss what makes them comically bad. The central flaw in all the entries is *overwriting*. Pay particular attention to the inept uses of figurative language and descriptive words, for these are devices that can produce good writing if used skillfully. Point out that there is often a fine line between the sublime and the ridiculous when description is concerned. Discuss mixed metaphor—the comparison of the same thing to several unrelated things in a short space. Good metaphors are thematically consistent. Also discuss cliché and overloaded imagery. Good imagery makes us see the thing described more clearly; it doesn't put a barrier of words between us and the thing described.

Invite your students to create comically overwritten paragraphs of their own. Have the writers read their entries aloud, and have their classmates evaluate them for skillful badness. As a follow-up, especially for advanced students, you might suggest that students look in published pieces of writing for passages that are unintentionally suited for the Bulwer Lytton contest.

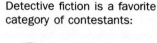

On the Lightside

THE BULWER-LYTTON FICTION CONTEST

Every year the Bulwer-Lytton Fiction Contest awards prizes for atrocious opening sentences of imagined wretched novels. Based on the famous opening sentence, "It was a dark and stormy night . . ." from a badly written Victorian novel by Edward George Earle Bulwer-Lytton, the contest requires the winners to skillfully control their mixed metaphors, hilarious *non sequiturs*, outrageous imagery, and meandering narratives.

Here are some bold and disgraceful contest entries.

"It was a dark and stormy knight who stood rigidly at the cliff's edge, scowling out over the cruel sea, and ruggedly bracing himself against the fierce winds which howled in from the west, where a ship had appeared suddenly on the horizon, silhouetted sharply in the long, snaking claws of lightning that crackled in over the cliff to freeze Sir Richard's saturnine, chiseled patrician features . . ."

Peter S. Ford

Detective fiction is a favorite category of contestants:

"There are things a good detective can feel in his bones, and Dillon Shane knew Jesimine Kimberly Collinsworth did not drown in her sleep on New Year's Eve."

Frances H. Shaw

"With the radio squawking that a 4711 was in progress at 37th and 127th, Murphy knocked car 495 into 3rd and headed up 5th at 70, little reckoning as he thumbed his .38, that this would be the day when his number came up."

R.B. Nelson

Can a Western be far behind?

"Rex Spurr sat so tall in the saddle that the Mexicans didn't know if he was a god or a saguaro cactus, and who could say that they cared, given the torturous temperature which the fireball sun beat down on the frying-pan flat landscape, like pellets of fire raining from the mouth of a volcano, but this was not Hawaii, no, this was Texas!"

Jim Heiden

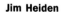

Sentence
COMPOSING

Adding Phrases and Clauses

Effective writers add detailed information to their sentences and variety to their writing by using phrases and clauses in different positions. In this lesson you will learn to add phrases and clauses to the beginning of sentences (openers), between the subject and the verb (s-v split), and at the end of sentences (closers).

Contrast the two sets of sentences below. The first set contains only the foundation of each sentence, the independent clause containing the main subject and predicate. The second set contains the original sentences. Notice their increased information, sophistication, and style.

MODELS

Foundations

1. He seemed more than ever like a gnome.
   s   v
2. The park had already disappointed him.
   s   v   v
3. He hung around L.A.
   s   v

Original Sentences

1. Opener added: With his yellowish stubbly low-growing hair, his stony unblinking eyes, his stoop, his feet planted apart and his knees bent, his clenched held-forward fists, he seemed more than ever like a gnome.
   Doris Lessing, *The Fifth Child*
2. S-v split added: The park, formal, unlovely, its amusements a mere glimmer of Palisades or Coney Island, had already disappointed him.
   Brian Moore, *The Lonely Passion of Judith Hearne*
3. Closer added: He hung around L.A., broke most of the time, working as an usher in movie theatres, getting an occasional part as an extra on the lots, or a bit on TV, dreaming and yearning and hungry, eating cold spaghetti out of the can.
   John Dos Passos, "The Sinister Adolescents"

Punctuation Note: Openers, s-v splits, and closers are generally set off by commas.

Objectives

1. To compose sentences that have phrases and clauses at the beginning, middle, or end
2. To combine sentences to form new sentences that have phrases and clauses at the beginning, middle, or end
3. To expand sentences by adding phrases and clauses at the beginning, middle, or end
4. To revise a paragraph using phrases and clauses.

Preteaching

These exercises focus on the use of phrases and clauses to achieve variety in sentence structure. Some students may need review of basic sentence parts and structure as well as the use of participial phrases, appositive phrases, and dependent clauses. Refer to the following sections of the Grammar Handbook for preteaching content:

Phrases and Clauses
Prepositional Phrases, pages 591–592
Verbals and Verbal Phrases, pages 594–596
Using Phrases Correctly, page 602
Clauses, pages 605–606
The Structure of a Sentence, pages 616–617
Adjective and Adverb Usage
Understanding Modifiers, pages 719–720

A. Imitating Sentences   Imitate each model, one sentence part at a time. Openers, s-v splits, and closers are underlined and labeled.

Model	Mr. Steffens,
	<u>borne upon the shoulders of four white rabbits</u>, (s-v split)
	was carried down a flight of stairs
	<u>which magically appeared in the floor</u>. (closer)

                            Ray Bradbury, *The Martian Chronicles*

Student Sentence   Louisa, secluded in the mountains of the Santa Lucia range, was camped in a meadow of wildflowers that rarely bloomed in the lowlands.

1. <u>Skirting the end of the willows</u>, (opener)
   he stealthily approached the trail further on.

                      Elliott Merrick, "Without Words"

2. <u>Cramped, cold, and worn out</u>, (opener)
   she went to her room.   **Mary Lavin, "One Summer"**

3. The shower curtain,
   <u>a pallid pastel pink</u>, (s-v split)
   was drawn protectively around the claw-footed tub.

                      Stephen King, *The Shining*

4. There she had to creep and crawl,
   <u>spreading her knees and stretching her fingers like a baby trying to climb the steps</u>. (closer)   **Eudora Welty, "A Worn Path"**

B. Combining Sentences   Use the first sentence in each set as the foundation. Insert the underlined parts of the other sentences into the foundation, using the positions indicated in parentheses. Punctuate correctly.

1. He built a small fire to boil the kettle. He built it <u>over a knoll in a thick clump of firs</u>. (opener)   **Elliott Merrick, "Without Words"**

2. Manuel kicked at the bull's muzzle with his slippery feet. Manuel was <u>lying on the ground</u>. (s-v split)   **Ernest Hemingway, "The Undefeated"**

3. Within a minute, it seemed, they were at the lakeside. That was <u>where they found her classmates gathered, timidly trying out the ice</u>. (closer)

                      Mary Lavin, "One Summer"

C. Expanding Sentences
Answers will vary.
Application
Answers will vary.

4. Jody straightened as the ranch hand sauntered out of the barn. It was Jody <u>who was helping Doubletree Mutt, the big serious dog, to dig out a gopher</u>. (s-v split)   **John Steinbeck, *The Red Pony***

C. Expanding Sentences Expand each sentence foundation by adding parts that start with the words provided. Write the complete sentence. Then compare your sentences with the originals on page 322.

Example	The old woman slid to the edge of her chair and leaned forward, shading . . . (closer)
Student Sentence	The old woman slid to the edge of her chair and leaned forward, shading herself with her faded pink parasol and fanning herself with her program.
Original	The old woman slid to the edge of her chair and leaned forward, shading her eyes from the piercing sunset with her hand.

**Flannery O'Connor,
"The Life You Save May Be Your Own"**

1. Wanting . . . , she turned and opened the door on her right and stepped into the dim crowded parlor. (opener)   **Shirley Jackson, "The Little House"**

2. Professor Kazan, wearing . . . , was the first ashore. (s-v split)   **Arthur C. Clarke, *Dolphin Island***

3. He moved restlessly, looking round . . . (closer)   **Richard Wright, *Native Son***

4. He had become part of the group of young unemployed, who . . . (closer)   **Doris Lessing, *The Fifth Child***

Application From something you have written recently, select five sentences to improve by adding information in the opener, s-v split, and closer positions. Use sentence parts similar to the ones in this lesson, and add at least one sentence part to each sentence. Notice how this elaboration increases the amount of detail in your sentences as well as the maturity of your writing style.

Grammar Refresher Some of the sentences in this lesson contain subordinate clauses. For more on dependent clauses, see Handbook 33.

Workshop Overview

Informative Exposition is writing that explains concepts and ideas, and it is one of the more common forms of student written expression. In this Workshop, students will concentrate on exposition that classifies a subject, either by examining it in relation to its characteristics or to some larger group of which it is a part. Such writing is excellent for developing clarity of expression and thinking skills, including classifying, defining, analyzing, and synthesizing. Workshop 4 includes the following Guided and Related Assignments:

1. **Guided: Explaining Concepts and Ideas** shows students methods for gathering and synthesizing information; also suggests different forms and methods of organization and outlines strategies to use in explaining ideas
2. **Related: Science Report** builds on research, analysis, synthesis, and explanatory skills introduced in the Guided Assignment by having students describe a scientific idea or development
3. **Related: Collaborative Writing** shows students ways to expand their potential for explaining concepts and ideas by sharing their skills in a joint or group writing project

Preparation Guide

1. Use the Overview above and the Teacher's Choice descriptions on page 113 as a basis for deciding which assignment(s) to teach.

2. Preview the assignment and the teacher's notes. The teaching suggestions and your knowledge of your class's abilities should allow you to identify quickly the concepts that may require preteaching or extra support. The Handbook mini-lessons suggested in the Preteaching notes within the lesson can also provide guidance in this area.

3. Preview the adjacent chart for support materials in the Teacher's Resource File that may be used with this Workshop. Resources are for use with the Guided Assignment unless otherwise noted.

Workshop Support Materials

Resources	For Use With
Ideas for Writing: Data Sheets, p. 7; Additional Ideas, p. 21	Look for ideas, p. 116
	Select a writing topic, p. 117
Thinking Skills Transparencies: Category Questions; *Worksheets,* p. 3	Gather information, p. 120
Elaboration/Proofreading, p. 7	Consider the form, p. 121
Peer Response Guides, p. 13	Review Your Writing, p. 124
Evaluating Writing, pp. 11, 29–31	Standards for Evaluation, p. 125
Student Revision Trans., pp. 15–18	Problem-solve, p. 125
Elaboration/Proofreading, p. 8	Proofread your work, p. 127
Tests and Assessment: Prompts, p. 4	

Professional Resources and Media

Books and Journals

Park, A. Franklin, et al. "Comparison and Contrast." *Structuring Paragraphs: A Guide to Effective Writing.* New York: St. Martin's Press, 1981. pp. 67–75.

Rorabacher, Louise E., and Georgia Dunbar. "Definition." *Assignments in Exposition.* New York: Harper & Row, 1985: pp. 265–278.

Films and Videos

Communication Skills—Expository Writing. Guidance Association, Mt. Kisco, New York. 1981. (60 min.) (reason/process, comparison/contrast)

Paper of Classification. Dallas Community College District, Mesquite, Texas (30 min.)

Linking Literature, Writing, and Grammar

The following options may be used to provide students with an integrated language experience. Begin by assigning and discussing any of the recommended pieces of literature, which can be found in most classroom anthologies. Use the suggested strategy to provide a link to the Guided Assignment.

Linking Literature and Writing

Option 1

Starting Point: "In Search of a Majority" by James Baldwin on pages 114–115 of *The Writer's Craft*

Strategy: Use the teaching suggestions on pages 114–115 to lead students into the Guided Assignment.

Option 2

Starting Point: "Shooting an Elephant" by George Orwell

Strategy: Have students focus on Orwell's explanation of imperialism and how the events he describes help create a complete portrait of his subject. As an outgrowth of the discussion, encourage students to state in their own words what Orwell's definition of imperialism might have been. Explain that students will have an opportunity to write about a concept and may choose to use narration as Orwell has done in part of their writing to help clarify their concept and create interest in it.

Option 3

Starting Point: section from Chapter IX of *1984* by George Orwell in which Winston reads in *The Theory and Practice of Oligarchical Collectivism* about the meaning of "doublethink"

Strategy: As part of your discussion, ask students to state in their own words what Orwell means by *doublethink*. Ask them to evaluate how completely and effectively Orwell has explained the concept. Then explain that they will have an opportunity to explain a concept that may or may not have as many ambiguities as *doublethink*.

Linking Writing and Grammar

Before the drafting or revision stage of this assignment, tell students that much writing, including writing involving the explanation of concepts, includes indefinite pronouns—pronouns that do not refer to a particular person, place, or thing. Encourage students to recognize that indefinite pronouns must agree with their verbs in number and to take special care with indefinite pronouns that can be either singular or plural, depending on the referent. Have students find examples of indefinite pronouns in their work as you write the following examples on the board:

> **SINGULAR:** No one knows why the fish suddenly died.
>
> **PLURAL:** Many are concerned about it.
>
> **SINGULAR:** Some of the criticism comes from environmentalists.
>
> **PLURAL:** Some of the newspapers blame pollution.

Go over the list of singular and plural indefinite pronouns on pages 673–674 of the Grammar and Usage Handbook. If problems with subject-verb agreement with indefinite pronouns continue to appear in students' work, assign the exercises on those pages for reteaching. Additional practice can be found in the Grammar and Usage Practice Book on pages 66–69.

Workshop Management Guidelines

The adjacent chart indicates the number of days recommended for each phase of the Guided and Related Assignments. Stars indicate portions of the assignment that may be completed outside the classroom if time is limited or if teachers wish the activity to be completed by students independently.

Explaining Concepts and Ideas

Starting from Literature—1 day
Prewrite—1–3 days*
Draft—1–2 days*
Revise—1–2 days
Publish—open
Learning—1 day*
Reteaching—open
Extension/Enrichment—open
Sentence Composing—1 day*

Science Report

Starting from Literature—1 day
Thinking About a Topic—1–3 days*
Drafting—1–3 days*
Reviewing—1–2 days
Publishing—open
Reteaching—open
Extension/Enrichment—open

Collaborative Writing

Starting from Literature—1 day
Planning a Collaboration—open*
Drafting—1–3 days*
Reviewing—1–2 days
Publishing—open
Reteaching—open
Extension/Enrichment—open

Sketchbook

Objective

To respond to humorous definitions as a springboard to informal writing

Using the Prompt

Remind students that Sketchbook activities will not be graded. Have students discuss why Bierce's definitions are funny and how their humor is compatible with his cynical views.

Invite students to think of alternative definitions to the words. Then have them brainstorm a list of words that have important meaning for them—for instance, "teacher" or "work" or "friend"—and freewrite definitions for each one in the style of Bierce. Encourage students to share their word choices and definitions with the class. Compare and contrast the meanings that different students attach to the same words. However, allow students to keep their writing private if they wish. Students who wish to use a prompt from the Additional Sketches may do so as an alternative to this activity.

Encourage students to save their definitions in their Writing Portfolios for possible use in the following workshop.

Sketchbook

English, n. A language so haughty and reserved that few writers succeed in getting on terms of familiarity with it.

Happiness, n. An agreeable sensation arising from contemplating the misery of others.

History, n. An account mostly false, of events mostly unimportant, which are brought about by rulers mostly knaves, and soldiers mostly fools.

Lawyer, n. One skilled in the circumvention of the law.

Year, n. A period of three hundred and sixty-five disappointments.

Ambrose Bierce,
THE ENLARGED DEVIL'S DICTIONARY

The nineteenth-century satirest Ambrose Bierce filled a dictionary with definitions showing how he felt words should be defined. We all attach personal meanings to certain words. Write definitions of words that have special meanings to you.

Additional Sketches

Describe the emotion you understand least.

A phobia is an extreme fear that often has no logical basis. Acrophobia is the fear of heights. Apiphobia is the fear of bees. Xenophobia is the fear of strangers. Describe any phobias that you have experienced.

Informative Exposition: Classification

Related Assignment

SCIENCE REPORT

Related Assignment

COLLABORATIVE WRITING

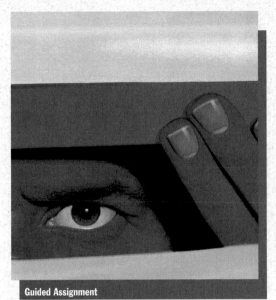

Guided Assignment

EXPLAINING CONCEPTS AND IDEAS

Start reading a newspaper or magazine and you're likely to encounter a variety of complex ideas and concepts: an article about the policies of *glasnost* and *perestroika,* an editorial about the *conservative* shift on the Supreme Court, or news about *apartheid* in South Africa. If a subject is unfamiliar to you, your understanding will depend largely on the effectiveness of the writer's explanation.

In this workshop, you will consider various ways to explain a complex idea or concept to someone who doesn't understand it. You will continue to sharpen your explanatory skills as you write a science report and try collaborative writing.

113

Writer's Workshop 4:

Informative Exposition: Classification

Objectives

Guided Assignment:
EXPLAINING CONCEPTS AND IDEAS
To recognize techniques used to explain and clarify concepts; to prewrite, draft, revise, proofread, and publish an explanation of a concept

Related Assignment:
SCIENCE REPORT
To analyze techniques used in effective science reports; to write a science report

Related Assignment:
COLLABORATIVE WRITING
To understand and use collaborative techniques to create a dramatic scene or in-depth report.

Teacher's Choice

The following information may help you choose the assignments that best fit the needs and interests of your students.

Guided Assignment
Explaining Concepts and Ideas This assignment calls for students to exercise thinking skills (classifying, defining, analyzing, comparing and contrasting, and synthesizing) in order to write an explanation of a concept. Have students complete this assignment before they attempt Workshop 6, in which they will apply similar skills to the more complex task of defining a problem and proposing a solution.

Related Assignments
Science Report Consider collaborating on managing the assignment with an interested science teacher.

Collaborative Writing This assignment will appeal to students interested in dramatics and students who learn best in social situations. However, try to promote the benefits of collaboration to all students.

Assignment Rationale

The ability to explain concepts and ideas is one of the foundations of clear thinking and effective communication in all areas of life. Explanation can also be applied to personal and persuasive essays that students will write throughout their careers.

Starting from Literature

Objective

To respond to a professionally-written explanation of a concept as a springboard to writing

Teaching Strategies

Motivate

Read aloud the following quotation "One man with courage makes a majority"—Andrew Jackson.

This is not the majority definition of *majority*. Yet it rings true, perhaps truer than the usual statistical definition. Lead students to see that in a free society, important ideas are always subject to discussion and redefinition.

Tap Prior Knowledge

Discuss the familiar phrase "The majority rules." Majorities decide elections, but does the majority really wield the most influence in most areas of life? Who determines what fashions are popular, what ideas and slang take hold? Ask whether students have heard the term "silent majority." After you or a volunteer have defined this term, discuss what it implies about the influence of a vocal minority.

Guided ASSIGNMENT

Explaining Concepts and Ideas

What is a *majority?* According to the dictionary, a majority is "a number greater than half of a total." This dictionary definition is adequate for everyday use. Yet when the term *majority* is applied to a complex society like the United States, it takes on a more complex meaning that is not so easily explained. Writer James Baldwin explored the concept of majority in a speech to a college audience. As you read this excerpt, notice the techniques he used to clarify the meaning of this complex concept.

114

In Search of a Majority

BY JAMES BALDWIN

AN ADDRESS

I am supposed to speak this evening on the goals of American society as they involve minority rights, but what I am really going to do is to invite you to join me in a series of speculations. Some of them are dangerous, some of them painful, all of them are reckless. It seems to me that before we can begin to speak of minority rights in this country, we've got to make some attempt to isolate or define the majority.

Presumably the society in which we live is an expression— in some way—of the majority will. But it is not so easy to locate this majority. The moment one attempts to define this majority one is faced with several conundrums. Majority is not an expression of numbers, of numerical strength, for example. You may far outnumber your opposition and not be able to impose your will on them or even to modify the rigor with which they impose their will on you, i.e., the Negroes in South Africa or in some counties, some sections, of the American South. You may have beneath your hand all the apparatus of power, political, military, state, and still be unable to use these things to achieve your ends. . . .

I suppose it can be said that there was a time in this country when an entity existed which could be called the majority, let's say a class, for the lack of a better word, which created the standards by which the country lived or which created the standards to which the country aspired. I am referring or have in mind, perhaps somewhat arbitrarily, the aristocracies of Virginia and New England. These were mainly of Anglo-Saxon stock, and they created what Henry James was to refer to, not very much later, as our Anglo-American heritage, or Anglo-American connections. Now at no time did these men ever form anything resembling a popular majority. Their importance was that they kept alive and they bore witness to two ele-

Set a Purpose

Have students read the side notes. Suggest they take note of sentences in Baldwin's explanation that they find especially effective or provocative.

Think and Respond

Elicit Personal Responses

Have students share their individual responses in small groups first, and then with the whole class. To prompt discussion, ask, "According to Baldwin's definition, who in American society today is the majority?" (Accept any answers that students can support with examples.)

Explore the Author's Techniques

Point out that Baldwin begins his definition by stating what the term to be defined is not. Then he gives a counterexample, defining what a majority is, but in terms very different from the usual. Discuss how and why this approach is effective for Baldwin's subject, and what kinds of other subjects it might be effective—or ineffective—in defining. For instance, Baldwin uses this method to clear up older, conventional misconceptions. If no one had ever defined the word *majority* before, he might have chosen a different technique.

Link Literature to Writing

In his explanation of the concept of a majority, James Baldwin tried to shake up people's thinking about American society by taking a commonly accepted idea—rule by the majority—and presenting it in a new light. Encourage students to think of other commonly accepted ideas that they could similarly recast. Suggest that students ask themselves if, like Baldwin in his essay, they could explain such an idea by first stating what it is *not,* and then by giving examples and counterexamples to prove their point.

ments of a man's life which are not greatly respected among us now: (1) the social forms, called manners, which prevent us from rubbing too abrasively against one another and (2) the interior life, or the life of the mind. These things were important; these things were realities for them and no matter how rough-hewn or dark the country was then, it is important to remember that this was also the time when people sat up in log cabins studying very hard by lamplight or candlelight. That they were better educated than we are now can be proved by comparing the political speeches of that time with those of our own day.

Now, what I have been trying to suggest in all this is that the only useful definition of the word "majority" does not refer to numbers, and it does not refer to power. It refers to influence. Someone said, and said it very accurately, that what is honored in a country is cultivated there. If we apply this touchstone to American life we can scarcely fail to arrive at a very grim view of it. But I think we have to look grim facts in the face because if we don't, we can never hope to change them.

Think AND Respond

How would you summarize, in your own words, Baldwin's explanation of the concept of a majority? How is Baldwin's view of the concept different from the dictionary definition? What strategies does Baldwin use to support his personal concept of majority? What concepts and ideas in today's world do you think are important for people to understand?

115

Literature Connection

Author Note Novelist, essayist, and playwright James Baldwin (1924–1987) grew up in New York City's Harlem. He wrote passionately about the injustice of racism and was perhaps the most important literary voice in the civil rights movements of the 1950's and 1960's. He spent much of his adult life in France.

Prewrite and Explore

Objectives

1. To use prewriting techniques to choose an idea or concept to explain
2. To use collaborative planning to clarify purposes, goals, and audience
3. To identify sources of information, gather information, and synthesize it

Preteaching

Preview the Prewrite and Explore section. If there are skills or concepts students may need help with, present them at this time. The mini-lesson references below may help you in your selection and instruction. The cross references in the pupil text will give students access to the same lessons for independent study.

> #### Handbook Mini-Lessons
> - Reflecting, p. 331
> - Thinking Techniques, pp. 333–334
> - Collaborative Planning, pp. 358–360
> - Finding the Best Source, pp. 493–494

INVITATION TO Write

James Baldwin's speech explained his concept of a majority. Now write your own explanation of a concept or idea so that its meaning and importance will be clear.

Concepts and ideas are usually abstract rather than concrete, and that makes them more challenging to explain. The Grand Canyon, for example, is a concrete thing. It has specific dimensions. It is made up of particular types of rock. You can show someone a picture of it. You can describe it down to its smallest detail. On the other hand, *perestroika* is an abstract concept. It has no dimensions, no physical substance. You can't take a picture of a concept or an idea. You can't touch it, smell it, taste it, hear it.

Nevertheless, as a writer you can use a wide variety of techniques to explain a complex concept or idea. You can construct a formal definition of it. You can describe its characteristics. You can give examples that show it in action. You can relate an anecdote that illustrates it. You can create an analogy that compares it to something more familiar. By doing so, you can increase your own understanding.

HANDBOOKS
FOR HELP & PRACTICE

Reflecting, pp. 331–332

Thinking Techniques, pp. 333–334

Collaborative Planning, pp. 358–360

Finding the Best Source, p. 493

PREWRITE AND EXPLORE

1. Look for ideas. What concepts or ideas intrigue you? Try one or more of the following exploratory activities to find interesting concepts and ideas you might want to explain.

Exploratory Activities

- **Listening** For the next several days, listen carefully to the evening news. Be alert for concepts and ideas that you'd like to learn more about, and write them down in your journal. Here are some you might hear. Add others you hear to this list.

socialism	liberalism	judicial restraint	diplomacy
due process	censorship	civil disobedience	monopoly

Humanities Connection

Art Note Marc Chagall (1889-1985) drew his inspiration for *Bouquet with Flying Lovers* (c. 1934–47), as well as for many other paintings, from the daily life and folklore of the Jewish community in his native Russia. Although he reworked this painting many times, he offered no explanations of it in the end, claiming that "everyone can interpret is as he wishes." Chagall achieved great success in his own lifetime, particularly with paintings such as this one illustrating the concept of romantic love. Ask: How would you illustrate the concept of romantic love in writing?

- **Reading** Your textbooks are a rich source of complex concepts and ideas. Look for such ideas as you read. For example, what is the *global village, homeostasis, plate tectonics, existentialism, superego?* List interesting terms as you come across them.
- **Reflecting and freewriting** Think about some area of the arts or humanities that you are especially interested in, and then do some freewriting about your interest. Look over your freewriting and highlight any concepts and ideas you would like to learn more about or would enjoy explaining to others.
- **Brainstorming and collaboration** Get together with some of your classmates and brainstorm a list of concepts and ideas that relate to moral or ethical matters. See how many terms you can add to this list: *honesty, tolerance, dignity, compassion, fairness, responsibility.*
- **Responding to literature** Use sayings that define concepts, such as these, as starting points for your own definitions.

> "What does education often do? It makes a straight-cut ditch of a free meandering brook."
>
> **Henry David Thoreau**

> "True love is like ghosts, which everyone talks about and few have seen."
>
> **François de la Rochefoucauld**

PROBLEM
S O L V I N G

How can I find a concept that intrigues me and would make a suitable paper?

Bouquet with Flying Lovers, (detail), Marc Chagall

2. Select a writing topic. Review the list of concepts and ideas you've been generating to discover a topic to explain. Which topic interests you the most? Perhaps you think it is especially important to clarify one of these ideas for a particular audience. For example,

Explaining Concepts and Ideas **117**

Personal Touch

Bring in your own list of terms that intrigue you from the evening news. Explain why you are curious about each concept or what aspect of it you would like to explore further.

Speaking and Listening

Invite students to share concepts and terms from the evening news that they have found intriguing. Have them tell in what context the term was used and what questions they have about the concept. Students who chose the same terms can compare responses.

Collaborative Opportunity

Students who work together on the fourth Exploratory Activity might each freewrite separate definitions and examples for the ethical concepts they have brainstormed, then compare and contrast them to arrive at a single synthesized definition for each concept.

Teaching Tip: Quotations

Suggest that students consult *Bartlett's Quotations* or similar compilations in the reference section of the library. Remind them to use the index to find quotations about ideas that interest them.

Social Studies Connection

The New York Times columnist and former Nixon administration official William Safire often writes about the changing meanings of words and ideas used by people in politics and government. Have pairs of students browse through one of his books such as *What's the Good Word?* or *I Stand Corrected.*

Humanities Connection

To guide artistically inclined students toward concepts to freewrite about, ask your librarian to make available magazines such as *The New Yorker, Dance,* and *Art News,* and the Entertainment and Book Review sections of the Sunday *New York Times.*

◆ *Individualizing Instruction*

ESL Students Students for whom English is a second language may enjoy taking a word from their native language that has no exact English equivalent and explaining its meaning.

Teaching Tip: Purpose and Goals

Remind students that although it may be helpful to have a vision of their goal at the beginning, it's just as common for a writer's goals to evolve in the course of prewriting and later stages of writing. Students working with partners should be especially open to new ideas from their partners as they go through the process. They do not have to agree on a final purpose and carve it in stone during prewriting.

you may want to educate a politically unaware group about apartheid. Perhaps you have always wanted to clarify in your own mind just what one of these concepts or ideas really means. If you are having trouble coming up with a topic, try reading several entries in your journal, look at the ideas you explored in the Sketchbook on page 112, or check the ideas listed under "Apply Your Skills" on page 131.

 Writer's Choice Do you want to write a straightforward report on a concept with an objective, widely agreed upon meaning? Would you prefer to write a more personal essay on a concept such as beauty or friendship, which means different things to different people?

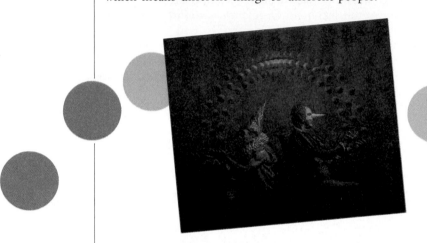

3. Try collaborative planning. Working with a partner, discuss your plans for your essay. Pay particular attention to the following issues.

- **Your purpose and goals** Your general purpose, of course, is to explain the meaning of the concept or idea you have chosen; however, do you want to take a serious approach, or write a humorous essay? Do you have specific goals as well? For example, do you want to clarify a term in preparation for an important presentation or debate? Do you want to suggest a new way of looking at an old idea, to break down a stereotype by examining a concept from a new perspective? Clarifying your goals will help you determine the focus and tone of your writing.

Springboard

Choose a word or concept that all your students can relate to, such as *school* or *seventeen* or *radio,* and do a cluster for that word on the board, inviting as many students as possible to supply related words. Encourage students to use clustering as they search for topics and information.

- **Your audience** Who are your readers and what do you want them to think or feel as a result of reading your essay? What do you have to do to make sure your readers understand you? How much background do you need to supply? What examples or comparisons would help them grasp your meaning?

As Susan began looking into careers she might pursue, she was struck by how widely pay scales seemed to vary. She was particularly concerned that some jobs requiring more training or experience paid less than simpler jobs. She had heard the term *comparable worth* used in discussions about this issue, so she decided to investigate what it really meant.

4. Identify sources of information. James Baldwin drew on his knowledge of American history and the civil rights movement for his speech on the idea of majority. There are many sources of information you can draw on as you plan your explanation. The following are a few possibilities.

- **Your own knowledge** Don't underestimate what you already know. Brainstorm or freewrite about your subject. Try to list everything you already know about it. You might try writing about it from different points of view.
- **Other people** Often you can gain interesting insights into the meaning of a term by comparing what different people have to say about it. For example, people have very different ideas and feelings about such concepts as *tradition, adventure, creativity,* and *solitude.*
- **Authorities** Sometimes you may wish to consult people who have a particular expertise in the area you are writing about. If you are explaining the idea of free markets, for instance, you might consult an economist. If your subject is Manifest Destiny, an American history professor might prove helpful. Also look for articles, studies, and books written by authorities.
- **Dictionary and thesaurus** These are logical places to look if you want to define a term. You might discover shades of meaning that hadn't occurred to you before. You'll also learn the history of a term, which can shed additional light on its meaning.
- **Other reference works** Don't overlook specialized reference works. There are many specialized dictionaries, for example, including dictionaries of science, philosophy, literary terms, music, arts, and so on. You'll find these in the reference section of your library.

Challenge students to cite occupations that are less well-paid than simpler or less important occupations. Almost everyone might cite major league baseball as an overpaid field even though it requires enormous skill.

Individualizing Instruction

LEP Students Students with limited English proficiency may need help interpreting dictionary definitions. You might pair them with proficient students who can give everyday examples to explain terms.

Individualizing Instruction

Basic Students Some basic students may need a reminder about research skills and practice in note taking before they are ready to do their own research. Review the basics of note taking with them and then refer them to Academic Skills Handbooks 24, Research Skills, pp. 479–489, and 25, "Library, Reference Works, and Other Sources," pp. 491–500.

Management Tip

If necessary, schedule time for your librarian to introduce students to the reference section of the library, focusing on the specialized dictionaries mentioned in the lesson.

Social Studies Connection

Have students research ideas that helped determine the course of American history and explain the impact each idea had. Possibilities include *Manifest Destiny, frontier, federalism, isolationism,* and *domino theory.*

Math Connection

Have interested students explain a complex mathematical concept in language that non-mathematicians can understand. Possible concepts include *irrational number, logarithm, algorithm, null set, information, transfinite number, imaginary number,* and *fractal.*

Managing the Paper Load

To limit the amount of reading you need to do at this stage, duplicate the following short form for students to fill out about the results of their prewriting activities:

WHAT I WANT TO EXPLAIN:

_____

WHY I WANT TO EXPLAIN IT:

_____

MY EXPLANATION WILL BE:
_____OBJECTIVE
_____SUBJECTIVE
WHO I WANT TO READ MY EXPLANATION:

_____

THREE IMPORTANT FACTS OR EXAMPLES
I HAVE FOUND ABOUT MY CONCEPT:
1.
2.
3.

Problem Solving

For students who are still having difficulty coming up with a topic, you may wish to provide the Data Sheet for this assignment. You may also want to refer them to the *Ideas for Writing* booklet.

Writing
—TIP—

Keep your eyes and ears open as you explore your topic. You may suddenly discover that many people on TV, in magazines, and in conversations are discussing the idea that interests you.

5. Gather information. Once you know where to look, decide what type of information you are after. Remember, your purpose is to explain your concept or idea as clearly and precisely as possible. Look for concrete examples, step-by-step explanations, interesting anecdotes, revealing analogies, historical definitions—any information that adds to your knowledge of your subject and that will make your explanation informative and compelling. Also, don't ignore your own feelings about the subject.

To gather information for her essay, Susan first looked up the term *equal pay* in the subject catalog at her library. The catalog referred her to listings on *comparable worth* and *pay equity*. There she found books such as Steven Willborn's *A Comparable Worth Primer* and Joan Acker's *Doing Comparable Worth,* as well as a number of studies that had been published by the federal and state governments and by private institutes. Susan wrote the following notes from the information she gathered.

ONE STUDENT'S PROCESS

Comparable worth theory says . . .
—people doing equally difficult or valuable jobs deserve equal pay
—women and minority groups have been historically "crowded" into certain fields (e.g., nursing)
—pay rates in these fields have reflected the discrimination against women

Advocates of comparable worth . . .
—want to evaluate various types of work whose contents have very little in common (e.g., nurse and tree surgeon)
—this would be likely to upgrade certain traditionally "female" professions and close the earnings gap between men and women

Opponents say . . .
—it's impossible to compare different fields of work scientifically
—bureaucratic nightmare would result
—downgrading of certain jobs would hurt women and children (e.g., wives of male factory workers)
—best way to close earnings gap is to recruit and promote women for currently high-paying jobs

Off the Record

The great naturalist Cuvier (coov-yay) was once asked to evaluate a definition of *crab* proposed by the French Academy: "Crab: a small red fish that walks backwards." Cuvier responded: "Your definition, gentlemen, would be perfect, but for three exceptions: the crab is not a fish, it is not red, and it does not walk backwards."

6. Synthesize your information. Simply put, *synthesize* means "combine various parts into a coherent whole." You've gathered a great deal of information about your topic, but what does that information suggest to you about the direction your explanation should take? Look over your information. Which details seem the most important or interesting? What theme seems to be emerging in your research, thoughts, and feelings about the subject? About what aspect of the subject have you gathered the most information? Think back to the goals you established. What information best supports those goals? Freewrite about what you know so far. As you synthesize, highlight the information you want to be sure to include in your explanation.

PROBLEM
S O L V I N G

How does all my information fit together? How can I draw generalizations about my information?

D RAFT AND DISCOVER

1. Consider the form. After thinking about your topic and synthesizing the information you've gathered, you are now ready to consider the form you want your explanation to take. Here are some possibilities.

- **Expository article** Write a straightforward, informative treatment of your concept or idea, the type of article that might appear in an encyclopedia.
- **Persuasive essay** Argue for or against a particular view of your topic. For example, you might argue that free expression must include tolerance for unpopular viewpoints as well as those in the mainstream.

HANDBOOKS
FOR HELP & PRACTICE

Graphics for Organizing,
pp. 343–347
Organizing Your Work,
pp. 349–357
Introducing Nonfiction,
pp. 365–367
Figurative Language,
pp. 435–436

Explaining Concepts and Ideas **121**

Objectives

1. To draft an explanation of a concept or idea, using examples and comparison and contrast
2. To respond to one's own writing and that of one's peers

Preteaching

Preview the Draft and Discover section to determine whether your students will need special help with some concepts or skills. The mini-lessons listed below may help you provide this instruction. Cross references in the pupil text will give students access to the same lessons for independent study.

Handbook Mini-Lessons
- Graphics for Organizing, pp. 343–347
- Organizing Your Work, pp. 349–357
- Introducing Nonfiction, pp. 365–368
- Figurative Language, pp. 435–437

Off the Record

"A committee consists of the unwilling selected from the unsuitable to do the unnecessary."—Anonymous

Teaching Tip: Form

To help students identify the appropriate forms to fit their goals, suggest they ask themselves the following questions:

- Do I simply want to give information? (expository)
- Do I want to convince someone of something? (persuasive)
- Do I want to let people know how I feel about this? (personal)
- Do I want to find out what I really think about this? (exploratory)

Modeling

The phrase *dominant impression* may need some clarification. Ask for a definition, but expect that students' definitions will be vague. Inform students that *dominant impression* is something like the "angle" in journalism and something like the "major idea" or "thesis" in essays without being exactly synonymous with them. Whenever we perceive a phenomenon, we're likely to perceive it in a complex way that contains numerous impressions, some of them conflicting with others. The dominant impression is the one that seems most important, remaining most powerfully with us and affecting our idea of the whole. To model this concept, say, "My dominant impression of this class is that it is hard-working," or "My dominant impression of _____ is that he/she is a responsible student." It doesn't necessarily mean that the class works hard every minute or that the student has never turned in homework late.

Teaching Tip: Figurative Language

Ask students to review the differences among similes, metaphors, and personification. Pick a subject—for instance, sadness or joy—and ask for an example of each of the three types of figurative language for it.

- **Personal essay**   Write an essay that explains what a concept means to you personally. Such essays usually include the widely accepted definition of the concept as well.
- **Exploratory article**   Write an explanation that examines an idea from several different points of view without endorsing any particular definition, or that explores problems in understanding or analyzing the idea.

 Writer's Choice   Sometimes the best form for your explanation will be immediately apparent to you. At other times, you may want to begin drafting to discover which form your writing seems to settle into.

2. Convey a dominant impression.   What is the main point you want to make with your explanation? Just as you would look for a specific angle in writing a journalistic narrative, you should present a dominant impression that captures the significance of your subject. For example, James Baldwin wanted to make the point that influence was more important in defining *majority* than physical numbers. Remember to keep your audience in mind as you draft. Which of the following techniques will add to their understanding of the subject?

PROBLEM

S O L V I N G

Which strategies can help me clarify my explanation?

Strategies

- **Examples**   Give specific examples that illustrate the point you are making about your subject. Examples are especially helpful to your readers when your subject is abstract. James Baldwin cited examples from American colonial history to make his point that a majority may not necessarily be the largest numerical group.
- **Comparison and contrast**   Compare your subject with something familiar to your readers. How are the two alike? How are they different?
- **Figurative language**   Metaphors, similes, and personification can be especially striking forms of comparison that will help you explain an abstract subject in a way that appeals to your readers' imagination.

Susan decided to compare the situations of a woman with a low-paying job to that of a man with a higher-paying job. Notice that she put the comparison in the form of a narrative, with specific characters, in order to enhance reader interest.

122   Workshop 4

Springboard

Guide students in generating illustrative examples by playing a game of "Illustrate that Concept." Divide the class into two teams. State an idea or concept (for example, loyalty or friendship or greed) and ask each team to provide an example or anecdote that supports the concept. You can reverse the process in the "lightning round" by providing an anecdote and calling on the teams to identify the concept. (You can adapt Aesop's fables or other well-known fables as sources of anecdotes. For example, the story of King Midas illustrates greed.)

ONE STUDENT'S PROCESS

Fran Katcavage is a nurse in the emergency room of a busy city hospital. Every day she uses her skills, education, and experience to save the lives of people who have been shot by strangers, injured by passing automobiles, or attacked by mysterious microorganisms. Doctors rely on her coolness and patients rely on her compassion. Fran, who makes twenty-one thousand dollars a year, lives in a two-bedroom house in an old, crowded surburb just across the city's border. Fran has called a local tree surgeon, Sam Robustelli, to prune the oak tree in her yard. With a few expert passes of the chain saw, Sam cuts off the sick branches in order to save the healthy ones. When Fran gets out her checkbook, however, she's embarrassed: she doesn't have enough money to pay Sam, who makes thirty-five thousand a year.

3. Consider ways to organize your information. In what order will you present the main ideas and details that explain your subject? Consider using one or more of the following strategies to organize your draft.

Strategies

- **General to specific** After you have introduced your subject with a broad definition, begin discussing the specific details that will develop your explanation. James Baldwin began his speech by stating his general goals for the evening. Then he progressed to an abstract discussion of the term *majority*. Finally, Baldwin developed his explanation through the use of specific examples.
- **Analysis** Can your subject be divided into parts or subgroups? If so, devote a paragraph to each of these specific aspects. Begin each paragraph with a sentence that both introduces the part or subgroup you want to discuss and links it with the part or subgroup that came before it. Be sure these parts or subgroups are logically presented.

Writing
TIP

Making an outline can help you analyze and classify the information you have gathered.

Explaining Concepts and Ideas **123**

Self-Evaluation

Suggest that students evaluate their work on their own before sharing it with a peer reader. Have them write one sentence describing its strongest feature and one sentence describing its weakest feature. Point out that having a clear sense of their own opinion of their work may help them deal confidently with feedback from others.

Managing the Paper Load

To save some time in evaluating drafts, have peer readers attach their comments to students' drafts. Mark those comments that you feel are especially helpful and perceptive rather than writing long evaluations of your own at this point.

• **Narration** If you choose to use narration, use chronological order to tell the story of your subject. Where does your subject originate? What is its history? Why or how is your subject important today?

• **Classification** Develop categories into which your subject can be placed and explain how it fits into each category.

4. Take a break. When you have a draft that you are reasonably satisfied with, put your work aside for a day or two. When you come back to it, you will be able to read it with a fresh eye, seeing both its strengths and its weaknesses. You may also want to share your draft with one or more of your peer readers. Use the following questions to help you evaluate your draft.

R E V I E W   Y O U R   W R I T I N G

Questions for Yourself

• Have I used concrete examples to illustrate my ideas?

• Is my explanation overly broad or overly specific? Is it clear enough to be readily understood by someone unfamiliar with my subject?

• Did I present a dominant impression?

• Is there anything in my explanation that I think might be unclear to my reader and that should be clarified with additional details, descriptions, definitions, or background information?

Questions for Your Peer Readers

• What ideas did you have about my subject before you began reading? Did my explanation clarify the subject for you or give you any new insights about it?

• Did you find my explanation interesting? What parts did you like best? What parts could be made more interesting, and how might I do this?

• Is there any part of the explanation that is not clear to you? Which part?

• Are you aware of any facts or points of view that I've overlooked? Would you change the central definition in any way? How?

R EVISE YOUR WRITING

1. Evaluate your responses. Consider your own responses and those of your peer readers. Use the responses to guide the revision of your draft. As you revise, keep in mind that explanations of concepts and ideas generally display these characteristics.

Standards for Evaluation

An effective explanation of a concept . . .

- includes an interesting introduction that clearly states the subject to be explained and a reason for explaining it.
- conveys a dominant impression of its subject.
- uses examples, comparisons, and figurative language, as appropriate, to present the information in a lively manner.
- presents information logically and effectively through the use of an appropriate organizational strategy.
- demonstrates an awareness and clear sense of audience through the use of appropriate language and details.

2. Problem-solve. Revise your draft, making whatever changes you consider necessary. The next page shows revisions Susan made in response to comments from her peer readers.

HANDBOOKS
FOR HELP & PRACTICE

Unity/Coherence, pp. 382–391
Avoiding Wordiness, pp. 406–408

Explaining Concepts and Ideas **125**

Revise Your Writing

Objectives

1. To evaluate responses to a draft of an explanation of a concept
2. To revise the draft based on responses
3. To proofread for errors in spelling, grammar, usage, and mechanics

Preteaching

Preview the Revise your Writing section. Based on this preview and on problems you may have noted in students' drafts, identify skills your students may need help with. The mini-lessons listed below may be helpful.

> **Handbook Mini-Lessons**
> - Unity/Coherence, pp. 382–391
> - Avoiding Wordiness, pp. 406–408

Guidelines for Evaluation

The following guidelines may be used for a close evaluation of a concept or idea explanation. See the Writing Evaluation Guidelines in the Teacher's Resource File for additional help with holistic or analytic scoring.

Ideas and Content
- clearly states the subject to be explained and gives a reason for explaining it
- conveys a dominant impression of the subject
- uses examples and comparisons to support the dominant impression
- uses vivid, precise words, including figures of speech when appropriate

Structure and Form
- includes an introduction
- displays a sound organizational structure using such strategies as analysis, classification, progression from general to specific, and chronological order
- uses transitions to show how ideas are related

Grammar, Usage, and Mechanics
- uses standard grammar and usage
- uses correct punctuation
- uses correct spelling

Managing the Paper Load

You may want to focus your evaluation of students' papers on how well students convey their dominant impression of the concept and support that impression with examples and comparisons. Various methods of evaluation are discussed on pages T28–T29.

ONE STUDENT'S PROCESS

Could you give examples?

Before reading your essay, I didn't really understand these implications.

This isn't clear to me. How do you "measure" these qualities?

Avocates of comparable worth claim that some
d   the   theory

such as nursing, teaching, and secretarial work
occupational fields have been historically undervalued.

People entering these occupations have earned less
, on the average,
money than people entering bussiness management or
                  d
it's no coincidence that the lower-paid jobs are ones
that have been predominantly filled by women.
skilled, unionized blue-collar jobs. Women have been

"crowded" into certain fields, and the pay rates in those

fields reflect the discrimination against women in

society as a whole.

d
  Avocates of comparable worth have tried in recent
  based on evaluations of jobs' worth. Such job
  evaluations usually involve the measurement of
years to establish new pay scales by measureing four

qualities: Skill, responsibility, effort, and working
        levels of the first three factors, and the more dangerous the conditions,
conditions. The higher the evaluation, the more pay

deserved, under this theory ⊙

Off the Record

"The Ten Commandments contain 297 words. The Bill of Rights is stated in 463 words. Lincoln's Gettysburg Address contains 266 words. A recent Federal directive to regulate the price of cabbage contains 26,911 words."— from a letter to the editor of the Atlanta *Journal*

3. Proofread your work. When you have finished revising your draft, make a final copy of your essay. Proofread it carefully for errors in grammar, spelling, usage, and mechanics. Neatly correct any errors you find.

LINKING
GRAMMAR AND WRITING

If a one-sentence definition is used to define a term or idea, the word to be defined and the definition should be a similar part of speech. For example, if the word to be defined is an adjective, the definition should be an adjective or an adjective phrase or clause.

Incorrect: *Supercilious* means "a haughty person."
Incorrect: *Supercilious* means "to be haughty."
Correct: *Supercilious* means "haughty."

If the word to be defined is a noun or another word acting as a noun, then the definition should also be a noun or a word, phrase, or clause acting as a noun.

Incorrect: A *foul* is "when you hit a ball outside the base lines."
Correct: A *foul* is "a ball hit outside the base lines."

PUBLISH AND PRESENT

- **Make a speech.** Present your explanation to the class as a speech. Augment your speech with appropriate charts, graphs, or illustrations.
- **Submit your work in another class.** If your explanation relates to math, science, history, art, or some other school subject, you may wish to share it with your teacher and classmates in that class.
- **Save your work in your writing portfolio.** Look over your earlier work in your portfolio. How is your explanation different? Is it better? Think about all of the ways you have grown as a writer.

Grammar
TIP

Remember to underline the word you are defining and to enclose the definition in quotation marks.

HANDBOOKS
FOR HELP & PRACTICE

Publishing, pp. 412–415

Explaining Concepts and Ideas **127**

Publish and Present

Objective

To publish and present an explanation of a concept or idea

Handbook Mini-Lessons
- Publishing, pp. 412–415

Reteaching

Assess the needs of students who were not successful developing an effective concept or idea explanation and identify two or three areas in which additional practice is needed. Assign the appropriate Handbook Mini-Lessons, along with the support materials listed for each lesson. Concepts commonly requiring reteaching for this assignment are

Elaborative Details: Handbook 9
Unity/Coherence: Handbook 10

The following suggestions and resources may also be useful.

1. Poor Support Vagueness and lack of support will be an endemic problem in explanatory student essays. Assign Handbook 4, Graphic Devices, and/or 9, Techniques for Elaboration. Then have each student return to the library and obtain at least two more research sources, and include at least one fact, example, or anecdote from each source in the paper.

2. Grammar and Usage: Parallel Structures Duplicate examples of faulty parallelism from students' papers and have the class revise them together. If necessary, help students by identifying parts of speech and sentence structures such as phrases and clauses that should be parallel.

If you have written a concept explanation along with the class, publish and present it at this point along with those of students.

Management Tip

If some students decide to present their explanations to another class, you might collaborate with the teacher of that class in evaluating the explanations. Have the content-area teacher evaluate the ideas in the explanation, while you evaluate the clarity of expression.

Introduction uses an example to make the subject come alive

States the subject to be explained

Uses examples and comparisons to present information

ONE STUDENT'S PROCESS

Equal Pay for Different Work?

Susan Miller

Fran Katcavage is a nurse in the emergency room of a busy city hospital. Every day she uses her skills, education, and experience to save the lives of people who have been shot by strangers, injured by passing automobiles, or attacked by mysterious microorganisms. Doctors rely on her coolness and patients rely on her compassion. Fran, who makes twenty-one thousand dollars a year, lives in a two-bedroom house in an old, crowded suburb just across the city's border. Fran has called a local tree surgeon, Sam Robustelli, to prune the oak tree in her yard. With a few expert passes of the chain saw, Sam cuts off the sick branches in order to save the healthy ones. When Fran gets out her checkbook, however, she's embarrassed: she doesn't have enough money to pay Sam, who makes thirty-five thousand a year.

How can a society decide what any given job is worth? Is a nurse more valuable to America than a tree surgeon? Does a secretary deserve to make as much money as a truck driver? Questions such as these mark the forefront of the debate on equal pay in the 1990's. Even among people devoted to correcting past employment discrimination, the answers are by no means obvious.

The key concept is that of equal pay for comparable worth. If two jobs have comparable worth, it means that they are equally valuable to society, even if the specific contents of the jobs are very different. For instance, if a teacher's job and an airline pilot's are equally valuable to society, they have comparable worth, and according to this theory they should be paid the same amount.

There's no problem in comparing worth when the two people involved are performing identical jobs. For instance, if a man and a woman graduate from the same police academy at the same time and both begin

128   Workshop 4

Literature Connection

Selections to Read   The poems of Robert Herrick, Andrew Marvell, and the other Cavalier Poets convey the concept of *carpe diem*—"seize the day." Have students read these poems aloud and explain and evaluate the concept.

as patrol officers in the same police department, it's obvious that they should receive the same salary. This has been national policy in the United States since the Equal Pay Act passed Congress in 1963.

However, what about the differences in pay between jobs in different fields? Advocates of the comparable worth theory claim that occupational fields such as nursing, teaching, and secretarial work have been historically undervalued. People entering these occupations have earned less money, on the average, than people entering business management or skilled, unionized blue-collar jobs. It's no coincidence that the lower-paid jobs are ones that have been predominantly filled by women. Women have been "crowded" into certain fields, and the pay rates in those fields reflect the discrimination against women in society as a whole.

Advocates of comparable worth have tried in recent years to establish new pay scales based on evaluations of jobs' value. Such job evaluations usually involve the

Explaining Concepts
and Ideas   **129**

Have students discuss how effectively Susan's final draft explains the concept of comparable worth. If they were Susan's classmates, what suggestions, if any, would they give her for improving her paper further? Did her paper increase or decrease their interest in the subject? What aspects of the subject that Susan did not write about do they wish she had? Also refer back to Questions for Your Peer Readers on page 124 as criteria.

Tapping Prior Knowledge

Invite students to recount anecdotes from the experiences of people they know that might either support or oppose the theory of comparable worth.

Learning from Your Writing Process

Objective

To analyze and reflect upon what has been learned about the writing process and the writing of an explanation of a concept or idea

Teaching Strategies

Critical Thinking

Expressing Opinions Have students voice their opinions of the quotation in the Writer to Writer box. Ask how important they think the writer's fascination with the subject is in determining the success of a piece of writing. To spark debate, you might offer the following quotation from Oscar Wilde that directly contradicts Pasternak's: "The value of an idea has nothing whatsoever to do with the sincerity of the man who expresses it." Have them use examples from their own writing experience to support either side.

Reflecting on the Process

As students answer the questions in *1. Reflect on Your Writing* and reflect on their writing process, ask them to consider how important the concept they wrote about is in their everyday lives. Have them think of ways they might continue their investigation of their topic, if they so desired.

Writing Portfolio

As students summarize their reflections for inclusion in their Writing Portfolios, ask them to assess their progress in dealing with the anxieties and uncertainties of the writing process. What techniques have they learned that help them relax and enjoy the process of discovery and self-expression? Encourage students to share tips with their classmates.

Explores the subject by presenting differing viewpoints

Conclusion reinforces dominant impression: that society must find way to recognize comparable worth

measurement of four qualities: skill, responsibility, effort, and working conditions. The higher the levels of the first three factors, and the more dangerous the working conditions, the more pay deserved, under this theory.

Opponents of comparable worth efforts usually applaud the goal of equal pay, but point to dangers in the proposed remedy. For one thing, they say, there is simply no scientific way to compare the value of two different jobs. It is always a matter of personal judgment, and the question is, "Who is to judge?" Should the government step in? If so, a bureaucratic behemoth is likely to arise, and the results of its findings will always be, to a significant extent, arbitrary and controversial.

Opponents of comparable worth theory claim that the evaluation of jobs according to comparable worth will ironically set back the cause of higher pay for women. For example, if an evaluation decrees that secretaries deserve higher pay, business's likely response will be to hire fewer secretaries. They argue that the best way to close the gap between men's earnings and women's is to recruit more women for higher-paying, traditionally male-dominated jobs, rather than to revamp the pay scale. They also point out that if some men's wages are lowered after a job evaluation, it will harm their wives and children.

In sum, then, the issue of equalizing men's and women's earnings is more complicated than just paying both sexes the same for the same jobs. Our society faces the task of comparing different occupations—the apples and oranges of the labor force. Even if comparative values were agreed upon, the medicine might be more harmful than the ailment. Nevertheless, the fact that this is a difficult issue does not mean we can shirk it. One way or another, the gap between men's and women's earnings must be closed in future years, or painful societal conflicts will result.

130 Workshop 4

LEARNING FROM YOUR WRITING PROCESS

WRITER TO WRITER

The greatness of a writer has nothing to do with subject matter itself, only with how much the subject matter touches the author.

Boris Pasternak, Russian poet and novelist

1. Reflect on your writing. Take a few minutes to write a journal entry or an introductory note for your paper reflecting on your experience in writing this essay. In reflecting on that experience, you may want to consider the following questions.

- In what ways did your own understanding of your subject change as a result of your work on the essay? Do you now see your subject as even more complicated or as less complicated than you had thought?
- How adequately did you define your subject? What would it take to define it adequately? A book? A lifetime? Assuming that much more might have been written on your subject, how did you decide where to stop? What would you do next with your subject if you had more time and space and desire?

2. Apply your skills. To further explore the skills involved in explaining a concept, try one or more of the following.

- **Cross curricular** Choose a favorite subject at school. Make a list of complex ideas that are part of that subject. For example, if biology is your favorite subject, your list might include *pollination, adaptation,* and *photosynthesis.* Write a brief definition of each idea you list that might lead to a longer, more detailed explanation.
- **General** What do the concepts *social responsibility* and *community service* mean to you? Submit an essay on this subject to your local United Fund or volunteer organization for use in their fund-raising or recruitment campaigns.
- **Related assignments** Follow the suggestions on pages 132–142 to write a science report or do collaborative writing.

Explaining Concepts
and Ideas   **131**

Summary and Closure

Before proceeding to the next lesson, be sure students have internalized the following concepts:

1. Ideas and concepts can often be defined or explained more fully than their dictionary definitions suggest.

2. An effective explanatory essay contains thoroughly researched information that has been organized and synthesized so as to convey a dominant impression of the concept.

3. The tone and form chosen for an explanation of a concept depend on the writer's goals and audience.

4. Concrete examples, comparisons, and anecdotes are valuable in explaining abstract ideas.

Allow time for students to summarize what they learned by describing the characteristics of effective explanations of concepts and by telling why knowing how to write one can help them in other areas of life.

Starting from Literature

Objective

To use a professional model of a science report as a springboard to exposition

Teaching Strategies

Motivate

Have students think of scientific concepts that they have learned about recently. Prompt with diverse examples, such as the greenhouse effect, the theory of relativity, the role of cholesterol in heart disease, the Pythagorean theorem. Discuss whether students usually find it difficult to learn such concepts. Is it ever simple? What makes the difference?

Tap Prior Knowledge

On the chalkboard, put a simple sketch of a cell, including the cell wall around the outside and nucleus in the middle. Tell students that it's a cell, and ask them to identify the nucleus and its function. They should know that the nucleus governs the cell's reproduction and contains its genetic material. Then ask what goes on between the nucleus and the outer cell wall. *(Specialized functions take place here, depending on the type of cell: in some cells, substances are manufactured and excreted; in others, material is taken in and converted.)* Explain that the discovery they will read of concerns our ability to change cells' the basic structure and function.

Set a Purpose

After the class has read and discussed the side-column notes, explain that understanding the difference between a virus and an ordinary cell is a key to understanding the comparison the notes refer to. Tell them to look for information about what a virus is and what it does, as well as for the comparison the author makes.

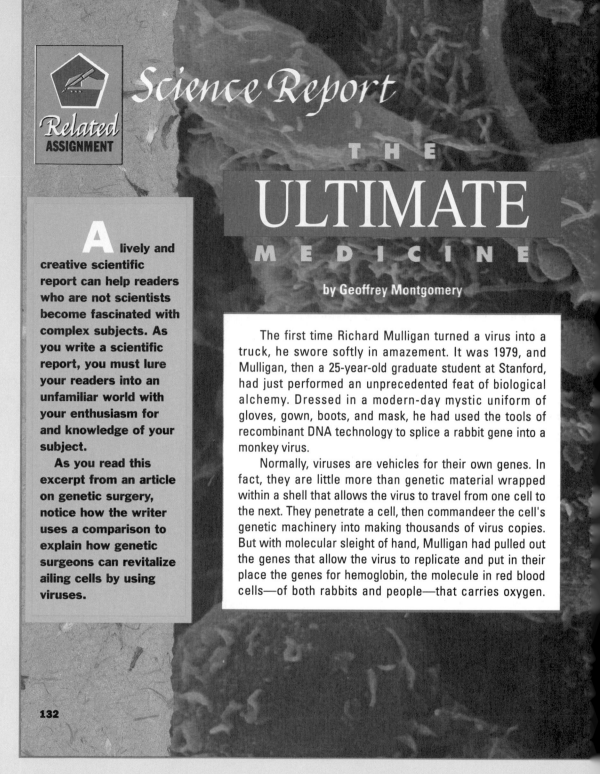

Related ASSIGNMENT

Science Report

THE ULTIMATE MEDICINE

by Geoffrey Montgomery

A lively and creative scientific report can help readers who are not scientists become fascinated with complex subjects. As you write a scientific report, you must lure your readers into an unfamiliar world with your enthusiasm for and knowledge of your subject.

As you read this excerpt from an article on genetic surgery, notice how the writer uses a comparison to explain how genetic surgeons can revitalize ailing cells by using viruses.

132

The first time Richard Mulligan turned a virus into a truck, he swore softly in amazement. It was 1979, and Mulligan, then a 25-year-old graduate student at Stanford, had just performed an unprecedented feat of biological alchemy. Dressed in a modern-day mystic uniform of gloves, gown, boots, and mask, he had used the tools of recombinant DNA technology to splice a rabbit gene into a monkey virus.

Normally, viruses are vehicles for their own genes. In fact, they are little more than genetic material wrapped within a shell that allows the virus to travel from one cell to the next. They penetrate a cell, then commandeer the cell's genetic machinery into making thousands of virus copies. But with molecular sleight of hand, Mulligan had pulled out the genes that allow the virus to replicate and put in their place the genes for hemoglobin, the molecule in red blood cells—of both rabbits and people—that carries oxygen.

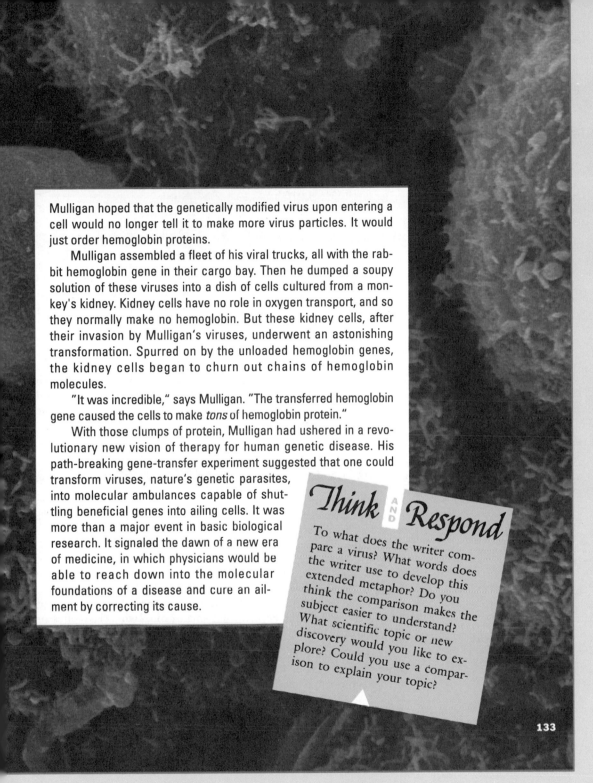

Mulligan hoped that the genetically modified virus upon entering a cell would no longer tell it to make more virus particles. It would just order hemoglobin proteins.

Mulligan assembled a fleet of his viral trucks, all with the rabbit hemoglobin gene in their cargo bay. Then he dumped a soupy solution of these viruses into a dish of cells cultured from a monkey's kidney. Kidney cells have no role in oxygen transport, and so they normally make no hemoglobin. But these kidney cells, after their invasion by Mulligan's viruses, underwent an astonishing transformation. Spurred on by the unloaded hemoglobin genes, the kidney cells began to churn out chains of hemoglobin molecules.

"It was incredible," says Mulligan. "The transferred hemoglobin gene caused the cells to make *tons* of hemoglobin protein."

With those clumps of protein, Mulligan had ushered in a revolutionary new vision of therapy for human genetic disease. His path-breaking gene-transfer experiment suggested that one could transform viruses, nature's genetic parasites, into molecular ambulances capable of shuttling beneficial genes into ailing cells. It was more than a major event in basic biological research. It signaled the dawn of a new era of medicine, in which physicians would be able to reach down into the molecular foundations of a disease and cure an ailment by correcting its cause.

Think *and* Respond

To what does the writer compare a virus? What words does the writer use to develop this extended metaphor? Do you think the comparison makes the subject easier to understand? What scientific topic or new discovery would you like to explore? Could you use a comparison to explain your topic?

133

Think and Respond

Elicit Personal Responses

This article, though written in relatively simple language, contains complex concepts, especially if students' background in life sciences is weak. Take time to ensure that students have understood its content before going on to the Think and Respond questions, which focus on the author's technique.

First, ask what students noted about the differences between a virus and a normal cell. *(There's no material between the viral nucleus and cell wall; the virus invades other cells' nuclei to reproduce itself.)* Then ask what Richard Mulligan's experiment was and what it implies. *(He put new genes into the DNA of a virus and got the virus to carry the new genes into living cells' nuclei, changing the cells' function. This implies that we can cure genetic diseases by using altered viruses to ferry new genes into certain cells.)*

Explore the Author's Techniques

With the class, work through the Think and Respond questions. Most students will have noticed Montgomery's first sentence, with its surprising statement that Richard Mulligan turned a virus into a truck. They may need guidance, however, to see that the author compares an unaltered virus to a vehicle. He develops the analogy by comparing Mulligan's altered viruses to trucks, vehicles capable of carrying cargo (in Mulligan's experiment, the cargo was the genes for producing hemoglobin). Further, in his conclusion, he envisions altered viruses in the role of ambulances, "shuttling beneficial genes into ailing cells."

Science Connection

To help students understand the gene-transfer experiment in the model, point out that all cells reproduce by division. On the chalkboard write, and elicit definitions for, the terms *chromosomes* ("small, paired bodies within the nucleus that contain DNA and initiate cell division"), *DNA* ("a long, double-helix shaped molecule chain that provides the coding for all inherited traits in the new cells"), and *genes* ("portions of the DNA chain that contain the coding for specific traits"). Then ask what might happen if, before a cell divided, a gene for a new trait were slipped into its DNA. The model will confirm students' guesses.

Guiding Your Writers

Objectives

1. To choose and research a topic for a science report
2. To draft and revise a science report
3. To publish or present a science report

Preteaching

Preview the content of the lesson. If there are skills or concepts that students may need help with, present them at this time. The mini-lesson references below may help you in your selection and instruction. The cross references in the pupil text give students access to the same lessons for independent practice.

Handbook Mini-Lessons

- Writing Variables, p. 329
- Figurative Language, pp. 435–437
- Presenting an Argument, pp. 474–476
- Using Source Material, pp. 482–489
- Finding the Best Source, pp. 493–494

Teaching Strategies

Teaching Tip: Personal Goals

After students have browsed through science textbooks and periodicals for topic ideas, encourage them to form groups, share their findings, and brainstorm a list of approaches to each student's topic. Students can then use the brainstormed lists to refine their topics and approaches according to their own goals.

INVITATION
TO
Write

Geoffrey Montgomery's article shows how one writer used an extended comparison to explain the difficult concept of gene transfer. Select a scientific topic and present it in a clear and concise report.

Science reports often require the writer to present new concepts and ideas clearly to a general audience. Given the advances that occur daily in science and medicine, this skill has become increasingly important, not just to scientists but also to reporters who must cover these advances. Like writing a definition, writing about a scientific concept requires you to explore your topic from a number of different angles, using a variety of techniques. More important, however, thinking and writing about science will open your mind to a fascinating world that you might otherwise have overlooked and that will play an increasingly important role in determining the future of our planet and its people.

HANDBOOKS
FOR HELP & PRACTICE

Writing Variables, pp. 329–330

Figurative Language, pp. 435–436

Presenting an Argument, pp. 474–476

Using Source Material, pp. 482–489

Finding the Best Source, pp. 493–494

THINKING ABOUT A TOPIC

1. Select an intriguing idea. The best ideas for science reports stem from topics that fascinate you. Do not rule out a difficult subject if it interests you; as you write about it, you will come to understand it better. Think about intriguing concepts you've discovered in your science class—quarks or antimatter, for example. You might also find ideas by browsing through newspapers; science magazines such as *Discover, Scientific American,* or *Science News;* or the science columns of general news magazines such as *Time* and *Newsweek.* You might even form a small group with classmates or friends and brainstorm a list of unusual research projects.

2. Research your topic thoroughly. A recent edition of an encyclopedia may cover your topic. Depending on the topic, current books on the subject may also be available. However, since new develop-

---

Literature Connection

Nonfiction   Students may enjoy reading examples of clear and engaging nonfiction literature dealing with medicine and/or the sciences. Invite them to find in the library Lewis Thomas's *The Lives of a Cell* and *The Medusa and the Snail,* Oliver Sack's *The Man Who Mistook His Wife for a Hat,* Loren Eiseley's *The Immense Journey,* Konrad Lorenz's *King Solomon's Ring,* David Macaulay's *The Way Things Work,* and Stephen W. Hawking's *A Brief History of Time.* These fascinating books might prove to be sources of ideas that could lead students to topics for their science reports.

ments in science occur so rapidly, the alphabetical subject headings in the *Readers' Guide to Periodical Literature* will probably be your best source of up-to-date information. Use at least three or four information sources for your report.

3. Envision your audience and your goal. Remember that your purpose is to explain your topic to an audience of your peers, not a group of scientists. As you take notes on your subject, your first goal is to understand the subject you are exploring yourself so that you can, in turn, explain it clearly to others.

DRAFTING YOUR REPORT

1. Set a purpose. Think about why you are fascinated with your topic. What aspect of your topic might your reader find most appealing? Write a controlling statement that sets a clear purpose for your report.

2. Evaluate your information. As you continue writing, keep your controlling purpose in mind so that you include only information that is relevant to your topic. Put yourself in the place of your reader. Are there any unfamiliar terms that need to be defined? Are there any gaps in logic or information in your report?

3. Look for ways to clarify or simplify your concept. Are there terms that should be defined in context? Can a difficult idea be paraphrased? Is there a comparison you could use, as Geoffrey Montgomery did, to make a difficult concept easier to understand?

Writing
─TIP─

You might find it easier to organize your notes if you write them on index cards. Use a separate card for each note.

 ## Individualizing Instruction

LEP Students Because reading and writing often take longer for LEP students than for others, they may need you to reduce the time they will devote to researching their topics, so that they will have enough time to draft and revise. You may wish to guide these students toward process analysis. They could, for example, explain the workings of anything from a light bulb to a laser. For many process analysis topics, they can observe or interview as part of their research, rather than depending entirely on printed references. In addition, the straightforward chronological order of a process analysis will free LEP students from worrying about complex organization and allow them to concentrate more on achieving an appropriate tone and style.

LD Students If students' topics are appropriate, you might ask them to produce a report in the form of sequential drawings with extensive captions.

Spot Check

As students finish their controlling statements, check to see that they focus on one topic and imply a specific purpose and approach. If a controlling statement is vague, the student is still groping for a specific way to approach the topic. Suggest a five-minute freewriting in which the student reflects on what he or she wants to convey and how best to convey it.

Science Report **135**

Social Studies Connection

Geoffrey Montgomery uses a second, more subtle comparison when he describes Mulligan as performing a "feat of biological alchemy," wearing a "modern-day mystic uniform," and using "molecular sleight of hand." Students who enjoy history and/or anthropology may be interested in researching cultures or time periods in which medicine and magic have merged. Some may want to investigate an aspect of the history of alchemy in medieval Europe; others may want to research shamanism in a specific culture of today or of the past.

Remind students that, though jargon can provide a concise way of referring to technical things, it can also confuse and distance the reader. Point out that writers have options for dealing with jargon. They can translate it into everyday language, perhaps with the help of comparisons to more familiar things. Geoffrey Montgomery demonstrates this option with his truck analogy. They can also combine key technical terms with definitions and ample context clues to their meaning. Montgomery demonstrates this option in paragraph 2, where he uses an appositive to define *hemoglobin*.

Managing the Paper Load

Consider focusing only on certain kinds of errors as you grade these papers. By now, you have an idea of each student's strengths and problem areas. You might remind each student of what he or she did well in the last assignment, then explain that you will focus, this time, on the area that needed improvement in the last assignment.

4. Use a lively style. Avoid writing that is dry or highly technical. Instead, use lively descriptions, quotations, and appropriate comparisons to convey your enthusiasm for your subject. Notice how Geoffrey Montgomery uses the extended metaphor to describe the virus's vehicular function in transferring genes from one cell to another. "Mulligan assembled a *fleet* of his viral *trucks,* all with the rabbit hemoglobin in their *cargo bay.*" Later in the article, Montgomery continues the metaphor by referring to the viruses as "molecular *ambulances* capable of *shuttling* beneficial genes into ailing cells."

 Writer's Choice You can present your material objectively, or you can personalize it with a more informal tone. Which approach is more appropriate to your subject and purpose?

5. Consider a graphic aid. You might use a diagram, chart, or illustration. If you include a graphic aid from one of your sources in your report, you must credit the source. Another option is to design a graphic aid of your own.

6. Document your sources. Be sure that you give credit to your sources, whether you paraphrase, summarize, or use direct quotations. Use parenthetical documentation in the body of your report, and include a bibliography of the sources you used at the end of the report.

R EVIEWING YOUR WRITING

1. Ask a classmate to read your report. Did your report immediately engage your reader's interest? Ask your reader to state the controlling purpose of your report. Does your reader clearly understand the scientific concept you are presenting? If not, you may need to simplify your presentation of the material or provide additional information about your topic. Did your reader find your comparison helpful? Were your details vivid and precise?

2. Evaluate your style and tone. Have you presented your topic in an exciting new way? Is your writing dry or overly technical?

3. Proofread your writing. Review your work for any errors in grammar, usage, spelling, and punctuation, and make any necessary corrections. Then prepare a neat final copy of your report.

136 Workshop 4

Literature Connection

Strong Verbs Point out that much of the strength and clarity of Geoffrey Montgomery's writing comes from his use of strong, simple verbs and verbals. (Examples include: *splice, dumped, spurred, churn, ushered, shuttling.*) In paragraph 2 he writes that Mulligan had *pulled out* (not *removed* or *extracted*) viral genes and *put in* (not *inserted* or *introduced*) hemoglobin genes. Let students choose any paragraph from their own reports, underline all the verbs and verbals, and evaluate them to see if they can be replaced with others that are simpler and more vivid.

The following guidelines may be used for a close evaluation of a science report. A good science report

- focuses on one topic and has a specific purpose
- contains enough detail to explain the topic clearly
- shows logical organization
- uses style and tone appropriately to appeal to a general audience
- documents sources
- displays standard grammar and mechanics

Reteaching

Assess the needs of students who were not successful developing an effective science report. Assign the appropriate Handbook Mini-Lessons. Concepts commonly requiring reteaching for this assignment are

Presenting an Argument: Handbook 23
Using Source Materials: Handbook 24

The following suggestions and resources may also be useful.

1. **Underdeveloped Analogies** If students fail to develop their comparisons, explain that an analogy can start as a simile: X is like Y. The writer then goes on to specify several ways (not just one or two) that X is like Y, illustrating each with details. Mark places where the analogy has been (or could be) extended, and direct students to develop further extensions.

2. **Inconsistent Style** Often students' style is influenced by the style of their sources, resulting in inconsistency. Put plus marks by sections that reflect the student's own style, and put arrows by sections that sound uneven or impersonal. Define style as a function of diction, sentence structure, and figurative language, and direct students to recast sections marked with arrows.

PUBLISHING AND PRESENTING

- **Make an encyclopedia.** Along with your classmates, use your science reports to create a science and technology encyclopedia. Divide your encyclopedia into sections that reflect different scientific and technological disciplines: medicine, astronomy, computers, transportation, flight, botany, biology, and so on. Enhance the look of your encyclopedia by adding illustrations—photographs, drawings, photocopies—and other graphic aids, such as charts, graphs, timelines, and so on. Your completed encyclopedia would be a great resource for other students and an important addition to your science classroom or school library.

- **Write a news story.** Imagine that the subject of your science report is a recent discovery, treatment, or advancement. Write a news story about it such as might appear in a major newspaper. Keep in mind that an effective news story tells *who, what, when, where,* and *why* about its subject. A news story also begins with an attention-getting "lead," the first few sentences that give the substance of the story.

Science Report **137**

Science Connection

Students interested in biology will enjoy James D. Watson's *The Double Helix.* This nonfiction work reads like a mystery or adventure novel. It is Watson's personal account of how he and Francis H. Crick, amid much international scientific intrigue, unlocked the secret of DNA's molecular structure and won the Nobel Prize for medicine.

Related Assignment:
COLLABORATIVE WRITING

Starting from Literature

Objective

To use a professional model of collaborative writing as a springboard to creating a collaborative passage

Teaching Strategies

Motivate

Most high-school seniors have definite ideas of the quality of life they'd like to achieve in adulthood, even if they haven't yet made career choices. Ask students to share some of their ideas about their future lives. How do they define success? What kinds of success do they most want to achieve?

Tap Prior Knowledge

Ask students to explain some of the ways that a character's speech can reveal his or her personality. By now, students have had experience with analyzing diction and speech mannerisms, as well as the content of spoken messages. They should mention not only content but also such elements as the level of formality the speaker chooses; the complexity of vocabulary and sentence structure; and the emotions, or lack of emotions, that the speaker conveys. Call on students to name favorite fictional characters and describe how their personalities are revealed in *what* they say and *how* they say it.

Set a Purpose

After the class has read and discussed the side-column notes, tell students that understanding the differences between the two characters in the dialogue will help them to form ideas about how the authors may have worked together on it.

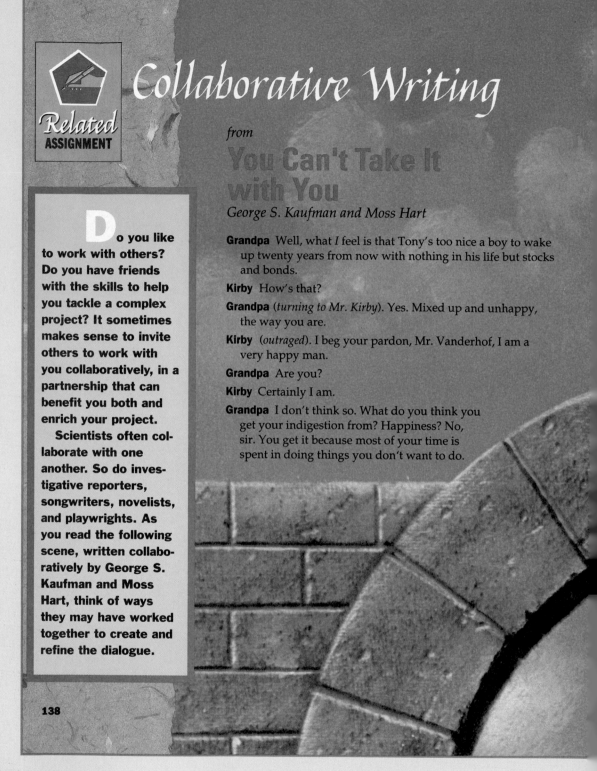

Related ASSIGNMENT

Collaborative Writing

from
You Can't Take It with You
George S. Kaufman and Moss Hart

Grandpa Well, what *I* feel is that Tony's too nice a boy to wake up twenty years from now with nothing in his life but stocks and bonds.

Kirby How's that?

Grandpa (*turning to Mr. Kirby*). Yes. Mixed up and unhappy, the way you are.

Kirby (*outraged*). I beg your pardon, Mr. Vanderhof, I am a very happy man.

Grandpa Are you?

Kirby Certainly I am.

Grandpa I don't think so. What do you think you get your indigestion from? Happiness? No, sir. You get it because most of your time is spent in doing things you don't want to do.

Do you like to work with others? Do you have friends with the skills to help you tackle a complex project? It sometimes makes sense to invite others to work with you collaboratively, in a partnership that can benefit you both and enrich your project.

Scientists often collaborate with one another. So do investigative reporters, songwriters, novelists, and playwrights. As you read the following scene, written collaboratively by George S. Kaufman and Moss Hart, think of ways they may have worked together to create and refine the dialogue.

138

Kirby I don't do anything I don't want to do.

Grandpa Yes, you do. You said last night that at the end of a week in Wall Street you're pretty near crazy. Why do you keep on doing it?

Kirby Why do I keep on—why, that's my *business*. A man can't give up his business.

Grandpa Why not? You've got all the money you need. You can't take it with you.

Kirby That's a very easy thing to say, Mr. Vanderhof. But I have spent my entire life building up my business.

Grandpa And what's it got you? Same kind of mail every morning, same kind of deals, same kind of meetings, same dinners at night, same indigestion. Where does the fun come in? Don't you think there ought to be something

more, Mr. Kirby? You must have wanted more than that when you started out. We haven't got too much time, you know—any of us.

Kirby What do you expect me to do? Live the way *you* do? Do nothing?

Grandpa Well, I have a lot of fun. Time enough for everything—read, talk, visit the zoo now and then, practice my darts, even have time to notice when spring comes around. Don't see anybody I don't want to, don't have six hours of things I *have* to do every day before I get *one* hour to do what I like in—and I haven't taken bicarbonate of soda in thirty-five years. What's the matter with that?

Kirby The matter with that? But suppose we *all* did it? A fine world we'd have, everybody going to zoos. Don't be ridiculous, Mr. Vanderhof. Who would do the work?

Think AND Respond

Notice the differences in temperament and point of view between the two characters in this scene. What fairly apparent method of collaborative writing does this scene suggest? If you were to write a play with one or more partners, how would you split up the tasks? What tasks would you perform as a group?

Collaborative Writing **139**

Guiding Your Writers

Objectives

1. To choose a writing task and a partner for collaborative writing
2. To use collaboration to plan and draft a piece of writing
3. To choose a forum and present a piece of collaborative writing

Preteaching

Preview the content of the lesson. If there are skills or concepts students may need help with, present them at this time. The mini-lesson references below may help you in your selection and instruction. The cross references in the pupil text give students access to the same lessons for independent practice.

> **Handbook Mini-Lessons**
> - Planning/Organizing Strategies, pp. 348–356
> - Collaborative Planning, pp. 358–360
> - Peer Response, pp. 397–401
> - Presenting/Publishing; pp. 412–415

Teaching Strategies

Teaching Tip: Personal Goals

Point out to students that this is an excellent opportunity for them to take on projects which they have been wanting to do but which have seemed overwhelming. Perhaps they could collaborate on a research paper or another major assignment for this class, or, with the consent of other teachers, on research projects for other classes. Or perhaps they have always wanted to try writing a play, a short story, a narrative poem, or a nonfiction article, but have been intimidated by the sheer bulk of work required. Encourage them to choose a project that has meaning for them, and help them to find partners whose interests and abilities match or complement their own. You and another teacher in the department may consider pairing students from one another's classes.

INVITATION TO Write

This excerpt from a Kaufman and Hart play shows the variety and depth that can be achieved through collaborative writing. With one or more partners, plan and develop a piece of writing, such as a dramatic scene or an in-depth report.

Collaboration provides you with an opportunity to expand your potential by joining your skills with those of your collaborators. Just as sports teams can accomplish more when all the players work together, a collaborative writing team may attain a richness and scope in its writing that one writer alone could not achieve.

PLANNING A COLLABORATION

HANDBOOKS
FOR HELP & PRACTICE

Planning/Organizing Strategies, pp. 348–357

Collaborative Planning, pp. 358–360

Peer Response, pp. 397–400

Presenting/ Publishing, pp. 412–413

1. Find a partner. Look for someone who has similar interests or a similar goal to achieve. For example, if you want to write a screenplay, you might choose to collaborate with a classmate who has some acting experience. If you want to collaborate on a specific research project, ask your teacher to steer you to someone else who would benefit from working on such a report. Discuss your ideas with several potential partners until you find someone with whom you can work well.

Writer's Choice You can work with a partner whose skills and interests parallel yours, or you can choose to work with someone whose abilities complement yours.

2. Explore your topic and goals. Determine with your collaborator what your writing goals are. For a screenplay, for example, you might decide you want to compose a comedy that would satirize some aspect of life in the 1990's. Next, brainstorm your topic from every angle. Entertain all related ideas, no matter how odd or unusual. Even a single word or phrase can trigger an interesting association, and therefore a potential new direction.

Literature Connection

Nonfiction Point out to students that three hundred years ago Addison and Steele were collaborating on *The Spectator*. Have students read articles from *The Spectator* excerpted in their literature text. Explain that, rather than dividing up the writing tasks, Addison and Steele each wrote their own articles. Yet the articles might never have been written if it were not for the ideas and energy the two friends generated in their discussions together. Suggest that students discuss with partners the goals and the projects they have in mind, noting how the discussions affect their ideas.

3. Plan your collaboration.   Think about how the individuals on your team can best work together. Will you discuss and shape ideas together verbally, then have one person draft and one or both revise? Or will you compose together, with one person acting as a scribe? In a creative piece such as a screenplay, you could role-play the characters with your collaborator, perhaps taping the exchanges for later analysis. You may want to consult the guidelines for Collaborative Planning on pages 358–360.

4. Assign different jobs.   Assign a partner to each task. In a research project, for example, all collaborators can be entirely responsible for one part of the report, including all research, organization, and drafting; or you can allot one complete stage of the writing task to each member of the group. If you are composing a song collaboratively, one person could be responsible for the words, the other for the music. Another exciting method of assigning collaborative writing, usually used for fiction, involves writers taking turns writing various chapters. This approach allows each writer to experience the surprise and challenge of building on the other's unexpected plot twists.

COMPUTER
——TIP——

Input each person's contribution in the same file on your word processor. Experiment with different arrangements of material on screen.

Collaborative
Writing   **141**

Guidelines for Evaluation

The following guidelines may be used for a close evaluation of a collaborative passage. A good piece of collaborative writing

- meets the goals of all collaborators
- has one main point or theme or a clear story line
- contains enough specific input from all collaborators
- shows appropriate organization with smooth transitions between segments
- uses sentence structures that suit its purpose and content
- uses correct grammar and mechanics

Reteaching

Assess the needs of students who were not successful developing an effective collaborative passage. Assign the appropriate Handbook Mini-Lessons. Concepts commonly requiring reteaching for this assignment are

Collaborative Planning: Handbook 6
Peer Response: Handbook 12

The following suggestions and resources may also be useful.

1. Uneven Style Pieces containing writing by two students may show a distracting unevenness in style. Underline conflicting elements of style. Direct partners to collaborate on choosing one suitable style, identifying its elements, and incorporating it throughout the piece.

2. Unclear Theme or Thesis This may be a signal that collaborators are not in agreement on topic and purpose. Mark the areas of confusion, saying something like "It's not clear whether you mean to focus on X or Y. Here it seems to be X, but here it seems to be Y." Instruct partners to clarify their ideas of topic and purpose, then clarify the writing.

DRAFTING YOUR MATERIAL

1. Organize the material. Gather together all your notes, research, or initial drafts and decide which material fulfills the group's purpose and goals. Then work together to discover an effective presentation. For a screenplay, you might discuss whether to experiment with flashbacks or to present events in chronological order.

2. Examine your options. Choose one person to read the prewriting aloud. Encourage others to elaborate on images and ideas. You might even create different versions of a segment or two and then discuss which version to use.

3. Draft your ideas. Write out a draft that incorporates everyone's comments. Use notations or symbols to mark the rough spots. Then read the draft aloud, discussing how to improve it.

Writing
—TIP—

As you read your writing aloud, have your collaborator mark the phrases or passages that sound awkward.

REVIEWING YOUR WRITING

1. Problem-solve. Read the completed draft aloud to make sure the pieces are now unified and the content or message is clear. Have you included all of the ideas or information each group member felt was important? Does the writing flow smoothly and logically? Look for problems in consistency. Do you need to create transitions between different segments? Work as a group to solve problems and answer questions.

2. Evaluate your work in relation to your goals. Review the group's stated goals and make revisions, if necessary, to meet those goals. If you have written a narrative or drama, stage readings or preliminary performances of your work.

PUBLISHING AND PRESENTING

- **Find a forum in which to present your collaborative work.** If it is a story or play, act it out. If it is a report, form a "panel of experts" and take turns speaking on the subject.
- **Create an anthology of collaborative works.** Illustrate, copy, and bind the anthologies.

Literature Connection

Translation   Inform students that many literary translations are collaborations. Some involve an author and a translator fluent in both languages. Others involve a scholar fluent in both languages and a translator fluent only in the target language. Suggest that bilingual and monolingual students collaborate to translate a short poem or prose piece.

Sentence

Varying Sentences

Various types of modifiers make up many of the sentence expanders used by professional writers to add detail and to create such effects as rhythm, suspense, and contrast. Notice the characteristics of each type of modifier below.

Adjectives and Adverbs

Adjectives and adverbs can be used singly or in combination.

Adverbs used singly — <u>Quickly, frantically</u>, he tried to slide back the hood with his left hand, but he had not the strength. **Roald Dahl, "Beware of the Dog"**

Adverb and adjective in combination — The vast, arid plain, <u>often deserted</u>, today teemed with game of all sorts.
Isak Dinesen, *Shadows on the Grass*

Prepositional Phrases

Prepositions are words that show relationships (for example, *over, under,* and *around*). A prepositional phrase contains a preposition and related nouns and modifiers.

<u>On the table in the middle of the</u> room lay the coffin.
Leo Tolstoy, *Childhood, Boyhood, Youth*

A. Combining and Imitating Sentences Use the first sentence in each set as the foundation. Join the underlined part(s) of the next sentence(s) with the foundation in the position indicated in parentheses. Place s-v splits directly after the subject, and set them off with commas. Finally, write a sentence whose structure imitates that of the combined sentence.

1. Beth had resisted leaving for the day-care center. Beth was <u>usually so pliable</u>. (s-v split) **Mary Higgins Clark, *A Cry in the Night***

2. A spring bubbled out of a rupture in the stone. The spring was <u>high in the grey stone mountains</u>. (opener) The spring was <u>under a frowning peak</u>. (opener) **John Steinbeck, *The Pearl***

3. Dr. Killgruel was visited by Miss M. This happened <u>on a summer day some months later</u>. (opener) **Joan Aiken, "Follow My Fancy"**

4. He got up. He was <u>vivid with excitement</u>. (closer) **F. Scott Fitzgerald, *The Great Gatsby***

Sentence Composing: Varying Sentences

Objectives

1. To combine sentences through the use of adjectives, adverbs, and prepositional phrases
2. To compose sentences that contain participial phrases, appositive phrases, and absolute phrases
3. To expand sentences by adding adjectives, adverbs, and modifying phrases

Preteaching

These exercises focus on the use of adjectives, adverbs, and modifying phrases to express more specific, detailed ideas. Some students may need review of basic sentence parts and structure as well as the proper placement of modifiers, prepositional phrases, participial phrases, appositive phrases, and absolute phrases. Refer to the following sections of the Grammar Handbook for preteaching content:

Phrases and Clauses
 Prepositional Phrases, pages 591–592
 Appositives and Appositive Phrases, page 593
 Verbals and Verbal Phrases, pages 594–596
 Using Phrases Correctly, page 602
Adjective and Adverb Usage
 Understanding Modifiers, pages 719–720

ANSWER KEY

12-4 Varying Sentences

A. Combining and Imitating Sentences
Imitations will vary.
 1. Beth, usually so pliable, had resisted leaving for the day-care center.
 2. High in the grey stone mountains, under a frowning peak, a spring bubbled out of a rupture in the stone.
 3. On a summer day some months later, Dr. Killgruel was visited by Miss M.
 4. He got up, vivid with excitement.

Present Participial Phrases

Present participial phrases contain a present participle and related words.

> Away she darted, <u>stretching close to the ground</u>.
> **Francis Parkman, *The Oregon Trail***

Past Participial Phrases

Past participial phrases contain a past participle and related words.

> The all-powerful auto industry, <u>accustomed to telling the customer what sort of car he wanted</u>, was suddenly forced to *listen* for a change.   **Jessica Mitford, *The American Way of Death***

B. Unscrambling and Imitating Sentences   Unscramble the parts of each set to form a sentence whose structure matches the model. Then write a second sentence whose structure also imitates the model.

1. <u>Craning his head back</u>, he looked up along the wall.
   Robb White, *Deathwatch*
   a. by the geraniums
   b. moving its body daintily
   c. the spider crawled down

2. Bigger laughed and approached the bed with the dangling rat, <u>swinging it to and fro like a pendulum, enjoying his sister's fear</u>.
   Richard Wright, *Native Son*
   a. apologizing right and left like a penitent
   b. the salesperson returned and presented Winston with the refund
   c. soliciting his patronage

3. The room, <u>shadowed well with awnings</u>, was dark and cool.
   F. Scott Fitzgerald, *The Great Gatsby*
   a. piled high with junk
   b. was forbidding but fascinating
   c. the attic

Appositive Phrases

An appositive is a noun or pronoun that identifies another noun or pronoun. Appositive phrases contain the appositive plus related modifiers.

> The face of Liliana Methol, <u>the fifth woman in the plane</u>, was badly bruised and covered with blood.   **Piers Paul Read, *Alive***

Absolute Phrases

An absolute is a sentence part, that, while related to the sentence as a whole, does not modify any specific word within the sentence.

> Then, very afraid, she shook her head warningly and touched a finger to her lips and shook her head again, <u>her eyes pleading with him</u>.
> **James Clavell, *Shogun***

C. Unscrambling and Imitating Sentences Unscramble the parts of each set to form a sentence whose structure matches the model. Then write another sentence whose structure also matches that of the model.

1. Alice, <u>a cousin of Frederick's, a widow down on her luck</u>, came to Dorothy. **Doris Lessing, *The Fifth Child***
   a. tried to get a weird haircut
   b. Dulcie
   c. a friend of mine, a person up on the latest styles

2. She returned to her bench, <u>her face showing all the unhappiness that had suddenly overtaken her</u>. **Theodore Dreiser, *An American Tragedy***
   a. that had always characterized him
   b. Odysseus lunged for the Cyclops
   c. his response showing all the cunning

3. <u>And the service over</u>, Shawn used to stay in his seat so that he might get one quick but sure look at her face as she passed out.
   Maurice Walsh, "The Quiet Man"
   a. Byrd had to huddle in his tent
   b. and the daylight waning
   c. before he pressed onward
   d. so that he might get a few cramped and damp hours of sleep

Application From a recent piece of writing, choose six sentences to expand by adding adjectives and adverbs and the five kinds of phrases you have studied in this lesson. Use adjectives and adverbs and each kind of phrase at least once, and place them where they make the most sense in your sentences.

Grammar Refresher For more on adjectives and adverbs, see Handbook 37; for more on prepositional phrases, see Handbook 33; for more on participial phrases, see Handbook 33; for more on appositives, see Handbook 33; for more on absolute phrases, see Handbook 33.

Workshop Overview

Informative exposition, writing that explains or informs, can take several forms: classification, as in Workshop 4, and, in this Workshop, analysis. Like classification, analysis is an important critical thinking skill. Students learn to examine a subject from all sides by breaking it down into its parts and noticing how the parts are alike and different and how they function together. This skill aids student comprehension of concepts and ideas in all subject areas. Workshop 5 includes the following Guided and Related assignments:

1. **Guided: Subject Analysis** shows students how to break a subject into its parts and how to focus an exploration of the subject; also helps students choose among appropriate methods of analysis for elaborating on the subject and its parts

2. **Related: Graphic Aid** helps students translate into the visual realm the skill of breaking down a subject into its parts

3. **Related: Project Analysis** builds on analysis skills by showing students how to examine and evaluate a school or business-related project

Preparation Guide

1. Use the Overview above and the Teacher's Choice descriptions on page 147 as a basis for deciding which assignment(s) to teach.

2. Preview the assignment and the teacher's notes. The teaching suggestions and your knowledge of your class's abilities should allow you to identify quickly the concepts that may require preteaching or extra support. The Handbook mini-lessons suggested in the Preteaching notes within the lesson can also provide guidance in this area.

3. Preview the adjacent chart for support materials in the Teacher's Resource File that may be used with this Workshop. Resources are for use with the Guided Assignment unless otherwise noted.

Workshop Support Materials

Resources	For Use With
Ideas for Writing: Data Sheets, p. 9; Additional Ideas, p. 23	Look for ideas, p. 150
	Choose a subject, p. 151
Thinking Skills Transparencies: Basic Category Chart; *Worksheets,* p. 6	Focus your exploration, p. 152
Elaboration/Proofreading, p. 9	Elaborate on ideas, p. 154
Peer Response Guides, p. 15	Review Your Writing, p. 156
Evaluating Writing, pp. 12, 32–33	Standards for Evaluation, p. 157
Student Revision Trans., pp. 19–22	Problem-solve, p. 157
Elaboration/Proofreading, p. 10	Proofread your work, p. 158
Tests and Assessment: Prompts, p. 5	

Professional Resources and Media

Books and Journals

Rorabacher, Louise E., and Georgia Dunbar. "Analysis." *Assignments in Exposition.* 8th Ed. New York: Harper & Row, 1985. pp. 181–205.

Films and Videos

Communication Skills—Expository Writing. Guidance Association, Mt. Kisco, New York. 1981. (60 min.)

"Process and Analysis." *The Write Course Series.* Dallas Community College District, Mesquite, Texas. 1984. (30 min.)

Computer Software

Write Approach II, The. The Write Approach to Editing Skills II. Intellectual Software, Bridgeport, Connecticut. Apple II, II+, IIc, IIe.

Linking Literature, Writing, and Grammar

The following options may be used to provide students with an integrated language experience. Begin by assigning and discussing any of the recommended pieces of literature, which can be found in most classroom anthologies. Use the suggested strategy to provide a link to the Guided Assignment.

Linking Literature and Writing

Option 1
Starting Point: "Stuttering" by Denise Grady on pages 148–149 of *The Writer's Craft*
Strategy: Use the teaching suggestions on pages 148–149 to lead students into the Guided Assignment.

Option 2
Starting Point: "Macbeth" by William Hazlitt
Strategy: As part of a discussion of the essay, have students identify the areas into which Hazlitt divides his analysis. Students should mention the play's opening, the "lofty imagination (the play) displays," "the tumultuous vehemence of the action," the character of Macbeth, the character of Lady Macbeth, and the Witches. Ask students how Hazlitt's analysis of these parts enhances the reader's understanding of the play. Encourage students to think of literary works they might analyze in a similar fashion.

Option 3
Starting Point: "The Unknown Citizen" by W. H. Auden
Strategy: After students have read the poem, ask them into what specific elements the speaker breaks down the unknown citizen's life. Based on the speaker's analysis, what does he conclude about the unknown citizen? Explain that the method of analysis used by Auden, the breaking down of an entity (here the unknown citizen's character) into specific elements, is often used in prose to clarify a subject. As an example, have them read the article on stuttering on pages 148 and 149 and lead them into the Guided Assignment.

Linking Writing and Grammar

Before the drafting or revision stage of this assignment, tell students that writers often use appositive phrases and adjective clauses to provide information about a subject. Have students look through their own papers for places in which they used appositive phrases or adjective clauses to add detail. As you write the following examples on the board, remind students that appositive phrases require commas and adjective clauses do not.

APPOSITIVE PHRASE: Lincoln, the sixteenth President of the United States, was born in modest circumstances in a small town in Kentucky.

ADJECTIVE CLAUSE: Lincoln is the man *who saved the American Union from splitting apart.*

Have students review the material about the correct use of appositive phrases on page 593 and adjective clauses on pages 608–609 of the Grammar and Usage Handbook. If students need further work with phrases and clauses, assign the exercises on those pages for reteaching. Additional practice can be found in the Grammar and Usage Practice Book on pages 22 and 28.

Workshop Management Guidelines

The adjacent chart indicates the number of days recommended for each phase of the Guided and Related Assignments. Stars indicate portions of the assignment that may be completed outside the classroom if time is limited or if teachers wish the activity to be completed by students independently.

Subject Analysis

Starting from Literature—1 day
Prewrite—3–4 days*
Draft—2–3 days*
Revise—1–2 days
Publish—1–2 days
Learning—1 day*
Reteaching—open
Extension/Enrichment—open
Sentence Composing—1 day*

Graphic Aid

Starting from a Model—1 day
Planning—2–3 days*
Creating—2–3 days*

Reviewing—1–2 days
Publishing—1–2 days
Reteaching—open
Extension/Enrichment—open

Project Analysis

Starting from Literature—1 day
Choosing and Investigating a Project—open*
Drafting—2–4 days*
Reviewing—1–2 days
Publishing—open
Reteaching—open
Extension/Enrichment—open

Sketchbook

Objective

To use a poster to stimulate exploration of an issue related to students' lives

Using the Prompt

Channel students' reaction to the poster (which may be strong) into a spirited exploration of this or another issue that touches on their own identity. Emphasize that they will not be graded on this activity and there are no wrong answers. Students should explore their ideas freely in whatever direction their writing takes them.

Begin by discussing the impression that current movies and television shows give of teenagers and have students compare this to the impression conveyed by the poster. Ask them to identify specific details in the poster that help create the overall impression. Then ask that students write their own description of teenagers. Suggest that they think of themselves as "answering" the challenge of the poster. Students who feel constricted by the poster can write about one of the ideas in Additional Sketches instead.

Encourage students to keep their writing in their writing portfolio for possible use in the workshop that follows.

Sketchbook

As this movie poster from 1955 shows, the stereotype of lawless, uncontrollable teenagers is nothing new. In your view, how would a teenager be described?

Additional Sketches

What is the secret of your success?

Choose an issue or topic with which you are quite familiar and write as many questions as you can about it. When you find a question that seems impossible to answer, stop and explore it.

146

Informative Exposition: Analysis

Guided Assignment
SUBJECT ANALYSIS

Related Assignment
GRAPHIC AID

Related Assignment
PROJECT EVALUATION

I f you have ever met people who like to tinker with machines, you know they are constantly taking things apart—radios, computers, cars, and other devices—just to "see how they work." Indeed, taking a thing apart and examining the separate parts is a good way to understand or explain anything from an electronic gadget to a concept in philosophy. In thinking and writing, such a process is called analysis. In the next three assignments you will use analysis to explore a complex subject, to create a graphic representation of a subject, and to evaluate a project.

147

Objectives

Guided Assignment:
SUBJECT ANALYSIS
To define and identify examples of analysis; to use prewriting activities to choose a topic and identify a purpose and audience for a subject analysis; to draft, revise, proofread, and publish a subject analysis

Related Assignment:
GRAPHIC AID
To identify graphic aids and understand how they convey complex information to create a graphic aid that conveys information about a complex subject

Related Assignment:
PROJECT EVALUATION
To identify the characteristics of a project analysis; to plan, draft, revise, and share a project analysis

Teacher's Choice

The following information may help you choose the assignments that best fit the needs and interests of your students.

Guided Assignment
Subject Analysis This assignment is a good introduction to objective exposition; it calls on students to write about an objective topic rather than about their own ideas, feelings, and experiences. It entails analysis, a thinking skill basic to most forms of expository and persuasive writing.

Related Assignments
Graphic Aid This assignment reinforces a skill useful in other school subjects, such as social studies and science, and gives visual learners a means to exercise their powers of analysis.

Project Evaluation This assignment gives students an opportunity to apply analytical skills to real-life issues and thus may offer cross-curricular ties to social studies.

Assignment Rationale

In a subject analysis the writer breaks a complex subject down to individual components in order to describe and explain it. Analysis is a key tool used by scientists, philosophers, critics, and other thinkers to understand and explain the world. Developing analytical skills will thus contribute to students' success in almost every intellectual endeavor from science to history to literature.

Starting from Literature

Objective

To respond to a professional analysis as a springboard to writing

Teaching Strategies

Motivate

Put a classic tongue twister up on the chalkboard such as "She sells sea shells" or "Peter Piper picked a peck of pickled peppers." Challenge volunteers to read the tongue twister. Ask them why they have difficulty enunciating the words.

Tap Prior Knowledge

Ask students if they are aware of unexplained medical phenomena such as crib death or Alzheimer's disease. In spite of intensive study, doctors do not know why these phenomena occur. Point out that stuttering is such a problem. Ask students why they think people stutter, and list speculations on the chalkboard.

Guided ASSIGNMENT

Subject Analysis

One way to understand a complex phenomenon is through analysis, the process of breaking down a subject into its constituent parts and studying how the parts fit together to make up the whole.

When writer Denise Grady's two-year-old son began to stutter, Grady decided to find out why, so she wrote a subject analysis about stuttering for a magazine. As you read this excerpt from the article, notice how Grady analyzes stuttering by identifying the various body parts involved and the many steps that lead to and comprise this complex behavior.

148

Nobody knows why people stutter. The disorder occurs in virtually every culture, and speech therapists estimate that it affects about one percent of the population around the world. The earliest explanations, dating from ancient Greece and persisting into the early 1800's, blamed the tongue: it was too weak, too wet, too dry, too hard, too cold, too large. By the early part of this

STUTT

by Denise Grady

century, the focus had shifted upward, and stuttering was seen first as a bad habit or the product of a neurosis, and later as the result of some unknown abnormality in the brain.

Today many speech researchers think that stuttering is both a physiological and a behavioral condition. The details may differ from one person to the next, but the basic scenario is that stuttering begins for an organic reason and persists, at least in part, because the anxiety generated by the stuttering then makes the stuttering worse, as do some of the habits that people fall into in their struggles to control their speech. Some experts believe that excessive concern with the mechanics of talking can throw the rhythm off, just as thinking too much about where to put your foot next can lead to a fall, and trying to perfect each sentence as you write it can lead to writer's block. Some researchers have even suggested that people become physically addicted to stuttering, perhaps to little jolts of adrenaline or other brain chemicals that may be released during stuttering.

In order to speak, one has to coordinate breathing, voice, and movements of the mouth, lips, and tongue. Almost a hundred muscles are involved, and all of them must receive nerve signals at certain instants to produce the right sequence of movements. Because the muscles are on both sides of the body, their movements must also be synchronized. The speech control center resides in the left half of the brain in most people; one popular theory suggests that in stutterers its control may be incomplete, and the right side may fire

ERING

out conflicting orders that throw the whole speech apparatus out of whack. The result may be a breakdown in timing—a failure of the mechanism that organizes the movements required for speech and that marks its rhythm. Some researchers say that mistiming may be a perpetual problem: stutterers may hear their own speech in a distorted way—with a delay, perhaps—that interferes with their ability to talk.

Male stutterers outnumber females by at least three to one, and the disorder often runs in families. It nearly always comes on during preschool years, when speech and language pass through their most intense phases of development. Many children, especially boys, have brief periods of stuttering or stumbling or fragmented speech. Most get over it. Why some never do remains a mystery. In one of his books, *The Nature of Stuttering*, Charles Van Riper describes a "monstrous collage of factors" of physiology, intelligence, personality, verbal skill, and environmental stress that may contribute to stuttering.

Think AND Respond

What steps lead to normal speech, according to Grady, and what steps lead to stuttering? What other aspects of the phenomenon does she consider? What evidence does she put forward to support her analysis? What subjects of personal interest to you could you explore in a subject analysis?

149

Set a Purpose

Before students read the excerpt, discuss the side-column notes with them. Point out that in this excerpt the author analyzes the phenomenon of stuttering with a view to explaining what it is and why it occurs. Have students read the excerpt to see how Grady analyzes stuttering and how her analysis helps explain the phenomenon.

Think and Respond

Elicit Personal Responses

Have students look through the questions and jot down their ideas. Then, using the questions as a point of departure, have them discuss what Grady's analysis revealed about stuttering: Did they find the analysis convincing? Why or why not?

Explore the Author's Techniques

To clarify how the selection may be used as a model for students' own writing, point out the elements of Grady's analysis: She looks at stuttering from three angles—(1) as an intellectual problem (paragraph 1); (2) as an individual behavior (paragraph 2); and (3) as a social phenomenon (paragraph 3). In paragraph 2 she breaks stuttering down to two components (line 3), identifies the mechanisms involved in normal speech (lines 21–28), and isolates steps that may account for stuttering (lines 20–21 and 30).

Link Literature to Writing

Grady wrote a subject analysis about stuttering because the phenomenon affected her life. Analyzing her son's speech problem helped her understand and cope with it. Most students face similarly baffling issues in their lives. Explain that the upcoming Guided Assignment will give them an opportunity to cut one such problem down to size by subjecting it to careful analysis.

Prewrite and Explore

Objectives

1. To use various prewriting techniques to select a topic of personal interest for a subject analysis
2. To explore a variety of approaches to a subject through "cubing"
3. To identify audience, purpose and personal goals for a subject analysis
4. To gather and organize information for a subject analysis

Preteaching

Preview the Prewrite and Explore section. At this time, present any skills or concepts students may need help with before they begin their prewriting activities. The mini-lesson references below, as well as the Thinking Skill Transparency and Worksheet on Analysis Frames from the Teacher's Resource File, may help you in your selection and instruction. The cross references in the pupil text will give students access to the same lessons for independent study.

Handbook Mini-Lessons

- Gathering Information, p. 332
- Limiting Your Topic pp. 337–338
- Analysis Frames, p. 343

Teaching Strategies

Modeling

Model the process for the first exploratory activity by suggesting a few topical ideas drawn from recent news events. For example: *Music*—The 1990's have seen the rise of rap music; what musicial traditions have affected this new sound? *Science*—Certain cosmic rays that used to stream from the core of the Milky Way have now stopped coming, astronomers report. What could it mean?

INVITATION TO Write

Denise Grady analyzed a subject that was important to her. Now it is your turn to choose a subject you consider important and analyze it by identifying and exploring its parts.

Even the most complicated subject is composed of simpler parts. Analysis can, therefore, be applied to almost any subject. A repair manual for an automobile shows thousands of parts and how they work together. A medical textbook may break a surgical procedure down to a series of steps. Each entry in an encyclopedia takes some whole subject and examines it part by part. A critic analyzes a play or movie to see how its various elements work—or fail to work—together. You, too, can take any topic and understand it better by writing a subject analysis, identifying the parts that comprise your subject and examining how they fit together.

PREWRITE AND EXPLORE

HANDBOOKS

FOR HELP & PRACTICE

Gathering Information, p. 332

Limiting Your Topic, pp. 337–338

Analysis Frames, p. 343

1. Look for ideas. You write best when you explore a subject that you care and know something about. Try one or more of the following exploratory activities to help you think of an interesting subject for analysis.

Exploratory Activities

- **Brainstorming** With a group of classmates, brainstorm a list of noteworthy recent events in such fields as science, technology, politics, art, music, or international affairs. What topics for analysis do these events suggest?
- **Questioning** Think of issues and topics that have raised questions in your mind recently, including ones mentioned at school, in conversation with friends, in your personal reading or research for school, or in the news. List your questions.

- **Interviewing** Talk to people with interesting occupations, hobbies, backgrounds, or fields of expertise. Listen for ideas you might like to write about.
- **Reading literature** Do you enjoy a particular type of literature—mysteries or science fiction, for example? How would you analyze the qualities of one genre of literature?

2. Choose a subject. Scan the ideas you have generated and choose a few that seem promising. Do a few minutes of freewriting to see where each one might lead. If you still can't choose a topic, look through your journal, review the writing you did for the Sketchbook on page 146, or check "Apply Your Skills" on page 161.

3. Explore your topic. Find out what you know and think about your subject by jotting down some notes about it. You might try "cubing" to discover new approaches to the subject. That is, picture your subject as a cube and let each of the six sides represent a different activity: *describe, compare, associate, analyze, apply,* and *argue for or against.*

One student, Zack, became fascinated with wolves after he observed them when he was on a wilderness trip. Here is how Zack cubed the subject of wolves. In this assignment you will follow Zack through the writing of his subject analysis of wolves.

PROBLEM
S O L V I N G

How can I discover the qualities or characteristics of my subject?

ONE STUDENT'S PROCESS

Describe   A wolf against a full moon, howling. Large mammals with
           thick dense fur, skinny legs, powerful jaws. Lupine family.

Compare   Wolves and people are alike: both are social. A wolf pack
           is like a large family and the whole pack raises the pups.

Associate When I think "wolf" I think of fierce animals. Also, of fairy
           tale wolves: the Big Bad Wolf in the "Three Little Pigs."
           Fables and sayings: the boy who cried wolf, a wolf in
           sheep's clothing.

Analyze   Aspects of a wolf's life: hunting, mating, raising pups,
           traveling, communicating, dying.

Apply   Wolves are an endangered species—what could I do to
           help preserve them? What can we learn from wolves?

Argue   I think wolves should be protected, not hunted. We
for or   should study the wolf for what it can teach us about
against   the ways of the wilderness—and about ourselves.

Subject Analysis   **151**

Use Zack's chart to help students distinguish between focusing and narrowing a topic. Focusing does not necessarily mean covering less content; it means approaching the subject from a distinct angle. For example, focusing on communication does not preclude Zack from touching on the social structure of wolves or their social behavior; but his focus on communication will guide and shape what he says about these subjects.

Stumbling Block

Some students may insist they cannot formulate personal goals for this writing because they would rather not be writing at all. Such students have probably been considering writing topics in which they have no personal investment. Help them adjust or replace their topic by asking them what they would rather be doing. Ask questions about the activity they cite until you lead them to an issue they find absorbing and would like to resolve. Suggest they shape this question or issue into a topic for their subject analysis.

4. Focus your exploration. Decide which aspect of your topic you want to focus on. After looking through his cubing notes, Zack decided he was most interested in the social life of wolves. He looked up wolves in an encyclopedia. Then he charted the main factors that make wolves social animals.

ONE STUDENT'S PROCESS

THE SOCIAL LIFE OF WOLVES

Social Structure	Live in packs	
	Dominant wolves	Submissive wolves
Communication	Facial contact	Rubbing
	Scent marking	Tickling
Social Behaviors	Hunting	Cub rearing
	Respect for other wolves' territory	

As he created his chart, Zack realized that wolf communication lay at the heart of all the issues he wanted to raise in his analysis. He decided to focus specifically on this topic.

5. Break your subject into parts. To analyze, you must explore the subparts of your subject. These parts may be steps in a process, characteristics, stages, or any other logical division. Zack, for example, has already broken *communication* into four parts.

6. Frame your purpose and specific goals. Having brought your specific topic into focus, consider your purpose. Do you want to inform your readers? prove a point? rally support for some cause? Denise Grady wrote her analysis of stuttering to provide information—but she also wrote to gain a better understanding of a problem affecting a member of her family. What specific goals might you achieve by writing your subject analysis?

7. Gather information. Once you have a working purpose, you can gather information from interviews, books, magazines, reference works, videotapes, and other sources. Before you start, make a list of

152 Workshop 5

questions to guide your research. What parts of your subject are not yet clear to you? What evidence do you need to support your analysis?

8. Write a forecast sentence. To further focus your purpose, you can write a thesis, or forecast, sentence. Such a sentence may provide a good point of departure for drafting, even though you may change or adapt it once you get into your actual writing.

Zack wrote the following forecast sentence for his essay on wolves. It helped him to see what he wanted to achieve and what material he needed to cover in order to achieve it.

ONE STUDENT'S PROCESS

Despite their reputation as savage loners, wolves communicate with each other in many ways in order to maintain a rich social life.

9. Consider your audience. Before you begin drafting, try to visualize your readers. Will they have any background in your subject? Will you need to define any terms to them? What tone should you use with this audience? You may want to spend a few minutes freewriting about your readers.

DRAFT AND DISCOVER

1. Begin your draft. Look over your prewriting notes and then begin writing, keeping your overall purpose in mind. Try to get into the flow of your writing and set down everything you want to say. You will have time later to cut what you don't need, add what you forgot, and improve what you didn't express perfectly. Remember that drafting is an experimental stage. You may go back to the prewriting stage at any time to find more information, reorganize your approach, or redefine your purpose.

 Writer's Choice A compelling first sentence is important but it doesn't have to be written first. You can finish your whole draft and then write your opening, or craft an opening and then write the rest of your draft.

HANDBOOKS

FOR HELP & PRACTICE

Introducing Nonfiction, pp. 365–367

Elaborative Details, pp. 376–378

Developing/ Presenting Arguments, pp. 474–477

Subject Analysis **153**

During prewriting, check students' notes and charts to make sure they are producing useful materials for drafting. However, do not collect or grade any of these materials. Students can discard any freewriting they do about their audience once they achieve a sense of that audience.

Draft and Discover

Objectives

1. To draft a precise and penetrating subject analysis
2. To respond to one's own writing and to that of a peer

Preteaching

Preview the Draft and Discover section and decide if your students need extra help with any of skills or concepts required to draft this piece. Present any such skills or concepts at this time. The mini-lesson references below, as well as the Elaboration Worksheet for this assignment, may help you in your selection and instruction.

Handbook Mini-Lessons
- Introducing Nonfiction, pp. 365–368
- Elaborative Details, pp. 376–378
- Developing/Presenting Arguments, pp. 474–477

Teaching Strategies

Stumbling Block

Students may get stuck because they have too many ideas rather than too few. Have such students unravel their confusion by explaining their ideas orally to you, following the three-part organizational plan suggested in the lesson (the subject, the components, their relationships).

2. Organize your draft. The specific qualities of your subject will determine how you proceed, but subject analyses often follow this general form.

1. Provide a provocative introduction calculated to engage your readers' interest.
2. Identify the subject you intend to analyze, either in a single sentence or in a short paragraph.
3. Describe the parts that comprise your subject.
4. Examine each part and its relationship to the others or to the subject as a whole.

3. Elaborate on ideas. Writing a subject analysis allows you to examine your subject from a variety of viewpoints using a variety of strategies. The unique characteristics of your subject will determine which strategies you use, but you may need to use one or more of the following.

Strategies

- **Description** Elaborate on each subpart by examining its distinguishing characteristics in detail.
- **Comparison** Show how your subject and its parts resemble or differ from another relevant subject. Denise Grady, for example, compared the process of stuttering with that of normal speech.
- **Process analysis** If you are analyzing an event or procedure, discuss how each action or step results from the previous step and leads to the next one. Denise Grady used cause and effect to explain why some people stutter.
- **Definition** For some complex or technical subjects, an analysis may consist, at least to some degree, of clear, explicit definitions of key parts, characteristics, or terms.

 Writer's Choice Will charts, diagrams, or illustrations help clarify your analysis or make it more interesting? Include any graphic elements that may help you communicate with your readers.

When Zack wrote his subject analysis, he began by evoking the stereotype of wolves familiar to everyone. Then he used a variation of his forecast sentence to introduce the analysis he hoped would change this stereotype. Here is the beginning of his unrevised draft.

ONE STUDENT'S PROCESS

When you think of wolves, you may think of the Big Bad Wolf who threatened the three little pigs in the fairy tale, or of the one who ate Little Red Riding Hood, or of the shepherd boy who cried "Wolf!" Or you might think of the lone wolf howling in the moonlight. All these images give a false picture. Wolves are not really vicious or mean animals at all, nor could you call them solitary hunters. In fact, wolves are very family- or pack-oriented and have a rich social life, which they maintain by communicating with each other in a variety of interesting ways. Some common wolf communication behaviors are facial contact, howling, and scent marking.

Visual Learners These students may do well to begin by creating a graphic representation of their analysis. Students could create a diagram, add explanatory notes and labels, and then expand these notes into the basis for a subject analysis.

Teaching Tip: Graphic Aids

Jot a list of possible graphic aids on the chalkboard as a reference for students who may wish to incorporate visuals in their analyses. These aids include maps, pie charts, bar graphs, line graphs, statistical tables, illustrations with labels or with numbered parts and footnotes, exploded diagrams, photographs, and drawings.

Critical Thinking

Evaluating Have students think back to Zack's forecast sentence and his purpose in writing about wolves and then discuss whether his beginning heads him in the right direction and where he might go from here. Students should apply their insights about Zack to their own writing.

Individualizing Instruction

LEP Students A limited vocabulary in English can prevent LEP students from achieving the fluency that marks sucessful drafting. Let these students know that they can plug in placeholder words whenever necessary during drafting and replace them later with the help of a dictionary and thesaurus.

Social Studies Connection

History is not just narrative; some historical writing is, in fact, analysis, which attempts to explain or account for such phenomena as wars, revolutions, and social movements. Ask students to find a passage in their history books that analyzes a historical event.

Peer Response

Have students meet in groups of four to discuss one another's papers. Ask the groups to formulate a brief written response for each paper that you can use as a touchstone for your own response when you join the group. You may want to provide students with the Peer Response Worksheet for this assignment to assist them in their review.

Revise Your Writing

Objectives

1. To evaluate the responses to a draft
2. To revise a draft based on the responses
3. To proofread for errors in spelling, grammar, usage, and mechanics

Preteaching

Decide what skills you need to review with students, based on the problems you noticed in their drafts. The mini-lessons listed below may be useful to you for instructional purposes.

Handbook Mini-Lessons
- Unity/Coherence, pp. 382–391
- Improving Sentences, pp. 402–411
- Varieties of Language, pp. 429–433

---

4. Take a break. Put your completed first draft away for a day or two to get some distance from it. Then read it over and see what you think of it. If possible, have a classmate read and respond to it as well. Here are some questions for you and your readers to keep in mind while evaluating your draft.

R E V I E W   Y O U R   W R I T I N G

Questions for Yourself
- Do I make my subject and purpose clear to the reader quickly?
- Have I covered all the points needed for a complete analysis of my subject? Should I leave out any of the information I have included?
- What could I add or change to make my analysis clearer? Do I need to explain any of the terms I have used? Would any graphic aids help the readers?
- Do I present the information in a logical order? Do the parts fit together smoothly?
- Have I achieved my purpose?

Questions for Your Peer Readers
- What did you learn about my subject? Did you find this information interesting?
- Are any parts of my essay unclear? Which parts? Do you understand all my terms or should I define any of them?
- Can you restate the main points of my analysis?
- Do you have any unanswered questions about my subject? What are they?

HANDBOOKS
FOR HELP & PRACTICE

Unity/Coherence, pp. 382–391
Improving Sentences, pp. 402–411
Varieties of Language, pp. 429–434

R E V I S E   Y O U R   W R I T I N G

1. Evaluate your responses. Think about your personal assessment of your draft and the responses you got from your peer readers. As you consider your draft, keep in mind that an effective subject analysis displays the characteristics listed on the following page.

Standards for Evaluation

An effective subject analysis . . .

- introduces the subject in an interesting and informative manner.
- identifies the individual parts that comprise the subject.
- uses appropriate strategies to examine and explain each part.
- presents information in a logical order.
- demonstrates an awareness of audience through the use of appropriate language and details.
- includes an effective and well-developed introduction, body, and conclusion.
- uses transitional words and phrases to illustrate the relationship among ideas, sentences, and paragraphs.

2. Problem-solve. Decide which responses you want to use and then rework your draft. Here are some of the changes Zack made as a result of the responses of one peer reader.

ONE STUDENT'S PROCESS

Howling is another way. ^important You may thing that wolves ^that wolves communicate

howl because they are lonely. ^,but in fact They usually howl for

social purposes. Barry Lopez ^, author of the book Of Wolves and Men, says that wolves probably

don't howl during a chase, but often do howl after a

hunt ^"perhaps to celebrate a successful hunt (the

presence of food), their prowess, or the fact that they

are all together again, that no one has been injured". (TR)

Wolves howl most often during breeding and courtship

times (in the winter), and more often in the evening or

early morning. However, they don't howl at the moon, and they don't howl any more often when there is a full moon.

Seems a little choppy here.

Nice quote but who is Barry Lopez? Some authority?

I always heard that wolves howl at the moon. Is that true?

Grammar TIP

When you quote a source directly, remember that the closing quotation mark normally goes to the right of a comma or period.

Teaching Strategies

Teaching Tip: Revision

Encourage students to attempt structural changes during revision—changes involving whole blocks of copy—rather than just single words or phrases.

Guidelines for Evaluation

The following guidelines may be used for a close evaluation of a subject analysis. See the Guidelines for Evaluating Writing in the Teacher's Resource File for additional help with holistic or analytic scoring.

Ideas and Content
- presents a complete analysis
- holds the reader's interest
- makes cogent, accurate points
- uses relevant and telling details
- has an appropriately formal tone

Structure and Form
- opens with a clear introduction
- follows a consistent, logical order
- makes effective transitions
- ends with a satisfying conclusion

Grammar, Usage, and Mechanics
- uses correct grammar and spelling
- uses correct punctuation
- uses correct spelling

Off the Record

Analyzing humor

Managing the Paper Load

From the list, choose two or three criteria to emphasize in grading, such as completeness and logical organization. Select one or two points of grammar and mechanics to stress as well. Various methods of evaluation are discussed on pages T28–T29. Before the students start revising, let them know what criteria you will be using for your evaluation.

Publish and Present

Objective

To publish and present an essay that analyzes a subject.

> **Handbook Mini-Lesson**
> • Publishing, pp. 413–414

Teaching Strategies

Speaking and Listening

Some students may have written on the same subject from different angles or may have analyzed the same subject in opposing ways. Have these students present their papers orally and use the opportunity to promote a class debate of the issue.

3. Proofread your work. Once you have finished revising your work, correct all errors in punctuation, grammar, and spelling. Make sure you have used appropriate punctuation marks to set off parenthetical definitions and other interrupting phrases. Then make a clean copy of your work that reflects all your changes.

GRAMMAR AND WRITING

Punctuating Parenthetical Definitions

A parenthetical definition is a phrase that interrupts a sentence to explain or define something. You can set off a parenthetical definition with commas, parentheses, or dashes.

COMMAS: "Cartography, the science of map-making, developed slowly and painfully out of obscure origins."

Willis Lloyd

PARENTHESES: "Deer have a tremendous biotic potential (ability to reproduce and increase their population)."

Paul Winks

DASHES: "At the so-called House of the Tragic Poet, a mosaic shows a barking dog, with the inscription *cave canem*— 'Beware of the dog.'"

Robert Silverberg

See Grammar Handbook 39, pages 766–772, for more information on punctuating sentence interrupters.

PUBLISH AND PRESENT

HANDBOOKS
FOR HELP & PRACTICE
**Publishing,
p. 413**

• **Prepare a mini-encyclopedia.** Get together with a group of classmates and prepare a mini-encyclopedia in which each student's analysis comprises one entry.
• **Submit your work to your school or community newspaper.** If your paper doesn't usually print articles like the one you have written, suggest that the editors try a "Readers' Page" feature where work like yours could be published.
• **Present your paper to another class.** Try presenting an oral report based on your subject analysis to an appropriate class.

ONE STUDENT'S PROCESS

Wolf Communication—Part of Wolf Society

Zack N. Pauly

The Big Bad Wolf who threatened the three little pigs . . . the wolf who disguised himself as a grandmother and ate Little Red Riding Hood . . . the story of the little shepherd boy who cried "Wolf!" . . . a lone wolf howling in the moonlight—all these familiar images of the wolf have one thing in common: they give a false picture. Contrary to stereotypes born out of human fear, the wolf is not a cold-blooded killer of humans, nor is it a solitary hunter. In fact, wolves are very family- and pack-oriented and have a rich social life, which they maintain by communicating with each other in a variety of interesting ways. These wolf communication behaviors include facial contact, howling, and scent marking.

Facial contact behaviors, the most intimate type of wolf communication, closely resemble what humans do when they nuzzle their babies or hug and kiss one another as a greeting. Wolves use nose pushing, cheek rubbing, facial licking, and jaw wrestling to greet one another, to give a friendly welcome, or sometimes to show dominance. For example, jaw wrestling—a behavior in which two wolves mouth one another's jaws—can be a greeting or it can be a way of intimidating another, lower-ranking wolf. If one wolf puts its mouth over another's muzzle, it is giving a sign of friendship. But if the first wolf has its teeth bared, the greeting is not so friendly—it is the wolf's way of establishing itself

Introduces the subject in an interesting way

Establishes the purpose of the analysis

Identifies the parts of the subject

Examines each part separately in a logical order

Uses classification and cause and effect to examine this aspect of the subject fully

Subject Analysis **159**

Literature Connection

Selection to Read   Students who enjoyed Zack's analysis of wolf communication might like to read Farley Mowat's narrative, *Never Cry Wolf*. Ask students to look for analytical writing in the book.

Reteaching

Assess the needs of students who were not successful in developing an effective subject analysis and identify two or three areas in which additional practice is needed. Assign the appropriate Handbook Mini-Lessons, along with the support materials listed for each lesson. Concepts commonly requiring reteaching for this assignment are

Unity and Coherence, Handbook 10
Introducing Nonfiction Writing, Handbook 8

The following suggestions and resources may also be useful.

1. Incompleteness Some students may get so involved in one aspect of their topic they lose sight of the overall picture. Remind students that analysis has three aspects: identification, description, and examination of relationships. Have students use a pie chart, creating a wedge for each aspect of the topic they cover. Then review the pie charts and indicate points in each wedge that students can elaborate on.

2. Grammar and Usage: Misplaced Clauses and Modifiers Select an example of a student sentence with misplaced clauses and modifiers and analyze it on the chalkboard. First, write the core simple sentence and then add clauses and modifiers to rebuild a graceful version of the original sentence. Discuss each decision as you go along. Then have students find and rework similarly faulty sentences from their own works.

Makes a smooth transition to a second aspect of the subject

Presents evidence to support analysis

Completes analysis of subject by examining its third major part

Closes analysis with an effective conclusion

---

as the more dominant, or more important, member of the wolf pack.

Howling is another important way that wolves communicate. You may think that wolves howl because they are lonely, but in fact they usually howl for social purposes. Barry Lopez, author of the book *Of Wolves and Men,* says that wolves probably don't howl during a chase, but often do howl after a hunt, "perhaps to celebrate a successful hunt (the presence of food), their prowess, or the fact that they are all together again, that no one has been injured." Wolves howl often during breeding and courtship times (in the winter), and more often in the evening or early morning. However, contrary to popular belief, they don't howl at the moon, and they don't howl any more often when there is a full moon.

Wolves also communicate by scent-marking. Wolves leave scent marks to define their territory as if to erect an invisible fence that only other wolves with their keen sense of smell can detect. They mark their territory partly for the same reasons that we put our names and initials on our books, mailboxes, sweaters, bracelets—to say, "This is mine." Scent marks help a wolf to know if it is in its own territory. They may even keep a pack together. How exactly do wolves leave scent marks? They urinate, defecate, or scratch the ground every few minutes as they are traveling. And wolves on the move stop every few minutes to inspect scent marks left by other wolves.

The more we learn about these and other forms of wolf communication, the better we understand the complex social structure of wolf packs. Perhaps by gaining insight into these magnificent animals—who form enduring relationships, just as humans do—we can learn more about ourselves and our place in the world of nature.

LEARNING FROM YOUR WRITING PROCESS

WRITER TO WRITER

There's something in life that's a curtain, and I keep trying to raise it.

Maxine Hong Kingston, novelist and memoirist

1. **Reflect on your writing.** Look back over your earliest writing on your topic and reflect on what you have learned in the course of completing your subject analysis. If you would like to pursue your topic further, how would you do it? On the other hand, are you now so tired of your topic that you hope never to think about it again? Finally, consider how satisfied you are with your paper and how you might be inclined to revise it further.

Use your reflections on the questions above to compose a brief introduction that tells something about what doing the paper has meant to you and where your interest might now take you.

2. **Apply your skills.** Try one or more of the following activities.

   - **Cross curricular** Make a list of important words you've run across in your history studies, such as *Crusade, Aztec, plague, Northwest Passage,* or *shogun.* Choose two and do some research about each word. Jot down notes that would be helpful if you were writing a subject analysis of each word.
   - **Literature** Look through magazines that publish nonfiction, such as *Discover, Smithsonian, Vanity Fair,* and *Travel & Leisure* and find articles that contain subject analyses. Take notes about any words, passages, or techniques the writers used that you found particularly effective. Find examples of how the writers considered the background and needs of their audiences. For example, write down their techniques for defining unfamiliar words. Also highlight the forecast sentence in each article if you can find one.
   - **Related assignments** Follow the suggestions on pages 162–172 to develop a graphic aid or write a project evaluation for a composition about some subject.

Literature Connection

Author Note Writer and English teacher Maxine Hong Kingston was born in 1940 and grew up in California. Her book *The Woman Warrior: Memoirs of a Girlhood Among Ghosts* won the National Book Critics Circle award for general nonfiction in 1976.

Learning from Your Writing Process

Objective

To analyze and reflect upon what has been learned about the writing process and the writing of a subject analysis

Teaching Strategies

Critical Thinking

Interpreting Ask students what Kingston might mean by "something in life that's a curtain" and how writing can lift it.

Reflecting on the Process

Discuss the questions with the class, eliciting responses to each one from more than one student. Encourage students to comment on one another's statements.

Writing Portfolio

Have students attach their finished introduction to their analysis; suggest that they save it in their Writing Portfolio.

Summary and Closure

Before beginning the next lesson, make sure that students have mastered the following concepts.

1. A subject analysis takes a close look at an issue or topic.

2. A subject analysis examines a topic by looking at its parts.

3. An effective subject analysis is coherent, complete, and logical.

Allow students to summarize what they learned by describing the characteristics of effective subject analyses and by telling why knowing how to write a subject analysis can help them in other school subjects.

Related Assignment:
GRAPHIC AID

Starting from Literature

Objective

To respond to a graphic aid as a spring-board for creating students' graphic aids

Teaching Strategies

Motivate

You might begin with a graphic example. For instance, draw a single line on the chalkboard, slanting upward from left to right, and ask the class to guess what it is. Encourage imaginative and humorous answers. The correct answer: It is a graph of the improvement you hope for in everyone's grades during the course of the year.

Tap Prior Knowledge

Most students will be familiar with graphic aids from math, science, and social studies courses. Ask students to supply instances from their own learning experience when difficult concepts were made easier to understand through the use of graphic aids.

Set a Purpose

Point out that students may not have seen graphic aids in English courses before (except in diagramming sentences) but that the creation of graphic aids is a practical skill that involves the abilities to gather, organize, summarize, and present information—the same skills they have been using in writing essays. In addition, graphic aids are usually found accompanied by explanatory text. As students read the U.N. chart, urge them to pay attention to how visuals and text work together, each performing a necessary task.

Related **ASSIGNMENT**

Graphic Aid

Graphic aids, such as charts, tables, graphs, diagrams, or maps, can help explain a complex subject by breaking it down into parts and presenting the parts visually. You probably have come across many graphic aids in newspaper and magazine articles, textbooks, and library reference material. You also may have used, or even made, graphic aids in connection with school activities such as fund raising drives and sporting events.

As you examine this chart, notice how visual representations help explain the subject.

162

The United Nations System

- Trusteeship Council
- Security Council
- General Assembly
- International Court of Justice
- Secretariat
- Economic and Social Council

- **Major UN organs**
- **Other UN organs and committees**
- Specialized agencies and other agencies related to the UN

- **Regional commissions**
- **Functional commissions**
- **Sessional, standing, and** *ad hoc* (special) **committees**

- United Nations Disengagement Observer Force (UNDOF)
- United Nations Interim Force in Lebanon (UNIFIL)
- United Nations Truce Supervision Organization (UNTSO)
- United Nations Peacekeeping Force in Cyprus (UNFICYP)
- United Nations Military Observer Group in India and Pakistan (UNMOGIP)

- Military Staff Committee

- Main committees
- Standing and procedural committees
- Other subsidiary organs of the General Assembly

- United Nations Relief and Works Agency for Palestine Refugees in the Near East (UNRWA)

- International Atomic Energy Agency (IAEA)

- United Nations Conference on Trade and Development (UNCTAD)
- United Nations University (UNU)
- World Food Council (WFC)
- United Nations Environment Program (UNEP)
- United Nations Development Program (UNDP)
- United Nations Industrial Development Organization (UNIDO)
- United Nations Institute for Training and Research (UNITAR)
- International Research and Training Institute for the Advancement of Women (INSTRAW)
- UNICEF (United Nations Children's Fund)
- Office of the United Nations High Commissioner for Refugees (UNHCR)
- World Food Program (WFP)
- United Nations Fund for Population Activities (UNFPA)
- United Nations Center for Human Settlements (UNCHS), or Habitat

- World Intellectual Property Organization (WIPO)
- International Labor Organization (ILO)
- Food and Agriculture Organization of the United Nations (FAO)
- UNESCO (United Nations Educational, Scientific and Cultural Organization)
- World Health Organization (WHO)
- International Monetary Fund (IMF)
- International Development Association (IDA)
- World Bank
- International Finance Corporation (IFC)
- International Fund for Agricultural Development (IFAD)
- International Civil Aviation Organization (ICAO)
- Universal Postal Union (UPU)
- International Telecommunication Union (ITU)
- World Meteorological Organization (WMO)
- International Maritime Organization (IMO)

- General Agreement on Tariffs and Trade (GATT)*

*GATT has no formal relationship with the UN but cooperates with it and is considered part of the UN system.

Think AND Respond

What can you learn about the United Nations by examining this diagram? What visual techniques did the writer use to present this information? Think of other ways you could visually present the information in the diagram.

163

Think and Respond

Elicit Personal Responses

A table of organization is likely to elicit less of a strong personal response than, for instance, a short story or personal essay. This reflects one of the strengths of graphic aids: they are objective; they do not ordinarily show us a personality to like or dislike. To stimulate student responses, you might ask them to spend five minutes attempting to summarize the information in the chart in a purely verbal form. Then, discuss their results. This will demonstrate the advantages of the visual form.

Explore the Author's Techniques

The U.N. chart is a particular type of graphic aid known as a table of organization. It shows where the various offices and functions belong in a bureaucratic system. Similar charts could be found for the job structures in any large corporation, government, military apparatus, or school administration. Ask how each department in the chart could be further broken down and charted. (Individual offices in, for instance, the World Food Council could be listed, from the people who head the council down to their deputies, assistants, and clerical workers.) Another type of table of organization is a genealogical chart, or family tree.

Link Literature to Writing

Explain that a graphic aid is one kind of subject analysis: it names the parts of something and shows how they are interrelated. In this assignment, students will create their own graphic aids.

Springboard

Challenge students to locate as many different kinds of graphic aids as they can in this textbook. An obvious one that might be overlooked is the Table of Contents. Discuss how graphic aids add to textbooks in teaching effectiveness and enjoyment.

Math Connection

There are inherent close connections between this assignment and mathematics. Have students look in their math textbooks for explanations of the various kinds of graphs. Encourage them to use, and expand on, this knowledge as they create their own graphic aids.

Guiding Your Writers

Objectives

1. To choose information for a graphic aid
2. To organize and create a graphic aid
3. To publish and present a graphic aid

Preteaching

Look over the remainder of the lesson. If there are concepts or skills you feel your students will need help with before starting, present them at this time. The mini-lesson references below may help you in your selection and instruction. Cross references in the pupil text will give students access to the same lessons for independent practice.

> **Handbook Mini-Lessons**
> - Limiting Your Topic, pp. 337–338
> - Graphics for Exploring, pp. 339–342
> - Informal Sharing, p. 412
> - Reference Works, pp. 495–498

Teaching Strategies

Teaching Tip: Goals

Remind students that in choosing a form of graphic aid, their aim is to clarify a complex subject for their audience—to create quick understanding. Therefore, they should try to use the simplest form that will adequately contain all the necessary information. They should avoid visual complexity if it is only for complexity's sake.

INVITATION TO Write

The chart you have just examined presents the organizational structure of the United Nations. Now create a graphic aid that explains a complex subject by analyzing its parts.

Sometimes a subject analysis can best be presented through, or with the help of, a graphic aid. In the chart you have just examined, the writer analyzes the structure of a complex organization. As in any type of analysis, the writer breaks down the subject into parts, examines those parts, and shows how they fit together.

HANDBOOKS
FOR HELP & PRACTICE

Limiting Your Topic, pp. 337–338

Graphics for Exploring, pp. 339–342

Informal Sharing, p. 412

Reference Works, pp. 495–498

UNDERSTANDING GRAPHIC AIDS

Many types of graphic aids can be used in a subject analysis. **Graphs** show relationships between groups, as well as development in time. **Tables** and **charts** are used to list and compare information. **Diagrams** show the parts or functions of the subject. **Maps** display geographical areas or distribution.

PLANNING YOUR GRAPHIC AID

1. Familiarize yourself with the variety of graphic aids. Look through books and magazines for examples of graphic aids that are used to help explain a complex subject. You may wish to get together with several classmates to share and discuss some of the more interesting examples you find.

2. Explore possible subjects for your graphic aid. Think about subjects in which a graphic aid might prove useful. Could a chart clarify a complex process in chemistry or biology class? Would a series of maps help explain territorial changes in a certain region of the world?

164 Workshop 5

Off the Record

In his legendary English Literature lectures at Cornell University in the 1950's, Vladimir Nabokov liked to poke fun at trends in literary criticism. During one lecture, he charted the structure of the novel he was analyzing, as was then fashionable. He started by outlining the book as a circle. With intricately drawn lines he added to the complexities of character and plot, while dozens of students copied the diagram in their notes. At last, when the structure of the novel had been followed to completion, Nabokov turned from the board, where students found he had drawn the smiling face of a cat.

3. Gather information. Carefully research the subject you will be presenting. This may be done through library research, brainstorming sessions, and interviews; or through firsthand observation or experience.

4. Analyze the information. How can your subject be broken down for easier understanding? For example, in the UN chart, large groups are broken down into major UN organs, then further broken down into smaller UN commissions and committees, and finally into specialized agencies and other related bodies.

5. Choose the type of graphic aid to use. In doing so, consider which type is best suited to your subject and purpose. In general, charts and tables are most effective when you want to compare or list information. Diagrams are helpful when showing parts or functions of the subject. Maps are the best choice for displaying geographical information, while graphs can present quantitative relationships and development over time.

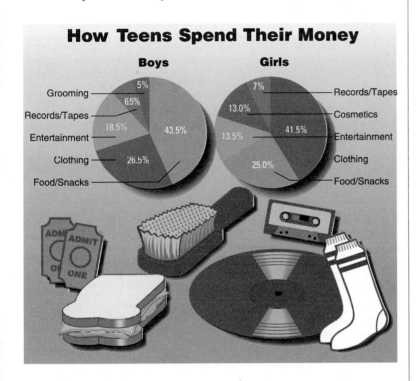

How Teens Spend Their Money

Boys
- Grooming — 5%
- Records/Tapes — 6.5%
- Entertainment — 18.5%
- Clothing — 26.5%
- Food/Snacks
- 43.5%

Girls
- Records/Tapes — 7%
- Cosmetics — 13.0%
- Entertainment — 13.5%
- Clothing — 41.5%
- Food/Snacks — 25.0%

Graphic Aid   **165**

Learning Styles Both global and analytic learners can contribute to a graphic aids project. Ideally, a cooperative pair will include one student with each learning style. Analytic learners will warm to the task of breaking information down into parts that can be labeled; global learners will be interested in grasping their whole subject as a single visible form.

Advanced Students Advanced students may be impatient with the simple task of transferring research data onto a chart or graph. Encourage them to think of original subjects and forms. A challenging heuristic question might be, "Can you think of any kind of information that *couldn't* be explained graphically?" Also, encourage students to try to objectify subjective phenomena—for instance, by graphing emotional ups and downs, charting the interactions in a family, or even tracking the entire course of a human life.

LD Students Encourage these students to select subjects that they know well. For example, they might create a bar graph to represent how much food they eat in a week or a pie graph to represent how they spend a typical day.

Teaching Tip: Computer Graphics

The graphics programs of your school's computers can be very valuable in helping your students create their graphic aids. You might want to combine this assignment with their work in computer lab.

Science Connection

Encourage students to consult their science textbooks and notebooks for graphic forms they can adopt. Examples include molecular diagrams, anthropological kinship diagrams, evolutionary charts, energy flow charts, star charts, circuitry diagrams, illustrations of organisms, and the Periodic Table of Elements.

Social Studies Connection

Economics is an area of social studies often presented graphically. Line graphs show market trends; pie and bar graphs show employment and production statistics. Demographic data are especially adaptable to graphic presentation. In history, time lines are frequently used; and of course, geography depends on the use of maps.

Guidelines for Evaluation

The following guidelines may be used for a close evaluation of a graphic aid. See the Guidelines for Evaluating Writing in the Teacher's Resource File for additional help with holistic or analytic scoring.

A good graphic aid . . .

- uses an appropriate form for its subject
- presents accurate data
- conveys all the necessary information on the subject
- is clearly labeled, neat, and easy to read
- enhances reader understanding of the subject

Reteaching

Assess the needs of students who were not successful developing an effective graphic aid. Assign the appropriate Handbook Mini-Lessons. Concepts commonly requiring reteaching for this assignment are

Limiting Your Topic: Handbook 3
Graphics for Exploring: Handbook 4

The following suggestions and resources may also be useful.

1. Ineffective Format Stress that the choice of format should be determined by the nature of the subject and the purpose. Direct students to Graphics for Organizing Ideas in Handbook 4. After students have reexamined their subjects, allow them to redo their graphic aids in different forms. For example, a student may want to switch from a pie chart to a line graph or vice versa.

2. Faulty Parallelism Explain that labels for similar parts of the graphic aid should be parallel in structure. Refer students to Handbook 13. Then have them rewrite their labels to show parallelism.

COMPUTER TIP

If you have access to a computer with appropriate software, you may wish to create your graphic aid on disk.

CREATING YOUR GRAPHIC AID

1. Organize your information. Decide what information to include in your graphic aid and how best to present it. You may want to experiment with various organizational methods before settling on the best one to use in your subject analysis.

2. Draft your graphic aid. Create the first draft of your graphic aid. As you draft, label your information where appropriate: in columns or rows for charts and tables, alongside graphs, and in keys or legends for diagrams and maps. Color-coding your graphic aid can also make interpretation easier for your readers. Give your graphic aid a title. The title should provide readers with a framework for interpreting the information.

 Writer's Choice Do you want to write a caption or other brief text to help explain or summarize the information in your graphic aid?

REVIEWING YOUR WRITING

1. Take another look at your graphic aid. Ask yourself questions such as the following: Does my graphic aid clearly convey all the necessary information? Does it accomplish the goal I had in mind? Is it attractive and easy to read?

2. Share your graphic aid with several classmates. To elicit helpful information from your classmates, ask them specific questions: Do you understand the information I am trying to communicate? Would a different organization make my graphic aid easier to understand? Would adding or eliminating color make the graphic aid clearer?

PUBLISHING AND PRESENTING

- **Copy your graphic aid onto a poster.** Display the poster as you orally present your graphic aid to the class.
- **Submit your graphic aid to a newspaper.** If your graphic aid deals with a subject of interest to the student body, submit it for publication in your school newspaper.

166 Workshop 5

On the Lightside

SNIGLETS

Here are some humorous additions to your vocabulary study. "Sniglets" are words that don't appear in the dictionary, but should.

Accordionated *(ah kor'de on ay tid) adj.* Being able to drive and refold a road map at the same time.

Anaception *(an a sep'shun) n.* The body's ability to actually affect television reception by moving around the room.

B+ Stampede *(bee' plus stam peed) n.* The attempt by half the classroom to claim the paper with no name on it.

Bleemus *(blee'mus) n.* The disgusting film on the top of soups and cocoa that sit out for too long.

Brattled *(brat'uld) adj.* The unsettling feeling, at a stoplight, that the busload of kids that just pulled up beside you is making fun of you.

Burgacide *(burg'uh side) n.* When a hamburger can't take any more torture and hurls itself through the grill into the coals.

Cinemuck *(si'ne muk) n.* The combination of popcorn, soda, and melted chocolate which covers the floors of movie theaters.

Eurfirstics *(yew fur'stiks) n.* Two people waiting on the phone for the other to hang up first.

Flopcorn *(flop'korn) n.* The unpopped kernels at the bottom of the cooker.

Greedling *(gree'dling) v.* Pretending to read the inscription on the birthday card when you really just want to know how much the check is for.

Gription *(grip'shun) n.* The sound of sneakers squeaking against the floor during basketball games.

Hystioblogination *(his' to o blahg in ay'shun) n.* The act of trying to identify a gift by holding it to your ear and shaking it.

Multipochoholes *(mul ti po'cho holz) n.* Wounds left in test papers from overerasing.

Pigslice *(pig'slys) n.* The last unclaimed piece of pizza that everyone is secretly dying for.

Puntificate *(puhn tih'fih kayt) v.* To try to predict in what direction a football will bounce.

Sark *(sark) n.* The marks left on one's ankle after wearing tube socks all day.

Scribblics *(skrih'bliks) n.* Warm-up exercises designed to get the ink in a pen flowing.

Waftic *(wahf'tik) adj.* Describes any person in whose direction campfire or barbeque smoke always blows.

Rich Hall and Friends

On the Lightside

This feature gives humorous definitions of nonsense words called "sniglets." These words do not exist, but according to the author they should exist. When discussing this feature, ask students to try to figure out the derivations of some of the words. Students might note, for example, that the first sniglet, *accordionated*, seems to be derived from both *accordion* and *coordinated*. Discuss how both roots relate to the meaning of the term. Encourage students to make up their own sniglets and share them with the class.

PROJECT EVALUATION

Starting from Literature

Objective

To respond to a project analysis as a springboard for writing

Teaching Strategies

Motivate

Discuss what differentiates a project from a mere activity. For example, a project has a goal; the workers on the project try to approach the goal systematically. In addition, analysis is important to a project as its planners and workers try to correct errors and maximize success.

Tap Prior Knowledge

Ask students to share memories of projects they have worked on, in or out of school. Discuss how they, as well as others, went about evaluating the projects. What criteria were used? What conclusions were formed?

Set a Purpose

Remind students that most projects combine elements of both success and failure. In "Kids with Causes" they will read about both elements. Remind them that in many cases throughout life, as much can be learned from failure as from success, and the former is a necessary preparation for the latter.

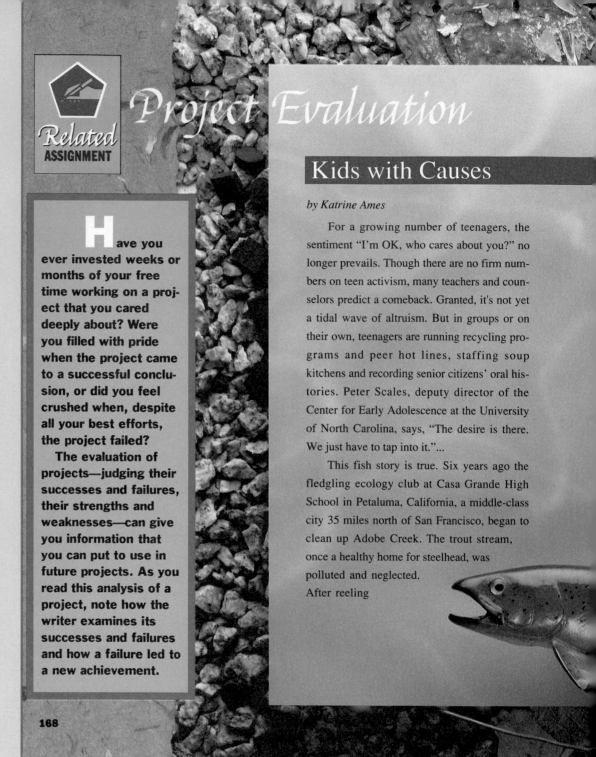

Related ASSIGNMENT

Project Evaluation

Have you ever invested weeks or months of your free time working on a project that you cared deeply about? Were you filled with pride when the project came to a successful conclusion, or did you feel crushed when, despite all your best efforts, the project failed?

The evaluation of projects—judging their successes and failures, their strengths and weaknesses—can give you information that you can put to use in future projects. As you read this analysis of a project, note how the writer examines its successes and failures and how a failure led to a new achievement.

Kids with Causes

by Katrine Ames

For a growing number of teenagers, the sentiment "I'm OK, who cares about you?" no longer prevails. Though there are no firm numbers on teen activism, many teachers and counselors predict a comeback. Granted, it's not yet a tidal wave of altruism. But in groups or on their own, teenagers are running recycling programs and peer hot lines, staffing soup kitchens and recording senior citizens' oral histories. Peter Scales, deputy director of the Center for Early Adolescence at the University of North Carolina, says, "The desire is there. We just have to tap into it."...

This fish story is true. Six years ago the fledgling ecology club at Casa Grande High School in Petaluma, California, a middle-class city 35 miles north of San Francisco, began to clean up Adobe Creek. The trout stream, once a healthy home for steelhead, was polluted and neglected. After reeling

168

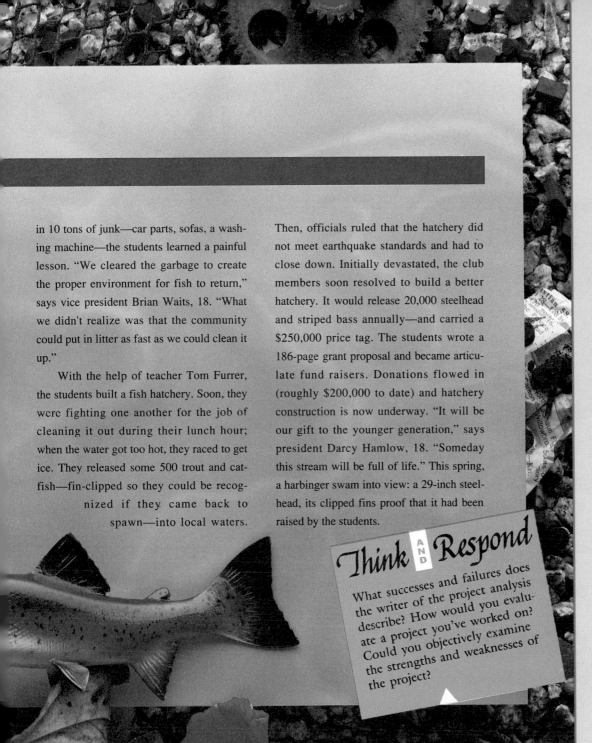

in 10 tons of junk—car parts, sofas, a washing machine—the students learned a painful lesson. "We cleared the garbage to create the proper environment for fish to return," says vice president Brian Waits, 18. "What we didn't realize was that the community could put in litter as fast as we could clean it up."

With the help of teacher Tom Furrer, the students built a fish hatchery. Soon, they were fighting one another for the job of cleaning it out during their lunch hour; when the water got too hot, they raced to get ice. They released some 500 trout and catfish—fin-clipped so they could be recognized if they came back to spawn—into local waters.

Then, officials ruled that the hatchery did not meet earthquake standards and had to close down. Initially devastated, the club members soon resolved to build a better hatchery. It would release 20,000 steelhead and striped bass annually—and carried a $250,000 price tag. The students wrote a 186-page grant proposal and became articulate fund raisers. Donations flowed in (roughly $200,000 to date) and hatchery construction is now underway. "It will be our gift to the younger generation," says president Darcy Hamlow, 18. "Someday this stream will be full of life." This spring, a harbinger swam into view: a 29-inch steelhead, its clipped fins proof that it had been raised by the students.

Think AND Respond

What successes and failures does the writer of the project analysis describe? How would you evaluate a project you've worked on? Could you objectively examine the strengths and weaknesses of the project?

Think and Respond

Elicit Personal Responses

Ask students to imagine that they participated in the Casa Grande High School ecology project. Have them jot down their feelings about working on the project—its frustrations and elations—and the analysis of its results. Discuss how the following might evaluate the project: (a) participating students, (b) nonparticipating students at the same school, (c) teacher Tom Furrer, (d) members of the community, (e) reporters, (f) fish.

Explore the Author's Techniques

Since this analysis is in the form of a newsmagazine article, its techniques are those of the journalistic feature story. Direct student attention to the use of interviews with participants, vivid description, and chronological narrative. Point out that many, but not necessarily all, project analyses may share these traits. Some may be more objective and statistics-oriented, less narrative and people-oriented.

Link Literature to Writing

Explain that a project analysis is a kind of subject analysis. In this assignment, students will create their own project analyses. Remind students that a project analysis has a practical aim: to enhance future project success. Therefore, like the author of "Kids with Causes," students should present both problems and successes of the project.

Guiding Your Writers

Objectives

1. To choose a project to analyze
2. To conduct a project analysis
3. To publish and present a project analysis

Preteaching

Preview the remainder of this lesson. If there are skills or concepts students may need help with, present them at this time. The mini-lesson references below may help you in your selection and instruction. The cross references in the pupil text give students access to the same lessons for independent practice.

> **Handbook Mini-Lessons**
> - Analysis Frames, p. 343
> - Questioning, pp. 376–377
> - Organizing Your Work, pp. 349–357
> - Introducing/Concluding Nonfiction, pp. 365–371
> - Developing/Presenting Arguments, pp. 474–476

Teaching Strategies

Teaching Tip: Audience

Encourage students to consider the audience for whom they are writing. They must also consider their relation to the project. Are they participants or outsiders? Are they writing for participants or outsiders? Are these outsiders proponents or opponents of the project? The answers may affect the amount of information it is necessary to provide, and the tone of the analysis.

INVITATION TO Write

The excerpt from a news article evaluated an ambitious ecology project initiated by high-school students like yourself. Write an evaluation of a school, community, or national project, one that you can investigate either firsthand or through research.

In the working world, the project evaluation is a common type of written report. Businesses and other groups use it to determine the success of projects, programs, and procedures and to determine if any changes are necessary. This type of analysis has three main parts: (1) an explanation of the project; (2) an analysis and evaluation of its successes and/or failures; and (3) a summarizing conclusion or recommendation.

CHOOSING AND INVESTIGATING A PROJECT

HANDBOOKS
FOR HELP & PRACTICE

Analysis Frames, p. 343

Questioning, pp. 376–377

Organizing Your Work, pp. 349–357

Introducing/ Concluding Nonfiction, pp. 365–371

Developing/ Presenting Arguments, pp. 474–476

1. Choose a project that interests you. It might be a class or club project in which you are currently active or interested, or, like students at Casa Grande High, perhaps you'd like to organize an environmental clean-up. Does the Student Council sponsor a community-service program, or has a history class created a school museum? The program does not have to be local. For example, you might investigate a national program like Headstart.

2. Make a list of questions. Think of what you want to know about the various aspects of the project or program. To explain the project, you need answers to certain basic questions. Who runs the project? What is the purpose of the project? How is it organized and operated?

3. Break down a complex project into its key parts or stages. Some projects or programs have many aspects. If you were investigating a volunteer tutoring program, for example, you might want

---

Springboard

Albert Einstein analyzed his own work as follows: "I think and think for months and years. Ninety-nine times, the conclusion is false. The hundredth time I am right." Ask students to respond orally to this. Was Einstein being excessively modest or simply telling the truth? What do his words mean for students in their own work? Finally, ask students to create their own "quotable quote" about their own writing and thinking habits. You may wish to have students create a class quotation booklet.

to examine such aspects as the selection of participants, the screening and training of volunteers, and the measurement of improvements made by participants.

4. Conduct your investigation. If you chose a project in your school or community, much of your investigation may consist of personal interviews and direct observations. If you chose a project outside your school or community, you will need to conduct library research.

5. Determine the criteria for evaluating the project. How will you judge whether a project, or an aspect of it, is successful? First, list any results or goals that the project, or one phase of it, was supposed to achieve. Then determine whether these goals were achieved. For some aspects, you may rely on the reports of those involved: find out what those people think of it and what benefits and drawbacks they see. In "Kids with Causes," the writer reported the setback to the project when the fish hatchery was closed because it did not meet earthquake standards. For other aspects, you might find useful statistics and other objective data: see if the data support people's opinions. Make your list of questions as specific and comprehensive as needed to achieve your goal, which is to explain clearly a particular project and analyze its successes and failures.

6. Organize your findings and draw some conclusions. Listen to your taped interviews and transcribe parts you can use. Read your notes and highlight the important parts. Draw conclusions and list the strengths and weaknesses of the project.

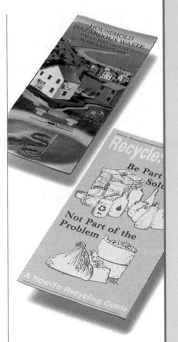

D RAFTING YOUR ANALYSIS

1. Write an introduction that provides a context. Let your readers know why the subject is important and why you are analyzing this project. Make your introduction interesting to capture your readers' attention. Notice how the writer of "Kids with Causes" both provided a context and captured your attention.

2. Organize the body of your analysis in a logical way. Begin by providing basic information about the project—what it is, why it was started, who runs it, and how it operates. Then proceed to describe the strengths and/or weaknesses of the project or each aspect of it. Include direct quotes and statistics or other data to support your evaluations.

Project Evaluation **171**

Speaking and Listening

Interviewing may be an important part of students' research into projects. Encourage them to record interviewees' words as accurately as possible, to listen for the tone and implications of statements, and to observe body language. Remind students to ask each interviewee for the names of other potential interviewees.

Stumbling Block

Many projects are neither clear successes nor clear failures. Some high school students may be troubled by this ambiguity. Emphasize that a project analysis does not have to contain a "thumbs up or thumbs down." It should strive to make a constructive contribution by presenting pluses and minuses fairly.

Individualizing Instruction

Advanced Students Encourage advanced students to choose offbeat projects and to approach them from unusual angles. They may wish to be ironic or satirical. They may wish to analyze large-scale projects undertaken by nations or civilizations, or personal projects of self-improvement.

Guidelines for Evaluation

The following guidelines may be used for a close evaluation of a project analysis. See the Guidelines for Evaluating Writing in the Teacher's Resource File for additional help with holistic or analytic scoring.

A good project analysis . . .

- explains the project
- analyzes and evaluates the successes and failures of the project
- contains enough data for the reader to form a knowledgable judgment about the project
- makes its evaluative criteria clear
- displays sound logical organization
- concludes by summarizing its findings or recommending action
- uses standard grammar and correct usage, and mechanics

Reteaching

Assess the needs of students who were not successful developing an effective project analysis. Assign the appropriate Handbook Mini-Lessons. Concepts commonly requiring reteaching for this assignment are:

Questioning: Handbook 3
Developing/Presenting Arguments: Handbook 23

The following suggestions and resources may also be useful.

1. Weak Conclusions Remind students that their analyses should end with a summary or a call to action. Refer them to Handbook 8, Concluding Nonfiction Writing. Let them reassess and revise their conclusions in light of what they have learned.

2. Loaded Words Point out to students that loaded words can destroy the objectivity of an analysis. Examine students' papers to find examples of sentences that contain loaded words. Display the (nameless) sentences on an overhead transparency and have students discuss whether these words are used justifiably in relation to the projects.

Writing TIP

As in "Kids with Causes," blend the factual data with information about the feelings of the people involved.

3. End by drawing a conclusion or making a recommendation. The writer of "Kids with Causes" concluded by noting that the fin-clipped steelhead came back in the spring, a sign that the stream was clean enough to support life. Conclude your analysis by describing the overall success or failure of your project or by recommending improvements.

REVIEWING YOUR WRITING

1. Reread your draft with your goal in mind. Did you clearly explain the project and evaluate its strengths and weaknesses? Did you blend facts and human interest well?

2. Ask project participants to read your evaluation. Were any important events or details left out? Are the goals of the project explained clearly and completely? Are participants' roles and titles described accurately?

3. Check for accuracy. After making sure the content is on target, reread your analysis with an eye for improving the word choice and writing style. Proofread for correct spelling of project and participant names. Also check that direct and indirect quotations have been punctuated correctly.

PUBLISHING AND PRESENTING

- **Prepare a final copy of your evaluation.** Share your report with the members of the project. Encourage them to discuss their reactions with you.
- **Submit your evaluation.** Send it to the school or community newspaper for publication.
- **Prepare an oral report for your classmates.** Use visual aids such as charts, graphs, or diagrams if possible.
- **Prepare a videotape of your evaluation.** Include segments of interviews with project members and scenes of people participating in the project. Share the videotape with the project members and your classmates. Submit your videotape to a local television station as a feature about your community.
- **Save your project evaluation in your writing portfolio.** Compare it to other works you have written. How is your project evaluation different? How are you growing as a writer?

Literature Connection

In discussion, compare and contrast projects and quests. The terms are nearly synonymous but *quest* implies adventure in search of a prized goal, while *project* has connotations of long, hard work. For example, King Arthur's Round Table was a project, but his knights' search for the Holy Grail was that particular type of project called a quest. Elicit other projects and quests from literature your stu-

dents have read this year or in recent years, such as the Canterbury pilgrims' journey, Odysseus' struggle to return home, and Professor Higgins's project of educating Eliza Doolittle in *Pygmalion*.

Sentence
COMPOSING

Varying Sentence Openers

Experienced writers know that, by varying sentence openers, they can not only add detail but also build suspense and increase readers' interest. In the sentences below, notice the varying degrees of detail and suspense achieved with each type of opener.

Single Word	<u>Sighing</u>, he sat down and put on the other. **Elizabeth Bowen, "Foothold"**
Prepositional Phrase	<u>To her astonishment</u>, she saw that the expression on his face was one of satisfaction. **Mary Lavin, "One Summer"**
Present Participial Phrase	<u>Changing into dry clothes from his cellophane pack</u>, Mr. Benjamin Driscoll lay down and went happily to sleep. **Ray Bradbury, *The Martian Chronicles***
Past Participial Phrase	<u>Amazed at the simplicity of it all</u>, I understood everything as never before. **Alphonse Daudet, "The Last Lesson"**
Absolute Phrase	<u>Pain shooting up my entire arm</u>, I lay panting on the edge of the pool and gingerly began to feel my wrist. **Theodore Taylor, *The Cay***

A. Imitating Sentences Write a sentence to imitate the structure of each model. Openers are underlined.

1. <u>Overhead</u>, the live oaks met, and it was as dark as a cave.
   Eudora Welty, "A Worn Path"

2. <u>Stupidly</u>, Eugie gazed around the room to see if morning had come into it yet. **Gina Berriault, "The Stone Boy"**

3. <u>At the gate</u>, the servant opened the door a trifle and looked out at the waiting people. **John Steinbeck, *The Pearl***

4. <u>Weaving in and out among the rocks</u>, they carried bamboo baskets on erect heads, unmindful of the salt water leaking down on their half-dried hair. **Kim Yong Ik, "The Sea Girl"**

5. <u>Enchanted and enthralled</u>, I stopped her constantly for details.
   Richard Wright, *Black Boy*

Sentence Composing: Varying Sentence Openers

Objectives

1. To compose sentences that contain a variety of types of introductory phrases
2. To expand sentences by adding introductory phrases

Preteaching

These exercises focus on the use of phrases. Before beginning the activities, some students may need review of basic sentence parts and structure as well as participles, participial phrases, prepositional phrases, absolute phrases, and dangling modifiers. Refer to the following sections of the Grammar Handbook for preteaching content:

Phrases and Clauses
  Prepositional Phrases, pages 591–592
  Verbals and Verbal Phrases, pages 594–596
  Using Phrases Correctly, page 602
Adjective and Adverb Usage
  Understanding Modifiers, pages 719–720

ANSWER KEY

12-5 Varying Sentence Openers

A. Imitating Sentences
  Imitations will vary.

B. Unscrambling and Imitating Sentences Sometimes, as in the models below, professional writers use a combination of openers. Unscramble each set of parts to form a sentence whose structure matches that of the model. Then write a sentence of your own whose structure also imitates that of the model. Follow each opener with a comma. Openers are underlined.

Example	There, in the tin factory, in the first moment of the atomic age, a human being was crushed by books. **John Hersey, *Hiroshima***
	a. the champions were defeated by Central High
	b. abruptly
	c. in the closing seconds of the fourth quarter
	d. on a freak play
Unscrambled	Abruptly, on a freak play, as time ran out in the fourth quarter, the champions were defeated by Central High.
Student Sentence	First, in the mortar, in the hooded work area of the chemistry lab, the dark chunks should be ground to powder.

1. Standing in the shadows, with the bright window behind him, he blazed with sunburned health.   **John Knowles, *A Separate Peace***
   a. with the difficult routine successfully behind her
   b. Monica finished with stunning grace
   c. tumbling across the gym floor

2. Pushing himself on up, pain throbbing into his legs, he looked around the outcrop.   **Robb White, *Deathwatch***
   a. Janet jackknifed from the high diving board
   b. her legs stretching to tautness
   c. arching her body way up

3. Oiled, with tube bones cut from bronze and sunk in gelatin, the robots lay.   **Ray Bradbury, *The Martian Chronicles***
   a. his car waited
   b. polished
   c. with its body double-coated in wax and gleaming in the sun

C. Expanding Sentences
Answers will vary.
Application
Answers will vary.

4. <u>In and out among the trees and bushes</u>, <u>across streams</u>, <u>over grassy places</u>, <u>now low to the ground</u>, <u>then just above my head</u>, the dodging butterfly led me far before I caught and held it with my hand.
   Frank Lindermann, "Interview with a Crow Chief"
   a. now plummeting from a steep peak
   b. up and down along the tracks
   c. then climbing to a new precipice
   d. across bridges
   e. the roller coaster car sped us all around before the ride was done
   f. over the water

C. Expanding Sentences Write an opener or a combination of openers to begin each sentence below. Each of your openers should start with the words in parentheses and should make sense within the context of the sentence. After you finish, compare your sentences with the originals on page 322.

1. (Filled . . .), Vera took the letter.   **Mary Lavin, "One Summer"**

2. (Sitting . . .), (gazing . . .), he spent a day in idleness.
   J. M. Coetzee, *Life & Times of Michael K*

3. Sometimes, (mounted . . .), (with . . .), Jody rode out beyond the room.   **John Steinbeck, *The Red Pony***

4. (Although . . .), they always felt an anxiety in the house.
   D. H. Lawrence, "The Rocking-Horse Winner"

5. There, (between . . .), (against . . .), was a figure from a dream, a strange beast that was horned and drunken-legged, but like something he had never even imagined.   **Doris Lessing, "A Sunrise on the Veld"**

6. (Trying . . .), (twirling . . .), (turning . . .), the officer, with his stalwart form and slight swagger, made a fine picture of a guardian of the peace.   **O. Henry, "After Twenty Years"**

Application From a recent piece of writing, select three sentences at random. Write each sentence three times, adding a different opener each time. Vary the openers in content, length, and structure. Note how each adds detail and interest.

Grammar Refresher An opening phrase that does not refer clearly to the correct noun may create a dangling modifier. For information on avoiding dangling modifiers, see Handbook 33.

Informative Exposition: Synthesis

Workshop Overview

Informative exposition is writing that explains or informs. In previous workshops, students have explored informative exposition in two of its forms: classification and analysis. In this Workshop, students will focus on informative exposition that is developed through synthesis; they will bring together ideas and information and process them to create a new whole using a variety of critical thinking strategies. Students will use the critical thinking skills they have been developing to examine and define problems and draw conclusions about how such problems should be addressed. They will also focus on the requirements of audiences they may not previously have addressed. Workshop 6 includes the following Guided and Related Assignments:

1. **Guided: Making Proposals**   shows students how to define a problem and develop a plan of action in light of requirements of a target audience; also discusses how to use a summary, definitions, argumentation, quotations, and documentation to support a proposal
2. **Related: Rebuttal**   builds on the skills developed in defining a problem and developing a plan of action by having students examine an opponent's position and build arguments against it
3. **Related: Oral Presentation**   develops speaking skills by having students apply the knowledge and techniques used in defining problems and developing plans of action to the creation and presentation of a speech

Preparation Guide

1. Use the Overview above and the Teacher's Choice descriptions on page 177 as a basis for deciding which assignment(s) to teach.

2. Preview the assignment and the teacher's notes. The teaching suggestions and your knowledge of your class's abilities should allow you to identify quickly the concepts that may require preteaching or extra support. The Handbook mini-lessons suggested in the Preteaching notes within the lesson can also provide guidance in this area.

3. Preview the adjacent chart for support materials in the Teacher's Resource File that may be used with this Workshop. Resources are for use with the Guided Assignment unless otherwise noted.

Workshop Support Materials

Resources	For Use With
Ideas for Writing: Data Sheets, p. 11; Additional Ideas, p. 23	Identifying a problem or topic, p. 180
Thinking Skills Transparencies: Problem-Solution; *Worksheets*, p. 14	Draft and Discover, p. 182
Elaboration/Proofreading, p. 11	Strategies, p. 183
Peer Response Guides, p. 17	Review Your Writing, p. 184
Evaluating Writing, pp. 13, 34–35	Standards for Evaluation, p. 185
Student Revision Trans., pp. 23–26	Problem-solve, p. 185
Elaboration/Proofreading, p. 12	Proofread your work, p. 186
Tests and Assessment: Prompts, p. 6	

Professional Resources and Media

Books and Journals

Jones, Ken. ''Simulations and Anxiety Related to Public Speaking.'' *Simulation and Games*. Vol. 17.3 (Sept. 1986): pp. 327–344.

Films and Videos

Write It Right—It All Starts with Paragraphs. Writing Skills Series, Films Education. Inc. (55 min.)

Computer Software

Thinking Cap. Broderbund Software, Inc., San Rafael, California. 1986.

Linking Literature, Writing, and Grammar

The following options may be used to provide students with an integrated language experience. Begin by assigning and discussing any of the recommended pieces of literature, which can be found in most classroom anthologies. Use the suggested strategy to provide a link to the Guided Assignment.

Linking Literature and Writing
Option 1
Starting Point: "The Clifton Awards for Innovative Learning Programs Request for Proposals (RFP)" on pages 178–179 of *The Writer's Craft*

Strategy: Use the teaching suggestions on pages 178–179 to lead students into the guided assignment.

Option 2
Starting Point: "Letter to Lord Chesterfield" by Samuel Johnson

Strategy: Ask students what Samuel Johnson's letter has to say about how writers and others with original ideas went about seeking support in his time.

Discuss how times have changed and how people today can often find support from private or public institutions by writing formal proposals outlining their ideas. As an example of how agencies often show their willingness to support innovative ideas, remind them of the Request for Proposals on pages 178–179 and then lead them into the Guided Assignment.

Option 3
Starting Point: "A Modest Proposal" by Jonathan Swift

Strategy: Remind students that Swift's "modest proposal" is a satire. Nevertheless, it illustrates many of the elements of a good proposal. Help students recognize these elements; Swift describes a problem, details his proposal, lists the advantages of his plan, discusses and dismisses objections, and finally summarizes the argument. Ask students what elements make the proposal forceful and convincing. Conclude by having students list the elements from Swift's proposal that they might want to incorporate into a proposal of their own.

Linking Writing and Grammar

Before the drafting or revision stage of this assignment, tell students that correct subject-verb agreement is very important in proposals; incorrect usages can lessen a proposal's impact by making the reader question the abilities of the writer. Singular verbs are used with singular subjects; plural verbs are used with plural subjects. Have students look through their papers for examples of correct subject-verb agreement as you write these examples on the board:

SINGULAR SUBJECT AND VERB:
The *mayor* is mistaken.
The *history* of ancient societies is fascinating.

PLURAL SUBJECT AND VERB:
The *libraries* close at eight.
The town *beaches* are too crowded.
The *city* and *county* need more funds.

Have students review the material about subject-verb agreement on pages 668–686 of the Grammar and Usage Handbook. If problems with subject-verb agreement continue in students' work, assign the exercises on those pages for reteaching. Additional practice can be found in the Grammar and Usage Practice Book on pages 48 and 49.

Workshop Management Guidelines

The adjacent chart indicates the number of days recommended for each phase of the Guided and Related Assignments. Stars indicate portions of the assignment that may be completed outside the classroom if time is limited or if teachers wish the activity to be completed by students independently.

Subject Analysis

Starting from a Request for Proposals —1 day
Prewrite—3–4 days*
Draft—2–3 days*
Revise—1–2 days
Publish—open
Learning—1 day*
Reteaching—open
Extension/Enrichment—open
Sentence Composing—1 day*

Rebuttal

Starting from Literature—1 day
Preparing—2–4 days*
Drafting—2–3 days*
Reviewing—1–2 days
Publishing—open
Reteaching—open
Extension/Enrichment—open

Project Analysis

Starting from Literature—1 day
Planning—1–2 days*
Getting Your Speech on Paper—3–5 days*
Reviewing—1–2 days
Publishing—1–2 days
Reteaching—open
Extension/Enrichment—open

Sketchbook

Objective

To use a quote from an advertising campaign as a springboard to informal writing

Using the Prompt

To encourage spontaneity and a sense of discovery, tell students that the Sketchbook activity will not be graded.

Begin by writing the following incomplete sentences on the board to help students generate ideas:

It's not fair for our school to—.
It's not fair for colleges to require—.
It's not fair for our town to—.
It's not fair for our country to—.

Ask volunteers to complete a sentence of their choice with a rule or issue that really concerns them. Have the class brainstorm ways that the rule might be changed. If students have trouble getting started, model the process by mentioning a rule in your town that you think is unfair to teenagers or others and telling how you think it might be changed. Then have students write a paragraph using one of the sentence starters and share their paragraphs orally with the class. Students who wish may use a prompt from Additional Sketches as an alternative.

Encourage students to save their writing in their writing portfolios for possible use in the workshop that follows.

Sketchbook

What rules would you like to change? How would you change them, and why?

Additional Sketches

What was the best advice you ever received? What was the worst?

How would you improve your school or your community?

Informative Exposition: Synthesis

Related Assignment
REBUTTAL

Related Assignment
ORAL PRESENTATION

Guided Assignment
MAKING PROPOSALS

Have you ever thought of a plan for something and then tried to get others to go along with your plan? This is essentially what is involved in writing a proposal. Proposal writers identify a need and offer a specific plan to meet that need. Since a proposal is an offer to do something, the proposal writer's main goal is to convince an audience to accept the offer, that is, to adopt the proposal. As you complete your writing for this workshop, you will first learn how to make a written proposal. Then you will develop your skills in presenting a proposal orally and in answering or rebutting objections to your proposal.

177

Writer's Workshop 6:

Informative Exposition: Synthesis

Objectives

Guided Assignment:
MAKING PROPOSALS
To analyze the essential elements of a proposal; to use prewriting activities to choose a topic for a proposal; to draft, revise, edit, proofread, and publish a proposal

Related Assignment:
REBUTTAL
To analyze the elements of a rebuttal; to write a rebuttal to an article, speech, proposal, or opinion

Related Assignment:
ORAL PRESENTATION
To analyze the elements of a persuasive speech; to write a persuasive speech

Teacher's Choice

Guided Assignment
Making Proposals This assignment calls for students to exercise skills of synthesizing, defining, problem-solving, researching, and writing persuasively to propose a solution to a problem. Students will probably be highly motivated by the opportunity to propose solutions to problems, but they will need adequately developed basic expository writing skills in order to complete the assignment successfully.

Related Assignments
Rebuttal Since rebutting anticipated objections is a skill needed for proposal writing, you may wish to cover this lesson before the Guided Assignment.
Oral Presentation Auditory learners may feel comfortable with this opportunity to write a speech to persuade others to take action. With its focus on public issues, the lesson offers strong cross-curricular ties to social studies.

MAKING PROPOSALS

Assignment Rationale

By making proposals, individuals formally present detailed solutions to problems in an effort to convince others to support them and their solutions. Proposal writing is a practical skill with many applications in the business world, the academic professions, and community service. The skills students will need in completing the assignment—synthesizing information, presenting a clear plan of action, and using persuasive techniques to win approval from a particular audience—will be invaluable in innumerable work, service, and personal situations.

Starting from Literature

Objective

To respond to a request for proposals as a springboard to writing

Teaching Strategies

Motivate

Ask students to recall a memorable educational experience and to explain why it made such a strong impression. Ask what arguments they would use to persuade their school system to make this experience available to more students.

Tap Prior Knowledge

Ask students to recount times they have proposed changes in the way things were done. Ask what techniques they used in presenting their idea and persuading others to try it and what techniques backfired or failed.

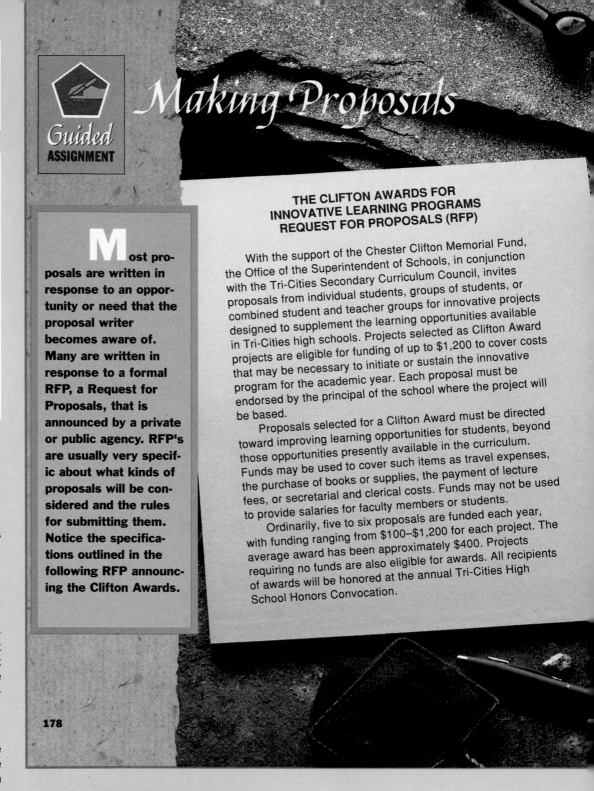

Guided **ASSIGNMENT**

Making Proposals

Most proposals are written in response to an opportunity or need that the proposal writer becomes aware of. Many are written in response to a formal RFP, a Request for Proposals, that is announced by a private or public agency. RFP's are usually very specific about what kinds of proposals will be considered and the rules for submitting them. Notice the specifications outlined in the following RFP announcing the Clifton Awards.

178

THE CLIFTON AWARDS FOR INNOVATIVE LEARNING PROGRAMS REQUEST FOR PROPOSALS (RFP)

With the support of the Chester Clifton Memorial Fund, the Office of the Superintendent of Schools, in conjunction with the Tri-Cities Secondary Curriculum Council, invites proposals from individual students, groups of students, or combined student and teacher groups for innovative projects designed to supplement the learning opportunities available in Tri-Cities high schools. Projects selected as Clifton Award projects are eligible for funding of up to $1,200 to cover costs that may be necessary to initiate or sustain the innovative program for the academic year. Each proposal must be endorsed by the principal of the school where the project will be based.

Proposals selected for a Clifton Award must be directed toward improving learning opportunities for students, beyond those opportunities presently available in the curriculum. Funds may be used to cover such items as travel expenses, the purchase of books or supplies, the payment of lecture fees, or secretarial and clerical costs. Funds may not be used to provide salaries for faculty members or students.

Ordinarily, five to six proposals are funded each year, with funding ranging from $100–$1,200 for each project. The average award has been approximately $400. Projects requiring no funds are also eligible for awards. All recipients of awards will be honored at the annual Tri-Cities High School Honors Convocation.

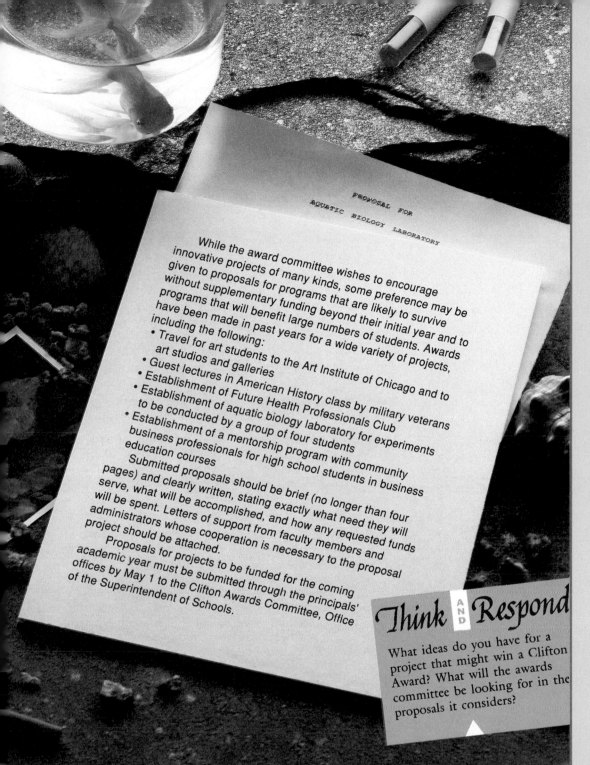

PROPOSAL FOR
AQUATIC BIOLOGY LABORATORY

While the award committee wishes to encourage innovative projects of many kinds, some preference may be given to proposals for programs that are likely to survive without supplementary funding beyond their initial year and to programs that will benefit large numbers of students. Awards have been made in past years for a wide variety of projects, including the following:

• Travel for art students to the Art Institute of Chicago and to art studios and galleries
• Guest lectures in American History class by military veterans
• Establishment of Future Health Professionals Club
• Establishment of aquatic biology laboratory for experiments to be conducted by a group of four students
• Establishment of a mentorship program with community business professionals for high school students in business education courses

Submitted proposals should be brief (no longer than four pages) and clearly written, stating exactly what need they will serve, what will be accomplished, and how any requested funds will be spent. Letters of support from faculty members and administrators whose cooperation is necessary to the proposal project should be attached.

Proposals for projects to be funded for the coming academic year must be submitted through the principals' offices by May 1 to the Clifton Awards Committee, Office of the Superintendent of Schools.

Think AND Respond

What ideas do you have for a project that might win a Clifton Award? What will the awards committee be looking for in the proposals it considers?

Set a Purpose

Before students read the excerpt, discuss the side-column notes. Point out that proposal writers must carefully consider the needs of their audience because they are depending on the audience to help them carry out their ideas. Have students read the excerpt to analyze the requirements and preferences of the award committee for the Clifton Awards.

Think and Respond

Elicit Personal Responses

Have the class brainstorm ideas for Clifton Awards, and write their ideas on the board. Then have the class evaluate the ideas, using the specifications and preferences outlined in the excerpt. Have them vote on the three ideas most likely to make good proposals for awards.

Link Literature to Writing

Based on their evaluations of Clifton Awards ideas, have students make generalizations about important factors to consider when planning a proposal. Accept such answers as the cost of the proposal, the number of people who might benefit, what support they can gather for the idea from influential people, whether they can present the idea in a few pages, and their ability to meet proposal deadlines. Tell students to keep these factors in mind as they plan their own proposals.

Prewrite and Explore

Objectives

1. To use prewriting techniques to find an idea for a proposal
2. To use collaborative planning to analyze the concerns of an audience
3. To evaluate the workability of ideas
4. To gather supporting evidence

Preteaching

Preview the Prewrite and Explore section. If there are skills or concepts students may need help with before prewriting, present them at this time. The mini-lesson references below may help you in your selection and instruction. The cross references in the pupil text will give students access to the same lessons for independent study.

Handbook Mini-Lessons

- Writing Techniques, pp. 334–335
- Interviewing, p. 336
- Collaborative Planning, pp. 358–360

You may also wish to use the Fine Art Transparencies: Starting Points for Writing, the Writing Prompts for Fine Art Transparencies, and the Data Sheet for this assignment as well as *Ideas for Writing* as resources during the Prewrite and Explore phase.

Teaching Strategies

 Individualizing Instruction

Gifted and Talented Instead of listing problems in the first Exploratory Activity, students gifted in photography may take photos to illustrate pressing problems or needs in the community. These may later be integrated into a proposal as documentation.

INVITATION TO Write

Think of an urgent problem or need in your school or community, and write a proposal for solving the problem or meeting the need. If you prefer, write a proposal for a project that meets the specifications for a Clifton Award.

The way a proposal is written is often important to its success. Your proposal may have to meet the following requirements. It must (1) define the problem or need you propose to address; (2) develop a clear plan of action for solving the problem or meeting the need; (3) meet the expectations and standards held by the readers who will evaluate your proposal and who will decide whether to grant or withhold their support.

HANDBOOKS

FOR HELP & PRACTICE

Writing Techniques, pp. 334–335
Interviewing, p.336
Collaborative Planning, pp. 358–360

▶ PREWRITE AND EXPLORE

1. Identify a problem or topic. A proposal must always answer an announced need or demonstrate that a need exists. Try one or more of the following activities to help you decide on the need or problem you would like to propose a solution for.

Exploratory Activities

- **Listing** Make a quick private list of problems, needs, or conditions that could use improvement in school or in your community. How might these problems be solved?
- **Researching and interviewing** Read recent issues of your school and community newspapers, looking for problems that need solutions. Then interview classmates, teachers, parents, and administrators. Ask them what they would like to see improved at school or in the community.
- **Sharing and collaborating** Share your more promising topics in a small group of writers and brainstorm ideas for solving those problems. Consider whether the solutions are realistic.

180 Workshop 6

Humanities Connection

Exhibit Jacob Riis's photographs of immigrants in New York City in the early twentieth century and Dorothea Lange's Depression-era photos, or show the documentary "Harvest of Shame" by Edward R. Murrow. Have students research and discuss the social changes these works inspired.

You should now have several possible ideas for a proposal. If you are still having difficulty finding a topic, look at the suggestions under "Apply Your Skills" on page 191. You might also consider the ideas you experimented with in the Sketchbook on page 176 or ideas you discover in your journal. List and evaluate all your ideas to see which ones you care about most, which ones seem most worthwhile for you to pursue, and which have the best chance of being adopted.

One student, Angela, listed and evaluated the following topics. In this workshop you will follow the development of her proposal.

PROBLEM
S O L V I N G

What should I look for in identifying a strong idea for a proposal?

ONE STUDENT'S PROCESS

Possible proposal ideas:

o Propose new sports team for girls so more girls can play team sports:
  I care about this topic. We don't get to travel or compete nearly as much as boys. Would like to make a league involving other schools. Too complicated for this assignment?
o Propose that Service Club hold a fund raising car wash in parking lot of downtown store, giving publicity to store. I really want to do this, but I could probably do it better by talking to them.
o Propose starting a health food snack bar in school to combat junk food addiction among students. This is a serious need and I really care about it. It could make money and be educational too. This is it!

2. Freewrite. Take ten minutes or so for some focused freewriting about your tentative proposal topic. Explain the problem, tell how you propose to solve it, and what sort of support you need.

3. Use collaborative planning. Working with a partner, share your freewriting and discuss your plans for a proposal. Pay special attention to the following areas.

- **Your audience** Who will be evaluating your proposal? What do they care about? What will it take to persuade them to give you what you are asking for?

Making Proposals **181**

Teaching Tip: More Sources

Use the Data Sheet for this assignment with those students who are having difficulty coming up with a proposal idea. You might also want to use the *Ideas for Writing Booklet* or the Fine Art Transparencies with these students.

Critical Thinking

Judging As students begin to judge the workability of their proposal idea, encourage them to talk out their ideas with a variety of people and to consider carefully any objections raised. Point out that responding to questions helps writers make judgments about their ideas and solve problems they might otherwise overlook.

Cooperative Learning

Because planning a proposal involves a variety of tasks, you may want to assign students with varying abilities and learning styles to work together on a proposal. If a cooperative learning group is having difficulty coming up with an idea for a proposal, you may wish to have them work together using the Data Sheet for this assignment.

Teaching Tip: Audience

Point out to students that in proposal writing they must keep their audience in mind at all times and consider its needs. As an example, ask how proposals submitted to a hypothetical Traditional Ways Society and Innovative Futures Association might differ.

Springboard

To broaden students' thinking about the value of proposals and grantsmanship in adult life, play a careers and proposals game. Write careers in which proposal writing is important on index cards. Include such careers as medical researcher, astronomer, social worker, artist, physicist, education researcher, and historian. Go around the class, showing students one card at a time and challenging students to suggest a topic for a proposal that the indicated professional might write in an effort to get funding.

Draft and Discover

Objectives

1. To draft a proposal, using persuasive argumentation and documentation
2. To respond to one's own writing and to that of one's peers

Preteaching

Review the Draft and Discover section to determine if there are skills or concepts students may need special help with. The mini-lessons listed below may help you provide this instruction.

Handbook Mini-Lessons
- Facts and Statistics, p. 379
- Voice, pp. 418–422
- Developing Arguments, pp. 474–476
- Research Skills, pp. 479–490
- Building Arguments, p. 504

- **The nature of the problem and its importance** How can you demonstrate its importance?
- **The details of your proposal** What, specifically, do you propose to do, and in what order?
- **The workability of your proposal** Will your proposal really work? How difficult will it be to put your plan into action? What are some arguments against it?
- **Your request** What are you asking for in order to implement your proposal, and how will you use what you are asking for? How will you spend any money that is given to you or use other resources (including time, materials, assistance) that you are requesting?
- **Research** What additional information might help you write a more effective proposal? Are there experts you ought to consult or books and articles you need to read? Could you conduct some research by doing your own observation, interviews, or surveys?

HANDBOOKS
FOR HELP & PRACTICE

Facts and Statistics, p.379

Voice, pp. 418–422

Developing Arguments, pp. 474–476

Research Skills, pp. 479–490

Building Arguments, p. 504

DRAFT AND DISCOVER

1. Think about the parts of your proposal. Look over your free-writing and your notes from your collaborative planning session, and then begin a rough draft of your proposal. As you draft, you may want to look at the outline below, which presents a standard way of organizing a formal proposal.

I. Preview summary of proposal (optional)
II. Statement of need, supported by examples, testimony, and data, when appropriate
III. Description of plan of action, detailing steps to be taken and describing benefits of the plan and how they will outweigh any disadvantages
IV. Your request: exactly what you are asking for in money or other resources and how it will be used

 Writer's Choice If you are missing information (for example, statistics, costs, expert testimony), you might do more research now or go ahead with your rough draft, flagging places where you need to fill in blanks.

182   Workshop 6

Off the Record

"I love being a writer. What I can't stand is the paperwork."—Peter de Vries

2. Employ effective writing strategies. You will probably want to use all or most of the following strategies at various points in writing your proposal.

Strategies

- **Summary** As a guide to readers, proposals often begin with a brief summary of what is being proposed.
- **Definition** Be sure to define any technical terms that your readers may not know.
- **Argumentation** A proposal makes two arguments: first, that a need exists and, second, that your plan can meet that need. To make your proposal persuasive, be sure to acknowledge any possible objections to it and refute those objections.
- **Quotation and documentation** An effective way to strengthen your argument is to present statistical data and expert testimony from books and articles or from your own original research through interviews and surveys.
- **Supplementary documentation** Proposal writers often attach to their proposals supplementary documents such as statistical charts, copies of published articles, letters of support, or résumés showing their qualifications and experience.

PROBLEM
SOLVING

What strategies can I use to strengthen my proposal?

Angela wrote her rough draft quickly; she knew that she would be able to add additional material later. Here is the beginning of the first draft of her proposal.

ONE STUDENT'S PROCESS

SUMMARY. This is a proposal to establish a health food snack bar on campus to provide students with a healthy alternative to junk food snacks and, through better nutrition, to improve their ability to concentrate and learn.

NEED. In the three years I've been in Roosevelt High School, there is one complaint I've heard from everyone, students and teachers alike. There is no place at school where you can get healthy snacks. The cafeteria sells chips and sodas and candy, but very little fruit. Moreover, the cafeteria isn't open except at lunchtime.

Making Proposals **183**

Teaching Strategies

 Individualizing Instruction

Basic Students Students may need to review elementary composition skills such as summarizing, defining, and supporting a thesis statement. Model these processes by taking the proposal ideas of individual students and telling how you might summarize, define, and support different aspects of the idea in a proposal. You may want to provide examples by using other students' work.

Critical Thinking

Analysis Before students read Angela's preliminary draft on page 183, say that one objection you can think of to the proposal is this: "Why does her school need a health food snack bar when they already have a cafeteria?" Then have students read the draft and tell whether and how Angela begins to refute this objection. Ask what other evidence Angela might add to strengthen her case.

Teaching Tip: Gathering Evidence

Make sure students understand that examples, testimony, and statistical data are three different types of evidence they can use to support arguments. To reinforce the point, ask them how they might gather each type of evidence to support a proposal for after-school care in the local elementary school (*example:* describe a case study of a latchkey child; *testimony:* interview a childcare expert on the importance of adult supervision; *data:* survey parents on their childcare needs).

Springboard

Ask students to decide if the following quotation provides a useful tip for drafting proposals:
"A problem well stated is a problem half solved."
—Charles Kettering

Making Proposals **183**

Peer Response

Encourage peer readers to think of themselves as partners with a stake in helping the proposal succeed. Ask them to focus on helping the writer think of persuasive evidence to strengthen arguments. You may want to use the Peer Response Worksheet for this assignment as students provide feedback on each other's work.

Stumbling Block

Point out the advantages of sharing a draft with more than one reader. If two or more readers express the same objection to some aspect of the writer's draft, the writer will have a clear indication that the material in question should be reevaluated.

 Individualizing Instruction

Advanced Students Advanced students may want to draw up a budget for their proposal and prepare computer-generated graphs and spreadsheets of their statistical data.

COMPUTER TIP

You may wish to enter the "Questions for Your Peer Readers" into a word processing file, adding blank response lines after each question. Print a copy of these questions for each reader.

3. Reread your draft and share it with others. After completing your rough draft, set it aside for a time. Then review it by yourself and share it with other readers. Ask yourself and your readers the following questions.

REVIEW YOUR WRITING

Questions for Yourself

- Have I made a strong case that my proposal is a response to an important need? What further examples or data might help demonstrate the need?

- Am I clear about exactly what I propose to do, and am I sure that it can really be done?

- Have I noted possible objections or obstacles to implementing my proposed plan and answered them or shown how they can be overcome?

- Have I shown the advantages of my plan and how they outweigh the disadvantages?

- Have I made clear what I need to implement my proposal and what I'll do with the resources I get?

- Have I provided information about people who are ready to work with me once the proposal is approved?

Questions for Your Peer Readers

- Are you persuaded by the case I present that there is a real need for this proposal? Can you think of any other evidence I could use?

- Do you think my plan will work? What problems do you think might make it difficult to implement? Can you think of ways to improve the plan?

- Can you think of additional advantages and disadvantages of adopting my plan?

- Can you suggest anything else I might ask for to support my plan? Do you think I should ask for more or less money, more or fewer resources, more or less assistance?

- Can you think of influential people who might oppose my plan? Why would they oppose it?

Math Connection

Some of your advanced students may be using computer-generated graphs and spreadsheets to support their proposals as suggested under Individualizing Instruction above. You may want to ask a math teacher in your school to work with these students.

R EVISE YOUR WRITING

1. Re-evaluate your proposal. Review your draft and reflect on your own response to it and on the responses of your readers. Decide how you want to revise your proposal. Before you begin rewriting, check the following list of features that reviewers usually look for in evaluating proposals.

Standards for Evaluation

An effective proposal . . .

- clearly defines a problem or describes a need, using such evidence as testimony, statistics, and examples.
- presents a clear plan for solving the problem or meeting the need, giving enough detail to demonstrate that the plan is workable.
- shows that the writer understands how to implement the plan and knows what expenditures it will entail.
- persuasively demonstrates how the advantages of the plan outweigh its disadvantages.
- addresses and respectfully refutes possible objections to the proposal.
- demonstrates a clear sense of the audience through the use of an appropriate tone and choice of details.
- makes clear how any requested funds will be spent and how other allocated resources will be used.

2. Problem-solve. Rework your draft to incorporate the changes you have decided to make.

HANDBOOKS
FOR HELP & PRACTICE

Emphasis/ Tone/Mood, pp. 423–428
Problem Solving, pp. 472–473

"First of all, let me congratulate everybody on the swell turnout and on the really bang-up job you all did on such short notice."

Drawing by Rowland B. Wilson; ©1964, The New Yorker Magazine, Inc.

Making Proposals **185**

Revise Your Writing

Objectives

1. To evaluate the responses to a draft proposal
2. To review the draft based on the responses
3. To proofread for errors in spelling, grammar, usage, and mechanics

Preteaching

Preview the Revise Your Writing section. Based on this preview and on problems you may have noted in students' drafts, identify skills you want to review. The mini-lessons listed below may be helpful.

> **Handbook Mini-Lessons**
> - Emphasis/Tone/Mood, pp. 423–428
> - Problem Solving, pp. 472–473

You may also wish to use the Student Revision Model Transparencies, the Revision and Proofreading Worksheets, and the Guidelines for Evaluating Writing for this assignment as teaching resources.

Teaching Strategies

Individualizing Instruction

Auditory Learners Auditory learners may find revising easier if they read their draft aloud to a partner or a group. Encourage these writers to stop reading whenever they find a section of their proposal that sounds ''wrong'' to them. Suggest they try out revision ideas on the group before writing the final draft.

LEP Students Students for whom English is a second language or students who speak in a dialect may need help in attaining an appropriate tone for their proposal. Read through their introductions, point out any slang or colloquial expressions that are inappropriate in a formal proposal, and suggest replacements. Then ask them to eliminate similar expressions in the rest of their proposal.

Guidelines for Evaluation

The following guidelines may be used for a close evaluation of a proposal. See the Writing Evaluation Guidelines in the Teacher's Resource File for additional help with holistic or analytic scoring.

Ideas and Content
- clearly defines a problem or need
- uses testimony, examples, and statistics as evidence
- presents a clearly described, realistic plan for solving the problem
- convincingly demonstrates that the plan's advantages outweigh its disadvantages
- refutes possible objections
- makes clear how requested resources will be used
- uses words that create a formal tone

Structure and Form
- includes a preview summary (optional), a statement of need, a plan of action, and a request for resources
- organizes ideas logically
- uses transitions to show how ideas are related
- includes charts and graphs of data, if appropriate

Grammar, Usage, and Mechanics
- uses standard grammar and usage
- uses correct punctuation
- uses correct spelling

Peer Response

You may want to use the Peer Response Worksheet for this assignment as students provide feedback for each other.

 Writer's Choice Keep in mind that you do not have to incorporate all (or even any) of your readers' suggestions. Before making a change, consider whether it will improve your draft.

Notice how Angela improved two paragraphs of her draft by incorporating some changes suggested by one reader.

ONE STUDENT'S PROCESS

Health–conscious students and teachers have long
~Everybody has always complained about the absence
where students can   Mrs. DiLeo, who
of any place at school~to buy nutritious snacks. ~Health
chairs the Health and Physical Education Department, is convinced that "student
~~teachers say that students in our school would~~
concentration in most classes would improve and hyperactivity would diminish if kids
~~concentrate more better if they could buy such snacks~~
could eat healthy snacks in place of the sweets they now bring with them to school."
~~instead of the candy and chips they bring to school now.~~
, she adds.Teenagers need
~Forbidding snacks altogether is not the answer.~
snacks during the day: they just need healthy snacks instead of junk food."
Some administrators have argued that the cafeteria

is responsible for providing food for students and that it

can provide healthy snacks as well as lunches. But this
because the cafeteria is open only at lunch-time and is far removed from the
would not work~. ~~And even if the cafeteria did offer~~
classroom areas.
~~healthy snack, it would not affect students' snacking~~

~~habits much.~~

*Sidebar notes:*

Maybe you should quote a health teacher to support your claim.

Why isn't forbidding snacks the answer?

You should tell why the cafeteria plan won't work.

3. Proofread your work. After you have revised your proposal, read it again. Look for typographical errors and errors in spelling, punctuation, grammar, and usage. Minor blemishes can prejudice a reviewer against your proposal, especially if you are competing with other proposal writers for support.

Off the Record

"There is no expedient to which man will not resort to avoid the real labor of thinking."
—Sir Joshua Reynolds

Affect and Effect

Affect is a verb meaning "to influence." *Effect,* when used as a verb, means "to bring about or accomplish." When used as a noun, *effect* refers to the result of an action.

Will eating junk food, snacks with little nutritional value, affect a person's mood? (verb)

The school cafeteria, which is a well-managed facility, effected changes in the kinds of snacks being purchased. (verb)

The changes will have a positive effect on student health. (noun)

PUBLISH AND PRESENT

Here are some ways you might share your completed proposal.

- **Present your proposal orally.** Present your proposal to your class, to a school assembly, or to a community group that might be interested in the problem you are trying to solve. Afterward, lead a discussion of possible sources of support for the plan.

- **Submit your proposal to the school or community newspaper.** Choose the newspaper whose readers are concerned about the issue and who might have the power to help you implement the proposal.

- **Show your proposal to an expert on the problem.** That person might be able to suggest places where you can submit your proposal.

- **Send a copy to someone who might help implement it.** Prepare a list of individuals or agencies that might be in a position to support your proposal. Then send it to the most likely supporter first, reserving the others as back-ups to be used as necessary.

- **Save your work in your writing portfolio.**

Grammar
TIP

Set off nonessential appositives and clauses with commas.

HANDBOOKS
FOR HELP & PRACTICE

Publishing, p. 413

Linking Grammar and Writing

Point out that the student model includes several complex sentences. Point out further that complex sentences can add a feeling of maturity and seriousness to a piece of writing. Encourage students to look for places in their drafts where combining sentences to create complex sentences would improve the work. Refer them to Grammar Handbooks 33 and 39 for rules on using commas in complex sentences.

Managing the Paper Load

Choose four or five points from the Guidelines for Evaluation on page 186, and tell students you will focus your grading on those points. Remind them that a clear plan, strong evidence, and persuasive arguments are the key elements of a proposal. Methods of evaluation are discussed on pages T28–T30. You may want to use the Guidelines for Evaluating Writing and the Student Revision Model Transparencies for this assignment to help students further recognize what goes into an effective proposal.

Publish and Present

Objective

To publish and present a proposal

Handbook Mini-Lesson
- Publishing, pp. 413–414

Social Studies Connection

Students who wrote a proposal about a community problem may enjoy sharing their work with someone who writes grant proposals for a nonprofit agency in your community. The professional may be able to evaluate the effectiveness of the proposal as well as share his or her own experiences in proposal writing.

Teaching Strategies

Using the Model

Have students evaluate Angela's final proposal by using the Questions for Your Peer Readers on page 184.

Teaching Tip: Assessment Prompts

Now that students have completed their proposals, you may want to use the Writing Prompts for Assessment for this assignment to give students practice in responding to assessment prompts that call for proposals.

Clearly defines a problem, using expert testimony and statistics

ONE STUDENT'S PROCESS

Food for Thought: A Proposal to Improve Nutrition and Student Learning

Angela Greentree

Summary

This proposal requests support for the establishment of a health food snack bar at Roosevelt High School to counteract the disabling effects of poor nutrition on student learning and, as a bonus, to contribute to student health education and business education.

Need

According to Nathan Pritikin, a noted researcher on nutrition, junk food (soft drinks, candy, and so on) "gives you quick energy," but "it also gives you a quick letdown." Junk food snacks result after a short while in "lightheadedness, weakness, loss of concentration, and fatigue." Yet it is precisely such snacks that Roosevelt High students typically consume between classes. In a recent survey of students in three English classes (two at grade 11 and one at grade 12—meeting in the second, third, and sixth periods), it was found that almost half the students claimed to be hungry. Half said that they had snacked before class; and 85% of the snacks reported were high-sugar foods. For these students who want and need a snack during school hours, there is no real alternative to junk food.

Health-conscious students and teachers have long complained about the absence of any place at school where students can buy nutritious snacks. Mrs. DiLeo, who chairs the Health and Physical Education Department, is convinced that "student concentration in most classes would improve and hyperactivity would diminish if kids could eat healthy snacks in place of the sweets they now bring with them to school." Forbidding snacking altogether is not the answer, she adds.

"Teenagers need snacks during the day; they just need healthy snacks instead of junk food."

Some administrators have argued that the cafeteria is responsible for providing food for students and that it can provide healthy snacks as well as lunches. But this would not work because the cafeteria is open only at lunchtime and is far removed from the classroom areas. Moreover, even if the cafeteria should begin to stock healthy snacks, few students would purchase them. The fact is that most students have become accustomed to the quick rush of energy that sugar gives them and are unaware of the way sugar's quick energy is followed by the letdown that will deprive them of their energy and ability to concentrate. That is why my proposal, detailed below, includes an aggressive but entertaining campaign to educate students.

Proposed Solution

The solution is to provide a centrally located health food snack bar (an ideal location would be the main hallway near the auditorium, where most students pass between classes during an ordinary day) and to conduct a vigorous, schoolwide advertising campaign to change the snacking habits of students. Such a store would allow students and teachers to buy items such as fruit, bran muffins, health food snacks, fruit juices, and naturally sweetened sodas between classes throughout the day. The store would also serve three important educational purposes, described below.

First of all, students would manage the store themselves and thus get practical business experience of a kind not ordinarily available through regular business courses or through after-school jobs, where they are unlikely to be given management responsibilities. The store would require a staff for ordering, stocking, and selling snacks, and for record keeping, so a great many students could be involved in the project. Students could be restricted to working in the store only during periods when they would otherwise be in study hall or during free periods, so they would not miss any of

Addresses and respectfully refutes possible objections

Presents a clear plan for solving the problem, giving enough detail to show that the plan is workable

Persuasively demonstrates how the advantages of the plan outweigh its disadvantages

Making Proposals **189**

Reteaching

Assess the needs of students who were not successful in developing an effective proposal, and identify two or three areas in which additional practice is needed. Assign the Appropriate Handbook Mini-Lessons, along with the support materials listed for each lesson. Concepts commonly requiring reteaching for this assignment are:

- Facts and Statistics: Handbook 9.
- Specific Examples: Handbook 9.

The following suggestions and resources may also be useful.

1. Inappropriate Tone Remind students that diction creates tone, and that tone is the writer's attitude toward either the topic or the audience. Assign Handbook 16, Emphasis/Tone/Mood. Then have students define the tone of their proposals and choose wording that will strengthen it.

2. Comma Errors To reinforce the correct punctuation of essential and nonessential clauses, write the following sentences on the board. Have students explain why the clause in sentence 1 is essential, but the clause in sentence 2 is not:

(1) The proposal that you wrote is wonderful.
(2) Your proposal, which I read this morning, is wonderful.

• Have students contact the local city or town council to find out how proposals are made to the locality and what process the proposals follow before they are adopted or rejected. Encourage students to list the steps of the process or to create graphic representations of the process.

• Show a documentary on a current social problem. Afterward, have students define the problem and brainstorm possible solutions. Emphasize that the way a problem is defined often determines the kinds of solutions that are proposed. Ask students to try to agree on how to define the problem before they begin proposing solutions.

Shows that the writer understands how to implement the plan

their regular academic classes. The store would also have academic supervision, because it would be operated under the general supervision of the Business Education Department, all of whose members have endorsed this proposal (see attached letters).

Another educational function of the snack bar would be to provide nutrition information for all students and staff at Roosevelt High. This would be accomplished through an advertising campaign conducted by the student managers, encouraging students to buy their snacks in the snack bar and to eat healthier foods in general. Mr. Gordon, in the English Department, has agreed to act as advisor to the snack bar on advertising strategies and Mrs. DiLeo will advise on the principles of nutrition (see attached letters).

The third educational function of the snack bar will be to improve learning in all classes at Roosevelt High by replacing junk food with healthy snacks in the diet of Roosevelt High students, thereby making those students better able to concentrate in class and more likely to learn whatever they are studying.

Support Requested

Implementing this proposal would entail relatively little expense on the part of the school administration. The establishment of a snack bar would cost approximately $600 for starting inventory, plus approximately $600 in lumber and supplies needed to build a structure that could be placed in the main hallway in front of the auditorium, where it would also be used for after-school events that are held in the auditorium. Mr. Kerwick, head of the Vocational Arts Department, has provided an estimate of construction costs and will guarantee that the snack bar can be built without any labor costs as a project of one or more shop classes (see attached memo). Once built and operating, the snack bar will be financially self-sufficient and should generate enough profit to repay construction and start-up costs and then provide additional income for other school activities.

LEARNING FROM YOUR WRITING PROCESS

WRITER TO WRITER

Grant writing has to be persuasive. You must be able to market and sell your organization. The writing should be direct, compelling and concise.

Michael Chapman, former director of the American Indian Business Association, Chicago, Illinois

1. Reflect on your writing. Review your prewriting materials and the various drafts you have written of your proposal. Reflect on how your proposal developed from your initial idea to a finished proposal. In what ways has your initial idea changed in this process? What were the influences that led to those changes? Summarize these reflections in a note that you attach to your proposal when you place it in your writing portfolio.

2. Apply your skills. Use the thinking and writing skills you have developed in writing your proposal to complete one or more of the following assignments.

- **Cross curricular** Identify a number of social problems that trouble or have troubled a society you are studying in history. Develop a proposal (with a clear sense of audience) that addresses one of the problems or needs of that society.
- **Literature** Consider the needs or problems of a character in a novel, play, or story you are studying. Try to describe the character's problem as if you were writing a "needs" section of a proposal. What proposal could you make to solve the character's problem? To what other character in the work would you address the proposal? Consider why proposals can't solve many important problems people have.
- **General** Use your proposal-writing experience to obtain funds or other support for a project that would be carried out by some group that you belong to.
- **Related assignments** Follow the suggestions on pages 194–202 to create a rebuttal and an oral presentation.

Learning from Your Writing Process

Objective

To analyze and reflect upon what has been learned about the writing process and the writing of a proposal

Teaching Strategies

Reflecting on the Process

Ask students to discuss what they would do differently now that they have had the experience of writing a proposal. How would their planning be different? In what ways would the actual writing be different?

Writing Portfolio

As students summarize their reflections for inclusion in their writing portfolio, ask them to include a comment about what they hope to do differently the next time they write a proposal.

Summary and Closure

Before proceeding to the next lesson, be sure students have internalized the following concepts:

1. Proposals are practical forms of writing for solving problems inside and outside the school environment.

2. An effective proposal convincingly documents a problem or need and persuasively presents a workable solution.

3. A proposal writer must keep in mind the needs, expectations, and biases of the audience in order to be persuasive.

Allow time for students to summarize what they learned by describing the characteristics of effective proposals and by telling why knowing how to write one can help them in other areas of life.

Starting from Literature

Objective

To respond to a published rebuttal as a springboard for writing

Teaching Strategies

Motivate

Ask students if they have ever felt like talking back to authorities—on television, in the news, in school, or other everday situations. Encourage them to share any appropriate experiences. Let them know that in this assignment, they will learn how to do so with greater effectiveness.

Tap Prior Knowledge

Encourage students to share what they know about blindness. How have they gained that information—through making assumptions or by learning about blindness in books and from personal narratives of those who are sightless?

Set a Purpose

As students discuss the side-column notes, emphasize that the letter they will now read is an example of rebuttal: a point-by-point reply based on reason, rather than a general response based on emotion. Direct them to identify the places where Joanne Lucas replies to specific points in Friedrich's article.

Related **ASSIGNMENT**

Rebuttal

Seeing Blindness

Letter to the Editor of Harper's, *May 1989*

Letters to the editor, editorials, and political debates are all examples of responses that argue with or try to refute a particular statement such as you might do in an argument with a friend. Such refutations are called *rebuttals*.

Joanne Lucas's letter to the editor of *Harper's* is a response to an article on temporary blindness that appeared in a previous issue of the magazine. As you read the letter, pay particular attention to how the writer responds to each of the points made by the author of the original article.

192

"**G**one Blind," an essay by Otto Friedrich in the March issue, perpetuates some of the worst stereotypes and misconceptions about blindness. The journal that Friedrich kept during his four days of blindness, undergone for medical reasons, offers an interesting account of the sudden loss of vision. The anxieties that he experienced are shared by many newly blind persons, as well as their families and friends. But his assumptions about blindness are holdovers from the Dark Ages and should not remain unchallenged.

Friedrich's chronicle exemplifies what a sighted person *imagines* blindness to be. The blind do need help initially in gaining the training and tools that will allow them to participate fully in society and to hold jobs appropriate to their abilities. Such training is available. But blind persons wishing to work still face a high unemployment rate. This needless waste of human potential is, perhaps, largely due to ignorance and fear on the part of prospective employers. Friedrich's journal only reinforces such fears. For example, word processing equipment that uses synthetic speech technology can free a blind writer from dependency on—to use Friedrich's dismal phrase— "some suburban stenographer."

The assumption that a blind person cannot write well is ludicrous. Some of the best writers in the Western canon wrote in spite of blindness or severe vision impairment. Even if we are not sure that there was a Homer, we do know about Milton, Joyce, Borges, and Thurber, to mention a few. On what grounds does Friedrich base his conjecture that blind, he would be reduced to writing potboilers?

Friedrich even insinuates that thinking is impaired by loss of vision. Yet during his brief confinement, he gained new insights from the familiar material with which he passed the time.

Vision, in a poetic sense, is more than a matter of eyesight.

Joanne Lucas
Waldport, Ore.

Elicit Personal Responses

You might have students imagine, first, that they are Lucas, reading Friedrich's article, and second, that they are Friedrich reading Lucas's letter. How would they feel and what would they think in each case? What rebuttal might Friedrich make to Lucas's letter?

Explore the Author's Techniques

Lucas's opening paragraph offers a strong statement of her thesis. She then goes on to support it with more specific points. Notice how she uses concrete facts, such as the names of authors, to counter Friedrich. Notice, too, that at times she gives partial credit to Friedrich's effort (''offers an interesting account of the sudden loss of vision'') without giving an inch on her own position. This makes her appear reasonable and fair.

Link Literature to Writing

Point out that a rebuttal uses elements of exposition as well as persuasion. You might ask the class what, in their conjecture, prompted Lucas to write her letter. Undoubtedly the answer is that she felt a strong emotional reaction to Friedrich's article. She perceived injustice and felt a need to argue for justice. Urge students to search for topics that make them feel similarly.

Think AND Respond

The writer of this letter argued that Otto Friedrich's essay reinforced common stereotypes that portray blindness in a misleading way. Which of Otto Friedrich's observations about the blind did the writer attack in her rebuttal? Notice how Joanne Lucas went beyond merely refuting Friedrich's points to providing convincing examples for her own argument. Can you think of an article or position to which you would like to offer a similar rebuttal?

Literature Connection

Have a student read Milton's ''On His Blindness'' aloud to the class, and have the class read the biographical sketch of Milton in their literature textbook. Have a student bring in biographical information on Joyce, Borges, and Thurber—focusing on their visual impairments. Discuss how they might have responded to Friedrich's article and Lucas's letter.

Guiding Your Writers

Objectives

1. To find an opinion to challenge
2. To collect evidence for a rebuttal
3. To draft and revise a rebuttal
4. To publish and present a rebuttal

Preteaching

Preview the remainder of the assignment. If there are skills or concepts your students will need help with, present them at this time. The mini-lesson references below may help you in selection and instruction. Cross references in the pupil text give students access to the same lessons for independent practice.

Handbook Mini-Lessons

- Analysis Frames, p. 343
- Order of Importance, pp. 353–354
- Developing/Presenting Arguments, pp. 474–478
- Rebuttals, pp. 505–506

Teaching Strategies

Personal Touch

Recount to the class an instance of your rebutting someone's position, particularly in an official setting such as a town meeting or in a letter. Express your feelings about the incident, including how you might have made your rebuttal more effective.

INVITATION TO *Write*

Joanne Lucas's letter refuted some common misconceptions about the blind that had appeared in a previous article in the magazine. Write your own rebuttal to an article, speech, proposal, or opinion that has provoked you.

Responding to ideas with which you disagree requires some of the same skills you use to present a proposal of your own ideas. To write a strong rebuttal, scrutinize your opponent's position and weigh the evidence he or she has used to build a case. Be sure to answer, or rebut, each argument with which you disagree with an example or counterargument that supports your own viewpoint.

PREPARING YOUR REBUTTAL

1. Find an issue that provokes you. A news or magazine article, an editorial, or a television documentary can provide you with a one-sided argument that invites rebuttal. You could also write a rebuttal to a commonly held position or point of view with which you disagree. For example, you may want to attack common stereotypes about the disabled or about a racial or ethnic group.

2. Analyze the opinion you intend to rebut. List all your opponent's arguments, whether you agree with them or not. Notice how Joanne Lucas commends Otto Friedrich's "interesting account of the sudden loss of vision." A rebuttal can gain credibility by conceding some advantages or good points to the opposing viewpoint.

3. Note the opposition's evidence. Find the main weapons for your rebuttal in your opponent's ideas, in the evidence he or she uses to support them, or in your opponent's credentials to argue a particular viewpoint. For example, Joanne Lucas attacks Otto Friedrich's essay because Friedrich is a sighted person who can only imagine what it would be like to be permanently blind.

HANDBOOKS

FOR HELP & PRACTICE

**Analysis Frames,
p. 343

Order of Importance,
pp. 353–354

Developing/Presenting Arguments,
pp. 474–476

Rebuttals,
pp. 505–506**

194 Workshop 6

Social Studies Connection

In addition to the literary authors Lucas mentions in her letter, two of America's greatest historians, Francis Parkman and William Prescott, became blind in early adulthood. This caused them considerable anguish but did not prevent either of them from writing volumes full of magnificent prose on the French and English colonies and the Spanish conquests, respectively.

4. Collect supporting evidence and examples. Your purpose is to answer every point made by your opponent and to add any further information that will persuade your audience. Friedrich's assumption that he would be unable to write if blind, for example, is cleverly countered by Lucas's reference to several blind or visually impaired authors who are commonly regarded as geniuses.

DRAFTING YOUR REBUTTAL

1. Introduce your rebuttal with a strong statement of purpose. Look at Lucas's opening sentence. Although some of the first paragraph and much of the second concede that Friedrich makes some valuable points, you can tell exactly where Lucas's rebuttal is heading from the author's very first statement. Make sure your introduction states your viewpoint with equal power.

2. If possible, point out flaws in your opponent's arguments. Lucas says Friedrich's assumption that blindness leads to thinking impairment is belied by the very insights Friedrich reveals in his article. You may agree with some of your opponent's arguments but feel that they do not go far enough, or perhaps you'll argue that your opponent draws the wrong conclusion from the examples.

Writing
—TIP—

Ask for assistance from a member of your school's debate team. Debaters are trained to structure rebuttals that refute each argument of the opposing side.

Teaching Tip: Prewriting

Encourage students to use graphic aids as part of prewriting. For instance, they may make point-by-point lists of their opponents' positions and of their own answers to each position. Alternatively, they may illustrate their own and opponents' positions in the forms of maps, tree diagrams, or Venn diagrams.

 Individualizing Instruction

LD Students You might suggest that students with severe reading problems such as dyslexia write a rebuttal to a movie review on television. Ask them to tape record the review.

Stumbling Block

Students presenting the problem, "I know what my position is but I can't find specific evidence," should be given practical tips on library research. For example, you might steer them toward the *Reader's Guide to Periodical Literature* to find articles on news topics or to biographical dictionaries and encyclopedias in the reference section to find information about famous persons. Also encourage them to consult your school librarian.

Social Studies Connection

Discuss the distinction between historical facts, which can't be rebutted unless overturned by more reliable evidence, and historical interpretations, which are normally rebutted and counterrebutted. For example, it is a fact that King John signed the Magna Carta at Runnymede in 1215. However, the statement, "King John was a compassionate and egalitarian ruler" is an interpretation, open to rebut – tal and debate. Interpretations usually change over the course of time, as values change or new facts become available.

Guidelines for Evaluation

The following guidelines may be used for a close evaluation of a rebuttal. See the Writing Evaluation Guidelines in the Teachers' Resource File for additional help with holistics or analytic scoring. A good rebuttal . . .

- addresses a provocative issue
- answers the opponent point by point
- employs factual supporting evidence
- uses the opponent's words and ideas against themselves
- begins with a strong statement of purpose
- develops points in order of ascending importance
- concludes with a forceful summary of major points

Reteaching

Assess the needs of students who were not successful developing an effective rebuttal. Assign the appropriate Handbook Mini-Lessons. Concepts commonly requiring reteaching for this assignment are:

Developing/Presenting Arguments: Handbook 23
Rebuttals: Handbook 26

The following suggestions and resources may also be useful.

1. Insufficient Support Draw circles around all poorly supported points in students' rebuttals. Call these ''holes in your arguments.'' Have students plug the holes by acknowledging and countering possible objections or by adding clarifying statements or supportive evidence.

2. Flawed Generalizations In students' rebuttals, underline generalizations that seem hasty, overly broad, or unsubstantiated. Instruct students to correct them by either limiting them or adding enough specifics to support them.

3. Develop your points in order of ascending importance. Notice that Lucas first takes issue with Friedrich's assumption that blind people encounter insuperable technical obstacles to accomplishment. Then she attacks his more serious argument that sightlessness condemns a person to intellectual inferiority. Saving your strongest arguments for the end keeps your audience interested and helps you build to a more compelling conclusion.

4. Conclude with a forceful summary of your main points. Lucas's distinction between vision and eyesight in her last sentence drives home the observation that while blind people have lost the physical ability to see, they need not suffer a more fundamental lack of vision or insight.

REVIEWING YOUR WRITING

1. Reread your rebuttal. List all the points you have included to argue your position. Have you answered every point made by your opponent? Can you think of any further examples that would strengthen your argument? Have you argued your points in ascending importance and ended with a strong conclusion?

2. Ask one or more classmates to read your rebuttal. Can your friend summarize your position in a one-sentence statement? Can he or she list all the points that prove your case? Are there any flaws in your ideas that your classmate can point out?

3. Rewrite your rebuttal. Proofread your draft for spelling, punctuation, and grammar. Incorporate your own and your friends' suggestions into a final draft that presents your rebuttal in the most compelling fashion.

PUBLISHING AND PRESENTING

- **Correspond with your opponent.** Send your rebuttal to the political figure, writer, or television commentator who presented the original viewpoint with which you disagreed. If you get a response, share it with your class.
- **Try to get your rebuttal into print.** Mail a copy of your rebuttal to your local or school newspaper.
- **Hold a debate.** If you are refuting a proposal made by one of your classmates, present your rebuttal as part of a structured debate.

196   Workshop 6

Social Studies Connection

You may want to bring in a videotape of the 1960 Kennedy-Nixon presidential debates, or distribute the text of the 1860 Lincoln-Douglas debates, for students to assess. Encourage students to provide rebuttals of their own to any and all points, including points they personally agree with.

On the Lightside

DENOTATIONS AND CONNOTATIONS

Many words have two kinds of meaning. The basic, direct meaning we call the *denotation*. The implied, suggestive meanings—*connotations*—are what give a word its individuality and color, its distinctive and unique personality.

Take the word *fist*. *Webster's Ninth New Collegiate Dictionary* defines *fist* as "the hand clenched with the fingers doubled into the palm and the thumbs doubled inward across the fingers." Okay, then, "The maiden held a white lily in her delicate fist" ought to be a perfectly effective sentence.

But it isn't; in fact, it's humorously incongruous. We smile at the clashing connotations of *maiden*, *white*, *lily* and *delicate* on the one hand, and *fist* on the other. The denotation of *fist* is correct, but its connotations make it a grotesque choice for a sentence about a maiden and a lily.

Giggle is defined in the dictionary as "to laugh with repeated short catches of the breath." But, because of its connotations, *giggled* is strikingly misplaced in a sentence like "The grizzled cowhand giggled at the tenderfoot's foolish suggestions."

Here are some entries from a magazine contest asking readers to create word-plays using connotation and denotation.

- I am traditional. You are old-fashioned. He is reactionary.
- I am beautiful. You have quite good features. She isn't bad-looking, if you like that type.
- I am righteously indignant. You are annoyed. He is making a fuss about nothing.

Try *your* hand at mixing the many hues of words. Create your own experiments in connotation and denotation by following these rules:

1. Each must proceed from *I* through *you* to *he* or *she*.
2. The basic denotation of the concept must be maintained. For example, "I am slender; you are skinny; he is a fat slob," would be unacceptable because the denotation changes.
3. In each grouping, the connotations must become increasingly mean as you move from first to second or third person.

The following examples were created by students.

- I have trouble keeping a tune. You can't sing. When he sings, all the female moose come running.
- I am good at procrastination. You are inactive. He is a lazy bum.
- I choose my friends with discrimination. You are standoffish. She is the snob of the century.

Richard Lederer

197

On the Lightside

If some students have trouble understanding the difference between denotation and connotation, you might have them look those two words up in the dictionary and read the definitions aloud. A very simple explanation is that connotations are the shades of a word's meaning.

Emphasize that most descriptive words, even the simplest, have connotations as well as denotations. The reason is that any given word is used by large numbers of individuals in widely different contexts, and in different cultures and historical eras. Each of us has a slightly different mental image of "fist" and "giggle," based on our experiences, our personalities, and the time and place we live in. Connotations are what make language a flexible, evolving thing.

To guide students in creating their connotative groupings, read the rules aloud and discuss any points that need clarification. In rule 2, ask students to provide a correct third term instead of "he is a fat slob" (it might be, "he is emaciated") and correct first and second terms for fatness (they might be "I am solidly built; you are pleasantly plump").

This Lightside provides a good opportunity for students to work as partners, brainstorming both their denotations and connotations. Have pairs or individual students read their creations aloud, and invite their classmates to suggest additional connotative phrases.

Starting from Literature

Objective

To respond to a professional oral presentation as a springboard to writing

Teaching Strategies

Motivate

Ask for a show of hands on how many students are nervous about speaking before a group. Raise your own hand as well, to show that even adults whose professions involve speaking to groups are often nervous about it. Some studies have shown this to be the type of fear that affects the most people. Tell students that this assignment will teach them skills that will improve their speech-making. It may not take away the butterflies in their stomachs—only practice can do that—but it will give the butterflies less reason to be there.

Tap Prior Knowledge

Ask students to share what they know about the recent economic problems of farmers and the decline of the family farm. If time permits, have a volunteer create a bibliography of newspaper and newsmagazine articles on the subject, especially ones from the mid-1980's, when Spacek spoke. This task can be efficiently completed using the *Reader's Guide to Periodical Literature*. Discuss with students what a quick glance at the *titles* of the articles reveals about the problem.

Set a Purpose

First, discuss why Spacek begins her speech by describing her background. The answer is doubtless that she wanted to assure the committee she was not an outsider who took up the farmers' cause when it became fashionable. As students read the speech, have them note how Spacek supports her facts with emotional appeals.

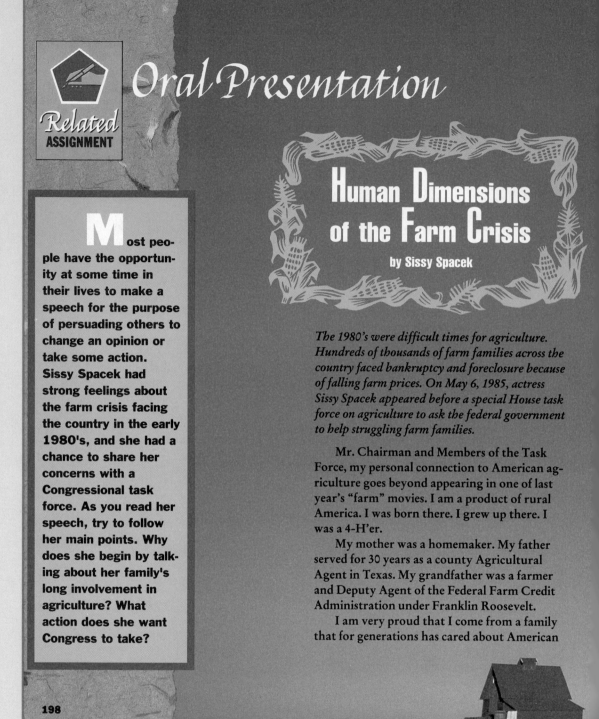

Related ASSIGNMENT

Oral Presentation

Human Dimensions of the Farm Crisis
by Sissy Spacek

Most people have the opportunity at some time in their lives to make a speech for the purpose of persuading others to change an opinion or take some action. Sissy Spacek had strong feelings about the farm crisis facing the country in the early 1980's, and she had a chance to share her concerns with a Congressional task force. As you read her speech, try to follow her main points. Why does she begin by talking about her family's long involvement in agriculture? What action does she want Congress to take?

198

The 1980's were difficult times for agriculture. Hundreds of thousands of farm families across the country faced bankruptcy and foreclosure because of falling farm prices. On May 6, 1985, actress Sissy Spacek appeared before a special House task force on agriculture to ask the federal government to help struggling farm families.

Mr. Chairman and Members of the Task Force, my personal connection to American agriculture goes beyond appearing in one of last year's "farm" movies. I am a product of rural America. I was born there. I grew up there. I was a 4-H'er.

My mother was a homemaker. My father served for 30 years as a county Agricultural Agent in Texas. My grandfather was a farmer and Deputy Agent of the Federal Farm Credit Administration under Franklin Roosevelt.

I am very proud that I come from a family that for generations has cared about American farmers and American farmlands, and it is our conviction that the American family farmer is the most efficient, stable and productive of all of the world's farmers.

So I'm not here today to defend them on nostalgic grounds, but to support them as the best and wisest of farmers.

Right now the future of American agriculture looks pretty bleak. Young farmers can't afford to get started, and in an effort to make up losses, existing farmers plant every available scrap of ground, contributing to the worst soil erosion in history.

And corporate farms are learning the hard way what the family farmer has known for centuries: farming is no easy road to short-term profits.

I would be naive to assume that this is a simple problem with simple answers, but one thing I'm sure of: we can't turn our backs on these people who have fed us all so abundantly and cheaply throughout our history.

Our largest and most vital industry is disintegrating. It is not marginal producers, speculators or bad managers who are being squeezed out, but the solid core of our agriculture which is threatened.

And trouble on the farm spreads without regard for performance. As bankruptcies mount, land values fall—and since production loans are secured by land, without borrowing another dime, all farmers fall deeper into debt.

If we think this catastrophe affects only the farmers, we are dangerously naive.

The drugstore, the implement dealer, the grocery store and the bank in every agricultural community in this country is in trouble, and that trouble arrives in the cities when homeless farmers with their wives and children come to town to look for a job.

We have a responsibility to insure that our farmers make not only a fair living, but [can] afford to put back into the soil what they take out.

And the American public recognizes our responsibility in this crisis: According to recent *USA Today* and *New York Times* polls, more than 70 percent believe that the federal government has a clear obligation to save financially distressed farm families–families who are endangered by forces beyond their control, families who are the stewards of our homelands, this fertile American earth. . . .

A century ago, William Jennings Bryan said, "Burn down your cities and leave your farms, and cities will spring up again as if by magic, but destroy our farms and the grass will grow in the streets of every city in the country."

Thank you for this opportunity to appear before you today.

Think AND Respond

Do you find Sissy Spacek's appeal on behalf of American farmers persuasive? What are some of the arguments and techniques she uses to influence her audience to take action? What public issues do you have strong opinions about?

Humanities Connection

Actress Sissy Spacek is noted for her starring appearances in the films *Carrie, Violets Are Blue,* and *Crimes of the Heart.* She won a Best Actress Oscar for her portrayal of country singer Loretta Lynn in *Coal Miner's Daughter. The River* is the "farm movie" she alludes to in her oral presentation.

Think and Respond

Elicit Personal Responses

Invite students to imagine that they are members of Congress who have just heard Spacek's speech or that they are citizens who have heard it from the gallery. Have them jot down their immediate responses, then discuss them as a class.

Explore the Author's Techniques

Point out that Spacek makes the farmers' problems seem personal. She first connects her own personal history to farming. Later, she speaks about farm problems as they affect human beings, rather than in terms of generalities or statistics. This is a good strategy to apply to many other topics as well.

Link Literature to Writing

Sissy Spacek spoke about farm problems because she cared deeply about them. Her emotions are evident in her speech even though it is hard-headed and practical. Encourage students to find topics they genuinely care about, and, like Spacek, to use that caring as a practical, unsentimental tool for achieving their goals. Mention that the oral presentation students will create uses both exposition and persuasion.

Guiding Your Writers

Objectives

1. To choose a topic for an oral presentation
2. To draft an oral presentation
3. To make an oral presentation

Preteaching

Preview the remainder of the lesson. If there are skills or concepts students may need help with, present them at this time. The mini-lesson references below may help you in your selection and instruction. The cross references in the pupil text give students access to the same lessons for independent practice.

Handbook Mini-Lessons
- Organize Your Work, pp. 349–357
- Collaborative Planning, pp. 358–360
- Introducing/Concluding Nonfiction, pp. 365–371
- Varieties of Language, pp. 429–433
- Outline Form, pp. 826–827

INVITATION TO Write

Sissy Spacek spoke out on an issue that was important to her. Think of some policy that you think needs changing—at school, in your local community, or for the entire nation. Write a speech in which you try to persuade others to join you in working for change.

Many efforts to persuade others are most effective when they are presented orally. A speaker has a more direct and immediate impact on an audience than a writer does, and can even change the delivery of the speech in response to the audience's reaction. Therefore, it is very important when preparing and delivering a speech to know your audience and to take advantage of your personal impact.

PLANNING AN ORAL PRESENTATION

HANDBOOKS
FOR HELP & PRACTICE

Organizing Your Work, pp. 349–357

Collaborative Planning, pp. 358–360

Introducing/ Concluding Nonfiction, pp. 365–371

Varieties of Language, pp. 429–433

Outline Form, pp. 826–827

1. Choose a topic about which you have strong feelings. Do you want to urge others to join you in changing a policy? Do you have a proposal for which you want support? Sissy Spacek, for example, knew that many farmers were facing a crisis in the early 1980's, and she believed that the federal government should help. Find an issue that really interests you. You might want to get together with a few classmates and examine the issues in your community—social, political, moral, or economic—which you would like to address.

2. Identify your audience. A speech is usually meant for a specific audience. For example, Sissy Spacek knew as she was planning her speech that she would be addressing a congressional committee. You may already have earmarked the group to whom you will be speaking. If not, now is the time to identify your listeners. Will they be young people or adults, or a mix of both? Choose your facts, tone, and approach with your intended audience in mind.

Springboard

One of the most enjoyable forms of comic entertainment is improv, in which audience members suggest topics to the performers, who then improvise comic routines about those topics. If your class has some natural performers in it, you might suggest an improv session in which members of the class toss out ideas to volunteers who will improvise thirty-second or sixty-second speeches. Alternatively, divide the class into improv teams and let them compete at improvising speeches on ideas you toss out to them.

3. Discuss your plans with a friend. Write the main idea you want to convey to your audience in a sentence or two. Then discuss with a friend some ways you might accomplish your goal. How can you get your audience's attention at the beginning of your speech? What key points should you cover? What tone, approach, and persuasive appeals would be most effective?

Getting Your Speech on Paper

1. Make an outline. Draw up an outline detailing what you want to say in the order you want to say it. Plan to cover only key points, since listeners may become confused by too long an introduction or too many arguments. If you find you are trying to cover too much, prune your outline.

2. Give some thought to the beginning of the speech. Sissy Spacek started her speech by presenting her "credentials" to speak —her family roots in the rural community. She then used vivid description to re-create the farmer's plight. How can you capture your audience's attention?

3. Write your first draft. Use your outline as a map or guide when you write your first draft. Be sure you include details and examples to support your arguments. Sissy Spacek, for example, showed that the economic trouble of some farmers led to bankruptcies and falling land values, which in turn affected other farmers and people in other occupations. As you write the first draft of your speech, try to build a case that clearly shows the importance of the issue you have chosen.

 Writer's Choice After making their outline, some people like to dictate their speech directly into a tape recorder. Then they transcribe the speech from tape to paper. You may want to prepare your first draft in this manner.

4. Provide an effective conclusion. In the last sentence or two of your speech, summarize your proposal, recap your main points, and request action. Spacek used a powerful quotation from William Jennings Bryan to accomplish these goals. In your conclusion, try not to trail off weakly, but end with a forceful restatement of your convictions on the issue.

Writing TIP

Speeches that attempt to persuade are most effective when they are short—three minutes is ideal. A typewritten speech of 1½ pages, double-spaced, is just about the right length for a three-minute speech.

◆ Individualizing Instruction

Learning Styles Professional speakers vary in their approaches to preparation. Some write out speeches word for word; others jot a few scribbled notes, trusting in their ability to speak off the cuff. Some outline in detail, others only note main headings. Some memorize their speeches; others, after writing them, never look at them again. Tape recorders and mirrors are essential tools for some speakers, not for others. Encourage students to test out more than one method at home and to use whichever makes them feel most comfortable and most effective.

Teaching Tip: Audience

If a student has tailored his or her speech for a specialized audience, have him or her invite the class to play the role of that audience. For instance, the student might say, "I wrote this speech with an audience of senior citizens in mind. Imagine that you're in your seventies or eighties and I'm giving this speech to you about improving the quality of life in nursing homes."

Teaching Tip: Writing

Let students know that, as a general rule, sentences in speeches are shorter than sentences in written works.

Social Studies Connection

The mid-1980's saw a wave of celebrity involvement in public issues such as the farm crisis, world hunger, saving the rain forests, and ending the sale of furs. The trend began when rock star Bob Geldof of the British group Boomtown Rats organized Band-Aid, an all-star group whose Christmas record benefited victims of the Ethiopian famine. In quick succession, multicelebrity events such as Live-Aid, Farm-Aid, and Comic Relief augmented the efforts of individual celebrities such as Spacek and Meryl Streep on behalf of various causes. Students may be interested in researching these benefits as they search for topics for their oral presentations.

Guidelines for Evaluation

The following guidelines may be used for close evaluation of an oral presentation. See the Writing Evaluation Guidelines in the Teacher's Resource File for additional help with analytic or holistic scoring.

A good oral presentation
- deals with a topic that interests speaker and audience alike
- is geared to a specific audience
- presents the speaker's credentials on the subject if they are not well known
- captures audience attention at the beginning
- moves listeners to agreement or action with its conclusion
- is delivered in a clear and direct manner appropriate to the audience
- is delivered with effective variations in rate, volume, tone, pitch, and emphasis

Reteaching

Assess the needs of students who were not successful developing an effective oral presentation. Assign the appropriate Handbook Mini-Lessons. Concepts commonly requiring reteaching for this assignment are:

Organizing Your Work: Handbook 5
Collaborative Planning: Handbook 6

The following suggestions and resources may be useful.

1. Faulty Analysis Mark any parts of students' speeches which betray too shallow a view of the issues they have chosen. Direct students to restate the issues, mentioning both long-range and short-range causes. Then have them rethink their proposals for change, listing both long-range and short-range effects.

2. Weak Presentation As students deliver their speeches, mark them with a check, plus, or minus for eye contact; clarity of diction; and effective variation in speech rate, volume, tone, pitch, and emphasis. Let them practice to correct weaknesses and then give their speeches again to a new audience.

5. Rehearse your presentation. After you finish your first draft, rehearse your speech. Stand up, face your imaginary audience, and deliver the speech orally. Practice varying your rate of delivery, volume, tone, pitch, and emphasis. Where can you pause for effect? Where could a soft or forceful tone help to communicate your meaning? Pay special attention to how you can deliver your opening remarks to capture the audience's attention and how you can deliver an effective conclusion that will move your listeners to agreement or action.

REVIEWING YOUR WRITING

1. Listen to your speech with a friend. Use a tape recorder to record your speech, and play it back with a friend. Is your message clear? Is it interesting? Can you think of ways to make it more persuasive?

2. Listen to the way the speech sounds. Remember that speaking is different from writing. Sissy Spacek used a conversational style for her speech, with many short sentences. She also made effective use of repetition. Could you improve your speech by using one of these techniques?

PUBLISHING AND PRESENTING

- **Participate in a round robin.** Schedule an informal round robin with other class members who are working on a speech. Take turns reading your speeches aloud. Discuss methods of making the speeches more effective.
- **Deliver your speech.** Recall the audience you had in mind when you first started to draft your speech. Make arrangements to deliver your speech to them.

202   Workshop 6

Literature Connection

As a warm-up before they give their own speeches, you might have students read speeches from plays they have read in your course or a previous English course, such as Shakespearean soliloquies or the "mind of God" speech from *Our Town*.

Sentence

Varying S-V Splits

Effective writers often add details in the subject-verb split position to elaborate on the subject or provide a context for the action that follows.

In the sentences below, notice how the various kinds of s-v splits (underlined) prepare the reader for the main ideas of the sentences.

Appositive Phrase   The real estate agent, <u>an old man with a smil-ing hypocritical face</u>, soon joined them.
Willa Cather, "The Sculptor's Funeral"

Present Participial Phrase   August, <u>gasping for breath</u>, melted into Septem-ber.   **Robert Lipsyte, *The Contender***

Past Participial Phrase   The tent, <u>illumined by candle</u>, glowed warmly in the midst of the plain.
Jack London, *The Call of the Wild*

Absolute Phrase   An Arab on a motorcyle, <u>his long robes flying in the wind of his speed</u>, passed John at such a clip that the spirals of dust from his turn-ings on the winding road looked like little tornadoes.
Elizabeth Yates, "Standing in Another's Shoes"

Delayed Adjectives   The head of the filing department, <u>neat, quiet, attentive</u>, stood in front of the old man's desk.   **James Thurber, "The Catbird Seat"**

A. Sentence Combining   In the first sentence in each set, locate the main sub-ject and verb. Then place the underlined part of the second sentence directly after the subject of the first sentence. Enclose each s-v split in commas. The kind of phrase you will be inserting is identified in parentheses.

Example   When the light went out, the old man peeped into the little window. The old man was <u>trembling from agita-tion</u>. (present participial phrase)

Combined   When the light went out, the old man, trembling from agitation, peeped into the little window.
Anton Chekhov, "The Bet"

1. An open book lay beside it. The book was <u>something called *Totem and Taboo*</u>. (appositive phrase)   **Ralph Ellison, *Invisible Man***

Sentence Composing: Varying S-V Splits

Objectives

1. To combine sentences to form new sentences that contain an intervening phrase between the subject and verb
2. To expand sentences by adding an in-tervening phrase between the subject and verb
3. To compose sentences that contain an intervening phrase between the subject and verb
4. To compose a paragraph with sen-tences that contain an intervening phrase between the subject and verb

Preteaching

These exercises focus on the appropri-ate use of phrases that appear between the subject and the verb. Some students may need review of basic sentence parts and structure as well as the use of appos-itive phrases, participial phrases, and ab-solute phrases. Refer to the following sec-tions of the Grammar Handbook for preteaching content:

Phrases and Clauses
    Appositives and Appositive Phrases, page 593
    Verbals and Verbal Phrases, pages 594–596
    Using Phrases Correctly, page 602

Adjective and Adverb Usage
    Understanding Modifiers, pages 719–720

ANSWER KEY

12-6 Varying S-V Splits

A. Sentence Combining

   1. An open book, something called *Totem and Taboo*, lay beside it.

2. Ethan, alerted now for signs of the wonderful in his daughter, was struck by the strange
fact that she was making conversation.
3. Gerard, tenacity showing itself in his attitude, was sticking to something.
4. High in the air, a little figure, his hands
thrust in his short jacket pockets, stood staring
out to sea.
5. A man, young and graceful and very much
preoccupied, walked through the church-goers
faced in the opposite direction.

B. Sentence Expanding
Answers will vary.

**C. Unscrambling and Imitating Sen-
tences**
Imitations will vary.
1. The small cat, terrified by a sudden streak
of blinding lightning, raced desperately toward
cover in a cave that jutted out of the hillside.

2. Ethan was struck by the strange fact that she was making conversation.
Ethan was <u>alerted now for signs of the wonderful in his daughter</u>.
(past participial phrase)   **John Updike, "Man and Daughter in the Cold"**

3. Gerard was sticking to something. Gerard had <u>tenacity showing itself
in his attitude</u>. (absolute phrase)   **Elizabeth Bowen, "Foothold"**

4. High in the air, a little figure stood staring out to sea. He had <u>his
hands thrust in his short jacket pockets</u>. (absolute phrase)
          Katherine Mansfield, "The Voyage"

5. A man walked through the church-goers faced in the opposite direction. The man was <u>young and graceful and very much preoccupied</u>.
(delayed adjectives)   **Esther Forbes, "Break-Neck Hill"**

B. Sentence Expanding   For each sentence below, write some details that
could be inserted in the s-v split position. Insert your addition at the (/) and
enclose it in commas. Compare your sentences to the originals on page 323.

1. There had followed then a time of such happiness that Chips (/)
   hardly believed it could ever have happened before or since in the
   world.   **James Hilton, Goodbye, Mr. Chips**

2. Old Mrs. Beal (/) was homeward bound from dinner with her
   daughter.   **Jessamyn West, "The Child's Day"**

3. Across an immense ethereal gulf, intellects (/) regarded this earth with
   envious eyes and slowly drew their plans against us.
          H. Koch, "Invasion from Mars"

4. The bride (/) stood between her parents (/) and their three faces were
   calm, grave, and much alike.   **Katherine Anne Porter, Ship of Fools**

C. Unscrambling and Imitating Sentences   Unscramble each set of parts to
form a sentence that matches the model. Then write a second sentence
imitating the model. Enclose s-v splits in commas.

1. A wooded amphitheater, surrounded on three sides by precipitous cliffs
   of naked granite, sloped gently toward the crest of another precipice
   that overlooked the valley.   **Bret Harte, "The Outcasts of Poker Flat"**
   a. raced desperately toward cover in a cave that jutted out of the hillside
   b. the small cat
   c. terrified by a sudden streak of blinding lightning

2. He had already done it, and another face, grey, wet, and sour, was pushing into his, knocking him down and back as it scraped out under the plank.   **Flannery O'Connor, "The River"**
   a. and the second horse
   b. as it tired out under the pressure
   c. Dandelion was clearly winning it
   d. out-classed, straining, and winded
   e. was slowing on the track, moving gradually behind and back

3. The class above, seniors, draft-bait, practically soldiers, rushed ahead of us toward the war.   **John Knowles, *A Separate Peace***
   a. screamed above us at the band
   b. middle-schoolers, teeny-boppers, almost fanatics
   c. the row behind

4. At eleven o'clock, a man in a raincoat, dragging a lawnmower, tapped at my front door and said that Mr. Gatsby had sent him over to cut my grass.   **F. Scott Fitzgerald, *The Great Gatsby***
   a. on the window seat
   b. a package in red ribbon
   c. and announced that Mike had sent a present to resolve their argument
   d. sat on a cushion
   e. gleaming in the sun

5. While we were waiting for coffee, the headwaiter, an ingratiating smile on his false face, came up to us bearing a large basket full of huge peaches.   **Somerset Maugham, "The Luncheon"**
   a. the car
   b. as she was driving through Dallas
   c. emitting a dense cloud of black exhaust
   d. a suspicious rattle in its untrustworthy engine
   e. slowed to a crawl

Application Write a paragraph explaining how you cheer yourself up when your spirits get low. Into three of the sentences in your paragraph, insert s-v splits, varying the s-v splits in length and structure. Notice how efficiently these constructions can provide information essential to the main idea.

Grammar Refresher Expanders in the s-v split position may create confusion about subject-verb agreement. For a review of subject-verb agreement and intervening phrases, see Handbook 35.

Sentence Composing **205**

2. Dandelion was clearly winning it, and the second horse, out-classed, straining, and winded, was slowing on the track, moving gradually behind and back as it tired out under the pressure.
3. The row behind, middle-schoolers, teeny-boppers, almost fanatics, screamed above us at the band.
4. On the window seat, a package in red ribbon, gleaming in the sun, sat on a cushion and announced that Mike had sent a present to resolve their argument.
5. As she was driving through Dallas, the car, a suspicious rattle in its untrustworthy engine, slowed to a crawl emitting a dense cloud of black exhaust.

Application
Answers will vary.

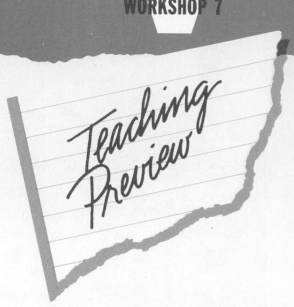

Teaching Preview

Workshop Overview

Writing that affirms an idea by setting forth and supporting a proposition is called persuasion. In this type of writing, the writer offers reasons why a belief should be held or an action taken, using arguments that are powerful enough to bring readers into agreement. In this Workshop, students are called on to present arguments from both sides of an issue in real-world and fictional contexts, and to remain impartial during fact-finding and analysis. This type of writing is excellent for further developing the critical thinking skills students have been applying and for helping students develop open minds about the opinions of others. Workshop 7 includes the following Guided and Related Assignments:

1. **Guided: Argument Analysis** shows students how to investigate and clarify two sides of an issue and how to recognize underlying assumptions
2. **Related: Establishing Conflict—Literature** builds on the skill of explicating both sides of an issue by showing students how to convey conflicts of ideas, attitudes, and temperament between fictional characters
3. **Related: Debate** extends speaking and critical thinking skills by having students write and present speeches on two sides of an issue

Preparation Guide

1. Use the Overview above and the Teacher's Choice descriptions on page 207 as a basis for deciding which assignment(s) to teach.

2. Preview the assignment and the teacher's notes. The teaching suggestions and your knowledge of your class's abilities should allow you to identify quickly the concepts that may require preteaching or extra support. The Handbook mini-lessons suggested in the Preteaching notes within the lesson can also provide guidance in this area.

3. Preview the adjacent chart for support materials in the Teacher's Resource File that may be used with this Workshop. Resources are for use with the Guided Assignment unless otherwise noted.

Workshop Support Materials

Resources	For Use With
Ideas for Writing: Data Sheets, p. 13; Additional Ideas, p. 25	Look for an issue, p. 210
	Evaluate your topics, p. 211
Thinking Skills Transparencies: Dialoguing Frame; *Worksheets,* p. 18	Freewrite, p. 212
Elaboration/Proofreading, p. 13	Begin your draft, p. 214
Peer Response Guides, p. 19	Review Your Writing, p. 216
Evaluating Writing, pp. 14, 36–39	Standards for Evaluation, p. 217
Student Revision Trans., pp. 27–30	Problem-solve, p. 217
Elaboration/Proofreading, p. 14	Proofread your work, p. 218
Tests and Assessment: Prompts, p. 7	

Professional Resources and Media

Books and Journals

Fahnestock, Jeanne and Marie Secor. *Rhetoric of Argument.* New York: Random House, 1985.

Films and Videos

"Argumentation." *The Write Course Series.* Dallas Community College District, Mesquite, Texas. 1984. (30 min.)

Communicating with a Purpose Series: Persuasive Essay. Alberta Educational Commission Corporation, Alberta, Canada. 1982. (30 min.)

Persuasive Writing. Effective Writing Series, Deltak, Inc. Naperville, Illinois. (40 min.)

Computer Software

Persuasive Essay. Intellectual Software, Bridgeport, Connecticut, Apple II, II+, IIc, IIe. (5 disks)

Linking Literature, Writing, and Grammar

The following options may be used to provide students with an integrated language experience. Begin by assigning and discussing any of the recommended pieces of literature, which can be found in most classroom anthologies. Use the suggested strategy to provide a link to the Guided Assignment.

Linking Literature and Writing

Option 1

Starting Point: "Owl vs. Man" by Ted Gup on pages 208–209 of *The Writer's Craft*
Strategy: Use the teaching suggestions on pages 208–209 to lead students into the Guided Assignment.

Option 2

Starting Point: "To His Coy Mistress" by Andrew Marvell
Strategy: As you discuss the poem, ask students to paraphrase and list the arguments the speaker makes to encourage his mistress to end her coy behavior. Encourage students to think of arguments that the mistress might make in response. Explain to students that they will have an opportunity to write an essay in which they explore both sides of a question.

Option 3

Starting Point: "Of Marriage and Single Life" by Francis Bacon
Strategy: Have students list the points Bacon makes in favor of married life and those he makes in favor of single life. Then encourage students to speculate about which life Bacon probably personally favored. Has Bacon presented a balanced view or does one point of view seem to prevail? Tell students that they will soon have an opportunity to analyze a question from two sides.

Linking Writing and Grammar

Before the drafting or revision stage of this assignment, tell students that persuasive writing often contains ideas that are contrasted using such words or phrases as *still, however, on the other hand,* or *instead* for emphasis. These introductory elements and interrupters should be set off by commas. Ask students to find examples of sentences containing introductory elements and interrupters in their work as you write the following examples on the board:

The seniors oppose the new fees. Instead, they support a reduction in service.

The spotted owl is fast disappearing. The lumber industry, however, shows little concern.

Go over the rules for commas with introductory elements and interrupters on pages 766–772 of the Grammar and Usage Handbook. If problems with commas with such expressions still appear in student papers, assign the exercises on those pages for reteaching. Additional practice can be found in the Grammar and Usage Practice Book on pages 86 and 87.

Workshop Management Guidelines

The adjacent chart indicates the number of days recommended for each phase of the Guided and Related Assignments. Stars indicate portions of the assignment that may be completed outside the classroom if time is limited or if teachers wish the activity to be completed by students independently.

Examining Arguments

Starting from Literature—1 day
Prewrite—2–4 days*
Draft—1–3 days*
Revise—1–2 days
Publish—open
Learning—1 day*
Reteaching—open
Extension/Enrichment—open
Sentence Composing—1 day*

Two Points of View—Literature

Starting from Literature—1 day
Developing a Conflict—2–4 days*
Reviewing—1–2 days
Publishing—1–2 days
Reteaching—open
Extension/Enrichment—open

Debate

Starting from Literature—1 day
Researching and Planning Your Speeches—3–5 days*
Drafting—1–2 days*
Reviewing—1–2 days
Publishing—1–2 days
Reteaching—open
Extension/Enrichment—open

Sketchbook

Objectives

To use a cartoon as a springboard for thinking and writing about the nature of argument

Using the Prompt

Cubist artists Picasso and Braque shattered long-standing conventions by representing objects from more than one point of view in space. The cartoon draws on this idea to lampoon Calvin's attachment to one-sided thinking. Using the cartoon as a springboard, have students explore the characteristics of an argument. Explain that they will not be graded on this writing: the purpose of the activity is strictly to help them examine the right and wrong ways to argue.

Begin by discussing what makes the cartoon funny and whether it reminds students of their own attitudes about arguing. Help students recognize the insight implied in the cartoon: that even though people argue to change each other's minds, they sometimes end up polarizing each other and clinging more tenaciously than ever to their original views. Have students freewrite to explore what they think about arguments in general and their own style of arguing. Students can respond to the questions listed with the cartoon, or they can use one of the ideas in the Additional Sketches section as a writing prompt.

Afterwards have students discuss what they have discovered from writing; allow them to quote passages from what they wrote. Ask students to save their work in their Writing Portfolio for possible use in the workshop that follows.

Can you see more than one side of issues? In an argument or debate, how do you decide who is right and who is wrong?

Additional Sketches

Resolved, that the United States should have a king. How would you debate this resolution?

Write a dialogue between yourself and a friend about some matter that perplexes both of you. Start your dialogue by describing what is bothering you. Then let your friend reply, and keep the dialogue going.

206

Persuasion

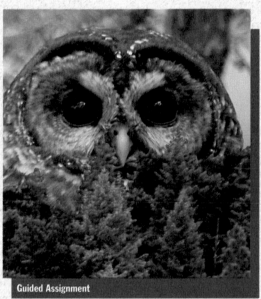

Guided Assignment
ARGUMENT ANALYSIS

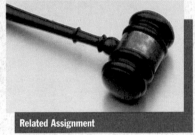

Related Assignment
ESTABLISHING CONFLICT

Related Assignment
DEBATE

Arguments can be used for many purposes. You are probably most familiar with persuasive arguments used to sway readers and argumentative arguments used to marshall evidence in support of one position. As long as you are intent on proving that your view is correct, however, you are not likely to come to see the point of view of the opposition—to look at your topic from an alternative perspective.

In the workshop that follows, you will learn to use arguments to look at a controversial issue from both sides with the intention of illuminating the issue, to develop a conflict between your own literary characters, and to engage in a debate.

207

Objectives

Guided Assignment:
ARGUMENT ANALYSIS
To recognize the characteristics of an argument analysis; to choose a topic, purpose, and audience for an argument analysis; to draft, revise, and proofread an argument analysis

Related Assignment:
ESTABLISHING CONFLICT
To identify realistic conflict in fiction; to write a scene depicting conflict between fictional characters

Related Assignment:
DEBATE
To recognize the elements of a debate; to plan and write a persuasive speech

Teacher's Choice

Guided Assignment
Argument Analysis In this assignment, students write an argument analysis. They build on skills acquired in Workshop 5 and develop their ability to see both sides of a question, an ability that will help them as they analyze and respond to current events. The skills developed in this workshop will help students construct a persuasive argument when they write a literary analysis in Workshop 8. For this reason, the workshop should be presented after Workshop 5 but before Workshop 8.

Related Assignments
Establishing Conflict By deepening students' appreciation of fictional conflict, this assignment supports work they may be doing in literature classes.
Debate This assignment will be beneficial for all students, especially auditory learners: students develop a persuasive speech, relying on their ability to see both sides of an issue to construct valid arguments.

ARGUMENT ANALYSIS

Assignment Rationale

An argument analysis elucidates a controversial issue by presenting the evidence on both sides fairly. In such an analysis, students must suspend judgment while evaluating arguments and evidence for and against various assertions. Skills developed in writing such an analysis can help with the issues students face as citizens of a complex, pluralistic society. In addition, because this kind of writing is common in newsmagazines and books on current affairs, this assignment will enable students to better understand and evaluate what they read.

Starting from Literature

Objectives

To respond to a professional argument analysis as a springboard to writing

Teaching Strategies

Motivate

Have students test the old saw that there are two sides to every question. Divide the class into two teams and challenge each team to come up with three statements of opinion that few people they know would argue with. Then have each team formulate a valid objection to one of the other team's positions.

Tap Prior Knowledge

Have students cite examples of threat or damage to the environment resulting from human activity. Focus on a problem students know and care about. Ask what action should be taken to resolve this problem and who should be responsible.

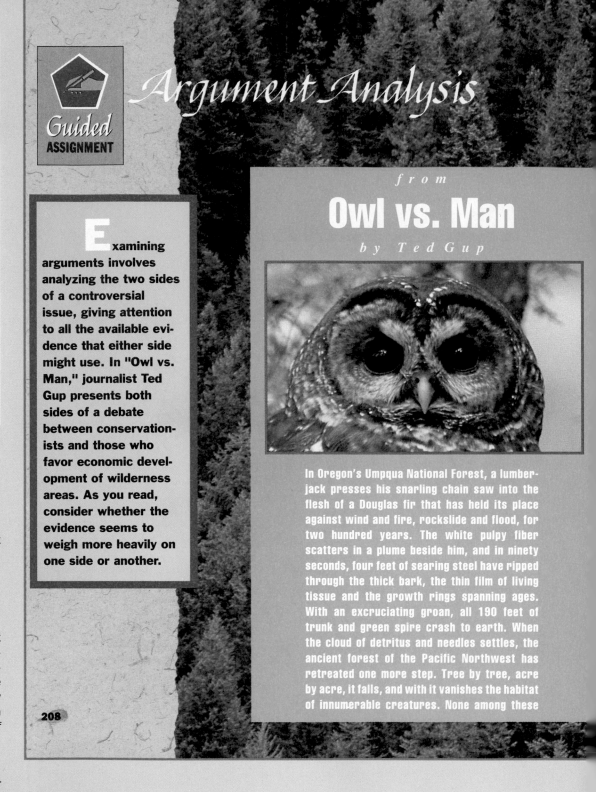

Guided ASSIGNMENT

Argument Analysis

Examining arguments involves analyzing the two sides of a controversial issue, giving attention to all the available evidence that either side might use. In "Owl vs. Man," journalist Ted Gup presents both sides of a debate between conservationists and those who favor economic development of wilderness areas. As you read, consider whether the evidence seems to weigh more heavily on one side or another.

208

from

Owl vs. Man
by Ted Gup

In Oregon's Umpqua National Forest, a lumberjack presses his snarling chain saw into the flesh of a Douglas fir that has held its place against wind and fire, rockslide and flood, for two hundred years. The white pulpy fiber scatters in a plume beside him, and in ninety seconds, four feet of searing steel have ripped through the thick bark, the thin film of living tissue and the growth rings spanning ages. With an excruciating groan, all 190 feet of trunk and green spire crash to earth. When the cloud of detritus and needles settles, the ancient forest of the Pacific Northwest has retreated one more step. Tree by tree, acre by acre, it falls, and with it vanishes the habitat of innumerable creatures. None among these

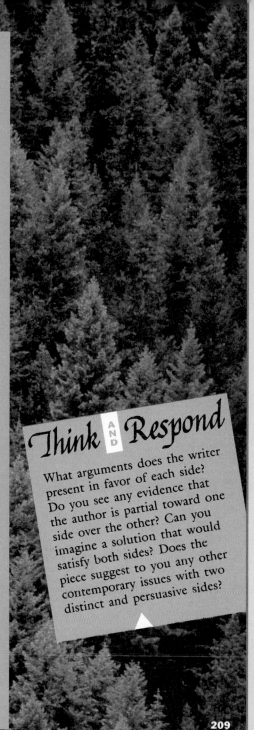

creatures is more vulnerable than the northern spotted owl, a bird so docile it will descend from the safety of its lofty bough to take a mouse from the hand of a man.

The futures of the owl and the ancient forest it inhabits have become entwined in a common struggle for survival. Man's appetite for timber threatens to consume much of the Pacific Northwest's remaining wilderness, an ecological frontier whose deep shadows and jagged profile are all that remain of the land as it was before the impact of man. But rescuing the owl and the timeless forest may mean barring the logging industry from many tracts of virgin timberland, and that would deliver a jarring economic blow to scores of timber-dependent communities across Washington, Oregon, and Northern California. For generations, lumberjacks and mill-workers there have relied on the seemingly endless bounty of the woodlands to sustain them and a way of life that is as rich a part of the American landscape as the forest itself. For many, all that may be coming to an end. . . .

More than a contest for survival between a species and an industry, the owl battle is an epic confrontation between fundamentally different philosophies about the place of man in nature. At issue: Are the forces—and by extension, nature itself—there for man to use and exploit, or are they to be revered and preserved? How much wilderness does America need? How much human discomfort can be justified in the name of conservation? In the Pacific Northwest the nation's reinvigorated environmental movement is about to collide head on with economic reality. What happens here will shape the outcome of similar conflicts between ecological and economic concerns for years to come. It will also enhance or diminish U.S. credibility overseas, as America tries to influence other nations to husband their natural resources and protect their endangered species. From Brazil to Japan, the decision will be carefully observed. The stakes are that high.

Think AND Respond

What arguments does the writer present in favor of each side? Do you see any evidence that the author is partial toward one side over the other? Can you imagine a solution that would satisfy both sides? Does the piece suggest to you any other contemporary issues with two distinct and persuasive sides?

209

Prewrite and Explore

Objectives

1. To use freewriting and other prewriting techniques to choose an argument for examination
2. To use collaborative planning to explore the arguments on either side of an issue
3. To identify audience, purpose, and goals for an analysis of an issue

Preteaching

Preview the Prewrite and Explore section and present any skills or concepts students may need help with in this stage. The mini-lesson references below may help you in your selection and instruction. The cross references in the pupil text will give students access to the same lessons for independent study.

Handbook Mini-Lessons

- Limiting Your Topic, pp. 337–338
- Collaborative Planning, 358–360
- Reading Strategies, p. 479
- Using Source Materials, pp. 482–489
- Research Skills, pp. 499–500

You may also wish to use the Thinking Skills Transparencies; Thinking Skills Worksheets; Fine Art Transparencies: Starting Points for Writing; Writing Prompts for Fine Art Transparencies; and the Data Sheet for this assignment along with *Ideas for Writing* as resources during the Prewrite and Explore phase.

Teaching Strategies

Management Tip

Students who decide to use monitoring as an exploratory activity may forget about it once they are out of class. As an incentive and reminder, ask them to turn in, at the next class session, a list of issues explored on news broadcasts they may be interested in pursuing as writing topics.

INVITATION TO Write

The excerpt you have just read presents both sides of a controversial environmental and economic issue. Write an essay in which you impartially examine both sides of some issue of interest to you.

When you examine arguments, your goal is to analyze both sides of a controversial issue. In some cases this examination will lead you to a proposal for a compromise solution—a solution that is satisfactory to both sides. In other cases you may be led to the conclusion that the arguments on one side are stronger than those on the other. It is your responsibility, however, to remain impartial in your analysis and refrain from drawing any conclusion until you have examined all of the evidence. Your assignment is not to choose a side or to solve a problem, but to illuminate an issue.

An argument analysis can be crucial to legislators who want to be sure that they understand an issue thoroughly before they pass legislation in a related area, to students or scholars who are more interested in understanding a controversial issue than in taking a side, and to judges who wish to make impartial rulings in cases with conflicting sides.

HANDBOOKS
FOR HELP & PRACTICE

Limiting Your Topic, pp. 337–338
Collaborative Planning, pp. 358–360
Reading Strategies, p. 479
Using Source Materials, pp. 482–489
Research Skills, pp. 499–500

PREWRITE AND EXPLORE

1. Look for an issue. Try one or more of the following suggestions to explore ideas for your essay.

Exploratory Activities

- **Monitoring** As you listen to news broadcasts on television or radio, identify issues that intrigue you. Note these issues in your journal.
- **Inquiring** Ask teachers of other subjects to suggest issues that are appropriate for argumentative writing.

Science Connection

Scientific Controversies The history of science is studded with controversies, and their resolutions have often marked great scientific breakthroughs. Have students explore an issue such as the Copernican challenge to the Ptolemaic theory, the wave vs. the particle theories of light, or the debate in biology between Darwinians and Lamarckians. Have them study these controversies as examples of argument analysis at work, and use the techniques of argument analysis to understand the accepted modern scientific position on these once hotly disputed issues.

- **Brainstorming and listing**   With a small group of classmates, brainstorm topics for argumentative writing in categories of your creation, such as current events, life at school, or teen concerns.
- **Scanning**   The excerpt you read at the beginning of this workshop comes from an article that appeared in *Time* magazine. Scan copies of *Time, Newsweek,* and other newsmagazines for possible topics. Also check the letters to the editor printed in newspapers and magazines.
- **Reading literature**   Make a list of issues in literature that have two sides. For example, is Stanley Kowalski, in Tennessee Williams's *A Streetcar Named Desire,* a hopeless, violent male chauvinist or just a man protecting his interests and those of his wife? Do some freewriting about the topics that interest you most.

2. Evaluate your topics.   After you have come up with a variety of topics, you must decide which are suitable for an essay. Do some freewriting about the topics that interest you the most. Share your ideas with classmates. If you are not satisfied with your topics, check your journal for possibilities, consider the ideas you experimented with in the Sketchbook on page 206, or check the "Apply Your Skills" section on page 222. Also ask yourself questions about your topics such as the ones below.

How can I determine if my issue is appropriate for an argumentative essay?

Questions for Evaluating Topics

- Does the issue have two clear sides?
- Do both sides appear reasonable? Can I find strong arguments in support of both sides?
- Can I treat the issue impartially, or am I prejudiced toward one side?
- Do I find the issue interesting enough to spend time on it?

Argument Analysis   **211**

Learning Styles   Although most students may generate ideas best by working in groups, some students work more effectively alone. Make both options available to students. Have magazines and other appropriate materials available in the classrooms for those who wish to work independently and who may, for example, wish to scan for topics while their classmates are brainstorming.

LD Students   Students with special learning problems may experience greater success if they are asked to supply only one side of an argument. You might have such students work with a partner who supplies the other side; the students would then produce a joint essay.

Teaching Tip: Bias

Emphasize that students need not reject out of hand an issue on which they feel biased; they can choose such a topic and approach it as an opportunity to work through or get beyond their bias.

Critical Thinking

Evaluating   Ask students to consider Jeremy's topic ideas and his comments about them. Do they agree with his comments? Which topic would they write about if they had to choose one from this list? How might they reshape any of these items into viable topics?

Teaching Tip: Topic

Point out two traits in Jeremy's topic that mark almost every good topic for an argument analysis: one, the issue is concrete (airport or forest?); and two, it embodies a larger question (conservation or development?). To aid students in their search for writing topics, you may also wish to provide the Data Sheet for this assignment, use the Fine Arts Transparencies, or refer students to the *Ideas for Writing Booklet*.

 Individualizing Instruction

Basic Students   Students may select topics of high current interest, only to discover as they begin their research that the topics are highly technical. This may present particular problems to basic students. Be especially careful with these students in making sure that they select topics suitable to their ability level.

Stumbling Block

If students have trouble getting started with their freewriting, suggest they begin by writing about why they can't get started and what it is about the topics at hand that leaves them baffled or blank.

Jeremy thought of several possible topics for his argumentative essay and evaluated them as follows.

ONE STUDENT'S PROCESS

Possible Essay Topics	Comments
Should a national health insurance program covering all U.S. citizens be created?	Too complicated. Would require more research than I have time for.
Should there be a permanent site for the Olympic Games?	Possible but not exciting to me.
Should employers of workers who handle hazardous materials be required to provide protective clothing?	Too one-sided; no real controversy.
Should conservation or economic development be given a higher priority in our city?	Too general, and I'm prejudiced in favor of conservation. I'm really interested, though.

Jeremy found he was most interested in his last topic. He knew he had to narrow the focus and find a particular issue he could deal with impartially. He decided to write about a controversy in his city. This issue had two clear sides: one favored conservation and opposed construction of a new municipal airport on the proposed forested site, while the other supported the new airport.

3. Freewrite.   Tentatively choose one topic and freewrite about it for ten minutes. Write what you know about the issue, the arguments advanced on both sides, and your questions about the issue.

4. Use collaborative planning.   Share your freewriting with a partner. Discuss and take notes on what you must do to complete an effective argument analysis. Be sure to consider these questions:

- **About your topic**   How can you find adequate information to present complete arguments on both sides? Do you need to make use of reading, interviews, observation, or your own experiences? Who are some experts you might consult?

Writing
—TIP—

It's a good idea to have two back-up topics in mind, in case your first, preferred topic turns out to be unsatisfactory for you.

Springboard

Before students use freewriting to explore their topic, read the following quote from Henriette Anne Klauser's book *Writing on Both Sides of the Brain:* "Giving yourself permission to write garbage is like having a compost pile in the backyard. It might smell a little and even look yucky, but it provides a fertile environment for some great stuff to grow."

Discuss with students how freewriting is like giving oneself permission to write garbage.

- **About your purpose** Aside from providing an impartial analysis of your issue, what do you hope to accomplish with your paper? Do you want to make up your own mind on a controversial topic or provide public officials with a clearer understanding of an important issue? Is it possible that an impartial airing of the issues could lead to a compromise or a solution that would satisfy all parties? How might your purposes influence how you proceed in conducting your analysis?
- **About your audience** Who will read your analysis and what might your readers' purposes be? How familiar are your readers with the general topic? Should you avoid or use technical terms? Will you have to define some terms for your readers? How much background information will you need to provide? How biased are your readers likely to be and to which side and why? What can you do to help your readers give a fair hearing to both sides?

 Writer's Choice Your planning efforts may have shown you unanticipated problems in pursuing your chosen topic. Do you now want to drop your initial choice of a topic and turn to one of your back-up choices?

5. Learn about your topic. Use the library, newspapers, and magazines to read about your topic. Also talk to people who are experts. As part of his research on the airport controversy, Jeremy began by reading newspaper accounts of the controversy, along with editorials and letters to the editor in his local paper. When he thought he understood the major issues, he arranged to interview two of the people he had learned about from newspaper articles as leaders of the two opposing sides: the director of a local conservation group and the president of a regional business association.

6. Look for underlying assumptions. See if you can classify the individual arguments advanced by both sides of your issue under the larger or deeper concerns that account for the arguments. Ted Gup, for example, in writing about the Oregon timberland controversy, found the roots of the controversy not in specific arguments about the fate of the northern spotted owl or the jobs of lumberjacks, but in "fundamentally different philosophies about the place of man in nature." Then he briefly explained the philosophies. What differences in values, philosophy, or outlook on life are at the root of the controversy you are analyzing? Will the differences allow for a meeting of the minds? Why can't a solution be worked out?

COMPUTER TIP

If you have access to a modem, you may be able to conduct some interviews by electronic mail.

 PROBLEM SOLVING

How can I uncover the roots of the controversy?

LEP Students Remind LEP students that they can research their topic by reading sources in their first language and by interviewing people who speak their language.

Collaborative Opportunity

Students writing about similar issues can work as partners to conduct interviews. While one student asks a question, the other takes notes, which frees the first student to listen to the answer and shape follow-up questions—a crucial skill for effective interviewing.

Spot Check

Review students' progress at this stage by making sure they have more than enough information needed for drafting.

Draft and Discover

Objectives

1. To draft a balanced argument analysis
2. To respond to one's own writing and that of a peer

Preteaching

Preview the Draft and Discover section and then present any skills or concepts with which students may need help during drafting. The mini-lesson references below may help you in your selection and instruction.

> ### Handbook Mini-Lessons
> - Comparison-Contrast Order, p. 352
> - Drafting Styles, pp. 361–362
> - Developing/Presenting Arguments, pp. 474–476

You may also wish to use the Elaboration Worksheet and the Peer Response Guide during the Draft and Discover phase.

Teaching Strategies

Critical Thinking

Comparison Have students decide if Jeremy's statement is balanced and then compare it to their own statement of opposing arguments. To check their statement, they might try recasting it with a deliberate bias, in one direction and then the other. Comparing the slanted versions may help them find the neutral point between them.

HANDBOOKS
FOR HELP & PRACTICE

Comparison-
Contrast Order,
p. 352
Drafting Styles,
pp. 361–362
Developing/
Presenting
Arguments,
p. 474–476

PROBLEM
SOLVING

How can I best present both sides of my issue?

DRAFT AND DISCOVER

1. Begin your draft. The next step is to begin writing your first draft. You may use a variety of strategies to elaborate on your ideas, such as the ones below.

- **Narration** You can use this strategy to dramatize the controversy you are analyzing. In the opening paragraph of "Owl vs. Man," for example, the writer presents a dramatic account of a lumberjack cutting down a 200-year-old fir tree.
- **Explanation and definition** Much of an argument analysis entails explaining or defining the grounds for the argument. Even more important than the arguments on both sides is an explanation of why people are arguing in the first place. What values, or underlying assumptions, separate them?
- **Quotation and documentation** You will probably want to use quotations from spokespersons for the two sides of the controversy and to cite facts, statistics, and opinions from pamphlets, newspapers, or magazines.
- **Comparison and contrast** Your analysis is likely to consist largely of an examination of how the claims, goals, and assumptions of two disputing parties compare and contrast.

2. Introduce the issue. You might begin your essay with a narrative, a case history, or a scene. Another alternative is to give the historical background of the issue. Some writers begin by stating the issue in the form of a question.

3. Clearly state the two sides of the issue. Since the purpose of your essay is to examine both sides of an issue, it's important to give a clear statement of what the two sides are. Notice how Jeremy did this in the following sentence from his essay.

ONE STUDENT'S PROCESS

On one side of the issue are those who favor construction of the airport on the proposed site; on the other side are those who want to preserve Millers Woods in its natural state.

---

4. Present evidence to support both sides of the issue. As evidence, you can use facts, examples, expert opinions, statistics, or anecdotes. Try to present all important arguments on both sides of the issue. Remember that your goal is to accurately portray both sides, not to persuade your readers to support one or the other.

 Writer's Choice Which side of the issue do you want to present first? Often the side presented last assumes greater importance simply because it remains fresh in the reader's mind.

5. Organize your draft. After clearly stating both sides of the issue, in what order will you then present the evidence? As you compare and contrast the two sides, will you present all the evidence on one side of the issue, then all the evidence on the other side? Or is an item-by-item organization better?

6. Draw a conclusion. You may find that your examination of the two sides and your analysis of the underlying disagreements (or agreements) has led you to a conclusion. Your conclusion might be an opinion favoring one side over the other, a recommendation for a compromise solution, or a recognition that the underlying assumptions of the disputing parties make any resolution of their differences impossible. You might also conclude by summarizing the issues, leaving the issue of resolution to others.

In the following excerpt from the end of Jeremy's essay, he identified what he believed to be the underlying assumptions dividing the disputants in the airport controversy. Note that his analysis led him to take a surprising stand—surprising because it runs counter to the prejudice with which he began his study.

As you check on students, see to it that they focus on two sides of a single issue, rather than on two different issues associated with opposing camps or styles of thought (conservation vs. development, rather than conservation vs. pollution).

Stumbling Block

Students who begin with no bias might develop one in the course of writing. Suggest that instead of trying to restrain their bias during drafting—which may inhibit their fluency—they should concentrate on giving equal time to the opposing view. They can edit for bias during revision, but during drafting they should concentrate on generating more material, not less.

 ## Individualizing Instruction

Learning Styles Some students have a global learning style: they need to see the big picture before they can focus on details. For these students scribbling off two or three quick rough drafts may work better than painstakingly putting together a single draft.

Teaching Tip: Conclusions

Point out that writers can conclude an argument analysis in many ways—for example, by delivering a verdict, summing up the evidence, or pointing the way for further study.

Critical Thinking

Analyzing Ask students what underlying issues are revealed in Jeremy's conclusion. Have students cite other cases and situations that may be rooted in these same issues.

 ## Individualizing Instruction

Auditory Learners Suggest that auditory learners listen to another student read their work to them aloud. Hearing the words in another person's voice may give them a sense of distance and help them hear the work as if it were new and unfamiliar, an important component of effective self-evaluation.

Managing the Paper Load

Let students who feel confident of their drafts assess each others' work. Spend your time with students who self-select themselves as needing help. Ask them to identify their problem areas as best they can before coming to you. After reviewing their drafts, discuss the major points they should address in revision. Record the advice you give now so you can key in on the same issues when you grade their finished papers.

In a contest between the economic survival of people and that of a woodland preserve I see no alternative to standing up for people—which, unfortunately, means supporting airport construction at Millers Woods. Every effort to find a suitable alternative to building on the Millers Woods site has failed. We have a pressing need to reduce local unemployment and to promote economic growth—both of which the construction of an airport will achieve. At least for the short run, then, I feel we must act on behalf of the basic well-being of people over environmental preservation. In time we may be able to serve both interests without conflict.

Writing
TIP

In your first draft, concentrate on ideas. You will have time to clean up your writing in subsequent drafts.

7. Put your draft aside for a day or so. This allows you to put some distance between yourself and your writing. When you reread your draft, you will be able to evaluate it more objectively. Ask yourself and peer readers the following questions.

R E V I E W   Y O U R   W R I T I N G

Questions for Yourself
- Have I clearly stated the two sides of the issue?
- Have I presented the main supporting evidence for both sides? Have I treated both sides fairly?
- Have I identified and examined the underlying assumptions of the opposing parties?

Questions for Your Peer Readers
- Did my introduction make the controversy clear?
- What are the two sides of the issue? Did my writing give you a greater understanding of each side?
- Have I fairly presented the arguments on both sides of the issue? Does my analysis favor one side or the other?

216   Workshop 7

REVISE YOUR WRITING

1. Evaluate your responses. Decide what changes you want to make. Keep in mind these qualities of good argumentative writing.

Standards for Evaluation

An effective argument analysis . . .

- clearly states the two sides of the issue.
- gives adequate background to understand the issue.
- impartially presents arguments on both sides of the issue.
- attempts to uncover basic underlying assumptions and values.
- concludes by summarizing the controversy or by stating the writer's conclusion about the issue.

2. Problem-solve. Now rework your draft, incorporating the changes you have decided to make.

Jeremy made the following changes to a paragraph from his draft.

ONE STUDENT'S PROCESS

Those who favor construction of the airport on the [concerned citizens] proposed site point to the 20% rate of unemployment. [our city's]

They note that construction of the airport would keep biulding trades workers in our city busy for more than a year. The airport also would provide many permanant [and] [at least 200] [e] new jobs for City residents. Either we build the airport or people will lose their jobs. A study showed that a new [According to] [done by the Chamber of Commerce,] airport would help make our city more attractive as a tourist, and convention center. An increase in the tourist and convention trade would bring more business to—and create more jobs in—local hotels, restaurants, and retail stores.

Can you tell how many new jobs would be created?

Be more specific. Who did the study?

Explain how our city would benefit from this.

HANDBOOKS
FOR HELP & PRACTICE

Unity/Coherence, pp. 382–391
Peer Response, pp. 397–400
Avoiding Wordiness, pp. 406–408
Emphasis, pp. 423–424
Sentence Variety, pp. 439–444
Avoiding Logical Fallacies, pp. 477–478

Revise Your Writing

Objectives

1. To evaluate the response to a draft
2. To revise a draft based on the responses
3. To proofread for errors in spelling, grammar, usage, and mechanics

Preteaching

Identify the skills you want to review based on problems you noted in students' drafts. The mini-lessons listed below may be useful to you for instructional purposes.

Handbook Mini-Lessons
- Unity/Coherence, pp. 382–391
- Peer Response, pp. 397–400
- Avoiding Wordiness, pp. 406–408
- Emphasis, pp. 423–424
- Sentence Variety, pp. 439–444
- Avoiding Logical Fallacies, pp. 477–478

You may also wish to use the Student Revision Model Transparencies, the Revision and Proofreading Worksheets, and the Guidelines for Evaluating Writing for this assignment as resources during the Revise Your Writing phase.

Teaching Strategies

Linking Grammar and Writing

Discuss conjunctive adverbs with those students who need stronger transitions. Help them generate a list of words, including *above all, accordingly, still, in fact,* and *thus.* Point out that such words are like signs on the highway: by signaling which way thought will flow next, they keep the readers from getting lost. See Grammar and Usage Handbook 31 for further details.

Springboard

Students whose work requires a great deal of revision may feel discouraged. Encourage them by sharing this quote from novelist James Michener: "I have never thought of myself as a good writer. Anyone who wants reassurance of that should read one of my first drafts. But I am one of the world's great rewriters."

Guidelines for Evaluation

The following guidelines may be used for a close evaluation of an argument analysis. See the Guidelines for Evaluating Writing in the Teacher's Resource File for additional help with holistic or analytic scoring.

Ideas and Content
- identifies the controversy
- states the case for each side fairly
- explores underlying issues
- presents useful background information

Structure and Form
- opens with a clear introduction
- presents ideas in logical order
- ends by summarizing the issue or stating the writer's position

Grammar, Usage, and Mechanics
- contains no grammatical errors
- uses correct mechanics

Managing the Paper Load

Read the material in the Student Revision Model Transparencies and the Revision and Proofreading Worksheets aloud, focusing on the virtues and problems they demonstrate. Have students use these materials as models to critique and evaluate their own papers. Before the class finishes revising, let them know the specific criteria you will be using for your evaluation.

Publish and Present

Objective

To publish and present an argument analysis

Handbook Mini-Lesson
- Presenting Arguments, pp. 474–475

---

3. Proofread your work. Make a clean copy of your essay. Then, read through it and correct errors in spelling, grammar, usage, and mechanics.

Writing
—**TIP**—
To check whether a word or phrase is redundant, cross it out and see if the sentence has exactly the same meaning without it.

LINKING
GRAMMAR **AND** WRITING
Avoiding Redundancy

Avoid using words and phrases that repeat the same idea as another word or phrase.

Original **People sit idly, doing nothing** and wondering if they ever will find work again.

Revised People sit idly, wondering if they will ever find work again.

HANDBOOKS
FOR HELP & PRACTICE

Presenting Arguments, pp. 474–476

PUBLISH AND PRESENT

- **Conduct a panel discussion on the issue you have chosen.** Meet with classmates who are interested in that issue to plan your discussion. Present your paper orally as a starting point for the discussion.
- **Present your paper as a speech.** Contact an organization that is concerned with your chosen issue and propose that you speak at an upcoming event. Ask your librarian to help you locate appropriate organizations.
- **Send a copy of your argument analysis to representatives of the two sides of the issue you examined.** Ask them if they think you presented the issues fairly and how they feel about any compromise or solution your conclusion may propose.
- **Save your work in your writing portfolio.**

Off the Record

"I read somewhere that Henry Luce hired poets to write on business subjects in *Fortune* on the theory that they could be taught economics easier than economists could be taught writing."
—A. M. Tibbets
from *To the Point*

ONE STUDENT'S PROCESS

To Build Or Not to Build

Jeremy Yu

It's a beautiful spring morning at Millers Woods. The sun is shining brightly and birds are chirping. Some fifth-graders from a nearby elementary school are walking one of the nature trails with their teacher, identifying the various wild flowers they see and eagerly watching for any signs of animal life.

In the Chatham neighborhood on the other side of the city, the sun is shining but the mood is anything but cheerful. People sit idly on their front porches, wondering if they ever will find work again. Some have been unemployed for as long as two years, having lost their jobs in the first wave of layoffs at the auto plant. Others have been out of work since January, when the plant closed permanently.

A proposal to build a new municipal airport on the land that is now Millers Woods pits the interests of schoolchildren and unemployed workers—as well as other groups—against one another. On one side are those who favor construction of the airport on the proposed site; on the other side are those who want to preserve Millers Woods. Although numerous alternate sites for the airport have been proposed, none has been found to be suitable. Nor have proposals to expand the present airport turned out to be feasible.

Effective introduction—utilizes vivid description of site of the controversy

Introduces both sides of the issue—the need to preserve a wild area and the need to create jobs

Have students read the model and list what works and doesn't work for them in Jeremy's analysis. Then have them check for the same elements in their own pieces. If you have not already done so, you may want to provide students with the Student Revision Model Transparencies and the Guidelines for Evaluating Writing for this assignment to help them with their analysis of Jeremy's work as well as their own.

Argument Analysis   **219**

Now that students have completed their argument analyses, you may want to use the Writing Prompts for Assessment for this assignment to give students practice in responding to assessment prompts that call for similar kinds of writing.

Uses statistics to explain one argument

Those concerned citizens who favor construction of the airport on the proposed site point to our city's 20% rate of unemployment. They note that construction of the airport would keep building trades workers in our city busy for more than a year and would provide at least 200 permanent new jobs for city residents. According to a study done by the chamber of commerce, a new airport would help make our city more attractive as a tourist and convention center. An increase in the tourist and convention trade would bring more business to —and create more jobs in—local hotels, restaurants, and retail stores.

City residents who want to preserve Millers Woods emphasize its value as an educational and recreational resource. Each year, thousands of people visit the area to hike, picnic, and observe its abundant plant and animal life. If an airport is built on the site, the habitat of many animals native to our region will be destroyed.

220   Workshop 7

Opponents of the airport also point out that the levels of noise and air pollution in our city will increase substantially if a new airport is built.

Underlying the debate are two different sets of priorities about what is important for our city. The question is whether aesthetic and environmental concerns take priority over the economic well-being of a large segment of our community, or vice versa. There is no doubt that if the airport is built, our city will lose a valuable educational and recreational resource and the habitat of many animals will be destroyed. In addition, we will have to deal with noise and air pollution. These are valid considerations and consequences to be avoided, even at great cost. But how do we weigh the seriousness of these consequences against the problem of chronic unemployment and underemployment for many of our city's residents? Their homes and lives are no less at risk than those of the woodland animals.

In a contest between the economic survival of people and that of a woodland preserve I see no alternative to standing up for people—which, unfortunately, means supporting airport construction at Millers Woods. Every effort to find a suitable alternative to building on the Millers Woods site has failed. We have a pressing need to reduce local unemployment and to promote economic growth—both of which the construction of an airport will achieve. At least for the short run, then, I feel we must act on behalf of the basic well-being of the people. In time we may be able to serve both interests without conflict.

Explains underlying assumption

Draws a conclusion from the analysis of the controversy

Argument Analysis **221**

Reteaching

Assess the needs of students who were not successful in developing an effective argument analysis and identify two or three areas in which additional practice is needed. Assign the appropriate Handbook Mini-Lessons, along with the support materials for each lesson. Concepts commonly requiring reteaching for this assignment are

Gathering Information: Handbook 2
Types of Details: Use Handbook 9

The following suggestions and resources may also be useful:

1. **Uneven Balance** Elaborate on the idea of giving equal time to two sides of an argument by drawing a balance on the chalkboard. Pose a simple premise, such as "Students should attend school all year round." Have students alternate offering arguments on each side of the question; write them on the different sides of the balance to give a graphic demonstration of what a balanced argument would look like.

2. **Faulty Parallelism** On the chalkboard, write examples of sentences from students' work that violate the rules of parallel construction. As a group, discuss what is wrong and how the errors should be corrected.

Literature Connection

Poem to Read For a passionately one-sided statement of a philosophic position, students should read Dylan Thomas's "Do Not Go Gentle into That Good Night." Ask them to look at the poem as one side of an argument, and have them formulate the argument for the other side. They could write it in the form of a poem titled "*Do* Go Gentle into That Good Night."

Learning from Your Writing Process

Objective

To analyze and reflect upon what has been learned about the writing process and the writing of an argument analysis

Teaching Strategies

Reflecting on the Process

After students have written their notes, ask them to share and discuss their answers to the questions.

Writing Portfolio

If students have completed the subject analysis in Workshop 5, ask them to compare their argument analysis to the subject analysis. Encourage them to reflect on how writing the earlier piece helped them write this one more effectively. Ask them to keep the argument analysis in their Writing Portfolio for future comparisons.

Summary and Closure

Before going on to the next lesson make sure students have fully mastered the following concepts:

1. An argument analysis is an objective look at a debatable issue.

2. An argument analysis presents the case for both sides of an argument.

3. An effective argument analysis provides information readers can use to make up their own minds about the issue.

Allow students to summarize what they learned by describing the characteristics of effective argument analyses and by telling why knowing how to write an objective argument analysis might help them in other school subjects.

WRITER TO WRITER

If everybody is thinking alike then somebody isn't thinking.
General George S. Patton, U.S. Army, World War II

1. Reflect on your writing. Write a note about your experience in writing your essay and your present view of what you accomplished. Attach your note to your paper when you submit it or place it in your writing portfolio. Try to address some of these issues:

• To what extent did your analysis lead you to change your understanding of and opinion on the issue you were examining? What new insights did you gain and how?

• Do you think your analysis is really impartial or does it favor one side? Why is that the case?

• How adequately do you think you presented the two sides? Did the need to present both sides prevent you from doing a thorough job with either?

• What part of writing this essay was most difficult and why?

2. Apply your skills. Draw upon the strategies you have used in your argument analysis to complete one or more of the following:

• **Social Studies/History** Write an argument analysis of any controversial issue or public policy debate you have studied in history or social studies class. Look for underlying assumptions that account for the opposition between the two sides.

• **General** Review the issues being debated in the letters to the editor in your local paper. Try to identify the assumptions underlying the arguments presented. What prospects for resolution or impasse are revealed to you through this analysis?

• **Literature** Write a brief analysis of an argument or conflict at the center of a short story, play, or novel you are studying. This might be a conflict between characters, between a character and an external force, or within a character.

• **Related assignments** Follow the suggestions on pages 224–232 in completing the related assignments in this workshop.

Literature Connection

Author Note General George S. Patton is one writer whose sword was mightier than his pen: A leading U.S. troop commander during World War II, he was considered a genius at tank warfare. His published works include a volume of poetry and the memoir *War As I Knew It*.

On the Lightside

DOUBLESPEAK

Please utilize a portable hand-held communications inscriber to input the digital readout that for each alphabetically identified episode will derive a positive informational response.

If you have not figured out that you're supposed to take a pencil and answer the following questions, you are already in danger of failing the doublespeak quiz. *Doublespeak* is a word for deceptive language and double talk. Also known as *gobbledygook* or *officialese,* it often conceals and obscures information rather than clarifying and communicating. See if you can match the governmental and institutional doublespeak below with plain English.

Unauthorized withdrawal

A. ___ frame-supported tension structure	1. toothpick
B. ___ safety-related occurrence	2. used car
C. ___ experienced automobile	3. accident
D. ___ terminal episode	4. firing employees
E. ___ revenue enhancement	5. greeting cards
F. ___ downsizing personnel	6. death
G. ___ unauthorized withdrawal	7. scared
H. ___ wood interdental stimulator	8. tent
I. ___ philosophically disillusioned	9. bank robbery
J. ___ social-expression products	10. taxes

Check the following answers to see if you are an incomplete success (a failure) at understanding doublespeak: A-8, B-3, C-2, D-6, E-10, F-4, G-9, H-1, I-7, J-5.

223

On the Lightside

Discuss with the class why people might use doublespeak. What is gained by using it? What is lost by using it? Have students find or recall other examples of doublespeak that they have seen or heard. Use the opening sentence of *On the Lightside* as a model and have students write their own extended examples of doublespeak. Ask students to make up original doublespeak phrases and to try them out on each other.

Related Assignment:
ESTABLISHING CONFLICT

Starting from Literature

Objective

To respond to a literary model of conflict as a springboard for writing

Teaching Strategies

Motivate

Before having students read the side notes and excerpt, ask them to define *conflict* orally. Then ask how and why conflict is important in literature.

Tap Prior Knowledge

Ask students to cite examples of literary works they have read this year in which conflict between characters has been prominent.

Set a Purpose

Have students read with an eye toward pinpointing the specific places in the passage where the conflict between Laura and Jose is defined most clearly—for example, their interchange about stopping the party.

Related ASSIGNMENT

Establishing Conflict

from
The Garden-Party
by Katherine Mansfield

Conflict is a part of everday life. People argue among themselves; individuals struggle to make important personal decisions; political, social, and religious ideologies clash. However broad or narrow their scope, all conflicts represent a struggle between opposing sides—people, ideas, principles, beliefs, hopes, ideals.

Conflict is a driving force in literature, too. Study the following scene from Katherine Mansfield's short story "The Garden-Party." As you read, think about the nature of the conflict between Laura and Jose.

"There's been a horrible accident," said Cook. "A man killed."

"A man killed! Where? How? When?"

But Godber's man wasn't going to have his story snatched from under his very nose.

"Know those little cottages just below here, miss?" Know them? Of course, she knew them. "Well, there's a young chap living there, name of Scott, a carter. His horse shied at a traction-engine, corner of Hawke Street this morning, and he was thrown out on the back of his head. Killed."

"Dead!"

Laura stared at Godber's man.

224

"Dead when they picked him up," said Godber's man with relish. "They were taking the body home as I come up here." And he said to the cook, "He's left a wife and five little ones."

"Jose, come here." Laura caught hold of her sister's sleeve and dragged her through the kitchen to the other side of the green baize door. There she paused and leaned against it. "Jose!" she said, horrified, "however are we going to stop everything?"

"Stop everything, Laura!" cried Jose in astonishment. "What do you mean?"

"Stop the garden-party, of course." Why did Jose pretend?

But Jose was still more amazed. "Stop the garden-party? My dear Laura, don't be so absurd. Of course we can't do anything of the kind. Nobody expects us to. Don't be so extravagant."

"But we can't possibly have a garden-party with a man dead just outside the front gate. . . . And just think of what the band would sound like to that poor woman," said Laura.

"Oh, Laura!" Jose began to be seriously annoyed. "If you're going to stop a band playing every time someone has an accident, you'll lead a very strenuous life. I'm every bit as sorry about it as you. I feel just as sympathetic." Her eyes hardened. She looked at her sister just as she used to when they were little and fighting

together. "You won't bring a drunken workman back to life by being sentimental," she said softly.

"Drunk! Who said he was drunk?" Laura turned furiously on Jose. She said, just as they had used to say on those occasions, "I'm going straight up to tell mother."

"Do, dear," cooed Jose.

"Mother, can I come into your room?" Laura turned the big glass door-knob.

"Of course, child. Why, what's the matter? What's given you such a color?" And Mrs. Sheridan turned round from her dressing table. She was trying on a new hat.

"Mother, a man's been killed," began Laura.

"*Not* in the garden?" interrupted her mother.

"No, no!"

"Oh, what a fright you gave me!" Mrs. Sheridan sighed with relief, and took off the big hat and held it on her knees.

"But listen, mother," said Laura. Breathless, half-choking, she told the dreadful story. "Of course, we can't have our party, can we?" she pleaded. "The band and everybody arriving. They'd hear us, mother; they're nearly neighbors!"

Think AND Respond

Explain the argument between Jose and Laura and the specific reasons each uses to rationalize the position she has taken. How does Katherine Mansfield establish, or set up, this conflict? Can you recall any experiences in your life that were marked by clear conflict between opposing sides?

Think and Respond

Elicit Personal Responses

Have students discuss their responses to the characters and the conflict. Ask which character they sympathize with more, and why. Have them predict the outcome of the story, and encourage them to find and read the complete story on their own.

Explore the Author's Techniques

The major technique Mansfield uses in presenting this conflict is dialogue. Her description is minimal, comparable to stage directions in a play. Discuss why this method is so effective, and invite students to suggest and evaluate alternative ways Mansfield might have used.

Link Literature to Writing

Point out that establishing conflict involves the use of persuasive writing techniques. In this assignment, students will have a chance to practice establishing conflict in fiction. While dialogue is a strong and direct means of presenting conflict, remind students that most short stories have a greater percentage of narrative and exposition than ''The Garden–Party.''

Off the Record

Katherine Mansfield and John Middleton Murry were close friends—and sometimes close enemies—of D. H. Lawrence, who used them as the models for Gudrun Brangwen and Gerald Crich in his masterpiece, *Women in Love*.

Literature Connection

Author Note Katherine Mansfield (1888–1923) helped revolutionize the English short story during her brief career by focusing on character and mood instead of plot. Raised in New Zealand and educated in London, she married the writer John Middleton Murry. She died of tuberculosis, brought on in part by an impecunious lifestyle.

Guiding Your Writers

Objectives

1. To invent a fictional conflict or fiction-alize a real-life conflict
2. To draft a narrative emphasizing con-flict
3. To publish and present a narrative em-phasizing conflict

Preteaching

Preview the remainder of the lesson. If there are concepts or skills students may need help with, present them at this time. The mini-lesson references below may help you in your selection and instruction. The cross references in the pupil text give stu-dent access to the same lessons for inde-pendent practice.

Handbook Mini-Lessons

- Analysis Frames, p. 343
- Peer Response, pp. 397–400
- Tone, pp. 424–425
- Point of View, pp. 446–449
- Developing/Presenting Arguments, pp. 474–476

Teaching Strategies

 Individualizing Instruction

Basic Students   Basic students may need refresher work in the essential elements of fiction, such as dialogue, speech tags, and description.

Advanced Students Encourage ad-vanced students to indicate characters' personalities and conflicts through impli-cation rather than direct statement and through the control of narrative tone.

A disagreement between fictional characters is usually based on opposing or at least strongly contrasting viewpoints. A realistic fictional disagreement must rise naturally out of the personalities and attitudes of the characters. Therefore, the arguments need not always be logical or reasonable. Instead, your characters may resort to fallacious reasoning and emotional appeals as real people do.

DEVELOPING A CONFLICT

HANDBOOKS
FOR HELP & PRACTICE

Analysis Frames, p. 343

Peer Response, pp. 397–400

Tone, pp. 424–425

Point of View, pp. 446–449

Developing/ Presenting Arguments, pp. 474–476

1. Choose an issue.   Brainstorm a list of situations and personal experiences involving conflict between two sides. Include examples of both internal and external conflicts. You might list arguments you've had, difficult decisions you've made, or meetings where opposing ideas clashed. Select two or three conflicts and do some freewriting about each one. As you freewrite, notice which conflict stirs your creative energies the most. Try to state this conflict in a sentence or two, and use it as the basis of your writing.

2. Investigate both sides of your conflict.   A diagram can help you to discover as much as possible about the conflict you have chosen. Start your diagram with two boxes, side by side. In each box, write one side of the conflict. Then draw additional boxes descending from the two main boxes. In each descending box, write an argument or reason to develop that side of the conflict.

3. Create a situation in which to present your conflict.   How will you present the conflict you're developing? Katherine Mansfield's conflict came to life in a story about a garden party. You too might choose a fictional setting. Another option is to recreate the conflict

---

Springboard

Have two or three volunteers role-play a con-flict of their choice. Then have the rest of the class discuss whether the conflict was pre-sented believably or not and how the presenta-tion could be strengthened. Tell students to keep those points in mind as they write their conflicts.

Social Studies Connection

Encourage students to write fictionalized scenes of conflicts from current events or his-tory. There are two basic approaches: writing about leaders and their decisions or writing about ordinary people caught in historical events.

situation from your life. If you choose the fictional approach, you must invent a setting, characters, and a plot. Be sure the characters representing each side of the conflict have contrasting personalities. Ask yourself, "What type of person would naturally take this position?" If you decide to write a nonfiction account, you still need a setting, characters, and a plot; these can be drawn from experience.

4. Consider an appropriate tone. What tone will your story have? Will it be serious? comic? melancholy? angry? satiric? Choose a tone that reflects the way you feel about the conflict.

5. Reveal information subtly as you draft. Provide necessary information about your characters gradually as they talk and react. Notice how in "The Garden-Party" Mansfield slowly reveals that Laura has a sister with whom she always disagrees, that an accident has occurred, and that a garden party is to take place. Also notice how the conflict is revealed entirely through dialogue. Introduce your own conflict and supporting arguments in a similar manner.

REVIEWING YOUR WRITING

1. Read your narrative to a friend. Ask for help in evaluating it. Does the dialogue make the conflict clear? Does it sound natural? Have you given the characters personalities that fit their points of view? Have you provided enough information about the characters to make them seem real? Have you presented both sides?

2. Revise your draft. Use your friend's comments and your own judgment to make your narrative clearer and more lifelike. When you've revised it, make a clean copy. Proofread for errors in grammar, usage, spelling, and mechanics.

PUBLISHING AND PRESENTING

- **Share your writing.** In a small group compare your writing with others. Which papers showed the most effective use of dialogue? Which conflicts seemed most realistic?
- **Perform the scene.** Stage a dramatic reading of your narrative, and record it on audiotape. Have the actors vary the pitch, tone, and volume of their voices to emphasize the drama of the conflict. Play your tapes as part of a class presentation.

Writing
—TIP—

Acting out the conflict with a partner can provide you with useful bits of dialogue.

Establishing Conflict **227**

Establishing Conflict **227**

Starting from Literature

Objective

To respond to a professional model as a springboard for writing debate speeches

Teaching Strategies

Motivate

Ask for a show of hands on how many students have taken part in debates, either in or out of school. Informal debates may count as well. Ask students to share their experiences, anecdotes, and emotions, and to state how they feel debating experience has helped them.

Tap Prior Knowledge

Ask students how they feel about laws requiring car seatbelt use. Both sides of the issue are likely to be represented in your class. After several students have presented their positions, point out that they have created the beginnings of a debate. Point out, too, that in a formal debate, they would have the benefit of more research and planning.

Set a Purpose

As you discuss the side-column notes, emphasize that the article students are about to read sets forth both sides of the motorcycle helmet issue. Reasons are cited, and proponents quoted, for each side, so that the article reads as if a debate were taking place within it. (Point out that, later in this lesson, students will also argue both sides of their issues, but in separate speeches.) Remind them to decide, as they read, which side of the helmet debate they support.

Debate

"It's a free country." This expression implies that, as a citizen, you're free to do whatever you want. Is this assumption true, or does government have the right to limit personal freedom in some circumstances?

This excerpt from a magazine article addresses these questions in the context of a dispute between motorcyclists and government leaders in California.

As you read the excerpt, think of the bikers and lawmakers as the two teams in debate about personal a freedom. Then decide which position you would argue in a debate.

228

In Bike-Happy Hollywood, Gary Busey's Crash Revs Up the Helmet Controversy Again

Jacob Young and Jack Kelley

Gary Busey couldn't wait to get rolling. The mechanics had finished installing a windscreen on his customized $15,000 [bike], and Busey wanted the big motorcycle right away. So even though Bartels' cycle showroom is closed on Sundays, salesman Gene Thomason opened the Culver City, California, shop to let Busey pick up his bike. The actor hit the starter, waved, then wheeled the custom-painted black-and-cream cycle into the traffic on Washington Boulevard.

As usual, Busey rode bareheaded. Hollywood's tough guys have had a long love affair with motorcycles, and the romance has recently heated up to the boiling point. . . . For many in the growing swaggering fraternity of bikers . . . helmets are for wimps. Barely 100 feet out of Bartels' door, Busey came face-to-face with the consequences of that macho style. As he tried to make a turn around a bus, his 625-pound [motorcycle] went into a skid. Instead of laying the bike down in the direction of the slide, as he should, "Gary high-sided," says Thomason. "The momentum threw him off. He landed on the curb on his back and his head hit."

Busey . . . was suddenly a statistic, one of an estimated 25,000 Californians to suffer serious injuries in biking accidents [that] year. Even as he struggled toward recovery, Busey also became the focus of a new battle over whether motorcyclists should have to wear helmets. . . . The day after Busey's accident, Assemblyman Richard Floyd angrily reintroduced his helmet bill. . . .

"Actors go out and buy these bikes because it's become a status symbol," says Marjoe Gortner, who owns four [motorcycles] and wears no helmet. "All this macho stuff comes into play. You feel invincible on a bike–you're Marlon Brando." . . . Salesman Thomason takes such play-riding philosophically. "We get a lot of celebrities," he shrugs. "They all ride; they all crash." And few wear headgear. . . .

Assemblyman Floyd doesn't care much for how bikers feel. By his estimate, the maimings and deaths from motorcycle accidents cost California $100 million each year, and helmets would cut both the carnage and the expense. The antihelmet forces argue that wearing headgear is a personal decision the government has no business legislating. They also claim that wearing a helmet cuts peripheral vision and muffles the senses, making accidents likelier. That may be so, but in a 1980 survey of Oklahoma crashes the fatality rate for riders who were not wearing helmets was almost six times that of those who were. . . .

Busey's manager and bike-riding partner, Herb Nanas, told a reporter that he believed "Gary would still take a position advocating freedom of choice" about helmets. In the end, however, Busey's injuries seemed a chilling price to pay just so he could feel the wind in his hair.

Think AND Respond

What is this particular controversy about? What position do the bikers take? How does the viewpoint of the lawmakers differ from that of the bikers? Which position comes closer to your own? In what other circumstances might government and citizens disagree about possible limits to personal freedom?

Guiding Your Writers

Objectives

1. To choose a subject for debate
2. To write constructive speeches for each side in a debate
3. To publish and present speeches for a debate

Preteaching

Preview the remainder of the lesson. If there are skills or concepts your students will need help with, present them at this time. The mini-lesson references below may be useful for your selection and instruction. Cross references in the pupil text give students access to the same lessons for independent practice.

> ### Handbook Mini-Lessons
> - Collaborative Planning, pp. 358–360
> - Unity/Coherence, pp. 382–391
> - Developing/Presenting Arguments, pp. 474–476
> - Research Skills, pp. 479–489
> - Debating Techniques, pp. 501–506

Teaching Strategies

Modeling

If there is a member of the school debating team in your class, enlist that student to model the debating process for the rest of the class. Ask the student to give a short talk outlining the debating process, including reading aloud an example of an especially good constructive speech.

INVITATION TO Write

The article summarizes a dispute between California bikers and lawmakers about personal freedom. Write a four-minute constructive (opening) speech for the affirmative and negative teams in a debate about the right to freedom.

Like the essay you wrote for the Guided Assignment, the opening speeches in a debate present the pros and cons of a controversial issue. Arguments, even heated ones like the dispute between the bikers and the California lawmakers, do not have to be disagreeable confrontations. Even strong differences of opinion can usually be resolved through discussion, persuasion, and negotiation. The **debate** is a formal discussion in which rational arguments are put forth on both sides of an issue. In a debate, two opposing groups—the affirmative and the negative teams—express their reasons for supporting or not supporting a controversial proposal or proposition. The constructive (opening) speeches set forth the evidence and reasoning that support each team's case. Participating in a debate is a very effective way to develop your thinking skills because it requires you to look at the same issue from more than one angle.

HANDBOOKS
FOR HELP & PRACTICE

Collaborative Planning, pp. 358–360

Unity/Coherence, pp. 382–391

Developing/ Presenting Arguments, pp. 474–476

Research Skills, pp. 479–489

Debating Techniques, pp. 501–506

RESEARCHING AND PLANNING YOUR SPEECHES

1. Write a proposition. Isolate the proposition, or controversial subject, the two teams will debate; for example:

> Resolved, that in certain circumstances government has the right to pass laws that limit personal freedom.

With some friends, brainstorm for subjects that have two clear sides about which people would disagree. The proposition you write

Springboard

After students have responded to the article about Busey, take a poll of the class's position on motorcycle helmet laws. Enlist a volunteer to write his or her debate speeches on this issue. Then, after that student's speeches have been presented, take another poll and see whether any students have changed their minds.

should state only one main idea. Furthermore, the proposition should be worded precisely so that the debate does not become a quibble over semantics.

2. Assemble your evidence. First, list all the arguments that support the proposition. Next, list all the arguments against the proposition. From these, choose the strongest arguments to serve as the main points of each speech. Then consult books, magazines, newspapers, and other references for facts, statistics, reasons, quotations, and examples to develop each main point.

3. Determine appropriate content. The constructive speech of the affirmative team should show the need for change and the way to change. If the debate were on the issue discussed in the article, the arguments in favor of legislation requiring bikers to wear helmets would be presented. The constructive speech of the negative team should defend current conditions and show why proposed changes would be unwise. Evaluate the information you gathered earlier, and select the material that lends the strongest support to the position of each speech.

4. Outline each speech. Develop outlines you can use to guide you as you draft each speech. Each speech should have an introduction that captures the listeners' interest and states the proposition as clearly as possible. The body of each speech should present the main points in the order of increasing importance, with each main point followed by the supporting evidence you developed and selected in steps 2 and 3. Finally, each speech should have a strong, convincing conclusion that summarizes the main points and restates the speaker's position.

DRAFTING YOUR SPEECHES

1. Use persuasive devices cautiously. A constructive speech is a type of persuasive speech. Therefore, you can utilize elements and techniques of persuasion to make your points. As you draft, you may use either inductive or deductive reasoning, explaining your assumptions and their bases as you go along. You may also choose words whose connotations will influence listeners to accept your position. However, remember that the strength of an effective constructive speech rests on an appeal to the audience's reason, rather than on an overdependence on loaded language and emotional appeals.

Individualizing Instruction

Cultural Differences Issues that are matters for debate in some cultures may be unarguable in others. Community consensuses on issues such as obscenity, school prayer, abortion, and equal rights vary widely within the United States, with some communities being unanimous on certain issues and others being divided. Be aware of such distinctions when you suggest or evaluate topics.

Guidelines for Evaluation
The following guidelines may be used for close evaluation of a debate. A good debate speech . . .
- states the proposition clearly
- captures audience attention at the beginning
- sets forth a rational argument for one side of a debate
- is built on factual evidence
- presents the main points in order of increasing importance in the body of the speech
- mentions major points the speaker expects the opposition to make and offers information or logic to weaken those points
- uses transitional devices to make reasoning clear
- contains a conclusion that summarizes the main points and restates the speaker's position

Science Connection

One of the most important debates in western civilization took place when Galileo defended his theory that the earth moves around the sun. You might bring in Bertolt Brecht's play *Galileo* and have students read the relevant speeches aloud.

Reteaching

Assess the needs of students who were not successful developing an effective debate. Assign the appropriate Handbook Mini-Lessons. Concepts commonly requiring reteaching for this assignment are

Developing/Presenting Argument: Handbook 23
Debating Techniques: Handbook 26

The following suggestions and resources may be useful.

1. Uneven Bias Some students may be hampered by a strong personal bias in favor of one side of their issue, preventing them from doing justice to the opposing view. Encourage them to confer with peers or outside experts who hold the opposing view and to ask their reasons.

2. Inappropriate Tone Too much levity and too much solemnity can both damage debate speeches. In speeches with inappropriate tone, point out examples of diction that create a tone either too flippant or too serious. Tell students that *tone* is another word for *attitude;* direct them to decide which attitude is appropriate to their topics, and to choose new wording conveying that attitude.

Extension and Enrichment

• Find out when the criminal court in your community is open to visitors and when debates are held in local government. Arrange a visit with your class so your students can observe debates that have real-world consequences. If you are near a state or national legislature, higher-level court, or international debating body, arrange a visit there if possible.

• Invite a trial lawyer or local legislator to give a talk to your class on debating technique and the rewards of a career in law or public service.

Writing TIP

Tape the drafts of your speeches and time them. Remember that each speech should take only about four minutes to deliver.

2. Respond to arguments of the opposing side. In a debate, each team tries to anticipate and parry the arguments of the opposing team. In your constructive speeches, you should mention the main points that you expect the opposing side will make, and offer information or logic that counters or at least weakens those points.

3. Make your reasoning clear. Include transitional words, phrases, or clauses that show how sentences and ideas are related. This technique not only helps the listener to follow your reasoning, but also helps you to think clearly and avoid logical fallacies. When you revise, you can remove any of these "links" that seem unnecessary.

REVIEWING YOUR WRITING

1. Ask for reactions. Read your speeches to several students. Ask them to comment on the clarity and effectiveness of each speech. Do the main points and supporting facts, reasons, and examples persuade the listener to accept the position you are arguing? Is the listener influenced by the persuasive techniques you have used? Which arguments seem weak or unconvincing? How could the persuasive thrust of each speech be improved? Can your presentation itself be improved to stress important points?

2. Incorporate suggestions as you reread. Revise your speeches to include helpful suggestions made by peer readers and any new ideas that have occurred to you that will strengthen your arguments.

3. Rehearse your speeches aloud. Are there any series of words that are difficult to say aloud? Are there any sentences that are too long to be said in one breath? Make any changes that will make an oral presentation of the speeches smoother and easier.

PUBLISHING AND PRESENTING

• Present one of your speeches orally to your class.
• If you have strong convictions about one side of the issue of personal freedom, submit your speech in support of that view to the school or community newspaper.
• Prepare a class debate on the proposition. Form affirmative and negative teams. For each team, select the most persuasive constructive speech from all the speeches written for this assignment.

Literature Connection

In *Macbeth,* Act I, Scene 7, Macbeth and Lady Macbeth engage in a debate over whether Macbeth should murder Duncan. Have a male and female student read the scene aloud. Have the class analyze it as a debate.

Sentence COMPOSING

Varying Sentence Closers

Effective writers use sentence closers to clarify or expand the information in a sentence and to add an interesting and unexpected rhythm. Notice the clarity and the differing rhythms provided by the kinds of closers underlined below.

Appositive Phrase	The room was empty, <u>a silent world of sinks, drainboards, and locked cupboards</u>.
	Frank Bonham, *Chief*
Present Participial Phrase	He turned and ran, <u>dodging through the trees</u>.
	Elliott Merrick, "Without Words"
Past Participial Phrase	I seem forever condemned, <u>ringed by walls</u>.
	Richard Wright, *Black Boy*
Absolute Phrase	The parrot was gone, <u>its cake a mess of crumbs and frosting on the ground</u>.
	Shirley Jackson, "Island"
Delayed Adjectives	Our father was younger than the landlord, <u>leaner, stronger, and bigger</u>.
	James Baldwin, *Tell Me How Long the Train's Been Gone*

A. Composing Sentences Use the first sentence in each set as a foundation. Use a comma to join the underlined part of the second sentence to the end of the first sentence.

1. She lay and drowsed. She was <u>hoping in her sleep that the children would keep out and let her rest a minute</u>.
   Katherine Anne Porter, "The Jilting of Granny Weatherall"

2. He had the appearance of a man who had done a great thing. It was <u>something greater than any ordinary man would do</u>.
   John Henrik Clarke, "The Boy Who Painted Christ Black"

3. They were diggers in clay. They were <u>transformed by lantern light into a race of giants</u>.   **Edmund Ware, "An Underground Episode"**

4. He trudged with his hands and tight fists in his pockets. He had <u>his head to the wind and the rain</u>.
   Walter Edmonds, "Water Never Hurt a Man"

Sentence Composing: Varying Sentence Closers

Objectives

1. To combine sentences to form new sentences that contain a variety of types of closing phrases
2. To compose sentences that contain a variety of types of closing phrases
3. To expand sentences by adding closing phrases

Preteaching

These exercises focus on the appropriate use of closing phrases. Some students may need review of the basic distinction between phrases, clauses, and sentences as well as the use of appositive phrases, participial phrases, and absolute phrases to achieve arresting sentences. Refer to the following sections of the Grammar Handbook for preteaching content:

Phrases and Clauses
    Appositives and Appositive Phrases, page 593
    Verbals and Verbal Phrases, pages 594–596
    Using Phrases Correctly, page 602

Adjective and Adverb Usage
    Understanding Modifiers, pages 719–720

ANSWER KEY

12–7 Varying Sentence Closers

A. Combining Sentences

1. She lay and drowsed, hoping in her sleep that the children would keep out and let her rest a minute.
2. He had the appearance of a man who had done a great thing, something greater than any ordinary man would do.
3. They were diggers in clay, transformed by lantern light into a race of giants.
4. He trudged with his hands and tight fists in his pockets, his head to the wind and the rain.

B. Unscrambling and Imitating Sentences

Imitations will vary.

1. The pup was sleeping, and Meg promptly tripped over it, stumbling with a lurching, twisting movement, falling with a desperate grab at the chair and table.

2. They now worked with tools in hand, their boots knee-deep in the muck, their mops sopping up the water, their shovels scooping the heavy mud into makeshift garbage pails.

3. You have to begin by trying to be a self-confident individual, a person fulfilling potential, a person who hopes that hard work and effort will eventually pay off, a person who wants to persist and struggle to achieve as many dreams and goals and longings as this earth can provide.

4. The calf waited listlessly for still more food, this from its mother, and it noticed across the field the large bull chewing lazily on some grass, watching the others.

B. Unscrambling and Imitating Sentences Professional writers often use a series of phrases to create a long sentence closer. Unscramble each set of parts to form a sentence whose structure matches that of the model. Then write an imitation of the model. Punctuate your sentences as the models are punctuated.

1. My mother is waiting, and I nearly run into her, <u>choking with pounding, aching emotions, trembling with a dizzy swirl of ecstasy and fear</u>.
   Richard E. Kim, *Lost Names*
   a. falling with a desperate grab at the chair and table
   b. stumbling with a lurching, twisting movement
   c. the pup was sleeping, and Meg promptly tripped over it

2. She was now standing arms akimbo, <u>her shoulders drooping a little, her head cocked to one side, her glasses winking in the sunlight</u>.
   Harper Lee, *To Kill a Mockingbird*
   a. their boots knee-deep in the muck
   b. their shovels scooping the heavy mud into makeshift garbage pails
   c. they now worked with tools in hand
   d. their mops sopping up the water

3. You have to start by wanting to be a contender, <u>the man coming up, the man who knows there's a good chance he'll never get to the top, the man who's willing to sweat and bleed to get up as high as his legs and brains and his heart will take him</u>. **Robert Lipsyte, *The Contender***
   a. a person who wants to persist and struggle to achieve as many dreams and goals and longings as this earth can provide
   b. a person fulfilling potential
   c. you have to begin by trying to be a self-confident individual
   d. a person who hopes that hard work and effort will eventually pay off

4. Katherine stood quietly at yet another window, this in the depot, and she saw in the distance the lantern mountains <u>glowing gold in all directions, catching the future sun</u>.
   Mark Helprin, "Katherine Comes to Yellow Sky"*
   a. and it noticed across the field the large bull
   b. the calf waited listlessly for still more food
   c. chewing lazily on some grass
   d. this from its mother
   e. watching the others

5. There he stood, <u>tall, handsome, rubbing his hands that were red with cold</u>.   **Virginia Woolf, "Lapin and Lapinova"**
   a. proud, confident
   b. up she strode
   c. accepting the plaque that was inscribed with her name

6. Her china blue eyes were bright as she watched the young couple go down the path, <u>he walking in an easy, confident fashion, with his wife on his arm</u>.   **D. H. Lawrence, "The Shadow in the Rose Garden"**
   a. Art singing in an off-key, cracked baritone
   b. the tall, dark trees seemed welcoming as we let the old trail lead us up the canyon
   c. without a care in the world

C. Sentence Expanding   Expand each sentence below by writing a closer that makes sense and joining it to the sentence with a comma. Write one each of the five types of closers you have been shown. Then compare your closers with the originals on page 323.

1. He grabbed the shield again.   **Martin Raim, "The Cell"**

2. Towser roused himself under Fowler's desk and scratched another flea.   **Clifford Simak, "Desertion"**

3. Halfway there he heard the sound he dreaded.   **John Steinbeck, *The Red Pony***

4. The other shoji slammed open, and unseen, Buntaro stamped away.   **James Clavell, *Shogun***

5. In the fishpond, the hippo belched.   **Leon Hugo, "My Father and the Hippopotamus"**

Application   From a piece of recent writing, select three sentences. Write each sentence three times, adding a different closer each time. Vary the content, length, and structure of your closers. Note how each affects the rhythm and clarity of the sentences.

Grammar Refresher   A phrase added to the end of a sentence but not clearly modifying the intended noun can become a misplaced modifier. To learn to avoid misplacing modifiers, see Handbook 33.

5. Up she strode, proud, confident, accepting the plaque that was inscribed with her name.

6. The tall, dark trees seemed welcoming as we let the old trail lead us up the canyon, Art singing in an off-key, cracked baritone, without a care in the world.

C. Sentence Expanding
Answers will vary.
Application
Answers will vary.

Workshop Overview

Written responses to literature can take many forms, from simple expressions of enjoyment or distaste to complex, scholarly analyses of symbolism or the psychological motivation of characters. In its broadest sense, this kind of writing also includes responses to plays, movies, television programs, works of art, and other creative endeavors. Such writing fosters a greater appreciation of a work by encouraging the writer to think more deeply and critically about its meanings and techniques. In this Workshop, students will analyze specific elements within works and exercise their personal judgment in critically reviewing a work. Workshop 8 includes the following Guided and Related Assignments:

1. **Guided: Literary Analysis**   shows students methods of reading, rereading, responding, and analyzing to arrive at an interpretation of a literary work
2. **Related: Exploring a Proverb**   builds on critical review and analysis skills developed in the Guided Assignment by helping students evaluate the truth of an old saying
3. **Related: Critical Analysis/Review**   extends critical analysis skills by having students evaluate a play, movie, painting, or other creative effort

Preparation Guide

1. Use the Overview above and the Teacher's Choice descriptions on page 237 as a basis for deciding which assignment(s) to teach.

2. Preview the assignment and the teacher's notes. The teaching suggestions and your knowledge of your class's abilities should allow you to identify quickly the concepts that may require preteaching or extra support. The Handbook mini-lessons suggested in the Preteaching notes within the lesson can also provide guidance in this area.

3. Preview the adjacent chart for support materials in the Teacher's Resource File that may be used with this Workshop. Resources are for use with the Guided Assignment unless otherwise noted.

Workshop Support Materials

Resources	For Use With
Ideas for Writing: Data Sheets, p. 15 Additional Ideas, p. 20	Choose a literary work to explore, p. 241
Thinking Skills Transparencies: Basic Category Chart; *Worksheets,* p. 10	Test a tentative interpretation, p. 245
Elaboration/Proofreading, p. 15	Begin drafting, p. 246
Peer Respnse Guides, p. 21	Review Your Writing, p. 248
Evaluating Writing, pp. 15, 40–43	Standards for Evaluation, p. 248
Student Revision Trans., pp. 31–34	Problem-Solve, p. 249
Elaboration/Proofreading, p. 16	Proofread your work, p. 250
Tests and Assessment: Prompts, p. 3	

Professional Resources and Media

Books and Journals

Gerrard, Lisa, Ed. *Writing at Century's End: Essays on Computer-Assisted Composition.* McGraw-Hill Publications, Manchester, Missouri. 1987. (technical writing, argumentative writing, writing about literature)

Matthews, Dorothy, et al. *Writing Assignments Based on Literary Works.* Urbana, Illinois: NCTE, 1985.

Films and Videos

Great Poets and Writers. ABC Wide World of Learning, New York, New York. (180 min.)

Computer Software

Writing an Opinion Paper. MECC Writing Series, Minnesota Educational Computing Corporation, St. Paul, Minnesota. 1983. Apple II, II+, IIe, IIc.

Linking Literature, Writing, and Grammar

The following options may be used to provide students with an integrated language experience. Begin by assigning and discussing any of the recommended pieces of literature, which can be found in most classroom anthologies. Use the suggested strategy to provide a link to the Guided Assignment.

Linking Literature and Writing

Option 1

Starting Point: excerpt from "A Sunrise on the Veld" by Doris Lessing on pages 238–240 of *The Writer's Craft*

Strategy: Use the teaching suggestions on pages 238–240 to lead students into the Guided Assignment.

Option 2

Starting Point: "The Rocking-Horse Winner" by D. H. Lawrence

Strategy: As part of your discussion, have students suggest themes, symbols, or elements of style in Lawrence's story that might make good subjects for literary analysis and encourage them to explain their reasoning. Students might suggest such subjects as luck, money, love, the supernatural, the use of irony, or the imagery used to describe Paul's eyes or Paul's mother's emotions. Emphasize that the story becomes ever richer as it is examined ever more closely. Explain that students may choose this story for literary analysis or another story or work of literature they enjoy.

Option 3

Starting Point: "Digging" by Seamus Heaney

Strategy: As part of your discussion, ask students what elements they would include in an analysis aimed at a deeper understanding of the meaning and impact of the poem. Also ask them to explain their reasoning. Students might mention such elements as the multiple meanings of *digging*, the contrast of past and present, the tactile imagery, and the use of rhyme, rhythm, and repetition. Tell students that they can choose this poem for literary analysis or another poem or literary work they particularly like.

Linking Writing and Grammar

Before the drafting or revision stage of this assignment, point out that literary analyses often contain comparisons. Stress that the words *more* and *most* should not be used with modifiers that are already in their comparative form nor should comparative forms of modifiers of more than two syllables be formed by adding -er or -est. Ask students to find examples of sentences containing comparisons as you write the following examples on the board:

WRONG: The symbolism is more stronger in the last paragraph.
RIGHT: The symbolism is stronger in the last paragraph.

WRONG: The interestingest element in the poem is the imagery.
RIGHT: The most interesting element in the poem is the imagery.

Have students review the material about comparisons on pages 723–726 of the Grammar and Usage Handbook. If problems with comparisons continue in students' work, assign the exercises on those pages for reteaching. Additional practice can be found in the Grammar and Usage Practice Book on pages 72 and 73.

Workshop Management Guidelines

The adjacent chart indicates the number of days recommended for each phase of the Guided and Related Assignments. Stars indicate portions of the assignment that may be completed outside the classroom if time is limited or if teachers wish the activity to be completed by students independently.

Literary Analysis

Starting from Literature—1 day
Prewrite—2–3 days*
Draft—1–2 days*
Revise—1–2 days
Publish—1–2 days
Learning—1 day*
Reteaching—open
Extension/Enrichment—open
Sentence Composing—1 day*

Exploring a Proverb

Starting from Literature—1 day
Exploring a Proverb—1–2 days*

Writing—1–2 days*
Reviewing—1–2 days
Publishing—1–2 days
Reteaching—open
Extension/Enrichment—open

Critical Analysis/Review

Starting from Literature—1 day
Choosing and Analyzing a
 Subject—1–2 days*
Drafting—1–2 days*
Reviewing—1–2 days
Publishing—1–2 days
Reteaching—open
Extension/Enrichment—open

Sketchbook

Objective

To use a series of quotations as a springboard to informal writing

Using the Prompt

This activity is an informal one; as such, it should be ungraded, giving students the freedom to experiment with ideas.

Before students survey the quotations, read them a newspaper or magazine review of a recent popular movie. Ask students who have seen the movie to comment on the critic's opinion and how it is presented. To expand the discussion, have students read the quotations and write the answers to the questions that follow. You might form cooperative learning groups of three students to discuss the quotations, with each student then responsible for answering one question.

Some students might prefer to work on the Additional Sketches, which focus more on their being "critics" as they offer their opinions.

Remind students to save their sketches in their Writing Portfolios for possible use in the workshop that follows.

Sketchbook

*T*he good critic is the one who tells of his mind's adventures among masterpieces.
Anatole France

*D*rooling, driveling, doleful, depressing, dropsical drips.
Sir Thomas Beecham

A true critic ought to dwell rather upon excellencies than imperfections, to discover the concealed beauties of a writer, and communicate to the world such things as are worth their observation.
Joseph Addison

*C*riticism is prejudice made plausible.
H. L. Mencken

What do you think a critic is? What do critics do? What *should* they do?

Additional Sketches

What books, films, or works of art have had a powerful impact on you? Why?

Would the story of your life be presented as a Broadway play, a major motion picture, a made-for-television movie, a situation comedy, or some other form of entertainment?

WRITER'S 8 WORKSHOP

Writing About Literature

Related Assignment
EXPLORING A PROVERB

Guided Assignment
LITERARY ANALYSIS

Related Assignment
CRITICAL REVIEW

Whenever people have finished experiencing a particularly powerful or moving work of literature or art, they often wish to compare notes and responses. Through conversations, groups of readers and writers become a literary community—a community where individual perceptions about literary and artistic works are honored and common values are expressed. In the next assignment, your classroom will function as a literary community as you analyze a literary work. You will then apply these same skills examining the message in a proverb and evaluating a motion picture or television work.

237

Response to Literature

Objectives

Guided Assignment:
LITERARY ANALYSIS
To recognize the characteristics of a literary analysis; to choose a literary work suitable for analysis; to draft, revise, proofread, and share a literary analysis

Related Assignment:
EXPLORING A PROVERB
To analyze a proverb; to write a persuasive argument that reinterprets a proverb

Related Assignment:
CRITICAL REVIEW
To identify the elements of a critical analysis or review; to write a critical review

Teacher's Choice

The following information may help you choose the assignments that best fit the needs and interests of your students.

Guided Assignment
Literary Analysis The Guided Assignment draws on students' writing skills of narration, description, and persuasion and their thinking skills of criticism and analysis. Thus, it may be best presented after Workshops 1, 2, 6, and 7. However, you may want to use the assignment while students are studying a particularly challenging literary selection.

Related Assignments
Exploring a Proverb This Assignment has wide appeal because it gives students the opportunity to prove familiar proverbs wrong.
Critical Review This assignment will be particularly useful for reluctant readers or students who are especially excited by the visual media.

LITERARY ANALYSIS

Assignment Rationale

An analysis is the division of an entity into its parts in order to understand the whole. Analysis is necessary for the understanding of ideas in all curricular areas. Chemists use it as they look at experiment results; home economists use it as they look for ways to run a home efficiently; historians use it as they try to figure out why events occurred. Analysis is also among the most common kinds of writing done in the English classroom. In using this assignment to write a literary analysis, students will hone this critical thinking skill as they break down and focus on specific elements of a work in order to clarify the meaning of the whole.

Starting from Literature

Objective

To respond to a professional model of a short story in preparation for writing a literary analysis

Teaching Strategies

Motivate

Ask students to remember and share times in their lives when they felt "grown-up," only to realize fairly quickly that they were not as grown-up as they thought. To initiate the discussion, you might want to share an event from your own life—perhaps having a "fender-bender" or borrowing jewelry from a parent and then losing it. Focus on the emotional high of feeling grown-up followed by the low of feeling vulnerable and childlike. As students share experiences, lead them to recognize that such experiences are universal.

Guided ASSIGNMENT

Literary Analysis

FROM **A SUNRISE ON THE VELD**

A literary analysis attempts to explain how a literary work communicates a particular set of meanings for a reader.

In the short story "A Sunrise on the Veld," Doris Lessing tells what happens early one morning when a fifteen-year-old sneaks away from his home in southern Africa to go hunting by himself on the nearby veld, or grassland. As you read this excerpt, write down phrases and sentences from the story that you find particularly significant, memorable, or striking in any way. Think about how these help you appreciate and find meaning in the story.

238

The first bird woke at his feet and at once a flock of them sprang into the air calling shrilly that day had come; and suddenly, behind him, the bush woke into song, and he could hear the guinea fowl calling far ahead of him. That meant they would now be sailing down from their trees into thick grass, and it was for them he had come: he was too late. But he did not mind. He forgot he had come to shoot. He set his legs wide, and he balanced from foot to foot, and swung his gun up and down in both hands horizontally, in a kind of improvised exercise, and let his head sink back till it was pillowed in his neck muscles, and watched how above him small rosy clouds floated in a lake of gold.

Suddenly it all rose in him: it was unbearable. He leaped up into the air, shouting and yelling wild, unrecognizable noises. Then he began to run, not carefully, as he had before, but madly, like a wild thing. He was clean crazy, yelling mad with the joy of living and a superfluity of youth. He rushed down the vlei under a tumult of crimson and gold, while all the birds of the world sang about him. He ran in great leaping strides, and shouted as he ran, feeling his body rise into the crisp rushing air and fall back surely on to sure feet; and thought briefly, not believing that such a thing could happen to him, that he could break his ankle any moment, in this thick tangled grass. He cleared bushes like a duiker, leaped over rocks; and finally came to a dead stop at a place where the ground fell abruptly

BY DORIS LESSING

away below him to the river. It had been a two-mile-long dash through waist-high growth, and he was breathing hoarsely and could no longer sing. But he poised on a rock and looked down at stretches of water that gleamed through stooping trees, and thought suddenly, I am fifteen! Fifteen! The words came new to him; so that he kept repeating them wonderingly, with swelling excitement; and he felt the years of his life with his hands, as if he were counting marbles, each one hard and separate and compact, each one a wonderful shining thing. That was what he was: fifteen years of this rich soil, and this slow-moving water, and air that smelled like a challenge whether it was warm and sultry at noon, or as brisk as cold water, like it was now.

There was nothing he couldn't do, nothing! A vision came to him, as he stood there, like when a child hears the word *eternity* and tries to understand it, and time takes possession of the mind. He felt his life ahead of him as a great and wonderful thing, something that was his; and he said aloud, with the blood rising to his head: all the great men of the world have been as I am now, and there is nothing I can't become, nothing I can't do; there is no country in the world I cannot make part of myself, if I choose. I contain the world. I can make of it what I want. If I choose, I can change everything that is going to happen: it depends on me, and what I decide now.

The urgency, and the truth and the courage of what his voice was saying exulted him so that he began to sing again, at the top of his voice, and the sound went echoing down the river gorge. He stopped for the echo, and sang again: stopped and shouted. That was what he was!—he sang, if he chose; and the world had to answer him.

And for minutes he stood there, shouting and singing and waiting for the lovely eddying sound of the echo; so that his own new strong thoughts came back and washed round his head, as if someone were answering him and encouraging him; till the gorge was full of soft voices clashing back and forth from rock to rock over the river. And then it seemed as if there was a new voice. He listened, puzzled, for it was not his own. Soon he was leaning forward, all his nerves alert, quite still: somewhere close to him there was a noise that was no joyful bird, nor tinkle of falling water, nor ponderous movement of cattle.

There it was again. In the deep morning hush that held his future and his past, was a sound of pain, and repeated over and over: it was a kind of shortened scream, as if someone, something, had no breath to scream. He came to himself, looked about him, and called for the dogs. They did not appear: they had gone off on their own business, and he was alone. Now he was clean sober, all the madness gone. His heart beating fast, because of that frightened screaming, he stepped carefully off the rock and went towards a belt of trees. He was moving cautiously, for not so

Tap Prior Knowledge

Ask students who have taken biology to explain Darwin's theory of natural selection, also sometimes called "survival of the fittest." Discuss how this principle operates on animals in their natural habitats. Tell students that in Doris Lessing's short story a fifteen-year-old boy witnesses a horrifying example of natural selection.

Set a Purpose

Have students read the side-column notes. Clarify that although the column begins with a definition of literary analysis, this selection is a short story, not an example of a literary analysis. Explain that as students read they should be looking for details that may help them analyze the meaning of the boy's experience.

Think and Respond

Elicit Personal Responses

Before students answer the Think and Respond questions, suggest they write down one or two things about the selection that seemed most striking to them. Use these responses to initiate a discussion about how these striking elements contribute to Lessing's message.

Explore the Author's Techniques

Help students recognize a few of the elements they might explore in a literary analysis of "A Sunrise on the Veld." Point out the sharp contrast between the boy's emotions at the beginning and end of the story. In addition, help students recognize the author's use of sounds to change the emotional tenor of the story. In the first paragraph, for example, birds call shrilly, the bush breaks into song, and the guinea fowl calls. In the second paragraph, the boy shouts "wild, unrecognizable noises." These reflect the joy and bustle of life. In contrast, the buck's scream reflects the pain and terror in life. Also encourage students to note how the author uses setting and events to convey such themes as control vs. lack of control and the notion of coming of age.

Link Literature to Writing

Point out that often people can write their way to an understanding of a literary work. A story like Lessing's has many layers of meaning and by writing an analysis, a reader can uncover layers beneath layers to gain a fuller appreciation of the work. Explain that students will soon have an opportunity to uncover the deeper meanings of a work through a literary analysis. They may base their analysis on Lessing's story or choose another literary work.

long ago he had seen a leopard in just this spot.

At the edge of the trees he stopped and peered, holding his gun ready; he advanced, looking steadily about him, his eyes narrowed. Then, all at once, in the middle of a step, he faltered, and his face was puzzled. He shook his head impatiently, as if he doubted his own sight.

There, between two trees, against a background of gaunt black rocks, was a figure from a dream, a strange beast that was horned and drunken-legged, but like something he had never even imagined. It seemed to be ragged. It looked like a small buck that had black rugged tufts of fur standing up irregularly all over it, with patches of raw flesh beneath . . . but the patches of rawness were disappearing under moving black and came again elsewhere; and all the time the creature screamed, in small gasping screams, and leaped drunkenly from side to side, as if it were blind.

Then the boy understood: it was a buck. He ran closer, and again stood still, stopped by a new fear. Around him the grass was whispering and alive. He looked wildly about, and then down. The ground was black with ants, great energetic ants that took no notice of him, but hurried and scurried towards the fighting shape, like glistening black water flowing through the grass.

And, as he drew in his breath and pity and terror seized him, the beast fell and the screaming stopped. Now he could hear nothing but one bird singing, and the sound of the rustling whispering ants.

He peered over at the writhing blackness that jerked convulsively with the jerking nerves. It grew quieter. There were small twitches from the mass that still looked vaguely like the shape of a small animal.

It came to his mind that he should shoot it and end its pain; and he raised his gun. Then he lowered it again. The buck could no longer feel; its fighting was a mechanical protest of the nerves. But it was not that which made him put down his gun. It was a swelling feeling of rage and misery and protest that expressed itself in the thought; if I had not come it would have died like this: so why should I interfere? All over the bush things like this happen; they happen all the time; this is how life goes on, by living things dying in anguish. He gripped the gun between his knees and felt in his own limbs the myriad swarming of the twitching animal that could no longer feel, and set his teeth, and said over and over again under his breath: I can't stop it. I can't stop it. There is nothing I can do.

Think AND Respond

How does the boy change during this scene? What causes the change? In what ways does this boy remind you of yourself at age fifteen, or of fifteen-year-olds you have known?

Literature Connection

Author Note Doris Lessing was born in 1919 and raised in Southern Rhodesia, moving to England in 1949. Known for her sensitivity to all kinds of exploitation, she wrote about feminist themes before it was fashionable to do so. *The Golden Notebook* is her most famous novel, written in the form of diaries and notebooks.

INVITATION TO Write

Literary works like Lessing's draw a variety of responses and interpretations from readers. Guided by the activities in this assignment, analyze a literary work in order to explain the meaning the whole work or any of its elements has for you.

Most essays of literary analysis address two fundamental questions about a work of literature: "What does it mean?" and "How does it communicate its meaning?" Through reading, rereading, response, and analysis, you can arrive at your own interpretation of a literary work and account for the ways in which the work produces the meanings you find in it.

The skills of analysis and interpretation are applicable any time you wish to understand a work of literature, a written text of any kind, or any complex situation. For example, social scientists analyze and interpret human behavior whereas marine biologists analyze and interpret the behavior of sea animals.

PREWRITE AND EXPLORE

1. Choose a literary work to explore. Think about works you are studying, writers and themes that interest you, or works that you have already read and found challenging or memorable. You might consider responding to "A Sunrise on the Veld," "The Handsomest Drowned Man in the World" by Gabriel Garcia Marquez, "Ode to My Socks" by Pablo Neruda, or "Miss Brill" by Katherine Mansfield.

2. Learn about the author. A reader's sense of the meaning of a text often depends upon knowing something about its author and the time when the text was written. Consult a reference work to see what you can find out about the author you choose.

HANDBOOKS
FOR HELP & PRACTICE

Reflecting/ Observing,
pp. 331–332
Writing Techniques,
pp. 334–335
Problem Solving,
pp. 472–473
Outline Form,
pp. 826–827

Literary Analysis **241**

Prewrite and Explore

Objectives

1. To select a literary work suitable for analysis
2. To use prewriting techniques to analyze the meaning of a literary work
3. To focus on literary elements to develop an interpretation of the work for the classroom community of readers

Preteaching

Preview the Prewrite and Explore section. If there are skills or concepts students may need help with before prewriting, present them at this time. The mini-lesson references below may help you in your selection and instruction. The cross references in the pupil text will give students access to the same lessons for independent study.

Handbook Mini-Lessons

- Observing/Reflecting, pp. 331–332
- Writing Techniques, pp. 334–335
- Point of View, pp. 446–451
- Problem Solving, pp. 472–473
- Outline Form, pp. 826–827

You may also wish to use the Thinking Skills Transparencies; Thinking Skills Worksheets; Fine Art Transparencies: Starting Points for Writing; Writing Prompts for Fine Art Transparencies; and the Data Sheet for this assignment along with Additional Ideas in *Ideas for Writing* as resources during the Prewrite and Explore phase.

Individualizing Instruction

Cultural Differences   Students may prefer to do an analysis of a work by an author of the same cultural background. If students have difficulty finding such a work, suggest they contact a public library.

Modeling

Whether or not you decide to write a literary analysis along with the class, do choose a literary work that the entire class is familiar with so that you can demonstrate how you would make decisions about the text if you were to write a literary analysis. To begin the process, tell the class which selection you have chosen and explain why you think that text would work well for analysis.

Collaborative Opportunity

Students who have chosen works by the same author might work together to gather information about the author. Suggest that students consult different sources and then pool their information.

Personal Touch

Explain to students how you personally "notice what you notice" while you're reading. For example, you might notice an unusual word or phrase that recurs. Point out that something that catches the attention of one reader often will catch the attention of others because it *is* significant in some way.

Writing
——TIP——

When you free-write, it is often helpful to limit yourself to writing for no more than ten minutes. If you try freewriting for longer periods of time, you may find yourself getting bogged down with decisions that you can make later.

Born Free, by Edwin Salomon (Publisher: Jacques Soussana Graphics, Jerusalem).

Readers of Lessing's story, for example, should know that from the time she was five years old until she was thirty, she lived on a farm in Rhodesia (Zimbabwe) in southern Africa. Her colonial experiences seem to have influenced her work, which characteristically reveals her concern with the experiences of exploited people.

3. Notice what you notice.   The best readers understand that what they notice and wonder about as they read is important and therefore worth recording and reflecting on. You may already be keeping a reading log in which you record your questions, critical responses, and interpretations of the text you read. The following activities are other techniques you can use to focus your thinking on what you, as a reader, notice.

Exploratory Activities

* **Double-entry journal**   Draw a line down the middle of a notebook page. On the left-hand side, write down short passages that strike you as you read. On the right-hand side, across from the passages, comment on what struck you.
* **Freewriting**   Write a quick response to your first reading of the text, commenting on what you found interesting, puzzling, or memorable. Share your freewriting in a small group.
* **Text rendering**   Work with others who have read the same text, and have each student read aloud interesting passages. If someone else chooses a passage you had picked, repeat it. A text can be heard best when it is read in different voices.

Jessica decided to write a literary analysis of "A Sunrise on the Veld." As she read the entire short story, she kept a double-entry journal. In this assignment you will follow Jessica's process in writing a literary analysis.

242   Workshop 8

Springboard

   If students are having difficulty coming up with a topic, suggest that they look through the Table of Contents of their literature book. You might also suggest that students focus on their favorite authors and go to the library to find new, different, or unfamiliar selections by those authors.

ONE STUDENT'S PROCESS

"All the great men of the world have been as I am now, and there is nothing I can't do; there is no country in the world I cannot make part of myself, if I choose. I contain the world. I can make of it what I want. If I choose, I can change everything that is going to happen: it depends on me, and what I decide now."

I guess this is just the way a young man might feel when he feels that his whole future is ahead of him and that he can conquer any obstacle. But something feels very immature about this. So he has to find out soon that he isn't in control of everything in his world. Why should he think he can make any country in the world a part of himself? What can he mean?

". . . and set his teeth, and said over and over again under his breath: I can't stop it. I can't stop it. There is nothing I can do."

Wow! Now I really see a theme clearly! What a contrast from the way the boy felt a minute before, when he thought he could control everything. I'm glad I wrote it down.

---

4. Examine the literary elements. In addition to examining your reactions, think about how the writer manipulated literary elements to create a character, achieve a certain effect, make a point, or convey a theme. To focus your thinking, consider the following elements of a story.

- **Plot** How predictable are the events in an unfolding story? Are there events that seem similar or contrasting? What is the central conflict? Are there events that don't relate to this conflict? Why not?
- **Characters** What meanings are suggested by their names, their descriptions, their way of talking, or their actions? For example, do you think it is significant that the boy in Lessing's story has no name?

PROBLEM
S O L V I N G

How can I explore the significance of literary elements?

Literary Analysis   **243**

Literature Connection

Stories to Read "The Rocking Horse Winner" by D.H. Lawrence and "The Demon Lover" are additional stories suitable for a literary analysis.

Stumbling Block

Students sometimes fall into the trap of giving a plot summary of the literary work instead of writing a literary analysis. To help them avoid this common pitfall, encourage them to focus on literary elements other than plot—such as character, setting, or tone—when they write their analysis.

Critical Thinking

Judging Students sometimes have difficulty in understanding that point of view affects the meaning of a work. Encourage students to classify the stance of a narrator as objective or subjective, truthful or misleading, and limited or omniscient and then judge how the reader's understanding of the text is influenced by the narrative stance.

 ## Individualizing Instruction

Basic Students Have these students work with stronger students who can help them find patterns of language and imagery that point to a larger meaning.

   Learning Styles Allow those students who prefer to work alone the option of using a tape player to record their retelling of the story rather than working with someone else.

- **Setting** Where and when does the story take place? What mood is created? How does the setting affect events? How are physical setting and psychological events related?
- **Point of view** From whose point of view is the story told? Why might the author have made that choice? How much does the narrator know? Is the narrator reliable? Notice that Lessing used an omniscient third-person narrator—one who sees, hears, and knows everything.
- **Language and imagery** What words, phrases, images, or figures of speech seem to be repeated? Do any objects or events seem to have symbolic value? For example, could Lessing's story be symbolic of the political situation that exists in southern Africa?
- **Theme and ideology** Does the story address any universal problem or experience, or does it teach a lesson? Are there other stories it reminds you of? Does it reflect any particular set of religious or political beliefs?

5. Reread and reflect. As you reread, notice how much more you are able to observe. In a five-minute freewrite, focus on how your understanding of the text changed on subsequent readings. Also record what remains unclear to you.

6. Develop an interpretation. To focus your thinking on an interpretation, try one or more of the following activities.

- **Retelling** Working with a partner, retell the story. Vary the story to fit your own style of retelling. After you have retold the story and have heard your partner's retelling, discuss how similar or different your two stories are from each other and from the original. Discuss how these differences may reflect or lead to different views of the meaning of the story.
- **Problem solving** Select a passage that you don't fully understand. In a focused freewriting, explain what you don't understand about it and what you do know about other parts of the text that surround the problem section. Share your writing with a small group who have read the same text.
- **A striking sentence** Select from the text a sentence or a short passage that strikes you or that seems to be very important. Use it as a starting point for a focused freewriting on why it stands out and how it influences your interpretation of the text.

Jessica used freewriting to focus her emerging interpretation.

ONE STUDENT'S PROCESS

I want to write about two closely related passages, and what strikes me about them is the way they almost repeat each other yet say opposite things. The passages are the one that says "there is nothing I can't become, nothing I can't do" and then the passage that echoes it, saying "I can't stop it. There is nothing I can do." These passages contain the whole idea behind the story. That is, the story is about a boy's experience of his adolescent fantasy of omnipotence and his recognition of his fantasy as a fantasy. So it's sort of about disillusionment. Yet it's not clear if the boy is actually disillusioned.

What else do I want to say? I don't think girls have such fantasies of power and control. So perhaps the story is trying to show the foolishness of male fantasies. I mean I think that Lessing is trying to mock male fantasies at the same time that she appreciates the boy who has the experience of growing up slightly. So it's not a put-down of males either, but a showing of their limitations. And maybe of some strength? I want to think more about this. Does the boy's having no name suggest that he could be any boy or all boys at a certain age?

7. Test a tentative interpretation. The value of your interpretation within a community of readers will depend on how much your interpretation can help others see the same text more clearly. This does not mean that your readers must agree with your interpretation, but that they must be able to see how you arrived at it—what evidence from the text will support the interpretation that you advance. To test your interpretive argument and the evidence available, try the following.

- **Nutshelling** Put your tentative interpretation in writing in a nutshell of two or three sentences.
- **Believing and doubting** Share your interpretation with a partner. Provide each other with reasons to support and reasons to doubt each other's interpretation. Consider how you might want to revise or clarify your interpretation.

COMPUTER TIP

Enter into your computer file your nutshell interpretation and all the supporting and contradictory information. Later you can organize the evidence for use in your essay.

Individualizing Instruction

Learning Styles As students choose a planning strategy for their essays, try to direct them to the strategy compatible with their learning style. For example, some students work best when every point has been laid out in front of them; for these students suggest the outline or tree diagram. You may wish to use appropriate Thinking Skills Transparencies and/or Worksheets with these students. Other students work best in a relaxed atmosphere where they are free to bounce ideas off others; suggest collaborative planning for those students.

Draft and Discover

Objectives

1. To draft a literary analysis, using quotations from the literary work to substantiate an interpretation
2. To respond to one's own writing and to that of one's peers

Preteaching

Preview the Draft and Discover section. If there are skills or concepts students may need help with before drafting, present them at this time. The mini-lesson references below may help you in your selection and instruction. The cross references in the students' books will give them access to the same lessons for independent study.

Handbook Mini-Lessons
- Drafting Styles, pp. 361–363
- Elaborative Details, pp. 376–378
- Emphasis/Tone/Mood, pp. 423–428
- Poetic Language, pp. 434–438

You may also wish to use the Elaboration Worksheet and the Peer Response Guide during the Draft and Discover phase.

PROBLEM SOLVING

How can I make sure my interpretation really makes sense?

HANDBOOKS

FOR HELP & PRACTICE

Drafting Styles, pp. 361–363

Elaborative Details, pp. 376–378

Emphasis/Tone/Mood, pp. 423–428

Poetic Language, pp. 434–438

- **Brainstorming for evidence** Using a cluster or a list, write down all the evidence in support of your interpretation. When you think of evidence that would be inconsistent with your interpretation, write it down too.
- **Evaluating the evidence** Review the evidence supporting and contradicting your interpretation. Try to figure out how you can use the contradictory information to revise or clarify your interpretation.

8. Plan your essay. As you think about ways to organize and present your essay, you may want to use one or both of the following strategies.

Strategies

- **Collaborative planning** Get together with a partner and discuss your plans for drafting your essay. Make sure you discuss the main point you want to make in your essay; the evidence in support of your point; the contradictory evidence and how to deal with it; and your plan for organizing your information and structuring your essay.
- **Outlining** Use an outline form or a tree diagram to organize your material into main points and subordinate points.

DRAFT AND DISCOVER

1. Begin drafting. Your writing plan or outline can help you organize your thoughts, but keep yourself open to new ideas and interpretations that occur to you as you draft. Writers often find their best ideas or even change their minds about what they are going to say while they are in the middle of writing.

Writer's Choice To start your draft, you might begin with a thesis statement, with a piece of freewriting you have already completed, or with a brief summary of the story.

2. Organize your draft. As you write your essay, keep in mind the following points for making your analysis effective.

- In the introduction to your literary analysis, identify the title and author of the work you are analyzing, and briefly state your main point.

Springboard

Discuss how these words of James Baldwin might relate to the drafting stage of a literary analysis: "When you're writing, you're trying to find out something which you don't know. The whole language of writing for me is finding out what you don't want to know, what you don't want to find out. But something forces you to anyway."

- Provide enough of a summary of the work so that your essay will be clear to readers unfamiliar with the work. Avoid giving a detailed plot summary.
- Show your reader how you get from the words in the literary text to your interpretation. Use quotations from the text to show that your claims are valid, but don't count on quotations alone. Explain how the quotations support the claims you make about the text.
- Don't misrepresent your understanding of a literary work for the sake of a convenient interpretation. Sometimes a work of literature will reflect two opposing value systems or suggest two contradictory views of human nature. Let your interpretation reflect such complexities; discuss and analyze the conflicting ideas you find.
- Don't avoid evidence that may seem to contradict your interpretation. Tell how you account for such evidence, or acknowledge the plausibility of an alternative interpretation. If you can dispute the evidence, do so.

Notice that Jessica began her draft with an opening paragraph that gave the title and author of the literary work and also stated her main point.

ONE STUDENT'S PROCESS

Doris Lessing's short story "A Sunrise on the Veld" is an initiation story about one dramatic moment during one morning in the life of a fifteen-year-old boy—a moment that forces the boy to begin the process of maturing into an adult. Although the story focuses on one person, the events in the boy's life represent experiences that are universal. During a moment of joy and confidence, the boy suddenly encounters pain and death, and he begins to change and mature. This experience is like the experiences that all persons must have in order to move into adulthood.

3. Reread and reflect. When you review your essay, ask yourself the following questions. Have your peer readers respond also.

Sunset over Lake Kou, Burkina Faso, West Africa

Literary Analysis **247**

Teaching Strategies

Individualizing Instruction

LD Students For those students who have difficulty writing with pencil or pen, have them dictate their draft to a volunteer or allow them to use a typewriter or word processor in class if possible.

Critical Thinking

Analysis Ask students to identify the salient points in Jessica's draft beginning. Guide students to recognize that she makes a transition from the one boy in the story to the more universal theme of all boys.

Revise Your Writing

Objectives

1. To review and evaluate the responses to the first draft of a literary analysis
2. To revise the draft based on an assessment of the responses
3. To proofread for errors in spelling, grammar, usage, and mechanics

Preteaching

Preview the Revise Your Writing section. Based on this preview and on problems you may have noted in students' drafts, identify skills you want to review. The mini-lessons listed below may prove helpful. The cross references in the pupil text will give them access to the same lessons for independent study.

Handbook Mini-Lessons
- Unity/Coherence, pp. 382–391
- Peer Response, pp. 397–400
- Using Source Materials, pp. 482–489

You may also wish to use the Student Revision Model Transparencies, the Revision and Proofreading Worksheets, and the Guidelines for Evaluating Writing for this assignment as resources during the Revise Your Writing phase.

Teaching Strategies

Individualizing Instruction

LEP Students After assessing individual needs, you might want to suggest that LEP students focus on only one or two of the evaluation criteria to keep them from being overwhelmed.

REVIEW YOUR WRITING

Questions for Yourself
- Does my essay say what I want it to say?
- Is the writing unified, or did I change my mind or wander as I wrote?
- Have I provided evidence from the text—including quotations—to support my interpretation?
- Have I acknowledged the possibility that the story can be interpreted in another way and explained why I have interpreted it my way?

Questions for Your Peer Readers
- Do I give enough of a summary of the story so you can follow it? Do I tell you more than you need to know?
- What is the main idea of my interpretation?
- Summarize the evidence I present for my interpretation.
- What confirming or contradicting evidence to my interpretation did I leave out?
- Are you persuaded that my interpretation is the most plausible one? Why or why not?
- What questions remain for you about my paper?

REVISE YOUR WRITING

HANDBOOKS
FOR HELP & PRACTICE

Unity/Coherence, pp. 382–391
Peer Response, pp. 397–400
Using Source Materials, pp. 482–489

1. Evaluate your responses. Be sure to treat the responses of your readers as information about their reading of your draft and not as the last word on what you need to do. Trust yourself as a reader too. As you decide what to do, keep in mind these guidelines, which are often used to evaluate literary analyses.

Standards for Evaluation

An effective literary analysis . . .

- identifies clearly the title and author of the literary text.
- presents an interpretation of a literary text that clarifies the meaning of the text or reveals how the text operates.

- provides textual evidence for the interpretation it advances and shows how the evidence supports the interpretation.
- takes into account any plausible alternative interpretations and any contradictory evidence.

2. Problem-solve. Taking into account your review of your paper and the responses of your readers, revise your paper. Jessica responded to suggestions from her peer readers this way.

ONE STUDENT'S PROCESS

Two particular passages in the story echo one another

ironically to reveal the theme of the story and the

—unnamed because he could be any boy—

content of the lesson that the unnamed boy has to learn.

Here is the first of these passages. *reflects the boy's sense of his own power and approaching manhood:*

"There was nothing he couldn't do, nothing! . . . He felt

his life ahead of him as a great and wonderful thing,

; and he said aloud, with the blood rising to his head: all the great men of the world have been as I am now, and there is nothing I can't become, nothing I can't do;

something that was his . . . If I choose, I can change

everything that is going to happen: it depends on me,

and what I decide now."

Almost immediately after uttering these words to

himself, he is drawn by a scream of pain to a nearby

being devoured alive by a thick swarm of black ants.

wooded area where he discovers a young buck. Moved by

pity for the helpless buck, he considers shooting it to end

its misery, but decides not to. Recognizing that he is
                                                        s
merely witnessing a natural event, one that perhaps he

no right to interfere with.

Is it significant that he is unnamed?

Nice choice of quotations. Could you include more to clarify the boy's feelings?

Shouldn't you tell why the buck is screaming?

Good that you've shown the conflict he's beginning to feel.

Using the comments written alongside Jessica's analysis, demonstrate for students how you would go about evaluating the comments and how (or whether) you would act upon them. You might also want to use the Student Revision Model Transparency and the Elaboration, Revision, and Proofreading Worksheets. The Guidelines for Evaluating Writing may also be useful in helping students recognize the elements of an effective literary analysis.

Guidelines for Evaluation

The following guidelines may be used for a close evaluation of a literary analysis. See the Guidelines for Evaluating Writing in the Teacher's Resource File for additional help with holistic or analytic scoring.

Ideas and Content
- gives a plausible interpretation that clarifies the meaning of a literary text
- provides adequate summary information for readers unfamiliar with the work
- reveals how the text operates
- provides evidence including quotations from the text to support interpretations
- accounts for alternative interpretations and contradictory evidence

Structure and Form
- identifies the title and author of the literary work
- states the main idea in a clear introduction
- uses a logical organization to convey interpretations and reasoning
- uses paragraphs in which key ideas are supported by clearly related, supporting ideas

Grammar, Usage, and Mechanics
- incorporates standard grammar and usage
- uses correct punctuation
- uses correct spelling

Speaking and Listening

Before students do their final proofreading, suggest that they read their analysis aloud to a peer. Being conscious of how their analysis sounds to an audience should help students find rough spots in their essays.

Publish and Present

Objective

To publish and present a literary analysis

Handbook Mini-Lesson
• Preparing Manuscript, pp. 414–415

Teaching Strategies

Cooperative Learning

Students who analyzed works by the same author might work together to produce a booklet of these essays. Each person in the group should be responsible for some aspect of the booklet. For example, a student with artistic tendencies could produce a cover; a student with good organizational skills could arrange the analyses and produce the table of contents; and a student with good manipulative skills could bind the book together.

Grammar —TIP—

Remember to place quotation marks at the beginning and end of short passages that you are quoting.

HANDBOOKS
FOR HELP & PRACTICE

Preparing Manuscript, pp. 414–415

3. Proofread your work. Reread your revised draft aloud at least twice, listening for places where your reading stumbles. Your ear can help you hear where your essay may need additional editing. Then correct any mechanical errors that you see.

LINKING
GRAMMAR AND WRITING
Long Quotations

In a literary analysis, long quotations—usually those of four lines or more—should be set off from the text. Double-space the quotation, indent from the left, do not use quotation marks, and place the page reference in parentheses after the final period.

> The urgency, and the truth and the courage of what his voice was saying exulted him so that he began to sing again, at the top of his voice, and the sound went echoing down the river gorge. (159)

See Grammar Handbook 41, pages 807–815 for additional help with quotations.

PUBLISH AND PRESENT

• **Collect essays on a particular author in a single volume.** Place it in the school or classroom library as a reference work for other interested students.
• **Exchange essays.** If students in another class have read and written about the same literary works, trade literary analyses and see how the interpretations of their community of writers differs from yours.
• **Read your essay aloud.** The best audience would be composed of people who have read your chosen literary work.
• **Participate in a read-around.** Meet with other writers who have written about the same text. Pass the papers around in a circle until everyone has had a chance to read one another's paper. Use the papers as the basis for a round-table discussion of the literary text.
• **Save your literary analysis in your writing portfolio.**

250   Workshop 8

Off the Record

"The only sensible ends of literature are, first, the pleasurable toil of writing; second, the gratification of one's family and friends; and, lastly, the solid cash."

—Nathaniel Hawthorne

ONE STUDENT'S PROCESS

The Dawning of Awareness

Jessica Schaeffer

Doris Lessing's short story "A Sunrise on the Veld" is an initiation story about one dramatic moment during one morning in the life of a fifteen-year-old boy—a moment that forces the boy to begin the process of maturing into an adult. Although the story focuses on one person, the events in the boy's life represent experiences that are universal. During a moment of joy and confidence, the boy suddenly encounters pain and death, and he begins to change and mature. This experience is like the experiences that all persons must have in order to move into adulthood. In addition, the story may have even a larger message since the boy is from a white family in southern Africa. Perhaps his story might be representative of the white males who govern southern Africa.

On the morning portrayed in the story, the boy comes across a young buck with a broken leg that is being eaten alive by ants. The boy is shocked and sickened by the sight of the suffering animal and is forced to recognize how little control he has over the world and its tragic and cruel forces.

Two particular passages in the story echo one another ironically to reveal the theme of the story and the content of the lesson that the unnamed boy—unnamed because he could be any boy—has to learn. The first of these passages reflects the boy's sense of his own power and approaching manhood.

> There was nothing he couldn't do, nothing! . . . He felt his life ahead of him as a great and wonderful thing, something that was his; and he said aloud, with the blood rising to his head: all the great men of the world have been as I am now, and there is nothing I can't become, nothing I can't do; . . . If I choose, I can change everything that is going to happen: it depends on me, and what I decide now. (25)

Mentions title, author, and theme immediately

Presents larger theme—the boy represents an exploitive government

Provides short summary of important plot event

Includes interpretation of subsequent quotation

Cites quotation that supports interpretation

Literary Analysis   **251**

Reteaching

Assess the needs of students who were not successful in developing an effective literary analysis and identify two or three areas in which additional practice is needed. Assign the appropriate Handbook Mini-Lessons, along with the support materials for each lesson. Concepts commonly requiring reteaching for this assignment are

Elaboration Details/Specific Examples/ Quotations: Handbook 9
Coherence Within Paragraphs: Handbook 10

The following suggestions and resources may also be useful.

1. Poor Support for Interpretations Point out that in explaining an interpretation writers should be able to break down their reasoning into a "what and why" format; they should be able to explain what they think and why they think it. Give students a concrete example of this, using a premise from Jessica's literary analysis. You might, for example, discuss Jessica's premise that "The first of these passages reflects the boy's sense of his own power" and the way she uses a quotation to support this premise. Ask students to list their key premises and the text references or ideas they can use to support them.

2. Ineffective Use of Quotations Some of your students may have used a series of quotes without effectively relating them to key ideas. Model for students the thinking process you would use to relate the passages Jessica has selected to the key ideas she presents. You might read the second quote, for example, and say: "I recall that just a few moments ago the boy felt all-powerful. When I read this passage, I see that he now realizes there are things he cannot prevent. I see that the boy has progressed from adolescence to a new maturity."

Gives descriptive details of pivotal event in plot

Almost immediately after uttering these words to himself, he is drawn by a scream of pain to a nearby wooded area where he discovers a young buck being devoured alive by a thick swarm of black ants. Moved by pity for the helpless buck, he considers shooting it to end its misery, but decides not to, recognizing that he is merely witnessing a natural event, one that perhaps he has no right to interfere with.

Supports interpretation of boy's growing awareness with quotation

> ... if I had not come it would have died like this: so why should I interfere? All over the bush things like this happen; they happen all the time; ... He gripped the gun between his knees and felt in his own limbs the myriad swarming that the twitching animal could no longer feel, and set his teeth, and said over and over again under his breath: I can't stop it. I can't stop it. There is nothing I can do. (26)

Relates two passages and draws conclusions

The last line of the passage above is an ironic echo of the boy's reflection a few moments earlier that "there is ... nothing I can't do." Moving from his adolescent fantasy of power to recognition of helplessness represents the beginning of his progression into manhood. Until that moment, Lessing seems to be saying, the boy's development was in the direction of a false sense of unlimited control and power.

Summarizes evidence that was given above

Uses author's background to substantiate interpretation

Given the southern African setting of the story and Lessing's position as an opponent of all forms of exploitation, it is almost impossible not to read the story as a political parable. Perhaps Lessing sees the adolescent, white, southern African boy as a representative of the society into which he was born—a society dominated by a distinctly male sense of power and control. The boy's identification with "all the great men of the world" links him with an even larger tradition of the male ambition for control over other humans and nature.

Provides symbolic interpretation

Concludes by tying the ideas in the essay together

Whether we read this story as an account of one boy's experience or of a country's experience, the character's recognition that he is not omnipotent indicates that the possibility for growth and change always exists in life.

252   Workshop 8

LEARNING FROM YOUR WRITING PROCESS

WRITER TO WRITER

Criticism, analysis, reflection is a natural response to the existence in the world of works of art. . . . Without it, works of art would appear in a vacuum, as if they had no relation to the minds experiencing them. It would be a dismal, unthinkable world with these shooting stars arousing no comment, leaving no trace.

Elizabeth Hardwick, novelist

Elizabeth Hardwick,
American novelist

1. Reflect on your writing. As an introduction to your essay, write a note to your reader telling the story of the writing of your essay. Tell about which activities helped you most in developing your interpretation, whose responses or ideas may have influenced you, and how your essay developed through the stages of the writing process. Now that you have read other literary analyses, tell what changes you would make to yours. Attach your note to your essay when you submit it to your teacher.

2. Apply your skills. Use your skills to do an interpretive analysis of one of the following:

- **General** Write an essay that analyzes and interprets the social significance of the seating pattern of students in the school cafeteria.
- **Cross-curricular** Write an essay that analyzes and interprets an eyewitness account of a historical event, such as the shots fired on Lexington Green, or a historical document, such as the Gettysburg Address.
- **Literature** Write an essay that analyzes and interprets a poem such as "The Tyger" by William Blake or "Hope" by Emily Brontë. Remember that interpreting symbols is often an important part of any analysis of a poem.
- **Related assignments** Using the suggestions on pages 256–264, write an analysis of a proverb or a review of a movie or television show.

Literary Analysis **253**

Social Studies Connection

The Media Students interested in current events might use their analysis skills to compare and contrast two articles about the same event. For example, students could compare the coverage in a newspaper with the coverage in a weekly magazine and explain the differences in the depth of analysis in each article.

Learning from Your Writing Process

Objective

To analyze and reflect on what students have learned about the writing process and about the writing of a literary analysis.

Teaching Strategies

Reflecting on the Process

You may want to model an introduction that reflects on your own process of writing a literary analysis.

Writing Portfolio

Have students write the note and attach it to their literary analysis. Before students place their work in their Writing Portfolio, suggest that they indicate the most important insight mentioned in their note, perhaps by starring the comment.

Summary and Closure

Before proceeding to the next lesson, be sure that students have internalized the following key points:

1. Analysis techniques are used in everyday life and in curricular areas other than literature.

2. Backing up an interpretation with evidence is necessary for an accurate literary analysis.

3. An effective literary analysis gives the writer and the readers meaningful insights into a literary text.

Allow students time to summarize what they learned by describing the characteristics of an effective literary analysis and by telling why knowing how to write a literary analysis might help them in other school subjects.

Starting from Literature

Objective

To respond to a professional model as a springboard for writing

Teaching Strategies

Motivate

Point out that a *proverb* is "a short saying expressing a well-known truth"; "Too many cooks spoil the broth" is one example. Ask students to discuss proverbs that have affected their lives. Which have they heard their parents and grandparents repeat? Which have affected the way they were raised?

Tap Prior Knowledge

Ask students to restate in their own words the proverb "Spare the rod and spoil the child." Encourage students who believe the proverb contains a large or small element of truth to provide illustrative examples. Ask students whether they believe that the proverb has affected the way some or many parents treated their children.

Set a Purpose

In discussing the side-column notes, point out that exploring proverbs allows us to probe and question the conventional wisdom of established authority. Explain that the article students will read evaluates a proverb to see whether it holds true in the light of modern findings. Tell students that the author states his main point at the beginning of the article; remind them that, after they have discovered it, they should note the facts and details he uses to support it.

Related ASSIGNMENT

Exploring a Proverb

"You Know What They Say..."

by Alfie Kohn, *Psychology Today*

"**A**ctions speak louder than words." "The early bird catches the worm." You have probably heard proverbs like these all your life. Such sayings seem to express undeniable truths about the way people act or feel. However, you may well wonder if these age-old sayings are still true. Do actions still speak louder than words? Does the early bird catch the worm every time?

The excerpt you are about to read questions the truth of a different proverb, "Spare the rod and spoil the child." As you read, notice the evidence the author uses to make his main point.

"Spare the rod and spoil the child." Few proverbs have been so thoroughly disproved—or have caused so much harm—as this one. Nearly 40 years of research have shown conclusively that the "rod" produces children who are more aggressive than their peers. "Physical punishment teaches that the way to solve problems is to beat up others," says Leonard Eron, a research psychologist at the University of Illinois at Chicago. He and others explain that having children focus on what they did wrong and why it was wrong encourages them to internalize control of their own actions. But physical punishment, while suppressing misbehavior in the short run, ultimately promotes nothing more than a determination to avoid getting caught.

In 1960 Eron and his colleagues studied 870 8-year-olds in rural New York and found a clear-cut relationship between the severity of the physical punishment they received—ranging from none at all to slaps and spankings—and how aggressive other children judged them to be. Twenty-two years later, the researchers tracked down some of these same people and found that the aggressive kids were now aggressive adults. And those adults now had aggressive children of their own.

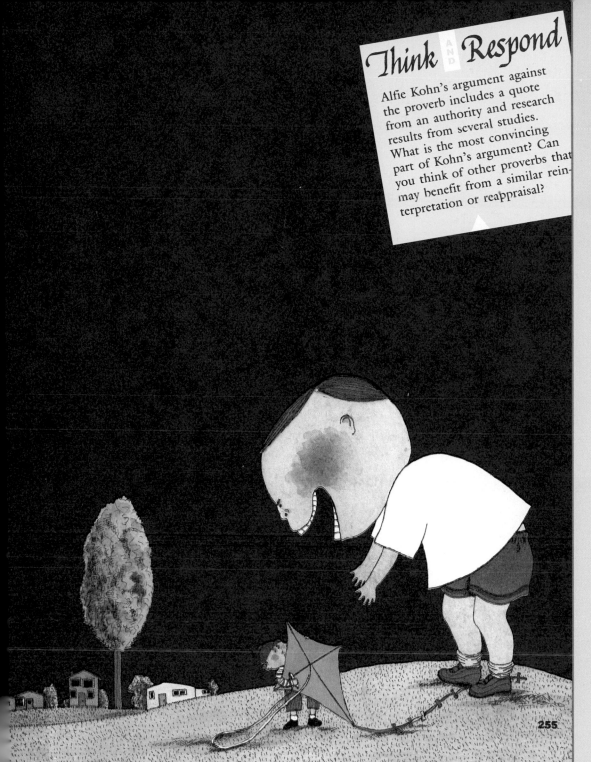

Think and Respond

Alfie Kohn's argument against the proverb includes a quote from an authority and research results from several studies. What is the most convincing part of Kohn's argument? Can you think of other proverbs that may benefit from a similar reinterpretation or reappraisal?

Elicit Personal Responses

Have students freewrite their responses to Alfie Kohn's article, including their feelings about the proverb "Spare the rod and spoil the child." Then discuss students' responses as a class.

Explore the Author's Techniques

To assist students in using the model, point out that Kohn structures his article as an inductive argument, presenting several specific pieces of evidence that support his general conclusion. As evidence, he includes a quotation from an expert in psychology, refers to the statements of other experts, and presents a synopsis of a study impressive in scope, following 870 subjects, some for a period of twenty-two years. Encourage students to structure their arguments with equal care, choosing either inductive or deductive logic and selecting strong evidence. Though they do not have time for an extensive review of psychological and sociological research, they can draw on news stories and on their own experiences.

Link Literature to Writing

Point out that exploring a proverb, like writing a literary review, involves the skills of analysis and evaluation. Stress the importance of applying those skills, rather than simply accepting an idea because it is familiar or traditional. As the Think and Respond questions imply, there is more than one way to explore a proverb; remind students that proverbs can be reinterpreted for modern times without being completely discarded. "Spare the rod and spoil the child," for example, can now be a call for firm discipline rather than corporal punishment.

Literature Connection

Many proverbs represent folk wisdom, but others were written by individual authors; for example, Oliver Goldsmith's "God tempers the wind to the shorn lamb" and Shakespeare's "This above all, to thine own self be true" and "Neither a borrower nor a lender be" (both from the same speech of Polonius in *Hamlet,* Act I, Scene 3). Encourage students to be alert for other proverbs as they read such classics of British literature as Sir Francis Bacon's essays, Shakespeare's plays and sonnets, and the writings of Alexander Pope.

Guiding Your Writers

Objectives

1. To use brainstorming to choose a proverb
2. To explore the proverb through writing
3. To publish and present an exploration of a proverb

Preteaching

Preview the remainder of the lesson at this time, and present any skills or concepts your students will need help with. The handbook mini-lessons listed below may help you in your selection and instruction. The cross references in the pupil text give students access to the same lessons for independent practice.

Handbook Mini-Lessons

- Sharing Techniques, pp. 335–336
- Introducing Nonfiction, pp. 365–368
- Peer Response, pp. 397–400
- Problem Solving, pp. 472–474
- Developing/Presenting Arguments, pp. 474–477

Teaching Strategies

Personal Touch

If there is a proverb that has guided you through life—or one that you decisively reject—share it with the class and discuss your reasons.

INVITATION TO Write

The excerpt you just read claims that the proverb "Spare the rod and spoil the child" has been thoroughly discredited by research. Analyzing a proverb of your own choice, present a persuasive argument that it, too, should be reinterpreted.

For generations, truths about human nature have been handed down in the form of proverbs. Human nature hasn't changed so much over the years, and many of the old sayings still ring true. However, our familiarity with these proverbs sometimes prevents us from taking a critical look at how traditional sayings apply to current situations. The skills of critical review and analysis can help you discover how much truth a particular proverb still contains.

HANDBOOKS
FOR HELP & PRACTICE

Sharing Techniques, pp. 335–336
Introducing Nonfiction, pp. 365–368
Peer Response, pp. 397–401
Problem Solving, pp. 472–474
Developing/ Presenting Arguments, pp. 474–477

EXPLORING A PROVERB

1. Brainstorm a list of proverbs. With a group of friends, or perhaps with your family, try to recall as many old sayings as possible. Here are a few examples: "Make hay while the sun shines." "You can't teach an old dog new tricks." "Look before you leap." A class brainstorming session will produce many proverbs, perhaps including parallel examples from different cultures. For example, a Nigerian proverb, "Seeing is better than hearing," echoes the Chinese saying "A picture is worth a thousand words." A Japanese equivalent of "Spare the rod" is "To pamper children is to desert them." Libraries also have books of proverbs.

2. Choose a proverb. It doesn't matter whether you agree or disagree with the proverb you select. You are looking for a saying that will benefit from analysis and interpretation.

Writer's Choice Could you analyze a proverb by comparing it to another similar proverb or to a contrasting version?

Springboard

Make a game out of inventing new proverbs based on contemporary lifestyles ("When all else fails, rent a video") or rewording old proverbs in contemporary idiom ("Neither a borrower nor a credit card user be").

3. Freewrite about the meaning of your proverb. Without imposing any order on your thoughts, begin to write about what the proverb seems to mean and your own reaction to it. Tell whether you agree with it. To what situations does the proverb refer? Is it always true? How might the words of the proverb be interpreted in a different way?

4. Determine your approach to the analysis. Your purpose is to persuade your reader that your proverb is not true, is still true, or is true but needs to be reinterpreted. Select the approach that you can support most effectively. You might choose to rely on research, as did the author of the excerpt, or you could argue from personal experience, telling a story to make your major point. Reading may provide you with more examples to support your argument. Consider taking an informal poll to determine if people agree or disagree with your proverb, and then use the results of your poll to bolster your conclusion.

WRITING YOUR ANALYSIS

1. Introduce your proverb in a way that suggests your approach. Depending on the approach you select, you could begin by stating your proverb as a question: "Is beauty really only skin deep?" Similarly, you can grab your readers' attention with a negative statement about a proverb with which you disagree: "Misery does not love company." If you are going to tell a story, you might choose a narrative hook such as, "Last summer I learned to my chagrin that honesty is not always the best policy."

2. Examine the commonly accepted meaning of your proverb. Even if you choose to disagree with your proverb, you should still explain what it means and explore why people have believed it for so long.

3. Analyze whether the accepted meaning still holds true. Present your research or your story, making clear how these examples support your main point.

4. Conclude your analysis. Summarize the arguments you have already presented or bring your story to its natural conclusion. Adding just one more example, as the author does in the excerpt, can leave your reader with something new to think about that cements the argument.

Writing
— **TIP** —

Readers will want to know the qualifications of researchers you quote.

Individualizing Instruction

Cultural Differences The study of proverbs is a good way to acquaint students with the wisdom of different cultures. Remember that proverbs represent cultural values, which may differ greatly. For instance, "Spare the rod and spoil the child" may still make excellent sense to some cultures but seem barbaric to others.

ESL Students Proverbs, like jokes, can be hard to understand in a second language. Encourage ESL students to learn English proverbs; at the same time, allow your ESL students to choose proverbs from their native cultures, translated into English. This will provide a learning opportunity for their classmates.

Cooperative Learning

Groups who have brainstormed proverbs together may wish to stay together for the remainder of the writing process. In determining an approach, some members of a group may wish to concentrate on reasons to follow a proverb, others on reasons to reject it, others on ways to reinterpret it.

Physical Education Connection

Many contemporary American proverbs come from sports; for example, Leo Durocher's "Nice guys finish last," Yogi Berra's "It ain't over till it's over," and Vince Lombardi's "Winning isn't the most important thing, it's the only thing" (often misquoted as "Winning isn't everything, it's the only thing"). Encourage the sports fans in your class to think of other examples.

Guidelines for Evaluation

The following guidelines may be used for a close evaluation of the exploration of a proverb. See the Writing Evaluation Guidelines in the Teacher's Resource File for additional help with holistic or analytic scoring. A good exploration of a proverb . . .

- states the proverb clearly and interestingly at the beginning
- displays a unified interpretation of the proverb
- examines the commonly accepted meaning of the proverb and whether it still holds true
- contains a conclusion that summarizes the arguments or brings the analysis to a fitting ending.

Reteaching

Assess the needs of students who were not successful developing an effective exploration of a proverb. Assign the appropriate Handbook Mini-Lessons. Concepts commonly requiring reteaching for this assignment are

Introducing Nonfiction: Handbook 8
Problem Solving: Handbook 23

The following suggestions and resources may also be useful.

1. Misinterpretation Some students may have had difficulty comprehending the meaning of their proverb. Have these students explain their interpretations of the proverb for the class. Then open the proverb up for discussion so the students' peers can help them comprehend.

2. Insufficient Support Students may have begun with one view of their chosen proverb, then have been unable to support their view with sufficient evidence. Such students may wish to reexamine their thoughts about the proverb and take a different view—perhaps accepting the proverb rather than rejecting it. Encourage such students to write about their rethinking process as part of their exploration of the proverb.

REVIEWING YOUR WRITING

1. Read your analysis. Have you anticipated and addressed all the possible criticisms of your approach? Do your examples or story support your conclusion? Have you omitted any possible examples that would strengthen your case?

2. Ask a classmate to read your paper. Have you accomplished your purpose, persuading your reader that your argument is sound? Can your friend think of additional examples that would help to prove your point, or arguments against it that you hadn't thought of? Solicit ideas about how to make your introduction or conclusion more arresting to readers.

3. Read your paper to an older person. You may learn something about why your proverb seemed to be true in an earlier time.

4. Proofread and rewrite your analysis. Check your paper for grammar, spelling, and punctuation. If you have told a story, make sure that you have been consistent in your use of tenses.

PUBLISHING AND PRESENTING

- **Create a booklet.** Compile your classmates' analyses along with your own into a booklet entitled "A New Look at Some Old Proverbs."
- **Enter your analysis in a nonfiction writing contest.**
- **Hold a debate.** If two students have written contradictory analyses, have them present their arguments in the form of a debate.

258   Workshop 8

Science Connection

For contemporary western civilization, science has become a source of proverbs. Some, appropriated by writers or musicians, use laws of nature as metaphors: "What goes up must come down" (line from a popular song) and "Everything that rises must converge" (title of a Flannery O'Connor short story) are two examples. Encourage students to find more.

On the Lightside

WHERE THERE'S A WILL

It is high time people realize the impact William Shakespeare had on the English language. *The long and the short of it* is that our everyday speech is filled with words and phrases that have been taken from his plays and poems. Anyone who underestimates his contribution is *living in a fool's paradise.*

Over the centuries Shakespeare's expressions—such as the ones in italics above—have become some of the most familiar in the English language. Some have been overused to the point that they are now clichés. A British journalist, Bernard Levin, once showed how much Shakepeare contributed to common speech by stringing together sixty of his phrases in one giant sentence. It reads, in part:

If you cannot understand my argument, and declare *"It's Greek to me,"* you are quoting Shakespeare; . . . if you have *played fast and loose,* if you have been *tongue-tied, a tower of strength, hoodwinked* or *in a pickle,* . . . why, *be that as it may, the more fool you,* for it is *a foregone conclusion* that you are *(as good luck would have it)* quoting Shakespeare; . . . even if you *bid me good riddance* and *send me packing,* if you wish I was *dead as a doornail,* if you think I am *an eyesore, a laughingstock, the devil incarnate,* . . . then—*by Jove! O Lord! Tut, tut! for goodness' sake! what the dickens! but me no buts*—it is all one to me, for you are quoting Shakespeare.

The genius of Shakespeare lives on, not only in his great plays and sonnets, but also in our common, everyday speech.

259

In discussing this feature, you might point out other examples of Shakespeare's lasting impact on the English language. In addition to expressions such as those that are italicized in the article, Shakespeare contributed many now-familiar quotations, such as "Friends, Romans, Countrymen," from *Julius Caesar;* "To be or not to be," from *Hamlet;* and "Tomorrow and tomorrow and tomorrow," from *Macbeth.* Some students may also be aware of other works that draw their titles from Shakespeare— for example, the novels *Winter of Our Discontent* (from *Richard III*), *Brave New World* (from *The Tempest*), and *The Sound and the Fury* (from *Macbeth*); and the musical comedy *Kiss Me Kate* (from *The Taming of the Shrew*).

Starting from Literature

Objective

To respond to a published model of a review as a springboard to writing

Teaching Strategies

Motivate

Ask how many students read reviews regularly, and in which art forms. Ask why they read reviews—to learn about the contents of shows and books? To decide whether to spend their money on particular shows? To learn what people are talking about? To read clever writing? All of the above are common reasons for reading reviews.

Tap Prior Knowledge

Ask students to discuss their reactions to any live performances—including plays, concerts, and dance events—they have attended. What reactions did they have to the performances? Had they read reviews of the event before or after attending it? Did the review shape their thinking in any way?

Set a Purpose

After you have gone over the side-column notes with students, remind them that the elements of a musical can include its origin, the writing, the direction, the music, the performance, and the set. Because the question posed in the side-column is complex, encourage students to take brief written notes about which of these elements Chris Sanders responded to, and how he responded, in his review of *The Merry Wives of Windsor, Texas.*

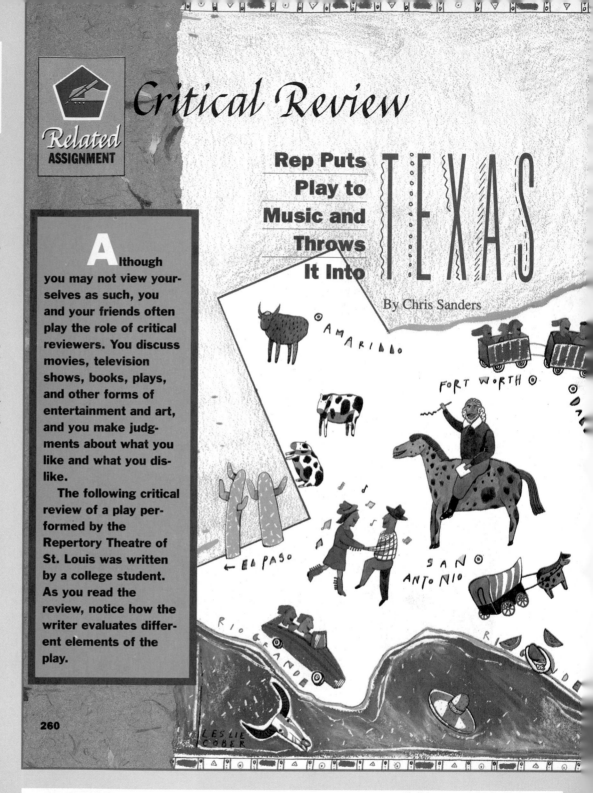

Related ASSIGNMENT

Critical Review

Rep Puts Play to Music and Throws It Into TEXAS

By Chris Sanders

Although you may not view yourselves as such, you and your friends often play the role of critical reviewers. You discuss movies, television shows, books, plays, and other forms of entertainment and art, and you make judgments about what you like and what you dislike.

The following critical review of a play performed by the Repertory Theatre of St. Louis was written by a college student. As you read the review, notice how the writer evaluates different elements of the play.

260

Literature Connection

Have students locate and discuss reviews of contemporary plays. Back issues of *The New Yorker* are one source of consistently insightful reviews, and major newspapers such as *The New York Times,* the *Chicago Tribune,* and the *Los Angeles Times* also publish in-depth drama reviews. You may want to further challenge students to research early reviews of classics; a handful of reviews, some in the form of diary entries, are still extant for the first performances of Shakespeare's plays.

A Shakespearean musical? Set in Texas circa 1870? With a live country and western band on stage?! When I first heard that the Rep was adapting one of Shakespeare's lesser known comedies into a musical, I was admittedly apprehensive. But, as this job requires, I put my preconceptions behind me and began my research.

The Merry Wives of Windsor, Texas, the Shakespearean comedy John L. Haber adapted for the Rep, has a curious history. A well-known theatrical legend explains that the play was commissioned by a royal mandate. To allegedly satisfy Queen Elizabeth's desire to see a play about Falstaff in love, Shakespeare wrote *The Merry Wives of Windsor* within a fortnight.

First performed in 1597, the play was a tremendous success and continued to be a popular favorite until the early 19th century when it fell into disfavor. It has since been considered critically as an aberration, too banal or trite to be taken seriously: Shakespearean fluff, if you will.

Which brings us to Mr. Haber's adaptation, although perhaps "adaptation" is too mild a word to describe the incredible transformation the play underwent. Although he borrows Shakespeare's plot, the characters and some of the dialogue, this stuff is more like *Bonanza* than Shakespeare, albeit a very amusing *Bonanza.*

Director Edward Stern has taken the otherwise weak script firmly in hand and created a comic world where barbecues, stampedes and a live band are just part of the fun. . . .Sight gags abound, and simply hearing the characters drawling Shakespeare's lines is good for an occasional guffaw.

The Rep has assembled a strong cast for the production. . . . Although country music is not one of my favorite musical spheres, I must confess that the sounds of the Red Clay Ramblers kept the action flowing briskly throughout and was quite infectious. The Ramblers. . . provide us with two, count 'em *two* hoedowns, as well as a hilarious second act curtain-opener entitled "The Moo Song." The musical highlight of the evening, however, was the performance by John Foley, who played (believe it or not) the yodelling cowboy. One of his two numbers, "Count On My Love," a ballad sung with Deborah Jean Culpin, was truly beautiful.

The set, designed by Kevin Rupnik, worked well on the Rep's thrust stage and created a Texan atmosphere through the use of an impressive array of eclectic southern curios. Candice Donnelly's costumes were similarly impressive, as was Peter Sargent's lighting design, which gave us neon beer signs and a lariat made of Christmas lights.

So if you're looking for an evening of fine Shakespeare, don't go see the Rep's season opener. But if you are looking for some light entertainment and musical fun, and a rib or two at the Bard, you just might enjoy *The Merry Wives of Windsor, Texas.*

Think AND Respond

What strengths and flaws in *The Merry Wives of Windsor, Texas* does the writer point out? What is the writer's overall conclusion about the play? Have you seen any plays or films recently about which you would like to comment?

Think and Respond

Elicit Personal Responses

Invite students to write a review of Chris Sanders' review. Did it make them want to see *The Merry Wives of Windsor, Texas?* Did it give them a clear idea of the production? Was it an entertaining piece of writing? Then have students share their opinions in discussion.

Explore the Author's Techniques

Note that the tone of Sanders' review is mainly subjective, except for objective statements of facts about the play ("First performed, in 1597, the play was a tremendous success . . ."). In writing reviews, students will want to maintain a similar balance between subjectivity and objectivity. They should avoid disguising personal reactions as objective truths. Indeed, subjectivity often makes reviews more entertaining.

Link Literature to Writing

Chris Sanders talks openly, in his review, about his preconceptions of the production, his feelings on attending it. Readers can tell that he is both emotionally and intellectually engaged in his subject. Encourage students to search the wide range of currently available arts and entertainment and to pick one in which they feel personally involved.

Guiding Your Writers

Objectives

1. To choose a subject for a critical analysis or review
2. To draft and revise a critical review
3. To publish and present a critical review

Preteaching

Preview the remainder of the assignment. At this time, present any skills or concepts your students may need help with. The handbook mini-lessons listed below may help you with selection and instruction. Cross references in the pupil text will give students access to the same lessons for independent practice.

Handbook Mini-Lessons

- Analysis Frames, p. 343
- Introducing/Concluding Nonfiction, pp. 365–371
- Elaborative Details, pp. 376–381
- Unity/Coherence, pp. 382–391
- Developing/Presenting Arguments, pp. 474–477

Teaching Strategies

Personal Touch

Tell the class about a performance you have recently seen or book you have recently read. Give your informal assessment of it—tell what you would have written if you were a reviewer. If you wish, go on to write a review and share it with the class.

INVITATION TO Write

Chris Sanders's critical review analyzes the strengths and shortcomings of a performance of *The Merry Wives of Windsor, Texas.* Write a critical review of your own, evaluating a play, movie, painting, or another work of art.

Like an analysis of any literary work, a critical review has three main parts: a description of the subject, an in-depth evaluation of the subject's various elements, and a conclusion about its overall value. The purpose of a critical review is to offer readers a useful analysis of the subject and to suggest whether seeing it, reading it, or listening to it is worth their time. That's why critical reviews most often appear in newspapers and magazines. Some critics also offer their views on radio and television programs, and others have had their work collected in books.

HANDBOOKS

FOR HELP & PRACTICE

Analysis Frames, p. 343

Introducing/ Concluding Nonfiction, pp. 365–371

Elaborative Details, pp. 376–381

Unity/Coherence, pp. 382–391

Developing/ Presenting Arguments, pp. 474–477

CHOOSING AND ANALYZING A SUBJECT

1. Choose a subject that engages you personally. Your subject might be a movie or a television show you enjoyed—or one that you disliked. You might also choose to review a live performance, such as a play, a rock concert, an opera, or a dance recital. Perhaps there is a painting, drawing, photograph, sculpture, or other work of art you have seen and admired. Do you have a favorite tape or CD?

Begin your search for a topic by brainstorming a list of specific subjects you might review. Discuss your list with friends, and write down any additional suggestions they may have. After reviewing your list, choose the subject that interests you the most, the one you feel most compelled to write about.

262 Workshop 8

Springboard

Choose a television program that is faddish or widely promoted right now or a popular song that is a smash hit. Before they begin to write this assignment, have students read a review of the program or song, then watch or listen to the work themselves. Discuss how their reactions agreed or disagreed with the reviews.

2. Identify key elements of your subject.
Theme is an element that is common to all forms of art. Beyond theme, however, each form of art has its own inherent characteristics. For plays, these elements include plot, dialogue, acting, staging, sets, lighting, and costumes. When evaluating paintings, you might look at color, technique, and composition. A review of a song or album would consider such elements as melody, rhythm, and lyrics. Think about your subject, and make a list of the key elements that relate to that specific art form.

3. Analyze each element of your subject. Examine each element on your list, and jot down some notes about how your subject expressed that element. You don't necessarily need to evaluate every element of a subject. You might instead choose to focus on just a few elements. Look for strengths or weaknesses in each area you want to evaluate. You might do this in chart form to use later as a guide to writing. Don't worry about searching for a "right" response. Critical reviews are largely a matter of opinion. Your review should give your honest, personal reactions.

DRAFTING YOUR REVIEW

1. Write an introduction. In the introduction, identify the subject, set the tone, and express your general opinion. Notice how the reviewer of *The Merry Wives of Windsor, Texas* identifies the subject and sets a lighthearted tone in the first two paragraphs. He also lets the audience know that he was "admittedly apprehensive." The tone of your review—whether it's objective, sarcastic, laudatory, humorous, or negative—will be shaped by your opinion of the subject.

2. Organize the body of your review logically. Let your subject guide the organization of your review. For a play or movie, you might first describe the plot and then discuss the merits and flaws of the script, acting, and staging. For a painting, you might describe the work as a whole first, and then evaluate color, technique, and composition in turn. Remember to support your opinions with specific details or examples.

Critical Review   **263**

Guidelines

The following guidelines may be used for a close evaluation of critical analyses or reviews. See the Writing Evaluation Guidelines in the Teacher's Resource File for additional help with holistic or analytic scoring. An effective review . . .

- identifies its subject at the beginning
- opens with a general opinion
- includes enough facts, examples, and specifics to support the general opinion
- displays logical organization
- quickly establishes a tone
- uses standard grammar and usage and correct mechanics

Reteaching

Assess the needs of students who were not successful developing an effective critical analysis/review. Assign the appropriate Handbook Mini-Lessons. Concepts commonly requiring reteaching for this assignment are

Introducing/Concluding Nonfiction: Handbook 8
Unity/Coherence: Handbook 10

The following resources and suggestions may be useful.

1. Insufficient Support Professional reviewers often pay more than one visit to the work reviewed, if publication deadlines don't forbid it. A music reviewer may listen to the same recording over and over; a restaurant reviewer may return to order other dishes. Students who had trouble formulating cogent criticisms may wish to go back to the works and see them again.

2. Vagueness Circle the empty adjectives, such as *good, okay, great, awesome, cool, boring,* or *terrible,* in students' reviews. Assign Finding Details for Elaboration in Handbook 9; then instruct students to replace each circled adjective with an adjective or phrase that is specific and concrete. *Boring,* for example, could be replaced with a reference to slow tempo or flat dialogue.

---

3. Be specific. In your descriptions and evaluations, avoid the use of vague adjectives, such as *great, good,* and *poor.* Instead, make your descriptions and evaluations meaningful by carefully choosing your words. Notice Chris Sanders's use of such descriptive words as *inventive, briskly, infectious, hilarious,* and *eclectic.*

4. Sum up your general impression. Reread the concluding paragraph of Chris Sanders's review, and note how he sums up his overall view of the play. Write a concluding paragraph to your review that reinforces the opinions you've expressed.

REVIEWING YOUR WRITING

1. Check your draft for specific, detailed evaluations. Did you clearly state your opinion of each element of your subject, using specific, expressive vocabulary? Did you support your evaluations with details and examples?

2. Be sure the tone of your review is consistent. Have you maintained the tone you intended throughout your review? If not, you may want to rewrite some sentences or change some vocabulary so that your tone remains consistent.

3. Make sure your criteria are clear. Have you clearly indicated the standards by which you are judging your subject? Can your readers understand the reasons for your reactions? If not, you may want to add further explanations to some parts of your review.

4. Prepare a final copy. After revising your review, prepare a final copy incorporating all of your changes. Proofread your final copy for errors in grammar, usage, spelling, and mechanics.

PUBLISHING AND PRESENTING

- **Collect all the reviews in a class binder.** Organize the binder by subject, so that classmates can read one another's reviews.
- **Submit your critical review to the school or community newspaper.**
- **Stage a Critic's Circle.** On many radio and TV shows, critics review and rate current movies. Form teams to stage similar presentations of your class's reviews.

Writing TIP

As you write a critical review of a performance, replay scenes in your mind. Keep asking yourself, "What *exactly* is it I liked or disliked? What *exactly* made me feel the way I did?"

Cross Curricular Connection

Have students write reviews of any of their textbooks, including this one. You might want to send copies to the publishers.

Sentence
COMPOSING

Combining Sentence Variations

Often, professional writers mix sentence expanders (openers, s-v splits, closers) within one sentence. Contrast the two versions of each sentence below. Notice not only the increased information and vividness, but also the changes in rhythm.

MODELS

Foundations
1. The two girls sank into the kitchen chairs.
2. Then Sylvia makes her perilous way down again.
3. Mr. Aaa heard the voices outside in the stone causeway.

Original Sentences
1. With opener and closer: <u>Laughing</u>, the two girls sank into the kitchen chairs, <u>their feet sprawled out in front of them</u>.   **Mary Lavin, ''One Summer''**
2. With s-v split and closer: Then Sylvia, <u>well satisfied,</u> makes her perilous way down again, <u>not daring to look far below the branch she stands on, ready to cry sometimes because her fingers ache and her lamed feet slip</u>.   **Sarah Orne Jewett, ''A White Heron''**
3. With opener and s-v split: <u>Half an hour later</u>, Mr. Aaa, <u>seated in his library sipping a bit of electric fire from a metal cup</u>, heard the voices outside in the stone causeway.   **Ray Bradbury, *The Martian Chronicles***

A. Unscrambling and Imitating Sentences Unscramble each set of parts to form a sentence whose structure matches that of the model. Follow the punctuation in the model. Then write a second imitation of the model. Openers, s-v splits, and closers are underlined in the models.

1. Two boys, <u>in gym clothes and boxing shoes,</u> were balancing themselves on their shoulders, <u>kicking their legs up in the air</u>.
   a. slowing their speed slightly at the sharp bend
   b. several stock cars
   c. with garish paint and donut tires
   d. were hurling themselves against the third turn

Objectives

1. To compose sentences with modifiers and phrases in the introductory position, between subject and verb, and in the closing position to vary sentence rhythm.
2. To combine sentences to form new sentences with modifiers and phrases in the introductory position, between subject and verb, and at the close of the sentence.

Preteaching

These exercises focus on varying sentence rhythms through the use of modifiers, participles, and phrases. Before assigning the activities, be aware that some students may need review of basic sentence parts and structure as well as the use of modifiers, participles, participial phrases, appositive phrases, and prepositional phrases. Refer to the following sections of the Grammar Handbook for preteaching content:

Phrases and Clauses
  Prepositional Phrases, pages 591–592
  Appositives and Appositive Phrase, 593
  Verbals and Verbal Phrases, pages 594–596

Adjective and Adverb Usage
  Understanding Modifiers, pages 719–720

ANSWER KEY

12-8 Combining Sentence Variations

A. Unscrambling and Imitating Sentences
  Imitations will vary.
  1. Several stock cars, with garish paint and donut tires, were hurling themselves against the third turn, slowing their speed slightly at the sharp bend.

2. Branwell, the only Bronte boy, spent the first weeks of his life lying peacefully in the old cradle, gurgling in contentment and being admired.

3. With a whir and a rattle, the ancient ceiling fan spun above the tourists, stirring and moving the air, ruffling the curtains, the bedclothes, the papers within the charming little room of the quaint hotel.

4. And so, bent and broken by the wind, with branches and trunk pummelled, the plum tree drooped, rather than stood, in the garden outside his window on Monday morning.

B. Combining Sentences

Answers will vary. Authors' original sentences below.

1. At the gate, I show the pass to a young Japanese private, the sentry.

2. Janet, pausing half-way down to say something to someone above, stood there as if painted, distinct and unreal.

---

2. Poppa, <u>a good quiet man</u>, spent the last hours before our parting <u>moving aimlessly around the yard, keeping to himself and avoiding me</u>.

Gordon Parks, "My Mother's Dream for Me"

   a. lying peacefully in the old cradle
   b. the only Bronte boy
   c. gurgling in contentment and being admired
   d. Branwell
   e. spent the first weeks of his life

3. <u>For a day and a night</u>, the great flakes drove down upon us, <u>swirling and swooping in the wind, blotting out the summit, the shoulder, everything beyond the tiny, white-walled radius of our tent</u>.

James Ramsey Ullman, *Top Man*

   a. stirring and moving the air
   b. the ancient ceiling fan spun above the tourists
   c. the papers within the charming little room of the quaint hotel
   d. with a whir and a rattle
   e. ruffling the curtains, the bedclothes

4. <u>And so, lost and wandering on the sea</u>, <u>with topsails and spritsails torn</u>, the rotten hulk drifted, rather than sailed, <u>into the harbor of Berehaven on Bantry Bay on June 11th, 1593</u>.

Bruce Chatwin, *In Patagonia*

   a. on Monday morning
   b. with branches and trunk pummelled
   c. the plum tree drooped, rather than stood
   d. and so, bent and broken by the wind
   e. in the garden outside his window

B. Combining Sentences Use the first sentence in each set as a foundation. Locate the subject and verb in the foundation. Next, insert the underlined parts of the following sentences into the foundation. Each combined sentence should contain expanders in two of the three positions, opener, s-v split, and closer. Compare your sentences with the originals on page 323.

1. I show the pass to a young Japanese private. I show it to him <u>at the gate</u>. The private is <u>the sentry</u>.   **Richard E. Kim, *Lost Names***

2. Janet stood there as if painted. She was <u>pausing half-way down to say something to someone above</u>. She seemed <u>distinct and unreal</u>.

Elizabeth Bowen, "Foothold"

3. He went about with a sort of stealth. He was <u>absorbed, taking no heed of other people</u>. He was <u>seeking inwardly for luck</u>.

D. H. Lawrence, "The Rocking-Horse Winner"

4. He slipped from the wooden ledge and fell onto his back on the windowsill. He slipped <u>after perhaps a seventh attempt</u>. He fell <u>fluttering his wings</u>.

Virginia Woolf, "The Death of the Moth"

C. Unscrambling Sentences Unscramble the parts in each set to form a sentence that makes sense. Each sentence should contain expanders in two of the three different positions, opener, s-v split, and closer.

1 a. she covered the tear
  b. her shoulders bunching to hide her face
  c. with a quick, guilty hand   **Zenna Henderson, "The Believing Child"**

2 a. braced for a new concussion
  b. brought him leaping out of bed
  c. pouring in on Father Kleinsorge's half sleep
  d. the sudden flood of light   **John Hersey, *Hiroshima***

3 a. she got up in an apologetic sort of way and moved toward the better protected rear of the car
  b. feeling the empty seats as she went in a palpable search for hot pipes
  c. at last, her teeth chattering   **Henry Sydnor Harrison, "Miss Hinch"**

4 a. looked neat and snug
  b. in the frosty December dusk
  c. with pale blue smoke rising from the chimneys and doorways glowing amber from the fires inside
  d. their cabins   **Harper Lee, *To Kill a Mockingbird***

Application From a piece of your recent writing, select six sentences at random. To each sentence, add expanders in two of the three different positions, opener, s-v split, and closer. Vary the content, length, and structure of your expanders. Notice the increased vividness and detail and the variations in rhythm that the various combinations of expanders bring to your writing.

Grammar Refresher For more on absolute phrases, see Handbook 33, page 599. For more on present and past participial phrases, see Handbook 33, page 598. For more on appositive phrases, see Handbook 33, page 593.

3. Absorbed, taking no heed of other people, he went about with a sort of stealth, seeking inwardly for luck.

4. After perhaps a seventh attempt he slipped from the wooden ledge and fell, fluttering his wings, onto his back on the windowsill.

C. Unscrambling Sentences

Answers may vary. Authors' original sentences below.

1. With a quick, guilty hand, she covered the tear, her shoulders bunching to hide her face.

2. The sudden flood of light, pouring in on Father Kleinsorge's half sleep, brought him leaping out of bed, braced for a new concussion.

3. At last, her teeth chattering, she got up in an apologetic sort of way, and moved toward the better protected rear of the car, feeling the empty seats as she went in a palpable search for hot pipes.

4. In the frosty December dusk, their cabins looked neat and snug with pale blue smoke rising from the chimneys and doorways glowing amber from the fires inside.

Application

Answers will vary.

WORKSHOP 9

Teaching Preview

Workshop Overview

Reports are a form of informative exposition based on detailed research and the synthesis of ideas from many sources. Report writing is the most common kind of writing done in school and differs from other forms of exposition in the way it poses questions and then molds and shapes responses based on research findings. In this Workshop, students will explain a subject in detail based on readings and analyses. As they work, students will apply many of the critical thinking skills they have developed in previous workshops. As a result, it is recommended that the Workshop be used toward the end of the year. Workshop 9 includes the following Guided and Related Assignments:

1. **Guided: The Research Paper** shows students methods for focusing research, evaluating and using sources of information, taking notes, organizing ideas, documenting sources, and organizing bibliographies
2. **Related: Career Search** extends research and analysis skills developed in the Guided Assignment to the realm of examining career options

Preparation Guide

1. Use the Overview above and the Teacher's Choice descriptions on page 269 as a basis for deciding which assignment(s) to teach.

2. Preview the assignment and the teacher's notes. The teaching suggestions and your knowledge of your class's abilities should allow you to identify quickly the concepts that may require preteaching or extra support. The Handbook mini-lessons suggested in the Preteaching notes within the lesson can also provide guidance in this area.

3. Preview the adjacent chart for support materials in the Teacher's Resource File that may be used with this Workshop. Resources are for use with the Guided Assignment unless otherwise noted.

Workshop Support Materials

Resources	For Use With
Ideas for Writing: Additional Ideas, pp. 21–24	Choose a topic, p. 273
Thinking Skills Transparencies: Analysis Frame; *Worksheets*, p. 9	Begin your research, p. 276
Elaboration/Proofreading, p. 17	Begin to write, p. 282
Peer Response Guides, p. 23	Review Your Writing, p. 285
Evaluating Writing, p. 16	Standards for Evaluaton, p. 286
Student Revision Trans., pp. 35–42	Problem-solve, p. 286
Elaboration/Proofreading, p. 18	Proofread your work, p. 291

Professional Resources and Media

Books and Journals

Jensen, Jean L. "Career Research: Researching for Real." *English Journal*, Vol. 78.5 (September 1989). pp. 39–40. (researching careers, observing and working with professionals)

Rorabacher, Louise E., and Georgia Dunbar. "The Research Paper." *Assignments in Exposition*. 8th Ed. New York: Harper & Row, 1985. pp. 320–340.

Films and Videos

Communicating with a Purpose Series: Research Paper. Alberta Educational Commission Corporation, Alberta, Canada. 1982. (30 min.)

"Research Papers." *The Write Course Series*. Dallas Community College Dist., Mesquite, TX. 1984. (30 min.)

Computer Software

Job Storming. Write On: Secondary Collection, Humanities Software, San Francisco, CA. Apple II, II+, IIc, IIe.

Linking Literature, Writing, and Grammar

The following options may be used to provide students with an integrated language experience. Begin by assigning and discussing any of the recommended pieces of literature, which can be found in most classroom anthologies. Use the suggested strategy to provide a link to the Guided Assignment.

Linking Literature and Writing

Option 1
Starting Point: from "Introduction to Medieval Literature" by John Steinbeck on pages 270–271 of *The Writer's Craft*
Strategy: Use the teaching suggestions on pages 270–271 to lead students into the Guided Assignment.

Option 2
Starting Point: "Introduction to *Frankenstein*" by Mary Wollstonecraft Shelley
Strategy: Have students imagine that they are focusing a research report on the writing of *Frankenstein*. Ask them why Shelley's "Introduction" would be an important primary source. Have them brainstorm other sources, both primary and secondary, that would be useful in researching the topic. Explain that they will be writing a research paper and, if they are allowed to choose any topics they wish, encourage them to suggest literary topics that might be of interest.

Option 3
Starting Point: speech by Winston Churchill on March 15, 1946
Strategy: As part of your discussion, help students recognize that this speech itself became an important part of post-World War II history as the source of the phrase "the iron curtain." Ask students what factual information Churchill includes in his speech. Ask them to suggest research papers for which the speech might be an important primary source. If students can choose whatever topics interest them, suggest that prominent world figures, either contemporary or from the past (like Churchill), might be interesting subjects as would World War II and its aftermath.

Linking Writing and Grammar

Before the drafting or revision stage of this assignment, point out that research reports, particularly those focusing on people, often contain pronouns in the nominative and objective cases. Nominative pronouns are used as subjects or as predicate pronouns; objective pronouns are used as objects of verbs or objects of prepositions. Encourage students to find examples of sentences containing nominative and objective pronouns as you write the following examples on the board:

NOMINATIVE PRONOUNS:
They gathered at Potsdam.
It was they who signed the peace treaty.

OBJECTIVE PRONOUNS:
The Allies feared them the most.
The treaty ended the war for them.

Have students review the material about the correct use of nominative and objective pronouns on pages 693–697 of the Grammar and Usage Handbook. If problems with nominative and objective pronouns continue in students' work, assign the exercises on those pages for reteaching. Additional practice can be found in the Grammar and Usage Practice Book on pages 60–62.

Workshop Management Guidelines

The adjacent chart indicates the number of days recommended for each phase of the Guided and Related Assignments. Stars indicate portions of the assignment that may be completed outside the classroom if time is limited or if teachers wish the activity to be completed by students independently.

Research Report

Starting from Literature—1 day

Prewrite—2–3 days*

Research—6–10 days*

Draft—3–5 days*

Revise—1–2 days

Publish—1–2 days

Learning—1 day*

Reteaching—open

Extension/Enrichment—open

Sentence Composing—1 day*

Career Search

—3–5 days*

Sketchbook

Objectives

To use a photograph to stimulate students' exploration of their own penchant for research

Using the Prompt

The photograph presents an image of a somewhat mysterious bygone culture. Use the photograph and the prompts below it to focus students on the purposes and pleasures of research and to have them explore what interests, inclinations, and strengths of their own they might bring to information-gathering as an enterprise. Emphasize that they will not be graded on this activity and should write to learn about their own thoughts.

Begin by asking students what the term "lost city" evokes for them. The discussion might roam over such topics as Pompeii, Machu Picchu, Atlantis, western ghost towns, or the Roanoke settlement. Ask students what they know about the place in the picture. You might mention that Stonehenge was built by the pre-Christian Druids of Great Britain, who were driven underground by the Roman invasion and the influx of Christianity. Tell students to use the picture and their thoughts about the prompts as springboards for writing about mysteries of the past they'd like to explore. Students can use the Additional Sketches as prompts for separate writing or as triggers to continue their response to the picture.

Tell students to save their work in their Writing Portfolio; they might find a use for it in the course of the workshop that follows.

Sketchbook

What purpose did the builders of Stonehenge have in mind? Why did the Anasazi abandon their cliff dwellings? Who built the Great Zimbabwe structures?

The past is filled with mysteries. Which ones would you like to explore?

Additional Sketches

What is your area of expertise?
How do you find things out?

268

WRITER'S 9 WORKSHOP

Reports

Guided Assignment
RESEARCH REPORT

A scientist peering through a telescope and comparing mathematical formulas makes a fascinating discovery about matter at the edge of the universe. A medical researcher studying data from dozens of experiments unlocks the mystery of a deadly disease. A scholar poring through ancient manuscripts compiles a startling picture of a lost civilization. All these people are conducting research to answer particular questions. Research can also give you access to the information discovered by humankind through the ages. In this workshop you will apply your research skills to write a research report and to learn about careers you might enter in the years to come.

Objectives

Guided Assignment:
THE RESEARCH PAPER
To plan, research, draft, revise, proofread, and share a research paper using appropriate documentation

Related Assignment:
CAREER SEARCH
To apply research techniques; to gather information about a career

Teacher's Choice

Guided Assignment
Research Paper In this assignment students are asked to gather and integrate information from many sources to support and elaborate an assertion about a particular topic. The task requires them to apply individual skills practiced in most of the other workshops; therefore, the research report makes an appropriate writing assignment for late in the year.

Related Assignment
Career Search This assignment provides students the opportunity to apply the research skills they acquire in the guided assignment to a topic of practical importance, choosing a suitable career.

269

RESEARCH REPORT

Assignment Rationale

A research report propounds and demonstrates an original thesis, using information drawn from a variety of sources. Research, summarizing, paraphrasing, and documentation skills have many practical applications in everyday life, from consulting sources to find out how to remove an unusual stain to learning how to contact a congressperson.

Starting from Literature

Objective

To respond to a description of an author's motivations for research as a springboard to writing

Teaching Strategies

Motivate

Have students discuss fictional adventures they enjoyed as children, whether in games, books, movies, or any other context. Ask what they now know about the reality behind these adventures. For example, did a love of science fiction lead them to find out about real space travel?

Tap Prior Knowledge

Find out what students know about the legend of King Arthur and where they derived their information.

Set a Purpose

Before students read the excerpt, go through the side-column notes. Point out that this excerpt is *not* a research report: rather, it explores how the desire for information begins and where it can lead. Encourage students to note the way Steinbeck describes how a piece of fiction affected him. Have they had similar experiences?

Guided ASSIGNMENT

Research Report

Research, or the systematic gathering of information from a variety of sources, can take us deep into new worlds of the future, present, and past.

Novelist John Steinbeck's childhood fascination with the legends of King Arthur led him to research the literature of medieval England, and this research led him eventually to write a new translation of Sir Thomas Malory's classic *Morte d'Arthur.* As you read this introduction to Steinbeck's translation, think about the impact Malory's work had on him and how he acted on his fascination.

270

FROM
Introduction to Medieval Literature

by John Steinbeck

Some people there are who, being grown, forget the horrible task of learning to read. . . . I remember that words—written or printed—were devils, and books, because they gave me pain, were my enemies.

Some literature was in the air around me. The Bible I absorbed through my skin. My uncles exuded Shakespeare, and *Pilgrim's Progress* was mixed with my mother's milk. But these things came into my ears. They were sounds, rhythms, figures. Books were printed demons—the tongs and thumbscrews of outrageous persecution. And then, one day, my aunt gave me a book and fatuously ignored my resentment. I stared at the black print with hatred, and then, gradually, the pages opened and let me in. The magic happened. The Bible and Shakespeare and *Pilgrim's Progress* belonged to everyone. But this was mine—it was a cut version of the Caxton *Morte d'Arthur* of Thomas Malory. . . .

Later, because the spell persisted, I went to the sources—to the *Black Book of Caermarthen*, to "The Mabinogion and Other Welsh Tales" from the *Red Book of Hergist*, to *De Excidio Britanniae* by Gildas, to *Giraldus Cambrensis Historia Britonum*, and to many of the "Frensshe" books Malory speaks of. And with the sources, I read the scholarly diggings and scrabblings—Chambers, Sommer, Gollancz, Saintsbury—but I always came back to Malory, or perhaps I should say to Caxton's Malory, since that was the only Malory there was until a little over thirty years ago, when it was announced that an unknown Malory manuscript had been discovered in the Fellows Library of Winchester College. The discovery excited me but, being no scholar but only an enthusiast, I had neither the opportunity nor the qualification to inspect the find until in 1947 Eugène Vinaver, Professor of French Language and Literature at the University of Manchester, edited his great three-volume edition of the works of Sir Thomas Malory, for Oxford University, taken from the Winchester manuscript. . . .

For a long time I have wanted to bring to present-day usage the stories of King Arthur and the Knights of the Round Table. . . . I wanted to set them down in plain present-day speech for my own young sons, and for other sons not so young—to set the stories down in meaning as they were written, leaving out nothing and adding nothing—perhaps to compete with the moving pictures, the comic-strip travesties which are the only available source for those children and others of today who are impatient with the difficulties of Malory's spelling and use of archaic words. If I can do this and keep the wonder and the magic, I shall be pleased and gratified. In no sense do I wish to rewrite Malory, or reduce him, or change him, or soften or sentimentalize him. I believe the stories are great enough to survive my tampering, which at best will make the history available to more readers, and at worst can't hurt Malory very much.

Think AND Respond

What drew Steinbeck to his subject? How did he go about researching the subject? What are some subjects in which you have a deep interest and which you would like to research?

Think and Respond

Elicit Personal Responses

Lead a class discussion focusing on the factors that inspired Steinbeck's research, the factors that might inspire the students to go on a similar search for information, and the types of information they might look for.

Explore the Author's Techniques

Go through the selection with students, tracing how research stemming from a passion for knowledge can lead step by step to worlds of previously unknown information. Point out how Steinbeck's love of Caxton's Malory began with his sense of ownership (Page 270, paragraph 2: '' . . . *Pilgrim's Progress* belong to everyone. But this was mine . . .''), which led him to study the literature of Malory's predecessors (Page 270, paragraph 3, lines 1–5), as well as scholarly studies of the times (lines 7–8), and new editions of Malory's work. Emphasize that Steinbeck finally applied the information he had gathered to a labor of love closely related to his original passion: translating Malory's work into modern English.

Link Literature to Writing

A research report originates from a writer's passions and personal interests. Steinbeck's interest in a book led him to research ancient Welsh literature. Every student has some analogous vital interest, though it may be in an item or activity rather than a book. Tell students that in the upcoming Guided Assignment they will identify such a topic and, like Steinbeck, set off on a quest for information triggered by that interest; then they will use the information to write a research report.

Literature Connection

Author Note   John Steinbeck was born in 1902 and worked as a hod carrier, house painter, ranch hand, and fruit picker before he found his calling as a writer. His novel *The Grapes of Wrath* won the Pulitzer prize in 1940, and Steinbeck won the Nobel Prize for Literature in 1962 (an award contested by his critics, who labeled his work sentimental).

Prewrite and Explore

Objectives

1. To choose and narrow a topic for a research report, using a variety of prewriting activities
2. To formulate personal goals and a controlling purpose for a report
3. To identify an audience for a research report

Preteaching

Preview the Prewrite and Explore section. Present skills and concepts needed for prewriting at this time if students need the help. The mini-lesson references below may help you in your selection and instruction. The cross references in the pupil text give students access to the same lessons for independent study.

> **Handbook Mini-Lessons**
> • Writing Variables, pp. 329–330
> • Tree Diagrams, pp. 339–340
> • Limiting Your Topic, pp. 337–338

You may also wish to use the Thinking Skills Transparencies; Thinking Skills Worksheets; Fine Art Transparencies; Starting Points for Writing and Writing Prompts for Fine Art Transparencies as resources during the Prewrite and Explore phase.

Teaching Strategies

Cooperative Learning

Brainstorming can be set up as a cooperative learning activity. Give each group a goal by asking it to generate a certain minimum number of topics. Have each student come to the brainstorming session with a few starter ideas and have students take turns using their ideas to trigger rounds of free-association.

INVITATION TO *Write*

You have read how John Steinbeck acted on his interest in the King Arthur legends. Now research and write a paper that examines in depth a subject that interests you. Use the suggestions in this workshop as guidelines.

A good research paper poses a question or problem and takes the reader on a purposeful quest for the answer. In writing such a paper you have to exercise your own thinking and judgment to locate relevant information and to mold and shape it into an interesting, readable form. The skills you acquire in this workshop will enable you to write papers on many academic topics. You also can apply these research skills in many situations outside of school, from deciding which brand of a particular product to buy, to investigating which college to attend or what career to pursue.

HANDBOOKS
FOR HELP & PRACTICE

Writing Variables,
pp. 329–330

Tree Diagrams,
pp. 339–340

Limiting Your Topic,
pp. 337–338

PREWRITE AND EXPLORE

1. Look for ideas. As Steinbeck's experience shows, personal interest can be your best guide in choosing a topic to research. Sometimes, however, a teacher may assign a general subject for your research paper. In either case, the following suggestions may help you explore ideas for your paper.

Exploratory Activities

• **Skimming your journal** If you are free to write about any subject you choose, read some of the entries in your journal, looking for broad areas that interest you. List these areas and then freewrite to find possible topics within them.
• **Brainstorming** Get together with several classmates and brainstorm ideas for your research paper assignment. Don't reject any of the ideas that come up or stop the discussion; just keep trying to generate more.

Springboard

If students need additional help in selecting a topic, suggest that they use recent newspapers to identify broad topics of current interest such as *computers, oil,* or *the environment,* and then write titles of books that might be found about this topic in a library or bookstore. Students should give free rein to their imaginations, inventing humorous or offbeat titles if they wish; in the process they may think of some good ideas for research papers.

- **Freewriting**   Start writing about your assigned subject, or a broad area of interest, and see where the words take you. Don't worry about logical progression: your purpose is simply to explore ideas. Decide beforehand how many minutes you will write and don't stop or look back until the time is up. Then review your writing to see if you generated any new research topics.
- **Tree diagraming**   Write your assigned subject or a broad area of interest as the trunk of a tree. Write any related ideas that come to mind as branches of the tree, and keep branching out as long as ideas keep coming to you. One of these idea branches may be refined into a writing topic for a research paper.
- **Reading literature**   What authors or literary works "speak" to you? Are you drawn to such writers as George Orwell, Nadine Gordimer, or Doris Lessing, or to the subjects they address? How might research help you explore any of these subjects further?

2. Share ideas.   After generating a list of topics, get together with a group of classmates to share and discuss ideas. Notice how your classmates react to your topics and see if the ones they suggest give you any fresh ideas.

3. Narrow your choice.   Identify the most promising topics on your list. Doing some preliminary reading in reference works, such as encyclopedias and specialized dictionaries, may help you decide which topic is most appropriate for your research paper. Also, try looking through the tables of contents and indexes of several books on the subjects you are considering. Ask yourself the following questions to help you evaluate a potential topic:

- Does the topic matter to me personally in some way?
- Is there enough information available on the topic?
- Is the topic narrow enough to be developed in a research paper of my assigned length?
- Is the topic too subjective, familiar, or technical?

4. Choose a topic.   If you find yourself unable to choose among several topics, try freewriting to explore your options. You may also wish to consult your journal, look back at the writing you did for the Sketchbook on page 268, or check the "Apply Your Skills" section on page 300 for possible topics.

PROBLEM SOLVING

How can I decide if my topic is suitable for a research paper?

Stumbling Block

Students who are having difficulty coming up with a research paper topic might profit from hearing how other students have arrived at their topics. You may also wish to provide undecided students the Fine Arts Transparencies, or refer them to the *Ideas for Writing Booklet*.

Teaching Tip: Purpose

Explain that a writer's purpose functions like the North Star during writing: it provides a fixed point of reference by which the writer can steer. Any piece of information can then be held to the same standard. Does it point directly toward the writer's purpose? Does it move the paper in that direction?

Critical Thinking

Classifying Discuss whether and how each of the examples of topics fits the purpose on its left. Ask students to come up with another example for each purpose. Use their responses to determine whether they understand the relationship between general purposes and particular topics and help clarify that relationship if necessary.

Richard Harris plays King Arthur in the film, *Camelot*.

Michele's English class was assigned to write a research paper examining the influence of history on literature. In this assignment you will follow Michele's process in developing and writing her paper. She did some freewriting to help her choose a topic.

ONE STUDENT'S PROCESS

Maybe I could write something about the King Arthur legends. I know what Steinbeck means—they're pretty neat. Not that I ever read Malory's book. Most of my impressions come from movies, I guess. I always liked the historical details that give the feeling of the times—the armor, the cups, the castles. Come to think of it, when exactly were those times? Was there ever really a king named Arthur? Or a court called Camelot? That might make a good topic for a paper—separate fact from fiction in the legend of King Arthur.

5. Identify your purpose. Formulating a provisional purpose for your paper can serve as a compass, guiding you through your research and giving you a sense of direction as you write. It may also help you find an interesting angle or approach to your topic. The chart below lists several possible purposes and examples of paper topics.

Purpose of Paper	Example of Topic
To inform	King Arthur: the many versions of an English legend
To examine cause and effect	How the legend of King Arthur influenced the work of John Steinbeck
To compare and contrast	Similarities and differences between King Arthur and Robin Hood
To analyze	Elements of historical fact in the legends of King Arthur

274   Workshop 9

Social Studies Connection

History   Suggest that students choose a period in history they have come to know through fiction—whether movies or novels—and then do some research to find out how accurate a picture the fiction gives of the period in question.

John Steinbeck had a goal for researching medieval British literature: to deepen his appreciation of the Arthurian legends he loved. Think of specific goals you might achieve by researching and writing your paper, such as settling an argument, exploring a career option, or increasing your expertise in an area that interests you. Specific goals can serve to keep you focused, even though, like your purposes, they may change as you go along.

6. Focus your research.   If you know what the gist of your paper will be, you are now in a position to write your controlling purpose, a formal statement of what your paper will be about. A controlling purpose can help you maintain a sense of direction throughout the writing process, giving you a standard by which to judge the relevance of your information and the effectiveness of your words. Keep in mind, however, that your controlling purpose may change as you research, write, and revise your paper.

By the time Michele had limited her topic, she felt fairly certain of the purpose of her paper. She wrote the following statement to guide her work.

> In this paper I will identify which parts of the story of King Arthur are actually historical and which are pure legend.

7. Identify your audience.   Although you will usually be writing for your teacher and classmates, you may have the occasion to write for another audience as well—if, for example, you decide to submit your research paper to a writing contest or present it to a local organization, club, or civic agency. Keeping your audience in mind will help you gather information more efficiently, write more effectively, and employ appropriate strategies to catch and hold your reader's attention.

RESEARCH YOUR TOPIC

1. Prepare to do research.   Before you can begin to write your paper, you will need to locate, analyze, evaluate, and organize a large body of information. As with any search, you have a better chance of success if you know what you're looking for. Before you go to the library, therefore, consider making a list of the questions you will try to answer through your research. Michele made the list of questions shown on the following page before she began researching her topic.

HANDBOOKS
FOR HELP & PRACTICE

Using Source Materials,
pp. 482–489
Finding the Best Source,
pp. 493–495
Reference Works,
pp. 495–498
Outline Form,
pp. 826–827

Research Report   **275**

Research Your Topic

Objectives

1. To use research techniques to gather information about a topic
2. To prepare a working bibliography
3. To organize information and prepare an outline

Preteaching

Preview the Research Your Topic section. If there are skills and concepts students need help with, present them at this time. The mini-lesson references below may help you in your selection and instruction.

Handbook Mini-Lessons
- Using Source Materials, pp. 482–489
- Reference Works, pp. 495–498
- Outline Form, pp. 826–827
- Finding the Best Source, pp. 493–495

You may also wish to use Thinking Skills Transparencies during this phase of the assignment.

Teaching Strategies

Critical Thinking

Analysis Have students consider Michele's questions in light of her controlling purpose. What information is each question likely to generate? How might this information contribute to her purpose? What questions would students add to the list? Which ones would they change or leave out? Why?

Management Tip

Schedule a meeting halfway through the time allotted for research to have students discuss their progress and problems with one another. Use this opportunity to assess which students need help and how you should redirect their efforts. Monitoring students' progress in some such way is crucial. Faulty research nearly automatically leads to a poor research report, and during research students have much opportunity to veer off course unnoticed.

Stumbling Block

Students may complain that they cannot find any sources of information about the topic they have chosen. Point out that this is probably a good sign: it means they have chosen an original topic. Emphasize that they will have to search out material pertinent to *their* purpose in books and articles written for a somewhat different purpose—the same procedure that all writers of original research books and papers use. Remind students that often they can track down information on unusual topics by checking entries in the index of books that deal with subjects related to their topic.

ONE STUDENT'S PROCESS

- What are the earliest known versions of the Arthur legend?
- How did the story change over the course of time?
- What was happening in British history at the time that Arthur supposedly lived?
- Was there really a King Arthur and if so, what is known about him?
- What parts of the story of King Arthur belong to legend rather than to history?

2. Begin your research. Doing research involves finding facts and ideas in a variety of reliable sources. Begin your library research by consulting one or more good encyclopedias and other reference works that contain entries on your general subject. Consulting such reference works will give you an overview of the subject and may suggest directions for further research and study. Next check the *Readers' Guide to Periodical Literature* for a list of articles on your subject. Your library's card catalog will provide you with titles and call numbers for books on your writing topic. Also ask your librarian for any specialized reference books geared to your topic.

In some fields, especially the social sciences, you will want to explore both primary and secondary sources. **Primary sources** provide direct or firsthand reports about events. Diaries, letters, journals, and original documents—such as the Constitution and the Emancipation Proclamation—all qualify as primary sources. **Secondary sources** provide indirect or secondhand information, including analyses of primary sources. Most newspaper and magazine accounts, encyclopedia articles, and research studies—such as your paper—are examples of secondary sources. Secondary sources are more plentiful and, in some cases, easier to obtain than primary sources, and they can provide a broad range of information and analysis about a topic.

You can also gather information on your topic through interviews, television and radio programs, recordings, and graphic aids. Sources like these often provide insights that can contribute to the freshness of a paper.

3. Evaluate your sources. As you discover potential sources, you need to evaluate them to determine whether they might contain useful and accurate information. The following guidelines can help you evaluate your materials.

Selecting Source Materials

- Is the author an authority on the subject? An author who has written several books or articles on your subject and whose name is included in various bibliographies may be an authoritative source.

- Is the source reliable, unbiased, and up-to-date? A book on a politician's economic policies written by a friend or relative may not be as accurate as one written by an authority on economics. A book on computers published in 1968 will not be as relevant or accurate as one published in 1990. A third edition of a book would be more valuable than the first or second edition. Finding the most recently published material is essential—particularly if your topic involves technology, science, or medicine.

- If the title of an article looks promising, in what kind of publication does it appear? Many popular-interest magazines generally are not suitable sources for a research paper. Scholarly journals or trade magazines are often sources of more credible information.

- If a book looks promising, for what audience is it intended? Many of the books you'll find are really intended for younger readers. Because they present information in an overly simplified form, they are not suitable sources of information for research papers. Books of a highly technical nature are also usually unsuitable. They are likely to be too detailed and complex for your purposes.

- Do the sources you've consulted contain bibliographies? Most secondary source books and articles will include a bibliography of resources the authors used in conducting their own research. Examine the bibliographies of your potential sources carefully. You may wish to investigate those authors and titles that appear in more than one bibliography. Chances are good they'll hold just the information you're looking for on your topic.

Learning Styles Students vary in their need for order and tolerance for structure. For students who need much order, establish a fixed work center where they can keep all important papers related to their research report, including a file box or even a rolodex for their working bibliography. Students at the other pole, who thrive on stimulus and spontaneity, might do better bundling their bibliography cards with a rubber band and carrying them along when they go questing for information.

Gifted and Talented Students Advise students to be on the alert for patterns of *disagreement* about their topic among the various sources they consult. By addressing themselves to one of these disputed areas, they may be able to contribute something original and important to the literature of their chosen topic.

COMPUTER TIP

Some libraries subscribe to one or more information services. Such services can call upon data banks of the most current information on a wide variety of topics. Ask a librarian if your library has these services and how you can use them in researching your paper.

4. Begin a working bibliography. A working bibliography is a list of potentially useful sources for your research paper. Recording information about sources you are sure to use on 3″ × 5″ index cards will help you when you are ready to write footnotes and your final list of works cited.

Guidelines for Source Cards

- **Books** List the author (or editor), last name first; the title; the name and location of the publisher; the year of publication; the library call number; and the location of the source.

- **Magazines** List the author, last name first; the title; the name and date of the magazine; the page numbers of the article; and the location of the source.

- **Encyclopedias** List the title of the entry; the name of the encyclopedia set; the year of the edition; the library call number; and the location of the source.

- **Other reference works** List the title of the article or entry; the name of the book or set; the volume and page numbers; the year of publication; and the location of the source.

It is important to number your sources in the upper right-hand corner of the cards for reference during notetaking and drafting; when you use a source, note the number, and your footnotes will then be easy to compile. Three of Michele's source cards are shown on the next page.

Le Morte D'Arthur by Thomas Malory is a 15th century French version of the Arthurian legend.

278   Workshop 9

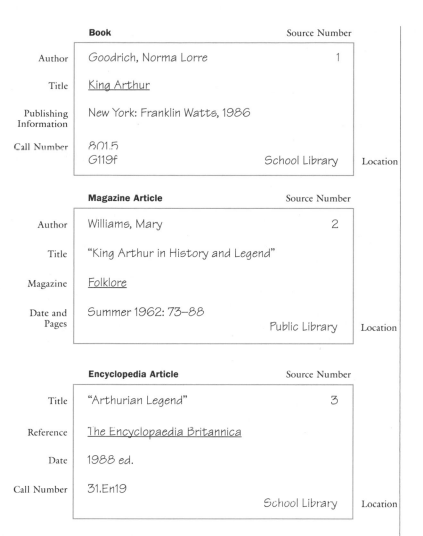

Book		Source Number
Author	Goodrich, Norma Lorre	1
Title	King Arthur	
Publishing Information	New York: Franklin Watts, 1986	
Call Number	801.5 G119f	School Library Location

Magazine Article		Source Number
Author	Williams, Mary	2
Title	"King Arthur in History and Legend"	
Magazine	Folklore	
Date and Pages	Summer 1962: 73–88	Public Library Location

Encyclopedia Article		Source Number
Title	"Arthurian Legend"	3
Reference	The Encyclopaedia Britannica	
Date	1988 ed.	
Call Number	31.En19	School Library Location

5. Take notes as you read your sources. As you go through the sources in your working bibliography, write down any information —paraphrases, summaries, or direct quotations—that you may include in the body of your paper. Take notes on 4″ × 6″ index cards, putting only one idea or fact on each card. That way, you can shuffle the cards later to experiment with various ways of organizing your paper.

PROBLEM SOLVING

How do I record the information I gather?

Teaching Tip: Taking Notes

Advise students to notice the context of any information they record from a source. If isolating it from the context will give it a misleading slant, they should include a few words about the context on the note card. Warn them *not* to assume they will remember anything they fail to write down. After all, they may take hundreds of notes in the course of their research.

 ## Individualizing Instruction

LEP Students Students who have difficulty expressing themselves in standard English should, for note-taking purposes, use whatever language suits them, including foreign words, drawings, or symbols. Emphasize that their notes are not for the public but for themselves.

Spot Check

Ask students how the information they have gathered so far has enlarged or changed their views. The absence of change may indicate a problem. Remind students that research should not be a process of gathering data to confirm what one knows. It should be a creative search for information that will enable one to draw fresh conclusions about a topic.

Modeling

Read a passage of information aloud to students and model how you would paraphrase it as a note. Demonstrate how to summarize information without distorting it or omitting any essential point.

Writing TIP

To take notes efficiently, look through the table of contents and index of each book, or the headings and subheadings of each encyclopedia or magazine article. Closely read and take notes on only the parts that pertain to your limited topic.

The following guidelines can help you take notes you will use as you draft your paper.

Guidelines for Note Taking

- Keep your controlling purpose and audience in mind so that you record only relevant material.

- Take notes quickly, omitting words or phrases that are not essential to meaning and using abbreviations when appropriate. However, be careful not to make your notes so brief that you can't understand them.

- Save time by paraphrasing information. However, when you summarize or paraphrase a writer's words, be sure you do not misinterpret or distort their meaning. Double check facts and statistics to make sure you have correctly recorded them.

- Distinguish between fact and opinion. Signal opinion by writing: "Dr. Schultz thinks that . . ." or "According to Gloria Steinem, . . ." Point out differences of opinion in your notes.

- Copy direct quotations word for word, including correct punctuation and spelling. Mark the beginning and end with quotation marks so that you can easily distinguish the quotation from paraphrased material. Indicate the omission of nonessential parts of a quotation with ellipses (. . .).

Here is one of the note cards Michele prepared for her research paper on King Arthur. The number in the upper right-hand corner of the note card corresponds to the source card that documents the source where Michele got her information.

Sample Note Card	Source Number
	4
Note	All the legends seem to agree on this point: King Arthur is going to wake up some day and ride forth to save his people just when they need him the most.
Page Reference	11–12

6. State your thesis. After completing your reading and note taking, you should have a good idea of what you want your paper to accomplish. Your purpose can now be refined into a thesis statement that will guide and focus your draft. You can use your thesis statement in the introduction of your paper, and you can work it into your conclusion as well.

7. Organize your material. Although you may not decide the final structure of your research paper until later, you should consider drawing up a provisional organization plan now. Group your note cards under major ideas, arrange these groups in an appropriate, logical order, and then make an outline based on this arrangement. For detailed information on making outlines, see the Appendix, pages 826–827.

Here is the outline Michele made for her paper.

ONE STUDENT'S PROCESS

The Real King Arthur
I. The legend of King Arthur
   A. Earliest versions
   B. Changes over time and place
   C. Geoffrey of Monmouth, Wace, Troyes
   D. Thomas Malory
   E. Summary of Malory's story
II. The historical King Arthur
   A. Early hints from historians and chronicles
   B. Arthur in the context of British history
III. Composite picture of King Arthur
   A. What he did and didn't look like
   B. What he did and didn't accomplish
IV. Value of myth versus reality

To help you keep your material organized, you may want to write the corresponding numerals and letters from your outline on your note cards. Keep in mind, however, that your outline is only a tool. You should feel free to reorganize your material at any time, collect new information if you feel the need, or even change your whole approach.

Research Report **281**

Draft and Discover

Objectives

1. To draft an informative research report
2. To document sources of information accurately
3. To respond to one's own writing and that of a peer

Preteaching

Preview the Draft and Discover section and present any skills and concepts students may need help with. The mini-lesson references below may help you in your selection and instruction.

Handbook Mini-Lessons

- Organizing Your Work, pp. 349–357
- Elaborative Details, pp. 376–378
- Problem Solving, pp. 472–474

You may also wish to use the Elaboration Worksheet and the Peer Response Guide during the Draft and Discover phase.

Teaching Strategies

Spot Check

Check to make sure that students are not stringing together quotations with transitions, thereby substituting research for original thought. Remind them that a research report should consist of the *writer's* own ideas and assertions, *supported* by information gleaned from others.

HANDBOOKS

FOR HELP & PRACTICE

Organizing Your Work,
pp. 349–357
Elaborative Details,
pp. 376–378
Problem Solving,
pp. 472–474

DRAFT AND DISCOVER

1. Begin to write. Now you are ready to begin working on your first draft. At this stage, just try to get your ideas down on paper, using your outline as a guide. Begin a new paragraph for every topic and subtopic on your outline. Don't worry about achieving an elegant style or about rules of grammar, spelling, and mechanics. You can make corrections during revision.

2. Think about the general organization of your paper. A typical research paper begins with an introduction, in which you present a central problem or question and explain how you will approach it. Next comes the body of the paper, a series of paragraphs in which you develop your main idea using supporting details from authoritative sources. The paper ends with a conclusion in which you may, for example, sum up your research, discuss the implications of your findings, or point the way for further study.

3. Support your analysis. During the research process you will gather a great deal of information. Keep in mind, however, that a good research paper does not just report the information; it makes

Stirling in the Time of the Stuarts, Johannes Vorsterman

282   Workshop 9

Humanities Connection

Art Note   *Stirling in the Time of the Stuarts,* by the Dutch artist Johannes Vorsterman (1643–c.1699) is a painting of the Scottish county Stirling during the reign of King Charles II, who was a member of the royal family Stuart. For many centuries, both kings and commoners commissioned artists like Vorsterman to provide images of their kingdoms and properties.

inferences, analyzes and interprets evidence, and reaches a conclusion. Use the facts, statistics, opinions, examples, and other evidence you have gathered to support your analysis. Direct quotations can often be used to support or prove your original ideas, but use them sparingly. They should give credibility to your analysis and interpretation, not replace it.

4. Document your sources.   All information in your paper except your own interpretations and ideas must be documented, or credited, to its original source. Documentation serves three basic purposes in your research paper: it indicates the source of material that is directly quoted; it gives credit for other people's ideas even if you've written them in your own words; and it gives the sources of graphic aids, figures, or statistics. You can document your sources with either footnotes or parenthetical documentation. Check with your teacher to see which method of documentation is preferred.

Make sure students understand that they do not need to document the source of commonly known or undisputed information, even if it happens to be a point they didn't know and were forced to look up, such as the latitude of Paris.

Management Tip

During drafting, the demand on your attention may outstrip the supply. Streamline the process by identifying students who are struggling with similar problems (such as introductions, unworkable outlines, or conclusions). Get these students together to discuss their problems and help each other find solutions, liberating you to work with students who are more deeply mired in problems and need individual help.

Speaking and Listening

Students may use a conversational tone in a research report, but should probably avoid cute, breezy, or slang language. To discover if they are striking the right tone, students might try reading passages from their papers aloud to a classmate. Merely reading their work to an attentive audience will enable them to sense how the words are being received. You may want to use the Peer Response Worksheets for this assignment as students provide feedback on each other's work.

Springboard

Have students write on index cards questions relating to how successful research reports should be approached and written. (For example, "What would be a reliable source of information for technical data about computers?"; "How should information about a quotation be given in a research paper?") Divide the class into two teams and have a "Research Paper Question Bee." Read the questions at random, alternately calling on each team. Evaluate the responses and assign points. The team with the most points at the end is the winner.

Stumbling Block

If students find themselves in a dead end, labyrinth, or swamp halfway through drafting (a distinct possibility no matter how tight and clean the outline seemed), suggest that they go through what they have written so far and circle every point they consider strong. Then they should copy these points onto a separate paper and use them as the basis for a fresh draft. At this time, students may also benefit from re-evaluating and if necessary rewriting their statement of controlling purpose.

 Individualizing Instruction

Learning Styles Students whose learning style led them to begin drafting with a minimal outline may benefit from making an outline now, as a prelude to revision, based on a consideration of what they have written. This will help them evaluate how logical and orderly their presentation of ideas is.

COMPUTER TIP

If you entered the first draft of your research paper into a computer, you should make a printout of your draft now. You will need this "hard copy" to share with your peer reader or readers.

Footnotes, the traditional method of documentation, are a numbered list of sources, placed either at the bottom of the page on which the reference appears or on a separate page at the end of the report. Number the quotations and paraphrased ideas consecutively in the text, using Arabic numerals directly after and slightly above the last word of the quotation or passage.

The most common way to cite a source is with **parenthetical documentation,** which cites a reference in parentheses after the quotation or paraphrased idea. A parenthetical note is sufficient since a full list of sources appears in the bibliography. Use these guidelines for parenthetical documentation.

Guidelines for Parenthetical Documentation

- **Works by one author** Give the author's last name in parentheses at the end of a sentence or quote, followed by the page numbers (Jones 58–60).

- **Works by more than one author** List all the last names in parentheses, or give one last name followed by *et al.* (Smith, Jones, and Wilcox 87) or (Smith *et al.* 87).

- **Works with no author listed** When citing an article that does not identify the author, use the title of the work or a shortened version of it ("Sir Lancelot" 398).

- **Two works by the same author** If you use more than one work by the same author, give the title, or a shortened version, after the author's last name (Jones, Holy Grail 398).

- **Two works cited at the same place** If you use more than one source to support a point, use a semicolon to separate the entries (Jones 398; Smith 87).

As you write your first draft, keep your central purpose in mind, but don't hesitate to expand your ideas. Don't worry if your views about the subject start to change or if you find yourself veering off the course charted in your outline. Drafting should be an opportunity to explore your topic and make new discoveries.

5. Take a break. Set your completed first draft aside for a while so that you will be able to review it with fresh eyes. Then read it again. If possible have a classmate read it as well. Use the following questions to help you and your peer readers evaluate your writing.

REVIEW YOUR WRITING

Questions for Yourself

- Does my paper cover all the information I want to present? What should be added, deleted, or changed?
- If this was an assignment, have I met the requirements?
- Does my introduction clearly state my thesis, or main idea?
- Does the body of my paper develop and support my controlling purpose?
- Have I documented my sources? Are my facts accurate?
- Do I communicate my interest in the subject?
- Are my ideas developed clearly and logically? How can I organize my material more effectively?
- Are my quotes too long? Should I paraphrase any of them?
- Have I achieved my overall purpose and personal goals for the paper? If my purpose and personal goals changed as I wrote, what changes do I need to make in the content, organization, or style of the report?

Questions for Your Peer Readers

- What did you like most about my paper?
- Why do you think I chose to write about this subject?
- Did you have trouble following any part of my paper?
- Is the main idea of my paper clear? Tell me its subject and purpose in your own words.
- What do you need more information about? What parts can I leave out?
- Did the introduction capture your interest? Did the conclusion satisfy you, or did it leave you hanging?

REVISE YOUR WRITING

1. Evaluate your responses. Think about your own reactions to your draft and the responses you got from your readers. What changes will you want to make? As you consider this question, keep in mind that a good research report has certain characteristics.

HANDBOOKS
FOR HELP & PRACTICE

Concluding Nonfiction, pp. 368–370
Unity/Coherence, pp. 382–391
Peer Response, pp. 397–401

Based on students' peer and self-evaluations, try to identify the single most important problem in each paper. Identifying the main problem students should attack during revision will lead to finished papers that are easier to read and evaluate.

Revise Your Writing

Objectives

1. To evaluate the responses to a draft
2. To revise a draft based on the responses
3. To prepare a final bibliography
4. To proofread for errors in spelling, grammar, usage, and mechanics

Preteaching

Assess students' problem areas based on their drafts and on a preview of the Revising section, and identify the skills you want to review. The mini-lessons listed below may be useful to you for instructional purposes.

Handbook Mini-Lessons
- Concluding Nonfiction, pp. 368–370
- Unity/Coherence, pp. 382–391
- Peer Responses, pp. 397–401
- Evaluating Media, pp. 539–540

You may also wish to use the Student Revision Model Transparencies, the Elaboration, Revision, and Proofreading Worksheets, and the Writing Evaluation Guidelines for this assignment as resources during the Revise Your Writing phase.

Teaching Strategies

Critical Thinking

Evaluating Ask students to decide what they like and don't like about Michele's first paragraph, what elements they might try to include or imitate in their own research reports, and what changes they would make during revision if this report were theirs.

Management Tip

As you confer with students during revision, notice which ones can be grouped together in terms of working styles, topics, and problems. Then when students reach a point at which they seek collaboration, you will know which ones to link up as partners.

Teaching Tip: Revision

Suggest that instead of working through a draft sequentially, students should first make major changes in content and organization—changes that involve whole blocks of text—and then attack more local problems of language and wording.

Grammar
—TIP—

When you're not sure whether to set off a word or phrase with commas, try saying the sentence without the words in question. If the sentence is clear and complete without those words, use commas.

Standards for Evaluation

An effective research report . . .

- begins with an interesting introduction that identifies the subject and establishes the author's approach.
- develops the author's thesis in the body of the paper.
- offers detailed and concrete information in support of the author's thesis.
- presents accurate facts about the topic drawn from a variety of sources.
- expresses all facts and ideas in the author's own words, except in the case of direct quotations.
- documents the sources of all facts, direct quotations, and opinions derived from others.
- uses exact quotations sparingly and always for a purpose.
- uses logical organization and effective transitional phrases to create a smooth flow of ideas.
- ends with a conclusion that effectively sums up the paper.

2. Problem-solve. Rework your draft, taking both your own and your readers' responses into account. Here are some of the changes Michele made in part of her first draft based on those responses.

ONE STUDENT'S PROCESS

I like the Arthur legend too, but aren't you overstating its importance?

I'm confused about your main point. "Truly a legend" makes it sound as if it has no basis in fact.

This story may sound familiar, for it retells part of the *what may be the most famous* greatest legend ever told—the tale of Britain's King, *in the Western world* Arthur. And a legend it truly is. Yet was there a real King Arthur? If so, what did he do to inspire such mystical legends? To find out, we will look at the legend *Untangling fact from myth in the Arthurian legends requires a close look at the legend in its many forms as well as* in its many forms. Next we will conduct an examination of British history to untangle the facts from the myth.

It has all the elements of a classic legend: a kind and noble king, magic spells, knights in armor, and a misty other world. Some legends, however, have a basis in fact.

Springboard

Students who keep revising their report and can't get it right might enjoy what writer and economist John Kenneth Galbraith had to say: "There are days when the result is so bad that no fewer than five revisions are required. In contrast, when I'm greatly inspired, only four revisions are needed."

Help students further understand the frustration and ultimate satisfaction of rewrites by encouraging them to keep track of the way a particular sentence or paragraph underwent various changes. Allow them to share their one, two, three, or more revisions of the passage with the class.

3. Prepare your list of works cited. At the end of your research paper, you must list the sources you actually used in writing the paper. Gather the cards for every source you have cited and prepare your final list of works cited in accordance with the following guidelines.

Guidelines for a List of Works Cited

- Arrange all works cited entries alphabetically by the last name of the author or editor.
- If you wish, divide the works cited list into separate sections for books, magazines, and other sources. Each section should be alphabetized separately, with a centered subheading reading, in upper- and lowercase letters, *Books, Magazines,* and *Other Sources.*
- If no author or editor is given, alphabetize each entry by the first word of the title. If the first word is *A, An,* or *The,* alphabetize according to the second word of the title.
- Begin the first line of each entry at the left margin. If the entry runs to a second or third line, indent those lines five spaces.
- Double-space each entry, and double-space between entries.
- Put a period at the end of each entry.
- Works cited entries contain page numbers only when they refer to parts within whole works. For example, an entry for a chapter in a book or an article in a magazine should contain page numbers for the complete chapter or article you used.

These guidelines are general rules for the Works Cited section of your paper. The following basic forms for entries will help you use correct punctuation and cite sources with different elements.

Books are not the only research sources. These details from a medieval tapestry show some 14th century amusements.

287

Speaking and Listening

The emphasis on content in a research paper can all too easily lead students to use dull, graceless language. As a corrective, have students read to a partner (or listen to a partner read) from a good *nonfiction* author, whether your choice or the students'. (V. S. Naipaul, Joan Didion, and John McPhee, for example, are excellent choices.)

Peer Response

After working on a passage too long, students may be unable to gauge their progress because older versions echoing in their mind interfere with their ability to judge how it sounds now. Suggest that at such a point students stop revising and read the passage in question to a peer for an objective response.

Linking Grammar and Writing

To cut through the clutter of a long sentence, students should ask, "Who (or what) does what?" Once they have identified the core of the sentence, the subject and the verb, they can rebuild it.

Literature Connection

Selection to Read For another example of ancient British literature based on legends, some students might enjoy reading the poem *Beowulf.* Point out that this poem was composed in the eighth century; it was as ancient to the 15th century Sir Thomas Malory as Malory's work is to us today.

Individualizing Instruction

Basic Students While they are making their final revisions to their reports, basic students may be in particular need of isolation and quiet. Create "total quiet" workstations for these students and make it clear that no one should disturb students in these workstations.

Teaching Tip: Writing Process

Remind students that writing is a recursive process: they may be able to solve seemingly intractable problems they are facing now, during revision, by going back to an activity from an earlier phase, such as brainstorming for ideas, freewriting on their topic, working on focusing their topic, doing more research, or tinkering with their outline. Use the Student Revision Model Transparency for this assignment to help students recognize the kinds of revisions that can improve a research report.

Basic Forms for Works Cited

Whole Books

A. One author

Wilson, Anne. The Magical Quest: The Use of Magic in Arthurian Romance. Manchester: Manchester UP, 1988.

UP is an abbreviation for University Press.

B. Two authors

Gilbert, Sandra M., and Susan Gubar. The Madwoman in the Attic: The Woman Writer and the Nineteenth Century Literary Imagination. New Haven: Yale UP, 1979.

C. Three authors

Heppelwhite, Charles W., Jeannette M. Meyerhoff, and Gerhardt B. Kassenbaum. The Effects of High Technology on Smokestack America. Litchfield: Litchfield, 1988.

D. Four or more authors

Gatto, Joseph, et al. Exploring Visual Design. 2nd ed. Worcester: Davis, 1987.

The abbreviation *et al.* is Latin for the phrase *and others*. You can use *et al.* instead of listing all authors.

E. No author given

Literary Market Place: The Directory of American Book Publishing. 1990 ed. New York: Bowker, 1990.

F. An editor, but no single author

Saddlemyer, Ann, ed. Letters to Molly: John Millington Synge to Maire O'Neill. Cambridge: Harvard UP, 1984.

This form may be used when you have cited several works from a collection. Instead of writing separate bibliography entries for each work, you may write one entry for the entire work, listing the editor or editors first.

G. Two or three editors

Emanuel, James A., and Theodore L. Gross, eds. Dark Symphony: Negro Literature in America. New York: Macmillan, 1968.

Parts Within Books

Page numbers of selections follow publication dates for entries citing parts within books, and magazines, newspapers, journals, encyclopedias, and reviews.

A. A poem, short story, essay, or chapter from a collection of works by one author

Angelou, Maya. "Remembering." Poems. New York: Bantam, 1986. 11.

B. A poem, short story, essay, or chapter from a collection of works by several authors

Welty, Eudora. "The Corner Store." Prose Models. Ed. Gerald Levin. New York: Harcourt, 1984. 20–22.

C. A novel or play from a collection of novels or plays published under one cover

Serling, Rod. Requiem for a Heavyweight. Twelve American Plays. Ed. Richard Corbin and Miriam Balf. New York: Scribner's, 1973. 299–327.

Cannery Row. The Short Novels of John Steinbeck. New York: Viking, 1963. 355–649.

Magazines, Newspapers, Journals, Encyclopedias, and Reviews

A. An article from a quarterly or monthly magazine

Batten, Mary. "Life Spans." Science Digest Feb. 1984: 46–51.

B. An article from a weekly magazine

Powell, Bill. "Coping with the Markets." Newsweek 27 Apr. 1987: 54.

C. A magazine article with no author given

"How the New Tax Law Affects America." Nation's Accountants 24 Sept. 1986: 66–69.

D. An article from a daily newspaper

Faust, Joan Lee. "Tulips: A History of Success." New York Times 12 Sept. 1990, sec. 2: 18.

If no author is given, begin with the title.

Research Report **289**

Research Report **289**

Teaching Tip: Reorganizing

Students should feel free to use scissors and tape or rubber cement to attack problems of structure and organization. Before cutting up their drafts, they should make a backup copy to keep as a reference. Advise them to use tape or paste sparingly so they can change their minds many times about any choices they make.

Stumbling Block

Some students may have a hard time cutting passages that contain good writing but which simply do not fit into the paper. Suggest that these students begin an "archives" box or file in which to keep deleted material for possible use in a future project.

Guidelines for Evaluation

The following guidelines may be used for a close evaluation of a research report. See the Writing Evaluation Guidelines in the Teacher's Resource File for additional help with holistic or analytic scoring.

Ideas and Content
- catches attention in the opener
- states a coherent problem or thesis
- presents interesting information
- is accurate and authoritative
- uses quotations effectively

Structure and Form
- contains an introduction, body, and conclusion
- presents ideas in logical sequence
- makes relationships between ideas clear
- documents information correctly

Grammar, Usage, and Mechanics
- uses correct grammar and usage
- uses correct spelling and punctuation

Managing the Paper Load

Divide the class into response groups, and ask them to formalize their assessment of each member's report in a brief written evaluation that identifies both strengths and weaknesses. Each assessment should represent the consensus of the group. Use these student assessments as a reference when you grade the papers.

E. An editorial in a newspaper

> "Is America Set for the Hypermarket?" Editorial. Chicago Tribune 4 Jan. 1988, sec. 1: 10.

If no author is given, begin with the title.

F. An article in a journal

> Aumiller, Emily P. "Lord of the Flies as a Musical." English Journal 71.8 (1982): 32.

The volume number, the number of the issue, the date, and the page number follow the title of the journal.

G. An encyclopedia article

> "Western Frontier Life." World Book Encyclopedia. 1990 ed.

H. An unsigned, untitled review

> Rev. of Harry and Son. American Film Mar. 1984: 78.

I. A signed, titled review

> Ludlow, Arthur. "Glass Houses." Rev. of Rolling Breaks and Other Movie Business, by Aljean Harmetz. Movies Aug. 1983: 76.

If a titled review is unsigned, begin the bibliographic entry with the title.

Other Sources

A. An interview

> Farquharson, Reginald W. Personal interview. 26 May 1988.

B. A letter that has not been published

> Reagan, Ronald. Letter to Professor Stephanie R. Somerville. 22 May 1988.

C. A thesis or dissertation

> Ortega, Miguel C. "The Acceptance and Rejection of the American Dream: 1960 to 1975." Diss., Southwestern Oklahoma State U, 1988.

D. Information in private files

> Students of Paul D. Schriener. Of Our Lives: A History of the 1960's and 1970's. Department of Social Studies, Munster High School, 1981.

4. Proofread your work. Finally, make a clean copy of your paper and read through it, checking for errors in grammar, spelling, usage, and mechanics. Correct any dangling modifiers so that your readers will always know to whom or what you are referring.

LINKING
GRAMMAR **A N D** WRITING
Avoiding Dangling Modifiers

When a modifier seems to refer to a word that is missing from the sentence, the modifier is said to dangle. Notice how Michele corrected the dangling modifier in the following sentence.

Original: After defeating the Saxons, much of Europe is conquered.

Revised: After defeating the Saxons, Arthur rides on to conquer much of Europe.

See Handbook 33, pages 602–603, for more information about this problem.

PUBLISH AND PRESENT

- **Present your paper to an interested organization.** Ask a librarian for help in finding a local association whose members might be interested in the topic of your paper. Contact the head of the association and request permission to present your research findings at an association meeting.
- **Present your paper orally to one or more of your classes.** Add models, charts or graphs, illustrations, video materials, or music to make your presentation more interesting.
- **Submit your paper to a publisher.** Consult a guide such as *Writer's Market* to find a magazine that specializes in the subject of your paper, and send it to the magazine. You also may wish to submit it to a local newspaper.
- **Save your work in your writing portfolio.** Look at it in a few months. See if you still agree with the ideas you have presented and if your writing style has changed.

HANDBOOKS
FOR HELP & PRACTICE

Manuscript Preparation, pp. 414–415

Research Report **291**

Individualizing Instruction

ESL Students ESL students may have trouble identifying dangling modifiers due to the differing conventions of syntax in their native languages. If you detect problems, review fundamental sentence structure, modifiers, and participial phrases. Use the Handbook materials to provide practice.

Publish and Present

Objective

To publish and present a research report

> *Handbook Mini-Lesson*
> - Manuscript Preparation, pp. 414–415

Teaching Strategies

Speaking and Listening

Work with other teachers to arrange a forum in which interested students can make oral presentations of their research reports.

Reteaching

Assess the needs of students who were not successful developing an effective research report, and identify two or three areas in which additional practice is needed. Assign the appropriate Handbook Mini-Lessons, along with the support materials listed for each lesson. Concepts commonly requiring reteaching for this assignment are:

Focusing Ideas: Handbook 3
Using Source Materials: Handbook 24

The following suggestions and resources may also be useful:

1. Insufficient Detail Research reports need both generalizations and details. Discuss the difference, using examples from students' writing. Have students identify generalizations in their reports, use freewriting to generate numerous concrete supporting details and examples, and then select from these appropriate ones to include in their papers when they revise.

2. Faulty Subject–Verb Agreement Review the rules for subject-verb agreement with compound subjects, indefinite pronouns, collective nouns, and singular subjects followed by prepositional phrases that contain plural nouns. Find examples of sentences embodying each problem situation in students' work, and ask students to identify the correct verb for each case.

Catches the reader's attention with an engaging introduction in the form of an exciting narrative

Documents the source of the information

States the central problem of the paper and establishes the author's approach: a comparison of the Arthur of legend and historical fact

ONE STUDENT'S PROCESS

Arthur: Britain's Elusive King

Michele King

The aging King Arthur gazed over the battlefield. A hundred thousand noble knights, allies and enemies alike, lay dead. Across the field the king saw the enemy leader, Mordred, in full armor. "Traitor," cried the king as he ran and plunged a spear into Mordred's belly. But at his dying breath, Mordred struck a mighty blow with his sword. The blade cut through the king's helmet and went into his skull. The king and Mordred fell.

"My time passes fast," said the wounded king to Sir Bedivere, his only surviving knight. "Take my good sword, Excalibur, and go with it to yonder water's side and throw it into the water." Sir Bedivere did so; and, as the sword flew, a mysterious hand reached up from the deep, caught it by the handle, waved it three times in farewell, and disappeared.

Then Bedivere set the king on a barge at the water's edge. On this barge, many beautiful ladies in black wept over the king. "I must go to the vale of Avalon to heal me of my grievous wounds," said King Arthur as he sailed off. Never again was he seen (Hibbert 54–56).

This story may sound familiar, for it retells part of what may be the most famous legend in the Western world—the tale of Britain's King Arthur. It has all the elements of a classic legend: a kind and noble king, magic spells, knights in armor, and a misty other world. Some legends, however, have a basis in fact. Was there a real King Arthur? If so, what did he do to inspire such mystical legends? Untangling fact from myth in the Arthurian legends requires a close look at the legend in its many forms as well as a careful examination of British history.

Literature Connection

Selection to Read Now that students have followed Michele through the writing of her paper about Arthurian legends, students might be interested in reading selections from Malory's *Le Morte d'Arthur*, the work that got both her and Steinbeck started.

For many centuries, people have told the story of King Arthur and his knights. During the 700's, and probably earlier, storytellers spread tales of the king's adventures across England, Scotland, Wales, Ireland, France, and into the rest of Europe (Hibbert 11; Ashe 14; Morris 117, 119). In each land, the tale changed. In England's Cornwall, the legend told of a land swarming with giants until Arthur vanquished them (Hibbert 11). One story from Wales describes Arthur's follower Kei, who could breathe under water for nine days (Williams 81). All the legends agree on one point, however: that one day, Arthur will return to save his people.

The tale of Arthur "the once and future king" probably gained its greatest popularity during the 12th century. In 1135 Geoffrey of Monmouth completed his twelve-volume <u>History of the Kings of Britain</u>, devoting three entire books to King Arthur (Hibbert 16–17). Scholars agree that Geoffrey's work is a "masterpiece," yet few think that the books recount true history. Most of his tales come from ancient stories and legends or from Geoffrey's own rich imagination. Geoffrey's purpose, many insist, was not to present historical fact, but to create a national hero (Hibbert 19–21; Williams 77, 88; Ashe 4, 25; Morris 118).

Filled with heroic adventure, spells of the wizard Merlin, and even a man-eating giant, Geoffrey's tales inspired other writers (Ashe 9, 12). In 1155, Wace of Jersey wrote a long poem in French retelling Geoffrey's story. Wace added the story of the Round Table where Arthur's chivalrous knights met (Hibbert 21; Williams 77–78). Twenty years later, the French poet Chrétien de Troyes created his version of the tale. It is set in a mystical land and tells stories of love between knights and ladies, of a new knight named Lancelot, and of the search by Arthur's knights for the Holy Grail, the cup

Develops the topic in an organized way by presenting a historical analysis

Uses information from a variety of sources

Uses concrete details and examples to develop the author's analysis

Extension and Enrichment

- Students interested in art and music might get together and create original record jackets for their favorite albums, with liner notes and graphics based on research into the background of the musicians and their music.

- Suggest that students use research techniques to compile an album documenting their family history and roots as a gift for a member of their family. Such an album might contain not only photographs and information about their specific forebears, but information, illustrations, and photographs about times and places important to their family, such as scenes from their country of origin or conditions on Ellis Island.

Humanities Connection

Art   Students interested in art might enjoy making illustrations for a book of stories about King Arthur and the Knights of the Round Table. Encourage them to write briefly about how they researched the clothing, weaponry, and background details they included in their illustrations.

Using the Model

Have students get together in small groups of three or four to read and discuss their own papers and the model by Michele. Have students identify points of similarity and difference among the various works. Ask them to consider what elements in Michele's paper might have strenghtened their own reports (and conversely, what elements in their papers might have strengthened Michele's).

Makes a smooth transition to the next main idea

Uses the author's own words to express information derived from a source

Uses an exact quotation to establish authenticity and flavor

used by Jesus at the Last Supper (Hibbert 21; Ashe 169; "Arthurian Legend" 603).

Over the next two hundred years the legend spread across Europe and even Asia. New writers added stories of lost loves, noble searches, chivalrous knights, and valiant battles (Hibbert 26; Morris 118).

Finally, in 1485, England's Sir Thomas Malory wove together many of these tales, legends, and poems. Malory's work, Le Morte D'Arthur (The Death of Arthur), became the classic English version of the legend, basically the tale as it is known today (Hibbert 33–34, 138–139; "Arthurian Legend" 604).

Malory tells of Uther Pendragon, King of England, who is in love with the beautiful Ingrayne, the wife of a mighty duke. Merlin, the king's wizard, helps Uther win Ingrayne's love. In return, however, Merlin demands that the king give him the son who is born to them. The wizard then sends the son, Arthur, to live with a knight named Sir Ector (Hibbert 35–36).

Years later, according to Malory's legends, King Uther dies with no heir. Merlin advises England's leaders to wait for a sign, a miracle. Suddenly, a rock appears with a sword plunged into it. Written on the sword are these words: "Whoso pulleth out this sword . . . is rightwise king." Powerful knights cannot loosen the sword, yet Arthur, a young page seeking a weapon for his squire, easily pulls the sword, the magical Excalibur, from the rock. "We will have Arthur for our king," the crowd cheers (Hibbert 36–37).

In this way, says Malory, Arthur becomes king and goes on to fight evil barons, kill a thirty-foot giant, and defeat the legions of Rome. At the height of his power, Arthur gathers the bravest, most honest knights to sit at his Round Table at the court of Camelot. The story turns tragic, however, when the king's queen, Guinevere, and his favorite knight, Lancelot, fall in love. Some of Arthur's knights ride off in search of the Holy Grail. Finally, Arthur is wounded in the battle of Camlann, and set on a barge headed for Avalon (Hibbert 38–53).

Returns to the central problem

Are these legends just myths created and embellished by storytellers and poets, or is there some truth in this tale of a powerful, noble king? Historical records are scanty, but they do provide a rough picture of a real historical King Arthur.

Around 600 a tribute to a fallen warrior stated, "still, he was no Arthur" (Hibbert 15; Morris 116). In 548, the monk-historian Gildas refers to a major victory over the German Saxons at Mount Badon that had taken place about 50 years earlier. He talks about a great leader of the battle, but never mentions Arthur by name. A later biography of Gildas suggests that Arthur had killed the monk's brother in battle. For that reason, Gildas most likely hated the king and refused to include his name in the account of the Mount Badon victory (Hibbert 91, 93, 95; Williams 74, 80–81).

Uses documented facts to support the author's thesis

Later historians do mention Arthur by name. In the early ninth century, the Welsh monk Nennius briefly refers to Arthur as the victor in twelve battles against the Saxon invaders, one of which was Mount Badon. Nennius, however, calls Arthur only a dux bellorum, or military commander (Hibbert 16, 81–82; Williams 74–75). A tenth-century chronicle, The Annals of Wales, lists King Arthur's victory at Mount Badon in the year 516, and his last battle against Mordred's forces in 537 ("Arthur" 602).

To be understood, however, these clues of Arthur's existence and accomplishments must be seen against the background of British history of the fourth through sixth centuries. Fourth-century Britain was the western boundary of the great Roman Empire. By

Presents background information important to the central problem

Peer Response

Remind students that in responding to a classmate's research report they should begin by mentioning what they liked about the paper. Also, although the temptation to give advice may be nearly irresistible, they should concentrate on reporting their own responses when they voice their criticisms, not on telling the writer what he or she should do.

Moves coherently through a chronological sequence of key ideas

the late fourth century, though, that empire had begun to crumble. Barbarian tribes, a general term for any people who did not adopt Roman ways, threatened the borders and even attacked Rome. By the fifth century, Roman forces could no longer defend the vast empire, and little by little, Rome released its grip over Britain (Hibbert 59; Ashe 28).

The British were not happy about their newfound freedom, however. Over the years they had become "civilized" and peaceful, and they felt unable to protect their lands without help from the mighty Roman troops (Hibbert 60; Ashe 27). Yet British lands were in danger. The Saxons of the Arthurian legends really did raid the island from Germany across the North Sea. These rugged, bearded warriors swarmed onto Britain's shores with short swords, iron spears, and axes (Hibbert 61). The invaders may, in fact, have looked like monstrous giants to the peaceable British. The British faced other "barbarian" enemies also: the fierce Picts from Scotland and the Scotti from Ireland (Hibbert 60; Ashe 28–29).

The British searched for powerful rulers to lead them against the invaders. The first of these warrior-kings was known as Vortigern, a powerful ruler who won control of vast lands in Britain, probably during the late 420's (Hibbert 70; Ashe 38). Vortigern made a serious mistake, however. He allowed a band of Saxons to settle in Britain in return for their help in fighting the Picts. The plan went well at first, but the Saxons soon brought more and more of their warriors to Britain who began to attack their neighbors; the country was devastated once again (Hibbert 70–71; Ashe 38–41).

Then, around 460, a new British ruler, Ambrosius, arose. Ambrosius halted the advance of the Saxons. The British again won control of the island. But Ambrosius's rule ended sometime between 470 and 480 (Ashe

49–50; Morris 108). Suddenly, the Saxons could no longer be stopped. They continued to invade Britain from Germany, extending their settlements as warriors won new lands (Ashe 57–58). Only a powerful new ruler could save the British from the devastation of the new Saxon advance.

The reign of Arthur began at this time, perhaps around 475. There is little historical evidence about this period, but records suggest that British forces began gaining ground over the Saxons. Mounted British troops defeated the Saxon foot-soldiers in a series of battles. Nennius lists twelve of these battles, led by a victorious Arthur. After the final victory at Mount Badon, sometime between 500 and 516, the Saxon threat was halted (Morris 110–114). Arthur had ended Britain's crisis.

After Mount Badon, Arthur ruled for about twenty years. Even Gildas, who refused to mention Arthur by name, described these as years of good government and stable rule, years of "truth and justice" (Morris 117). Arthur ensured stability by subduing raiders from Ireland and establishing his power over local kings and barons. These years of stable, just government were the basis of tales of a "golden age" under Arthur. This golden age would last until Arthur's death at Camlann, in the 530's (Morris 117, 123, 132, 140).

Can this historical background help reveal a picture of the true, historical king Arthur? He surely was not the medieval king in shining armor of Malory's story. The real Arthur probably wore the brown leather tunic of a fifth century warrior. His "helmet" was not dragon-shaped, but most likely a simple, fifth-century iron headpiece. For weapons, he would have carried a heavy iron sword and a wooden spear with an iron point. His home was not a grand castle, but more likely

Ties the background information to the central problem

Brings together different strands of information to draw a new conclusion about the topic

Research Report   **297**

Help students recognize that even though a comma represents a pause, commas cannot be inserted wherever a pause occurs naturally in speech—too often these are simply places where speakers pause for breath. Have volunteers read aloud the first two paragraphs on this page so that the class can note the difference between breathing pauses and comma pauses. Review correct use of commas with appositives (paragraph 2, line 1), with introductory words (paragraph 2, line 5), and with conjunctions separating independent clauses (paragraph 1, line 8). Direct students to Grammar Handbook 39 for specific information.

Speaking and Listening

Ask a student to read Michele's final three paragraphs aloud while the other students listen for the tone of her language. Ask them to decide if the conclusion sustains readers' interest, and how Michele's language accounts for the success or failure of her conclusion.

a squat stone fortress. And his companions, rather than the courteous knights of the Round Table, were probably rugged cavalrymen like Arthur himself (Hibbert 129; Ashe 14; Goodrich 9).

Steers the reader toward closure

Still, the historical picture of Arthur does show that there are bits of truth in the legend. Arthur, it seems, truly did rescue his land from devastation and barbarian rule. He did rule as the powerful but honorable leader of a just government. Most likely, jealous lords like Mordred finally did succeed in killing Arthur and ending his "golden age."

Brings the paper to a satisfying conclusion by summing up the implications of the author's research

They would never kill the people's memory of King Arthur, however. "The future needed a legend, not a history" (Morris 87, 119). And the story of Arthur provided that legend, of a good and noble ruler and the everlasting "gleam of a golden age" (Morris 87).

<u>Works Cited</u>

"Arthur." <u>The Encyclopaedia Britannica</u>. 1988 ed.

"Arthurian Legend." <u>The Encyclopaedia Britannica</u>.
    1988 ed.

Ashe, Geoffrey. <u>The Discovery of King Arthur</u>. Garden
    City: Doubleday, 1985.

Goodrich, Norma Lorre. <u>King Arthur</u>. New York: Frank-
    lin Watts, 1986.

Hibbert, Christopher. <u>The Search for King Arthur</u>. New
    York: American Heritage, 1969.

Morris, John. <u>The Age of Arthur</u>. New York: Scribner's,
    1973.

Williams, Mary. "King Arthur in History and Legend."
    <u>Folklore</u>. Summer 1962: 73–88.

Critical Thinking

Generalizing Discuss James Michener's work and ask students how (or whether) his observation on p. 300 relates to the experience they went through in writing a research report.

Learning from Your Writing Process

Objective

To analyze and reflect upon what has been learned about the writing process and the writing of a research report

Teaching Strategies

Reflecting on the Process

Have students use the questions as a trigger for free association about the process they went through. Ask them to jot down whatever thoughts they have, whether related to the questions or not.

Writing Portfolio

Have the class discuss their thoughts about writing a research report, focusing on what they learned and what other uses they might find for these skills. Ask them to compare their research report to other writings in their Portfolio and to think about how they have grown as writers over the course of the year.

Summary and Closure

To end the workshop, check that students have internalized the following concepts:

1. A research report integrates information from many sources.

2. A research report reflects the writer's own interests and concerns.

3. A good research report makes a point.

4. Techniques used to gather information for a research report can be used to gather information for many different purposes.

Allow students to summarize what they learned by describing the characteristics of effective research reports and by telling why knowing how to write a research report might help them in other school subjects.

LEARNING FROM YOUR WRITING PROCESS

WRITER TO WRITER

(I)n effect, since my college days, what I do in my life is more or less give myself a seminar in advanced studies when I work. So my education has really taken place after college.

James Michener, novelist

1. Reflect on your writing. Think about the process you used in writing your research paper. Read the questions below to see what thoughts they stimulate. Note your answers and insights in your writing log or in an afterword that you can attach to your paper and keep in your portfolio.

- What did you learn about gathering information during the process of writing your research paper? What other applications could you find for this skill?
- How did your view of your topic change as you researched and wrote your paper? What caused your view to change?
- Are there aspects of your subject that you would like to research further?
- What did you learn about yourself from researching and writing this paper?

2. Apply your skills. Try one or more of the following activities.

- **Cross curricular** Choose any current event or circumstance that raises questions in your mind—such as a dispute between two countries, a government policy, or the rising cost of music concerts. Gather enough information to arrive at an opinion about the issue and then defend your position in a debate or discussion.
- **Literature** Think of a nonfiction book you have read that you found interesting. Do some research to see if you can independently confirm the position or point of view presented by the author of that book.
- **Related assignments** Follow the suggestions on pages 301–302 to write a plan for a career search.

Literature Connection

Author Note One of the world's best-selling writers, James Michener won a Pulitzer Prize for his story collection *Tales of the South Pacific*. He is best known, however, for meticulously researched novels about various cultures or places, novels that include *The Source* (about Israel), *Centennial* (about a Colorado town), *Caravans* (about Afghanistan), and *Hawaii*.

Career Search

You can apply the skills you have acquired in completing this Guided Assignment to many other types of research tasks, both inside and outside of school. For example, at this time you may be getting ready to make a career choice. Before making a decision about which career to pursue, it's a good idea to do some research on the career or careers that interest you. Many of the research techniques you used in this workshop can be applied to doing research on a variety of professions that interest you. Suggestions for using these techniques appear below.

1. Examine your goals.   Begin your career search by taking a good look at yourself. How important do you think a satisfying career will be to your future happiness? What are you looking for in a job or career? Where do you want this career to take you? Write in your journal about your personal goals and what types of careers you might pursue to fulfill them.

2. Examine your skills.   What do you do well? What do you enjoy doing most? Make a list of your skills, and then think about which skills you'd like to use on the job. For what jobs and careers are your skills most suited?

3. Choose careers to explore.   Use your goals and skills to identify careers you would like to know more about. Then choose one or more and begin your search.

4. List career search questions.   Think about what you want to find out about your chosen field and make a list of questions such as the following:

- What responsibilities does a professional in this field have?
- What level of education or training is required?
- Where must people live to pursue this career?
- What is the starting salary? What is the earning potential of this career?
- What is the employment outlook for this career?
- What are the opportunities for advancement and growth in this career?
- Is there an opportunity for travel on the job?
- How satisfied are people currently working in the field?
- What political issues or economic trends are challenging people in the profession?

Related ASSIGNMENT

HANDBOOKS
FOR HELP & PRACTICE

Interviewing,
p. 336
Sources,
pp. 482–489
Evaluating Sources,
pp. 493–494
Evaluating Your
Career Options,
pp. 507–509

Career Search   **301**

Reteaching

Assess the needs of students who were not successful developing an effective Career search. Assign the appropriate Handbook Mini-Lessons. Concepts commonly requiring reteaching for this assignment are

Interviewing: Handbook 2
Evaluating Options: Handbook 27

The following suggestions and resources may also be useful.

1. Insufficient Material For students unable to find information about their chosen careers, write a "Personal Prescription" directing them to one specific library reference source, periodical, or member of the community. Then direct them to Investigating Job Opportunities in Handbook 27. Tell them that this prescription is a starting point, and that they are to use it to find not only career information but also more information sources.

2. Lack of Skills Some students may report that they have no skills. Instruct them to list activities they have enjoyed during the last two months, specifying which readings, movies, TV shows, sports events, hobbies, gatherings, or outings have most interested them. Work with them to identify one or two areas of interest that recur in this list, and suggest careers that could develop those interests.

Extension and Enrichment

• Ask students what kinds of work their parents, relatives, and older friends do. Some of those people may be willing to give talks to the class.

• A contemporary self-help adage says, "Do what you love—the money will follow." Have a panel or the whole class discuss this. Is it true? Is it good advice for contemporary teenagers? Why or why not?

5. Begin searching. As with researching a school report, you will probably want to consult a variety of sources. Your school counseling office can direct you to many sources. Here are some additional suggestions:

• **Library sources** Consult your librarian to find out what employment reference works your library has, such as career encyclopedias and the *Occupational Outlook Handbook*. Libraries often carry professional and trade journals and magazines as well. These are helpful for finding out the latest issues, concerns, and trends in a given field.

• **Professional, trade, and union associations** Associations often produce brochures and other materials about vocational career opportunities.

• **Interviews** Talk to people in the career you are exploring. If you know people who do this type of work, ask them about it. If not, contact a company directly. The personnel director can give you information over the phone or make an appointment with you for an informational interview.

6. Record your findings. Since the information you gather is for your own use, you may not choose to make a formal presentation of your findings. However, you will probably find it helpful to write about your experiences in your journal as a way of reviewing and evaluating what you have learned. This process can help you decide whether to pursue a particular career or whether to search for alternatives. You also might consider writing up your findings as a report for the school guidance office that could be useful to other students researching careers.

Literature Connection

For extra credit, ask volunteers to report on the careers of authors and poets whose work they especially like. If the authors are still alive, encourage students to write letters asking them how they became writers.

Sentence
COMPOSING

Reviewing Sentence Composing Skills

In the preceding sentence composing exercises, you have studied how professional writers use openers, s-v splits, and closers singly and in combination to increase the information in their writing, to provide variety, and to create the rhythms of their style. In this lesson, you will review and practice the skills you have learned. You will also apply those skills to a piece of your own writing.

REVIEWING VARIETY IN SENTENCE OPENERS

Skill 1: Single Words as Sentence Openers (pages 173–175)

<u>Sighing</u>, he sat down and put on the other shoe.
Elizabeth Bowen, "Foothold"

Skill 2: Phrases as Sentence Openers (pages 173–175)

Prepositional Phrase — <u>To her astonishment</u>, she saw that the expression on his face was one of satisfaction.
Mary Lavin, "One Summer"

Present Participial Phrase — <u>Changing into dry clothes from his cellophane pack</u>, Mr. Benjamin Driscoll lay down and went happily to sleep.
Ray Bradbury, The Martian Chronicles

Past Participial Phrase — <u>Amazed at the simplicity of it all</u>, I understood everything as never before.
Alphonse Daudet, "The Last Lesson"

Absolute Phrase — <u>Pain shooting up my entire arm</u>, I lay panting on the edge of the pool and gingerly began to feel my wrist. **Theodore Taylor, The Cay**

REVIEWING VARIETY IN S-V SPLITS

Skill 3: Phrases as S-V Splits (pages 203–205)

Appositive Phrase — The real estate agent, <u>an old man with a smiling, hypocritical face</u>, soon joined them.
Willa Cather, "The Sculptor's Funeral"

Present Participial Phrase — August, <u>gasping for breath</u>, melted into September. **Robert Lipsyte, The Contender**

Sentence Composing: Reviewing Sentence Composing Skills

Objectives

1. To compose sentences using a variety of types of modifiers and phrases in the opening position, between the subject and verb, or in the closing position to increase sentence variety
2. To analyze types of modifiers and phrases in sentences
3. To write a paragraph composed of sentences that contain modifiers or phrases in the opening position, between the subject and verb, or in the closing position

Preteaching

These exercises focus on the use of modifiers, participles, and phrases. Before assigning the exercises, be aware that some students may need review of basic sentence parts and structure as well as the use of modifiers, participles, participial phrases, appositive phrases, prepositional phrases, and absolute phrases. Refer to the following sections of the Grammar Handbook for preteaching content:

Phrases and Clauses
  Prepositional Phrases, pages 591–592
  Appositives and Appositive Phrases, page 593
  Verbals and Verbal Phrases, pages 594–596
  Using Phrases Correctly, page 602

Adjective and Adverb Usage
  Understanding Modifiers, pages 719–720

Past Participial Phrase	The tent, <u>illumined by candle</u>, glowed warmly in the midst of the plain. **Jack London, *The Call of the Wild***
Absolute Phrase	An Arab on a motorcycle, <u>his long robes flying in the wind of his speed</u>, passed John at such a clip that the spirals of dust from his turnings on the winding road looked like little tornadoes. **Elizabeth Yates, "Standing in Another's Shoes"**
Delayed Adjectives	The head of the filing department, <u>neat, quiet, attentive</u>, stood in front of the old man's desk. **James Thurber, "The Catbird Seat"**

REVIEWING VARIETY IN SENTENCE CLOSERS

Skill 4: Phrases as Sentence Closers   (pages 233–235)

Appositive Phrase	The room was empty, <u>a silent world of sinks, drainboards, and locked cupboards</u>. **Frank Bonham, *Chief***
Present Participial Phrase	He turned and ran, <u>dodging through the trees</u>. **Elliott Merrick, "Without Words"**
Past Participial Phrase	I seem forever condemned, <u>ringed by walls</u>. **Richard Wright, *Black Boy***
Absolute Phrase	The parrot was gone, <u>its cake a mess of crumbs and frosting on the ground</u>. **Shirley Jackson, "Island"**
Delayed Adjectives	Our father was younger than the landlord, <u>leaner, stronger, and bigger</u>. **James Baldwin,** ***Tell Me How Long the Train's Been Gone***

A. Imitating Sentences The sentences below are from *My Left Foot,* the autobiography of modern Irish writer Christy Brown. Born with cerebral palsy, Brown was never capable of moving his hands, arms, or legs. In fact the only part of his body he could move was his left foot. Remarkably, Brown learned to write with his left foot, creating such novels as *Down All the Days* and *Where the Wild Lilies Bloom.*

Each of the sentences below illustrates one or more of the sentence composing skills you have studied. Using your own words, write sentences that imitate the structures of the underlined openers, s-v splits, and closers as well as the other parts of the sentences.

1. <u>Curious</u>, I managed to stumble to the pantry window.

2. <u>On Thursday evening, about seven or eight days after my return from Lourdes</u>, I was sitting at my window gazing gloomily out into the gathering autumn dusk that was slowly covering the street outside in a dark purple haze.

3. <u>Pushing out my box of lead soldiers toward him with my foot</u>, I asked him, in grunts, to swap them for his paints.

4. <u>Scrawled on the floor with a broken bit of yellow chalk gripped between my toes</u>, that one letter was my road to a new world, <u>my key to mental freedom</u>.

5. <u>His face lit by flames</u>, across the open hearth sat my father, <u>leaning forward</u>, <u>hands outspread on his knees</u>, <u>shoulders tense</u>.

6. <u>A little grey man with an unkempt mustache and watery eyes</u>, the proprietor leaned on the counter, <u>reading a newspaper</u>.

7. A few minutes later, Father, <u>happening to go into the yard for something</u>, saw her.

8. Four men, <u>armed with rifles</u>, piled out.

9. Mona, <u>her black curls framing her chubby little face</u>, stared at me with great big eyes and open mouth.

10. Robbie Collis, <u>the doctor's tall, fair-haired, powerful, medical-student son</u>, said he would steer me in through a door at the back of the hotel and get me into my seat before the show started.

11. She, <u>pale and worn</u>, lay prone on a stretcher, <u>moaning feebly now and then</u>.

12. I often sat up in my bed at night, <u>thinking of Jenny and the way she kissed me that day in the garden</u>.

13. I sat on the edge of the bank, <u>fascinated as I looked down into the sun-flecked water to see the forms of fish flitting like shadows in and out of the bottom</u>.

14. Paddy was no longer a schoolboy in short trousers and catapult sticking out of his back pocket, but an apprentice bricklayer who marched in proudly every Friday night with his pay packet and handed it with great pomposity to Mother, <u>his boots and overalls begrimed with dust and mortar</u>.

15. I was now just ten, <u>a boy who couldn't walk, speak, feed or dress himself</u>.

16. I was at peace, <u>happy</u>.

17. <u>Thinking of the same things</u>, <u>feeling the same things</u>, <u>dreading the same things</u>, I felt as if I was merely moving along a groove.

18. Ruthie, <u>her hair down over her eyes and her dress wrinkled and twisted</u>, came wriggling out like a snake.

19. It was a beautiful night, <u>calm</u>, <u>gentle</u>, <u>yet alive</u>.

20. <u>My heart beating quickly</u>, <u>waiting desperately for the verdict</u>, I sat alone on the couch.

21. <u>Of this total of twenty-two babies</u>, seventeen lived, but four died in infancy, <u>leaving thirteen still to hold the family fort</u>.

22. <u>Toward the end of spring</u>, Mother became bed-ridden and was shifted to the Rotunda Hospital where a few weeks later she gave birth to her last child, <u>completing the total of twenty-two</u>.

22. opener, prepositional phrase; closer, present participial phrase

23. s-v split, present participial phrase

24. closer, series of absolute phrases

25. opener, prepositional phrase, present participial phrase; closer, series of absolute phrases

Application
Answers will vary.

Application
Answers will vary.

23. My brother's voice, <u>sounding very suspicious</u>, spoke from within.

24. In it was a little boy in short trousers, <u>his thin legs bent under one another</u>, <u>his eyebrows cocked up rather snobbishly</u>, and <u>his twisted hand held tightly to keep it still</u>.

25. <u>Writing them down on paper with my left foot to look at them in sort of wonder</u>, I played with words like a child fascinated with a new toy.

B. Identifying Sentence Composing Skills   For each sentence in Exercise A, identify the sentence composing skills the underlined parts illustrate. Some sentences illustrate more than one of the four skills.

Application   Like Christy Brown, you can play with words. Without using models or writing imitations, write four sentences, each illustrating a different sentence composing skill. You may write four unrelated sentences, or you may include your sentences within a longer piece of writing.

Application   The sentences below are from *Grendel,* a modern retelling of the Beowulf epic from the monster's point of view, by John Gardner. They give portions of the sequence of events when the monster Grendel raids the hall of the king. Imitate each sentence. Then choose one of your imitations and use it as the first sentence in a paragraph. Your paragraph should explain the sequence of events in an activity you have performed often, perhaps doing a household chore, practicing one technique in a sport, or going from your house to a friend's house. Use varying openers, s-v splits, and closers as you write your paragraph.

1. Behind my back, at the world's end, my pale slightly glowing fat mother sleeps on, old, sick at heart, in our dingy underground room.

2. Eleven years now and going on twelve I have come up to this clean-mown central hill, dark shadow out of the woods below, and have knocked politely on the high oak door, bursting its hinges and sending the shock of my greeting inward like a cold blast out of a cave.

3. The old Shaper, a man I cannot help but admire, goes out the back window with his harp at a single bound, though blind as a bat.

Workshop Overview

Writing for assessment is a type of writing in which students demonstrate their skill, within a controlled environment, at interpreting and responding to specific, focused prompts. The situation, usually a test, requires that students work quickly and in a focused manner. To be successful they must recognize exactly what they are being asked to write as well as apply critical thinking, analysis, and organizational skills. In this Workshop students will apply not only their test-taking skills but also their reading comprehension skills. Workshop 10 contains the following Guided Assignment:

Guided: Responding to Readings shows students how to understand and interpret a reading passage and to apply effective strategies for responding to questions about the passage

Preparation Guide

1. Use the Overview above and the Teacher's Choice descriptions on page 309 as a basis for deciding which assignment(s) to teach.

2. Preview the assignment and the teacher's notes. The teaching suggestions and your knowledge of your class's abilities should allow you to identify quickly the concepts that may require preteaching or extra support. The Handbook mini-lessons suggested in the Preteaching notes within the lesson can also provide guidance in this area.

3. Preview the adjacent chart for support materials in the Teacher's Resource File that may be used with this Workshop.

Workshop Support Materials

Resources	For Use With
Thinking Skills Transparencies: Cluster Diagram; *Worksheets,* p. 2 Compare/Contrast: *Worksheets,* p. 16	Strategies, p. 315
Elaboration/Proofreading, p. 19	Draft and Discover, p. 317
Evaluating Writing, p. 17	Standards for Evaluation, p. 318
Elaboration/Proofreading, p. 20	Evaluate your response, p. 318
Tests and Assessment: Prompts, p. 8	

Professional Resources and Media

Books and Journals

Chaika, Glori. "Teaching Test-taking Techniques to the Gifted." *Clearing House.* Vol. 59.4 (December 1985): pp. 182–184.

O'Keefe, Michael. "The Role of Tests in the Transition from High School to College." *NAASP Bulletin.* Vol. 68 (October 1984): pp. 54–68.

Pratt, John Clark. "Writing Under Pressure: Examinations and Other Timed Indignities." *Writing from Scratch.* Lanham, Maryland: Hamilton Press, 1987: pp. 85–94.

Films and Videos

Diagnosis. PBS Video, Alexandria, Virginia. (29 min.) (assessment, analysis of writing, and diagnosis)

Epistemology and Logic. Writing for a Reason Series, Dallas Community College District, Mesquite, Texas. (30 min.)

Computer Software

Answering Essay Questions. Write On: Secondary Collection, Humanities Software, San Francisco, California. Apple II, II+, IIe, IIc.

Linking Literature, Writing, and Grammar

The following options may be used to provide students with an integrated language experience. Begin by assigning and discussing any of the recommended pieces of literature, which can be found in most classroom anthologies. Use the suggested strategy to provide a link to the Guided Assignment.

Linking Literature and Writing

Option 1

Starting Point: excerpt from *The Life and Times of Chaucer* by John Gardner and excerpt from *Home: A Short History of an Idea* by Witold Rybczynski on pages 310–312 of *The Writer's Craft*
Strategy: Use the teaching suggestions on pages 310–312 to lead students into the Guided Assignment.

Option 2

Starting Point: "Sonnet 130" by William Shakespeare and "She Walks in Beauty" by George Gordon, Lord Byron
Strategy: After students have read the poems closely, write the following prompt on the board: "Compare the ways in which the two poets describe their loved ones. Include a discussion of tone, form, imagery, and meaning in your response. Include as well a comment on which way you think a woman would prefer to be described and why." Have students discuss how they would respond to the prompt and how they might organize their response. They may want to use the prompt as the basis for their Guided Assignment.

Option 3

Starting Point: "Dulce et Decorum Est" by Wilfred Owen
Strategy: Have students read the poem closely. Then write the following prompt on the board: "Explain what the poem says about a soldier's life and how the poem uses irony to convey its ideas. Include a comment about the impact of the poem and explain your reasoning." Have students discuss the way they would go about responding to the prompt, including how they would take notes and how they would organize their response.

Linking Writing and Grammar

Before the drafting or revision stage of this assignment, point out that people who evaluate responses to assessment questions are concerned with the way ideas are related to each other. Transitional words and phrases can provide necessary links between ideas and help writers achieve coherence within and between paragraphs. Have students review their work for transitional words and phrases as you write the following examples on the board:

TO SHOW TIME RELATIONSHIPS: The rain began to fall. Later, the wind picked up.

TO SHOW LOGICAL RELATIONSHIPS: The story does not state its theme directly. Therefore, readers must judge the author's intentions for themselves.

TO SHOW CONTRAST: Wolfe uses a casual style. Priestley's style, on the other hand, is more formal.

Have students review the material about transitional words and phrases on pages 766–772 of the Grammar and Usage Handbook and in the Writing Handbook on pages 384–387. If problems with transitions continue in students' work, assign the exercises on those pages for reteaching. Additional practice can be found in the Grammar and Usage Practice Book on page 86.

Workshop Management Guidelines

The adjacent chart indicates the number of days recommended for each phase of the Guided Assignment. Stars indicate portions of the assignment that may be completed outside the classroom if time is limited or if teachers wish the activity to be completed by students independently.

Responding to Readings

Starting from Literature—1 day

Prewrite—1 day

Draft—1 day

Revise—1 day

Apply Your Skills—1 day*

Reteaching—open

Extension/Enrichment—open

Sentence Composing—1 day*

Sketchbook

Objective

To use literary and visual prompts as springboards to informal writing

Using the Prompt

Remind students that Sketchbook activities are opportunities for students to experiment with their writing. They are intended to encourage creative thinking and risk-taking, and they will not be graded.

Point out that the image is a famous drawing by Pablo Picasso of Don Quixote, the classic picaresque hero. Ask students to discuss what they know about the adventures of Don Quixote. Then tell them to set their minds free to play with ideas and adventures for a picaresque hero of their own.

Students may choose to write about either of the Additional Sketches instead. Have students keep their writing in their Writing Portfolios for possible use in other writing projects.

Sketchbook

Since the sixteenth century, the picaresque novel has been a popular literary form. This type of novel recounts the zany adventures of a sharp-witted rogue, or *picaro,* who often unwittingly gets into trouble. Create a picaresque hero of your own. Relate one episode from your hero's story.

Additional Sketches

Newspaper columnists often give personal accounts of or opinions about current events. Find a short, objective newspaper article about an event or incident of interest to you. Write a personal, subjective account of the event or give your opinion of the event described.

Think of a celebration that you have either participated in or seen covered in newspapers, magazines, or on television, such as a Fourth of July picnic or a Chinese New Year parade. Write a description of the celebration.

308

Writing for Assessment

Guided Assignment

RESPONDING TO READINGS

By now, you have quite a bit of experience using your writing skills to answer test questions. Sometimes, however, you need to call on more than your writing skills; you must use your reading comprehension skills as well. In this workshop you will study ways you can develop your ability to interpret written selections and then write effective essays about them.

Objectives

Guided Assignment:
RESPONDING TO READINGS
To learn and apply techniques that are useful in interpreting written selections and in responding to assessment prompts about them; to learn and apply strategies for responding to different kinds of prompts; to draft, revise, and proofread a response to an assessment prompt about written selections

Teacher's Choice

Guided Assignment
Responding to Readings Students will often be called on to respond to assessment prompts like the one in this Guided Assignment. In addition, students will encounter this kind of prompt in writing assessments and college placement tests that are taken nationally. Use this assignment either toward the beginning or in the middle of the year to prepare students for the many essay tests they will be taking during the remainder of the year.

309

Guided Assignment:
RESPONDING TO READINGS

Assignment Rationale

Assessment is a critical part of academic life, allowing both students and teachers to evaluate student progress and competence. In their own best interests, students need to recognize strategies that will help them help others see their strengths. Often assessments ask students to apply their reading skills and background knowledge to specific reading passages. This assignment focuses on this kind of assessment and fosters both reading for comprehension and response skills. Note that a non-language arts topic was purposefully chosen since many assessments are cross-curricular in nature.

Starting from Literature

Objective

To make initial responses to two selections in preparation for responding to an assessment prompt about them

Teaching Strategies

Motivate

Begin with a discussion of assessments. Ask students how they feel when faced with a writing assessment. First invite them to share some of their concerns and/or fears about such a process. Then ask if they can think of any benefits of assessments. Reassure them that there are strategies to be learned through assessments.

Guided ASSIGNMENT

Responding to Readings

Reading, as well as writing, is an essential skill for test taking. In many instances, you must apply your skills at comprehending texts before you can use your writing skills to convey the meaning you have discovered.

The two reading selections on these pages deal with the idea of "home." John Gardner describes the medieval English home, and Witold Rybczynski examines the modern home. As you read each selection, think about the similarities and differences in what each writer describes.

From
THE LIFE and TIMES of CHAUCER
by John Gardner

A modern visitor might be distressed, too, by the living arrangements: no glass windows except in the houses of the rich—places like John Chaucer's house on Thames Street and, better yet, John of Gaunt's palace on the Savoy, where the glass was stained. At night all light that might have labored in through the coarse glass windows, or the parchment windows or nothing-covered windows in poorer houses, was tightly sealed out by wooden shutters. (It made, of course, for a coziness we miss.) There were no chairs, only benches or cushioned trunks for a lady or a gouty old gentleman to sit on; at mealtimes the servants brought out trestles and table boards. There was no privacy, even in a vintner's big house. Whereas the poor lived in only one room, or at most two, in company with their chickens, pigs, geese, cats, and mice, a vintner's house might have numerous rooms, but none to be alone in. A house like Chaucer's father's would be a large building with a high stone wall and gardens around it, perhaps a few fruit trees, a house with a steeply pitched tile roof and leaded-glass bay windows projecting from the second and third floors. There were various outbuildings, including a pigpen (the livestock of the citizenry was a persistent problem for town magistrates, who repeatedly issued ordinances forbidding the inhabitants to let their horses, swine, and geese run loose in the streets); and inside the house lay a labyrinth of corridors and chambers, dark arches, stairs. There would be a garret, or coalhouse, set over the great gate opening onto Thames Street and extending over whatever humble tenantries were built into the wall; there would be a "pastry house" or bakehouse, connected with the kitchen, which stood next to the central hall; a vaulted cellar and a larder house, with a buttery above, and above that a chamber, all connected by stairs; beyond the hall, the great parlor, with small chambers around it, a chapel, perhaps a privy; and there would probably be, elsewhere, a cloth house with closets, a bolting house, third floor garrets, and various chambers for storage, laundry, and so forth. A rich splay of rooms; but the rooms—queerly small, from a modern point of view—were for working in, never for getting away by oneself. For living there was only the great parlor and the hall, which doubled as a dining room. In the bedrooms the inhabitants slept several to a bed, usually naked, though sometimes in heavy, long nightgowns and nightcaps. (Nightgowns and nightcaps are frequently mentioned in medieval wills.) Though today we might object to sleeping several in a bed, no objection seems to have crossed medieval minds; even the gentlemen-servants to the king slept two to a bed, as Edward's Ordinances show. It may be, however, that we pay dear for our privacy. The loneliness, ennui, and alienation now so common seem to have been rare diseases in the late Middle Ages.

Tap Prior Knowledge

Ask students what they think the perfect home would be like. Encourage students to suggest what the atmosphere of the home would be like as well as the layout and furnishings. Explain that in the excerpts they are about to read, novelist John Gardner and architecture professor Witold Rybczynski compare the look and feel of homes during different time periods.

Set a Purpose

Prior to having students read the excerpts, discuss the side-column notes, being sure students recognize that these excerpts will be the basis for an essay question. As students read, ask them to watch carefully for the ideas the authors share and the ideas on which they differ.

In 1977, on the other hand, when *Better Homes and Gardens* magazine surveyed its readers, only 15 percent preferred furniture in the "latest modern style." What the majority wanted, and continue to want, was old-fashioned—not necessarily old—furniture and traditional decor. . . . If department stores or home-decorating magazines are any indication, most people's first choice would be to live in rooms that resemble, as much as their budgets permit, those of their grandparents.

No one finds this peculiar. But, as Adolf Loos pointed out, such nostalgia is absent from other aspects of our everyday lives. We do not pine for period cuisine. Our concern for health and nutrition has altered the way that we eat, as well as what we eat; our admiration for the slim physique would be puzzling to the corpulent nineteenth century. We have changed our way of speaking, our manners, and our public and private behavior. We do not feel the need to revive the practice of leaving visiting cards, for example, or of indulging in extended, chaperoned courtship. A return to eighteenth-century decorum would ill suit our informal way of life. Unless we are collectors, we do not drive antique cars. We want automobiles that are less expensive to operate, safer, and more comfortable, but we do not imagine that these improvements can be achieved by resurrecting car models from previous periods. We

311

Think and Respond

Elicit Personal Responses

Have students write their personal responses in their journals or reading logs before taking part in a class discussion of the excerpts. Focus discussion on general responses to the authors' writing styles and unusual details (such as the idea that in Chaucer's time people slept several to a bed) and on whether or not students generally agree or disagree with the authors' overall ideas.

Link Literature and Writing

Help students recognize that in the assignment that follows they will be asked to compare the two excerpts. Ask students what the theme of both selections is (the idea of home) and what idea both writers support (homes from previous periods, though not always comfortable, provided a sense of well-being and community). Encourage students to discuss the facts both Gardner and Rybczynski use to support their conclusions and to tell what qualities they most appreciate in a "home." Explain that the Guided Assignment that follows will help students apply their understanding of the excerpts and their own ideas about "home" as they write an essay response to an assessment prompt.

would feel as odd in a Model T as we would in plus fours or a hooped skirt, yet although we would not think of dressing in period clothes, we find nothing strange in dressing our homes in period decor. . .

Nostalgia for the past is often a sign of dissatisfaction with the present. I have called the modern interior "a rupture in the evolution of domestic comfort." It represents an attempt not so much to introduce a new style—that is the least of it—as to change social habits, and even to alter the underlying cultural meaning of domestic comfort. Its denial of bourgeois traditions has caused it to question, and reject, not only luxury but also. . . intimacy. Its emphasis on space has caused it to ignore privacy just as its interest in industrial-looking materials and objects has led it away from domesticity. Austerity, both visual and tactile, has replaced delight. What started as an endeavor to rationalize and simplify has become a wrong-headed crusade; not, as is often claimed, a response to a changing world, but an attempt to change the way we live. It is a rupture not because it does away with period styles, not because it eliminates ornament, and not because it stresses technology, but because it attacks the very idea of comfort itself. That is why people look to the past. Their

nostalgia is not the result of an interest in archaeology, like some Victorian revivals, not a sympathy for some particular period, like Jeffersonian classicism. Nor is it a rejection of technology. People appreciate the benefits of central heating and electric lighting, but the rooms of a Colonial country home or of a Georgian mansion—which had neither—continue to attract them, for they provide a measure of something that is absent from the modern interior. People turn to the past because they are looking for something that they do not find in the present—comfort and well-being.

Think AND Respond

What themes do the selections explore? What similar ideas do Gardner and Rybczynski present? How do the selections differ? What qualities do *you* think are important about the concept of "home"?

312

Art Connection

Today's Home Encourage students to look through such magazines as *Architectural Digest*, *House Beautiful*, and *Better Homes and Gardens* and write their own responses to the kinds of architecture and furnishings that are popular today.

> **SAMPLE TEST QUESTION: Read the two passages carefully and then write a well-organized essay in which you examine the concerns that Gardner and Rybczynski seem to share in their accounts of home life. To what extent do these two accounts suggest similarities or differences in human needs in different periods or cultures? Feel free to comment on the degree to which your own view of human needs agrees or disagrees with theirs.**

A number of essay tests that are administered by classroom teachers, school districts, state agencies, colleges, and national testing organizations require you to demonstrate your ability to understand and interpret difficult reading passages at the same time that you show yourself proficient in English composition. Rather than measuring what facts you have learned and retained, such tests reveal whether you can analyze, interpret, or evaluate material. Although traditional study techniques may not be helpful, you can take several steps that will help you present your thoughts clearly within a limited time period.

This workshop will provide you with guidance and practical strategies you can use to perform effectively on tests that require you to read one or more passages and to write an essay dealing in specific ways with those passages.

PREWRITE

1. Read the question.   Before you turn to the reading selection, read the question or "prompt" that will direct your writing. The prompt will give you guidance about what to look for as you read the passage.

2. Read the passage carefully.   A deliberate reading is a good investment of your time. Make sure you understand the passage as you read. Don't hesitate to go back over complicated sentences or paragraphs, and don't feel discouraged by the difficulties the passage may pose for you—it was probably selected to provide a challenge. The test of a good reader is in his or her willingness to accept that challenge and to keep trying.

HANDBOOKS
FOR HELP & PRACTICE

**Writing Prompts,
pp. 327–330**
**Graphics for
Organizing,
pp. 343–347**
**Reading Strategies,
p. 479**
**Testing,
pp. 521–532**

Responding to
Readings   **313**

Objectives

1. To use prewriting techniques in preparation for responding to an assessment prompt
2. To understand strategies useful in responding to different assessment prompts
3. To plan a response to the assessment prompt

Preteaching

Preview the Prewrite and Explore Section. If there are skills or concepts students may need help with before prewriting, present them at this time. The mini-lesson references below may help you in your selection and instruction. The cross references in the pupil text give students access to the same lessons for independent study. In addition, because students will be asked to compare and contrast two readings, you may decide to preteach this strategy using the Compare-and-Contrast Chart in the Thinking Skills Transparencies in the Teacher's Resource File.

Handbook Mini-Lessons
- Writing Prompts, pp. 327–330
- Graphics for Organizing,
  pp. 343–347
- Reading Strategies, p. 479
- Testing, pp. 521–532

Teaching Strategies

Modeling

To help students recognize an effective reading of an assessment prompt, read the prompt aloud, pausing to identify key words and phrases and thinking aloud about what you would look for in the passages in order to respond effectively to the prompt.

Springboard

Use the following quote from Winston Churchill, who was well known for his wit, to promote discussion about feelings toward taking exams: "It is very much better, sometimes, to have a panic feeling beforehand, and then be quite calm when things happen, than to be extremely calm beforehand and go into panic when things happen."

Modeling

If possible, copy the excerpts onto an overhead transparency. Read through the first excerpt, showing students how you would annotate it and explaining your reasoning. Allow students to annotate the second excerpt independently.

Management Tip

Make copies of the excerpts and assessment prompt so that students can make their own underlinings and annotations in preparation for writing their responses.

Stumbling Block

Some students may complain that the excerpts are too difficult and that they are unable to recognize the main points. To enable these students to proceed through the assignment, you may want to read the excerpts aloud with them, stopping from time to time to have students summarize what has been read.

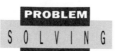

What techniques can I use to probe the meaning of a selection?

3. Annotate the text. As you read, mark up the text—unless you are directed not to—and make notes to help you keep track of the ideas in it. Keep these guidelines in mind.

- Look for the thesis or main idea and underline it or draw a box around it to help you refer to it later.
- Underline or put check marks next to key points and important details.
- Write your comments and questions in the margins.
- Use notes or arrows to show connections or similarities between ideas or important distinctions.
- Write brief definitions of unfamiliar terms that you figure out from context.

4. Re-read the passage. Unless it is a very long passage or a very short test, you will probably have time to re-read the reading selection. You may be surprised about how many details and important ideas slipped your attention on your first reading. Don't be surprised if your re-reading changes your mind about what the passage means.

5. Re-read the question or prompt. One key to answering essay questions is to understand what you are expected to do. Look for the words in the prompt that give you directions: *compare and contrast, define, explain, analyze, discuss.* The following lists include most of the tasks you are likely to be asked to perform in an essay test and what such tasks may entail. Note that most of the suggestions listed are really strategies for writing.

Social Studies Connection

Analyzing Prompts Have students focus on the prompts in their history, geography, or economics books, looking for the key words that specify the tasks to be carried out. Have them relate the key words to the categories of tasks on these pages, and ask them to identify those tasks that could be profitably used in developing responses to the prompts.

Strategies

Descriptive Tasks

If you are asked to *describe, show,* or *tell about* your subject, follow these guidelines.

- Identify the major characteristics of your subject.
- Gather details from the reading to describe your subject.
- Use a logical method of presenting your description (such as top to bottom, left to right, near to far, or most important to least important).

Explanatory and Analytic Tasks

If you are asked to *explain, analyze, interpret, examine,* or *discuss* a text or subject, use one of these methods.

- Break your subject down into its component parts or its main and subordinate ideas and then examine these parts to determine how each works or to determine the meaning of the whole.
- Analyze your subject in terms of causes and effects, problem and solution, advantages and disadvantages, or pros and cons.
- Show how the evidence presented in the text supports or fails to support the main idea or how it is sometimes contradictory.
- Explain how some parts of the passage are difficult to understand or unclear to you.

Defining, Classifying, and Evaluating Tasks

If you are asked to *define,* to *compare and contrast,* to *classify,* or to *evaluate* a text or subjects, use one of these approaches.

- Define a subject by describing its features and showing what distinguishes it from similar subjects.
- Classify a subject by placing it in a larger class along with other members of that class and describing the key features that unify them.
- Evaluate a topic by comparing it against a standard or set of criteria for judging.
- Compare and contrast subjects, that is, discuss their similarities and differences either feature by feature or by describing all the features of one and then of the other.

PROBLEM SOLVING

Which strategies should I use to respond to the prompt?

Individualizing Instruction

Learning Styles Encourage students to work to their strengths as they plan responses to the prompt. Global learners, those who need to see the whole picture before they can concentrate on details, should be encouraged to list their main points and broad conclusions before filling in the details. Analytic learners, those who learn successively and in small steps, should be encouraged to list details that relate to the prompt and then draw their broader conclusions.

Critical Thinking

Analyzing Ask students to evaluate Paula's notes. What can students learn from the way Paula has written her notes? How might students write their own notes differently?

Managing the Paper Load

To cut down on teacher review time, have the students work in pairs to respond to each other's planning notes. Encourage students to check each other's work for important points that may have been overlooked or for possible errors in interpretation.

Argumentative Tasks

If you are asked to *argue for a point of view, persuade* somebody, *agree or disagree, take a side,* or *give your opinion* on a controversial question, use one of these methods.

- State your position and then give clear and logical reasons to support your position.
- Acknowledge opposing arguments and deal with them.
- Acknowledge complexity and ambiguity—that neither position may be entirely right or the issues not clear.
- Show the strengths and weaknesses of both sides and refuse to take a side, if you think neither is more correct.

Reflective Tasks

If you are asked to *reflect on, respond to, comment on, give your opinion on* or *discuss* a subject, you might use any of the following approaches.

- Elaborate on your own point of view on your subject.
- Talk about how your view of the subject changed from your first reading to the second.
- Discuss other texts that illuminate or might be illuminated by your text.
- Discuss how the text influenced your thinking, surprised you, made you angry, or moved you in some other way.
- Agree or disagree with the position taken in the text and give your reasons.

6. Plan your response. Some students find it helpful to jot down words and phrases without worrying about logical order. Then they organize their notes by numbering them. Others like to take notes in a modified outline form. Reread the selection as necessary to increase your understanding and gather pertinent details.

Whatever organizational method you use, keep the time factor in mind. Pacing is very important. Plan out how much time you can devote to each part of your outline or each point you will cover. In this way, you will not be left with a great deal to say and no time to respond.

To respond to the prompt on page 312, Paula first identified her basic writing decisions. Then, because she was asked to compare and contrast, she made notes by listing information in two columns and in order of their importance.

ONE STUDENT'S PROCESS

Gardner
describes medieval house–not
comfortable in modern sense–
purpose not to provide a place
of comfort but to provide rooms
for working–point is that homes
did not foster privacy but
community and warmth

Rybczynski
writes about the modern
home and how we furnish
our homes in ways that
evoke the past.

DRAFT AND DISCOVER

1. Develop a thesis statement. A thesis statement contains your main idea and shows that you understand the question. It keeps you on track as you write. Paula wrote this thesis statement.

> Both Gardner and Rybczynski agree that although home life in the past was not physically comfortable or convenient, it provided a sense of well-being and intimacy that, according to Rybczynski, we try to recreate in our homes today.

2. Organize your draft. Compose your answer in three parts: an introduction, a body, and a conclusion. The introduction includes your thesis statement and briefly previews points you will cover. The body supports each point with specific details, appropriate facts, and opinions from the selection. Use transition words to connect ideas smoothly. You may end in one of these ways:

- referring to your thesis statement (in different words);
- summarizing your points;
- drawing a conclusion about the importance of your points; or
- making a recommendation or stating your opinion.

3. Write to your audience. Remember that one goal of assessment is to determine how effectively you can communicate in standard formal English. Therefore, you should use a friendly straightforward style. Avoid trying to impress your readers with unnaturally inflated diction. The use of slang or trite expressions is also inappropriate.

HANDBOOKS
FOR HELP & PRACTICE

Thesis Statements,
p. 349
Elaborative Details,
pp. 376–378
Unity/Coherence,
pp. 382–391

Responding to
Readings   **317**

Draft and Discover

Objectives

1. To draft a response to an assessment prompt related to reading selections
2. To respond to one's own writing

Preteaching

Look through the content of the Draft and Discover section for skills or strategies students may need special help with. The mini-lessons listed below, as well as the Elaboration Worksheet for this assignment, may be useful in providing this instruction.

> **Handbook Mini-Lessons**
> - Thesis Statement and Supporting Details, p. 349
> - Finding Details for Elaboration, pp. 376–378
> - Achieving Unity and Coherence, pp. 382–391

Teaching Strategies

Critical Thinking

Evaluating Ask students how effective Paula's thesis statement is. Encourage students to suggest modifications they might make or to come up with alternative thesis statements.

Individualizing Instruction

LD Students You may want to give extra support to students who are learning disabled as they organize their drafts. Provide topic sentences for the introduction, body, and conclusion and ask students to complete the paragraphs.

Off the Record

There's no "quick fix" for succeeding at exams although lots of students would like to find one. Here's a story David Mallery related in *High School Students Speak Out*. A student heard that you could significantly raise your College Board aptitude scores by doing extra reading. He passed this information along to a friend of his. According to him, "she was crazy to get her scores up," but she said, "Isn't there some workbook or something? I hate to *read!*"

Revise Your Writing

Objectives

1. To revise a draft based on one's own responses
2. To proofread for errors in spelling, grammar, usage, and mechanics

Preteaching

Based on problems you may have noted in students' drafts or on a preview of the revising section, identify the skills you want to review. The mini-lessons listed below may be useful to you for instructional purposes.

Handbook Mini-Lessons

- Introductions and Conclusions, pp. 365–375
- Revising Effectively, pp. 392–395
- Improving Sentences, pp. 402–411
- Varieties of Language, pp. 429–433
- Avoiding Logical Fallacies, pp. 477–478

Teaching Strategies

 Individualizing Instruction

Basic Students Evaluate how effectively your basic students have formed their paragraphs. You may find that they will benefit from reviewing Writing Handbook 9, "Techniques for Elaboration and Development", pp. 376–381.

Teaching Tip: Additional Resources

Use the Writing Evaluation Guidelines and Sample Papers to help students recognize what goes into an effective response to a reading selection. Use the Student Revision Model Transparency to help students see the kinds of revisions that one student used to improve a response to a reading selection.

PROBLEM SOLVING

How can I organize my response essay?

HANDBOOKS

FOR HELP & PRACTICE

Introductions/
Conclusions,
pp. 365–375
Revising Effectively,
pp. 392–396
Improving Sentences,
pp. 402–411
Varieties of
Language,
pp. 429–433
Avoiding Logical
Fallacies,
pp. 477–478

4. Reread your draft. Once you complete your draft, take time to look it over. Ask yourself the following questions.

REVIEW YOUR WRITING

- Does my response directly address the reading selections?
- Have I included specific evidence from the selections?
- Is my response in an appropriate form?
- Is my response organized effectively?

REVISE YOUR WRITING

1. Compare your work against criteria for evaluation. Because you are writing specifically for evaluation, keep in mind the qualities most evaluators will be looking for.

Standards for Evaluation

An effective essay on a reading selection . . .

- demonstrates an understanding of the reading selection or selections at more than a superficial level.
- fulfills the task assignment specified in the prompt.
- is organized around a clear, single, central idea or thesis or main idea.
- is expressed clearly, using precise language and a style that is neither overly casual nor pretentiously academic.
- demonstrates a willingness to think seriously and honestly about a subject rather than to sacrifice intellectual honesty to presumptions about what readers want to hear.
- shows a willingness to learn from a writing assignment, even if it entails acknowledging changes in thinking in the middle of an essay.

2. Evaluate your response. You won't have much time to change your essay, but you should take time to reread the question and be sure you understood and responded to the key words. Also review your prewriting notes to make sure you included everything you planned to. You can neatly strike out passages or insert additional words or lines with a carat. As a last step, go back and correct any spelling and punctuation errors. Paula's final essay follows.

NAME Paula Guajardo   GRADE   12

In these passages, both John Gardner and Witold Rybczynski write about the idea of home. Gardner describes how people lived in the late Middle Ages, and Rybczynski writes about contemporary homes. They agree that, although home life in the past was not physically comfortable or convenient, it provided a sense of well-being and intimacy that, according to Rybczynski, we are trying to recreate in our homes today.

Explores similarities and differences between two essays

Gardner depicts the medieval house as dark and small and sometimes airless—but cozy. The rooms were small and tacked on to one another haphazardly; and there were, in the houses of the rich, numerous rooms to provide space for work and storage but not for providing individuals with privacy. There were no designated areas for public and for private space. Gardner suggests, though, that the lack of privacy and enforced community were not necessarily bad. He notes that people in the Middle Ages seemed not to have suffered from the boredom and loneliness so common in modern American life.

Uses specific detail from the selection

Rybczynski agrees with Gardner that contemporary Americans are seeking peace at home. He says that is why we look to the past when we furnish our homes— to recreate the sense of well-being and satisfaction missing from modern home life with its clinical-looking stark colors and sharp interiors. We don't want to give up electricity and central air, he argues, but we are trying to create more liveable environments.

Identifies point of agreement between the two selections

These ideas appeal to me because I am most comfortable when I have the happy clutter of my things about me and when people I care about are near. I see the desire to create intimacy more and more—in the dentist's waiting room that looks like a den and in classrooms that feel warm and cozy. Although no one would want the total lack of privacy characteristic of Medieval home life, it is psychologically important for humans to feel comfortable and connected to others at home— and both Gardner and Rybczynski seem to agree.

Interior of a Kitchen, Beuckelaer, The Louvre, Paris

Responding to Readings   **319**

Guidelines for Evaluation

The following guidelines may be used for a close evaluation of a response to an assessment prompt. See the Guidelines for Evaluating Writing in the Teacher's Resource File for additional help with holistic or analytic scoring.

Ideas and Content
- shows understanding of the selections
- responds directly to the prompt
- displays interpretation or analysis of ideas in the passage rather than simple restatement
- uses precise language and a direct style

Structure and Form
- develops ideas from one central thesis
- contains an introduction, body, and conclusion

Grammar, Usage, and Mechanics
- uses standard grammar and usage
- punctuates sentences correctly
- uses correct spelling

Using the Model

After students read Paula's completed essay, encourage them to discuss what they think Paula has done especially well and what might need improvement. Ask them how their approach to the essay differed from Paula's.

Humanities Connection

Art Note   *Interior of a Kitchen,* by the Belgian painter Joachim Beuckelaer (c.1530– c.1574) represents a kind of domestic subject that was quite popular among painters in the northern Belgian region of Flanders during the late Middle Ages and the early Renaissance. Ask: How is this kitchen different from a modern American kitchen?

Reteaching

Assess the needs of students who were not successful developing an effective response to an assessment prompt and identify two or three areas in which additional practice is needed. Assign the appropriate Handbook Mini-Lessons, along with the support materials listed for each lesson.

Concepts commonly requiring reteaching for this assignment are

Writing Prompts: Handbook 1
Reading Strategies: Handbook 24

The following suggestions and resources may also be useful.

1. Poor Test-Reading Skills If students have failed to respond directly to the prompt, help them reread it, focusing their attention on key words. Talk with them about how they might have written their response differently if they had focused on exactly what was called for and then have them revise their responses.

2. Sentence Fragments and Run-on Sentences Select specific errors in sentence formation from students' writing and copy them (with no names) onto overhead transparencies. Have students discuss as a group how these sentences should be corrected.

APPLY YOUR SKILLS

The more you practice responding to written prompts the more comfortable you will feel. Try these topics for practice.

Topic 1

This passage from Willa Cather's *A Lost Lady* introduces the character Ivy Peters. Describe the kind of person Ivy seems to be and explain how the passage achieves this impression. Finally, predict what kind of activity Ivy will involve himself in.

> George and Niel hated to look at Ivy,—and yet his face had a kind of fascination for them. It was red, and the flesh looked hard, as if it were swollen from bee-stings, or from an encounter with poison ivy. This nickname, however, was given him because it was well known that he had "made away" with several other dogs before he had poisoned the judge's friendly water spaniel. The boys said he took a dislike to a dog and couldn't rest until he made an end of him. Ivy's red skin was flecked with tiny freckles, like rust spots, and in each of his hard cheeks there was a curly indentation, like a knot in a tree-bole,—two permanent dimples which did anything but soften his countenance. His eyes were very small, and an absence of eyelashes gave his pupils the fixed, unblinking hardness of a snake's or a lizard's. His hands had the same swollen look as his face, and were deeply creased across the back and knuckles, as if the skin were stretched too tight. He was an ugly fellow, Ivy Peters, and he liked being ugly.

Topic 2

Edward Abbey writes about his home state of Arizona in the following passage. Analyze Abbey's attitude toward his home state and explain how the style and tone of the passage function in expressing that attitude.

> But Arizona is something different. Or was. There is nothing in Arizona that much resembles Europe or the East except the slums along the railroad tracks in Flagstaff. Arizona has some pretty mountains too, like Colorado, but mostly and essentially, Arizona is desert country. High desert in the north, low desert in the south, ninety percent of my state is an appalling burnt-out wasteland, a hideous Sahara with a few oases, a grim bleak harsh overheated sun-blasted . . . inferno. Arizona is the

native haunt of the scorpion, the solpugid, the sidewinder, the tarantula, the vampire bat, the conenose kissing bug, the vine-garroon, the centipede, and three species of poisonous lizard: namely, the Gila monster, the land speculator, and the real estate broker. Arizona is where the Apaches live, who used to suspend their prisoners head-down above a slow fire . . . . Arizona is where the vultures swarm like flies about the starving cattle on the cow-burnt range. In Arizona the dust storms carry lung fungus . . . . Arizona is the land-fraud capital of the world. Keep a firm grip on your shirt. Because of the parched air and the hard water, Arizonans come down with more kidney stones per pelvis than any place outside of Chad and southern Libya. In Arizona the trees have thorns and the bushes spines and the swimming pools are infested with loan sharks, automobile dealers and Mafiosi. The water table is falling and during a heavy wind you can see sand dunes form on Central Avenue in Phoenix. We have the most gorgeous sunsets in the Western World—when the copper smelters are shut down. I am describing the place I love. Arizona is my natural native home. Nobody in his right mind would want to live here.

Objective

To apply writing skills in responding to additional assessment prompts

Writing Portfolio

Encourage students to compare their responses to the prompt for this assignment to other assessment responses they may have in their Writing Portfolios. In what ways is this response clearer and more effective? Then have students add the responses done for this assignment to their Writing Portfolios.

Application

Before students respond to either one of the prompts, have them identify the key words within the prompts. Then have them refer to pages 315 and 316 to identify those tasks that would be useful in planning responses to the prompts.

Summary and Closure

Be sure students have internalized the following concepts:

1. A response to a reading selection requires a thorough understanding of the selection itself.

2. A response to a reading selection must be well organized around a central idea.

3. Information in a response to a reading selection must be clearly stated in language appropriate to the reader.

Allow students time to summarize what they learned by describing the characteristics of effective responses to a reading selection and by telling why knowing how to write an effective response to a reading selection might help them in other school subjects.

Sentence

Author's Expansions
Adding Phrases and Clauses, Exercise C, page 111

1. Wanting to whistle, to do something to bring noise and movement into the house, she turned and opened the door on her right and stepped into the dim crowded parlor.

2. Professor Kazin, wearing a spotlessly white tropical suit and a wide-brimmed hat, was the first ashore.

3. He moved restlessly, looking round as though expecting to see some-one sneaking up on him.

4. He had become part of the group of young unemployed, who hung about on pavements, sat around in cafés, sometimes did odd jobs, went to the cinema, rushed about on motorbikes or in borrowed cars.

Varying Sentence Openers, Exercise C, page 175

1. Filled with joy, Vera took the letter.

2. Sitting in the mouth of his cave, gazing up at the farther peaks on which there were still patches of snow, he spent a day in idleness.

3. Sometimes, mounted on an old saddle, with shrill cries of encourage-ment, Jody rode out beyond the room.

4. Although they lived in style, they always felt an anxiety in the house.

5. There, between two trees, against a background of gaunt black rocks, was a figure from a dream, a strange beast that was horned and drunken-legged, but like something he had never even imagined.

6. Trying the doors as he went, twirling his club with many intricate and artful movements, turning now and then to cast his watchful eye down the pacific thoroughfare, the officer, with his stalwart form and slight swagger, made a fine picture of a guardian of the peace.

Varying S-V Splits, Exercise B, page 204

1. There had followed a time of such happiness that Chips, remembering it long afterward, hardly believed it could ever have happened before or since in the world.

2. Old Mrs. Beal, her Sunday black billowing in the wind, was homeward bound from dinner with her daughter.

3. Across an immense ethereal gulf, intellects vast, cool, and unsympathetic, regarded this earth with envious eyes and slowly drew their plans against us.

4. The bride, in her bridelike traveling dress, surrounded by her maids, stood between her parents, each of them holding her by a hand, and their three faces were calm, grave, and much alike.

Varying Sentence Closers, Exercise C, page 235

1. He grabbed the shield again, twisting it as he pulled.

2. Towser roused himself under Fowler's desk and scratched another flea, his leg thumping hard against the floor.

3. Halfway there he heard the sound he dreaded, the hollow, rasping cough of a horse.

4. The other shoji slammed open, and unseen, Buntaro stamped away, followed by the guard.

5. In the fishpond the hippo belched, not softly.

Combining Sentence Variations, Exercise B, pages 266–267

1. At the gate, I show the pass to a young Japanese private, the sentry.

2. Janet, pausing half-way down to say something to someone above, stood there as if painted, distinct and unreal.

3. Absorbed, taking no heed of other people, he went about with a sort of stealth, seeking inwardly for luck.

4. After perhaps a seventh attempt he slipped from the wooden ledge and fell, fluttering his wings, onto his back on the windowsill.

Travel Alphabet, Alan Nils Adler, 1983

Writing Handbook

The mini-lessons in this Handbook may be used for a variety of purposes.

Preteaching—to introduce specific writing concepts and skills before beginning a Guided or Related Assignment

Reference—to provide extra help and practice as students problem-solve their way through a piece of writing

Reteaching—to remedy specific problems noted in student writing

To match mini-lessons to an assignment, see teaching notes under Preteaching in the Writers Workshop, and Handbook cross-references on the pupil page.

Sketchbook

Objective

To use a painting as a springboard to informal writing

Using the Prompt

Before beginning the activity, remind students that Sketchbook activities are ungraded and are meant as opportunities to experiment with writing

Explain that Edvard Munch (1863–1944) focused much of his work on pain, death, and unhappy love. Many of his pictures presented the tensions, anguish, and loneliness of modern life. Ask students how the artist used color and line to convey the idea of a dreadful fear and a scream "passing through nature." Help students recognize that the strong colors and the long, wavy lines carry the horror of the scream into every corner of the picture, permeating the entire canvas with panic and misery.

Ask students what their first response to the painting was and whether this response changed as they studied it. Then have them jot down ideas or write a paragraph or two describing the emotions and memories the painting triggers.

Use the ideas in Additional Sketches with those students who find these ideas to be better starting points for writing. Encourage students to keep their writing in their Writing Portfolios. Point out that there may be ideas in their Sketchbook writing that they will want to develop at a later time.

Sketchbook

*O*ne evening I was walking along a path, the city was on one side and the fjord below. I felt tired and ill. I stopped and looked out over the fjord—the sun was setting, and the clouds turning blood-red. I sensed a scream passing through nature; it seemed to me that I heard the scream. I painted this picture, painted the clouds as actual blood. The colour shrieked.

Edvard Munch
DIARY

The Scream, by Edvard Munch, 1893

For Norwegian artist Edvard Munch, the surrounding landscape and his own state of mind combined to produce a powerful emotional response—so powerful that he "sensed a scream passing through nature." Have you ever experienced anything like that? Have you ever felt like the figure in the painting? What emotions does this painting stir in you?

Additional Sketches

Think of a color. Then think of a memory you associate with that color.

The humorist Roy Blount once wrote a song entitled, "I'm just a Bug on the Windshield of Life." What are you?

Writing Prompts and Writing Decisions

Before beginning a writing project, you probably will find it helpful to analyze the activity as a whole and the individual parameters you will have to consider. Questions such as the following may help you focus your thinking.

- What is my purpose in writing this piece? Who will read it?
- What do I already know about the topic, and what do I need to research?

WRITING PROMPTS

There are three major categories of writing: self-prompted, prompted by others, and done for assessment. Self-prompted writing is personal writing done to fulfill your own purposes or for your own pleasure. Writing prompted by others includes class assignments, reports, and memos. Writing done for assessment purposes includes college entrance examinations and job applications.

Self-Prompted Writing Some writing that you do for yourself is utilitarian, or practical, such as filling out forms and writing letters of complaint. Other self-prompted writing you will do simply because you enjoy it. This type of writing includes poems, journal entries, and personal letters.

The variables of practical self-prompted writing are largely predetermined. If you write a letter requesting information about summer-school programs at a local college, for example, your topic, form, purpose, audience, and tone are already established. In doing creative self-prompted writing, on the other hand, you have complete freedom to determine all of the variables of your work.

WRITER TO WRITER

Each time I write, no matter what the form or subject, it is an expression of me.

Brandy Barton, student
Cedar Rapids, Iowa

WRITING
HANDBOOK
1

Writing Prompts and Writing Decisions

Objectives

1. To define and respond to a writing prompt
2. To analyze and make decisions about the writing variables

Handbook Mini-Lessons

For information related to writing prompts and writing decisions, see the following mini-lessons.

- Organizing Your Work, pp. 349–357
- Your Unique Voice, pp. 418–419
- Applying for a Job, pp. 516–518
- Types of Tests, pp. 521–522

Teaching Strategies

Motivating

Ask students if they have ever filled out job application forms. Have volunteers describe the process, including the information they need to know and the writing style they used in filling out the form. Discuss with students the importance of filling out such a form correctly and intelligently. Help students recognize that they can present the information to enhance their employment prospects. Point out that this is only one example of the many everyday situations in which they are asked to respond to a writing prompt.

Writing for Others In school, you often write in response to prompts supplied by your teachers. Some of the writing you do after you graduate will also be prompted by others. Some jobs, including newspaper reporting and writing advertising copy, require people to write all the time. Even nonwriting jobs involve writing: for example, scientists write proposals, lab reports, and articles for journals; accountants and salespeople write business letters and reports.

Writing for Assessment A unique kind of writing prompted by others is writing done for assessment purposes. This kind of writing occurs throughout your academic life—on essay tests, college entrance examinations, and entrance exams for many training programs. Often, job applicants also must submit letters explaining their qualifications for employment. Many jobs require people to pass written examinations for promotions to higher positions. The following guidelines should help you respond to a writing prompt on a test or application.

Guidelines: Writing for Assessment

1. Read the question over until you understand all of its parts. Look for key words, such as *explain, describe, analyze,* and *classify* that give specific directions.

2. Briefly consider your topic, purpose, form, and audience.

3. Make some notes or an informal outline on a piece of scrap paper or in your head.

4. Develop a thesis statement that sets a goal for your writing, and state it at the beginning of the piece.

5. Make a list of the main points that you will present to support the thesis statement.

6. As you write, use transitions to connect your ideas.

7. End with a strong conclusion.

8. If you have time, reread and revise your work.

ESL Students These students may have trouble determining key words on a test or in an assignment. Provide a list of key words in addition to those provided in the student book, such as *tell about, list, compare, contrast, complete,* for these students to use as reference.

Career Connection

Have students pick a field that interests them—anything from football coach to open-heart surgeon to AIDS researcher. Have them discuss and write a thesis statement that would begin a letter of application for the job they have chosen. Encourage them to explain in their thesis statement why they feel their services are needed in the field.

WRITING VARIABLES

Analyzing a writing prompt by breaking it down into its parts, or variables, enables you to make decisions about each variable separately, and then to examine the relationships of all the variables to one another. Some of the key writing variables are listed in the following chart.

Writing Variable	Definition	Examples
Topic	what you write about	*perestroika*, recycling
Form	the shape of the piece of writing	research paper, radio script, memo, blank verse
Purpose	overall goal to be accomplished by the piece of writing	to explain, to entertain, to persuade, to teach, to figure something out
Personal Goals	specific goal(s) that you want the writing to accomplish	to work out a problem, to create a particular mood, to impress your boss
Audience	the people for whom you are writing	your co-workers, yourself, your classmates, your friends and neighbors
Voice	your tone and personal writing style	objective or subjective, formal or informal, serious or mocking, disapproving or supportive

Although writing involves making decisions about these variables, there are no strict rules about when in the writing process you should consider them. In fact, some decisions may not be made until you are well into the drafting process. However, when you examine a writing prompt, identify which variables have already been specified and which you can select.

Writing Prompts and
Writing Decisions **329**

Personal Touch: Writing Variables

Describe a piece of writing that you have done yourself. Break down your work into the six variables described, and explain to the class why you decided on the variables you chose and how they affected your writing.

Springboard

Have students choose pieces of fiction from a book they have at hand—a novel, book of short stories, or literature text. Working in pairs, students can read aloud the first paragraph from the piece they have chosen. Their partners can then try to analyze the piece in terms of the variables, using the chart. Explain that the first paragraph may not make all six of the charted variables clear; students may need to skim the piece further. Encourage students to discuss how fully the opening of the fictional piece illustrates the variables the author chose.

Answers will vary. Possible responses to the exercises include the following:

Topic: given. Form: research paper. Purpose: to inform. Personal goal: to learn about the civil rights movement. Audience: given. Voice: objective.

Topic: given. Form: given. Purpose: given. Personal goal: to fulfill boss's expectations. Audience: given. Voice: formal.

Topic: your summer plans. Form: given. Purpose: to entertain. Personal goal: to continue a friendship. Audience: your best friend. Voice: informal; humorous.

Additional Resources

- Writing Resource Book, p. 1
- Thinking Skills Transparencies:
  Analysis Frame
  Basic Category Chart
- Writing About Literature
- Fine Art Transparencies and Writing Prompts
- Ideas for Writing

Writing
TIP

The most effective way of improving your writing skills is to write on a regular schedule, every day if possible.

PROBLEM-SOLVING AND THE WRITING VARIABLES

Sometimes a predetermined writing variable can make the task of writing seem impossible. For example, what can you do if you must write about a topic that doesn't interest you or for an audience that intimidates you?

Try not to let your writing process be undermined by a topic that bores you. Instead, look for an aspect of the topic that has some interest for you and start writing about that aspect. Getting involved in part of an assigned topic may help you find a personal approach to the topic as a whole.

"Fellow octopi, or octopuses ... octopi? ... Dang, it's hard to start a speech with this crowd."

If you must write for a difficult audience, before you write ask yourself, "What is hard for me about this audience?" Many people find it easier to write for classmates or for a teacher they know than for strangers. You might try writing a draft for your favorite audience first, and then revise it for the audience you find difficult.

Remember that your most important audience is *yourself*. It is often helpful to write early drafts just for *yourself*—so you can feel safe to experiment with new techniques. Then you can revise these drafts to suit the needs of other audiences.

Practice Your Skills

For each of the following writing prompts, decide which writing variables are given and which still need to be determined. Then provide the missing writing variables for each prompt, including reasons for your choices. If any of the variables is problematic for you, indicate how you would deal with the problem.

- Your history teacher asks you to write about the civil rights movement.
- Your boss tells you to write a memo briefing other employees on changes in the sick-day policy.
- You decide to write a personal letter.

330 Writing Handbook

Generating Ideas for Writing

Have you ever wondered where the really successful writing ideas come from — the ones behind popular books, movies, and television programs? There's really nothing mysterious about the process of coming up with writing ideas. You can generate compelling ideas for your own writing by learning a few simple techniques for stimulating creative thinking.

REFLECTING AND OBSERVING

Two basic approaches to idea generation are (1) recalling and reflecting and (2) observing and responding. The first is directed inward; the second, outward.

Recalling and Reflecting

If you sit quietly and let your mind drift back into the past, you can often **recall** vividly the sights, sounds, smells, tastes, and feelings of a previous event in your life. If you start to **reflect** about the significance of the event, relating your recollection to your present-day experience and observations, you will often experience the surprise of discovery and find the germ of a writing idea starting to take shape in your mind.

To illustrate, suppose you begin by thinking about a camping trip you once took in the mountains. Soon you might start asking yourself what made the trip so memorable. After reflection, you might decide that camping always brings out the best in people. Now you have the glimmer of a writing idea. Perhaps you could write a play in which two enemies find themselves in a situation where they must camp in the woods together.

WRITER TO WRITER

For me the initial delight is in the surprise of remembering something I didn't know I knew. . . . There is a glad recognition of the long lost, and the rest follows. Step by step the wonder of unexpected surprise keeps growing.

Robert Frost, writer and poet

Generating Ideas
for Writing   **331**

Writing Handbook 2:
Generating Ideas for Writing

Objectives

1. To use various techniques of reflecting and observing to generate ideas
2. To elaborate on observations in a variety of ways

Handbook Mini-Lessons

For information on topics related to generating writing ideas, see the following mini-lessons.
- Applying Graphic Devices, pp. 339–347
- Collaborative Planning, pp. 358–360

Teaching Strategies

Personal Touch: Recall and Reflect

To help your students better understand the technique of recall and reflect, describe for them a scene from your past in terms of the five senses. Then reflect on the scene, relating it to your present-day experiences. Suggest one or two writing ideas you could generate from the scene.

Observing and Responding

When you **observe** and **respond,** you see beyond the surface of things. You might look at a friend as she talks and hear her words but not recognize what she is thinking. If you are a sensitive observer, however, you will watch her eyes, listen to the tone of her voice, and draw inferences about what she is feeling. Such active, responsive observation can lead you to new insights and provide you with new ideas for writing.

Suppose that you are at an aquarium and you notice a child watching a brightly colored fish swim in and out of the tentacles of an anemone. Observing this child might lead you to think about how people often lose their sense of wonder as they grow up. Later, in a quiet moment of contemplation, you might decide to write a poem on that subject.

GATHERING INFORMATION

You can learn to supplement your own reflections and observations with those of other people. Several techniques can help you tap this information as a new source of writing ideas.

Gleaning

When you **glean,** you gather bits and pieces of information from conversations, newspapers, television programs, and other sources you encounter. You can glean at any time and in any place. All you need to do is collect interesting details, looking for a "writable" idea. You then examine all its different facets and ramifications.

Browsing

Casually leafing through books and magazines, called **browsing,** often helps you find new ideas for writing. You can browse through subject area sections of bookstores, libraries, or even computer information services.

Clip Files

If you come across an article that you want to keep for future reference, you might clip it out and file it, or else photocopy it. It's a good idea to record the name, date, and page number on the clip so that you can document quotations you may later use.

ELABORATING ON YOUR OBSERVATIONS

There are many techniques for "mining" your observations and reflections for ideas, including thinking techniques, writing techniques, sharing techniques, and others. At first you may choose to respond simply by thinking. Later, you may want to write your ideas down, share them, or interpret them with graphics, questioning, and research.

Thinking Techniques

The most immediate way you can expand upon what you've observed or recalled is through creative thinking processes such as imaging, conducting a knowledge inventory, and using trigger words and pictures.

Imaging Much of what you've experienced is stored in your brain as mental images. You can respond to what you've observed, recalled, or reflected on by using a technique called **imaging.** When you image, you recall ideas and memories by clearing your mind of distractions and concentrating only on the sensory qualities of your remembered subject—its look, sound, feel, taste, and smell. List all the details you can envision.

Knowledge Inventory A **knowledge inventory** helps you discover what you already know about a subject, which will often be much more than you are aware of knowing. You complete a knowledge inventory by jotting down, in list form, every fact you can think of regarding a subject. Then you can list questions you still have about the subject.

Trigger Words and Pictures **Trigger words** are words that stimulate your idea-generation process. Finding trigger words can be as simple as flipping through a dictionary or browsing through a magazine. To use a trigger word, start by thinking about its traditional meaning. Then free-associate or cluster to discover alternate meanings, metaphorical relationships, or other less ordinary meanings. Here are some examples of trigger words.

blackout	treasure	detention	masquerade
cult	crisis	graduation	solstice
xenophobia	fantasy	hoax	avalanche
ingenuity	accomplice	opportunity	waterhole

Generating Ideas
for Writing **333**

Modeling

Some students may have trouble with the concept of free association. Illustrate the concept for the class by choosing an evocative word and modeling free-association of other meanings and connotations for it.

Springboard

Read this quotation by Thomas Hobbes aloud to the class: " . . . After the object is removed or the eye shut, we still retain an image of the things seen, though more obscure than when we see it. . . . Imagination, therefore, is nothing but decaying sense." Ask students to write their own definition of imagination in their journals. Do they agree or disagree with Hobbes? Then discuss with students the meaning of the last part of the quotation. What does Hobbes mean by "decaying sense"? What implication does this statement have for the practice of imaging? for generating ideas?

Just as words can trigger your imagination, so can visual images in the world around you or in fine art or photographs. Look at a picture and ask yourself questions such as the following: How could I describe what I see in this picture? How does this picture make me feel? What might have occurred just prior to the scene shown? Could the people in this picture make good characters in a story?

Breeze at Work, Sandy Skoglund, 1987

Writing Techniques

Once you've discovered ideas through reflecting and responding to your observations, you can use the following prewriting techniques to build on those ideas: using a journal, freewriting, looping, listing, and internal dialogue.

Journals A **journal** is your creation, your own place to record your thoughts. It can also become one of the most powerful writing tools you will ever use. As your entries accumulate, your journal becomes a sourcebook for your writing ideas, a place to collect memorable passages from other people's writing, and a laboratory for trying out ideas and writing styles.

334 Writing Handbook

Freewriting and Looping **Freewriting** is the written equivalent of letting your mind wander. Without paying attention to grammar, mechanics, or logic, you write continuously for a given amount of time. Freewriting helps you find new approaches to a topic. **Looping** takes freewriting a step farther. After you freewrite, you examine what you wrote to find your best idea. This idea then becomes a new subject for a second loop of freewriting. Repeat the loop at least once. By the end of your third or fourth loop, you should be able to identify and narrow your writing topic.

Listing Making a **list** can help you organize ideas, examine them, and identify areas where you need to do further research. Listing parts of a whole or steps in a process will help you determine order and relationships as well as provide you with an outline for your writing. By annotating the list with questions, you can often discover other possible ideas for writing.

Internal Dialogue Here are three different ways to use **internal dialogue** to generate writing ideas.

1. Interview yourself thoroughly about a topic. Write down your questions and answers.
2. Hold a dialogue between two parts of yourself—between your mind and your emotions, your studious self and your playful self, your angry self and your loving self.
3. Take on the roles of two characters, or of a character and some idea or object, to debate an issue.

   Regardless of whether or not the conversation makes sense, it will still help you generate ideas and see ideas and issues from different perspectives.

Sharing Techniques

   Other people can often provide valuable perspectives on your ideas. Some effective sharing techniques that you can use to generate useful ideas include brainstorming, interviewing, discussion, and idea exchanges.

Brainstorming Free generation of ideas in a group setting, or **brainstorming,** can be an exciting way to expand on your observations. When you brainstorm, you and others simply come up with as many ideas as you can without stopping to critique or examine them. A brainstorming session should have the atmosphere of a free-for-all, and no idea should be discarded.

Generating Ideas
for Writing   **335**

Teaching Tip: Internal Dialogue

Some students may have trouble with the idea of interviewing themselves. Encourage these students to imagine that the person they are interviewing is someone else—either someone they know or someone in the public eye. Tell them that, as they write down the answers to the interview questions they have prepared, they can think about the way their "subject's" answers might differ from answers they themselves would give. By looking at two possible points of view on a topic, they will gain even more from the interview.

Answers will vary. Good answers should meet the following criteria.

1. Students should generate a wealth of multisensory details—not merely one or two—describing a place.

2. The three writing ideas should show a clear distinction in *purpose*.

3. The dialogue should show adequate elaboration—with each character's point of view clearly stated.

4. The interview questions should indicate that the interviewer has a clear sense of purpose. The writing ideas should allow for elaboration from the interview materials.

Cooperative Learning

Students can gain new ideas for Exercise 2 by working in pairs to brainstorm a list of ideas related to the object they have chosen. Encourage them to use their brainstorming session to determine at least one writing idea in addition to the three required.

Additional Resources

- Writing Resource Book, pp. 2–3
- Thinking Skills Worksheets, p. 2, Generating Ideas
- Fine Art Transparencies and Writing Prompts
- Ideas for Writing
- Writing About Literature

Writing TIP

Before interviewing an expert about a topic, research the topic thoroughly so you can ask informed, substantive questions. During the interview, listen carefully and record the answers accurately.

Interviewing One of the most useful ways to explore a topic is **interviewing.** Simply find someone who knows a great deal about your topic, and talk to him or her about it. The interview can be informal, or it can involve elaborate planning, with questions written out beforehand and a formal appointment for a question-and-answer session.

Discussion A **discussion,** of course, is simply the act of getting together with others to talk about a topic. Perhaps you will have a discussion leader, who helps the group define key terms, keeps order during the conversation, and summarizes the main points.

Idea Exchange You may wish to organize a group of friends or classmates into a writing group that meets frequently and exchanges ideas. You might also set up a file of writing ideas to which everyone contributes and from which everyone can draw. Such a file is called an **idea exchange.**

Practice Your Skills

Follow the directions given below. After completing each activity, record your writing ideas in your journal or write them on a page to be saved in your writing portfolio. You can refer to your collection of writing ideas later when you need a subject about which to write.

1. Think about a special place you have visited. Make a chart listing your memories of the place. What sights, sounds, smells, and feelings do you associate with the place?
2. Browse through an encyclopedia or dictionary and choose some physical object that interests you. Conduct a knowledge inventory to investigate what you already know about the object. Then come up with at least three different writing ideas—one for a factual piece, one for a persuasive piece, and one for a literary work such as a poem or short story.
3. Choose an important decision or crisis currently facing politicians in your city or state, or in the country as a whole. Write a dialogue in which two characters take opposing viewpoints on your subject. Based on your dialogue, jot down three or four ideas for pieces that you might write.
4. Imagine that you are going to write an article for your school newspaper on an aspect of the arts in your school—dance, art, film, or music. Interview a teacher or student involved in the art program you have chosen to investigate. Use the results of the interview to write down several ideas for your article.

Humanities Connection

Students may wish to make a visual idea exchange—that is, a file that includes photographs and illustrations that might stimulate ideas for writing. Encourage students to bring in any art they find that they feel might be useful in such a file; students can consult the file when they feel that visual stimulation might aid them in writing.

Social Studies Connection

Students can further focus their writing ideas in Exercise 3 by preparing an interview with a politician involved in the issue they have chosen. Encourage them to write a list of questions they would like to ask the politician about the issue. If possible, encourage them to follow through with an in-person interview or letter.

Focusing Ideas

Once you have generated some writing ideas and have reflected, observed, and expanded on your observations, you can begin to focus on a topic suitable for your writing activity.

LIMITING YOUR TOPIC

Is it better to write about African music or about the group Ladysmith Black Mambazo? The answer depends on what kind of writing you want to do.

Determining Factors

The principal factors that determine how you should limit a topic are your purpose, intended audience, and length and format requirements.

Purpose If your purpose is to provide a general survey of a topic, you can choose a fairly broad topic. Usually, however, you will want to include as much detailed information as possible, so you will need to narrow your topic.

Audience If your audience is well informed about your subject, you can either present your topic in broad terms or focus on very specialized information. If your audience is unfamiliar with your subject, you will need to focus on a narrow aspect of the topic, providing a great deal of detailed information.

Length and Format Requirements When you are writing in response to a classroom or publication prompt, you must consider length and format requirements. Usually you will want to limit your topic so that you can elaborate it fully in the available space.

Techniques for Limiting a Topic

Several techniques that you can use to explore and elaborate on a topic can also help you focus your topic. These techniques include brainstorming, questioning, browsing in books and magazines, and using graphic devices.

Brainstorming Enlist the help of other writers in a brainstorming session. Present your general topic to your group and see what specific aspects of the topic occur to them.

Writing Handbook 3:
Focusing Ideas

Objectives

1. To identify how to limit a topic by considering purpose, audience, and assignment requirements
2. To identify and use questioning, brainstorming, and various graphic devices as tools for limiting a topic

Handbook Mini-Lessons

For information on topics related to focusing ideas, see the following mini-lessons.

- Applying Graphic Devices, pp. 339–347
- Techniques for Elaboration and Development, pp. 376–381

Teaching Strategies

Motivating

Have students brainstorm nature programs they have enjoyed and jot down "what they were about." Responses to the latter will probably range from very general topics ("African animals") to specific ones ("the social life of a hyena pack in the Serengeti"). When the list is completed, point out that in some cases they have cited broad subjects while in others they have named the specific topic of a show. Point out that when they write, they generally need to zero in on a specific topic in order to be productive.

Personal Touch

Tell students about a time in college when you began working on a writing topic that turned out to be too broad. How did you discover you needed to limit your topic? What paths did you follow to change to one that suited your needs?

Organize students into groups and have each group use brainstorming to come up with a specific and focused writing topic. Have all the groups begin with the general subject of sports, decide on a writing format, and focus on a topic that would be appropriate for a ten-page paper. Set a time limit for the brainstorming session. Circulate from group to group to suggest strategies for improvement. When time runs out, each group should choose a spokesperson to present its topic to the class. Have the class decide whether each topic is sufficiently focused to write about.

ANSWERS TO PRACTICE YOUR SKILLS

Answers will vary. However, a topic appropriate for each format will correspond with the purpose, intended audience, and length requirements.

Additional Resources
- Writing Resource Book, p. 4
- Thinking Skills Tranparencies
- Thinking Skills Worksheets

Questioning Asking questions about a general topic can help you generate a list of more focused topics related to it. For example, you might ask yourself the following questions.

- What issue or aspect of this topic matters most to me?
- What is at stake for me or my audience with regard to this topic?
- What is the most interesting aspect of this topic?

Other types of questions that can help you focus a topic—action questions, category questions, and creative questions and Aristotelian invention—are discussed in "Using Questioning Techniques," pages 376–378.

Browsing and Research Sometimes, just leafing through books, magazines, or reference works can give you ideas for a focused topic. If you are writing a factual piece, make a list of questions for research. As you use reference works to find answers, you may discover an aspect of your topic that you want to pursue further.

Graphic Devices Charting, clustering, and mapping are a few of the graphic devices that might help you to narrow a topic. For more specific information on using graphic devices like these, see Writing Handbook 4, pages 339–347.

W R I T E R   T O   W R I T E R

As soon as I pick a topic, I write that topic in the center of my paper and make a cluster map.

Ryan Fiel, student
San Marcos, California

Practice Your Skills

Match each broad topic from the list on the left with a writing format from the list on the right. Then, limit each broad topic by questioning, brainstorming, or using a graphic device.

Broad Topics	Writing Formats
Careers	six-page short story
The Future	fifteen-page story
Community Problems	three-minute speech
Other Cultures	ten-minute oral report

338 Writing Handbook

Social Studies Connection

Have students analyze and compare various elements in their social studies textbooks such as chapter overviews, biographical features, and general text copy. The topics of these elements range from broad to narrow. Have students infer possible reasons for the various types of topics within one book.

Applying Graphic Devices

A **graphic device** is a visual representation of things, ideas, and the relationships among them. Writers often use graphic devices throughout the writing process to limit or focus topics, to gather or generate ideas, and to organize their material.

Each graphic you'll learn about can function in more than one way and at different stages of your writing process. The usefulness of all types of graphic devices is limited only by your imagination.

GRAPHICS FOR EXPLORING IDEAS AND FOCUSING TOPICS

Some graphic devices are useful for exploring ideas—for developing writing topics, gathering general information and specific details, and limiting and focusing topics. These graphics include cluster maps, tree diagrams, observation charts, pro-and-con charts, and evaluation matrices.

Cluster Maps and Tree Diagrams   Graphic devices that help you explore ideas related to a general topic or central idea include **cluster maps** and **tree diagrams** (or spider maps). Graphics like these can help you both broaden the range of your thinking and limit the focus of your ideas. In a cluster map, the central idea is broken down into subordinate or related ideas connected to it with lines.

Cluster Map

- both sides of head
- intense pain
- eyes teary, nose clogged
- Cluster
- 20 minutes to 2 hours
- once a day for weeks or months
- **Headaches**
- 4 hours to 2 days
- Migraine
- throbbing
- one side of head
- nausea and aversion to lights and noise
- Tension
- intermittent or chronic
- both sides of head
- dull ache

Applying Graphic Devices   **339**

Writing Handbook 4:
Applying Graphic Devices

Objectives

1. To use graphic devices to explore and focus ideas
2. To use graphic devices to organize ideas

Handbook Mini-Lessons
For information on topics related to graphic devices in writing, see the following mini-lessons.
- Generating Ideas for Writing, pp. 331–336
- Collaborative Planning, pp. 358–360

Teaching Strategies

Motivating

Set up a brainstorming session in which students call out ideas (for a writing topic, or a solution to a practical problem) as you write them on the chalkboard. But use a graphic device, such as an idea tree or cluster, to arrange the ideas on the board. Later, focus on the graphic device you used. Ask students how they think it might have helped move the creative thinking process along. Ask if any students have ever used graphic devices to help them think through a problem. Invite respondents to tell about their methods.

Individualizing Instruction

LEP Students Cluster-type graphics are often the most suitable kind of graphic device for students who have limited English proficiency because the visual display is easy to understand and descriptors can be written as words and abbreviations. Encourage these students to try a cluster using a familiar topic.

LD Students Moving from one column to the next and then back again while working with two-column graphics might cause students to reverse information. When learning disabled students use two-column graphics, suggest they complete one column before they place information in a second column.

Teaching Tip: Purpose

Remind students that when their purpose is to persuade, a pro-and-con chart is a valuable tool because it will enable them to recognize the kinds of objections to their point of view that they are likely to face. By knowing the possible objections, students can then plan strategies to deal with them.

340 Writing Handbook

Writing
—**TIP**—
Remember that you can alter these standard graphic devices to make them more useful for you.

A tree diagram differs from a cluster map in certain respects, but it functions in the same way. The main idea is at the bottom or top, and the related ideas "branch out" from there.

Tree Diagram

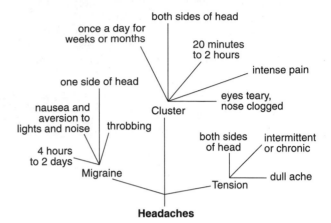

Pro-and-Con Charts You can explore and compare the positive and negative aspects of an idea or course of action by making a **pro-and-con chart.** This type of chart can help you explore two sides of an issue. If you were preparing for a debate on the subject of nuclear energy, for example, you could list arguments in a chart as shown below.

Pro-and-Con Chart Nuclear Energy	
Pros	**Cons**
Decreases dependence on foreign oil.	Produces hazardous wastes that cannot be disposed of safely.
Does not create adverse greenhouse effects like the burning of fossil fuels.	Creates potential for a major accident (as at Chernobyl).
Can be abundantly produced.	Is associated with leaks of radiation into environment.

Observation Charts If you plan to write about a place or situation, you can make an **observation chart** to record information gathered through the five senses. The following chart was created by a student who was planning to write about her scuba-diving experience.

Observation Chart Diving on a Coral Reef	
Sight	Underwater things appear closer and larger; as you descend, lose colors: first the reds, then the yellows, finally, the blues
	Elkhorn, staghorn, and other corals; enormous multicolored sponges; starfish; urchins; angelfish; burrfish; porcupine fish; puffers; giant flounder; trumpetfish; moray eels; bull shark, lemon shark, tiger shark
Touch	Weightlessness in water, like an astronaut (hydronaut?); tightness of dive mask; caution not to touch anything under water because of damage that can be done to the marine life
Taste	Taste of salt water; bitter rubber of mouthpiece
Hearing	Sound amplified under water; faraway boat sounds as if it is about to run over you; wonderful quiet of the deeper water—no conversation, no cars, no telephones, no loud radios—just a meditative calmness and the sound of your own breathing through the regulator
Smell	Smell of salt sea air; diving equipment (rubber and silicone); fish

Evaluation Matrices An **evaluation matrix** is used for making evaluations, or judgments. Begin by listing the parts of the subject or idea that you want to evaluate. Then list criteria by which each part should be judged. Finally, make judgments based on each of your criteria. Suppose, for example, that you want to write a review of a short story you've read. You might make an evaluation matrix like the one shown on the next page.

Individualizing Instruction

Learning Styles Students who are not visual learners may have difficulty using or understanding some of the graphic devices in this lesson. You may want to use examples on the chalkboard or on a transparency to explain aloud the relationship between ideas. You might want to point out that the observation chart is a good graphic device because it forces the writer to record all kinds of observations—not just those perceived through sight.

Critical Thinking

Making Inferences Ask students when they might find an observation chart most useful *(When they are doing any kind of writing that requires the use of descriptive detail such as in a journalistic narrative or in a lab report)*. Mention that grouping observations systematically in a chart can reveal patterns that would not otherwise be obvious.

Critical Thinking

Judging To illustrate the effectiveness of an evaluation matrix, suggest that students use the criteria to judge a story that most students know such as ''Sunrise on the Veld'' or ''The Handsomest Drowned Man in the World.''

 Individualizing Instruction

Gifted and Talented Students Suggest that these students add two more elements and criteria to the chart before they judge one of the short stories.

Evaluation Matrix
Short Story by Classmate

Narrative Element	Criteria	Evaluation
Character	1. Dialogue is natural, distinct.	1. Yes, especially dialect of main character.
	2. Characters have distinct personalities, histories, values, and motivations.	2. Antagonist is a bit weak.
	3. Interactions are interesting.	3. Yes!
Setting	1. Time and place are clear.	1. & 2. Could make setting clearer with fewer and more precise details.
	2. Details are included that create the texture, the feel, of the setting.	
	3. The setting evokes a mood.	3. Yes—of hilarity.
Plot	1. A conflict is introduced and resolved.	1. Yes.
	2. Twists in the plot are surprising.	2. The resolution is particularly surprising— well done.
Theme	1. The message of the story is significant and original, not a cliché.	1. Yes—humorously depicts human nature.
	2. Theme grows out of the events in the story.	2. Yes— characters' interactions make it clear.

Humanities Connection

Art Students interested in art might create an evaluation matrix to judge the quality of a piece of art. Working in small groups, students can produce several evaluation matrices: for paintings, for photographs, and for sculptures.

Graphics for organizing ideas

Graphic devices are useful for organizing ideas and information during the writing process. Graphics that are particularly useful for organizing ideas include analysis frames, category charts, compare-and-contrast charts and Venn diagrams, flowcharts, inductive reasoning frames, plot diagrams, and time lines. Organizing your information in one of these graphics may help you get ready to write. You may, however, prefer to organize your ideas visually in the middle of the drafting process or when you're ready to make revisions.

Analysis Frames You can use an **analysis frame** to break down a subject into its component parts. To construct an analysis frame, write the subject at the top of the chart. Then list its parts as column headings, and describe each part in the appropriate column.

If you were writing a report on different ways the media handle a major news item, you might first break the subject into its parts as in the following analysis frame to ensure your full coverage of the topic.

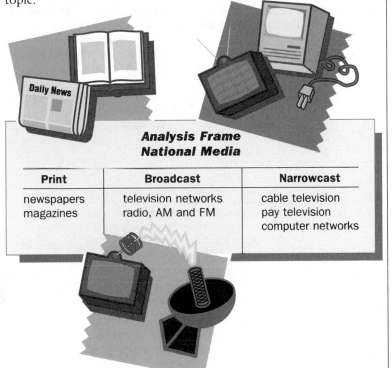

Analysis Frame
National Media

Print	Broadcast	Narrowcast
newspapers magazines	television networks radio, AM and FM	cable television pay television computer networks

Critical Thinking

Division Suggest that students create an analysis frame for the topic *travel*. Invite students to come up with column heads like *air*, *sea*, *rail*, and *roads*.

Critical Thinking

Classifying Have students classify hit prime-time television programs in the 1990's. Before they begin, discuss whether the categories used in the model are appropriate for the 1990's.

 Individualizing Instruction

Learning Styles Although both graphic devices present the same information, students with different learning styles may favor one over the other. For example, more verbal students will probably be more comfortable with the comparison-and-contrast chart while more visual students may favor the Venn diagram.

Category Charts You can use a **category chart** to classify things or ideas according to their qualities, characteristics, or membership in a group. Note how the following chart categorizes some of the most popular television shows of the 1970's.

Category Chart Hit Prime-Time Television Programs in the 1970's		
Serial Comedy	**Serial Drama**	**Variety Shows**
All in the Family	The Waltons	Sonny and Cher
The Brady Bunch	Family	The Carol
Sanford and Son	Little House on	Burnett Show
Happy Days	the Prairie	Hee Haw
The Odd Couple	Kojak	Donny and Marie
Laverne and Shirley	Mission Impossible	Captain and
	Marcus Welby, M.D.	Tenille

Comparison-and-Contrast Charts and Venn Diagrams To organize ideas by their similarities and differences, use either a **comparison-and-contrast chart** or a **Venn diagram.** Like the cluster map and tree diagram, these two graphics have different structures but function in the same way. Note how similarities and differences between the novel and the epic poem are organized in the following graphics.

Comparison-and-Contrast Chart Epic Poem Versus Novel	
Similarities	1. Narrative 2. Relatively long 3. Subplots 4. Room for character development
Differences	1. Novel originally and most often deals with realistic material; epic usually fantasy. 2. Divine forces often intervene in epics; gods usually don't play a role in novel. 3. Epic usually told in poetry; novel in prose.

Mathematics Connection

Venn Diagram Students interested in mathematics might research the origin, history, and uses of the Venn diagram in the field of mathematics.

Venn Diagram

Epic Poem   *Novel*

- fantasy
- divine forces often intervene
- poetry

- narrative
- relatively long
- subplots
- room for character development

- often realistic
- gods usually don't play a role
- prose

Flowcharts   You can use a **flowchart** to help you organize the stages in a process or the steps necessary to complete an activity. In flowcharts used by professionals such as businesspeople and computer scientists, an oval usually stands for start or stop, a diamond for a question or point of decision, and a rectangle for an action. Use these symbols or any other shapes you like. In a flowchart like the one shown below, the stages or steps are listed in order and are connected by arrows that show direction of movement.

Flowchart
*Portion of Videogame: Finding the Safe
in Lord Grimley's Castle*

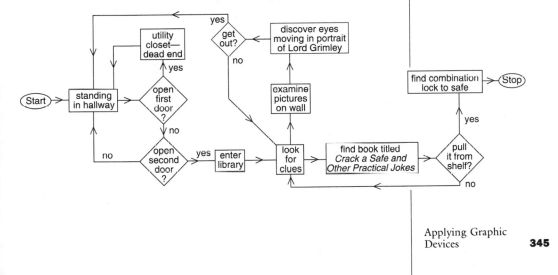

Applying Graphic Devices   **345**

Modeling

Of all the graphic devices presented in this lesson, the flowchart may be the most daunting to students who have never worked with one. Using the flowchart in the text or one of your own construction, demonstrate to students how a portion of it works. You may also wish to change several steps in the flowchart into sentences to demonstrate dramatically how much more effective the graphic is in presenting the information.

Collaborative Opportunity

Suggest that students work in small groups to develop a flowchart that demonstrates the process of class assignments, the workings of the school cafeteria or library, or any other appropriate topic.

Teaching Tip: Time Lines

Remind students that time lines are arranged chronologically, but within the chronological order other patterns of organization are possible, especially when time lines are used in planning personal writing. For example, positive events in a person's life might be placed above the line and negative events below the line; events that lead to a certain goal might be placed higher above the line than less significant events. Suggest that students try making a personal time line.

 Individualizing Instruction

Cultural Differences Students from other cultures may be reluctant to share personal experiences. Assure these students that they may keep their time lines for themselves.

Writing
─TIP─

A diagram like this is only one way to plan a work of fiction. Some people prefer just to begin writing without knowing how the story will end; for them, writing becomes a process of discovery.

Plot Diagrams If you were writing a short story or a play, you might make a **plot diagram** showing all the major events in your plot. A plot diagram can help keep you on track during the drafting process.

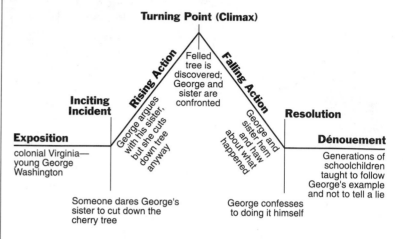

Plot Diagram:
Story Idea—History as It Might Have Happened

Time Lines Although a time line doesn't show story development in the same way a plot diagram does, this graphic can help you keep track of the order of major developments or discoveries. Whether you are writing a mystery or an essay on the history of comic strips, a **time line** can help you organize information in chronological order.

Time Line
Development of the Comic Strip in the United States

Social Studies Connection

Time Lines Time lines are a useful way to present a chronology of historical events. Suggest that students do research to continue the time line of the development of the comic strip or create a time line of another development that interests them, such as air travel or the personal computer.

Inductive-Reasoning Frames You can use an **inductive-reasoning frame** to list separate facts or examples that support a general conclusion, or induction. To make an inductive-reasoning frame, list the specific facts and draw an arrow to the conclusion based on these facts. Do not make overgeneralizations in your conclusions.

Inductive-Reasoning Frame
Writers' Early Work

Fact 1: *A Portrait of the Artist as a Young Man,* James Joyce's first novel, is, in part, an autobiographical work in which the protagonist comes of age and asserts his identity as an artist.

Fact 2: Ernest Hemingway's first major work, *In Our Time,* is a collection of stories revolving around Nick Adams, a character whose experiences roughly parallel those of young Hemingway.

Fact 3: F. Scott Fitzgerald's first novel, *This Side of Paradise,* deals with a young Princeton man like himself.

▼

Conclusion: Novelists sometimes begin their careers by writing about what they know best—themselves.

Practice Your Skills

A. Make an observation chart that could be used to plan a piece of writing about one of the following topics.

- auditioning for the school play
- gridlock on the city streets

B. Make a pro-and-con chart for one of the following topics.

- campaigning for political candidates
- making long-range career plans

C. In small groups, discuss which type of graphic device would be most helpful for planning an essay on each of the following topics.

- a description of a vista seen from a helicopter
- ways of dealing with poverty in the U.S.
- the history of papermaking
- an analysis of recent Supreme Court decisions on an issue
- a comparison of network newscasts

Applying Graphic Devices   **347**

Planning and Organizing Strategies

Objectives

1. To recognize patterns of organization
2. To choose appropriate planning and organizational strategies based on writing purpose

Handbook Mini-Lessons

For information on topics related to strategies for planning and organizing, see the following mini-lessons.

- Applying Graphic Devices, pp. 339–347
- Writing Introductions and Conclusions, pp. 365–375
- Mastering Unity and Coherence, pp. 382–391

Motivating

Ask students to think about how they plan activities or projects. Do they ever make lists? Sketch out a plan, timeframe, or flowchart of responsibilites? Then ask how many students use a standard outline whenever they tackle a writing assignment. Few students will probably respond in the affirmative, so have students discuss other methods that they use to organize their writing. Point out that students will be studying additional methods of organization in this lesson.

WRITING HANDBOOK **5**

Planning and Organizing Strategies

A novelist may begin writing with only a sketchy idea of the plot, characters, and setting of a story. A news reporter may make a list of questions and interview several people before writing an article. A student may make a detailed outline and do extensive research before beginning a report. Different writing activities—and different writers—require different types of planning. Knowing the various strategies that writers often use can help you choose an approach that is right for you and your writing situation.

PLANNING YOUR WORK

It usually is helpful to plan your writing carefully before drafting if you are constrained by predetermined requirements. For example, if you are writing an essay for a history class, the material you use and its organization may be determined by the topic you have been asked to cover. You might therefore decide to outline your topic and gather information to support each point in the outline before you begin writing. However, if you are writing an original story, play, or poem, you may want to begin drafting immediately and see where your ideas take you.

The amount of initial planning that you do also depends on your personal style. Some people feel more secure when they have a careful plan to follow. Others prefer the challenge of working out their structure as they go along. Use the method that works for you and for the particular activity you are working on.

WRITER TO WRITER

My first draft is generally a jumble of all my ideas on a given subject. In my next draft, I choose those ideas that are most important and pertinent to each other. From there on, it is simply a matter of refining the paper.

Adam Shoughnessy, student
Watertown, Massachusetts

Whether you organize your ideas before you draft, as you draft, or as you revise, you will at some point want to order the presentation of your material. Writing that is well-organized has unity and coherence—each idea is relevant and leads logically and smoothly into the next. See "Unity and Coherence," pages 382-391, for more information.

There are many different ways to organize your writing. Generally, your material itself will suggest the most effective method. As you write, ask yourself how your ideas are related to one another. Try not to force them into a preconceived organizational mold. The form of organization that is closest to the natural relationships among your ideas probably also will be the most natural, and the most effective, way to organize your paper.

Some common types of organization include thesis statement and supporting details; chronological, spatial, and comparison-and-contrast order; organization by classification and division and by degree; and cause-and-effect, dialectic, and inductive and deductive organization.

Thesis Statement and Supporting Details

Many types of writing are best organized by stating a main idea, or thesis, and supporting it with examples or reasons. This organizational method works especially well if you are writing to inform or persuade. You may choose to begin with your thesis statement and follow it with supporting details, or you can present the details first and conclude with the main idea. Here is an example of expository writing that opens with a thesis statement followed by supporting details.

Friendship appears to be a unique form of human bonding. Unlike marriage or the ties that bind parents and children, it is not defined or regulated by law. Unlike other social roles that we are expected to play—as citizens, employees, members of professional societies and other organizations—it has its own subjective rationale, which is to enhance feelings of warmth, trust, love, and affection between two people.

Mary Brown Parlee and the Editors of *Psychology Today*

PROFESSIONAL
M O D E L

Planning and Organizing
Strategies   **349**

Teaching Tip: Thesis Statement

Students sometimes misunderstand or confuse the terms *thesis*, *topic sentence*, and *main idea*. To clarify, you might tell students that a *thesis* is the statement that expresses the main idea of an entire essay; a *topic sentence* expresses the *main idea* of one paragraph. Emphasize that although every piece of writing must have a main idea, that idea does not have to be stated explicitly. Elicit that both a thesis and a topic sentence need supporting details to be effective.

If you choose to use flashback or foreshadowing, be sure that you give your reader clear signals that you have temporarily suspended the normal chronological presentation of events.

LITERARY MODEL

Chronological Order

Many types of writing that present a series of events—short stories, biographies, and historical accounts, for example—are most effectively presented using chronological order. Notice how the following paragraph from a science fiction story uses chronological order to dramatize the hardship of the characters' journey:

The summer was waning when Shann took his two sons and went ahead to explore the way. For three days they climbed, and for three nights slept as best they could on freezing rocks, and on the fourth morning there was nothing ahead but a gentle rise to a cairn of gray stones built by other travelers, centuries ago.

Arthur C. Clarke, "History Lesson"

Writers sometimes follow chronological order strictly, starting with the first event. Variations on this order are possible, however. In the **flashback,** a writer interrupts the forward movement in time to relate an event that occurred in the past. In **foreshadowing,** a writer hints about something that may happen in the future. Foreshadowing can help build suspense or arouse curiosity.

Spatial Order

Physical descriptions of persons and places are most naturally organized by spatial order. When describing a medieval cathedral, for example, you might describe it first as seen from a distance and then up closer; you might describe it from the top down; or you might describe it from the inside out. Notice how the following description uses both top-down and bottom-up spatial order.

The sky too has its changes, but they are less marked than those of the vegetation and the river. Clouds map it up at times, but it is normally a dome of blending tints, and the main tint blue. By day the blue will pale down into white where it touches the white of the land, after sunset it has a new circumference—orange, melting upwards into tenderest purple.

E. M. Forster, *A Passage to India*

Zoom in and zoom out are two camera techniques that also can be particularly effective in writing an introduction or conclusion. If you are using a zoom-in organization, you begin by describing a panoramic view. Then you describe the same scene as you move closer, focusing on progressively finer and finer details. You end with a close-up description of one aspect of the scene. In the following excerpt, the author uses the zoom-in technique to describe the main character's home.

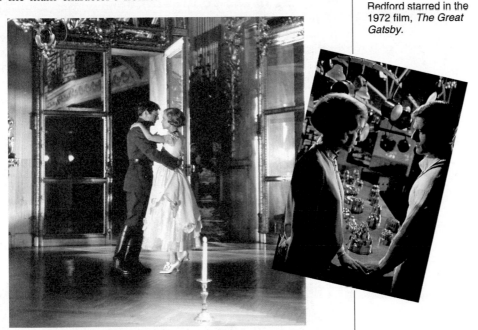

Mia Farrow and Robert Redford starred in the 1972 film, *The Great Gatsby.*

> The lawn started at the beach and ran towards the front door for a quarter of a mile, jumping over sundials and brick walks and burning gardens—finally when it reached the house drifting up the side in bright vines as though from the momentum of its run. The front was broken by a line of French windows, glowing now with reflected gold and wide open to the warm windy afternoon, and Tom Buchanan in riding clothes was standing with his legs apart on the front porch.
>
> **F. Scott Fitzgerald,** *The Great Gatsby*

LITERARY
· · · · · · · · · · · · · · ·
M O D E L

Planning and Organizing
Strategies   **351**

To illustrate the techniques of "zoom in" and "zoom out," you might bring in some photographs or videos that show the same scene but with a progressively closer image. Have students study the photographs and freewrite about how the distance influences the spatial description.

Modeling

Choose an object visible to all students—perhaps something as simple as the classroom bulletin board—and model how you would describe it using the order of impression, beginning with the most interesting aspect. Also ask students to describe the object by order of impression to show that this can vary. Then suggest another object that students can use to practice organizing by impression.

Critical Thinking

Drawing Conclusions Ask students which of the three organizational patterns of comparison and contrast can best be visualized by using a Venn diagram. (If students seem unsure of what a Venn diagram is, refer them to Writing Handbook 4.) *(#2, similarities and differences, because all the similarities would appear in the parts of the circles that intersect and the differences would remain outside the intersecting area.)*

Collaborative Opportunity

Suggest that students work in small groups to compare and contrast two subjects such as two local teams, two "boom boxes," or rail versus bus transportation. Have each group decide on one of the three organizational patterns, outline that approach, and then explain the choice to the rest of the class. Elicit that there is no one right way to organize writing that compares and contrasts.

PROFESSIONAL
M O D E L

Another variation of spatial order is **order of impression.** In this type of organization, the writer begins with the image that creates the most powerful impact and then describes the peripheral or less compelling images. For example, if you were describing a crying child, you might describe his face first, then his drooping shoulders and clenched hands.

Comparison-and-Contrast Order

In expository and persuasive writing, you will often want to discuss the similarities and differences between two or more persons or things. You can do this by using comparison-and-contrast order, organizing your information in any of three ways: by subject, by similarities and differences, or by features.

1. When organizing your material by **subject,** you discuss one subject completely and then the other.

2. When organizing your material by **similarities and differences,** you discuss the similarities between the two subjects first and then describe all their differences (or vice versa).

3. When organizing your material by **features,** you compare and contrast the two subjects with respect to each characteristic.

Here is a review that compares and contrasts two television programs by feature.

> NBC's "Cosby Show" and Fox's "In Living Color" are very different half-hour comedy shows controlled primarily by black performers. Bill Cosby's humor tends to be warm and gently didactic: eat your veggies; stay in school. Keenen Ivory Wayans's approach is hip-hop brash and iconoclastic; neither whites nor blacks are exempt. But both shows share a distinctively black sensibility. . . .
>
> **John J. O'Connor, *The New York Times***

Organization by Classification and Division

If you are writing about a number of related subjects, you can classify the subjects into groups according to criteria such as related characteristics or membership in a specific class. The following excerpt from *Moby Dick* uses classification to describe porpoises.

Literature Connection

Spatial Organization A particularly vivid model of spatial organization can be found in the opening paragraph of Joseph Conrad's "The Secret Sharer."

DUODECIMOES—These include the smaller whales. I. The Huzza Porpoise. II. The Algerine Porpoise. III. The Mealy-mouthed Porpoise.

To those who have not chanced specially to study the subject, it may possibly seem strange that fishes not common-ly exceeding four or five feet should be marshalled among WHALES—a word, which, in the popular sense, always con-veys an idea of hugeness. But the creatures set down above as Duodecimoes are infallibly whales, by the terms of my def-inition of what a whale is—i.e. a spouting fish, with a horizon-tal tail.

Herman Melville, *Moby Dick*

Organization by Degree

When you are describing a number of persons or things that share a particular characteristic, you might organize your material by degree—either from more to less of the characteristic or from less to more. For example, you might describe a variety of jobs by the amount of creativity required to do each one. You might describe a group of actors according to their ability to play a wide variety of roles. Notice how the following excerpt from *Sports Illustrated* is organized by degree.

Wayne Gretsky of the Los Angeles Kings will make $3 mil-lion this season, counting deferred payments. Mario Lemieux of the Pittsburgh Penguins will earn $2.3 million. But these two players are in a separate universe—nobody fills seats the way they do. The next-highest-paid player last season in straight salary—bonuses, deferred payments and perks promised by handshakes not included—was the Edmonton Oilers' Mark Messier, the league MVP, who made $832,000.

Jay Greenberg, *Sports Illustrated*

Variations on the organization-by-degree format include **organi-zation by order of importance** and **organization by familiarity.** For example, a report on types of seashells could be organized by familiarity—from most familiar to less well known.

Suggest that students imagine that they are writing an article about musical groups for a teenage audience. Ask students to use an outline or cluster to show how they would classify the musical groups.

Remind students that when they order their writing by degree or by importance, they want to be sure that they use the cor-rect comparative and superlative forms of adjectives and adverbs. Refer students who need help with this concept to Gram-mar and Usage Handbook 37, pp. 723–731.

The inverted pyramid is a special type of organization by order of importance. Newspaper articles are often organized this way so readers can get information quickly. The "lead" typically answers six questions about the event being described: *who, what, where, when, why,* and *how.* In subsequent paragraphs the writer presents background details in the order of their importance. In a newspaper article, paragraphs are often no more than three sentences long. Here is a graphic representation of the inverted pyramid.

Inverted Pyramid Organization

Who, What, Where, When, Why, How
Most important detail
Next most important detail
Next most important
detail
Least important
detail

Notice how this organization is used effectively in the following paragraphs from a classic news report.

PROFESSIONAL
M O D E L

> HOUSTON, July 20—Man stepped out onto the moon to-night for the first time in his two-million-year history.
>
> "That's one small step for a man," declared pioneer astronaut Neil Armstrong at 10:56 P.M. EDT, "one giant leap for mankind."
>
> Just after that historic moment in man's quest for his origins, Armstrong walked on the dead satellite and found the surface very powdery, littered with fine grains of black dust.
>
> A few minutes later, Edwin (Buzz) Aldrin joined Armstrong on the lunar surface and in less than an hour they put on a show that will long be remembered by the worldwide television audience.
>
> **Thomas O'Toole,** *Washington Post*

The first paragraph of this story explains **who** the event is about (man), **what** happened (he set foot on the moon), **where** it took place (the surface of the moon), and **when** it occurred (July 20). The subsequent paragraphs provide additional details about **why** and **how** this historic event took place.

354 Writing Handbook

Cause-and-Effect Order

Events—personal, historical, political, or scientific—often form causal chains. For example, the discovery of atomic structure led eventually to the development of the hydrogen bomb. The novelist Jack London used this type of organization to describe the causes and effects of a famine on a northern tribe.

▼

In the summer the salmon run had failed, and the tribe looked forward to the winter and the coming of the caribou. Then the winter came, but with it there were no caribou. Never had the like been known, not even in the lives of the old men. But the caribou did not come, and it was the seventh year, and the rabbits had not replenished, and the dogs were naught but bundles of bone. And through the long darkness the children wailed and died, and the women, and the old men; and not one in ten of the tribe lived to meet the sun when it came back in the spring.

Jack London, "The Law of Life"

Planning and Organizing Strategies **355**

The failure of the salmon run and the disappearance of the caribou are causes; the effects include intense suffering and the death of ninety percent of the population.

Cause-and-effect writing is often organized into one of the following patterns.

Cause-to-Effect Pattern   **Effect-to-Cause Pattern**

In the **cause-to-effect pattern,** you state the cause or causes first and then proceed to describe the effect or effects. In the **effect-to-cause pattern,** you begin with an effect and gradually reveal its cause or causes.

Dialectic Organization

In **dialectic organization,** you present one position (the thesis), then its opposite (the antithesis), and finally describe a compromise position between the two (the synthesis). The Greek philosopher Aristotle proposed this method of seeking the "Golden Mean," or middle ground, as the basis of all ethics. In writing, this organization is particularly useful in persuasion or argumentation. Dialectics are often used for working out solutions to dilemmas or other difficult problems.

You might, for example, use dialectic organization in a report on a dispute between renters and landlords in your community. You might first present the renters' position—that they want to establish a renters' rights commission to protest landlords' raising rents, demanding too much rent in advance, and refusing to return security deposits. Then you would discuss the property owners' stance—that the renters' allegations are untrue and that a commission would make it more difficult for owners to pay their taxes and make a profit. Finally, you could present a compromise solution—establishment of a renters' commission composed of both renters and landlords so that the rights of both groups could be protected.

Inductive and Deductive Organization

Inductive and deductive organization are two other means of presenting an argument. **Inductive arguments** begin by presenting

---

Visual Learners To make the dialectic organization more obvious to these students, suggest they use the information to make a Venn diagram, labeling one circle *renters,* the other circle *landlords,* and placing the compromise position in the middle.

Modeling

Since an example of an inductive argument is not given in the text, you might want to model one for students. For example, you might say that when you got home last night your house was cold, your digital clock was blinking, and the lamp attached to your electric timer was not on although it should have been. From this information you concluded that there had been a power outage in your neighborhood yesterday. Ask students if they can supply other examples of inductive arguments.

specific facts or examples and end with a general conclusion based on the facts and examples. **Deductive arguments** begin with a general statement and then present facts and examples that support the generalization. An example of deductive argumentation follows.

▼

[A] host of studies have found many children with low social competence are at risk for adverse effects [on their academic performance]. One of the most striking findings was a study of 200 kindergarteners reported in the August issue of *Child Development* by Gary Ladd at the University of Illinois.

Those kindergarteners who were socially rejected in October, Dr. Ladd found, did only half as well as other children on tests of academic readiness when tested the following May. At the start of the year both groups were at the same level.

Daniel Goleman, *The New York Times*

Practice Your Skills

A. Tell what method of organization you might use for each of the following pieces of writing and why you would choose it.

1. A humorous play about an ordinary high school student who is mistaken for a famous rock-and-roll star.

2. An essay that presents the reasons why, in your opinion, all beachfront property should (or should not) be government owned.

3. A newspaper story about an automobile accident caused by a flock of Canada geese strolling across a freeway.

4. A review of events that brought about the Solidarity-led revolution in Poland.

5. An essay that argues that the nation swings between periods of conservatism and periods of liberalism.

6. A description of Loch Ness in Scotland.

B. Read two articles from contemporary magazines that are appropriate for a general audience. Think about the method of organization used in each article. Bring the articles to class and, in small groups, discuss the methods used by the writers of the articles to organize their material.

PROFESSIONAL
M O D E L

Planning and Organizing
Strategies   **357**

As students work independently on exercise **A**, circulate through the class, offering aid to students who seem stuck. Help students to focus on key words in the prompt that might point to an appropriate organizational strategy to use.

ANSWERS TO PRACTICE YOUR SKILLS

A. Answers will vary. Suggested answers and reasons follow.
1. chronological order; in narration the order of events is usually important.
2. thesis statement and supporting ideas; the supporting ideas can be points in favor of the thesis
3. inverted pyramid; the standard format for most newspaper stories
4. cause and effect; need to show how the events led to the revolution
5. dialectic organization; presents reasons for both sides
6. spatial organization; describes a scene
B. Answers will vary.

Additional Resources
- Writing Resource Book, pp. 8–9
- Thinking Skills Transparencies
- Thinking Skills Worksheets

Collaborative Planning

Objectives

1. To understand the role of collaborative planning in writing
2. To recognize the elements of a planner's blackboard
3. To use collaborative planning as a prewriting strategy

Handbook Mini-Lessons

For information on topics related to collaborative planning, see the following mini-lessons.
- Planning and Organizing Strategies, pp. 348–357
- Peer Review, pp. 397–401

Motivating

Ask students to share experiences they have had working on committees. To initiate the discussion, you might want to describe an experience of yours. Elicit from students that when committee members cooperate, both the quantity and the quality of work may surpass that which can be done by an individual.

WRITING
HANDBOOK
6

Collaborative Planning

Whether you make a formal plan for your writing before you begin, or plan as you work, you often complete this aspect of your writing process alone. However, if you choose to plan before you begin, you may prefer to engage in a process called **collaborative planning.** This process involves sharing or "talking out" your writing plan with someone else. Explaining your plan aloud allows you to see your writing from a larger perspective and gives you the opportunity to test ideas before you put them in writing.

USING THE PLANNER'S BLACKBOARD

Every writing situation demands a different kind of plan. Nevertheless, all good writing plans address these elements: topic, purpose, audience, form, and the connections among them.

One useful way to consider the relationships among these writing variables is by using a graphic representation called a **planner's blackboard.**

As a writer, you can use the planner's blackboard to remind you to consider all the components of planning as you explain and develop your writing plan. Information about your topic serves as the background of your plan, and as you assess the purpose, audience, and form of your writing, you consider how each decision you make affects the other variables. In doing so, you work forward and backward as the arrows in the diagram indicate to elaborate your writing plan.

Once you understand how the writing variables work together, you'll be able to make decisions that result in an effective piece of writing. You will become a more flexible and confident writer by using the planner's blackboard alone and in collaboration with others.

ENLISTING SUPPORT FOR YOUR WRITING PLAN

A collaborator, or partner, can help you create and formalize your writing plan by giving you encouragement, objectivity, and a fresh perspective. He or she can read your plan and then ask probing questions or make suggestions to improve it. You can also identify the plan's weak points by reading it aloud to your collaborating partner.

Your collaborator may also notice that you have forgotten a certain writing consideration—such as the characteristics of your audience, for example. He or she may then offer suggestions for resolving that specific problem, suggesting, for example, that you establish a checkpoint in your planning process for evaluating the needs of your readers.

Your Role as a Writer   The most important thing to remember in the collaborative planning process is that you, the writer, are in charge. Your collaborator can help you by facilitating your efforts to develop your writing plan. Your role is to present your plan clearly and to listen carefully to your collaborator's responses and questions about your plan. However, you evaluate all responses and decide if and how you will change your plan.

The planner's blackboard can be very useful to you in presenting your plan to your partner. It will give you a framework for explaining your ideas about your writing and clarifying the relationships among your topic, form, audience, and purpose.

COMPUTER
TIP

If you have a computer with a graphics program, you can save the planner's blackboard on your computer and use it whenever collaborative planning seems most appropriate.

Collaborative
Planning   **359**

Collaborative Planning **359**

Critical Thinking

Decision Making   Ask students what they would do if their collaborator did not like the approach they took to a particular subject. Elicit that they should find out their partner's objections, evaluate them, and possibly get feedback from a second person.

Modeling

Using a planner's blackboard, model the role of the supporter. Have students work together to create the blackboard. As students suggest information for the components, model each of the four ways to give support.

Science Connection

Role of Collaboration   Great strides in science would be impossible without collaboration. Suggest that students research an achievement or discovery that interests them to determine how scientists worked together to produce the result.

Peer Response

After students have completed "Practice Your Skills," suggest they work in pairs to give one another feedback using the strategies outlined in the lesson.

> ### Additional Resources
> - Writing Resource Book, p. 10
> - Peer Response Guides

Your Role as a Supporter Supporters are neither teachers nor critics. A supporter neither tells you how to write nor criticizes your work; rather, he or she helps and supports your effort to develop and elaborate your writing plan. As a supporter, you can also help the writer by using the following guidelines.

Guidelines for Providing Collaborative Support

- Listen carefully to what the writer has to say. Afterward, try to summarize the writer's plan in a few words. For example, you might say, "What I hear you saying is that _____. Is that what you mean?"

- Ask the planner to elaborate. "You just said _____. Tell me more about what you mean or why you said that."

- Ask about key parts of the blackboard planner that the writer has not explained fully. "If your purpose is _____, what form will you use? Is it the best choice? What are your specific personal goals?"

- Ask the writer to consider how different parts of his or her writing plan are connected, especially if you detect weak links or potential problems. For example, you might ask, "If your key point here is _____, how do you think your readers will respond?" You might also encourage the writer to think about each of the writing variables individually in relation to his or her writing purpose, considering whether each best serves that purpose. Mention any problems you notice, and offer suggestions if the writer asks for your advice.

Practice Your Skills

Imagine that you are going to collaborate with a writer who has made the following initial statement about her writing: "I think I want to write about the process new immigrants to this country must go through in becoming citizens in order to explain the complexities of this privilege we take for granted."

Write out a list of questions or responses that will help the writer pinpoint missing variables, inconsistencies, or potential problems in her plan. To assess this plan objectively, prepare a planner's blackboard based on her statement.

Literature Connection

Literary Analysis   Point out to students that both the planner's blackboard and the strategies for giving support are particularly valuable when they are writing an analysis of a poem or story and need to test the effectiveness of their ideas.

Drafting to Discover Meaning

Drafting is the process of making meaning with your writing. Therefore, when you draft, concentrate on what you have to say, not on how you are saying it. Don't worry about matters such as spelling or mechanics, and don't think that you have to have everything worked out beforehand. In fact, you may have only a vague idea of what you want to say as you begin.

Perplexity, not certainty, is the ideal state in which to start writing. As you draft, explore your confusion. Raise questions and see where they lead. Don't be afraid to experiment. Concentrate on getting your thoughts down on paper. You will have the chance to bring your writing into sharper focus later, when you start to revise.

W R I T E R   T O   W R I T E R

When you write, you lay out a line of words. The line of words is a miner's pick, a woodcarver's gouge, a surgeon's probe. You wield it, and it digs a path you follow. Soon you find yourself deep in new territory. Is it a dead end, or have you located the real subject? You will know tomorrow, or this time next year.

Annie Dillard, *The Writing Life*

Although drafting is important, that doesn't mean that when you're writing a critical or informative piece you don't have to plan beforehand. However, with any type of writing, you need to leave yourself open to new ideas that emerge.

DRAFTING STYLES

Certain general patterns—drafting, getting feedback from others, rereading, rewriting—are all part of the writing process. However, writers and writing styles differ widely. Some writers begin by writing freely; others make plans and follow them carefully. Still others combine planning and experimentation.

Drafting   **361**

Writing Handbook 7:
Drafting to Discover Meaning

Objectives

1. To understand the process of drafting
2. To recognize various styles of drafting
3. To write a quick draft in response to a prompt

> **Handbook Mini-Lessons**
> For information on topics related to drafting, please see the following mini-lessons.
> - Writing Introductions and Conclusions, pp. 365–375
> - Revising Effectively, pp. 392–395
> - Peer Review and Response, pp. 397–401

Teaching Strategies

Motivating

Choose a familiar subject such as the school cafeteria menu, the football team, or a well-publicized community issue and tell students you are giving them ten minutes to write about the topic. Stop them after five minutes and ask them to describe what they're doing. At the end of ten minutes, discuss the various methods students used to complete the task. Elicit that everyone has his or her own way to approach and fulfill a writing assignment.

Critical Thinking

Interpreting In these days of instantaneous communication and quick gratification, students sometimes have difficulty understanding and accepting that writing is a process that unfolds gradually. Discuss Annie Dillard's words, focusing on what she meant by "You will know tomorrow, or this time next year."

Drafting   **361**

LEP Students   Students who have limited proficiency in English sometimes are afraid to commit their ideas to paper for fear of making a mistake and therefore take the "careful approach" to drafting, often losing what they want to say in the process. Encourage these students to use "adventuresome drafting," pointing out it is a well accepted way of writing.

Personal Touch

To defuse the myth that English teachers are natural writers, honestly share with students the way you approach writing. Discuss writer's block, false starts, and rewrites.

Writing TIP

Underline any phrases and sentences in the raw draft that you want to be sure to include in your next draft.

STUDENT MODEL

Adventuresome Drafting   When you aren't sure what you want to say or how to organize your information, you may choose simply to set your thoughts freely down on paper. Don't worry about form, style, audience, or purpose at this point. Just concentrate on getting all of your ideas out. Writing of this kind, done without much planning, is called **adventuresome drafting.** One expert on composition calls it *raw writing*. Raw writing is worth doing in the early stages of your work because it frees you from the constraints of form and lets you concentrate on finding meaning.

Raw writing often produces fresher, more evocative language than does careful writing. Give yourself the freedom to use some of this livelier writing in your final product. Consider, for example, the informal tone that this student retained in the final draft of these paragraphs.

> My mother was a writer? The thought made me laugh when I first considered it, but as I sat at the kitchen table with her that Sunday evening . . . listening to her talk, that silly thought I had quickly diminished.
>
> I have to admit now that I wasn't very excited about doing the interview, just because I didn't think that my mother would have anything interesting to say about writing. Wrong again. My mother's always been one who loves to talk, so it turned out that I'd ask a simple question, and she'd go on supplying me with such a long, elaborate answer that I couldn't keep up with her!

Careful Drafting   The direct opposite of adventuresome drafting is **careful drafting.** When writing a careful draft, you work slowly, getting each paragraph the way you like it before moving on to the next one.

As you might expect, careful drafting requires extensive planning. You must decide beforehand what you are going to say and how you are going to say it. For example, you might prepare a formal outline and an elaborate set of notes before you start to write. Some writers always prepare a set of 3″ × 5″ note cards that they can arrange and rearrange as they work out an organization.

Intermediate Drafting   If you are like most writers, you often have a rough idea of what you are going to say before you start a piece of writing. In that case, you will probably be most comfortable with a

362   Writing Handbook

Literature Connection

Autobiography   Advanced students interested in the Annie Dillard feature on p. 361 might enjoy reading her autobiography, *An American Childhood*.

drafting process that lies somewhere between adventuresome and careful.

Bridge-building is an excellent way of writing an intermediate draft, because it allows you to organize your ideas as you write. You start by identifying the key ideas, sections, or events that you want to include in your writing. Then you begin writing your draft. As you work, ask yourself questions like these: How can I get from point A to point B? What details do I need to include to make the connections among my ideas clear? Martha Grimes, the well-known mystery writer, uses the bridge-building technique. She jots down notes about characters, plot, and setting over the course of several months, traveling to various places in England to get ideas. Then she goes back home and weaves her notes together into an intricately plotted, evocatively written novel.

Drafting is a process of constant self-discovery. When you begin, you can never be quite sure what your finished piece of writing will look like. Because they often make surprising discoveries about themselves and their topics, many writers say that drafting is the most enjoyable part of writing. Once you learn to draft without inhibition and restraint, you will experience the true joy of writing.

DRAFTING AND REVISION

Overlapping Processes Rarely do writers wait until they have completed a draft before they begin to revise. Some revise and shape their writing as they draft, blending the two processes into one. Others draft a few paragraphs, revise, and then go on to draft some more. Still others wait until they have a complete draft before doing any revisions. Draft and revise in the manner that works best for you.

Knowing When to Stop Strange as it might seem, knowing when to stop is an important part of the drafting process. Typically, you will revise your draft several times, do more research, and perhaps rethink your entire topic before you decide it's time to stop. Ultimately you will stop drafting and begin to fine-tune your piece.

It is a good idea to take a break between drafts; when you return to your writing, you will be able to evaluate it with a fresh eye. When you have worked on a piece for some time and cannot look at it objectively anymore, a peer reader can provide you with new perspectives on your writing. For more help on working with peers during the writing process, see "Peer Review and Response," pages 397–401.

Drafting   **363**

Individualizing Instruction

Learning Styles Students with different learning styles need to find methods of organization that work best for them. Suggest that to get the most benefit from the bridge-building approach, students might use some of the graphic devices illustrated in Writing Handbook 4 or record their thoughts on an audio tape.

Teaching Tip: Self Evaluation

Knowing when to revise and when to stop is important. Suggest to students that each time they finish a version of their draft, they should read it aloud so they can hear what it sounds like. Whenever they come to a place that doesn't sound quite right or where they feel a little uneasy, they should make a note of it because others are probably going to respond the same way.

Springboard

Tell students to imagine that they are taking an important exam and are running out of time when they come to the final essay question: *If you could live anywhere in the world, where would you choose?* Have students discuss how they would approach this question.

Drafting When You Can't Revise You probably will not have time to revise your draft when you are writing an answer to an essay question during an examination. The best strategy for answering essay questions on tests is to spend a few minutes drawing up a quick but explicit writing plan.

Begin by jotting down the main ideas that you want to cover in a brief, informal outline. This will help guide your writing and remind you to include all the important points in your answer. If you cannot write a brief outline or list, make one up in your head.

Begin by restating the question as a topic sentence or thesis. Then, use a simple method of organization, such as chronological order, order of importance, or the inverted pyramid form. Use transitions that indicate the form of organization you are using, such as *first . . . second* and *least important . . . more important.* Readers of essay exams are impressed by good organization.

Practice Your Skills

A. Meet with a group of three or four students to discuss the following questions.

1. What drafting technique did each person in your group use on his or her last piece of writing? What drafting technique does each writer generally prefer? Why?
2. Have you ever switched from one topic to another in the middle of the drafting process? Discuss how and why this happened.

B. Choose one of the following writing prompts and draft a response to it. Then, in a small group, share your writing with other students. Discuss any difficulties that you had during the drafting process. Solicit suggestions for alternative ways you might have proceeded.

1. Briefly discuss three people whom you admire, and explain what personal and professional qualities or attributes make these people worthy of respect.
2. Imagine you were Secretary of Education of the United States and write a short speech discussing the two issues you would make priorities and why.
3. Think of a part-time, after-school job for which you would like to apply. Write a short letter of application discussing your qualifications.
4. Write a critique of a book you have recently read and enjoyed or a popular song that you like. Include specific reasons why you think others might enjoy it too.

364 Writing Handbook

Collaborative Opportunity

Before students form groups to discuss Exercise *A,* suggest that they jot down the answers to the questions as they pertain to themselves so that they will be prepared to discuss one another's approaches to drafting.

Spot Check

If some students seem to have difficulty responding to the writing prompts, suggest that they try "adventuresome drafting."

ANSWERS TO PRACTICE YOUR SKILLS

A. Answers will vary.
B. Answers will vary. However, since students will not have time to revise, they might want to jot down their main ideas first and choose a simple method of organization.

Additional Resources
• Writing Resource Book, p. 11

Writing Introductions and Conclusions

Making a good impression is as important in your writing as it is in your personal life. Creating an effective introduction and conclusion will leave your reader with a powerful impression of your writing.

W R I T E R   T O   W R I T E R

I have noticed that the hardest part about writing anything, from a short essay to a short story, is the beginning.

Andy Ness, student
Seattle, Washington

INTRODUCING NONFICTION

An introduction should engage the reader's interest, state the main idea, or both. Every piece of writing begins somewhere, so the writer must create a suitable introduction. For example, most newspaper and magazine articles begin with a direct statement of the topic or main idea. In journalism, this type of introduction is called a **lead.** However, starting with the main idea is only one of many ways to begin a nonfiction piece.

Make a Startling Statement One way to begin a piece is with a surprising, unusual, or interesting fact or opinion. For example, Guy Davenport introduces an essay about the power of the imagination with a list of comparisons and a surprising conclusion about the list.

> The difference between the Parthenon and the World Trade Center, between a French wine glass and a German beer mug, between Bach and John Philip Sousa, between Sophocles and Shakespeare, between a bicycle and a horse, though explicable by historical moment, necessity, and destiny, is before all a difference of imagination.
>
> **Guy Davenport, "The Geography of the Imagination"**

Introductions and
Conclusions   **365**

WRITING
HANDBOOK
8

Writing Introductions and Conclusions

Objectives

1. To identify techniques for writing effective introductions and conclusions in nonfiction
2. To identify techniques for writing effective introductions and conclusions in narrative works
3. To plan introductions and conclusions for both nonfiction and fiction

Handbook Mini-Lessons

For information on topics related to writing introductions and conclusions, see the following mini-lessons.
- Drafting to Discover Meaning, pp. 361–364
- Techniques for Elaboration and Development, pp. 376–381

Critical Thinking

Expressing Opinions Ask students to explain why they agree or disagree with the student writer's statement. Point out that in this lesson students will be learning a number of techniques that should make writing a beginning easier.

Relate an Anecdote Beginning with a brief story, or anecdote, can set a tone and make a point in a dramatic way. Notice how Douglas Hofstadter uses two anecdotes to introduce an essay about our misconceptions about enormous numbers.

PROFESSIONAL
M O D E L

The renowned cosmogonist Professor Bignumska, lecturing on the future of the universe, had just stated that in about a billion years, according to her calculations, the earth would fall into the sun in a fiery death. In the back of the auditorium a tremulous voice piped up: "Excuse me, Professor, but h-h-how long did you say it would be?" Professor Bignumska calmly replied, "About a billion years." A sigh of relief was heard. "Whew! For a minute there, I thought you'd said a *million* years."

John F. Kennedy enjoyed relating the following anecdote about a famous French soldier, Marshal Lyautey. One day the marshal asked his gardener to plant a row of trees of a certain rare variety in his garden the next morning. The gardener said he would gladly do so, but he cautioned the marshal that trees of this size take a century to grow to full size. "In that case," replied Lyautey, "plant them this afternoon."

Douglas R. Hofstadter, "On Number Numbness"

Present a Description Sometimes you want to create a mood. In the following example, Scott Frier uses an introductory description to evoke the lush atmosphere of the Virgin Islands.

PROFESSIONAL
M O D E L

They look like a tropical paradise is supposed to look: the steep, green hills of sun-drenched islands rising out of a clear blue sea. Tucked into the nooks and crannies of the irregular coastline of these islands are small secluded white-sand beaches washed by a warm crystal-clear sea. An almost constant breeze wafts in from the ocean, rustling the palms and cooling the beach. **Scott Frier, "Island in the Sun"**

Draw an Analogy An analogy is a comparison between your subject and something else. A creative analogy can draw the reader's interest into your subject. The following essay begins with an analogy comparing people who plant trees to gods and poets.

366 Writing Handbook

Springboard

Challenge students to choose a favorite piece of writing and draft a new opening sentence for it. Have the class compare and contrast the two versions.

> Acts of creation are ordinarily reserved for gods and poets, but humbler folk may circumvent this restriction if they know how. To plant a pine, for example, one need be neither god nor poet; one need only own a shovel. By virtue of this curious loophole in the rules, any clodhopper may say: Let there be a tree—and there will be one.
>
> **Aldo Leopold, "Pines Above the Snow"**

Pose a Question A question draws your readers into your writing because they become involved in answering the question.

> From birth to death, gravity pervades our life. Our every step, day in, day out, is a struggle against this relentless force. It cuts our baby knees when we fall. It pulls on our limbs so that every motion is burdened by its enervating presence. It sucks our bodies into the mud, preventing us from soaring into the skies like the birds.
>
> Is there some future-magical method to control gravity? Can we somehow find a way to "turn off" or "nullify" the gravity field of the earth? Could we possibly arrange for a mass to push us gently away into the skies instead of hugging us firmly to its crushing bosom?
>
> **Robert L. Forward, "Magic Gravity"**

Cite a Quotation Readers respond particularly well to introductions that contain interesting quotations. The writers of this article chose a question and two quotations to elicit the reader's attention.

> What is the fuss about? Glen George, manager of Kansas City's country radio KCKN, says: "Anything that Grandma can hum, whistle, or sing is country." Its traditional message is one of despair, hope, loss, death, the land, and . . . love . . . . Says Moon Mullins, program director of the all-country WINN in Louisville: "If you listen to our station long enough, one of our songs will tell your story."
>
> **Sylvan Barnet and Marcia Stubbs, *Practical Guide to Writing***

Writing TIP

You can look for quotations in magazines, books, newspapers, or books of quotations. Poetic quotations are often effective and evocative.

Introductions and Conclusions   **367**

Linking Grammar and Writing

Remind students that citing a quotation is a valuable technique in writing an introduction, but if the quotation is not punctuated correctly, the reader can become distracted and the value of the quotation will be lost. Refer students who need help punctuating quotations to Grammar and Usage Handbook 41.

Critical Thinking

Interpreting Ask students what the use of quotations in the model contributes to the success of the passage. *(The quotations provide a partial answer to the question, make the writing seem more personal, and lend authenticity to the ideas.)*

Teaching Tip: Conclusions

Point out that the three characteristics of a good conclusion given here are not equally important and that their importance varies according to the piece and its purpose. In fiction, for example, the conclusion is a vital piece of the whole work, and the third characteristic—making a lasting impression—is of great importance. However, in a news story this characteristic is scarcely important at all, since news stories are often cut from the bottom to fit a space at the last minute. In a news story, therefore, the second characteristic—not introducing anything new—is the most important characteristic of a good conclusion. Have students discuss what characteristics might be especially vital in other kinds of writing, such as persuasive essays or science reports.

Critical Thinking

Generalizing   Ask students why a restatement of the main idea is an effective way to conclude a piece of writing. *(The writer reinforces the main point by repeating it and leaves that idea with the reader since it is the last point he or she reads.)*

PROFESSIONAL
· · · · · · · · · · · ·
M O D E L

State Your Main Idea Directly   This technique can be used in many types of writing other than journalism. The following paragraph opens a report by stating the main idea—the conclusion of a study.

▼

Ultimately, death is inescapable. But a recent study shows that people can postpone their dates with the Grim Reaper until important events in their lives are over.
"Death Delayed," *Journal of the American Medical Association*

CONCLUDING NONFICTION

After reading a conclusion, the reader should have a sense of closure and resolution. A conclusion that gives a reader this kind of satisfaction usually has the following characteristics.

- It follows logically from what has been presented or covered.
- It does not introduce new, unrelated material.
- It makes a lasting impression by leaving the reader with something to think about.

There are, of course, many ways of meeting these criteria. The following are some useful methods of writing conclusions.

Restate Your Main Idea   One straightforward way to conclude a piece of writing is with a restatement of your main idea. In the following piece, the main idea is that pines, and woodlands in general, are of great spiritual and emotional value to human beings.

PROFESSIONAL
· · · · · · · · · · · ·
M O D E L

▼

It is in midwinter that I sometimes glean from my pines something more important than woodlot politics, and the news of the wind and weather. This is especially likely to happen on some gloomy evening when the snow has buried all irrelevant detail, and the hush of elemental sadness lies heavy upon every living thing. Nevertheless, my pines, each with his burden of snow, are standing ramrod-straight, rank upon rank, and in the dusk beyond I sense the presence of hundreds more. At such times I feel a curious transfusion of courage.
Aldo Leopold, "Pines Above the Snow"

Science Connection

Technical Reports   Technical reports often do more than state the main idea in the introduction. Many technical reports begin with a summary of the results. Students might find books on technical writing in the library and determine how introductions and conclusions vary from the standards presented in this lesson.

Summarize the Ideas of Your Body Paragraphs When you present a series of ideas in a piece of writing, your reader may find it useful to read a summary of these ideas in the conclusion. You might begin the conclusion by summarizing the ideas of the body paragraphs and then end it by summarizing, in a single sentence, the main point, or thesis, of the entire piece.

▼

> As we have seen, coral reefs take thousands and thousands of years to build. However, they can be destroyed within a matter of years, days, or even minutes by pollutants, by untrained divers, by anchors, and by ships going aground. Given these perils and the extraordinary fragility of the coral environment, it is vital that protected marine parks be established to preserve the living coral reef.

Generalize About the Information You Have Given At times you may wish to end by drawing a general conclusion from the specific information that you have presented. In the following example, Bill Lovin reaches a general conclusion about a moving experience and about the photographer's need to make visual records.

▼

> I overcame the romanticism of the moment enough to hold my camera out as far as I could and let the film roll, filming Jovita [his dive buddy] and the manta's point of view. I almost wish I hadn't.
>
> In 25 years of diving with whales, dolphins, sharks, to name but a few, I had never felt such a kinship with any of the ocean's creatures. The whole experience lasted for 280 feet of film, 7 minutes and 42 seconds. It might seem absurd for an underwater photographer to suggest leaving the camera at home in order to feel the experience and not be compelled to record it. You do not need a camera at Cocos Island to remember it forever.   **Bill Lovin, "Impressions of Cocos"**

Make a Prediction Readers are interested in matters that are going to affect them and are therefore moved by conclusions that predict the future. The conclusion on the following page was written for a photographic essay on endangered species. In it the author makes a thought-provoking prediction.

Introductions and
Conclusions   **369**

Learning Styles Students who need a great deal of formal structure in order to work productively might benefit from making an "after-the-fact" outline of their work before they summarize it in a conclusion. If these students are highly visual, they might like to use some of the graphic devices suggested in Writing Handbook 4 to summarize the content of their writing before writing their conclusion.

Critical Thinking

Analyzing Have students analyze the student model of a conclusion to determine what the body paragraphs covered and what the main point, or thesis, was of the entire paper. *(The body paragraphs probably give a detailed explanation of how coral reefs are formed, and named and described various forces and elements that have destroyed and are destroying them; the thesis is that marine parks should be established to protect the reefs.)*

Teaching Tip: Purpose

Remind students that when they choose a strategy for writing a conclusion, they need to keep the purpose of their essay in mind. For example, if they are writing to persuade, they might end with a call to action, but if they are writing to entertain, some other type of conclusion would probably be more appropriate.

Critical Thinking

Making Inferences Ask students why they think Anthony did not end her speech by leaving the question for the reader to answer but instead went on to answer it herself. *(To leave the question unanswered might have caused people not to take the question seriously; by answering the question, she showed that as foolish as the question may have seemed, the answer was, in fact, both logical and important.)*

PROFESSIONAL MODEL

Perhaps these images can play a small part in helping us find our way home out of that long exile from nature. But until we become much more skilled at listening to the voices of nature in and around us, all animals—including the one we call human—are in jeopardy. The unspeakable tragedy is that our learning process will be too slow to prevent some of the extraordinary animals on these pages from being among the last survivors of their species.
James Balog, "A Personal Vision of Vanishing Wildlife"

Issue a Call for Action Writers of persuasive pieces often use their conclusions to ask readers to take action. Coretta Scott King, for example, urges people to support a full-employment statute.

PROFESSIONAL MODEL

For myself, if the alternative to full employment is simply to wait, to tolerate in silence the shattered dreams of jobless youth and the broken hearts of laid-off men, then my choice is clear.
America's jobless cannot "wait," not only because waiting is no solution and not only because waiting has social consequences that are frightening to contemplate, but because to do nothing when we have the capacity to act is morally and socially wrong.   **Coretta Scott King, "Why We Still Can't Wait"**

Ask a Question Just as beginning a piece of writing with a question can engage readers' attention, concluding with a question can make your readers think about the issues you have raised.

PROFESSIONAL MODEL

The only question left to be settled now is: Are women persons? And I hardly believe any of our opponents will have the hardihood to say they are not. Being persons, then, women are citizens; and no State has a right to make any law, or to enforce any old law, that shall abridge their privileges or immunities. Hence, every discrimination against women in the constitutions and laws of the several states is today null and void.   **Susan B. Anthony, "A Woman's Right to Suffrage"**

370 Writing Handbook

Social Studies Connection

Speeches Since speeches are heard rather than read, introductions and conclusions must capture the audience's attention. Suggest students read a speech such as Kennedy's inaugural address or Martin Luther King's "I Have a Dream" speech and analyze the techniques used to introduce and conclude the speech.

End with a Quotation As in an introduction, a quotation is a good way of focusing readers' thinking. To conclude an essay about accepting losses in sports, Charles Kuralt uses an apt quotation.

> Winning isn't the only thing, Coach Lombardi. Defeat is not like death, Coach Allen. I noticed the daffodils came up in my garden the morning after the Marquette game, even though North Carolina lost. Life goes on, even for us losers. I have a new maxim for the dressing room walls: Berton Brayley's sportsman's prayer, which says, "If I should lose, let me stand by the side of the road and cheer as the winners go by."
>
> **Charles Kuralt, *Dateline America***

INTRODUCING AND CONCLUDING NARRATIVES

The introduction of a narrative should draw readers into the story; the conclusion of a narrative should leave readers with something to think about.

Introducing a Narrative

Most narratives follow this advice: "Begin at the beginning . . . and go on till you come to the end: then stop." However, some stories start in the middle of the action, or *in medias res*.

> Basil Duke Lee shut the front door behind him and turned on the dining-room light. His mother's voice drifted sleepily downstairs:
> "Basil, is that you?"
> "No, mother, it's a burglar."
>
> **F. Scott Fitzgerald, "The Captured Shadow"**

Other types of introductions provide readers with information that will help them to understand and enjoy the story. This information will often establish an important story element or theme. The following are some ways to introduce a narrative.

Writing
—TIP—

Changing an introduction can completely alter the focus of a story. Be sure that the opening you choose is suitable for the tale that follows it.

LITERARY
M O D E L

Introductions and Conclusions   **371**

Critical Thinking

Interpreting Point out to students that Kuralt could have ended his essay with the sentence "Life goes on, even for us losers." Instead he added the Berton Brayley quotation. Ask students how concluding with a quotation changed the tone of the paragraph. *(Up until that point the tone seems biting, almost sarcastic. With the addition of the quotation, Kuralt inserts a positive note: "let me . . . cheer as the winners go by.")*

Personal Touch

Most people have a favorite way in which to start a narrative whether it is at the beginning of things, in the middle of things, or at the end of things. Share your preference for a narrative beginning and discuss with students their preferences.

Teaching Tip: Introductions in Fiction

Before students read about introductions in fiction ask them which, if any, of the introductions discussed for nonfiction would work equally well for fiction. Lead them to recognize that a good writer *might* use any of the techniques mentioned for nonfiction in the first few sentences, since fiction and nonfiction both have to start by hooking the reader. After "the hook," however, the introduction has a different job to do in fiction than it does in nonfiction.

Individualizing Instruction

Advanced Students Point out that even if students did not know that this excerpt came from *Sir Gawain and the Green Knight,* they would know from the introductory description that the story is set long ago and unusual happenings are going to occur. Suggest that students write an introduction that sets the scene in another time frame and then have students guess in what century the story is set.

Individualizing Instruction

Learning Styles For those students who have artistic ability, you might suggest that if they plan to introduce a narrative by describing the main character, they first sketch their character in action and then transfer their drawing into words.

LITERARY
M O D E L

372 Writing Handbook

LITERARY
M O D E L

Set the Scene Writers often choose to begin a piece of writing by setting the scene for their readers. Consider the following introductory paragraph from the Middle English romance *Sir Gawain and the Green Knight.*

> Winter lay upon the land. Cold held forest and field in its grim clutch, and in the night sky the stars glittered like gems. The wolf slid from shadow to shadow, stalking hapless prey, falling upon the unwary with death in his fangs. Deep in caverns the great trolls and other monsters mumbled in uneasy sleep, seeking warmth. Over the moor and fen the mists rose and fell, and strange sounds troubled the chill silence.
>
> **Y. R. Ponsor, translator, *Sir Gawain and the Green Knight***

Describe the Main Character Many narratives begin with a revealing description of the main character. Remember that a character can be described by a narrator, by another character, or by his or her own words. Charles Dickens's characterizations are considered to be among the most vivid and well drawn in all of literature. The following characterization is the first paragraph of "The Madman's Manuscript," a chapter from Dickens's novel *The Pickwick Papers.* Notice how the reader learns about the character from his speech patterns, his exclamations, and the frightening thought processes they reveal.

> Yes!—a madman's! How that word would have struck to my heart many years ago! How it would have roused the terror that used to come upon me sometimes, sending the blood hissing and tingling through my veins, till the cold dew of fear stood in large drops upon my skin, and my knees knocked together with fright! I like it now though. It's a fine name. Show me the monarch whose angry frown was ever feared like the glare of a madman's grip. Ho! ho! It's a grand thing to be mad! to be peeped at like a wild lion through the iron bars— to gnash one's teeth and howl through the long still night, to the merry ring of a heavy chain—and to roll and twine among the straw, transported with such brave music. Hurrah for the madhouse! Oh, it's a rare place!
>
> **Charles Dickens, "A Madman's Manuscript"**

Literature Connection

Setting James Joyce's short story "Araby" begins with a description of the setting. Suggest that students read the story, determine the mood or atmosphere suggested by the setting at the beginning of the story, and compare it to the mood at the end of the story.

Introduce the Central Conflict Most stories are based on the working out of a conflict, and a narrative may begin by introducing this conflict. The following newspaper article begins by establishing the alignment of countries in a potential confrontation.

▼

WASHINGTON, Aug 3—Powerful Iraqi forces wheeled into position for a possible attack on Saudi Arabia today, while the United States and its allies continued to search, so far without discernible success, for a way to force Iraq to pull back from its rapid conquest of Kuwait on Thursday.

R. W. Apple, Jr., ''U.S. Weighs Action''

Present a Major Symbol Sometimes an image that appears in the introduction of a story will later be developed into a major symbol. For example, in the course of William Saroyan's story "Gaston," the peaches come to symbolize the liveliness and compassion that a girl discovers in her father and for a time also experiences within herself. In the introductory paragraph, the writer both presents the symbol and gives a description of the main characters, the narrator and her father.

▼

They were to eat peaches, as planned, after her nap, and now she sat across from the man who would have been a total stranger except that he was in fact her father. They had been together again (although she couldn't quite remember when they had been together before) for almost a hundred years now, or was it only since day before yesterday? Anyhow, they were together again, and he was kind of funny. First, he had the biggest mustache she had ever seen on anybody, although to her it was not a mustache at all; it was a lot of red and brown hair under his nose and around the ends of his mouth. Second, he wore a blue-and-white striped jersey instead of a shirt and tie, and no coat. His arms were covered with the same hair, only it was a little lighter and thinner. He wore blue slacks, but no shoes and socks. He was barefoot, and so was she, of course. **William Saroyan, "Gaston"**

PROFESSIONAL
. . . .
M O D E L

LITERARY
. . . .
M O D E L

Introductions and
Conclusions   **373**

Analyzing Tell students that while this news story begins with a central conflict, it gives other pertinent information in the lead as well. Have students identify the 5 W's—*who, what, when, where,* and *why*—of journalistic writing *(who: Iraqi forces; what: wheeled into position; why: for a possible attack; when: today, August 3; where: near Saudi Arabia).*

(I) ## Individualizing Instruction

Gifted and Talented Students Discuss the Saroyan excerpt; then challenge these students to write a short story in which they present an image in the introduction that turns out to be a significant symbol later in the story.

Stumbling Block

Remind students that a number of techniques for writing introductions and conclusions have been presented in this lesson. Ask students how they will determine which ones to use the next time they are faced with a writing task. Elicit that their choice of techniques should be based on their purpose, goals, and audience.

Critical Thinking

Making Comparisons Ask students how writing a conclusion for a fictional narrative would differ from writing a conclusion for a nonfiction narrative. *(In fiction the conclusion is another event—the final one—in the chain of events that constitutes the story and is usually selected to emphasize a theme or emotional element in the work; in nonfiction, on the other hand, the conclusion may recap the main points in the essay or call on the reader to take some action.)*

LITERARY
M O D E L

LITERARY
M O D E L

Concluding a Narrative

Did you ever find that you were enjoying reading a story, only to be sadly disappointed by the ending? Just as there are many ways to begin a story, there are many ways to end one. Consider the following methods to conclude a narrative.

Present the Last Event Often a story simply ends with the last event. The interpretation of the event is left to the reader's imagination. One famous American novel, for example, ends with the event that comes immediately after the death of the narrator's beloved.

▼

> But after I had got them [the doctors and nurses] out and shut the door and turned off the light it wasn't any good. It was like saying good-by to a statue. After a while I went out and left the hospital and walked back to the hotel in the rain.
>
> **Ernest Hemingway, *A Farewell to Arms***

End with a Climactic Event The climax is the point in a story where the conflict reaches its highest suspense or tension. Some narrative conclusions are especially effective because they end at the height of the story's plot. Edgar Allan Poe's famous story "The Tell-Tale Heart" ends with a murderer's confession.

▼

> I could bear those hypocritical smiles no longer! I felt that I must scream or die!—and now—again!—hark! louder! louder! louder! *louder!*—
>
> "Villains!" I shrieked, "dissemble no more! I admit the deed!—tear up the planks!—here, here!—it is the beating of his hideous heart!" **Edgar Allan Poe, "The Tell-Tale Heart"**

Resolve the Conflict Many stories show the resolution of the central conflict in the conclusion. Often, the resolution follows the climactic event. In the conclusion to his short story "The Long Winter," writer Walter Havighurst resolves a conflict between his two main characters, a rancher and his son. In the story, the rancher has been estranged from his son, whom he has blamed for his wife's death. At the end of the story, the rancher has saved his son's life, and the rift between the man and boy has begun to close.

"Summer is getting here at last," the rancher said. "It's late season. We had a long winter, but it's over now." He turned in the saddle. "You're not saying much, Danny. What's on your mind?"

The boy smiled. "Oatmeal and corn bread," he said, "bacon and pancakes. I'm starved."

Walter Havighurst, "The Long Winter"

Practice Your Skills

Read the following ideas for pieces of writing. Think of a possible introduction and conclusion for each writing idea. Take some notes on your ideas for introductions and conclusions. Share your notes with your classmates in a group discussion.

1. You are writing a short story, and the setting, characters, and conflict are the following.

   • *Setting:* sleepy town in New Hampshire, in the present.
   • *Characters:* two restless high-school seniors, approaching graduation with a long, empty summer ahead of them.
   • *Conflict:* a camping trip turns into a life-and-death struggle as the two young people become hostages of a cult group.

2. Assume that you have a developmentally disabled brother and that you have decided to write a personal essay about him. The essay will give an honest account of your feelings and opinions about your brother. You plan to give examples of how people sometimes patronize and ignore him. You will explain that he has a strong need for companionship, but that people are sometimes repelled by his handicap and so miss out on the opportunity to be his friend. You will also explain that while having a sibling with special needs can be a trying experience, you think that you have grown considerably in your understanding of people through sharing life with your special brother.

3. Assume that you are writing a report on the subject of energy alternatives. You plan to describe the progress made in research over the past twenty years toward finding alternative energy sources to replace or supplement oil and nuclear energy. You want to give objective examples of various alternatives. You also want to make the point that more research in this field is necessary.

COMPUTER
═TIP═

As you revise, remember to print a hard copy of your story every so often, or else save your drafts on disks. That way you won't lose material if you change your text and then decide to go back to your original version.

Introductions and
Conclusions   **375**

Techniques for Elaboration and Development

Objectives

1. To identify and understand techniques for elaboration
2. To use elaboration techniques to develop a piece of writing

Handbook Mini-Lessons

For information on topics related to elaboration, see the following mini-lessons.

- Generating Ideas for Writing, pp. 331–336
- Applying Graphic Devices, pp. 339–347
- Collaborative Planning, pp. 358–360
- Using Poetic Language, pp. 434–438

Teaching Strategies

Motivating

Provide students with a "teaser" statement such as "I had a terrible experience last night" or "I can't believe what happened this morning." Instead of elaborating further, immediately move into class work. When students object, discuss with them the frustration everyone feels when others do not give enough details about an event. Suggest that you feel the same frustration when students do not elaborate in their writing.

WRITING
HANDBOOK
9

Techniques for Elaboration and Development

Elaboration is the process of developing a writing idea by generating specific supporting details. Elaboration can take place at any point during the writing process.

FINDING DETAILS FOR ELABORATION

To find details to elaborate your writing, you can use any of the information-gathering techniques in Writing Handbook 2, pages 331–336, or the graphic devices described in Writing Handbook 4, pages 339–347. Questioning is another useful technique.

Using Questioning Techniques

Questioning is a particularly useful method for determining the types of details that will help you elaborate your topic. The following list suggests types of questions you might consider.

Action Questions These questions, which begin with the words *who, what, where, when, why,* or *how,* are particularly useful in generating detailed descriptions of events or actions. Examples of these questions are listed below.

- What is happening? What has happened? What will happen?
- Who is, was, or will be responsible? Who else is involved?
- Where does, did, or will it happen?
- Why did, does, or will it happen?
- How did, does, or will it happen?

Category Questions You can use category questions, such as those listed below, to explore and analyze various aspects of a topic.

- **Definition**
  How does the dictionary define my subject? How would I define it?
  To what group does it belong?
  What are some specific examples of it?
  What are its parts? How might they be divided?

- **Comparison**

  What is my subject similar to? In what ways?

  What is it different from? In what ways?

  What is it worse than? In what ways?

- **Cause and Effect**

  What causes my subject?

  What effects does it have?

  What is its purpose?

- **Conditions and Events**

  Is this subject possible? Why or why not?

  Is it practical? Why or why not?

  Has it happened before? When? How? To whom?

- **Documentation**

  What facts or statistics do I know about my subject?

  What have I seen, heard, or read about it?

  What saying, proverb, song, or poem do I know about it?

  How could I find out more about it?

Creative Questions These can help you shift your perspective and stretch your imagination by considering fanciful approaches to your subject.

- What if I combined two objects that are normally separate?
- What if I used something in a new or unusual way?
- What if something had never happened?
- What if someone had never existed?
- What if I changed the material, shape, color, or location?
- What if I put unlikely or opposing ideas together?
- What if people changed their roles or actions?

Aristotelian Invention Questions based on techniques developed by the Greek philosopher Aristotle can also help stimulate creative thinking about your subject. Some of the most useful techniques are listed below and on the following page.

- Compare and contrast your subject with other things.
- Think of synonyms for your subject and of the differing implications, or connotations, of these synonyms.
- Consider your subject over time.
- Relate the subject to yourself.
- Define your subject; think of the different meanings of words used to name your subject.
- Think of the parts of your subject.
- Look for examples and see if you can generalize from them.
- Look for causes, effects, pros, and cons.

Elaboration and Development   **377**

Collaborative Learning

The creative questions are particularly appropriate for students working together because students can take turns reading the questions aloud (also good for auditory learners) and then brainstorming possible answers.

Modeling

Some of the invention techniques may seem abstract and overwhelming to students. Select a topic, perhaps something as simple as choosing a car to buy, and then use appropriate techniques from the list to demonstrate the process.

Listening and Speaking

Suggest that when students use this strategy they might like to use a cassette player to record their dialogues. Then they can listen to themselves to critique and clarify their ideas.

Writing TIP

Use phone directories or local government listings to find experts in the topic you are researching.

- Look for analogies and draw conclusions based on them.
- Contrast the actual or current state of your subject with its possible future state.
- Consider common opinions concerning your subject, and determine whether these opinions are factually based.

Finding Answers to Your Questions

You can find the answers to your questions in several ways, including holding a dialogue, conducting an interview, and checking reference works such as encyclopedias, almanacs, dictionaries, and collections of short biographies.

Holding a Dialogue You can use internal dialogue in several ways to develop writing ideas. Holding a dialogue allows you to consider more than one side of an issue. Here are some ways to use dialogue to generate ideas.

- Interview yourself about the subject. Write down both your questions and answers.
- Hold a dialogue between two parts of yourself, such as your confident side and your insecure side, or your brave self and your frightened self. Use your contradictory feelings to explore different sides of an issue or idea.
- Take on the roles of two characters, or one character and an inanimate object or abstract idea.

Conducting an Interview You can gather up-to-date information on a topic by interviewing. Quoting experts or experienced persons can add interest and authenticity to your writing. You should prepare for an interview by doing research beforehand and compiling a list of questions to ask your expert. This will allow you to focus on the information you need when you are conducting the interview.

Using Library Resources Checking reference works can help you answer questions you might have about a topic. Don't allow the number and size of reference works to daunt you. Take the following steps to save time and energy when trying to locate information.

- Begin by **skimming.** Move your eyes quickly over the page to find out if the information you need is there.
- **Scan** promising material, again moving your eyes quickly until you locate the information you want.
- Do **in-depth reading** of the relevant information.

Science and Humanities Connection

Aristotle The Techniques for Invention are part of the philosopher Artistotle's work in the field of logic. But Aristotle was also a scientist and a writer. Students might use some of the techniques in this lesson to find out more about Aristotle, an uncommon man.

INCORPORATING DETAILS

The types of details that you need to elaborate a piece of writing depend on your purpose, audience, and form.

Facts and Statistics   A **fact** is a statement that can be verified, and **statistics** are simply facts expressed as numbers.

> According to the *1990 Universal Almanac,* edited by John W. Wright, there are currently 1.5 million Native Americans and 64,000 Native Alaskans (Eskimos and Aleuts) living in the United States. This represents a significant increase since the 1960 census, when only 524,000 Native Americans and 42,500 Native Alaskans were counted.

WRITER TO WRITER

Include many specific details and examples so that the reader knows exactly what you are saying and can visualize the images you describe.

**Jason Moneymaker, student
DeSoto, Texas**

Sensory Details   Details that appeal to the senses are particularly helpful in enlivening descriptions. Notice how they are used below.

▼

LITERARY MODEL

The village matchmaker came to my family when I was just two years old. No, nobody told me this, I remember it all. It was summertime, very hot and dusty outside, and I could hear cicadas crying in the yard. We were under some trees in our orchard. The servants and my brothers were picking pears high above me. And I was sitting in my mother's hot sticky arms. I was waving my hand this way and that, because in front of me floated a small bird with horns and colorful paper-thin wings. And then the paper bird flew away and in front of me were two ladies. I remember them because one lady made watery "shrrhh, shrrhh" sounds. When I was older, I came to recognize this as a Peking accent, which sounds quite strong to Taiyuan people's ears.   **Amy Tan, *The Joy Luck Club***

Elaboration and
Development   **379**

Teaching Tip: Library

Even advanced students sometimes feel uneasy when they go to a library to do research. Often students immediately head for the familiar—encyclopedias—and leave a wealth of information untouched. Prepare and post a list of resources that are available in your school library and encourage students to ask about unfamiliar resources. If time permits, you may wish to draw up a list of research questions, the answers to which *require* students to use the unfamiliar resources. Refer students to Library, Reference Works, and other Sources," pp. 491–500.

Critical Thinking

Analyzing   Have students read the Tan excerpt. Ask students to identify sensory details, the senses appealed to, and the effect the elaborative details had on them. *(Sight: people picking pears, small bird with horns and colorful paper-thin wings, two ladies; Hearing: cicadas crying, "shrrhh, shrrhh" sounds; Touch: hot and dusty, hot sticky arms; Possible effect: emphasizes the importance of the moment because the little girl remembered so many details.)*

Social Studies Connection

Statistics   It has been said that statistics can be used to prove anything. Suggest that students read the newspaper, looking for examples of the use of statistics. Have students share their examples with the class and discuss how the same statistics could be used to support other points of view.

Incidents An incident—an interesting or significant event—can illustrate a persuasive argument very well.

Average United States consumers continue to face what appears to me to be more direct and blatant overcharges in phone rates. . . . A recent attempt to place a call on a pay phone from Lower Manhattan directly across the Hudson River to Jersey City—a distance of perhaps one mile—brought a request to deposit $1.90 for one minute. The charge seemed ludicrous, given that I could have physically delivered my message by train for $1.
Mark Solof, *The New York Times*

Specific Examples Examples are often effective in building a convincing thesis, as in the following paragraph.

That's the individual she is: neither Kennedy nor Onassis nor even her own glamorous public image, but a woman who remains serious, hardworking, sensitive, funny, and even slightly outrageous. (In conversation, she's the sort of person to whom you find yourself saying things you had previously only thought, indiscreet things that her own gentle rebelliousness encourages you to say.)
Gloria Steinem, *Outrageous Acts and Everyday Rebellions*

Quotations A pertinent quotation can breathe life into nonfiction.

The time-honored methods of teaching home economics are changing in high schools across the country. As family structures and eating habits change from the two-parent, mother-at-home, meat-and-potatoes form on which the original curriculum was based, home ec classes move with the times. "Two out of three meals are eaten away from home; everybody works," points out Jewell Deene Ellis, director of Home Economics Education for the Kentucky Department of Education.

Opinions Many different kinds of opinions—including judgments and proposals—can be used for elaboration.

There is no reason that a country with one of the highest standards of living in the world, the United States, should be

Linking Grammar and Writing

Quotations You might want to remind students that while quotations are an effective way to give information and authenticity to an account, they can be distracting to a reader if they are not punctuated correctly. Suggest students refer to Grammar and Usage Handbook 41 whenever they use quotations as a means of elaboration.

Critical Thinking

Present this problem to students: "You have been given many strategies for elaboration and development. When someone tells you that your writing lacks detail, how will you know which strategy to use?" Elicit from students that there is no one right answer, but the technique chosen should depend on their goals, purpose, and audience.

nineteenth in its infant mortality rate. Clearly, this problem should be a top priority among human-service professionals and legislators. We need better prenatal care, better education for young mothers, and more financial support for indigent mothers and their children.

Visual Aids Charts, graphs, maps, and tables can sometimes illustrate a complicated point more effectively than words. For example, the following table might help you discuss the comparative amounts spent on defense by various NATO countries.

$281.10 Billion	$27.33 Billion	$19.84 Billion	$7.90 Billion	$2.17 Billion
$1,164.00	$481.00	$163.00	$308.00	$520.00
United States	Britain	Japan	Canada	Norway

Practice Your Skills

A. Consider each of the following main ideas, and choose the three you can elaborate into a paragraph most effectively. Follow the suggestions for elaboration in parentheses.

1. Some of the most important work is that for which people usually do not get paid. (Elaborate with examples.)

2. The developing countries of the world suffer under a great burden of debt. (Consult some almanacs to find statistics.)

3. The opening of the film _____ established a mood of _____. (Fill in the blanks. Use sensory details to re-create the event.)

4. Few things in life are irrevocable. However . . .(Elaborate with an incident from your life.)

B. Read the following statistics. Then use them to create a pie chart, a bar chart, or a table. Write a brief report in which you draw a conclusion from the statistics. Use the graphic aid in your report.

Region	Population
Asia	3,031 million
Africa	615 million
North America	413 million
South America	282 million

Elaboration and Development   **381**

 Individualizing Instruction

LD Students Since these students sometimes reverse numbers, you might want to check their graphs or have them work with another student so that their conclusions will be based on accurate figures.

ANSWERS TO PRACTICE YOUR SKILLS

A. Answers will vary.
B. Answers will vary. Students might conclude that the population of Asia is more than double the combined population of the other three continents.

Off the Record

Definition
conjunction (con + junction) *n.,* The point at which both teacher and student recognize that the excuse offered for not having done a homework assignment is not believable.

Writing Handbook 10:
Mastering Unity and Coherence

Objectives

1. To recognize and apply techniques for achieving unity
2. To recognize and apply techniques for achieving coherence
3. To revise paragraphs so that they are unified and coherent

Handbook Mini-Lessons

For information on topics related to unity and coherence, see the following mini-lessons.

- Techniques for Elaboration and Development, pp. 376–381
- Revising Effectively, pp. 392–395
- Improving Your Sentences, pp. 402–411
- Refining Critical Thinking and Writing Skills, pp. 472–478

Motivating

Tell students that you are going to talk about today's topic "Mastering Unity and Coherence." Instead of giving them a straightforward "lecture," ramble on about other matters, occasionally coming back to the topic. After a few minutes of this type of presentation, ask students whether they understand the lesson on unity and coherence. Elicit that your "lecture" was not unified and coherent and therefore was hard to follow and proved frustrating to them.

 Individualizing Instruction

Basic Students Review the definition of "topic sentence." Then work with these students to produce a simple paragraph that will begin with a topic sentence followed by sentences containing supporting details. You might start them off with a topic sentence about a favorite sport or activity.

WRITING HANDBOOK 10

Mastering Unity and Coherence

What makes one piece of writing seem solid and well-crafted and another seem patched together and makeshift? The answer is unity and coherence. Writing has **unity** when all the sentences and paragraphs work together toward the same goal and are directly related to the main idea. Writing has **coherence** when all the sentences and paragraphs are clearly and logically linked together.

TECHNIQUES FOR ACHIEVING UNITY

In a unified piece of writing, all sentences support the main idea. Unity is important both in individual paragraphs and in longer pieces of writing.

Unity Within Paragraphs

Here are some specific techniques to help you unify your paragraphs.

Write a Topic Sentence State the main idea of a paragraph in a topic sentence, and then make sure each subsequent sentence supports it.

Relate All Sentences to a Single Controlling Idea Write a paragraph that does not have a formal topic sentence but in which all the sentences support one implied idea. In the following paragraph, for example, all the sentences are about the stress of moving to a new place, although no topic sentence specifically states this.

> You're not sure what lies ahead in your new home. You don't know who your new friends will be, what your new school will be like, or even what your new room will be like. You try to be philosophical, but somehow you feel like a small, frightened child.

Delete Unrelated Ideas During revision, delete any sentences that clearly don't contribute to your main idea.

> If you carefully consider what animals people find attractive, an interesting pattern emerges. People generally love young mammals—baby seals, kittens, chimpanzees, and so on. ~~Chimpanzees are especially astonishing, since they can be~~

Writing **TIP**

Remember that you don't have to have a topic sentence in every paragraph. Using a topic sentence is only one way of creating paragraph unity.

taught to communicate through sign language. People also love adult creatures that look like babies—big-eyed, small-nosed animals like pandas and koala bears. Some inborn, instinctive urge draws us to animals that resemble, however distantly, our own young. That's why cute little greeting card animals usually have, in proportion to body size, big heads, eyes, and ears but small noses, feet, and hands. That's also why we so despise harmless but alien-looking creatures—long-nosed rats and many-eyed spiders.

Create Two Paragraphs from One A paragraph lacks unity if it contains more than one main idea. During revision, analyze each paragraph to make sure it is built around a single idea. Create new paragraphs wherever necessary.

> Rosa climbed the stairs to her ballet class with no particular enjoyment that day. She knew that she would have to hear about how Inéz was going to dance the part of Giselle, and she didn't relish the thought. I'll never get a break, she thought to herself. It's almost enough to make me hate her.
> ¶ Meanwhile, Inéz had started to board the Fifth Avenue bus when a man in a business suit, obviously in a hurry, pushed by her. She didn't know what hit her. She fell back onto the sidewalk, her left leg twisted in one direction, her foot in the other. She would be in a cast for six weeks.

Unity in Description

A good description creates a unified impression. Consider the following example from the story of a poor woman whose husband and children die of starvation. On the way to a temple, where there is supposed to be food, the woman's husband falls, obviously near death. Notice how all the details in this passage work together to create a unified impression of the extreme mental anguish the woman is suffering.

Writing
—**TIP**—
Review the unity of your essay before reviewing individual paragraphs, since you may decide to delete some paragraphs altogether.

Critical Thinking

Making Inferences Point out that the deleted sentence contains a reference to chimpanzees and that chimpanzees are mentioned in the preceding sentence. Ask students why the sentence was deleted. *(It spoils the unity of the paragraph by not sticking to the point of why people find certain animals attractive.)*

Critical Thinking

Analyzing Ask students why the paragraph should be divided. *(The first part of the paragraph is about Rosa; the second is about Inéz.)* Then ask students whether the two paragraphs seem to be part of a unified story. *(Yes, because Inéz's leg injury will have an impact on what happens to Rosa's aspirations.)*

Listening and Speaking

For students to get the full impact of the unified description, you might have a speech or drama student practice the literary model and then perform it for the class. Have students discuss the words and phrases that make the description unified.

Teaching Tip: Coherence

Point out that unity and coherence work together and that a composition that is not unified usually lacks coherence as well. Tell students that coherence is the stick-to-itiveness of a composition. It helps to relate the ideas and cement the unity.

Critical Thinking

Interpreting Have students discuss the quotation and suggest how it relates to the concepts of unity and coherence. *("Wise men" use logical patterns to determine where their ideas are going; "fools" ignore the logic, and their ideas become muddled. Compositions that are unified and coherent follow logical patterns providing a beacon for readers.)*

LITERARY
M O D E L

> What do I remember? Every word, every detail. I remember walking along the wet deserted street by the wall of the temple; I remember looking up for the flare that had ever burnt on the top of the temple, and it was quenched; and the black demons of fear came shrieking at my ear and would not be silenced, for all that I repeated like a madwoman, "Fire cannot burn in water." I saw the faces of men who were not there and of children from whom the life had been filched, and yet it was black night, blacker than black since the stars were hidden.
>
> **Kamala Markandaya, *Nectar in a Sieve***

TECHNIQUES FOR ACHIEVING COHERENCE

A piece of writing is coherent when the ideas flow smoothly from one to the next, with no gaps in logical organization. The reader should be able to follow the ideas and readily understand the connections between them. Like unity, coherence is important both within single paragraphs and in longer writing as a whole.

WRITER TO WRITER

> Logical consequences are the scarecrows of fools and the beacons of wise men.
>
> **Thomas Henry Huxley, British biologist**

Coherence Within Paragraphs

A paragraph is coherent when each of its sentences logically flows to the next. Three major techniques help achieve coherence.

- Present your ideas in a logical order.
- Use pronouns, synonyms, and repeated words to show that ideas previously mentioned are connected.
- Use transitional devices to show the relationships among ideas.

384 Writing Handbook

Humanities Connection

Art Just as a piece of writing must be unified, so must a work of art be unified. Interested students might enjoy analyzing a work of art by identifying the artistic details that lead to the unifying, dominant impression.

Word Chains One way to create coherence in a piece of writing is by repeating key words from sentence to sentence or by referring to a previously stated idea in different words. As you read the following passage, notice how the repetition of the word *crab* creates a chain within the first paragraph and also between the first paragraph and the second.

> I was not too fond of **crab,** ever since I saw my birthday **crab** boiled alive, but I knew I could not refuse. That's the way Chinese mothers show they love their children, not through hugs and kisses but with stern offerings of steamed dumplings, duck's gizzards, and **crab.**
> I thought I was doing the right thing, taking the **crab** with the missing leg. But my mother cried, ''No! No! Big one, you eat it. I cannot finish.''
> **Amy Tan, *The Joy Luck Club***

Another way to structure a word chain is by using synonyms, near synonyms, or pronouns instead of a key word. This technique creates coherence and adds interest and variety to your writing. Notice how the last two paragraphs of the passage that follows are linked by repetition of the word *dress,* by use of the near synonyms *red taffeta* and *green velvet,* and by use of the pronoun *it* in place of *red taffeta.*

Grammar
—TIP—

Be sure your reader can tell which nouns are referred to by the pronouns you choose.

> ''He's a nice young man, a scholar, from college. You'll like him.''
> ''I won't.'' Naomi glared. ''You're wearing my favorite **dress** for him.''
> **The red taffeta. It** was the only nice **dress** Ruthie had, although she had put a dollar down on a **green velvet** now in layaway.
> **Marge Piercy, *Gone to Soldiers***

Transitional Devices Another way to achieve coherence in your writing is to use words and phrases that indicate specific relationships and provide necessary links between ideas. Such words and phrases are called **transitional devices.** They can be used to achieve coherence both within a paragraph and between paragraphs in a longer piece of writing.

Unity and Coherence **385**

Some students may say that former teachers instructed them never to repeat words but to use synonyms instead. Affirm that what their former teachers told them is valid because the overuse of some words can make writing sound boring and repetitious; however, as their writing becomes more sophisticated, students can *choose* to repeat words for emphasis, thus contributing to coherence.

Modeling

To illustrate the importance of making pronoun references clear, write the following sentence on the chalkboard: *My mother gave Sarah her ring.* Ask students to whom the word *her* refers. Have them suggest ways to revise the sentence to make the reference clear.

Occasionally, two ideas are so obviously connected that no transitional device is needed. In the following example, no transition is necessary because the reader can infer the connection between the bad weather described in the first sentence and the postponement of the trip reported in the second.

> The surf was pounding and there was a storm brewing. We decided to postpone our snorkeling trip.

More often, however, you need to add a specific word or phrase to show how two ideas are connected. In the next example, the word *nevertheless* signals the contrast between the idea in the first sentence and the idea in the second.

> Many people suffer from phobias—such as fear of heights, dogs, or driving—that make their lives very difficult. **Nevertheless,** through therapy, a person suffering from a phobia can gradually learn to deal with the object of his or her fear.

A transition can, of course, connect two paragraphs as well as two sentences. In the next passage, the transition *for example* shows how the second paragraph is connected to the first—it gives an example of the idea the first paragraph expresses.

PROFESSIONAL
M O D E L

> Persi Diaconis and Frederick Mosteller of Harvard have spent ten years collecting thousands of stories of coincidences. They have concluded that nearly all the coincidences were statistically likely events.
>
> **For example,** a few years ago a New Jersey woman won her state lottery twice within four months. This was widely reported as a one in 17 trillion long shot. But the odds were actually closer to one in 30. Why? One in 17 trillion is the odds that a given person who buys a single ticket for each of two lotteries will win both times. But the odds that *somebody*, out of all the millions who buy lottery tickets in the United States, will win twice in her lifetime are better than one in 30.
>
> *The New York Times*

Some of the most common transitions are those that show relationships of time or sequence. Other transitions show more abstract relationships, such as cause and effect, similarity, degree, or contrast. The following chart lists some of the most useful transitional devices.

Linking Grammar and Writing

Remind students that transitional devices are words added to a sentence to show a relationship between ideas. As such, many transitional devices are set off by commas. Refer students to Grammar and Usage Handbook 39 for more information on the use of commas.

Transitional Devices

	Words or Phrases	Example
Time or Sequence	before, during, after, earlier, then, later, soon, first, next, finally, once, eventually, in time	My legs felt heavier and heavier as the marathon continued. **Finally,** I saw the finish line.
Logical Relationships	since, therefore, as a result, because, inevitably, besides, consequently	Construction of the new reactor began that summer. **Inevitably,** public reaction was mixed.
Similarity	as, like, and, again, too, also, likewise, equally, similarly, another, moreover, in addition	The candidate's campaign workers were quite effective in delineating the issues. **Equally** important were their efforts to get the voters to vote.
Degree	better, best, more, most, worse, worst, less, least, greater, greatest	The story I wrote won a prize! **Even better,** it was published!
Contrast	but, yet, not, still, nevertheless, however, in contrast, otherwise, although, on the other hand, nonetheless	Smith's book treats its subject lightheartedly. **In contrast,** Vonnegut's novel treats the same topic with dark humor.

Cooperative Learning

You might want to have students form small groups to create pairs of sentences that illustrate the use of some of the transitional devices. Circulate through the class and when you find a group having difficulty with a transition, have the rest of the class suggest related sentences.

Linking Grammar and Writing

Since *but* and *however* are sometimes used synonymously, students may erroneously punctuate sentences joined by these words in the same way. Remind students that *but* is a coordinating conjunction and is preceded by a comma when two independent clauses have been joined. *However* is a conjunctive adverb and is preceded by a semicolon and followed by a comma when two independent clauses have been joined.

In addition to showing relationships, transitions can signal that an example is about to be given, that the material following the transition is being emphasized, that additional information follows, or that explanation or clarification is being offered to the reader.

Transitions That Introduce Examples

as	for example	for instance
like	such as	to illustrate
that is	namely	in particular

Transitions That Signal Emphasis

indeed	in fact	in other words

Transitions That Signal More Information

in addition	besides	furthermore
moreover	also	as well

Transitions That Signal Explanation

for example	that is	in other words

UNITY AND COHERENCE IN LONGER WRITING

The same techniques you use to achieve unity and coherence within single paragraphs are useful for creating unity and coherence in longer pieces of writing such as essays and reports. In longer pieces, not only should each sentence build on the topic of its paragraph but each paragraph should also clearly contribute to the main idea of the composition. In addition, each paragraph should develop logically from the one that precedes it.

As you consider the following passage, notice how the sentences within each paragraph and the paragraphs themselves contribute to the writer's thesis. In addition, observe the various techniques the writer uses to create coherence in the piece.

According to a recent survey conducted by the Center for the Study of Public Information, a full 60 percent of American voters get all their information about political issues from nightly television programs. A democracy that gets most of its news from such shows is a democracy in great jeopardy, for half-hour news programs provide the public with the illusion of information, not the substance. This insubstantiality is the result not of a conspiracy to misinform or underinform; it is an inherent shortcoming of television as an information medium, at least as it is currently organized.

The importance of solid information to a democracy did not escape Thomas Jefferson, who felt most strongly that a democracy could survive only when the public was well informed. In his view, an informed public would have the ability to evaluate political issues and make political decisions on the basis of reason, not as a result of preconceptions or whims. He feared a public that received false or inadequate information; people would be unable to make intelligent decisions. Jefferson could not have foreseen television, but he clearly anticipated its impact.

To achieve coherence, the writer makes particularly effective use of repeated words such as *democracy,* of synonyms such as *not the substance* and *insubstantiality,* and of pronouns. The transition between paragraphs is provided by the phrase *the illusion of information,* the subject of the first paragraph, and the contrasting phrase, *the importance of solid information,* that begins the second.

Practice Your Skills

A. Revise the following paragraphs for unity and coherence. Delete unrelated ideas, reorganize the paragraphs, and add transitions so that the relationships among the ideas are clear.

Unity and Coherence **389**

Critical Thinking

Analyzing Ask students to analyze the passage to explain how it achieves unity and to identify other transitional devices. (*The first paragraph is unified because it is focused on the problems with nightly news programs. The second paragraph is unified because it is focused on Thomas Jefferson's views. Other transitions used are for, at least, not as a result of, instead, but.*)

Literature Connection

Coherence D. H. Lawrence's "The Rocking-Horse Winner" is a particularly good example of the use of repeated words and phrases to achieve coherence. Suggest that students read the short story and identify the repeated words and phrases.

A. Answers will vary. Revisions, however, should show applications of the techniques of unity (details that contribute to one idea) and coherence (logical order, repetition, and transitional devices), as shown in the examples below.

1. Adopting a child from another country usually involves several steps. First, you must contact an agency that deals with international adoptions. This agency will do a home-study report on your family. After the home study has been done, you have to compile many documents, including health, birth, and marriage certificates, letters of recommendation, police checks, and immigration and naturalization papers. These documents have to be notarized, certified, and sent to the country before you can travel there to adopt a child. After all the paper work has been completed, you can travel to the country, go through the legal adoption process there, and then bring the child back to the United States. Once back in the United States, you must go through additional legal procedures so that the adoption can be finalized under U.S. law.

2. There are many approaches to painting a landscape in oils, but the following is the approach I usually take. First, assemble the materials—oil paints, a palette knife, cloths, canvas, an easel, and charcoal. Then begin with a careful charcoal sketch, working directly on the canvas. (A good sketch is hard to spoil with paint, and the paint will cover the sketch.) When applying the paint, work from back to front. Paint first any large background areas such as mountains, bodies of water, the ground, or the sky. Then paint the smaller middle-ground features such as grasses, trees, and clouds. Finally, add the finishing details like branches, birds, fence posts, ice caps, ripples on the water, highlights, and shadows.

1. Adopting a child from another country usually involves several steps. You travel to the country, go through the legal adoption procedure there, and then bring the child back to the United States. Once back in the United States, you go through additional legal procedures so that the adoption can be finalized under U.S. law. The first thing that happens, though, is that you contact an agency that deals with international adoptions, and this agency does a home study report on your family. After the home study is done, you have to get together many, many documents, including health certificates, birth certificates, marriage certificates, letters of recommendation, police checks, immigration and naturalization papers, and many others besides. These documents have to be notarized, certified, and sent to the country before you can travel there to adopt the child. To call this a complicated procedure is an extreme understatement. Marrying someone from another country is quite easy.

2. There are many, many approaches to painting a landscape in oils. You paint any large, background areas such as mountains, bodies of water, the ground, or the sky. You then add on smaller, middle-ground features such as grasses, trees, and clouds. Turner was a master at painting clouds. So was Winslow Homer. You add finishing details like branches, birds, fence posts, ice caps, ripples on the water, highlights, and shadows. Basically, you work from back to front. Begin with a really careful sketch. (If your sketch is good, it's hard to spoil it with paint.) Assemble your materials—oil paints, a palette, paint thinner, turpentine, brushes, a palette knife, cloths, canvas, an easel, and charcoal. Do your background sketch in charcoal. This is the approach that I usually take. Sketch right on the canvas. Your paint will cover up the sketch.

Breezing Up,
Winslow Homer

Humanities Connection

Art Note   When the noted American painter and illustrator Winslow Homer (1836–1910) exhibited *Breezing Up* in 1876, the critics praised its "youthful freshness and spirited optimism." Homer excelled in capturing the qualities of outdoor light and color, which may partly explain why he was a "master at painting clouds."

3. Until recently, the main source of information in the United States was the newspaper. By its very nature as a print medium, the newspaper can be read at the reader's own pace. Many people have even taken speed-reading courses to help them read faster. The newspaper provides long and careful analyses of issues and events. Recent polls show a sharp decline in readership. Some people read only the cartoons or the sports section. The in-depth analyses newspapers provide require higher levels of literacy and longer attention spans. Each year, more Americans get most of their information from television. Television is an inadequate medium for communicating information in depth. Because television is a visual medium, relying on stories that can be filmed, it cannot probe the subtlety of the issues that confront the citizens of a complex world. Television news programs must take periodic commercial breaks and the brief stories can never provide the depth that is possible in newspapers. The visual image encourages a focus on personalities rather than issues, a preoccupation that is demonstrated by the newscasters themselves, since they make tremendous amounts of money.

B. Read the following pairs of sentences. The first sentence of each pair comes at the end of one paragraph and the second comes at the start of the next. Identify the type of transitional device that links each pair.

1. [This system of streets] persisted in the Roman [town], the medieval eastern German towns, and the [towns] of southern France, in certain European cities of the seventeenth and eighteenth centuries, and, of course, in the modern cities of North America.

   Even more important than those practical criteria for the design of cities were the habits that governed the lives of their inhabitants.

   René Dubos

2. The nights are always cold on Thorn. There's no fog there up on the mountainside, but the wind always blows.

   But Thorn was behind me now.

   Ursula Le Guin

3. If you just press ENTER instead of keying in numbers for the day, month, and year, the robot will interpret this as an instruction to perform the requested tasks at the same time every day.

   After you enter the time, [it] will ask you to confirm that you entered the date and time correctly, and will then say, "Next."

   Mike Higgins

3. Until recently the main source of information in America was the newspaper. The newspaper provides long and careful analyses of issues and events. By its nature as a print medium, the newspaper can be read at the reader's own pace. Nevertheless, recent polls show a sharp decline in readership.

Instead of reading the newspaper, more and more Americans are getting most of their information from television. Television, however, is an inadequate medium for communicating information in depth. For example, television news programs must take periodic commercial breaks, and their brief stories can never provide the coverage that is available in newspapers. Because television is a visual medium that relies on filmed stories, it cannot probe the subtlety of the issues that confront the citizens of a complex world. In addition, the visual image encourages a focus on personalities rather than issues, a preoccupation that is demonstrated by the newscasters themselves.

B.
1. Even more important (degree)
2. But (contrast)
3. After (sequence)

Additional Resources

- Writing Resource Book, pp. 17–18
- Student Revision Model Transparencies
- Elaboration, Revision, and Proofreading Worksheets

Social Studies Connection

Magazine Articles Suggest that students find articles of interest in weekly news magazines and analyze them by identifying techniques of unity and coherence. Students might like to write their own articles about a current event, emulating the techniques in the magazine.

Revising Effectively

Objectives

1. To recognize issues critical to revising for content
2. To improve structure by focusing on organization, logic, and sentence structure
3. To revise a rough draft for mechanics

Handbook Mini-Lessons

For information on topics related to revising effectively, see the following mini-lessons.

- Mastering Unity and Coherence, pp. 382–391
- Peer Review, pp. 397–401
- Improving Your Sentences, pp. 402–411
- Refining Critical Thinking and Writing Skills, pp. 472–478

Teaching Strategies

Motivating

Ask students to write at least three sentences describing the classroom—its size, lighting, furniture, windows, bulletin boards, and so on. Tell them they have only 30 seconds in which to write. After 30 seconds, have students form groups of three or four and read their descriptions aloud. Without allowing time for discussion, ask each student to decide whether his or her description is perfect or could be improved. Tell students they may have 60 (or 90) seconds to make any changes or additions. After 60 (or 90) seconds, have students discuss the kinds of changes they made and why. Point out that the more time students had to think about the topic, the more additions and corrections they wanted to make.

WRITING HANDBOOK 11

Revising Effectively

Revision is an integral part of the writing process entailing three different types of changes: rethinking content, reworking structure, and refining mechanics, or proofreading. You don't have to wait until you have completed a draft to begin revision, and you can often do more than one type of revision at a time.

REVISING FOR CONTENT

Rethinking content is the most important part of the revision process. You must make sure that your work has a clear focus, that the ideas are developed fully, and that all material included is relevant to your thesis. Consider the following issues as you revise.

Checklist for Rethinking Content

- **Is my thesis clear? Does my writing have a central focus?** Check that you have expressed your main idea clearly and that you have provided all the information your readers need.
- **Have I incorporated adequate detail?** See where you can insert a telling detail, a revealing statistic, or a vivid example.
- **Have I eliminated material that is unnecessary, irrelevant, or confusing?** Check your writing for unity, making sure that all the ideas and supporting details advance your thesis.

As you read the following first draft of an editorial for a high school newspaper, think of ways the content could be made stronger.

392 Writing Handbook

Three cheers for the Durfee Ecology Club! A few months ago some students at Durfee Community High decided that they wanted to improve their environment. They organized the Durfee Ecology Club, and one of their first projects was an extremely successful Clean-Up-Durfee Day on March 13. Last year fourteen trash containers were placed throughout the school. This constituted a major effort to keep Durfee clean; but how did all that litter get in the halls in the first place? And on the grounds. The answer is obvious, of coarse. Students put it there—careless, inconsiderate, thoughtless students. A lot of students prefer littering the school with trash and didn't make much use of the containers.

The student body should feel honored to have such civic-minded students in their school.

In rereading his draft, the writer realized that it lacked specific details about the number of students involved in the cleanup campaign and the number of trash bags they filled. He also decided to elaborate on the results of the campaign and to add a concluding paragraph urging students to make an ongoing commitment to the ecology effort.

REVISING FOR STRUCTURE

In addition to considering the content of your writing, you must examine its organization and sentence structure. The following questions will help you focus your structural review.

Remind students that they should not use the "Rethinking Content Checklist" without considering the needs of their audience. For example, before they can determine whether material is unnecessary or irrelevant, they have to identify what their audience already knows. You might want them to contrast the typical content of an article about hurricanes written for elementary schoolchildren with that written for civil defense workers or for readers of a scientific magazine.

Personal Touch

No matter how many times students have heard that writing is a process, some students still believe that good writers are able to get it "right" the first time. Whenever you can, share some of your writing experiences with the class, either by showing them drafts of your work or by telling them about revising you have had to do for course work, business, or pleasure. Encourage students to discuss their feelings about getting writing "right" the first time.

Springboard

Have students brainstorm and then discuss all the ways in which computers and word-processing programs have changed the way people write and revise their work.

Individualizing Instruction

Visual Learners   Suggest that these students use some of the graphic devices in Writing Handbook 4 to determine whether their ideas are logically connected. You may want to post a list of transitional devices in the classroom for their use.

Auditory Learners   Emphasize to these students the importance of reading their drafts aloud to themselves to evaluate the effect of their words.

Individualizing Instruction

ESL Students   Punctuating sentences can be confusing to students whose primary language is not English. For example, a student whose primary language is Spanish may both begin and end a sentence with a question mark. Suggest that these students work with a partner to proofread for errors in sentence punctuation.

LD Students   To aid students who reverse letter patterns, pair each student with a partner to help find spelling errors.

Teaching Tip: Proofreading Spelling

Some students have difficulty spotting spelling errors because they do not read each word. You might suggest that those students go through their essay backward, one word at a time, to identify misspelled words.

Checklist for Reworking Structure

- **Is the organization of my writing clear and coherent?** An easy way to check your draft for logical organization is to outline the material. Use the main ideas of the piece as major heads and the supporting ideas as subheads.

- **Are my ideas logically connected to one another?** Make sure you have clearly communicated the logical relationships among your ideas—such as chronology, juxtaposition in space, cause and effect, or order of importance—by using appropriate transitional words.

- **Are my sentences well constructed?** Strive for a natural, rhythmic cadence, with one sentence flowing smoothly into the next. Combine sentences where possible to eliminate unnecessary repetition, and prune sentences that ramble.

In considering the structure of his editorial, the writer realized that the last six sentences of the first paragraph were out of place, and he moved them to a more logical position. He also created paragraphs, added transitional words to clarify relationships, and reworded several sentences to eliminate unnecessary repetition.

REVISING FOR MECHANICS

When you proofread, or refine the mechanics of your writing, you look for and correct errors in grammar, usage, and mechanics. The following questions can help you identify these errors.

Checklist for Refining Mechanics

- Have I used capital letters and punctuation marks appropriately? Have all run-ons or sentence fragments been corrected?

- Have I checked the spelling of all unfamiliar words?

- Have I used all parts of speech correctly? Do all my subjects and verbs agree in number? Are my verb forms appropriate and my tenses consistent?

As the writer proofread his editorial, he indicated all content, structural, and mechanical alterations using the following standard editorial symbols.

Revising and Proofreading Marks

- ∧ Insert a letter or word
- ⊙ Insert a period
- ═ Capitalize a letter
- / Make a capital letter lowercase
- ___ Delete letters or words
- ⌒ Close up
- ¶ Begin a new paragraph
- ∧ Insert a comma
- ∿ Transpose the position of letters or words

TIP

As you proofread, have a dictionary, thesaurus, and style book available for easy reference.

Three cheers for the Durfee Ecology Club! A few months ago

twenty-six

~~some~~ students at Durfee Community High decided that they

wanted to improve their environment. They organized the Durfee

Ecology Club, and one of their first projects was an extremely

successful Clean-Up-Durfee Day on March 13. ¶ This was not the first clean-up effort at Durfee, however. ∧ Last year fourteen

in

trash containers were placed throughout the school, This constitut-

ed a major effort to keep Durfee clean, but how did all that litter get

in the halls in the first place? And on the grounds. The answer is (tr)

u

obvious, of coarse. Students put it there—careless, inconsiderate,

Apparently

thoughtless students. A lot of students prefer littering the school

to using

with trash ~~and didn't make much use of~~ the containers.

The student body should feel honored to have such civic-

minded students in their school.

∧ ¶ It is time that all Durfee students take a look at their environment. The Ecology Club challenged students to participate in a clean-up day. Now I am challenging them to eliminate the need for clean-up days.

Critical Thinking

Analyzing Discuss with students the revisions in the student model. Have students explain how the changes in content (the additional paragraph), structure (the moving of an entire section), and mechanics contribute to a stronger essay.

Collaborative Opportunity

Sometimes students have difficulty understanding a hand-marked edited version of a draft. Have students work in small groups to produce a version of the student model that demonstrates their understanding of the editing process. For example, students might make a fresh copy of the model, which incorporates the changes, or they might record an oral version of the revised model.

Revising Effectively **395**

Literature Connection

Revisions Samuel Taylor Coleridge's "The Rime of the Ancient Mariner" is a ballad that went through several revisions after it was published in *Lyrical Ballads* in 1798. Students might like to try to locate varying versions of the ballad and compare them.

Answers will vary. However, a good revision will address problems in content, structure, and mechanics, as shown in the example below.

Have you ever seen someone snatch a tablecloth from a dining room table, leaving all the dinnerware intact on the table? That experiment demonstrates the principle of inertia, the tendency of a physical body to stay in motion or to remain at rest until it is acted upon by an outside force. If you tried the experiment yourself, you probably found that everything fell off the table because the friction between the tablecloth and the dinnerware created enough force to overcome the effects of inertia.

Recently I demonstrated the effects of inertia by doing a different experiment using a cup filled with water, a broom, an 8-inch cake pan, a small, empty box that had a slick surface, and a hard-boiled egg. First, I put a cup of water on a table, two inches from the edge. Next, I centered the cake pan on the cup of water and put the box in the middle of the cake pan. Then I balanced the hard-boiled egg on top. Finally, I positioned the broom upright in front of the table, pinning the brush part on the floor with my foot.

Once everything was ready, I pulled back the broom handle, aimed for the center of the cake pan, and let it go. Thwack! Clatter! The cake pan flew across the table, crashing to the floor—pushing the egg into the cup of water. Because of inertia, the egg did not fly off the table but dropped into the cup.

If you would like to demonstrate the principle of inertia, you can duplicate my experiment. Just be sure to hit the cake pan squarely in the middle. If you're truly adventurous, you can even use a raw egg; my advice, however, is don't.

Additional Resources

- Writing Resource Book, pp. 19–20
- Student Revision Model Transparencies
- Elaboration, Revision, and Proofreading Worksheets

Practice Your Skills

Revise the following expository piece, making content, structural, and mechanical changes as necessary.

Inertia is the tendensy of a physical body to stay in motion or at rest until it is acted upon on by an outside force. I have always been fascinated by that old parlor trick. You know, the one where someone snatches a tablecloth from a dining room table. That will work in principle, but in practice, you would find that friction between the dinnerware and the tablecloth creates enough force to overcome the effects of inertia. It starts everything moving right off the table.

Last night I tried a little experiment. It demonstrates the effects of inertia just as dramaticly but with far less mess! I followed these steps: I put a cup of water on the table, two inches from the edge. I centered a cake pan on the cup. I set a box in the middle of the cake pan. I balanced a hard-boiled egg on top. I positioned a broom in front of the setup and pinned it to the floor with my foot. Of course, I had to gather all the material first: a cup, a broom, an 8-inch cake pan, and a small, empty box with a slick surface. And don't forget the hard-boiled egg.

Once everything was ready, I pulled back the broom handle and aimed for the center of the cake pan. Then I let fly. Thwack! Clatter! The cake pan flew across the table. It crashed to the floor. Where was the egg? Sitting in the water. Because of inertia, the egg did not fly off the table, it just dropped into the cup.

I had to try the experiment several times before I could make it work. The trick is to hit the cake pan in the middle. Squarely. Some people like to use a raw egg. It makes the experiment more dramatic. My advice is don't.

Peer Review and Response

Although you are ultimately responsible for your own writing, you will find that a peer reader can be a valuable asset, serving as a sounding board when you want to try out ideas and providing feedback when you get stuck and need help in getting back on track.

WORKING WITH A PEER READER

Both you and your peer reader will find the relationship profitable, but you have to be clear about the ground rules at the outset. You want your reader to act as an audience, not as an editor. You want to know what he or she thinks about your writing, but it is up to you to decide what changes to make—or even whether to make changes at all. You may not agree with what your reader says. In that case, you may decide to keep your writing as it is.

It is not always easy to establish a satisfactory working relationship with a peer reader. Communication is crucial. You have to be specific in telling your reader just what kind of feedback you need. Here are a few suggestions for working with a peer reader that others have found effective.

Using a Peer Reader as a Sounding Board Ask your peer reader to listen as you read your piece aloud. You can tell a great deal about your writing by sharing it this way. When someone is listening to you, you are more aware of what you're saying. Using your reader as a sounding board is especially useful in the early stages of the writing process, when you have just started to explore a topic and are not yet ready for criticism. Similarly, you may not want your reader to offer criticism after you finish a piece of writing. You will certainly hope that your reader likes the finished product, but you may be more interested in just having your work heard.

Focusing on the Positive At times, you may become discouraged about a piece of writing. That's when you can go to your peer reader for some positive feedback, saying, "I need help. I want you to point to specific things in the piece that work especially well for you or that stick in your mind."

You may even be able to read between the lines of your reader's positive response to learn what doesn't work. For example, if you've

Peer Review
and Response   **397**

Writing Handbook 12:
Peer Review and Response

Objectives

1. To understand the concept of peer review and response
2. To work with a peer reader
3. To act as a peer reader

> ### *Handbook Mini-Lessons*
> For information on topics related to peer review, see the following mini-lessons.
> - Collaborative Planning, pp. 358–360
> - Revising Effectively, pp. 392–396
> - Presenting and Publishing Your Writing, pp. 412–415

Teaching Strategies

Motivating
Ask students to describe times in their lives when feedback from a trusted friend has helped them. Elicit ideas about what kinds of feedback and response are most helpful: advice, questions, sharing of feelings, criticism, silent listening? Focus on the idea that different personalities and situations require different kinds of feedback.

written a story and your reader has not commented on one important character, you may wonder if that character is as effectively portrayed as he or she might be.

Clarifying Your Purpose   You can ask your peer reader to help you with your writing purpose by asking questions like this: "Can you help me see what my words actually accomplish?" One benefit of this is that you might find out whether you are saying what you think you're saying. Another is that you might come up with new ideas about your purpose that will take you in interesting directions.

Honing Your Ideas   You may want to ask your peer reader to ignore your language and focus only on your ideas. Phrase your questions something like this: "Talk to me about *what* I've said, not about *how* I've said it. What are your ideas on this topic? Where do you agree or disagree with me? What do you want to hear more about?" These questions will probably elicit some of your most valuable peer responses. They may help you establish your audience and purpose more clearly as well as find out whether your current ideas work.

Analyzing Specific Features   At some point, you may want to ask your peer reader for help in a specific area, such as word choice, organization, sentence structure, or mechanics. For example, you might ask for help on something concrete like transitions, saying: "Would you check this piece to see if you can find ways I can connect my ideas more closely?" Or you might ask for help on something more general like organization, saying: "What do you think about my organization? Is it easy to follow? Does it make sense?"

Here are other types of questions you could direct to your peer reader.

1. Listen as I read this speech aloud. Have I included enough examples to support my main point? Does the speech sound convincing?

2. Will you read this editorial I wrote for the school newspaper? Does it help you see my position, or at least make you question your own?

3. Will you check the paragraphing in this report? I tried to begin a new paragraph each time I began a new idea, but I am not sure of myself.

4. I really feel nervous about writing this letter of application. I want to appear calm and confident. Will you read the letter for me and tell me how I come across?

398   Writing Handbook

Writing TIP

Listen carefully as your peer reader offers constructive criticism. Later, when you are alone and have time to think, you can sort out which ideas you think are really helpful.

◆ Individualizing Instruction

Learning Styles   Students with different learning styles can approach interpreting peer response in different ways. **Auditory learners** might benefit from oral feedback from peer readers, but some students will not process oral feedback as well. Encourage students to ask for the type of response that they feel would benefit them most—oral or written.

Springboard

Read this quotation by George Jean Nathan aloud to the students: "Impersonal criticism is like an impersonal fist fight or an impersonal marriage, and as successful." Have them discuss what is meant by the word *impersonal*. Do they agree that impersonal criticism is unsuccessful, and if so, why? Finally, ask each student to write his or her definition of the best kind of criticism for a writer.

Encourage students to keep these definitions in their Writing Portfolios, reviewing and modifying them as the semester progresses.

Eliciting Spontaneous Feedback Give your peer reader your piece of writing, saying: "Let me stop you a few times as you read so you can tell me what's going on in your mind—moment to moment." This type of response is trustworthy because it gives you your reader's immediate, unmodified reactions. Your reader might respond this way, for example: "Well, I was a little confused in the first paragraph because you quoted someone I've never heard of. Just now, though, I was really getting interested in this idea about America's changing demographics."

Here are some specific issues to consider when asking for spontaneous feedback from your reader.

1. You need to know your reader fairly well and trust him or her before you ask for this kind of honesty. The reader may feel something negative at the moment when you ask for a comment. He or she may say, "I'm really annoyed about this disorganized paragraph because it's interrupting my train of thought." Be sure you are prepared for the possibility of a negative response.

2. Your reader may say something too general, such as, "I pretty much like it." Try to find out exactly what caused this response. For example, ask, "What do you like in the sentence you just finished reading?"

3. Your reader may not want to be interrupted while reading. One alternative is for you to read your piece aloud, stopping once in a while to ask, "What are you thinking or feeling now?" Another option is to ask your reader to read silently, stopping to comment after each paragraph or page. A third option is to ask the reader to jot down brief responses as you read your piece aloud or to take marginal notes as he or she reads silently. You can then ask the reader to share those comments with you.

Teaching Tip: Self-Evaluation

Remind students that when they are acting as peer readers, they should remember that their job is to criticize constructively. They can be more constructive if they put themselves in their peer's shoes. Have them ask themselves, "How would I feel about this criticism?" "Will my criticism help to create a better piece of writing?"

MAKING THE MOST OF PEER RESPONSE

You may get many varied or even contradictory responses to your writing. Not only do different readers respond differently to one piece of writing, but the same reader may respond differently to the same piece at different times. When you get multiple responses, the best strategy is to wait until you've heard all the responses. Take them all in, ponder them, and then make up your own mind.

Again, you're in control of your own writing. Don't feel that you have to argue with your peer reader or defend your own choices. Eventually, you will probably become relatively comfortable with peer response and find it an essential component of your writing process.

WRITER TO WRITER

The writer should receive another writer's opinion before trashing questionable ideas.

Kathleen O'Brill, student
Northfield, Illinois

ACTING AS A PEER READER

Try to take your responsibilities seriously when you act as a peer reader. Remember that the person whose writing you read today may be the one who reads yours tomorrow. Be constructive, and try to frame your criticisms diplomatically. For example, instead of saying, "Your grammar is abominable," say, "You might want to check the usage in this sentence. I don't think the subject agrees with the verb."

When you act as a peer reader, think of the type of feedback you find most helpful in your own writing, and respond accordingly. Here are some specifics.

- **Acting as a sounding board** Listen when your writer feels the need to read his or her piece aloud. Don't interrupt, and don't volunteer comments unless the writer asks for them.

Humanities Connection

Point out to students that film endings are often reworked according to the criticisms of preview audiences. Have them think of a movie ending they found unsatisfactory and write a criticism of it, using the techniques they have learned. Students can share their critiques with each other.

- **Focusing on the positive** Whenever possible, comment on some aspect of the writing that you think is particularly effective. Volunteer suggestions for improving the piece only when asked.
- **Analyzing specific features** Follow the writer's lead in deciding what specific feature to focus upon. If the writer asks you to read the dialogue in a short story to see if it sounds natural, do it. If the writer just asks for help in punctuating the dialogue, however, don't offer unsolicited advice about whether or not it sounds realistic.

Practice Your Skills

In a small group, practice responding to the following rough draft in each of the six ways described in this lesson. Afterward, revise the piece of writing based on the group's comments.

> Have you ever been to a stand-up comedy show in which the comic was not at all funny? You squirm in your chair and look the other way, trying to pretend that you don't notice anything wrong. Though you're thoroughly embarrassed, you know that the comic would like to be in another galaxy right now.
>
> I believe that comedians, though they can make the audience believe they are artless and flaky, are actually the hardest-working, most courageous, and most talented of all performers. They have to be willing to do lots of stuff other performers don't have to worry about. Like actors on pretaped soaps.
>
> Like Rodney Dangerfield, comedians rarely get any respect. But put yourself in their shoes. I wouldn't try to do it. No way.

The Far Side Cartoons by Gary Larson are reprinted by permission of Chronicle Features, San Francisco, CA.

"Larry? Betty? . . . Stand up, will ya? . . . These are some friends of mine, folks, who flew all the way in from the dump."

Peer Review and Response **401**

Answers will vary.
  Students should keep in mind the peer response techniques they have learned:
    using reader as sounding board
    focusing on the positive
    clarifying purpose
    honing ideas
    analyzing specific features
    eliciting spontaneous feedback
Their discussion should take into account the importance of a writer's asking for specific types of responses and deciding which to use.

Cooperative Learning

Students might approach the exercise by working in groups with each student focusing on one of the peer response techniques. The group can then discuss how they could use their responses to revise the passage effectively.

Additional Resources
- Writing Resource Book, pp. 21–22
- Student Revision Model Transparencies
- Peer Response Guides
- Writing Evaluation Guidelines
- Elaboration, Revision, and Proofreading Worksheets

Springboard

Provide students with book reviews from newspapers or magazines. Challenge students to identify which of the response techniques—if any—each reviewer has incorporated into the review and whether the review would be helpful for the book's author in planning and writing his or her next book.

Improving Your Sentences

Objectives

1. To correct empty and overloaded sentences
2. To avoid wordiness and awkward beginnings
3. To link sentence parts

Handbook Mini-Lessons

For information on topics related to sentence improvement, see the following mini-lessons.
- Revising Effectively, pp. 392–396
- Understanding Voice and Style, pp. 417–422
- Establishing Sentence Variety, pp. 439–444

Teaching Strategies

Motivating

Tell students that one of the longest sentences ever written is by the French writer Marcel Proust, from his novel *Cities of the Plain*. It is 958 words long and runs for over three pages. Have students discuss possible problems in reading such a sentence, but stress that Proust's sentence is perfectly and brilliantly constructed.

Improving Your Sentences

Some carpenters work on large, rough structures such as frames for houses. Other carpenters do more delicate work such as building cabinets, stairways, and wood moldings. Drafting is like rough carpentry. It's all about putting up the rough overall structure. After drafting you start to do the delicate work—the fine-tuning that will make your writing exceptional. One important part of this fine-tuning is the process of revising individual sentences.

CORRECTING EMPTY SENTENCES

To create effective sentences, you need to revise sentences that are grammatically correct, yet lack substance. Empty sentences often contain the following problems.

Circular Reasoning This problem occurs when the second part of a sentence merely restates what was said in the first part. Circular reasoning cheats the reader, who is led to expect details and reasons that are never supplied.

Circular	The increase of traffic problems in major urban areas results from having too much traffic congestion on the roads in the city.
Analysis	The writer promises to tell why traffic problems have increased, but then says in effect that there are traffic problems because there are traffic problems.
Revised	Traffic problems in major urban areas have increased because the number of vehicles on most roads and highways now dramatically exceeds the volume that city planners had anticipated.

Unsupported Opinions Sentences that contain opinions without reasons, facts, or examples force the reader to guess at the writer's full meaning. Such sentences need further development.

Unsupported	Automobile insurance rates are unfair.
Analysis	No reasons or facts are supplied to support the claim.
Revised	Automobile insurance rates are unfair because they discriminate against male drivers under the age of twenty-five.

Statement of the Obvious Some statements are so obvious that they do not need to be made. Everyone knows, for example, that Shakespeare was an important writer or that mountain climbing is difficult and dangerous. Your writing will be more effective if you learn to weed out the obvious.

Obvious   Dickens was a popular writer.

Revised   Dickens's popularity was due to his wide range of memorable characters and his intricate and suspenseful plots.

Practice Your Skills

Rewrite the following sentences to correct problems of circular reasoning, unsupported opinions, or statement of the obvious.

1. Leonardo da Vinci, a demanding perfectionist, never finished many of his artistic projects because he found it difficult to complete a work of art.
2. School sports can be dangerous.
3. Martin Luther King, Jr., received a doctorate in systematic theology from Boston University in 1955, the same year that people began to call him "Doctor."
4. The extremes in contemporary fashion are interesting.
5. Since its founding, the United States has always been a nation of immigrants.
6. Ambition can be potentially harmful.
7. Some critics argue that the poetry of Edgar Allan Poe sounds better when translated into French because the poems achieve a more musical quality in French.
8. Cross-country skiing, a popular recreational sport in many countries, is enjoyed during the winter.
9. Abraham Lincoln was a remarkable President.
10. *Mrs. Dalloway* was the most challenging novel I have ever encountered, owing to its complexity.

REDUCING OVERLOADED SENTENCES

For the same reason that a machine should have no unnecessary parts, a sentence should have no unnecessary words. Lively writing is concise. For example, consider the following statement written by Barley T. Campbell.

Distance lends enchantment to the view.

Stumbling Block

Students may need reference materials to complete the Practice Your Skills exercise. Have one or more single-volume encyclopedias on hand.

ANSWERS TO PRACTICE YOUR SKILLS

Answers will vary.
  Be sure students correct the following problems:
  1. circular reasoning
  2. unsupported opinion
  3. circular reasoning
  4. unsupported opinion
  5. stating the obvious
  6. unsupported opinion
  7. circular reasoning
  8. stating the obvious
  9. unsupported opinion
  10. circular reasoning

Speaking and Listening

Students might be challenged in this section by working in pairs to correct overloaded sentences. One student can read aloud the overloaded sentence from the lesson and the other can listen carefully and provide an oral revision of the sentence. Students can then discuss their revised sentences and how they improve on the originals.

Writing
─TIP─

You may find it helpful to list all the ideas in a sentence you suspect of being wordy. Then you can decide which ideas belong in the sentence and which should be deleted or put in another sentence.

Now read the same idea expressed in another sentence.

> Sometimes you have to step back from a scene in order to really see it, because if you are too close you may not appreciate it as fully as possible.

In the first sentence, the writer focused precisely on his idea. The second sentence, with five times the number of words, is **overloaded.**

Overloaded sentences may contain unrelated details, too many ideas or details, or unclear relationships among ideas.

Unrelated Details   Unrelated details interrupt the main ideas and distract the reader.

Overloaded   The poet Carl Sandburg, who once lived in Kansas, was the author of a biography of Abraham Lincoln.

Revised   The poet Carl Sandburg wrote a biography of Abraham Lincoln.

Too Many Ideas   Putting too many ideas or details in a sentence can make you forget what you started to write and will confuse the reader. When you find overloaded sentences in your writing, you will need to eliminate some details or put them in a new sentence.

Overloaded   Everyone should learn a second language because this knowledge will expand his or her cultural horizons, while it may lead to practical career benefits as well, considering our need for businesspeople who are fluent in more than one language.

Revised   Everyone should learn a second language to expand his or her cultural horizons. Bilingual ability may also have practical benefits, since many businesses need bilingual employees.

Stringy Sentences   Some sentences become overloaded when the writer strings a series of ideas together with *and*'s. In the resulting run-on sentence, no single idea stands out, and the reader will find it difficult to understand how the ideas are related. When revising, you can correct a stringy sentence in two ways:

1. Choose conjunctions that will show a more precise relationship between your ideas. A subordinating conjunction such as *because, in order that, although,* or *whenever* is more specific than *and.* For more information, see Grammar Handbook 31, pages 562–564.

2. Divide the sentence into two or more statements.

Stringy   There is a water shortage in many parts of the country, *and* this shortage is causing concern, *and* the U.S. Department of the Interior is trying to find economical methods of changing sea water to fresh water.

Revised   The water shortage in many parts of the country is causing concern; *consequently,* the U.S. Department of the Interior is trying to find economical methods of changing sea water to fresh water.

Stringy   Scientists today are working in an invisible world, *and* they are dealing with atoms, ions, electrons, and quarks, *and* no one has ever seen these things, *and* some of them may not even exist in the usual sense of the word.

Revised   Scientists today are working in an invisible world of atoms, ions, electrons, and quarks. No one has ever seen these things; *indeed,* some of them may not even exist in the usual sense of the word.

Practice Your Skills

Rewrite the following overloaded sentences by choosing more precise conjunctions, eliminating details, or creating new sentences.

1. She had just been promoted to book critic for our newspaper, and she decided to write her own novel and quit her job, and we were in a quandary about who could be hired to replace her.
2. Building a tunnel beneath the English Channel is a sensible idea though a difficult engineering feat, and also expensive, because the tunnel will ease travel between England and the Continent.
3. Scientists dreamed long ago of transmitting power through the air without the use of wires, and they experimented for many years, developing their ideas, and at last they seem to be near the realization of their dream.
4. San Francisco, the famed "City by the Bay," with its breathtaking hills, scenic waterfronts, and pastel-colored houses that excite the senses, not to mention the russet-hued majesty of the Golden Gate Bridge, is one of America's most enchanting cities.
5. We usually finish our chores on Saturday, which is the last day of the week, and buy groceries for the next week.
6. Art lovers enjoy Florence, Italy, which my aunt Florence says she was named after, because of the city's great art treasures.
7. Our first day of traveling brought us to the outskirts of Houston, and just as we were about to stop for the night, the car stalled, and we later learned that it would need extensive repairs.

Improving Your Sentences   **405**

Art Connection

Point out to students that art can appear overloaded. Show them examples of late Baroque or Rococo architecture, and point to the ornamentation of the buildings in question. Have students discuss whether these structures would be more visually appealing with less ornamentation.

8. Ryan went skiing in the Colorado Rockies with his friends.
9. The emergency crew was able to tow away the truck that had burned; no one but the owner thought it could be repaired.
10. Ben Jonson wrote one of his most famous poems to mourn his seven-year-old son, who died of the plague in 1603.

Stumbling Block

Some students may have trouble differentiating between an elaborate writing style and wordiness. Point out that certain writers write long, complex sentences, but they do not include unnecessary words or ideas in their writing. You may wish to reproduce a long sentence from a work students are studying (Mary Shelley's *Frankenstein* would provide lively examples); then help students recognize that although the sentences are long, each word serves a purpose and to delete a word would alter the meaning. Explain that students must be critical of imprecise writing, but must allow their writing style to come through.

8. Ryan, who won the soccer award last year after recuperating from an extended illness early in the season, went skiing in the Colorado Rockies with his friends.
9. The emergency crew was able to tow away the truck that had burned, since the tires had not been damaged, though no one who saw it thought the truck could be repaired, despite the owner's hopes to the contrary, which probably reflected an understandable lack of perspective.
10. Ben Jonson wrote one of his most famous poems to commemorate the death of his seven-year-old son, who died after he became a victim of the plague in 1603, and this loss was deeply mourned by the father, who considered his son his "best piece of poetry."

AVOIDING WORDINESS

A sentence containing unnecessary words is usually hard to read because the extra words obscure the meaning. Consider the following sentence.

> The world is full of both advantages and disadvantages, and for every advantage that we enjoy we have to compensate for it by accepting some disadvantage at the same time.

Now read a sentence by Ralph Waldo Emerson in which the same idea is expressed more concisely.

> Every advantage has its tax.

You can correct wordiness in your writing in two ways: by eliminating repetition and by reducing sentences.

Redundancy One kind of wordiness results from needless repetition. Correct redundancies by deleting words, using pronouns, or rewriting.

Wordy	We thought we had provided an adequate supply of food with enough for everyone to eat.
Revised	We thought we had provided an adequate supply of food.
Wordy	I have chosen a topic that is a frequent topic of debate. My topic is the exploitation of our natural resources.
Revised	I have chosen a topic that is frequently debated today— the exploitation of our natural resources.

406 Writing Handbook

Literature Connection

Students might enjoy reading more of Emerson's concise prose in volumes such as *Essays: First and Second Series,* and his poetry, collected in *Poems.* Encourage them to notice his precise and economical use of words as they read.

Off the Record

You might find amusing Mark Twain's cynical, tongue-in-cheek comment on how he chose the correct word when writing for pay: "I never write *metropolis* for seven cents because I can get the same price for *city.* I never write *policeman* because I can get the same money for *cop.*"

Wordiness can result from using several words instead of one.

Wordy *At the present time* she thinks that she will be able to join us, but since her schedule may change, she cannot be certain until *a later point in time.*

Revised Now she thinks that she will be able to join us, but since her schedule may change, she can't be certain yet.

Sentence Reduction Sometimes you need to reduce a sentence to avoid wordiness. At other times you may want to reduce one for stylistic reasons. You can often convert wordy sentences into shorter ones in one of three ways:

1. Change a clause to a phrase.
2. Change a clause to an appositive.
3. Change a phrase to a single modifier.

Clause *When pajamas were brought from India to England,* they caused a tremendous sensation.

Phrase *Bringing pajamas from India to England* caused a tremendous sensation.

Clause My cousin Leslie likes to hear me tell "The Three Bears," *which is a favorite story of many children.*

Appositive My cousin Leslie likes to hear me tell "The Three Bears," *a favorite story of many children.*

Phrase One of the *players on the team that represents Detroit* was hurt badly.

Modifier One of the *Detroit players* was hurt badly.

If the clauses of a compound sentence have the same subject, you can reduce the sentence by changing it to a simple sentence with a compound predicate. If, on the other hand, the clauses of a compound sentence have the same verb, you can reduce the sentence by using a compound subject.

Compound Sentence The quarterback's feeble pass floated lazily, and it was easily intercepted.

Simple Sentence The quarterback's feeble pass floated lazily and was easily intercepted.

Compound Sentence All the cups of the new china set shattered upon falling, and the saucers shattered too.

Simple Sentence All the cups and saucers of the new china set shattered upon falling.

Improving Your
Sentences   **407**

Springboard

Read aloud this quotation by Thomas Jefferson: "The most valuable of all talents is that of never using two words when one will do." Have students discuss how this talent might be useful in other fields besides literature, such as politics and advertising.

A. Answers may vary. Possible responses include the following.

1. Humans have been trying to predict the weather with accuracy for many years.

2. More than three hundred years ago, people believed that they would be able to predict changes in patterns of weather.

3. The thermometer was invented in 1593, and a simple barometer in 1643.

4. With these two instruments, humans were able to measure temperature and air pressure.

5. In 1686, the English astronomer Edmund Halley made the first weather map.

6. Weather maps of the early 1800's showed how weather systems moved with the prevailing winds.

7. At that time scientists could predict approaching storms but could not warn people of them.

8. Because radio and television had not been invented at that time, reports of weather observations were sent by mail.

9. Unfortunately, the storms often arrived before the mail.

10. Now we have better methods of forecasting and relaying weather information.

B. Answers may vary. Following is a typical response.

On May 25, 1981, Dan Goodwin dressed in a Spiderman costume and set off to climb Sears Tower in Chicago, the world's tallest building. Dan used a homemade claw and suction cups to climb the 110-story building. His stunt violated city trespassing laws; officials were not amused. As Goodwin was climbing, firefighters were lowered from the top of the building in an attempt to stop him. He evaded them successfully, and when he reached the top, he was arrested.

Practice Your Skills

A. Rewrite the following sentences, eliminating wordiness.

1. The activity of weather forecasting is not new, for humans have been trying or attempting to predict the weather correctly with accuracy for many years.

2. Three hundred years ago, people believed that with confidence that they would be able to predict changes in patterns of weather.

3. In 1593 the thermometer had been invented, and less than a hundred years later a simple barometer was invented in 1643.

4. With these two instruments, which measured temperature and which measured air pressure, humans were able to tell how cold the air was and how heavy the air was that they were measuring.

5. In the year 1686, the Englishman Edmund Halley, who was an English astronomer, made the first weather map in existence.

6. Weather maps of the early 1800's showed weather systems, and those maps showed and indicated that the weather systems moved with the prevailing winds.

7. At that time scientists could predict the approach of storms, but scientists could not warn people about the approaching storms.

8. Because there was no radio or television available or possible at that time, reports of weather observations were then sent by mail through the postal system.

9. Unfortunately, the storms often arrived, as luck would have it, before the mail had a chance to arrive.

10. Now, we have better and more accurate methods of forecasting weather, and we have better methods of relaying our weather forecast information.

B. Rewrite the following paragraph. Avoid wordiness by eliminating redundancies and reducing overloaded sentences.

On May 25, 1981, Dan Goodwin dressed in a Spiderman suit, which he wore as a costume, and set off to climb Sears Tower in Chicago, the city which is on Lake Michigan, and which is also the tallest of the world's tall buildings, or skyscrapers. Dan used a homemade claw and cups that had a suction capacity to climb the 110-story building, and officials were not amused, and Dan's stunt or process of climbing violated city laws which prohibited trespassing. As Goodwin was climbing the skyscraper, people who were permanent employees of the fire department were lowered from the top of the building in an attempt to stop him, but he evaded them successfully, and when Dan Goodwin finally reached the top of the Sears Tower, he was arrested and taken into police custody.

Mathematics Connection

Point out to students that mathematics is one of the most precise disciplines. Have students find examples of mathematical formulae in their math textbooks and rewrite them in words. They can then have classmates try to determine the concise statement of the formulae in mathematical symbols and rewrite them correctly.

PREVENTING AWKWARD BEGINNINGS

Just as first impressions are difficult to alter, it is hard to regain the attention of a reader who has been bored by a weak beginning.

WRITER TO WRITER

Fiction writing is very seldom a matter of saying things; it is a matter of showing things.

Flannery O'Connor, short story writer and novelist

A less skillful writer than Flannery O'Connor might have begun the sentence above with *It is a commonly recognized fact that* or *In my opinion.* Avoid beginning sentences with phrases that unnecessarily delay expressing the main ideas. The most common of such phrases are *the fact that, due to the fact that, what I believe is, in my opinion,* and *the reason is.* Also be careful of overusing phrases such as *there are* and *here is,* which are often unnecessary.

Study these solutions to the problem of awkward beginnings.

Awkward	There are many useful experiments being conducted at the University of Michigan.
Revised	Many useful experiments are being conducted at the University of Michigan.
Awkward	Due to the fact that Joan's injury is serious, she was unable to compete in the race.
Revised	Because Joan's injury was serious, she was unable to compete in the race.
Revised	Joan's injury was serious, so she was unable to compete in the race.

Practice Your Skills

Rewrite the following sentences to avoid awkward beginnings.

1. What a waterfall is, is a sudden and steep descent of a stream or river from one level to another.
2. The reason that a waterfall exists is because the soft rock of the stream bottom has worn away, and the water plunges over the ledge of hard rock that remains.

ANSWERS TO PRACTICE YOUR SKILLS

Revised sentences should begin as follows.
1. A waterfall is a . . .
2. A waterfall exists because . . .

Improving Your
Sentences   **409**

3. A small volume of falling water . . .
4. Niagara Falls is one of the . . .
5. Niagara's fame can be . . .
6. At least twelve cataracts in North America are . . .
7. The drop of Ribbon Falls . . .
8. Six waterfalls in Yosemite alone are . . .
9. At least fourteen other cataracts in the world are . . .
10. Angel Falls in Venezuela . . .

3. What a small volume of falling water is called is a cascade, while a large volume of falling water is called a cataract.
4. There is Niagara Falls, one of the most spectacular cataracts in the world, but this is due to the volume of water and not the depth of the drop.
5. In my opinion, Niagara's fame can be partially attributed to the daredevils who have attempted death-defying stunts there.
6. The fact of the matter is that there are at least twelve cataracts in North America that are higher than Niagara Falls.
7. What I want to point out is that the drop of Ribbon Falls in Yosemite, California, is almost twice as steep as that of Niagara.
8. In point of fact, there are six waterfalls in Yosemite alone that are higher than Niagara Falls.
9. Then, too, it should also be recognized that there are at least fourteen other cataracts in the world higher than Niagara Falls.
10. You can believe it when I tell you that Angel Falls in Venezuela has a total drop of 3,212 feet, while Tugela Falls in South Africa has a total drop of 2,014 feet.

LINKING SENTENCE PARTS

Anyone reading your writing has certain expectations because of the way you have constructed your sentences. If your sentence parts are not linked correctly, your sentences will be awkward or difficult to understand.

Parallel Sentence Parts Parts of a sentence that have parallel meanings should be parallel in structure. When *and* is used to join sentence parts of equal value, such as noun and noun, verb and verb, or phrase and phrase, the constructions are said to be **parallel.** One error in parallel structure occurs when *and* is used to join unequal constructions.

Not Parallel   I like *football, soccer,* and *playing softball.* (two nouns and a gerund)

Parallel   I like *football, soccer,* and *softball.* (three nouns)

A particular type of faulty parallelism occurs with *which* and *who*. *And* should never appear before these words unless *which* or *who* appears earlier in the sentence.

Incorrect   Shanghai, China, one of the world's largest cities, *and which* has a densely populated city center has a high standard of living by Chinese standards.

Literature Connection

One of the most famous speeches in American history is Martin Luther King's "I Have a Dream" speech. It features several different kinds of parallelism, most markedly parallelism among sentences (each beginning with "I have a dream . . ."). Have students read the speech and discuss why parallelism is particularly effective in oral presentations.

Correct   Shanghai, China, *which* is one of the world's largest cities, *and which* has a densely populated city center, has a high standard of living by Chinese standards.

Related Sentence Parts   Certain sentence parts derive much of their meaning from their relation to each other: subject and verb, verb and complement, the parts of a verb phrase. When these related sentence parts are separated by intervening words, the resulting sentence is confusing. Keep closely related sentence parts together.

Confusing   The Seminoles *were,* after several fierce wars with the U.S. Army, *defeated* and *moved* to reservations. (parts of verb phrase separated)

Revised   After several fierce wars with the U.S. Army, the Seminoles *were defeated* and *were moved to* reservations.

Confusing   In 1970, the U.S. government *awarded* to the Seminoles, as partial compensation for lands taken from their ancestors 150 years earlier, *twelve million dollars.* (verb and direct object separated)

Revised   In 1970, the U.S. government *awarded twelve million dollars* to the Seminoles as partial compensation for lands taken from their ancestors 150 years earlier.

Practice Your Skills

Rewrite the following sentences to make sentence parts parallel or to connect related sentence parts.

1. I sat and watched and was hoping she would not drop the baton.
2. The kneeling chair has an unconventional design and which is quite comfortable was developed in Scandinavia.
3. After we arrived, we took a cab to the train station, had lunch, and were looking at the train schedule.
4. As in a Chagall painting, people had the ability to fly and floating in space.
5. On the trip to Belize, the students were able to try scuba diving and to snorkel.
6. The dog trainer was able, after several classes on heeling and staying, to help Geoffrey control the spaniel.
7. In Rome we bought, as a present for Julia's birthday, a purse.
8. Liane practiced long-distance running, swimming, and the bicycle for the triathlon.
9. New arrivals to San Juan crowd its streets and who search for jobs often live in substandard housing.
10. We were, as the sun set slowly, completely satisfied just to watch.

Improving Your Sentences   **411**

Springboard

Divide the class into two groups to compete at correcting sentences with separated parts. Have each group compose four sentences with each of the following parts separated: subject and verb, verb and complement, verb and direct object, parts of verb phrase. Then groups can exchange their sentences and race to correct the sentences.

Writing Handbook 14:
Presenting and Publishing Your Writing

Objectives

1. To share writing informally
2. To formally publish writing

Handbook Mini-Lessons

For information on topics related to presenting and publishing, see the following mini-lessons.

- Writing Prompts and Writing Decisions, pp. 327–330
- Collaborative Planning, pp. 358–360
- Peer Review and Response, pp. 397–401

Teaching Strategies

Personal Touch

Relate to students an experience you have had sharing and publishing your own work. You may wish to discuss a positive experience or a more troubling one and how you dealt successfully with it.

Presenting and Publishing Your Writing

Through writing, you can teach people, persuade them, make them laugh, or move them to tears. You already know how rewarding it can be to have people read and respond favorably to your work. Until now, though, you may have limited your writing audience to your teachers and closest family and friends. There are many ways, however, for you to expand your audience.

WRITER TO WRITER

What I love about writing is the finished product.

**Victoria Reilly, student
Bethpage, New York**

IDEAS FOR INFORMALLY SHARING YOUR WRITING

You can share your writing at any point during the writing process. Here are some ways to share your writing with others.

Sharing Your Writing in Process

- Have someone sit at your word-processing terminal, reading and responding to what you have written.

- Have someone read your manuscript and comment on it in the margins, and then return it to you.

- Meet with your teacher to discuss a particular piece of writing or your writing portfolio as a whole.

- Form a writing exchange group with friends or classmates. Meet regularly to read and comment on one another's work.

- Keep a portfolio of your writing. When you want to share your work, find there the pieces that you want others to read.

IDEAS FOR PUBLISHING YOUR WRITING

If you feel ready to share your writing with an audience, take steps to get your work published. Here are some options you might consider for self-publication and for formal publication.

Self-Publishing Options

- Make copies of your work to distribute to friends, relatives, classmates, and teachers.
- Present your work orally at speech tournaments or in similar situations.
- Save your work on a computer diskette and give the diskette to others who have access to a computer.
- Write pieces for production or interpretation by a drama club or other fine-arts groups.
- Make a home video or cassette recording of your work.
- Through collaboration with others, create a class anthology, magazine, or newspaper, and distribute it.

Formal Publishing Options: Publishing at Your School

- Submit writing to your school newspaper. Some school papers publish short stories, essays, and poems as well as news stories and features.
- Yearbook editors sometimes need short pieces to accompany photographs of various school activities.
- Your school may publish a literary magazine that contains poems, essays, and short stories by student writers. If not, consider starting one yourself, with a faculty sponsor and a staff of fellow students.
- Give a multi-media presentation of your work at a school assembly or special-interest club meeting.

COMPUTER TIP

If you have access to the necessary software, try experimenting with the layout of your writing. See how various designs can affect the dramatic impact or reading of your work.

Presenting and Publishing **413**

Teaching Tip: Audience

Stress to students that they should consider their audience when thinking of ways to publish their work. Urge them to ask themselves these questions: Whom do I want to reach with my writing? What is the most effective medium with which to reach my audience? Encourage students to think of the various markets and publishing options that might be available to them.

Springboard

Tell students that many famous writers published their first work in unusual ways or had trouble getting published. For example, suspense writer Elmore Leonard received 84 rejections before his first novel was published. Encourage students to look in writers' autobiographies for other examples of unusual first publication experiences.

Manuscript Preparation

For formal publication, you will need to prepare your writing in standard manuscript format. Here are some basic guidelines.

- Type or word-process your piece double-spaced.
- Place your name and the page number in the upper right-hand corner of each page.
- Leave ¾-inch margins all around the page.
- If you have a title for your piece, center it on the top line.
- Keep your pages together with a staple or paper clip at the upper left-hand corner.

There are some variations in manuscript preparation guidelines, so check to find out what your prospective publisher prefers. It is important to follow these guidelines meticulously. Doing so will increase the chances of your manuscript being given adequate consideration and even being accepted for publication.

414 Writing Handbook

Art Connection

Show students, or have students bring in, magazines with unusual and eyecatching layout and design. Discuss with them how layout and design appeal to specific audiences and how they work to move the eye through the magazine.

Beyond manuscript preparation, you may be interested in designing your own work, that is, doing your own layout and graphic design. **Layout** is the process of preparing a printed page in which you divide the page into carefully measured columns and indicate space for pictures and art. **Graphic design** is the art of designing a printed page. A graphic designer makes decisions about layouts, typefaces, borders, art, photographs, and graphic elements such as symbols and bars. Some computer programs make it possible for writers to experiment with various graphic elements and influence the way their work will look on the page. Consult your local computer dealer or the manuals for the software programs to which you have access for further information about how you can design and style the look of your writing.

Practice Your Skills

A. Think of an idea for a short story or a nonfiction article. Choose a local newspaper or a magazine to which you'd like to submit the piece and find out what specific guidelines the publisher requires writers to follow. Write your piece, prepare a final copy following the guidelines, and mail it to the appropriate office.

B. Working with your classmates, publish a newsletter of students' stories, essays, poems, and dramatic sketches. First, develop a design for your newsletter; decide on its overall size, the size of its margins, the number and width of the columns, whether it will have photos or illustrations and other graphic features. Collect writing from classmates typed to fit your column sizes, and then cut and paste the writing onto pieces of paper. Also paste up artwork to accompany the writing. Finally, make copies of your finished newsletter and distribute them.

Presenting and
Publishing   **415**

Sketchbook

Objective

To use a cartoon as a springboard to informal writing

Using the Prompt

Be sure students understand that the writing activities suggested in the Sketchbooks were designed to be informal in order to allow risk taking and experimentation and will not be graded.

Focus students' attention on the shoes the man is wearing in the cartoon. What makes them funny? In what way are the shoes a humorously jarring or incongruous element? What do the shoes suggest about the wearer? Then ask students what is meant by "personal style." Most students will probably recognize "personal style" as the special way individuals do things—the way individuals reflect their personalities and ideas through such things as behavior, dress, and decorating. Ask students to characterize the personal style of the man in the cartoon.

Have students make quick lists of ways of talking, dressing, and acting that make them different from others. Then ask them to develop their ideas into short descriptions. Encourage them to use language in ways that "show" their style rather than "tell" about it.

Ideas in the Additional Sketches section can be used as alternatives if some students find these ideas a better starting point.

Encourage students to keep their writing in their Writing Portfolios. They may wish to use some of the ideas they have developed in later writing.

416

Sketchbook

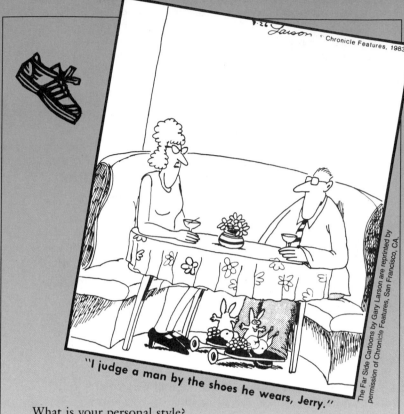

"I judge a man by the shoes he wears, Jerry."

The Far Side Cartoons by Gary Larson are reprinted by permission of Chronicle Features, San Francisco, CA.

What is your personal style?

Additional Sketches

Can you remember a time when something you said was completely misunderstood? Tell about the experience.

Think of a person whose style you admire. You could select a writer, actor, musician, artist, or someone from any walk of life. Why does this person's style appeal to you?

416

Understanding Voice and Style

No two people use language in exactly the same way. A given writer or speaker's particular way of using language is known as his or her **style.** Writers often find that the more they write, the stronger and more distinctive their writing style becomes. Most professional writers have developed styles that are as distinct and recognizable as their signatures.

WRITER TO WRITER

Interest and style vary between people, just as much as people themselves vary.

**Alison Elgin, student
Seattle, Washington**

YOUR UNIQUE STYLE

The following elements work together to create a writing style. To develop a style that is distinctly your own, you need to make choices about how you want these elements to work in your writing. Of course, you may make different choices with each piece of writing, depending on your audience and purpose. However, your individual writing style will be the basis of every set of decisions.

Sentence Structure Certain aspects of sentence structure help define the style of each piece of your writing. Will you write short, simple sentences or long ones with several phrases and clauses? Will the verb always follow the subject or will you vary the sentence structure?

Diction Your diction, or word choice, greatly affects your writing style. In some circumstances—and for some audiences—common, general words like *brave* or *dog* are most appropriate. In other situations, precise words like *intrepid* or *terrier* are best. If your diction is good, you'll consistently choose strong nouns and verbs rather than modifiers, and you'll avoid redundancy, jargon, and clichés.

Imagery The way you use images or descriptive pictures affects the style of your writing. Will you describe things in a direct, literal way? Or will you draw on figures of speech to color your descriptions?

COMPUTER TIP

If your word-processing program has a thesaurus, it will help you choose the best word by offering you a list of synonyms. Choose the synonym that is most appropriate for your context and the voice you have chosen.

Voice and Style   **417**

Writing Handbook 15:
Understanding Voice and Style

Objectives

1. To understand the components of style
2. To understand and choose different voices

Handbook Mini-Lessons

For information on topics related to understanding voice and style, see the following mini-lessons.
- Improving Your Sentences, pp. 402–411
- Creating Emphasis, Tone, and Mood, pp. 423–428
- Varieties of Language, pp. 429–433
- Examining Point of View, pp. 446–451

Teaching Strategies

Teaching Tip: Figures of Speech

Remind students of the various figures of speech they can use to create imagery, such as simile, metaphor, and personification. Refer to Writing Handbook 18, pages 434–438, for more information on figures of speech.

Mechanics Will you use exclamation points often in your composition? Are you fond of the dash? The way you use punctuation is also part of your writing style.

Tone What is your attitude toward the subject you are writing about? Sympathetic? Curious? Lighthearted? Ironic? Outraged? The way you feel about your subject influences the language you use and sets the tone of your writing.

Voice Voice is the individual "sound" of your writing, closely interwoven with all the previously mentioned elements of style. Note how the author's voice comes through even in the following paragraph about iguanas.

PROFESSIONAL
M O D E L

> They stare at the surf, beneath which their pastures of algae are now buried by the risen tide. They shift their positions as the sun shifts, as their bodies warm, and seldom otherwise move. I want to see them swim. But they don't oblige. Occasionally the big male bobs his head, a quick series of three or four jerky nods that seem to say: *Believe it, Jack, I'm the baddest dude on this piece of beach.*
>
> **David Quammen, *The Flight of the Iguana***

Together, Quammen's varied sentence structure, precise language, evocative imagery, humorous slang, and lighthearted tone contribute to the voice of the paragraph.

YOUR UNIQUE VOICE

Writing is like having your own private canyon in New Mexico where you can go to be alone with your thoughts, to shout your ideas and feelings without inhibition, and then to listen to their echoes. Writing allows you to hear yourself clearly and to recognize your own uniqueness. Discover your true voice in your writing and see what makes it different from anyone else's. The following guidelines will help you assert your individual voice in your writing.

Write for yourself. When you write without thinking about an audience, you are not tempted to change your voice to impress other people. The voice that emerges is your own. Write often just for yourself. Journal writing is an excellent vehicle for this.

418 Writing Handbook

Literature Connection

Students might enjoy seeing an unusual use of mechanics by reading the poetry of e.e. cummings. Urge them to notice how the poet's unconventional use of capitalization and punctuation affects the tone and meaning of the poems.

Write about things you care about. If you feel passionately about your subject, your caring will be evident in your voice. Even when your choice of writing topics is limited, you can usually find some part of the topic that you care about.

Use everyday language. Don't upgrade your vocabulary to impress your audience. Avoid the fifty-cent word when a nickel word will convey your meaning just as well. Try to capture the flavor of your own conversational tone.

Delete superfluous words. Many deadwood expressions and wordy phrases can be whittled down for more effective writing. For example, you can change phrases such as the following to make your prose clear and precise.

make an attempt to	>	*try*
in a hasty manner	>	*hastily*
owing to the fact that	>	*because*
gain an understanding of	>	*understand*

Read your work aloud. The best way to hear how your writing voice sounds is to read your words aloud. Revise passages that sound silly, wooden, or phony. Also replace words or phrases that are difficult to pronounce aloud with language that can be spoken smoothly.

Use other writers' voices. You can actually develop your own style of writing by imitating other writers' voices. Try imitating writers whose styles you admire. You'll soon be integrating the elements you feel most comfortable with into your own work.

CHOOSING DIFFERENT VOICES

Inevitably, your style will change to suit the purpose of each piece of writing you do. You must find the most appropriate stylistic options in every writing circumstance. In some writing situations, for example, you may need to choose a voice other than your own or to use a voice that exaggerates some of the characteristics of your own voice. If you were writing a poem about a young child, you might choose to speak in the child's voice, using short sentences and simple vocabulary. You might also use nonstandard speech to present your child speaker realistically. On the other hand, if you were writing a scientific report, you might decide to use careful, precise language and an objective tone to reflect the seriousness and reliability of your content.

—TIP—

Tape-record your ideas before writing to help you retain some of the natural elements of your spoken language.

Voice and Style   **419**

 Individualizing Instruction

LEP Students   LEP students might benefit from reading their work aloud to other students. Classmates can listen to be sure they've used language correctly and in a way that sounds smooth and natural.

Springboard

Challenge your students to pick authors with well-known and easily imitated styles, such as Ernest Hemingway or Emily Dickinson, and write a brief description of a place in the style of the author they choose. A panel of student judges can then decide which description is the most like the style of the original. The judges should identify the stylistic criteria they used.

As you read the following two passages by E.B. White, listen to the two different voices of the writer. Both passages are descriptions of summer, but one comes from a book White wrote for children, and the other comes from an essay he wrote for adults.

LITERARY

M O D E L

> The early summer days on a farm are the happiest, fairest days of the year. Lilacs bloom and make the air sweet, and then fade. Apple blossoms come with lilacs, and the bees visit around among the apple trees. The days grow warm and soft. School ends, and children have time to play and to fish for trouts in the brook. Avery often brought a trout home in his pocket, warm and stiff and ready to be fried for supper. . . .
>
> In early summer there are plenty of things for a child to eat and drink and suck and chew. Dandelion stems are full of milk, clover heads are loaded with nectar, the Frigidaire is full of ice-cold drinks. Everywhere you look is life; even the little ball of spit on the weed stalk, if you poke it apart, has a green worm inside it. And on the underside of the leaf of the potato vine are the bright orange eggs of the potato bug.
>
> **E.B. White, *Charlotte's Web***

LITERARY

M O D E L

> Summertime, oh, summertime, pattern of life indelible, the pasture with the sweet fern and the juniper forever and ever, summer without end; this was the background and the life along the shore was the design, the cottages with their innocent and tranquil design, their tiny docks with the flagpole and the American flag floating against the white clouds in the blue sky, the little paths over the roots of the trees leading from camp to camp and the paths leading back to the outhouses and the can of lime for sprinkling, and at the souvenir counters at the store the miniature birch-bark canoes and the postcards that showed things looking a little better than they looked.
>
> **E.B. White, "Once More to the Lake"**

In *Charlotte's Web,* White uses short, simple sentences; monosyllabic, familiar words; and concrete images. In "Once More to the Lake," he uses a very long, complex sentence; less common words; and poetic images. By modifying various stylistic elements in each passage, White adapts his voice to his audience.

420 Writing Handbook

Literature Connection

E.B. White (1899–1985) was a humorist who wrote for the *New Yorker, Harper's,* and other magazines. He was also known for his essays, his book on writing style, *Elements of Style,* and his children's books, among which are *Charlotte's Web* and *Stuart Little*. Remind students that White wrote humorous works for both adults and children. Challenge interested students to compare and contrast two humorous passages from White's work and to make a generalization about the way White's voice and style contribute to the humor.

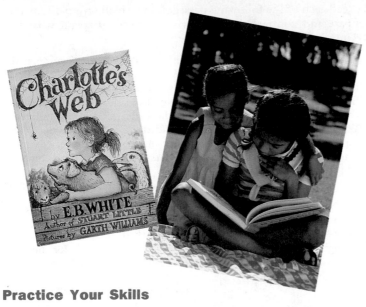

Practice Your Skills

A. Read each of the following passages. Consider the sentence structure, diction, imagery, mechanics, and tone of each. Write a paragraph comparing and contrasting the two writers' styles.

1.   To an anomalous species of terror I found him a bounden slave. "I shall perish," said he, "I must perish in this deplorable folly. Thus, thus, and not otherwise, shall I be lost. I dread the events of the future, not in themselves, but in their results. I shudder at the thought of any, even the most trivial, incident, which may operate upon this intolerable agitation of the soul. I have, indeed, no abhorrence of danger, except in its absolute effect—in terror. In this unnerved—in this pitiable condition—I feel that the period will sooner or later arrive when I must abandon life and reason together, in some struggle with the grim phantasm, FEAR."

         Edgar Allan Poe, *The Fall of the House of Usher*

2.   The woman of Pablo could feel her rage changing to sorrow and to a feeling of the thwarting of all hope and promise. She knew this feeling from when she was a girl and she knew the things that caused it all through her life. It came now suddenly and she put it away from her and would not let it touch her, neither her nor the Republic, and she said, "Now we will eat. Serve the bowls from the pot, Maria."   **Ernest Hemingway, *For Whom the Bell Tolls***

B. Answers will vary. Students should note that Amy Tan's voice is that of a grown woman looking back with nostalgia and perhaps regret; Garrison Keillor's is straightforward and humorously self-mocking; and Jane Austen's is formal and complex.

Additional Resources
- Writing Resource Book, pp. 29–30
- Writing About Literature

B. Read each of the following passages. In a small-group discussion, compare and contrast the three writers' voices. Explain what you like most about each writer's voice.

1. My life changed completely when I was twelve, the summer the heavy rains came. The Fen River which ran through the middle of my family's land flooded the plains. It destroyed all the wheat my family had planted that year and made the land useless for years to come. Even our house on top of the little hill became unlivable. When we came down from the second story, we saw the floors and furniture were covered with sticky mud. The courtyards were littered with uprooted trees, broken bits of walls, and dead chickens. We were so poor in all this mess.

    Amy Tan, *The Joy Luck Club*

2. Nobody in this family lies in the sun. You work in the sun, you lie in the shade. We don't have air-conditioning, of course. "If you'd work up a little sweat out there, the shade ought to feel good enough for you" is Dad's thinking. Air-conditioning is for the weak and indolent. This isn't the Ritz, you know. Be thankful for a little breeze.

    Garrison Keillor, *Lake Wobegon Days*

3. Elizabeth, however, had never been blind to the impropriety of her father's behaviour as a husband. She had always seen it with pain; but respecting his abilities, and grateful for his affectionate treatment of herself, she endeavoured to forget what she could not overlook, and to banish from her thoughts that continual breach of conjugal obligation and decorum which, in exposing his wife to the contempt of her own children, was so highly reprehensible. But she had never felt so strongly as now, the disadvantages which must attend the children of so unsuitable a marriage, nor ever been so fully aware of the evils arising from so ill-judged a direction of talents; talents which rightly used, might at least have preserved the respectability of his daughters, even if incapable of enlarging the mind of his wife.

    Jane Austen, *Pride and Prejudice*

4. Polly sat for a little time on the side of the bed, crying. Then she dried her eyes and went over to the looking glass. She dipped the end of the towel in the water jug and refreshed her eyes with the cool water. . . . Then she went back to the bed again and sat at the foot. . . . She rested the nape of her neck against the cool iron bedrail and fell into a reverie. There was no longer any perturbation visible on her face.

    James Joyce, "The Boarding House"

422 Writing Handbook

Springboard

Read the students this statement on style from the Roman writer Tacitus: "Style, like the human body, is specially beautiful when the veins are not prominent and the bones cannot be counted." Have students discuss what is meant by the "veins" and "bones," and determine if they agree that style is most beautiful when it does not show.

Creating Emphasis, Tone, and Mood

The process of writing is more than just an intellectual activity. It is an emotional one as well—both for you as a writer and for your audience who shares your artistry. Emphasis, tone, and mood work together to create the emotional impact of all writing.

WRITER TO WRITER

Write your heart out.

Bernard Malamud, fiction writer

EMPHASIS

Good writers have an appreciation for sentence rhythm and an ability to create varied and interesting effects in their writing. **Emphasis** is the special stress given to words and phrases to make them stand out and have an impact on the reader. Good writers avoid relying on exclamation points, underlinings, and words like *very, really,* and *quite* to achieve emphasis.

By changing your syntax, or word order, you can make a whole paragraph or certain parts of it emphatic. You can, for example, repeat important words and phrases or use parallel or varied sentence structure.

Repetition   Repeating words and phrases can create emphasis within a sentence or paragraph. To be effective, repetition must not simply be a lack of variety. Use repetition only when the repeated word underscores an idea you want to emphasize. Notice how the repetition of the word *hunger* serves to unify the following passage. The reader can actually feel the narrator's urgency.

> Hunger stole upon me so slowly that at first I was not aware of what hunger really meant. Hunger had always been more or less at my elbow when I played, but now I began to wake up at night to find hunger standing at my bedside, staring at me gauntly.   **Richard Wright, *Black Boy***

Writing Handbook 16:

Creating Emphasis, Tone, and Mood

Objectives

1. To create emphasis
2. To create tone
3. To create mood

Handbook Mini-Lessons

For information on topics related to creating emphasis, tone and mood, see the following mini-lessons.

- Improving Your Sentences, pp. 402–411
- Understanding Voice and Style, pp. 417–422
- Varieties of Language, pp. 429–433
- Using Poetic Language, pp. 434–438

Teaching Strategies

Motivating

Tell students that in acting classes, students are often given a sentence to say and told to deliver the statement in as many different ways as possible. Have students do this with the statement "I wouldn't do that, if I were you," placing emphasis on both *I*'s, on *that*, on *wouldn't*, and so on. Discuss how the meaning of the sentence changes as it is said with different emphasis.

Parallelism By expressing related concepts in similar structural and grammatical forms, parallelism achieves emphasis. Note how Gwendolyn Brooks uses parallelism and the repetition of phrases to emphasize the importance of ritual at Christmastime.

> The world of Christmas was firm. Certain things were done. Certain things were not done.
>
> **Gwendolyn Brooks, *Report from Part One***

Position One of the simplest ways to achieve emphasis and make your writing more interesting is to change the position of words or phrases. When a modifier is moved to the front of the sentence as shown below, it immediately gains importance.

> Instinctively, I pulled my quilt over my face to stifle a cry of terror. **Nien Cheng, *Life and Death in Shanghai***

A second possibility is to invert a sentence's customary word order; a subject can follow a verb, or a verb can follow an adverb.

> In the high heavens rode a veiled moon, magnified by the mist of an early spring day. **Colette**

Notice how Katherine Mansfield uses this technique successfully in the passage on page 427 of this handbook.

TONE

Tone is the expression of the attitude you have toward the subject of your writing. You communicate tone through your choice and placement of words and the complexity of your sentence structure. The tone of a piece of writing is conveyed through the voice of the narrator, the speaker, or the actual writer.

A list of various tones you can communicate through your writing would be virtually endless. The following box, however, includes a few of the more common ones.

Types of Tone in Writing

formal	amused	admiring	humorous
informal	condescending	bitter	sympathetic
romantic	optimistic	ironic	serious
satirical	critical	pessimistic	cynical

Writing —TIP—

Remember that your tone must remain consistent throughout a piece of writing. During revision, check to be sure that your attitude —or that of your narrator—has not changed.

424 Writing Handbook

I Individualizing Instruction

ESL Students Students for whom English is a second language might find the idea of changing word position confusing, since in many languages word position determines meaning. Work with those students to be sure they understand how words and phrases can be moved in English without changing meaning.

Teaching Tip: Audience

For students to gain a broader understanding of what tones are appropriate for different audiences, have them consider the following audiences: a class of sixth graders; readers of a neighborhood newsletter; readers of an environmental magazine; judges in a funny-anecdote contest; recipient of a love letter. Have them determine which of the boxed tones would be appropriate for each audience and encourage them to suggest other suitable tones.

Literature Connection

Students who want to learn about Gwendolyn Brooks might be interested to know that she is an African-American poet, born in 1917, who won the Pulitzer Prize for poetry in 1950 for her volume *Annie Allen*. She writes of the struggles and dreams of African Americans, often using humor to make her point. Encourage interested students to find a poem by Brooks that appeals to them and analyze how the poet creates emphasis, tone, and mood. Other volumes of her poetry include *The Bean Eaters* and *To Disembark*.

Your audience and writing purpose should help you determine your tone. For research reports, you will want to adopt a fairly objective or scientific tone that focuses attention on the content of your writing and allows the reader to make his or her own judgments. For essays and for fiction writing, you can use a more informal, subjective tone.

The following passage from an encyclopedia illustrates the use of objective tone.

> The Indian Meteorological Department recognizes four seasons. . . . In effect, however, there are only three noticeable seasons—the cold season, from about November to the end of February; the hot season (when it can be intensely warm, particularly in central and northern India), from about March to June; and the rainy season, from about June to October, by which time the southwest monsoon expends itself.
>
> **Encyclopaedia Britannica**

In contrast, a writer crafting an essay on the same general subject may adopt a highly subjective tone.

> I cannot describe the *oppression* of such afternoons. It is a physical oppression—heat pressing down on me and pressing in the walls and the ceiling and congealing together with time which has stood still and will never move again. And it is not only those two—heat and time—that are laying their weight on me but behind them, or held within them, there is something more which I can only describe as the whole of India.
>
> **Ruth Prawer Jhabvala, *An Experience of India***

In this highly personal account, Ruth Jhabvala expresses a pessimistic attitude toward her adopted land. Her choice of words like *oppression, pressing, congealing, weight,* and phrases like *time which has stood still and will never move again,* leaves no mistake that on afternoons like these, the writer feels oppressed by India—its summers, its past, its present.

Fiction, editorials, magazine articles, biographies, and autobiographies are usually written with an identifiable tone that can range from sarcastic and critical to admiring and even lighthearted. The author's diction provides the most important clue to tone.

For example, if you describe the chemistry laboratory of your school as "bursting with creative energy," you are conveying a positive, enthusiastic tone. On the other hand, if you describe that same classroom as "disorganized and chaotic," your tone becomes critical and disapproving.

Emphasis, Tone, and Mood **425**

Literature Connection

Students might be interested in reading one of Ruth Prawler Jhabvala's novels about India, such as *Heat and Dust,* which was made into a successful motion picture.

MOOD

While tone is the deliberate stance the writer takes toward the subject of his or her writing, mood is the overall climate of feeling or emotional setting a writer creates as a backdrop for the action.

Mary Shelley creates a powerful mood in the following excerpt from her novel *Frankenstein*. Read the passage slowly, and consider how it makes you feel.

> It was on a dreary night of November that I beheld the accomplishment of my toils. With an anxiety that almost amounted to agony, I collected the instruments of life around me, that I might infuse a spark of being into the lifeless thing that lay at my feet. It was already one in the morning; the rain pattered dismally against the panes, and my candle was nearly burnt out, when, by the glimmer of the half-extinguished light, I saw the dull yellow eye of the creature open; it breathed hard, and a convulsive motion agitated its limbs.
>
> **Mary Shelley, *Frankenstein***

Shelley creates a mood of gloom, horror, and suspense with words and phrases such as *dreary night, lifeless thing, pattered dismally, dull yellow eye,* and *convulsive motion.* She chooses words whose connotations will evoke these feelings in her audience.

A writer's diction affects both tone and mood. Word choice, details, images, figurative language, and repetition all contribute to the mood of a piece of writing; these elements invite the reader to participate in the moment, to become part of a scene, and to feel the same feelings. Notice how strong adjectives determine the melancholy mood of the following paragraph.

426 Writing Handbook

Critical Thinking

Classifying Students might have difficulty differentiating between mood and tone. Read aloud the excerpt from *Frankenstein* to the class and discuss the deliberate word choices and other elements of diction that determine its mood. Then have students discuss the tone of the piece. Remind them that *tone* is synonymous with *attitude*: the author's attitude toward the reader, in this case. Is it formal or informal? Romantic? Bitter? Despairing? Encourage students to think about the persona of the narrator and about the author's purpose in writing as they discuss the tone.

Art Connection

Point out to students that works of art also convey mood, just as writing does. Show students reproductions of paintings by artists such as Rembrandt, Picasso, Van Gogh, and Turner, and have them determine the mood of each painting. Ask them if they can identify specific elements or aspects of the artist's style that contribute to the mood.

There was a cold bitter taste in the air, and the new-lighted lamps looked sad. Sad were the lights in the houses opposite. Dimly they burned as if regretting something. And people hurried by, hidden by their hateful umbrellas.

Katherine Mansfield, "A Cup of Tea"

Practice Your Skills

A. Identify the tone and mood and any devices used for emphasis in the following passages. How effective is the use of each device?

1.   It was a beautiful college. The vines and the roads gracefully winding, lined with hedges and wild roses that dazzled the eyes in the summer sun. Honeysuckle and purple wisteria hung heavy from the trees. . . . I've recalled it often . . . How the grass turned green in the springtime and how the mocking birds . . . sang, how the moon shone down on the buildings, how the bell in the chapel tower rang out the precious, short-lived hours; how the girls in bright summer dresses promenaded the grassy lawn.

Ralph Ellison

2.   Some experts believe that teen-agers' nuclear fears are greater today than at any time since the first atom bombs were dropped on Japan in 1945. One reason is pretty obvious, says Tony Wagner, executive director for Educators for Social Responsibility: Nuclear weapons are more powerful and more numerous than they have ever been before.

Sara E. Lewis

3.   Oh, yes, . . . I know what they all say about our "youthful exuberance"—our music, our clothes, our freedom and energy and go-power. And it's true that, physically, we're strong and energetic, and that we dance and surf and ride around on motorbikes and stay up all night while the parents shake their heads and say "Oh, to be young again. . . ." What sticks in my head, though, is another image. I hear low, barely audible speech, words, breathed out as if by some supreme and nearly superhuman effort, I see limp gestures and sedentary figures. Kids sitting listening to music, sitting rapping, just sitting. Or sleeping—that, most of all. Staying up late, but sleeping in later. We're tired, often more from boredom than exertion, old without being wise, worldly not from seeing the world but from watching it on television.

Joyce Maynard

Emphasis, Tone,
and Mood   **427**

Springboard

Read the first paragraphs of several famous works of fiction aloud. Challenge students to identify the mood created in each and the stylistic elements that create the mood.

4.   Suddenly it all rose in him; it was unbearable. He leaped up into the air, shouting and yelling wild, unrecognizable noises. Then he began to run, not carefully, as he had before, but madly, like a wild thing. He was clean crazy, yelling mad with the joy of living and a superfluity of youth.

Doris Lessing

5.   Then he rose, lightly, and, as always now when he left me, stooped to kiss me. Usually he made stay there by the fire, while he went out into the night, but this time I got up and followed him to the cave entrance, and waited there to watch him go. The light was behind me and my shadow stretched, thin and long. . . . It was almost night, but over beyond Maridunum in the west, a lingering bar of light hinted at the dying sun. It threw a glint on the river skirting the palace wall where I was born, and touched a jewel spark on the distant sea. Near at hand the trees were bare with winter, and the ground crisp with the first frost. Arthur trod away from me across the grass, leaving ghost-prints in the frost. He reached the place where the track led down to the grove, and half turned. I saw him raise a hand.

Mary Stewart

B. Choose one of the passages from exercise A and rewrite it, using a different tone or mood from the original. For example, if the original paragraph has a serious tone, rewrite it with a humorous or ironic one. If the mood is quiet and reminiscent, make it sad or melancholy.

C. Choose a special place in nature or a favorite city street corner. Observe the place carefully at different times of day—in the morning and again at sunset, for example. Write a description contrasting the place at those two times, choosing evocative images and details to establish two different moods.

Varieties of Language

Because communication involves both *what* we say and *how* we say it, good writers understand and draw on all the varieties of English, using them to communicate effectively with different audiences for different purposes. For example, in factual writing such as for reports, you generally would use straightforward, formal language to present ideas clearly to your reader. In narrative writing, on the other hand, you might use different levels of language such as slang and dialect to create vivid and believable characters.

Standard English is language that is acceptable in any writing or speaking situation. It falls into two categories—formal and informal. **Nonstandard English** is language that does not conform to the conventional rules of grammar, usage, and mechanics, and is generally not used in writing.

FORMAL AND INFORMAL

ENGLISH

Formal English This level of language is suitable for serious lectures and speeches, scholarly journals, business reports, legal documents, and textbooks. It has a serious tone and is devoid of contractions and slang. Notice how the use of formal English conveys the serious tone and purpose of the following passage.

> The language we use about war is inappropriate, and its inappropriateness is designed to conceal a reality so odious that we do not wish to know it. The language we use about politics is also inappropriate; but here our mistake has a different purpose.
> **Aldous Huxley, *The Language of War***

Informal English This is the language that is used in casual, everyday circumstances. Also known as **colloquial English,** it is the language of conversation and informal writing and is characterized by a relaxed tone; generally nontechnical, simple words; and use of contractions and sentence fragments. Newspaper and magazine journalists often use informal language, as you can see in the example on the next page.

LITERARY
MODEL

Varieties of
Language   **429**

Varieties of Language

Objectives

1. To distinguish between standard and nonstandard English
2. To identify formal and informal language and use them appropriately in writing
3. To recognize special varieties of language: idioms, slang, euphemisms, clichés, jargon, gobbledygook, and dialect
4. To eliminate inappropriate varieties of language from writing

Handbook Mini-Lessons

For information on topics related to varieties of language, see the following mini-lessons.
- Understanding Voice and Style, pp. 417–422
- Using Poetic Language, pp. 434–438

Teaching Strategies

Motivating

Introduce the lesson by addressing your students in language that is heavily studded with slang expressions current in your school today. Allow students to correct and criticize your use of the slang. Then ask them to describe and explain their reaction to your use of such language. Students will probably express surprise and puzzlement at the very least. Lead them to recognize that they associate this language with conversations among themselves and with contexts other than the classroom. Point out that there are many varieties of English and that each variety or level of the language is appropriate to certain contexts and not to others.

Have students work with partners to identify and list the words and phrases in the excerpt that mark the language as informal. Have students share items from their list with the class and have the class discuss whether each example counts as informal. Students may be surprised to learn that they don't all have the same criteria for what constitutes formal and informal language.

Individualizing Instruction

ESL Students Students whose first language is not English may have trouble understanding and using American idioms. Encourage them to work with other students to become familiar with American idioms. In turn, they can tell their classmates what phrases are idioms in their native language.

PROFESSIONAL
M O D E L

▼

It wasn't an ideal way to study nature. Last month Alvaro Garza, Jr., decided to take a close look at a dead squirrel on a frozen river near his Minnesota home, fell through the ice, and spent 45 minutes submerged. At the time of his rescue he was considered clinically dead, yet within days he was acting like an ordinary kid.　　　　*Newsweek*

SPECIAL LANGUAGE

A writer or speaker can also use special varieties of language such as idioms, slang, euphemisms, clichés, jargon, and gobbledygook to create specific effects. Because these varieties of language can be confusing or inappropriate, they should be used with caution.

Idioms An idiom is a group of words whose intended meaning differs from the literal meanings of the individual words. For instance, in the sentence "After a heated discussion, we voted to *turn down* the proposal," the words *turn down* are an idiom meaning "to veto or decline." Some common idioms are listed below. Avoid using idioms in formal writing or when they may cause confusion, such as when speaking with people from another country.

bottle up [one's] feelings	*in the same boat*
called on the carpet	*lock, stock, and barrel*
good ear	*sitting pretty*

Slang This informal, vivid language is created by a particular group within a culture, becomes popular within that group, and then either passes out of use or becomes part of the standard vocabulary. Expressions such as *groovy, dig* (as in "Can you dig it?"), and *cool cat* were popular in the middle part of this century but have mostly fallen out of use. However, although the word *rap* (meaning "talk"), for example, is of the same vintage as the words *groovy* and *dig,* it has been accepted into general use.

Because of the specialized nature of slang, it is best to consider your audience and your intention before using it. Slang is inappropriate in formal writing, but it is often used in informal conversation and in the dialogue of fiction and drama.

430 Writing Handbook

Music Connection

Have students give examples of current popular songs that use slang and tell what the various slang expressions in the songs mean. You may wish to give the class examples of older songs that use slang, such as Simon and Garfunkel's "Feelin' Groovy" from the 1960's.

Euphemisms Euphemisms are expressions that sound less offensive than the words they replace. For example, *sanitation engineer* is a euphemism for *garbage collector.* You may decide to use a euphemism out of courtesy, but avoid using euphemisms to hide the truth.

Clichés Expressions that have lost their descriptive power through overuse are called **clichés.** Phrases such as *sad but true, pretty as a picture, cold as ice, clear as a bell,* and *chip off the old block* detract from good writing. Replace clichés with fresh, precise words.

W R I T E R   T O   W R I T E R

The difference between the right word and the wrong word is the difference between lightning and a lightning bug.

Mark Twain, American novelist and humorist

Jargon The specialized, technical vocabularies of particular professions or activities are called **jargon.** For example, medical professionals use words such as *infarction, peritonitis,* and *toxin.* Computer operators use words like *mainframe, access, printout, hardware,* and *software.* Such words provide a shortcut to meaning for those within the profession but may confuse others. Unless you define your terms, do not use specialized vocabulary if your audience will not understand it. Study the following example.

Jargon	The plaintiff's legal representative was shocked to learn that her client had brought suit against the company prior to the present litigation.
Standard English	The man's lawyer was shocked to learn that her client had sued the company before.

Gobbledygook Language that is inflated, pretentious, and often intentionally confusing is called **gobbledygook**. It is often found in legal, technical, and business writing and is characterized by overloaded sentences and vague, abstract, uncommon, or technical words.

> In view of the previous and projected voluntary personnel reductioning, we anticipate no unilaterally enforced retirement except under the most compelling circumstances unforeseen at this point in time.

Varieties of
Language   **431**

Avoid gobbledygook by using direct and understandable language such as the following.

Because enough people have resigned, we will not have to lay off anyone.

Dialects A **dialect** is a version of a language that is spoken by people of a particular region or social group. Everyone speaks a particular dialect, and although dialects can differ in vocabulary, pronunciation, and even grammar and punctuation, each is entirely adequate and "correct." Examples of dialects include the Hispanic dialect of English spoken in American cities such as Miami, the dialect spoken by educated people from Great Britain, and the Midland dialect spoken in the American Midwest.

In recent years, widespread education and national media have tended to reduce the differences between regional dialects in the United States. However, differences in regional dialect still remain. In major urban areas distinct English dialects are used by people of different economic, racial, and ethnic backgrounds.

Not only the pronunciations of words, but the words themselves, may vary from dialect to dialect. The lowly earthworm is a good example. In various parts of the United States it is called *angle dog, angleworm, bait worm, dew worm, fish bait, fishing worm, fish worm, mud worm, rain worm*, or *red worm*.

Writers such as William Faulkner used dialect very effectively to evoke the setting of a story and to create vivid, memorable characters. Here is a passage from one of his novels set in the rural South of the 1920's.

LITERARY MODEL

"Is you all seen anything of a quarter down here," Luster said.
"What quarter."
"The one I had here this morning," Luster said. "I lost it somewhere. It fell through this here hole in my pocket. If I dont find it I cant go to the show tonight."
"Where'd you get a quarter . . ."
"Got it at the getting place," Luster said. "Plenty more where that one come from. Only I got to find that one. Is you all found it yet."
"I aint studying no quarter. I got my own business to tend to."
William Faulkner, *The Sound and the Fury*

432 Writing Handbook

Practice Your Skills

A. Below is the first draft of a factual paragraph written in informal English. Identify examples of clichés, slang, idioms, and dialect. Then rewrite the paragraph in formal English.

> There's like about 800 ponies living free, all by themselves, on this fab island called Assateague, somewhere off the coast of Maryland. I'm not putting you on. Every year, the Chincoteague Volunteer Fire Department like herds the ponies across the water to another island, it's called Chincoteague. This way, some of the foals can be sold as pets and the rest of the herd can be checked for illness or injury. And that keeps the population stable so the ponies have enough vittles and water on their island, Assateague. Really it's the Chincoteague Volunteer Fire Department that owns the ponies, like officially. But the ponies be free as the wind on their own island all through the year, except for roundup week at the end of July. After the July roundup, the firemen swim the ponies back to their island for another year of sitting pretty in freedom and protection.

B. Below is a brief glossary of jargon used in the world of the theater. Choose another discipline, such as medicine, law, psychology, or sports, and create a similar glossary of specialized vocabulary used in that field. Then write a paragraph using terms from your list or the list below.

stage left	the actor's left as he or she faces the audience
block	to plan the movement and placement of the actors
mug	overact, especially with facial expressions
cross upstage	to move away from the audience

C. Find some technical or government pamphlets or official regulations in your local library. Among these publications, you should be able to find examples of gobbledygook. Copy them, and then rewrite them in simple, straightforward English.

Varieties of Language **433**

ANSWERS TO PRACTICE YOUR SKILLS

A. Answers will vary. Students should note the following examples: "there's" (should be "there are")—informal; "like about"—slang; "all by themselves"—idiom; "fab"—slang; "somewheres"—dialect; "I'm not putting you on"—idiom; "like"—slang; "it's called"—informal; "vittles"—dialect; "really"—informal; "like"—slang; "free as the wind"—cliché; "sitting pretty"—idiom.

B. Answers will vary.

C. Answers will vary.

Additional Resources

- Writing Resource Book, pp. 34–35

Springboard

Divide the class into two groups and give each group a dictionary of slang or a list of slang terms from the past. Each student can choose one slang term and use it in a sentence. The other group can then try to determine the meaning of the term from its context.

Using Poetic Language

Objectives

1. To recognize the characteristics and purposes of imagery
2. To identify and use various types of figurative language: metaphor, simile, personification, symbolism, hyperbole, understatement, and synesthesia
3. To recognize various sound devices: rhyme, onomatopoeia, alliteration, assonance, and consonance
4. To use imagery, figurative language, and sound devices in writing

Handbook Mini-Lessons

For information on topics related to using poetic language, see the following mini-lessons.
- Varieties of Language, pp. 429–433
- Developing Your Vocabulary, pp. 457–471

Teaching Strategies

Motivating

Transcribe a stanza from a poem into prosaic language. Then read both versions to students, beginning with the prosaic one. For example:

"I think I know the guy that owns this wooded property. But he lives in town, so he won't see that I've stopped here to look at it snowing in his woods."

Whose woods these are, I think I know.
His house is in the village though;
He will not see me stopping here
To watch his woods fill up with snow.

Discuss which version is more interesting to hear and what elements make it more attractive. Use the discussion to introduce the lesson.

WRITING HANDBOOK **18**

Using Poetic Language

WRITER TO WRITER

I think that to transfuse emotion—not to transmit thought but to set up in the reader's sense a vibration corresponding to what was felt by the writer—is the peculiar function of poetry.

A. E. Housman, poet

Poetry is the oldest form of literature. Long before people learned how to communicate through written symbols, they shared information by chanting it in rhythmic patterns that could be easily remembered. Because of this long tradition, it is not surprising that poets have developed many effective techniques for using language to communicate moods and emotions. You can use these techniques, or **poetic devices,** to enrich your own writing of both poetry and prose.

IMAGERY

As a writer you should attempt to show your readers what you mean rather than just tell them. In other words, your writing is most effective when it vividly creates a concrete experience or picture in your readers' minds. One way you can give your readers this concrete experience is by using images.

An **image** is a representation in words of a sensory experience—a sight, sound, touch, taste, or smell. Collectively, the images used by a writer are called **imagery.** As the poet Archibald MacLeish eloquently exemplified in his poem "Ars Poetica," the way to enable readers to feel an emotion—in this case, grief—is to present them with images that evoke that feeling.

For all the history of grief an empty doorway and a leaf.
Archibald MacLeish, "Ars Poetica"

Now suppose you read the following sentence in an essay about the Okefenokee Swamp.

I assumed that hiking across the swamp would be difficult.

434 Writing Handbook

This statement doesn't give readers enough sensory information to engage their imaginations and enable them to re-create the difficult experience. Compare the following passage.

> I had imagined that five days of slogging across the Okefenokee Swamp would offer such heights of discomfort and travail that the experience would be exhilarating for its pure intensity. Tangled vegetation, oppressive heat, no solid ground for miles, fetid water, biting insects, ten thousand alligators, and the continent's foremost selection of poisonous snakes— that sort of thing. I had to put it to Red like one of those old recruiting ads for the Peace Corps: "Bad pay and long hours, but at least you'll be hungry and in danger."
>
> **David Quammen, "Swamp Odyssey"**

The second passage provides many sensory details and images that allow the reader to form a lively picture of the swamp—insects, poisonous snakes, and all.

FIGURATIVE LANGUAGE

As you have seen, one way to create a powerful experience for a reader is to use sensory language, or imagery. Another way is to use **figurative language,** language that evokes associations that go beyond the literal meaning of the words. Some specific types of figurative language are **simile, metaphor, personification, symbolism, hyperbole, understatement,** and **synesthesia.**

Simile   A simile is a comparison using the words **like** or **as** that enriches the reader's understanding. Consider the following line by the novelist Joseph Conrad.

> The mysterious East faced me, perfumed like a flower, silent like death, dark like a grave.   **Joseph Conrad, "Youth"**

Notice how, by using three similes, Conrad provides a concrete sensory experience of the East in a single sentence.

Metaphor   Like a simile, a metaphor also compares something with something else that is concrete and familiar. However, it merely implies the comparison, rather than stating it explicitly through the use of the words *like* and *as*. In the following passage, the main character in a play describes the play and its setting to the audience before the action begins, using two metaphors.

Teaching Tip: Clichés

Point out to students that many similes are used so much in everyday speech that they have become clichés, and no longer provide a powerful image for the reader. Examples include "cool as a cucumber" and "pretty as a picture." Have students give examples of other such overused similes and encourage discussion of similes that may work better.

Poetic Language   **435**

Literature Connection

The Polish-born twentieth-century novelist Joseph Conrad wrote exclusively in English, using an extremely rich poetic language. You might suggest that students read his short novel *Heart of Darkness,* paying special attention to his language. Ask them to collect examples of each of the types of figurative language mentioned here.

If everything goes well for me tonight, this should be a
waltz, one-two-three, one-two-three; a no-holds-barred romantic story, and since I'm not a romantic type, I'm going to
need the whole valentine here to help me: the woods, the
willows, the vines, the moonlight, the band.

Lanford Wilson, *Talley's Folly*

By comparing the story to a waltz and the sets to a valentine, the
character helps to create a romantic mood for the action that will
follow in the play.

Personification Writers often provide an additional dimension to
their readers' experience by using **personification,** the attribution of
human qualities to animals or inanimate objects. Notice how the
poet Shelley uses personification to convey the desolate sound of
the wind.

Rough wind, that moanest loud
    Grief too sad for song **Percy Bysshe Shelley, "A Dirge"**

Symbolism A word functions as a **symbol** when it is used to
indicate not only its usual referent, but also something quite
different. Some symbols have traditional associations. For example,
the word *flag* refers not only to a cloth banner, but it also
symbolizes the country that flies it. Other conventional symbols
include a circle—perfection; the sun—power or reason; greenery—
youth; winter—old age; and a road—the path of life. For example,
when Walt Whitman used the symbol of the "ship of state" in his
poem "O Captain! My Captain!" readers knew that the poem was
actually referring to the ship of the United States and its lost
captain, Abraham Lincoln.

Writers can also create their own associations between unlike
things, establishing **personal symbols.** For example, notice in the
following lines how the poet Dylan Thomas uses opposing symbols
—both conventional and personal—to express a basic paradox of
human experience.

Time held me green and dying
Though I sang in my chains like the sea.

Dylan Thomas, "Fern Hill"

The conventional symbol for youth and life—greenery—is
combined with its opposite—death, and the personal symbol—the
sea—both sings freely and is chained. These powerful symbols
convey Thomas's deep understanding of the mingled joy and
despair of life.

Writing
──TIP──

You can use sym-
bols as the frame-
work of an entire
work, as Herman
Melville did in
Moby-Dick, or as a
way of supporting
a single point in
your writing.

Critical Thinking

Analyzing Point out to students that writers often use symbols for the most important of life's themes: love and death. Have
them think of symbols other writers have
used for these experiences, such as a river
(Byron) or a rose (Wordsworth) for love, or
the evening (Eliot) or a crown of yewberries
(Keats) for death. Discuss with students
how effectively these objects symbolize
love and death.

Literature Connection

For an extreme example of personification,
students might enjoy reading George Orwell's
Animal Farm. Encourage them to note which
human characteristics have been given to each
animal in the novel and to explore the author's
purpose in personifying the animals as he does.

Hyperbole The word *hyperbole* is derived from the Greek word meaning "excess." It denotes the use of exaggeration to say something in a highly dramatic way that captures the reader's attention. For example, the writer Constance Urdang uses hyperbole in the lines "Papa's got a job in a miracle factory . . . in an old building taller than God." Notice that the hyperbole establishes a dramatic contrast between an ordinary, man-made object, a building, and the boundlessness and otherness of God.

Understatement Writers often use understatement, the opposite of hyperbole, for comic effect. For example, in James Goldman's play *The Lion in Winter,* King Henry II of England is threatening to disown his sons, who are conspiring for the throne, and to have his wife put to death. In a masterful example of understatement, Queen Eleanor sums up the situation: "Well, what family doesn't have its ups and downs?"

Synesthesia In using this type of figurative language, writers describe a sensory experience as if it were perceived through another sense. For example, people often describe a painter's colors—a visual experience—in auditory terms—as clashing or loud. The following lines from William Blake's poem, "London," use synesthesia to describe an auditory phenomenon—a soldier's sigh—in visual terms: "And the hapless soldier's sigh/Runs in blood down palace walls."

SOUND DEVICES

In addition to imagery and figurative language, you can use the sounds of words to make your writing lyrical and to reinforce an idea, create a mood, or express a theme. These sound devices include **rhyme, onomatopoeia, alliteration, assonance,** and **consonance.** Since these poetic devices are used mainly to create special effects, use them judiciously in your prose writing.

Rhyme This common sound device involves the repetition of syllables with the same consonant and vowel sounds. Writers usually use this repetition at the end of a line of poetry for maximum effect. Notice how rhyme enhances these lines in the modern English rendering of Chaucer's *The Canterbury Tales:* "When in April the sweet showers fall/And pierce the drought of March to the root, and all/The veins are bathed in liquor of such power/As brings about the engendering of the flower. . . ."

Poetic Language **437**

Onomatopoeia When writers use a word with a sound that suggests its meaning, they are using **onomatopoeia.** For example, in the sentence "The telephone wires *whined* a reply," the word *whined* suggests the actual sound of a whine. Other onomatopoeic words include *crack, hiss, rumble,* and *pop.*

Alliteration Repetition of the initial sounds in words, **alliteration,** lends a musicality and depth to writing. The repeated *s* and *h* sounds create rhythm and lilt in this line: "The **s**ecret **s**ide of the **h**unted **h**eart."

Assonance Repetition of a vowel sound usually preceded and followed by unlike consonant sounds is called **assonance.** The poet Richard Wilbur used assonance to enrich the reader's experience in the following line: "F**oa**m was in upr**oa**r where he dr**o**ve bel**ow**."

Consonance This sound device involves the repetition of a consonant sound internally in words, as in this line by the poet John Keats: "Much ha**v**e I tra**v**eled in the realms of gold."

Practice Your Skills

A. Identify the poetic device used in each example—simile, metaphor, personification, symbolism, hyperbole, understatement, or synesthesia.

1. Because I could not stop for Death—
   He kindly stopped for me—   **Emily Dickinson**
2. Your absence has gone through me
   Like thread through a needle   **W. S. Merwin**
3. A work in progress . . . is a lion you cage in your study.
                                            Annie Dillard

B. Identify the use of rhyme, onomatopoeia, alliteration, assonance, or consonance in the following examples.

1. Give me the splendid silent sun with all his beams
        full dazzling.   **Walt Whitman**
2. Many times man lives and dies
   Between his two eternities.   **William Butler Yeats**
3. My husband and child smiling out of the family photo;
   Their smiles catch onto my skin, little smiling hooks. **Sylvia Plath**

C. Write two paragraphs describing a scene at a carnival. In the first paragraph, create a mood of festivity and frivolity. In the second, create a mood of suspense and horror. Use imagery, figurative language, and sound devices that contribute to each mood.

Literature Connection

   Students might enjoy making a tape recording of poetry that exemplifies the poetic language discussed in the lesson. Have them work in small groups, with each group finding an example of a different poetic device. Students can read their poems chorally, or take turns reading stanzas.

Establishing Sentence Variety

Read the following paragraph, and notice your response to it.

> The community has been divided by politicians' tactics. The campaign has been extremely negative. The commercials have concentrated on name-calling and mudslinging. The climate has been aggressive, and the voters have been the victims. The election has represented a triumph of sensationalism and publicity antics over well-reasoned debate and decision.

The paragraph sounds choppy because the sentences all have the same structure—subject followed by verb. They all begin with *the*. The sentences are correct, but they give the passage no life. The following suggestions will help you avoid this problem.

VARIETY IN SENTENCE OPENERS

When every sentence begins the same way, a paragraph is dull. Avoid beginning too many sentences with a subject followed by a verb. This most common sentence structure is often overused.

Varying Sentence Openers

- **Begin with a subject and verb.**
  Alicia worked conscientiously at the job until evening.
- **Begin with a single-word modifier.**
  Conscientiously, Alicia worked at the job until evening.
- **Begin with one or more prepositional phrases.**
  Until evening, Alicia worked conscientiously at the job.
- **Begin with a participial phrase.**
  Working conscientiously, Alicia stayed at the job.
- **Begin with an appositive.**
  A model employee, Alicia worked at the job until evening.
- **Begin with an infinitive phrase.**
  To finish the job, Alicia worked at it until evening.
- **Begin with a subordinate clause.**
  Since Alicia was determined to finish, she worked conscientiously at the job until evening.

WRITING HANDBOOK 19

COMPUTER TIP

When using a word processor for revisions, try underlining, boldfacing, or otherwise highlighting any sentence you plan to adjust to create more variety.

Objectives

1. To vary sentence openers for greater reader interest
2. To vary sentence structure for variety and flow
3. To vary sentence length to reduce choppiness and monotony

Handbook Mini-Lessons

For information on topics related to sentence variety, see the following mini-lessons.
- Varieties of Language, pp. 429–433
- The Parts of a Sentence, pp. 569–589
- Phrases and Clauses, pp. 591–627

Teaching Strategies

Motivating

Choose a long sentence from a work of literature. (A novel of Henry James would be a good source.) Read the sentence aloud, and ask students to describe the effect of the long sentence on them. Next, choose a passage that contains several short sentences. (The work of Ernest Hemingway provides good examples.) Again, have students describe the effect the shorter sentences had on them.

Practice Your Skills

A. Rewrite the following sentences, beginning each with the form suggested in parentheses.

1. Wanda walked over to the bank in the morning to cash the check. (prepositional phrase)
2. Someone evidently notified the Coast Guard that our boat had not returned. (adverb)
3. The value of gold usually increases when the value of the U.S. dollar decreases. (subordinate clause)
4. Virginia Woolf used the stream-of-consciousness technique to reveal a character's thoughts. (infinitive phrase)
5. John Maynard Keynes was an English economist, and he profoundly influenced economic policy in the United States during the Roosevelt administration. (appositive)

B. Identify the italicized structure as Prepositional Phrase, Participial Phrase, Appositive, Infinitive Phrase, or Subordinate Clause.

1. *Although they lived in style,* they felt always an anxiety in the house.   **D. H. Lawrence**
2. *To judge by the goat and sheep pens,* this was the den of a giant, and this was no mild vegetable-eater.   **Iain Finlayson**
3. *Breathing slowly,* Peter Lake stared at the ceiling.   **Mark Helprin**
4. *One of eleven brothers and sisters,* Harriet was a moody, willful child.   **Langston Hughes**
5. *At daybreak on the next morning* all hands were roused out to weigh anchor.   **W. H. G. Kingston**

VARIETY IN SENTENCE STRUCTURE

Writing is repetitious if too many sentences have the same structure. Basically, there are four different kinds of sentences.

- A **simple sentence** has one independent clause.
- A **compound sentence** has two or more independent clauses.
- A **complex sentence** has one independent clause and one or more subordinate clauses.
- A **compound-complex sentence** has two or more independent clauses and one or more subordinate clauses.

Notice how the overuse of compound sentences in this passage produces a monotonous, singsong rhythm.

> The storm arose without warning, and waves started to bounce our boat around. Herb pulled in the anchor, and I reeled in the lines. It was impossible to get back to the dock, so Herb steered for the point. The wind was behind us, or we never would have made it. We sailed into the beach, and then we jumped into the water and pulled the boat ashore.

You can achieve more variety in sentence structure by applying strategies such as the following.

Varying Sentence Structure

- **Create a simple sentence with a compound predicate.**
  We were delayed by a flat tire and missed the first inning.
- **Create a simple sentence with a participial phrase.**
  Delayed by a flat tire, we missed the first inning.
- **Create a complex sentence with a subordinate clause.**
  Because we were delayed by a flat tire, we missed the first inning.
- **Create a compound-complex sentence with two independent clauses and one or more subordinate clauses.**
  We were delayed because we had a flat tire, and we missed the first inning.

Notice how applying these strategies improves the sample paragraph.

> The storm arose without warning. As waves started to bounce our boat around, Herb pulled in the anchor and I reeled in the lines. It was impossible to get back to the dock, so Herb steered for the point. With the wind behind us, we sailed into the beach, jumped into the water, and pulled the boat ashore.

Practice Your Skills

A. Revise the following compound sentences by following the directions in parentheses.

1. Jon shot the puck into the goal, and he raised his arms in joy. (Create a simple sentence with a compound predicate.)

Sentence Variety **441**

Linking Grammar and Writing

It may be helpful to review the terminology used in this Handbook—such as *independent clause, subordinate clause, participial phrase*—by referring to Grammar Handbook 33, Phrases and Clauses.

ANSWERS TO PRACTICE YOUR SKILLS

A. 1. Jon shot the puck into the goal and raised his arms in joy.

Off the Record

The complex sentence structure used by some German writers is amusingly summed up by Mark Twain in this quotation from *A Connecticut Yankee in King Arthur's Court:* ''Whenever the literary German dives into a sentence, that is the last you are going to see of him till he emerges on the other side of his Atlantic with his verb in his mouth.''

2. Speaking about cancer, the lecturer said that this illness could turn out to be several diseases.

3. Since I know the radius, I can compute the diameter.

4. Although spices can be hard to digest if they have been used too generously, they enhance taste.

5. Influenza vaccine is available to everyone, but epidemics still occur because some people do not bother to get the vaccine.

B. Answers will vary but should employ many of the the seven sentence-varying techniques identified on the page.

2. The lecturer spoke about cancer, and she said that this illness could turn out to be several diseases. (Create a simple sentence with a participial phrase.)
3. I know the radius; I can compute the diameter. (Create a complex sentence with one subordinate clause.)
4. Spices such as pepper enhance taste, but they can be hard to digest if used too generously. (Create a complex sentence with two subordinate clauses.)
5. Influenza vaccine is available to everyone, but some people do not bother to get a shot, and epidemics still occur. (Create a compound-complex sentence with two independent clauses and one subordinate clause.)

B. Revise the following paragraph. Vary the sentence structure to include at least one simple sentence and one complex sentence.

> We reached Trinidad, Colorado, in the evening, and in the morning we headed south through Raton Pass. We ate lunch at Eagle's Nest, New Mexico, and then we took a roundabout route through the mountains. The gravel road was better than we expected, and the mountains were strikingly beautiful.

VARIETY IN
SENTENCE LENGTH

Using variety in sentence length can create powerful writing. Notice how Ernest Hemingway varied the length of his sentences in the following paragraph. Notice how the mix of long and short sentences mimics the rhythm of the hiker's physical activity.

LITERARY
MODEL

> He walked along the road feeling the ache from the pull of the heavy pack. The road climbed steadily. It was hard work walking uphill. His muscles ached and the day was hot, but Nick felt happy. He felt he had left everything behind, the need for thinking, the need to write, other needs.
>
> **Ernest Hemingway, "Big Two-Hearted River"**

Sometimes writers deliberately use a series of short sentences, a device that can be especially effective in building suspense or emphasizing action. However, the unintentional use of short sentences often produces the opposite effect—dullness. When you

Literature Connection

Ernest Hemingway (1899–1961) was an American short story writer, novelist, and journalist. He developed his style of short, compact sentences while working as a foreign correspondent and used his experiences in World War I and his travels around the world as the basis for much of his writing. Challenge students to find a sentence in Hemingway's work that is short, compact and even out of context but still delivers a powerful punch. Suggest *The Old Man and the Sea*, *The Sun Also Rises*, or *For Whom the Bell Tolls*.

detect this problem, you can easily combine some of the short sentences in a passage by using the strategies suggested in the following chart.

Varying Sentence Lengths

- **Use a single-word modifier.**
  Weak   Quietly we walked into the hall. It was dark.
  Revised   Quietly we walked into the dark hall.

- **Use a prepositional phrase.**
  Weak   The concert will be held at The Civic Forum. The date is May 7.
  Revised   The concert will be held at The Civic Forum on May 7.

- **Use a participial phrase.**
  Weak   The Van Allen belts are two fields of charged particles. They extend 600 miles to 15,500 miles above the earth.
  Revised   The Van Allen belts are two fields of charged particles extending 600 miles to 15,500 miles above the earth.

- **Use an appositive.**
  Weak   Susan Stein won first prize in the state competition. She is a violin soloist in our orchestra.
  Revised   Susan Stein, a violin soloist in our orchestra, won first prize in the state competition.

- **Use a simple sentence with a compound predicate.**
  Weak   I stained the cabinet. Then I coated it with shellac.
  Revised   I stained the cabinet and coated it with shellac.

- **Use a compound sentence.**
  Weak   The plane stopped in Okinawa for repairs. We landed in Tokyo three hours late.
  Revised   The plane stopped in Okinawa for repairs, so we landed in Tokyo three hours late.

- **Use a subordinate clause.**
  Weak   Yuki sprained her right ankle. She was practicing fencing.
  Revised   Yuki sprained her right ankle while she was practicing fencing.

Teaching Tip: Audience

Remind students to think of their audience when considering the length of their sentences. For example, if they are writing a short story for a literary magazine, they may want to use a variety of sentence lengths. If they are writing a newspaper article or an advertisement for a school function, they will find that short sentences serve them best in getting information across.

Sentence Variety   **443**

ANSWERS TO PRACTICE YOUR SKILLS

A. 1. Ellen paged carefully through the old book.
2. When the judge came in, the spectators stood up.
3. Traveling at the speed of light, you can reach the planet Jupiter in about two seconds.
4. When Grover Cleveland was elected to a second term, the country was on the verge of financial panic.
5. In the dead of winter, the engineers landed their helicopters on Ellesmere Island.
B. Answers will vary.
C. Answers will vary.

Additional Resources
• Writing Resource Book, pp. 39–41

W R I T E R   T O   W R I T E R

A writer may err by making his sentences too compact and periodic. An occasional loose sentence prevents the style from becoming too formal and gives the reader a certain relief. Consequently, loose sentences are common in easy, unstudied writing. The danger is that there may be too many of them.

William Strunk, Jr., and E. B. White, *The Elements of Style*

Practice Your Skills

A. Combine each set of short sentences by using the form suggested in parentheses.

1. Ellen paged carefully through the book. It was old. (single-word modifier)
2. The judge came in. The spectators stood up. (subordinate clause beginning with *when*)
3. You can reach the planet Jupiter in about thirty minutes. You must travel at the speed of light. (participial phrase beginning with *traveling*)
4. Grover Cleveland was elected to a second term. The country was on the verge of financial panic. (subordinate clause beginning with *when*)
5. The engineers landed their helicopters on Ellesmere Island. It was the dead of winter. (prepositional phrase beginning with *in*)

B. Revise the following paragraph to create more variety in sentence structures and lengths.

A chinook is a dry wind that blows down from the Rocky Mountains in winter and early spring. It is an unseasonably warm wind. The wind's temperature increases as the chinook moves down the slopes. The temperature increases about 1 degree for every 180-foot drop. A chinook helps grazing cattle. It melts snow in the lowlands and exposes grass. Chinooks can cause snow to melt very rapidly. Lowland areas are often flooded.

C. Revise the paragraph about an election on page 439. Create a natural rhythm by varying the sentences. Use the guidelines suggested in this handbook to help you make appropriate revisions.

Springboard

Invite students to write the longest sentence they can. It should express a clear thought and contain no unnecessary words. Discuss each sentence with the class to see whether there is consensus that the sentence contains no extraneous verbiage.

On the Lightside

THE DING-DONG THEORY

Listen to the sound of *bash, clash, crash, lash, mash, slash,* and *thrash.* The short *a* sound and the hiss of the *-sh* give them all the sound of violence.

Sense the rapid movement the *fl* sound gives to *flicker, flutter, flurry, fly,* and *fling.*

Notice how your nose wrinkles from the *sn* in *snort, sneer, sniff, snarl,* and *snout.*

Hear the metallic resonance of *bong, gong, ring, clang,* and *ding-dong.*

All these words seem to echo their meanings. Such **echoic** words have fascinated people throughout history. The eighteenth-century British poet Alexander Pope marveled at them, writing that "the sound must seem an echo to the sense."

The ancient Greek philosophers Pythagorus, Heraclitus, and Plato went even further. They subscribed to the theory that the universe is like a great bell, and every object in it has a special ring. Speaking a word is like ringing a bell—the word's own special sound rings out. The theory has been called the "ding-dong" theory of language origin. The name may sound like a nursery school concept, but for many words, it has the ring of truth.

445

Although students may not have heard of the "ding-dong" theory of language origin, most will have heard of the related concept of onomatopoeia. Discuss the relationship of the two theories, eliciting from students that onomatopoeia is a label given only to a word that imitates the sound of a thing or action. Echoic words, on the other hand, are described as words that "echo their meanings" and can be related to other senses. Ask students to choose the words in the selection that are onomatopoeic as well as echoic.

Examining Point of View

Objectives

1. To identify the first-, second-, and third-person points of view in writing
2. To identify appropriate uses of various points of view in nonfiction and fiction
3. To use point of view appropriately in writing

Handbook Mini-Lessons

For information on topics related to point of view, see the following mini-lessons.
- Understanding Voice and Style pp. 417–422
- Mastering Dialogue pp. 452–455

Teaching Strategies

Motivating

Read aloud an excerpt from *Grendel,* John Gardner's retelling of part of the Beowulf epic employing the first-person point of view—with the monster as narrator. Let students discuss the differences between the way Beowulf sees the story and the way Grendel sees it. Then explain that point of view is one of the writer's most powerful tools, and that in this lesson students will hone their skills at using it.

WRITING HANDBOOK 20

Examining Point of View

The **point of view** in a piece of writing is the perspective from which a story or a nonfiction account is told. You may write from the first-person, second-person, or third-person point of view. Read each example below. How do you react to each point of view?

First-Person Point of View	
The bases are loaded. If I strike out, we'll lose the game. I feel paralyzed.	*Narrator participates in the action and uses the pronoun* I *to refer to himself or herself.*

Second-Person Point of View	
When you're up to bat, you've got to forget the crowd. Just concentrate on the ball.	*Narrator uses the imperative mood and the pronoun* you *to refer to the reader. The narrator does not refer to himself or herself.*

Third-Person Point of View	
It's the bottom of the ninth inning. The Sox are winning 3–2, but the Jets have the bases loaded. Smith is coming up to bat.	*Narrator does not participate in the action. Instead, the action is described "at a distance," as happening to some he, she, or it.*

IDENTIFYING POINT OF VIEW IN NONFICTION

First-Person Point of View A writer will choose to write in the first person when he or she wants to let readers know that the personal experiences or ideas expressed are his or her own. Typically, writers make this choice when writing personal essays, letters, and autobiographies or memoirs. The following letter is an example of nonfiction writing from the first-person point of view. Samuel Johnson writes in a wry tone to an earl who claimed to be his benefactor.

446   Writing Handbook

> Seven years, my Lord, have now passed, since I waited in your outward rooms, or was repulsed from your door; during which time I have been pushing on my work through difficulties, of which it is useless to complain, and have brought it at last to the verge of publication, without one act of assistance, one word of encouragement, or one smile of favor. Such treatment I did not expect, for I never had a patron before.
>
> **Samuel Johnson, from his letter to**
> **Lord Chesterfield dated February 7, 1755**

Second-Person Point of View The second-person point of view is often used in nonfiction, especially in speeches, essays, and educational materials. In speeches and essays, the writer often tries to elicit a personal response or action from individuals in the audience. Many writers find the second-person point of view very effective in these cases. Technical writing, such as a computer- or bicycle-repair manual, also commonly uses the second-person perspective. Below is an example of second-person nonfiction taken from a travel guide.

> *Pack light.* Lay out everything you think you'll need, pack only half of it, and take more money. Remember that you can buy almost anything you'll need in Europe, and that the more luggage you carry, the more you'll look and feel like a tourist.
>
> ***Let's Go: The Budget Guide to France***

Third-Person Point of View Writers of nonfiction use the third-person point of view when the emphasis is on the message rather than on the message-giver. Most general nonfiction is written from this point of view. The following passage is an example.

> Several years ago, *Time* photographer Steve Northup, who had covered Vietnam and Watergate, took a group of students around Cambridge shooting pictures. He quietly insisted that they ask every [subject] for permission. His attitude toward private citizens was one of careful respect for the power of "exposure."
>
> **Ellen Goodman, *Close to Home***

Point of View   **447**

Linking Literature to Writing

Explain that one of the writer's tasks is to choose a point of view appropriate to the purpose of the writing and keep to it consistently. That is, a writer should not inadvertently mix together sentences using differing points of view such as a sentence from the first-person point of view in a paragraph written from the third-person point of view. However, professional writers of reflective essays sometimes shift point of view deliberately in order to achieve a particular effect. For example, George Orwell's *The Road to Wigan Pier,* about inhumane working conditions in coal mines, alternates third-person narrative passages with first-person commentary, but does so purposefully and skillfully, rather than inadvertently, in order to convey objective information and yet bring it home to the reader and make it dramatically personal.

Collaborative Opportunity

Have students work in groups to rewrite passages of nonfiction found in their literature texts or elsewhere, changing the point of view. For example, they might rewrite the text excerpt from Samuel Johnson's "Letter to Lord Chesterfield" in the third-person point of view. Let the groups share their results with the class. Then, in a class discussion, elicit students' ideas about the effects of the changes in point of view in nonfiction. They should notice that shifting to the first-person point of view brings the personality of the narrator into sharper relief, while shifting to the third person moves the focus more to the content or point of the writing.

Basic Students   To be sure that students understand the distinction between the *author* and the *narrator* of first-person fiction, you might ask them to think about a stand-up comedian who presents an obvious persona to the audience. (Have students suggest such a comedian and focus your explanation on their example.) Discuss the fact that as we listen to a comedian telling funny stories, we know we are listening to a character he or she has created and is "speaking as." Explain that the person who exists offstage is akin to the author in fiction. The character who speaks and tells the stories and cracks the jokes on stage is akin to the narrator in fiction.

Advanced Students   To deepen students' understanding of the *persona* as a role taken on by the author of first-person fiction, explain that the author must use characterization techniques to develop the narrator's personality. Swift, for example, in the excerpt from *Gulliver's Travels,* indirectly establishes the "wit" and "good sense" of his narrator by mentioning that they impressed the queen of the giants. In addition, you might point out that even authors of first-person nonfiction create personas. Remind students that the persona they take on when writing in their journals is often quite different from the persona they would take on when writing a letter applying for a job, for example.

▣DENTIFYING POINT
OF VIEW IN FICTION

First-Person Point of View   In fiction, the first-person point of view can be very powerful. The speaker is not the writer, but rather a character created by the writer's imagination. In first-person fiction, everything is seen from the perspective of that character, who is also the narrator. In the following passage, the narrator is Lemuel Gulliver, a ship's surgeon who describes his adventures in an imaginary land.

▼

> The Queen, giving great allowance for my defectiveness in speaking, was however surprised at so much wit and good sense in so diminutive an animal. She took me in her own hand, and carried me to the King, who was then retired to his cabinet.
> **Jonathan Swift, *Gulliver's Travels***

You might compare first-person fiction to acting. The writer takes on the role, or persona, of someone else and expresses that person's thoughts, emotions, and reactions. The writer is limited to expressing only what that character can see, hear, or experience. By inhabiting the world of one character fully, a writer can use first-person narration to create intimate and moving portrayals of individuals and their stories.

Third-Person Point of View   When writing fiction from a third-person perspective, a writer must decide whether to use a limited or omniscient point of view. In writing from the **third-person limited point of view,** the narrator speaks from the perspective of one character. For example, the point of view in the following passage is limited to the perspective of Louise Mallard as she anticipates the news that her husband has been killed in a train accident.

▼

> There was something coming to her and she was waiting for it, fearfully. What was it? She did not know; it was too subtle and elusive to name. But she felt it, creeping out of the sky, reaching toward her through the sounds, the scents, the color that filled the air.   **Kate Chopin, "The Story of an Hour"**

448   Writing Handbook

Springboard

Divide the class into groups of four or five students. Have each student adopt a persona and interact with the group as this character. (Possible personae include soft-spoken and retiring, witty and flippant, demanding and impatient.) Then ask the students to write a sentence or two from the first-person point of view as the personae they have developed. Share the work with the class as a whole and have the class describe the persona revealed in each piece of writing.

In writing from the **third-person omniscient point of view,** the narrator is able to reveal the unspoken thoughts of all the characters. The word *omniscient* simply means "all-knowing." In the following passage, three brothers and their sister discuss their plans for the future. An omniscient narrator records the scene.

> But the consultation amounted to nothing. There was a strange air of ineffectuality about the three men, as they sprawled at table, smoking and reflecting vaguely on their own condition. The girl was alone, a rather short, sullen-looking young woman of twenty-seven. She did not share the same life as her brothers. She would have been good-looking save for the impressive fixity of her face, "bulldog," as her brothers called it.   **D. H. Lawrence, "The Horse-Dealer's Daughter"**

EXPERIMENTING WITH POINT OF VIEW

Point of view is one of the writer's most powerful tools. Investigating different points of view can help you write imaginatively and effectively.

Write in the third person about yourself. Attribute your own experiences to a character with a name other than your own. Many fiction writers have done this. For example, in *A Portrait of the Artist as a Young Man,* James Joyce writes about his own boyhood in Ireland, giving himself the name Stephen Dedalus.

Use an omniscient first-person narrator. Write a story told by someone who knows everything that goes on in the other characters' minds. This is only possible, of course, in fiction about really exceptional characters—as in a science fiction story about a person with telepathic powers.

Use the first person to explore a nonhuman narrator. You might choose an animal, a mountain, a river, even a cockroach, as in Don Marquis's *archy and mehitabel.* This is often done in poetry.

Write from a point of view unlike your own. This experiment can help you to grow both as a writer and as a citizen. It can broaden your awareness and understanding of others.

Point of View   **449**

Teaching Tip: Third-Person Point of View in Fiction

To demonstrate the differences between a third-person limited point of view and a third-person omniscient point of view, ask students how the excerpt from "The Horse Dealer's Daughter" would have been different if it had been written from the girl's point of view (third-person limited). Would she have known what was going on in the men's minds? Would she be likely to know that she was sullen-looking or that "she would have been good-looking save for the impressive fixity of her face"? What would she have seen, and what might she have been thinking?

  Individualizing Instruction

ESL Students As students experiment with writing from various points of view, remind them to be sure that the pronouns and verb endings they use are in agreement and are consistent with the point of view they have chosen.

Teaching Tip: Second-Person Point of View in Fiction

Tell students that the modern French author Michel Butor also uses the second-person point of view in his 1957 novel, *A Change of Heart*. He employs the indicative mood, rather than the imperative. To get an idea of the effects of this unusual point of view in fiction, let students work in groups to rewrite the Kate Chopin excerpt on p. 448 so that it shows the second-person point of view, retaining the indicative mood. (The first sentence would be ''There was something coming for you and you were waiting for it fearfully.'') You might also encourage students to use their imaginations to continue Chopin's story from this point of view. Let them discuss the effects of the new viewpoint; some may find its immediacy almost eerie.

Writing —TIP—

Try writing different drafts of a work from different points of view. When you revise for your final draft, choose the point of view that works best.

LITERARY
MODEL

Tell a story from several different points of view. You can investigate different perspectives by shifting point of view within a story. In her novel *Gone to Soldiers,* Marge Piercy tells different parts of her story from different characters' points of view.

Use the second person in fiction. The second-person point of view is seldom used in fiction, though some authors such as Italo Calvino and Jay McInerny have used it effectively.

Use an unreliable narrator. Edgar Allan Poe, for example, often wrote from the point of view of narrators who were portrayed as insane. A villain like the narrator of Ring Lardner's story "Haircut" is another kind of unreliable narrator.

Use the first person to tell someone else's story. Ghostwriting is a common example of this. Autobiographies are not always written by the people they're about. Some celebrities ask professional ghostwriters to tell their stories for them.

ANALYZING VANTAGE POINT

The physical location from which a writer views a subject is called the **vantage point.** In the essay "Shooting an Elephant," George Orwell recalls when he was called upon to deal with a rampaging elephant. By the time he arrived, the elephant was grazing placidly. Orwell uses the vantage point of a narrator surrounded by two thousand hostile villagers.

> But at that moment I glanced round at the crowd that had followed me. It was an immense crowd, two thousand at the least and growing every minute. It blocked the road for a long distance on either side. I looked at the sea of . . . faces above the garish clothes—faces all happy and excited over this bit of fun, all certain that the elephant was going to be shot. They were watching me as they would watch a conjurer about to perform a trick. They did not like me, but with the magical rifle in my hand I was momentarily worth watching. And suddenly I realized that I would have to shoot the elephant. . . . The people expected it of me and I had got to do it; I could feel their two-thousand wills pressing me forward, irresistibly.
>
> **George Orwell, "Shooting an Elephant"**

Telling the story from this vantage point helps the reader gain a greater appreciation of the pressures and circumstances that led Orwell to shoot the elephant. How would the emotional impact of the passage differ if Orwell had made the decision from the safety of the police station?

Vantage point can also refer to a distancing in time. For example, George Orwell wrote "Shooting an Elephant" long after the incident took place. Looking back at the event from the vantage point of time contributes to the ironic tone and sense of shame that permeate the essay.

Practice Your Skills

A. Read the following passages by Annie Dillard and Stephen Crane. Identify the point of view used in each excerpt. Then discuss why you think it might have been chosen and what impact it makes on the reader.

1.   I do not so much write a book as sit up with it, as with a dying friend. During visiting hours, I enter its room with dread and sympathy for its many disorders. I hold its hand and hope it will get better.   **Annie Dillard, *The Writing Life***

2.   The oiler, steering with one of the two oars in the boat, sometimes raised himself suddenly to keep clear of water that swirled in over the stern. It was a thin little oar, and it seemed often ready to snap.
    The correspondent, pulling at the other oar, watched the waves and wondered why he was there.
    The injured captain, lying in the bow, was at this time buried in that profound dejection and indifference which comes, temporarily at least, to even the bravest and most enduring when, willy-nilly, the firm fails, the army loses, the ship goes down.   **Stephen Crane, "The Open Boat"**

B. Write a poem or short story using one of the unusual points of view discussed in "Experimenting with Point of View" on pages 449–450.

C. Describe a tornado from two different vantage points. First describe it from the vantage point of a weather forecaster tracking it on radar. Then describe the same tornado from the vantage point of someone caught in its path. Remember to determine the response you want to elicit in your readers and choose an appropriate point of view for describing the tornado.

Point of View   **451**

Stumbling Block

If your students have no experience of tornadoes, you might have them substitute a natural disaster more familiar in their area (an earthquake, flood, blizzard, or hurricane, for example) for the tornado in part C of the Practice Your Skills exercise. Explain that it is difficult to produce honest writing about things with which one has no experience.

Additional Resources
- Writing Resource Book, pp. 42–43
- Writing About Literature
- Thinking Skills Worksheets
- Ideas for Writing

Off the Record

Really, I did write an essay on the topic "Our Life at Home." It was confiscated at breakfast.

Mastering Dialogue

Objectives

1. To identify the elements of dialogue and note its conventions
2. To analyze the uses of dialogue in fiction, drama, poetry, and nonfiction
3. To use dialogue appropriately in an original piece of writing

Handbook Mini-Lessons

For information on topics related to dialogue, see the following mini-lessons.

- Techniques for Elaboration and Development, pp. 376–381
- Understanding Voice and Style, pp. 417–422
- Varieties of Language, pp. 429–433
- Apostrophes and Quotation Marks, pp. 802–815

Teaching Strategies

Motivating

Have two students read aloud the dialogue between The Flower Girl and The Note Taker on p. 453 of this lesson. (You may want to explain that The Flower Girl's first line is a Cockney pronunciation of "Oh!" and that "Garn!" is "Go on!") Then ask how students felt about the characters after hearing the brief exchange. Prompt them, if necessary, by asking, "Which one would you rather have as a friend? Why?" Explain that, in this handbook, they will learn how dialogue functions to provide insights into character.

WRITING HANDBOOK **21**

Mastering Dialogue

When you skim a page of a novel or magazine article, **dialogue** is one element in the writing that draws you in. Dialogue adds life to all kinds of writing. In fiction, dialogue reveals subtleties of character, moves the action, and provides information. In poetry, conversation adds variety. In nonfiction, quotations give articles authenticity as well as a human dimension.

W R I T E R   T O   W R I T E R

For me as an author, cultivating an astute ear for dialogue is a lifelong process.

Anne Chamberlain, fiction writer

U S I N G   D I A L O G U E   I N   F I C T I O N

Any kind of imaginary prose narrative—a play, short story, legend, myth, or novel—is **fiction.** In any given piece of fiction, three modes of writing are woven together: **narration,** which presents events; **description,** which presents details of setting and character; and **dialogue,** which presents characters' words. Through dialogue the characters reveal themselves directly.

The passage below is from a short story by Katherine Mansfield. Notice how the dialogue reveals the insensitivity of the two young people to the older woman.

LITERARY **MODEL**

> Just at that moment a boy and a girl came and sat down where the old couple had been. They were beautifully dressed; they were in love. The hero and heroine, of course, just arrived from his father's yacht. And still soundlessly singing, still with that trembling smile, Miss Brill prepared to listen.
>
> "No, not now," said the girl. "Not here, I can't."
>
> "But why? Because of that old stupid thing at the end there?" asked the boy. "Why does she come here at all—who wants her? Why doesn't she keep her silly old mug at home?"
>
> **Katherine Mansfield, "Miss Brill"**

452 Writing Handbook

For information about punctuating dialogue, see Grammar Handbook 41, "Apostrophes and Quotation Marks," on pages 808–810.

USING DIALOGUE IN DRAMA

Dialogue is the main component of drama. Therefore it must provide information about the setting and plot, as well as the characters. Notice how George Bernard Shaw uses dialogue in the following passage to reveal character, provide background information, and move the story line forward. We learn that the note taker is self-confident, even smug, and that he makes his living by teaching millionaires how to speak proper English. We also get a hint of the conflict to come when the note taker boasts that he could transform the way the flower girl speaks in just three months.

▼

THE FLOWER GIRL *(quite overwhelmed, looking up at him in mingled wonder and deprecation without daring to raise her head).* Ah-ah-ah-ow-ow-ow-oo!

THE NOTE TAKER *(whipping out his book).* Heavens! what a sound! *(He writes; then holds out the book and reads, reproducing her vowels exactly.)* Ah-ah-ah-ow-ow-ow-oo!

THE FLOWER GIRL *(tickled by the performance, and laughing in spite of herself).* Garn!

THE NOTE TAKER. You see this creature with her kerbstone English: the English that will keep her in the gutter to the end of her days. Well, sir, in three months I could pass that girl off as a duchess at an ambassador's garden party. I could even get her a place as lady's maid or shop assistant, which requires better English. That's the sort of thing I do for commercial millionaires. And on the profits of it I do genuine scientific work in phonetics, and a little as a poet on Miltonic lines.

George Bernard Shaw, *Pygmalion*

In the script of a play, each new passage of dialogue is signaled by the speaker's tag. Stage directions in parentheses convey information about gestures and tone of voice, and they provide suggestions for staging, music, and sound effects.

Writing
—**TIP**—

To write realistic dialogue, have your characters speak in relatively short exchanges, not in long sentences or paragraphs.

. . . .
L I T E R A R Y
M O D E L

Individualizing Instruction

LEP Students These students may find it especially difficult to recognize the elements that make dialogue sound natural; bridging auditory stimuli (the sound of language) and visual stimuli (the printed word) may be unusually challenging for them. For LEP students, you may wish to select additional examples of dialogue in each genre and read them aloud as students follow along.

Teaching Tip: Personal Goals

You might tell students that they will use dialogue to write a short story, a one-act play or a nonfiction piece as part of this lesson. Suggest that they begin thinking about which genre they would like to use. Further, suggest that as they read these models, they pay special attention to the way the dialogue functions in each of the various genres. (In fiction and nonfiction, it provides directness and emphasis; in drama it carries most of the story as well.)

Social Studies Connection

Remind students that dialogue is often used to enliven biographies and autobiographies. Challenge students to skim autobiographies of historical figures that interest them to find passages that contain touching, humorous, or thought-provoking insights into the subject of the autobiography and his or her times and experiences.

Critical Thinking

Interpreting Challenge the class to translate the excerpt from "Channel Firing," including the dialogue, into standard, modern prose. Write their prose sentences on the board as they formulate them. This group practice session in creating dialogue will be helpful to students later as they work at their individual writing assignments.

Teaching Tip: Dialogue

To help students become familiar with the sounds of dialogue and understand the character nuances that dialogue can convey, suggest that they take notes of some of the dialogue they hear over a 24-hour period, being careful not to invade others' privacy. Let them read their notes (not naming the speakers) to class members, who can then assess what the dialogue tells about the speakers. Take dialogue notes yourself and participate in this exercise. Point out the short, even fragmentary nature of most everyday exchanges. Students may be able to use their notes or their insights from the class discussion to help them complete the Practice Your Skills exercise.

USING DIALOGUE IN POETRY

Poets often use dialogue in narrative poetry to give their readers a sense of immediacy and involvement. In his poem "Channel Firing," Thomas Hardy describes the terrible disruption of warships firing their guns through the voices of the dead, whom it has awakened. Notice in the concluding lines of the poem shown below how the dead speak not only for themselves, but for the living as well.

LITERARY
M O D E L

So down we lay again. "I wonder,
Will the world ever saner be,"
Said one, "than when He sent us under
In our indifferent century!"

And many a skeleton shook his head.
"Instead of preaching forty year,"
My neighbour Parson Thirdly said,
"I wish I had stuck to pipes and beer."

Again the arms disturbed the hour,
Roaring their readiness to avenge,
As far inland as Stourton Tower,
And Camelot, and starlit Stonehenge.

Thomas Hardy, "Channel Firing"

GUIDELINES FOR WRITING DIALOGUE IN FICTION

- Use words and expressions that reveal your characters' backgrounds, ages, personalities, and feelings. When appropriate, use special language like dialect, jargon, or slang.
- Make your characters sound natural. People often use sentence fragments, idioms, and contractions when speaking.
- In your speaker tags, use verbs that describe emotions. If a speaker is annoyed, it is more revealing to write "Nelson snapped" than "Nelson said."
- In a play, you can use stage directions to describe a character's voice, facial expression, body language, and actions.
- Test your dialogue by reading it aloud. If it sounds unnatural when you say it, then it needs to be revised.

454 Writing Handbook

Springboard

Invite students to bring to class a favorite piece of literature that contains character-revealing dialogue. Ask students to read the dialogue aloud—without giving the title or the name of the character. Challenge the class to determine what the dialogue reveals about the character. Allow the student who brought in the piece—and who should know it best—to determine if the class has correctly analyzed the character from the dialogue.

USING DIALOGUE IN NONFICTION

News stories, histories, biographies, and most essay writing—all forms of **nonfiction**—often contain dialogue. Dialogue in nonfiction is a transcription of the actual words of actual people and must, therefore, accurately reflect what was said.

Journalists add human interest to news stories by using dialogue. The following excerpt from a newspaper article describes a ~~   ~~ of wills between New Jersey's Governor Florio and the chai~~   ~~ of Hartford Insurance Company, who threatened to refuse car insurance to New Jersey drivers.

▼

What the state did was tell ITT Hartford, one of the biggest insurers in the nation, that if it wanted to pull out of the auto insurance business in New Jersey, it would have to give up lucrative business in lines like health and homeowner's policies as well. "If they won't play by the rules," an angry Mr. Florio said, "we won't let them sell anything."

Wayne King, "Going Toe-to-Toe Over Car Insurance Bills"

Practice Your Skills

Complete one of the following activities. Work alone or with a partner, as your teacher directs.

1. Write a short story. Create a strong beginning, and give your characters dialogue that reveals their personalities.

2. Write a one-act play. Create stage directions and dialogue that will convey the setting and mood and carry the plot forward.

3. Write a newspaper article about an event or issue of local interest. Interview participants, witnesses, and people affected by the event or issue, and include quotes from them.

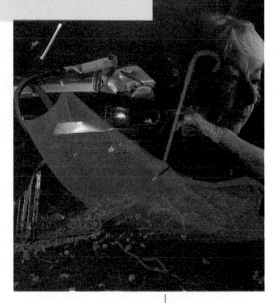

Stumbling Block

Remind students that dialogue should show the point of view of only the character who is speaking it and that in fiction a character's speech should only include information that he or she could logically know.

Managing the Paper Load

You might want to tell students that you will consider the quality, content, and mechanics of only the dialogue in grading the Practice Your Skills assignments.

ANSWERS TO PRACTICE YOUR SKILLS

1. Answers will vary. Dialogue should consist of short exchanges, rather than long sentences or paragraphs. Speaker tags should employ verbs or other words showing emotion: " . . . giggled the girl," " . . . said the boy in an angry whisper." Dialogue should be punctuated correctly.

2. Answers will vary. Dialogue should sound natural and reveal character and setting as well as advancing the plot. Stage directions in parentheses should give further clues to character. Form and punctuation should follow standard dramatic conventions.

3. Answers will vary. The article should use several quotes, ideally from more than one person, to add human interest and to illuminate pertinent parts of the story. Quotes should be accurate, skillfully blended into the surrounding sentences, and correctly punctuated.

Additional Resources
- Writing Resource Book, pp. 44–45
- Writing About Literature

Social Studies Connection

To familiarize themselves with the sound of one formal kind of dialogue and with the details of character it conveys, students interested in political science may enjoy perusing the transcripts of the Watergate hearings or the Iran-Contra hearings.

PROFESSIONAL **MODEL**

Sketchbook

Objective

To use lines from a song as a springboard to informal writing

Using the Prompt

Remind students that Sketchbook activities are meant to encourage risk taking and experimentation and are not graded.

Ask students to name people who they believe to be successes. List their names on the chalkboard. Encourage students to include people from their daily lives as well as celebrities. Then ask students for characteristics that make these people successes. Encourage students to go beyond notions of fame and wealth and to include such qualities as ability to help or inspire others, ability to face unfavorable odds to get a job done, and willingness to risk failure to achieve a worthy goal.

If possible, play a recording of Allen Toussaint's "What Is Success." Have students discuss their responses to the questions in lines 2–3 and in lines 4–7 in the section of the song on p. 456. Then have them write a paragraph giving their own definition of success.

Use the ideas from the Additional Sketches section as an alternative for students who prefer a different starting point. Have students keep their writing in their Writing Portfolios for possible use in later writing.

Sketchbook

What is success?
Is it doing your own thing
or to join the rest?
Or should you truly believe
and keep trying over and over again
living in hopes
that some day you'll be in with the winners?

Allen Toussaint
"WHAT IS SUCCESS"

What is success?

Additional Sketches

What will you be doing ten years from today?

Write a letter of complaint about something that has been bothering you.

Developing Your Vocabulary

A calligrapher dips into his pot of ink and his handwriting flows elegantly from the brush. That fluidity, however, was developed only after much practice with the tools of his trade. In the same way, by immersing yourself in words, you can develop the fluidity that will enable you to express your thoughts clearly and elegantly.

You can begin by applying the following techniques for analyzing words from their component parts and their context. Then, just practice, practice, practice.

MAKING A PERSONAL PLAN

You have two distinct vocabularies. Your **passive vocabulary** contains words that you understand when you hear or read them. Your **active vocabulary** contains words that you comprehend well enough to use yourself.

Both of your vocabularies grow over time. A word enters your passive vocabulary when you first encounter it in the speech or writing of others. You recognize and understand the word in context but do not yet use it yourself. By applying certain strategies you can integrate the word into your active vocabulary and begin to use it in your speech.

By following a personal plan for vocabulary improvement, you will gain precision in expressing yourself. Your higher degree of sophistication in the use of language will benefit you in job and college interviews. By using the techniques discussed below, you can also improve your performance on the standardized tests that are part of the college and job application process.

Develop Curiosity Instead of passing over an unfamiliar word in your reading, or ignoring a new word you hear on the evening news, jot it in a special section in your journal. The list that you collect becomes the basis for your personal program of vocabulary improvement. Also take the opportunity to explore new words while using a thesaurus.

Learn the Definitions Familiarity with a word begins with understanding its meaning. Look up unfamiliar words in a dictionary. In addition to discovering the definition, research the background of a new word. A colorful **etymology,** or word history, may help you remember the definition.

WRITING
HANDBOOK
22

Writing
TIP

If a somewhat unfamiliar word pops into your head while you are writing, use it and keep going. When you have finished writing, you may go back and look up the word in the dictionary.

Objectives

1. To plan a personal strategy for vocabulary development
2. To identify types of context clues and use them to infer word meanings
3. To recognize word parts: prefixes, suffixes, base words, and word roots
4. To use structural analysis as an aid to identifying word meanings

Handbook Mini-Lessons

For information on topics related to developing vocabulary, see the following mini-lessons.
- Improving Your Sentences, pp. 402–411
- Understanding Voice and Style, pp. 417–420
- Library, Reference Works, and Other Sources, pp. 491–500
- Testing for College Admission, pp. 521–533

Teaching Strategies

Personal Touch

Share with students several new words that you have learned recently, and explain how you learned them. Discuss why you think those particular words caught your notice.

Suggest that students use a section of their journals to collect the words that they like best and to explore why they like them. Explain that the sounds of words engage some people; novelist Betty Smith, for example, liked *antimacassar, samovar,* and *windowsill* for their sounds. The poet Donald Hall prefers short, strong words: "Think of the richness in *hogwash,*" he writes, "or the exact strength in *rasp.*" For others, a word's etymology is what makes it interesting; the author Isak Dinesen, who felt more at home in forests than in cities, loved the fact that *trust* and *truth* could both be traced back to an Indo-European root meaning *tree.* Encourage students to browse through literature and dictionaries like collectors, examining at leisure any interesting words they encounter.

Put New Words to Use Once you have discovered a new word and researched its meaning, try to work the word into your speech and writing as soon as possible. It's been said that if you use a word twice, it is yours.

Set Goals The list of new words you gather in your journal is only the beginning for your vocabulary-improvement plan. In addition, set a goal of learning a specific number of words in a particular time period. Remember to set reasonable goals—perhaps two new words a day—to ensure that you continue your plan.

Make a Plan Establish a personalized method for acquiring and practicing new words. You might begin with the following list of sixty-nine words for vocabulary study. Apply your personal program for vocabulary development to make these words a part of your passive and active vocabularies.

Words for Vocabulary Study

abstruse	exigency	onerous
acquisitive	fatuous	overt
aesthetic	frenetic	paucity
anachronism	germane	pedantry
banal	histrionic	penchant
cacophonous	ignominy	propitious
chronic	impecunious	quintessence
coalition	importune	raze
collusion	incumbent	rebuff
congeal	inexorable	rectitude
conjecture	laconic	recumbent
credence	manifest	sequester
decimate	mélange	somnambulist
demur	mesmerize	taciturn
deprecate	misanthrope	tirade
derogatory	monotheism	unequivocal
disarray	mutable	unremitting
dissident	myopic	utopian
ebullient	nadir	vacillate
eclectic	neologism	verbiage
efficacy	non sequitur	viscous
errant	nuance	visionary
ethereal	obtuse	zealot

Humanities Connection

Point out that the oldest words in English, those that come from the Proto-Indo-European language, have been in use for over 7,000 years—since around 5,000 B.C. By studying these words, linguists have pieced together a great deal of information about the Indo-Europeans, the prehistoric people who used the earliest form of our language. Suggest that students research the Indo-Europeans and report what is known, or surmised, about their civilization and their travels. Interested students could also research the relationships of languages within the Indo-European group or could trace the development of another major world language group.

In addition, start browsing through books on vocabulary available in the library and in bookstores. Pay attention to books specifically designed to help you with the vocabulary portions of the college entrance examinations.

Build a strategy for practice into your vocabulary-improvement plan. You may wish to write new words on index cards so that you can review them at free moments, or you might record new words on tape to listen to and review.

W R I T E R   T O   W R I T E R

Our words must seem to be inevitable.
William Butler Yeats, Irish poet and dramatist

Extend Your Plan   Integrate your pursuit of new words into as many of your activities as possible. For example, word games and crossword puzzles are enjoyable activities to help build and review vocabulary.

Practice Your Skills

A. For the next five days, work on your own personal vocabulary-development program. Follow the steps in this list.

1. Each day record two unfamiliar words in your journal.
2. Use a dictionary to find the meaning of each word and learn its definition.
3. Use index cards or a tape recorder to drill each word; then introduce it into your speaking and writing.
4. Every week write a sentence for each of your new words.

B. Read this passage, then follow the directions on the next page.

> The side of the ship made an *opaque* belt of shadow on the shimmer of the sea. But I saw at once something elongated and pale floating very close to the ladder. Before I could form a guess a faint flash of *phosphorescent* light, which seemed to issue suddenly from the naked body of a man, flickered in the sleeping water with the *elusive,* silent play of summer lightning in a night sky. With a gasp I saw revealed to my stare a pair of feet, the long legs, a broad *livid* back *immersed* right up to the neck in a green *cadaverous* glow. One hand, *awash,* clutched the bottom rung of the ladder.

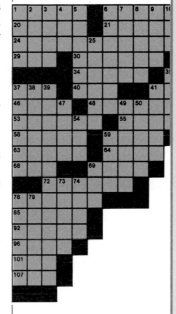

Developing Your
Vocabulary   **459**

Literature Connection

Author Note   W. B. Yeats (1865–1939), Irish, won the Nobel Prize for literature in 1923 for his poetry. Students may find his poems "The Second Coming" and "Sailing to Byzantium" especially memorable.

Literature Connection

Author Note   Joseph Conrad (1857–1924) was born in Poland and raised in Russia; he took British citizenship as an adult. He is considered a master of psychological realism. His many novels include *The Secret Sharer, Lord Jim,* and *Heart of Darkness* (which inspired the Francis Ford Coppola film *Apocalypse Now).*

Linking Grammar to Writing

Remind students that, in their own writing, using appositive phrases to explain unfamiliar terms will allow them to achieve both conciseness and sentence variety. For a review of appositives and appositive phrases, see Grammar and Usage Handbook 39. For practice in using appositive phrases for sentence variety and conciseness, see Sentence Composing: Varying Sentences, pp. 143–145, and Sentence Composing: Varying S-V Splits, pp. 203–205.

He was complete but for the head. A headless corpse! The cigar dropped out of my *gaping* mouth with a tiny plip and a short hiss quite *audible* in the stillness. . . . The moment of *vain* exclamations was past. . . . I only . . . leaned over the rail as far as I could, to bring my eyes near to the mystery floating alongside.

Joseph Conrad, *The Secret Sharer*

1. Make five columns on your paper and label them *Word, Definition, Unknown, Passive Vocabulary, Active Vocabulary.*
2. Enter each italicized word from the passage in the column marked *Word.* Check the appropriate place in the last three columns to indicate whether the word is unknown, in your passive vocabulary, or currently in your active vocabulary.
3. Under *Definition* write a complete meaning for each word. If a word is unknown to you, use a dictionary.
4. Reread the passage noting any words that were unknown.
5. Write a sentence using each of the italicized words.

EXTRACTING MEANING FROM CONTEXT

You can use a dictionary to find the meanings of unknown words. However, you can also get a clue to the meanings of an unfamiliar word from its **context,** the sentence or the group of sentences in which the word appears. Using context clues is a simple but powerful method for increasing your passive vocabulary. Six common types of context clues are definition, restatement, example, comparison, contrast, and cause and effect.

Definition and Restatement The most obvious type of context clue is direct **definition.** Clues of this type are usually signaled by a form of the verb *to be* (*am, is, are, was, were*).

> A *sycophant* **is** someone who tries to win favor by using flattery.

Sometimes a writer will explain a term by restating it in other words. Be alert for such words or phrases as *in other words, that is, to put it another way, or,* and *this means,* which may often signal **restatements.** The demonstrative pronouns *this, that, these,* and *those* may also indicate restatements. Finally, a restatement may be signaled by the use of commas, parentheses, or dashes. Such restatements are called *appositives.*

Jane Eyre was *ambivalent* about Mr. Rochester; **that is,** her feelings about him were contradictory.

Irv is studying *topology*. **This** branch of mathematics deals with those properties of geometric figures that do not change even when the figure is distorted.

The symbols etched on the magnificent sword were *runes,* characters from an early German alphabet.

Example Sometimes a writer will give examples that reveal the meaning of a word. Words that signal examples include *such as, like, especially, particularly, for example,* and *for instance.*

All *arachnids*—scorpions and ticks, **for example**—have four pairs of legs.

When the example word itself is unfamiliar, you must examine the words that precede the example, and even the whole sentence, for context clues.

Nicole's poise, particularly her *composure* when speaking to an audience, made her an ideal student leader.

Comparison Occasionally a writer will make a comparison that enables you to grasp the meaning of an unfamiliar word. Words often used to indicate comparisons include *similar, like,* and *as.*

He approached his work *meticulously,* **like** a landscape painter who must render every leaf in precise detail.

Contrast Sometimes a writer will supply a contrast, allowing you to determine a word's meaning. Contrasts may be signaled by words such as *but, although, unlike,* and *on the contrary.*

Although she strode confidently up to the horse and grasped the bridle, Ann was a complete *novice* at horseback riding.

Cause and Effect When a writer sets up a cause-and-effect relationship between the ideas in a sentence, you often can deduce the meaning of one word from its effect on another. Cause-and-effect relationships are signaled by the words *because, since, when, consequently, therefore,* and *as a result.*

Because the candidate had lied so often in the past, the public suspected that he was *mendacious.*

When the chemist noted that the acid had not damaged the metal, he concluded that the metal was *impervious* to acid.

Developing Your Vocabulary **461**

Critical Thinking

Making Inferences Point out that drawing inferences about word meanings is a bit like reaching an inductive conclusion: One collects all the facts and details available and then makes an "inductive leap" to arrive at a reasonable definition. As with inductive reasoning, one must beware of jumping to a conclusion, arriving too hastily at a definition that fails to take into account all the facts. For example, in the lesson passage containing the word *talisman,* a reader who overlooked the detail that a talisman could fit into a pocket might have arrived at the erroneous conclusion that it was a device for supporting a skier's arm. Remind students to be sure they have noted all available information before making inferences about the meanings of words in context.

Managing the Paper Load

After completing Practice Your Skills, students may learn more from exchanging papers with their peers and checking one another's work than from having you correct and grade the exercise. Consider allowing them to exchange, review and score one another's papers. Direct them to use classroom dictionaries as well as the lesson material for reference; if they are in doubt after consulting both these sources, they should ask you for assistance.

Stumbling Block

Point out that the words *infer* and *imply* are often confused, though their meanings are very different. To *imply* is to state something indirectly or to hint at something. To *infer* is to draw a conclusion or make a guess based on facts or clues.

INFERRING WORD MEANINGS

The six types of context clues that you have just studied provide direct information concerning the meanings of words. Sometimes, however, context clues are more subtle. Often, you must study an entire paragraph to **infer** the meaning of a word; that is, you must draw a conclusion from specific facts.

When you encounter an unfamiliar word, search the context to see what information is provided. Then try to determine the connection between those facts and the unknown word.

Supporting Details Notice how details in the following passage lead you to a definition of the italicized word.

> He always kept the *talisman* in his pocket. Once he'd gone skiing without it and had broken his arm. It didn't pay to take chances.

The context tells you that the object called a *talisman* can be kept in a pocket and that the owner once thought going out without it brought bad luck. Therefore, you can infer from the details that a talisman must be something like a good luck charm.

Context Clues Inferences can also be drawn from any of the context clues discussed earlier. The following passage develops a series of contrasts that help you to infer the meaning of *scrupulous*.

> She was such a *scrupulous* housekeeper that her neighbors were suspicious when her windows remained open during a rainstorm. Their concern grew when the newspapers began to pile up at her door. Finally, someone called the police.

You note the contrast that is developed between a scrupulous housekeeper and one who would allow windows to remain open in the rain or newspapers to accumulate. Therefore, you can infer that *scrupulous* means "careful and exacting."

Structure Clues Occasionally the structure of the writing offers clues to word meaning. An intentionally repeated sentence pattern, such as the one in the example below, may suggest an association between familiar and unfamiliar words.

> The speech *slandered* the senatorial candidate. Suggestions of dishonesty *defamed* his character.

The parallel placement of *slandered* and *defamed* as verbs suggests that *slander* means "to speak ill of."

Practice Your Skills

A. Define the italicized words by using context clues. Identify the method by which the clue reveals the meaning.

1. Since his last case of severe indigestion, Pat has *eschewed* his own cooking.
2. Charlene did not resist the suggestion. On the contrary, her *acquiescence* was immediate and enthusiastic.
3. Louis Pasteur investigated *rabies,* the disease that makes dogs, bats, and other animals go mad.
4. Our unusual neighbor, Mr. Robson, is generally known for his *eccentricity*. Thus we were not surprised to learn that he has over seventy-five pet cats and dogs.
5. The points at which bones make contact or unite with one another are called *articulations*.
6. This *burgeoning* community is quickly depleting its water supply. Its growing population must look to a new source.
7. The fact that lower vertebrates do not depend very much on the *cerebrum* can be demonstrated by removing that part of the brain and observing the general behavior of the animal.
8. Their drafting technician requested the *calipers,* several protractors, and a ruler.
9. Like a child who is reluctant to go to bed, Elizabeth *dawdled* all the way up the stairs.
10. Many *Porifera,* including the elephant-ear sponge, are used commercially for cleaning and cosmetic purposes.

B. Infer the meaning and write your own definition for each italicized word in the following sentences. Check your definition in a dictionary.

1. Eleanor, who has always suffered from *acrophobia,* could not be induced to go to the top of the Washington Monument when her class toured the capital.
2. In my hometown there is a law against smoking in public, but the law has fallen into *desuetude*. Until recently, people have not felt it was their concern whether another person was smoking or not, and the law has not been used in forty years.
3. Since the days of President Johnson's War on Poverty in the United States, many Americans have improved their standard of living: yet it is still possible to find people living in *destitution* in our wonderful land of plenty.
4. An *indefatigable* worker, Thomas Edison spent days and nights on his experiments, not even taking time to eat and sleep.

Developing Your
Vocabulary **463**

7. *disparaged*—spoke ill of
8. *prodigy*—gifted person
9. *jeopardize*—endanger
10. *public domain*—available for free use by the public
11. *extolled*—praised
12. *decelerate*—slow down
C. (Definitions may vary slightly)
1. *visionary*—seer, prophet one who fore-sees the future
intricate—finely detailed
mesmerized—spellbound, hypnotized

5. After trying countless fad diets without success, Mom found that the most *efficacious* way to lose weight was to take smaller portions and to avoid snacking between meals.
6. Lawrence's *effrontery* at the Christmas party surprised everyone. He asked my grandfather's guests personal questions, though he had scarcely made their acquaintance.
7. Frustrated and jealous because he believed himself less talented than the younger composer, Antonio Salieri belittled Mozart at every opportunity. He *disparaged* both Mozart's talent and his personal habits.
8. Each of the pianists is an erstwhile *prodigy*. Gould is supposed to have been able to read notes before he could read the printed word. He started playing the piano at the age of three and gave his first recital at fourteen.
9. Jogging lost some of its popularity as people realized that it was not without risk. Many former joggers have taken up race walking instead, an activity that does not *jeopardize* the knees and joints.
10. The first national parks were established because people feared that commercial development of all lands would leave nothing in the *public domain* and would eventually destroy the magnificent scenic wealth of the continent.
11. Coach Hernandez *extolled* the benefits of aerobic exercise as a way to maintain fitness. As a way to achieve flexibility and suppleness, he praised yoga.
12. Suddenly the brake lights of the car in front flashed. Seeing this, Sam prepared to *decelerate*.

C. Examine the following passages, and write your own definitions for each italicized word. Check your definitions in a dictionary.

1. One of the great *visionaries* of the architectural world is Paolo Soleri, who came to the United States from Italy thirty-one years ago. Soleri's fame does not rest on the structures he has actually built, for these are few in number: a striking glass-domed house, a ceramics factory on the Amalfi coast, and the so-called earth colony where he and his followers lived in Arizona. His impact on the world of design has been made almost entirely through his *intricate,* detailed drawings for the city of the future—in which he fully intends to live. These drawings have astonished and *mesmerized* visitors to museum shows around the country.
Joseph J. Thorndike, Jr.

2. Mr. Bingley had soon made himself acquainted with all the principal people in the room; he was lively and *unreserved,* danced every dance, was angry that the ball closed so early, and talked of giving

one himself at Netherfield. Such *amiable* qualities must speak for themselves. What a contrast between him and his friend! Mr. Darcy danced only once with Mrs. Hurst and once with Miss Bingley, *declined* being introduced to any other lady, and spent the rest of the evening in walking about the room, speaking occasionally to one of his own party. His *character* was decided. He was the proudest, most disagreeable man in the world, and everybody hoped that he would never come there again.   **Jane Austen**

3. Although it is difficult to generalize, too many of our universities have become huge circuses in which the sideshows overshadow the main attraction. "When a university president makes a speech calling for intellectual leadership," writes Dr. Hutchins, "he cannot be heard over the din his publicity man is making about the newest campus queen." Our colleagues have involved themselves in activities that have only the most *tenuous relation* to the *academic function*.   **Martin B. Margolies**

4. Jade was the link in China between earth and heaven, the bridge from life to immortality. A Chinese gentleman paced his life by altering his *gait* to make jades dangling from his belt tinkle to a measured beat. Confucius compared the *virtues* of such a gentleman with the virtues of jade, applying such traits as intelligence, loyalty, justice, humanity, truth, and more. Just as we use the word gold to *embellish* a phrase, the Chinese *incorporate* jade into thousands of expressions: "Jade person" is a beautiful woman; "fragrant jade" is a woman's skin; "jade shattered" is a beauty's death.   **Fred Ward**

A NALYZING WORD PARTS

You have already learned how to use context clues to determine the meanings of unfamiliar words. Another technique that you can use for the purpose of unlocking word meaning is the analysis of **prefixes, suffixes, base words,** and **roots.** These are the **word parts** from which words are made.

- **Prefix** a word part added to the beginning of another word or word part
- **Suffix** a word part added to the end of another word or word part
- **Base Word** a complete word to which a prefix and/or suffix can be added
- **Root** a word part that can never stand alone but to which a prefix and/or a suffix is added

Developing Your
Vocabulary   **465**

 Individualizing Instruction

ESL Students Recognizing English word parts may be especially difficult for these students because the same English root or prefix can take many different forms. Explain, however, that studying word parts can be extremely useful for them, and that their English fluency will probably increase more quickly if they resist looking up unknown words in the dictionary until they have first attempted to define the words on their own, even if these attempts do not at first seem successful. While they can infer meaning from context clues, a knowledge of word parts is essential because it can often be used to confirm or disprove guesses that they have based on context. Suggest that if prefixes and roots are confusing, students begin by developing an eye for base words and suffixes, which remain more consistent.

Critical Thinking

Classifying Point out that several of the prefixes in this list have similar or identical meanings. To make the prefixes easier to learn, have students rewrite the list, grouping the prefixes by meaning. Then challenge students to create other classifications for grouping the prefixes. For example, they might group together all prefixes having to do with spatial arrangement (ones meaning *around, with, through, upon, under, in*); prefixes with negative connotations (ones meaning *excessive, bad, wrong,* or *not*); or prefixes having to do with description (ones meaning *large, many, equal, bad, good,* etc.). Classifying the prefixes in various ways can help students gain a fuller understanding and mastery of them.

Prefixes

A careful reader or listener can apply several strategies, such as analyzing prefixes to unlock the meanings of unfamiliar words. When using this technique, remember that many prefixes have more than one meaning. If you encounter an unfamiliar word with such a prefix, decide which of the meanings fits the context or consult a dictionary. The following is a list of common prefixes in English.

Common English Prefixes

Prefix	Meaning	Example
bene-	good	benefit
circum-	around	circumscribe
com-, con-	with	compassion consequence
dia-	through, across	dialogue
dis-	the opposite of	disapprove
epi-	upon	epidermis
equi-	equal, even	equidistant
eu-	good	eulogy
hyper-	excessive	hypercritical
hypo-	under	hypodermic
il-, im-, in-, ir-	not, in	illogical, impossible, input, irregular
inner-, intra-	within	innermost, intramural
intro-	into	introspection
macro-	large, long	macrocosm
mal-	bad	malnutrition
mis-	wrong	mismatched
non-	not	nonflammable
omni-	all	omnivorous
pan-	all	panorama
para-	beside	parallel
poly-	many	polysyllabic
re-	again	recover
sub-	under, less than	substandard
super-	above, beyond	supersonic
sym-	together	sympathy
trans-	across	transoceanic

Science Connection

A knowledge of roots and affixes is indispensable for understanding the terms used in such sciences as biology, zoology, anatomy, and physiology. Suggest that students taking life science courses list new terms introduced in whichever chapter of their science text they are now studying. Have them find the meanings of the roots and affixes that make up each term.

Suffixes

Suffixes affect the function as well as the meaning of a word. **Noun suffixes,** for example, are used to create nouns from other parts of speech. **Adjective suffixes** can be used to create adjectives.

You can increase your vocabulary considerably by analyzing suffixes you encounter on unfamiliar words and by adding suffixes to familiar words. If you have any doubts, consult a dictionary to assure yourself that the suffix you are using fits the context and the meaning you wish to convey.

Noun Suffixes

Suffix	Meaning	Example
-ade	act, condition	blockade
-age	act, condition, collection, home	marriage, parsonage
-an	belonging to, born in	American
-archy	form of government	monarchy
-ary	member, doer	missionary
-cide	killer, killing	insecticide
-dom	state, condition	freedom
-ectomy	surgical removal	tonsillectomy
-ee	recipient	appointee
-eer, -er	doer, maker	puppeteer, winner
-hood	condition	priesthood
-ician	doer	diagnostician
-ics	science, skill	mathematics
-ism	ideology	Romanticism
-ist	doer, maker	violinist
-itis	inflammation	tonsillitis
-ization	state, quality	colonization
-ment	result, agency, state, condition	government, internment
-mony	result, condition	testimony
-ness	quality	happiness
-or	doer	director
-ster	doer, member	youngster
-ion, -sion, -tion	state, condition	inflation
-tude	state, quality	quietude
-ure	act, result	censure

Stumbling Block

Be sure students understand that the grammatical inflections added to nouns, verbs, and modifiers are different from suffixes. For example, though -er is a noun-forming suffix, *higher* is not a base with a suffix; it is a modifier inflected to form the comparative. Similarly, -en, an adjective-forming suffix, is different from the inflection that forms the past participles *broken* and *forgotten*.

Teaching Tip: Suffixes

To give students practice in the correct use of words with suffixes, have them work in pairs or groups to write a brief (one-page) narrative that incorporates ten words from the list showing examples of words with noun suffixes. Point out that they will need to use their creativity and senses of humor to work ten of these unrelated words into a single narrative. After they finish, have them exchange their narratives with those of another group or pair.

Divide the class into teams and tell them to name two examples, other than those given in the lesson, of words that demonstrate the use of each suffix on the lists. Let students do this exercise orally, with teams competing by taking turns as they go down the suffix lists. Words whose authenticity is disputed by members of the opposing team can be checked in the dictionary.

Writing ═TIP═

When using a thesaurus, notice the different word roots within the selection. Knowing the definitions of the roots will enable you to select the perfect word to express your thoughts.

Adjective Suffixes

Suffix	Meaning	Example
-able	able, capable	washable
-al	like, suited to	musical
-ar	of, pertaining to	solar
-en	made of	wooden
-esque	relating to	statuesque
-fic	causing	honorific
-ful	having qualities of	wonderful
-ic	pertaining to	volcanic
-ish	like, similar to	impish
-ive	tending to or toward	instructive
-less	without	penniless
-like	similar to	lifelike
-oid	relating to	humanoid
-ose	full of, having	verbose
-ous	full of, having	nervous
-some	like, showing	worrisome
-ward	in the direction of	homeward

Base Words

Words that can stand by themselves or be used with suffixes and/or prefixes are called **base words.** When a prefix or suffix is added to a base word, the meaning of the base word will alter slightly. Notice how the meaning of the base word *provision* changes when different suffixes are added to it:

provision   provisional   provisioner

Once you fully comprehend the meanings of prefixes and suffixes, you will be able to discern the complete definitions of words comprised of a base word and word parts.

Word Roots

Sometimes, when a prefix or suffix is removed from a word, the part remaining will not stand by itself. Such a word part is a **root.** A root has a specific meaning that can help you determine the meaning of the entire word. Many English words are derived from Greek and Latin roots. The following two charts list some of these common roots.

Literature Connection

Nonfiction   Point out that, just as words can be used to clarify ideas, they can also be used to obscure them. Assign George Orwell's essay "Politics and the English Language." After students have read it, let them discuss Orwell's points and examples. Emphasize that a knowledge of the way roots and affixes function can enable us to decipher "bureaucratese."

Roots Derived from Greek

Root	Meaning	Example
aesthet, esth	perception	aesthetic
anthrop	human	anthropology
arche, archae	ancient	archaeology
bibl	book	Bible
bio	life	biography
cryptos	secret, hidden	cryptic
dogma	opinion	dogmatism
dynamo	power	dynamo
ge, geo	earth	geology
gnos	know	diagnostic
graphein, gram	writing, write	graphic
homo	same	homogeneous
kine, cine	movement	cinema
log	word, thought	dialogue
mania	madness	maniac
paleo	old	paleolithic
patho	suffering	sympathy
phil	love	philharmonic
phobe	fear	phobia
pneum	air, breath	pneumonia
scope	seeing, look at	oscilloscope
sophos	wise, wisdom	sophisticated
therme	heat	thermometer

Developing Your
Vocabulary   **469**

Teaching Tip: Word Roots

To further enhance students' word analysis skills and to allow them to complete the Practice Your Skills exercise more easily at the end of the lesson, teach the additional Latin roots (*fac-, fic-* (make or do); *flux-* (flow); *ten-* (hold); and *tend-, tent-* (stretch or strive); and the Greek root *psycho-* (mind). Examples of words containing these roots are *manufacture, influx, tenable, tentacle,* and *psychology.* Let students use their knowledge of prefixes, suffixes, and other roots to explain how the meanings of these examples can be determined.

Managing the Paper Load

Consider allowing students to exchange papers and grade each other's work on the Practice Your Skills exercise. As they do so, they should refer to the dictionary as well as to the material in the lesson. If they are still in doubt about an answer after consulting both these references, they should ask you for help. By evaluating one another's answers in this way, students will gain additional independent practice both in analyzing the structure of words and in using the dictionary to deepen their word comprehension.

ANSWERS TO PRACTICE YOUR SKILLS

A. Definitions may vary slightly.
1. (prefix—bene; root—fac; suffix—or) doer of good deeds
2. (prefix—in; root—gratia; suffix—tude) lack of thankfulness
3. (prefix—in; root—juris; suffix—ous) causing harm
4. (prefix—can; root—flux; suffix—ence) place where two streams join
5. (root—geo; root—therm; suffix—al) having to do with heat generated by the earth
6. (prefix—in; root—alius; suffix—able) not to be taken away
7. (root—paleo; root—log) the study of fossils and ancient life forms
8. (prefix—super; root—flux; suffix—ous) excessive
9. (root—archae; suffix—ic) ancient
10. (root—phil; root—anthrop; suffix—ist) giver of charitable gifts
11. (prefix—eu; root—phon; suffix—ous) melodic, pleasant-sounding
12. (root—patho; root—log) the study of disease
13. (root—malus; root—fac; suffix—or) wrongdoer
14. (root—demos; root—graphein; suffix—ic) concerning population statistics
15. (base—technique; suffix—ician) an expert in a certain skill or process

Roots Derived from Latin

Root	Meaning	Example
alius	other	alien
amo, ami	love	amity
animus	mind, life	animate
cogn	know	recognize
corpus, corporis	body	corporeal
credere, creditus	believe	creed
dicere, dictus	say, tell	dictate
gratia, gratus	kindness, favor	gratitude
grex, gregis	flock	segregate
init	beginning	initiate
just, juris	law, right	injury
lumen, luminis	light	illuminate
mandare	command	reprimand
manus	hand	manipulate
mon	advise, warn	premonition
mut	change	mutate
rid	laugh	ridicule
rumpere, ruptus	break	rupture
sequor, secutus	follow	sequence
tact, tang	touch	tangible
unus	one	universe
ver	truth	veracity
videre, visus	see	visit
void	empty	devoid

Word Families

The same root may serve as the source for a large number of related words. A group of words with a common root is called a **word family.** For example, the word *logic* belongs to a word family that includes *logistics, monologue, dialogue, logo,* and *logarithm.* This family contains the Greek root *log* and each word has a meaning that includes the ideas "word" or "thought." By combining this knowledge with the fact that the suffix *-ic* means "science or skill," you arrive at "the science or skill of thought" as a definition for *logic.* This approximates the formal meaning of *logic,* which is "the science of correct reasoning." By adding word families to your personal vocabulary plan, your word power will grow rapidly.

470   Writing Handbook

Springboard

Suggest that students note the roots and affixes they encounter as they work with the following buzz-phrase generator. They may also enjoy scanning newspapers and news magazines for words they can use to construct similar buzz-phrase generators of their own. Ask students to explain what the generator parodies.

Directions: choose one word from each column to make an impressive, all-purpose buzz phrase.

resurgent	economic	indicator
burgeoning	technological	expansion
unparalleled	global	upswing
comprehensive	retrograde	trend
significant	governmental	variable

Practice Your Skills

A. Each of the words given below contains two or more of the following word parts: a prefix, a base word, a suffix, or a root. First, write the word and then identify these word parts. Write a definition for each whole word based on the meanings of its parts. Check the meaning of each word in a dictionary and alter your definition if necessary. Finally, use each word in a sentence.

1. benefactor	11. euphonious	21. tenacious
2. ingratitude	12. pathology	22. cryptography
3. injurious	13. malefactor	23. inconsequential
4. confluence	14. demographic	24. symmetrical
5. geothermal	15. technician	25. paraprofessional
6. inalienable	16. geopolitical	26. contender
7. paleontology	17. nonconformist	27. psychopath
8. superfluous	18. germicide	28. pneumatic
9. archaic	19. bibliographer	29. incognito
10. philanthropist	20. kinetic	30. gregarious

B. Read the following passage, list the italicized words, and identify prefixes, roots, and suffixes. Use your knowledge of word parts, context clues, and inference to write a definition of each word. Examine the etymological portion of a dictionary entry for assistance with word parts. Check your definitions in a dictionary.

Up in her bedroom window Sally Carrol Happer rested her nineteen-year-old chin on a fifty-two-year-old sill and watched Clark Darrow's ancient Ford turn the corner. The car was hot—being partly *metallic* it *retained* all the heat it *absorbed* or *evolved*—and Clark Darrow bolt upright at the wheel wore a pained, strained expression as though he considered himself a spare part, and rather likely to break. He *laboriously* crossed two dust ruts, the wheels squeaking *indignantly* at the *encounter,* and then with a terrifying expression he gave the steering gear a final wrench and deposited self and car approximately in front of the Happer steps. There was a *plaintive* heaving sound, a death-rattle, followed by a short silence; and then the air was rent by a startling whistle.

Sally Carrol . . . continued to silently regard the car, whose owner sat brilliantly if *perfunctorily* at attention as he waited for an answer to his signal. . . . Sally Carrol sighed *voluminously* and raised herself with *profound inertia* from the floor. . . .

F. Scott Fitzgerald

16. (root—geo; base—politic; suffix—ic; suffix—al) concerning the relationship between politics and geography

17. (prefix—non; prefix—con; base—form; suffix—ist) one who does not follow standard procedures

18. (base—germ; suffix—cide) a substance that kills germs

19. (root—bibl; root—graphein; suffix—er) one who compiles a booklist

20. (root—kine; suffix—tic) concerning body movement

21. (root—ten; suffix—ous) stubborn

22. (root—crypt; root—graphein) the study of codes

23. (prefix—in; prefix—con; root—sequor; suffix—al) unimportant, having little effect

24. (prefix—sym; suffix—ic; suffix—al) having similar or equal forms on either side of a dividing line

25. (prefix—para; base—profess; suffix—ion; suffix—al) one who assists a professional

26. (prefix—con; root—tend; suffix—er) one who competes or strives

27. (root—psycho; root—patho) a mentally ill person

28. (root—pneum; suffix—ic) concerning air or other gases

29. (prefix—in; root—cogn) under an assumed name

30. (root—gregis; suffix—ious) sociable

B. Definitions may vary slightly.

1. metallic: (base—metal; suffix—ic) made of metal

2. retained: (prefix—re) held

3. absorbed: took in

4. evolved: developed, turned out

5. laboriously: (base—labor; suffix—ous) with difficulty

6. indignantly: (prefix—in) angrily

7. encounter: meeting

8. plaintive: (base—plaint; suffix—ive) mournful

9. perfunctorily: without enthusiasm

10. voluminously: (base—volume; suffix—ous) fully

11. profound: extreme, deep

12. inertia: (base—inert) resistance to motion, action, or change

---

Additional Resources

- Writing Resource Book, pp. 46–49
- Vocabulary Development

Refining Critical Thinking and Writing Skills

Objectives

1. To identify problem-solving techniques and apply them to writing
2. To identify inductive and deductive reasoning and logical fallacies
3. To compose written arguments displaying critical thinking skills

Handbook Mini-Lessons

For information on topics related to critical thinking and writing skills, see the following mini-lessons.

- Writing Prompts and Writing Decisions, pp. 327–330
- Planning and Organizing Strategies, pp. 348–357
- Correcting Empty Sentences, pp. 402–403
- Research Skills, pp. 479–489
- Debating Techniques, p. 501
- Understanding and Evaluating the Media, pp. 534–541

Teaching Strategies

Motivating

Invite students to share with the class some of their favorite anecdotes about situations in which they devised unusual or outrageous solutions to problems—for example, using a hair dryer to dry an article of clothing when a clothes dryer was unavailable. If you wish, begin the discussion by sharing an anecdote of your own. Encourage students to explain how they devised their methods. Then tell them that the skills they used to devise their methods are problem-solving skills. In this lesson, they will learn to apply problem-solving skills in their writing processes.

WRITING HANDBOOK 23

Refining Critical Thinking and Writing Skills

You can't write without thinking; therefore, whenever you are writing, you are also developing your thinking skills—particularly the skills of hypothesis testing and problem solving.

W R I T E R   T O   W R I T E R

How do I know what I think until I see what I say?

E. M. Forster, British novelist

WRITING AS HYPOTHESIS TESTING

Writing is a process that enables you to explore what you know and to try new ideas. Every writing idea is an untested **hypothesis** or assumption, an experiment that may or may not work.

As you draft, you test ideas, developing them to see where they lead. If they take you somewhere you don't want to go or if they don't lead anywhere, you can revise your draft or begin again.

Not every writing idea leads to a successful piece of writing. However, every time you experiment with an idea, you can learn something valuable.

WRITING AS PROBLEM SOLVING

When reality is different from your expectations, a problem exists. For example, you have a problem if you can't find the car keys where you thought you left them and you need to drive to the airport. You also have a problem if you must write a paper for your social studies class and you have no idea where to begin. Any writing activity can be viewed as a problem to be solved.

You can apply the following strategies to any kind of problem, but consider, specifically, applying them to writing problems.

Strategies for Understanding and Solving Problems

Understanding Problems

1. **State the problem.** Putting the problem into simple, clear language is an important step toward solving it.

2. **Explore the problem.** Describe the problem in detail. Analyze it, freewrite about it, and ask questions about it. Make a sketch, diagram, chart, or map to explore the problem graphically.

3. **Define the problem.** Use the goal-oriented method to zero in on components of the problem. Ask yourself, "What is the situation like now?" Then, ask yourself, "What will the situation be like when the problem is solved?"

Solving Problems

1. **The trial-and-error method.** Think of all the possible solutions that you can and list them. Then look at each solution and imagine its consequences. Beginning with the most promising solution, try each one successively until the problem is solved.

2. **The divide-and-conquer method.** Divide the problem into parts and solve each part, one at a time.

3. **The past-experience method.** Think of similar problems that you have solved before. Evaluate your past solutions to see if any can be applied to the new problem.

4. **The simplification method.** Determine the core of the problem and solve it first; then work on the details.

5. **The "what-if" method.** Ask "what-if" questions to stimulate your imagination. This process may lead you to a creative solution you would not have seen otherwise.

6. **The "two-heads-are-better-than-one" method.** Include friends, relatives, and teachers in your problem-solving process.

7. **The pros-and-cons method.** Make a pro-and-con chart listing possible solutions. You may want to assign a number value to each pro and con so that you can evaluate the relative "weight" of each and not just the number of items in your chart.

Teaching Tip: Problem-Solving Techniques

Be sure students understand that some problem-solving techniques may seem more natural to them than others or more appropriate to a given writing task. They are free to choose the approaches that they are most comfortable with and that best fit a particular problem.

Personal Touch

Share with students your own experiences and preferences in regard to problem-solving techniques. Perhaps you usually resort to trial and error; perhaps you prefer to consult others whenever possible, to list pros and cons, or to use your imagination and creativity to generate unusual solutions. Whatever your approach, let students know about it, perhaps recounting an anecdote concerning a time when one approach worked especially well for you.

Springboard

Have students discuss the Forster quote. Ask them whether they ever discovered their thinking only after putting it in writing. Encourage them to share personal examples.

Science Connection

Students interested in science will recognize that the scientific method can draw on several or all of the problem-solving techniques. You might ask students to write a one-page account of an experiment they performed in a recent science lab. Then have them identify the problem-solving technique(s) they used at each stage of the experiment.

1. Answers will vary but should involve trying each of the three conclusions and analyzing their effects.
2. Answers will vary but should involve dividing the topic into many subtopics and perhaps further dividing certain subtopics. Graphic techniques such as clustering can be helpful.
3. Answers will vary but should involve speculative questioning and imaginative answers.
4. Answers will vary but should involve listing pros and cons of employer-provided day care.

Suppose Jill is writing a letter to her congressional representative to voice her concerns about impending restrictions in government guidelines for granting student loans. After reading over the first draft of her letter, Jill identifies a serious problem: her main point—that students from middle-income families may no longer be eligible for education loans—has gotten lost among several other ideas, including that there is no community college in her area.

Jill can use various problem-solving strategies in the process of revision. For example, she might first state the problem in writing, using simple, clear language. "I have lost the focus of my letter." Once she defines the problem clearly for herself, she might use the simplification method, stating her main point and then listing and prioritizing other ideas that support and clarify that point. If she still feels unsure of the clarity of her argument, she might use the "two-heads-are-better-than-one" method, asking friends or relatives how she could make her letter more focused and convincing.

Practice Your Skills

In a small group discuss each of the following writing problems and their possible solutions.

1. You have three ideas for the conclusion of a human-interest story that you are writing for your school paper. How might you use the trial-and-error method to decide which to use?
2. For a comparative government class, you must write a paper on similarities and differences between the Soviet Union and the United States. Use the divide-and-conquer method to help you come up with a narrower topic.
3. You are trying to come up with an idea for a science-fiction story. Use the "what-if" method to come up with some ideas that might work for your story.
4. You are preparing a persuasive speech about requiring companies to offer day care to employees with children. Use the pros-and-cons method to gather information.

DEVELOPING AND PRESENTING AN ARGUMENT

Critical thinking skills play a major role in persuasive writing, or argumentation. Many situations, in and out of school, call for the ability to argue persuasively in writing. For example, a student may

474 Writing Handbook

write a paper for science class, arguing that the songs of whales are a form of communication but do not meet certain criteria necessary to be classified as a true language; or a film critic may review a new movie, arguing that it is trite and predictable. Each piece of writing must clearly convey the writer's point of view.

Types of Arguments

Drawing conclusions from available information—and finding the appropriate structure for it—is a key to producing effective argumentative writing. Deduction and induction are two logical processes of argumentation with opposite structures.

Deductive Arguments   A **deductive argument** begins with a general statement of fact. Following that generalization is a specific conclusion that can be deduced, or derived, from it, as in the example below.

Generalization	A winning team is one that wins more games than it loses.
Specific fact	Our softball team has a 9–8 record.
Specific conclusion	Our softball team should be recognized as a winning team.

Inductive Arguments   An **inductive argument,** on the other hand, begins with specific observations that lead to a general conclusion, as in the following example.

Specific fact	In every softball game we've won this year, the pitcher rested three days between games.
Specific fact	In every softball game we've lost this year, the pitcher rested only two days between games.
General conclusion	Pitchers need at least three days rest between games for them to be most effective and to win games for the team.

Notice, however, that this general conclusion is not necessarily true. It doesn't take into account other factors that contribute to winning and losing games, such as the quality of the team's offense. The conclusion needs to be qualified: *Some* pitchers need at least three days rest between games for them to be most effective. Be sure to use qualifiers such as *some, few, often, many,* or *most* to limit the scope of the generalizations you derive in an inductive argument.

Writing TIP

Test the clarity and completeness of your argument by reading it aloud to a reliable listener who is unfamiliar with your topic. Then ask the person to restate your main point.

Individualizing Instruction

Basic Students   Be sure that these students recognize the difference between a generalization and a specific fact. Ask them to identify the generalization and the specific fact in each pair.

1. A mouse is a vertebrate. (specific)
   All vertebrates have backbones. (general)
2. Cyanide is a poisonous substance. (general)
   Apricot seeds contains cyanide. (specific)
3. All Key Club members wear white shirts on Tuesdays. (general)
   Lee wore a white shirt last Tuesday. (specific)
4. The two tadpoles in Tank A have gills. (specific)
   All fish have gills. (general)

Advanced Students   Challenge advanced students to state a conclusion that can be deduced reasonably from each set of statements above. If no reasonable conclusion is possible for a set of statements, ask students to explain why. Stress that they need not know the terminology or techniques of formal logic to do this; their common sense can tell them which conclusions are reasonable and why. (1. Mice have backbones. 2. Apricot seeds contain a poisonous substance. 3. Lee *may* be a member of the Key Club. 4. No reasonable conclusion is possible.)

Teaching Tip: Induction

Point out that in inductive reasoning many items of specific evidence are needed before one can reasonably draw a general conclusion. The more evidence, the stronger the possibility is that the generalization will be correct. However, an inductive generalization is disproved when only one piece of evidence contradicts it. For example, if a student examined 100 fish from a certain lake and found that all of them contained mercury, a reasonable inductive conclusion would be that all fish from that lake were tainted with mercury. But the discovery of a single mercury-free fish from the lake would disprove the conclusion. Hence the need for qualifiers in most inductive conclusions.

Linking Grammar to Writing

Point out that sentences stating conclusions to logical arguments often begin with conjunctive adverbs such as *therefore*, *thus*, or *consequently*. Remind students that any clause introduced by a conjunctive adverb is independent; it should never be joined to another clause with only a comma. Suggest that students proofread carefully to be sure that when they use clauses beginning with *therefore, thus,* and so on, they do not inadvertently create comma splices or run-ons.

Application of Induction and Deduction to Writing You can use both inductive and deductive thinking processes as you write argumentative essays. You can use induction when you begin to gather material for your writing, since you don't always know what hypothesis you will prove or what conclusion you will draw before you begin your research. If you wanted to write about the efficacy of job-internship programs, you might begin by gathering facts.

Specific fact   Of the students who go to work, 80 percent are rehired by the companies they interned for while still in high school.

Specific fact   Nineteen percent of those who go to work are hired by companies that receive written recommendations from intern employers.

What generalizations can you draw from your list of facts? You might come up with the following.

General conclusion   Participating in a job-internship program helps students to succeed after graduation.

You can use the deductive process as you write your draft. Begin with your general conclusion, which becomes the thesis of your paper, then provide your audience with enough information and specific details to prove your point. You can expand the range of the specific facts and details you initially have gathered by adding information about students who do not participate in the program, or by adding case histories and interviews with graduates. When you write, each specific fact should be fleshed out with details in full paragraphs. Your conclusion—a restatement of your original premise—is inevitable if you've provided convincing evidence.

Practice Your Skills

A. Tell whether each of the following arguments is inductive or deductive. Change the conclusions if necessary to make them true.

1. Environmentalists want to preserve the natural environment.
   Development damages the natural environment.
   Environmentalists want to restrict development in order to preserve the natural environment.

2. Any level of dioxin is unsafe.
   Wood preservatives with penta (pentachlorophenol) contain dioxin.
   Wood preservatives with penta are unsafe.

476   Writing Handbook

Math Connection

Challenge students who enjoy math to identify the pattern in the following series of numbers (Fibonacci's series):

$$1,1,2,3,5,8,13,21,34, \ldots$$

(Solution: Each number after the first is the sum of the two preceding numbers.) Then encourage students to analyze their thinking processes; ask whether, in solving this problem, they used induction or deduction or a combination to arrive at their answers. Interested students may want to explore or research Fibonacci's series further, looking for patterns within it or learning of its applications.

B. Choose a controversial issue that interests you as a topic for an argumentative essay. Explore the issue using inductive reasoning, gathering facts and information that will support your point of view. Then, using deduction, write an outline for your essay.

AVOIDING LOGICAL FALLACIES

Mistakes in reasoning are **logical fallacies.** Because persuasive writing must be logical, you need to evaluate your logic to avoid the following types of fallacious arguments.

Circular Reasoning Supporting a statement by repeating it in different terms is **circular reasoning,** as in the following example: "Experts prefer Gothic architecture to modern architecture because people who know about architecture believe Gothic architecture is superior." The second part of this sentence rephrases but does not support the first part.

Evasion of Issues Supporting an opinion with arguments that do not address its central point is **evading the issue.** For example, substantial evidence indicates that exhaled smoke—or secondary smoke—may be harmful to nonsmokers. Imagine a smoker opposing a ban against smoking in enclosed public areas, saying, "Smokers have rights, too. Why should a smoker put out a cigarette just to make a short pass through a lobby? Nonsmokers can stay out of lobbies if they are offended." The smoker's argument evades the central issue: secondary smoke may be harmful to nonsmokers.

False Analogy A **false analogy** assumes that two things share a similarity that they do not actually share, as in this example: "People in cities are like rats crowded in cages. When subjected to high levels of stress, they instinctively attack one another." The analogy is not totally false, because—like rats—people do respond to a stressful environment. However, reason, as well as instinct, guides human behavior. The analogy between rats and humans is false because it implies that human behavior is guided only by instinct.

Overgeneralization A generalization that is too broad is an **over-generalization.** A visitor to the United States who observes overflowing garbage cans on the streets of five large cities may conclude: "All large cities in the United States have inadequate garbage collection." However, this conclusion would be an overgeneralization because it is based on a limited sample.

THE FAR SIDE   By GARY LARSON

"Wait a minute! Isn't anyone here a real sheep?"

Critical Thinking
and Writing Skills   **477**

Critical Thinking

Analyzing To give students practice in recognizing flawed logic, you might point out that propaganda techniques and advertising gimmicks rely on logical fallacies. Bring a supply of old magazines to class, and let students choose advertisements that they would like to work with. Challenge students to identify the techniques used in the ads (for example, the bandwagon approach, the plain folks appeal, the false testimonial, flag waving, card stacking, transfer) and to identify the logical fallacies inherent in each technique. Point out that circular reasoning is a problem that can result in empty sentences.

Social Studies Connection

Students interested in political science may enjoy uncovering logical fallacies in election campaign material. Let them work with material from a recent election that interests them; this could be anything from a vote on local bond issues to the campaigns of the current President and the candidate who opposed him.

A. Revisions will vary
  1. Either/Or
  2. Overgeneralization
  3. Oversimplification
  4. Circular reasoning
  5. False cause *or* only reason
B. Answers will vary but should show an understanding of the logical fallacy selected and should propose a way to avoid it.

Additional Resources
- Writing Resource Book, pp. 50–52
- Thinking Skills Transparencies
- Thinking Skills Worksheets

Stereotyping   The most dangerous type of overgeneralization is the **stereotype.** Stereotypes are broad generalizations made about people on the basis of their gender; ethnicity; race; or political, social, professional, or religious group. Stereotyping not only prevents people from responding authentically to each other as individuals, but it also can provide justification for repressive social and political policies.

Oversimplification   Explaining a complex situation by omitting relevant information is **oversimplification.** For example, saying that heart disease is strictly inherited overlooks other factors that may influence susceptibility, such as diet, smoking, and exercise.

Either/Or Fallacy   Advocating a polarized position, leaving no room for alternatives, is the **either/or fallacy.** For example, believing that a decision must be based on either reason or emotion—not on a combination—is fallacious.

False Cause   Attributing a specific response to the wrong stimulus is citing a **false cause.** The statement "The pilot landed his plane in the cornfield because the straight rows provided him with a visual runway," contains a false cause. He landed in the cornfield because he didn't have enough fuel to get to the airport.

Only Reason   Attributing an event with more than one cause to a single reason is an instance of **only reason.** Note the following example, "Professional football team owners say they want the instant-replay rule abolished because it takes away a referee's authority." The argument is fallacious if the owners also have unstated reasons for wanting to abolish the rule.

Practice Your Skills

A. Identify the error in logic in each of these statements, and revise each statement to correct the error.

1. America. Love it or leave it.
2. Everyone enjoys a good comedy.
3. If you can read this, thank a teacher.
4. Europeans love soccer because that's the sport they enjoy in every European country.
5. Rita was late due to heavy commuter traffic.

B. Write a paragraph based on a logical fallacy. Exchange paragraphs with a classmate, identify the fallacy, and rewrite your classmate's paragraph so that it makes sense.

Research Skills

As you face exams, research projects, and preparing for college or a career, the work may often seem overwhelming. However, even if you have a stack of textbooks to review or a dozen library books to consult, you can manage the reading and the documentation of source materials in an efficient and straightforward way. The following guidelines for reading rapidly, studying effectively, and using source materials in your writing should help.

APPLYING READING STRATEGIES

You have different purposes in reading—whether in school, at work, or at home—and it is important that you match your reading method to your material and purpose. The three primary methods of reading are *skimming, scanning,* and *slow, careful reading.*

Skimming   This type of rapid reading involves moving your eyes quickly over a text, glancing at headings, topic sentences, highlighted phrases, and graphic aids. Skimming is useful when you want to get a general idea of what the material is about and whether it will be useful to you. For example, you might want to skim a newspaper to see if you can find information about a particular current event. You can also skim possible source materials for a research paper.

Scanning   You scan materials to find a specific fact or piece of information, such as a percentage or a definition. Scanning is particularly useful when you review for a test or when you are trying to find a specific item of information to use in a paper.

To scan, place a card over the first line of a page and then move the card down the page quickly, taking in whole lines or groups of lines at a time. You will notice key words and phrases that indicate that you are close to the information you need. Then you can slow down and read carefully.

Slow and Careful Reading   When you must thoroughly understand material in depth, you will want to read slowly and carefully. This process involves taking notes, asking questions, identifying main ideas, finding relationships between ideas, and drawing inferences, or conclusions, about what you read.

Writing Handbook 24:
Research Skills

Objectives

1. To identify and apply the reading techniques of skimming, scanning, and intensive reading
2. To identify and apply the study techniques of questioning, note-taking, analyzing, and evaluating
3. To recognize and use quoting, summarizing, and paraphrasing as techniques for incorporating source material into writing
4. To recognize and apply conventions for documenting sources correctly

Handbook Mini-Lessons

For information on topics related to research skills, see the following mini-lessons.
- Developing Your Vocabulary, pp. 457–471
- Refining Critical Thinking and Writing Skills, pp. 472–478
- Library, Reference Works, and Other Sources, pp. 491–500

Teaching Strategies

Motivating

Ask students how many times they have put off a term paper or a research project until the last possible minute, then stayed up most of the night or "gotten sick" the day it was due to buy a little extra time. Let them share their experiences in a class discussion. Then tell them that learning efficient approaches to research can actually make them less likely to procrastinate—and can certainly help them to make the most of their available time if they do get a late start on a project.

Personal Touch

Share with students some of the study skills that you found most useful as you completed your degree and credential. You might want to tell students which courses or areas you had the most trouble with and which study skills helped you to master them.

Teaching Tip: Previewing

Explain that, in previewing a reading assignment, students should be looking for the big picture: how the reading is laid out, which main areas it will cover. In addition, they should be thinking about how this piece of reading fits into the larger context of their studies. For what purpose are they reading it? How will it help them achieve their purpose?

Stumbling Block

Emphasize that in order to make it easier to write their notes in their own words, students should write without looking at the book, even closing the book or setting it aside if necessary, at least until they establish good note-taking habits. You might also suggest they take notes at set intervals during reading, perhaps at the end of every paragraph or subsection. Students who find it distracting to take notes as they read may be more comfortable dictating important details into a tape recorder at fixed intervals. Remind them that they should look away from the text while doing this. Whatever their method of note-taking, students should be sure to reword the material. This serves two purposes: First, it ensures that they are processing it mentally and will remember it; and, second, it minimizes the chances of inadvertent plagiarism.

BUILDING STUDY SKILLS

Study skills will be important to you all your life, in school and at work. Now, more than ever, professionals need to study manuals, reports, memoranda, specifications, and other written materials to do their jobs well.

The most effective way to study an assignment is to divide it into manageable sections and approach it systematically using the study and research techniques described on this and the following page.

Preview the Assignment When you preview an assignment, you prepare to learn by getting a general idea of what the material is about and establishing a context for what you will learn by recalling what you already know. In previewing written material, take the following steps.

1. Read the first two paragraphs of the assignment.

2. Read the first sentence of each paragraph that follows.

3. Read the last two paragraphs.

4. Read any information presented in special type—such as captions, headings, and boldfaced words—or in graphics, such as photos, graphs, diagrams, and charts.

Take Notes as You Read Even if you don't refer to the notes after you take them, the note-taking itself will help fix what you read in your mind. Translating what you read into your own words and then writing them down involves more of your brain than just reading does. Consequently, taking notes increases the likelihood that you will remember what you are studying.

Predict As you read, try to guess what will happen next. When you're studying literature, you may find predicting especially useful and enjoyable. Ask yourself questions like these: "What will this character do next? How will these characters get along? What will happen to this character as a result of his or her personality and actions? What will result from this event? How will this conflict be resolved?" By making predictions, you will become more involved in your reading and improve your retention of what you read.

Question Before reading, make a list of questions that you hope to answer. Write down the answers as you find them. As you read, add questions as they occur to you. Questions that remain unanswered

Social Studies Connection

Suggest that students use the Study Skills steps as they complete a reading assignment for their history or political science classes. Afterwards, ask them how the Study Skills steps differ from their usual study techniques, and whether the results of their studying also differed.

after you've finished reading can be raised in a class discussion or in a conference with your teacher.

Identify Main Ideas Don't get sidetracked by details as you read: it's important to recognize the main ideas in the material. Topic sentences of paragraphs, particularly in introductory or concluding paragraphs, often state main ideas. Because main ideas are sometimes implied rather than directly stated, however, be particularly attentive to the total context of a passage.

Identify Relationships As you read, look for passages that either imply or specifically state relationships between things or ideas. Common types of relationships include sequence, cause and effect, part to whole, spatial order, order of importance, order of value, comparison and contrast, and negation.

Make Inferences You make inferences when you draw conclusions based on what you know or observe. For example, if you read in a newspaper that unemployment and prices are rising while wages and sales are falling, you can infer that the economy is heading toward a recession. Write down any inferences you draw from the material you read.

Respond with Your Own Ideas and Opinions As you read, you may want to write comments to yourself about the material you're reading. For example, if you disagree with an author, make a note of the reason for your disagreement. Remember, you don't have to accept everything that you read as fact. Use your own experience, knowledge, and opinion to challenge the author.

Review What You Have Read Review your notes and skim over the material again to get an overview of it after you have familiarized yourself with the details. You may decide to organize your notes into questions and answers, main ideas and key terms, and ideas or opinions that you plan to follow up on later.

Practice Your Skills

At the top of the following page is a passage from a book called *The Minutemen and Their World.*

1. Skim the passage. Does the passage contain any information about the American Revolution?
2. Scan the passage. What powers did the colonial town have?
3. Now read the passage carefully. How was the town run? How much power did it have? How does it compare with towns today?

Research Skills   **481**

Research Skills   **481**

Critical Thinking

Expressing Opinions Remind students that when they disagree with material they read, they should try to pinpoint the exact words or identify the implications they don't accept. In formulating reasons for their disagreement, they should be as specific as possible, since vague, general disagreement has little credibility. If the problem is not that they disagree with the material but find it inconsistent or confusing, they should, again, identify the words or implications that are causing the problem and then make a note, stating explicitly the inconsistency or ambiguity.

Teaching Tip: Reacting to Published Works

If students find errors in a textbook or have serious objections to its content, suggest that they write a letter to the author or publisher, explaining their concerns. Refer them to Handbook 28, Business Writing, for correct letter form.

Managing the Paper Load

In order to give students experience with the critical thinking skills of evaluating and judging, consider allowing them to check their own work on this Practice Your Skills exercise. After they complete the exercise, read aloud the sample answers provided in the teacher's edition. Instruct students to give themselves credit if their answers resemble the sample answers in both scope and content. You may also wish to allow volunteers to read their answers aloud for purposes of comparison.

1. No

2. Answers will vary in wording but should convey the following information: it had power over all matters within its borders including people's private affairs and behavior.

3. Good answers should go beyond the literal information in the text, presenting inferences and conclusions drawn from, and reflecting, a close reading of the passage. For example: Colonial towns were similar to towns today in that their leaders were elected by public vote. Public vote also set taxes and made decisions about such community affairs as the construction of roads, the operation of schools, and providing for the poor. But unlike towns today, these matters were decided in town meetings, so colonial towns had a more direct democracy. Also, unlike modern towns, colonial towns had broad authority over people's private affairs. They could hire ministers, compel church attendance, control public uses of private property, and oversee the morals of their citizens.

Cooperative Learning

Let students practice choosing appropriate material to quote. Explain that usually, direct quotations either can add emphasis to important points in a piece of writing, or they can add general color to engage the reader's interest. Allow students to form groups; each group should select a passage from a piece of literature that they have all read and enjoyed. They should then write a brief (one-page) review, explaining what they liked about the passage. They should choose two significant quotations from the passage to include in their writing, and they should be ready to explain how the quotations function in the review. Remind them to follow the correct forms for using quotations.

Grammar
TIP

Use single quotes to indicate quotations within quotations.

When the eighteenth-century Yankee reflected on government, he thought first of his town. Through town meetings, he elected his officials, voted his taxes, and provided for the well-ordering of his community affairs. The main business of the town concerned roads and bridges, schools, and the poor. . . . But the colonial New England town claimed authority over anything that happened within its borders. It hired a minister . . . and compelled attendance at his sermons. It controlled public uses of private property. . . . And it gave equal care to the moral conduct of its inhabitants.

USING SOURCE MATERIALS IN WRITING

In addition to culling information from books, you must be able to incorporate material written by others into your own writing. You can do this three ways: by quoting directly, by paraphrasing, or by summarizing. The method you choose depends on the nature of the material and how you are using it.

Direct Quotation

Citing a writer's words exactly can be very effective if they are particularly important or well stated. Notice how Pearl Bailey's own words make a point forcefully and succinctly.

> As Pearl Bailey said, "There's a period of our lives when we swallow a knowledge of ourselves and it becomes either good or sour inside." In other words, at some point we come to terms with ourselves; we either make peace with who we are, or we struggle against our nature.

If a direct quotation is longer than four lines, set it off from the text by beginning the quote on a new line and indenting it ten spaces from the left margin. Because the quote is already differentiated from the text, you do not need to add quotation marks.

WRITER TO WRITER

By necessity, by proclivity, and by delight, we all quote.
Ralph Waldo Emerson, American essayist and poet

Literature Connection

Quotations Encourage students to browse through their literature text to find quotations they might like to incorporate into their writing in the future. Suggest that they record each quotation they find in their journals, along with its source and their thoughts concerning it.

Paraphrase

Sometimes you will want to **paraphrase,** or rewrite a passage from someone else's work in your own words, instead of quoting it directly. You might want to paraphrase material rather than quote it directly in order to simplify the material or to maintain a consistent style in your writing. You can use paraphrasing to incorporate material into your writing or to review material that you have read. For example, compare the following passage from *The Flamingo's Smile* by Stephen Jay Gould with a paraphrase of the material done by a student.

Original Passage

> In most birds (and mammals, including us), the upper jaw fuses to the skull; chewing, biting, and shouting move the mobile lower jaw against this stable brace. If reversed feeding has converted the flamingo's upper jaw into a working lower jaw in size and shape, then we must predict that, contrary to all anatomical custom, this upper beak moves up and down against a rigid lower jaw. The flamingo, in short, should feed by raising and lowering its upper jaw.
>
> **Stephen Jay Gould, *The Flamingo's Smile***

Paraphrase

> For the most part, birds and mammals have rigid, immobile upper jaws and loose, mobile lower jaws. This is the situation with humans, for example. However, the flamingo is a special case. It typically feeds with its head upside down, and its upper jaw looks like a lower jaw in both size and shape. Therefore, it would be reasonable to expect the flamingo's upper jaw, since it acts like other animals' lower jaws, to move like other animals' lower jaws (Gould 85).

Notice that the paraphrase in the example above is approximately the same length as the original passage and that the source is cited in parentheses. Consider the paraphrasing guidelines in the box at the top of the following page when you are writing a paraphrase.

Research Skills   **483**

Social Studies Connection

For an upcoming social studies assignment, encourage students to evaluate sources as part of their review of the material. Questions they should ask themselves include the following.

1. Is this a primary source (for example, a diary entry, a letter, a memoir, or an interview) or a secondary source (for example, a biography, a magazine article, or a news report)?

2. How reliable is this source? Are its sources acknowledged? Does it show bias?

3. How valuable is this source? What are the reputation and expertise of the author?

Critical Thinking

Generalizing Point out that, in order to find the main idea of a passage they wish to paraphrase, students must be able to conceive a generalization covering what the passage is about. One way to generalize is to consider the specifics in a passage, deciding what they have in common or how they are related. Suggest that students practice by reading the Gould excerpt again. Point out that the specifics in the passage concern the workings of the upper and lower jaws in birds and mammals. In addition, point out how these specifics are related: Gould uses them to build to a deductive conclusion. Then have students cover the excerpt and write a generalization in their own words that states Gould's main idea. Let them share their generalizations with their classmates.

Summary

Like a paraphrase, a summary, or précis, presents the basic meaning of a piece in your own words. Whereas a paraphrase is about the same length as the original, a summary condenses a passage to about one-third of its original length without sacrificing its basic meaning.

You read and listen to summaries daily. The lead paragraph of a news article that appears in a newspaper or magazine is a summary.

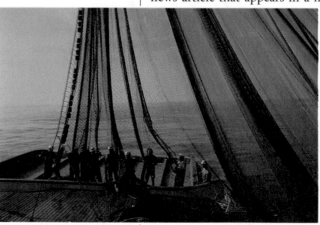

Radio and television broadcasts present the important events of the day in brief, summarized form. Summaries also often serve as the conclusions of compositions, reports, and research papers.

In addition to summarizing source materials in your writing, you can write summaries as you are reading to help you understand complex material.

Read the following passage by Jacques Costeau and compare it with the summary on the following page.

Science Connection

Students who enjoyed the excerpt from *The Flamingo's Smile* may enjoy other books of essays on natural history by Stephen Jay Gould. Suggest *The Panda's Thumb* and *Hen's Teeth and Horse's Toes*. Challenge interested students to identify a particularly striking passage by Gould or another science writer and paraphrase it. Allow the class to read the original passage and the paraphrase. Then ask the class to judge the effectiveness of the paraphrase, using the Guidelines for Paraphrasing to establish criteria.

Original Passage

About a hundred years ago, Thomas Henry Huxley, the English biologist, could say with confidence: "I believe that probably all the great sea fisheries are inexhaustible; that is to say that nothing we do seriously affects the number of fish." Huxley, of course, did not foresee the technological advances that would be made and applied within a century to fishing, as well as to every other aspect of man's activities. Sadly, Huxley's prediction has proved wrong. Today's fishing fleets consist of entire flotillas equipped with electronic devices and include floating ships that process the catch at sea. Planes are often used as spotters to locate schools of fish. Radio telephones direct boats to the fish. Radar and echo sounders find schools that cannot be seen from the air or on the water's surface. Moreover, oceanic sciences have determined the conditions of salinity and temperatures required for various species to thrive. Today, thermomometers and salinometers are used by fishing fleets. These ultramodern fishing fleets can stay in the open water almost indefinitely, sweeping the sea of much of its life. The herring population in the Atlantic, the most heavily fished area of the world, is decreasing. Haddock may have been wiped out. Similarly, modern whaling methods have all but eliminated several types of whales from the face of the earth. Helicopters and swift, engine-driven catcher boats with sounding equipment spot the whales. Explosive harpoons fired from guns mounted on the catchers find their marks. Humans have become by far the greatest predators of all time. **Jacques Cousteau**

Research Skills **485**

To model summarizing for students, place a brief magazine article on the overhead projector and circle the main ideas and details you would incorporate into a summary. Draw lines through the material that you would omit from your summary, and discuss portions that you would shorten or simplify.

Springboard

To develop summarizing skills in a lively way, play "Literature in a Nutshell." Ask students to write the shortest possible summary of a work with which they are familiar. For example, *Romeo and Juliet* might be abbreviated: Boy meets girl, boy loses girl, girl loses boy. Then point out that such a condensation, though funny, is not a true summary because it could describe hundreds of stories. Challenge students to add the minimum amount of detail needed to make the summary recognizably about *Romeo and Juliet* and no other work.

Critical Thinking

Judging Ask students to evaluate the model summary of the Cousteau excerpt. Let them begin by developing criteria for evaluation; if they have trouble with this, suggest questions (Is the length appropriate? Does it cover all main points? Does it omit unnecessary details? Is the wording significantly different from the author's?) and direct students to rank them in order of importance. Have students refer to specific parts of the summary as they make their evaluations. If they can see ways to improve the summary, encourage them to rewrite it, incorporating the necessary changes.

S T U D E N T
M O D E L

Summary

> A hundred years ago, the English biologist Thomas Henry Huxley predicted that despite anything we might do, our supply of fish would remain inexhaustible. Technological and scientific advances have proved him wrong. Today's year-round fleets are aided by electronic detectors, radio telephones, radar, echo sounders, and spotter planes. Advances in oceanic sciences have further improved their efficiency. As a result, the herring population has been seriously decreased; haddock and several kinds of whales have been almost wiped out. Humans are the greatest destroyers of all time (Cousteau 131).

Follow these steps when writing a summary.

Guidelines for Summarizing

1. **Locate the important points.** Identify the core of the writer's argument.

2. **Reduce the information.** Look for ways to reduce or eliminate unnecessary details, examples, anecdotes, and repetition. Also shorten long phrases and combine sentences.

3. **Revise the summary.** Check to make sure that all essential ideas in the original are contained in the summary.

Documentation of Sources

Whenever you use material from another writer, whether you are quoting directly, paraphrasing, or summarizing, you must document your source.

Using Parenthetical Documentation In using **parenthetical documentation,** you list the author's last name and the page number from the source in parentheses after the paraphrased, summarized, or quoted material. Notice, for example, the following documentation from a research paper about baseball.

> Baseball was played in a form called rounders in England in the early eighteenth century, and until 1845 was popular in various forms in America (Voigt 11).

If you use the author's name in the sentence introducing the quotation, you need to supply only the page number in the parenthetical reference.

> David Voigt refers to the decade of the 1880's as baseball's "Golden Age" (11).

To cite two or more works in one reference, separate the works with a semicolon. For example: (Voigt 25–27; Mackie 166). If you use two or more works by the same author in your paper, put the author's name and the title of the source—or an abbreviation—in the parenthetical note. For example: (Voigt, Baseball 64).

When citing the source of a brief quotation that ends a sentence, place the reference between the closing quotation mark and the final punctuation.

> The popularity of the sport had ramifications in other aspects of life: "baseball sold newspapers" (61).

A source may be attributed to a corporate author, such as the Department of the Treasury or the Environmental Protection Agency. In such a case, use the corporate author in your documentation (Environmental Protection Agency 17) or simply mention the corporate author in the text.

Sometimes you will find that your source contains a quotation from another source that you want to use. If the second source is not available, you may simply begin your parenthetical reference with the abbreviation *qtd. in* for "quoted in."

When you use an in-text parenthetical citation, be sure to document the complete source in your bibliography. See "Research Report," pages 287–290, for detailed information on preparing a bibliography.

Using Footnotes   Another form of documentation is the **footnote,** which can be used instead of parenthetical references. The information to be documented by footnotes should be numbered consecutively throughout the paper. Use Arabic numerals placed in the text of your paper, usually after the last word of a sentence or a direct quotation. The footnote number should be superscripted, that is, placed slightly above the line on which it appears.

> . . . Sometimes, however, a forest fire may actually play a useful ecological role in preventing the buildup of excess brush and debris, and also in allowing the development of certain types of seeds.[6]

 Individualizing Instruction

Basic Students   To give students practice with parenthetical documentation, have them quote and paraphrase brief paragraphs of instructional material from this textbook and document it correctly. (Instruct them to treat the textbook as a work by a corporate author.) Then have them use the instructions on pp. 287–290 to prepare a complete bibliography entry for this textbook.

Advanced Students   Let students apply their documentation skills by writing a brief review of one of the chapters in this textbook. The review should include at least three direct quotations. Some of the sentences containing quotations should also incorporate part of the documentation, so that the parenthetical references will differ in form. Then refer students to the instructions on pp. 287–290, and have them prepare a bibliography entry for this textbook.

Humanities Connection

MLA Handbook   Explain to students that the Modern Language Association sets the standards for documentation followed by most scholars and researchers in the humanities. Bring to class a copy of the MLA Handbook and let students scan it for details about documentation and other information concerning research.

Critical Thinking

Making Comparisons Explain that footnotes were once the only acceptable form for documentation, but today they are used infrequently, whereas parenthetical documentation is widely used. Point out that it is useful to know how footnotes are constructed, both because students may at some point in their studies be required to use footnotes, and because they will probably encounter them in reference material and will need to know how to interpret them. Invite students to compare the footnote method of documentation with the parenthetical method of documentation. Encourage them to notice the differences and similarities in form and to consider the advantages and disadvantages of each method.

Stumbling Block

Mention that, aside from the problems of plagiarism, it can be especially difficult to find one's own writing voice when working with researched material because the scholarly tone, technical terminology, and/or strong voices of the professional writers of the source material are distracting. When writing up research, if students find themselves sounding more like reference works than like themselves, they should stop for a while and try writing in their journals about their subject matter. They can explore why they like their topic, which parts they find most interesting, and why. This will give them a chance to catch the sound of their own voices again. Another tactic is to tape-record themselves as they explain to a good friend the concepts they are writing about.

Footnotes in a paper may appear at the bottom of each page or on a separate page at the end. If you do on-page footnotes, allow enough space at the bottom for all the footnotes on that page. When you have typed the last line of text on a page, skip one line. Then type a solid line that extends across the page, from the left margin to the right. Skip another line, and then type your first footnote. Single-space each footnote, but double-space between them. Here is a footnote and its corresponding documentation.

> . . . Sometimes, however, a forest fire may actually play a useful ecological role in preventing the buildup of excess brush and debris, and also in allowing the development of certain types of seeds.[6]

---

6. Rene Dubos, <u>The Wooing of Earth</u> (New York: Charles Scribner's Sons, 1980), 134.

Avoiding Plagiarism The act of presenting someone else's words or ideas as your own is known as **plagiarism.** Plagiarism is a serious offense and is avoided by all responsible writers. Follow these procedures when gathering source material to avoid plagiarism.

- Write complete bibliographic information on $3'' \times 5''$ index cards for each source you are likely to use. Give each card a source number. Write down the number beside the notes you take from each source so you can document your information.
- Write material from your sources on note cards. If you copy material from a source word for word, be sure to put quotation marks around it.
- If you write a summary or paraphrase on a note card, indicate that fact on the card.

When writing your paper follow these guidelines:

- **Do not document ideas or phrases that are common knowledge.** Material is considered common knowledge if it can be found in many different sources or if it is knowledge that many people have.

- **Document all direct quotes.**

- **Document all original ideas.** While it is not always clear what constitutes an original idea, you will be reasonably safe if you follow this guideline: *If you didn't think of it and you haven't heard of it before, then document it.*

Practice Your Skills

A. Write a paraphrase of the following passage. Try to retain all the basic ideas of the original, but make sure you use your own words.

Americans seem to live and breathe and function by paradox; but in nothing are we so paradoxical as in our passionate belief in our own myths. We truly believe ourselves to be natural-born mechanics and do-it-yourself-ers. We spend our lives in motor cars, yet most of us—a great many of us at least—do not know enough about a car to look in the gas tank when the motor fails. Our lives as we live them would not function without electricity, but it is a rare man or woman who, when the power goes off, knows how to look for a burned-out fuse and replace it. We believe implicitly that we are the heirs of the pioneers; that we have inherited self-sufficiency and the ability to take care of ourselves. . . . There isn't a man among us in ten thousand who knows how to butcher a cow or a pig and cut it up for eating, let alone a wild animal. . . . Americans treasure the knowledge that they live close to nature, but fewer and fewer farmers feed more and more people; and as soon as we can afford to we eat out of cans, buy frozen TV dinners, and haunt the delicatessens.
John Steinbeck, *America and Americans*

B. Write a summary of this passage. Condense it to one-third its original length without sacrificing its essential meaning.

[Dinosaurs] were unintelligent machines; their actions were automatic, and lacking in the flexibility needed to cope with unfamiliar situations. Flexibility means intelligence, and the dinosaurs had little. Their small brains held a limited repertoire of behavior, with no room for varied response. The brain of the dinosaur was devoted mainly to the control of his huge bulk; it served simply as a telephone switching center, receiving signals from his body and sending out messages to move his head and limbs in unthinking reaction. If the eye of Tyrannosaurus registered a moving object, he pursued it; but his hunt lacked cunning. If the eye of Brontosaurus registered movement, he fled; but his flight was mechanical and mindless. And some other dinosaurs were still less intelligent; Stegosaurus, a ten-ton vegetarian, had a brain the size of a walnut. Dinosaurs were stupid animals; incapable of thought, moving slowly and ponderously, they waded through life as walking robots. . . . There was no need for greater intelligence in their lives, and therefore it never evolved.
Robert Jastrow, *Until the Sun Dies*

Springboard

Suggest that students try rewriting the following scholarly sentences using their own words and their own writing voices.

1. The tendency to endow lowly vocations with names presumably dignified goes back to the Revolution, and has been frequently noted by English travelers, beginning with Thomas Anburey in 1779.

2. Either we continue whaling policies as they now exist in order to acquire what the whale affords, until we have exterminated all remaining whales, or we develop alternative sources for the products now supplied by the whaling industry.

This feature by Dave Barry treats the subject of college testing in a humorous manner. Guide students to realize that humor, as illustrated by this essay, is a good way to alleviate the tension that often accompanies test taking and making major decisions about the future. Encourage students to bring in other examples of the subject of applying to colleges. Post these in a "College Corner" on the class bulletin board.

On the Lightside

CLAW YOUR WAY TO THE TOP

Humorist Dave Barry's educational plan for a successful future

ELEMENTARY SCHOOL

This is where you should learn to add, subtract, multiply, and divide, which are skills that are essential for filling out expense reports; you should also develop lifelong chumships with anybody whose name ends in "II," or, even better, "III." You might also consider learning to read. This is not really necessary, of course, inasmuch as you will have a secretary for this purpose, but some businesspersons like to occasionally do it themselves for amusement on long airplane trips.

HIGH SCHOOL

The point of high school is to get into a good college. The way you do this is by being well rounded, which is measured by how many organizations you belong to. Many college admissions officers select students by actually slapping a ruler down on the list of accomplishments underneath each applicant's high school yearbook picture. So you should join every one of the ludicrous high school organizations available to you, such as the Future Appliance Owners Club and the National Honor Society. If they won't let you into the National Honor Society, have your parents file a lawsuit alleging discrimination on the basis of intelligence.

Another thing you need to do in high school is to get good SAT scores, which are these two numbers you receive in the mail from the Educational Testing Service in Princeton, New Jersey. They have a whole warehouse filled with numbers up there. To get yours, you have to send some money off by mail to Princeton, then you have to go sit in a room full of other students with number-two pencils and answer questions like "BRAZIL is to COMPENSATE as LUST is to . . ." Then you have to figure out what kind of mood the folks up at the Educational Testing Service were in on the day they made up that particular question.

Nobody has the vaguest idea anymore how this elaborate ritual got started, what it has to do with anything in the real world, or how the Educational Testing Service decides what numbers to send you. My personal theory is that it has to do with how much money you send them in the mail. I think the amounts they tell you to send are actually just Suggested Minimum Donations, if you get my drift.

Dave Barry

490

Library, Reference Works, and Other Sources

REVIEWING CLASSIFICATION SYSTEMS

Most of the important human accomplishments have come about because someone asked a question and got an answer. In fact, this simple process is the basis for all research. Libraries hold the answers to so many important questions that they need their own unique organizational system.

Card and Computer Catalogs

Any search for materials in the library should start with the catalog listings. The card catalog allows you to locate a listing for a book by **title**, by **author**, and, for nonfiction books, by **subject.** Next to every listing in a card catalog, you will find an identification number, the **call number,** which will help you locate the book. Some libraries have recently supplemented or replaced the card catalog with a computer catalog, where the search process is the same as it is with the more familiar cards.

The Classification of Books

All libraries organize books similarly. The most elementary categorization of books in libraries is as fiction or nonfiction.

Fiction In most libraries, novels are arranged alphabetically by the author's last name. Books by the same author are shelved alphabetically by title. Short-story anthologies may be shelved with novels by the author's last name, placed in a separate section at the end of fiction, or classified as literature in the nonfiction section.

Nonfiction Factual material, or nonfiction, is organized in one of two ways. Many libraries use the Dewey Decimal System to classify their nonfiction. Major disciplines—technology, for example—are further divided into subcategories, such as 608 for inventions and patents. The Dewey Decimal numbers form the call number that is displayed on the book spine to help you locate the book on the library shelves.

COMPUTER TIP

When using a computer catalog, print out the sources you find listed. This saves time, ensures accuracy, and eliminates having to come back to find more sources.

Library and
Other Sources   **491**

Writing Handbook 25:

Library, Reference Works, and Other Sources

Objectives

1. To use card catalogs and the *Reader's Guide* to locate library materials
2. To identify and use the parts of a book
3. To identify and use encyclopedias, almanacs, atlases, indexes, and other reference sources
4. To vary research techniques

Handbook Mini-Lessons

For information on topics related to the library, reference works, and other sources, see the following mini-lessons.
- Research Skills, pp. 479–489
- Understanding and Evaluating the Media, pp. 534–539
- Occupational Interests and Career Choices, pp. 507–515

Teaching Strategies

Motivating

Start the class by presenting two or three mysterious events or phenomena from various fields. For example, the Egyptian pyramids were built of stones weighing many tons. How did people with no sophisticated technology carry these stones for miles and lift them up to build the pyramids? Jot student suggestions of additional mysteries on the board and discuss where information about these phenomena could be found. Lead students to recognize that the single most fruitful source of all such information is the library.

Collaborative Opportunity

Allow students to form groups and increase their familiarity with the Dewey Decimal System by deciding under which classification each of the following nonfiction works would be found. Groups can exchange their work and check one another's answers. (Correct answers appear in parentheses.)

1. *The Short-Cut Cookbook* (600–699)

2. *Simone de Beauvoir: A Biography* (900–999)

3. *Ever Since Darwin: Reflections in Natural History* (500–599)

4. *An Anthology of Spanish Poetry,* (800–899)

5. *Norse Mythology* (200–299)

6. *Philosophy and the Mirror of Nature* (100–199)

7. *Who's Who in America* (000–099)

8. *Photography for Beginners* (700–799)

9. *A History of the Moors in Spain* (900–999)

10. *The Official Baseball Rule Book* (700–799)

Dewey Decimal Classifications

000–099	General Works (encyclopedias, bibliographies)
100–199	Philosophy (conduct, psychology)
200–299	Religion (the Bible, mythology, theology)
300–399	Social Science (law, education, economics)
400–499	Language (grammars, dictionaries, foreign languages)
500–599	Science (mathematics, biology, chemistry)
600–699	Technology (medicine, inventions, cooking)
700–799	The Arts (painting, music, theater, sports)
800–899	Literature (poetry, plays, essays—but not novels)
900–999	History (biography, geography, travel)

Melvil Dewey, American librarian, 1851-1931

Some libraries use the Library of Congress, or LC, system. This system has twenty-one broad categories, designated by letters of the alphabet. Subcategories are identified with a second letter. Fiction is shelved in the P section in the LC system.

P1880 G672.1 A701.3 P934.41 Q434.0 T114.91

Library of Congress Classification

A	General Works	M	Music
B	Philosophy, Psychology, Religion	N	Fine Arts
C-F	History	P	Language and Literature
G	Geography, Anthropology, Recreation	Q	Science
		R	Medicine
H	Social Science	S	Agriculture
J	Political Science	T	Technology
K	Law	U	Military Science
L	Education	V	Naval Science
		Z	Bibliography and Library Science

Literature Connection

Biography   Students may enjoy browsing in the library's biography section for works that interest them. You might want to guide them toward biographies of literary figures, such as Deirdre Bair's recent and illuminating *Simone de Beauvoir,* Vladimir Nabokov's *Speak, Memory,* Eudora Welty's *One Writer's Beginnings,* and Scott Elledge's *E.B. White.*

LOCATING MATERIALS

Your research will be more efficient if you learn about the special sections or rooms that libraries have.

Sections of the Library

Stacks The stacks, or shelves, in a library may be open or closed. Although only library personnel can use **closed stacks,** you can browse freely in open stacks to locate resources.

Periodicals Current magazines and newspapers are often displayed on open racks in a separate section or room. Back issues of periodicals may be bound and shelved in the periodical room.

Nonprint Microfilm and microfiche, photographic reductions of printed material, are often housed in a separate room, along with machines for reading them. Filmstrips, films, cassettes, records, compact discs, art prints, and framed photographs also may be found there.

Reference, Biography, and Vertical File These areas are discussed later in this handbook.

FINDING THE BEST SOURCE

Although browsing in the stacks can help you find sources of information, following some proven research methods will save you effort and produce more reliable results.

Indexes

Indexes are sources that lead to other sources. Indexes list names, places, topics, people, titles, and first lines of works alphabetically, and they supply the titles of specific reference books that contain information on the listing.

Readers' Guide to Periodical Literature Suppose that you are writing a publicity article for the school paper on an upcoming sixties dance and you need some background on the twist. Skimming subject entries in the bound volumes of the *Readers' Guide* for the sixties would provide you with a list of magazine articles on the twist.

Library and
Other Sources   **493**

Springboard

From your community library, you can obtain a catalog of available audio/video material. Bring it to class, and encourage students to read it and to go to the library to investigate any audio or video material that interests them. You might want to offer extra credit if a student writes a summary of the material and how it was located.

Teaching Tip: Library

To gain familiarity with the way the school or local library is arranged, suggest that students work in groups to create a basic guide to it. Their guide should cover whether stacks are open or closed; where current periodicals are displayed, and where back issues are shelved; where microfilm and microfiche materials are found; how to operate a microfilm reader; where films, cassettes, records, and art prints can be located, and whether they can be checked out. You may want to specify an audience for this guide; perhaps incoming freshmen, local seniors, or even elementary-school children. Remind students to choose content and diction that will engage the interest of the audience.

Teaching Tip: Personal Goals

Point out that the library has more information than most people realize. It is an excellent source of help with any project students may have, from do-it-yourself car repair to selecting a university, *if* students know how to use it. Suggest that students use their journals to explore what they hope to accomplish within the next five years, the next year, and the next six months. When they have done so, they should jot down the kinds of information they will need to accomplish their goals. Direct them to be alert for instructions on how to find that information in the library or in other reference sources.

To give students practice in using the *Readers' Guide* to locate periodical articles, divide the class into groups and give each group a photocopy of pages from the *Readers' Guide*. Instruct each group to write five questions that can be answered only by using their own pages from the *Readers' Guide*. Then have groups exchange their sets of questions and their *Readers' Guide* pages, and answer the questions their peers have written. After students have finished and the writers of the questions have confirmed the answers, consider asking students to share anything new they may have learned about the *Readers' Guide*.

Modeling

Students may not know that *The New York Times Index* goes back to the years long before they were born. Use *The New York Times Index* to find abstracts of the major news articles that appeared on the day you were born. Copy the abstracts and show them to students; suggest that they use *The New York Times Index* as you did, locate information about what happened on their dates of birth, and report on it in class.

The excerpt from the *Readers' Guide* below shows typical listings.

The New York Times Index   If you are researching an incident or an issue that made the national news, *The New York Times Index* will have abstracts of articles about your topic. This index lists articles by subject in chronological order for each year.

Biography and Genealogy Master Index   There are over 350 commonly used biographical dictionaries. The *Biography and Genealogy Master Index* tells you which biographical sources contain information on the person you are researching. The index lists pseudonyms as well as real names.

Granger's Index to Poetry   Suppose your literature text does not include Shelley's poem "Ozymandias," but you need a copy of the poem by tomorrow. *Granger's Index to Poetry* lists this poem by author, title, and first line and identifies books containing it.

Other Indexes   Similar to *Granger's,* the *Short Story Index* and the *Play Index* help you locate books that contain a certain literary work. The *National Geographic Magazine Cumulative Index* can help you locate articles in *National Geographic* magazine published from 1899 to 1976. The *American Heritage Cumulative Index* is useful for research of American history.

Social Studies Connection

Students with an interest in social studies may find it interesting to use *The New York Times Index* as primary source material. For example, by scanning the abstracts of articles that appeared in the months before a historical event (such as the U.S.'s entry into World War II), students can get an unusually broad view of the range of the event's immediate causes.

Parts of a Book

An examination of the parts of a book will help you decide if the book is going to be useful to you.

Title Page   The title page lists the full title, author or editor, and publisher. Publication by a special-interest group may affect the credibility of the material.

Copyright Page   The publication date will help you determine if the information in the book is current enough for your purpose.

Foreword, Preface, Introduction   Skim this preliminary material to learn how the author approached the subject.

Contents   This chapter outline of the book's contents will indicate coverage of your topic.

Index   This detailed alphabetical list of subjects, found in the back of the book, directs you to the page(s) you need.

Text   Sample the text itself. A useful source will treat the subject thoroughly in language that you can understand.

End Matter   You may find that one source is superior to others because it includes maps and charts in an **appendix** or because it contains a **glossary** of special terms. **Notes** and **bibliographies** list the author's sources. If one source is mentioned repeatedly in the bibliographies that you check, this source may be an especially reliable one for you to consult.

Reference Works

Dictionaries, encyclopedias, yearbooks, atlases, and almanacs are usually cataloged as reference works. Such sources are often located in a separate room or section of the library and are marked with an *R* or *Ref* above the call number.

Dictionaries

Abridged dictionaries, sometimes called college or desk dictionaries, are useful for discovering the meanings of unfamiliar words. **Unabridged dictionaries,** like the *Oxford English Dictionary* and *Webster's Third New International Dictionary,* contain longer, more detailed entries than those in abridged dictionaries.

Specialized Dictionaries

You might consult one of the many specialized dictionaries available if you are researching a topic that requires specialized or technical knowledge.

Dictionaries About Language You can trace the origin of a word in either an abridged or an unabridged dictionary, but if you try to learn the etymology of a phrase such as "heavens to Betsy," you may need one of several dictionaries that treat specific aspects of language. These aspects include phrases, idioms, slang, jargon, rhyme, etymologies, and elements of usage.

Thesaurus The word *thesaurus* comes from a Greek word meaning "treasure." This dictionary of synonyms and antonyms is indeed a treasure to a writer who is looking for a word with just the right shade of meaning.

Special-Purpose Dictionaries Special-purpose dictionaries are available for many subjects, such as music, law, and medicine. If you wanted to explain the distinction between watercolor, gouache, and casein paints, for example, you probably would find a dictionary of art terms to be most helpful.

Encyclopedias

Encyclopedias, like dictionaries, can provide either general or specialized information.

General Encyclopedias The word *encyclopedia* comes from a Greek word meaning "general education." Thus, the alphabetically arranged collection of articles on nearly every subject that makes up the volumes of an encyclopedia provides a quick reference on a subject. Yearbooks provide updated supplementary information.

The respected *Encyclopaedia Britannica* is composed of three parts: the *Propaedia,* or Outline of Knowledge and Guide to the *Britannica;* the *Micropaedia,* an index and short-entry encyclopedia; and the *Macropaedia,* which contains knowledge in detail.

Specialized Encyclopedias Just as you may need to consult a specialized dictionary for technical vocabulary, you may need to consult a specialized encyclopedia on a specific subject for more exact, more detailed information than a general source offers. For example, a discussion in your economics class centers around monopolies and how they differ from cartels. Your assignment is to write a comparison-contrast paper. You might supplement what you learn from a general encyclopedia with material from a specialized work such as Donald Greenwald's *Encyclopedia of Economics.*

Almanacs, Yearbooks, and Atlases

Because almanacs and yearbooks are published annually, they provide an excellent source for current facts and statistics. They also cover matters of historical record in government, economics, sports, and other fields. Examples include the *Statistical Abstract of the United States* and the *World Almanac and Book of Facts.*

Atlases, such as the *National Geographic Atlas of the World,* are books of maps that also contain information about weather, global statistics, and geography.

Biographical References

In some libraries, biographies are part of the 900 Dewey Decimal classification and are marked with a number that begins with 92. Other libraries create a separate biography section and mark each book with a *B* and the first letter of the last name of the person the book is about.

If you want only to learn or confirm simple facts, such as someone's birth date or career history, a special dictionary such as *Webster's Biographical Dictionary* would be a good choice. If you require more information but do not need a full-length biography, consult sources such as the following for information on your subject: *Who's Who, Who's Who in America, Current Biography,* and *Dictionary of American Biography.*

Literary Reference Works

Literary research may involve a variety of tasks. You may need to learn about writers and their works or investigate some aspect of literary history. Occasionally, you might need to identify a quotation or locate a poem or short story. Literary reference works meet these needs.

Books About Authors   Sources such as *Twentieth Century Authors* and *Contemporary Authors* provide biographical information about authors. More extensive entries in *American Writers: A Collection of Literary Biographies and Writers at Work* also identify the connections between the authors' own experiences and those of their fictional characters.

Library and
Other Sources   **497**

on pp. 497–498

Many students are unaware of the range of information included in literary reference works. To enhance their awareness, ask them to decide which of the sources listed on pp. 497–498 would provide answers to the following questions. (Correct answers are in parentheses.)

1. What were the last words of the American author Gertrude Stein? *(American Writers: A Collection of Literary Biographies)*
2. Which American author wrote the short story "A Good Man Is Hard to Find"? *(The Oxford Companion to American Literature)*
3. What is the title, and who is the author, of the novel in which the main character is called Meursault? *(Cyclopedia of Literary Characters)*
4. Who won the Booker Prize for British literature in 1981? *(The Oxford Companion to English Literature)*
5. What is the actual wording of the Biblical phrase that many people quote as "Spare the rod and spoil the child"? *(Bartlett's Familiar Quotations)*

Literature Connection

Encyclopedia   Assign students to research one of the earliest encyclopedias: the French author Denis Diderot's *Encyclopédie,* whose first volume came out in 1751. (A modern encyclopedia might be a good place to begin researching.) Students will be interested to learn that some of the volumes were so controversial that they—the books—were locked up in a prison, and that they have been cited as contributing to the unrest that culminated in the French Revolution. Challenge students to determine what it was about the *Encyclopédie* that sparked such controversy.

Problem Solving Point out to students that flexibility and creative thinking are keys to success in research. Instruct them to work in groups to brainstorm ways they might use the Altering Your Techniques strategies (p. 499) if they could find no heading in the card catalog for the topics you are going to hand out. Then give each group a slip of paper on which is written a topic like the following: gene transfer; Dadaism; agribusiness; scoliosis; cinnabar; levitation; tektites; Circe; golden macaques. (If students do not know the meanings of the terms on the slips, their first step will be to consult a dictionary.) Allow the groups fifteen minutes to explore their topics and brainstorm; then ask them to report their findings and ideas to the class.

Book Review Digest Suppose that you are responsible for writing the book reviews in your school newspaper. By consulting articles in the *Book Review Digest,* arranged alphabetically by author, you can compare your reviews with those of professional reviewers.

Cyclopedia of Literary Characters The *Cyclopedia of Literary Characters* identifies the main characters in 1,300 novels, dramas, and epics from world literature. For example, a glance at the listing "Uriah Heep" in the character index leads you to a listing for Charles Dickens's *David Copperfield* and tells you that Heep was a hypocritical embezzler.

Books of Quotations *Bartlett's Familiar Quotations* is a popular source for identifying quotations and well-known sayings. You may search for a quotation by author, subject, or first line. *Bartlett's* also contains a short section with often-quoted passages from religious works, such as the Bible, the Koran, and the Book of Common Prayer.

Bergen Evans's *Dictionary of Quotations* is another useful source. It extends beyond *Bartlett's* to include the comments of contemporary literary, political, and scientific figures.

Other Literary Sources Your library offers many reference works on the history of literature. Among them you will find the Oxford Companion Series. Suppose you know that the character John Falstaff appears in a number of Shakespearean plays. How can you quickly learn which ones? You will find this kind of information in *The Oxford Companion to English Literature*. You will also find short biographies of authors, discussions of literary movements, awards and lists of winners, and explanations of literary allusions. Other books in the Oxford series focus specifically on American literature, classical literature, and the theater.

Literature Connection

Quotations Ask students to list five abstract concepts that have meaning for them (for example, love, friendship, independence, etc.). They can then use *Bartlett's* or the *Dictionary of Quotations* to locate quotations that deal with these concepts and that appeal to them. Instruct them to record quotations and sources in their journals; they may yield writing topics.

EXPANDING RESEARCH SKILLS

The process of research, like a road map, suggests a network of possible directions for you to follow. At times, you may decide to alter your techniques or explore sources beyond the library.

Altering Your Techniques

If you seem to have reached a dead end in your research, try some of the following strategies.

1. Examine how your topic fits a category. Suppose you fail to find a listing in the card catalog for the topic *chaos theory*. Chaos theory is a subcategory of the cosmos. You may be able to find information about chaos theory listed under the entry for *cosmos*.

2. Expand your search words. Consult a specialized dictionary or a thesaurus for additional terms related to your topic. For example, if you are investigating genetically transmitted diseases, you could start by looking for source material about genetics. Then you could look for information listed under the related headings *heredity* and *inherited traits*.

3. Follow up cross-references. Catalog listings and encyclopedia articles often include related subject headings called **cross-references**. DNA and Mendel's law, for example, might be cross-reference leads for the genetic disease topic.

4. Be alert to possible sources in bibliography lists. Skim the bibliographies found at the end of encyclopedia and journal articles and in the backs of nonfiction books.

5. Remember: the librarian is a valuable resource. Your library is staffed with knowledgeable people who are anxious to help you with your research.

WRITER TO WRITER

The single most important thing to remember when using the library is this: *if you have a question, ask someone.* A reference librarian can help you match your needs to the sources of information available in the library.

Milton H. Crouch, librarian

Library and Other Sources **499**

Cooperative Learning

Consider letting students work in groups to complete the Practice Your Skills exercise on p. 500. To ensure that each group member understands how to locate a wide variety of reference information, direct the groups to start by going down the list of Practice Your Skills questions together and writing down the most likely reference source for finding the answer to each question. Groups can then divide up the research tasks and share the information they discover.

Managing the Paper Load

Peer grading of the Practice Your Skills exercise on p. 500 may be especially beneficial in this lesson because many of the questions have a variety of answers that can be considered correct. If the groups exchange papers with other groups, they can divide up the tasks of checking their peers' answers, and they will add to their own knowledge in the process.

COMPUTER TIP

Find out if your library offers modem services—computer telephone connections to central data banks providing current information on many topics.

Exploring Sources Beyond the Library

The U.S. government and special-interest groups may be able to provide information not available elsewhere.

U.S. Government as a Source The Government Printing Office and many government agencies publish material on a multitude of subjects. Consult the *United States Government Organizational Manual,* which gives the purpose of each government agency and indicates the agencies to consult for special information. Also examine the *Selected List of United States Publications* to obtain the titles of possible useful publications.

Information Networks Special-interest groups or organizations often distribute excellent pamphlets. These are sometimes housed in a set of library file cabinets called the **vertical file.** Names and addresses of special-interest organizations may be found in the *Encyclopedia of Associations.*

Practice Your Skills

A. Choose a suitable topic for a research paper. Use the card catalog or computer catalog in your library to compile a working bibliography for the topic. List at least three books.

B. Continue researching the topic you chose for Exercise A by finding two related listings in the *Readers' Guide* and one listing in another index mentioned in this handbook. Copy the entry information for each listing.

C. Use reference works to complete the following items.

1. List the almanac, yearbook, or atlas that supplies the following statistics: (a) last year's PGA winner; (b) average rainfall in Buenos Aires, Argentina; (c) primary export of the United States.
2. What does a computer user mean by saying that a program needs "handshaking"?
3. How favorable were the reviews of John Steinbeck's *The Grapes of Wrath* when it was first published?
4. What is the plot of Frank Norris's novel *The Pit?*
5. Complete this quotation, and identify the speaker: "Let us never negotiate out of fear . . ."

D. List three sources found in the card or computer catalog that provide information on the French Revolution. You may need to search alternative headings and cross-references.

Springboard

Invite a reference librarian, perhaps from a nearby university library, to come and speak to the class. Suggest that the librarian offer personal anecdotes in describing the education it takes to become a librarian; what he or she likes best (and least) about the job; and which library resources he or she considers most useful. You may want students to use their journals, before the librarian comes, to record their expectations of what the librarian will be like. After the visit, they can compare their expectations to the reality; they may be surprised.

Debating Techniques

A **debate** consists of two opposing teams arguing a controversial subject called the question, or **proposition.** In a formal debate, the proposition is stated as a **resolution.** That is, it begins with the words, "Resolved, that. . . " and then makes a positive statement that advances an opinion, a solution, or an action. A typical proposition might be: "Resolved, that Puerto Rico should become the fifty-first state."

The speakers in a debate are divided into two teams. The **affirmative team** argues that the resolution should be upheld and accepted. The **negative team** argues that the resolution should be rejected. Each team tries to collect enough reasons and evidence to convince an audience that its stand is the correct one.

Debating helps sharpen your ability to analyze facts, evaluate evidence, and see logical connections. It also teaches you how to support your own views and to listen critically to the ideas of others. The following guidelines and techniques will enable you to argue your position on any subject effectively according to the rules of formal debate.

THE DEBATE PROPOSITION

All debates concern one of three types of propositions.

- **Propositions of fact** make a claim that a particular state of affairs can be proved to exist.

    Resolved, that acid rain is destroying forests.

- **Propositions of value** state that something is good or ethical.

    Resolved, that reporters are justified in maintaining the confidentiality of their sources.

- **Propositions of policy** recommend particular actions. Almost every topic for high-school debate is a proposition of policy.

    Resolved, that grades in elective classes should be abolished.

Debating
Techniques   **501**

Writing Handbook 26:
Debating Techniques

Objectives

1. To identify the format and elements of formal debate
2. To identify types of debate propositions and their characteristics
3. To identify and apply techniques of preparing for a debate
4. To identify and apply techniques for writing and delivering a constructive speech and rebuttal

Handbook Mini-Lessons

For information on topics related to debating techniques, see the following mini-lessons.

- Writing Introductions and Conclusions, pp. 365–375
- Developing Critical Thinking and Writing Skills, pp. 472–478
- Library, Reference Works, and Other Sources, pp. 491–500

Teaching Strategies

Motivating

Bring up a controversial issue familiar to students and ask what their position is on it. The issue could be an international, national, local, or school matter. Play devil's advocate, disputing students' contentions and provoking them to argument. Then as the discussion becomes louder and less rational, bring it to a halt and ask students to think about the way they have been arguing: is there any chance of arriving at any useful conclusions or agreements this way? Ask students to suggest rules and regulations that might be used to govern a conversation of this type to keep it calm and rational. Use students' suggestions to introduce the lesson.

Every debate proposition must have the following characteristics.

1. The proposition must be stated in the affirmative. For example, a proposition might state that "Warren High School should abolish its dress code," but would never state that "Warren High School should not have a dress code."

2. The proposition should state only one main idea.

3. The proposition should be arguable. Neither side should be obviously right or wrong.

4. The proposition should be expressed in precise language so that the debate does not become a quibble over words.

THE DEBATE FORMAT

Following is a traditional debate format.

1. The affirmative and negative teams have the same number of debaters and the same amount of time to speak.

2. Members of the two sides alternate speaking. The affirmative team opens and closes the debate.

3. Each of the team's speakers gives an opening speech called the **constructive speech** and a closing speech called the **rebuttal.** The constructive speech contains the evidence and reasoning that support the speaker's case. The rebuttal contains a defense of each team's arguments and an attack on the opposition's.

Constructive Speeches (8 minutes each)

First Affirmative	First Negative
(Speaker 1)	(Speaker 2)
Second Affirmative	Second Negative
(Speaker 3)	(Speaker 4)

Rebuttals (4 minutes each)

First Negative	First Affirmative
(Speaker 1)	(Speaker 2)
Second Negative	Second Affirmative
(Speaker 3)	(Speaker 4)

A chairperson presides and maintains order during the debate. A speaker may appeal to the chairperson if he or she feels that the opposing team has violated legitimate procedures. Either a panel of judges or the audience votes to decide which team wins.

Speaking and Listening

Point out that skillful listening is vital to preparing an effective rebuttal during a debate. To help students develop and practice listening skills, read or play a tape of a relatively brief speech (perhaps one of Winston Churchill's speeches from the 1940's); have students take notes on main points as they listen. Their notes should include (1) what each main point is, (2) whether it has adequate support, and (3) whether the support is logical. (If it is not, they should note, if possible, which errors in logic it displays.) Afterwards, let students discuss their notes, writing on the board the information they gathered in each of the three categories.

Literature Connection

Nonfiction   Let students read Jonathan Swift's "A Modest Proposal." Point out that Swift uses both logical reasoning and irony in the arguments he presents: He sets up his arguments (in favor of his proposal) by using logic, but simultaneously refutes these arguments by using irony. Challenge students to locate examples in the essay of both.

PREPARING FOR DEBATE

The debate itself may take only an hour or so, but many hours of studying, planning, and practicing must come first. The box below describes these steps as they relate to debate preparation.

Steps in Preparing for Debate

1. Research the proposition
2. Plan your case.
3. Write a constructive speech.
4. Practice your constructive speech.
5. Prepare for rebuttal.

Researching the Proposition

The first step in preparing for debate is to learn as much as possible about the subject. The more you know, the better you can argue either side of the proposition. To ensure systematic and thorough research, use the following guidelines.

Researching the Proposition

1. Do preliminary reading to gain background information on the proposition. Consult books, encyclopedias, atlases, magazines, newspapers, and other reference works.

2. Prepare a bibliography. Since most debate topics are current issues, current sources of information are most important. Consult such indexes as the *Readers' Guide to Periodical Literature,* the vertical file index, and the *Monthly Catalog of U.S. Government Publications.*

3. Collect as much material on your topic as you can find in the resources available to you.

4. Study the material you have collected. Record any facts, examples, or reasons that support your arguments. Be sure to gather a variety of materials.

5. Organize your notes by topic for easy access.

Debating
Techniques   503

Literature Connection

Poetry   Students may enjoy learning of two Renaissance writers who engaged in a form of poetic debate. Assign Christopher Marlowe's "The Passionate Shepherd to His Love" and Sir Walter Raleigh's "The Nymph's Reply to the Shepherd." Let students list Marlowe's points and then find Raleigh's rebuttals of them.

Collaborative Opportunity

You may wish to allow students to form small groups and divide up the research tasks. For example, a group of five could research the proposition concerning animal experimentation from Practice Your Skills, exercise B. Two members could consult the *Readers' Guide,* each checking under a different heading; another could consult the vertical file; another could research the pamphlet file; and another might interview local people involved in the issue. Group members could then pool the information they have discovered.

Teaching Tip: Supporting Evidence

Remind students that each of their main points should, ideally, be supported by more than one item of evidence. Point out that each item of evidence should contain specific details (names, numbers, or dates, for example) rather than generalizations, and that it should be based on fact rather than on opinion.

 Individualizing Instruction

Basic Students Point out that the evidence students choose to use must consist of facts, not opinions. To be sure that these students understand the differences between fact and opinion, remind them that statements of fact can be objectively verified (by consulting reference works or authorities), whereas statements of opinion are based on personal judgment. Ask students to determine whether each of the following is a fact or an opinion.

1. Mikhail Gorbachev won the Nobel Peace Prize in 1990. *(fact)*
2. Mikhail Gorbachev is one of the Soviet Union's greatest leaders. *(opinion)*
3. The people of Soviet Georgia are warm and friendly. *(opinion)*
4. Tbilisi is the capital of Soviet Georgia. *(fact)*

Building an Argument

Once you have researched and studied your subject, you are ready to plan your case and build an argument.

1. Analyze the proposition. Go over every important word of the proposition to make sure you know what you are to prove or disprove.

2. Determine the issues. The issues are the main differences between the affirmative and the negative positions. To determine the issues, list all the reasons you have for supporting your side of the proposition. Then list what your opponents' contrasting reasons might be. Devise a list of questions to help determine the issues.

Affirmative	Negative
a. Why does the current state of affairs need changing?	a. Why is there no need to change?
b. Why will the proposed change improve conditions?	b. Why will the proposal not improve conditions?
c. What other advantages will the change bring?	c. What bad effects would the change bring?
d. Why is it wrong to attack this proposition?	d. What more desirable idea could be suggested?

3. Choose your contentions, or main points. From the reasons you have for supporting your position, choose the ones you will use to build your case.

4. Select your evidence. Go over the notes from your reading to select items of evidence that support each of your points. Record each item of evidence and its source on a separate note card. Your case will appear stronger if you use various types of evidence, including statistics, examples from past experience, quotations from recognized authorities, and analogies to similar situations.

5. Prepare an outline. Separate your note cards according to topic. Your main points should become the main topics of your outline and the pieces of evidence the subtopics. Arrange the arguments in your outline in an order you think would have the greatest impact.

Social Studies Connection

Students with an interest in political science may enjoy reading transcripts of the debates that take place in the United States Senate and House of Representatives as bills are introduced, discussed, and put to the vote. Suggest that students locate copies of the *Congressional Record* in the library and follow the debates concerning any bills that interest them.

PREPARING CONSTRUCTIVE SPEECHES AND REBUTTALS

Once you have an outline, you can prepare your constructive speech and take notes to help in your rebuttal.

Constructive Speeches

The constructive speech should include an introduction, a body, and a conclusion. Avoid long, convoluted sentences that are difficult for the judges to follow. Use transitions between points to keep your speech flowing smoothly.

Introduction   The introduction should arouse interest by presenting questions, facts, illustrations, or anecdotes. It should also state the debate proposition as clearly and precisely as possible.

Body   The body of an affirmative or negative speech states the main points of the argument and presents evidence to support each point. However, affirmative and negative speeches differ in the following two ways.

1. The constructive speeches of an affirmative team show the need for change, the way to change, and the advantages of change.

2. The constructive speeches of a negative team defend the current conditions, show how proposed changes will be harmful, and suggest possible counterplans.

Conclusion   The conclusion of a constructive speech should simply summarize the main points listed in the body. Conclusions should never introduce new material, and they should not repeat the evidence used to support the main points. A clear restatement of the main position should end the constructive speech.

Rebuttal

The rebuttal affords debaters a final opportunity to attack their opponents' arguments and defend their own. Rebuttals do not include new issues, although they may introduce new evidence. Unlike constructive speeches, which are completely written ahead of time, rebuttals must be prepared while the debate is in progress.

Methods of Rebuttal   Each debater listens carefully to the opponents' constructive speeches, takes notes, organizes the material in

Debating Techniques   **505**

Teaching Tip: Parallel Structure

Point out that the organization of a constructive speech is similar to that of a persuasive essay, but that the sentence patterns in speeches differ significantly from those in written persuasion. For clarity, writers of speeches use shorter sentences and rely more on such devices as parallel structure and selective repetition to convey their points to listeners. If necessary, review parallel sentence parts (Handbook pp. 410–411). Then, to give students practice in using parallel structure and selective repetition, let them write sentences whose structure imitates each of the following.

1. It was the best of times; it was the worst of times.   —Charles Dickens
2. The Highlands of Vietnam are spooky, unbearably spooky, spooky beyond belief.
                              —Michael Herr
3. Slang is a language that rolls up its sleeves, spits on its hands, and goes to work.   —Carl Sandburg
4. Lock up your libraries if you like; but there is no gate, no lock, no bolt that you can set upon the freedom of my mind.
                              —Virginia Woolf

Critical Thinking

Drawing Conclusions   As students build and evaluate the conclusions of their constructive speeches, remind them to be wary of the "either/or" fallacy. Speeches displaying this common but subtle error in logic will present complex situations in polarized, black-and-white terms. For example, "In the country of Kurain, capitalistic enterprises are prohibited. This means that Kurain is a communist country." The speaker here is assuming, or trying to force others to assume, that an economy that is not capitalistic must be communistic; this assumption ignores many other alternative or mixed possibilities. Suggest that students be alert for the either/or fallacy as they evaluate their own conclusions and as they analyze the constructive speeches of others.

A. 1. No—stated in the negative. Revisions will vary but should be stated in the affirmative.

2. No—imprecise language. The terms *sufficient, the work world,* and *the last few years* are all too vague. Revisions will vary but should replace those terms with specific ones.

3. No—stated in the negative. Revisions will vary but should be stated in the affirmative.

B. Answers will vary, but should consist of two outlines, note cards with pertinent details to support main outline points, and an appropriate bibliography.

C. Answers will vary, but should begin with a "grabber" introduction, have main points logically organized, provide appropriate support for each point, and conclude with a summary of the body of speech.

his or her head, and prepares an extemporaneous rebuttal. This can be done in the following ways.

1. Prove that the opponents' evidence is not sufficient.

2. Prove that the evidence is inaccurate.

3. Prove that the evidence is from an unreliable source.

4. Prove that the evidence could lead to a different conclusion.

Rehearsing and Presenting the Debate

You and your partner should rehearse your constructive speeches many times. Presenting your speeches to parents or friends and asking them to list arguments against your position helps you find gaps in your thinking. For more help in evaluating arguments, see "Developing and Presenting an Argument," pages 474–476.

During the debate, stand so that you can see your audience. Vary the speed, pitch, and volume of your voice, and speak clearly and confidently. Avoid sarcasm and arrogance.

Practice Your Skills

A. Decide whether each of the following statements is a valid, well-worded proposition. If not, explain why and revise it.

1. Resolved, that public employees do not have the right to strike.
2. Resolved, that women have made sufficient gains in the work world in the last few years.
3. Resolved, that TV debates between political candidates do not change voters' opinions.

B. Choose one of the following propositions. Prepare to debate this proposition, taking either the affirmative or the negative side. Research the proposition, prepare a bibliography, gather evidence, and prepare an outline for your constructive speech and for a hypothetical rebuttal.

1. Resolved, that states should eliminate parole for prisoners who commit violent crimes.
2. Resolved, that medical and scientific experimentation with animals should be outlawed.

C. Write a constructive speech based on one of the propositions from Exercise B, or on another proposition of your own choice. Make sure that your introduction states the proposition and arouses a significant amount of interest among your listeners.

506 Writing Handbook

Occupational Interests and Career Choices

About this time, people may start asking you, "What are you going to do after graduation?" This may seem like a simple enough question, but when you give it some thought you just might find the entire issue a bit overwhelming. After all, you're being asked to map out your future, to make decisions that will affect the course of your life.

Here is some help. The following techniques for self-evaluation, preparing résumés and letters of application, and choosing a college or career will help you to plan the next few years of your life carefully and intelligently.

EVALUATING YOUR OPTIONS

You may have already identified an occupational interest or a definite career choice. Perhaps, however, your future goals are more general: to become independent, to provide for yourself or for a family, to find a challenging job, to work in an area of service to others. To clarify your goals, you will find it worthwhile to sit down and evaluate your options for the future.

Analyzing Your Interests, Abilities, and Needs

Your research and critical thinking skills are as valuable in finding answers to what to do with your life as they are in solving problems in school, at work, and with friends. Carefully consider the questions below. Discuss your answers to the questions with your guidance counselor, your parents, and anyone else whose opinion you value.

Identifying and Evaluating Your Interests   The following questions may help you to identify and evaluate your interests.

- What school subjects do I enjoy most and least? why?
- Which hobby, extracurricular activity, or volunteer work gives me the greatest satisfaction?
- What types of leisure reading do I choose?
- What have I enjoyed most and least about a job I've had?
- Do any of my interests relate to a possible career?

Occupational
Interests   **507**

Writing Handbook 27:
Occupational Interests and Career Choices

Objectives

1. To evaluate and research career options
2. To recognize ways to find jobs and prepare for job interviews
3. To identify criteria for selecting a college and techniques for completing an application for admission

> ### Handbook Mini-Lessons
> For information on topics related to occupational interests and career choices, see the following mini-lessons.
> - Testing for College Admission, pp. 521–533
> - Business Writing, pp. 516–520
> - Library, Reference Works, and Other Sources, pp. 491–500

Teaching Strategies

Motivating

Ask students to describe the life they would like to be living eight years from now. Have them discuss what they would like to be doing for a job, where they would like to be living, and any other factors that form parts of their dream for their future. Then ask students to get practical and talk about the steps they would have to go through to achieve this dream—would they need to go to college? Get into an apprenticeship program? Get started in a particular job? What steps would be needed for these? Guide the discussion closer to students' present circumstances until they are discussing what steps they can take right now to help achieve their ultimate goals. Use this discussion to introduce the lesson.

Suggest that students read over their journals to help them pinpoint their interests. They should note any topics that recur and any activities they consistently enjoy. They should also note anything they have written concerning their feelings about school and about jobs or volunteer work they have been involved with. After reading over their journals, they might want to do a five-minute freewriting in which they bring into focus not only their interests but also any fields they would like to avoid.

Collaborative Opportunity

Allow students to form small groups and brainstorm orally about the options open to them after high school, not only discussing the options presented in the text but any additional ones they know of. They will enjoy hearing each other's ideas and may develop an awareness of new options that would not otherwise have occurred to them. During the brainstorming session, students should jot down all the ideas that interest them. Later, students may want to explore some of these ideas further in their journals.

Identifying Your Strengths and Preferences The following questions will aid you in identifying your strengths and weaknesses, your special skills and personal preferences.

- How do I view myself as a student? Have I been an underachiever or an overachiever? What is my grade-point average and class rank?
- What are my strongest and weakest school subjects?
- How well have I done on college entrance tests (SAT, ACT)?
- Do I enjoy working with ideas, numbers, people, machines, tools, plants, or animals?
- Do I enjoy working independently or with others?
- Do I prefer variety or routine? indoor or outdoor work? sedentary work or physical activity and/or travel?

Exploring Your Options The following questions will aid you in exploring your options after high school.

- Shall I take a year off to work or travel after graduation?
- Shall I join the armed forces as a career or as a way to obtain training?
- Shall I attend college full time? Should I attend a community college and live at home to save money?
- Would a trade or technical school give me the training I need?
- Does a specialized school—in the arts, design, mechanical arts, or computers—match my interests and goals?

Considering Your Financial Options The following questions will be helpful as you consider your financial options.

- After graduation, how much of my living expenses must I provide?
- How much financial help will or can my parents provide? What savings or other financial resources do I have?
- Will I need additional help in financing my education?
- Can I qualify for any scholarship money?
- Am I willing to apply for and repay loans?
- Can I work part-time or apply for work-study programs?
- Can I finance my education through the armed forces?

After you have answered the preceding questions, examine your answers with care. Then begin to narrow your choices about possible careers and fields of study. Base your choices on a realistic look at your options, your interests, and your abilities.

Literature Connection

Novels Students may enjoy reading perceptive fictional accounts of young people seeking a direction for their lives. Suggest contemporary works, such as Frank Conroy's *Stop Time* and Sandra Cisneros's *The House on Mango Street,* as well as classics like Joyce's *Portrait of the Artist as a Young Man* and Salinger's *Catcher in the Rye.*

Researching Your Prospects

The following are some valuable sources of information about occupations and schools. Most of the books listed are available in either counseling offices or libraries.

1. *Dictionary of Occupational Titles* and *Occupational Outlook Handbook*
2. Career-planning manuals, such as *What Color Is Your Parachute?*
3. Parents, guardians, and friends who have attended college and pursued various careers
4. College catalogs or school bulletins
5. *Comparative Guide to American Colleges*
6. Peterson's Guides, including *After Scholarships, What?* and *Creative Ways to Lower Your College Costs and the Colleges That Offer Them*

INVESTIGATING JOB OPPORTUNITIES

You may decide that you want to get a job immediately after graduation. Looking for a job can be a stressful experience, but you'll probably find that thinking about it is worse than doing it. The best way to combat your anxiety is to plunge into job-search activities with as much enthusiasm as possible.

Ways to Find Jobs Once you know what sort of job you want to pursue, there are a number of ways you can learn what jobs are available.

- Check the classified ads in a local newspaper.
- Contact local employment agencies.
- Network with people whom you know.
- Write letters to possible employers.
- Arrange to talk with potential employers informally, without requesting a job, to gather information.

When you are seeking information about a particular job, it's sometimes better to find out the name and title of the person who is responsible for the department in which you want to work rather than talking to someone in the human resources or personnel department. By contacting the department directly, you'll be speaking to people with whom you might be working. It's important to find out what those people are like.

Occupational Interests **509**

Remind students that doing volunteer work is an excellent way to discover whether a job in a given field might be right for them. In addition, the fact that a job applicant has done volunteer work often influences a prospective employer in the applicant's favor, and the experience that volunteers gain is invariably helpful when they begin working at paying jobs. Most city chambers of commerce will mail out lists of organizations in the community that are in need of volunteers.

You might be surprised to find how willing people are to talk with you about what they do. Most managers welcome an opportunity to discuss how they became interested in their professions and what they like and dislike about their jobs.

Writing Résumés and Letters of Application   In preparing your résumé or letter of application, be sure you conform to one of the commonly accepted formats. Once you've done that, you can infuse your letter or résumé with your own individuality. For additional information about writing résumés and letters of application, see "Applying for a Job" on pages 516–518.

Job Application Forms   If an employer asks you to come to his or her place of business for a job interview or to complete a job application, ask whether any tests will be a part of the application process.

When you visit the potential employer, you will want to bring with you all the information necessary to complete an application. Have on hand, for example, the names, titles, addresses, and telephone numbers of people who will give you personal and professional references. You will want to read the entire application form before filling in the blanks. In fact, it's a good idea to write your answers on a sheet of scrap paper first before completing the form.

Interviewing   The following guidelines will help you in an interview.

1. Prepare yourself beforehand. Employers will probably ask you about the information in your résumé. They may also ask you questions that will reveal your interpersonal skills and your plans for the future.

2. Dress appropriately for the interview.

3. Arrive at the interview on time. Make sure you have good directions.

4. Come prepared. Bring with you any information that you might need, including extra copies of your résumé.

5. Be courteous and enthusiastic during the interview. Greet the interviewer with a friendly handshake. During the interview, maintain eye contact and good posture. Think about what you are going to say before you say it. At the end of your interview, thank the interviewer for his or her time.

6. Write a follow-up letter. Thank the interviewer for considering you for the position. Follow proper business letter form.

510   Writing Handbook

Springboard

After you have an idea of which fields each of your students is interested in, invite professionals in several of those fields to come to a class session. Ask them each to speak for 5–7 minutes about how they chose their fields and about the advantages and drawbacks of their work. They might also tell students which qualities they especially value in job applicants seeking to enter their fields.

Have students prepare questions to ask speakers whose fields are of special interest to them.

INVESTIGATING COLLEGES

You may decide that you want to go to college before settling on a career. To learn more about a particular college, send a letter or a postcard to its admissions office, requesting a catalog and an application for the academic year in which you plan to attend.

Handling a College Interview and a Visit to the Campus Some colleges and universities recommend an interview as part of the formal application process. Use the interview to help you decide whether to apply to that particular college.

If you schedule an interview, be sure to allow enough time to tour the campus. Most colleges offer scheduled campus tours for prospective students and their parents. Try to allow some extra time for exploring the campus on your own so that you can begin to get a "feel" for the place and some idea about whether you would be comfortable there.

Evaluating College Information After you have gathered information on various schools that interest you and perhaps visited a few of them, it's time to narrow the field and select a handful of colleges or universities to which you will apply.

The following lists of questions should help you narrow down your choice of schools.

Occupational
Interests   **511**

If students have not already prepared résumés, refer them to pp. 516–520, Business Writing, and have them work in pairs to compile the facts they will need for their résumés and to draft them in an appropriate form.

Next, instruct students to tell each other which job they would most like to have, and let them practice being interviewed. Direct students to review the guidelines for interviews listed on p. 510. The student who is the interviewer should take a few minutes to read the applicant's résumé and decide which questions to ask. The student who is the applicant should decide which personal strengths to emphasize and which questions, if any, to ask the interviewer. After one interview, students can switch roles. When everyone has finished, let them analyze their experiences in a class discussion. Students can either work as a class to compile the list, with one or two students recording ideas on the board, or they can work in small groups and then put the groups' lists together to form one main list. After the list is finished, make a copy of it for each class member.

Springboard

Ask students to write a list of interview do's and don'ts for job applicants. Ask any students who have had real-life job interviews to incorporate their experiences into the list as well.

Teaching Tip: Choosing a College

Invite several alumni of this high school, who are now attending a college or university, to come and speak to your class. Ask them to describe how they chose their colleges, to give their impressions of the college experience, and to offer any tips they can think of to your seniors. Schedule an informal discussion session afterwards so that students can talk individually with the alumni if they wish. Alternatively, you might invite several recent graduates of colleges students may be considering, whether or not they are alumni of this school, to come and speak to the class.

Critical Thinking

Judging Point out that, before they choose a college, students need to know what their criteria are for choosing. Suggest that they spend five minutes mapping out a list of at least six things that would be very important to them in a college. The questions on p. 512 can guide them, but they should not neglect to consider honestly their own desires and needs. After they have a list of criteria, instruct them to rank the criteria in order of importance. Tell them to keep this list in their journals and to add to it or modify it as time goes by. They can use it, in conjunction with the chart mentioned on p. 512, to evaluate colleges and universities they are considering.

Choosing a School: Questions to Ask Yourself

Academics
- What is the academic reputation of the school?
- Does my record make this a realistic prospect?
- Does the school offer quality programs in my fields of interest?

Costs
- What is the cost of tuition, fees, and housing?
- Does the school offer scholarships, loans, work-study programs, or other financial opportunities?

Size
- Are students given individual attention, or is the freshman year a "sink-or-swim" experience?
- How large are the lecture courses? If a class is too large for a student to get to know a professor, are teaching assistants easily accessible?

Facilities
- Are the dormitory and dining facilities adequate?
- Does the school have a good library?
- Do the departments in my areas of interest have any special facilities?
- Does the school have adequate recreational and sports facilities? Are these facilities open to all students?

In addition to the preceding questions, keep your personal needs and preferences in mind. Ask yourself whether you want—or need—to attend a school close to home. If you are considering a college located far from home, remember to include travel costs for at least two or three trips home as part of your annual expenses. Would you prefer a school located in a big city, or is a quiet college town more appealing? If you have your heart set on a particular college, is your goal realistic?

One effective way to compare colleges is to construct a chart that contrasts their important features. Across the top of a sheet of paper, list the names of the schools. In a left-hand column, write the

Literature Connection

Memoir Students may enjoy Susan Allen Toth's *Ivy Days* (1984), a penetrating memoir centered on her experiences of leaving home to attend college in another state.

headings *Academics, Costs, Size,* and *Facilities.* Then fill in the spaces under each school's name.

From the information on your chart, make a list of the schools that best fit your needs. Many guidance counselors suggest that this list number no more than six to eight. Include both the school you would most like to attend and a "safety" school that you would be satisfied to attend—one to which you feel certain of gaining admission.

Completing a College Application   After narrowing your prospects to no more than six schools, the next step is to complete your admissions applications. Since your college application is your formal presentation to the admissions committee, you will want to make sure it represents you well.

Preview the entire application before you even pick up a pen. An overview will give you the chance to plan what you want to emphasize about yourself and your accomplishments.

Many schools require written recommendations from teachers and/or school counselors. Select your references carefully. Choose people who know you well and who will write positively and informatively about you.

As you fill out your application, keep these points in mind.

1. Read and follow all the application's instructions carefully. A completely accurate application tells the reader that you are a candidate for whom detail is important.

2. If possible, photocopy the application before you fill it out. Use this copy as a draft and then copy the information onto the actual form. Carefully type or print your final form.

3. Note all application deadlines on a calendar, or list deadlines on a flowchart. Allow plenty of time for the school to receive transcripts, test scores, and recommendations.

4. Emphasize your key interests and those activities to which you devote the most time and energy. Highlight areas in which you excel and activities or attributes that make you unique.

Writing an Essay   Your application may require an entrance essay. A well-written one can help tip the balance toward admission in cases where the decision could go either way. Other than a personal interview, the entrance essay is the only place in the application procedure where you can convey a real sense of your personality, values, and style.

Writing
═TIP═

Make photocopies of everything you submit to the admissions office in case your application is lost in the mail.

Occupational
Interests   **513**

Teaching Tip: Completing a College Application

Remind students that, whereas many colleges and universities now charge fees for mailing out catalogs or applications, libraries often have college catalogs and sample college applications available for perusal in the reference area. Point out that library reference materials usually cannot be checked out; they can, however, be reproduced on library copy machines.

Cooperative Learning

Let students work in pairs to complete copies of sample college applications that you (or they) have brought to class. They can help each other with many of the small questions that come up, and this joint practice session will provide them with experience and confidence. It will also facilitate their work on the Practice Your Skills exercise at the end of this lesson, as well as their work on their own college application forms.

Teaching Tip: Entrance Essays

Let students practice writing a brief (250–500 word) entrance essay of the sort that might be required with a college application. First, write on the board a question students should answer in their essays. For example:

1. Describe a person who has influenced your values, and explain how this person has affected you.
2. Explain your reasons, both personal and academic, for wanting to attend this university.

Remind students that the admissions officers who read their essays will be looking for a clear thesis statement, adequate details to elaborate the thesis; a logical progression of ideas; mature and varied sentences and appropriate diction; and correct grammar, usage, and mechanics.

After students have written their essays, have them form peer response groups and evaluate one another's essays, using the five criteria mentioned above.

Practice Your Skills

A. Answer the questions on pages 507–508 under the heading "Analyzing Your Interests, Abilities, and Needs." Then analyze your answers and write a short paragraph that summarizes what you find out about yourself.

B. Write down three careers in which you are interested. Research each one by consulting sources such as those listed on page 509. Then answer the following questions.

1. What specific academic skills and personality traits are required for the job?
2. What special training or education must a person receive before entering this career?
3. What is the typical work environment for someone in this job? Are there any health restrictions?
4. What financial return can someone working in this job expect to receive, both immediately and over the long run? What types of benefits are offered?
5. Is there a demand for new workers in this field? Will that demand remain steady?

C. The following chart is taken from the Common Application, an admissions form currently used by more than 100 private colleges. Complete this section as if you were applying for college admission. Write your answers on a separate sheet of paper.

EXTRACURRICULAR AND PERSONAL ACTIVITIES

Please list your principal extracurricular, community, and family activities and hobbies in the order of their interest to you. Include specific events and/or major accomplishments such as musical instruments played, varsity letters earned, awards from clubs or organizations, etc.

Activity	Grade levels	Hours per week	Weeks per year	Positions held, Honors won

D. On a separate sheet of paper, complete the following part of an application for admission to a fictitious school. Save the information you provided on the form to use as a guide when completing your real applications.

Humanities Connection

Suggest that students research Michel de Montaigne, the French author generally credited with having developed the essay form. They may be interested in the fact that the term *essay* comes from Montaigne's "essai," from the French verb meaning to attempt, try, or weigh; Montaigne conceived of his "essais" as a trying out or weighing of ideas.

Application for Admission to General University

Please return to Office of Admissions, General University, College Junction, Idaho 83539, with an application fee of $30.

1. _____
   Last name (type or print)   First (legal)   Middle

2. _____
   Permanent address   City   State   Zip

3. _____
   Social Security number   Telephone (area code)

4. Place and date of birth _____

5. Name of parent or guardian _____

6. Permanent address of parent or guardian _____

7. Father's occupation _____ Employer _____

   Mother's occupation _____ Employer _____

8. What college did your father attend? _____

   Your mother? _____

9. Name of any relative who is now attending or has attended General University _____

10. Name of high school _____

11. City and state of high school _____

12. Date of graduation _____

13. Have you taken the ACT? _____ When? _____

    SAT? _____ When? _____

14. What semester do you wish to enter?

    Fall _____ Winter _____

15. Division and major _____

16. On a separate sheet of paper, write an essay that gives us a personal statement about yourself. Choose one of the topics below.

    a. Explain and discuss the significance of a personal experience or achievement that has special meaning for you.

    b. Identify and describe a person who has had a significant influence on you and explain that influence.

E. Answer this Common Application essay question: "Briefly discuss which of these activities (extracurricular and personal activities or work experience) has had the most meaning for you, and why." Limit your answer to no more than one typed page.

Occupational
Interests   **515**

Managing the Paper Load

Students will benefit greatly from checking one another's work after completing this exercise. Let them know beforehand that they will be doing this. After they complete the exercise, direct them to form small groups and exchange papers within the group. Instruct them to check the answers in sections B, C, and D first. Then let them form peer response groups to go over the paragraph written for Section A and the essay written for Section E.

Additional Resources
- Writing Resource Book, pp. 63–64
- Thinking Skills Worksheets
- Thinking Skills Transparencies
- Taking Standardized Tests

Business Writing

Objectives

1. To recognize the purposes and characteristics of successful business letters
2. To identify that correct format for a cover letter and a résumé in a job application
3. To identify the correct format for memoranda and technical writings
4. To write effective and correctly formatted business communications

Handbook Mini-Lessons

For information on topics related to business writing, see the following mini-lessons.

- Varieties of Language, pp. 429–433
- Occupational Interests and Career Choices, pp. 507–515

Teaching Strategies

Motivating

Ask students to recall and discuss encounters they have had with someone who wanted to conduct business with them—for example, people who wanted to sell them a product or service or solicit money or signature for a cause. Have students discuss and describe both ''pitches'' that worked and those that didn't work. Lead them to recognize that a polite, direct approach usually works best in business encounters. Explain that this handbook discusses ways to achieve the effect of a polite, direct approach in business writing.

WRITING
HANDBOOK
28

Business Writing

The writing you do in school prepares you for the kind of writing you'll need to do after you graduate—in the job application process, in your work, and in conducting your day-to-day affairs. One of the most common types of business writing is the letter, which incorporates many of the elements of persuasive writing. Whether you are writing to request information, order or return products, state your opinions, complain, or say thank you, business letters attempt to get the reader to agree with you and comply with your requests.

To ensure that your letter has the desired effect on your reader, you must first realize that every business letter sends a double message: the factual information conveyed in the letter and the impression it makes about you, the writer. You can control the impact of your letter's content by using proper grammatical form, present tense, and accurate, clearly-stated facts. You can control the reader's impression of you by always using a businesslike tone—straightforward and polite, but not overly formal and stodgy. These simple, yet crucial, guidelines should be followed in all types of business writing, including job applications or cover letters, follow-up letters, and the writing you do on the job.

APPLYING FOR A JOB

Your first contact with a prospective employer usually will be a cover letter, accompanied by a résumé. Prepare these documents with care and make sure they are error-free.

Cover letters   When writing a **cover letter** or letter of application, follow proper business letter format (see the Appendix, pages 828–829.) Address your letter to a specific person, such as a personnel director, and make certain that the person's title and the spelling of his or her name are correct. State the purpose of your letter in your first sentence. Briefly explain why you want the job and outline your special qualities or qualifications that make you the perfect candidate.

Type your letter single-spaced—double-spaced between paragraphs—on 8 1/2 × 11-inch paper. If your letter is very brief, double space the entire letter to improve its appearance. A sample letter of application is shown on the next page.

1402 Welles Avenue
Grover's Mill, New Jersey 04562
January 28, 19—

Ms. Marion Robinson
Director of Human Services
Grover's Mill Telegraph
566 Main Street
Grover's Mill, New Jersey 04562

Dear Ms. Robinson:

I would like to apply for an internship as a copy editor
for the Grover's Mill Telegraph. I hope to work for your
paper this summer before entering the Indiana University
School of Journalism in the fall.

As you will see from the enclosed résumé, I have
considerable experience as a writer and copy editor on the
staff of the Grover's Mill High School newspaper, the
Clarion. I have written news stories on school and
community events and features on bicycle racing, toxins in
the home, and Outward Bound programs for high-school
students. I have enclosed clippings of my writing from the
school paper for your review.

In addition to my experience on the school paper, I have
many other skills that qualify me for this job. I am
familiar with several word processing programs and my
communication skills are superb. I can provide excellent
recommendations from teachers, previous employers, and
co-workers who will attest to my industriousness and
dependability.

Thank you for considering my application. Please write
or call to let me know when I can come in for an
interview. My telephone number is (201) 555-1616. I look
forward to hearing from you soon.

Sincerely,

Philip Yani

Enc: Résumé; clippings

Teaching Tip: Addressee

Point out why it is important that cover letters be addressed to a specific person and that his or her name and title be correct. Emphasize that by getting these details right, students show respect for their readers. The personnel director or other recipient of the letter will feel a closer personal responsibility to read the material, take it seriously, and respond appropriately if it is addressed directly to him or her. In addition, the entire process of presenting themselves on paper as they apply for a job is a test of their attention to detail.

Springboard

Have students suggest questions an employer might ask when hiring for a particular job opening. They may wish to choose partners and take turns acting as prospective employee and employer, while other students offer feedback.

Tell students that almost everyone, even people with a great deal of education and work experience, finds the prospect of writing a résumé intimidating. Suggest that as with any first draft, they forget about the final product at the outset and simply start anywhere. Some students may find it helpful to brainstorm before they start writing, jotting down their work experience, hobbies, interests, travel, etc. on a separate sheet of paper. Once their ideas are flowing, they may discover material that will be appropriate to include in a résumé.

Personal Touch

Students might be interested in seeing a résumé you have written. The best one to show them might not be your current one but rather—if you still have copies—one you wrote in high school and another that you wrote some years later. Explain your purposes for writing each résumé and the circumstances in which you wrote it. Then discuss why you set your résumé up the way you did and what you would do differently if you could write those résumés again.

Teaching Tip: Active Verbs

It will be helpful to list active verbs on the board for use as students work on their own résumés. Begin by having students identify active verbs used in the sample résumé. Have them continue brainstorming other active verbs. Afterwards you may want to suggest the following: *adapted, advised, arranged, communicated, compiled, conducted, created, designed, developed, directed, followed, generated, guided, improved, increased, led, managed, organized, performed, planned, proposed, reorganized, scheduled, simplified, solved.*

Résumé A résumé is a list of information about you that would be of interest to potential employers. It should be a self-advertisement, highlighting your experience and qualifications in the best possible way.

A clear, easy-to-read résumé is divided into separate sections, each with its own heading. If you know exactly what kind of job you are looking for, you can say so under the job objective heading which always falls at the beginning of a résumé as shown in the sample below. If you are applying for a variety of jobs, you can write a general résumé without an objective. Both forms are accepted in the business world.

Philip Yani
1402 Welles Avenue
Grover's Mill, New Jersey 04562
(201) 555-1616

OBJECTIVE	Summer intern at a local newspaper
QUALIFICATIONS	• Three years' experience as writer and copy editor, Grover's Mill High School <u>Clarion</u> • Knowledge of Associated Press Stylebook • Thorough understanding of newspaper production process
WORK EXPERIENCE	September 1990–Present Part-time cashier/stockboy, Best Food Market August 1988–Present Writer and copy editor for Grover's Mill High School <u>Clarion</u>. Researched, wrote, and edited a variety of news, features, and sports stories. Wrote headlines, assisted in layouts, trained new staff members.
EDUCATION	Grover's Mill High School, Grover's Mill, New Jersey, 1988–1992; B+ average.
AWARDS	Winner of Tri-State "Young Authors" Composition Contest, 1990.
INTERESTS	Journalism, modern American literature, history, tennis
REFERENCES	Available on request.

Organize your résumé to emphasize your strong points. For example, if you have held several important jobs, list your work history in reverse chronological order immediately after your job objective. If you have little work experience, emphasize your education, including any awards or specialized training you may have received, and your skills, such as leadership, business or teaching.

A résumé should be written in phrases or clauses, not in complete sentences. Use positive, active verbs to describe your work and achievements. Do not include references to your gender, weight, height, age, race, or religion, since they are legally irrelevant to your job qualifications. Including wage or salary expectations on a résumé is also considered inappropriate. Type your résumé on good-quality 8 1/2 × 11-inch stationery, preferably white, off-white, or buff, or have it professionally typeset. Proofread the final copy carefully. To make the best impression, your résumé must be clear, concise, and completely error-free.

The writing you do to apply for a job gives employers an idea of the skills you will bring to writing activities required on the job. Of all the different types of writing you are likely to do in the business world, memoranda and technical writing are two of the most common.

Memoranda   Written communications to convey information and make announcements to company employees are called **memoranda,** or **memos.** When writing a memo, include the mandatory header information as shown in the example below. Although the tone of a memo may be more informal than a business letter, the message should still be brief, clear, and concise.

```
                            Memo
TO:           Newspaper staff
FROM:         Mary Rutkowski, Production Dept.
SUBJECT:      Deadlines for special "Graduation Day"
              issue
DATE:         April 23, 1992

All copy for the special "Graduation Day" issue is to be
submitted on or before April 30th. Please let me know if
you anticipate any problems in meeting this deadline. We
expect this to be our finest "Graduation Day" issue ever.
```

W R I T E R   T O   W R I T E R

The greatest thing a human soul ever does in this world is to see something and tell what it saw in a plain way.
Galileo, Italian astronomer and physicist

Technical Writing   **Technical writing** is a broad term used to cover various types of writing done in science, industry, and other specialized fields. Assembly instructions, on-line documentation, and manuals are all forms of technical writing. Use the following guidelines when doing technical writing.

Critical Thinking

Making Comparisons Have students compare the tone appropriate for memoranda with that appropriate for business letters. *(Both need to be clear and concise, but a less formal tone is appropriate for memoranda, because they generally are used to communicate within an already established group.)*

Science Connection

Have students investigate science textbooks and other books to analyze the types of directions presented. Have them bring examples that fulfill the requirements for good technical writing and share them with the class.

Business Writing   **519**

Managing the Paper Load

Students will learn more from using peer response or peer grading for all exercises in this lesson. Have them share suggestions for improving their letters, résumés, memos, and directions. In Exercise B have each student revise and complete a résumé; other activities do not require revision.

ANSWERS TO PRACTICE YOUR SKILLS

A. Answers will vary. However, a good business letter will state its business clearly and directly, present accurate, relevant facts, and use businesslike tone, traditional business letter format, proper grammatical form, present tense, and accurate, clearly-stated facts.

B. Answers will vary. However, a good cover letter and résumé will be appropriate to the requirements of the position being advertised as well as using the proper formats, tone, and grammatical form. The résumé will highlight experience and qualifications in the best possible way.

C. Answers will vary. A good memo will use the proper format and be brief, clear, and concise.

D. Answers will vary. However, good directions will use second-person imperative, break down the process into separate steps presented in chronological order, and use simple sentences and familiar vocabulary. If appropriate, the directions will include visual aids.

Additional Resource
- Writing Resource Book, pp. 65–67

Technical Writing Guidelines

1. When possible, use the second-person imperative. For example, write "Tighten the bolt," not "The bolt should be tightened."

2. Break a process down into separate steps, and include in your writing every step that the reader must take to complete it. Assume that the reader will do nothing unless specifically told to do it.

3. Present the steps in chronological order. Use transitions such as *first, second, third,* and *finally.*

4. Use simple sentences and familiar vocabulary. Make sure that everyone who reads your directions can follow them.

5. Use visual aids such as diagrams and flowcharts. Good technical writing uses all means available to make complex information clear and understandable. A picture sometimes says a thousand words.

6. Try your directions as part of the revision process. This will test whether or not your directions are clear, logical, and complete.

Practice Your Skills

A. Write a business letter of complaint (about damaged merchandise, late delivery, or a cockroach in a plate of spaghetti served at a restaurant, for example); a letter of apology (for a missed appointment or a late report, for example); or a letter of request (for college brochures, time extension, or information for a research report).

B. Find a job in the "Help Wanted" ads that might be appropriate for a high-school student. Then prepare a job application letter and a résumé that you might use if you were applying for this job.

C. Imagine that you are the director of a student production of *South Pacific.* Write a memo to the cast members announcing a change of opening night from May 4th to May 9th.

D. Choose an activity that you are good at but not everyone can do, such as videotaping a scene, changing a tire, or preparing a meal. Write directions for completing that activity.

Testing for College Admission

College-bound students usually take one or more college entrance exams. Two widely used tests are the Scholastic Aptitude Test (SAT) and the test of the American College Testing Program (ACT). You already may have taken one of these tests. However, you should be aware that you can retake either one in the fall of your senior year and still receive your scores in time to meet college admission and scholarship deadlines.

TYPES OF TESTS

The Scholastic Aptitude Test and the ACT Assessment are the two most common entrance tests taken by college applicants. Many students, however, will also take achievement tests and advanced-placement tests during high school, and most colleges and universities give placement tests to incoming freshmen.

The Scholastic Aptitude Test   The SAT is a multiple-choice test. Its format is being revised during the early 1990's, but it currently contains two verbal and two math sections.

The ACT Assessment   The ACT has multiple-choice questions measuring skills in English, mathematics, social studies, and natural sciences, and requires some knowledge of American history, chemistry, and biology. The ACT is divided into four sections: English usage, mathematics usage, social studies reading, and natural sciences reading.

Achievement Tests   The College Entrance Examination Board offers one-hour achievement tests in such subjects as English, foreign languages, history and social studies, mathematics, and sciences.

Advanced-Placement Tests   Some students are able to pursue the equivalent of college-level studies while they are still in high school. Advanced-placement tests measure students' understanding and in some cases award them college credit and appropriate placement at participating colleges. These examinations are offered each May. The tests contain an essay or a problem-solving section and a multiple-choice section on a wide range of subjects.

Testing for College Admission   **521**

Objectives

1. To identify types of tests used for college admissions
2. To recognize types of questions found on standardized tests: antonyms; analogies; sentence completion; reading comprehension; English usage; sentence correction; constriction shift; and content-specific questions
3. To identify and use strategies for answering test questions of various types

Handbook Mini-Lessons

For information on topics related to testing for college admission, see the following mini-lessons.
- Developing Your Vocabulary, pp. 457–471
- Refining Critical Thinking and Writing Skills, pp. 472–477

Teaching Strategies

Motivating

Have students brainstorm the various types of preparation a professional football team makes for a particular game (*physical conditioning; practicing specific moves such as blocking, tackling, passing, receiving; watching films of themselves playing; watching films of the team they will play; developing a game plan*). Tell students that all this preparation takes place for an event that will last only a few hours. Similarly, college entrance exams take only a few hours, yet the amount of preparation they do can make an important difference in their test scores.

Critical Thinking

Analyzing Students who score well on advanced-placement tests normally receive credit in one or more areas of strength, but students who score well in a *variety* of subjects can sometimes enter college with a second-year, or sophomore, standing. Have students discuss the possible advantages and disadvantages of skipping their first year of college by means of advanced placement tests. For example, advanced placement may allow students to begin focusing on their area of major interest sooner and get through college faster, thereby saving money and perhaps securing other advantages; but students should note, too, that the first year of college allows a period of social orientation that students may be ill-advised to hurry through. Also, the first year often exposes students to a wide range of subjects. Some students discover new interests they want to pursue in college.

Stumbling Block

Some students may have great anxiety about taking college entrance exams, especially if they are under pressure to be admitted to schools with very high standards. They may find it difficult to sleep the night before a test, to understand written instructions, or to follow their own pacing plan for completing a section of the test. Ask students to discuss their anxieties and to help each other think of positive strategies for dealing with nervousness. *(One solution for students is to use a test-preparation program. If this isn't possible, students might work together simulating testing situations and answering sample questions within fixed amounts of time.)*

PREPARING FOR AND TAKING STANDARDIZED TESTS

Last-minute cramming does not help you on aptitude tests such as the ACT and the SAT. The best scores are achieved through regular reading, writing, and studying in the courses that are part of your high-school curriculum. However, practicing with commercially prepared manuals or with sample tests from the testing organization will familiarize you with the test content and formats, and will help you develop strategies for answering the questions. On the day of the test, follow these guidelines.

1. Bring to the test center all required materials named in the booklet you receive with your registration form. Typically, you need several sharpened number-two pencils, an admission ticket, a form of personal identification, and a watch (to help you budget your time).

2. Plan to arrive at the test center thirty minutes before the test is scheduled to begin.

3. Listen carefully to all instructions given by the test supervisor. Begin as soon as the command to begin is given.

4. Completely darken each appropriate space on the answer sheet. Thoroughly erase any stray marks or changed answers. Check your answer sheet periodically to make sure that the numbers on the spaces you are marking coincide with the numbers of the questions you are answering in the booklet.

5. Approach each test section with a comprehensive strategy. Note the number of questions and the time available. Answer all the easy questions on a quick first read-through. Then go back for the more difficult questions, keeping an eye on your time.

QUESTIONS AND STRATEGIES

Standardized tests typically contain questions of the following types: antonyms, analogies, sentence completion, reading comprehension, usage, sentence correction, and construction-shift. In order to be well prepared for taking standardized tests, you should learn specific strategies for answering questions of each kind.

Antonyms Antonym questions provide a single word and ask you to choose from five words the one most nearly opposite in meaning.

FERMENTING: (A) improvising (B) stagnating (C) wavering
(D) plunging   (E) dissolving

You will find the following strategies helpful for answering antonym questions.

1. Try to determine the meaning of the given word before you look at the answer choices. Note any prefixes, suffixes, base words, or roots. Think of a synonym (a word that has most nearly the same meaning) for the given word, or create a sentence that uses this word.

2. Once you have determined the meaning of the given word, look carefully at the answer choices. Remember to look only for words with *opposite* meanings. Do not be thrown off by synonyms. In some test items, synonyms are deliberately included, and they can fool students who automatically choose the first related word they find.

3. If you cannot readily identify the correct answer, try to eliminate any obviously incorrect answers. Also, since most words have multiple meanings, try looking for antonyms of the word's other meanings.

4. Remember that few words are exact opposites; find the word most nearly opposite in meaning. In the example, both *dissolving* and *stagnating* can be related to *fermenting,* which signifies a kind of chemical breakdown or turbulence and unrest. However, *dissolving* implies a melting or disintegration into a liquid, not the molecular simplification of fermentation. *Stagnating,* meaning "becoming sluggish or inactive," is a much clearer opposite.
    The correct answer is *B.*

Practice Your Skills

Each of the following antonym examples consists of a word in capital letters, followed by five lettered words or phrases. Choose the word or phrase most nearly opposite in meaning to the word in capital letters.

1. VERSATILE: (A) unadaptable (B) mediocre
    (C) impatient (D) egocentric (E) vicious
2. FRAUDULENT: (A) rather pleasing (B) extremely beneficial
    (C) courteous (D) authentic (E) simplified

Testing for College Admission   **523**

Teaching Tip: Follow-up

For students having difficulty with antonym questions, you may want to suggest that they review Handbook 22, Developing Your Vocabulary.

Teaching Tip: Analogies

Review for students that in analogy questions colons are used to represent relationship. The single colon represents *is to* and the double colon represents *as*. Suggest that when students see an analogy notated with these symbols, they try saying the phrase in their minds (or out loud, if practical), replacing the colon and double colon with ''is to'' and ''as,'' in order to help them understand exactly what they are to do.

Critical Thinking

Generalizing Check that students have really understood each item in the box as a general type of relationship by asking them to think of another analogy of the same type. You can do this orally with the whole class, eliciting suggestions from a range of volunteers.

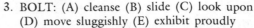

3. BOLT: (A) cleanse (B) slide (C) look upon (D) move sluggishly (E) exhibit proudly
4. IMPUGN: (A) speak well of (B) describe in detail (C) forget to complete (D) dissociate (E) stimulate
5. EPHEMERAL: (A) lasting (B) inhumane (C) contemporary (D) destructive (E) appropriate

Analogies   Analogy questions ask you to note the relationship in a pair of words, to understand the basis of the relationship, and to recognize a parallel relationship in another word pair.

TERRESTRIAL : LUNG :: (A) marsupial : pouch (B) floral : root (C) perennial : seed (D) aquatic : gill (E) canine : mouth

The following strategies will help you to complete analogies.

1. Determine the relationship between the first two words, and state the relationship in a sentence: *Terrestrial* creatures breathe by means of their *lungs*.

2. Decide which of the choices expresses a similar relationship: *Aquatic* creatures breathe by means of their *gills*.

The correct answer is *D*.

Types of Relationships in Analogy Questions

Type of Analogy	Example
object to its function	BRUSH : PAINTING :: scissors : cutting
object to its material	STREET : ASPHALT :: memorial : granite
cause to effect	ICE : COOLING :: acid : etching
action to object	HURL : DISCUS :: fire : cannon
part to whole	THREAD : FABRIC :: brick : wall
item to category	MACBETH : DRAMA :: Lord Jim : novel
item to characteristic	MERCURY : LIQUID :: diamond : hard
worker and tool	ARTIST : BRUSH :: dentist : drill
worker and creation	SCULPTOR : STATUE :: composer : sonata
worker and workplace	CHEMIST : LABORATORY :: actor : theater
word to antonym	GLORIOUS : INFAMOUS :: haughty : meek
word to synonym	OMINOUS : SINISTER :: succinct : concise
time sequence	PREMATURE : TIMELY :: punctual : late

Practice Your Skills

Each of the following analogy items begins with a related pair of words. Select the lettered pair whose relationship most closely resembles that of the original pair.

1. VOLUME : SPHERE :: (A) altitude : triangle
   (B) diagonal : square (C) area : circle
   (D) angle : rectangle (E) length : cube
2. RAMSHACKLE : COLLAPSE :: (A) intact : explode
   (B) threadbare : hem (C) waterlogged : sink
   (D) dilapidated : repair (E) flammable : quench
3. TRICK : ROGUE :: (A) stratagem : friend
   (B) sentence : criminal (C) accident : witness
   (D) conspiracy : traitor (E) novel : reader
4. CALIPERS : MEASURING :: (A) nails : hammering
   (B) crops : harvesting (C) glasses : polishing
   (D) decisions : weighing (E) scissors : cutting
5. WHEEDLE : FLATTERY :: (A) inspire : creations
   (B) accuse : denials (C) scrutinize : clues
   (D) intimidate : threats (E) appreciate : offers

Sentence Completion To answer sentence-completion questions successfully, you must recognize relationships among parts of a sentence, and you must recognize and know the meanings of key words. A sentence-completion question consists of a sentence from which one or two words have been removed. You must choose the lettered word or set of words that completes the meaning of the sentence most logically. Study the following example.

> Although Spalding _____ the importance of the physical necessities of life, her most successful endeavor was the _____ of the condition of the impoverished.
> (A) deprecated . . . alleviation
> (B) emphasized . . . investigation
> (C) accentuated . . . amelioration
> (D) epitomized . . . delineation
> (E) disregarded . . . desecration

Use these strategies to answer sentence-completion questions.

1. Read the incomplete sentence carefully, noting any key words that show the following relationships: contrast (*but, although, however*); similarity (*another, the same as, and*); cause and effect (*therefore, as a result, consequently, because*). In the example, *although* suggests a contrasting relationship.

Testing for College Admission **525**

 Individualizing Instruction

Advanced Students You may wish to ask these students to supplement their answer by framing a statement that explains why the two relationships are similar. For example, in item 1, choice C is correct because *volume* names the amount of space a *sphere* contains, just as *area* names the amount of space a *circle* contains.

Teaching Tip: Sentence Completion

Point out that syntax—the structure of relationships between words in a sentence—often provides important clues that students can use to help them answer sentence completion questions. Emphasize that any speaker of English has an instinct for English syntax, which students can tap into by repeating an incomplete sentence out loud and actually saying "blank" wherever a blank appears. Have students try this with the example.

ANSWERS TO PRACTICE YOUR SKILLS

1. A
2. B
3. A
4. E
5. C

2. Try each choice in the sentence, eliminating those that are nonsensical or grammatically incorrect.

3. Make sure that *both* words fit the sentence logically. In the example on the preceding page, the second word in answer *C* makes sense, but the first word does not.

4. Make sure that *both* words are the correct part of speech and form.

The answer to the sample question is *A*.

Practice Your Skills

The blanks in these sentences indicate an omission. Following each are five lettered words or sets of words. Choose the answer that best fits the meaning of the sentence.

1. In the North Pacific, the number of whales has been so drastically reduced that the sighting of even one is _____ event.
   (A) a newsworthy   (B) a treacherous   (C) an everyday
   (D) an elaborate   (E) an expected

2. Musicians' salaries have risen so much faster than concert admission prices and donations that some famous _____ are threatened with _____.
   (A) composers . . . silence   (B) orchestras . . . bankruptcy
   (C) works . . . oblivion   (D) conductors . . . strikes
   (E) soloists . . . taxation

3. In view of the _____ value of the new treatment for this complicated case, _____ with another physician is advisable.
   (A) questionable . . . a consultation
   (B) necessary . . . an interlude
   (C) accepted . . . an exploration
   (D) impossible . . . a confrontation
   (E) presumed . . . an argument

4. Parental devotion, especially if too solicitous, has its _____, one of which is _____ a child's progress toward maturity.
   (A) delusions . . . envisioning (B) excesses . . . abetting
   (C) targets . . . ensuring   (D) rewards . . . ameliorating
   (E) pitfalls . . . protracting

5. The validity of her experimental findings was so _____ that even the most _____ investigators could not refrain from extolling her scientific genius.
   (A) enigmatic . . . officious   (B) fallacious . . . credulous
   (C) unassailable . . . disputatious   (D) inevitable . . . convivial
   (E) dubious . . . skeptical

526   Writing Handbook

Springboard

Suggest that students write letters requesting information about the SAT and Achievement tests. They should address the letters to the College Entrance Examination Board, 45 Columbus Avenue, New York, NY 10023. To obtain information about the ACT test, they should write to the American College Testing Program, Box 168, Iowa City, IA 52243.

Reading Comprehension Reading-comprehension questions test your ability to read and understand passages of various kinds. Typically, a reading passage is followed by five questions, which may ask the student to (1) identify a central idea, a specific detail, or a specific technique used by the author; (2) interpret meanings of words; (3) see relationships between ideas in the passage; (4) draw a conclusion based on information in the passage; or (5) apply information given in the passage.

Study the following reading-comprehension passage.

> However one chooses to define weather and climate, there is a simple, practical distinction between them: weather is a matter of everyday experience, whereas climate is a statistical generalization of that experience. Weather is what usually interests us, but to interpret it correctly we must first determine what the underlying climate is in general; otherwise, we have no yardstick for comparison. In a sense, climate is like the carrier wave in radio broadcasting on which the irregular signals of programming—weather—are superimposed. We have to study the "normal" distribution of the meteorological elements before we can begin to understand the "variability around the norm" that constitutes weather.

Which of the following comparisons most closely parallels the relationship between weather and climate in this paragraph?

(A) A particular game to a team's season record
(B) A heat-seeking missile to a fighter plane
(C) A bacterium to its colony
(D) An element to a compound
(E) A waterfall to a lake

To answer reading-comprehension questions, use the following strategies.

1. Identify the main idea as you read. Pay attention to transitions and words that show relationships.

2. Read all the choices before you select an answer.

3. Do not choose an answer just because it's a true statement; make sure it answers the question being asked.

4. Base your answer on the information in the passage, not on your knowledge or opinion.

The answer to the sample question is *A*.

Testing for College Admission **527**

Read the following passage. Then answer the reading-comprehension questions on the next page.

My grandmother's notorious pugnacity did not confine itself to the exercise of authority over the neighborhood. There was also the defense of her house and her furniture against the imagined encroachments of visitors. With my grandmother, this was not the gentle and tremulous protectiveness of certain frail people who infer the fragility of all things from the brittleness of their own bones and hear the crash of mortality in the perilous tinkling of a teacup. No, my grandmother's sentiment was more autocratic: she hated having her chairs sat in or her lawns stepped on or the water turned on in her sinks; for no reason but pure administrative efficiency, she even grudged the mailman his daily promenade up her sidewalk. Her home was a center of power, and she would not allow it to be insulted by easy or democratic usage. Under her jealous eye, its social properties had withered, and it functioned in the family structure simply as a political headquarters. Family conferences were held there, consultations with the doctor and the clergy; unruly grandchildren were there for a lecture or an interval of thought-taking; wills were read and loans negotiated. The family had no friends, and entertaining was held to be a foolish and unnecessary courtesy required only by the bonds of a blood relationship. Holiday dinners fell, as a duty, on the lesser members of the organization; sons and daughters and cousins respectfully offered up baked Alaska on a platter, while my grandparents sat enthroned at the table, and only their digestive processes acknowledged the festal nature of the day.

Springboard

Have students work in groups, assuming the roles of college admissions board members. It is their responsibility to design supplementary admissions procedures to be used in addition to standardized tests to determine admissions to a state college or university. Their discussions should focus first on what qualities are important for success at college and then on how to determine whether applicants possess the qualities needed to succeed. Encourage students to present their decisions to the class as a whole, explaining their reasoning.

1. The author's main purpose in this passage is to
   (A) review childhood impressions and fears
   (B) mourn the vanishing unity of the nuclear family
   (C) create a vivid portrait of a strong personality
   (D) revive the memory of a dimly recalled ancestor
   (E) commend some of a grandmother's firmly held principles

2. It can be inferred from the passage that all of the following are characteristic of the author's grandmother EXCEPT
   (A) desire for order   (B) pride in authority
   (C) disdain for sentiment   (D) reluctance to compromise
   (E) jealousy of youth

3. The tone of the passage is best described as
   (A) sympathetic and sentimental   (B) restrained and cautious
   (C) apathetic and aloof   (D) satirical and candid
   (E) bitter and loathing

English Usage   English-usage questions test your ability to recognize errors in word choice, punctuation, capitalization, grammar, and usage. Study the following example.

> An idealist is not always <u>as</u> <u>ignorant</u> of realities as <u>their</u> critics
>   **A**   **B**   **C**
> would <u>like to</u> believe. No <u>error</u>
>   **D**   **E**

To answer English-usage questions, keep these points in mind.

1. Read the entire sentence slowly and carefully, not just the underlined parts.

2. Look for errors in word choice, punctuation, capitalization, grammar, and usage.

In the example, since the possessive pronoun *their* does not agree with its antecedent, *idealist,* the correct answer is *C.*

Practice Your Skills

In each sentence, four words or phrases are underlined. Choose the underlined word or phrase that contains an error in usage. If the sentence is correct, choose *E, No error.*

1. It is <u>rumored that</u> the names <u>of them</u> <u>to be promoted</u> will be
             A   **B**   **C**
   announced today, but the choices <u>have not been made</u> yet. <u>No error</u>
                              D   **E**

 Individualizing Instruction

LEP Students   You may wish to circulate through the classroom working through problem questions individually or in small groups with the students. It may be helpful to review grammar and usage concepts in the Grammar and Usage Handbook. Encourage students to review the strategies for answering English usage questions as they work through the exercise.

ANSWERS TO PRACTICE YOUR SKILLS
1. B

Springboard

You may want to have students work in groups to discuss whether standardized tests are a good way to decide if students should be admitted to a certain school. Encourage them to explain their reasoning. Have students who question the validity of standardized tests suggest alternative means of evaluation.

2. C
3. C
4. B
5. C

2. For <u>many people</u>, hang gliding, an <u>increasingly</u> popular sport, seems
   <u>A</u>   <u>B</u>
   <u>satisfying</u> the urge <u>to fly</u>. <u>No error</u>
   <u>C</u>   <u>D</u>   <u>E</u>

3. Late in the war, the Germans, <u>retreating</u> <u>in haste,</u> <u>left many</u> of <u>their</u>
                                  <u>A</u>   <u>B</u>   <u>C</u>   <u>D</u>
   prisoners go free. <u>No error</u>
                       <u>E</u>

4. <u>Throughout</u> the Middle Ages, women <u>work</u> <u>beside</u> men, knowing
   <u>A</u>   <u>B</u>   <u>C</u>
   that the efforts of men and women alike were <u>essential</u> to survival.
                                                <u>D</u>
   <u>No error</u>
   <u>E</u>

5. <u>Because of</u> extreme weather conditions, starvation <u>exists</u> in some
   <u>A</u>   <u>B</u>
   countries where <u>they</u> must struggle every day <u>to stay alive</u>. <u>No error</u>
                    <u>C</u>   <u>D</u>   <u>E</u>

Sentence Correction   Sentence-correction questions test your ability to identify errors in different parts of a sentence. All or part of a sentence is underlined. Following the sentence are five ways of changing the underlined part. Select the answer that produces the most effective, grammatically correct sentence. The first choice always repeats the underlined words. The correct answer will be the one that best expresses the meaning of the sentence. A typical sentence-correction question follows.

<u>Because she was a woman was why Sharon Frontiero, a lieutenant in the United States Air Force, felt that she was being treated unfairly.</u>

(A) Because she was a woman was why Sharon Frontiero, a lieutenant in the United States Air Force, felt that she was being treated unfairly.
(B) Sharon Frontiero, a lieutenant in the United States Air Force, felt that she was being treated unfairly because she was a woman.
(C) Because she was a woman, Sharon Frontiero felt that this was why she was being treated unfairly as a lieutenant in the United States Air Force.
(D) Sharon Frontiero, a lieutenant in the United States Air Force, feeling that was being treated unfairly because she was a woman.
(E) A woman, Sharon Frontiero, felt that because she was a lieutenant in the United States Air Force, that she was being treated unfairly.

Even if you believe that the sentence is correct as written, read all of the suggested answers. In this case, the original sentence is awkwardly stated, so answer *A* is incorrect. Answer *C* is wrong because it begins with a misplaced adverb clause. Answer *D* is incorrect because it is a sentence fragment. Answer *E* is incorrect because it changes the meaning of the sentence.

The correct answer is *B*.

When answering a sentence-correction question, try to decide which version sounds best. Avoid wordy versions, unnecessary shifts of verb tense, run-on sentences, and expressions that are not considered acceptable in standard written English.

Practice Your Skills

Each of the following sentences contains an underlined portion. Following each sentence are five ways of rephrasing the underlined part. Select the answer that produces the most effective and grammatically correct sentence. Answer *A* always repeats the original sentence.

1. In the nineteenth century, trains were more than <u>machines they were</u> expressions of the greatness of the United States.
   (A) machines they were
   (B) machines and were
   (C) machines; they were
   (D) machines; although they were
   (E) machines, but were

2. The widespread slaughter of buffalo for their skins profoundly <u>shocked and angered Native Americans</u>.
   (A) shocked and angered Native Americans
   (B) shocked Native Americans, angering them
   (C) shocked Native Americans, and they were also angry
   (D) was a shock and caused anger among Native Americans
   (E) was shocking to Native Americans, making them angry

3. <u>Many memos were issued by the director of the agency that</u> had an insulting tone, according to the staff members.
   (A) Many memos were issued by the director of the agency that
   (B) Many memos were issued by the director of the agency who
   (C) The issuance of many memos by the director of the agency which
   (D) The director of the agency issued many memos that
   (E) The director of the agency, who issued many memos that

Testing for College
Admission   **531**

4. <u>Joseph Conrad was born and educated in Poland and he</u> wrote all of his novels in English.

(A) Joseph Conrad was born and educated in Poland and he
(B) Joseph Conrad, being born and educated in Poland,
(C) Although being born and educated in Poland, Joseph Conrad
(D) Although Joseph Conrad was born and educated in Poland, he
(E) Being from Poland, where he was born and educated, Joseph Conrad

Construction-Shift Sentences Construction-shift sentences, found in the English Composition Test given by the College Board, ask you to rephrase sentences according to specific directions without changing the meaning of the original.

Although the composer Ethel Smyth was famous in England in the early years of this century for her operas and symphonies, she is almost unknown in this country.
Begin with <u>Almost unknown</u>.

(A) country, despite being famous for
(B) country, the composer
(C) country, the English
(D) country, although she was famous
(E) country and famous

The rephrased example sentence would read as follows: Almost unknown in this country, the composer Ethel Smyth was famous in England in the early years of this century for her operas and symphonies. Thus the correct answer is *B*.

Practice Your Skills

Rephrase each of the following construction-shift sentences according to the directions that follow it. Make only those changes that the directions require. Keep the meaning of the revised sentence as close as possible to the meaning of the original sentence.

1. The appreciation of painting, as well as of other forms of art, demands the interplay of judgment and imagination.
Begin with <u>The interplay</u>.

(A) demands
(B) is demanded by
(C) is essential to
(D) are essential to
(E) demand

Modeling

You may wish to read and discuss this section aloud with the class. Emphasize that it is important for them to rephrase the sentence *before* they look at the possible answers.

ANSWERS TO PRACTICE YOUR SKILLS

1. C

Math, Social Studies, Science Connection

Have students use textbooks and information from other subject areas and the formats they have learned to create test questions. They should cover each subject area and include the following types of questions: antonyms, analogies, sentence completion, reading comprehension, English usage, and sentence completion. Afterwards, organize students in pairs or small groups to exchange questions and take the sample tests. Allow them to discuss questions and answers afterwards.

2. Gandhi started out with the normal ambitions of a young Indian student and adopted his nationalist opinions only by degrees as he grew older.
Begin with <u>Starting</u>.

(A) he only adopted
(B) Gandhi adopted
(C) only adopting
(D) Gandhi had only adopted
(E) and only adopted

3. The supervisor was able, or so he thought, to make the decision himself.
Change <u>able</u> to <u>capable</u>.

(A) to be making
(B) of having made
(C) of making
(D) to have made
(E) to make

4. The computer's most profound impact arises less because of its usefulness as a calculating machine than because of its potential for communication.
Eliminate both occurrences of <u>because</u>.

(A) not only is it useful
(B) and it has the potential
(C) as well as its potential
(D) more from being useful
(E) more from its potential

Content-Specific Questions Content-specific questions, found in the College Board achievement tests, measure your knowledge of facts and concepts in subjects such as English, history, mathematics, science, and foreign language. The following is an example of a content-specific question.

The Marshall Plan can best be described as an attempt to achieve

(A) military goals through political means.
(B) political goals through economic means.
(C) economic goals through military means.
(D) political goals through military means.
(E) economic goals through political means.

The correct answer is *B*.

Critical Thinking

Analysis Tell students that while this type of question may seem particularly difficult, it is actually a format that is typical in many classroom tests. Have them discuss strategies they have developed for answering multiple choice tests.

Additional Resources
• Writing Resource Book, pp. 68–69

Understanding and Evaluating the Media

Objectives

1. To compare the advantages and disadvantages of broadcast and print media
2. To identify the criteria for evaluating the media
3. To evaluate broadcast and print media

Handbook Mini-Lessons

For information on topics related to understanding and evaluating the media, see the following mini-lessons.

- Examining Point of View, pp. 446–451
- Refining Critical Thinking and Writing Skills, pp. 472–478
- Research Skills, pp. 479–489

Teaching Strategies

Motivating

Read the opening paragraphs from an article or an editorial about a controversial topic in a recent issue of a school or local newspaper. Ask students to evaluate its purpose and audience, language, objectivity, and content. Students should recognize how these variables are interrelated.

Teaching Tip: Personal Experience

Before students read "Understanding Broadcast Media," have them list their favorite television and radio news programs. After they complete the section, have them classify the programs they listed.

WRITING
HANDBOOK
30

Understanding and Evaluating the Media

Information about the world—in the form of radio and television news reports and written stories in newspapers and news magazines—is available twenty-four hours a day, seven days a week. Keeping abreast of current events, as well as ongoing social, political, and economic trends, can seem like an impossible chore. However, once you learn to think critically about the sources of news stories, you may find that understanding the news is not only possible, but is essential to being an informed citizen.

UNDERSTANDING BROADCAST MEDIA

Broadcast media include radio and television programs. Broadcast news reports can be short and succinct, providing only headlines and brief details, or long and analytic, providing in-depth discussion and varying points of view.

Radio News

Nearly all radio stations report the news at different times during the day. News broadcasts range in length from roughly five minutes every hour during morning and afternoon rush hours to around-the-clock news broadcasting.

News Briefs Brief, five-minute reports include abbreviated local and international news stories—complete with short quotes taken from interviews with eyewitnesses and experts—as well as sports, weather, and traffic information.

Advantage
- News briefs give you basic, essential information you can investigate more fully through other broadcast or print media.

Disadvantages
- Radio news only informs through one of the senses; it provides no visual images or photographs to enhance the text of the stories.

- Short news stories do not provide any in-depth coverage.

News Analysis Public radio and all-news stations provide news analysis, often conducting lengthy interviews with experts and providing a forum for discussion and debate.

Advantage
- Analytical reports provide more perspectives than you can usually find in another single source of news.

Disadvantage
- Although they provide depth of coverage on selected issues, news analysis programs do not present a broad overview of important issues of the day.

Television News

Like all television programming, newscasts compete for your viewership. Newscasts hold viewers' interest with captivating video pictures, eyewitness interviews, and warm, congenial newscasters. However, news stories often are selected for their potential to increase the ratings of the network, and may be sensationalized accordingly. Television news coverage, therefore, can provide a distorted impression of what is really important.

Several kinds of news programs—each with unique advantages and disadvantages—can be seen throughout the day.

Local Newscasts The coverage provided by half-hour news programs focuses primarily on local, city, or statewide news, providing only a few world headlines.

Advantages
- Powerful visual information supports and extends the text of the reporters' stories.
- Live and on-tape reports include brief interviews with news-makers, experts, and eye-witnesses to bolster interest and provide comprehensive analysis of events.

Disadvantage
- Newscasts are limited to short reports on selected local stories.

National Newscasts Broadcast nightly from such cities as Washington, D.C., and New York, these newscasts focus on national and international events, sometimes providing several sides to a single story.

Advantage
- On-the-scene reporters stationed all over the country and around the world provide viewers with international perspectives on the news.

Understanding and
Evaluating the Media **535**

Individualizing Instruction

Learning Styles Encourage auditory learners to discuss the advantages of radio news, explaining to visual learners its effectiveness for them. If any students prefer radio to television newscasts, ask them to explain their reasons.

Critical Thinking: Analyzing

Tell students that careful thought goes into the choice of the lead story on national evening news programs. Ask them to suggest questions the news planners might consider in determining which story to use as an opener.

Tell students that if they have trouble concentrating when they are watching news analysis shows, they might find it helpful to think about how they would explain the point that is being made to someone who isn't watching. In order to get a more in-depth understanding of discussions, students can focus on determining the points of view of the various participants. Students may also find it helpful to take brief notes as they watch news analysis programs.

Personal Touch

Display copies of your favorite newspaper or newspapers to the class. Evaluate them in terms of the depth and breadth of coverage, accuracy, and editorial philosophy.

Disadvantage
- Network newscasts sometimes fail to supply adequate background information.

News Analysis Programs Public television stations—as well as some networks—air news analysis shows which provide a forum for in-depth discussion and debate on topical events.

Advantages
- News analysis shows provide a comprehensive analysis of selected issues from a variety of perspectives.
- Viewers can gather information from primary sources and make judgments for themselves.

Disadvantage
- News analysis programs do not provide a broad sense of daily local, national, or international news.

UNDERSTANDING PRINT MEDIA

Print media include news transmitted to an audience in writing. The primary sources are newspapers and news magazines.

WRITER TO WRITER

He had been kicked in the head by a mule when young, and believed everything he read in the Sunday papers.

George Ade, humorist

Newspapers

Major daily newspapers report not only local and world news, but most also offer editorials and cover sports, business, employment opportunities, cultural events, and human interest stories.

Advantage
- Newspapers can be scanned quickly for an overview of news issues; headlines flag articles of particular interest.

Disadvantage
- Some papers are perceived to be liberal or conservative; the editorial philosophy of the paper can affect the way news events are explained and which events are included.

News Magazines

News magazines are published weekly or monthly, rather than daily, like newspapers. They contain objective news reporting, in-depth analyses of major issues, and subjective reviews and editorials. They also include articles on topics of general interest, such as art, music, dance, medicine, science, economics, and politics.

Advantages
- News magazines provide colorful visual and graphic information to supplement each story.

- News magazines often include well-rounded stories that explain the broad personal and social effects of news events.

- You can browse through a news magazine at your leisure, reading the stories that are of particular interest while ignoring the rest.

Disadvantage
- Like newspapers, some magazines are perceived to be liberal or conservative; the editorial philosophy can affect the way news events are explained and which events are included in the coverage.

EVALUATING THE MEDIA

Since there are so many different kinds of news stories, written from a range of perspectives, you need to evaluate news sources in your pursuit of the truth.

Understanding Angles

No single news story could begin to capture all aspects of an issue—nor should it try. Just as you often begin with a broad, general idea and then narrow your focus to a manageable size in your own writing, journalists narrow their focus for stories by choosing an angle, or perspective, for each report. If you piece together reports on an event from a number of different news sources, you will get a more complete picture than if you examine only one. The following guidelines can help you analyze the news you see and hear.

Analyzing Ask students to think of recent news events that initially were reported inaccurately. Have them analyze the stories in terms of the questions in the lesson. Ask them to discuss any changes that became apparent as time passed and reporters were able to investigate more fully before revising their stories.

Critical Thinking

Expressing Opinions Have students make a note of the medium—broadcast or print—on which they depend most for factual accounts of current events and of the medium on which they depend for analysis or interpretation of current events. Encourage them to recall stories or items that were particularly effective. As they report their choices to the class, have students evaluate them according to angle, timing, and content.

Writing
TIP

Any editorial you write will be more convincing if you understand perspectives other than your own before you begin. Conduct interviews with several people so that you understand the range of thinking about your topic.

538 Writing Handbook

Consider Timing Journalists often want to be the first to report on a breaking news event. Initial reports of events—ranging from local warehouse fires, to outbreaks of disease, to federal budgets—often include only rough outlines of the news with few, sketchy details. Sometimes initial reports turn out to be highly inaccurate. When you hear news reports, ask the following questions.

- When did the event happen?
- How soon after the event are the media revealing it to the public?
- How many and what kinds of details does the story include?
- What information seems to be missing from the initial reports? What do I still want to know?

It is very important that you follow the developments of news stories over time. If you first read a story in a newspaper, watch for related stories in the same paper through the following weeks. See what initial information turned out to be true, and what information was revised.

Consider Content When you read or listen to a news story, think carefully about the facts and details presented. You may find a story to be deficient because a journalist has not fully investigated his or her story; or an insignificant story may be blown out of proportion for its entertainment or shock value. Ask these questions as you consider the content of news stories.

- What information does each news story include? What information does it exclude? What can I infer by reading between the lines?
- Did the writer interview representatives from more than one side of a controversial issue? Does the story seem balanced? If not, is it an editorial representing the views of a particular columnist?

Consider Style The language a journalist uses to report the news is critical to your understanding events as they truly happen. It's one thing for language that reflects value judgments to be used on the editorial page, but quite another for it to be used on the front page. Know what you're reading, and ask questions like these as you evaluate news styles.

- Who is the intended audience for the story?
- Does the writer use value-laden language, or is the writing style objective and matter-of-fact?

To most effectively interpret and evaluate the media, you must combine what you already know with what you learn from the news. Decide what to accept, what to reject, and what to find out more about. Remember, too, that no two news sources are alike, since the news is investigated, written, and reported by different people who bring their own perspectives to each story and who write from different angles on the same topic. Gather your news, then, from a variety of sources to get the most complete story possible.

Practice Your Skills

A. Over the course of a week, take in as much broadcast news as you can. Try to listen to an analytical news program on the radio in the morning or pay special attention to the headlines presented on shorter radio newscasts. Watch television news in the late afternoon, and listen to another radio news program in the early evening, perhaps on a public broadcasting station. Compare the pros and cons of these media and write about your preferences in your journal. Answer these questions.

- How does the presence or absence of pictures influence the way you understand news reports?
- How are your emotions affected by radio and TV news?
- Did you respond differently to the same news story presented on radio and television?
- What information does your imagination supply when you listen to radio news?

B. Choose a local, national, or international story that interests you and follow it in print for a week. Read as much as you can about the issue in your city's daily newspaper, in national newspapers, and in news magazines. Check to see if that story is also covered in broadcast news and compare the information you get from different sources.

C. Some analysts say that the news media serve three vital functions with regard to the government.

- gatekeeper—deciding which stories get attention
- watchdog—reporting waste, mismanagement, criminal activity
- scorekeeper—making judgments about politicians, policies, bills, and the like.

For one week, study various kinds of news coverage on the air and in print. Find two examples of each of these functions.

LEP Students Since some students may not have English print media readily available in their homes, provide newspapers and news magazines for students to use to complete Exercises B and C. You also might encourage students to use the school library and local libraries to find news stories.

Peer Response

Organize students into small groups, and have them exchange any articles they have collected for Exercise C without labeling them. Have students categorize the articles as gatekeeper, watchdog, or scorekeeper and analyze them for their effectiveness within the categories.

ANSWERS TO PRACTICE YOUR SKILLS

A. Answers will vary but should reflect the four elements addressed in the bulleted questions.
B. Answers will vary.
C. Answers will vary but must contain two or more examples of these three media functions: gatekeeper, watchdog, and scorekeeper.

Additional Resources
- Writing Resource Book, p. 70

Literature Connection

Autobiographies Criteria for evaluating the media can also be useful in analyzing autobiographies. For example, such questions as what is the writer's angle or perspective, who is the intended audience for the book, is the style objective or highly personal, and does the book deal with current time or with the past will help students evaluate autobiographies. Remind them that the author's purpose determines the answers to most evaluation questions. Have them brainstorm a list of purposes for which people write autobiographies.

Drought, Kenneth Noland, 1962

Humanities Connection

Art Note *Drought* (1962) is an acrylic painting by the modern American abstract painter Kenneth Noland (b. 1924). Noland has painted many abstract compositions made up of color bands. Much of the "meaning" of these paintings is in the texture, transparency, density, and coolness or warmth of their colors.

Grammar and Usage Handbook

The mini-lessons in this Handbook may be used for a variety of purposes.

Direct Teaching—to cover a specific language skill in depth

Preteaching—to introduce a specific language skill before the revision stage of an assignment (see Teaching Preview pages in this Teacher's Edition for suggestions).

Reteaching—to remedy specific problems noted in student papers

These exercises enable you to discover the areas of strengths and weaknesses in your students' backgrounds. The items are constructed similarly to some standardized tests that students will encounter as they move through high school. The range of errors tested include those of grammar, usage, spelling, punctuation, and capitalization. Use this assessment as a formal diagnostic tool or as an informal means of deciding what grammar handbooks you will emphasize.

Skills Assessment Pretest
1. A—Doesn't anyone
2. B—he
3. E
4. A—encyclopedia
   C—it doesn't
5. C—twentieth century
   D—aristocrats; today, or aristocrats. Today
6. A—Gilbert and Sullivan's

Skills
A S S E S S M E N T

Directions One or more of the underlined sections in the following sentences may contain errors of grammar, usage, punctuation, spelling, or capitalization. Write the letters of each incorrect section. Then rewrite the item correctly. If there is no error in an item, write E.

> **Example** Renoir, the <u>artist,</u> told his son, <u>whom</u> later became a
>   **A**   **B**
> <u>filmmaker,</u> that to know people one <u>need</u> to study their hands
>   **C**   **D**
> and faces. <u>No error</u>
>   **E**
>
> **Answer** B—who; D—needs

1. "<u>Don't no one</u> know <u>who</u> invented the <u>wheel?</u>" the student <u>asked,</u> incredulously.
        A   **B**   **C**   **D**
   <u>No error</u>
    E

2. <u>Jacques Cousteau</u> is a great innovator; <u>him</u> and Emil Gagnan <u>invented</u> the aqua-
        A   **B**   **C**
   lung <u>used in scuba diving.</u> <u>No error</u>
          D   **E**

3. Whether <u>a real, verifiable</u> <u>King Arthur</u> ever lived <u>is</u> a subject of <u>considerable</u> debate
             A   **B**   **C**   **D**
   among historians. <u>No error</u>
             E

4. The <u>Encyclopedia</u> article describes estivation <u>as similar</u> to hibernation, but
        A   **B**
   <u>they don't</u> say <u>what the difference is.</u> <u>No error</u>
    C   **D**   **E**

5. The first <u>Arabian horses</u> were brought to the <u>West</u> in the early <u>Twentieth Century</u>
           A   **B**   **C**
   by two English <u>aristocrats, today,</u> the descendants of those Arabians are being bred
              D
   and raised on a horse farm in Arizona. <u>No error</u>
                           E

6. <u>Gilbert's and Sullivan's</u> operetta *The Pirates of Penzance* became widely popular
     A   **B**
   again because of a <u>Broadway</u> production starring Kevin Kline and the
                 C
   <u>pop singer Linda Ronstadt.</u> <u>No error</u>
     D   **E**

7. Executing fantastic pirouettes, loops, and tumbles in the clear skies of Washington,
                              A
   the audience watched the stunt pilot, David Rahm, perform. No error
       B   **C**   **D**   **E**

8. Long ago, well before the invention of the Printing Press, poets often sung their
           A   **B**   **C** **D**
   poetry to small, interested audiences. No error
                              E

9. Sanskrit, the ancient language of India, is a distant relative of english,
              A   **B**
   which is evident when two common words such as "brother" and "phrater" are
      C   **D**
   compared. No error
            E

10. One wonders whether the artist who sculpted Mount Rushmore might have began
         A   **B**   **C**
    to have second thoughts when he realized that the work was going to take him an
                              D
    entire lifetime. No error
                     E

11. Belize's many atractions include the following tropical jungles, Mayan ruins, and
     A   **B**   **C**
    magnificent coral reefs. No error
         D   **E**

12. Colors that are opposite one another on a color wheel—red and green, for
     A   **B**   **C**
    example—are known as complimentary colors. No error
       C   **D**   **E**

13. Most of the desserts of the world lie in two bands, north and south of the tropics.
             A   **B**   **C**   **D**
    No error
     E

14. Many studies have tried to determine whether seeing violence on television makes
             A   **B**   **C**
    children behave more violent. No error
            D   **E**

15. Archbishop Desmond Tutu recieved the Nobel Peace Prize for his efforts to end
     A   **B**   **C**
    the system of apartheid in South Africa. No error
                     D   **E**

7. A—The audience watched the stunt pilot, David Rahm, executing fantastic pirouettes, loops, and tumbles in the clear skies of Washington.
8. B—printing press
   C—sang
9. B—English
   D—brother and phrater
10. C—begun
11. B—attractions
    C—following: tropical
12. D—complementary
13. A—deserts
14. D—more violently
15. B—received

16. B—well
    D—chose
17. E
18. B—don't
19. C—rising from
20. E
21. A—Those
22. D—record for the greatest number of
    fumbles in a career
23. E
24. B—magnifying
    D—beautifully
25. A—set
    D—laid

16. Marion <u>didn't</u> feel too <u>good</u> after her <u>accident, but</u> she <u>choose</u> to keep an optimis-
          A   B   C   D
    tic attitude. <u>No error</u>
                  E

17. The <u>Museum of Man</u> in Paris <u>is</u> a major source of <u>scientific</u> information about
              A   B   C
    <u>human anatomy.</u> <u>No error</u>
       D   E

18. <u>Researchers</u> concluded that chimpanzees like Nim Chimpsky <u>doesn't</u> really <u>have</u> the
     A   B   C
    ability <u>to learn language.</u> <u>No error</u>
          D   E

19. A crowd <u>gathered,</u> hoping <u>to see</u> the huge rocket ship <u>raising from</u> <u>its</u> launch pad.
            A   B   C   D
    <u>No error</u>
      E

20. Thomas <u>Hardy's</u> novel <u>was called</u> <u>*Far from the Madding Crowd,*</u> <u>not</u> *Far from the*
           A   B   C   D
    Maddening Crowd. <u>No error</u>
               E

21. <u>Them</u> place names throughout California <u>such as Los Angeles and San Luis Obispo</u>
     A   B
    <u>reflect</u> the <u>Spanish</u> heritage of the state. <u>No error</u>
      C   D   E

22. Roman Gabriel, <u>who</u> played football for <u>Los Angeles and Philadelphia,</u> <u>holds</u> the
                A   B   C
    <u>record. For the greatest number of fumbles in a career.</u> <u>No error</u>
                 D   E

23. In <u>500 B.C.</u> Iran <u>was called</u> Persia and <u>was</u> the <u>nucleus</u> of a vast empire. <u>No error</u>
       A   B   C   D   E

24. Archimedes, <u>the Greek mathematician,</u> invented a giant <u>magnifiing</u> glass that was
                A   B
    used to set fire to enemy <u>ships;</u> according to ancient historians, this ship burner
                           C
    worked <u>beautiful.</u> <u>No error</u>
           D   E

25. The adobe bricks were <u>sat</u> in the sun to <u>dry,</u> and then, after a few days, the bricks
                   A   B
    <u>were</u> <u>lain</u> to make the foundation and walls. <u>No error</u>
     C   D   E

Sketchbook

*T*omorrow, and tomorrow, and tomorrow
Creeps in this petty pace from day to day
To the last syllable of recorded time

William Shakespeare
MACBETH, act 5, sc. 5, lines 21–23

Think of something that you would love to do but have always postponed. Devise a plan to do it. To express a sense of urgency, use only simple sentences.

Additional Sketches

When was the last time you watched clouds roll by, enjoying the parade of weightless and ever-changing forms, perhaps imagining that they were something else? Look up in the sky and write down what you see, using expressive adjectives and verbs.

Create a detailed sketch of a character for a story. Make notes describing his or her appearance and personality. Include in your sketch things your character might say or do.

545

Objective

To use a quotation as a springboard to informal writing

Using the Prompt

Before beginning the activity, be sure students understand that Sketchbook writing is ungraded. It is designed to be informal and to offer opportunities for experimenting with writing techniques.

Explain that the quotation from *Macbeth* is spoken by Macbeth after he has heard about the death of his wife. In this speech, he anticipates his own death and laments the swift passing of life. Although students are not in Macbeth's dire and tragic situation, they will no doubt still appreciate that in time's swift and relentless march, opportunities can be missed and things that are postponed often never happen at all.

Have students brainstorm things they would love to do. You might begin by sharing something that you yourself have postponed and would really like to do. List on the board the things the students mention. Groups of students might then pick ideas on which they would like to do planning and work collaboratively to figure out how to make them happen. Stress the importance of listing the steps of the plans in order, so that the plans will be easy to follow and carry out.

Use the ideas in the Additional Sketches section with students who prefer a different starting point. Encourage students to keep their writing in their Writing Portfolios for possible use in future writing projects.

Grammar Handbook 31:
Review of Parts of Speech

Parts of Speech

Objectives

- To identify the parts of speech
- To use context to determine parts of speech

Teaching Strategies

This handbook has been designed so that students can independently check their understanding of the parts of speech. The first part provides a diagnostic exercise that students can complete and check themselves. Before they take the test, you may want to use the following Individualizing Instruction activity to provide practice.

 Individualizing Instruction

Basic Students To reinforce the importance of examining context, offer additional examples of words that can function as a number of parts of speech. For example: *inside* (preposition, adverb, adjective, noun).

- *Inside* the operating room stood a team of surgeons. (preposition)
- When it began to rain, we hurried *inside.* (adverb)
- The secretary escorted us to an *inside* office. (adjective)
- The *inside* was soft and mushy. (noun)

Additional Resources
- Tests and Assessment, Pretests, pp. 9–12
- Grammar and Usage Practice Book, p. 1

GRAMMAR HANDBOOK 31

Review of Parts of Speech

PARTS OF SPEECH

This handbook reviews the eight parts of speech. The first section contains a test that will enable you to check your knowledge of these basic elements of the English language. Each of the following sections reviews one of the parts of speech: **nouns, pronouns, verbs, adjectives, adverbs, prepositions, conjunctions,** and **interjections.**

First, do the following diagnostic exercise and compare your answers with the answer key at the bottom of page 567. If you find that you need review on any part of speech, study the appropriate section in this handbook. Then, use the Application and Review on pages 566 and 567 to recheck your skills.

As you complete the exercises in this handbook, keep the following rule in mind:

The part of speech of any particular word is determined by the function of the word in the sentence.

For example, the word *photograph* can function as a number of different parts of speech. Its use in context determines its part of speech.

Jo took a *photograph* of the food-laden picnic table. (Noun)

Many parents *photograph* their babies often. (Verb)

The *photograph* album belongs to my family. (Adjective)

Diagnostic Exercise Write the italicized words from the following literary excerpt. After each word, write its part of speech as it is used in the context of the story.

When you have completed the exercise, check your answers with the key on page 567.

(1) "*Oh*, this heat!" said Mrs. Baumgartner, *and fanned herself gracefully* with her straw hat. (2) *Something* had alarmed the children on the beach *below, and* Mrs. Otis, turning to look at them again, saw them abruptly immobilized; then, as *silently* and as swiftly as sharks, they led the horse away and disappeared *into* the *pine* grove, leaving *no traces* of themselves behind. (3) *Until* she saw them go, she had not been *aware* that the skies *were darkening,* and she wondered how long ago the transforma-

tion *had begun*. (4) Now, *from* miles away, there rolled up a *thunderclap, and,* as always in the tropics, the rain came *abruptly,* battling the trees and lashing the vines, beheading the flowers, crashing onto the *tin* roofs, and belaboring the jalousies of Captain Sundstrom's pretty house. (5) *Blue* blossoms *showered* the head *of* Pan. (6) Wrapping the field glasses in *her* sash to protect *them* from the rain, *Mrs. Otis* returned *to* the gallery.

(7) "See?" said Captain Sundstrom to his guests, *with* a *gesture toward* the storm. (8) "We told *you this* heat *was* only an interlude." **Jean Stafford, *A Modest Proposal***

N OUNS

A noun is the name of a person, place, thing, quality, or action.

Nouns can be classified in several ways. Notice that all nouns can be placed in at least two classifications, and some nouns can be placed in more than two.

All nouns are either *common* or *proper*. A **common noun** is the general name for a person, place, thing, or idea. It is common to an entire group: *comedian, city, organization, religion*. A **proper noun** names a specific person, place, thing, or idea. It always begins with a capital letter and may consist of more than one word: *Charlie Chaplin, Rome, League of Women Voters, Mormonism*.

All nouns are either *concrete* or *abstract*. A **concrete noun** names something that can be perceived by the senses—sights, sounds, odors, tastes, and textures: *mountain, pizza, jeans, sand, waves, lizard*. An **abstract noun** names something that cannot be observed by the senses, such as ideas and beliefs: *intelligence, loneliness, theory*.

A **collective noun** is a singular noun that names a group of people or things: *audience, clan, jury, crew, herd, class*.

A **compound noun** is a noun formed from two or more words that express a single idea. Compound nouns can be written as one word, as separate words, or with hyphens: *backpack, night owl, Fifth Avenue, sister-in-law*. A dictionary gives the correct form for compound nouns.

Grammar Note Gerunds are verbals ending in *-ing* that function as nouns:

Laura did the *organizing* of the library books; we all helped with the *shelving*.

Writing
—TIP—

Precise, accurate word choice contributes to strong writing. Use specific rather than general nouns— *terrier* for *dog*, or *canoe* for *boat*.

Nouns

Objectives

- To identify nouns as common, proper, concrete, abstract, collective, or compound
- **Writing** To use specific nouns to add clarity to writing

Teaching Strategies

Teaching Tip: Concrete and Abstract Nouns

Certain nouns can be classified as either concrete or abstract, depending on their context. To illustrate, write these sentences on the board:
- The performance of *Hamlet*, Shakespeare's classic *tragedy*, was superb. (concrete)
- In his treatise *The Poetics*, Aristotle described the nature of *tragedy*. (abstract)

Linking Grammar and Writing

Remind students that careful writers avoid using nouns as verbs in formal writing. Suggest that students consult a dictionary when they are unsure of any noun usage that seems questionable.

> *Additional Resources*
> - Grammar and Usage Practice Book, p. 2

Practice Your Skills

A. CONCEPT CHECK

Nouns List the nouns in this literary excerpt. Identify the *Collective, Abstract,* and *Proper* nouns.

(1) "Uranium," said the captain. (2) "Uranium 235." (3) The words glittered on his tongue like sparks from a gold-stopped tooth.

(4) There was no crew. (5) The only answer came from the wind, which sang in the rigging of his crazy old ship like the music of Orpheus. . . . (6) The decks were clear. (7) The sails were stowed, since there would be no need for them. (8) Insofar as was possible, old *Argo* was trim and ready for the voyage.

Joan Aiken, "Follow My Fancy"

B. DRAFTING SKILL

Precise Word Choice A writer's choice of specific words contributes to effective writing. Replace the vague italicized nouns in the passage below with more exact nouns. You may wish to experiment with the effect achieved by more than one set of answers.

(1) The *person* huddled over the table in the almost deserted *room*. (2) *Items* scattered about gave testimony to the morning's *activity*. (3) Outside the *weather* continued, giving no signal of *change*. (4) In the distance were *sounds* of *things*. (5) Unmistakable was the *feeling* that lay over the entire scene. (6) A *smell* permeated the air of the *place*. (7) Suddenly a loud *noise* was heard outside. (8) The *person* at the table walked to the door and peered out at the *surroundings*.

PRONOUNS

A pronoun is a word used in place of a noun or another pronoun.

The noun to which a pronoun refers is called its **antecedent.**

Kim said that *she* would win a bowling trophy. (*Kim* is the antecedent of the pronoun *she*.)

The horses rushed past the farmer and kept on running until *they* reached the meadow. (*Horses* is the antecedent of the pronoun *they*.)

There are seven main categories of pronouns.

Personal Pronouns

Personal pronouns are pronouns that change their form to express person, number, gender, and case. All these pronouns are listed in the box below.

Singular

	Nominative	Objective	Possessive
First Person	I	me	my, mine
Second Person	you	you	your, yours
Third Person	he, she, it	him, her, it	his, her, hers, its

Plural

	Nominative	Objective	Possessive
First Person	we	us	our, ours
Second Person	you	you	your, yours
Third Person	they	them	their, theirs

Person When a personal pronoun refers to the person speaking, it is a **first-person** pronoun. If a pronoun refers to the person being spoken to, it is a **second-person** pronoun. A pronoun that refers to a person or thing spoken about is a **third-person** pronoun.

Number Pronouns that refer to one person, place, thing, or idea are **singular** in number. Pronouns that refer to more than one are **plural.**

Gender Pronouns that refer to males are in the **masculine** gender. Pronouns that refer to females are in the **feminine** gender. Pronouns that refer to things are in the **neuter** gender.

Writing
TIP

Avoid ambiguity in your writing by checking for clear antecedents of pronouns.

Pronouns

Objective

- To identify pronouns as personal, reflexive, intensive, demonstrative, interrogative, indefinite, or relative

Teaching Strategies

Individualizing Instruction

ESL Students In Spanish as well as in other languages, personal pronouns change form according to their gender, number, and case. Invite students to compare the forms of personal pronouns in their native language with the English equivalents.

Stumbling Block

Point out that possessive pronoun forms such as *yours, hers, its, ours,* and *theirs* never take an apostrophe to show possession because they are already possessive. Remind students that they should avoid confusing the pronoun *its* with the contraction *it's* in their writing.

 Individualizing Instruction

Advanced Students Occasionally, pronouns are used as indirect objects. (We bought ourselves some supplies.) Encourage students to give other examples based on this model.

Case Personal pronouns change form to show how they function in a sentence. This change in form is called **case.** The three cases are nominative, objective, and possessive. Nominative pronouns are used as subjects or as predicate pronouns. Objective pronouns can be used as objects of verbs and objects of prepositions.

Possessive pronouns show ownership. The forms *mine, yours, hers, his, its, ours,* and *theirs* can be used in place of nouns: The bright blue umbrella is *mine.* The forms *my, your, her, his, its, our,* and *their* are used to modify nouns: *Their* umbrella is striped.

For more information on pronoun case, see Grammar Handbook 36, pages 693–694.

Reflexive and Intensive Pronouns

Intensive and reflexive pronouns are formed by adding *-self* or *-selves* to certain personal pronouns.

Reflexive and Intensive Pronoun Forms	
First Person	myself, ourselves
Second Person	yourself, yourselves
Third Person	himself, herself, itself, themselves

Although reflexive and intensive pronouns look alike, each is used in a different way; neither can be used without an antecedent.

A **reflexive pronoun** is a pronoun used as the object of a verb or preposition.

> During the Boston Tea Party, the colonists disguised *themselves* for protection. (The reflexive pronoun *themselves* is the object of the verb *disguised.*)

An **intensive pronoun** is used in apposition to a noun or pronoun to add emphasis.

> Theseus *himself* found the way out of the maze.

Demonstrative Pronouns

The **demonstrative pronouns** are *this, that, these,* and *those.* They are used to point out or identify specific people or things.

> *That* is the path to the lake.
> Are *these* the horseshoes that you were looking for?

550 Grammar Handbook

Interrogative Pronouns

The **interrogative pronouns,** which are used to ask questions, are *who, whom, whose, which,* and *what.*

> *What* are the ingredients in shish kebab?
> *Who* painted that picture of knights in armor?

Indefinite Pronouns

Pronouns that do not refer to a specific person or thing are called **indefinite pronouns.** Indefinite pronouns usually have no antecedent.

> *Everyone* was on the edge of his or her seat at the movie's end.

> *All* of Alfred Hitchcock's films have conclusions that are full of suspense.

Commonly Used Indefinite Pronouns

Singular			Plural	Singular or Plural	
another	everybody	no one	both	all	most
anybody	everyone	nothing	few	any	none
anyone	everything	one	many	more	some
anything	much	somebody	several		
each	neither	someone			
either	nobody	something			

Grammar Note Demonstrative, interrogative, and some indefinite pronouns can also function as adjectives: *These* jumping beans are lively.

Relative Pronouns

The relative pronouns *who, whose, whom, which,* and *that* introduce a subordinate clause and relate it to a word in the sentence.

> Jane Goodall is the naturalist *who* studied the behavior of chimpanzees. (The antecedent of the relative pronoun *who* is the noun *naturalist.*)

> The statesman *whom* everyone admires is the nominee. (The antecedent of the relative pronoun *whom* is *statesman.*)

Parts of Speech **551**

Individualizing Instruction

Basic Students If students are puzzled by the use of some pronouns as either singular or plural, provide these sample sentences:
- Some of these vegetables are fresher than others. (plural)
- Some of this food is simply inedible. (singular)

Individualizing Instruction

LD Students Since the exercise requires students to classify pronouns in seven categories, you may want to suggest a useful strategy for mastering the different types of pronouns. Urge students to assign a "typical" pronoun of their own choice to each classification: for example, *I* (personal), *myself* (reflexive), and *anyone* (indefinite).

Additional Resources
- Grammar and Usage Practice Book, pp. 3–4

Suggest that students explore the idea of writing a news article or a science fiction story about robots.

Concept Check

Pronouns

1. What—Interrogative
2. many—Indefinite
3. One—Indefinite; these—Demonstrative
4. itself—Reflexive
5. it—Personal; which—Relative; itself—Intensive; its—Personal
6. themselves—Intensive; they—Personal
7. these—Demonstrative; each—Indefinite; itself—Reflexive
8. it—Personal; its—Personal
9. that—Relative; us—Personal
10. Who—Interrogative; that—Demonstrative

Verbs

Objective

- To identify verbs as action and linking, transitive and intransitive, main and auxiliary

Practice Your Skills

CONCEPT CHECK

Pronouns   Write the pronouns in the following sentences. Identify each pronoun according to kind: *Personal, Reflexive, Intensive, Demonstrative, Interrogative, Indefinite,* or *Relative.*

1. What is the state of "robotics," or robot technology, today?
2. Already many of the more technologically innovative companies are using "service" robots for cleaning offices and guarding buildings.
3. One of these uses the "Hansel and Gretel principle" to sweep a floor.
4. The robot first circles a room, using sonar to place itself correctly.
5. Then it goes around the room again, leaving a trail of fluorescent paper, which the robot itself follows and sweeps up, along with dirt and dust, on its next circuit.
6. If robotics researchers are successful, robots themselves will be able to "see" and "sense" where they are.
7. Robots such as these would be capable of humanlike movements, and each would be able to adjust itself to an environment.
8. Eventually a service robot will deliver meals in hospitals; it will "memorize" and negotiate hospital corridors on its regular rounds.
9. There may also be house robots that serve us breakfast and do chores.
10. Who wouldn't like a robot like that?

V ERBS

A verb is a word or group of words that expresses an action, a condition, or a state of being.

The verb is the key part of every sentence. There are two main categories of verbs: action verbs and linking verbs.

Action Verbs

An **action verb** tells what the subject does. The action may be physical or mental.

Physical Action	The albatross *landed* awkwardly on the beach. We *flung* ourselves into the icy stream.
Mental Action	Most people *dream* every night. Amanda *considered* her father's promise again.

Linking Verbs

A **linking verb** does not express action. Instead, it links the subject of a sentence to its complements. A complement may be one of the following: a predicate noun, a predicate pronoun, or a predicate adjective.

> The Everglades *are* swamplands in Florida. (The verb *are* links the subject *Everglades* with the predicate noun *swamplands*.)

> The audience walking out of the theater *seemed* pleased with the performance. (The verb *seemed* links the subject *audience* with the predicate adjective *pleased*.)

The most common linking verb is *be* in its various forms. Many linking verbs relate to the senses: *sound, taste, appear, feel, look, smell*. Others express the condition or placement of the subject: *become, remain, seem, stay, grow*.

Although some linking verbs such as *be* and *seem* are never action verbs, others can function as either linking or action verbs depending on how they are used.

Linking Verb	**Action Verb**
The avocado *tasted* bland.	We *tasted* the guacamole dip.
Ed *felt* tired today.	Lee *felt* the wind on her face.
The casserole *smelled* spicy.	George *smelled* the pine trees.

Auxiliary Verbs

In many sentences the verbs—whether action or linking—consist of more than one word. They are a combination of a **main verb** and one or more **auxiliary verbs.** A main verb with its auxiliaries is called a **verb phrase.** The main verb is always the last word in the phrase.

Auxiliary	+	**Main Verb**	=	**Verb Phrase**
was		driving		was driving
should have		remembered		should have remembered
will have been		doing		will have been doing
can		embroider		can embroider

The most frequently used auxiliaries are the forms of *be, have,* and *do*. These are other common auxiliaries:

must	may	shall	could	would
might	can	will	should	

Writing
—TIP—

Look for opportunities to strengthen your writing by replacing linking verbs with action verbs.

Teaching Strategies

Critical Thinking

Analyzing Point out a pattern that will help students to recognize linking verbs. Within a sentence, linking verbs are always followed by a word or words that identify or describe the subject. You may want to have students find examples of linking verbs in their own writing. It may also be helpful to point out that verbs are classified as linking verbs only when they actually link the subject and its predicate word.

 Individualizing Instruction

ESL Students In some languages, the verb *be* is regularly used to form auxiliaries with certain main verbs that require the use of *have* in English. For example, English: *I have arrived;* French: *Je suis arrivé;* German: *Ich bin gekommen.* Point out that English uses forms of *be* for auxiliaries in quite a different way.

The verbs in a verb phrase are often separated by one or more words that are not part of the verb phrase.

The hinges *haven't been oiled* in years.

The orchids *could* probably *benefit* from more frequent spraying.

Did you *participate* in the school talent show?

Should they *have been waiting* in the rain?

Transitive and Intransitive Verbs

Action verbs may be transitive or intransitive. A **transitive verb** is a verb that has a direct object. The verb carries the action from the subject to the object. An **intransitive verb** has no object.

Transitive	**Intransitive**
Polo players *hit* a wooden ball.	The players *ride* expertly.
Elena *bought* an oboe.	Elena *practiced* in the garage.
You *forgot* your ticket.	Ian *arrived* today.

A few verbs in English are only transitive; a few others are only intransitive. Most verbs, however, can be either.

Transitive	**Intransitive**
Sudi *moved* the furniture.	Sudi *moved* to Phoenix.
I *packed* my suitcase.	I *packed* for the trip hastily.
We *ran* a fast race.	We *ran* down the block.

Grammar Note Linking verbs do not have objects and so may be considered intransitive. When passive voice verbs are changed to their active form, they are always transitive.

For more information on verbs, see Grammar Handbook 34, "Verb Usage," pages 631–667.

Practice Your Skills

CONCEPT CHECK

Verbs and Verb Phrases Write all of the verbs or verb phrases in the following sentences. Then label each verb either *Action* or *Linking*. Identify each action verb as *Transitive* or *Intransitive*. Most sentences will have more than one verb.

1. The Chinese were probably the first users of fireworks since they had already invented the gunpowder necessary for pyrotechnics.
2. Between the sixteenth and eighteenth centuries in Europe, fireworks became the toys of kings, who often used them in court celebrations.

554 Grammar Handbook

Individualizing Instruction

LEP Students You may need to explain the passive voice to these students and provide an example of its use. (We were invited to their home for dinner.)

Additional Resources
• Grammar and Usage Practice Book, pp. 5–6

WRITING THEME Fireworks

You might want to suggest that fireworks would make an exciting subject for a first-person narrative.

Concept Check

Verbs and Verb Phrases
1. were—Linking; had invented—Action, Transitive
2. became—Linking; used—Action, Transitive
3. would construct—Action, Transitive; served—Action, Intransitive; added—Action, Intransitive

3. Court fireworks masters would construct elaborate decorated "machines," stage settings that served as background for the fireworks explosions and added to the excitement.

4. King Louis XIV of France was a lover of fireworks, and once he ordered a show that continued for five days.

5. Handel wrote his famous "Fireworks" music for a display in England; its fireworks machine was 410 feet long and 114 feet high and included eleven thousand fireworks.

6. Before the 1830's, fireworks must have seemed dull because their colors included only amber and greenish blue; since then, however, the use of new chemicals has produced many other vibrant colors.

7. Today, Fourth of July celebrations all over the United States sparkle and reverberate with the sights and sounds of sophisticated pyrotechnic displays.

8. Americans specialize in "multi-shell fireworks" that explode in one cluster of light after another as the shells fall.

9. We also like "willow" fireworks, which emit long, thin tendrils of light that bloom in the sky with just the smallest puff, while the Chinese prefer round fireworks that produce a quick burst of stars like a spread of chrysanthemums.

10. Fireworks specialists are always seeking even more extraordinary effects so that they can further amaze and thrill us spectators.

ADJECTIVES

An adjective is a word that modifies a noun or a pronoun.

Adjectives change or limit the meaning of nouns or pronouns by answering one of the following questions:

Which One?	*this* keyboard, *that* suggestion, *those* test tubes
What Kind?	*thick* sandwich, *hasty* decision, *portable* computer
How Many?	*twelve* eggs, *many* floats, *few* comedians
How Much?	*little* experience, *enough* money, *abundant* rainfall

Position of Adjectives An adjective generally precedes the word it modifies. Sometimes, for variety, a writer will place adjectives after the words they modify.

> The house, *isolated* and *eerie*, resembled a set for a horror movie.

> Last week's weather, *hot* and *humid,* forced us to stay indoors.

Writing
—TIP—

Keep your writing lively by using fresh, imaginative adjectives and avoiding trite expressions.

4. was—Linking; ordered—Action, Transitive; continued—Action, Intransitive

5. wrote—Action, Transitive; was presented—Action, Transitive; was presented—Linking; included—Action, Transitive

6. must have seemed—Linking; included—Action, Transitive; has produced—Action, Transitive

7. sparkle—Action, Intransitive; reverberate—Action, Intransitive

8. specialize—Action, Intransitive; explode—Action, Intransitive; fall—Action, Intransitive

9. like—Action, Transitive; emit—Action, Transitive; bloom—Action, Intransitive; prefer—Action, Transitive; produce—Action, Transitive

10. are seeking—Action, Transitive; can amaze—Action, Transitive; thrill—Action, Transitive

Adjectives

Objectives

- To identify adjectives, their types, positions, and functions
- **Writing** To use adjectives to add details and create variety in writing

Teaching Strategies

Speaking and Listening

Have students read the sample sentences aloud. Make sure that they note the comma pauses that set off adjectives placed after the noun they modify.

Teaching Tip: Position of Adjectives

Remind students that predicate adjectives do not always directly follow linking verbs. A linking verb and its predicate adjective may be separated by intervening words. (While she was ill, she seemed to her friends almost continually impatient.)

Personal Touch

Share with students a descriptive passage from your own writing, and invite them to comment on the use of adjectives. Some students may want to share descriptions that they have written.

 Individualizing Instruction

ESL Students Some foreign languages, including French, Spanish, and Italian, also display variations in the forms of articles, depending on the sound of the initial letter in the word that follows. Invite students to offer some examples from their native language.

Vietnamese and Russian are examples of two languages that contain no articles. Students who speak these languages will need help in using definite and indefinite articles correctly.

Linking Grammar and Writing

Remind students that the use of nouns as adjectives can help writers to be more concise. When overused, however, this usage can lead to jargon or inflated diction: for example, *her labor routine* for *her routine at work.*

Additional Resources
- Grammar and Usage Practice Book, p. 7

Predicate Adjectives A **predicate** adjective is an adjective that follows a linking verb and modifies the subject.

> The bench was *wet* from the rain. (The predicate adjective *wet* modifies the subject *bench*.)

> The acoustics in the auditorium seemed *excellent*. (The predicate adjective *excellent* modifies the subject *acoustics*.)

Proper Adjectives Proper adjectives are formed from proper nouns and are always capitalized.

Hawaiian pineapples	*Chaucerian* age
Atlantic coast	*French cooking*

Articles The most common adjectives are the articles *a, an,* and *the*. Articles modify the nouns they precede.

The word *the* is called the **definite article** because it usually refers to a specific person, place, or thing.

The words *a* and *an* are the **indefinite articles.** They indicate that a noun is not unique but is one of many of its kind. Use *a* before a word beginning with a consonant sound: *a* diary, *a* union. Use *an* before a word beginning with a vowel sound: *an* apricot, *an* understanding. Remember, it is the sound and not the spelling that determines the correct choice.

Other Words Used as Adjectives Many words that are generally thought of as other parts of speech can also function as adjectives. These include nouns and certain classes of pronouns including possessive, demonstrative, interrogative, relative, and indefinite pronouns. Certain verbals ending in *-ed* and *-ing* may also function as adjectives. The following list shows some examples.

Nouns	*cattle* drive, *tennis* racket, *traffic* jam, *wall* phone, *desk* pad, *graduation* cap
Pronouns	*her* chopsticks, *this* parabola, *which* idea, *some* artifacts, *all* legends
Verbals	*sparkling* icicles, *wilting* flowers, *congested* streets, *fast-paced* comedy, *often-visited* spot

Practice Your Skills

A. CONCEPT CHECK

Adjectives Find at least twenty-five adjectives in the following passage from a novel by Mark Twain. Do not include articles.

Writing Theme
Mark Twain

(1) Now when I had mastered the language of this water and had come to know every trifling feature that bordered the great river as familiarly as I knew the letters of the alphabet, I had made a valuable acquisition. (2) But I had lost something, too. . . . (3) All the grace, the beauty, the poetry had gone out of the majestic river! (4) I still keep in mind a certain wonderful sunset which I witnessed when steamboating was new to me. (5) A broad expanse of the river was turned to blood; in the middle distance the red hue brightened into gold, through which a solitary log came floating, black and conspicuous; in one place . . . the surface was broken by boiling, tumbling rings, that were as many-tinted as an opal; . . . the shore on our left was densely wooded, and the sombre shadow that fell from this forest was broken in one place by a long, ruffled trail that shone like silver; and high above the forest wall a clean-stemmed dead tree waved a single leafy bough that glowed like a flame in the unobstructed splendor that was flowing from the sun. **Mark Twain, *Life on the Mississippi***

B. DRAFTING SKILL

Using Adjectives Rewrite the following paragraph, inserting adjectives for the blanks. Insert proper adjectives as indicated.

(1) Samuel Clemens grew up in the _____ Midwestern town of Hannibal, Missouri, on the Mississippi River. (2) Clemens was fascinated by the _____ life that the river offered. (3) _____ towns such as St. Louis and New Orleans with their (<u>Proper</u>) names seemed _____ to him. (4) The _____ chance he got, Clemens left home to become a cub pilot on a steamboat. (5) Although he was _____ as a pilot, he eventually grew restless. (6) He spent three years as a pilot, and then the _____ year he went west to _____ frontier country. (7) In Nevada, Clemens began to write _____ short stories, which were so amusing they earned him a job on a (<u>Proper</u>) newspaper; these stories, which he signed "Josh," were the beginning of a _____ career. (8) Later, he took the pen name of Mark Twain from the _____ term for "two fathoms."

Parts of Speech   **557**

The Champions of the Mississippi, Currier and Ives print, 1866

C. APPLICATION IN WRITING

Describing a Scene In the passage at the top of page 557, Mark Twain shows himself to be a skillful painter with words. Write a paragraph in which you describe a scene that you have experienced. It could be a path in a forest, a view from a mountaintop, or even the view from your window.

ADVERBS

An adverb modifies a verb, an adjective, or another adverb.

Adverbs tell *where, when, how,* or *to what extent* about the words they modify. Note that nouns can sometimes function as adverbs.

Where?	floated *away,* went *home* (noun), sauntered *forward*
When?	worked *late,* heard *before,* left *already*
How?	fell *noisily,* wrote *legibly,* cooks *well*
To What Extent?	*very* rare, *rather* hot, *hardly* begun

Many adverbs are formed by adding *-ly* to an adjective: *foolish*—adjective, *foolishly*—adverb.

Writing —TIP—

Strong adverbs, used sparingly, describe, expand, and focus your adjectives and verbs.

558 Grammar Handbook

Adverbs

Objective

• To identify adverbs and their function

Humanities Connection

Art Note This Currier and Ives print, *The Champions of the Mississippi* (1866), depicts two prominent subjects in Mark Twain's works—paddleboats and the Mississippi River. Nathaniel Currier (1813–1888) and James Ives (1824–1895), the most popular and successful of all American printmakers, produced some 7,000 lithographs of landscapes, historical and sporting events, sentimental scenes, and portraits that together form a catalog of American tastes and culture in the 19th century.

Intensifiers Adverbs that modify, and add emphasis to, adjectives and other adverbs are called **intensifiers.** Some common intensifiers are *too, very, quite, rather, really, fully, barely, completely, scarcely,* and *little.*

Directive Adverbs Adverbs that tell *where* (place or direction) about the verb are **directive adverbs.** Many directive adverbs combine with verbs to make idioms: *put through, break off, check in.* An idiom's meaning cannot be understood from the meanings of its separate words.

For more information about adverbs, see Grammar Handbook 37, "Adjective and Adverb Usage."

Practice Your Skills

CONCEPT CHECK

Adverbs Write the adverbs in the following sentences and tell which word or words each modifies. Then find and label the idioms in the sentences.

1. Arthur Ferguson, of Scotland, was a phenomenally successful salesman; he was also extraordinarily dishonest.
2. In the 1920's Ferguson quite deviously pulled off a series of cons that made him one of history's most notorious flim-flam artists.
3. One day in the early 1920's, Ferguson saw a tourist gazing admiringly at Nelson's column, a monument in Trafalgar Square, in London.
4. Ferguson immediately approached the tourist and explained very sadly that England was going to have to sell the monument in order to pay its debts.
5. Then Ferguson formally introduced himself as a government broker officially commissioned to carry out the sale of the monument.
6. The apparently wealthy tourist, excited at the news, rather foolishly gave Ferguson a $30,000 check for the valuable monument.
7. The tourist gradually realized that he had been completely duped. Ferguson had already cashed the check at the nearest bank.
8. For several years Ferguson ran a quite steady business selling monuments to tourists.
9. Ferguson sold, among other monuments and national treasures, Big Ben, Buckingham Palace, and even the White House in the United States, but he was eventually caught and imprisoned.
10. Ferguson's schemes broke down when he tried, totally unsuccessfully, to sell the Statue of Liberty to a man who wisely reported Ferguson to the New York police.

Writing Theme
Deception

Parts of Speech   **559**

Linking Grammar and Writing

We all tend to overuse intensifiers like *very, rather,* and *really* in casual conversation. The careless use of intensifiers in formal writing, however, should be avoided since too many intensifiers weaken sentence structure rather than strengthen it. Adjectives that express an absolute condition should not be used with intensifiers at all. One example is the word *unique.*

Have students scan selections from their own writing to check for the correct use of intensifiers.

> **Additional Resources**
> • Grammar and Usage Practice Book, p. 8

WRITING THEME   Deception

This writing theme may serve as the basis for a newspaper account of one of Ferguson's deceptions. Suggest that students explore this idea and make notes in their journal.

Concept Check
Adverbs
1. phenomenally—successful; also—was; extraordinarily—dishonest
2. quite—deviously; deviously—pulled off; most—notorious (pulled off—idiom)
3. admiringly—gazing
4. immediately—approached; very—sadly; sadly—explained
5. Then—introduced; formally—introduced; officially—commissioned (carry out—idiom)
6. apparently—wealthy; rather—foolishly; foolishly—gave
7. gradually—realized; completely—duped; already—had cashed
8. quite—steady
9. even—sold; eventually—was caught
10. totally—unsuccessfully; unsuccessfully—tried; wisely—reported (broke down—idiom)

Prepositions

Objective

- To identify prepositions and their objects

A preposition is a word used to show the relationship between a noun or a pronoun and another word in a sentence.

Men of fashion commonly wore three-cornered hats during the 1700's. (The preposition *of* relates the noun *fashion* to the noun *men;* the preposition *during* relates the verb *wore* to the noun *1700's.*)

The relationships most often expressed by prepositions are location (*by, near*), direction (*up, off*), and association (*of, with*). Some prepositions are **compound,** formed by combining two or more words. Study these lists carefully.

Commonly Used Prepositions

about	before	down	of	throughout
above	behind	during	off	to
across	below	except	on	toward
after	beneath	for	onto	under
against	beside	from	out	underneath
along	between	in	outside	until
among	beyond	inside	over	up
around	but	into	past	upon
as	by	like	since	with
at	despite	near	through	without

Commonly Used Compound Prepositions

according to	in place of
as well as	in relation to
because of	in response to
by means of	in spite of
by way of	inside of
except for	instead of
in accordance with	on account of
in addition to	

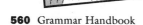

"Wait a minute! ... McCallister, you fool! *This* isn't what I said to bring!"

560 Grammar Handbook

Objects of Prepositions

A preposition is always followed by a word or a group of words called the **object of the preposition.** The preposition, its object, and any modifiers of the object form a **prepositional phrase.**

> Black peppercorns are the dried berries *of a woody climbing vine.* (*Of* is a preposition; *vine* is its object; *woody* and *climbing* modify *vine.*)

The object of a preposition may be a noun, a pronoun, or a clause.

> The first diesel engine was invented by *Rudolf Diesel.* (Noun)
> A thick fog swirled around *me.* (Pronoun)
> Extra test tubes are here for *whoever needs them.* (Clause)

For more information on prepositional phrases, see Grammar Handbook 33, pages 591–592.

Practice Your Skills

CONCEPT CHECK

Prepositions Write the prepositions from each of the following sentences. For each preposition, write its object.

1. Places on earth are often named after famous people or by geographic features, but how are places in space named?
2. In the past, each observatory chose its own names for planetary features and then battled for its choices with other observatories.
3. Because of these arguments, in 1919 it was decided that the naming would be done by a union of astronomers.
4. After years of haggling, the union has developed rules for naming.
5. The features on Venus, itself named for the Roman goddess of love, are named for women from myths and literature in accordance with the decision.
6. The names of many of Saturn's features are based upon characters from the King Arthur legend.
7. Many places on Mars are named after science-fiction writers like Edgar Rice Burroughs and H. G. Wells.
8. Ray Bradbury, who wrote the *Martian Chronicles,* probably also will appear on Mars.
9. According to the established rules, if satellites discover any new moons orbiting Neptune, these will be named after sea spirits from cultures throughout the world.
10. The decision seems to be an appropriate one since Neptune, a Roman diety, ruled the world beneath the sea.

Conjunctions

Objective

- To identify coordinating, correlative, and subordinating conjunctions and conjunctive adverbs

CONJUNCTIONS

A conjunction is a word that connects words, phrases, or clauses.

The three kinds of conjunctions are coordinating, correlative, and subordinating conjunctions. In addition, conjunctive adverbs function as conjunctions.

Coordinating Conjunctions

A **coordinating conjunction** is used to connect words or groups of words that have the same function in a sentence. The following are coordinating conjunctions:

and	but	or	for	so	yet	nor

Coordinating conjunctions can join various parts of speech or sentence parts: nouns, pronouns, verbs, adjectives, adverbs, prepositions, phrases, or clauses.

The attic was dark, airless, *and* dusty. (Adjectives)
The play's plot was old, *but* the dialogue was witty. (Clauses)

Correlative Conjunctions

Correlative conjunctions function like coordinating conjunctions, but they are always used in pairs. These are correlative conjunctions:

both . . . and	neither . . . nor	whether . . . or
either . . . or	not only . . . but (also)	

Both Monet *and* Renoir were impressionist painters.

Subordinating Conjunctions

Subordinating conjunctions introduce subordinate clauses. They connect clauses that are not complete sentences to clauses that are. A subordinating conjunction expresses relationships of time, manner, cause or reason, comparison, condition, or purpose.

┌──independent clause──┐ ┌──subordinate clause──┐

Many students take chemistry, although it is not required.
(The subordinating conjunction *although* connects the subordinate clause to the independent clause and shows their opposition.)

Subordinating Conjunctions	
Time	after, as, as long as, as soon as, before, since, until, when, whenever, while
Manner	as, as if
Place	where, wherever
Cause or Reason	because, since
Comparison	as, as much as, than, whereas
Condition	although, as long as, even if, even though, if, provided that, though, unless, while
Purpose	in order that, so that, that

For more information about clauses, see Grammar Handbook 33, "Phrases and Clauses," pages 605–615.

Conjunctive Adverbs

Conjunctive Adverbs are used to connect clauses that can stand by themselves as sentences.

> The number of apples to pick seemed endless; *nevertheless,* we continued at the task steadily.

> Under Kublai Khan, China extended its empire from the Pacific Ocean into Poland; *furthermore,* China flourished culturally at that time.

> Rita spent long hours in the chemistry laboratory at the university; *consequently,* she was far better prepared for the exam than her classmates.

Conjunctive Adverbs			
accordingly	finally	indeed	still
also	furthermore	moreover	then
besides	hence	nevertheless	therefore
consequently	however	otherwise	thus

Punctuation Note A conjunctive adverb is usually preceded by a semicolon and followed by a comma.

Writing
—TIP—

A skillful writer clarifies relationships between ideas by choosing appropriate subordinating conjunctions.

Teaching Strategies

Linking Grammar and Literature

The following passage from James Boswell's *Life of Samuel Johnson* illustrates a complex yet clear use of coordinating conjunctions and subordinating conjunctions. Discuss how the writer has used conjunctions to link sentence parts.

That the most minute singularities which belonged to him, and made very observable parts of his appearance and manner, may not be omitted, it is requisite to mention that while talking or even musing as he sat in his chair, he commonly held his head to one side toward his right shoulder and shook it in a tremulous manner, moving his body backward and forward, and rubbing his left knee in the same direction with the palm of his hand.

WRITING THEME Dragons

Students may want to brainstorm ideas for writing stories about dragons as either friendly or ferocious beasts. Students should record the ideas in their journals.

Concept Check

Conjunctions
1. and—Coordinating
2. when—Subordinating
3. accordingly—Conjunctive Adverb
4. neither . . . nor—Correlative; and—Coordinating; however—Conjunctive Adverb
5. but—Coordinating
6. and—Coordinating
7. because—Subordinating
8. and—Coordinating; not only . . . but also—Correlative; and—Coordinating
9. and—Coordinating; because—Subordinating
10. whereas—Subordinating

Practice Your Skills

CONCEPT CHECK

Conjunctions Write each conjunction and identify it as *Coordinating, Correlative,* or *Subordinating,* or as a *Conjunctive Adverb.*

1. Dragons appear in the Old English epic *Beowulf* and in many other medieval English tales.
2. These stories were probably brought to England when the Danes invaded, during the years following A.D. 750.
3. In Old English, the word *wyrm* "worm" referred to any creeping, crawling thing; accordingly, the word was used to refer to dragons.
4. In *Beowulf* neither warriors nor the monster Grendel can match the strength and cunning of the hero; however, in the end a fire-breathing "wyrm" overcomes the hero.
5. The dragons in *Beowulf* are well known, but even more famous is the dragon who fought with England's patron saint, St. George.
6. According to legend, St. George saved his own life and that of a princess by killing a dragon during a crusade.
7. During the Middle Ages, St. George became a favorite of the crusaders because they believed he could protect them in battle.
8. The episode of St. George and the dragon came to be celebrated not only in English literature, but also in painting, sculpture, and architecture.
9. Dragons appeared in medieval literature and art so often because they represented the evils fought by humans in every land.
10. In European stories, dragons are ferocious beasts, whereas in Asian legends the animals are considered friendly—an interesting contrast in cultures.

INTERJECTIONS

An interjection is a word or word group used to express surprise or other emotions. It has no grammatical relationship to the other words in a sentence.

Some common interjections are *oh, o, great, hello,* and *ouch.* An interjection may be followed by an exclamation point, or it may be included in a sentence but set off by commas.

Great! I bowled two strikes.   *Well,* what's wrong now?
You heard me. *Never!*   *Hurrah!* We won.

Practice Your Skills

A. DRAFTING SKILL

Using Interjections Fill in the blanks in the following passages with appropriate interjections.

"_____" Michiko said, stopping her friend. "Want to hear something weird?"

"Sure," Carmen responded. "What's up?"

"_____, in science class we were talking about meteorites. It seems that in 1902, in a rural part of the Soviet Union, a crash occurred that leveled the trees in a fifty-mile-diameter circle."

"_____! Can a meteor do that?"

"_____, that's what's really strange. There wasn't an impact crater. In fact, all the trees at the center of the circle were still standing."

"_____! So it wasn't a meteor."

"No one knows. It's one of the great unexplained mysteries of science."

"_____! The idea gives me goose bumps!"

B. APPLICATION IN WRITING

Creating a Dramatic Scene Try your hand at mystery writing. Imagine that you have been hired to create a drama for television. First, think of a general plot line and characters. Then focus on a scene showing a moment of tension and excitement, such as the discovery of the crime or the unmasking of the criminal. After briefly describing your characters and setting, write a dialogue for this emotional scene using at least four interjections. Make sure the interjections are appropriate and natural for your characters.

Writing —TIP—

Overuse of interjections results in loss of impact.

Writing Theme
Mysteries

Interjections

Objective
- To identify and use interjections

Teaching Strategies

Speaking and Listening

Remind students that the punctuation following an interjection is a guide to the emphasis intended by a writer. Have students experiment with writing emphatic sentences with interjections and then reading their sentences aloud in different tones of voice.

> **Additional Resources**
> - Grammar and Usage Practice Book, p. 11

WRITING THEME   Mysteries

To generate ideas for writing their own mystery stories, students may want to discuss mystery stories they have heard about or read. Encourage students to record their ideas for later use.

A. Drafting Skill
Using Interjections
Answers will vary. See typical answers below.
   Hey; Oh; Wow; Well; Incredible; Ugh

B. Application in Writing
Creating a Dramatic Scene
Answers will vary.

Application and Review

These activities allow students to apply concepts in this handbook. Exercise A requires students to identify parts of speech. Exercise B requires students to identify the parts of speech of words and then to use the same words as different parts of speech in original sentences. Exercise C challenges students to find examples of grammatical elements in a poem.

Additional Resources

- Grammar and Usage Practice Book, p. 12
- Tests and Assessment, Mastery Test, pp. 39–42
- Elaboration, Revision, and Proofreading, p. 22

WRITING THEME   Native American Culture

A. Recognizing the Parts of Speech
1. Pronoun
2. Adverb
3. Adjective
4. Preposition
5. Noun
6. Verb
7. Adverb
8. Article
9. Verb
10. Conjunction
11. Pronoun
12. Conjunction
13. Adverb
14. Adjective
15. Preposition
16. Noun
17. Adjective
18. Adverb
19. Adjective
20. Noun

B. Using Parts of Speech
Answers will vary. See typical answers below.
1. sports—Adjective. Football and soccer are contact sports. Noun
2. many—Adjective. Many have summer jobs. Pronoun
3. train—Verb. I like to travel by train. Noun
4. one—Pronoun. One day I decided to become a writer. Adjective
5. in—Preposition. She flies in today for a meeting. Adverb
6. ball—Adjective. I like to play ball. Noun
7. touch—Verb. This sweater is soft to the touch. Noun

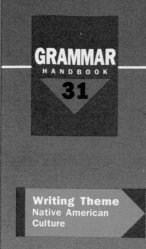

GRAMMAR
HANDBOOK
31

Writing Theme
Native American Culture

A. Recognizing the Parts of Speech   Identify the part of speech of each italicized word as it is used in the following literary excerpt. Then write *Noun, Pronoun, Verb, Adjective, Adverb, Article, Preposition,* or *Conjunction.*

(1) *I* have heard talk and talk, but nothing is done. (2) Good words do not last *long* unless they amount to something. (3) Words do not pay for my *dead* people. (4) They do not pay for my country, now overrun *by* white men. (5) They do not protect my father's *grave.* (6) They *do* not *pay* for all my horses and cattle. (7) Good words will not give me *back* my children. (8) Good words will not make good *the* promise of your War Chief General Miles. (9) Good words will not give my people good health and *stop* them from dying. (10) Good words will not get my people a home *where* they can live in peace and take care of themselves. (11) I am tired of talk *that* comes to nothing. (12) It makes my heart sick *when* I remember all the good words and all the broken promises. (13) There has been *too* much talking by men who had no right to talk. (14) Too *many* misrepresentations have been made. (15) Too many misunderstandings have come up *between* the white men about the Indians. (16) If the white man wants to live in *peace* with the Indian he can live in peace. (17) There will be *no* trouble. (18) Treat all men *alike.* (19) Give them the *same* law. Give them all an even chance to live and grow. (20) All men were made by the *Great Spirit Chief.* They are all brothers.

**Chief Joseph of the Nez Percé,
"Nez Percé Surrender and Outcome"**

B. Using Parts of Speech   Identify the part of speech of each italicized word. Then write a new sentence using the word as a different part of speech. Indicate which part of speech you have used.

1. Early inhabitants of the Americas valued *sports* activities.
2. Even though there were *many* different Native American societies, almost all played games.
3. Some would *train* warriors to win honor by requiring them to engage in competitive games.
4. *One* of the most popular sports was the footrace.
5. *In* the southwestern United States some footraces were thirty miles long.
6. Native Americans also played many different kinds of *ball* games.
7. In these games, the players did not *touch* the ball with their hands.

8. The game of lacrosse developed from one of *these* games.
9. In another game the players rolled a hoop *along* the ground and threw spears or sticks at it.
10. Of course, shooting arrows at a target was very popular and was also *good* for training hunters and warriors.

C. Understanding Parts of Speech Read the poem and locate within it the items listed below. Write the word or words for each item.

1. compound noun
2. verbal as an adjective
3. possessive pronoun as an adjective
4. adverb
5. subordinating conjunction

6. interjection
7. abstract noun
8. verb phrase
9. three pronouns
10. three prepositions

> O our Mother the Earth, O our Father the Sky,
> Your children are we, and with tired backs
> We bring you the gifts you love.
> Then weave for us a garment of brightness;
> May the warp be the white light of morning,
> May the weft be the red light of evening,
> May the fringes be the falling rain,
> May the border be the standing rainbow.
> Thus weave for us a garment of brightness,
> That we may walk fittingly where birds sing,
> That we may walk fittingly where grass is green,
> O our Mother the Earth, O our Father the Sky.
>
> **A Tewa Indian ballad, ''Song of the Sky Loom''**

Answer Key for Diagnostic Exercise, Pages 546–547

1. Oh—interjection; and—Conjunction; fanned—Verb; herself—Pronoun; gracefully—Adverb
2. Something—Pronoun; below—Adverb; and—Conjunction; silently—Adverb; into—Preposition; pine—Adjective; no—Adjective; traces—Noun
3. Until—Conjunction; aware—Adjective; were darkening—Verb; had begun—Verb
4. from—Preposition; thunderclap—Noun; and—Conjunction; abruptly—Adverb; tin—Adjective
5. Blue—Adjective; showered—Verb; of—Preposition
6. her—Adjective or Pronoun; them—Pronoun; Mrs. Otis—Noun; to—Preposition
7. with—Preposition; gesture—Noun; toward—Preposition
8. you—Pronoun; this—Adjective; was—Verb

Your students may not be among those who object to the verb *contact,* as in sentences like *I'll contact you later,* and they may not understand the title "When Nouns Go Bad." You might read the usage note under the entry *contact* in the *American Heritage Dictionary* to establish the fact that many people object to this usage. Remind students that they need not agree with the Usage Panel, but the majority's opinion can help them decide when or if they will use *contact* as a verb. The usage note can also help them understand the idea behind this article.

You might ask volunteers to look up unfamiliar words, such as *licentiousness* and *malodorous.* Talk about the article's humorous use of personification and how it contributes to a tongue-in-cheek tone of voice. Point out that the ease with which certain words can be changed to a different part of speech is one of the strengths and delights of our English language. Finally, ask questions like these: What other words can you think of that started as nouns but are also used as verbs? Can all nouns be used as verbs?

On the Lightside

WHEN NOUNS GO BAD

Let's face it: . . . If language wore clothing, nouns would be the nonstarters in horn-rimmed glasses and cardigan sweaters who loiter on the threshold of ambition, discussing abstracts, and whether their modifiers have dangled lately. In the versatile English language, however, nothing is impossible, and nouns have been known to yearn for a walk on the wild side. But when they aspire to linguistic licentiousness, nouns don't just swap their specs and sweaters for sunglasses and leather jackets. No, when nouns go bad, they go where the action is: They become verbs.

Take, for example, the opening of this essay: *Let's face it.* The principal verb there is *face*—a verb because it conveys an action. *Face* began in English as a noun signifying that area at the front of your head viewed in the mirror every morning. . . .

Actually, no law—save for that of good taste—prevents nouns from opting for life in the fast lane. In fact, the fast lane is congested with the malodorous traffic of the exotic models that whiz by. People are *ambulanced* to the hospital, where physicians *office, source* their medical libraries, and *chair* committees and *debut* expensive operations. Once there, patients are *impacted* by treatments, *gifted* by visitors, maybe even *flowered* by relatives. . . . Then it's back to the fast lane to *motor* the patients home, where cars are *garaged,* and their human cargo once again *hosts, parties, romances,* [and] *parents.* . . .

Of the nominal or nounal verbs (or maybe just *nerbs,* a suitably nerdy word) in the above paragraph, the *American Heritage Dictionary* gives whole-hearted recognition only to *chair, motor, garage, and parent.* . . . What does all this expert opinion mean? Not much.

The English language is one of the purest forms of active democracy. . . . In other words, if a sufficient bloc of delegates in the electoral college of language . . . nerbs the noun *contact*—as in "I'll contact you tomorrow"—then let the experts rail and wail for all they're worth. *Contact* becomes a working nerb in the marketplace of the language, where only the fit survive.

Charles Marsh

The Parts of a Sentence

SUBJECTS AND PREDICATES IN SENTENCES

A sentence is a group of words that expresses a complete thought. Every complete sentence has two parts: the subject and the predicate.

The subject of the sentence is the person, place, thing, or idea about which something is said.

The predicate tells what the subject did or what happened to the subject.

Subject	Predicate
Lava	flows.
The lava from a live volcano	flows hot and smooth.

The **complete subject** includes all the words that name the person, place, thing, or idea the sentence is about. The **complete predicate** includes all the words that tell what the subject did or what happened to the subject.

Each complete subject contains a **simple subject** that names exactly whom or what the sentence is about, and each complete predicate contains a **simple predicate,** hereafter referred to as the **verb.** The simple subject and the verb are the key words that express the core idea of each part of the sentence.

The simple subject (most often called the **subject**) tells whom or what the sentence is about. The subject may be a single word or a group of words, but it does not include modifiers.

The verb tells what the subject does or is. It may be one word or a verb phrase. The verb phrase may be interrupted by modifiers, but the modifiers are not part of the verb.

In each of the following sentences, a vertical line separates the complete subject and complete predicate. The simple subjects and the verbs are in bold type.

The **flowers** in Ms. Rivera's garden | **perished** in the frost.

This broken **camera** | **will** not **take** any pictures.

Which **bus** | **can take** me to the stadium?

Sentence Diagraming   For information on diagraming the subjects and verbs of sentences, see page 834.

Grammar Handbook 32:
The Parts of a Sentence

Subjects and Predicates in Sentences

Objectives

- To identify subjects and predicates in sentences
- To distinguish complete subjects and predicates from simple subjects and predicates
- To identify compound subjects and compound verbs

Teaching Strategies

Stumbling Block

Students may be confused by intervening words between the simple subject and the simple predicate of a sentence. Point out that words between the simple subject and the predicate are not part of the simple subject. (The flowers *in Ms. Rivera's garden* perished in the frost.) Words that interrupt the verb phrase are not part of the simple predicate. (The bus did *not always* run on schedule.)

LEP Students Emphasize the typical pattern for an English sentence: a subject followed by a verb.

ESL Students In some Asian languages, including Japanese, the verb always occurs at the end of the sentence. Compare English with the students' own languages, asking them to explain what the basic subject-verb pattern is in their native tongues.

Additional Resources
- Tests and Assessment, Pretests, pp. 13–15
- Grammar and Usage Practice Book, p. 13

Individualizing Instruction

Basic Students Students may need help with the last sentence in the exercise directions. Point out that verbals are easy to confuse with verbs. Before students do the exercise, you may want to direct attention to the verbals, all of which are infinitives: *to improve* in 3, *(to) find* in 4, and *to produce* in 8.

LD Students With these students, go over the exercise directions carefully. Write the first three sentences on the board. Help students find each subject by asking: *Whom* or *what* is it about? Help them find each verb by asking *What about it?* or *What happened?* After they complete the remaining sentences independently, review them with students.

WRITING THEME Resourcefulness

Discuss with students what resourcefulness means to them. Have students record their ideas in their journals for a future writing assignment.

Concept Check
Subjects and Predicates
Abbreviations: CS—Complete Subject; CP—Complete Predicate
Simple subjects and verbs are shown in italics.

1. CS: *L.T. Felty;* CP: *is* the official Chili Adviser to the governor of Texas.
2. CS: *Felty;* CP: also *acts* as vice-president of Waxahachie Bank and Trust Company.
3. CS: This remarkable *man;* CP: *discovered* and *pursued* an unusual way to improve the ailing economy of his town.
4. CS: *He;* CP: *helps* movie producers find sets and extras in the area.
5. CS: One downtown *building;* CP: *can be converted* overnight into a jailhouse, a barbershop, or a haberdashery.
6. CS: Three Academy Award-winning *movies;* CP: *were shot* there in just four years.
7. CS: *Horton Foote;* CP: *won* an Academy Award for best screenplay for *Tender Mercies.*
8. CS: *He;* CP: *returned* to Waxahachie to produce three more films.
9. CS: More than twenty *movies* and hundreds of TV *shows;* CP: *have been filmed* in Waxahachie in the past twenty years.
10. CS: *Waxahachie;* CP: today *calls* itself "the Hollywood of Texas."

Writing TIP

Avoid repetition. Combine ideas from two sentences into one by using compound sentence parts.

Writing Theme
Resourcefulness

Robert Duvall starred in the 1982 film, *Tender Mercies.*

Compound Sentence Parts

The subject, the verb, or both can be compound. A compound subject consists of two or more subjects that share the same verb. The subjects are joined by a conjunction.

Firefighters and *paramedics* worked to free the victim.

A **compound verb** has two or more verbs that share the same subject and are joined by a conjunction.

The contractor *erected* the walls and *installed* insulation.

Sentence Diagraming For information on diagraming sentences with compound subjects and verbs, see page 836.

Practice Your Skills
CONCEPT CHECK

Subjects and Predicates Rewrite the following sentences. Label the complete subject and complete predicate. Then underline the simple subject and the verb. Watch for compounds. Notice that some sentences contain verbals (see pages 594–601 for explanation); do not confuse these with verbs.

1. L. T. Felty is the official Chili Adviser to the governor of Texas.
2. Felty also acts as vice-president of Waxahachie Bank and Trust Company.
3. This remarkable man discovered and pursued an unusual way to improve the ailing economy of his town.
4. He helps movie producers find sets and extras in the area.
5. One downtown building can be converted overnight into a jailhouse, a barbershop, or a haberdashery.
6. Three Academy Award-winning movies were shot there in just four years.
7. Horton Foote won an Academy Award for best screenplay for *Tender Mercies.*
8. He returned to Waxahachie to produce three more films.
9. More than twenty movies and hundreds of TV shows have been filmed in Waxahachie in the past twenty years.
10. Waxahachie today calls itself "the Hollywood of Texas."

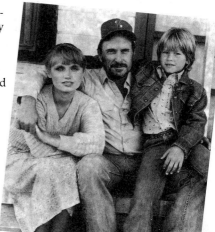

In English sentences, the subject generally precedes the verb. In some types of sentences, however, this order is reversed. This part of the handbook presents different kinds of sentences and points out unusual subject-verb patterns. Sentences can be classified into four types according to the purpose of the speaker or writer.

Declarative Sentences

A **declarative sentence** states a fact, wish, intent, or feeling and ends with a period. Most declarative sentences are in subject-verb order. However, the sentence order may be inverted to signal special emphasis or effect.

Normal Order   One extra <u>second</u> <u>was added</u> to 1987 to adjust for the slowing rotation of the earth.

Inverted Order   Just one mile from the cottage <u>was</u> a sandy <u>beach</u> with a lifeguard on duty.

In sentences beginning with *here* or *there,* the subject-verb order is often inverted, with the verb before the subject. *Here* and *there* are adverbs. *There* can also be an **expletive,** a word that helps to get the sentence started but has no other grammatical function in the sentence.

Here is the street I live on. (*Here* is an adverb.)

There are the books you ordered. (*There* is an adverb.)

There was no gas in the car. (*There* is an expletive.)

Interrogative Sentences

An **Interrogative** sentence asks a question and ends with a question mark. The subject of an interrogative sentence may appear before the verb, after the verb, or between parts of a verb phrase.

Which <u>pianist</u> <u>will perform</u> at the White House?

Why <u>is</u> the economic <u>forecast</u> so uncertain?

<u>Will</u> postage <u>rates</u> <u>go</u> up again this month?

Sentence Diagraming   For information on diagraming interrogative sentences, see page 834.

The Parts of a Sentence   **571**

Subjects in Different Types of Sentences

Objectives

- To identify declarative, interrogative, imperative, and exclamatory sentences
- To recognize the subject and verb in sentences that express inverted order
- **Writing** To use revision skills to correct the end punctuation of sentences

Teaching Strategies

Teaching Tip: Sentence Types

Ask students which sentence type they think is the most common (declarative). Then ask them to think of places or situations in which they would see or hear a great number of interrogative sentences (in tests, for example), imperative sentences (in directions), or exclamatory sentences (at athletic events).

 Individualizing Instruction

LD Students   After discussing the material in the text, you might say or read aloud a number of short, uncomplicated sentences and use them to reinforce understanding of the four sentence types.

ESL Students   Help students compare English with their native languages. Discuss similarities and differences in the way the two languages form and punctuate questions, commands, and exclamations. For example, discuss the advantage of alerting a reader to a question by beginning an interrogative sentence with an inverted question mark, as in Spanish.

Additional Resources
- Grammar and Usage Practice Book, p. 14

572 Grammar Handbook

Linking Grammar and Literature

The following lines from Thomas Gray's poem ''Elegy Written in a Country Church-yard'' exemplify the use of inverted order in declarative sentences:

Now fades the glimmering landscape on the sight,
And all the air a solemn stillness holds.

You may want to have students find other examples in poetry of inverted word order. Discuss the impact of writing sentences in this way.

Teaching Tip: Interrogative Sentences

Remind students that a declarative sentence may be converted into an interrogative sentence by adding a question mark and pronouncing the words with a rising inflection; for example, This train will arrive in Providence at noon?

WRITING THEME   Unusual Creatures

Point out that unusual animals might make an interesting topic for a writing assignment. Encourage students to brainstorm ideas on this subject and record them in their journals.

A. Concept Check

Types of Sentences
   1. Interrogative, Question mark
   2. Exclamatory, Exclamation mark
   3. Declarative, Period
   4. Interrogative, Question mark
   5. Declarative, Period
   6. Declarative, Period

Writing
━━TIP━━

In most writing, use exclamatory sentences sparingly. Overuse dilutes the impact.

Writing Theme
Unusual Creatures

Imperative Sentences

An **imperative sentence** gives a command, request, or direction. It usually ends with a period, but if the command is strong, the sentence may end with an exclamation point. The subject of an imperative sentence is usually not expressed, but it is understood to be the pronoun *you*.

(You) Leave a deposit for the videotape rental.

(You) Be home by eleven!

Don't (you) play in the park.

Sentence Diagraming   For information on diagraming imperative sentences, see page 834.

Exclamatory Sentences

An **exclamatory sentence** expresses strong feeling or excitement. It ends with an exclamation point unless it begins with an interjection such as *oh* or *hey,* in which case it can end with either an exclamation point or a period.

Hey! This boat is leaking!

Oh no! I can't find my keys.

Any declarative, interrogative, or imperative sentence can be considered exclamatory when it expresses strong feeling. Even if it is interrogative, it will end with an exclamation point.

Will you stop making that noise!

Practice Your Skills

A. CONCEPT CHECK

Types of Sentences   Identify each sentence in the following selection as *Declarative, Interrogative, Imperative,* or *Exclamatory,* and name the end punctuation it needs.

(1) Have you ever watched a flying squirrel fly (2) What a wonderful sight it is (3) The little animal doesn't really fly, of course, but it executes amazing glides (4) How can it glide 20, 60, or even 150 feet (5) A fold of loose skin, called a patagium, connects the wrist of each foreleg to the ankle of each hind leg (6) The squirrel glides by extending its legs, using the patagium as an airfoil

(7) Do you think that, as you get to know this delightful animal, you might want to adopt a flying squirrel as your pet (8) Don't do it (9) Though flying squirrels are often interesting and amusing, they can also be messy, and they sometimes bite (10) Enjoy them in their natural habitat

B. PROOFREADING SKILL

Sentences and End Punctuation Rewrite the following passage, correcting any <u>errors</u> that you find. Be sure to pay particular attention to end marks.

In 1825, on the island of St. Vincent in the <u>caribbean</u>, someone discovered what seemed to be a snai<u>l. W</u>ithout a shell. Picture a creature with <u>too</u> antennae like those of a snail, thirty pairs of legs <u>and</u> a length of about three inches After <u>carefull</u> study, scientists decided it wasn't related to the <u>snail_</u> but they couldn't determine what it was related <u>too</u> The mystery remained unsolved for eighty-six years.

What finally produced the answe<u>r A</u> fossil found in <u>canada</u> in 1911 provided the ke<u>y A</u> comparison of the fossil with the snail-like creature proved both to be members of a group of prehistoric sea creatures called peripati that are neither arthropods nor true worms, but organisms that have their own <u>seperate</u> branch on the evolutionary tree. Others of this family can be found in tropical regions toda<u>y</u> think of i<u>t T</u>hese creatures have remained in <u>existance</u>, relatively unchanged, for 450 million <u>years_</u>

Complements

Some sentences use just a subject and a verb to express a complete thought. Other sentences require another word or group of words to complete their meaning. These words are called complements.

A complement is one or more words used to complete the meaning of the verb in a sentence.

Since it completes the meaning of the verb, the complement is considered part of the predicate.

In this part of the handbook, you will study the four kinds of complements: direct objects, indirect objects, objective complements, and subject complements.

7. Interrogative, Question mark
8. Imperative, Period *or* Exclamatory, Exclamation mark
9. Declarative, Period
10. Imperative, Period

B. Proofreading Skill
End Punctuation
Errors are underlined on page.
In 1825, on the island of St. Vincent in the Caribbean, someone discovered what seemed to be a snail without a shell. Picture a creature with two antennae like those of a snail, thirty pairs of legs, and a length of about three inches. After careful study, scientists decided it wasn't related to the snail, but they couldn't determine what it was related to. The mystery remained unsolved for eighty-six years.
What finally produced the answer? A fossil found in Canada in 1911 provided the key. A comparison of the fossil with the snail-like creature proved both to be members of a group of prehistoric sea creatures called peripati that are neither arthropods nor true worms, but organisms that have their own separate branch on the evolutionary tree.
Others of this family can be found in tropical regions today. Think of it! [*or.*] These creatures have remained in existence, relatively unchanged, for 450 million years. [*or!*]

Complements

Objectives

- To identify direct objects, indirect objects, objective complements, and subject complements
- To identify two kinds of subject complements: predicate nominatives and predicate adjectives
- **Writing** To use objects and other complements to add details to written explanations

Teaching Strategies

 Individualizing Instruction

Basic Students A direct object receives the action of a verb, but some action verbs do not need anything to complete them. Display sentence pairs like these and discuss them:
Jeff walked around the block. (has no direct object)
Jeff walked the dog around the block. (has a direct object)

The Parts of a Sentence **573**

Direct Objects

A **direct object** is a word or group of words that receives the action of an action verb in a sentence. The direct object answers the question *whom?* or *what?*

> Tanya debated *Juan* on American foreign policy. (debated *whom?*)
>
> In 1990 the Germans reunited their *country*. (reunited *what?*)

The direct object may be just one word, as in the sentences above. It may also be a phrase or a clause, as shown below.

> Each day, Kim practices *swimming a mile* for next month's triathlon. (phrase)
>
> Rosa knows *how the word-processor operates*. (clause)

Sentence Diagraming   For information on diagraming direct objects, see page 835.

Direct Object or Adverb?   Do not mistake an adverb after an action verb for a direct object. Adverbs serve a different function in the sentence. A direct object following an action verbs tells *whom* or *what*. An adverb tells *where, when, how,* or *to what extent*.

> The salesperson called *customers* all day. (direct object—called *whom?*)
>
> The salesperson called *patiently* all day. (adverb—called *how?*)

Indirect Objects

An **indirect object** is a word or group of words that tells *to whom, to what, for whom,* or *for what* the action of the verb is performed. A verb can have an indirect object only if it also has a direct object. The indirect object comes before the direct object.

> The proctor gave each *student* two sharpened *pencils*. (*Student*, the indirect object, answers the question *to whom? Pencils* is the direct object.)
>
> José built his *beagle* a new *dog house*. (*Beagle*, the indirect object, answers the question *for what? Dog house* is the direct object.)
>
> The tour guide told *us* wonderful *stories*. (*Us*, the indirect object, answers the question *to whom? Stories* is the direct object.)

Cooperative Learning

Verbs that take indirect objects often express the semantic idea of "giving" or "sharing." Examples of such verbs include *give, send, bring, grant, show, offer,* and *promise*. Have pairs of students generate sentences with these verbs followed by both indirect and direct objects. Then have students share their work with the class.

Do not mistake a noun or pronoun preceded by *to* or *for* for an indirect object. Such a noun or pronoun is the object in a prepositional phrase. The word *to* or *for* does not appear before a noun or pronoun used as an indirect object.

> The subway conductor gave the *visitors* directions. (*Visitors* is an indirect object.)

> The subway conductor gave directions to the *visitors*. (*Visitors* is the object of the preposition *to*.)

Sentence Diagraming For information on diagraming indirect objects, see page 835.

Practice Your Skills

A. CONCEPT CHECK

Direct and Indirect Objects Make three columns on your paper. Label them *Verb, Indirect Object,* and *Direct Object.* For each sentence, write the verb and any objects in the appropriate columns. Watch for compound objects.

1. A *pascal* measures the pressure or force of an area.
2. A religious philosopher as well as a scientist, Blaise Pascal gave the scientific world this term and many other important contributions.
3. Pascal's father controlled what the boy learned.
4. The elder Pascal taught his son only certain subjects.
5. Curiously, his father would not teach Pascal mathematics or science.
6. However, Pascal gave his father quite a surprise.
7. At age twelve he taught himself nearly all the principles of Euclid's geometry.
8. At age sixteen he wrote *The Geometry of Conics*.
9. Some years later he developed the theory of probability and also a calculating machine.
10. With this calculating machine, Pascal may have provided future generations the prototype of the modern computer.

B. APPLICATION IN WRITING

Explaining a Process Blaise Pascal was known for his ability to explain complex concepts very clearly and simply. Choose a process you understand well. Write a short explanation of the process that a young child could understand. Use a variety of precise direct and indirect objects to help make your explanation clear.

Writing Theme
Blaise Pascal

Additional Resources
- Grammar and Usage Practice Book, p. 15

WRITING THEME   Blaise Pascal

Students may want to research the life of Blaise Pascal to write a historical narrative as a Writer's Workshop assignment.

A. Concept Check
Direct and Indirect Objects

Verb	Indirect Object	Direct Object
1. measures		pressure, force
2. gave	world	term, contributions
3. controlled		what the boy learned
4. taught	son	subjects
5. would teach	Pascal	mathematics, science
6. gave	father	surprise
7. taught	himself	principles
8. wrote		*The Geometry of Conics*
9. developed		theory, calculating machine
10. may have provided	generations	prototype

B. Application in Writing
Explaining a Process
Answers will vary.

Writing TIP

Hold your readers' attention by varying sentence types, subject placement, and types of complements.

Objective Complements

Another type of complement that can occur in a sentence with a direct object is the **objective complement.** An objective complement is always a noun or an adjective; it follows the direct object and identifies or describes it. Any of these verbs (or synonyms for any of them) may take an objective complement: *appoint, call, choose, consider, elect, find, make, keep, name, think.*

> This extreme cold makes some **people** *fearful.* (The objective complement, *fearful,* describes the direct object, *people.*)

> Ruth considers the **Alvin Ailey Dance Company** *a unique troupe.* (The objective complement, *a unique troupe,* describes the direct object, *Company.*)

Subject Complements

A **subject complement** comes after a linking verb and identifies or describes the subject. (For information on *be* and other linking verbs, see page 553.) The subject complement can be a *predicate nominative* or a *predicate adjective.*

Predicate Nominatives   A **predicate nominative** is a word or group of words that comes after a linking verb and renames or identifies the subject of a sentence. Predicate nominatives are either *predicate nouns* or *predicate pronouns.*

> The lead guitarist is also the group's *singer.* (predicate noun)

> The newest member of the team is *she.* (predicate pronoun)

Predicate Adjectives   A **predicate adjective** is an adjective that follows a linking verb and modifies the subject of a sentence.

> Darlene seems *happy* with her new after-school job.

Sentence Diagraming   For information on diagraming subject complements, see page 836.

Usage Note   Gerunds sometimes act as predicate nominatives, and participles sometimes act as predicate adjectives. Do not confuse such gerunds and participles with progressive (*-ing*) verb forms.

> The most exciting part of our vacation last summer was *rafting through the Grand Canyon.* (gerund phrase as predicate nominative)

> The senator's speech was hardly *inspiring.* (participle as predicate adjective)

Practice Your Skills

A. CONCEPT CHECK

Object and Subject Complements Identify each italicized word as *Direct Object, Objective Complement, Predicate Nominative,* or *Predicate Adjective.*

1. The horse is *unique* in its connection to the history of the Americas.
2. First appearing in North America about 55 million years ago, the earliest ancestor of the modern horse stood only about fifteen inches high, and it had *toes,* not hooves.
3. Scientists have labeled this earliest horse *Eohippus.*
4. The descendants of Eohippus grew *larger* and crossed into Asia and the Middle East.
5. Meanwhile, horses became *extinct* in the Americas.
6. No one knows who first made horses *beasts* of burden.
7. However, by early historic times, the horse had become an important *element* in warfare in the Middle East and throughout Asia.
8. When the Greeks first saw warriors from the east on horseback, they called these people *centaurs,* thinking that they were half-human and half-horse.
9. To Arabs and Spaniards of the Middle Ages and Renaissance, the horse was especially *important.*
10. The Arabs and the Spaniards were outstanding *riders* who displayed remarkable horsemanship.
11. During their exploration of North America, the Spaniards brought *horses* back to the continent of their origin.
12. Horses that were lost or released in New Spain, as the area of Spanish exploration was called, eventually became *wild.*
13. Today we call the descendants of these wild horses *mustangs.*
14. For the settlers of the American West, the horse was both a draft animal and an indispensable *means* of transportation.
15. Historians agree that the horse played a central *role* in Native American culture.

577

B. Drafting Skill

Sentence Imitation

1. Predicate Nominative
2. Direct Object
3. Objective Complement
4. Direct Object
5. Objective Complement
6. Direct Object
7. Direct Object
8. Objective Complement
9. Direct Object
10. Direct Object
11. Direct Object
12. Direct Object
13. Predicate Adjective
14. Direct Object
15. Predicate Nominative

Sentences will vary. See typical answers below.

1. Among those qualified to run for the office, John F. Kennedy was the youngest *President* of the United States.

2–5. They baptized *him John Fitzgerald Kennedy,* but many called *him Jack.*

6. He sought *office* at a time when the country honored youth.

7–10. World powers found *him* a *leader* determined to weather times of conflict with other countries; in the 1960's he achieved an *agreement* with the Soviet Union and a *settlement* of the Cuban missile crisis.

11. History records *how he waited,* like a chess player, for the Soviets to withdraw their missile threat.

12. History also records *what was achieved* when the crisis was over.

13. The stakes were *high* and involved a strong possibility of armed conflict.

14. Kennedy's face showed *signs* of stress and tension.

15. His problems, his decisions, and his actions in this crisis were *ones* upon which the fate of the world hung.

CHECK ✔ POINT
PAGES 569–578

WRITING THEME   Lobsters

Objects of Verbs, Object Complements, and Subject Complements

Little Blue Horse, A Children's Picture, 1912, Franz Marc

578 Grammar Handbook

B. DRAFTING SKILL

Sentence Imitation Identify each italicized word or phrase as *Direct Object, Objective Complement, Predicate Adjective,* or *Predicate Nominative.* Then write a sentence of your own that has the same structure as the one containing the italicized word(s).

Among those competent to judge, Don Vito Cantú was the best (1) *horseman* ever seen in New Spain. . . .

They christened (2) *him* (3) *Evaristo Rodrigo Cantú,* but they called (4) *him* (5) *Vito.* He rode (6) *horses* from the time his infant hands could hold reins. Destiny made (7) *him* a (8) *man* of consequence to savage spaces of a new world across an Ocean Sea: in the year 1552 he brought from Spain to the City of Mexico two Barbary (9) *stallions* and five (10) *mares* of exceptional worth. . . . I remember (11) *how he rode,* like a god of horsemanship. I remember (12) *how he looked when he dismounted.* . . . His hair was (13) *gray* and so were his spiked mustachios. His face bore (14) *marks* of hard years and hard weathers. . . . His quilted buff-leather doublet, his leathern and baize trunk hose, his tall jackboots were (15) *those* of a soldier familiar with rough employment and open sky.

Tom Lea, *The Hands of Cantú*

Humanities Connection

Art Note   Franz Marc (1880–1916) painted *Little Blue Horse, a Children's Picture* (1912) for a two-year-old. The German post-Impressionist painted many horses, often in blue. His dreamlike, slightly abstracted images of animals shocked the critics when they were first exhibited. Ask: What qualities do you associate with a horse?

Make two columns on your paper. For each sentence write the complete subject in one column and the complete predicate in the other. Underline each complement and identify it by writing *Direct Object (D.O.), Indirect Object (I.O.), Objective Complement (O.C.),* or *Subject Complement (S.C.).*

1. The waters off the coast of New England are cold and murky year-round.
2. Divers find this area attractive because of its marine life.
3. Cape Ann is a favorite diving spot in New England.
4. Two outstanding dive spots—Folly's Cove and Back Bay—give Cape Ann a solid reputation among divers.
5. One denizen of these waters is especially popular with divers.
6. Scientists call this creature *Homarus americanus.*
7. Divers simply call it tasty.
8. This creature is the famous East Coast lobster.
9. The succulent flesh of the lobster's tail and claws makes it a prized catch.
10. The laws of the New England states regulate lobstering by divers.
11. Limits on lobstering give the lobsters a chance to maintain their populations.
12. Many divers allow themselves lobster-watching holidays in the waters off Cape Ann.
13. Viewing underwater life affords them great pleasure.
14. Divers today are more ecology-minded than in the past.
15. Many consider the lobster a great but endangered resource.

Writing Theme
Lobsters

A VOIDING SENTENCE

FRAGMENTS

By definition, there are two requirements for a sentence: it must express a complete thought and have both a subject and a verb. A sentence fragment fails to satisfy one or both requirements.

A sentence fragment is only part of a sentence.

In some fragments, either the subject or the verb is missing.

Fragment   Seems difficult to complete. (What seems difficult? The subject is missing.)

Sentence   This new tax *form* seems difficult to complete.

The Parts of a Sentence   **579**

Complete Subject	Complete Predicate
1. The waters off the coast of New England	S.C. S.C. are <u>cold</u> and <u>murky</u> year-round
2. Divers	D.O. find this <u>area</u>
	O.C. <u>attractive</u> because of its remarkable marine life
3. Cape Ann	is a favorite diving S.C. <u>spot</u> in New England
4. Two outstanding dive spots—Folly's Cove and Back Bay—	I.O. give <u>Cape Ann</u> a solid D.O. <u>reputation</u> among divers
5. One denizen of these waters	S.C. is especially <u>popular</u> with divers
6. Scientists	D.O. call this <u>creature</u> O.C. <u>Homarus americanus</u>
7. Divers	D.O. simply call <u>it</u> O.C. <u>tasty</u>
8. This creature	is the famous East S.C. Coast <u>lobster</u>
9. The succulent flesh of the lobster's tail and claws	D.O. makes <u>it</u> a prized O.C. <u>catch</u>
10. The laws of the New England states	regulate D.O. <u>lobstering</u> by divers
11. Limits on lobstering	give the I.O. D.O. <u>lobsters</u> a <u>chance</u> to maintain their populations
12. Many divers	I.O. allow <u>themselves</u> lobster-watching D.O. <u>holidays</u> in the waters off Cape Ann
13. Viewing underwater life	I.O. affords <u>them</u> great D.O. <u>pleasure</u>
14. Divers	today are more S.C. <u>ecology-minded</u> than in the past
15. Many	consider the D.O. <u>lobster</u> a great but O.C. endangered <u>resource</u>

Avoiding Sentence Fragments

Objectives

- To identify sentence fragments
- **Writing** To correct sentence fragments by rephrasing incomplete thoughts or by correcting period faults

Teaching Strategies

Stumbling Block

Students are sometimes urged to write as they speak. This can be useful advice if the goal is a natural, conversational writing style. Students should be aware, however, that the casual style of most spoken English, which often contains fragments, can create confusion when read instead of spoken. In the following example, the fragment could be part of either the sentence it follows or the sentence it precedes: We stayed home all day. Because we were tired. We sent out for pizza instead of cooking supper. Lead students to see that the fragment could modify the verb in either sentence and that the meaning may be clear in speech but confusing in writing. Explain that in speech, pauses help to clarify meaning. Correct punctuation can serve the same function in writing as pauses do in speaking.

 Individualizing Instruction

LD Students These students tend to lack "sentence sense." Provide extra practice by asking them to listen as you read some sentences and sentence parts aloud, using your voice to provide clues about whether each one is complete or incomplete.

ESL Students In some languages, including Spanish and Vietnamese, it is grammatically correct for the subject to drop out. Explain to students that in English the subject cannot be inferred from the inflected verb and must be stated.

Linking Grammar and Writing

Remind students that sentence fragments are perfectly acceptable for such writing occasions as freewriting, note taking, and list making. In formal writing, however, sentence fragments are to be avoided since they are confusing for readers.

Writing TIP

Writers of advertisements often deliberately use fragments for effect.

Emperor Ming-Huang's Journey to Shu, later copy of an 8th-century original

Fragment	In the *Arabian Nights,* the queen Scheherazade. (What did the queen do? The verb is missing.)
Sentence	In the *Arabian Nights,* the queen Scheherazade *saved* her life with 1,001 suspenseful tales.

In other fragments, both subject and verb are missing.

Fragment	Popular among bikers and joggers.
Sentence	Tiny tape *players* with earphones *are* popular among bikers and joggers.

Sentence fragments result from incomplete thoughts or incorrect punctuation.

Fragments Resulting from Incomplete Thoughts

When you think faster than you can put your thoughts on paper, you may end up writing fragments and confusing your readers. For example, you may intend to express these complete thoughts:

> Calligraphy, the art of beautiful handwriting, began in China more than two thousand years ago. Today, many Americans study calligraphy and use it to make personalized invitations and greeting cards.

As your thoughts move quickly and your hand struggles to keep up, however, you may write something like the following:

> Calligraphy, the art of beautiful handwriting, began in China more than two thousand years ago, using calligraphy to make personalized invitations and greeting cards.

Humanities Connection

Art Note *Emperor Ming-Huang's Journey to Shu,* by an anonymous Chinese painter, probably of the 10th century, is executed in the traditional ink brush and color wash on a silk scroll. The three arts most highly regarded in China are poetry, calligraphy, and painting. In fact, the greatest Chinese painters have also been fine calligraphers.

The example passage on the previous page contains a confusing fragment. Readers may think you meant that the main use of calligraphy in China is for invitations and greeting cards—which was not your meaning at all.

Practice Your Skills

DRAFTING SKILL

Correcting Sentence Fragments Combine each incomplete thought in Column A with an incomplete thought in Column B to make a complete sentence.

Column A

1. The Nazca people of ancient Peru
2. Little is known
3. However, they left an astonishing memorial of their existence
4. The giant plateau in an extremely dry area of southern Peru
5. One of the most impressive of these designs shows a spider,
6. The shapes of giant lizards, cats, birds,
7. Perplexed by these ancient markings,
8. Only from a point in the air high above the earth
9. Since the Nazca left no written explanations of their design,
10. Perhaps sometime during the twenty-first century

Column B

a. scientists are investigating how they might have been carved by a primitive people who had no way of viewing the designs they were making.
b. it is highly likely that these astonishing designs will remain shrouded in mystery for a long time.
c. inhabited the Nazca desert more than a thousand years ago.
d. the mystery may eventually be solved.
e. on a high, forty-mile-long plateau.
f. and other creatures can also be found on the high Nazca Plateau.
g. about these mysterious people.
h. can these designs be seen clearly!
i. contains enormous designs the Nazca or some other ancient people carved into the surface of the earth.
j. its eight legs stretching along the plateau for an extraordinary 150 feet.

Drafting Skill
Correcting Sentence Fragments

1. The Nazca people of ancient Peru (c) inhabited the Nazca desert more than a thousand years ago.
2. Little is known (g) about these mysterious people.
3. However, they left an astonishing memorial of their existence (e) on a high, forty-mile-long plateau.
4. The giant plateau in an extremely dry area of southern Peru (i) contains enormous designs the Nazca or some other ancient people carved into the surface of the earth.
5. One of the most impressive of these designs shows a spider, (j) its eight legs stretching along the plateau for an extraordinary 150 feet.
6. The shapes of giant lizards, cats, birds, (f) and other creatures can also be found on the high Nazca Plateau.
7. Perplexed by these ancient markings, (a) scientists are investigating how they might have been carved by a primitive people who had no way of viewing the designs they were making.
8. Only from a point in the air high above the earth (h) can these designs be seen clearly!
9. Since the Nazca left no written explanations of their design, (b) it is highly likely that these astonishing designs will remain shrouded in mystery for a long time.
10. Perhaps sometime during the twenty-first century, (d) the mystery may eventually be solved.

WRITING THEME Llamas

A. Concept Check

Eliminating Sentence Fragments

Answers will vary. See typical answers below.

1. The largest mountain range in the world is the Andes. It stretches north to south along the entire western edge of the continent of South America.

2. This astonishing mountain range is being raised by the collision of geological plates along the western coasts of the South and North American continents.

3. Inhabiting the Andes are three relatives of the camel that are especially adapted to living at high elevations.

4. Sentences

5. The guanaco is a wild beast, but the alpaca and the llama, which may be descendents of the guanaco, have long been domesticated by the inhabitants of the Andes.

6. Sentences

7. Some say a llama looks like a small camel. Unlike a camel, however, it has no humps.

8. The llama serves as a beast of burden, carrying great loads to enormous heights.

9. It is also prized for its meat and milk, which are consumed mainly by local peoples.

10. In addition, the people harvest the llama's fine wool, which is dried, spun, and woven into wonderful designs for hats, scarves, and sweaters.

Fragments Resulting from Incorrect Punctuation

A complete sentence begins with a capital letter and ends with a period, a question mark, or an exclamation point. Many sentence fragments are caused by the period fault, which occurs when a writer inserts an end punctuation mark before he or she finishes writing a complete thought.

Fragment   *On this notebook-size computer.* Jan does all her accounting

Sentence   On this notebook-size computer, Jan does all her accounting.

Practice Your Skills

A. CONCEPT CHECK

Eliminating Sentence Fragments   Write *Sentences* after the number of each item that contains only complete sentences. Rewrite the other items, eliminating the fragment(s) by adding necessary words or correcting a period fault.

1. The largest mountain range in the world is the Andes. North to south along the entire western edge of the continent of South America.
2. This astonishing mountain range is being raised by the collision of geological plates. Along the western coasts of the South and North American continents.
3. Inhabiting the Andes are three relatives of the camel. That are especially adapted to living at high elevations.
4. These interesting creatures are the guanaco, the alpaca, and the llama. Two of these animals have proved most useful to Andean peoples.
5. The guanaco is a wild beast, but the alpaca and the llama, which may be descendents of the guanaco, have long been domesticated. By the inhabitants of the Andes.
6. A llama is four feet tall at the shoulders. It resembles a large, long-necked sheep.
7. Some say a llama looks like a small camel. Unlike a camel, however, no humps.
8. Serves as a beast of burden. Carrying great loads to enormous heights.
9. Also prized for its meat and milk. Which are consumed mainly by local peoples.
10. In addition, the people harvest the llama's fine wool. Which is dried, spun, and woven into wonderful designs for hats, scarves, and sweaters.

B. PROOFREADING SKILL

Sentence Fragments Rewrite the following passage, correcting all errors. Correct all sentence fragments, adding words and changing punctuation as necessary.

Helen Bodington operates an unusual school in San Francisco. An obedience school for llamas. She started her business nearly fourty years ago by training dogs. She taught her first llama to carry backpacks on hiking trips. And to jump into the bed of her pickup truck. Some other things she teaches llamas are how to pull a cart, jump, walk with their owners. And respond to simple commands.

For five thousand years the Incas bred llamas as beasts of burden. Llamas are work animals. Not really suitable as pets. Ms. Bodington says her own llama is a dignified companion, a "nice person." Llama ownership is an expensive proposition. With llamas selling for $1,000 to $7,000 depending on there gender and age. A person needs at least an acre of land to give a llama proper excercise. According to Ms. Bodington, llamas can live for twenty-five years. On one bale of hay a Month.

AVOIDING RUN-ON SENTENCES

Sometimes a writer fails to use an end mark to signal the end of a sentence. The result is a run-on sentence.

A run-on sentence is made up of two or more sentences written as though they were one sentence.

Run-on Cross-country skiing is more than just an invigorating winter activity it provides excellent conditioning for all major muscles.

Correct Cross-country skiing is more than just an invigorating winter activity. It provides excellent conditioning for all major muscles.

The Comma Fault or Comma Splice

A writer sometimes mistakenly separates two sentences with a comma instead of a correct end mark. This error is called a **comma fault** or **comma splice.** It results in the most common type of run-on sentence.

B. Proofreading Skill
Sentence Fragments
Answers will vary. See suggested answers below. Errors are underlined on page.

Helen Bodington operates an unusual school in San Francisco. It is an obedience school for llamas. She started her business nearly forty years ago by training dogs. She taught her first llama to carry backpacks on hiking trips and to jump into the bed of her pickup truck. Some other things she teaches llamas are how to pull a cart, jump, walk with their owners, and respond to simple commands.

For five thousand years the Incas bred llamas as beasts of burden. Llamas are work animals. They are not really suitable as pets. Ms. Bodington says her own llama is a dignified companion, a "nice person." Llama ownership is an expensive proposition, with llamas selling for $1,000 to $7,000, depending on their gender and age. A person needs at least an acre of land to give a llama proper exercise. According to Ms. Bodington, llamas can live for twenty-five years on one bale of hay a month.

Avoiding Run-on Sentences

Objectives

- To identify run-on sentences and comma faults
- To use a variety of strategies to correct run-on sentences

Linking Grammar and Literature

Share with students the fact that many twentieth-century authors, notably James Joyce, Virginia Woolf, and William Faulkner, deliberately used run-on sentences in their writing to convey the illusion of timelessness. This technique is called stream of consciousness. Tell students that Exercise B provides an example of this technique.

If any students have read *The Sound and Fury,* they should be especially helpful in discussing the effect that Faulkner was trying to create. Students should be able to see that this passage presents thoughts, sensory experiences, and actions as the narrator experiences them, in an unbroken flow, not neatly divided as they would be in separate sentences.

 Individualizing Instruction

Basic Students In Exercise A, students will need to decide which commas lead to run-on sentences. Remind these students that one useful strategy is to check to see which words in each item convey a single, complete thought.

LD Students These students are likely to have problems in knowing when to end one sentence and begin another. They will benefit from additional practice at correcting run-ons, especially using examples taken from their own writing and that of other students.

LEP Students You might want to omit Exercise B with these students, substituting some additional examples for practice in correcting fragments and run-ons.

Additional Resources
• Grammar and Usage Practice Book, pp. 18–19

Writing TIP

Vary the ways you join clauses. Too many *ands* sound childish; too many semicolons seem stiffly formal.

Comma Fault	Why is the main street in town blocked off today, is there going to be a parade?
Correct	Why is the main street in town blocked off today? Is there going to be a parade?
Comma Fault	Homeless people must find shelter in public buildings on nights like this one, no one should be exposed to this bitter cold.
Correct	Homeless people must find shelter in public buildings on nights like this one. No one should be exposed to this bitter cold.

Correcting Run-on Sentences The run-on sentences above were correctly rewritten as two separate sentences. In other cases, it is more appropriate to create one compound sentence. Several ways to correct run-on sentences by creating compounds are explained below. Notice that each correct example is a compound sentence with two independent clauses.

1. You can combine related ideas in one sentence by using a comma and a coordinating conjunction.

Run-on	Snowshoes seemed awkward at first, we grew used to them.
Correct	Snowshoes seemed awkward at first, but we grew used to them.

2. You can combine related ideas in one sentence by using just a semicolon.

Run-on	During the late 1800's, huge herds of cattle grazed on the open range they were tended and guarded by hired cowhands.
Correct	During the late 1800's, huge herds of cattle grazed on the open range; they were tended and guarded by hired cowhands.

3. You can combine related ideas by using a semicolon, a conjunctive adverb, and a comma.

Run-on	Long exposure to below-zero temperatures often makes car batteries go dead, my car started in this morning's record cold without any problem.
Correct	Long exposure to below-zero temperatures often makes car batteries go dead; nevertheless, my car started in this morning's record cold without any problem.

Practice Your Skills

A. CONCEPT CHECK

Run-on Sentences   Correct each run-on sentence below, using one of the following methods: (1) a capital letter and a period, (2) a semicolon alone, (3) a comma and a conjunction, or (4) a semicolon and one of these conjunctive adverbs followed by a comma: *however, nevertheless,* or *moreover.*

1. William Faulkner was born in Mississippi in 1897, that state was destined to be his home for most of his life.
2. He lived in the town of Oxford, Mississippi, where his house still stands, every year it is visited by crowds of tourists.
3. Some consider Faulkner the greatest novelist that America has produced he is one of the few Americans to win the Nobel Prize in literature.
4. Faulkner never finished college, as a young man he worked odd jobs and trained as a military pilot.
5. While working as a journalist in New Orleans, Faulkner met Sherwood Anderson the older novelist encouraged the young Faulkner to write novels.
6. In 1926 Faulkner wrote his first novel, *Soldier's Pay,* he followed this with a second novel, *Sartoris.*
7. *Sartoris* began a series of novels, all of them dealt with Faulkner's major theme— the decline of the Old South.
8. One fascinating aspect of Faulkner's novels is that he made up his own mythical Mississippi city, Jefferson, he created a mythical county, Yoknapatawpha.
9. Each novel is complete in itself, readers enjoy the fact that the same people, families, and places turn up in novel after novel.
10. Some readers find Faulkner's prose occasionally difficult to follow they invariably discover that his work is richly rewarding.

The Parts of a Sentence   **585**

WRITING THEME   William Faulkner

You may want to suggest that students consider reading and reviewing one of Faulkner's novels as a writing assignment.

A. Concept Check

Run-on Sentences

Answers will vary. See suggested answers below.

1. William Faulkner was born in Mississippi in 1897. That state was destined to be his home for most of his life.
2. He lived in the town of Oxford, Mississippi, where his house still stands. Every year it is visited by crowds of tourists.
3. Some consider Faulkner the greatest novelist that America has produced; he is one of the few Americans to win the Nobel Prize in Literature.
4. Faulkner never finished college, but as a young man he worked odd jobs and trained as a military pilot.
5. While working as a journalist in New Orleans, Faulkner met Sherwood Anderson. The older novelist encouraged the young Faulkner to write novels.
6. In 1926 Faulkner wrote his first novel, *Soldier's Pay;* he followed this with a second novel, *Sartoris.*
7. *Sartoris* began a series of novels. All of them dealt with Faulkner's major theme—the decline of the Old South.
8. One fascinating aspect of Faulkner's novels is that he made up his own mythical Mississippi city, Jefferson; moreover, he created a mythical county, Yoknapatawpha.
9. Each novel is complete in itself; however, readers enjoy the fact that the same people, families, and places turn up in novel after novel.
10. Some readers find Faulkner's prose occasionally difficult to follow; nevertheless, they invariably discover that his work is richly rewarding.

B. APPLICATION IN LITERATURE

Run-on Sentences   Sometimes a writer will break the customary rules of usage to create particular effects. Read the following passage from one of William Faulkner's great novels. Notice that Faulkner wrote the passage as one long run-on sentence, omitting all punctuation, even apostrophes. Rewrite the passage, adding or deleting words and inserting punctuation and capitalization as necessary to make complete sentences. Compare your version with the original. Discuss with your classmates why Faulkner might have written the passage as he did. What effect is created by his use of the run-on?

> I didnt look back the tree frogs didnt pay me any mind the grey light like moss in the trees drizzling but still it wouldnt rain after a while I turned went back to the edge of the woods as soon as I got there I began to smell honeysuckle again I could see the lights on the courthouse clock and the glare of town the square on the sky and the dark willows along the branch and the light in mothers windows the light still on in Benjys room and I stooped through the fence and went across the pasture running.
>
> **William Faulkner, *The Sound and the Fury***

CHECK POINT
PAGES 579–586

Correct the following fragments and run-on sentences, adding, changing, or dropping words, punctuation, and capital letters wherever necessary.

1. On the plain of Judea, near the Dead Sea, there is a huge, mesalike rock. Known as Masada.
2. There, about 160 B.C., a Jewish leader built a fort, this was later expanded into a great citadel.
3. In A.D. 66 the people of Judea rose against the Romans. Who were ruling their land.
4. At the time of the revolt, Masada was occupied by a garrison of Roman soldiers, however, Jewish patriots drove this first group of soldiers out.
5. The Romans crushed the rebellion elsewhere in Judea, to their great dismay, though, Masada held out against them.
6. In A.D. 72, therefore, an entire Roman legion marched against Masada. Included three to six thousand experienced soldiers.

Writing Theme
Masada

7. Massed against a small force of Jewish men, women, and children. Fewer than a thousand in all.
8. Despite their meager numbers, the people of Masada held out against the Romans, their strong beliefs and leadership sustained them.
9. Unable to take the citadel by sheer force of numbers, the Romans devised a plan they decided to build a ramp and to erect on it a stone siege tower, catapults, and a battering ram.
10. One can only imagine the feelings of the defenders of Masada. As they watched this fateful construction progressing.
11. Eventually it became clear that the Romans would succeed in their efforts, the people of Masada chose to take their own lives rather than be captured and killed by their enemies.
12. Of the original 967 Masadans, only seven survived. Two women and five children.
13. When they finally breached the walls of Masada in A.D. 73. The Romans were amazed at what they found, they marveled at the courage of their slain enemies.
14. Gazing upon their bodies, the Romans could only "wonder at their immovable contempt of death." As a contemporary Jewish historian put it.
15. Over the centuries some people claimed that the story of Masada was simply a legend. Only one contemporary written account of it.
16. However, in 1838 an American expert identified an enormous rock near the Dead Sea. As the legendary Masada.
17. Then, between 1963 and 1965, the area was excavated by a team led by an Israeli archaeologist. Modern techniques used in the task.
18. These modern excavations proved the Jewish historian correct the siege of Masada had actually taken place.
19. Many important finds have been made at Masada, these include ancient scrolls and fragments of scrolls.
20. However, the most important find was the place itself. A site that has become symbolic of human determination in the face of overwhelming odds.

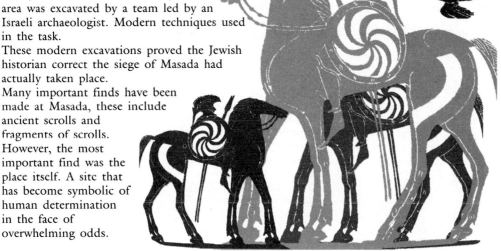

The Parts of a Sentence   **587**

8. Despite their meager numbers, the people of Masada—sustained by their strong beliefs and leadership—held out against the Romans.
9. Unable to take the citadel by sheer force of numbers, the Romans devised a plan; they decided to build a ramp and to erect on it a stone siege tower, catapults, and a battering ram.
10. One can only imagine the feelings of the defenders of Masada as they watched this fateful construction progressing.
11. Eventually it became clear that the Romans would succeed in their efforts; therefore, the people of Masada chose to take their own lives rather than be captured and killed by their enemies.
12. Of the original 967 Masadans, only seven survived. The survivors were two women and five children.
13. When they finally breached the walls of Masada in A.D. 73, the Romans were amazed at what they found, and they marveled at the courage of their slain enemies.
14. Gazing upon their bodies, the Romans could only "wonder at their immovable contempt of death," as a contemporary Jewish historian put it.
15. Over the centuries some people claimed that the story of Masada was simply a legend because there was only one contemporary written account of it.
16. However, in 1838 an American expert identified an enormous rock near the Dead Sea as the legendary Masada.
17. Then, between 1963 and 1965, the area was excavated by a team led by an Israeli archaeologist. Modern techniques were used in the task.
18. These modern excavations proved the Jewish historian correct; the siege of Masada had actually taken place.
19. Many important finds have been made at Masada; these include ancient scrolls and fragments of scrolls.
20. However, the most important find was the place itself, a site that has become symbolic of human determination in the face of overwhelming odds.

Application and Review

These activities have been designed to allow students to apply concepts presented in this handbook. Exercise A requires students to identify sentences types and to add end punctuation. Exercise B requires students to identify complements in sentences. Exercise C requires students to correct sentence fragments and run-on sentences.

Additional Resources
- Tests and Assessment, Mastery Tests, pp. 43–46
- Elaboration, Revision, and Proofreading, p. 22

WRITING THEME   Whales and Whaling

A. Sentence Types
1. Interrogative; Question mark
2. Imperative; Period
3. Declarative; Period
4. Declarative; Period
5. Interrogative; Question mark or Exclamatory; Exclamation Mark
6. Declarative; Period
7. Imperative; Period or Exclamatory; Exclamation point
8. Declarative; Period
9. Exclamatory; Exclamation point
10. Interrogative; Question mark

B. Identifying Complements
1. Predicate Nominative
2. Predicate Adjective
3. Objective Complement
4. Objective Complement
5. Predicate Adjective
6. Direct Object
7. Indirect Object
8. Predicate Nominative
9. Indirect Object
10. Predicate Adjective

Writing Theme
Whales and Whaling

A. Sentence Types Identify each sentence as *Declarative, Interrogative, Imperative,* or *Exclamatory.* Then name the appropriate end punctuation for each sentence.

1. Who has not heard of the great white whale, Moby Dick
2. Go to Nantucket, the island off Massachusetts
3. There, it's not hard to imagine the whaler *Pequod* and her crew preparing to set sail
4. In his epic novel *Moby Dick,* author Herman Melville captures the spirit of the whalers
5. How many a whaler has, like Melville's young seaman Ishmael, felt a "damp, drizzly November" in the soul
6. However, the novice Ishmael was certainly in for a few surprises as he set out to sea
7. Think about waking up to find that your roommate is a tattooed Polynesian prince named Queequeg
8. There is the matter of what Queequeg carries in his sack
9. How Ishmael's eyes bulge when Queequeg pulls out a shrunken head
10. How would you like to find that your captain is ready to risk the whole crew to satisfy his own obsession

B. Identifying Complements Identify each italicized complement as *Direct Object, Indirect Object, Objective Complement, Predicate Nominative,* or *Predicate Adjective.*

1. The blue whale is the largest *animal* that has ever lived.
2. To many people, such size is *intimidating.*
3. Adventure tales, such as the story of Moby Dick, have made whales *villains* in the eyes of many.
4. For example, because of its name, most people mistakenly consider the killer whale *ferocious;* the killer whale is, in fact, a large dolphin.
5. Actually whales, and even killer whales, are quite *harmless* to humans.
6. Moreover, whales of all kinds exhibit rather sophisticated social *behavior.*
7. Consider that humpback whales occasionally give *each other* affectionate hugs.
8. Although whales generally travel in herds, their basic social unit is the *family.*
9. Whales, like other mammals, bear their young live and feed *them* milk.
10. Furthermore, as you might expect, a mother whale is highly *protective* of her young.

588 Grammar Handbook

C. Sentence Fragments and Run-ons Rewrite any fragments and run-ons to make complete sentences. Write *Sentence* for any numbered item that is correct.

1. Because many of the larger whales face extinction.
2. Since the 1970's the United States, Canada, and some European countries. Have protested the continuation of whaling.
3. In the past few years, only a few countries have continued widespread whaling operations, one of the most active of these is the Soviet Union.
4. The Soviets have maintained a large whaling fleet. Since the end of World War II.
5. Therefore, it came as a surprise a few years ago. When the Soviets rescued some beluga whales in the frigid Bering Sea, off Alaska.
6. The weather had grown sharply colder, the belugas had become trapped in an ever-shrinking area of open water in the middle of an ice field. While they were feeding on a school of fish.
7. The whales thrashed about in the water, unable to escape, they faced inevitable doom as the ice closed in.
8. News media publicized the giant creatures' plight around the world; people from many nations expressed concern and sympathy for the imperiled whales.
9. For days the situation made the headlines, it concerned environmentalists and casual observers alike.
10. Fortunately for the whales, the Soviets sent an icebreaker to the area. To clear a channel to open water.
11. The Soviet ship broke through the ice and then, to the sound of classical music from its loudspeakers, led the whales to freedom in the open sea.
12. Proved to be a very difficult and expensive undertaking.
13. Altogether, the Soviets spent well over $80,000 to free the belugas. A fact that surprised many observers since the Soviets have been among the world's leading killers of whales.
14. Praise came from around the world, this was for the captain and crew of the Soviet icebreaker.
15. This was one whaling adventure with a happy ending.

Answers will vary. See suggested answers below.

1. Because many of the larger whales face extinction, whaling is being viewed in a new light.
2. Since the 1970's the United States, Canada, and some European countries have protested the continuation of whaling.
3. In the past few years, only a few countries have continued widespread whaling operations. One of the most active of these is the Soviet Union.
4. The Soviets have maintained a large whaling fleet since the end of World War II.
5. Therefore, a few years ago it came as a surprise when the Soviets rescued some beluga whales in the frigid Bering Sea, off Alaska.
6. The weather had grown sharply colder; consequently, the belugas had become trapped in an ever-shrinking area of open water in the middle of an ice field while they were feeding on a school of fish.
7. The whales thrashed about in the water, unable to escape. They faced inevitable doom as the ice closed in.
8. Sentence
9. For days the situation made headlines. It concerned environmentalists and casual observers alike.
10. Fortunately for the whales, the Soviets sent an icebreaker to the area to clear a channel to open water.
11. Sentence
12. It proved to be a very difficult and expensive undertaking.
13. Altogether, the Soviets spent well over $80,000 to free the belugas, a fact that surprised many observers since the Soviets have been among the world's leading killers of whales.
14. Praise came from around the world for the captain and crew of the Soviet icebreaker.
15. Sentence

On the Lightside

HEADLINE BLOOPERS

New Vaccine May Contain Rabies
Daily Press (Newport News, Va.) 5/1/78

Complaints about NBA referees growing ugly
Chicago Sun-Times 5/23/79

Squad helps dog bite victim
Grant County (Wisc.) *Herald Independent* 4/29/76

Dr. Tacket Gives Talk On Moon
Indiana Evening Gazzette 3/13/76

Bill Would Permit Ads on Eyeglasses
Tulsa World 11/30/76

Shouting Match Ends Teacher's Hearing
Newsday 7/13/77

Child teaching expert to speak
Birmingham Post-Herald 3/28/77

Farmer Bill Dies In House
The Atlanta Constitution 4/13/78

Jumping bean prices affect poor
Eugene (Ore.) *Register-Guardian* 2/27/74

Bond issue is readied for city incinerator
The Berkshire Eagle (Pittsfield, Mass.) 10/21/78

27 dental hygiene students to receive caps at MCC
Woodbridge (N.J.) *News Tribune* 2/5/74

Solar system expected to be back in operation
Libertyville (Ill.) *Herald* 3/15/78

PLO invited to raid debates
Dallas Morning News 12/5/77

Branch Avenue Bridge To Be Fixed Before Fall
Providence Evening Bulletin 8/8/74

Air head fired
Chicago Sun Times 9/18/90

Phrases and Clauses

PREPOSITIONAL PHRASES

A phrase is a group of related words that does not have a subject and predicate. It functions in a sentence as a single part of speech. A **prepositional phrase** is one of several kinds of phrases.

A prepositional phrase consists of a preposition, its object, and any modifiers of the object in the phrase.

Charlie Chaplin has long been a favorite *of filmgoers.*

The object of a preposition may be a noun, a pronoun, or a word or group of words used as a noun.

Margaret Mitchell's masterpiece is about the American Civil War *era.* (The noun *era* is the object of *about.*)

A preposition may take a compound object. A conjunction joins the parts of the compound object.

Aside from her famous *novel* and a *collection* of her letters, Mitchell published nothing else.

In some sentences, a prepositional phrase modifies the object in a phrase that precedes it.

Concerned citizens are protesting the excess *of violence in some TV programs.*

Prepositional phrases can function as adjectives or adverbs.

Adjective Phrases

An **adjective phrase** is a prepositional phrase that functions as an adjective, modifying a noun or a pronoun. Usually an adjective phrase immediately follows the noun or pronoun it modifies.

Modifying a Noun	Details *about Shakespeare's private life* are obscure. (Which details?)
Modifying a Pronoun	Few *of his works* shed much light on the author. (Few what?)

Adverb Phrases

An **adverb phrase** tells *where, when, how, why,* or *to what extent.* Like an adverb, it can modify a verb, an adjective, or another adverb. Study the following examples.

Charlie Chaplin in the silent film, *The Kid,* 1921

Grammar Handbook 33:
Phrases and Clauses

Prepositional Phrases

Objective

- To identify prepositional phrases and their function as adjectives or adverbs

Teaching Strategies

Linking Grammar and Writing

Occasionally, writers use two prepositions to govern a single object: for example, The joy inside and outside Germany was great when the Berlin Wall was demolished, or Cooperation both with and by the public is essential. Encourage students to offer similar examples.

◆ Individualizing Instruction

Basic Students Remind students that an adjective phrase usually answers the question *Which one?* or *What kind?* Suggest that they use these questions to distinguish between adjective phrases and adverb phrases.

LEP Students

Make sure these students do not confuse *to* as the sign of the infinitive with *to* as a preposition. The infinitive *to* is always followed by a verb; the preposition *to* is always followed by a noun or a pronoun. You might write these example sentences on the chalkboard and help students to distinguish between the two: A medical team rushed to aid the survivors. (infinitive) A police officer drove a doctor to the scene. (preposition)

Additional Resources

- Tests and Assessment, Pretests, pp. 16–19
- Grammar and Usage Practice Book, p. 21

WRITING THEME   The American South

Concept Check

Adjective and Adverb Phrases

1. to Fayetteville, Adverb; at the end, Adverb; of the year, Adjective; for her, Adverb
2. at Greenville, Adverb; to home, Adverb; through the Arkansas delta, Adverb
3. In Little Rock, Adverb; at a Waffle House, Adverb; for an omelet, Adverb; over the eggs, Adverb; like a bad child, Adverb; with her fingers, Adverb; of some outlandish feeling, Adverb; of freedom, Adjective
4. from her fingers, Adverb; of her journey, Adjective
5. At Alma, Adverb; in the United States, Adverb
6. into the mountains, Adverb; to her, Adverb
7. about the lay, Adjective; of the land, Adjective; to her, Adverb

Modifying a Verb	The incriminating letter was found *inside a book*. (Found where?)
Modifying an Adjective	The *Apollo* moon flights were successful *beyond anyone's dreams*. (Successful to what extent?)
Modifying an Adverb	The smoke alarm sounded late *in the morning*. (Late when?)

Sentence Diagraming   For information on diagraming prepositional phrases, see page 837.

Practice Your Skills

CONCEPT CHECK

Adjective and Adverb Phrases   Write each prepositional phrase in the numbered sentences in the following literary excerpt. Then write the word *Adjective* or *Adverb* to identify how the phrase functions. Notice how the use of phrases adds detail to the passage.

(1) When Katie went back to Fayetteville at the end of the year Amanda was lonely for her. Within a month she had gotten in the habit of going up there to visit.

The first time she drove to Arkansas she left before dawn, planning on making the long drive in one day. (2) She crossed the Mississippi River at Greenville so close to home she could smell it, then drove on up through the Arkansas delta . . . .

(3) In Little Rock she stopped at a Waffle House for an omelet, pouring maple syrup all over the eggs like a bad child, eating the last bites with her fingers, full of some outlandish feeling of freedom. (4) She licked the syrup from her fingers and began the last leg of her journey.

(5) At Alma the real hills began, the Boston Mountains, the oldest mountains in the United States. (6) As Amanda drove up into the mountains they reached out to her and took her heart away . . . . (7) Something about the lay of the land seemed exactly right to her . . . .

Ellen Gilchrist, *The Annunciation*

Leonardo da Vinci's *Angel of the Annunciation* (detail) appears on the front cover of the novel *The Annunciation* by Ellen Gilchrist.

Humanities Connection

Art Note   Leonardo da Vinci (1452–1519) was still an apprentice to a master painter when he produced the *Angel of the Annunciation*. Most critics agree that this Italian Renaissance painter, sculptor, architect, engineer, and inventor was a genius. The detail from the painting here shows the angel Gabriel as he appears to the Virgin Mary to tell her of the coming birth of Jesus Christ. Western artists—writers, painters, musicians—have often been inspired by Biblical stories. Some have retold these stories, whereas others have explored their symbolic or allegorical significance. Ask: Why is it important to know what "the annunciation" refers to in Ellen Gilchrist's novel and Leonardo da Vinci's painting?

APPOSITIVES AND APPOSITIVE PHRASES

An **appositive** is a noun or pronoun that usually comes directly after another word in a sentence to identify or provide further information about that word.

> The English poet *Elizabeth Barrett* secretly married Robert Browning. Her father, *a tyrant,* was very angry and vigorously opposed the marriage.

An **appositive phrase** is made up of an appositive and all of its modifiers. The modifiers may be single words, phrases, or clauses.

> The California Institute of Technology, *a famous university that is located in Pasadena,* attracts students from all over the world. (The adjective *famous* and the clause *that is located in Pasadena* are both modifiers of the appositive *university.*)

Appositives occasionally precede the noun or the pronoun to which they refer.

> *A strong skier,* Meera won a medal in the slalom.

An appositive or appositive phrase may be either essential or nonessential. An **essential appositive** must be included in a sentence to make the meaning clear.

> The singer *Bruce Springsteen* was born in New Jersey and continued to live there as an adult. (The appositive is necessary to identify the singer.)

A **nonessential appositive** is one that is not needed to make the meaning of a sentence clear. In the following example, the italicized appositive is nonessential. If it were omitted, the basic meaning of the sentence would be the same.

> January, *the coldest month in many northern regions,* is named for the Roman god Janus.

Punctuation Note   Use one or two commas to set off a nonessential appositive from the rest of the sentence. Do not use commas with an essential appositive.

Sentence Diagraming   For information on diagraming appositives and appositive phrases, see page 839.

Writing
━TIP━

Appositives provide a means of achieving emphasis and streamlining your writing.

Appositives and Appositive Phrases

Objectives

- To identify appositives and appositive phrases
- To distinguish between essential and nonessential appositives

Teaching Strategies

 Individualizing Instruction

Basic Students   You might explain that the word *appositive* comes from the same Latin root as *position* and means "to put near." Emphasize that an appositive usually follows a noun or a pronoun. The two words in apposition have roughly the same meaning, and both words have the same relation to the other elements in the sentence.

Teaching Tip: Appositional Or

Appositives or appositive phrases are often introduced by *or*. Such words, defining the preceding term, should be set off with commas. Help students distinguish between appositional *or* and alternative *or* by discussing these sentences:

An aquarelle, or painting done in transparent watercolors, won first prize. (appositional)

He usually paints in oils or acrylics. (alternative)

> **Additional Resources**
> - Grammar and Usage Practice Book, p. 22

Individualizing Instruction

LD Students   Model how to do the first three items in the exercise. Then have students complete the exercise independently.

LEP Students   Before assigning the exercise, preview any unfamiliar vocabulary.

WRITING THEME   Benjamin Banneker

Some students may want to research the life of Benjamin Banneker as a topic for a future research report.

Concept Check
Appositives and Appositive Phrases
   1. Benjamin Banneker, an inventor, surveyor, mathematician, and astronomer, was a prominent person in early U.S. history.
   2. His grandmother, an Englishwoman and a former indentured servant, taught him to read and write.
   3. In 1753, with only two models, an old pocket watch and a picture of a clock, he constructed a clock that kept nearly perfect time for more than fifty years.
   4. An amateur astronomer, Banneker accurately predicted a solar eclipse on April 14, 1789.
   5. In 1791, he assisted Major A. Elliott, the surveyor appointed by George Washington to design the city of Washington, D.C.
   6. None
   7. Other material, antislavery essays and medical advice, was also included.
   8. Other people, often prominent Americans, contributed articles for Banneker's publication.
   9. The almanac, evidence of the accomplishments of African Americans, was especially important in an age of discrimination.
   10. A supporter of the rights of African Americans, Banneker also advocated free public education and elimination of the death penalty.

Verbals and Verbal Phrases

Objectives

- To identify the three kinds of verbals: infinitives, participles, and gerunds
- To determine the function of verbals in sentences
- **Writing.** To use infinitives to streamline sentences and eliminate wordiness

Writing Theme
Benjamin Banneker

Practice Your Skills
CONCEPT CHECK

Appositives and Appositive Phrases   Rewrite each of the following sentences that contains an appositive or appositive phrase. Underline the appositive construction, inserting *commas* where needed. If a sentence has no appositive, write *None*.

1. Benjamin Banneker an inventor, surveyor, mathematician, and astronomer was a prominent person in early U.S. history.
2. His grandmother an Englishwoman and a former indentured servant taught him to read and write.
3. In 1753, with only two models an old pocket watch and a picture of a clock he constructed a clock that kept perfect time for more than fifty years.
4. An amateur astronomer Banneker accurately predicted a solar eclipse on April 14, 1789.
5. In 1791, he assisted Major A. Elliott the surveyor appointed by George Washington to design the city of Washington, D.C.
6. Later, he made all the astronomical calculations and weather predictions for an almanac he published.
7. Other material antislavery essays and medical advice was also included.
8. Other people often prominent Americans contributed articles for Banneker's publication.
9. The almanac evidence of the accomplishments of African Americans was especially important in an age of discrimination.
10. A supporter of the rights of African Americans Banneker also advocated free public education and elimination of the death penalty.

VERBALS AND VERBAL PHRASES

A **verbal** is a verb form that is used as a noun, an adjective, or an adverb. A group of words made up of a verbal, its modifiers, and its complements is called a **verbal phrase.**

In this section, you will review the three kinds of verbals and verbal phrases: **infinitive, participle,** and **gerund.**

Infinitives and Infinitive Phrases

An **infinitive** is a verbal that is made up of *to* (called the sign of the infinitive) and the base form of a verb. An infinitive may be used as a noun, an adjective, or an adverb.

Noun	*To write* demands discipline, time, and great effort. (subject)
	The only ambition Lian has in life is *to write*. (predicate nominative)
Adjective	I don't understand Alan's obsession *to succeed*. (modifies the noun *obsession*)
Adverb	The basketball team was playing *to win*. (modifies the verb *was playing*)

Auxiliary verbs are added to the present infinitive to form three other kinds of infinitives.

We are expecting *to be invited.* (passive present)

To have invited them was a mistake. (active perfect)

Frank was surprised *to have been invited.* (passive perfect)

Sometimes an infinitive is used without the word *to.*

Sylvia did not dare question the judge's statement. (Sylvia did not dare *to* question. . . .)

An infinitive phrase is a group of words made up of an infinitive, its modifiers, and its complements.

Subject of an Infinitive	The committee wanted Rosita to run for office. (*Rosita* is the subject of *to run.*)
Object of an Infinitive	A delegation went to greet the senator at the airport. (*Senator* is the object of *to greet.*)
Complement of an Infinitive	No one expected the winner to be Robert. (*Robert* is the predicate nominative identifying *winner.*)

Because it is a verb form, the infinitive in an infinitive phrase may take one or more complements.

I will try *to save her a seat near the stage.* (*Her* is the indirect object of *to save,* and *seat* is the direct object.)

Usage Note The objective form of the pronoun is used as *the subject, the object,* or *the predicate pronoun* of an infinitive.

The coach signaled *us* to play. (*Us* is the subject of the infinitive *to play.*)
We wanted to beat *them.* (*Them* is the object of the infinitive *to beat.*)

As a verb form, the infinitive in an infinitive phrase can have adverbs and adverb phrases as modifiers.

> *To walk briskly* is one of the best forms of exercise. (The adverb *briskly* modifies the infinitive *to walk*.)

> Flight 309 to Paris will be ready *to board in approximately fifteen minutes*. (The adverb phrase *in approximately fifteen minutes* modifies the infinitive *to board*.)

An infinitive phrase can function as a noun, an adjective, or an adverb.

Noun   On Inauguration Day, the President swears *to execute the laws of the United States faithfully*. (object)

Adjective   An optometrist or an ophthalmologist is the specialist *to see about eye problems*.

Adverb   The students hurried *to board the bus*.

In most cases, a skilled writer avoids placing words between *to* and the verb form in an infinitive. Such placement creates a **split infinitive,** a form that is usually awkward.

Awkward   Good comedians get their audience *to frequently laugh*.

Better   Good comedians get their audience *to laugh frequently*.

Usage Note Experts disagree about split infinitives. Some say a split infinitive is always incorrect. Others feel that a split infinitive sounds better, as in "The corporation expects *to very nearly double* its earnings." Discuss these opinions with your teacher.

Sentence Diagraming For information on diagraming infinitives and infinitive phrases, see page 839.

Practice Your Skills

A. CONCEPT CHECK

Infinitive Phrases Write the infinitives or infinitive phrases in the quotations below and identify the functions of each as *Adjective, Adverb,* or *Noun.* Label the use of each noun infinitive as *Subject, Object,* or *Predicate Nominative.*

1. There is a great difference between an eager man who wants to read a book and a tired man who wants a book to read.

   G. K. Chesterton

2. Almost anyone can be an author; the business is to collect money and fame from this state of being. **A. A. Milne**

3. Writers, if they are worthy of that jealous designation, do not write for other writers. They write to give reality to an experience.

   Archibald MacLeish

4. You must not suppose, because I am a man of letters, that I never tried to earn an honest living. **George Bernard Shaw**

5. To write books is difficult. To read books is more difficult still, because of the tendency to go to sleep.

   Felix Dahn, paraphrased by Sir Stanley Unwin

6. The greatest part of a writer's time is spent in reading, in order to write. A man will turn over half a library to make one book.

   Samuel Johnson

7. Nothing you write, if you hope to be any good, will ever come out as you first hoped. **Lillian Hellman**

8. Biography is to give man some kind of shape after his death.

   Virginia Woolf

9. What I like . . . is to treat words as a craftsman does his wood or stone or what-have-you. **Dylan Thomas**

10. When anyone sits down to write, he should imagine a crowd of readers looking over his shoulder. **Robert Graves**

B. REVISION SKILL

Sentence Combining Combine each of the following sentences by adding to one sentence an infinitive phrase taken from the other sentence. Eliminate unnecessary words. Some rewording of the base sentences may be needed.

1. William Faulkner traveled to Sweden in 1949. He went to accept the Nobel Prize for literature.

2. In his acceptance speech, Faulkner spoke about the duty of a writer. According to Faulkner, this duty is to celebrate the nobility of the human spirit.

Writing Theme
Writers on Writing

3. Faulkner said that writers serve an important purpose, to remind other people of "the courage and honor and hope and pride and compassion and pity and sacrifice" of which people are capable.

4. He said that "the poet's voice" can help mankind "to endure and prevail."

5. By reminding people of qualities like courage, honor, and pride, writers give their fellow human beings the strength to overcome the fears and anxieties of modern life.

C. Application in Writing

A Maxim

Answers will vary. Answers should include one infinitive phrase in each maxim.

Linking Grammar and Writing

Since participial phrases function as adjectives, they answer these questions: What kind? Which one or ones? How many? How much? Have students review a selection from their writing portfolios, using these questions to add participial phrases as descriptive details. Point out that a comma always follows a participial phrase that begins a sentence.

3. Faulkner said that writers serve an important purpose. He said this purpose is to remind other people of "the courage and honor and hope and pride and compassion and pity and sacrifice" of which people are capable.

4. He said that "the poet's voice" can help mankind. It can help mankind "to endure and prevail."

5. By reminding people of qualities like courage, honor, and pride, writers give their fellow human beings strength. This strength is needed to overcome the fears and anxieties of modern life.

C. APPLICATION IN WRITING

A Maxim   Maxims are wise sayings that express truths that most people believe, for example: There is a time *to speak* and a time *to keep silence*; *To err* is human, *to forgive* divine. Like many others, these maxims include infinitives. Write five maxims, each with an infinitive phrase. As your teacher directs, combine your ideas with those of other students to create a class booklet entitled *Maxims for Moderns*.

Participles and Participial Phrases

A participle used as an adjective is another type of verbal.

A participle has various forms: *encouraging* (present), *encouraged* (past), *having encouraged* (perfect), and *having been encouraged* (passive perfect).

Since participles act as adjectives, they can modify either nouns or pronouns.

Modifying a Noun	The magazine editor sent an *encouraging* letter to the young writer.
	Encouraged, the writer continued writing short stories.
Modifying a Pronoun	*Having been encouraged,* she developed more confidence in her ability to write.

Do not confuse a participle with the verb of a sentence. A present participle or a past participle can be used with an auxiliary verb to form a verb phrase. (See pages 552–554.) The participle in a verb phrase acts as a verb. A participle used as a verbal acts as an adjective. Study the following examples.

Verb	The young writer *had completed* another story before receiving the editor's letter.
Verbal	She submitted the *completed* short story to the magazine for publication.

A participle with its modifiers and complements is called a participial phrase. A participial phrase acts as an adjective.

> *Waiting anxiously for the editor's reaction,* the writer tried to begin another story.

Participles are verb forms and may be modified by both adverbs and adverb phrases. In the example sentence above, the adverb *anxiously* and the adverb phrase *for the editor's reaction* modify the participle *waiting*.

Like verbs, participles may have complements.

> The editor, *having received the writer's manuscript,* read it immediately. (In the participial phrase, *manuscript* is the direct object of the participle *having received.*)

Absolute Phrases An **absolute phrase** is made up of a participle and the noun or pronoun it modifies. Although an absolute phrase has no direct grammatical connection with a particular word in the rest of the sentence, it does modify the independent clause by indicating time, reason, or circumstance.

Time	*Our discussion finished,* we all shook hands.
Reason	*Her wallet having been stolen,* Nadine could not pay the dinner check.
Circumstance	The child dutifully answered the questions, *his eyes filling with tears.*

Sentence Diagraming For information on diagraming participles and participial phrases, see page 838.

Practice Your Skills

A. CONCEPT CHECK

Participles, Participial Phrases, and Absolute Phrases Write the participles and participial phrases in the following sentences. If the participle or participial phrase modifies a particular word, write the word that it modifies. If the participial phrase is an absolute phrase, write *Absolute.*

1. Hanged as a spy, Nathan Hale was nonetheless a famous patriot.
2. Hale was a member of a small, respected group of patriots known to history as the Rangers.
3. Their fighting skills and daring exploits were legendary.
4. The captain of the Rangers, having asked for a volunteer, chose Hale to spy on the British.

Writing
TIP

Participial phrases may be essential or nonessential. Set off nonessential phrases with commas.

Writing Theme
Espionage

Teaching Tip: Absolute Phrases

Alert students that absolute phrases are sometimes called nominative absolutes.

WRITING THEME Espionage

A. Concept Check
Participles, Participial Phrases, and Absolute Phrases
1. Hanged as a spy, Nathan Hale
2. respected, group; known to history as the Rangers, group
3. fighting, skills; daring, exploits
4. having asked for a volunteer, captain

5. Hale being untrained, Absolute
6. Pretending to be a Dutch schoolmaster, he
7. dedicated to the British cause, cousin
8. Stopped by a British officer, Hale
9. arresting, officer
10. his face betraying his fear, Absolute
11. condemned to hang, Hale
12. Facing death bravely, Hale
13. dangling from a rope, body
14. revered, heroes
15. believed to be the site of his capture, place

B. Drafting Skill

Sentence Combining

Answers will vary. See typical answers below.

(1) Elizabeth Van Lew, known to history as a spy for the Union forces, lived in Richmond, Virginia, during the Civil War.

(2) She helped runaway slaves and escaped Northern prisoners.

(3) She sent letters telling officials in Washington what was happening in Richmond. While her neighbors knitted for the men in gray, Van Lew sent intelligence reports to help the men in blue.

(4) Gathering information all the while, Van Lew tended prisoners at Libby Prison in Richmond.

(5) She sent coded messages to General Grant.

Runaway slaves, such as those helped by Elizabeth Van Lew, went north to join one of the 166 black Union regiments.

5. Hale being untrained, the espionage attempt was sure to fail.
6. Pretending to be a Dutch schoolmaster, he crossed British lines.
7. A cousin dedicated to the British cause may have betrayed him.
8. Stopped by a British officer, Hale did not know what to do.
9. The arresting officer questioned him.
10. Hale answered the questions, his face betraying his fear.
11. Hale, condemned to hang, was refused a trial.
12. Facing death bravely, Hale reportedly said, "I only regret that I have but one life to lose for my country."
13. His body, dangling from a rope, served as a grim message to other patriots.
14. Several monuments honor Hale as one of America's most revered heroes.
15. A boulder in Halesite, New York, marks the place believed to be the site of his capture.

B. DRAFTING SKILL

Sentence Combining   Rewrite the following paragraph, adding information or combining sentences according to the directions given in parentheses.

(1) Elizabeth Van Lew lived in Richmond, Virginia, during the Civil War. She is known to history as a spy for the Union forces. (Combine the sentences using a participial phrase.) (2) She helped runaway slaves and Northern prisoners who escaped. (Use *escaped* as a participial modifier.) (3) She sent letters to Washington. The letters told officials in Washington what was happening in Richmond. (Combine the sentences using a participial phrase.) While her neighbors knitted for the men in gray, Van Lew sent intelligence reports to help the men in blue. (4) Van Lew tended prisoners at Libby Prison in Richmond. She gathered information all the while. (Combine the sentences using a participial phrase.) (5) She sent messages to General Grant. The messages were coded. (Use *coded* as a participle.)

Gerunds and Gerund Phrases

A gerund is the *-ing* form of a verb used as a noun.

Gerunds can perform many of the functions of nouns.

Subject	Fast *driving* is dangerous on any road.
Direct Object	Most people really enjoy *sailing.*
Object of a Preposition	Before *leaving,* the senator called her office.
Predicate Nominative	Ted's most irksome habit is *interrupting.*
Appositive	A fairly new hobby, *spelunking,* is increasing in popularity.

A gerund, its modifiers, and its complements make up a gerund phrase.

Since the gerund in a gerund phrase is a verb form, it is often modified by an adverb or an adverb phrase.

> *Eating sensibly in the morning* is a wise practice. (The gerund *eating* is modified by the adverb *sensibly* and the adverb phrase *in the morning.*)

Practice Your Skills

CONCEPT CHECK

Gerunds and Gerund Phrases Write the gerunds and gerund phrases in the following sentences. Tell whether each is a *Subject, Direct Object, Predicate Nominative, Object of a Preposition,* or *Appositive.* If there is no gerund or gerund phrase, write *None.*

1. In ancient China, watching the heavens was the responsibility of court astrologers.
2. Another responsibility of court astrologers was informing the Emperor, in advance, about exceptional heavenly events.
3. One day, legend has it, a dragon began eating the sun.
4. The people drove the dragon away by beating drums and gongs.
5. The people's actions, making noise and frightening the dragon, saved the sun from certain destruction.
6. However, the Emperor was not at all pleased.
7. He had his two astrologers, Hsi and Ho, beheaded for failing to warn him about the sun-eating dragon.
8. At that time, foretelling any future event was based on magic.
9. Today predicting an eclipse is not difficult at all.
10. Astronomers wait for the periodic alignment of the earth, the sun, and the moon.

Writing Theme
Eclipses

Phrases and Clauses **601**

Stumbling Block

Some students may have difficulty distinguishing the uses of the *-ing* form of the verb: as part of a verb phrase, as a participial modifier, and as a gerund. You might present an oral exercise in which you use the *-ing* form in sentences in these three ways. Ask students to identify for each sentence the way the *-ing* form is used and to explain their choice.

 Individualizing Instruction

LD Students Give students this easily remembered example of gerunds: *Seeing is believing.* Then pair each with a partner who can help identify the gerund and gerund phrases in the exercise.

> ### Additional Resources
> • Grammar and Usage Practice Book, p. 25

WRITING THEME Eclipses

Concept Check
Gerunds and Gerund Phrases
  1. watching the heavens, Subject
  2. informing the Emperor, in advance, about exceptional heavenly events, Predicate Nominative
  3. eating the sun, Direct Object
  4. beating drums and gongs, Object of a Preposition
  5. making noise and frightening the dragon, Appositive
  6. None
  7. failing to warn him about the sun-eating dragon, Object of a Preposition
  8. foretelling any future event, Subject
  9. predicting an eclipse, Subject
 10. None

Teaching Strategies

Linking Grammar and Writing

Remind students that dangling modifiers usually occur at the beginning of long, complex sentences. In many cases, the writer, concentrating on the introductory phrase, momentarily forgets to identify the subject of the sentence. If you have heard or seen any dangling modifiers lately, share them with the class.

Additional Resources
- Grammar and Usage Practice Book, p. 26

Writing
—TIP—

Dangling phrases occur most often when the verb is in the passive voice. Using the active voice may make dangling modifiers less likely.

USING PHRASES CORRECTLY

It is usually best to place every modifier as close as possible to the word it modifies. Also, it should be obvious which word in a sentence is being modified.

Misplaced Modifiers

A **misplaced modifier** is one that is placed so far away from the word it modifies that the intended meaning of the sentence is unclear and perhaps even humorous. The examples below show how misplaced modifiers can distort the meaning of a sentence.

Misplaced	The helpful librarian pointed out the book to the boy *on the shelf.* (The prepositional phrase *on the shelf* seems to modify *boy.*)
Clearer	The helpful librarian pointed out the book *on the shelf* to the boy.
Misplaced	Tourists see many historic sites *walking the Freedom Trail in Boston.* (The participial phrase *walking the Freedom Trail in Boston* seems to modify *sites.*)
Clearer	Tourists *walking the Freedom Trail in Boston* see many historic sites.

Dangling Modifiers

Like misplaced modifiers, dangling modifiers can distort meaning or cause unintended humor. A **dangling modifier** does not clearly modify any noun or pronoun in a sentence. Dangling modifiers often appear at the beginnings of sentences. To correct a dangling modifier, make sure the sentence names the thing modified.

Dangling	*To land human beings on the moon,* huge amounts of time and money were expended. (Who or what expended huge amounts of time and money?)
Clearer	*To land human beings on the moon,* the *United States* expended huge amounts of time and money.
Dangling	*Studying the American Revolution,* Paul Revere was captured before he could complete his historic ride. (Who was studying the American Revolution?)
Clearer	*Studying the American Revolution,* the *students* learned that Paul Revere was captured before he could complete his historic ride.

Practice Your Skills

A. CONCEPT CHECK

Misplaced and Dangling Modifiers Rewrite each sentence that contains a misplaced or dangling modifier, correcting the error. If a sentence has no error, write *Correct.*

1. Known for ruthless efficiency, spy novels about the Cold War often feature the KGB.
2. The KGB was created in 1954 in the Soviet Union, as the "Committee for State Security."
3. Acting as the Communist Party's watchdog the KGB's responsibilities include both domestic and international security.
4. In fact, composed of seventeen directorates, the KGB is the largest secret police and intelligence organization in the world.
5. Discredited for its part in a political purge, the KGB undertook a campaign in the eyes of Soviet citizens to revamp its image.
6. Acclaimed as heroes of Soviet espionage, the Soviet government in the 1950's proudly admitted to using spies.
7. In fact, some agents were secretly sent to the United States to gain information from the Soviet Union.
8. Using the alias of Emil Goldfus, in 1957 the United States captured and convicted a KGB agent.
9. To transmit military secrets, shortwave radio equipment had been installed in his Brooklyn apartment.
10. The spy, whose real name was Rudolf Abel, had worked in New York City for nine years as an artist and a photographer.

B. PROOFREADING SKILL

Using Phrases Correctly Rewrite the following sentences, eliminating <u>misplaced and dangling participles</u> and correcting <u>errors</u> in capitalization, punctuation, and spelling.

The Central Intelligence Agency (CIA) <u>an</u> organization that was founded in <u>1947 does</u> intelligence work for the United States. Wishing to learn the secrets of <u>freinds</u> as well as enemies, <u>more than a million agents</u> are employed worldwide. <u>To carry out</u> its secret missions, many electronic devices are used. For example, tiny microphones called *bugs* are planted by <u>agents in walls and telephones.</u> CIA Agents obtain useful intelligence from overheard conversations <u>listening on receivers located far away from the bugs.</u> Among other devices used by agents are hidden cameras, secret codes, and disguises. The life of a CIA agent is <u>fasinating</u> but the possibility of discovery or even death is always present.

You may wish to use the following Checkpoint exercises as an informal evaluation of student mastery of the kinds of phrases and modifiers covered in this handbook.

WRITING THEME   Settling the West

Settling the West is a broad topic. Have students explain what the topic means to them and how they might treat the subject as a writing assignment.

A.

1. Gerund Phrase; from their lands
2. Appositive Phrase; of the Oglala Sioux
3. Participial Phrase; along the Oregon Trail
4. Appositive Phrase; of the Powder River Indian country
5. Gerund Phrase
6. Participial Phrase; to Red Cloud, by the Great Spirit
7. Participial Phrase; from the nearby hills
8. Infinitive Phrase
9. Infinitive Phrase; with the United States
10. Infinitive Phrase; as restitution, for the illegal seizure, of Sioux land, in 1877

Writing Theme
Settling the West

A. Tell whether the italicized phrase in each of the following sentences is an *Appositive Phrase,* an *Infinitive Phrase,* a *Participial Phrase,* or a *Gerund Phrase.* Also list any prepositional phrases used as modifiers in the italicized phrases.

1. *Pushing Native Americans from their lands* was a dark aspect of westward expansion.
2. Red Cloud, *war chief, medicine man, and popular leader of the Oglala Sioux,* believed that his land should not be taken from him.
3. His land had become a highway for homesteaders *traveling along the Oregon Trail.*
4. The Oregon Trail and the nearby Bozeman Trail, *both parts of the Powder River Indian country,* were located in the territory of the mighty Sioux.
5. *Protecting these sacred lands and hunting grounds* became the consuming purpose of the Sioux.
6. These hunting grounds, *given to Red Cloud by the Great Spirit,* were crucial to the Sioux culture.
7. *Swarming down from the nearby hills,* Red Cloud and the Sioux fiercely defended their land.
8. After many years of fighting, Red Cloud signed a treaty *to make the Powder River country Sioux land forever.*
9. He was the first—and only—Native American *to win a war with the United States.*
10. In 1980, the Supreme Court ordered the federal government *to pay the Sioux 122.5 million dollars as restitution for the illegal seizure of Sioux land in 1877.*

Caroline Kills in Water (below), resident at the Sioux Indian Reservation, Rosebud, South Dakota (right)

604 Grammar Handbook

B. Write each verbal phrase in the following sentences and label it *Infinitive Phrase, Participial Phrase,* or *Gerund Phrase.* Identify its function by writing *Noun* or *Modifier.*

1. Not all Native Americans believed in resisting with violence.
2. The Navajos, for example, chose not to fight the American settlers.
3. Peacefully raising sheep in the American Southwest, the Navajos did not believe in war.
4. When American soldiers rounded up the Navajo people, most of their leaders did not seriously consider fighting the troops.
5. Destroying crops and canyon homes, however, the soldiers terrorized the Navajos.
6. The soldiers thus made it impossible for the Navajos to return to their homes.
7. A tragic chapter in history continued when the Navajos, forced by the soldiers, endured a 300-mile march to Fort Sumner.
8. Exhausted from the long journey and uprooted from their homeland, many Navajos did not survive.
9. To make the Long Walk required more strength than some of the young and old people had.
10. Others found adjusting to new lands and a new culture impossible.

C. Rewrite each sentence to eliminate the misplaced or dangling modifier.

1. Rushing westward in the mid-1800's, Indian lands were crossed on the route to California.
2. To seek instant fortune, many hardships were endured and untold dangers were faced.
3. Eastern farmers joined the thousands of "forty-niners" seeking gold along the Oregon Trail.
4. In wagons called "prairie schooners," historians estimate that more than 80,000 people headed west to California.
5. Squalid living conditions and lawlessness prevailed as fortunes in gold were mined in the hastily built towns.

CLAUSES

A clause is a group of words that contains a subject and a verb.

A clause always has a subject and a verb; a phrase never does. Remembering this will help you differentiate between phrases and clauses.

In this section, you will study and use two kinds of clauses: **independent clauses** and **subordinate clauses.**

Clauses

Objectives

- To identify clauses
- To distinguish independent from subordinate clauses

Teaching Strategies

Linking Grammar and Writing

Since the theme of the exercise below is writers who overcame adversity, you might want to have students research one of their favorite writers and then write a biographical summary of the author's life. Students should check their use of independent and subordinate clauses.

 ### Individualizing Instruction

LD Students You may wish to write on the chalkboard the italicized items in the first four sentences and help students find the prepositions and their objects in the prepositional phrases and the subjects and verbs in the clauses.

LEP Students Consider asking advanced students to volunteer to act as resource persons for LEP students, answering any vocabulary or cultural questions that may arise as they work through the exercise.

Additional Resources
• Grammar and Usage Practice Book, p. 27

WRITING THEME   Overcoming Adversity

Discuss with students what overcoming adversity means to them. Encourage them to record their thoughts on this subject as a possible topic for a writing assignment.

Concept Check
Types of Clauses
1. P
2. P

Writing
—TIP—

To avoid faulty subordination, place important ideas in independent clauses and lesser ideas in subordinate clauses.

Writing Theme
Overcoming Adversity

Independent Clauses

An independent clause can stand alone as a sentence.

There are two independent clauses in the following sentence. The subject of each clause is underlined once; the verb is underlined twice.

A young West German <u>pilot</u> <u>landed</u> his plane in Moscow's Red Square, and the <u>police</u> <u>arrested</u> him immediately.

Each clause in the sentence above can stand alone as a sentence because each clause has a subject and a predicate and expresses a complete thought. The conjunction *and* is used to join the two clauses. Notice that independent clauses can be written as sentences.

A young West German <u>pilot</u> <u>landed</u> his plane in Moscow's Red Square.
The <u>police</u> <u>arrested</u> him immediately.

Subordinate Clauses

A subordinate clause cannot stand alone as a sentence.

The following subordinate clause has a subject and a verb. However, since it does not express a complete thought, it cannot stand alone as a sentence.

After Nansen and his partner had survived the Arctic winter in a hand-built stone hut . . . (What happened then?)

To use the subordinate clause in a sentence, add an independent clause to complete the thought.

After Nansen and his partner had survived the Arctic winter in a hand-built stone hut, *they were rescued by a party of British explorers.*

Practice Your Skills

CONCEPT CHECK

Types of Clauses Identify each italicized word group in the following sentences. Write *P* for each phrase, *I* for each independent clause, and *S* for each subordinate clause.

1. Many writers of great literature have had *to overcome physical or psychological adversity.*
2. The poet John Keats wrote some of his best-known works while suffering from tuberculosis, *a common disease of his era.*

3. The epileptic seizures of the Russian novelist Feodor Dostoevski were so severe that it took him days to recover; for much of his career *he was also overwhelmed with debts.*

4. *At various stages in her career,* Virginia Woolf experienced bouts of mental illness that prevented her from writing.

5. *John Milton wrote his most famous poem* after he had completely lost his sight.

6. The novelist Richard Wright overcame a childhood of hunger and prejudice, *and he became a powerful writer.*

7. Flannery O'Connor continued *writing short stories,* though she had an incurable disease which eventually took her life.

8. O. Henry, *who became a master of the short story,* continued his writing career while in prison.

9. While *working as a hotel busboy,* Langston Hughes showed Vachel Lindsay his poems; soon a book of Hughes's poems was published.

10. The power *of Elie Wiesel's novels* can be traced to his childhood experience in concentration camps.

11. *After his father was imprisoned for debt,* the twelve-year-old Charles Dickens went to work in a factory.

12. *As a child Alice Walker was blinded in one eye;* writing fiction helped her escape from the taunts of her classmates.

13. *How the young orphan Jerzy Kosinski survived in war-torn Europe* became the subject for his highly praised novel.

14. *Katherine Mansfield spent her last years as an invalid,* yet during that time she wrote some of her best stories.

15. The Argentine writer Jorge Luis Borges wrote many of his finest short stories *after he became totally blind.*

Phrases and Clauses **607**

Objectives

- To distinguish the three types of subordinate clauses: adjective, adverb, and noun
- To identify the relative pronouns or subordinating conjunctions that introduce subordinate clauses
- **Writing** To use subordinate clauses to enhance sentence structure

KINDS OF
SUBORDINATE CLAUSES

The three kinds of subordinate clauses are **adjective clauses, adverb clauses,** and **noun clauses.**

Adjective Clauses

A subordinate clause that is used to modify a noun or a pronoun is called an **adjective clause.**

Like an adjective, an adjective clause answers the questions *Which one?* or *What kind?* Usually the adjective clause follows the noun or pronoun it modifies.

> The man *who examined the mummy* was Myron Marx, a hospital radiologist. (Which man?)
>
> Marx X-rayed the mummy of Ta-bes, a woman *who lived in Egypt 3,000 years ago.* (What kind of woman?)

Words That Introduce Adjective Clauses Many adjective clauses begin with **relative pronouns** such as *who, whom, whose, that,* and *which.* The relative pronoun relates the adjective clause to the noun or pronoun it modifies. The modified noun or pronoun is the antecedent of the relative pronoun. An adjective clause that begins with a relative pronoun is sometimes referred to as a **relative clause.**

In an adjective clause, the relative pronoun may function as the subject, the direct object, the object of a preposition, or a modifier.

Subject	Rosa Bonheur was the French artist *who created those wonderful paintings of horses.* (*Artist* is the antecedent of *who. Who* is the subject of the verb *created.*)
Direct Object	Her father, *whom she greatly respected,* taught her the basics of painting. (*Father* is the antecedent of *whom. Whom* is the direct object of the verb *respected.*)
Object of a Preposition	The painting *for which Rosa Bonheur is most admired* is called *The Horse Fair.* (Painting is the antecedent of *which. Which* is the object of the preposition *for.*)
Modifier	She also painted a portrait of Buffalo Bill, *whose Wild West Circus toured Europe in the 1800's.* (*Whose* modifies the noun *Wild West Circus.*)

Some adjective clauses begin with relative adverbs such as *after, before, since, when, where,* and *why.* Like a relative pronoun, a **relative adverb** relates the adjective clause to the word it modifies. The relative adverb also modifies the verb in the clause.

> The house *where President John F. Kennedy was born* is in Brookline, Massachusetts. (*Where* relates the clause to the noun *house* and modifies the verb *was born.*)

In some cases, the relative pronoun or adverb can be omitted from the sentence.

> Paris is a city *I want to see someday.* (*That* has been omitted from the clause.)

Essential and Nonessential Clauses An adjective clause can be essential or nonessential. An **essential adjective clause** must be included to make the intended meaning of a sentence complete. Do not set off essential clauses with commas.

> Fish *that swim in the waters of totally dark caves* have no eyes. (Without the clause, the intended meaning would be incomplete.)

A **nonessential adjective clause** is one that adds additional information to a sentence whose basic meaning is already complete. One or two commas are needed to set off nonessential clauses from the rest of the sentence.

> The tour guide on the African camera safari spoke Swahili, *which we do not understand.*

Sentence Diagraming For information on diagraming adjective clauses, see page 840.

Practice Your Skills

A. CONCEPT CHECK

Adjective Clauses Write each adjective clause and identify the introductory word as a *Relative Pronoun* or a *Relative Adverb*. If the introductory word is omitted, write *Omitted.* Last, write the word in the independent clause that is modified by the adjective clause.

1. Belladonna, which is also known as "poison cherry" and "deadly nightshade," is a poisonous herb.
2. According to Greek myth, it was Hecate who first cultivated deadly nightshade.

Writing
TIP

In formal speech and writing, use *that* to introduce essential adjective clauses and *which* to introduce nonessential clauses. (The antecedent of *which* can never be a person.)

Additional Resources
• Grammar and Usage Practice Book, p. 28

WRITING THEME   Exotic Plants

A. Concept Check
Adjective Clauses
   1. which is also known as "poison cherry" and "deadly nightshade"; Relative Pronoun; Belladonna
   2. who first cultivated deadly nightshade; Relative Pronoun; Hecate

Phrases and Clauses   **609**

3. who was a goddess; Relative Pronoun; Hecate

4. where the plant grew; Relative Adverb; garden

5. which is a compound of two Italian words meaning "beautiful woman"; Relative Pronoun; *Belladonna*

6. Italian women tried to achieve; Omitted; "look"

7. which caused the pupils to dilate; Relative Pronoun; drops

8. into which the drops were placed; Relative Pronoun; Eyes

9. before the dangers of belladonna were widely recognized; Relative Adverb; age

10. that can bring on madness or even death; Relative Pronoun; plant

B. Revision Skill

Sentence Combining

Answers will vary. See suggested answers below.

1. Sundews, bladderworts, and Venus' flytraps are meat-eaters that trap insects.

2. A sundew has many little hairs, which are sweet and sticky, on its leaves.

3. Any insect *that* stands on the sticky leaf will get stuck.

4. Another meat-eater, the bladderwort, fascinates botanists, who study its little hollow holes, or bladders.

5. Each bladder has a kind of trap door that is surrounded by tiny hairs.

6. The trap door, which is very sensitive to the touch of passing insects or fish, opens; and the bladder sucks in the prey.

7. A third carnivorous plant is the Venus' flytrap, which is familiar to most people.

8. The flytrap's leaves, which lock together, encircle the prey.

9. The insect is then trapped in a place within the plant where it is slowly digested.

10. Stories that have no basis in fact have been told about people being eaten by huge meat-eating plants.

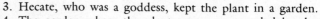

3. Hecate, who was a goddess, kept the plant in a garden.

4. The garden where the plant grew was guarded by demons and could not be entered by mortals.

5. *Belladonna,* which is a compound of two Italian words meaning "beautiful woman," is the plant's scientific name.

6. At one time, having large eyes was a popular "look" Italian women tried to achieve.

7. Women treated their eyes with belladonna drops, which caused the pupils to dilate.

8. Eyes into which the drops were placed appeared larger and therefore more beautiful.

9. However, this was an age before the dangers of belladonna were widely recognized.

10. Now belladonna is recognized as a plant that can bring on madness or even death.

B. REVISION SKILL

Sentence Combining Combine each of the following sentence pairs into one sentence that contains an adjective clause. When using relative pronouns, remember to use *that* for essential clauses and *which* for nonessential clauses. Punctuate all clauses correctly.

Example   There are some very unusual plants. These plants are meat-eaters.
      There are some very unusual plants that are meat-eaters.

1. Sundews, bladderworts, and Venus' flytraps are meat-eaters. They trap insects.

2. A sundew has many little hairs on its leaves. The hairs are sweet and sticky.

3. Any insect will get stuck. The insect stands on the sticky leaf.

4. Another meat-eater, the bladderwort, fascinates botanists. These botanists study its little hollow holes, or bladders.

5. Each bladder has a kind of trap door. This trap door is surrounded by tiny hairs.

6. The trap door opens and the bladder sucks in the prey. The door is very sensitive to the touch of passing insects or fish.

7. A third carnivorous plant is the Venus' flytrap. The Venus' flytrap is familiar to most people.

8. The flytrap's leaves encircle the prey. The leaves lock together.

9. The insect is then trapped in a place within the plant. In that place it is slowly digested.

10. Stories have been told about people being eaten by huge meat-eating plants. These stories have no basis in fact.

Adverb Clauses

An adverb clause is a subordinate clause that is used as an adverb to modify a verb, an adjective, or an adverb.

Verb   Kareem carries his calculator *wherever he goes.*

Adjective   Marian's cold got worse *after she walked in the rain.*

Adverb   Can any animal run faster *than a gazelle can?*

An adverb clause can also modify a verbal.

Infinitive   The team members vowed *to practice* harder *as soon as exams were over.*

Participle   *Proud* of herself *after she won,* Janet smiled.

Gerund   *Arguing* with Peter *because he refused to work* accomplished nothing.

Words That Introduce Adverb Clauses   Most adverb clauses begin with a **subordinating conjunction** that relates the clause to the word it modifies and establishes a specific relationship between them.

Time	as, as soon as, after, before, since, until, when, whenever, while
Cause	because, since
Comparison	as, as much as, than
Condition	if, although, as long as, though, unless, provided that
Purpose	so that, in order that
Manner	as, as if, as though
Place	where, wherever

Adverb clauses answer these questions: *Where? When? How? Why? To what extent?* and *Under what circumstances?*

Follow your dreams *wherever they take you.* (Follow *where?*)

When you visit Tokyo, shop along the Ginza. (Shop *when?*)

Since she has a bad cold, the mayor postponed her meeting. (Postponed *why?*)

The agitated lion acted *as if it might attack.* (Acted *how?*)

Myra plays the guitar much better *than most professionals do.* (Better *to what extent?*)

If the snow continues, all flights will be canceled. (Will be canceled *under what circumstances?*)

Writing
—TIP—

Use a comma after an adverb clause that begins a sentence.

Phrases and Clauses   **611**

Linking Grammar and Writing

Elliptical Clauses   When there is no possibility that readers and listeners will misunderstand the meaning, one or more words may be left out of an adverb clause. A clause from which a word or words have been omitted is called an **elliptical clause.**

> When competing in a chess tournament, the champion was totally absorbed. (The words *she was* have been dropped: When *she was* competing in a chess tournament. . . .)

> She usually wins because she can concentrate on the game far more intently than her opponents. (The word *can* has been omitted: . . . than her opponents *can*.)

Sentence Diagraming   For information on diagraming adverb clauses, see page 840.

Practice Your Skills

A. CONCEPT CHECK

Adverb Clauses   Write the adverb clause in each sentence, and underline the subordinating conjunction. Then write the word, or words, modified by the clause. If the clause is elliptical, write *E*.

1. When Pearl Buck's novel *The Good Earth* was published in 1931, no one suspected that it would gain worldwide popularity.
2. If Buck had not grown up in China, she might not have written so movingly about the poor Chinese peasant named Wang.
3. Because Buck's parents were Presbyterian missionaries, the family lived in a Chinese community.
4. Though Buck was an American, Chinese was the first language she learned.
5. She returned to the United States to attend college when she was seventeen years old.
6. After she had graduated from college, she went back to China to teach.
7. While living in a small village with her missionary husband, she formed the ideas and impressions she would later use in *The Good Earth*.
8. *The Good Earth* has been translated into more than fifty languages so that people the world over can enjoy the story of Wang and his life.
9. None of Pearl Buck's later works became as popular as *The Good Earth*.
10. Before she died, Buck had published over sixty books and had become the first woman to win the Nobel Prize for literature.

A Chinese River with a
Figure on the Bank,
George Chinnery

B. DRAFTING SKILL

Sentence Expansion Expand each sentence by adding an adverb clause. Begin each clause with a subordinating conjunction that expresses the relationship indicated in parentheses. Do not always place the adverb clause at the beginning of the sentence.

1. Remember that good books can vicariously transport you. (place)
2. Try a good mystery or adventure novel. (condition)
3. Don't sneak a look at the ending. (time)
4. Some readers enjoy competing with a fictional detective to solve a crime. (cause)
5. Perhaps science fiction suits your tastes better. (cause)

Noun Clauses

A noun clause is a subordinate clause that is used as a noun in a sentence.

A noun clause can perform all the functions of a noun: subject, direct or indirect object, predicate nominative, object of a preposition.

Subject	*What the committee suggested* was an outdoor beautification project.
Direct Object	Scientists may have determined *where Noah's Ark landed.*
Indirect Object	The teacher gave *whoever had been absent from class* a review of the lesson.
Predicate Nominative	An unsolved mystery is *where Atlantis was located.*
Object of a Preposition	The reporter offered scanty proof for *what he claimed in his article.*

Phrases and Clauses **613**

B. Drafting Skill

Sentence Expansion
Answers will vary but should contain elements shown below.
1. Remember that good books can vicariously transport you wherever their stories take place.
2. If you ever find yourself with time on your hands, try a good mystery or adventure novel.
3. Don't sneak a look at the ending before you finish reading what precedes it.
4. Because some readers like to imagine themselves as amateur detectives, they enjoy competing with a fictional detective to solve a crime.
5. Perhaps science fiction suits your tastes better because it takes you into the future.

Teaching Tip: The Word That

Explain that when it introduces a noun clause, the word *that* has no meaning in itself. It simply marks the beginning of the clause. Frequently the word *that* is omitted, especially in speaking. It should not be omitted, however, if misreading would result. The word *that* is not omitted when it introduces a noun clause used as the subject of the sentence. (That the world is round is a fact.)

Noun clauses also function as direct objects of verbals.

> Spanish explorers of the Americas tried unsuccessfully to discover *where the fabled El Dorado was.* (The noun clause is the direct object of the infinitive *to discover.*)

> Hearing *what the second baseman called him,* the umpire threw the player out of the game. (The noun clause is the direct object of the participle *hearing.*)

Words That Introduce Noun Clauses A pronoun or a subordinating conjunction can introduce a noun clause.

Pronouns	who, whom, whose, which, that, whoever, whomever, what, whatever
Subordinating Conjunctions	how, that, when, where, whether, why (More subordinating conjunctions are on pages 562–564.)

Some words that introduce noun clauses may also introduce adjective and adverb clauses. To avoid confusing one type of clause with another, consider the context and determine how the clause functions within the sentence.

> April 4, 1968, was *when Martin Luther King, Jr., was assassinated.* (functions as a noun—a predicate nominative.)

> It is the anniversary of the day *when Martin Luther King, Jr., was assassinated.* (functions as an adjective modifying *day*)

> The whole nation grieved *when Martin Luther King, Jr., was assassinated.* (functions as an adverb modifying *grieved*)

The introductory pronoun in a noun clause can act as a subject or an object within the clause.

> *What is needed in the world* is a little more love and laughter. (*What* is the subject of the verb *is needed* in the clause.)

> *What the world needs* is a little more love and laughter. (*What* is the direct object of the verb *needs* in the clause.)

Usage Note At times, the introductory word *that* may be omitted from a noun clause.

> Did you know *the numeral representing a trillion has twelve zeros? (That* has been omitted at the beginning of the clause.)

Sentence Diagraming For information on diagraming noun clauses, see page 840.

Writing
TIP

When a noun clause follows verbs such as *see, feel, think,* and *say,* it is often necessary to retain the word *that* for clarity.

Practice Your Skills

A. CONCEPT CHECK

Noun Clauses Write whether each italicized noun clause is used as a *Subject, Indirect Object, Direct Object, Object of a Preposition,* or *Predicate Nominative.*

1. The Taj Mahal is *what many people describe as the most beautiful tomb in the world.*
2. The Indian ruler Shah Jahan knew *that he wanted a spectacular monument to his favorite wife and constant companion.*
3. *That Mumtaz Mahal (Chosen One of the Palace) had died in childbirth* brought great sorrow to the Shah.
4. Agra, in northern India, is *where the Taj Mahal is located.*
5. The Taj Mahal affords *whoever sees it* great pleasure and ·delight.
6. Part of *what makes this great tomb so astoundingly beautiful* is the intricate carving and inlaid precious stones.
7. It is staggering to think of *how many workers were needed to complete the building.*
8. *That the whole complex of buildings took twenty-two years to complete and cost 40 million rupees* is well known.
9. Visitors can see *that the tomb is built of pure white marble.*
10. To preserve this impressive complex, Indian authorities spend *whatever it takes to keep the Taj Mahal in perfect condition.*

B. DRAFTING SKILL

Sentence Combining Combine each of the following sentence sets. Form one sentence with a noun clause that has the introductory word and function indicated in parentheses.

Example   Love, murder, or deception are story elements. These can make a story intriguing. (*what,* subject)
What can make a story intriguing is love, murder, or deception.

1. Something fooled Sampson. It was Delilah's deceptive charm. (*what,* subject)
2. Everybody knows about Romeo and Juliet. They were caught in a web of tragic misunderstanding. (*that,* direct object)
3. Cleopatra brought about the downfall of Mark Antony. Several ancient Roman authors tell this story. (*how,* direct object)
4. An event caused the ruin of Eleanor of Aquitaine. It was the betrayal of her husband, King Henry II. (*what,* predicate nominative)
5. Lady Macbeth became a victim. She became a victim of the things guilt can do. (*what,* object of a preposition)

Phrases and Clauses   **615**

Individualizing Instruction

LD Students Make sure that these students understand the directions for each exercise. You may want to have advanced students work in pairs with LD students.

Additional Resources
- Grammar and Usage Practice Book, p. 30

WRITING THEME   Stories of Love and Grief

A. Concept Check
Noun Clauses
1. Predicate Nominative
2. Direct Object
3. Subject
4. Predicate Nominative
5. Indirect Object
6. Object of a Preposition
7. Object of a Preposition
8. Subject
9. Direct Object
10. Direct Object

B. Drafting Skill
Sentence Combining
Answers will vary. See suggested answers below.
1. What fooled Sampson was Delilah's deceptive charm.
2. Everybody knows that Romeo and Juliet were caught in a web of tragic misunderstanding.
3. Several ancient Roman authors tell how Cleopatra brought about the downfall of Mark Antony.
4. The betrayal of her husband, King Henry II, is what caused the ruin of Eleanor of Aquitaine.
5. Lady Macbeth became a victim of what guilt can do.

The Structure of a Sentence

Objectives

- To identify simple, compound, complex, and compound-complex sentences
- **Writing** To combine sentences to enhance and vary sentence structure

Teaching Strategies

Linking Grammar and Literature

Some writers use a semicolon followed by the conjunction *for,* rather than a comma, to indicate a more emphatic break between the two independent clauses of a compound sentence or a compound-complex sentence. This usage is illustrated in the following famous lines from Shakespeare's *Macbeth.* Discuss how the use of this construction enhances the flow of words:
Hear it not, Duncan; for it is a knell
That summons thee to heaven or to hell.

You already know that sentences are classified according to purpose and may be declarative, interrogative, imperative, or exclamatory. In this part of the chapter, you will learn that sentences are also classified according to structure, that is, by the number and kinds of clauses they have. There are four kinds of sentences included in this classification: **simple, compound, complex,** and **compound-complex.**

Simple Sentences

A simple sentence has one independent clause but no subordinate clauses.

The trains made ninety-seven stops.

A simple sentence contains no subordinate clauses, but it may contain a number of phrases.

Carrying passengers and freight, *the trains* of the Trans-Siberian Railway *made ninety-seven stops* at large and small stations on their trips across the vast expanses of Asian Russia.

Some simple sentences have compound parts.

Turkey and pumpkin pie may not have been part of the original Thanksgiving feast. (compound subject)

Compound Sentences

A compound sentence has two or more independent clauses that are joined together.

The independent clauses in a compound sentence may be connected (1) by a comma and a coordinating conjunction such as *and, but, or, nor, for, so,* or *yet;* (2) by a semicolon; or (3) by a semicolon and a conjunctive adverb followed by a comma.

The people of ancient times built the Seven Wonders of the World, *but* only the Great Pyramid of Khufu still stands.

Sonja Henie won three Olympic figure-skating championships; this led to her being given starring roles in Hollywood films.

Mary Martin played Nellie Forbush in the Broadway version of *South Pacific; however,* she did not play this role in the film version.

Sentence Diagraming For information on diagraming simple and compound sentences, see pages 834 and 841.

Practice Your Skills

A. CONCEPT CHECK

Sentences Write *Simple* or *Compound* to describe each sentence. Also tell if a sentence has a *Compound Subject, Compound Predicate, Compound Direct Object*, or *Compound Predicate Nominative*.

1. Both the original Indian culture of the Aztecs and the Spanish culture from Europe influenced the Mexico of today.
2. In fact, the past seems to be present everywhere in Mexico, and the present seems to be deeply rooted in the past.
3. In Mexico today, the three main groups of people are those with Spanish ancestry, those with Indian ancestry, and those with mixed Spanish and Indian ancestry.
4. The majority of Mexicans are mestizos (of mixed ancestry), but some follow an Indian way of life and are considered Indians.
5. Most Indians live in isolated groups in remote areas; therefore, their traditional ways of life define them.
6. For example, many Indians wear traditional clothing, follow the customs of their ancestors, and worship ancient gods.
7. The people of Spanish descent are the smallest and wealthiest group; the mestizos comprise the middle class.
8. Skilled workers, government workers, and businesspeople make up the middle class.
9. Mexico is a large country and a rapidly growing one, and it benefits from its basically homogeneous population.
10. Most Mexicans share their common Indian-Spanish heritage, their religious beliefs, and their language.

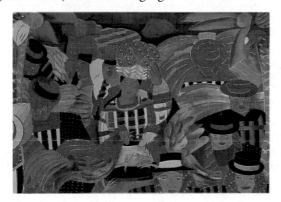

Writing Theme
Mexico

Additional Resources
- Grammar and Usage Practice Book, p. 31

WRITING THEME Mexico

Students may want to think about writing a story set in modern or ancient Mexico. Suggest that they record story ideas in their journals.

A. Concept Check
Sentences
1. Simple, Compound Subject
2. Compound
3. Simple, Compound Predicate Nominative
4. Compound, Compound Predicate
5. Compound
6. Simple, Compound Predicate
7. Compound
8. Simple, Compound Subject
9. Compound, Compound Predicate Nominative
10. Simple, Compound Direct Object

B. REVISION SKILL

Sentence Combining   Compound sentences and sentence parts can be used to express ideas efficiently. Rewrite each of the following sentence sets, combining each set to form a compound sentence or a sentence with compound parts.

1. Mexico is a modern, industrialized nation. It is also an ancient land.
2. Mexico City is the capital of Mexico. It is one of the largest urban centers in the world.
3. For years this city was the world's largest. Now Tokyo holds that position.
4. All the glories of modern Mexico can be seen in Mexico City. A great deal of rich local color can be seen in Mexico City.
5. You can also see all the overwhelming problems of rapid population growth. All the problems of poverty are also evident.
6. Mexican citizens have been drawn to the city in increasing numbers for years. Now the city has become the industrial center of the nation.
7. More than 50 percent of Mexico's industry is located in Mexico City. Almost all of Mexico's leading banks and businesses are located there.
8. Some people live in great comfort. Others have inadequate housing, housing without plumbing, or no housing at all.
9. Wealthy neighborhoods can be found in Mexico City. Slums can also be found in this city of fourteen million people.
10. For the tourist, Mexico City offers picturesque plazas. It also offers open market places. The extraordinary cultural attractions make it a magnet for tourism.

Complex Sentences

A complex sentence has one independent clause and one or more subordinate clauses.

> The passengers grumbled *when the airline announced the third postponement of their flight.*

In a complex sentence, a subordinate clause functions as a *noun* or a *modifier*. As a modifier, it modifies a word in the independent clause.

> W. C. Fields was the film comedian *who wore a tall top hat and had a large red nose.* (The clause modifies the noun *comedian.*)

When Whoopi Goldberg participated in the television program "Comic Relief", she donated her talents to raise funds for the homeless. (The clause modifies the verb *donated*.)

If the subordinate clause functions as a noun in a complex sentence, it can be the subject, object, or complement in the independent clause.

Subject	*What we saw on our whirlwind vacation* is just a blur in my memory.
Direct Object	We photographed *whatever looked important or interesting*.
Predicate Nominative	Scuba diving was *what we wanted to try first*.
Object of a Preposition	I will tell you about *where we were* if I can remember.

In each of the preceding examples, the subordinate clause is a part of the independent clause; the two cannot be separated. Each sentence has one independent clause and at least one subordinate clause. Therefore, all the sentences are complex.

Sentence Diagraming For information on diagraming complex sentences, see page 841.

Practice Your Skills

CONCEPT CHECK

Types of Sentences Identify each sentence as *Simple, Compound,* or *Complex.* If it is complex, write the subordinate clause or clauses.

1. In the great hall of a French castle, servants light torches signaling that the evening meal is about to begin.
2. A long board has been laid on a series of trestles and covered with cloths.
3. On one side, the cloth goes all the way to the floor so that the dogs can't crawl under the table in search of scraps.
4. The year is 1200, and neither permanent tables nor individual chairs are common yet.
5. On a side table sits a bronze container called an *aquamanile,* which means it is used for washing hands.
6. Hands are publicly washed so that everyone knows fingers are clean when they are dipped into serving bowls.
7. There are no utensils, bowls, or napkins to greet diners.
8. Instead of plates, diners are handed trenchers, thick slices of bread.

Complex yet simple, the humor of W. C. Fields and Whoopi Goldberg delights movie audiences.

Writing Theme
Life in the Middle Ages

Phrases and Clauses **619**

Linking Grammar and Writing

Point out to students that although subordinate clauses are extremely helpful tools for showing the relationship of ideas in a complex sentence, writers who value clarity avoid accumulating too many of them in one sentence.

9. The guests help themselves with bare hands to the many platters, and they put the food on their trenchers.
10. An occasional carved or cast spoon may be used for serving, but the fork isn't yet known in Western Europe.

Compound-Complex Sentences

A compound-complex sentence has two or more independent clauses and one or more subordinate clauses.

Independent clauses are joined (1) by a coordinating conjunction preceded by a comma, (2) by a conjunctive adverb preceded by a semicolon and followed by a comma, or (3) by a semicolon alone.

Subordinate clauses either modify a word in one of the independent clauses or act as a noun in one of the independent clauses.

Each of the following compound-complex sentences has two independent clauses. The second independent clause in each sentence has one subordinate clause, which is italicized.

> The crew from the United States entered the sailing race off the coast of Perth, Australia, and they won the cup *that the Australian crew coveted so much.*
> Perth is normally a quiet place; however, it became a beehive of frenzied activity *while the America's Cup race was in progress.*

The following compound-complex sentence has two independent clauses, each of which contains a subordinate clause.

> Holmes asked Watson what clues suggested a solution to the mystery, but he smiled condescendingly when his doctor companion nervously hazarded a guess.

Independent Clause 1	Holmes asked Watson what clues suggested a solution to the mystery
Independent Clause 2	he smiled condescendingly when his doctor companion nervously hazarded a guess
Subordinate Clause 1	what clues suggested a solution to the mystery (a noun clause that functions as the direct object of independent clause 1)
Subordinate Clause 2	when his doctor companion nervously hazarded a guess (an adverb clause that modifies the verb *smiled* in independent clause 2)

Sentence Diagraming   For information on the diagraming of compound-complex sentences, see page 841.

Practice Your Skills

CONCEPT CHECK

Kinds of Sentences Identify each of the following sentences as *Simple, Compound, Complex,* or *Compound-Complex.* Write each subordinate clause and indicate its function as *Noun* or *Modifier.*

(1) No one could remember when the tribe had begun its long journey. (2) The land of great rolling plains that had been its first home was now no more than a half-forgotten dream. (3) For many years, Shann and his people had been fleeing through a country of low hills and sparkling lakes, and now the mountains lay ahead. (4) This summer they must cross them to the southern lands. (5) There was little time to lose. (6) The white terror that had come down from the Poles, grinding continents to dust and freezing the very air before it, was less than a day's march behind. (7) Shann wondered if the glaciers could climb the mountains ahead, and within his heart he dared to kindle a little flame of hope. (8) This might prove a barrier . . . which even the remorseless ice would batter in vain. (9) In the southern lands of which the legends spoke, his people might find refuge at last.   **Arthur C. Clarke, "History Lesson"**

AVOIDING PHRASE AND CLAUSE FRAGMENTS

A **sentence** is a group of words that contains a subject and a predicate and that expresses a complete thought. Keep this definition in mind to avoid mistaking fragments for complete sentences.

Phrases as Fragments

Prepositional phrases, appositive phrases, and verbal phrases are sometimes used incorrectly as sentences; however, they are fragments because they have no subjects or verbs.

Fragment	*After their appearance on the Ed Sullivan Show in the United States* (a series of prepositional phrases)
Sentence	*The Beatles became world-famous* after their appearance on the *Ed Sullivan Show* in the United States. (An independent clause has been added.)

Phrases and Clauses **621**

WRITING THEME   Ice Age

A description of life during the Ice Age might be a possible writing assignment for your students.

Concept Check
Kinds of Sentences
   1. Complex; when the tribe had begun its long journey—Noun
   2. Complex; that had been its first home—Modifier
   3. Compound
   4. Simple
   5. Simple
   6. Complex; that had come down from the Poles, grinding continents to dust and freezing the very air before it—Modifier
   7. Compound-Complex; if the glaciers could climb the mountains ahead—Noun
   8. Complex; which even the remorseless ice would batter in vain—Modifier
   9. Complex; of which the legends spoke—Modifier

Avoiding Phrase and Clause Fragments

Objective

- To recognize and correct phrase and clause fragments

Teaching Strategies

Stumbling Block

Students may have noticed sentence fragments in professional writing. Stress that when good writers use fragments, they do so to achieve a special effect, which does not affect the clarity of their meanings. In most of the writing that students are asked to do, they should not use sentence fragments.

Auditory Learners Since these students may recognize sentence fragments more easily when they are read aloud, have pairs of students do Exercise A orally.

Additional Resources
- Grammar and Usage Practice Book, p. 33

WRITING THEME Defense Mechanisms

Suggest that students may want to research the defense mechanisms of an animal for one of their writing assignments or for a science project.

A. Concept Check
Types of Fragments

Answers will vary. See suggested answers below.

1. Armadillos are small burrowing animals with armored coats of overlapping plates and scales. Prepositional
2. *Armadillo* is a word in the Spanish language meaning "little armored one." Participial
3. Having a strong suit of armor protects the armadillo from its enemies. Gerund
4. Unlike the protective shell of the turtle, the armadillo's "armor" is flexible and moves with its body. Prepositional
5. Armadillos also have powerful claws to dig their way into their burrows. Infinitive
6. When an armadillo senses danger, it will dig quickly into the ground and out of sight. Prepositional
7. Rolling itself up into a ball is another technique necessary for protection. Gerund
8. Hoping its armor alone will protect it, the armadillo might simply crouch on the ground. Participial
9. It takes an animal with extremely strong teeth or claws to penetrate the tough scales and plates of an armadillo's hide. Infinitive
10. To fight off an attacker, an armadillo will also use its claws as a last resort. Infinitive

> **Writing Theme**
> Defense
> Mechanisms

Fragment	*Madame Tussaud's, a wax museum located in London* (appositive phrase)
Sentence	Madame Tussaud's, a wax museum located in London, *features a Chamber of Horrors.*
Fragment	*Still standing on the north bank of the Thames River* (participial phrase)
Sentences	*The Tower of London,* still standing on the north bank of the Thames River, *is a reminder of England's past.* (The phrase is used as a modifier in a sentence.)
	The Tower of London is still standing on the north bank of the Thames River. (The participle in the phrase is used as part of the main verb in a verb phrase.)

Practice Your Skills

A. CONCEPT CHECK

Types of Fragments Each example below contains a sentence and a fragment. Write a new sentence, joining the two parts. Then tell what kind of phrase the fragment has become in the new sentence: *Prepositional, Participial, Gerund,* or *Infinitive.*

1. Armadillos are small burrowing animals. With armored coats of overlapping plates and scales.
2. *Armadillo* is a word in the Spanish language. Meaning "little armored one."
3. Having a strong suit of armor. The armor protects the armadillo from its enemies.
4. Unlike the protective shell of the turtle. The armadillo's "armor" is flexible and moves with its body.
5. Armadillos also have powerful claws. To dig their way into their burrows.
6. When an armadillo senses danger, it will dig quickly. Into the ground and out of sight.
7. Rolling itself up into a ball. This is another technique necessary for protection.
8. Hoping its armor alone will protect it. An armadillo might simply crouch on the ground.
9. It takes an animal with extremely strong teeth or claws. To penetrate the tough scales and plates of an armadillo's hide.
10. To fight off an attacker. An armadillo will also use its claws as a last resort.

B. DRAFTING SKILL

Correcting Fragments Expand each fragment by adding details to make a complete sentence. Add any needed punctuation.

 1. A defense mechanism called "protective coloration"
 2. To hide from predators by blending with the surroundings
 3. On land and in the water all over the world
 4. For example, the chameleon's ability to change color
 5. The walking stick, an insect resembling a twig
 6. Spotted like the bottom of a stream bed
 7. With the coloration of coral reefs
 8. Changing from brown fur to white fur in winter
 9. Unnoticed against the white of the Arctic winter
10. To blend with the tall grasses of the African plain

Subordinate Clauses as Fragments

A subordinate clause can be mistaken for a sentence because the clause has a subject and a verb. The introductory word in a subordinate clause, however, makes the clause a fragment.

Sentence The Star of Africa and Cullinan II are diamonds of enormous value.

Subordinate Clause Because the Star of Africa and Cullinan II are diamonds of enormous value.

A capitalized word at the beginning of a subordinate clause and an end mark after it do not make the clause a sentence. The clause is always a fragment until it is combined with an independent clause.

Fragment Before the diamond cutter began to divide the huge stone. She examined it from various angles.

Sentence Before the diamond cutter began to divide the huge stone, she examined it from various angles.

The fragment above was combined with a related independent clause in order to make it a sentence. A subordinate-clause fragment can also be corrected by rewriting the clause as a sentence.

> The diamond cutter divided the large stone into six pieces. All of which would be polished and set in a new tiara for the princess.

> The diamond cutter divided the large stone into six pieces. All of them would be polished and set in a new tiara for the princess.

Phrases and Clauses **623**

WRITING THEME Sports

Brainstorm with students the many kinds of sports to write about. Have them jot down ideas in their journals.

Concept Check

Correcting Clause Fragments

Answers will vary. See typical answers below.

1.,2. Orienteering is a sport that the entire family can enjoy.

3.,4. Although it resembles cross-country running, orienteering involves finding one's way through an unknown area to a pre-selected place by using a map and a compass.

5.,6. Long before the contestants gather their equipment, the course planner has marked control points along the route.

7.,8. Teams and individual competitors must proceed along the course to these marked points, where they have a score card punched.

9.,10. A winner's prize is awarded to whoever has the fastest time.

11.,12. Because participants will be navigating around obstacles, they must plan a strategy.

13.,14. One big help is the topographical map, which shows the lay of the land, including features such as stone walls, buildings, and streams.

15. Correct

16. Correct

17.,18. Because courses vary in difficulty, an event may last from one to three hours.

19.,20. Although most participants proceed on foot, some adventurers orienteer on skis, in canoes, in wheelchairs, and even on horseback.

C H E C K   P O I N T
PAGES 605–623

You may wish to use the following Checkpoint exercises as an informal evaluation of student mastery of the types of subordinate clauses and the types of sentences covered in this handbook.

WRITING THEME The Far East

A.

1. who need to get around; Adjective

2. which has a population of over three and a half million; Adjective

3. Wherever they need to go; Adverb

4. What is hard to obtain; Noun

5. that three years passed; Noun; before she could get her bicycle coupon; Adverb

6. Whoever does not want to be fined; Noun

Writing Theme
Sports

Writing Theme
The Far East

Practice Your Skills

CONCEPT CHECK

Correcting Clause Fragments Rewrite the fragments in the paragraph below as complete sentences. In some cases the fragment may be combined with the word group that precedes it. If a sentence is correct, write *Correct*.

(1) Orienteering is a sport. (2) That the entire family can enjoy. (3) Although it resembles cross-country running. (4) Orienteering involves finding one's way through an unknown area to a pre-selected place by using a map and a compass. (5) Long before the contestants gather their equipment. (6) The course planner has marked control points along the route. (7) Teams and individual competitors must proceed along the course to these marked points. (8) Where they have a score card punched. (9) A winner's prize is awarded. (10) To whoever has the fastest time. (11) Because participants will be navigating around obstacles. (12) They must plan a strategy. (13) One big help is the topographical map. (14) Which shows the lay of the land, including features such as stone walls, buildings, and streams. (15) The contestant must get oriented to the landmarks and find a path. (16) It should be the fastest route to the next control point. (17) Because courses vary in difficulty. (18) An event may last from one to three hours. (19) Although most participants proceed on foot. (20) Some adventurers orienteer on skis, in canoes, in wheelchairs, and even on horseback.

C H E C K   P O I N T
PAGES 605–623

A. Write each subordinate clause in the following sentences. Tell whether the clause functions as a *Noun,* an *Adjective,* or an *Adverb.*

1. In the United States, cars are necessary for people who need to get around.
2. However, bicycles are the main transportation in Beijing, which has a population of over three and a half million.
3. Wherever they need to go, the Chinese rely on their bicycles.
4. What is hard to obtain is a bicycle coupon.
5. One factory worker complained that three years passed before she could get her bicycle coupon.
6. Whoever does not want to be fined must obtain a license as well as a license plate.

7. Accidents happen frequently, although police officers and volunteer traffic wardens are everywhere.
8. Whenever riders do not obey the regulations, the police are required to issue fines.
9. Giving someone a ride and not obeying the lights are what police officers watch for.
10. Also, bicycle owners must have government-specified equipment, which includes a bell, brakes, and a lock.

B. Write *Simple, Compound, Complex,* or *Compound-Complex* to identify each of the following sentences. Then label each italicized group of words as an *Adjective Clause, Adverb Clause, Noun Clause,* or *Phrase.*

1. The first emperor *of China* was an extraordinary man.
2. He is credited with many great reforms *that changed his empire.*
3. *That he unified the system of writing* is in itself an enormous accomplishment.
4. *To foster better communication and trade,* he also standardized the currency system and the system of weights and measures.
5. *In an age of travel by wagon,* his legislation of a uniform length for wheel axles advanced transportation.
6. *Obsessed with immortality,* he drank potions *to prolong his life,* and he had an enormous mausoleum built for himself.
7. The potions, *which contained mercury,* arc probably *what killed him.*
8. Excavation *of his tomb* has been ongoing *in China for years.*
9. An entire army of six-foot-tall terracotta figures and three-foot-tall bronze figures has been found *surrounding the perimeter of the burial area.*
10. Each of these figures was meticulously cast, carefully painted, and equipped with weapons *to protect the entombed emperor in the afterlife.*
11. The wooden weapons have crumbled, but styles of clothing and hairdos are details *that have endured over the centuries.*
12. *What this tomb will yet reveal about life in early China* cannot be guessed.
13. *After a farmer found a terracotta figure on his land,* the site was established, and archaeological research began.
14. The site is so large *that it is housed in an airplane hangar,* and only a small part has been excavated so far.
15. *Since the excavation began,* thousands of tourists have visited the site *where the buried emperor rests amid the glories of his empire.*

7. although police officers and volunteer traffic wardens are everywhere; Adverb
8. Whenever riders do not obey the regulations; Adverb
9. what police officers watch for; Noun
10. which includes a bell, brakes, and a lock; Adjective

B.
1. Simple; Phrase
2. Complex; Adjective Clause
3. Complex; Noun Clause
4. Simple; Phrase
5. Simple, Phrase
6. Compound; Phrase, Phrase
7. Complex; Adjective Clause, Noun Clause
8. Simple; Phrase, Phrase, Phrase
9. Simple; Phrase
10. Simple; Phrase, Phrase
11. Compound-Complex; Adjective Clause
12. Complex; Noun Clause
13. Compound-Complex; Adverb Clause
14. Compound-Complex; Adverb Clause
15. Complex; Adverb Clause, Adjective Clause

Application and Review

These activities have been designed to allow students to apply concepts presented in this handbook. Exercise A requires students to identify types and functions of phrases. Exercise B requires students to identify and correct misplaced or dangling modifiers. Exercise C requires students to identify types and functions of clauses. Exercise D requires students to identify types of sentences. Exercise E requires students to label sentence fragments and complete sentences; students are then challenged to expand each fragment into a complete sentence.

Additional Resources

- Tests and Assessment, Mastery Tests, pp. 47–50
- Elaboration, Revision, and Proofreading, p. 23

WRITING THEME   Money

A. Identifying Phrases
1. Gerund, Noun
2. Infinitive, Adverb
3. Infinitive, Adverb; Prepositional Phrase, Adjective
4. Gerund, Noun
5. Prepositional, Adverb
6. Prepositional, Adverb
7. Infinitive, Noun
8. Participial, Adjective
9. Infinitive, Adjective
10. Gerund, Noun; Prepositional, Adjective

B. Placing Modifiers Correctly
Answers will vary. See typical answers below.
1. Dangling; To prohibit the printing of paper money in the American colonies, the British government imposed strict regulations on the colonists.
2. Dangling; Defying the British, the colonists still printed the money even though it was not backed by gold or securities.
3. Misplaced; In 1787 the United States minted the first coin, the Fugio cent, that bore the country's name.
4. Dangling; Having engraved the coin with the motto "Mind Your Business," the United States sent a clear message of independence.
5. Misplaced; The U.S. Treasury mints all paper money and coins, now engraved with the motto "In God We Trust."

C. Recognizing Clauses
1. Independent Clause
2. Subordinate Clause, Adjective

GRAMMAR
HANDBOOK
33

Writing Theme
Money

A. Identifying Phrases Write *Prepositional, Participial, Gerund,* or *Infinitive* to identify each italicized phrase in the following sentences. Identify the function as *Noun, Adjective,* or *Adverb.*

1. *Counterfeiting money* is not a new practice.
2. Since about the fourth century B.C., counterfeiters have worked hard *to distribute fake money.*
3. *To demonstrate the seriousness of the crime,* the Chinese cut off the hands of counterfeiters.
4. The Romans took a different approach by *offering handsome rewards* to reporters of the crime.
5. If a Roman reported a counterfeiter, his taxes were waived for life *as a reward.*
6. A slave was rewarded *with freedom* for such a report.
7. On the other hand, the jailer paid with his own life if a counterfeiter was allowed *to escape.*
8. In England during the early 1800's, counterfeiters *hanging from the gallows* were a common sight.
9. The English felt that this was the most certain way *to send a message* about the seriousness of the crime.
10. In contrast, *abolishing the death penalty for counterfeiting* became a focus of crusaders who didn't view it as harshly.

B. Placing Modifiers Correctly Identify each modifier error as *Misplaced* or *Dangling.* Then rewrite the sentence, correcting the error.

1. To prohibit the printing of paper money in the American colonies, strict regulations were imposed on the colonists.
2. Defying the British, the money was still printed even though it was not backed by gold or securities.
3. In 1787 the United States minted the first coin that bore the country's name, the Fugio cent.
4. Having engraved the coin with the motto "Mind Your Business," a clear message of independence was sent.
5. Now engraved with the motto "In God We Trust," the U.S. Treasury mints all paper money and coins.

C. Recognizing Clauses Identify each group of italicized words as an *Independent Clause* or a *Subordinate Clause.* Then show how each subordinate clause functions by writing *Adjective, Adverb,* or *Noun.*

1. Before the Revolutionary War, *the most popular currency in the United States was the Spanish dollar.*
2. This silver dollar, *which was stamped with a large 8,* was known as a "piece of eight."

---

3. *The silver dollar was worth eight Spanish coins,* which were called "reals."
4. Eventually these pieces of eight were cut *so that coins of smaller denomination could be used.*
5. *The results were halves and quarters* called "bits."
6. Today, *"two bits" is an Americanism for a quarter.*
7. These bits also produced the colloquial expression "two bit," *which means cheap or inferior.*
8. *How Great Britain got the halfpenny* is not hard to guess.
9. A halfpenny was one piece of a penny *that had been cut in half.*
10. *When a penny was quartered,* it became a farthing.

D. Identifying Sentence Types Identify each sentence as *Simple, Compound, Complex,* or *Compound-Complex.*

1. One of the oldest forms of money is shells.
2. The most valuable shell is the cowry, and the rare white-toothed variety is the most valuable of all.
3. Historians know that Native Americans used shells called "wampum" as currency.
4. Bread was used as currency in ancient Egypt, and pictures of bakeries served as symbols of wealth in the occupant's tomb.
5. The Romans used salt as a form of money, and the word *salary* comes from *salarium,* which is the Latin word for "payments of salt" to the soldiers of Julius Caesar.
6. Because pepper was a highly valued spice during the Middle Ages, in some towns it could be used to pay taxes.
7. At one time, dried codfish served as money in Newfoundland, and sugar served as money in the West Indies.
8. Even tobacco, the mainstay of the economy of the southern colonies, was used as currency for a short time in Virginia.
9. In Iran, people use money, or they negotiate with fine carpets, which can be used as collateral.
10. In Australia, some groups still use bird feathers as currency!

E. Identifying Fragments Label each of the following groups of words *Phrase Fragment, Clause Fragment,* or *Complete Sentence.* Then expand each fragment into a complete sentence.

1. To destroy all damaged or old currency.
2. Seven denominations of U.S. paper money are in use today.
3. That no living person be portrayed on a denomination of U.S. paper money.
4. On the front of the dollar bill.
5. Which bears the signature of the Secretary of the Treasury.

Phrases and Clauses **627**

These exercises allow your students to practice skills acquired in Handbooks 31–33. You may wish to use the exercises to provide a thorough review of the material in these chapters or to evaluate student mastery of the concepts.

Additional Resources
- Grammar and Usage Practice Book, pp. 36–38
- Standardized Test Practice

Skills Assessment Test 1
1. C—people. This
2. E
3. D—folklore?
4. A—Covering an area of over sixty-four million square miles, the
   B—Pacific
5. C—car, which he promptly ran
6. A—Isaac Newton, formulator of much of classical physics,
   C—religion

Skills
ASSESSMENT

Directions One or more of the underlined sections in the following sentences may contain errors of grammar, usage, punctuation, spelling, or capitalization. Write the letters of each incorrect section. Then rewrite the item correctly. If there is no error in an item, write E.

Example Reduced to the lowest possilbe price, the sales clerk
               A   B
put the shoes on display. No error
 C   D   E

Answer A—The sales clerk put the shoes, reduced to the lowest possible price, on display.

---

1. Ethnocentrism is the tendency to believe that one's own group or culture is supe-
                                      A   B
   rior to that of other people, this is one explanation that is often given for the fre-
                                C   D
   quency of war. No error
                   E

2. An amoeba does not die the way a multicellular organism does; it simply splits in
                 A   B
   two and becomes two juvenile organisms. No error
       C   D   E

3. Is it true that storms are often preceded by periods of calm, or is that just another
   A   B   C
   bit of meteorological folklore. No error
                          D   E

4. Covering an area of over sixty-four million square miles. The pacific is by far the
                                              A   B
   largest ocean on the earth. No error
   C   D   E

5. In 1769 Nicholas Cugnot invented a three-wheeled motor car; which he promptly ran
             A   B   C
   into a stone wall. No error
   D   E

6. Isaac Newton formulator of much of classical physics became increasingly interested
   A   B
   in mysticism and Religion in his old age. No error
                    C   D   E

7. The defense <u>attornies</u> argued that the <u>prosecutor's</u> case was <u>ilogical</u> because the
A   B   C
defendant <u>could not have been</u> in two places at the same time. <u>No error</u>
D   E

8. <u>At the beginning</u> of <u>most published plays</u> is the *dramatis personae*. <u>A list of</u>
A   B   C
<u>characters</u> <u>appearing in the play.</u> <u>No error</u>
C   D   E

9. <u>Stewed to her complete satisfaction,</u> grandmother <u>removed</u> the <u>tomatoes</u> from the
A   B   C
stove and poured them <u>into a casserole dish.</u> <u>No error</u>
D   E

10. The <u>tour</u> guide <u>pointed out</u> <u>the many small islands</u> to the tourists <u>out in the bay.</u>
A   B   C   D
<u>No error</u>
E

11. The <u>British</u> royal family had the <u>German</u> surname <u>Hanover.</u> Until strong anti-
A   B   C
German feeling forced them to change it to <u>Windsor</u> during World War I.
D
<u>No error</u>
E

12. <u>Looking directly up,</u> thousands <u>of</u> stars were spread <u>across the sky,</u> like so many
A   B   C
lights on a <u>Christmas</u> tree. <u>No error</u>
D   E

13. Scientists <u>have bred</u> a strange animal called a <u>geep, it</u> is a combination <u>of a goat</u>
A   B   C
and <u>an</u> angora sheep. <u>No error</u>
D   E

14. <u>What</u> gave <u>director</u> <u>Alfred Hitchcock</u> the <u>idea? To make a brief appearance in more</u>
A   B   C   D
<u>than thirty of his own spine-chilling movies?</u> <u>No error</u>
D   E

15. <u>Trapped in a well for more than a day,</u> the <u>child</u> came <u>close</u> to dying
A   B   C
<u>before she was finally rescued.</u> <u>No error</u>
D   E

16. The surface <u>of Venus</u> reaches temperatures of over <u>900° Fahrenheit;</u> <u>moreover the</u>
A   B   C
atmosphere is <u>a thick soup of toxic gases.</u> No error
D   E

17. C—radiation
18. B—times; moreover,
    D--Midwest and West
19. A—Wow!
    D—butter?
20. E
21. E
22. D—Emily, and
23. B—arts. For
24. D—space
25. C—road, thousands

17. The <u>Van Allen belts</u> <u>are</u> belts of <u>Radiation</u> circling the <u>earth.</u> <u>No error</u>
          A   B   C   D   E

18. By the late nineteenth century enough track <u>had been laid in the United States</u> to
                                                A
    reach around the globe two <u>times moreover,</u> trains <u>were bringing</u> thousands of
                                  B   C
    settlers into the <u>midwest and west.</u> <u>No error</u>
                  D   E

19. <u>Wow.</u> Did you know that a neutrino <u>can travel</u> right through the earth as though
      A   B
    <u>it</u> were traveling through a thin cake of <u>butter.</u> <u>No error</u>
    C   D   E

20. The color pictures <u>that</u> <u>one sees</u> printed in books and magazines <u>are made up</u> of
                  A   B   C
    tiny dots of <u>cyan, magenta, yellow, and black.</u> <u>No error</u>
                   D   E

21. <u>Cross-country skiing</u> <u>is</u> wonderful <u>exercise and allows</u> the skier <u>to view the</u>
             A   B   C   D
    <u>countryside</u> close-up. <u>No error</u>
      D   E

22. Nearby <u>lived</u> the three <u>talented,</u> intelligent Bronte <u>sisters</u>—Charlotte, <u>Emily and</u>
             A   B   C   D
    Anne. <u>No error</u>
         E

23. The <u>Medici family</u> were patrons of the <u>arts for</u> two centuries they made <u>Florence</u> a
        A   B   C
    <u>golden city</u> of intellectual and artistic life. <u>No error</u>
      D   E

24. Scientists prior to the <u>nineteenth century</u> were <u>altogether</u> wrong in their <u>belief</u> that
                      A   B   C
    empty <u>Space</u> was filled with ether. <u>No error</u>
        D   E

25. As soon as the <u>World Bank</u> lent <u>Brazil</u> the money for the <u>road thousands</u> of set-
                A   B   C
    tlers began to pour into the rain forest, <u>bringing disease and death to the native</u>
                                                  D
    <u>Indians.</u> <u>No error</u>
      D   E

Verb Usage

THE PRINCIPAL PARTS OF VERBS

A **verb** is a word that expresses an action, a condition, or a state of being. **Action verbs** describe physical or mental actions. **Linking verbs** do not describe actions; they link, or relate, the subject of a sentence with a word in the predicate that renames or modifies the subject. See Handbook 31, pages 552–554, for additional information about verbs.

Every verb has different forms. Speakers and writers construct these forms by using the four **principal parts** of the verb: the **present infinitive** (or **present**), the **present participle**, the **past**, and the **past participle**.

Present	Present Participle	Past	Past Participle
know	(is) knowing	knew	(have) known
steal	(is) stealing	stole	(have) stolen
jump	(is) jumping	jumped	(have) jumped
laugh	(is) laughing	laughed	(have) laughed

Note that forms of the auxiliary verbs *be* and *have* are given in parentheses before each present and past participle. Participles cannot be used alone as the main verb of a clause or sentence. They must always be used with auxiliary verbs.

The present participle of every verb is formed by adding the ending *-ing* to the present infinitive form. The past and the past participle, however, may be formed in a number of different ways. The ending of the past and the past participle of a verb determines whether a verb is classified as regular or irregular.

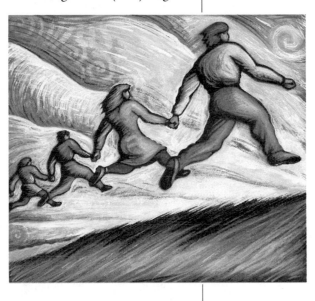

Verb Usage   **631**

The Principal Parts of Verbs

Objectives

- To review the function of verbs
- To identify the principal parts of regular and irregular verbs
- To use revision skills to correct errors in verb usage

Teaching Strategies

Linking Grammar and Literature

Read aloud the following lyrics from John Prine's song "Angels from Montgomery."

> I am an old woman
> Named after my mother
> My old man is another
> Child that's grown old
> If dreams were lightning
> And thunder were desire
> This old house would have burnt down
> A long time ago
> Make me an angel that flies from Montgomery
> Make me a poster of an old rodeo
> Just give me one thing that I can hold on to
> To believe in this living is a hard way to go

Elicit from students that the verbs in these lyrics do more than express action or condition. By varying the mood (inflection) of the verbs, Prine makes statements, indicates unfulfilled possibilities, and gives directions. He uses tense to create a sense of time.

Stumbling Block

Students may not understand why verbs are considered regular even though the spellings of some of the forms change when various verb endings are added. Lead students to notice that though the spellings of certain forms change, the stem of the verb (the present) is identical in pronunciation for all four parts.

Drafting Skill

Verbs

Student answers (principal parts) should be in columns. Sentences will vary but should relate to decision-making.

1. panic; (is) panicking; panicked; (have) panicked
2. tarry; (is) tarrying; tarried; (have) tarried
3. debate; (is) debating; debated; (have) debated
4. worry; (is) worrying; worried; (have) worried
5. plan; (is) planning; planned; (have) planned
6. mimic; (is) mimicking; mimicked; (have) mimicked
7. stir; (is) stirring; stirred; (have) stirred
8. vote; (is) voting; voted (have) voted

Teaching Strategies

Teaching Tip: Irregular Verbs

Some students may tend to regard this group of irregular verbs as the simplest since the principal parts display three identical forms. Remind them that the relatively few verbs in this list are sources of numerous errors, particularly when students mistakenly add -ed to the past participle.

Individualizing Instruction

LD Students   Model how to use the verb charts to select the correct verb form for the first three sentences in Exercise A. Then have students work in pairs to complete the exercise. For Exercise B, ask advanced students to help LD Students correct the sentences.

Writing Theme
Moments of Decision

Regular Verbs

Most verbs in the English language are regular. The past and past participle of all regular verbs are formed by adding the ending -*d* or -*ed* to the present. However, the spelling of the present form of some regular verbs is changed before adding -*ing* or -*ed*. Study such spelling changes in the chart below.

Present	Present Participle	Past	Past Participle
smile	(is) smiling	smiled	(have) smiled
drop	(is) dropping	dropped	(have) dropped
carry	(is) carrying	carried	(have) carried
picnic	(is) picnicking	picnicked	(have) picnicked
cruise	(is) cruising	cruised	(have) cruised
hope	(is) hoping	hoped	(have) hoped

Practice Your Skills

DRAFTING SKILL

Verbs   Make four columns, each headed with the name of a principal part, and write the principal parts of each verb below. Then use each verb in a sentence that relates to making a decision.

1. panic	2. tarry	3. debate	4. worry
5. plan	6. mimic	7. stir	8. vote

Irregular Verbs

The past and past participle forms of irregular verbs are not formed by adding -*d* or -*ed* to the present. The irregular forms of each of these verbs can be found in a dictionary entry for the present form of the verb. You may decide to memorize these forms, however, since irregular verbs occur frequently in reading and writing. Memorizing will be easier if you divide the verbs into the following five groups.

Group 1   The present, past, and past participles of the first group of irregular verbs have the same form.

Present	Present Participle	Past	Past Participle
burst	(is) bursting	burst	(have) burst
cost	(is) costing	cost	(have) cost
cut	(is) cutting	cut	(have) cut
hit	(is) hitting	hit	(have) hit
hurt	(is) hurting	hurt	(have) hurt
set	(is) setting	set	(have) set
shut	(is) shutting	shut	(have) shut

632 Grammar Handbook

Group 2 The past and past participle of each verb in this group are spelled alike. Notice that *get* has a second past participle form, *gotten*. In American speech and writing, *gotten* is the preferred form.

Present	Present Participle	Past	Past Participle
bring	(is) bringing	brought	(have) brought
catch	(is) catching	caught	(have) caught
fight	(is) fighting	fought	(have) fought
flee	(is) fleeing	fled	(have) fled
fling	(is) flinging	flung	(have) flung
get	(is) getting	got	(have) got *or* gotten
lead	(is) leading	led	(have) led
lend	(is) lending	lent	(have) lent
lose	(is) losing	lost	(have) lost
say	(is) saying	said	(have) said
shine	(is) shining	shone	(have) shone
sit	(is) sitting	sat	(have) sat
sting	(is) stinging	stung	(have) stung
swing	(is) swinging	swung	(have) swung
teach	(is) teaching	taught	(have) taught

Practice Your Skills

A. CONCEPT CHECK

Verbs Write the past or past participle form of the verb indicated in parentheses.

1. Louis Braille (bring) the gift of sight to many blind people.
2. At age three, a serious accident (cost) Louis his eyesight.
3. Later, while at the National Institute for the Blind in Paris, Louis learned of a dot code punched on cardboard that (lend) itself to use by the blind.
4. Captain Charles Barbier, a French military officer, had (teach) his soldiers to use such a dot code to send messages at night.
5. The idea (burst) on young Braille: the blind might be able to use a raised dot system to read by touch.
6. In 1829 Braille's own dot system (catch) the world's attention.
7. A light had suddenly (shine) in the darkness; the invention of braille provided hope for blind people everywhere.
8. Later in life, Braille adapted the code for musical notation; the sightless would no longer be (shut) out of the world of music.
9. Braille's inventiveness has since (lead) to the use of the dot system in mathematics, science, and computer technology.
10. Recently, medical science has (set) new standards in combating diseases of the eye.

Concept Check
Verbs
1. brought
2. cost
3. lent
4. taught
5. burst
6. caught
7. shone
8. shut
9. led
10. set

Additional Resources
- Tests and Assessment, Pretests, pp. 20–22
- Grammar and Usage Practice Book, p. 39

Writing Theme
Overcoming Handicaps

Verb Usage **633**

11. lost
12. hurt
13. fought
14. cut
15. brought

B. Proofreading Skill

Verbs

Errors are underlined on page.

Martine Kempf brought new mobility to many handicapped people with her creation of voice-activated computer technology in the early 1980's. At that time Kempf set up her Katalavox computer program on a home computer. She quickly adapted it to control wheelchairs, and she taught some armless teenagers to direct the chairs by using their voices. She was inspired to do this by her father, who had fought the effects of polio and developed a business customizing automobiles for himself and other people with mobility problems.

Doctors have found that Kempf's Katalavox also lends itself to microsurgery. Using the voice-activated computer controller, surgeons can move their delicate magnifying equipment simply by saying where they need it. With this procedure, they do not lose precious time swinging the lenses around manually.

11. Before, diabetics with retinopathy often (lose) their sight.
12. This disease often (hurt) the retina of the eye, and sometimes caused the retina to detach from the rest of the eye.
13. For many years doctors (fight) retinopathy with surgery.
14. Surgeons (cut) into the wall of the eye to reattach the retina.
15. By the early 1960's, the advent of the laser (bring) eye surgery to new levels of safety and success.

B. PROOFREADING SKILL

Verbs Rewrite the following paragraphs, correcting <u>errors</u> in spelling, punctuation, capitalization, and verb forms.

Martine Kempf <u>brang</u> new mobility to many <u>handicaped</u> people with her creation of voice-activated computer technology in the early 1980's, at that time Kempf set up her Katalavox computer program on a home computer. She <u>quikly</u> adapted it to control wheelchairs, and she <u>teached</u> some armless teenagers to direct the chairs by using their voices. She was inspired to do this by her father, who had fought the <u>efects</u> of polio and had developed a <u>busness</u> customizing automobiles for <u>hisself</u> and other people with mobility problems.

Doctors have found that Kempf's Katalavox also <u>lend</u> itself to microsurgery. Using the voice-activated computer <u>controler</u>. <u>Surgoens</u> can move their delicate magnifying equipment simply by saying where they need it. With this procedure, they do not lose <u>prescious</u> time swinging the lenses around manually.

Group 3 To the past forms of the verbs in this group, add *-n* or *-en* to form the past participle. The one exception is the past participle of *bear*. Note also spelling changes in the past participle forms of *bite, swear, tear,* and *wear.*

Present	Present Participle	Past	Past Participle
bear	(is) bearing	bore	(have) borne
beat	(is) beating	beat	(have) beaten
bite	(is) biting	bit	(have) bitten
break	(is) breaking	broke	(have) broken
choose	(is) choosing	chose	(have) chosen
freeze	(is) freezing	froze	(have) frozen
speak	(is) speaking	spoke	(have) spoken
steal	(is) stealing	stole	(have) stolen
swear	(is) swearing	swore	(have) sworn
tear	(is) tearing	tore	(have) torn
wear	(is) wearing	wore	(have) worn

Practice Your Skills

A. CONCEPT CHECK

Verbs Write the past or the past participle form of the verb in parentheses.

1. For many centuries, troubadors and poets have (speak) of the legends of the Trojan War and the adventures of Odysseus.
2. In this epic poem, the great bard Homer (speak) of glory, danger, and pride.
3. In the *Iliad,* Aphrodite, the Greek goddess of love, had (swear) to the Trojan prince Paris that she would grant him whatever he wished if he judged her the fairest of the immortals.
4. Granted his wish, Paris had (choose) to marry the most beautiful mortal woman on earth.
5. When visiting the Greek city of Sparta, Paris met and fell in love with Helen, the wife of King Menelaus; and the prince (steal) away with her to Troy.
6. Menelaus (tear) his hair in grief when he discovered that his wife had left.
7. Paris had not only insulted him gravely, but he had also (break) the divinely sanctioned laws of hospitality.
8. Menelaus's brother, King Agamemnon of Mycenae, (raise) a great army to avenge the insult.
9. Two of the heroes of this army, Achilles and Ajax, (wear) glorious armor into battle against Troy.
10. After nearly ten years of fighting, the Greeks had won several battles, but the Trojans had (beat) them in others.
11. Complaining that they had nearly (freeze) to death in their tents, the Greeks eventually began to criticize their leaders.
12. Furthermore, the Greeks were upset because the great hero Achilles had (choose) to withdraw from battle.
13. The gods, however, (swear) to Achilles that he would achieve undying fame if he remained with the Greeks to fight at Troy.
14. Achilles finally returned to battle, and before long he had (beat) the Trojan champion Hector in a fierce contest.
15. After that confrontation, the clever hero Odysseus (speak) in council and recommended that the Greeks deceive the Trojans by pretending to sail home.
16. The Greeks left behind a wooden horse, which the Trojans foolishly (bear) into their city as an offering to the gods.
17. Then Odysseus and his troops, hiding inside the horse, suddenly (break) out and attacked the Trojan soldiers.
18. After they had (tear) open the gates of Troy, the Greeks proceeded to destroy the city of their enemies.

A. Concept Check
Verbs
1. spoken
2. spoke
3. sworn
4. chosen
5. stole
6. tore
7. broken
8. raised
9. wore
10. beaten
11. frozen
12. chosen
13. swore
14. beaten
15. spoke
16. bore
17. broke
18. torn

Verb Usage   **635**

B. Proofreading Skill

Verbs

Errors are underlined on page.

After the Trojan War, the hero Odysseus and his companions chose to return to their native Ithaca. Homer's *Odyssey* recounts how two of the gods, Poseidon and Helios, swore that they hated Odysseus. The sea god Poseidon was angry because Odysseus had beaten Poseidon's son, the man-eating monster Cyclops. The sun god Helios became furious when Odysseus' men broke their leader's command. The sailors stole the sun god's special oxen and then cooked and ate them. After Helios had destroyed the hero's companions in a storm, Odysseus was borne on the waves, all alone, clinging to a single spar. This spar, which had been torn from his sinking ship, probably saved Odysseus' life. When he finally returned to Ithaca ten years after the end of the Trojan War, Odysseus prudently wore a disguise. When he discovered that some insolent young men in Ithaca had been courting his wife, Penelope, and were hoping to depose him from power, he bit his tongue to keep from divulging his identity and spoiling his revenge. By his own wits and with the aid of his son Telemachus, however, Odysseus froze the suitors in their tracks; his glorious homecoming has been spoken of for thousands of years.

C. Application In Writing

Myth

Answers will vary but should include at least four of the verbs from the Group 3 list on page 634.

---

19. The sudden surprise had (freeze) many Trojans in fear, and they could not halt the attacking Greeks.
20. Helen, who had been (steal) away by Paris so many years before, returned to Greece and Menelaus.

B. PROOFREADING SKILL

Verbs Rewrite the following summary of Homer's epic poem, the *Odyssey*. Correct all <u>errors</u> in spelling, punctuation, capitalization, and verb forms.

After the Trojan <u>War. The</u> hero Odysseus and his companions chose to return to their native Ithaca. Homer's *Odyssey* recounts how two of the <u>gods</u> Poseidon and Helios <u>sweared</u> that they hated Odysseus. The sea god <u>poseidon</u> was angry because Odysseus had <u>beat</u> Poseidon's son, the man-eating monster Cyclops. The <u>sun</u> god Helios became furious when Odysseus' men <u>breaked</u> their leader's command. The sailors <u>stealed</u> the sun god's special oxen and then cooked and ate them. After Helios had destroyed the <u>heroes</u> companions in a <u>storm</u> Odysseus was borne on the waves, all alone, clinging to a single spar.

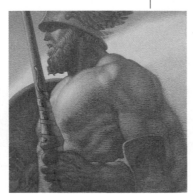

This spar, which had been <u>tore</u> from his sinking ship, probably saved Odysseus <u>life</u>. When he finally returned to Ithaca ten years after the end of the Trojan War, Odysseus prudently wore a disguise. When he discovered that some insolent young men in <u>ithaca</u> had been courting his wife, Penelope, and were hoping to depose him from <u>power.</u> <u>He</u> bit his tongue to keep from divulging his identity and spoiling his revenge. By his own wits and with the aid of his son Telemachus, however, Odysseus <u>freezed</u> the suitors in their tracks; his glorious homecoming has been <u>spoke</u> of for thousands of years.

C. APPLICATION IN WRITING

Myth The purpose of many ancient myths was to explain the origins of natural phenomena. For example, according to the myth of Phaëthon, the deserts of the world were formed when the sun god's mortal son, Phaëthon, took the reins of his father's fiery chariot and drove too close to the earth. Write your own myth, using either imaginary characters or ones from ancient mythology. In your myth, explain the origin of some natural phenomenon, such as bees, thistles, or pebbles at the bottoms of streams. Use at least four of the verbs from the Group 3 list on page 634.

Group 4 In this group of irregular verbs, the vowel *i* in the present changes to *a* in the past and *u* in the past participle. Notice the two past forms of *spring. Sprang* is the preferred form.

Present	Present Participle	Past	Past Participle
begin	(is) beginning	began	(have) begun
drink	(is) drinking	drank	(have) drunk
ring	(is) ringing	rang	(have) rung
shrink	(is) shrinking	shrank	(have) shrunk
sing	(is) singing	sang	(have) sung
sink	(is) sinking	sank	(have) sunk
spring	(is) springing	sprang *or* sprung	(have) sprung
swim	(is) swimming	swam	(have) swum

Practice Your Skills

A. CONCEPT CHECK

Verbs Write the past or the past participle form of the verb in parentheses to complete each sentence below. Then write the name of the principal part.

1. Pachio Lopez, a resident of San Ignacio Lagoon, had (begin) to worry.
2. The grey whales were late, and with each day's delay his hopes (sink) a little more.
3. As long as he could remember, each January they had come, had (swim), and had borne their young here in Baja, California.
4. Last year, one (swim) so close that Pachio could touch it.
5. He also recalled with sadness that the number that had come last year had (shrink) noticeably.
6. As he mused, the lonely cries of the gulls (ring) out around him.
7. All morning long the bell on the buoy at the mouth of the bay had (ring) mournfully, adding to his gloom.
8. Pachio tried to shake off the sadness as he waved to Miguel, who had just (begin) to repair his panga, a twenty-foot motorboat.
9. It had (spring) a leak and was useless for fishing.
10. Fortunately, Miguel had acted quickly when it happened or the boat might have (sink).
11. Watching Miguel, Pachio (sing) to himself to raise his spirits.
12. Then he (drink) some steaming coffee to ward off the dampness.
13. Suddenly a welcome sight (spring) into view.
14. First a spout, and then the whales' blowing (begin).
15. Pachio beamed with joy when a cow (swim) right in front of him, showing off her calf.

Writing Theme
Aquatic Pastimes

Verb Usage   **637**

B. PROOFREADING SKILL

Verbs Rewrite the following passage, and correct errors in verb usage, spelling, punctuation, and capitalization.

On September 21, 1961, Antonio Abertondo begun an unprecedented feat. His challenge was to swim the English channel. Others before him had swam the twenty two miles from Dover to calais France; but he was going to accomplish a round trip, 44 miles, without rest. As he greased his body to protect himself from the icey water, the cry of a lonely gull rung out above him. his mind sprung back to a time a few years before when he swum 262 miles down the mississippi river.

The first half of his English Channel swim went well, and he made good time. When he reached shore, he paused only two minutes and drunk a hot bevrage. He plunged in for the return trip, but extreem weariness had began to take it's toll. Waves buffeted his face and stinged his eyes. He fought his way onward. After more than fourty three hours in the water and over a day since he had touched land, Abertondo stagered ashore and collapsed.

C. APPLICATION IN WRITING

A Historical Account Research one of the following water sports, and write a brief history telling when, where, and how the sport originated. Use at least three verbs from the Group 4 list on page 637.

jet skiing	scuba diving	snorkeling
surfing	water skiing	wind surfing

638 Grammar Handbook

Group 5 These verbs are grouped together because the past participle is formed from the present rather than the past form.

Present	Present Participle	Past	Past Participle
blow	(is) blowing	blew	(have) blown
come	(is) coming	came	(have) come
do	(is) doing	did	(have) done
draw	(is) drawing	drew	(have) drawn
drive	(is) driving	drove	(have) driven
eat	(is) eating	ate	(have) eaten
fall	(is) falling	fell	(have) fallen
give	(is) giving	gave	(have) given
go	(is) going	went	(have) gone
grow	(is) growing	grew	(have) grown
know	(is) knowing	knew	(have) known
ride	(is) riding	rode	(have) ridden
rise	(is) rising	rose	(have) risen
run	(is) running	ran	(have) run
see	(is) seeing	saw	(have) seen
shake	(is) shaking	shook	(have) shaken
slay	(is) slaying	slew	(have) slain
take	(is) taking	took	(have) taken
throw	(is) throwing	threw	(have) thrown
write	(is) writing	wrote	(have) written

Practice Your Skills

A. CONCEPT CHECK

Verbs Write the past or the past participle form of the verb in parentheses.

1. In 1816 in the northeastern United States, the cold April weather (give) no hint of anything especially unusual.
2. By May, however, when the temperature still had not (rise), people became concerned.
3. The icy winds that had (blow) from January to April continued to lash the countryside.
4. A snowstorm in early June (drive) flocks of grazing sheep to take cover.
5. When twelve inches of snow (fall) in New York City on June 5, people suspected that something very strange was happening.
6. No crops (grow) that summer, as they had all been destroyed by the unusually cold weather.
7. On July and August mornings that year, people (shake) in temperatures that plunged to the low thirties.

Writing Theme
Volcanoes

Verb Usage **639**

8. wrote
9. drawn
10. known
11. come
12. seen
13. taken
14. thrown
15. did

B. Proofreading Skill

The Principal Parts of Verbs

Errors are underlined on page.

Another terribly destructive volcanic eruption took place on the Caribbean island of Martinique in 1902. On the morning of May 8, the residents of the beautiful port town of St. Pierre ate their breakfasts as usual. The calm was broken, however, when Mount Pelée erupted violently. Ironically, the volcano had given clear signals of an eruption for over a month.

Nevertheless, because of an important election scheduled for May 10 that year, the government had urged people to remain in St. Pierre; the governor himself had gone there to reassure them. The wife of the American consul, in fact, had written to her family in Boston, assuring them that her city was in no danger. When the volcano finally did its damage, a fiery cloud of superheated gases raced directly toward the city, six miles away. When they saw it coming, the inhabitants of St. Pierre ran for safety, but to no avail.

The disaster slew about 30,000 people. Although the zone of destruction was less than ten square miles, the eruption of Mount Pelée remains one of the greatest disasters in the annals of volcanic eruption.

8. Some scholars of the day (write) articles blaming the deceased Benjamin Franklin for the weird spell of weather.
9. According to their theories, lightning rods developed by Franklin had (draw) all the heat from the air, depriving the earth of summer!
10. If Franklin had been alive in 1816, he might actually have (know), or at least suspected, what was causing the phenomenon.
11. In 1784, Franklin had (come) to recognize a connection between volcanic eruptions and sudden changes in weather.
12. Franklin had (see) that volcanic dust could block out sunlight for months at a time.
13. In agreement, scientists now believe that the cause of the unusual weather in 1816 had (take) place the year before, in the faraway Dutch East Indies of the Pacific Ocean.
14. A huge volcanic eruption of Mount Tambora in that area had (throw) tremendous amounts of volcanic dust into the atmosphere, and that dust had encircled the earth blocking out the warmth of the sun.
15. The long-term damage that this eruption (do) was widespread, affecting European countries as well as the United States.

B. PROOFREADING SKILL

The Principal Parts of Verbs Rewrite the following passage, and correct errors in verb usage, spelling, punctuation, and capitalization.

Another terribly destructive volcanic eruption taken place on the Caribbean island of Martinique in 1902. On the morning of may 8, the residents of the beautiful port town of St. Pierre eaten their breakfasts as usual. The calm was broken, however. When Mount Pelée erupted violently. Ironically, the volcano had gave clear signals of an eruption for over a month. Nevertheless because of an important election scheduled for May 10 that year the government had urged people to remain in St. Pierre; the governor himself had went there to reassure them. The wife of the American consul, in fact, written to her family in Boston, assuring them that her city was in no danger. When the volcano finally done its damage, a fiery cloud of superheated gases raced directly toward the city, six miles away. When they saw it coming, the inhabitants of st. pierre ran for safety, but to no avail. The disaster slay about 30,000 people. Although the zone of destruction was less than ten square miles, the eruption of Mount Pelée remains one of the greatest disasters in the annals of volcanic eruption.

C. APPLICATION IN WRITING

A News Story Use reference sources to research the destruction of Pompeii by the eruption of Mount Vesuvius in A.D. 73. Then write a newspaper account of the destruction as if it had just happened. Use at least four verbs from the Group 5 list on page 639.

VERB TENSES

A verb has different forms to show when an action occurs. These forms are called **tenses.** Every verb has three *simple tenses*—the present tense, the past tense, and the future tense—as well as three *perfect tenses*—the present perfect, the past perfect, and the future perfect. As you study this part of the handbook, you will learn how to form the tenses and when to use them.

Verb Conjugation

A **conjugation** is a presentation of all the tenses of a verb. The conjugation of the regular verb *pull* appears below.

Principal Parts

Present	Present Participle	Past	Past Participle
pull	(is) pulling	pulled	(have) pulled

Simple Tenses

	Singular	Plural
Present Tense		
First Person	I pull	we pull
Second Person	you pull	you pull
Third Person	he, she, it pulls	they pull
Past Tense		
First Person	I pulled	we pulled
Second Person	you pulled	you pulled
Third Person	he, she, it pulled	they pulled
Future Tense (*will* or *shall* + the present form)		
First Person	I will (shall) pull	we will (shall) pull
Second Person	you will pull	you will pull
Third Person	he, she, it will pull	they will pull

Writing
TIP

Use proper verb tenses to show logical sequence in your writing.

Verb Usage   **641**

C. Application In Writing
A News Story
Answers will vary but should include at least four verbs from the Group 5 list on page 639.

Verb Tenses

Objectives

- To understand the forms of the three simple and the three perfect tenses of verbs
- To understand the uses of the different verb tenses
- To study special problems in the use of tenses
- To conjugate verbs using the present tense, the past tense, the future tense, and the perfect tenses
- To use tenses correctly

Teaching Strategies

Linking Grammar and Literature

From literature, select a variety of passages that have one or more tenses, or use the models below. Read the passages aloud, and ask students to discuss when the action took place from the point of view of the narrator. Students should tell you how they have distinguished the time frames in each passage. Point out that in most passages, time is indicated by the tense of the verbs.

> Suddenly the young girl began to play, and the whole room hung on the notes that she extracted from the keyboard. Off-pitch, metallic, horrible notes. The Oliveiras anxiously studied the faces of their visitors. The redheaded man remained utterly impassive. . . . The newly arrived lady made a wry face. The perfumed old lady seemed more tolerant and looked indulgently at the old piano case.
> It was a jury trial and the piano was the accused.
>
> —Anibal Monteiro Machado
> From ''The Piano''

(past tense)

Something strange I do not comprehend
Is this: I start to write a certain verse
But by the time that I come to its end
Another has been written that is worse
Or possibly better than the one I meant,
And certainly not the same, and differ-
ent.
I cannot understand it—I begin
A poem and then it changes as I write,

. . .

                —Merrill Moore
From ''Literature: The God, Its Ritual''
(present tense and present perfect
tense—passive voice)

 ## Individualizing Instruction

LD Students Review the principal parts of verbs with these students. Point out how the parts are used in each of the tenses. You may also want to go over the conjugation of the auxiliary verbs *be* and *have* to help students form the different tenses.

ESL Students Explain the rules for using each of these tenses. If possible, translate the tenses into each student's native language. Let the students compare the use of the tenses in their native language with the way in which the tenses are used in English. Emphasize that different languages use tenses in slightly different ways.

Personal Touch

If students seem overwhelmed by the conjugation chart, write the Turkish verb *sevmek* (meaning ''to love'') on the board, and explain that the full conjugation of this verb involves more than 1,900 different inflections.

Additional Resources
- Grammar and Usage Practice Book, p. 41

Perfect Tenses

Present Perfect Tense (*has* or *have* + the past participle)

First Person	I have pulled	we have pulled
Second Person	you have pulled	you have pulled
Third Person	he, she, it has pulled	they have pulled

Past Perfect Tense (*had* + the past participle)

First Person	I had pulled	we had pulled
Second Person	you had pulled	you had pulled
Third Person	he, she, it had pulled	they had pulled

Future Perfect Tense (*will have* or *shall have* + the past participle)

First Person	I will (shall) have pulled	we will (shall) have pulled
Second Person	you will have pulled	you will have pulled
Third Person	he, she, it will have pulled	they will have pulled

Using the Simple Tenses

Rules for forming and using the three simple tenses and the three perfect tenses are presented on the next several pages. Review these rules so that you use tense correctly in your writing.

The Present Tense Add *-s* or *-es* to the present—the first principal part—to form the third-person singular form of the present tense: he *wishes,* she *acts.* Use the unchanged present form for all other singular and plural forms of the present tense: I *wish,* you *act,* we *wish,* they *act.*

Use the present tense to express any of these actions: (1) a present action, (2) a regularly occurring action, or (3) a constant or generally true action.

Present Action	Although this apple *looks* ripe and juicy, it *tastes* quite sour.
Regular Action	The ticket office *opens* at nine each weekday morning.
Constant Action	Water *freezes* at zero degrees Celsius and thirty-two degrees Fahrenheit.

Use the **present historical tense** to express a past action as if it were happening now. This tense is also used frequently for writing about a piece of literature.

> General Pershing places a wreath on the tomb and says, "Lafayette, we are here."

> Juliet steps onto her balcony and proclaims her love to the night.

The Past Tense To form the past tense of a regular verb, add *-d* or *-ed* to the present: she *joked,* they *laughed,* they *pushed,* we *pulled.* The past tense of an irregular verb is the third principal part of the verb: it *sank,* I *swam.*

To express an action that began and ended in the past, use the past tense.

> In *Forgotten People,* George Sanchez *spoke* out against inadequate education for Mexican-American children.

The Future Tense To form the future tense, place the auxiliary verb *shall* or *will* before the present form of a verb: I *shall investigate,* you *will investigate,* they *will investigate.*

Use the future tense to express an action that will occur some time after this moment.

> We *shall visit* the ruins of Tikal.

> They *will tour* Guatemala City and the surrounding countryside before heading back to Mexico City.

Usage Note In formal writing many writers use the auxiliary verb *shall* for the first-person future and the auxiliary verb *will* for the second- and third-person future. In informal writing situations, however, *will* can be used with all subjects.

© DIGICON, INC.

Verb Usage **643**

ESL Students In some languages many common verbs, especially verbs of motion, regularly form the perfect tenses with an auxiliary form of the verb *be*. Stress to students that the perfect tenses in English verbs are always formed with the auxiliary verb *has* or *have*.

Teaching Tip: Past Perfect Verb Forms

Because of their function of establishing a sequential relationship between two past actions, past perfect verb forms are often used in complex sentences. One past action is expressed in the main clause, the other in the subordinate clause. Encourage students to use subordinate conjunctions such as *before, after,* and *although* to write complex sentences containing past perfect forms.

Additional Resources
- Grammar and Usage Practice Book, p. 42

You can also express a future action by using the **present tense** of a verb with an adverb or a group of words that indicates a future time.

> The awards dinner *starts* at 7:00 this evening. (The phrase *at 7:00 this evening* indicates a future time.)

Using the Perfect Tenses

Following are the rules for forming and using the **present perfect,** the **past perfect,** and the **future perfect** tenses.

The Present Perfect Tense To form the present perfect tense, place the auxiliary verb *has* or *have* before the past participle of a verb: she *has arrived,* we *have seen* her. Use the present perfect tense to express (1) an action completed at an indefinite time in the past or (2) an action that started in the past and continues at the present time.

> The commercial jet *has made* the world a smaller place. (action completed at an indefinite time)

> These swift planes *have carried* passengers and cargo since the 1950's. (action continuing into the present)

The Past Perfect Tense To form the past perfect tense, place the auxiliary verb *had* before the past participle of a verb: I *had shouted,* she *had heard.* Use the past perfect tense to express a past action that took place before another past action.

> Thomas Jefferson *had supported* the French Revolution until he heard of its excesses.

The Future Perfect Tense To form the future perfect tense, place the auxiliary verbs *shall have* or *will have* before the past participle of a verb. Use the future perfect tense to express a future action that will take place before another future action.

> The play *will have run* for six years when it closes next week.

Problems in Using Tenses

Study the following guidelines to avoid special problems related to the use of tenses.

Special Uses of the Past Perfect In some sentences, two verbs express actions that happened at different times: one action happened before the other. To express the action that happened first, use the past perfect tense. Use the simple past tense to express the other action.

Incorrect	In the 1970's, many airline pilots *reported* they *sighted* UFO's.
Correct	In the 1970's, many airline pilots *reported* they *had sighted* UFO's.

The incorrect sentence below tells about two past actions. The past action in the *if* clause occurred before the past action in the other clause. This error is corrected by omitting *would have* and using the past perfect of the verb in the *if* clause.

Incorrect	If the detectives *would have discovered* the fingerprints earlier, they might have apprehended the criminal responsible for the robbery sooner.
Correct	If the detectives *had discovered* the fingerprints earlier, they might have apprehended the criminal responsible for the robbery sooner.

Using *Having* with a Past Participle To show that one action was completed before another, use *having* with the past participle in a participial phrase.

Incorrect	*Completing* the application, Todd mailed it to the admissions office.
Correct	*Having completed* the application, Todd mailed it to the admissions office.

Using Present and Perfect Infinitives The present infinitive (*to sign*) and the perfect infinitive (*to have signed*) are used to express actions that take place at different times.

Use the present infinitive form to express an action that happens *after* another action.

Incorrect	The leaders of the two countries had hoped *to have signed* the treaty before the end of the year. (The perfect infinitive is incorrect. The action it is intended to express happened after the action expressed by *had hoped*.)
Correct	The leaders of the two countries had hoped *to sign* the treaty before the end of the year.

Use the perfect infinitive form to express an action that happens before another action.

> I am sorry *to have missed* your party last week. (The perfect infinitive is used correctly to express an action that happened *before* the action the verb *am* expresses.)

The moon has been a subject of study throughout the ages. Suggest that students use this topic as the subject of a research report, a science fiction story, or another type of writing.

A. Concept Check

Verb Tenses
1. have measured—Present Perfect
2. recorded—Past
3. use—Present
4. had honored—Past Perfect
5. will find—Future
6. has inspired—Present Perfect
7. had speculated—Past Perfect
8. observed—Past
9. had identified—Past Perfect
10. describe—Present
11. have written—Present Perfect
12. wrote—Past
13. challenged—Past
14. set—Past
15. watched—Past; orbited—Past
16. landed—Past
17. had become—Past Perfect
18. will seem—Future

Practice Your Skills

A. CONCEPT CHECK

Verb Tenses   Write the verbs in the following sentences. Remember to include any auxiliary verbs. Then identify the tense of each verb.

1. For most of recorded history, people have measured time according to the phases of the moon.
2. Native Americans recorded the times of harvests and hunts by designating "moons" as units of time.
3. Muslims and Jews still use the lunar calendar as the basis for religious holidays.
4. Before the time of the Romans, many ancient peoples, including the Egyptians, the Babylonians, and the Greeks, had honored the moon as a goddess.
5. In a dictionary, you will find an etymological link between the word *moon* and Old English words for *month* and *Monday*.
6. The moon has also inspired musical compositions, including a sonata by Beethoven and the popular song "Moon River."
7. For centuries, astronomers had speculated about the moon's shape, size, and motion.
8. In 1609, Galileo observed the moon's surface for the first time through a crude telescope.
9. Galileo had identified dark patches on the moon as "seas" before the invention of more powerful telescopes.
10. Today, scientists describe these "seas" as dry, rocky lowlands on the near side of the moon.
11. Many science fiction writers have written about imaginary space flights to the moon.
12. Jules Verne, the author of *Twenty Thousand Leagues Under the Sea*, also wrote a story called *From the Earth to the Moon*.
13. In the early 1960's, President Kennedy challenged the country to make the ancient dream of space travel a reality.
14. Kennedy set up the National Aeronautics and Space Administration to direct America's space program.
15. On Christmas Eve, 1968, as the whole world watched on television, the *Apollo 8* spacecraft with Frank Borman, William Anders, and James Lovell orbited the moon.
16. On July 20, 1969, Neil Armstrong and Buzz Aldrin of the *Apollo 11* crew landed on the moon.
17. President Kennedy's dream of reaching the moon had become a reality at last.
18. Perhaps this marvelous achievement will seem ordinary to scientists of the future.

19. By that point in time, however, missions such as *Apollo 8* and *Apollo 11* will have provided volumes of invaluable information.
20. After the successful completion of a mission to the planet Mars early in the next century, our body of knowledge about the entire solar system will have become quite impressive.

B. REVISION SKILL

Verb Tenses Revise the following paragraphs, correcting any errors in verb tenses to clarify the order of events. If the verb tense is correct, write *Correct*.

(1) Ideas are like a line of dominoes standing on end; their flow, or their toppling, underline{continue} until they reach an obstacle. (2) Such an obstacle stopped the flow of ideas for almost thirteen centuries. (3) Nicolaus Copernicus was the man who removed the obstacle and allows ideas to flow again.

(4) In the sixteenth century, Copernicus and others have become dissatisfied with the theory that Earth was the center of the universe. (5) Aristotle had devised this theory, and Ptolemy's models in the second century supports it. (6) For centuries this theory have helped philosophers and religious leaders to explain the importance of Earth and humanity in relation to the universe. (7) However, once astronomers learned to make more accurate observations, the theory no longer explains all observed phenomena.

(8) Copernicus looked for an alternative explanation. (9) He reads many works of ancient Greek writers and discovered that an alternative had already been proposed. (10) In fact, to this day, no one was sure why such early ideas were discarded. (11) Copernicus then made observations and performs many computations. (12) Gradually, he becomes convinced that the planets spin around the sun. (13) Had his friends not coaxed and nagged him, Copernicus might never have published his theory. (14) In fact, his pupil Georg Joachim Rhaticus undertook the task of having the manuscript printed. (15) The manuscript, *On the Revolutions of the Celestial Spheres,* starts the "Copernican Revolution" and unblocks a flow of ideas that will continue today.

C. APPLICATION IN WRITING

A Poem Write a poem comparing the stages in a person's life to the phases of the moon. Experiment with line breaks and elements of sound such as rhyme and alliteration. When you have finished, write the verbs that you used and the tenses of these verbs.

Verb Usage **647**

19. will have provided—Future Perfect
20. will have become—Future Perfect

B. Revision Skill
Verb Tenses
Errors are underlined on page.
1. Ideas are like a line of dominoes standing on end; their flow, or their toppling, continues until they reach an obstacle.
2. Correct
3. Nicolaus Copernicus was the man who removed the obstacle and allowed ideas to flow again.
4. In the sixteenth century, Copernicus and others had become dissatisfied with the theory that Earth was the center of the universe.
5. Aristotle had devised this theory, and Ptolemy's models in the second century supported it.
6. For centuries this theory had helped philosophers and religious leaders to explain the importance of Earth and humanity in relation to the universe.
7. However, once astronomers learned to make more accurate observations, the theory no longer explained all observed phenomena.
8. Correct
9. He read many works of ancient Greek writers and discovered that an alternative had already been proposed.
10. In fact, to this day, no one is sure why such early ideas were discarded.
11. Copernicus then made observations and performed many computations.
12. Gradually, he became convinced that the planets spin around the sun.
13. Correct
14. Correct
15. The manuscript, *On the Revolutions of the Celestial Spheres,* started the "Copernican Revolution" and unblocked a flow of ideas that continues today.

C. Application In Writing
A Poem
Answers will vary.

Progressive and Emphatic Verb Forms

Objectives

- To identify and form the progressive and emphatic forms of verbs
- To avoid improper shifts in tense and form of verbs
- **Writing** To use progressive and emphatic verb forms in original writing

Teaching Strategies

 Individualizing Instruction

ESL Students These students may require special help because in many languages there are no equivalents for English progressive and emphatic verb forms: A single present tense verb form conveys all these shades of meaning. If necessary, write the simple present, the present progressive, and the present emphatic forms of several common verbs on the board, and discuss their different meanings with these students.

Additional Resources
- Grammar and Usage Practice Book, p. 43

In the preceding section, you learned that every English verb has six basic tenses. In this section, you will study and use other special forms of a verb—six progressive forms and two emphatic forms.

Using the Progressive Forms

The **progressive forms** of a verb are used to express progressive, or ongoing, actions. As you can see in the examples below, the six progressive forms are constructed by combining simple and perfect tenses of *be* with the present participle of a verb.

> I *am pulling* the weeds. (present progressive)
>
> I *was pulling* the weeds. (past progressive)
>
> I *shall be pulling* the weeds. (future progressive)
>
> I *have been pulling* the weeds. (present perfect progressive)
>
> I *had been pulling* the weeds. (past perfect progressive)
>
> I *shall have been pulling* the weeds. (future perfect progressive)

The **present progressive** form should be used to express an ongoing action that is happening at the present time.

> Soccer *is becoming* a popular sport with high schools all over the country.

When used with an adverb or with a group of words that indicates a future time, the **present progressive** form can also express a future action.

> The flight from Denver *is arriving* in one hour.

The **past progressive** form should be used to express an ongoing action that occurred in the past.

> In the late 1800's, the women's rights movement *was gaining* momentum in the United States.

The **future progressive** form should be used to express an ongoing action that will take place in the future.

> Halley's comet *will be rushing* through the solar system for millennia.

The **present perfect progressive** form should be used to express an ongoing action that began in the past and is continuing in the present.

> The fate of the dinosaurs *has been puzzling* scientists for years.

The **past perfect progressive** form should be used to express an ongoing past action that is interrupted by another past action.

> Maria Martinez *had been making* pottery in the old pueblo style for many years before she received the American Ceramic Society Award in 1969.

The **future perfect progressive** form should be used to express an ongoing future action that will have taken place by a designated future time.

> By the time your great-grandchildren are adults, people *will have been exploring* other planets for decades.

Using the Emphatic Forms

The **emphatic forms** of the present tense and past tense lend force and emphasis to verbs. To form the **present emphatic,** place the auxiliary *do* or *does* before the present tense of the verb. To form the **past emphatic,** place the auxiliary *did* before the present tense.

Present	The ozone layer above the South Pole *seems* to be disintegrating.
Present Emphatic	The ozone layer above the South Pole *does seem* to be disintegrating.
Past	Phillis Wheatley, the first important African-American poet, *impressed* both British and American readers.
Past Emphatic	Phillis Wheatley, the first important African-American poet, *did impress* both British and American readers.

The present emphatic and past emphatic often appear in questions and negative statements. In these cases, emphasis is ordinarily not intended.

> A rain shower usually *does*n't *last* long in the tropics.

> *Did* Euclid *create* a form of geometry?

Writing
—TIP—
Use emphatic forms to add force to your writing.

Hold a brief discussion on the subject of how students might like to change the world in which they live. Encourage them to use those ideas for a future writing assignment.

A. Concept Check

Progressive and Emphatic Verbs
1. were wondering
2. did appear
3. did prevent
4. had been drafting
5. were envisioning
6. are recognizing
7. has been expanding
8. does promote
9. does seem
10. will be doing
11. will be joining
12. have been preparing
13. are abandoning
14. are creating
15. will have been affecting

Writing Theme
A Changing World

Practice Your Skills

A. CONCEPT CHECK

Progressive and Emphatic Verbs Rewrite each of the following sentences, adding the verb form named in parentheses.

1. In 1945, after the end of World War II, many European nations _____ how to pool their resources for more efficient trade and economic development. (*wonder*—Past Progressive)
2. In the early 1950's, in spite of national borders and loyalties, the desire for cooperation _____ strong. (*appear*—Past Emphatic)
3. Their different languages _____ not _____ these countries from entering negotiations. (*prevent*—Past Emphatic)
4. Two French statesmen, Robert Schuman and Jean Monnet, _____ plans for European economic development for some time. (*draft*—Past Perfect Progressive)
5. At the time, Schuman and Monnet _____ a united Europe. (*envision*—Past Progressive)
6. Although this dream may have seemed farfetched to some observers of the period, today economists and historians _____ these French leaders' farsightedness. (*recognize*—Present Progressive)
7. For nearly four decades, their original idea _____ first into the Common Market and then into the European Economic Community. (*expand*—Present Perfect Progressive)
8. The European Economic Community has been in existence since 1967; now as then, it _____ the gradual elimination of tariff and customs barriers. (*promote*—Present Emphatic)
9. The Community, currently numbering twelve European countries, _____ extremely successful. (*seems*—Present Emphatic)
10. Recently, nations such as Turkey have applied for membership, and no doubt more _____ the same. (*do*—Future Progressive)
11. The nations of the European Economic Community _____ together to create a single market of 325 million consumers. (*join*—Future Progressive)
12. To prepare for this change, many international companies _____ "Eurobrands" for their products. (*prepare*—Present Perfect Progressive)
13. Advertisers for these companies _____ national brands in an effort to create pan-European candy bars and sportswear. (*abandon*—Present Progressive)
14. These advertisers _____ messages that can be recognized throughout the European continent, regardless of language differences. (*create*—Present Progressive)
15. By the year 2000, the Community _____ the European way of life for almost a decade. (*affect*—Future Perfect Progressive)

B. DRAFTING SKILL

Progressive and Emphatic Verbs   Many areas of the world, such as Europe and Africa, have seen ongoing change in recent times. Write ten sentences using the verb forms indicated below to describe some of these changes.

1. expect (future progressive)
2. count (present progressive)
3. study (present perfect progressive)
4. watch (past perfect progressive)
5. live (future perfect progressive)
6. carry (past perfect progressive)
7. plan (past progressive)
8. report (past emphatic)
9. hope (present progressive)
10. know (present emphatic)

Improper Shifts in Tense and Form

Use the same tense to express two or more actions that occur at the same time.

Avoid a shift in tenses within a sentence or between consecutive sentences, except when a shift is needed to make the meaning clear. In most compound sentences and in sentences with a compound predicate, be sure that all the verbs are in the same tense.

Incorrect	Hamlet *feigns* insanity but *did* not *deceive* his father's murderer.
Correct	Hamlet *feigns* insanity but *does* not *deceive* his father's murderer.
Incorrect	Maria Cadilla de Martinez *worked* to preserve the literary and cultural traditions of Puerto Rico, and she *receives* many awards for her achievements.
Correct	Maria Cadilla de Martinez *worked* to preserve the literary and cultural traditions of Puerto Rico, and she *received* many awards for her achievements.

Sometimes a shift in tense is necessary to show a logical sequence of actions or the relationship of one action to another.

The Beatles *had performed* (past perfect) in small German clubs before they *rocketed* (past) to international fame.

By the time our team *wins* (present) a world championship, the Ice Age *will have returned* (future perfect).

Writing
—TIP—

Have a good reason for each change in tense you make. Be sure your reader can follow the change.

B. Drafting Skill
Progressive and Emphatic Verbs
Answers will vary but should contain the elements shown below.
1. will be expecting
2. am/is/are counting
3. has/have been studying
4. had been watching
5. will have been living
6. had been carrying
7. was/were planning
8. did report
9. am/is/are hoping
10. do/does know

Teaching Strategies

Linking Grammar and Writing

Students may not know when to use a shift in tense to make the meaning of a sentence clear. Choose various examples expressing a shift in tense, and discuss why the tense changes are necessary. You may want to use the literary model by Merrill Moore on page 642.

Additional Resources
- Grammar and Usage Practice Book, p. 44

A. Concept Check

Tenses
1. did decree—Past Emphatic; ran—Past
2. have desired—Present Perfect; fail—Present; flies—Present; blow—Present
3. had come—Past Perfect; had been endured—Past Perfect (Passive Voice); told—Past
4. sought—Past
5. shall go—Future; shall fly—Future
6. shall find—Future; will seek—Future (understood)

B. Revision Skill

Shifts in Verb Tense and Form
1. In August 1909, paleontologist Earl Douglass found eight tailbones of a brontosaurus that had died in the arid hills of eastern Utah.
2. Correct
3. People who visit this interesting site today begin their tour in a skylit building that surrounds the quarry, the Dinosaur National Monument Visitor Center.

Writing Theme
Destinations

Practice Your Skills

A. CONCEPT CHECK

Tenses   Write each underlined verb in the following lines of poetry. Then identify its tense.

1. In Xanadu <u>did</u> Kubla Khan a stately pleasure dome <u>decree</u>
   Where Alph, the sacred river <u>ran</u>
      through caverns measureless to man
   Down to a sunless sea.   **Samuel Taylor Coleridge**

2. I <u>have desired</u> to go
   Where springs not <u>fail</u>,
   To fields where <u>flies</u> no sharp and sided hail
   And a few lilies <u>blow</u>.   **Gerard Manley Hopkins**

3. The first Day's Night <u>had come</u>—
   And, grateful that a thing
   So terrible <u>had been endured</u>,
   I <u>told</u> my soul to sing.   **Emily Dickinson**

4. O Captain! My Captain! our fearful trip is done,
   The ship has weather'd every rack, the prize we
      <u>sought</u> is won.   **Walt Whitman**

5. Carriages without horses <u>shall go</u>,
   And accidents fill the world with woe.
   Around the world thoughts <u>shall fly</u>
   In the twinkling of an eye.   **Martha "Mother" Shipton**

6. Shall I find comfort, travel-sore and weak?
      Of labour you <u>shall find</u> the sum.
   Will there be beds for me and all who <u>seek</u>?
      Yea, beds for all who come.   **Christina Rossetti**

B. REVISION SKILL

Shifts in Verb Tense and Form   Rewrite each sentence to correct any error in the use of verb tenses. If the sentence is correct, write *Correct*.

1. In August 1909, paleontologist Earl Douglass found eight tailbones of a brontosaurus that died in the arid hills of eastern Utah.
2. Since then, archaeologists have exhumed thousands of bones from the area and reconstructed entire dinosaur skeletons from them.
3. People who visit this interesting site today begin their tour in a skylit building that surrounded the quarry, the Dinosaur National Monument Visitor Center.

4. Many people end their visit there, but the entire monument covered a 320-square-mile area.
5. The triangle-shaped area, which includes two rivers and a considerable number of canyons, cliffs, valleys, ridges, and buttes, is best traversed by bicycle.
6. From a bicycle, visitors not only gain an unparalleled perspective on the monument's wildlife and foliage, but they will also get an excellent workout on its varied terrain.
7. Cyclists riding on thin tires may prefer the paved, thirty-one-mile ride from Monument Headquarters up to Harper's Corner Overlook, with views of a hundred miles and more most of the way.
8. Some mountain bike riders take the steep Echo Park route from Harper's Corner that wound around in the canyons for thirteen miles.
9. The dinosaurs represented in this park actually lived millions of years ago.
10. Now, however, bicycling explorers can wander the cliffs and canyons and visualize how those dinosaurs roam the arid countryside.

C. PROOFREADING SKILL

Verb Tenses and Forms   Rewrite the following paragraphs, correcting errors in verb usage, capitalization, punctuation, and spelling.

The destination of the lowly hedgehog is often, simply, the other side of the road. Until recently, however, hedgehogs in england, were loseing the battel of the roadways. For quite some time. Cars, trucks, and buses had been killing 100,000 of the spiny creatures each year, thousands more have been crippled by fast-moving moter vehicles. often the injured hedgehogs managed to drag themselves from the roads into the woods genrally, however, after a few days, the animals die of there injuries.

Things were looking less than hopeful for the prickly hedgehogs. Then along comes Sue and Les Stocker. Witnessing the slaughter on the highways over the years, the Stockers had long wanted to have done something about it. Eventually they did do something. They opened St. Tigglywinkle's, a hospital for hedgehogs. Most of the patients at St. Tigglywinkle's has been hurt in highway accidents. A few have lost scrapes with dogs and cats. One patient might never have saw the inside of the hedgehog hospital. If it would have stayed out of the rhino cage at the zoo. Not surprisingly, one of the rhinos stepped on the careless creature.

Verb Usage   **653**

4. Many people end their visit there, but the entire monument covers a 320-square-mile area.
5. Correct
6. From a bicycle, visitors not only gain an unparalleled perspective on the monument's wildlife and foliage, but they also get an excellent workout on its varied terrain.
7. Correct
8. Some mountain bike riders take the steep Echo Park route from Harper's Corner that winds around in the canyons for thirteen miles.
9. Correct
10. Now, however, bicycling explorers can wander the cliffs and canyons and visualize how those dinosaurs roamed the arid countryside.

C. Proofreading Skill

Verb Tenses and Forms
Errors are underlined on page.
The destination of the lowly hedgehog is often simply the other side of the road. Until recently, however, hedgehogs in England were losing the battle of the roadways. For quite some time, cars, trucks, and buses had been killing 100,000 of the spiny creatures each year. Thousands more have been crippled by fast-moving motor vehicles. Often the injured hedgehogs manage to drag themselves from the roads into the woods. Generally, however, after a few days, the animals die of their injuries.

Things were looking less than hopeful for the prickly hedgehogs. Then along came Sue and Les Stocker. Having witnessed the slaughter on the highways over the years, the Stockers had long wanted to do something about it. Eventually they did do something. They opened St. Tigglywinkle's, a hospital for hedgehogs. Most of the patients at St. Tigglywinkle's have been hurt in highway accidents. A few have lost scrapes with dogs and cats. One patient might never have seen the inside of the hedgehog hospital if it had stayed out of the rhinoceros cage at the zoo. Not surprisingly, one of the rhinos stepped on the careless creature.

You may wish to use the following Checkpoint exercises as an informal evaluation of student mastery of principal parts, correct verb forms, verb tenses, and progressive and emphatic verb forms.

WRITING THEME Australia

A.

Student answers should be in columns.
1. sits—Present
2. beginning—Present Participle
3. lived—Past Participle
4. comes—Present
5. set—Present
6. chosen—Past Participle
7. led—Past
8. taught—Past
9. wore–Past
10. slew—Past
11. ate—Past
12. cost—Past
13. sprang—Past
14. seeking—Present Participle
15. drawing—Present Participle
16. spring—Present
17. caught—Past Participle
18. becoming—Present Participle

Writing Theme
Australia

CHECK ✔ POINT
PAGES 631–653

A. On a piece of paper, write four column headings with the names of the principal parts of verbs: *Present, Present Participle, Past,* and *Past Participle*. Write each of the italicized verbs below in the appropriate column.

1. Australia is the world's only island continent, and it *sits* between the Indian and Pacific oceans.
2. Scientists estimate that people were *beginning* to settle there forty thousand years ago.
3. Aborigines had *lived* in Australia long before the first Europeans set foot on the continent.
4. The word aborigine *comes* from a Latin phrase meaning "from the beginning."
5. Now, as before, Australian Aborigines *set* great value on family relationships.
6. For example, before they were influenced by European customs, Aborigines had *chosen* to live in tribal groups that were joined by marriage ties.
7. Although the tribes had no formal government, tribal elders *led* their people in matters of law and custom.
8. The elders *taught* the people the importance of cooperation in hunting and food collecting.
9. Because of the continent's warm climate, ancient Aborigines *wore* little clothing.
10. For food, Aborigines *slew* large sea animals with harpoons and land animals with boomerangs.
11. Scientists speculate that Aborigines also *ate* shellfish, fruits, vegetables, and turtle eggs.
12. The task of finding sufficient food and shelter probably *cost* the Aborigines much effort.
13. Gradually, the art of making stone tools *sprang* up among the tribes.
14. Before they moved to more modern types of housing, Aborigines had been *seeking* shelter in caves for decades.
15. Recently, the designs drawn by Aborigines on cave walls have been *drawing* attention.
16. Even after tens of thousands of years, freshness and vitality still *spring* forth from this cave art.
17. In recent years, the beauty and power of these paintings have *caught* the eye of the international art world.
18. Now, Aboriginal art is *becoming* better known in countries throughout the world.

19. At the same time, some Aborigines *have been taking* a public stand to promote interest in Aboriginal history.
20. They *speak* to others about the richness and dignity of the Aboriginal past.

B. Write the correct form of the two verbs in parentheses.

1. By the eighteenth century, the modern history of Australia had (began, <u>begun</u>).
2. By then, Portuguese, Spanish, and Dutch explorers had already (<u>taken</u>, took) their ships through the strait between New Guinea and Australia.
3. None of these sailors, however, knew that the land they had (saw, <u>seen</u>) was a huge continent.
4. In 1770, the British naval captain James Cook (<u>came</u>, come) to Australia's fertile east coast and claimed the region for Great Britain.
5. It was not until 1788, however, that British ships actually (brang, <u>brought</u>) the first settlers to the new land.
6. Until the American colonies (<u>rose</u>, risen) in rebellion against the British in 1776, England had been shipping many of its convicts to America.
7. People (<u>knew</u>, known) this policy as "transportation," and it had helped to relieve overcrowding in British jails.
8. Therefore, the British needed to find a new place to ship their convicts once America had declared its independence and (broke, <u>broken</u>) its ties with England.
9. The British government finally (<u>hit</u>, hitted) upon the idea of a convict settlement in Australia.
10. In May 1787, Captain Arthur Phillip (<u>set</u>, sat) out from England with a convoy of eleven ships.
11. These vessels (<u>bore</u>, borne) about 470 male and 160 female convicts, as well as 200 British guards.
12. Under the severe laws of eighteenth-century England, some people were prisoners simply because they had (stole, <u>stolen</u>) a chicken or a few loaves of bread.
13. By the end of January 1788, all of Phillip's ships had (sail, <u>sailed</u>) into Botany Bay, near what is now Sydney.
14. In his book *The Fatal Shore,* Australian Robert Hughes (<u>wrote</u>, written) eloquently of the early settlers' hardships in trying to establish homes in the new land.
15. In 1988, two hundred years after its unique beginning, Australia proudly held its bicentennial, and bells (<u>rang</u>, rung) out in celebration.

Verb Usage   **655**

C.
1. will speak
2. broke
3. have grown
4. will have seen
5. have known
6. hit
7. ride
8. have borne
9. will eat
10. has swung

D.
1. will be seeing
2. has been growing
3. are bringing
4. was leading
5. had been going; did regain
6. will be ending
7. will have been fighting
8. do take

C. Write the verb in parentheses in the tense indicated.

1. If questioned, most Australians (*speak*—Future) proudly about the distinctive animal life of their continent.
2. About 200 million years ago, the Australian landmass (*break*—Past) away from the other continents.
3. As a result, Australian animals (*grow*—Present Perfect) and developed differently from those in other areas of the world.
4. Within days of their arrival, most visitors (*see*—Future Perfect) examples of Australia's world-famous marsupials.
5. Australians (*know*—Present Perfect) for a long time that koalas, wallabies, wombats, and kangaroos draw tourists.
6. Observers are intrigued, for example, by the fact that kangaroos move in amazingly long hops when they (*hit*—Present) the ground and quickly spring forward.
7. Kangaroo babies are also an interesting sight as they (*ride*—Present) comfortably in a pouch on their mother's abdomen.
8. Not only are they an interesting sight, but these young that the kangaroos (*bear*—Present Perfect) are also well protected.
9. Another uniquely Australian animal, the koala, (*eat*—Future) up to two pounds of leaves from a eucalyptus tree on a typical day.
10. A visitor to Australia might look up into a tree in a hotel garden only to find that a cuddly looking koala (*swing*—Past Perfect) into a position directly above his or her head.

D. Write the form of the verb indicated in parentheses.

1. If you visit Australia in the summer, chances are that soon after your arrival you (*see*—Future Progressive) a cricket match.
2. Cricket, a game with British origins, (*grow*—Present Perfect Progressive) in popularity with the Australians for years.
3. Australian sports fans continually (*bring*—Present Progressive) one another up to date on the scores of the big matches.
4. Recently, Australia (*lead*—Past Progressive) New Zealand in an important test match.
5. When the game (*go*—Past Perfect Progressive) on for a while, however, New Zealand (*regain*—Past Emphatic) the lead with a surprise move.
6. "Doubtless," a visitor remarked to a fan, "this match (*end*—Future Progressive) in a few hours."
7. "Oh, no," chuckled the native. "By the time a cricket match is finally decided in Australia, normally the two sides (*fight*—Future Perfect Progressive) it out for several days!"
8. "My goodness," remarked the visitor, "you (*take*—Present Emphatic) your cricket seriously."

VOICE AND MOOD

Speakers and writers can choose from several tenses to express present, past, and future actions. They can also choose from among several progressive and emphatic forms. Verbs also have other more subtle forms that speakers and writers can use for special purposes.

Active and Passive Voice

The voice of a verb indicates whether its subject is the performer or the receiver of the action the verb expresses. When the subject is the performer of the action, the verb is in the **active voice.** When the subject is the receiver of the action, the verb is in the **passive voice.**

Active Voice	The quarterback *threw* the football past the rushing linemen. (The subject, *the quarterback,* is the performer of the action.
Passive Voice	The football *was thrown* past the rushing linemen by the quarterback. (The subject, *the football,* is the receiver of the action.)

The verb *threw* in the first sentence is transitive because it has a direct object. When this verb is changed to the passive voice, the direct object *football* becomes the subject. Only transitive verbs can be changed from active voice to passive voice.

Retained Objects   Verbs in the active voice can have indirect objects as well as direct objects. Either of the two objects can become the subject of the sentence when a transitive verb is changed from the active to the passive voice. The object that does not become the subject continues to function as an object and is called a **retained object**.

Active Voice	The citizens of France gave the American *people* the *Statue of Liberty*. (*People* is the indirect object; *Statue of Liberty* is the direct object.)
Passive	The American people were given the *Statue of Liberty* by the citizens of France. (*Statue of Liberty* is a retained object.)
Passive	The Statue of Liberty was given the American *people* by the citizens of France. (*People* is a retained object.)

If a retained object sounds overly formal, use a prepositional phrase instead: The Statue of Liberty was given *to the American people* by the citizens of France.

Verb Usage   **657**

Objectives

- To distinguish between the active and passive voice
- To identify retained objects
- To identify the indicative, imperative, and subjunctive moods of verbs
- **Writing** To use revision skills to recast passive sentences in active voice

Teaching Strategies

Speaking and Listening

You may wish to call on volunteers to read aloud the sample sentences for active and passive voice. Be sure that students are able to identify the performers and receivers of the action in each case. Also, be sure that students recognize the use of the past participle in the passive voice.

Stumbling Block

Students may have trouble distinguishing between a retained object and a prepositional phrase substituted for a retained object. Remind them that a prepositional phrase begins with a preposition such as *to, from, with,* followed by a noun. A retained object is a noun that is not preceded by a preposition. Although a sentence containing a retained object differs grammatically from a sentence in which a prepositional phrase is substituted for a retained object, there is no difference in meaning between such sentences.

Linking Grammar and Writing

You may want to reinforce this section by giving students some examples of the awkward use of active voice and passive voice in the same sentence, especially in parallel constructions; for example: The actors memorized their lines, participated in rehearsals, and were assisted by a talented director. Have students suggest ways to improve this sentence.

A. Concept Check

Active and Passive Voice.
1. was started—Passive; On the morning of April 3, 1860, a young horseback rider from St. Joseph, Missouri, started a journey of two thousand miles.
2. began—Active
3. marked—Active
4. was delivered—Passive
5. was reduced—Passive; The new system reduced the mail delivery period to ten days.
6. included—Active
7. rested—Active
8. were given—Passive: Employment recruiters gave candidates for the Pony Express posters that read: "Orphans preferred"!
9. has been exaggerated—Passive; Hollywood movies and television dramatically exaggerated the legend of the Pony Express.
10. was killed—Passive; ran—Active

Writing TIP

Active voice verbs are more natural, vigorous, and emphatic than passive verbs.

Writing Theme
American Legends

Using Voice in Writing

Active voice verbs are more forceful and direct than passive voice verbs. Avoid weak, wordy expressions by using the active voice rather than the passive voice. Also avoid using both active and passive voice verbs in the same sentence and in related consecutive sentences.

However, the passive voice need not always be avoided. It can be used effectively when a speaker or a writer wants to call attention to the person or thing receiving the action of a verb or does not know who or what is performing an action.

Arguments for and against nuclear power plants *are heard* frequently.

Many books and articles *have been written* on the subject.

Practice Your Skills

A. CONCEPT CHECK

Active and Passive Voice   Write the verbs in the following sentences. Identify each verb according to its voice: *Active* or *Passive*. Then, if a sentence can be made more direct by rewriting the verb in the active voice, do so.

1. On the morning of April 3, 1860, a journey of two thousand miles was started by a young horseback rider from St. Joseph, Missouri.
2. On the same day in Sacramento, California, another rider began a trip in the opposite direction.
3. These journeys marked the beginning of an American legend, the Pony Express.
4. Before the Pony Express, mail from coast to coast often was not delivered for six months.
5. The delivery period was reduced by the new system to ten days.
6. The Pony Express system included about eighty riders and between four hundred and five hundred horses.
7. Every twelve miles or so, the riders rested for two minutes at one of the relay stations.
8. Candidates for the Pony Express were given posters by employment recruiters that read: "Orphans preferred"!
9. The legend of the Pony Express has been dramatically exaggerated by Hollywood movies and television.
10. Despite the dangers, only one rider was actually killed, and his horse ran on to the next station with the mail intact!

B. REVISION SKILL

Using the Active Voice   Rewrite the following passage, using the active voice where possible.

> (1) On the night of September 13, 1814, the British bombardment of Fort McHenry was witnessed by a young American lawyer detained on a British ship. (2) The rockets that were fired by the British were the first ever seen in America. (3) These rockets had been designed by Sir William Congreve, the royal fire master, to streak across a range of two miles and to explode on impact. (4) The rockets were guided by polelike rudders; on impact, a shower of deadly shrapnel was thrown out by the rockets. (5) Francis Scott Key, the young lawyer, was inspired by the rockets' blazing trails to write the lines "And the rockets' red glare/The bombs bursting in air."

Understanding and Using Mood

Mood is a grammatical term that identifies the manner in which a verb expresses an idea. Verbs have three moods: the indicative, the imperative, and the subjunctive. Speakers and writers use the **indicative mood** most frequently. This mood states a fact or asks a question.

> *Did* Dorothea Dix *work* for proper treatment of the mentally ill in the mid-1800's?

> Environmental activists *work* to enact strict laws regulating pollution.

Use the **imperative mood** to give a command or make a request. Remember that verbs in this mood are always in the present tense and second person.

> *Participate* in conservation activities.
> Please *save* our planet from extinction.

Use the **subjunctive mood** (1) to express a wish or a condition that is contrary to fact or (2) to express a command or request after the word *that*.

> I wish I *were* a billionaire. (to express a wish)

> If I *were* that wealthy, I would help needy people. (to express a condition contrary to fact)

> I would order that the hungry *be* fed. (to express a command after the word *that*)

B. Revision Skill
Using the Active Voice
Answers will vary.
See typical answers below.
(1) On the night of September 13, 1814, a young American laywer detained on a British ship witnessed the bombardment of Fort McHenry. (2) The rockets that the British fired were the first ever seen in America. (3) Sir William Congreve, the royal fire master, had designed these rockets to streak across a range of two miles and to explode on impact. (4) Polelike rudders guided the rockets; on impact, the rockets threw out a shower of deadly shrapnel. (5) The rockets' blazing trails inspired Francis Scott Key, the young lawyer, to write the lines "And the rockets' red glare/The bombs bursting in air."

Speaking and Listening

Call on volunteers to read aloud the sample sentences and to make up sentences containing the same structure. Be sure that students "hear" the semantic patterns of contrary-to-fact conditions and indirect commands and requests. Also, be sure that students recognize the omission of the final -s in third-person singular subjunctive verbs.

 Individualizing Instruction

ESL Students Although the uses of the subjunctive are limited in English, this mood is used more commonly in many foreign languages. Have students offer examples for the uses of subjunctive verbs from their native language.

Additional Resources
- Grammar and Usage Practice Book, p. 45

WRITING THEME   Traditional Tales

Concept Check

Identifying Mood
1. Indicative
2. Subjunctive
3. Subjunctive
4. Indicative
5. Imperative
6. Subjunctive
7. Imperative, Imperative
8. Indicative
9. Subjunctive
10. Imperative, Imperative
11. Indicative

Writing Theme
Traditional Tales

The indicative and subjunctive moods have exactly the same forms, except for the following.

1. The *-s* is omitted from verbs in the third-person singular.

   Indicative   The President *holds* a news conference frequently.

   Subjunctive   The networks asked that the President *hold* a news conference next week.

2. In the present subjunctive mood, the form of the verb *to be* is always *be*.

   Present Subjunctive   The President suggested that the news conference *be* on Tuesday.

3. In the past subjunctive mood, the form of the verb *to be* is always *were*.

   Past Subjunctive   If TV time *were* available, the President would hold a news conference every week.

Practice Your Skills

CONCEPT CHECK

Identifying Mood   Read the following folk tale. Then write the mood of each italicized verb.

(1) Once upon a time, in a certain village in Nagaland, a wise old man *lived* with his grandson. (2) "If I *were* you," the old man advised his fellow villagers, "I would spend all my time cultivating rice." (3) Many of the villagers, however, suggested that the old man *be* ignored. (4) They therefore *continued* to gather wild yams and fruits, to hunt wild animals, and to fish in the streams. (5) One day, the grandson said to the old man, "Please *allow* me to hunt and fish in the forest." (6) The old man refused, insisting that the boy *accompany* him every day to the rice fields. (7) Soon afterward, the old man said to a friend of his grandson, "*Bring* me back a small fish, and *make* sure that it is still alive." (8) The boy *returned* later that day with a fish. (9) Then, to prove a point, the old man asked that his grandson *put* the fish into a wooden trough filled with water. (10) "Now, my boy, *catch* the fish and *give* it to me," he ordered. (11) However, no matter how hard he *tried,* the boy was unable to catch the fish.

660 Grammar Handbook

(12) The grandfather dryly told him, "If fishing *were* as easy as you had thought, you would grow up to be a rich man; let us tend to our rice cultivation instead!"

(13) When harvest time *came,* the old man and his grandson sold their plentiful harvest of rice for fish, game, yams, and fruits.

(14) "Do you *understand* now why rice is magic food?" the old man asked the child. (15) The villagers, impressed by the grandfather's wisdom, soon asked that he *consent* to be their chief.

COMMONLY CONFUSED VERBS

The verb pairs *lie* and *lay, rise* and *raise,* and *sit* and *set* can be confusing because the spelling and the meanings of the verbs in each pair are similar. Learn to use these verbs correctly.

Lie and Lay

Lie and *lay* are two different words. Here are the principal parts.

Present	Present Participle	Past	Past Participle
lie	(is) lying	lay	(have) lain
lay	(is) laying	laid	(have) laid

The meaning of the intransitive verb *lie* is "to rest in a flat position." *Lie* never takes a direct object.

> The Great Barrier Reef *lies* off the northeast coast of Queensland, Australia.

> The remains of the *Titanic* had *lain* on the floor of the Atlantic undisturbed until 1986.

Usage Note   Do not mistake the verb *lie* for its homonym meaning "to tell an untruth." The principal parts of the homonym are *lie, lying, lied, lied.*

Lay is a transitive verb meaning "to place." Except when it is in the passive voice, it usually has a direct object.

Active Voice   A skillful worker can *lay* wall-to-wall carpeting in a short time.

Passive Voice   A carpet can be *laid* in a short time by a skillful worker.

Occasionally *lay* can be used as an intransitive verb.

> The hens *are laying* well this year.

Verb Usage   **661**

12. Subjunctive
13. Indicative
14. Indicative
15. Subjunctive

Commonly Confused Verbs

Objective

- To understand the correct uses of the commonly confused verb pairs *lie* and *lay, rise* and *raise,* and *sit* and *set*

 Individualizing Instruction

LD Students   These students may have difficulty completing exercise B. Allow them to do the exercise orally by using a tape recorder. They should read the passage aloud, correcting mistakes in the choice of verbs. Let them point out incorrect spelling, punctuation, and capitalization during a conference with you or with another student.

Additional Resources
- Grammar and Usage Practice Book, p. 46

Rise and Raise

Rise and *raise* are two different words. Here are their principal parts.

Present	Present Participle	Past	Past Participle
rise	(is) rising	rose	(have) risen
raise	(is) raising	raised	(have) raised

Rise is an intransitive verb meaning "to go upward." It never takes a direct object.

> Cream *rises* to the top of a container of milk that has not been homogenized.

> The water level of the world's oceans *rose* after the glaciers of the Ice Age melted.

The transitive verb *raise* means "to lift" or "to make something go up." *Raise* nearly always has a direct object; it does not have a direct object when it is in the passive voice.

Active Voice   The builders *will raise* the entire house and put a new foundation under it.

Passive Voice   The many flags in front of the United Nations headquarters *are raised* ceremoniously each day.

Sit and Set

Sit and *set* are two different words. Here are their principal parts.

Present	Present Participle	Past	Past Participle
sit	(is) sitting	sat	(have) sat
set	(is) setting	set	(have) set

The intransitive verb *sit* means "to occupy a seat." It usually does not take a direct object.

> Some airline passengers are so superstitious they *will* not *sit* in row 13.

> Queen Elizabeth II *sat* on the Stone of Scone during her coronation.

If *sit* is used to mean "position in a seat," it is transitive and can take a direct object.

> *Sit* the patient carefully in that chair.

> *Sit* the baby in the safety seat and strap her in.

Set is a transitive verb meaning "to place." It usually has a direct object.

> The Archbishop of Canterbury *set* the royal crown onto the new queen's head.

> Many science-fiction writers *have set* the action of their stories on distant planets.

In certain situations, *set* is intransitive, taking no object.

> The sun *sets* early in the winter.

Practice Your Skills

A. CONCEPT CHECK

Commonly Confused Verbs   Write the <u>correct verb form</u> of the two verbs in parentheses.

1. Deserts (<u>lie</u>, lay) across one seventh of the earth's land surface.
2. Daytime temperatures in a desert may (raise, <u>rise</u>) to over 120 degrees Fahrenheit.
3. Some plants, such as the saguaro cactus, can (<u>sit</u>, set) happily in the severe surroundings for a lifetime.
4. In fact, even with little water this plant can (raise, <u>rise</u>) to heights of fifty feet and live nearly two centuries.
5. The cactus (lies, <u>lays</u>) down a shallow, broad root system just beneath the surface of the soil.
6. This root network acts as a pump, rapidly absorbing rainwater and (<u>raising</u>, rising) the plant's water level.
7. Desert-dwelling people such as the Bedouins, however, usually (sit, <u>set</u>) their tents near an oasis.
8. They do not (rise, <u>raise</u>) crops but keep herds of animals.
9. Very sociable, they can often be seen (<u>sitting</u>, setting) in a village marketplace telling stories or reciting poems.
10. A few desert settlements, mostly mining areas, have (<u>laid</u>, lain) pipelines to get water, but this is difficult and costly.

B. PROOFREADING SKILL

Errors in Verb Usage   Proofread the following paragraphs for <u>errors</u> in verb usage, spelling, punctuation, and capitalization. Then rewrite the paragraphs correctly.

> Scientists had known for centuries that some plants <u>rise</u> their temperatures as they mature. Then, in 1937, A. W. H. van Herk <u>sat</u> forth the idea that the flowers warmed them-

Verb Usage   **663**

leasing a chemical that he called calorigen. Fifty years later, botanists in the United States announced that they had discovered the chemical.

The voodoo lily is one plant that exhibits this chemical "magic." It produces salicylic acid—part of the compound that composes aspirin—as part of its reproduction process. That aspirin substance lowers the temperature of the human body, but it raises the temperature of the beautiful voodoo lily by as much as twenty-five degrees Fahrenheit.

The voodoo lily blooms immediately after it manufactures the salicylic acid. Then the interaction of the sun with the acid creates heat, and four-and-a-half hours later the temperature of the lily has risen to its peak.

Biologist Ilya Raskin explains that the carrion beetles that pollinate the voodoo lily are attracted by the smell of the nitrogen compounds emitted as the lily's temperature rises. Once a beetle enters the lily's pollination chamber, it lies there as the lily goes through another warming phase. The beetle gathers sticky pollen on its feet, and then it moves to sit on the next lily and unwittingly deposit its reproductive contribution.

CHECK POINT
PAGES 657–664

You may wish to use the following Checkpoint exercises as an informal evaluation of student mastery of voice, mood, and form of verbs.

WRITING THEME   The Vikings

A.
Answers will vary. See suggested answers below.
1. More than a thousand years ago, the Vikings dominated present-day Scandinavia.
2. Historians have explained the word *viking* as a form of *Vik.* the name of a pirate center in southern Norway.
3. Other Europeans called the Scandinavians Norsemen or Northmen.
4. Although *to go a-viking* meant "to fight as a pirate," the Vikings did not center all of their activities around warlike pursuits.
5. Most Vikings favored farming.
6. Archaeologists have made a number of interesting discoveries about Viking customs.
7. A king or a chief ruled each Viking community.
8. The *skalds,* or royal poets, praised in song Viking gods and battles.
9. Viking tradition accorded women considerable freedom.
10. For example, Viking communities permitted married women to divorce their husbands whenever they wished.

Writing Theme
The Vikings

selves by releasing a chemical that he <u>calls</u> calorigen. Fifty years later, <u>B</u>otanists in the United States announced that they had discovered the chemical.

The voodoo lily is one plant that exhibits this chemical "magic." It produces salicylic acid—part of the compound that composes aspirin—as part of its reproduction process. That aspirin substance <u>lowered</u> the temperature of the human body, but it <u>rises</u> the temperature of the beautiful voodoo lily by as much as twenty-five degrees <u>Farenheit</u>.

The voodoo lily blooms immediately after it <u>manufactured</u> the salicylic acid. Then the interaction of the sun with the acid creates heat, and four-and-a-half hours later the temperature of the lily has <u>raised</u> to its peak.

Biologist Ilya Raskin explains that the carrion beetles that <u>polinate</u> the voodoo lily are attracted by the smell of the nitrogen compounds emitted as the <u>lilys</u> temperature rises. Once a beetle enters the lily's pollination chamber, it <u>lays</u> there as the lily goes through another warming phase. The beetle gathers sticky pollen on its feet, and then it moves to <u>set</u> on the next lily and unwittingly deposit its reproductive contribution.

CHECK POINT
PAGES 657–664

A. Rewrite the following sentences, changing the verbs from the passive voice to the active voice.

1. More than a thousand years ago, present-day Scandinavia was dominated by the Vikings.
2. The word *viking* has been explained by historians as a form of *Vik,* the name of a pirate center in southern Norway.
3. The Scandinavians were called Norsemen or Northmen by other Europeans.
4. Although *to go a-viking* meant "to fight as a pirate," not all of the Vikings' activities were centered around warlike activities.
5. The occupation that was favored by most Vikings was farming.
6. A number of interesting discoveries about Viking customs have been made by archaeologists.
7. Each Viking community was ruled by a king or a chief.
8. Viking gods and battles were praised in song by the *skalds,* or royal poets.
9. Women were accorded considerable freedom by Viking tradition.
10. For example, married women were permitted by Viking communities to divorce their husbands whenever they wished.

664 Grammar Handbook

Additional Resources
• Grammar and Usage Practice Book, p. 47

B. Identify the mood of each italicized verb as *Indicative, Imperative,* or *Subjunctive.*

1. Viking warriors were especially *renowned* for their ferocity.
2. If a soldier *were* more fearsome than most, he might be called a "berserker."
3. This term *gave* the English language the word *berserk,* a descriptive term for someone who acts wildly.
4. Many Europeans were so terrified of the Vikings, they urged that special prayers *be* recited in churches.
5. The text of one prayer was as follows: "God, *deliver* us from the fury of the Northmen!"
6. Viking chiefs ordered that raids *be* launched to acquire food, cattle, horses, gold, and silver.
7. Ordinarily, Viking warfare was *waged* by small raiding parties.
8. Occasionally, however, Vikings *organized* fleets of several hundred warships to gain control of large territories.
9. In the year 886, for example, the King of France implored that a Danish Viking chieftain *end* his year-long siege of Paris.
10. "*Convince* me; *pay* me a huge treasure," the warrior might have retorted, "and I will command that my army *withdraw* from the city."

C. For each sentence, write the correct <u>verb form</u> of the two verbs in parentheses.

1. In the age of the Vikings, shipbuilding (<u>rose</u>, raised) to new heights of skill.
2. Shipbuilders improved vessels by (lying, <u>laying</u>) a keel.
3. By reducing the rolling motion of a ship underway, the keel helped the crews to (rise, <u>raise</u>) their speed.
4. The keel was also helpful to the steersman who (<u>sat</u>, set) at the helm.
5. It was easier to steer the ship and to maintain a consistent course that had been (sat, <u>set</u>) in advance.
6. Viking navigators used the (<u>rising</u>, raising) and (sitting, <u>setting</u>) of the sun and the stars to determine their ships' locations.
7. Sophisticated navigation charts helped them determine at any point the latitude where their ships (<u>lay</u>, laid).
8. The Viking chief Leif Ericson (<u>raised</u>, rose) an expedition for a voyage of discovery.
9. Ericson believed that a vast new territory (<u>lay</u>, laid) somewhere across the ocean to the west.
10. After a long voyage, Ericson and his crew finally (lay, <u>laid</u>) anchor in North America, which they called Vinland.

Application and Review

These activities have been designed to allow students to apply concepts presented in this handbook. Exercise A requires students to supply correct past and past participle verb forms. Exercise B requires students to identify verb tense or verb form. Exercise C challenges students to change verbs to a different form.

WRITING THEME   Television

As a future writing assignment, students may want to use the theme of television. To spark interest, you may want to ask students how television has affected their lives.

A. Verbs

Answers are underlined on the page.

GRAMMAR
HANDBOOK
34

Writing Theme
Television

A. Using Verbs Correctly   Write the correct verb form of the two given in parentheses.

1. Over the past half century, television has (grew, grown) into one of the most important communications media.
2. Experimental television broadcasts (taken, took) place in the 1930's.
3. In 1936, the Radio Corporation of America (led, lead) the way to widespread use by installing special receivers in 150 homes in New York City.
4. A New York City station (begun, began) transmitting programs to these homes.
5. The first program that home viewers (saw, seen) was a cartoon presentation of Felix the Cat.
6. World War II temporarily (drew, drawn) public attention away from television.
7. By 1950, however, the demand for television receivers had (set, sat) new records.
8. The number of television sets in the United States had (rose, risen) to about sixty million by 1960.
9. By today's standards, early TV shows (cost, costed) very little to produce, but fans loved them.
10. In those early days, some fans watched their favorite shows on neighbors' sets; the importance (lay, laid) in the viewing!
11. The first television entertainer who (caught, catched) the nation's attention was Milton Berle.
12. Berle's hilarious comedy routines (ran, run) on the *Texaco Star Theater* from 1948 to 1956.
13. Huge audiences (burst, bursted) into spontaneous laughter.
14. The immensely popular series *I Love Lucy* (gone, went) on the air in 1951.
15. Most viewers agreed that Lucille Ball (shone, shined) as the star of the show.
16. On Ed Sullivan's variety show, another audience hit, the Beatles (sang, sung) their first songs on television in the United States.
17. This appearance (brung, brought) the group wide exposure.
18. By 1960, it was clear that television had (sprang, sprung) into the political arena as a major force.
19. The presidential candidates John F. Kennedy and Richard M. Nixon (chose, chosen) to debate each other on TV.
20. It seemed that the clothing the candidates (wore, worn) and the way they looked were almost as important as the words they (spoke, spoken).

B. Verb Tenses and Forms   Write the italicized verbs and identify the tense and/or the form of each verb.

1. By the mid-1950's, many technological improvements *were affecting* television.
2. For example, specialists *had added* the feature of color to television by the end of 1953.
3. The videotaping of programs gradually *replaced* live productions.
4. Unlike film, videotape *did* not *require* time to develop.
5. Videotape also *produces* good quality sound and pictures.
6. Since the 1970's, commercial communications satellites orbiting the earth *have been making* worldwide broadcasting possible.
7. For example, sports fans in Japan *will be watching* the coverage of the next Olympics as the events unfold thousands of miles away.
8. The popularity of videocassette recorders *has grown* enormously.
9. People *enjoy* taping their favorite shows on these machines.
10. By the end of this century, high-definition television (HDTV) *will have improved* picture and sound quality even more.

C. Understanding Verb Forms   Rewrite each of the following sentences, changing the italicized verb to the form shown in parentheses. Rewrite the sentence if necessary.

1. Undoubtedly, television *exerted* a major impact on many aspects of life in the United States. (present perfect progressive)
2. Typical present-day adults *have spent* more time watching TV than on almost anything else. (present)
3. It is clear that TV *has* many beneficial effects on learning and on cultural enrichment. (present perfect)
4. Many home viewers *will have widened* their experience considerably by watching television. (present emphatic)
5. For example, the important acts of government officials *are presented* by the networks to vast audiences. (active voice)
6. Until the televised presentation in 1969, the public never *saw* a historic event like the moon landing before. (past perfect)
7. Experts, however, believe that viewers *had experienced* harmful effects from viewing certain kinds of programs. (future)
8. For example, some programs set up the expectation of a world that *will* always *seethe* with violence. (future progressive)
9. Another objection to TV viewing is that, by the end of an average week, viewers *will see* hundreds of commercial messages urging them to buy various products. (future perfect)
10. Some sociologists fear that, over the years, commercials *will be tending* to raise people's expectations unrealistically. (future)

B. Verb Tenses and Forms
1. Past Progressive
2. Past Perfect
3. Past
4. Past Emphatic
5. Present
6. Present Perfect Progressive
7. Future Progressive
8. Present Perfect
9. Present
10. Future Perfect

C. Understanding Verb Forms
Answers will vary.
See suggested answers below.

1. Undoubtedly, television has been exerting a major impact on many aspects of life in the United States.
2. Typical present-day adults spend more time watching TV than watching almost anything else.
3. It is clear that TV has had many beneficial effects on learning and on cultural enrichment.
4. Many home viewers do widen their experiences considerably by watching television.
5. For example, the networks have presented the important acts of government officials to vast audiences.
6. Until the televised presentation in 1969, the public had never before seen an historic event like the moon landing.
7. Experts, however, believe that viewers will experience harmful effects from viewing certain kinds of programs.
8. For example, some programs set up the expectation of a world that will always be seething with violence.
9. Another objection to TV viewing is that, by the end of an average week, viewers will have seen hundreds of commercial messages urging them to buy various products.
10. Some sociologists fear that, over the years, commercials will tend to raise people's expectations unrealistically.

Agreement of Subject and Verb

Agreement in Number

Objectives

- To use verbs that agree in number with their subjects
- To identify forms of the irregular verb *be*

Teaching Strategies

Linking Grammar and Literature

Read aloud the following excerpt from James Joyce's "The Dead."

Literary Model

"Oh, then," said Gabriel gaily, "I suppose we'll be going to your wedding one of these days with your young man, eh?"

The girl glanced back at him over her shoulder and said with great bitterness: "The men that is now is only all palaver and what they can get out of you."

Gabriel coloured, as if he felt he had made a mistake. . . ."

Elicit from students that part of the excerpt "sounds funny." The relationship between the plural subject (men) and the singular verb (is) sounds inappropriate. Point out that in formal English, the correct usage would be *men are,* but that this is dialect.

 Individualizing Instruction

ESL Students Since the forms of the verb *be* are irregular in most languages, these students should have no difficulty in singling out this verb for special attention and memorization if necessary. Encourage students to share some of the peculiarities of the inflection of the verb *be* in their native language.

GRAMMAR
HANDBOOK
35

Agreement of Subject and Verb

AGREEMENT IN NUMBER

In grammar, there are two numbers: **singular** when a word refers to one person or thing and **plural** if a word refers to more than one.

The subject and verb of a sentence must agree in number.

A singular verb is used with a singular subject; a plural verb is used with a plural subject. This is called **agreement.**

This <u>calculation</u> (singular) accurately <u>demonstrates</u> (singular) the scientist's theory.

These <u>equations</u> (plural) <u>demonstrate</u> (plural) the chemist's understanding of the substances.

Most verbs change form to show singular or plural only in the third-person present tense, where the singular form ends in *-s*. All verb forms are the same in the past tense.

Present Tense Verb Forms			
Singular		**Plural**	
I	race	we	race
you	race	you	race
he, she, it, Juan	races	they, the joggers	race

Singular and Plural Forms of *Be* The box below presents all conjugations of the irregular verb *be.*

Forms of *Be*				
	Present Tense		**Past Tense**	
	Singular	*Plural*	*Singular*	*Plural*
First Person	I am	we are	I was	we were
Second Person	you are	you are	you were	you were
Third Person	he, she, it is	they are	he, she, it was	they were

Usage Note The expressions *you was, we was,* and *they was* are nonstandard English and should be avoided in writing and speaking.

Writing TIP

One exception to the use of nonstandard forms involves dialogue. The use of such forms may add realism to a character's voice.

Words Between Subject and Verb

A verb agrees only with its subject.

Sometimes a word or phrase separates the subject from its verb. Such interruptions do not change the need for agreement between the verb and its subject.

> The <u>lawyers</u> in the public defender's office <u>have</u> excellent credentials. (*Lawyers,* not *office,* is the subject.)

> The <u>lawyer</u>, according to the newspapers, <u>has</u> questions for the witnesses. (*Lawyer,* not *newspapers,* is the subject.)

Beware of the prepositions *according to, along with, as well as, together with,* and *with.* The objects of such prepositions have no effect on the number of the verb. These prepositions may cause confusion since they appear to create a compound subject with which you would expect to use a plural verb.

Practice Your Skills

CONCEPT CHECK

Agreement in Number of Subject and Verb   Write the form of the verb that agrees in number with the subject of each of the following sentences. Then tell whether the verb form is *Singular* or *Plural.*

1. Unusual competitions around the United States (captures, capture) the public's imagination.
2. During summer, sand sculptors with their buckets of sand and water (vies, vie) to create compelling sculptures or castles.
3. Wood cutting, as well as pole climbing, (is, are) featured in annual contests of skill and daring for lumberjacks.
4. In contrast, a participant in hog-calling or yodeling contests (needs, need) more lung power than physical strength.
5. Young contestants from all over the country (competes, compete) in the International Rope Skipping Organization championships.
6. On the other hand, a frog, together with its owner, (wins, win) the Calaveras County Jumping Frog Jubilee held every year.
7. The most effective bird calls, according to a panel of judges, (is, are) given recognition in bird-calling contests.
8. Fairs in most rural areas (has, have) a variety of different tests of skill, including pie-eating and tractor pulling contests.
9. A cash prize, along with ribbons or trophies, (is, are) usually presented to the most skilled contestants.
10. Indeed, people of all ages (enjoys, enjoy) trying to set records or to win awards.

Writing Theme
Contests and Records

Agreement of
Subject and Verb   **669**

Students may have trouble determining whether a subject is singular or plural when it is followed by a prepositional phrase. Have students generate a list of prepositions to look for when checking subject-verb agreement.

Some students may also be confused by the fact that many nouns form their plurals by adding -s, whereas many verbs form the singular by adding -s.

Additional Resources

- Tests and Assessment, Pretests, pp. 23–25
- Grammar and Usage Practice Book, pp. 48–49

WRITING THEME   Contests and Records

Encourage students to consider using the subject of contests and records as a topic for writing a personal narrative.

Concept Check
Agreement in Number of Subject and Verb
1. capture, plural
2. vie, plural
3. is, singular
4. needs, singular
5. compete, plural
6. wins, singular
7. are, plural
8. have, plural
9. is, singular
10. enjoy, plural

Compound Subjects

Objective

- To identify verbs that agree with compound subjects

Teaching Strategies

Stumbling Block

If students seem confused by subjects that appear to be compound but are actually single units, offer them additional examples such as the following: Ham and eggs is a delicious breakfast or The give and take among the panelists was lively. You might also analyze sentences such as the following: Liver and bacon is a filling dish and Liver and bacon are foods rich in cholesterol. Point out that the subject in the first sentence refers to one dish and, therefore, requires a singular verb. The subject in the second sentence refers to two distinct foods and requires a plural verb.

 Individualizing Instruction

LEP Students   Give these students a list of compound subjects that are habitually used to refer to a single thing in English. You might elicit the list during a class discussion. Encourage students to memorize the compound subjects on the list.

Additional Resources
- Grammar and Usage Practice Book, p. 50

WRITING THEME   What's in a Name?

A. Concept Check
Agreement with Compound Subjects
1. Both creativity and dedication have inspired colorful epithets.
2. Neither wizardry nor magic tricks were the stock in trade of "the Wizard of Menlo Park."
3. Correct
4. The give and take of inventing by teamwork requires the organization and skill of a genius such as Edison.
5. Skill and genius also mark the prolific writings of the "Bard of Avon."
6. Many a writer aspires to the greatness of William Shakespeare, who is credited with writing more than one hundred sonnets and thirty-seven plays.

COMPOUND SUBJECTS

Use a plural verb with most compound subjects joined by the word *and*.

> <u>Oil</u> and <u>natural gas</u> <u>are</u> the most common heating fuels in the United States.

Use a singular verb with a compound subject joined by *and* that is habitually used to refer to a single thing.

> <u>Snow</u> and <u>ice</u> <u>creates</u> slippery roads.

Use a singular verb with any subject that is preceded by *each*, *every*, or *many a*.

> <u>Each</u> member and officer of the organization <u>gets</u> one vote.

> <u>Many a</u> writer at the beginning of a project <u>has needed</u> a source of inspiration.

When the words in a compound subject are joined by *or* or *nor*, the verb agrees with the subject nearer the verb.

> The editor or <u>proofreaders</u> <u>find</u> any errors in the final copy. (The plural verb *find* agrees with *proofreaders,* the subject nearer the verb.)

Practice Your Skills

A. CONCEPT CHECK

Agreement with Compound Subjects   Rewrite these sentences, correcting all errors in subject-verb agreement. If a sentence is correct, write *Correct*.

1. Both creativity and dedication has inspired colorful epithets.
2. Neither wizardry nor magic tricks was the stock in trade of "the Wizard of Menlo Park."
3. Every scientist and amateur inventor considers Thomas Edison's laboratory at Menlo Park, which was staffed by assistants who helped Edison, the first industrial research facility.
4. The give and take of inventing by teamwork require the organization and skill of a genius such as Edison.
5. Skill and genius also marks the prolific writings of the "Bard of Avon."
6. Many a writer aspire to the greatness of William Shakespeare, who is credited with writing more than one hundred sonnets and thirty-seven plays.

7. Each byname and nickname describe the individual.
8. For example, her voice and appearance were so distinctive that Jenny Lind was called "the Swedish Nightingale."
9. Each modern nurse and doctor have probably heard of Florence Nightingale, called "the Lady with the Lamp" because she made nightly rounds of hospital wards.
10. Both the fans and the general public still refer to entertainer Elvis Presley as "the King."

B. PROOFREADING SKILL

Errors in Agreement Rewrite the following paragraphs on your paper, correcting any errors. Be sure all subjects and verbs agree in number.

Many an essayist and novelist have published his or her writing under a pseudonym. Baroness Karen Blixen and Isak Dinesen, for example, is the same woman. Samuel Langhorne Clemens and Mark Twain are one man.

The aim and intent of writer's using other names have differed. In century's past, many a female novelist and poet were known to use a mans name to avoid public criticism of their feminine authorship. Currer Bell and Ellis Bell, who wrote the novels *Jane Eyre* and *Wuthering Heights* respectively, was actually two sisters. Neither the publisher nor the critics at the time was able to give Charlotte and Emily Brontë credit under her own names. Critics questioned whether both sensitivity and vigor was possible in a females work. Today each reader form his or her own standards based on the quality of the writing rather then the writer's gender.

Male novelists and essayists who wrote in more than one medium has sometimes used pen names as well. Charles Lamb and Charles Dickens was known by their *noms de plume*. Lamb published essays in *The London Magazine* under the name of Elia. Likewise, Dickens published sketches in the *Evening Chronicle* under the name Boz. Both Dickens and Lamb was recognized by thier true names when they wrote more serious novels and other works.

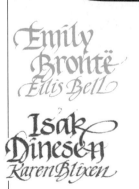

7. Each byname and nickname describes the individual.
8. Correct
9. Each modern nurse and doctor has probably heard of Florence Nightingale, called "the Lady with the Lamp" because she made nightly rounds of hospital wards.
10. Correct

B. Proofreading Skill
Errors in Agreement
Errors are underlined on page.

Many an essayist and novelist has published his or her writing under a pseudonym. Baroness Karen Blixen and Isak Dinesen, for example, are the same woman. Samuel Langhorne Clemens and Mark Twain are one man.

The aim and intent of writers using other names has differed. In centuries past, many a female novelist and poet was known to use a man's name to avoid public criticism of feminine authorship. Currer Bell and Ellis Bell, who wrote the novels *Jane Eyre* and *Wuthering Heights* respectively, were actually two sisters. Neither the publisher nor the critics at the time were able to give Charlotte and Emily Brontë credit under their own names. Critics questioned whether both sensitivity and vigor were possible in a female's work. Today each reader forms his or her own standards based on the quality of the writing rather than the writer's gender.

Male novelists and essayists who wrote in more than one medium have sometimes used pen names as well. Charles Lamb and Charles Dickens were known by their *noms de plume*. Lamb published essays in *The London Magazine* under the name of Elia. Likewise, Dickens published sketches in the *Evening Chronicle* under the name Boz. Both Dickens and Lamb were recognized by their true names when they wrote more serious novels and other works.

You may wish to use the following Checkpoint exercises as an informal evaluation of student mastery of the rules for subject-verb agreement covered in this handbook.

Managing the Paper Load

To limit the number of exercises to correct, provide an answer key for students to self-correct Exercise A. Then pair LEP students with partners to correct all subject-verb errors in Exercise B.

WRITING THEME Flora and Fauna of the Sea

A.
Answers are underlined on page.

B.
1. Wrapped in powerful tentacles, the drowning sailor, along with his rescuers, fights the monster octopus.
2. Many a science-fiction film and sea yarn has given cephalopods, or octopuses and squids, a bad reputation as vicious sea monsters.
3. In reality, the docile octopus, along with squids, is harmless to humans.
4. Correct
5. Many a shy member of the cephalopod group changes color to hide amid rocks and coral.
6. Both the octopus and the squid eject an inky fluid.
7. Correct

Writing Theme
Flora and Fauna of the Sea

A. Write the <u>form of the verb</u> that agrees in number with the subject of each of the following sentences.

1. Probably every gourmet and connoisseur of Japanese cuisine (<u>has</u>, have) eaten dried seaweed fronds.
2. Surprisingly, many plants from the oceans of the world (contributes, <u>contribute</u>) to a variety of foods.
3. For example, kelp, along with other kinds of seaweed, (<u>is</u>, are) harvested and processed.
4. Both seaweed fronds and the stipe, or stem, (has, <u>have</u>) practical uses.
5. More importantly, giant kelp plants, growing to a length of 215 feet, (produces, <u>produce</u>) algin, a jellylike substance.
6. In addition, many seaweeds in the Pacific Ocean, such as red algae, (yields, <u>yield</u>) agar, a substance similar to gelatin.
7. Either algin or agar (<u>is</u>, are) usually added to foods such as ice cream and salad dressings to prevent crystallization, to make them smooth, or to help them retain moisture.
8. In the 1800's, kelp and other types of seaweed (was, <u>were</u>) an important source of the minerals potash and iodine.
9. The life and death of some food, cosmetics, and drug industries (<u>depends</u>, depend) on the harvesting of seaweeds.
10. Many a food product or medicine (<u>uses</u>, use) kelp and other forms of algae, an important yet little-known ingredient in the human diet.

B. Rewrite the following sentences, correcting all errors in subject-verb agreement. If a sentence contains no error, write *Correct*.

1. Wrapped in powerful tentacles, the drowning sailor, along with his rescuers, fight the monster octopus.
2. Many a science-fiction film and sea yarn have given cephalopods, or octopuses and squids, a bad reputation as vicious sea monsters.
3. In reality, the docile octopus, along with squids, are harmless to humans.
4. Neither the octopus, with its eight arms, nor the squid, with its ten arms, eats anything larger than crabs and lobsters.
5. Many a shy member of the cephalopod group change color to hide amid rocks and coral.
6. Both the octopus and the squid ejects an inky fluid.
7. This fluid, according to experts, acts as a protective screen.

8. These gentle creatures, together with the cuttlefish, is more likely to end up as the dinner rather than the diner.
9. The economic "bread and butter" of many restaurants rely on octopuses and their cousins.
10. Either octopus appetizers or a squid entrée is a special treat in the Mediterranean, the Orient, and other areas.

INDEFINITE PRONOUNS AS SUBJECTS

Indefinite pronouns vary in number: some are always singular, others are always plural. Yet others may be singular or plural, according to their particular use in a sentence.

Singular Indefinite Pronouns

another	either	neither	other
anybody	everybody	nobody	somebody
anyone	everyone	no one	someone
anything	everything	nothing	something
each	much	one	

Use a singular verb with a singular indefinite pronoun.

No one from the jury is allowed to go home.

Everything in the store costs less than twenty dollars.

Does anyone on the committee agree with the principal?

Plural Indefinite Pronouns

both	few	many	several

Use a plural verb with a plural indefinite pronoun.

Both of our class projects are due on the same day, and there is no compromise on either deadline.

Many of the students in our class do their research at the university library.

Agreement of Subject and Verb **673**

8. These gentle creatures, together with the cuttlefish, are more likely to end up as the dinner rather than the diner.
9. The "bread and butter" of many restaurants relies on octopuses and their cousins.
10. Correct

Indefinite Pronouns As Subjects

Objective

- To identify subject-verb agreement with singular and plural indefinite pronouns

Teaching Strategies

Spot Check

Some students may mistake such singular indefinite pronouns as *each, either, everyone, everything,* and *neither* for plural pronouns because they are often followed by prepositional phrases referring to a group of people or things. You may wish to supplement the sample sentences in the text by writing these sentences on the board:

Each of the children loves ice skating.
Neither of them has a pen.
Everything in the stores is expensive this year.

Erase the prepositional phrase in each sentence and then have students read the shortened sentences aloud. Be sure that students understand that plural nouns or pronouns in the intervening prepositional phrases do not affect the singular number of the indefinite pronoun used as the subject.

Individualizing Instruction

LD Students You may wish to have these students work in pairs using flashcards to memorize singular and plural indefinite pronouns. To create these flashcards, write or type an indefinite pronoun on the front of an index card; on the back identify whether the indefinite pronoun is singular or plural.

LEP Students You may wish to pair these students with native speakers of English to give the LEP students extra practice with indefinite pronouns. Encourage them to work with a set of flashcards, as described for LD students. After these students have mastered the flashcards, encourage them to compose sample sentences using the indefinite pronouns.

Critical Thinking

Analyzing Students may have trouble understanding the meaning of the sample sentences on page 674 that use *none* and *any*. Explain that the first sentence using *none* may be paraphrased as follows: Not one of the tickets was returned. The second sentence using *any* may be paraphrased as follows: All of these interesting subjects have potential for further research.

Additional Resources
- Grammar and Usage Practice Book, p. 51

WRITING THEME Fire Testing

A. Concept Check
Agreement with Indefinite Pronouns
  1. Everybody, agrees
  2. many, are

Writing Theme
Fire Testing

Singular or Plural Indefinite Pronouns			
all	enough	most	plenty
any	more	none	some

These indefinite pronouns are singular when they refer to a quantity or a part of something. They are plural when they refer to a number of individual things. In some cases you may need to refer to an intervening prepositional phrase or a prior sentence to determine whether an indefinite pronoun is singular or plural.

Some of the stolen money was retrieved. (quantity)

Some of their trigonometry answers were wrong. (number)

Mrs. Chang ordered several items from the catalog. Some were defective. (*Some* refers to items in the previous sentence.)

Most of the mail was incorrectly addressed. (*Mail*, the object of the preposition, is singular.)

Most of the informational brochures were about basketball camps. (*Brochures,* the object of the preposition, is plural.)

None and *any* may be either singular or plural depending on whether the writer intends to refer to one thing or to several. In such cases you need to examine the context of the sentence.

None of the unused tickets was returned. (not one)

None of the unused tickets were returned. (no tickets)

Any of these interesting subjects has potential for further research. (any one)

Any of these interesting subjects have potential for further research. (any subjects)

Practice Your Skills

CONCEPT CHECK

Agreement with Indefinite Pronouns Write the subject of each sentence. Then write the form of the verb that agrees with the subject.

1. Everybody in the United States (agrees, agree) that the country needs protection from tragic fires.
2. According to experts, many of the fire-prevention regulations today (is, are) based on intuition and guesswork.

3. One of the problems (lies, lie) in the lack of scientific knowledge about fire and how it spreads.
4. Much of the current testing (focuses, focus) on the dynamics of fire, such as what affects how quickly it ignites and spreads.
5. In one test conducted by the National Bureau of Standards, several of the testers (watches, watch) as a match ignites a newspaper.
6. In one and a half minutes, plenty of thick smoke (spreads, spread) close to the floor.
7. In the same test, most of the objects in the room (has, have) caught fire within four minutes, and the temperature is 1,300° F.
8. Given the test results, few on the research team (questions, question) the need for educating the public about fire safety.
9. Everyone in the testing field (studies, study) computer models that re-create actual fires.
10. Nearly all of the existing fire codes (is, are) updated according to scientific knowledge gained from these tests.

OTHER AGREEMENT PROBLEMS

Although subject-verb agreement rules are simple, some situations often lead to errors. This section will help you avoid those errors.

Inverted Sentences

Agreement problems may occur in inverted sentences where the verb precedes the subject, as in some questions and in sentences beginning with *here* and *there*. To ensure agreement, think ahead and determine whether the verb should be singular or plural.

Incorrect   Near the smoldering wreck stands the dazed victims.

Correct   Near the smoldering wreck stand the dazed victims.

Incorrect   There was no bus services during the blizzard.

Correct   There were no bus services during the blizzard.

Incorrect   What's the scientific names for these bacterial strains?

Correct   What are the scientific names for these bacterial strains?

Notice the misuse of the contraction *what's* in the last example above. Contractions such as *what's, here's, there's,* and *who's* contain the singular verb *is* and should be used only with singular subjects.

Other Agreement Problems

Objectives

- To identify subject-verb agreement in inverted sentences, sentences containing predicate nominatives, sentences containing *don't* and *doesn't*, and sentences containing the following as subjects: collective nouns, singular nouns with plural forms, and groups of words or titles
- **Writing** To use subject-verb agreement in writing

Teaching Strategies

Linking Grammar and Writing

Encourage students to select a piece of writing from their own portfolios or from a newspaper or magazine article and then scan it for sentences containing predicate nominatives. Ask them to focus on sentences in which the number of the predicate nominative is different from the number of the subject and verb. Have students share these sentences with the class.

Sentences with Predicate Nominatives

Use a verb that agrees in number with the subject, not with the predicate nominative.

> Strong <u>muscles</u> <u>are</u> one sign of a fit body. (*Muscles* is the subject and takes a plural verb.)

> One <u>sign</u> of a fit body <u>is</u> strong muscles. (*Sign* is the subject and takes a singular verb.)

Sentences with *Don't* and *Doesn't*

Use *doesn't* with singular subjects and with the personal pronouns *he*, *she*, and *it*. Use *don't* with plural subjects and with the personal pronouns *I*, *we*, *you*, and *they*.

Singular   <u>Doesn't</u> the <u>governor</u> always have bodyguards?

  She <u>doesn't</u> always need protection.

Plural   <u>Don't</u> the <u>campers</u> need a ground cloth under their tent in case it rains?

  They <u>don't</u> want to sleep on the wet ground.

Practice Your Skills

A. CONCEPT CHECK

<u>Other Agreement Problems</u>   Write the <u>form of the verb</u> that agrees in number with the subject of each of the following sentences.

1. (<u>Doesn't</u>, Don't) everyone dream?
2. From modern sleep-research laboratories (<u>comes</u>, come) important information about dreams.
3. Recent events (is, <u>are</u>) one contributor to dreams—emotions, another.
4. However, (there's, <u>there are</u>) conflicting theories between the psychological and physiological sciences.
5. According to early twentieth-century psychoanalyst Sigmund Freud, dreams "(is, <u>are</u>) the royal road to the unconscious."
6. After all, (doesn't, <u>don't</u>) dreams often seem to reveal a person's problems, wishes, and anxieties?
7. On the other hand, physiological studies have shown that a dream (<u>is</u>, are) electrical impulses and chemical changes in the brain.
8. However, if each researcher (<u>doesn't</u>, don't) use accurate machines, then the findings are questionable.

9. Then (there's, <u>there are</u>) the careful physical measurements and the dreamer's oral report which make the data complete.
10. On some machines (<u>is</u>, are) recorded a subject's brain wave activity during sleep.
11. (There's, <u>There are</u>) also measurements of the dreamer's eye movement and muscle response.
12. The ultimate goal (<u>remains</u>, remain) the understanding of the content and the purpose of dreams.

B. PROOFREADING SKILL

Errors In Subject-Verb Agreement   Rewrite the following paragraph to correct any <u>errors</u> in subject-verb agreement. Also correct <u>errors</u> in capitalization, punctuation, and spelling.

(1) In the writings of Homer <u>are</u> evidence of early <u>beleifs</u> about dreams. (2) <u>There's</u> dreams of <u>prophesy</u> in which <u>zeus</u> hands down instructions. (3) However, this <u>gods</u> instructions <u>doesn't</u> always seem clear to the dreamer. (4) Asclepius <u>are</u> an expert who interprets dreams. (5) Through his explanations <u>come</u> the method for <u>destinguishing</u> significant from ordinary dreams.

Agreement of
Subject and Verb   **677**

B. Proofreading Skill
Errors in Subject-Verb Agreement
Errors are underlined on page.
    (1) In the writings of Homer is evidence of early beliefs about dreams. (2) There are dreams of prophecy in which Zeus hands down instructions. (3) However, this god's instructions don't always seem clear to the dreamer. (4) Asclepius is an expert who interprets dreams. (5) Through his explanations come the method for distinguishing significant from ordinary dreams.

Speaking and Listening

To help students distinguish between a group as a single unit and a group as a number of individual members, you may wish to read the sample sentences aloud. For each sentence you read, call on volunteers to give a similar sentence using a collective noun as the subject.

 Individualizing Instruction

ESL Students   Point out to these students that English is not unique in possessing singular nouns that require plural forms. Some examples from other languages include the following: French *colis* (package), Spanish *Dios* (God), and German *Schatten* (shadow). Invite students to share additional examples from their native languages.

Collective Nouns as Subjects

A **collective** noun such as *band, committee,* or *bunch* takes a singular verb when the group acts as a single unit, and a plural verb when the members of the group act separately.

> The <u>flock</u> of sheep <u>is grazing</u> on the mountainside. (The whole flock is grazing.)

> The <u>flock</u> of sheep <u>are running</u> from the sheep dog. (Individual sheep are running.)

> Our <u>club</u> <u>ratifies</u> all of its rules and the fee structure annually. (The whole group ratifies rules and the fee structure.)

> Our <u>club</u> <u>voice</u> dissent and <u>disagree</u> on every item on the agenda. (The individual members of the club voice dissent and disagree.)

Usage Note   Like other collective nouns, *number* is sometimes singular and sometimes plural. When *number* is preceded by *the* and followed by *of,* it is singular; when it is preceded by *a* and followed by *of,* it is plural.

> The <u>number</u> of blood donors from our school <u>is growing</u> each year.

> A <u>number</u> of blood donors <u>give</u> blood every month during the school year.

Singular Nouns with Plural Forms

Not every noun ending in *-s* is plural. A few nouns appear to be plural, but they are actually singular because they stand for only one thing. Examples are *molasses, measles,* and *news,* all of which take a singular verb.

> <u>Molasses</u> <u>is</u> a commodity that changed the pattern of world trade with the American colonies.

> Once <u>news</u> of the British duty <u>was known</u>, smugglers began to sell molasses.

A few nouns that end in *-s* refer to only one thing but still take a plural verb: *congratulations, eyeglasses, pliers, scissors, trousers.*

> <u>Scissors</u> <u>are</u> best <u>kept</u> out of the hands of small children.

> My <u>sunglasses</u> <u>fall</u> into the ocean every time I sail.
> <u>Congratulations</u> <u>were offered</u> to the finalists.

Nouns that end in *-ics,* such as *academics, aesthetics,* and *genetics,* can be either singular or plural. They are singular when they refer to a school subject, a science, or a general practice. In the plural form they usually follow a singular modifier or a possessive pronoun.

Economics is more than just dollars and cents.

World economics operate on a base of complicated relationships.

A geographic name or an organization ending in *-s* is singular even though it appears to be a plural form.

The Philippines consists of thousands of islands and islets.

The *Times* names all the contestants in the primary election.

Titles and Groups of Words as Subjects

Use a singular verb with a title.

The title of a book, play, story, poem, TV show, musical composition, painting, piece of architecture, or other work of art is singular and therefore requires a singular verb.

O Pioneers! was written by Willa Cather, a great American novelist who captured the heroic, creative spirit that was so much a part of the nineteenth century.

The Four Seasons represents Antonio Vivaldi in the repertoire of many chamber orchestras.

Any group of words referring to a single thing or thought is used with a singular verb.

"Rose is a rose is a rose is a rose" is an often-quoted line from a poem by Gertrude Stein that illustrates her use of repetition.

How people will respond to a crisis depends on their experience and temperament.

Illustration by Robert Crawford

Agreement of
Subject and Verb   **679**

Individualizing Instruction

Basic Students Help these students understand that a singular verb is used with the *exact words* of a title that is italicized or placed between quotation marks but not necessarily with paraphrases that may refer to the title. You may wish to draw this distinction by using the following examples: (a) *The Four Seasons* represents Antonio Vivaldi in the repertoire of many chamber orchestras; (b) Vivaldi's melodic evocations of the four seasons are often performed by many chamber orchestras.

Additional Resources
• Grammar and Usage Practice
  Book, p. 53

WRITING THEME   The Twenties

A. Concept Check
Agreement Problems
Answers are underlined on page.

Words of Amount and Time as Subjects

Words stating amounts are usually singular.

Use a singular verb with subject words or phrases that express periods of time, weights, measurements, fractions, or amounts of money.

> Three hours *is* longer than anyone should have to wait to see a doctor.
>
> Fifty dollars *seems* like a lot to spend on a gift.
>
> Eight tons *is* the weight limit of many local streets and highways.

If the subject is a period of time or an amount that is thought of as a number of separate units, use a plural verb.

> Four companies of fire trucks *come* to every alarm at a hospital.
>
> Twenty-four players *stay* on the active roster during the football season.

Practice Your Skills

A. CONCEPT CHECK

Writing Theme
The Twenties

Agreement Problems   Write the <u>form of the verb</u> that agrees in number with its subject.

1. It is the turn of the century, and the Roaring Twenties (<u>is</u>, are) a golden age of dizzying prosperity.
2. The United States (<u>enjoys</u>, enjoy) great industrial growth, as seen in the automobile industry.
3. Thanks to mass production, three hundred dollars (<u>is</u>, are) enough to buy a Model T Ford.
4. "You can get a Model T in any color, so long as it is black" (<u>becomes</u>, become) a familiar witticism of the day.
5. In 1933 the President's Research Committee on Social Trends (<u>reports</u>, report) 150 ways the automobile has changed the American way of life.
6. With new mobility gained from the use of automobiles, the American family (<u>moves</u>, move) away from the city to create the suburbs.
7. During the Roaring Twenties, radio also comes of age; at this time, nearly one-half the homes in the United States (has, <u>have</u>) radio sets.

8. A group of broadcasters (<u>airs</u>, air) the first commercial radio program in 1920 at station KDKA in Pittsburgh.
9. Within six years, the number of radio stations in the United States (<u>grows</u>, grow) to 732.
10. In addition, the movie *The Jazz Singer* (<u>makes</u>, make) history as the first talking movie.
11. Unfortunately, this is also a time when America's ethics (is, <u>are</u>) questioned as people bemoan an apparent decline in moral standards.
12. A number of writers (describes, <u>describe</u>) the disillusionment and alienation of a society trying to learn a new and vastly different role in the machine age.
13. "A vast . . . herd of good-natured animals" (<u>is</u>, are) how writer H. L. Mencken characterizes society.
14. T. S. Eliot's poem "The Hollow Men" (<u>predicts</u>, predict) that everything civilization has accomplished will end "not with a bang but a whimper."
15. Indeed, for good or bad, the economics of the era (<u>inspires</u>, inspire) great changes in American life.

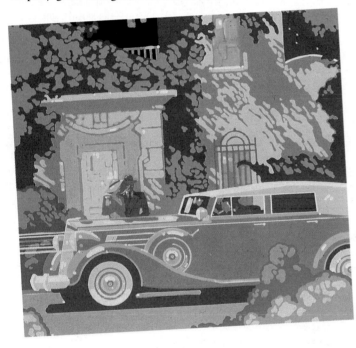

B. Revision Skill

Problems of Subject-Verb Agreement

(1) A few hours is enough time for readers to become entranced with the Jazz Age of the 1920's.

(2) Correct

(3) It is a time when almost three million copies of the popular magazine the *Saturday Evening Post* are sold each week.

(4) A number of Fitzgerald's short stories first appear in the *Post* and other popular magazines of the time.

(5) "Winter Dreams," published in *Metropolitan Magazine*, is among the pre-*Gatsby* short stories.

(6) In one scene of "Winter Dreams," the news of a boyfriend's penniless state upsets a selfish but beautiful young woman.

(7) Her family is very wealthy and belongs to the country club where the hero formerly worked as a caddy.

(8) Correct

(9) During his youth, the elite group of rich families fans his imagination.

(10) How to acquire the trappings of the rich becomes his obsession.

(11) Knickerbockers are the fashion on the golf course; elegant Pierce Arrows fill the parking lots.

(12) Correct

(13) The rich crowd is portrayed as selfish and superficial in another of Fitzgerald's short stories.

(14) "Dice, Brassknuckles & Guitar" explores the cultural differences that exist between the rich and the poor.

(15) "You're better than all of them put together" is a line from this short story that forecasts a later line in *The Great Gatsby*, reassuring the hero of his worth despite what he sees as his shortcomings.

C. Application in Writing

Comparison and Contrast

Answers will vary.

B. REVISION SKILL

Problems of Subject-Verb Agreement Rewrite the following sentences, correcting all errors in subject-verb agreement. If a sentence has no errors, write *Correct.*

(1) A few hours are enough time for readers to become entranced with the Jazz Age of the 1920's. (2) Through F. Scott Fitzgerald's short stories and his novel *The Great Gatsby,* wealthy society comes to life. (3) It is a time when almost three million copies of the popular magazine the *Saturday Evening Post* is sold each week. (4) A number of Fitzgerald's short stories first appears in the *Post* and other popular magazines of the time. (5) "Winter Dreams," published in *Metropolitan Magazine,* are among the pre-Gatsby short stories.

(6) In one scene of "Winter Dreams," the news of a boyfriend's penniless state upset a selfish but beautiful young woman. (7) Her family are very wealthy and belong to the country club where the hero formerly worked as a caddy. (8) Doing the laundry of the rich is how the hero, Dexter Green, now makes a living. (9) During his youth, the elite group of rich families fan his imagination. (10) How to acquire the trappings of the rich become his obsession. (11) Knickerbockers is the fashion on the golf course; elegant Pierce Arrows fill the parking lots. (12) Both Fitzgerald's Jay Gatsby and Dexter suffer years of disillusionment after trying to obtain the unattainable.

(13) The rich crowd are portrayed as selfish and superficial in another of Fitzgerald's short stories. (14) "Dice, Brassknuckles & Guitar" explore the cultural differences that exist between the rich and the poor. (15) "You're better than all of them put together" are a line from this short story that forecasts a later line in *The Great Gatsby,* reassuring the hero of his worth despite what he sees as his shortcomings.

C. APPLICATION IN WRITING

Comparison and Contrast Think about the time in which you are living. In what ways do you think the 1920's and this decade are similar? How are they different? Think about what people owned, what they believed about getting rich, and what they bought during the 1920's. Then think about the same things as they apply to society today. Compare and contrast the two time periods. Be sure your subjects and verbs agree.

RELATIVE PRONOUNS AS SUBJECTS

When a relative pronoun is used as a subject, it may be either plural or singular, depending on the number of its antecedent.

A relative pronoun agrees with its antecedent in number. When a relative pronoun is used as the subject of an adjective clause (see page 608), the verb of the clause must agree in number with the antecedent of the relative pronoun.

Singular   Amelia Earhart was a famous aviator <u>who</u> <u>has</u> the distinction of being the first woman to fly solo across the Atlantic. (*Who* refers to the singular antecedent *famous aviator* and takes the singular verb *has*.)

Plural   It is Richard Byrd and Floyd Bennett, two Americans, <u>who</u> <u>rank</u> as the first aviators to fly over the North Pole. (*Who* refers to the plural antecedent *Richard Byrd and Floyd Bennett* and requires the plural verb *rank*.)

In some sentences, it may be difficult to determine whether the verb should take the singular or plural form because there seems to be more than one possible antecedent. Sentences with the expressions *one of the* or *one of those* often prove confusing, as illustrated by the following examples.

Incorrect   Susan Glaspell is one of those playwrights <u>who</u> <u>has</u> won the Pulitzer Prize for drama.

Correct   Susan Glaspell is one of those playwrights <u>who</u> <u>have</u> won the Pulitzer Prize for drama. (Other playwrights have won the award besides Glaspell. Therefore, *who* refers to the plural antecedent *playwrights*.)

When the expression *the only one of those* is used, the relative pronoun modifies *one* and is therefore singular.

Eugene O'Neill is the only one of those playwrights <u>who</u> <u>has</u> been awarded four Pulitzer Prizes for drama. (The other playwrights did not win four Pulitzer Prizes; only O'Neill did. *Who* refers to the singular antecedent *one*.)

Always consider the context of the sentence. Usually the context will allow you to determine the correct antecedent and ensure that subject-verb agreement is correct.

Agreement of
Subject and Verb   **683**

Relative Pronouns As Subjects

Objective

- To identify subject-verb agreement when a relative pronoun is used as the subject

Teaching Strategies

Cooperative Learning

Form the class into several teams. Challenge each team to write as many sentences as possible patterned on the sample sentences on page 683. Remind students to use a relative pronoun as the subject of an adjective clause. At a set time, have the teams display and check one another's work to make sure that each verb agrees in number with the antecedent of the relative pronoun. As a class, decide on the winning team.

Linking Grammar and Writing

Have pairs of students look through their writing portfolios to find sample sentences illustrating the concepts taught in this handbook. Have volunteers use those sentences to make a poster illustrating the rules for subject-verb agreement.

Additional Resources
- Grammar and Usage Practice Book, p. 54

WRITING THEME   Inventors of Everyday Things

Encourage students to research a famous inventor and take notes in preparation for a writing assignment.

A. Concept Check
Agreement with Antecedents of Relative Pronouns
Answers are underlined on page.

B. Proofreading Skill
Agreement with Antecedents of Relative Pronouns
Errors are underlined on page.

Elevators, which provide vertical transportation, have been around in some form for over 2,000 years. It is believed that Archimedes, who was an ancient Greek mathematician, created one of the first elevators. By the 1840's anyone who was riding a steam-powered or hydraulic elevator would probably enjoy the convenience but might worry about safety. In a steam-powered elevator, when one of the ropes was broken, nothing could stop the elevator car from crashing. Fortunately, Elisha G. Otis was one of those people who see a solution where others see only a problem. It is his invention of the automatic safety device that has made traveling in elevators the safest form of human transportation.

Writing Theme Inventors of Everyday Things

Practice Your Skills

A. CONCEPT CHECK

Agreement with Antecedents of Relative Pronouns   Write the form of the verb that agrees in number with the subject of the adjective clause.

1. Edwin Budding is one of those inventors who (remains, remain) unsung heroes of modern technology.
2. All the people who (mows, mow) lawns in the summer can thank him for making their job easier.
3. Picture a British textile mill in the 1800's and a rotary shearing machine that (trims, trim) the nap off cotton cloth.
4. Budding tinkers with the cutters that (rotates, rotate) around a fixed cutter.
5. It is this tinkering that (leads, lead) Budding to the idea for his invention, the push mower.
6. Budding was the only one of those inventors of his day who (was, were) to apply for a patent on a rolling mower.
7. Before Budding's invention, English gardeners used a scythe, which (is, are) a long sharp blade with a handle.
8. Today we use mowers that (is, are) gasoline-powered.
9. Edwin George, an American army colonel, was one of the tinkerers who (was, were) responsible for the gasoline mower.
10. One of those people who never (wastes, waste) things, George used an old washing machine motor to power his mower.

B. PROOFREADING SKILL

Agreement with Antecedents of Relative Pronouns   Rewrite this paragraph, correcting all agreement errors and all errors in capitalization, punctuation, and spelling.

Elevators, which provides vertical transportation, have been around in some form for over 2,000 years. It is believed that Archimedes, who were an ancient greek mathematician, created one of the first elevators. By the 1840's anyone who were riding a steam-powered or hydraulic elevator would probably enjoy the convenience but might worry about safety. In a steam-powered elevator, when one of the ropes were broken, nothing could stop the elevator car from crashing. Fortunately, Elisha G. Otis was one of those people who sees a solution where others see only a problem It is his invention of the automatic safety devise that have made traveling in elevators the safest form of human transportation.

A. Select the <u>form of the verb</u> that agrees with its subject.

1. No one who (<u>studies</u>, study) English literature (<u>denies</u>, deny) the influence of the Bloomsbury Group.
2. In the inner borough of Camden north of the Thames (<u>lies</u>, lie) Bloomsbury, from which the group (<u>takes</u>, take) its name.
3. This group of noted writers, artists, and philosophers (<u>was</u>, were) known to hold spirited discussions.
4. Their aesthetics (is, <u>are</u>) still a significant influence on modern writers and thinkers.
5. (Who was, <u>Who were</u>) some of the group's members?
6. The noted author and frequent hostess of the Bloomsbury Group (<u>was</u>, were) Virginia Woolf.
7. Economist John Maynard Keynes, along with others, (<u>is</u>, are) one of the most illustrious guests who (was, <u>were</u>) invited.
8. Keynes's *The General Theory of Employment, Interest, and Money* (<u>contains</u>, contain) theories that (is, <u>are</u>) said to have influenced the policies of President Franklin D. Roosevelt.
9. Several in the group, such as E. M. Forster and Victoria Sackville-West, (was, <u>were</u>) prominent writers.
10. Three decades (<u>seems</u>, seem) a long time for a group to meet regularly, but meet it did from 1907 to 1930.

B. Rewrite the following paragraph to correct all <u>errors</u> in subject and verb agreement. If a sentence contains no errors, write *Correct.*

> (1) <u>There's</u> very few artists whose interests were as diverse as Leonardo da Vinci's. (2) His versatility amazes those admirers of his genius who <u>studies</u> his work. (3) All of his life's energies <u>was</u> devoted to understanding the world around him. (4) Worthy of our praises <u>are</u> his research in mathematics, music, optics, aeronautics, and anatomy—a few of the fields that <u>was</u> to capture his curiosity. (5) Optics, for example, benefits from his inventiveness. (6) His *Code on the Eye* <u>describe</u> a water-filled tube sealed at the end with a flat lens, which <u>were</u> a precursor of the modern soft contact lens. (7) Twenty-one such manuscripts are his legacy to humanity. (8) Everyone who <u>examine</u> these detailed notebooks marvels at his notes and sketches. (9) In addition, his paintings, the *Virgin and Child with St. Anne,* for example, serve as models that <u>inspires</u> artists to this day. (10) <u>Don't</u> such a versatile and creative genius seem amazing?

These drawings by Leonardo da Vinci depict the workings of an automated spool-winding machine.

Agreement of Subject and Verb **685**

You may wish to use the following Checkpoint exercises as an informal evaluation of student mastery of the rules for subject-verb agreement covered in this handbook.

Managing the Paper Load

To limit the number of exercises to correct, you may wish to do exercise A orally in class. Then have pairs of students rewrite the paragraph in exercise B to correct errors in subject-verb agreement. Discuss the answers.

> **Additional Resources**
> • Grammar and Usage Practice Book, p. 55

WRITING THEME Creative Genius

A.
Answers are underlined on page.

B.
Errors are underlined on page.
(1) There are very few artists whose interests were as diverse as Leonardo da Vinci's.
(2) His versatility amazes those admirers of his genius who study his work.
(3) All of his life's energies were devoted to understanding the world around him.
(4) Worthy of our praises is his research in mathematics, music, optics, aeronautics, and anatomy—a few of the fields that were to capture his curiosity.
(5) Correct
(6) His *Code on the Eye* describes a water-filled tube sealed at the end with a flat lens, which was a precursor of the modern soft contact lens.
(7) Correct
(8) Everyone who examines these detailed notebooks marvels at his notes and sketches.
(9) In addition, his paintings, the *Virgin and Child with St. Anne,* for example, serve as models that inspire artists to this day.
(10) Doesn't such a versatile and creative genius seem amazing?

Humanities Connection

Art Note Leonardo da Vinci (1452–1519) was one of the great creative geniuses of all time. This sketch, taken from one of his notebooks, demonstrates his inventiveness. You might point out the fine detail and careful perspective of the sketch. You might also note da Vinci's remarkably linear handwriting. Ask: What do you learn about da Vinci from these details? The class might mention the following points: he had excellent powers of observation, had the ability to create a sense of depth, was organized as well as creative, etc.

Application and Review

These activities have been designed to allow students to apply concepts presented in this handbook. Exercise A requires students to choose the correct form of a verb to make it agree with its subject. Exercise B challenges students to rewrite sentences to correct problems of subject-verb agreement. Exercise C challenges students to identify and correct errors of subject-verb agreement in a passage.

Additional Resources

- Tests and Assessment, Mastery Tests, pp. 55–57
- Elaboration, Revision, and Proof-reading, p. 25

WRITING THEME   Special Achievers

A. Making Subjects and Verbs Agree
Answers are underlined on page.

B. Solving Problems of Subject-Verb Agreement

1. It is 1810, and a way of life and traditions are disappearing.
2. Neither cholera nor measles threatens native people as much as the American settlers' greed for land.
3. The increasing number of confrontations with settlers gives rise to the leadership of Tecumseh of the Shawnee.
4. Most of his family has been killed by settlers and soldiers.
5. Certainly he is one who has reason to mistrust, yet he risks his life on behalf of white prisoners held by the Shawnee.
6. Tecumseh proves to be one of those leaders who strive to unite people under a single cause.
7. His strong convictions, as well as his eloquent oratory, convince some of the tribal leaders to unite.
8. Yet few in the American government understand Tecumseh's defense of the land.
9. What he states in his arguments is that no one can own the air and water; likewise, no one can possess the land.
10. Tecumseh's rise and fall is a subject of interest to both his admirers and critics.

GRAMMAR
HANDBOOK
35

Writing Theme
Special Achievers

A. Making Subjects and Verbs Agree   Choose the correct form of the verb in parentheses.

1. It is the early twenties, and DeWitt Wallace, who (is, are) recovering from serious war wounds, (ponders, ponder) an idea for a magazine.
2. Three months in the hospital (produces, produce) a plan.
3. "(Doesn't, Don't) men and women in the Twenties have too much to do and too little time?" he wonders.
4. Plodding through many a long magazine article (takes, take) time; a digest that (condenses, condense) them would be helpful.
5. At home, Lila Bell Acheson (is, are) the only one of his acquaintances who (believes, believe) in his idea.
6. DeWitt is convinced that there (is, are) readers for such a digest.
7. However, none of the New York publishers (expresses, express) interest in publishing the magazine.
8. DeWitt, together with his bride Lila Bell, (publishes, publish) the magazine independently.
9. Out of a Greenwich Village basement, the *Reader's Digest* (sallies, sally) forth in February 1922.
10. Neither the general public nor the Wallaces (anticipates, anticipate) the overwhelming success of the magazine.

B. Solving Problems of Subject-Verb Agreement   Rewrite the following sentences to correct all problems of subject and verb agreement.

1. It is 1810, and a way of life and traditions is disappearing.
2. Neither cholera nor measles threaten native people as much as the American settlers' greed for land.
3. The increasing number of confrontations with settlers give rise to the leadership of Tecumseh of the Shawnee.
4. Most of his family have been killed by settlers and soldiers.
5. Certainly he is one who have reason to mistrust, yet he risks his life on behalf of white prisoners held by the Shawnee.
6. Tecumseh proves to be one of those leaders who strives to unite people under a single cause.
7. His strong convictions, as well as his eloquent oratory, convinces some of the tribal leaders to unite.
8. Yet few in the American government understands Tecumseh's defense of the land.
9. What he states in his arguments are that no one can own the air and water; likewise, no one can possess the land.
10. Tecumseh's rise and fall are a subject of interest to both his admirers and critics.

C. Correcting Errors in Agreement Read the passage and identify errors of subject-verb agreement. Write the correct verb for each sentence. If a sentence has no errors, write *Correct*.

(1) "You must do the thing you think you cannot do" <u>are</u> a famous saying of Eleanor Roosevelt's. (2) Few of the people who hear these words today <u>realizes</u> that they were spoken by a woman who had to surmount enormous fears. (3) As a young girl, Eleanor Roosevelt <u>were</u> painfully shy and frightened "of practically everything," as she later recalled. (4) She was one of those students who <u>fears</u> even the simple task of standing up at her desk and spelling a word aloud in front of one's classmates.

(5) None of her childhood fears, however, <u>was</u> as crippling as her fear of water. (6) When she was three, Eleanor and her parents were involved in a serious steamship accident while traveling to Europe. (7) As her father, along with other passengers, <u>were</u> standing in a lifeboat beneath, a crew member tried to throw the young girl overboard. (8) The terrified child clutched so fiercely that her fingers had to be pried loose before she <u>were</u> thrown to safety.

(9) Later in her childhood, Eleanor almost drowned again, but neither the traumatic steamship incident nor these ocean immersions <u>was</u> enough to defeat her.

(10) Though she realized that her anxieties could not be dispelled completely, she knew that she could overcome a portion of the fear that <u>were</u> gnawing at her self-esteem. (11) She decided to deal with her problem one step at a time. (12) First, she learned to sail; then she learned to swim; and finally, when she was fifty-six years old, she learned to dive.

(13) In these small acts of personal heroism <u>reside</u> the key to her life's achievement. (14) There's a lesson here that all of us can still profit from today. (15) As she herself wrote near the end of her life: "We do not have to become heroes overnight, just one step at a time, meeting each thing that comes up, seeing it is not as dreadful as it appeared, discovering we have the strength to stare it down."

C. Correcting Errors in Agreement
Errors are underlined on page.
1. is
2. realize
3. was
4. fear
5. were
6. Correct
7. was
8. was
9. were
10. was
11. Correct
12. Correct
13. resides
14. Correct
15. Correct

To stimulate student interest in medical history, point out that in 1900 most people in the United States did not live past the age of 50. The average life expectancy of Americans today is about 74 years, due partly to medical progress. Most people today take vaccines and antibiotics—comparatively recent medical discoveries—for granted.

Encourage students to research the origin of a medical term and the history surrounding the term. You might allow students to give brief oral reports to the class.

On the Lightside

INFLUENTIAL MEDICAL TERMS

Medical terms are much more than labels. They can be keys to unlocking bits and pieces of medical history. *Flu*, for instance, is a shortened form of the term *influenza*, which doctors borrowed from the Italian *influenza*. *Influenza* came from the medieval Latin word *influentia*, meaning "inflowing" and refering to "ethereal power or fluid flowing from the stars and believed by astrologers to affect the characters and actions of people." Thus we can speculate that when doctors first identified the illness we now call the flu, they may have believed that it was caused by some astrological or occult influence.

Penicillin, too, is much more than just a label. The man who discovered this antibiotic, Alexander Fleming, gave it the name *penicillin* because he derived it from the mold *Penicillium notatum*. *Penicillium* got its name from the Latin word *penicillus,* meaning "paintbrush," because its spore-bearing structures are brushlike in appearance.

Finally, even the term *vaccine* provides a clue to its interesting origins. *Vaccine* comes from the Latin word *vacca* meaning "cow." The first preparation introduced into a body to prevent an illness was made from the cowpox virus and introduced into the body of a boy.

So, the next time you're scanning the rows of medicines at the local pharmacy, you might think twice about the names on those labels. Each one of those names just might have a fascinating story to tell.

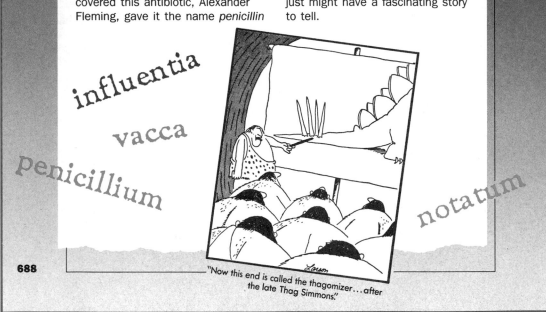

influentia
vacca
penicillium
notatum

"Now this end is called the thagomizer...after the late Thag Simmons."

688

Sketchbook

Developments in transportation have dramatically changed the way people get around. Automobiles and airplanes are as common in this country now as horse-drawn carriages once were. Think about how you might have traveled from Boston to Seattle 150 years ago, how you would make the trip today, and how you might make the trip 150 years from now. Then write a three-paragraph essay describing each trip as you imagine it taking place. Be sure to use verb tenses correctly.

Additional Sketches

Suppose that you have been appointed principal of your school. A national news magazine has asked you to write an article about your new position, in which you would discuss the following: highlights of your school's history, your school's present status, and your plans for making improvements. Write the article, making sure you use appropriate verb tenses.

The senior class is trying to decide on an appropriate and memorable gift to give the school. Write a letter to the school newspaper in which you present an idea and attempt to persuade others to go along with it. Use compound subjects and correlative conjunctions in your letter whenever possible.

689

Sketchbook

Objective

To use the theme of changes in transportation as a springboard to informal writing

Using the Prompt

Remind students that Sketchbook activities are ungraded and are meant to give them opportunities to experiment with writing techniques.

Have students look at a map of the United States and discuss how they might want to travel between Boston and Seattle. Would they like to travel from one place to the other as quickly as possible using one kind of vehicle, or would they want to make a leisurely trip, stopping at interesting sites and changing the kind of vehicle they are traveling in?

Share with students pictures of transportation vehicles from 150 years ago. These are easily accessible in articles on transportation in encyclopedias or in books on the history of transportation. Then encourage students to create and share sketches of what ground, air, and sea vehicles might look like 150 years from now.

Have students write their paragraphs based on the kind of trip—hurried or leisurely—they would like to take. Encourage them to use vivid verbs to describe the experience of traveling in the different vehicles they would use at different times.

Use the ideas in the Additional Sketches section with students who find that these ideas offer a better starting point. Encourage students to put their writing and any sketches they have made in their Writing Portfolios. They may wish to refer to them during future writing projects.

These exercises allow your students to practice skills acquired in Handbooks 34–35. You may wish to use the exercises to provide a thorough review of the material in these chapters or to evaluate student mastery of the concepts.

Skills Assessment Test 2
1. B—rung
   C—time
2. C—caught
   D—striped
3. D—were
4. C—sets
5. B—is
   C—misspellings
6. A—subscribes
7. E

Skills
A S S E S S M E N T

Directions One or more of the underlined sections in the following sentences may contain errors of grammar, usage, punctuation, spelling, or capitalization. Write the letters of each incorrect section. Then rewrite the item correctly. If there is no error in an item, write E.

Example Late in the battle, the Huns, <u>retreating</u> <u>in haste,</u> <u>left</u>
                                                         A   B   C

many of <u>their</u> prisoners go free. <u>No error</u>
          D   E

Answer C—let

---

1. Big Ben, <u>the bell in the tower of the British House of Parliament,</u> has <u>rang</u> out the
                                    A   B
   <u>Time</u> of day <u>since 1859.</u> <u>No error</u>
      C   D   E

2. Al McReynolds <u>received</u> a <u>$250,000</u> prize when he <u>catched</u> a 78-pound <u>stripped</u>
                    A   B   C   D
   bass. <u>No error</u>
            E

3. At the age of <u>fourteen,</u> the <u>young Albert Einstein</u> asked <u>himself,</u> "How would the
                    A   B   C
   world look if I <u>was</u> able to ride on a beam of light?" <u>No error</u>
                      D   E

4. At <u>extremely</u> <u>high or low latitudes,</u> the sun never <u>sits</u> during <u>the summer.</u> <u>No error</u>
         A   B   C   D   E

5. The <u>length</u> of these articles <u>are</u> not a problem, but the <u>mispellings</u> in them are
          A   B   C
   another matter <u>altogether.</u> <u>No error</u>
                      D   E

6. My family <u>subscribe</u> to two newspapers, but we <u>rarely</u> listen to <u>television news</u>
                A   B   C
   programs such as *Sixty Minutes* and *The MacNeil, Lehrer News Hour.* <u>No error</u>
                        D   E

7. <u>Economics</u> <u>is</u> one of the most fascinating and practical of all the sciences <u>because</u>
      A   B   C
   it deals with <u>how people go about making a living.</u> <u>No error</u>
                      D   E

8. <u>Neither</u> the most important financial center <u>nor</u> the most productive industrial
     A   **B**

   center <u>are based</u> in the <u>nation's</u> capital. <u>No error</u>
         C   **D**   **E**

9. During <u>World War II,</u> the Nazis <u>stealed</u> the crown of <u>Charlemagne,</u> but American
             A   **B**   **C**

   soldiers eventualy recovered it. <u>No error</u>
         D   **E**

10. <u>Because</u> the <u>Greek Goddess</u> Persephone had <u>ate</u> some pomegranate <u>seeds,</u> she had
      A   **B**   **C**   **D**

    to spend half her time on earth and half in Hades. <u>No error</u>
                                           E

11. According to <u>some</u> geologists, <u>known</u> petroleum reserves <u>run</u> out sometime
                   A   **B**   **C**

    <u>before the end of this century.</u> <u>No error</u>
                 D   **E**

12. Born in 1910, <u>Colonel Harlan Sanders</u> <u>founds</u> the chain of restaurants and was
                          A   **B**

    very successful, leaving fried chicken restaurants all over the <u>United States</u> and the
                                                          C

    world <u>when he died.</u> <u>No error</u>
            D   **E**

13. Each of these poems by Robert Frost—<u>"Stopping by Woods on a Snowy Evening,"</u>
                                                          A

    in particular—<u>seem</u> simple <u>but</u> <u>are</u> actually quite sophisticated. <u>No error</u>
                   B   **C** **D**   **E**

14. If Catherine Littlefield Green <u>would have got</u> the credit <u>she deserved</u> for helping
                                 A   **B**

    Eli Whitney design the cotton <u>gin,</u> she might <u>have become</u> as famous as he.
                                   C   **D**

    <u>No error</u>
      E

15. <u>Don't</u> stalactites grow up <u>from the floor,</u> and don't stalagmites <u>grow</u> down
      A   **B**   **C**

    <u>from the ceiling?</u> <u>No error</u>
        D   **E**

16. <u>Neither Lincoln nor his generals</u> <u>was</u> able <u>to come up with</u> an acceptable plan for
                 A   **B**   **C**

    bringing a quick end to the <u>hostilities.</u> <u>No error</u>
                              D   **E**

17. <u>In June of 1986,</u> a woman told us <u>that she sighted</u> the <u>Loch Ness</u> monster
      A   **B**   **C**
<u>a month before.</u> <u>No error</u>
      D   **E**

18. <u>One can only imagine</u> what life might be like today if the Nazis <u>would have won</u>
      A   **B**
<u>world war II</u> <u>in Europe.</u> <u>No error</u>
      C   **D**   **E**

19. <u>In the early 1960's</u> <u>President John F. Kennedy</u> had promised <u>to have sent</u> American
      A   **B**   **C**
astronauts to the moon <u>by the end of the decade.</u> <u>No error</u>
                          D   **E**

20. <u>Did</u> Werner von Braun really <u>say,</u> "I just build them. <u>I'm</u> not responsible for
      A   **B**   **C**
where they come <u>down?</u>" <u>No error</u>
                  D   **E**

21. The speaker <u>implied</u> that <u>most</u> of the animals <u>that apeared</u> during the Cambrian
                  A   **B**   **C**
era <u>became</u> extinct. <u>No error</u>
      D   **E**

22. Early in the novel <u>Huck</u> fakes his own <u>death</u> and then <u>slipped</u> away <u>down the river</u>
                         A   **B**   **C**   **D**
on a raft. <u>No error</u>
              E

23. Firefighters worked <u>furiously</u> after the great <u>quake,</u> but before they could put the
                          A   **B**
flames <u>out,</u> most of the city <u>were</u> destroyed. <u>No error</u>
          C   **D**   **E**

24. The density <u>of</u> a human body <u>and</u> the density of water <u>is</u> almost <u>exactly</u> the same.
                  A   **B**   **C**   **D**
<u>No error</u>
  E

25. Until the first <u>debate,</u> the candidate <u>had hoped</u> <u>to have avoided</u> the issue of <u>higher</u>
                      A   **B**   **C**   **D**
taxes. <u>No error</u>
          E

Pronoun Usage

CASES OF PRONOUNS

A pronoun is a part of speech that may take the place of a noun. A pronoun changes form, or **case,** according to its function in the sentence.

The three cases in English are the **nominative case,** the **objective case,** and the **possessive case.** Nominative case pronouns act either as subjects or as predicate nominatives. Objective case pronouns act as objects of verbs or as objects of prepositions. Possessive case pronouns show ownership or possession.

Personal pronouns have the most varied forms of all the categories of pronouns (see Handbook 31 for the categories of pronouns). The forms of the personal pronouns are shown in the box below.

Singular Personal Pronouns

	Nominative	Objective	Possessive
First Person	I	me	my, mine
Second Person	you	you	your, yours
Third Person	he, she, it	him, her, it	his, her, hers, its

Plural Personal Pronouns

	Nominative	Objective	Possessive
First Person	we	us	our, ours
Second Person	you	you	your, yours
Third Person	they	them	their, theirs

Personal pronouns change form, not only according to case but also according to number, person, and gender. The possessive forms *my, your, his, her, its, our,* and *their* function as adjectives that modify nouns: *my* suggestion.

The forms for the pronouns *who* and *whoever* are shown by case below.

Nominative	Objective	Possessive
who	whom	whose
whoever	whomever	whosever

Grammar Handbook 36:
Pronoun Usage

Cases of Pronouns

Objective

- To identify the cases of pronouns

Teaching Strategies

Linking Grammar and Literature

On the chalkboard, write the following excerpt from F. Scott Fitzgerald's "The Rich Boy."

> Let me tell you about the very rich. They are different from you and me. They possess and enjoy early, and it does something to them, makes them soft where we are hard, and cynical where we are trustful, in a way that, unless you were born rich, it is very difficult to understand.

Ask students to identify the pronouns and their cases. Establish that by determining a pronoun's function in a sentence, students can determine its case.

 Individualizing Instruction

LD Students When assigning Exercise B, you may want to simplify the instructions by asking students to do only part of the task.

Additional Resources

- Tests and Assessment, Pretests, pp. 26–28
- Grammar and Usage Practice Book, p. 59

WRITING THEME Family Memories

Some students may want to use family memories as the subject of their next writing assignment.

Concept Check

The Cases of Pronouns

   1. whom—Objective; we—First Person, Plural, Nominative;
us—First Person, Plural, Objective;
her—Third Person, Singular, Objective
   2. we—First Person, Plural, Nominative;
us—First Person, Plural, Objective
   3. I—First Person, Singular, Nominative;
her—Third Person, Singular, Objective
   4. She—Third Person, Singular, Nominative;
my—First Person, Singular, Possessive Case
   5. her—Third Person, Singular, Possessive;
she—Third Person, Singular, Nominative;
I—First Person, Singular, Nominative
   6. They—Third Person, Plural, Nominative;
her—Third Person, Singular, Objective;
their—Third Person, Plural, Possessive;
I—First Person, Singular, Nominative;
they—Third Person, Plural, Nominative;
who—Nominative;
her—Third Person, Singular, Possessive;
her—Third Person, Singular, Possessive; anyone, nominative
   7. We—First Person, Plural, Nominative
   8. It—Third Person, Singular, Nominative
   9. It—Third Person, Singular, Nominative
   10. We—First Person, Plural, Nominative;
our—First Person, Plural, Possessive
   11. No pronoun
   12. I—First Person, Singular, Nominative
   13. We—First Person, Plural, Nominative;
it—Third Person, Singular, Nominative;
I—First Person, Singular, Nominative

Writing Theme
Family Memories

Most indefinite pronouns, such as *anyone* and *no one,* change form only in the possessive case. The possessive case form ends in *'s: someone's, no one's.* For a list of indefinite pronouns, see page 551.

The pronouns *this, that, these, those, which,* and *what* do not change form to indicate case.

Practice Your Skills

CONCEPT CHECK

The Cases of Pronouns In the following passage, identify each personal pronoun as *First, Second,* or *Third Person;* as *Singular* or *Plural;* and as *Nominative, Objective,* or *Possessive Case.* Also, identify the case of indefinite pronouns and forms of *who.* If the sentence does not contain a personal pronoun, write *No pronoun.*

(1) Occasionally Mother, whom we seldom saw in the house, had us meet her at Louie's. . . . (2) While we sat on the stiff wooden booths, Mother would dance alone in front of us to music from the Seeburg. (3) I loved her most at those times. (4) She was like a pretty kite that floated just above my head. . . .

(5) The Syrian brothers vied for her attention as she sang the heavy blues that Bailey and I almost understood. (6) They watched her, even when directing their conversation to other customers, and I knew they too were hypnotized by this beautiful lady who talked with her whole body and snapped her fingers louder than anyone in the whole world. (7) We learned the Time Step at Louie's. (8) It is from this basic step that most American Black dances are born. (9) It is a series of taps, jumps and rests, and demands careful listening, feeling and coordination. (10) We were brought before Mother's friends, . . . to show our artistry. (11) Bailey learned easily, and has always been the better dancer. (12) But I learned too. . . . (13) We were applauded, . . . but it was to be years later before I found the joy and freedom of dancing well.

Maya Angelou, *I Know Why the Caged Bird Sings*

Maya Angelou

694 Grammar Handbook

PRONOUNS IN THE NOMINATIVE CASE

Pronouns, like nouns, may function as subjects or as predicate nominatives. Pronouns used in these ways are in the nominative case.

Pronouns as Subjects

The nominative form of the pronoun is used as the subject of a verb.

Choosing the proper case for pronouns used as subjects usually causes difficulty only in compounds. To decide which pronoun form to use, try each part of the compound by itself with the verb.

> Rena and (I, me) played a duet. (Rena played; I played, *not* me played. *I* is a nominative case pronoun used as part of a compound subject.)

The plural forms *we* and *they* often sound awkward in compound subjects. The problem can be eliminated by recasting the sentence.

Awkward	They and we waited in line for the ticket office to open.
Better	We all waited in line for the ticket office to open.

Pronouns as Predicate Nominatives

A predicate pronoun is linked to the subject by a form of the verb *be*.

The nominative form is used for a predicate pronoun.

The rule above also applies to verb phrases in which the main verb is a form of *be*, such as *could have been, can be,* and *should be.*

> It *was she* waving from the pier.

> The winners of the band contest *should have been they.*

Sometimes the use of the nominative case after the verb *be* sounds awkward. This awkwardness can be avoided by recasting the sentence.

Awkward	The acrobat at the top of the human pyramid was I.
Better	I was the acrobat at the top of the human pyramid.

Writing
—TIP—

Use the nominative case for predicate pronouns in all formal writing.

Pronouns in the Nominative Case

Objective

- To identify pronouns in the nominative case as subjects and as predicate nominatives

Teaching Strategies

Teaching Tip: Compound Subjects

Point out that in writing compound subjects that involve a first-person pronoun, students should place the first-person pronoun last in the series. For example: Rena and I played a duet; She and I played a duet; Rena, Tanya, Jane, and I played a quartet.

Linking Grammar and Writing

The use of nominative-case pronouns in these contexts is required in formal writing. You may wish to point out, however, that objective-case pronouns are used by an overwhelming number of English speakers in dialogue, especially in short exclamatory sentences such as *It's me.* Students writing dialogue for creative assignments should be encouraged to use natural-sounding and appropriate forms.

> **Additional Resources**
> - Grammar and Usage Practice Book, p. 60

WRITING THEME   Circus Jargon

Concept Check
Nominative Case Pronouns
Answers are underlined on page.

Writing Theme
Circus Jargon

Pronouns in the Objective Case

Objectives

- To identify the use of pronouns in the objective case as objects of verbs, objects of prepositions, and pronouns that are used with infinitives
- **Writing** To use pronoun cases correctly in original writing

Practice Your Skills

CONCEPT CHECK

Nominative Case Pronouns   Write the <u>correct form of the pronoun</u> for each sentence. Choose from those given in parentheses.

1. Luisa and (<u>I</u>, me) are among 300 eager applicants to the clown training school in Venice, Florida.
2. The other applicants and (<u>we</u>, us) are enchanted with the colorful language used by circus people.
3. For starters, neither (<u>she</u>, her) nor (<u>I</u>, me) want to be "jossers."
4. Jossers are (<u>they</u>, them) who are not part of the circus business.
5. Of course, the clowns are best; in the words of P. T. Barnum (<u>they</u>, them) are "the pegs to hang the circus on."
6. The "Auguste" clown is (<u>he or she</u>, him or her) who gets a pie or seltzer water in the face.
7. The "Joeys" are the regular clowns; (<u>they</u>, them) are the main attractions for the "flatties," or spectators.
8. Of the two of us, it is (<u>I</u>, me) who most wants to become an Auguste.
9. The other applicants and (<u>we</u>, us) hope to graduate and then be chosen to receive a two-year contract with the circus.
10. Luisa and (<u>I</u>, me) hope that we will be the students most likely to join the graduate clowns.

PRONOUNS IN THE OBJECTIVE CASE

Like nouns, pronouns can function as objects of verbs, as objects of prepositions, and as part of infinitive phrases.

Pronouns as Objects of Verbs

The objective pronoun form is used as a direct or indirect object.

When the object of the verb is a compound object consisting of a noun and pronoun, it is often difficult to decide which pronoun form to use. It is helpful to try each part of the object by itself.

Direct Object   Dennis joined Maria and (I, me) at the bandshell. (joined Maria; joined me, *not* joined I.)

Indirect Object   John gave the mayor and (she, her) a tour of his garden. (gave the mayor; gave her, *not* gave she)

Pronouns as Objects of Prepositions

The objective form of a pronoun is used as the object of a preposition.

Again, the dilemma of deciding which pronoun form to use as the object of a preposition occurs chiefly when an object is compound. To decide, try each pronoun separately in the sentence.

> The note on the door was addressed to Katie and (I, me).
> (to Katie; to me, *not* to I)

Usage Note In informal speech, people often incorrectly use nominative case pronouns as objects of prepositions. This misuse is particularly common with the preposition *between: between you and I.* Use only objective case pronouns for objects of prepositions. The correct form, then, is *between you and me.*

Pronouns with Infinitives

The infinitive is a verb that is preceded by *to.* See Handbook 33 for more information about infinitives.

The objective form of the pronoun is used as the subject, object, or predicate pronoun of an infinitive.

Subject of Infinitive	The clerk asked *me to complete* this form. (*Me* is the subject of *to complete.*)
	We helped *him find* his keys. (*Him* is the subject of *find,* an infinitive in which *to* is omitted.)
Object of Infinitive	Neil went *to meet them* at the airport. (*Them* is the object of *to meet.*)
Predicate Pronoun	We didn't expect the first guest *to be her.* (*Her* is the predicate pronoun after *to be.*)

Practice Your Skills

A. CONCEPT CHECK

Objective Case Pronouns Choose the <u>pronoun</u> that makes each of the following excerpts of poetry correct.

1. And the afternoon, the evening, sleeps so peacefully!/Smoothed by long fingers,/Asleep . . . tired . . . or it malingers,/. . . here beside you and (I, <u>me</u>). **T. S. Eliot**
2. In a field by the river my love and (<u>I</u>, me) did stand,/And on my leaning shoulder she laid her snow-white hand. **W. B. Yeats**

Writing Theme
Modern Poetry

Teaching Strategies

Personal Touch

You may wish to point out that faulty constructions such as *between you and I* result from substituting incorrect nominatives for correct objective-case pronouns. Perhaps you can recall an instance in which this or another pronoun construction caused you difficulty.

Additional Resources
- Grammar and Usage Practice Book, pp. 61–62

WRITING THEME   Modern Poetry
Students may want to research and write about a modern poet as the topic of a future writing assignment.

A. Concept Check
Objective Case Pronouns
Answers are underlined on page.

3. It was not (<u>I</u>, me) who began it./Turned out into draughty caves,/hungry so often, having to work for our bread,/hearing the children whining, I was nevertheless not unhappy. **Judith Wright**

4. Well, I would like to make,/thinking some line still taut between (I, <u>me</u>) and (they, <u>them</u>),/poems direct as what the bird said,/ . . . mysterious as the silence when the tailor/would pause with his needle in the air. **Denise Levertov**

5. Ah, love, let (we, <u>us</u>) be true/To one another! for the world, which seems/to lie before (we, <u>us</u>) like a land of dreams, . . ./Hath really neither joy, nor love, nor light. . . **Matthew Arnold**

6. The instructor said,/*Go home and write/a page tonight./And let that page come out of you—/Then it will be true* . . ./It's not easy to know what is true for you or (I, <u>me</u>) at twenty-two, my age. But I guess I'm what I feel and see and hear, Harlem, I hear you. . . . **Langston Hughes**

7. if i heard/a voice/coming from/a rock/i'd know/and her words/would flow inside (I, <u>me</u>)/like the light/of someone/stirring ashes/from a sleeping fire/at night. **Ray Young Bear**

8. Self-reliant like the cat—/that takes its prey to privacy,/the mouse's limp tail hanging like a shoelace from its mouth—/(they, <u>them</u>) sometimes enjoy solitude, and can be robbed of speech/by speech which has delighted (they, <u>them</u>). **Marianne Moore**

9. Each child seemed a child, like (I, <u>me</u>), on a loose perch,/Holding to childhood like some termless play. **Hart Crane**

10. Great Nature has another thing to do/To you and (I, <u>me</u>); so take the lively air,/And, lovely, learn by going where to go. **Theodore Roethke**

B. PROOFREADING SKILL

Objective Pronouns Rewrite the following paragraph, correcting any <u>errors</u> in pronoun use, in spelling, or in mechanics.

Emily Dickinson was a quiet, somewhat shy young woman. Critics consider <u>she</u> to be one of the greatest of the <u>Modern Poets</u>. Her poems tell <u>we</u> and any future readers of her intense concern for the <u>mysterys</u> of life and death. Most of her works explore the relationship between <u>she</u> and the external world. Although Dickinson lived primarily in seclusion, she had a few close <u>freinds</u>. In general, she preferred to see only <u>they</u> and her family. Some sources link <u>she</u> and the <u>Reverand</u> Charles Wadsworth romantically. <u>However</u> she <u>reguarded</u> him only as "her dearest earthly friend." His move to <u>san francisco</u> ended any chance for <u>he</u> and her to have a future together <u>which</u> <u>sugests</u> one reason for her reclusive lifestyle.

B. Proofreading Skill
Objective Pronouns
Answers will vary.
  See suggested answers below.
  Emily Dickinson was a quiet, somewhat shy young woman. Critics consider her to be one of the greatest of the modern poets. Her poems tell us and any future readers of her intense concern for the mysteries of life and death. Most of her works explore the relationship between her and the external world. Although Dickinson lived primarily in seclusion, she had a few close friends. In general, she preferred to see only them and her family. Some sources link her and the Reverend Charles Wadsworth romantically. However, she regarded him only as "her dearest earthly friend." His move to San Francisco ended any chance for him and her to have a future together, which suggests one reason for her reclusive lifestyle.

C. APPLICATION IN WRITING

A Poem Write a diamond-shaped poem to compare and contrast two people: for example, two friends or two athletes. The top half of the diamond should describe the traits of one person, and the bottom half, the other person. Start the poem with a one-word line, continue with a second line of three words, a third of five words, and so on. The middle or longest line might be a summary or transitional statement about the people. The line lengths of the bottom half then begin to decrease. Use pronouns correctly.

CHECK POINT
PAGES 693–697

Write the correct pronoun from those given in parentheses. Then tell the case of the pronoun you chose.

1. We British and Americans were never closer as allies than (we, us) were during World War II.
2. At that time, Winston Churchill was Prime Minister, and it was (he, him) who united the British to fight Adolph Hitler.
3. Churchill and President Franklin D. Roosevelt formed a strong bond; Churchill asked (he, him) to aid Great Britain.
4. "Give (we, us) the tools and (we, us) will finish the job," he said.
5. Londoners were suffering nightly German bombing raids; for (they, them) life had become a nightmare.
6. Over a million women and children left London because the government strongly urged (they, them) to evacuate the city.
7. Churchill's walking tours of London to inspect damage and boost morale were, for (he, him), a fraction of his work.
8. It was (he, him) who inspired the people with his oratory.
9. Journalist C. L. Sulzberger wrote about (he, him); "(He, Him) fancied . . . oratory, at which (he, him) was magnificent."
10. In one of his most famous speeches, Churchill said, "(I, Me) have nothing to offer but blood, toil, tears, and sweat."
11. "(We, Us) have before (we, us) an ordeal of the most grievous kind," he continued.
12. The British sorely needed inspiring words; a much beleaguered people were (they, them) after the bombing started.
13. Roosevelt and Churchill remained in close contact; Roosevelt agreed to meet (he, him) off the coast of Newfoundland.
14. When the two leaders met, Roosevelt and (he, him) renewed their warm, personal, and official relationship.
15. The Atlantic Charter, issued jointly by (they, them), outlined policies on which (they, them) based hopes for a better future.

C. Application in Writing
A Poem
Answers will vary.

CHECK POINT
PAGES 693–697

You may wish to use the following Checkpoint exercise as an informal evaluation of student mastery of pronouns in the nominative and objective case.

WRITING THEME Winston Churchill
1. we—Nominative
2. he—Nominative
3. him—Objective
4. us—Objective; we—Nominative
5. them—Objective
6. them—Objective
7. him—Objective
8. he—Nominative
9. him—Objective; He—Nominative; he—Nominative
10. I—Nominative
11. We—Nominative; us—Objective
12. they—Nominative
13. him—Objective
14. he—Nominative
15. them—Objective; they—Nominative

Pronoun Usage **699**

Pronouns in the Possessive Case

Objective

- To identify the use of possessive pronouns modifying gerunds

Teaching Strategies

 Individualizing Instruction

Basic Students Point out that although they show possession, possessive personal pronouns never take apostrophes.

Additional Resources

- Grammar and Usage Practice Book, p. 63

PRONOUNS IN THE POSSESSIVE CASE

Personal pronouns that show possession take the possessive case. The possessive pronouns *mine, yours, his, hers, its,* and *theirs* are used in place of nouns: The red towel is *mine. Yours* is striped. *My, our, your, his, her, its,* and *their* are used as adjectives to modify nouns: *My* beach towel is red. *Your* beach towel is striped.

Possessive Pronouns Modifying Gerunds

The possessive pronoun is used when the pronoun immediately precedes a gerund.

> *His running for the train* told us that the hour was late. (*Running for the train* is a gerund phrase functioning as the subject. The possessive form *His* modifies the gerund phrase.)

Remember that present participles also end in *-ing*. However, the possessive case is not used for pronouns that precede participles.

> When we saw *him* running for the train, we knew it was late. (*Him* is the object of the verb. *Running for the train* is a participial phrase modifying *him*.)

If the *-ing* word is used as a noun, it is a gerund; used as a modifier, it is a participle. A gerund often functions as the subject or object in a sentence. Check to see how the *-ing* word is used.

> The neighbors objected to *their* playing the drums at midnight. (*Playing the drums at midnight* is a gerund phrase, the object of the preposition *to*. The possessive pronoun *their* should be used before the gerund. The act of playing is focused on.)

> The neighbors heard *them* playing the drums at midnight. (*Playing the drums* is a participial phrase modifying *them*. The persons playing the drums are focused on.)

In some sentences, either form of the pronoun can be used, depending on the meaning and the emphasis desired.

> Imagine *his ice-skating in the Olympics*. (emphasizes action)

> Imagine *him ice-skating in the Olympics*. (emphasizes person)

For more about gerunds and participles, see Handbook 33.

Writing
—**TIP**—

Proofread your writing to be sure you have not used an apostrophe with a possessive pronoun.

Practice Your Skills

CONCEPT CHECK

Possessive Pronouns   Choose the <u>correct pronoun</u> in parentheses.

1. Sofia, a computer programmer, found that (she, <u>her</u>) researching the history of computers led her to a book about Charles Babbage.
2. She learned about (him, <u>his</u>) trying to eliminate errors in logarithmic tables during the early 1800's.
3. Babbage wanted to build a complicated machine to eliminate the necessity of (him, <u>his</u>) doing all calculations by hand.
4. Over the course of a long lifetime, Babbage devoted many hours to (him, <u>his</u>) working out the details of his marvelous machine.
5. Babbage's machine was an early attempt at a computer; (it's, <u>its</u>) parts could manipulate numbers to solve a variety of problems.
6. He approached the government and scientific societies for money; he promised (<u>them</u>, their) programming and calculating devices.
7. Babbage assured his sponsors that not only would his machine have a "memory," but (<u>his</u>, him) attaching the machine to a printer would result in (<u>its</u>, it's) printing answers.
8. His demonstration of the use of punch cards led to sponsors giving (them, <u>their</u>) support.
9. Babbage never did come up with anything that worked like (us, <u>our</u>) computing devices of today.
10. Nevertheless, (<u>his</u>, him) pioneering laid some of the groundwork for exciting computer developments that were to come later.

Writing Theme
Pioneers

PROBLEMS IN PRONOUN USAGE

The most common problems in pronoun usage occur in deciding whether the nominative or the objective form is the correct one.

Who and *Whom* in Questions and Clauses

In choosing whether to use *who* or *whom* in a question, it is necessary to understand the function of the pronoun.

Who, the nominative form of the pronoun, is used as the subject of a verb or as a predicate pronoun. *Whom,* the objective form, is used as the direct object or as the object of a preposition.

> *Who* auditioned for the lead role? (*Who* is the subject of *auditioned.*)

> *Whom* did the director choose for the lead role? (*Whom* is the direct object of *did choose.*)

Pronoun Usage   **701**

Problems in Pronoun Usage

Objectives

- To identify the proper use of *who, whom, whose, whoever,* and *whomever* in questions and clauses
- To identify and use pronouns correctly with *and* as appositives, in reflexive and intensive form, and in comparisons
- **Writing**   To use pronouns correctly in writing

Teaching Strategies

Critical Thinking

Analyzing   Have students analyze the function of the pronouns in the subordinate clauses of the sentences. *Whoever* and *whomever* are likely to give students special difficulty. Encourage them to analyze the context of the sample sentence about the Holy Grail. Students should recognize that the preposition *by* governs the whole clause. If necessary, review adjective and noun clauses. (See Grammar Handbook 33, pages 605–614).

Basic Students When discussing the usage problems in this section, stress that not all dialects follow the patterns and usages of standard English. Remind these students, however, that correct usage is important in contexts in which standard English is considered appropriate (such as academic writing, job applications and interviews, and work).

ESL Students Have these students complete the exercises in this section as a group. Encourage them to discuss how pronoun usage differs in other languages. Also, encourage them to discuss the English usage problems they find most troublesome.

Additional Resources
- Grammar and Usage Practice Book, p. 64

WRITING THEME   History of Rock-and-Roll

A. Concept Check
Who and Whom
Answers are underlined on page.

Writing
— **TIP** —

In formal writing, use *whom* whenever the objective case of *who* is needed.

Writing Theme
History of Rock-and-Roll

The pronouns *who, whoever, whom, whomever,* and *whose* may be used in noun or adjective clauses. These pronouns have a function within the clause.

Who and *whoever* are nominative case forms and can act as subjects or predicate pronouns in a clause. *Whom* and *whomever* are objective forms and can be direct objects or objects of a preposition.

In determining which pronoun you should use, first isolate the subordinate clause. Next determine how the pronoun functions in that clause.

> The writer (who, whom) we just studied was Thomas Malory. (The adjective clause is *[who, whom] we just studied.* The pronoun functions as the direct object of *studied* in the clause. *Whom,* the objective case pronoun, is needed.)

> The Holy Grail would be found by (whoever, whomever) was the most worthy person. (The noun clause is *[whoever, whomever] was the most worthy.* The entire clause is the object of the preposition *by.* The pronoun acts as the subject of the verb *was* within the clause. The nominative case pronoun *whoever* is the correct choice.)

In determining whether to use *who* or *whom,* do not be misled by parenthetical expressions in the subordinate clause.

> In one version of the legend, it is Perceval who, *I think,* finds the Holy Grail. (*Who* is the subject of *finds* in the subordinate clause. *I think* is a parenthetical expression.)

The pronoun *whose* functions as a possessive pronoun.

> The knight *whose* destiny was to find the Holy Grail was Galahad. (*Whose* is a possessive pronoun modifying *destiny.*)

Practice Your Skills

A. CONCEPT CHECK

Who and Whom   Choose the correct pronoun from those given in parentheses.

1. Rock-and-roll became familiar to the American public through Bill Haley and the Comets, (who, whom, whose) combined a heavy beat with a call to dance.
2. There were few teens of the fifties for (who, whom) the Comets' "Rock Around the Clock" was not a favorite.
3. It is Alan Freed, a Cleveland disc jockey, to (who, whom, whose) credit is given for popularizing the term *rock-and-roll.*

702 Grammar Handbook

4. (<u>Whoever</u>, Whomever) listened carefully to early rock-and-roll recognized its origin in rhythm and blues.
5. There is one musician, Chuck Berry, (who, <u>whom</u>) critics consider important to the early history of this music.
6. Berry was a trailblazer (who, whom, <u>whose</u>) virtuoso electric guitar playing helped set the style of rock.
7. (<u>Who</u>, Whom) does not think of the name Elvis Presley when rock is mentioned?
8. There was no one before him (<u>who</u>, whom) mixed country with rhythm and blues to produce songs such as "Heartbreak Hotel."
9. (Who, <u>Whom</u>) do people think of when they hear "I Want to Hold Your Hand"?
10. The sixties brought the Beatles, (who, whom, <u>whose</u>) new harmonies and effective lyrics transformed rock.
11. This British group, (who, <u>whom</u>) American audiences flocked to hear, had its first US hit in 1964.
12. All of these artists (<u>who</u>, whom) helped shape rock-and-roll contributed to what has become a popular musical style in our culture.

B. DRAFTING SKILL

Sentence Combining   Rewrite the following paragraph by drafting combined sentences by using forms of *who, whom,* or *whose.*

(1) In the sixties, musicians helped form popular culture. Their music appealed to the youth of the decade. (2) P. F. Sloan was one of the songwriters. He stirred consciousness of social issues in the United States. (3) Barry McGuire was a singer. With him, Sloan worked on the song "Eve of Destruction." (4) Others sang of many other social issues and problems. To them music was meant to convey a message. (5) British bands, such as the Rolling Stones, were also among the groups. Their music and messages influenced the youth movement. (6) One member of the Rolling Stones was Mick Jagger. People are likely to recognize Mick Jagger today. (7) The Rolling Stones and the Doors were especially popular with young people. Some of the young people considered themselves part of the counterculture. (8) Other youths listened to the message music of Peter, Paul, and Mary and of Simon and Garfunkel. These youths were not necessarily part of the counterculture. (9) They were among the many groups. They sang thought-provoking songs with gentle rhythms. (10) Overall, the music of the sixties offered myriad messages set to various beats. Anyone would listen for its meaning.

B. Drafting Skill
Sentence Combining
Answers will vary. See typical answers below.
  (1) In the sixties, musicians *whose* music appealed to the youth of the decade helped form popular culture. (2) P. F. Sloan was one of the songwriters *who* stirred consciousness of social issues in the United States. (3) Barry McGuire was a singer with *whom* Sloan worked on the song "Eve of Destruction." (4) Other singers, to *whom* music was also meant to convey a message, sang of many other social issues and problems. (5) British bands, such as the Rolling Stones, were also among the groups *whose* music and messages influenced the youth movement. (6) Mick Jagger was one member of the Rolling Stones *whom* people are likely to recognize today. (7) The Rolling Stones and the Doors were especially popular with young people, some of *whom* considered themselves part of the counterculture. (8) Other youths, *who* were not necessarily part of the counterculture, listened to the message music of Peter, Paul, and Mary and of Simon and Garfunkel. (9) They were among the many groups *who* sang thought-provoking songs with gentle rhythms. (10) Overall, to *whoever* would listen for its meaning, the music of the sixties offered myriad messages set to various beats.

C. Application in Writing
A Biography
Answers will vary but should include clauses beginning with *who* or *whom* to identify actions of people in the subject's life.

Teaching Strategies

Speaking and Listening

To highlight the use of pronouns, you may wish to read aloud the sample sentences. Use a number of different techniques; for example, omit the appositives or deliberately substitute the wrong pronouns. Help students distinguish between the correct and incorrect versions of each sentence.

WRITING THEME   Ballet

Concept Check
Appositives
Answers are underlined on page.

Writing Theme
Ballet

C. APPLICATION IN WRITING

A Biography   Choose a famous figure from the history of rock-and-roll, such as Chuck Berry or Grace Slick. Do some research and write a biographical sketch of this person. Use *who* or *whom* to add clauses identifying the actions of influential persons in your subject's life.

Pronouns Used with and as Appositives

Appositives are words or phrases that immediately follow another word for the purpose of identifying that word. A pronoun can be the appositive, part of the appositive, or the word identified.

Pronouns Used with Appositives   The pronouns *we* and *us* are often followed by appositives. To decide whether to use the nominative case *we* or the objective case *us,* read the sentence without the appositive.

> The usher told (we, us) Ranger fans to return to the stadium. (told us, *not* told we)

> (We, Us) Rangers trounced the Tigers in both games. (We trounced, *not* us trounced)

Pronouns as Appositives   The correct form of a pronoun used as an appositive is determined by the use of the noun to which the pronoun is in apposition.

> The children, *Jerry and she,* were riding on the carousel. (*Jerry* and *she* are in apposition to *children,* which is the subject of *were riding.* The nominative form *she* is required.)

To determine which form of the pronoun to use in apposition, try the appositive by itself in the sentence.

> The usher guided the latecomers, Gina and (he, him), to their seats with a flashlight. (guided him, *not* guided he)

Practice Your Skills

CONCEPT CHECK

Appositives   Choose the correct pronoun from those in parentheses.

1. (We, Us) reviewers do not often rave about performances.
2. Nevertheless, the production of Tchaikovsky's *Swan Lake* left the audience, ballet aficionados and (we, us), breathless.
3. Liv Ullman explained to (we, us) members of the audience that the ballet was a cooperative effort of the Soviet and U.S. citizens.

Dancers Climbing a Stairway, Edgar Degas

4. The producers, (they and we, them and us), combined the best in the ballet world.
5. The choreography was done by Konstantin Sergeyev; two brilliant minds, Natalia Dudinskaya and (he, him), staged the ballet.
6. The finest part of the production was the dancing of Nina Ananiashvili; Devon Carney and (she, her) danced the leads.
7. Needless to say, both dancers, (he and she, him and her), brilliantly portrayed the prince and the beautiful swan.
8. After the performance, (we, us) spellbound viewers loudly proclaimed, "Bravo! Brava!"
9. All the participants in this collaboration, both (we and they, us and them), were delighted with the response.
10. A hope held by many, including my fellow reviewers and (I, me), is that the future holds other Soviet–United States productions—*Sleeping Beauty*, perhaps?

Reflexive and Intensive Pronouns

A pronoun ending in *-self* or *-selves* can be used intensively for emphasis or reflexively to refer to a preceding noun or pronoun.

> I *myself* completed the one thousand piece jigsaw puzzle. (intensive)

> Richard locked *himself* out of his car. (reflexive—direct object)

Pronouns ending in *-self* or *-selves* cannot be used alone. Each must have an antecedent—the word to which it refers—in the same sentence.

Incorrect   Sara and myself are interested in robotics.(There is no antecedent for *myself*.)

Correct   Sara and I are interested in robotics.

The forms *hisself* and *theirselves* are nonstandard. Do not use them.

Pronoun Usage   **705**

Humanities Connection

Art Note   *Dancers Climbing a Stairway* (1885-90) is one of some 1500 works on the subject of ballet dancers by Edgar Degas (1834-1917), a French Impressionist painter and sculptor. Note the off-center placement of the dancers, the half-hidden views, and the unusual vantage point in this painting, all innovations of Degas' compositional style.

Writing Theme
Irish Storytelling

Practice Your Skills

CONCEPT CHECK

Reflexive and Intensive Pronouns   Write the correct pronoun from those given in parentheses.

1. The Irish pride (them, themselves) on their flair for highly imaginative storytelling.
2. An Irish storyteller, Lord Dunsany, provided (us, ourselves) with stories described as credible fantasy.
3. In one story, a young man dining at a restaurant has an animated conversation, seemingly with (him, himself).
4. The young man asks his "guest" if he has actually seen Helen of Troy (her, herself).
5. Between (them, themselves), the conversation ranges from Cheops to Cleopatra.
6. The reader senses that the guest (hisself, himself) knew them all personally.
7. One also wonders if the young man might be lovesick over a woman busy amusing (her, herself) elsewhere.
8. After dinner, the young man cryptically tells his guest, "I (me, myself) haven't taken (you, yourself) much out of your way."
9. With this the young man drinks the coffee he (him, himself) poisoned, and falls to the floor.
10. Discerning readers praise (them, themselves) for guessing that Death was the young man's guest.

Pronouns in Comparisons

A clause that begins with *than* or the sequence *as . . . as* can be used to establish a comparison.

> Marie is more musical *than* Lillian is.
> I did *as* many push-ups *as* Francisco.

The final clause in a comparison is sometimes elliptical; that is, some words are omitted. The omission of words makes it difficult to determine the correct pronoun.

> Marie is more musical than she.
> I did as many push-ups as he.

To decide which pronoun form to use in an elliptical clause, fill in the words that are not stated.

> The noise scared Phyllis more than (I, me). (The noise scared Phyllis more than it scared *me*.)

Teaching Strategies

Linking Grammar and Writing

Emphasize the importance of avoiding ambiguity in elliptical clauses that contain pronouns. Remind students that careful writers avoid ambiguity by supplying all the words instead of an elliptical clause, which might be misread.

Additional Resources
- Grammar and Usage Practice Book, p. 65

Sometimes either the nominative case or the objective case pronoun form may be correct, depending on the meaning.

> She writes her sister more often than he. (This means "She writes to her sister more often than he does.")

> She writes her sister more often than him. (This means "She writes to her sister more often than she writes to him.")

Practice Your Skills

A. CONCEPT CHECK

Pronouns in Comparisons   Choose the <u>correct pronoun</u> from those given in parentheses.

1. Mickey, Minnie, Donald, and Goofy—no characters in the world are as beloved as (<u>they</u>, them).
2. No fans have ever been more devoted than (<u>we</u>, us).
3. Their creator, Walt Disney, was a man of many talents; perhaps no one other than (<u>he</u>, him) could have built such an empire.
4. The success in 1928 of *Steamboat Willie* made Disney famous; audiences as well as (<u>he</u>, him) were enchanted with "talking films."
5. No one in the business worked harder than (<u>he</u>, him) and his brother Roy, who was the company's business manager.
6. Together they built a successful industry involving much more than short cartoons, which surprised their audiences as much as (they, <u>them</u>).
7. Moviegoers of the 30's were not as accustomed to products tied to movies as (<u>we</u>, us).
8. No one foresaw the possibilities of licensed products as well as (<u>they</u>, them), the founders of the Disney empire.
9. From cartoons to amusement parks, Disney has delighted fans in the past as much as (we, <u>us</u>) audiences today.
10. For a man who built an empire on fantasy, a realist more astute than (<u>he</u>, him) would be hard to find.

WRITING THEME   The Business of Film

A. Concept Check
Pronouns in Comparisons
Answers are underlined on page.

Pronoun Usage   **707**

B. Proofreading Skill

Pronouns

Answers will vary. See suggested answers below.

We movie spectators see many special effects, from dogfights in space to poltergeists in houses. In one longstanding movie technique, a piece of film is superimposed over another. It was the film pioneer Georges Méliès who first exploited this process in narrative films of the early 1900's. In the recent *Star Wars* movies by George Lucas, his special-effects team and he advanced the technique. Computers were used to track two cameras so that, after shooting, separate exposures could be put together into one final film. This method allowed him and his team to produce such classic scenes as the flight through the forest in *Return of the Jedi,* where both the characters and the background move. In fact, the computers worked so well that to him and his team the results seemed too perfect. Therefore, they introduced random movements into the computer program for variety.

C. Application in Writing

A Movie Review

Answers will vary.

B. PROOFREADING SKILL

Pronouns Rewrite the following paragraph. Correct <u>all errors</u> in pronoun usage, as well as any errors in spelling, capitalization, and punctuation.

<u>Us</u> movie spectators see many special effects, from dogfights in <u>Space</u> to poltergeists in houses. In one longstanding movie technique, a <u>peace</u> of film is superimposed over another. It was the film pioneer Georges Méliès <u>whom</u> first exploited this process in <u>narritive</u> films of the early 1900's. In the recent *Star wars* movies by George Lucas, his special-<u>affect</u> team and <u>him</u> advanced the technique. Computers were used to track two <u>camaras</u> so that, after shooting separate exposures could be put together into one final film. This method allowed <u>himself</u> and his team to produce such classic scenes as the flight through the forest in *return of the jedi,* where both the characters and the background move. In fact the computers worked so well that to <u>he</u> and his team the results seemed too perfect. Therefore, they introduced random movements into the computer program for variety.

C. APPLICATION IN WRITING

A Movie Review Think of a movie you have seen recently that included special effects. Describe the effects and compare them with similar effects you have seen in other movies. Think about the ways in which the effects were unique or fascinating and might be of special interest to other moviegoers. You might also want to speculate on how some of these effects were created. Use pronouns correctly as you write.

CHECK POINT
PAGES 700–708

Choose the <u>correct pronoun</u> of the two given in parentheses.

Writing Theme
Sherlock Holmes

1. (<u>We</u>, Us) mystery fans know well the address 221B Baker Street, in London.
2. The person (<u>who</u>, whom) lived at this address was Sherlock Holmes, the most famous detective in all fiction.
3. Many mystery fans know that Sir Arthur Conan Doyle, (<u>who</u>, whom) created Holmes, based some of (<u>his</u>, him) writing on the actual life of Dr. Joseph Bell, a surgeon and teacher.
4. Bell was renowned for (<u>his</u>, him) careful analytic thinking.
5. Few were better at deductive reasoning than (<u>he</u>, him).
6. Another person (who, <u>whom</u>) Doyle used as a model for Holmes was a cricket-playing friend named Sherlock.
7. In addition, Doyle modeled after (him, <u>himself</u>) some aspects of the character, Holmes.
8. In the Sherlock Holmes stories, Holmes works for (<u>whoever</u>, whomever) comes to him with an interesting case.
9. At the famous Baker Street address, Dr. Watson and (<u>he</u>, himself) discuss many a crime.
10. Holmes is a smart, capable man, but Watson is more amiable and good-natured than (<u>he</u>, himself).
11. In case after case, Holmes and Watson prove (them, <u>themselves</u>) superior to their adversaries, the craftiest criminals of the day.
12. Watson is a loyal friend, and part of practically every story is devoted to (<u>his</u>, him) extolling Holmes's virtues or exclaiming over Holmes's powers of reasoning.
13. (<u>Whoever</u>, Whomever) reads the Sherlock Holmes stories will find that Watson serves as a foil for Holmes.
14. Watson is a foil because (<u>his</u>, him) plodding makes Holmes's brilliance seem even more spectacular by contrast.
15. The Sherlock Holmes stories have given (we, <u>us</u>) mystery readers untold pleasure for many years.
16. Some readers have even formed clubs that discuss the situations Holmes gets (hisself, <u>himself</u>) into.
17. The members of one such club in New York call (theirselves, <u>themselves</u>) the "The Baker Street Irregulars."
18. A similar group, (<u>who</u>, whom) meet in London, have a more traditional name: "The Sherlock Holmes Society."
19. Few writers have had more demanding fans than (<u>he</u>, him).
20. Tiring of his hero, the author wrote Holmes' death scene; however, the public would not stand for (<u>his</u>, him) killing Holmes off.

You may wish to use the following Checkpoint exercise to evaluate student mastery of the rules for using pronouns covered in this handbook.

WRITING THEME   Sherlock Holmes
You may wish to encourage students who have read some of the Sherlock Holmes mysteries to discuss them in class. Those students may want to write about the famous detective as a topic for a writing assignment.
Answers are underlined on page.

Pronoun Usage   **709**

Pronoun–Antecedent Agreement

Objective

- To identify correct agreement of pronouns with their antecedents in gender, number, and case

Teaching Strategies

Linking Grammar and Writing

Stress that prepositional phrases that intervene between the simple subject and the verb can momentarily sidetrack even careful writers from focusing on proper pronoun agreement. You might discuss examples such as the following: *Everyone* on both teams played to the limit of *his* ability; It was so hot that *many* in the audience removed *their* jackets.

PRONOUN-ANTECEDENT AGREEMENT

An antecedent is the noun or pronoun to which a pronoun refers.

A pronoun must agree with its antecedent in number, gender, and person.

Agreement in Number   If the antecedent of a pronoun is singular, a singular pronoun is required. If the antecedent is plural, a plural pronoun is required.

The following indefinite pronouns are singular. When one of these is an antecedent, the second pronoun must be singular.

another	anything	everybody	neither	one
anybody	each	everyone	nobody	somebody
anyone	either	everything	no one	someone

Each (singular) of the violinists brought *his* (singular) violin. (*Each* is the antecedent of *his*.)

Everyone (singular) indicated *his or her* (singular) preferences in the marketing opinion survey.

Remember that a prepositional phrase following a singular indefinite pronoun does not affect the number of any other word in the sentence.

The following indefinite pronouns are plural and are referred to by the plural possessive pronouns *our, your, their*.

both	few	many	several

Both of the candidates had given *their* speeches by ten o'clock.

Many of us have taken all *our* required math courses.

The indefinite pronouns *all, some, any, most,* and *none* may be referred to by a singular or plural pronoun, depending on the meaning.

All of the play had *its* setting in a steam bath.

All of the networks are showing *their* best shows.

In the preceding examples, the indefinite pronouns are used as subjects. Note that the verb, as well as any pronouns referring to the subject, agrees in number with the subject.

Notice the other pronouns and the verbs in the following sentences that contain the indefinite pronoun *none*.

Incorrect   None of the debaters *has* made *their* rebuttal.

Correct   None of the debaters *has* made *his or her* rebuttal.

Correct   None of the debaters *have* made *their* rebuttals.

Two or more singular antecedents joined by *or* or *nor* are referred to by a singular pronoun. When any part of a compound antecedent joined by *or* or *nor* is plural, use the noun nearer the verb to determine whether the pronoun is singular or plural.

> Either *Kate* or *Geraldine* will lend me *her* skis.

> Neither *Marty* nor the *other gymnasts* have met *their* new coach.

Collective nouns may be referred to by either a singular or plural pronoun, depending on the meaning intended.

> The committee has made *its* decision on the location of the new park. (The committee is thought of as a singular whole.)

> The committee made *their* position speeches on the location of the new park. (The committee members are considered as individuals.)

Agreement in Gender   A pronoun must be of the same gender as the word to which it refers. *He, his,* and *him* are masculine pronouns. *She, her,* and *hers* are feminine pronouns. *It* and *its* are neuter.

When a singular pronoun refers to an antecedent that includes both males and females, the phrase *his or her* is acceptable. In fact, it is preferred to the use of *his* by many who want to avoid sexist language.

Correct   Each climber should bring *his* survival kit.

Correct   Each climber should bring *his or her* survival kit.

Agreement in Person   A personal pronoun must be in the same person as its antecedent. *One, everyone,* and *everybody* are in the third person. They should be referred to by the third-person pronouns.

Incorrect   Everyone should clean up your own lab area.

Correct   Everyone should clean up his or her own lab area.

A. Concept Check

Pronoun-Antecedent Agreement

1. In medieval times, neither a knight nor his page was likely to be seen without one of his weapons—a lance, a dagger, or a spear.
2. In fact, most of the people judged their favorite knights by the type and number of their weapons.
3. When knights engaged in jousting, the combat between two horsemen, each rider carried a lance tucked under his arm.
4. Correct
5. Each of the knights who jousted spent many hours of his day in careful training and practice.
6. Correct
7. Correct
8. Anyone who fought on foot knew his lance was too long.
9. All of the French knights who fought on foot shortened their lances.
10. Most of the knights also took off their foot-armor; that way, the army could handle its task of fighting on foot more efficiently.

B. Proofreading Skill

Pronoun-Antecedent Agreement

Answers will vary. See typical answers below.

One of the most romantic sports—fencing—has a long history. There is even an ancient Egyptian carving of fencers. Unlike fencing in centuries past, none of the modern fencers try to wound their opponents. Both women and men are modern practitioners of the sport, which involves the skillful use of swords for attack and defense. Most maintain that fencing is more like a game of live chess. Each of the fencers tries to outwit his or her opponent. The object for a fencer is to touch his or her opponent with a foil—without being touched himself or herself. Since a fencer needs to strike quickly and to know when to strike, both physical and psychological skills have their place in the sport. For the fencer's protection, each of the foils has a blunted tip at the end of its blade. All of the equipment—a canvas jacket, a mesh mask, and the foil—is available for him or her to rent in fencing classes.

712 Grammar Handbook

Writing Theme
Fencing and Jousting

Practice Your Skills

A. CONCEPT CHECK

Pronoun-Antecedent Agreement   Find and correct the errors in agreement in these sentences. Write *Correct* if there is no error.

1. In medieval times, neither a knight nor his page was likely to be seen without one of their weapons—a lance, a dagger, or a spear.
2. In fact, most of the people judged his or her favorite knight by the type and number of his weapons.
3. When knights engaged in jousting, the combat between two horsemen, each rider carried a lance tucked under their arm.
4. Not everyone, however, was able to control both his horse and his heavy lance at the same time.
5. Each of the knights who jousted spent many hours of their day in careful training and practice.
6. Both of the combatants in a joust had to be ready to aim and thrust their lances as well as to deflect blows.
7. Despite all of this rigorous training, many of the knights who fought in actual combat did not use their lances at all.
8. Anyone who fought on foot knew their lance was too long.
9. All of the French knights who fought on foot shortened his lances.
10. Most of the knights also took off their foot-armor; that way, the army could handle their task of fighting on foot more efficiently.

B. PROOFREADING SKILL

Pronoun-Antecedent Agreement   Rewrite the paragraph. Correct <u>all errors</u> in pronoun usage, spelling, capitalization, and punctuation.

One of the most romantic sports—fencing—<u>have</u> a long history. There is even an ancient <u>egyptian</u> carving of fencers. Unlike fencing in centuries past, none of the modern fencers try to wound <u>his</u> opponents? Both women and men are modern practitioners of the sport, which involves the <u>skilful</u> use of swords for attack and <u>defence</u>. Most <u>maintains</u> that fencing is more like a game of live chess. Each of the fencers tries to outwit <u>their</u> opponent. The object for a fencer is to touch <u>their</u> opponent with a foil—without being touched <u>yourself</u>. Since a fencer needs to strike quickly and know when to strike, both physical and psychological skills have <u>its</u> place in the sport. For the <u>fencers</u> protection, each of the foils has a blunted tip at the end of <u>their</u> blade. All of the equipment—a canvas jacket, a mesh mask, and the foil—is available for <u>you</u> to rent in fencing classes.

PRONOUN REFERENCE

A writer must be sure that pronouns have clear antecedents. If the pronoun reference is vague or ambiguous, the resulting sentence may be confusing to the reader. This section covers some of the common kinds of errors that occur with pronoun reference.

Unidentified and Indefinite Reference

To avoid any confusion for the reader, each personal pronoun should have a clear antecedent.

If no antecedent for the pronoun is present, or if the antecedent is vague or indefinite, the reader will be misled.

Unidentified Reference The words *it, they, this, which,* and *that* can create problems because in some cases they appear without a referent. Often the problem can be solved by reworking the sentence.

Unidentified	It says in the introduction that the story is true.
Better	The introduction states that the story is true.
Unidentified	In New Guinea they used large stones as money.
Better	People in New Guinea once used large stones as money.

The pronoun *you* is sometimes used to refer to people in general, rather than to the person spoken to. Avoid this confusing use of *you.*

Weak	In pioneer days you had to travel on horseback, by covered wagon, or on foot.
Better	The pioneers had to travel on horseback, by covered wagon, or on foot.

Indefinite Reference When the idea to which the pronoun refers is only weakly or vaguely expressed, a clear antecedent must be supplied. Sometimes the solution is to replace the pronoun with a noun.

Weak	Richard juggles at children's parties. It takes up much of his free time on weekends. (There is no clear antecedent for the pronoun *It.* The pronoun vaguely relates to the verb *juggles,* but a verb cannot be the antecedent for a noun.)
Better	Richard juggles at children's parties. Juggling takes up much of his free time on weekends.

Teaching Strategies

Cooperative Learning

Have pairs of students write sentences containing unclear pronoun references such as those in the sample sentences. Then have the pairs switch sentences and correct the work. Discuss the improvements in sentence clarity made by the corrections.

> **Additional Resources**
> - Grammar and Usage Practice Book, pp. 68–69

Weak	Hiking is my favorite sport although I haven't been on one yet this summer. (There is no clear antecedent for *one;* the verbal *hiking* cannot be a replacement for *one.*)
Better	Hiking is my favorite sport although I haven't yet been on a single hike this summer.
Vague	Computers are used to give farmers data on prices. This helps them track the profitability of their operations. (There is no clear antecedent for *This.*)
Better	The use of computers to get data on prices helps farmers track the profitability of their operations.
Vague	We arrived at the theater twenty minutes early, which meant we had time to read the program. (There is no clear antecedent for *which.*)
Better	Because we arrived at the theater twenty minutes early, we had time to read the program.

Ambiguous Reference

The word *ambiguous* means "having two or more possible meanings." The reference of a pronoun is ambiguous if the pronoun may refer to more than one word. This situation can arise when a noun or pronoun falls between the pronoun and its true antecedent, as shown in the following examples.

Ambiguous	Before putting the car in the garage, Beth cleaned it. (What did she clean? the car? the garage?)
Better	Beth cleaned the car before putting it in the garage.
Ambiguous	Barry told Kev that his camera was defective. (Whose camera? Barry's or Kev's?)
Better	Barry examined Kev's camera and told him it was defective.

Practice Your Skills

A. CONCEPT CHECK

Pronoun Reference   Rewrite the sentences to remove all indefinite or ambiguous pronoun references.

1. They tell a story about a famous Indian elephant that was brought to the United States in 1920.
2. It states in one source that the elephant was a present for a little girl.

Writing
TIP

When you proof-read your writing, make sure that each pronoun has a clear, specific antecedent preceding it.

Writing Theme
Famous Animals

3. The elephant was taken to its new home in a taxi, where it was deemed too difficult to handle.
4. From there, the elephant was given to a circus and entrusted to a trainer; he learned to do tricks.
5. The elephant, whose name was Ziggy, pleased the crowds by playing "Yes, Sir, That's My Baby" on the harmonica, and they loved it.
6. Nevertheless, you can lose your popularity at any time, and the day came when Ziggy was sent to the zoo.
7. The press reported that Ziggy and his keeper did not get along, and that he tried to kill him.
8. Ziggy spent the next thirty years in a cage apart from the other elephants; it was an isolation that aroused a great outcry of public sympathy.
9. Eventually, children raised enough money to "save" Ziggy. This enabled them to get a larger cage in a sunny location for the elephant.
10. By 1970 Ziggy was leading the good life again, romping with the other elephants. It filled the old elephant's time and seemed to bring him happiness.

B. REVISION SKILL

Revising to Correct Errors in Pronoun Usage Revise the following paragraph, correcting any unidentified, indefinite, or ambiguous references. One sentence in the paragraph contains no error; label that sentence *Correct*.

(1) "I don't know which is more high strung, my horse Bucephalus or my son Alexander. I ought to have him destroyed," mused Philip II, leader of Macedonia, "especially since no one can ride him." (2) It says in legend that Philip had sought a horse for combat. (3) It described the high-spirited horse, Bucephalus, who was brought by a clever horse trader. (4) Philip immediately realized he was unusual. (5) In Bucephalus you found speed, daring, and beauty—and a horse that was afraid of its own shadow. (6) Alexander bet Philip that he could ride the horse. (7) Philip took the bet because it seemed certain that Alexander would not win. (8) However, Alexander had never ridden one he couldn't master. (9) This enabled him to discover a way to break the steed. (10) Alexander turned Bucephalus to face the sun so that the horse would not see its own shadow, jumped on its back, and galloped across the field, thus winning the bet.

3. The elephant was taken by taxi to its new home, where the elephant was deemed too difficult to handle.
4. From there, the elephant was given to a circus and entrusted to a trainer who taught it to do tricks.
5. The elephant, whose name was Ziggy, played "Yes, Sir, That's My Baby" on the harmonica, a performance the crowds loved.
6. Nevertheless, Ziggy's popularity was bound to decrease sooner or later, and the day came when Ziggy was sent to the zoo.
7. The press reported that Ziggy and his keeper did not get along, and that Ziggy tried to kill his keeper.
8. Ziggy spent the next thirty years in a cage isolated from the other elephants, a situation that aroused a great outcry of public sympathy.
9. Eventually, children raised enough money to "save" Ziggy. The money they raised enabled the zoo to get a larger cage in a sunny location for the elephant.
10. By 1970 Ziggy was leading the good life again, romping with the other elephants. This fun filled the old elephant's time and seemed to bring him happiness.

B. Revision Skill
Revising to Correct Errors in Pronoun Usage
Answers will vary. See typical answers below.
(1) "I don't know which is more high strung, my horse Bucephalus or my son Alexander. I ought to have the horse destroyed," mused Philip II, leader of Macedonia, "especially since no one can ride him." (2) According to the legend, Philip had sought a horse for combat. (3) The legend described the high-spirited horse, Bucephalus, that was brought by a clever horse trader. (4) Philip immediately realized Bucephalus was unusual. (5) In Bucephalus Philip found speed, daring, and beauty—and a horse that was afraid of its own shadow. (6) Alexander bet Philip that he himself could ride the horse. (7) Philip took the bet because he felt certain that Alexander would not win. (8) However, Alexander had never ridden a horse he couldn't master. (9) His skill enabled him to discover a way to break the steed. (10) Correct

CHECK POINT
PAGES 710–715

You may wish to use the following Checkpoint exercise as an informal evaluation of student mastery of the rules for avoiding unclear pronoun references.

WRITING THEME   Georgia O'Keeffe

Answers will vary. See typical answers below.

1. Each of the great artists can be said to have his or her own personal vision, and the American artist Georgia O'Keeffe found hers.

2. One article about O'Keeffe states that she worked between realism and abstraction.

3. O'Keeffe's paintings often contain gigantic flowers and the haunting images of bleached bones against the dark earth and sky.

4. Her artistic talent was recognized in her early teens, and she knew she wanted to become an artist.

5. O'Keeffe's fame came almost by accident in 1916 when she sent charcoal drawings to a friend who was impressed by them.

6. Because her friend showed the drawings to an art gallery director, the drawings were put on display and O'Keeffe's work came to public attention.

7. In the late 1920's O'Keeffe visited New Mexico, and this visit had a strong effect on her personal artistic vision.

8. Her later paintings have their inspiration in the New Mexican landscape.

9. Some of her cityscapes have large forms that occupy most of the canvas. These forms make a strong impact on the viewer.

10. That O'Keeffe stands as one of the great artists of the twentieth century is fitting, for she gave her individual expression to the American spirit.

Additional Resources
• Grammar and Usage Practice Book, p. 70

Writing Theme
Georgia O'Keeffe

CHECK POINT
PAGES 710–715

Rewrite the following sentences, correcting any errors in pronoun usage.

1. Each of the great artists can be said to have their own personal vision, and the American artist Georgia O'Keeffe found hers.
2. In an article about O'Keeffe, it says that she worked between realism and abstraction.
3. In O'Keeffe's paintings you find gigantic flowers and the haunting images of bleached bones against the dark earth and sky.
4. Her artistic talent was recognized in her early teens, and she knew she wanted to become one.
5. O'Keeffe's fame came almost by accident in 1916 when she sent to a friend some charcoal drawings which she liked.
6. Her friend showed the drawings to an art gallery director, and they were put on display, which first brought her work to public attention.
7. In the late 1920's O'Keeffe visited New Mexico, and this had a strong effect on her personal artistic vision.
8. Her later paintings has its inspiration in the New Mexican landscape.
9. Some of her cityscapes have large forms that occupy most of the canvas, and they make a strong impact on the viewer.
10. O'Keeffe stands as one of the great artists of the twentieth century, which is fitting for one who gave her individual expression to the American spirit.

Near Abiquiu, New Mexico, 1941, Georgia O'Keeffe

Humanities Connection

Art Note   *Near Abiquiu, New Mexico* (1941) is one of many haunting Southwestern landscapes by Georgia O'Keeffe (1887-1986). The strong, clear colors and sensuous lines are typical of the work of this American painter. Ask: What aspects of her work do you think inspire critics to describe O'Keeffe's paintings as both austere and sensual?

GRAMMAR
HANDBOOK
36

Writing Theme
Codes and
Code-Breaking

A. Choosing Correct Pronouns Choose the <u>correct pronoun</u> from those given in parentheses.

1. When a person uses an automated teller machine, an ATM, (<u>he or she</u>, him or her) is involved in cryptology.
2. A personal identification number, or PIN, is issued to (<u>whoever</u>, whomever) is authorized to use the card.
3. The PIN is coded either on the card or in the bank's computer in (<u>its</u>, their) encrypted form.
4. Between (<u>you</u>, yourself) and (I, <u>me</u>, myself), few thieves are smart enough to figure out the special cipher (theirselves, <u>themselves</u>).
5. Clever criminals need the bank's key to the code and the customer's PIN in order for (they, <u>them</u>) to steal funds by computer.
6. Cryptologists, however, are more clever than (<u>they</u>, them).
7. By (them, <u>their</u>) devising this special coding, cryptologists have rendered the cardholder's code totally protected.
8. It is impossible for anyone (<u>who</u>, whom) breaks into the computer file to figure out the ciphered PIN, even if (<u>he or she</u>, they) knows the key.
9. Thus, the average cardholders, you and (<u>I</u>, me), are protected from computer hacks (who, whom, <u>whose</u>) designs are dishonest.
10. Likewise, phone signals from the automatic teller machines to the bank's central computer are encrypted; (they, them, <u>their</u>) transmitting of a transaction is completely secure.
11. (<u>We</u>, Us) would-be millionaires are also protected by codes from lottery-ticket forgers.
12. All of the lottery ticket numbers are printed on the cards in (its, <u>their</u>) encrypted forms.
13. People to (who, <u>whom</u>) the winning cards have been sold must turn in cards that have both the real and the encrypted numbers.
14. (<u>Whoever</u>, Whomever) has the equipment available can probably forge a card (hisself, <u>himself</u>, themselves).
15. However, if forgers do not include the correct cipher, the real losers will be (<u>they</u>, them).

B. Correcting Pronoun Errors Rewrite the sentences, eliminating pronoun errors. If there are no errors, write *Correct*.

1. The historian was interested in the early history of secret codes; it was either her or her assistants whom found *The Codebreakers*.
2. Whoever is an expert on codes knows that they are all based on two fundamental principles—transposition and substitution.
3. One of Julius Caesar's first military achievements was his creation of a substitution cipher, but he soon abandoned it.

Application and Review

These activities have been designed to allow students to apply concepts presented in this handbook. Exercise A requires students to choose the correct pronoun. Exercise B challenges students to rewrite sentences that contain pronoun errors. Exercise C challenges students to proofread a paragraph, correcting all errors in pronoun usage, spelling, capitalization, punctuation, and agreement.

Additional Resources
- Tests and Assessment, Mastery Tests, pp. 58–61
- Elaboration, Revision, and Proofreading, p. 26

WRITING THEME   Codes and Code-Breaking

A. Choosing Correct Pronouns
Answers are underlined on page.

B. Correcting Pronoun Errors
Answers will vary. See typical answers below.
1. The historian was interested in the early history of secret codes; it was either she or her assistants who found *The Codebreakers*.
2. Correct
3. One of Julius Caesar's first military achievements was his creation of a substitution cipher, but he soon abandoned the code.

4. He did not trust Cicero, with whom he had shared the secret of the code.
5. Cicero himself had his scribe, a man named Tyro, invent a form of secret writing.
6. Tyronian characters that looked like modern shorthand evolved; several of them are still familiar to us today.
7. Lysander of Sparta, who was a famous Greek warrior, is also associated with a device for breaking codes.
8. Surrounded by traitors, Lysander knew that one false move could mean that Sparta and he were both lost.
9. He tested the truthfulness of whoever came before him.
10. When a traitor with a secret message entered Lysander's presence, Lysander decoded the message through the use of a cylindrical staff known as a scytale.
11. Few generals were as distrustful and wary as he.
12. Correct
13. Anyone living during the Middle Ages probably would not have recognized the Zodiac Alphabet as a code or deciphered it by himself or herself.
14. Correct
15. A Frenchman named Vignère evolved a similar table; both of these men claimed that their ciphers were indecipherable.

C. Proofreading for Pronoun Errors
Answers will vary. See typical answers below.

Each of the greats in the history of cryptanalysis—code breaking—has had his triumphs; but William Friedman, whom experts called the "Harry Houdini" of code breakers, had an exceptionally brilliant mind. It was Shakespeare who indirectly started Friedman on his career.

Friedman was hired by an eccentric millionaire who believed that all of Shakespeare's plays had been written by another sixteenth-century writer, Francis Bacon. In fact, the millionaire thought that Bacon had left coded secret messages in the plays. Friedman set out to find and decipher the messages, and breaking codes became his career. He distinguished himself during both World War I and World War II by applying statistical analysis to cryptanalysis and became the chief code breaker for the War Department. Moreover, the fact that Friedman's achievements occurred before the age of computers, makes his accomplishments even more surprising.

4. He did not trust Cicero, with who he had shared the secret of the code.
5. Cicero hisself had his scribe, a man named Tyro, invent a form of secret writing.
6. Tyronian characters that looked like modern shorthand evolved; several of them are still familiar to we today.
7. Lysander of Sparta, whom was a famous Greek warrior, is also associated with a device for breaking codes.
8. Surrounded by traitors, Lysander knew that one false move could mean that Sparta and him were both lost.
9. He tested the truthfulness of whomever came before he.
10. When a traitor with a secret message entered Lysander's presence, he decoded the message through the use of a cylindrical staff known as a scytale.
11. Few generals were as distrustful and wary as him.
12. The art of cryptography faded for many centuries; the monks revived it during the Middle Ages.
13. Anyone living during the Middle Ages probably would not have recognized the Zodiac Alphabet as a code or deciphered it by themselves.
14. Centuries later, Giovanni Baptista della Porta devised the Porta Table; the Father of Modern Cryptography is said to be him.
15. A Frenchman named Vignère evolved a similar table; both of these men claimed that his cipher was indecipherable.

C. Proofreading for Pronoun Errors Rewrite the following paragraphs. Correct <u>all errors</u> in pronoun usage as well as any errors in spelling, capitalization, punctuation, or agreement.

Each of the greats in the history of cryptanalysis—code breaking—have had their triumphs; but it is William Friedman who experts called the "harry Houdini" of code breakers. Interestingly, it was Shakespeare whom indirectly started Friedman on his career.

An eccentric millionair hired Friedman because he believed that all of Shakespeares plays had been written by another sixteenth-century writer, Francis Bacon. In fact, the millionaire thought that Bacon had left coded secret messages in them. Friedman set out to find and decipher the messages, and it became his career. He distinguished hisself during both World War I and World War II by applying statistical analysis to cryptanalysis and became the chief code breaker for the War Departmint. Moreover, the fact that Friedman's achievements occurred before the age of computers makes it even more surprising.

Adjective and Adverb Usage

UNDERSTANDING MODIFIERS

Before examining the usage rules for modifiers, you may wish to review their basic definitions and functions. You will recall that an **adjective** is a modifier that describes or limits a noun or pronoun. An **adverb** is a modifier that describes a verb, adjective, or other adverb. A modifier can be identified as an adjective or an adverb by determining the part of speech of the word it modifies.

Adjective and Adverb Forms

Most adjectives have no identifying form or ending. Many adverbs, however, can be recognized by their *-ly* endings. These adverbs are formed by adding *-ly* to adjectives.

Adjective	Adverb
close	closely
fearless	fearlessly
respectful	respectfully
moody	moodily

A few adjectives and adverbs have identical forms.

Adjective	Adverb
a *rough* surface	play *rough*
the *first* act	arrive *first*
a *low* bush	threw *low*
your *left* hand	turn *left*

Most adjectives and adverbs that have only one syllable have the same form. Adjectives with more than one syllable usually add an *-ly* ending if they are to form an adverb.

> The *violent* storm made us nervous.
> The storm raged *violently* and made us nervous.

> The lifeguard pulled the *hysterical* swimmer out of the powerful surf.
> The swimmer shrieked *hysterically* as the lifeguard pulled her from the powerful surf.

Grammar Note Some adjectives end in *-ly*. For example, *lively, deadly, friendly, manly, costly,* and *beastly* are adjectives. Do not assume that all words that end in *-ly* are adverbs.

Writing
—TIP—

Use modifiers with economy. One precise modifier can often replace two general ones, as *minuscule* replaces *very small*.

Adjective and
Adverb Usage **719**

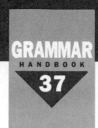
Grammar Handbook 37:
Adjective and Adverb Usage

Understanding Modifiers

Objectives

- To recognize the functions of adjectives and adverbs
- To distinguish between adjectives and adverbs in sample sentences

Teaching Strategies

Linking Grammar and Literature

Ask students to identify adjectives and adverbs in literary excerpts or samples of professional writing. You may want to start by giving students copies of the literary selection below. Ask them to identify the modifiers, which are underlined, in the selection.

When Martha Hale opened the storm-door and got a cut of the <u>north</u> wind, she ran <u>back</u> for <u>her big woolen</u> scarf. As she <u>hurriedly</u> wound that round her head, <u>her</u> eye made a <u>scandalized</u> sweep of her kitchen. It was no <u>ordinary</u> thing that called her <u>away</u>—it was <u>probably farther</u> from <u>ordinary</u> than anything that had <u>ever</u> happened in Dickson County. But what <u>her</u> eye took in was that <u>her</u> kitchen was in <u>no</u> shape for leaving: <u>her</u> bread <u>all ready</u> for mixing, half the flour <u>sifted</u> and half <u>unsifted</u>.

Susan Glaspell
From "A Jury of Her Peers"

Teaching Tip: Adjectives Ending in -ly

Point out that adverbial forms cannot be created for adjectives ending in *-ly*. Adverbial usages with these words have to be rephrased so that the adjective can be used in a prepositional phrase that acts like an adverb. They greeted us in a friendly manner, not: They greeted us friendlily.

Several adverbs have two forms, one with the *-ly* ending, the other without. Both forms are acceptable, but the longer form is used in formal writing. In a few instances, the two forms have completely different meanings and applications: for example, *late, lately; near, nearly.*

He always arrives *late.*	He hasn't come to any meetings *lately.*
Come *near.*	They ran *nearly* a mile.
Go *slow!*	He drove *slowly* on the snow-covered streets.
Reach down *deep.*	She appeared *deeply* troubled about the problem.

Modifiers That Follow Verbs

A word that modifies an action verb, an adjective, or another adverb is always an adverb.

Original thinkers experience ridicule *often.* (The adverb *often* modifies the action verb *experience.*)

Ridicule can be *terribly* demoralizing. (The adverb *terribly* modifies the adjective *demoralizing.*)

Original thinkers *very* definitely need self-confidence. (The adverb *very* modifies *definitely,* another adverb.)

Action verbs are frequently followed by adverbs. Modifiers that follow linking verbs are predicate adjectives. Choosing the correct modifier after a linking verb usually causes no problem when the linking verb is a form of *be.*

Remember, however, that most other linking verbs can also function as action verbs. If you are unsure whether to use the adjective or adverb form following a verb, determine whether the verb is linking or action.

Linking Verb	Action Verb
The man *looked* suspicious.	The detective *looked* suspiciously at the man.
The ship *appeared* damaged.	The ship *appeared* suddenly in the fog.
The crowd *sounds* angry.	The timekeeper *sounded* the buzzer to end the game.
You'll *feel* better if you exercise daily.	*Feel* the luxurious texture of this velvet cloth.

720 Grammar Handbook

Practice Your Skills

A. CONCEPT CHECK

Adjectives and Adverbs Write the correct modifier of the two given in parentheses. Label it *Adjective* or *Adverb*. Then write the word or words it modifies.

1. Interest in late Medieval and early Renaissance music has increased (considerable, considerably) in the past few decades.
2. This increased interest is (large, largely) due to the efforts of one person—Christopher Hogwood.
3. Hogwood, who himself plays the harpsichord (beautiful, beautifully), founded the Academy of Ancient Music.
4. The Academy performs and records Medieval and Renaissance music on original instruments—ones that are (clear, clearly) museum pieces.
5. These recordings and performances sound (wonderful, wonderfully) because of the authenticity of the instruments.
6. Even in recent years, some of these ancient instruments have been in (common, commonly) use by musicians such as Wanda Landowska, who has performed and recorded extensively on the harpsichord.
7. Others, such as the cornet, the krummhorn, the sackbut, and the shawm, have become (rare, rarely).
8. The Academy members are known, not only for their use of restored or reconstructed ancient instruments, but also for the (authentic, authentically) manner of their playing.
9. A listener can almost imagine being in the court of a great duke or earl, watching an (elaborate, elaborately) staged performance.
10. The recordings made by the Academy are (brilliant, brilliantly) and well worth adding to any music collection.

Writing Theme
Medieval and Renaissance Music

Harmony,
Bartolomeo Bettera

Humanities Connection

Art Note *Harmony* is a painting by Bartolomeo Bettera (1639–1699), an Italian painter who is chiefly known for his still life paintings of musical instruments. Art students often practice their skills in composition, color, and form by painting still life subjects.

WRITING THEME   Medieval and Renaissance Music

A. Concept Check

Adjectives and Adverbs
1. considerably, Adverb, has increased
2. largely, Adverb, due
3. beautifully, Adverb, plays
4. clearly, Adverb, are
5. wonderful, Adjective, recordings and performances
6. common, Adjective, use
7. rare, Adjective, Others
8. authentic, Adjective, manner
9. elaborately, Adverb, staged
10. brilliant, Adjective, recordings

B. Revision Skill

Adjectives and Adverbs

1. Reproducing historically accurate musical instruments is a very demanding craft.
2. Musicians insist that the reproduced musical instruments appear and sound authentic.
3. Correct
4. Each step must be completed deliberately.
5. First, the artisan studies carefully the musical instrument to be reproduced.
6. Correct
7. Finding wood that is appropriate may be very difficult.
8. One determined craftsman painstakingly searched the South American rain forests for snakewood.
9. Such devotion to detail may seem foolish, but it is crucial to the creation of a fine instrument.
10. With their commitment, skill, and pride, these artisans have been steadily opening a window to the music of the great composers of the past.

C. Application in Writing

Historical Fiction

Answers will vary.

B. REVISION SKILL

Adjectives and Adverbs Rewrite the following sentences to correct all errors in the use of adjectives and adverbs. If a sentence contains no errors, write *Correct*.

1. Reproducing historical accurate musical instruments is a very demanding craft.
2. Musicians insist that the reproduced musical instruments appear and sound authentically.
3. Skilled artisans strive diligently to achieve the original look and feel of the instruments they reproduce.
4. Each step must be completed deliberate.
5. First, the artisan studies careful the musical instrument to be reproduced.
6. The original instrument may be made of a rare wood.
7. Finding wood that is appropriately may be very difficult.
8. One determined craftsman painstaking searched the South American rain forests for snakewood.
9. Such devotion to detail may seem foolishly, but it is crucial to the creation of a fine instrument.
10. With their commitment, skill, and pride, these artisans have been steady opening a window to the music of the great composers of the past.

C. APPLICATION IN WRITING

Historical Fiction Historical fiction helps people imagine what it would have been like to live in a different place and time. Some historical fiction is told by means of letters. Choose some real or imaginary historical event, such as a concert at the court of Elizabeth I of England, and write a letter to a friend describing the event from the point of view of someone who attended the event. In your letter, use at least three adjectives and two adverbs.

COMPARING ADJECTIVES AND ADVERBS

Adjectives and adverbs have three forms, or degrees. The first form, the **positive degree,** is used to describe people, places, things, actions, or groups. This form of the modifier is the one used as the entry word of a dictionary definition.

Positive   Umberto Boccioni is considered a *great* Italian sculptor.

The **comparative degree** of a modifier is used to compare the thing modified with something else.

Comparative   Umberto Boccioni is considered *greater* than any other Italian sculptor of the early twentieth century.

To decide whether to use the comparative degree of the modifier, watch for clues such as "the other one," "any other," "of the two," and "of the pair." These clues signal that two things are being compared.

The **superlative degree** of an adjective or adverb should be used to compare the thing modified with two or more other things.

Superlative   Umberto Boccioni is considered the *greatest* Italian sculptor of the early twentieth century.

Notice that the context of a superlative often does not contain a number clue, but it does imply that a comparison is being made among more than two things. In the first example below, Humphrey Bogart is compared to all other actors who have played gangster roles. In the second example, the air conditioner is compared to all other inventions of this century.

Humphrey Bogart was one of the *most* popular gangster actors of all time.

Perhaps the *best* invention of this century is the air conditioner.

Development of the Bottle in Space, Umberto Boccioni

Adjective and Adverb Usage   **723**

LEP Students These students may need help recognizing the number of syllables in a word. Give them extra practice in counting the syllables in modifiers that are regular. Then ask them to form the comparative and superlative degrees of each of these modifiers by following the rules listed on page 724.

Regular Comparisons

Like verbs, adjectives and adverbs have both regular and irregular forms. However, most of these modifiers are regular, and their comparative and superlative degrees can be formed in one of these two ways.

1. **A one-syllable modifier forms the comparative and superlative by adding -*er* and -*est*. A few two-syllable modifiers also form the comparative and superlative in this way.**

Positive	Comparative	Superlative
straight	straighter	straightest
thin	thinner	thinnest
pale	paler	palest
wealthy	wealthier	wealthiest
pretty	prettier	prettiest
sleepy	sleepier	sleepiest
fast	faster	fastest
clear	clearer	clearest

Spelling Note Spelling changes must be made in the positive of some modifiers before adding the comparative and superlative endings. Such spelling changes are indicated in the dictionary under the positive form of the modifier.

2. **Most modifiers with two syllables and all modifiers with three or more syllables use *more* and *most* to form the comparative and the superlative.**

Positive	Comparative	Superlative
careless	more careless	most careless
powerful	more powerful	most powerful
hastily	more hastily	most hastily
ignorant	more ignorant	most ignorant
impressively	more impressively	most impressively
ambiguously	more ambiguously	most ambiguously

Negative comparisons of modifiers are formed by placing the words *less* and *least* before the positive form.

Positive	Comparative	Superlative
disastrous	less disastrous	least disastrous
precisely	less precisely	least precisely
fragrant	less fragrant	least fragrant
bravely	less bravely	least bravely
colorful	less colorful	least colorful
skillful	less skillful	least skillful

Irregular Comparisons

Some commonly used modifiers have irregular comparative and superlative forms. You may wish to memorize them.

Modifiers with Irregular Forms

Positive	Comparative	Superlative
bad	worse	worst
far	farther *or* further	farthest *or* furthest
good	better	best
ill	worse	worst
late	later *or* latter	latest *or* last
little	less *or* lesser	least
many	more	most
much	more	most
well	better	best

Usage Note *Farther* and *farthest* compare distances; *further* and *furthest* compare times, amounts, and degrees: Boston is *farther* from San Francisco than Minneapolis is. We will discuss this matter *further* at a later time.

Practice Your Skills

A. CONCEPT CHECK

Comparative and Superlative Forms Write the correct comparative or superlative form of the modifier given in parentheses.

1. Swimming is one of the (old) of all sports.
2. An Egyptian hieroglyph for swimming, from 2500 B.C., shows a man doing a form of the crawl, considered by many to be the (efficient) stroke of all.
3. References to swimming mentioned in epic and legend include the Anglo-Saxon hero Beowulf's boast that he was (strong) than his foe and could swim better—even fully armed.
4. The (early) swimming competition in history took place in 36 B.C.
5. Later, during the Middle Ages, swimming became (little) popular because people feared that the bubonic plague could be spread through the water.
6. When swimming made its comeback in the 1700's, the crawl had been forgotten and (slow) styles were used—the side stroke and the breast stroke.

Writing
—TIP—

Look for opportunities to replace overused adjectives such as *nice, pretty, good, bad, big,* and *little* with fresh, lively modifiers.

▶ **Writing Theme**
Sports History

Adjective and
Adverb Usage   **725**

7. faster
8. most
9. most healthful
10. better

B. Revision Skill

Comparative Forms of Adjectives and Adverbs
Answers will vary. See suggested answers below.

1. Which is the *more* difficult game, lawn bowling or curling?
2. The games are similar, but curling, which is played on the ice, demands the *greater* sense of balance.
3. Correct
4. The stones or irons vary in weight, the *heaviest* weighing seventy pounds.
5. Correct
6. Correct
7. Of all curling games played in America, the *earliest* ones were those played during the Revolutionary War by British soldiers stationed in Canada.
8. They played using flattened cannon balls—probably devising the *least* destructive use of cannonballs in history.
9. Today, Canada hosts the world's *largest* curling competition.
10. Even so, following World War II, women's curling associations increased *more* rapidly in the U.S. than in other countries.

C. Application in Writing

A Recommendation
Answers will vary.

---

7. In the late 1800's, the crawl was rediscovered when an Australian coach observed a twelve-year-old boy from a Pacific island who had a much (fast) style than the coach's swimmers.
8. Of all the strokes, the once-forgotten crawl again became the stroke (much) favored by racers.
9. Perhaps the (healthful) of all sports, swimming strengthens the muscles and develops the cardiovascular system.
10. Because the weight of the body is buoyed in the water, swimmers have a (good) chance of training without injury than do other athletes.

B. REVISION SKILL

Comparative Forms of Adjectives and Adverbs Rewrite the following sentences to correct all errors in the use of comparative and superlative modifiers. If a sentence has no errors, write *Correct*.

1. Which is the most difficult game, lawn bowling or curling?
2. The games are similar, but curling, which is played on the ice, demands the greatest sense of balance.
3. Curling also requires more precise aim, because the player must grip a heavy stone or iron by its handle and cast it off by sliding it on the ice.
4. The stones or irons vary in weight, the most heaviest weighing seventy pounds.
5. Both teams try to place their stones within a circle around a distant tee, and the team that places more stones in the circle wins.
6. Even in the 1500's curling was played in various regions of the British Isles, but Scotland promoted the game most actively.
7. Of all curling games played in America, the earlier ones were those played during the Revolutionary War by British soldiers stationed in Canada.
8. They played using flattened cannon balls—probably devising the less destructive use of cannonballs in history.
9. Today, Canada hosts the world's most large curling competition.
10. Even so, following World War II, women's curling associations increased most rapidly in the U.S. than in other countries.

C. APPLICATION IN WRITING

A Recommendation Imagine that you are a talent scout for a sports team. You have found three potential superstars whom you want to recommend. Write a report describing and comparing your three prospects. Use various forms of adjectives and adverbs to compare their physical characteristics, personalities, and performances.

A. Choose the correct form of each modifier to restore the excerpt to the original. Label the modifier *Adjective* or *Adverb*.

1. She looks (younger, youngest) than I do, her eyebrows are (thicker, thickest), her lips (fuller, fullest). Her (natural, naturally) curly hair is parted on the left, one wisp tendrilling off to the right. She wears a scholar's white gown, and she is not thinking about her appearance. She stares (straight, straightly) ahead as if she could see past me to her grandchildren and her grandchildren's grandchildren.

   Maxine Hong Kingston

2. He went into the rickety barn and brought out a rope, and he walked the horse (agile, agilely) enough up the hill to catch the horse. When he was ready and mounted before the door . . . Mama brought out the round black hat with the tooled leather band and she reached up and knotted the green silk handkerchief about his neck. Pepe's blue denim coat was much (more darker, darker) than his jeans for it had been washed much (less, lesser) often. The black hat, covering the high pointed head and black thatched hair of Pepe, gave him dignity and age. He sat the rangy horse (good, well).

   John Steinbeck

3. We had a good week at camp. The bass were biting (well, good) and the sun shone (endless, endlessly), day after day. We would be tired at night and lie down in the accumulated heat of the little bedrooms after the long hot day and the breeze would stir almost (imperceptible, imperceptibly) outside and the smell of the swamp would drift in through the rusty screens. Sleep would come (easy, easily) and in the morning the red squirrel would be on the roof, tapping out his merry routine.

   E. B. White

4. Evenings were spent mainly on the back porches where screen doors slammed in the darkness with those (real, really) very special summertime sounds. And, sometimes, when the Chicago nights got too steamy, the whole family got into the car and went to the park and slept out in the open on blankets. Those were, of course, the (better, best) times of all because the grownups were (invariable, invariably) reminded of having been children in the South and told the (better, best) stories. And it was cool and sweet to be on the grass and there was (usual, usually) the scent of (fresh, freshly) cut lemons or melons in the air.

   Lorraine Hansberry

5. The country is lyric,—the town dramatic. When mingled they make the (most perfect, more perfect) musical drama.

   Henry Wadsworth Longfellow

Writing Theme
Writers and
Their Craft

Adjective and
Adverb Usage   **727**

C H E C K **P O I N T**
PAGES 719–726

You may wish to use the following Checkpoint exercises as an informal evaluation of student mastery of the correct forms of adjectives and adverbs covered in this handbook.

WRITING THEME   Writers and Their Craft

A.

   1. younger, Adjective; thicker, Adjective; fuller, Adjective; naturally, Adverb; straight, Adverb

   2. agilely, Adverb; darker, Adjective; less, Adverb; well, Adverb

   3. well, Adverb; endlessly, Adverb; imperceptibly, Adverb; easily, Adverb

   4. really, Adverb; best, Adjective; invariably, Adverb; best, Adjective; usually, Adverb; freshly, Adverb

   5. most perfect, Adjective

B.

1. less clearly, Adverb
2. primarily, Adverb
3. odd, Adjective
4. easier, Adjective
5. exclusively, Adverb
6. serious, Adjective
7. really, Adverb
8. usually, Adverb
9. best, Adjective; suddenly, Adverb
10. more practical, Adjective

C.

1. The two *most* famous awards for writing are the Nobel Prize in Literature and the Pulitzer Prize.
2. The Nobel and the Pulitzer prizes were established by Alfred Nobel and Joseph Pulitzer, *respectively.*
3. The lists of award winners appear very *impressive.*
4. Of the two, the Pulitzer offers the *wider* variety of awards: eight for journalism and six for literary works.
5. Some of the *most* famous writers in the world have received awards.
6. In 1950, after publishing *Annie Allen,* a collection of poems about an African-American woman growing up, Gwendolyn Brooks felt *proud* to receive the Pulitzer Prize in Poetry.
7. Correct
8. *Earlier* in her career she had won awards at Writer's Conferences as well as grants of money called Guggenheim fellowships.
9. Although Brooks's poetry features *ordinary* black people and their everyday lives, Richard Wright said, "It is the honesty in her poems that makes them true for all people."
10. Correct

B. Write the correct form of the modifier given in parentheses. Then label the modifier as either an *Adjective* or an *Adverb.*

1. The writing profession is probably (less clearly, least clearly) understood than any other.
2. Robert Penn Warren thought of writing (primary, primarily) as a compulsion, like an itch that needs to be scratched.
3. This compulsion explains why James Michener kept very (odd, oddly) working hours when he wrote *Tales of the South Pacific.*
4. Writing was (easier, more easy) for him at night because he had another job during the day.
5. Now he writes almost (exclusive, exclusively) in the day.
6. Hortense Calisher, another writer, believes writers must feel (serious, seriously) about their work in order to succeed.
7. According to Calisher, she works (real, really) well in the morning.
8. By contrast, Eudora Welty (usual, usually) works whenever a story demands to be written.
9. Sometimes the (better, best) ideas come to her (sudden, suddenly) in the dead of night.
10. Instead of getting up to work, her (more practical, most practical) solution is to jot down the idea.

C. Rewrite each sentence to correct any error in the use of an adjective or adverb. If a sentence has no error, write *Correct.*

1. The two more famous awards for writing are the Nobel Prize in literature and the Pulitzer Prize.
2. The Nobel and the Pulitzer prizes were established by Alfred Nobel and Joseph Pulitzer, respective.
3. The lists of award winners appear very impressively.
4. Of the two, the Pulitzer offers the widest variety of awards: eight for journalism and six for literary works.
5. Some of the more famous writers in the world have received awards.
6. In 1950 after publishing *Annie Allen,* a collection of poems about an African-American woman growing up, Gwendolyn Brooks felt proudly to receive the Pulitzer Prize in poetry.
7. Brooks was the first African-American woman to receive this highly prestigious award.
8. Earliest in her career she had won awards at writer's conferences as well as grants of money called Guggenheim fellowships.
9. Although Brooks's poetry features ordinarily black people and their everyday lives, Richard Wright said "It is the honesty in her poems that makes them true for all people."
10. In particular, Wright praised Brooks for her ability to depict "the tiniest incidents that plague the lives of the desperately poor."

Avoid making double comparisons and illogical comparisons by keeping the following guidelines in mind.

Avoid Double Comparisons

As you know, the comparative degree of a modifier is formed either by adding *-er* to the positive form or by placing *more* before the positive form. Using *-er* and *more* together is incorrect. Similarly, the superlative is made by adding either *-est* or *most*. Using both is incorrect.

Incorrect	The Cahow is a *more rarer* sea bird than the sea gull.
Correct	The Cahow is a *rarer* sea bird than the sea gull.

Incorrect	The Nile Valley is the *most fertilest* part of Egypt.
Correct	The Nile Valley is the *most fertile* part of Egypt.

Avoid Illogical Comparisons

An illogical or confusing comparison results if two unrelated things are compared or if something is compared with itself.

The word *other* or the word *else* should be used in a comparison of an individual member with the rest of the group.

Illogical	This band has won more competitions than any band in the state. (Is this band in the state?)
Clear	This band has won more competitions than any *other* band in the state.

Illogical	Julius Caesar was as brilliant as any general in the history of Rome. (Was Julius Caesar a Roman general?)
Clear	Julius Caesar was as brilliant as any *other* general in the history of Rome.

The word *than* or *as* is required after the first modifier in a compound comparison.

Illogical	Ian's grades are better or at least as good as Kim's.
Clear	Ian's grades are better *than,* or at least as good as, Kim's.

Illogical	Felicia scored as many goals if not more than Steve.
Clear	Felicia scored as many goals *as* Steve, if not more.

Adjective and Adverb Usage **729**

Using Comparisons Correctly

Objectives

- To recognize and avoid double comparisons
- To eliminate confusing or illogical comparisons

Teaching Strategies

Linking Grammar to Literature

Point out that though usage of such forms as *more unique* and *more perfect* can be thought of as illogical, they are sometimes used in writing and in speech. Students may be familiar with the example below or may come up with other examples. Guide students to realize that the words from the Constitution might be paraphrased, " . . . in order to form a more nearly perfect union. . . ." Let students discuss why the framers of the Constitution might have used the term *more perfect*. You may want to emphasize that, in general, using comparative or superlative forms of absolute modifiers tends to weaken the original meaning of the modifier.

We the people of the United States, in order to form a more perfect Union, . . . and secure the blessings of liberty to ourselves and our posterity, do ordain and establish this Constitution for the United States of America. From *The Constitution of the United States*

Cooperative Learning

Remind students that there are a number of absolute modifiers in common usage. Additional examples include *full, empty, flawless, unique, peerless,* and *indeterminate.* Invite pairs of students to make a list of examples. Then have students share their lists and work as a class to write sentences using the words.

 ## Individualizing Instruction

LD Students Some of these students may have trouble completing Exercise C in paragraph form. You may wish to make a worksheet for these students by numbering the sentences and writing each on a separate line.

> **Additional Resources**
> • Grammar and Usage Practice
>   Book, p. 73

WRITING THEME   World War II

Discuss what students have learned about World War II from reading the exercises. Then encourage them to conclude that the discussion has given them ideas for writing.

A. Concept Check
Double and Illogical Comparisons
See suggested answers below.
  1. In 1922, Japan stated that it respected China's autonomy as much *as any other country did.*
  2. However, in 1931, in one of the *bloodiest* takeovers in history, Japan invaded the Chinese province of Manchuria.
  3. This act upset Europe *as much as* it upset the United States, *if not more.*
  4. After Japan's all-out invasion of China in 1937, a peaceful solution to the problem seemed *impossible.*

Writing Theme
World War II

730 Grammar Handbook

Certain modifiers cannot logically be used in the comparative or superlative forms because they are absolute.

Incorrect	*Twelfth Night* is a more perfect play than is *As You Like It.* (*Perfect* is absolute and cannot logically be compared.)
Correct	*Twelfth Night* is almost a perfect play, but *As You Like It* has many weaknesses.
Incorrect	The number of stars is more infinite than the number of grains of sand. (*Infinite* is absolute and cannot be logically compared.)
Correct	The number of stars and the number of grains of sand are infinite.
Incorrect	Calculus is more impossible than algebra. (*Impossible* is absolute and cannot be compared.)
Correct	Calculus is a more difficult form of math than is algebra.

Both parts of a comparison must be stated completely if there is any chance of its being misunderstood.

Unclear	I see Karen more often than Carla.
Clear	I see Karen more often than Carla *does.*
Clear	I see Karen more often than *I see* Carla.
Unclear	The Lakers beat the Celtics worse than the Knicks.
Clear	The Lakers beat the Celtics worse than the Knicks *did.*
Clear	The Lakers beat the Celtics worse than the Lakers *beat* the Knicks.

Practice Your Skills

A. CONCEPT CHECK

Double and Illogical Comparisons   Find the errors in comparison in the following sentences. Rewrite the sentences correctly.

1. In 1922, the nation of Japan stated that it respected China's autonomy as much as any country did.
2. However, in 1931, in one of the most bloodiest takeovers in history, Japan invaded the Chinese province of Manchuria.
3. This act upset Europe as much if not more than the United States.
4. After Japan's all-out invasion of China in 1937, a peaceful solution to the problem seemed more impossible.
5. Japan needed land and resources more than anything to bolster its economy.

6. At the same time in Europe, Hitler's Germany was becoming as aggressive if not more than Japan.
7. The threat of war seemed much more greater in Europe.
8. However, during the Great Depression, America thought its own problems were more important than any country's.
9. Americans felt more sympathy for Europe than China.
10. The U.S. was in a most unique situation.
11. Americans' most fiercest debate was over isolation versus intervention.
12. On December 7, 1941, the Japanese proved that the United States was as vulnerable as any target.
13. Tiny Japan, in the most boldest attack imaginable, bombed the American naval base at Pearl Harbor.
14. The attack resolved the Americans' debate more quickly than any action could.
15. Likewise, Hitler's attacks on U.S. escort ships more finally resolved the issue: America would go to war.

Ready for take-off, World War II pilot-in-training Nancy Nesbit of Pomona, California, checks with the control tower for instructions, 1943

B. PROOFREADING SKILL

Double and Illogical Comparisons The following paragraph has errors in the use of comparisons, spelling, capitalization, and punctuation. Rewrite the paragraph, correcting all errors.

(1) World War II probably created more changes in our society than any event in History. (2) On the home front, factries produced war materials more than anything. (3) In fact, the most proudest time in many americans lives was during their "service" in the factories at home. (4) Victory depended on well-made goods as much as productive workers

5. Japan needed land and resources *more than anything else* to bolster its economy.
6. At the same time in Europe, Hitler's Germany was becoming as aggressive as Japan, *if not more aggressive*.
7. The threat of war seemed *much greater* in Europe.
8. However, during the Great Depression, America thought its own problems were more important than *any other* country's.
9. Americans felt more sympathy for Europe *than they felt for* China.
10. The U.S. was in a *unique* situation.
11. Americans' *fiercest* debate was over isolation versus intervention.
12. On December 7, 1941, the Japanese proved that the United States was as vulnerable as *any other* target.
13. Tiny Japan, in the *boldest* attack imaginable, bombed the American naval base at Pearl Harbor.
14. The attack resolved the Americans' debate more quickly than *any other* action could.
15. Likewise, Hitler's attacks on U.S. escort ships *finally* resolved the issue: America would go to war.

B. Proofreading Skill
Double and Illogical Comparisons
Answers will vary. See suggested answers below.
(1) World War II probably created more changes in our society than *any other* event in history.
(2) On the home front, *factories* produced more war materials than *anything else*.
(3) In fact, the *proudest* time in many Americans' lives was during their "service" in the factories at home.
(4) Victory depended on well-made goods as much *as it depended on* productive workers.

(5) Some imported natural resources were as valuable as many domestic resources, *if not more valuable.*

(6) Because of the war, imports of rubber, silk, and tin *had stopped* completely.

(7) Goods made from these materials *were rationed,* which affected families as much as *it affected* industry.

(8) Among the *scarcest* items were canned foods, shoes, and gasoline.

(9) Canadians rationed consumer goods as much as Americans *rationed them.*

(10) Conservation of resources became a patriotic duty as important as buying war bonds, if not *more important.*

C. Application in Writing
A Biography
Answers will vary.

Special Problems with Modifiers

Objectives

- To recognize and avoid misusing the modifiers *this, that; them, those; bad, badly; good, well*
- To recognize and avoid double negatives

Teaching Strategies

Linking Grammar and Writing

Remind students that *them* is used as an adjective in some dialects. (*Them* dishes are on the table.) Thus this nonstandard form is perfectly suitable to create a realistic effect in some forms of written dialogue.

---

(5) Some imported natural resources were as valuable if not more than many domestic resources. (6) Because of the war, imports of rubber, silk, and tin had stoped more completely. (7) Families suffered from the rationing of goods made from these materials as much as industry. (8) Among the most scarcest items were canned foods, shoes, and gasoline. (9) Candians rationed consumer goods as much as Americans. (10) Conservation of resources became a patriotic duty as important if not more than buying war bonds.

C. APPLICATION IN WRITING

A Biography   Choose two figures from some period in American history and do some brief research about their lives. Write a paragraph comparing and contrasting these figures.

SPECIAL PROBLEMS WITH MODIFIERS

Certain adjectives and adverbs are often misused. Study the following information to avoid problems.

This and These; That and Those

This and *that* are adjectives that modify singular nouns and pronouns. Similarly, the adjectives *these* and *those* modify plural nouns and pronouns. *This* and *these* are used to refer to nearby things; *that* and *those* are used to refer to things at a distance. Notice how *kind* and *sort* signal that a singular adjective should be used.

Incorrect	*These* kind sold faster than *those* kind.
Correct	*This* kind sold faster than *that* kind.

Incorrect	*Those* sort of argument are a waste of time.
Correct	*That* sort of argument is a waste of time.

Them and Those

Those can act as either a pronoun or an adjective. However, *them* is always a pronoun, never an adjective.

Incorrect	Where did you get *them* sunglasses?
Correct	Where did you get *those* sunglasses? (adjective)
Correct	Where did you get them? (pronoun)
Correct	Those are fantastic sunglasses! (pronoun)

Bad and Badly

Bad is an adjective. It is used before nouns and after linking verbs in standard English. The word *badly* is an adverb. It can only modify action verbs, adjectives, and other adverbs—never a noun.

> Justin feels *bad* (not *badly*) about the disagreement. (adjective)
> Rhoda cut her knee *badly*. (adverb)
> The doctor treated the *badly* burned firefighters. (adverb)

Good and Well

The word *good* is always an adjective. It can modify only a noun or a pronoun.

> Barry has developed a *good* serve.

When *good* is used after a linking verb in a sentence, it functions as a predicate adjective that modifies the subject. As a predicate adjective, *good* can mean either "pleasant," "comfortable," or "in a happy state of mind."

> Barry's serve has become *good*.
> *He feels good* about it.
> He will be *good* at tennis some day.

Well can be used as an adverb to modify an action verb. Used as an adverb, *well* means that the action expressed by the verb is performed expertly or properly.

> Nikia writes *well* when she puts her mind to it.

Well can also be used as a predicate adjective after a linking verb. As a predicate adjective, *well* means "in good health."

> Although Danielle appeared *well,* she was really quite sick.

Adjective and
Adjective and Adverb Usage   **733**

Stumbling Block

Students may have difficulty distinguishing when to use the adjective *bad* and when to use the adverb *badly*, especially in sentences that contain linking verbs. Stress that in the sentence *Justin feels badly*, the adverb *badly* modifies the action verb *feels*. Thus this sentence suggests that Justin has an inadequate sense of touch (and it is unlikely that the speaker or writer of the sentence intends that meaning). In the sentence *Justin feels bad*, *feels* is a linking verb, and the adjective *bad* modifies the noun *Justin*. Thus this sentence suggests that Justin is upset, regretful, or ill. By determining whether they are using a verb as an action verb or as a linking verb, students can figure out whether to use *bad* or *badly* in particular sentences.

Individualizing Instruction

ESL Students   In some languages, including French and Spanish, two or more negatives are grammatically correct. Invite students to share examples from their native language.

Remind students that in English, one negative marker makes a sentence negative. Two or more technically make it positive, or at least ambiguous, and thus confusing.

Additional Resources
• Grammar and Usage Practice Book, p. 74

WRITING THEME   Art and Creativity
Suggest that art and creativity makes a good topic for writing. Have students brainstorm a few ideas about this topic, which they might want to write about.

A. Concept Check
Correct Use of Modifiers
Answers are underlined on page.

The Double Negative

If you add a negative word to a sentence that is already negative, the result will be an error known as a **double negative.**

Incorrect	He did*n't* tell me *nothing.*
Correct	He did*n't* tell me *anything.*
Correct	He told me *nothing.*

Incorrect	I did*n't* get *no* news from him.
Correct	I did*n't* get *any* news from him.
Correct	I got *no* news from him.

Using *hardly, barely,* or *scarcely* with a negative word is also incorrect.

Incorrect	There was*n't hardly* any juice in the pitcher.
Correct	There was *hardly* any juice in the pitcher.

Incorrect	The little juice that was left in the pitcher did*n't scarcely* wet my throat.
Correct	The little juice that was left in the pitcher *scarcely* wet my throat.

Certain expressions with the word *but* sometimes have the effect of creating a double negative. Study the examples below.

Incorrect	I *can't* help *but* feel sorry for him.
Correct	I *can't help feeling* sorry for him.

Incorrect	I have*n't but* one true friend.
Correct	I have *only* one true friend.

Incorrect	There are*n't* only *but* seven countries that don't allow women to vote.
Correct	There are *only* seven countries that don't allow women to vote.

Practice Your Skills

A. CONCEPT CHECK

Correct Use of Modifiers   Choose the <u>correct</u> modifier from the two given in parentheses.

1. Vasari, an Italian Renaissance biographer, chronicles (good, <u>well</u>) an unusual side to Leonardo da Vinci.
2. It seems Leonardo liked (those, <u>that</u>) sort of activity characteristic of a mad scientist.

3. As a young man, he (didn't enjoy nothing better, <u>enjoyed nothing better</u>) than shutting himself up in a secret part of the house so that he could create a composite monster.

4. Leonardo didn't feel (<u>bad</u>, badly) about using bits and pieces of lizards and bats.

5. The biographer also tells us that he (didn't hardly notice, <u>hardly noticed</u>) the stench around him.

6. (One can't help but, <u>One can hardly help</u>) picturing a reptilian Frankenstein's monster.

7. In some ways, Leonardo's creative genius can be compared to the fertile imaginations of (them, <u>those</u>) people who write science fiction.

8. There (aren't but a few, <u>are only a few</u>) minds that could envision a submarine or a vehicle capable of flight years before such things were technically possible.

9. Both Leonardo and writer Jules Verne accomplished this feat (good, <u>well</u>).

10. Think about what someone with an imagination that worked that (good, <u>well</u>) could dream up in our time!

B. REVISION SKILL

Problems with Modifiers   Rewrite the following sentences to correct misused modifiers and double negatives.

1. Mary Cassatt, like many other nineteenth-century American artists, didn't want to study art nowhere but in Europe.

2. Her father, who was a very stern man, didn't hardly approve of her aspirations.

3. Cassatt had always been an obedient daughter, and she felt badly about opposing her father.

4. However, she wouldn't allow nobody's objections to discourage her.

5. While living in Europe, she couldn't help but be inspired by the exploding Impressionist movement in art.

6. The Impressionists were them painters who try to show what the eye sees at a glance about a scene or object.

7. In these type of painting, tiny splashes of primary colors placed on the canvas simulate the vibration of reflected light.

8. Cassatt's paintings of mothers and children demonstrate her talent and techniques good.

9. With those sort of subject, she used flat, delicate colors and strong, clear lines.

10. Edward Degas, another of them artists who mastered impressionism, became a close friend and mentor to Mary Cassatt.

Il Profeta Zaccaria, (detail), Michelangelo, Sistine Chapel, The Vatican

C. PROOFREADING SKILL

Errors in Modifier Usage   Rewrite the paragraph to correct errors in capitalization, punctuation, and spelling.

Them paintings on the cieling of the Sistine chapel are the work of the Italian Renaissance artist, Michelangelo Buonarotti. There isn't scarcely a painter or sculptor of the human form whose work has not been influenced by Michelangelo. Interestingly, Michelangelo didn't hardly want to be a painter. In fact, he felt badly when he had to take time away from sculpting to paint. His statues show that he hadn't but one true love. Watching forms emerge from marble.

Michelangelo prefered sculpting those kind of heroic, larger-than-life work, typified by his *David*. If Pope julius hadn't comissioned him to do the Sistine chapel frescoes, Michelangelo might have continued to produce nothing but sculpture. Some sources indicated that in later years his hands became stiff and crippled bad. Yet, even when due to advanced age he wasn't feeling good, he produced the giant fresco, "The last Judgment."

CHECK POINT
PAGES 729–736

A. Write the correct word or phrase from the two in parentheses.

1. In 1974, the high school in Roseville, California, (had only, didn't have but) one girl on its track team—Evelyn Ashford.
2. This girl, destined to become the (faster, fastest) woman runner in the world, attracted recruiters from the University of California at Los Angeles, who offered her a track scholarship.

Writing Theme
Running Sports

Humanities Connection

Art Note   Michelangelo Buonarroti (1475–1564) spent 1508 to 1512 painting the ceiling of the Sistine Chapel in Rome, of which a detail is shown here. The Prophet Zachariah, depicted in this detail, and other Old Testament prophets and sibyls make up the borders of the ceiling. Its center features scenes from the Bible.

3. One track coach who thought her stopwatch had malfunctioned (couldn't hardly, couldn't) believe Ashford was capable of such speed.
4. In the years that followed, Ashford won several events in the World Cup Games, and she felt really (good, well) about breaking the world record for the 100-meter dash in both 1983 and 1984.
5. She did not reach her (ultimate, most ultimate) goal until the 1984 Olympics, when she won the gold medal for the 100-meter dash.

B. Rewrite each of the following sentences, correcting all errors in the use of modifiers.

1. Many people feel badly because they do not exercise.
2. They can't hardly force themselves to do the same old exercises every day.
3. Perhaps they should try joggling, one of the most unique new sports.
4. These kind of activity combines jogging and juggling.
5. In joggling, the ability to juggle is as important if not more than the ability to jog.
6. Learning to juggle is more complicated than some activities.
7. Good eye-hand coordination is required to keep them balls in the air without dropping them.
8. Top jugglers say that they can joggle as good as they can run.
9. Jogglers also say they can't help but improve their lower body muscles as well as their coordination.
10. However, the aerobic benefits of joggling can be greater than any benefits.
11. One joggler discovered that by juggling with heavier balls, he received a much more perfect workout.
12. The more heavier the balls he juggled, the more his heart rate increased.
13. Albert Lucas is one of them jogglers who love to compete.
14. In 1986, when he entered the Los Angeles Marathon as a joggler, no one there had never heard of joggling.
15. Representatives from the *Guinness Book of World Records* were as interested in the marathon as Lucas.
16. They wanted to be sure that the record for joggling would be recorded and verified good.
17. Lucas didn't do bad in 1986; he ran the 26.2 miles in 3 hours, 29 minutes, 17 seconds.
18. Even while joggling, he finished the race as fast if not faster than most of the other runners.
19. In 1988, he had a far more better finish, beating his old record.
20. Who knows? Someday, people may prefer joggling to any form of exercise.

Application and Review

These activities have been designed to allow students to apply concepts presented in this handbook. Exercise A requires students to choose the correct modifier. Exercise B requires students to rewrite sentences that contain errors in the usage of modifies. Exercise C challenges students to rewrite a paragraph, correcting all errors in the use of modifiers and in capitalization, spelling, and punctuation.

WRITING THEME   Cities Lost and Found

A. Using Modifiers Correctly
Modifiers are underlined on page.

B. Choosing the Correct Modifier
Answers will vary. See suggested answers below.

1. When he was only seven years old, Heinrich Schliemann looked *regularly* at an illustrated book that was very special to him.
2. Young Heinrich *could hardly* contain his excitement each time he looked at the book's picture of the city of Troy in flames.
3. When he grew up, this boy was destined to become more famous than *any other* archaeologist in history.
4. Throughout his youth, Heinrich looked *radiant* whenever the subject of Troy came up.
5. There was *scarcely any* aspect of the story of Troy that did not fascinate him.
6. The *most* famous of all the cities of the ancient world, Troy was the site of a great battle described by the Greek poet Homer in his epic work titled the *Iliad.*
7. Young Heinrich learned to read classical Greek really *well* so that he could study Homer's works in their original language.

GRAMMAR
HANDBOOK
37

Writing Theme
Cities Lost
and Found

A. Using Modifiers Correctly Write the <u>correct</u> form of the two modifiers given in parentheses.

1. The provincial Roman city of Pompeii is perhaps more famous than (any, <u>any other</u>) ruin from ancient Rome.
2. The people of Pompeii lived (prosperous, <u>prosperously</u>) in their seaside community prior to A.D. 79.
3. Then, on August 24, A.D. 79, they suffered a disaster (<u>as destructive as</u>, as destructive), if not more destructive than, the wars that destroyed other ancient cities.
4. Nearby Mount Vesuvius erupted, burying the city in ash and leaving (<u>scarcely any</u>, scarcely no) survivors.
5. (Them, <u>Those</u>) ruins of Pompeii lay buried under ash for almost 1,700 years.
6. After the site was discovered, early excavations were done somewhat (careless, <u>carelessly</u>).
7. Johann Winckelmann studied the ruins of Pompeii (careful, <u>carefully</u>), sorting them out and making sense of them.
8. Modern archaeologists have gone (slow, <u>slowly</u>) in order to preserve and catalog the buried secrets.
9. Over the past two centuries, excavations at Pompeii have proceeded quite (good, <u>well</u>), yielding exciting results.
10. Today, tourists find the ruins of Pompeii (as popular, <u>as popular as</u>), if not more popular than, the Roman Forum.

B. Choosing the Correct Modifier Rewrite each of the following sentences, correcting any errors in the use of modifiers.

1. When he was only seven years old, Heinrich Schliemann looked regular at an illustrated book that was very special to him.
2. Young Heinrich couldn't hardly contain his excitement each time he looked at the book's picture of the city of Troy in flames.
3. When he grew up, this boy was destined to become more famous than any archaeologist in history.
4. Throughout his youth, Heinrich looked radiantly whenever the subject of Troy came up.
5. There was scarcely no aspect of the story of Troy that did not fascinate him.
6. The more famous of all the cities of the ancient world, Troy was the site of a great battle described by the Greek poet Homer in his epic work titled the *Iliad.*
7. Young Heinrich learned to read classical Greek really good so that he could study Homer's works in their original language.
8. He believed that Homer's poems, the *Iliad* and the *Odyssey,* were more beautiful and inspiring than any poems ever written.

738 Grammar Handbook

9. He also believed something that hardly no one else at that time believed: that Homer's stories were true and Troy was real.
10. These sort of behaviors made many people consider Heinrich a bit eccentric.
11. Professional archaeologists scoffed: they had never heard of a more impossible theory.
12. Nevertheless, Heinrich persisted in his belief that them poems contained clues to the location of the ancient city.
13. Once he reached adulthood, Schliemann became enormous wealthy through activities as a merchant.
14. He married a Greek woman whom he thought more beautifuller than Helen of Troy herself.
15. Schliemann and his wife, along with a hundred hired workers, set out to find Troy, following them clues from Homer's poems.
16. It would be difficult to say who was most zealous about the attempt to find Troy, Schliemann or his new wife, Sophia.
17. There wasn't hardly a piece of evidence from the poems that they overlooked.
18. Surprisingly, Schliemann's literary approach to archaeology succeeded quite good, for in 1871 he found an ancient city on the Turkish coast.
19. At this site, Schliemann and later archaeologists dug up ten layered ancient cities; of these, the ninth from the top was considered the most likeliest site for the Troy of Homer's poem.
20. Doubtless, this discovery was the more exciting in the history of modern archaeological investigation.

C. Errors in Modifier Usage The following paragraph contains errors in the use of modifiers as well as errors in capitalization, spelling, and punctuation. Rewrite the paragraph to correct all of these errors.

By the mid-1500's, Pizzaro and his Spanish *conquistadores* thought there wasn't no city in the Incan Empire they had not conquered. However, the invaders from Spain were bad mistaken, there was one Incan city they didn't never find. This city was as grand if not more grander than any settlement built by the skillful incan artisans. The city straddles the 9,000-foot peek of Machu Picchu, a mountain in the Peruvian Andes. For hundreds of years after the Spanish conquest, the secret of the existence of Machu Picchu was kept good. However on July 24, 1911 the city was discovered by a young American explorer named Hiram Bingham. Today, the sight is one of the most popular tourist attractions in south America.

8. He believed that Homer's poems, the *Iliad* and the *Odyssey*, were more beautiful and inspiring than *any other* poems ever written.
9. He also believed something that hardly *anyone else* at that time believed: that Homer's stories were true and Troy was real.
10. *This sort of behavior* made many people consider Heinrich a bit eccentric.
11. Professional archaeologists scoffed: they had never heard of such an impossible theory.
12. Nevertheless, Heinrich persisted in his belief that *those poems* contained clues to the location of the ancient city.
13. Once he reached adulthood, Schliemann became *enormously* wealthy through activities as a merchant.
14. He married a Greek woman whom he thought more *beautiful* than Helen of Troy herself.
15. Schliemann and his wife, along with a hundred hired workers, set out to find Troy, following *those clues* from Homer's poems.
16. It would be difficult to say who was *more* zealous about the attempt to find Troy, Schliemann or his new wife, Sophia.
17. There *was hardly* a piece of evidence from the poems that they overlooked.
18. Surprisingly, Schliemann's literary approach to archaeology succeeded quite *well*, for in 1871 he found an ancient city on the Turkish coast.
19. At this site, Schliemann and later archaeologists dug up ten layered ancient cities; of these, the ninth from the top was considered the *likeliest* [or *most likely*] site for the Troy of Homer's poem.
20. Doubtless, this discovery was the *most* exciting in the history of modern archaeological investigation.

C. Errors in Modifier Usage
Answers will vary. See suggested answers below.
By the mid-1500's, Pizzaro and his Spanish *conquistadores* thought there *was no* city in the Incan Empire they had not conquered. However, the invaders from Spain were *badly* mistaken. There was one Incan city they *never* found. This city was as grand as any other settlement built by the skillful Incan artisans, *if not grander*. The city straddles the 9,000-foot *peak* of Machu Picchu, a mountain in the Peruvian Andes. For hundreds of years after the Spanish conquest, the secret of the *existence* of Machu Picchu was *well* kept. However, on July 24, 1911, the city was discovered by a young American explorer named Hiram Bingham. Today, the sight is one of the most popular tourist attractions in South America.

These exercises allow your students to practice skills acquired in Handbooks 36–37. You may wish to use the exercises to provide a thorough review of the material in these chapters or to evaluate student mastery of the concepts.

Additional Resources
- Grammar and Usage Practice Book, pp. 36–37
- Standardized Test Practice

Skills Assessment Test 3
1. E
2. D—they
3. C—as
4. C—he and she
5. A—whom
   C—who
6. C—himself

Skills
ASSESSMENT

Directions   One or more of the underlined sections in the following sentences may contain errors of grammar, usage, punctuation, spelling, or capitalization. Write the letters of each incorrect section. Then rewrite the item correctly. If there is no error in an item, write E.

> **Example**   <u>Them</u> postponing the vote <u>until</u> the next session of
>   A   B
> the <u>legaslature</u> increases the likelihood of the <u>bill's</u> defeat.
>   C   D
> <u>No error</u>
> E
>
> **Answer**   A—their, C—legislature

1. <u>Fats Waller</u> wrote the song "Ain't Misbehavin'"; <u>he</u> and Jelly Roll Morton <u>were</u>
      A   B   C
   influential jazz <u>pianists</u> and composers. <u>No error</u>
                D   E

2. The <u>Flying Wallendas</u> were tightrope walkers <u>who created the first high-wire pyramid,</u>
        A   B
   and few performers <u>were</u> as daring as <u>them.</u> <u>No error</u>
                    C   D   E

3. The astronaut <u>claimed</u> that no one who has only seen the earth from the ground
               A
   <u>can feel</u> <u>like</u> an astronaut <u>does</u> about the beauty and fragility of our planet.
     B   C   D
   <u>No error</u>
   E

4. In Sophocles' play, when Creon <u>forbade</u> the burial of <u>Antigone's</u> brother,
                                 A   B
   <u>him and her</u> <u>became antagonists.</u> <u>No error</u>
      C   D   E

5. Alexander Selkirk, on <u>who</u> Daniel Defoe <u>based</u> his character of Robinson Crusoe,
                      A   B
   was a British sailor <u>whom</u> was actually shipwrecked <u>for several years.</u> <u>No error</u>
                C   D   E

6. Although Socrates <u>is regarded</u> as the originator of Western <u>thought,</u> he <u>hisself</u> did
                    A   B   C
   not write down his <u>ideas;</u> they were written down by one of Socrates' famous pupils, an aristocratic youth named Plato. <u>No error</u>
                     D

7. His discovering the more-than-two-thousand-year-old tomb of Tutankhamen
   A
   in 1922 made Howard Carter a worldwide celebrity. No error
   B   C   D   E

8. In Maria Montessori's method of education for young children, each of the chil-
                                                            A
   dren are treated like an individual who brings a great deal of talent and knowledge
        B   C   D
   to the learning situation. No error
                              E

9. The two russian dancers, Mikhail Baryshnikov and him, dance in a style called
              A   B   C
   bravura, with brilliant, daring moves. No error
                 D   E

10. Jacob Grimm and his brother Wilhelm collaborated on writing fairy tales, and it
                            A   B
    was he who also developed a basic law of linguistics. No error
        C D   E

11. The finch is a spirited bird that sings beautiful and is often kept as a pet. No error
              A   B   C   D   E

12. Of all the actresses who have played Juliet, Olivia Hussey performed the part more
                        A   B   C   D
    sensitively. No error
                 E

13. Queen Anne's lace, which is really a wild carrot, is as beautiful as or more beautiful
                       A   B   C
    than any wild plant. No error
    C   D   E

14. Michelangelo painted so good that he was commissioned by the Pope to paint the
                        A   B   C
    ceiling of the Sistine Chapel. No error
    D   E

15. Them humorous, delicate, exquisitely beautiful paintings of monkeys on display
    A   B
    at the De Young Museum were painted by a twelve year old girl. No error
    C   D   E

16. The ancient Romans, who we respect for their culture, regularly practiced
                 A   B   C
    bribery and infanticide. No error
    D   E

17. <u>All of</u> the locations proposed for <u>the disposal</u> of these nuclear wastes have <u>its</u>
    　　A　　　　　　　　　　　　　　　B　　　　　　　　　　　　　　　　　　C
<u>disadvantages.</u> <u>No error</u>
　　　D　　　　　　　　E

18. Although it is a <u>one-celled</u> <u>animal,</u> the amoeba <u>can't barely</u> be seen
    　　　　　　　　　　A　　　　　　B　　　　　　　　　C
<u>by the naked eye.</u> <u>No error</u>
　　　D　　　　　　　　E

19. Between bites of his <u>hot dog,</u> Gene chatted with the players <u>who</u> <u>were waiting</u> for
    　　　　　　　　　　　A　　　　　　　　　　　　　　　　　　B　　C
<u>their</u> turn at batting practice. <u>No error</u>
　D　　　　　　　　　　　　　　　　E

20. Mark told Sara <u>that</u> Jane should take <u>her</u> sculpture <u>to the crafts fair</u> in
    　　　　　　　A　　　　　　　　　B　　　　　　C
<u>Peterborough New Hampshire.</u> <u>No error</u>
　　　D　　　　　　　　　　　　　E

21. The police pulled the car over <u>because</u> its driver looked <u>suspiciously,</u> and they
    　　　　　　　　　　　　　　A　　　　　　　　　　　B
<u>found</u> that the driver was only <u>seven years old!</u> <u>No error</u>
　C　　　　　　　　　　　　　　　D　　　　　　　E

22. The <u>giant</u> octopuses along the <u>pacific coast</u> <u>are becoming</u> <u>more and more rarer</u> be-
    　　A　　　　　　　　　　　B　　　　　C　　　　　D
cause of human disturbance of their habitat. <u>No error</u>
　　　　　　　　　　　　　　　　　　　　　E

23. Jake feels <u>that</u> <u>"Macbeth"</u> is more suspenseful and dramatic than <u>any play</u> by
    　　　　A　　B　　　　　　　　　　　　　　　　　　　C
<u>William Shakespeare.</u> <u>No error</u>
　　　D　　　　　　　　E

24. One <u>principle</u> that is central to <u>American democracy</u> <u>is the notion</u> that there <u>is</u>
    　　A　　　　　　　　　　　B　　　　　　　C　　　　　　　D
strength in diversity. <u>No error</u>
　　　　　　　　　　E

25. The <u>Department of Public Works</u> <u>announced</u> that the project <u>would be awarded</u> to
    　　A　　　　　　　　　　　B　　　　　　　　　C
<u>whomever</u> was the lowest bidder. <u>No error.</u>
　D　　　　　　　　　　　　　　　E

Sketchbook

Satellite communications permit almost instantaneous transmission of news from one part of the world to another. A century ago, news could take months, or even years, to travel around the globe. The advantages of increased speed in the transmission of news are obvious. Have you ever thought, though, of some of the disadvantages? Write an essay in which you compare methods of news transmission used in the past with the super fast technologies used today. Use precise adjectives and adverbs in your essay.

Additional Sketches

Imagine that you are moving to another area, but that you will be able to take three of your favorite places with you, such as a particular room in your house, a local snack shop, or a park. Write three paragraphs in which you describe these places and why they are important to you. Use pronouns correctly.

To what groups do you belong? Write about one group, explaining the characteristics that members of the group have in common and how members differ from nonmembers. Use pronouns and comparative modifiers clearly and effectively.

743

Sketchbook

Objective

To use the theme of changing methods of transmitting news as a springboard to informal writing

Using the Prompt

Before beginning the activity, underscore that Sketchbook activities are designed to be informal in order to encourage risk taking and experimentation; they are not graded.

Share with students pictures of communications devices and systems from a century ago and devices used today. You should be able to locate these easily in encyclopedia articles on communications or in books about the history of communications. Discuss with students how the devices and systems are used and how rapidly they can transmit information.

Have students brainstorm the advantages and disadvantages of almost instantaneous news transmissions. List students' ideas in a chart containing columns headed "Advantages" and "Disadvantages." Have students write their essays using the ideas from the chart that they think are the most important. Remind students that additional ideas frequently come to people as they write, and stress that students should not feel limited to the ideas in the chart.

Present the Additional Sketches as alternative topics for students who prefer a different starting point. Encourage students to keep their writing in their Writing Portfolios. They may wish to refer to it during future writing projects.

Capitalization

Personal Names and Titles, Nationalities, and Religions

Objective

- To capitalize correctly personal names and titles, nationalities, and religions

Teaching Strategies

 Individualizing Instruction

ESL Students In many foreign languages, proper adjectives that are derived from the names of countries are not capitalized. (Italian, *italiano;* German, *deutsche;* French, *français;* Spanish, *español*) You may want to ask ESL students to discuss how capitalization rules for names and other categories discussed in this lesson vary in their languages.

Stumbling Block

Remind students that there are no hard-and-fast rules for particles in foreign names. Capitalization conventions vary from country to country, and they also vary according to personal preference. Students should consult a reference source or ask the person directly for the correct form of address.

Teaching Tip: Titles

Encourage students to think of some titles that would *not* be capitalized if used without a person's name. (senator, congressman, archbishop, professor, judge) You might encourage students to explain the following examples:
- In the last election, Senator Todd was reelected.
- The senator attended the fund-raising event.

GRAMMAR HANDBOOK 38

Capitalization

PERSONAL NAMES AND TITLES, NATIONALITIES, AND RELIGIONS

A **common noun** is the name of a person, place, thing, or idea. A **proper noun** is the name of a particular person, place, thing, or idea. Proper nouns are capitalized. A **proper adjective** is also capitalized.

Common Noun	Proper Noun	Proper Adjective
philosopher	Socrates	Socratic method
city	Rome	Roman fountain

A prefix and a proper noun or adjective may form a hyphenated compound. Capitalize the prefix if the word falls at the beginning of a sentence or if it is part of a title.

pre-Nixon   anti-Communist   mid-September   non-European

Personal Names and Titles

Capitalize personal names and initials standing for names.

E. B. White   Gertrude Stein   Lydia H. Palmer-Watson

Capitalization rules for particles in foreign names vary widely. If you are unsure about the spelling of a foreign name, consult a reference source. Accepted capitalization includes the following:

Daphne du Maurier   Flannery O'Connor   Vincent van Gogh

Capitalize a title or an abbreviation for a title when it immediately precedes a name or when it is used in direct address.

Cardinal Krol   Professor Rodriguez   Senator Simon

I think you will agree, Dr. Ortega, that we must act soon.

Usage Note Capitalize all words except *the* in a nickname.

the Great Emancipator   William "the Refrigerator" Perry

Capitalize the abbreviations *Jr., Sr., II,* or *III* after a person's name. The abbreviations *Jr.* and *Sr.* are preceded by a comma, and they are followed by a comma if they do not fall at the end of the sentence.

John Littleton, Jr., performed a piano concert.

He was named Victor Garcia III after his father and grandfather.

Abbreviations for academic degrees, such as *Ph.D., M.S.,* and *B.A.,* are capitalized when used with or without a proper name.

> It took him three years to earn his **M.S.**
> Kay Monroe Smith, **Ph.D.,** will instruct the class next week.

In general, do not capitalize a title when it follows a name or when it is used alone.

> Tamara Richards, the president, called the meeting to order.
> Call the professor for an appointment.

Capitalize a title used alone only when it refers to a head of state or to a person in some other uniquely important position.

> the **P**resident and **V**ice-**P**resident of the United States
>
> the **Q**ueen of **E**ngland   the **S**ecretary of **S**tate
> the **J**oint **C**hiefs of **S**taff   the **P**ope

Do not capitalize the prefix *ex-,* the suffix *-elect,* or the word *presiding* when it is part of a title.

> ex-President Reagan   Governor-elect Sara Kole
> presiding Judge Jones

Kinship Names

Capitalize kinship names when they are used before a proper name or when they are used in place of one.

> We visited **A**unt Josie, my father's sister.
> Will **G**randma meet us for lunch after she plays golf?

Do not capitalize kinship names when they are preceded by articles or by possessive nouns or adjectives.

> Her aunt and my grandmother were both living in Detroit.
> The mother of the boy was not available for comment.

Names of Races, Languages, Nationalities, Tribes, and Religions

Capitalize the names of races, languages, nationalities, tribes, and religions. Capitalize any nouns or adjectives that are derived from such names.

> **A**ztec   **H**ispanics   **Y**iddish
> **I**nuit   **M**ethodist   **L**atin
> **G**reek alphabet   **P**arisian cafés   **A**ustralian banks

The Supreme Being, Other Deities, and Sacred Writings

Capitalize all words referring to God, the Holy Family, other deities, and religious scriptures.

Jesus	**B**ook of **M**ormon	**K**oran
Revelations	**V**irgin **M**ary	**Y**ahweh
Messiah	**H**oly **S**pirit	**A**llah

Capitalize the names of mythical deities.

Jupiter	**A**starte	**Z**eus
Gaia	**T**hor	**H**era

Do not capitalize the words *god* and *goddess* when they refer to mythological deities. Capitalize personal pronouns that refer to God as the supreme deity but not those that refer to mythological figures.

> They pray to **G**od and ask **H**im to answer their prayers.
> Diana was a Roman goddess, and women often worshiped her.

The Pronoun *I* and the Interjections *O* and *Oh*

Always capitalize the pronoun *I*.

> When **I** reached safety, **I** heaved a sigh of relief.

Capitalize the interjection *O*, which often appears in poetry, the Bible, and prayers or petitions. Capitalize the interjection *oh* only when it is the first word in a sentence.

> Help us, **O** mighty king!   My, oh my, what a mess!

Practice Your Skills

A. CONCEPT CHECK

Using Capital Letters   For each of the following sentences, rewrite the words that have capitalization errors, capitalizing or lower-casing as necessary.

1. At first the audience was disappointed that the vice-president of the United States was unable to attend.
2. Everyone in the crowded meeting room, including mayor chun, was delighted that the explorer, grover "the rover" burke, jr., had agreed to speak.
3. Burke, whose Grandfather had been a friend of president teddy roosevelt, held an m.a. and a ph.d. in anthropology.

4. "Today," he began, "the people of Easter Island speak the spanish language and are chilean citizens.
5. However, the Prehistoric wanderers who first arrived with their panoply of ancient Gods and Rituals were polynesian.
6. In 1722, a dutch Admiral, jacob roggeveen, was the first european to set foot on this remote Volcanic Island.
7. When i was a boy, grandfather burke told me about the mystery of Rapa Nui, the polynesian name for the island.
8. Questions concerning the Giant Stone Statues found on the Island still baffle Archaeologists.
9. One theory suggests that chief hotu matu's tribe made them; another, that people of a pre-incan peruvian culture did.
10. Archaeologist dr. w. mulloy believed that those who made them, whether polynesian or non-polynesian, were Masters of Masonry."

B. PROOFREADING SKILL

Capitalization   Rewrite the following paragraphs, correcting errors in capitalization, punctuation, and spelling.

After Easter Island's initial exploration by the dutch, british adventurer James Cook visited the mysterious isle. On behalf of the king of England. In 1862, the Population was nearly wiped out by a peruvian Slave raid and a Smallpox epedemic. With the introduction of christianity in 1868, the population moved to the Village of Hanga Roa on the west coast.

At the time of the arrival of the dutch, the easter islanders ate primarily their own Fish and sweet potatoes now they depend on supplies brought by the chilean Navy. Visitors to this part of the South Pacific are drawn to the mystereous statues for which the island is famous. Carved from the rock of the volacano rana Roraka, these eyeless forms take the shape of heads fourty feet tall. Were they intended to honor some Diety as the parthanon honors athena. We can only guess.

C. APPLICATION IN WRITING

A Travel Brochure   Do some research on one of the following islands or some other exotic destination. Put your findings in the form of copy for a travel brochure that might be sent out by the island's tourism bureau. Describe the people, language, culture, sights, and any other special features.

Aruba   Jamaica   Bermuda   Madagascar

Statues, Easter Island, Chile. These ancient statues, as well as other archaeological remains, are of unknown origin.

Capitalization   **747**

Objective

- To capitalize correctly place names, directions, regions, astronomical terms, and vehicles

Teaching Strategies

 Individualizing Instruction

ESL Students The capitalization of place names and adjectives referring to directions and regions differs in many foreign languages. Encourage ESL students to compare the rules in this lesson with those for their native languages.

LEP Students Have these students refer to the rules and examples in this lesson as they complete the exercises.

> *Additional Resources*
> - Grammar and Usage Practice Book, p. 80

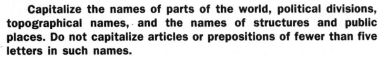

PLACE NAMES, DIRECTIONS AND REGIONS, ASTRONOMICAL TERMS, AND VEHICLES

Place Names

Capitalize the names of parts of the world, political divisions, topographical names, and the names of structures and public places. Do not capitalize articles or prepositions of fewer than five letters in such names.

Parts of the World	Asia, South America, Antarctica, Africa, the Northern Hemisphere, the Orient, the New World
Political Divisions	Orange County, the Dominion of Canada, the Province of Quebec, Saudi Arabia
Topographical Names	Death Valley, Mount Ranier, Ohio River, Channel Islands, the Gobi Desert, the Grand Tetons
Structures and Public Places	Vietnam War Memorial, Blarney Castle, Magnificent Mile, Pennsylvania Turnpike, the Capitol

Usage Notes Such words as *lake, mountain,* and *river* are capitalized when they are part of an official or formal name but not when they stand alone or when they follow two or more proper names.

> Lake Michigan   the lake   Indian and Tupper lakes

In official documents, such as a constitution, words such as *city, state,* and *country* are capitalized when they are part of the name of a political unit.

> the City of Houston (official document)
> the city of Houston (regular usage)

Directions and Regions

Capitalize the names of regions of the country but not of directions of the compass.

> Driving to the East Coast will be expensive.
> During spring break many college students migrate south to enjoy the warm weather.

Capitalize proper adjectives derived from names of regions of the country. Do not capitalize adjectives derived from words denoting direction.

a **W**estern city   a **S**outheastern college
a northbound train   an easterly wind

Astronomical Terms

Capitalize the names of stars, planets, galaxies, constellations, and other heavenly bodies. Do not capitalize *sun* and *moon*.

Mars	eclipse of the sun	**A**lpha **C**entauri
Saturn	moon's orbit	**M**ilky **W**ay
Mercury	sunset	**U**rsa **M**inor

Usage Note The word *earth* is capitalized only when it is used in context with other astronomical terms. *Earth* is never capitalized when it is preceded by the article *the*.

The earth is the fifth largest planet.

Mercury, **V**enus, and **E**arth are the planets nearest the sun.

Vehicles

Capitalize the names of ships, trains, automobiles, airplanes, and spacecraft.

Orient Express   *U.S.S. Enterprise*
Empress of Ireland   **E**dsel

Practice Your Skills

A. CONCEPT CHECK

Using Capitalization Rewrite the following sentences, capitalizing words as necessary. Use the rules you have studied in this chapter.

1. On the atlantic coast of central florida, just east of the city of orlando, is a promontory known as cape canaveral.
2. Cape canaveral, one of the most famous places in the western hemisphere, is the location of the john f. kennedy space center.
3. This east coast space center is the primary launching site for missions of the american space program.
4. It was from this site that the *apollo 11* mission, the first manned mission to the moon, was launched.
5. The first flight of the space shuttle *columbia* took place in 1981 under the direction of commander john young.

Writing
──TIP──

Underline the names of ships, trains, airplanes, and spacecraft (but not the names of automobiles) in a typed or handwritten manuscript. On a word processor, use italics.

Writing Theme
Space Exploration

6. The space shuttles have been used to launch, retrieve, and repair many satellites, including <u>indonesia</u>'s *<u>palapa b</u>* communications satellite and Western Union Corporation's *<u>westar</u>* satellite.
7. Space shuttle missions have also carried devices used to study <u>mars</u> and other planets, the sun, the moon, and the stars.
8. The <u>nile river</u> in <u>egypt</u> and the <u>great wall</u> in the <u>people's republic</u> of <u>china</u> can be seen quite clearly from space at times.
9. During the *<u>apollo</u>* 7 mission, the people of <u>brisbane</u>, <u>australia</u>, turned their lights on all at once as the spacecraft passed over.
10. Through space exploration, much can be learned about our galaxy and perhaps about galaxies beyond the <u>milky way</u>.

B. PROOFREADING SKILL

Correcting Errors in Capitalization Rewrite the following paragraph, correcting all <u>errors</u> in capitalization.

(1) In the summer of 1983, <u>sally</u> <u>ride</u> became the first <u>american</u> woman to lift off into space. (2) Ride and four other astronauts blasted off in the *<u>challenger</u>* from the launch pad at <u>cape</u> <u>canaveral</u>, <u>florida</u>, and orbited the earth for seven days before landing in <u>california</u>. (3) Traveling at five miles per second, circling the earth once every ninety minutes, <u>ride</u> and her fellow astronauts had magnificent views. (4) As they looked at <u>north</u> <u>america</u>, they could clearly see <u>los</u> <u>angeles</u> and, to the north, <u>puget</u> <u>sound</u>. (5) Within minutes, they would be admiring <u>florida</u>'s distinctive coastline and the city of <u>new</u> <u>york</u>. (6) Their panoramic view included huge dust storms blowing over deserts in <u>africa</u> and smoke spewing from active volcanoes in <u>hawaii</u>. (7) The astronauts spotted enormous chunks of ice floating in <u>antarctic</u> waters and electrical storms raging over the <u>atlantic</u>. (8) Looking eastward toward <u>wales</u> and <u>england</u>, they saw the <u>english</u> <u>channel</u>, <u>cardigan</u> <u>bay</u>, and the <u>bristol</u> <u>channel</u>. (9) Natural and artificial wonders dazzled <u>ride</u> during her orbits around the earth. (10) Through books, talks, and television appearances, she has shared her excitement about space travel with people in all parts of the <u>united</u> <u>states</u>.

C. APPLICATION IN WRITING

Science Fiction If you could travel throughout the universe, where would you go? What might you see there? Let your imagination soar. Use existing facts, names, and theories, or create your own. Write a brief essay in which you describe your imaginary universe. Remember to use correct capitalization.

B. Proofreading Skill
Correcting Errors in Capitalization
Words that need capital letters are underlined on page.

C. Writing Application
Science Fiction
Answers will vary.

Other terms that are to be capitalized include the names of organizations and institutions, certain historical and cultural terms, and calendar and time designations.

Organizations and Institutions

Capitalize the names of organizations and institutions and their abbreviations.

Capitalize all the words in the name of an organization or institution with the exception of prepositions and conjunctions. Capitalize the abbreviations and acronyms for such names.

> the **B**oard of **R**egents of the **U**niversity of **T**exas
> **W**ashington **N**ational **S**ymphony
> **A**merican **S**tock **E**xchange
> **B**ureau of **I**ndian **A**ffairs (**BIA**)
> **H**ome **B**ox **O**ffice (**HBO**)
> **F**irst **B**aptist **C**hurch

Do not capitalize words such as *school, company, church, college,* and *hospital* unless they are part of a proper noun.

> She finished high school and applied to **B**oston **C**ollege.

Historical Events, Periods, and Documents

Capitalize the names of historical events, periods, and documents.

> **N**avigation **A**ct
> **T**reaty of **V**ersailles
> **B**oston **T**ea **P**arty
>
> **B**lack **F**riday
> **C**ivil **W**ar
> the **D**ark **A**ges

A Visit from the Old Mistress, Winslow Homer, National Museum of American Art. Homer illustrated various aspects of the Civil War, including the living conditions of slaves.

Capitalization   **751**

Humanities Connection

Art Note   Winslow Homer painted *A Visit from the Old Mistress* (1876) after touring postwar Virginia. His belief in equality for blacks and his impressions of the South's changed way of life after the Civil War inspired Homer to devote a number of paintings to the subject of freed slaves. Ask: What thoughts and feelings do you imagine freed slaves and their former masters might have had on seeing each other again? Do you think Homer's painting captures these thoughts and feelings?

Linking Grammar and Writing

Suggest that students can help remember the capitalization rules in this section by composing sentences showing correct usage. Give an example such as the following: On New Year's Day, which fell on a Thursday this year, we arrived at my uncle's house for lunch at 1:00 P.M., just in time to watch the Cotton Bowl.

Additional Resources
• Grammar and Usage Practice Book, p. 81

Months, Days, and Holidays

Capitalize the names of months, days, and holidays, but not the names of seasons.

> We always go to my uncle's house for **T**hanksgiving.
> In **O**ctober, autumn colors reach their peak in this area and by late **M**ay spring flowers appear.
> On the fourth **T**hursday in **J**une, we'll pick strawberries.

Time Abbreviations

Capitalize the abbreviations B.C., A.D., A.M., and P.M.

> The Roman historian Livy lived from 59 B.C. to A.D. 17.
> Football replays will be shown at 10:00 A.M. and 2:00 P.M.

Capitalize the abbreviations for time zones.

> **PDT** (Pacific Daylight Time)　　　**EST** (Eastern Standard Time)

Awards, Special Events, and Brand Names

Capitalize the names of awards and special events.

> **S**uperbowl　　**G**rammy **A**wards　　**H**eisman **T**rophy　　**M**ardi **G**ras

Capitalize the brand name of a product but not a common noun following the brand name.

> **D**azzle nail polish　　　　**D**are **T**o **B**e **D**ifferent ties and shirts

School Subjects and Names of School Years

Do not capitalize the general names of school subjects. Do capitalize the names of specific courses, including those designated by numbers. The name of a language course is always capitalized.

> history　　　　　　　　　　**W**orld **H**istory II
> physical education　　　　**E**nglish 101

Capitalize the words *freshman*, *sophomore*, *junior*, and *senior* when they are used as adjectives referring to specific classes (or class events). Also capitalize them when they are used as nouns in direct address.

> The **S**enior **C**lass excelled in raising money for a new gym.
> College recruiters hoped to impress the juniors and seniors.
> Now is the time, **S**eniors, to complete college applications and submit applications fees.

Practice Your Skills

A. CONCEPT CHECK

Capitalization   Rewrite the following sentences, capitalizing words as necessary. You may use a dictionary for guidance.

1. History can be cruel, as many a college freshman enrolled in engineering 100, introduction to engineering, has learned.
2. As if it were unimportant, history has lost the name of the remarkable Mesopotamian inventor who, about 3000 b.c., invented the chariot.
3. The thousands of New Yorkers who ride the subway on the fourth thursday of every november to macy's thanksgiving day parade give little thought to the engineers who created the underground train.
4. Few, if any of them, realize that tammany hall and "Boss" Tweed stifled a revolutionary subway system in 1866.
5. Alfred ely beach would surely have won an award titled inventor of the decade had his air-powered subway train not been scuttled.
6. From 6:00 p.m. to 12:00 a.m. for 58 days, Beach's men built the block-long model that was later legislated into oblivion.
7. In february, 1912, construction workers accidentally uncovered Beach's pneumatic subway train.
8. Who in San Francisco thanks the inventors of bart (bay area rapid transit) for the first completely automated transit system?
9. Did engineers earn an award during the civil war when their confederate submarine sank a union ship on february 17, 1864?
10. Perhaps the freshman class should research forgotten inventors from 2000 b.c. to a.d. 2000.

B. REVISION SKILL

Using Capitalization   Correctly write the words in each sentence that need capital letters.

(1) Several of the majestic automobiles built during the twenties and thirties, such as the american duesenberg, the english rolls-royce, and the french hispano-suiza and bugatti, are considered classic cars. (2) According to the classic car club of america, a classic is one that was made between 1925 and 1942, of a limited series, and with special technical features. (3) The only exceptions are the lincoln continentals of 1946–48, which are also considered classics. (4) The quality of the classic car engine is exemplified by the hispano-suiza that was driven 1,100 miles from paris to nice and back and then parked over white paper; not a trace of oil or water dropped from the engine.

Charles S. Rolls and Henry Royce produced the Rolls-Royce Silver Ghost, known by its distinctive grill, the double-R trademark, and the flying-lady radiator ornament.

Capitalization   **753**

(5) Ettore bugatti, an italian, built his famous cars in molsheim, a small town in eastern france. (6) the haughty bugatti, who liked to be called "*le patron*," once refused to sell a car to a king, the king of albania in fact, because he disapproved of the ruler's table manners.

(7) At the age of 40, henry royce built his first car because he was dissatisfied with the one he had just bought. (8) In 1904, royce began the manufacture of rolls-royces with a london car dealer, charles rolls. (9) Rolls-royce factories produced the classic silver ghost, the phantom I, and the phantom II.

(10) Sometimes mistakenly thought of as a german car, the duesenberg is a classic american-built car. (11) Racing duesenbergs won the indianapolis 500 in three different years —1924, 1925, and 1927. (12) The j cars, built primarily between 1930 and 1936, could only be afforded by the very rich. (13) The chassis alone cost as much as ten thousand depression-era dollars.

(14) Classic cars are on display at the following places: harrah's automobile collection in reno, nevada; briggs cunningham automotive museum in costa mesa, california; and the early american museum in silver springs, florida. (15) A number of other classic-car museums are scattered throughout the united states.

C. PROOFREADING SKILL

Capitalizing Correctly   Imagine that you are a reporter for a news magazine directed toward high-school students. You have written a story about a new sport—one of the many that have grown out of unusual modes of transportation—a sport called snowboarding. The following is your rough draft. Rewrite the draft, correcting all errors in spelling, punctuation, and capitalization.

Snowboarding, a fairly young Sport invented in the mid-1960's, is a great way for Hill Riders to hang ten when snow falls. From vermont to california, Snowboarders are traveling the slopes on a cross between a Surfboard and a Ski. It is a five-foot-long, ten-inch-wide piece of laminated Wood or Fiberglass, with fixed bindings that strap around any sturdy boot. No Poles are needed for this cousin sport to Surfing and Skateboarding. Boarders shoot down a slope in a surf-style sideways stance, boarders can ride on anything from a tiny hill in new england to a giant mountinside in the rocky Mountins.

CHECK POINT
PAGES 744–755

A. Rewrite the following sentences, capitalizing or lower-casing as necessary.

1. In 1498, the portuguese Explorer vasco da gama, who commanded the Ships the *berrio,* the *saint gabriel,* and the *saint raphael,* became one of the first europeans to visit the exotic Land of india.
2. The vast Subcontinent stretches from the hindu kush mountains in the north to cape comorin in the south.
3. In the Northern Region, the People depend heavily on the ganges, indus, and brahmaputra rivers, especially during the Monsoon Season from june to september.
4. The earliest indian civilization dates from about 2500 b.c.
5. Today, india is larger than any other Democracy in the western world.
6. The streets of new delhi are crowded at 3:00 p.m. or 3:00 a.m.
7. More than 200 languages are spoken, including telugu, tamil, and bengali; the official languages are hindi and english.
8. Historically, the two largest religious groups in india, the hindus and the moslems, have disagreed on many issues.
9. The islamic, or moslem, sects worship allah.
10. Hindus worship many Gods, two of whom are vishnu and shiva.
11. Mohandas karamchad gandhi—who was called mahatma, or "Great Soul"—made efforts to reconcile religious differences.
12. Gandhi led the indian national congress in a policy of non-cooperation with british rule.
13. He wrote: "i believe nonviolence is infinitely superior to violence."
14. In 1947, independence from britain resulted from the efforts of prime minister jawaharlal nehru, gandhi's follower.
15. Nehru's Daughter, indira gandhi, became prime minister in 1966.

B. Application in Literature Rewrite the following paragraph, restoring capital letters or lower-casing where necessary.

> Anything is possible on a Train: a great Meal, a Binge, a Visit from card players, an Intrigue, a good night's Sleep, and strangers' Monologues framed like Russian Short Stories. It was my intention to board every Train that chugged into view from victoria station in London to tokyo central; to take the branch line to simla; then go through khyber pass and the line that links indian railways with those in ceylon; the *mandalay Express,* the malaysian *golden arrow,* the Locals in Vietnam, and the trains with bewitching names, the *orient express,* the *north star,* the *trans-siberian.*
>
> **Paul Theroux, *The Great Railway Bazaar***

Writing Theme
Faraway Places

Capitalization   **755**

CHECK POINT
PAGES 744–754

You may wish to use the following Checkpoint exercises as an informal evaluation of student mastery of the rules for capitalization covered in this handbook.

WRITING THEME   Faraway Places

A.

1. In 1498, the Portuguese explorer Vasco da Gama, who commanded the ships the *Berrio,* the *Saint Gabriel,* and the *Saint Raphael,* became one of the first Europeans to visit the exotic land of India.
2. The vast subcontinent stretches from the Hindu Kush Mountains in the north to Cape Cormorin in the south.
3. In the northern region, the people depend heavily on the Ganges, Indus, and Brahmaputra rivers, especially during the monsoon season from June to September.
4. The earliest Indian civilization dates from about 2500 B.C.
5. Today, India is larger than any other democracy in the Western world.
6. The streets of New Delhi are crowded at 3:00 P.M. or 3:00 A.M.
7. More than 200 languages are spoken, including Telugu, Tamil, and Bengali; the official languages are Hindi and English.
8. Historically, the two largest religious groups in India, the Hindus and the Moslems, have disagreed on many issues.
9. The Islamic, or Moslem, sects worship Allah.
10. Hindus worship many gods, two of whom are Vishnu and Shiva.
11. Mohandas Karamchad Gandhi—who was called Mahatma, or "Great Soul"—made efforts to reconcile religious differences.
12. Gandhi led the Indian National Congress in a policy of noncooperation with British rule.
13. He wrote: "I believe nonviolence is infinitely superior to violence."
14. In 1947, independence from Britain resulted from the efforts of Prime Minister Jawaharlal Nehru, Gandhi's follower.
15. Nehru's daughter, Indira Gandhi, became Prime Minister in 1966.

B. Application in Literature
Errors are underlined on page.

Anything is possible on a train: a great meal, a binge, a visit from card players, an intrigue, a good night's sleep, and strangers' monologues framed like Russian short stories. It was my intention to board every train that chugged into view from Victoria Station in London to Tokyo Central; to take the branch line to Simla; then go through Khyber Pass and the line that links Indian railways with those in Ceylon; the *Mandalay Express,* the Malaysian *Golden Arrow,* the locals in Vietnam, and the trains with bewitching names, the *Orient Express,* the *North Star,* the *Trans-Siberian.*

Capitalization   **755**

First Words and Titles

Objective

- To capitalize correctly first words and titles, direct quotations, letter parts, and outlines

Teaching Strategies

Linking Grammar and Writing

Occasionally poets experiment for special effect with long, run-on lines of verse, without following the rules for capitalization. Display this excerpt from "Prayer Before Birth" by Louis MacNeice:

Literary Model
I am not yet born; provide me
With water to dandle me, grass to grow
   for me, trees to
talk to me, sky to sing for me, birds and
   a little white light
in the back of my mind to guide me.

Encourage students to write some lines of poetry modeled on this example of free verse.

Capitalize the first words of sentences, lines of poetry, and direct quotations.

Sentences and Poetry

Capitalize the first word of every sentence.

Graduation marks the beginning of new life choices.

In general, capitalize the first word of every line of poetry.

In the deserted moon-blanch'd street
How lonely rings the echo of my feet!

Matthew Arnold, "A Summer Night"

Quotations

Capitalize the first word of a direct quotation.

Rev. King said, "We have no alternative but to protest."

In a **divided quotation,** the first word of the second part of the quotation is capitalized only when it begins a new sentence.

"I like football," Vito said, "because it is action-packed."
"I like football," Vito said. "It's action-packed."

Parts of a Letter

Capitalize the first word in the greeting and complimentary close of a letter. Capitalize the title and name of the person addressed or words such as *Sir* and *Madam* that take the place of a name.

Dear Manager: Dear Ms. Macon,   Sincerely yours,

Outlines and Titles

Capitalize letters that introduce major subsections in an outline, and capitalize the first word of each item.

I. Solar system
   A. Planets
      1. Mars
      2. Jupiter
   B. Moons

Writing TIP

In modern poetry, first words are not always capitalized. When you write your own poetry, choose the style that suits your subject.

Capitalize the first, last, and all other important words in titles. Do not capitalize conjunctions, articles, or prepositions with fewer than five letters.

Book Title	*The Prince of Tides*
Newspaper	*Los Angeles Free Press*
Magazine	*Sports Illustrated*
Play	*King Lear*
Movie	*Sophie's Choice*
TV Series	*Nightline*
Long Musical Composition	*William Tell Overture*
Short Story	"The Sojourner"
Poem	"The People, Yes"
Magazine Article	"College Tuitions on the Rise"
Chapter	Chapter III: "Colonial America"
Cartoon	*Calvin and Hobbes*
Song	"Let It Be"
Work of Art	*Silence*

Capitalize the words *the* and *magazine* only when they are part of the title.

The Wall Street Journal	the *California Farmer*
Texas Homes Magazine	*Seventeen* magazine

Usage Note Always capitalize the first element of a hyphenated compound used in titles. Capitalize the second element if it is a proper noun or if it has equal force with the first element. Do not capitalize the second part if it is a modifying participle.

Eighteenth-Century Art   Japanese-made Automobiles

Practice Your Skills

A. CONCEPT CHECK

Capitalization Errors Rewrite the following items, capitalizing words as necessary. Underline the words that are italicized.

1. s. s. osgood's painting *poe* depicts a gentle young man.
2. tam mossman writes: "edgar allan poe's name is now synonymous with horror, mystery, and the macabre."
3. Few know that poe wrote tall tales, such as "the angel of the odd."
4. There is nothing sinister about his romantic poems, such as "to the river."
5. Poe even pokes fun at the literary magazines and writers of his day in "the literary life of thingum bob, esq., late editor of the *goosetherumfoodle*."

Capitalization   **757**

Linking Grammar and Literature

Write the following excerpt or another of your own choice on the chalkboard, omitting all capitalization. Then ask students to determine where capitalization is needed both in the excerpt and the title.

Literary Model
"Mother," said the boy Paul one day, "why don't we keep a car of our own? Why do we always use uncle's, or else a taxi?"

"Because we're the poor members of the family," said the mother.

"But why are we, Mother?" he asked, rather timidly.

"Well—I suppose," she said slowly and bitterly, "it's because your father has no luck."

D. H. Lawrence
From "The Rocking-Horse Winner"

 Individualizing Instruction

Advanced Students Suggest that these students read the works of such poets as Allen Ginsberg, Nikki Giovanni, Edwin Morgan, Denise Levertov, and Lawrence Ferlinghetti. Ask them to think about the role that capitalization (or the lack of it) plays in the style and message of these poets. You might also suggest that these students try writing a poem in which capitalization (or the lack of it) plays a part. Then ask them to share their poems and discuss the part that capitalization plays.

> **Additional Resources**
> • Grammar and Usage Practice Book, p. 82

WRITING THEME   Edgar Allan Poe

A. Concept Check
Capitalization Errors
Words that need capital letters are underlined on page.

6. "He virtually created the detective story," writes critic <u>robert regan</u>. "<u>he</u> also produced some of the most influential literary criticism of his time."

7. In 1835, he was editor of the *<u>southern literary messenger</u>*.

8. The following stanza from "<u>annabel lee</u>" shows his romantic nature:

> <u>it</u> was many and many a year ago,
> <u>in</u> a kingdom by the sea,
> <u>that</u> a maiden there lived whom you may know
> <u>by</u> the name of <u>annabel lee</u>;
> <u>and</u> this maiden she lived with no other thought
> <u>than</u> to love and be loved by me.

9. His poem "<u>the raven</u>" was so popular that he once apologized for not keeping a pet raven.

10. <u>an</u> encyclopedia might outline his biography as follows:

> I. <u>poe</u>'s life
> a. <u>youth</u> in <u>virginia</u>
> b. <u>work</u> as writer and critic
> c. <u>problems</u> in his adult life

B. PROOFREADING SKILL

Capitalization Rewrite this letter, capitalizing <u>words</u> as necessary.

> 5050 <u>west</u> <u>third</u> <u>street</u>
> <u>normal</u>, <u>illinois</u> 61761
> <u>october</u> 19, 19—
>
> James <u>rankin</u>
> 555 <u>north</u> <u>sycamore</u>
> Joplin, Missouri 64802
>
> <u>dear</u> Mr. <u>rankin</u>:
>   <u>please</u> reserve for me the first-edition copies of <u>poems</u> <u>by</u> <u>edgar</u> <u>a.</u> <u>poe</u> and <u>tales</u> <u>of</u> <u>the</u> <u>grotesque</u> <u>and</u> <u>arabesque</u> advertised in <u>bookbuyers'</u> <u>bulletin</u>.
>
>   <u>sincerely</u> yours,
>
>   c.a. <u>dupin</u>

C. APPLICATION IN LITERATURE

Capitalization   Rewrite the following passage, capitalizing words as necessary.

> i am not a son of charleston. nor could i be if i wanted to. i am always a visitor, and my allegiance lies with other visitors, sons and daughters of accident and circumstance. edgar allan poe was a son by visitation. it was no surprise to me when i was a freshman at the institute to discover that poe was once stationed at fort moultrie and that he wrote "the gold bug" about one of the sea islands near charleston. . . . i like to think of the city shaping this agitated, misplaced soldier, keening his passion for shade, trimming the soft edges of his nightmare, harshening his poisons and his metaphors, deepening his intimacy with the sunless wastes that issued forth from his kingdom of nightmare in blazing islands, still inchoate and unformed, of the english language. whenever i go back to charleston, i think of poe.
>
> **Pat Conroy, *The Lords of Discipline***

D. APPLICATION IN WRITING

A Movie Review   Thrillers remain as popular today as they were in Poe's time. Moviemakers profit from this fact. Think about a spine-tingling movie you have recently seen. If you have not seen an exciting movie lately, invent your own idea for one. Write a brief review of the film. Include some quotations from your friends about the movie. You might wish to put your review in the form of a letter to a motion-picture studio. Use correct capitalization throughout.

C H E C K   P O I N T
PAGES 756–759

A. Rewrite the following sentences, capitalizing words as necessary.

1. The july 1990 issue of the magazine *rural new england* included a feature on an interesting book.
2. "each page," the magazine tells us, "contains a short poem of rhymed couplets and a freehand illustration."
3. subtitled *a manual of flornithology for beginners,* this little book on distinguishing birds from flowers is a masterpiece of pre-depression light verse and cartooning.
4. published in 1907 by paul elder and company of san francisco, the book was written and illustrated by robert williams wood.

Writing Theme
Cartoons and
Cartooning

Capitalization   **759**

C. Application in Literature
Capitalization
Words that need capital letters are underlined on page.

D. Application in Writing
A Movie Review
Answers will vary.

C H E C K P O I N T
PAGES 756–759

You may wish to use the following Checkpoint exercises as an informal evaluation of student mastery of the rules for capitalization covered in this handbook.

> **Additional Resources**
> • Grammar and Usage Practice Book, p. 83

Managing the Paper Load

To limit the number of exercises to correct, you may wish to have students write their answers to exercise A. Then do exercise B orally in class.

WRITING THEME   Cartoons and
Cartooning

A.
Words that need capital letters are underlined on page.

5. the poems have whimsical names such as "the clover and the plover," "the carrot and the parrot," "the quail and kale," and "catbird and catnip."
6. one poem from the book, "the cowbird and the cowslip," goes as follows:

   growing in mires, in gold attired,
   the cowslip has been much admired,
   altho' its proper name, we're told,
   is really the marsh marigold:
   the cowbird picture, i suspect,
   is absolutely incorrect,
   we make such errors now and then,
   a sort of cowslip of the pen.

7. "wood's book of drawings and poems is important," says historian richard shenck. "for one thing, it is one of but a few examples of non-political cartooning produced before world war i."
8. Indeed, most nineteenth-century cartoons, such as those done by Thomas Nast for *harper's weekly,* were political.
9. One exception was one of the first cartoon strips, James Swinnerton's *the little bears* and *tigers*.
10. this strip appeared in the *san francisco examiner* in 1892.

B. For each numbered sentence, rewrite the words that need capitalization and those that are incorrectly capitalized.

(1) in gary larson's comic strip, *the far side,* animals act like Humans and humans act like animals. (2) the One-Panel Cartoon, run in Seven Hundred Daily Newspapers, is loaded with animals making fun of people, and people making fools of themselves.

(3) "*the far side* is a Collage of Charles addams and the politics of the Green Party," said peter richmond, a reporter for *the miami herald.* (4) "it's rod serling crashing at the ozzie nelson household, george romero produced by disney."

(5) in a Second-story Studio in seattle, washington, gary larson produces seven editions a week of *the far side*. (6) a former Music-Store Clerk, larson wanted to make people laugh and thought his cartooning might make him a living. (7) through Newspapers, Books, and other Media, larson's potential readership is eighty million people.

(8) "i'm a little worried that too many people appreciate the cartoon," larson said. (9) "when people don't get the strip, i like that. (10) i like that *the far side* can be confusing, because that means i'm still being experimental."

Gary Larson, American cartoonist and creator of *The Far Side*

760 Grammar Handbook

B.
  1. In Gary Larson's, *The Far Side,* humans
  2. The one-panel cartoon, seven hundred daily newspapers
  3. *The Far Side,* collage, Addams, Peter Richmond, *The Miami Herald*
  4. It's Rod Serling, Ozzie Nelson, George Romero, Disney
  5. In, second-story studio, Seattle, Washington, Gary Larson, *The Far Side*
  6. A, music-store clerk, Larson
  7. Through, newspapers, books, media, Larson's
  8. I'm, Larson
  9. When, I
  10. I, *The Far Side,* I'm

A. Capitalization Rewrite the following sentences, capitalizing words as necessary.

1. sophocles, who lived from 497 to 406 b.c., was one of the great writers of greek tragedy.
2. only seven plays by sophocles remain; most of them are taught in either world literature or western civilization.
3. sophocles lived in athens, located in southeastern greece on a peninsula between the aegean and mediterranean seas.
4. he lived in athens during the golden age of greece.
5. records indicate that he was a general during the samian revolt and the peloponnesian war, and he was treasurer of the delian league in athens.
6. his plays were staged at the theater of dionysus; the building's remains can still be seen on the southern slope of the acropolis near the center of modern athens.
7. theater originated in greece as part of the springtime celebrations honoring dionysus, the god of wine and fertile crops; such festivities were held at about the time that christians celebrate easter.
8. each year in athens, a play-writing contest, which can be considered an olympics of drama, was held.
9. sophocles won this contest twenty-four times, with such plays as *antigone, oedipus rex, ajax,* and *electra.*
10. the play *antigone* tells of a woman torn between loyalty to her dead brother and the dictates of the state.
11. "the ideal condition," wrote sophocles in the play, "would be, i admit, that men should be right by instinct."
12. in the play *oedipus rex,* oedipus unknowingly kills his father, king laius, and marries his mother, queen jocasta.
13. the greek philosopher aristotle, writing in his *poetics,* praised *oedipus rex* as the ideal model for tragedy.
14. in *ajax,* a father says, "my son, may you be happier than your father."
15. however, ajax's pride leads him to his downfall, on a course as unerring as the orbit of the planet earth.
16. one might begin an outline on sophocles' life as follows:

    i. sophocles the man
       a. his youth in colonus
       b. his education
       c. his family

17. the plays of ancient greece greatly influenced the dramas written in the days of the roman empire, but they were unknown to most european scholars during the middle ages.

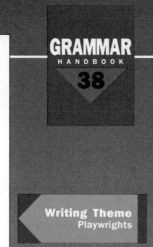

GRAMMAR
HANDBOOK
38

Writing Theme
Playwrights

Capitalization   **761**

18. <u>interest</u> in <u>greek</u> drama was revived throughout <u>europe</u> during the <u>renaissance</u>.
19. <u>the</u> birth of opera in the late sixteenth century resulted from the rediscovery of information that confirmed the importance of music in the performances of the ancient <u>greeks</u>.
20. <u>today</u>, people in the <u>united states</u> enjoy plays by <u>aeschylus, sopho</u>-<u>cles, euripides,</u> and <u>aristophanes</u>, writers who lived and worked in the fifth century <u>b.c.</u>, more than 2,000 years before the founding of our nation.

B. Correct Capitalization   After each sentence number, rewrite the words from the sentence that have errors in capitalization. Capitalize or lower-case each word as necessary.

(1) Eugene O'neill is one of america's greatest Playwrights. (2) He was born in 1888 in New York city and attended princeton university before deciding to strike out on his own as a Seaman.

(3) Traveling on Ships, o'neill visited Africa, south america, and many Islands. (4) His experiences at Sea and his observations of Islanders and crew are reflected in many of his works, including the Trilogy entitled *mourning becomes electra,* which is based on a greek trilogy by aeschylus. (5) O'neill used Greek forms, themes, and Characters, but set the drama in new england during the civil War.

(6) eugene o'neill suffered from tb (tuberculosis) early in life and parkinson's disease later on; nevertheless, he wrote forty-five plays during his lifetime. (7) These included One-Act plays, Full-Length plays, and Extended plays, such as his Trilogy. (8) Some of the playwright's Works, such as *the great god brown,* were experimental, but other plays were more traditional in form. (9) His play entitled *long day's journey into night* was Autobiographical.

(10) Most of o'neill's plays show compassion for the characters and at the same time demonstrate their faults. Walter f. Kerr, a writer for the *New York herald tribune,* once wrote that O'Neill wrote his play about his family as "An Act of Forgiveness." (11) O'neill himself once stated, "to me, the Tragic alone has that significant Beauty which is Truth."

(12) Although eugene o'neill died in 1953, he remains a vital part of American Culture. (13) He gave american Literature some of its greatest tragedies. (14) During his lifetime, He was honored with the nobel prize for literature and three Pulitzer prizes. (15) After his Death, his memory was honored with a fourth Pulitzer prize.

B. Correct Capitalization

1. O'Neill, America's, playwrights
2. City, Princeton University, seaman
3. ships, O'Neill, South America, islands
4. sea, islanders, trilogy, *Mourning Becomes Electra*, Greek, Aeschylus
5. O'Neill, characters, New England, Civil
6. Eugene O'Neill, TB, Parkinson's
7. one-act, full-length, extended, trilogy
8. works, *The Great God Brown*
9. *Long Day's Journey into Night*, autobiographical
10. O'Neill's, F., *Herald Tribune*, "an act of forgiveness"
11. O'Neill, To, tragic, beauty, truth
12. Eugene O'Neill, culture
13. American, literature
14. he, Nobel Prize, Prizes
15. death, Prize

End Marks and Commas

END MARKS

Using end marks correctly is an important skill for satisfactory communication. The first part of this handbook reviews the proper use of the period, the question mark, and the exclamation point.

The Period

Use a period at the end of all declarative sentences and most imperative sentences.

> The Food and Drug Administration has approved the use of irradiation as a safe method of keeping food fresh longer.

> Turn on the floodlight when it gets dark.

Use a period at the end of an indirect question.

An indirect question is repetition without the direct quotation of something asked or requested. (See page 807 for punctuation used with direct questions.)

> Mark asked whether Sylvia Plath was a poet or a novelist.

> Aunt Caterina requested that we arrive at her house early.

Use a period at the end of an abbreviation or initial.

Mr.	M.D.	Inc.	Jan. 16	7:30 A.M.
Ms.	Rev.	Sgt.	Fri.	100 B.C.

Do not use periods for abbreviations of metric measurements, acronyms, the initials of company or organization names, the abbreviations for some nations, or the two-letter abbreviations for states.

m	Kg	SADD	AT&T	US	TX

Use a period after each number or letter in an outline or a list.

Outline	List
I. Volcanoes	1. labels
A. Central-vent	2. manila folders
1. Shield	3. typing paper
2. Composite	4. typewriter ribbons
B. Fissure	5. eraser

Use a period with decimals.

> $32.75   7.135%   0.3334 second

Writing
TIP

A polite request in a business letter may be followed by a period or a question mark.

ESL Students All languages have their own conventions for punctuating a sentence. Spanish, for example, uses an inverted exclamation point to introduce an exclamation or an inverted question mark to introduce a question; for example, *¿Como esta usted?* (How are you?) Remind students who use inverted introductory punctuation marks to omit them in writing English.

LEP Students Ask these students to read the example sentences aloud. Point out that they naturally pause at the end of a sentence. Explain that end punctuation marks correspond to the pause at the end of the sentence. Demonstrate the rising inflection of a question by asking a native speaker of English to read a question aloud. As the student speaks, draw a line on the board that shows changes in pitch.

> **Additional Resources**
> - Tests and Assessment, Pretests, pp. 33–34
> - Grammar and Usage Practice Book, p. 84

WRITING THEME   Historic Events

Encourage students to consider an important world event as a possible subject for a Writer's Workshop assignment.

A. Concept Check
End Marks
   1. It's a miracle!
   2. Reporters asked whether people could believe their eyes.
   3. What was the cause of their amazement? The Berlin Wall was coming down. (or !)
   4. In 1948, Berlin was divided into two sectors, East Berlin and West Berlin.

Writing
═══**TIP**═══

Check the end punctuation of sentences that begin with *what* or *how*. They may be exclamatory sentences.

▶ **Writing Theme**
Historic Events

764 Grammar Handbook

The Question Mark

Use a question mark at the end of an interrogative sentence or fragment.

> Did Han Suyin write *The Crippled Tree*?
> The cat? It's asleep in the window as usual.

Use a question mark after a declarative sentence that is expressed as a question by being pronounced with rising inflection.

> Rita scored ten points. (declarative, falling inflection)
> Rita scored ten points? (interrogative, rising inflection)

The Exclamation Point

Use an exclamation point at the end of an exclamatory sentence. Use an exclamation point after a strong interjection or any other forceful expression.

> This is wonderful!
> No! Don't open the lion's cage!

Although an imperative sentence usually ends with a period, it can end with an exclamation point when strong emotion or excitement is expressed.

> Grab onto that life preserver!
> Watch out for that candle flame!

The sentence following an interjection may end with a period, a question mark, or an exclamation point.

> Oof! Akim's fall knocked the wind out of him.
> Wow! Is that for me?
> Ouch! That really hurts!

Practice Your Skills

A. CONCEPT CHECK

End Marks Rewrite the following sentences, adding periods, question marks, and exclamation points where needed.

1. It's a miracle
2. Reporters asked whether people could believe their eyes
3. What was the cause of their amazement The Berlin Wall was coming down
4. In 1948, Berlin was divided into two sectors, East Berlin and West Berlin

5. Work began on the Berlin Wall's 850 miles of concrete and barbed wire in Aug 1961

6. How tall was the Berlin Wall

7. Over the years, it rose to about 10 ft, or 305 (three and five-hundredths) meters in height

8. What led to the dramatic changes on Nov 9, 1989

9. The following factors contributed to the historic event:
   a Mikhail Gorbachev, the leader of the Soviet Union, instituted widespread reform, called *perestroika*
   b Other East European countries were opening their borders
   c The May elections and demonstrations that followed in East Germany urgently called for reforms

10. After US President George Bush attended a NATO meeting in May, he encouraged East Germany to tear down the wall

11. Bush urged West Germany to be "partners in leadership" with us

12. Reporters at the scene exclaimed, "The atmosphere is one of great rejoicing and festivity It's incredible"

13. "I shall return to East Berlin," said one West Berliner, Mrs Schmidt She said that it was home for her.

14. Soon TV commercials sold pieces of history for less than fifty dollars, blaring, "Own a piece of the Berlin Wall for only $3995!"

15. What a happy day

B. PROOFREADING SKILL

Punctuation Errors   Rewrite the following passage, correcting errors in end marks, spelling, and capitalization.

Didn't the war end imediately when Berlin was captured in World War II No In fact, the Nazi troops, under Grand Adm Karl Doenitz, fought for one week longer. Many Nazi soldiers didn't know that Hitler had taken his own life at 3:30 PM on May 1, 1945 The chaos in Berlin was horible Mr Claus Fuhrmann, a Berlin civilian, wrote that the 2-cm. antiaircraft guns were useless and people were desperate for supplies. Even two lbs of potatos was impossible to get? Russian planes would machine-gun people waiting in lines When the firing stopped on may 2 people cried, "At last" Berlin civilians were glad to see the Russian and US troops?

C. APPLICATION IN WRITING

An Eyewitness Report   Choose an exciting event from recent news reports. Write a brief news story as if you were an eyewitness to the event. Use end marks and punctuation with abbreviations correctly.

End Marks and Commas   **765**

5. Work began on the Berlin Wall's 850 miles of concrete and barbed wire in Aug. 1961.
6. How tall was the Berlin Wall?
7. Over the years, it rose to about 10 ft., or 3.05 (three and five-hundredths) meters in height.
8. What led to the dramatic changes on Nov. 9, 1989?
9. The following factors contributed to the historic event:
   a. Mikhail Gorbachev, the leader of the Soviet Union, instituted widespread reform, called *perestroika*.
   b. Other East European countries were opening their borders.
   c. The May elections and demonstrations that followed in East Germany urgently called for reforms.
10. After US President George Bush attended a NATO meeting in May, he encouraged East Germany to tear down the wall.
11. Bush urged West Germany to be "partners in leadership" with us.
12. Reporters at the scene exclaimed, "The atmosphere is one of great rejoicing and festivity. It's incredible!"
13. "I shall return to East Berlin," said one West Berliner, Mrs. Schmidt. She said that it was home for her.
14. Soon TV commercials sold pieces of history for less than fifty dollars, blaring, "Own a piece of the Berlin Wall for only $39.95!"
15. What a happy day!

B. Proofreading Skill
Punctuation Errors
Errors are underlined on page.
Didn't the war end immediately when Berlin was captured in World War II? No. In fact, the Nazi troops, under Grand Adm. Karl Doenitz, fought for one week longer. Many Nazi soldiers didn't know that Hitler had taken his own life at 3:30 P.M. on May 1, 1945. The chaos in Berlin was horrible! Mr. Claus Fuhrmann, a Berlin civilian, wrote that the 2-cm antiaircraft guns were useless and people were desperate for supplies. Even two lbs. of potatoes was impossible to get! Russian planes would machine-gun people waiting in lines. When the firing stopped on May 2, people cried, "At last!" Berlin civilians were glad to see the Russian and US troops.

C. Application in Writing
An Eyewitness Report
Answers will vary.

Commas: Series, Introductory Elements, and Interrupters

Objectives

- To apply rules for using commas in a series, setting off introductory elements, and setting off interrupters
- **Writing** To use commas correctly in combining sentences to eliminate wordiness

Teaching Strategies

Critical Thinking

Analyzing Without pausing at each comma, read aloud the first sample sentence under Commas in a Series. Then re-read the sentence, pausing at each comma. Lead students to conclude that the commas indicate natural pauses that make the sentences easier to read and understand. Ask volunteers to read the remaining sentences aloud.

Stumbling Block

Students might mistake words customarily used in pairs for individual items in a series. For example: *bread and butter, table and chairs*. Point out how commas are used to separate the word pairs in this sentence:

> On the table they placed the salt and pepper, macaroni and cheese, and franks and beans.

A comma is used to add clarity to a sentence and to enable a reader to understand the relation of its parts more quickly.

Commas in a Series

Use a comma to separate the elements in a series.

A series consists of three or more words, phrases, or clauses. When one or more of the elements contain a comma, semicolons instead of commas are used to separate the elements in a sentence. (See page 784.)

Words	The Japanese syllabic, the Chinese logographic, and the Korean alphabetic writing systems look similar.
Phrases	The Chinese language is pronounced differently in many provinces of the country, in Taiwan, and in Hong Kong.
Clauses	Some people believe that Japanese is difficult to pronounce, that its writing system is complicated, and that learning the language takes many years of study.

No commas are used in the series if all of the items are joined by *and, or,* or *nor.*

> The icy wind numbed the climber's face *and* feet *and* hands.

Use commas after the words *first, second,* and so on when these words introduce items in a series. (Note the use of semicolons in the example below.)

> The word *aborigine* refers to three groups of people: first, an ancient mythical people of Italy; second, the aboriginal tribes of Australia; and third, any original inhabitants of a country.

Use commas between coordinate adjectives that modify the same noun.

Coordinate adjectives are adjectives of equal rank. To determine whether adjectives are coordinate, try placing *and* between them. If *and* sounds natural, and if you can reverse the order of the adjectives without changing the meaning, then a comma is needed. Study the examples on the next page.

The cold, exhausted climbers returned to their camp. (*And* sounds natural between *cold* and *exhausted,* and the meaning is not changed by reversing their order. Therefore, a comma is needed.)

Many animals grow a thick winter coat. (*And* does not sound natural between *thick* and *winter,* and the adjectives cannot be reversed. No comma is necessary.)

Do not use a comma before the final adjective in a series if the adjective is thought of as part of the noun.

As the horns blared, the marchers formed a colorful, shimmering American flag. (*American flag* is considered one item. *Colorful* and *shimmering* modify *American flag,* not just *flag.* Thus, there is no comma between *shimmering* and *American.*)

If one word in a series modifies another word in the same series, no comma separates them.

Incorrect   A dark, brown coat was left in the closet.

Correct   A dark brown coat was left in the closet. (*Dark* modifies *brown,* telling what shade of brown. It does not modify the noun *coat.*)

In general, no comma is needed after numbers and after adjectives of size, shape, and age.

an old Italian custom   five small round windows

Practice Your Skills

A. CONCEPT CHECK

Commas   Write the word before each missing comma and place the comma correctly. If the sentence is correct, write *Correct.*

1. Natural habitats include such areas as wetlands deserts grasslands and deciduous forests.
2. A grassland is defined as a habitat in which most of the plants are grasses rather than woody shade-giving trees and shrubs.
3. Grasslands are known by various names: as prairies in North America as steppes in Asia and as savannas in tropical Africa.
4. The vast spectacular grasslands of South America are the pampas.
5. Australia's grasslands provide a home for such unusual animals as emus and dingoes and red kangaroos.
6. In North America, the symbol of the flat open prairie has long been the buffalo, or plains bison.

Writing Theme
Natural Habitats

End Marks
and Commas   **767**

WRITING THEME   Natural Habitats

You may wish to encourage students with an interest in ecology to use the subject of natural habitats in a research report.

A. Concept Check

Commas

1. Natural habitats include such areas as wetlands, deserts, grasslands, and deciduous forests.
2. A grassland is defined as a habitat in which most of the plants are grasses rather than woody, shade-giving trees and shrubs.
3. Grasslands are known by various names: as prairies in North America, as steppes in Asia, and as savannas in tropical Africa.
4. The vast, spectacular grasslands of South America are the pampas.
5. Correct
6. In North America, the symbol of the flat, open prairie has long been the buffalo, or plains bison.

7. Scientists have described three types of North American prairie: first, tall-grass prairie near the Mississippi River; second, mixed-grass prairie somewhat farther west; and third, short-grass prairie, farther west still.

8. Grasses on the African savannas develop a beautiful light golden color, and the savannas abound with lions, cheetahs, and wildebeest.

9. Correct

10. Correct

B. Revision Skill

Sentence Combining

Answers will vary. See typical answers below.

The tropical rain forests of the world are located in the Amazon region of South America, central and western Africa, and southeast Asia. Rain forests are natural habitats containing many species of tall, shady evergreen trees. The treetops form an unbroken shield against the sunlight. There are several levels, or strata, of vegetation in the rain forest. The highest level, the canopy, provides a food supply of flowers, fruits, and nuts for many animals. Below the canopy are the understory, the shrub level, and the forest floor.

C. Application in Writing

A Personal Essay

Answers will vary.

7. Scientists have described three types of North American prairie: first tall-grass prairie near the Mississippi River; second mixed-grass prairie somewhat farther west; and third short-grass prairie, farther west still.

8. Grasses on the African savannas develop a beautiful light golden color, and, the savannas abound with lions cheetahs and wildebeest.

9. It is not unusual to see three or four tall giraffes together there, munching the distinctive thorny leaves of the acacia tree.

10. Bird lovers are familiar with these facts: the ostrich is found on African savannas; the emu lives on Australian grasslands; and the habitat of the long-legged, swift-running rhea is the dry South American pampas.

B. REVISION SKILL

Sentence Combining Reduce the repetition in the paragraph below by combining sentences and eliminating unnecessary words. Use commas correctly.

The tropical rain forests of the world are located in the Amazon region of South America. There are rain forests in central and western Africa. They also exist in southeast Asia. Rain forests are natural habitats containing many species of tall evergreen trees. The evergreen trees are shady. The treetops form an unbroken shield against the sunlight. There are several levels, or strata, of vegetation in the rain forest. The highest level, the canopy, provides a food supply of flowers. Fruits and nuts are also part of the food supply at this level for many animals. Below the canopy are several additional levels. The second level is the understory. The next level is called the shrub level. Then there is the forest floor.

C. APPLICATION IN WRITING

A Personal Essay The natural habitats of many species are being threatened or destroyed by residential and industrial development. Write a brief essay on this topic or another of your choice in which you express your opinions or offer a solution to a problem.

The Snake Charmer (detail), Henri Rousseau

768 Grammar Handbook

Humanities Connection

Art Note *The Snake Charmer* (1907), which depicts Eve in the garden of Eden, is by Henri Rousseau (1844-1910), a French painter. Because he emphasized psychological symbolism, Rousseau is considered to be a precursor of the Surrealist movement. Ask: Why do you think Rousseau set this story of creation in a rain forest?

Commas with Introductory Elements

Use a comma after an introductory word, mild interjection, or adverb at the beginning of a sentence.

Well, the meeting is about to start.

Wait, I think I can access this encoded computer file.

However, the suspect refused to answer Holmes's question.

Use a comma after a series of prepositional phrases at the beginning of a sentence.

From his seat in the senate, the Emperor Augustus listened intently.

Under a table by the window, our puppy curled up for a nap.

A single prepositional phrase at the beginning of a sentence need not be followed by a comma unless the comma is needed for clarity.

On Saturday I work until noon.

Before the new hit, *Grease* was the group's best production.

Use a comma after an introductory infinitive phrase or introductory participial phrase used as a modifier.

To activate the system, pull the toggle switch.

Erupting violently, Mount St. Helens spewed volcanic ash for miles.

Use a comma after an adverb clause at the beginning of a sentence.

Although asparagus is used as a vegetable, it is actually a member of the lily family.

Since Melody visited the museum, she has been interested in Asian art.

For more information on verbals and adverb clauses, see Handbook 33, pages 594–612.

Use a comma after a word or phrase that has been moved to the beginning of a sentence from its usual position.

The crime was apparently committed at night. (usual order)

Apparently, the crime was committed at night. (transposed order)

End Marks
and Commas   **769**

. . . His nephew at fifteen, an overgrown farm boy, had a farm boy's love of the sea, though he could not swim a stroke and was often sick in choppy weather. That was the reason his father, the fisherman's brother, was a farmer and chose to sleep in on the holiday morning at his brother's house.

Discuss the nonessential appositives in the passage (an overgrown farm boy, the fisherman's brother). Then have students read the passage aloud, omitting the appositives. This strategy will demonstrate that commas help to identify appositives as unnecessary elements.

Commas with Interrupters

Use commas to set off nonessential appositives.

A **nonessential appositive** is a word or phrase that adds additional information to a sentence that is already complete.

Mercury, a heavy metal, is also known as quicksilver.

San Angel, a Mexico City suburb, has a colorful craft market.

An **essential appositive** qualifies or limits the word it modifies in such a way that it could not be omitted without affecting the meaning. Do not set off an essential appositive with commas.

The opera *La Traviata* was written by the Italian composer Giuseppe Verdi.

The sculptor Lois Nevelson works predominantly in wood.

Use commas to set off words of direct address.

Nguyen, will you direct this year's holiday talent show?

Ghosts, my gullible friend, have no basis in reality.

Use commas to set off parenthetical expressions.

A **parenthetical expression** is a word or phrase inserted in a sentence as a comment or exclamation. The sentence is complete without it, and it should always be set off with commas. The following expressions are often used parenthetically:

after all	by the way	for instance
of course	as a matter of fact	for example
on the other hand	I believe (hope, suppose)	however

The train, after all, is over an hour late.

When these words and phrases are used as basic parts of the sentence, they are not set off by commas.

The train was late after all our rushing to be on time.

When adverbs such as *however, therefore,* and *consequently* are used parenthetically in a sentence, they are set off with commas.

His older brother, however, is a much better athlete than he.

When these same adverbs modify a word in a sentence, they are an essential part of the sentence and are not set off by commas.

We must repair the broken generator however long it takes.

When these adverbs are used to join two independent clauses, they are called **conjunctive adverbs.** A conjunctive adverb is preceded by a semicolon and followed by a comma.

> The climate in Denmark is generally mild; however, some winters there have been bitterly cold.

Practice Your Skills

A. CONCEPT CHECK

Commas Rewrite the following sentences, adding commas where needed. If no additional commas are needed, write *Correct.*

1. It's a cravat child and a beautiful one, as you say.
2. Humpty Dumpty Lewis Carroll's fictional character points out the importance of using just the right word.
3. Clearly vocabulary was very important to Carroll.
4. The book *Through the Looking-Glass* uses several invented words.
5. To describe words that are formed by telescoping two words into one Carroll coined the term *portmanteau.*
6. The term is the French name for a stiff leather suitcase.
7. Such a suitcase by the way opens into two compartments.
8. Thus Carroll derived the idea of blending two words into one.
9. Blending *chuckle* and *snort* for example resulted in *chortle.*
10. Such blending is not limited to Carroll's work *Through the Looking-Glass;* indeed several words in English—such as *smog, motel,* and *brunch*—were formed in this way.

B. APPLICATION IN LITERATURE

Using Commas Some commas have been omitted from these passages. Write the word before each missing comma, and place the comma correctly. Use the rules you have learned in this chapter.

1. If it is any use to know it I always try to write on the principle of the iceberg. There is seven-eighths of it under water for every part that shows.   **Ernest Hemingway**
2. Biography like a game is one of the recognized forms of sport, and is as unfair as only a sport can be.   **Philip Guedalla**
3. I never told you mother that if I can ride my horse and *get there,* then I'm absolutely sure . . . Mother did I ever tell you? I am lucky!   **D. H. Lawrence**
4. [Dorothy Parker's] wit of course was delicate, clear, and sharp.   **Lillian Hellman**
5. Art it seems to me should simplify. That indeed is very nearly the whole of the higher artistic process. . . .   **Willa Cather**

Additional Resources
- Grammar and Usage Practice Book, pp. 86–87

WRITING THEME   Writers and Words

A. Concept Check
Commas
1. It's a cravat, child, and a beautiful one, as you say.
2. Humpty Dumpty, Lewis Carroll's fictional character, points out the importance of using just the right word.
3. Clearly, vocabulary was very important to Carroll.
4. Correct
5. To describe words that are formed by telescoping two words into one, Carroll coined the term *portmanteau.*
6. Correct
7. Such a suitcase, by the way, opens into two compartments.
8. Thus, Carroll derived the idea of blending two words into one.
9. Blending *chuckle* and *snort,* for example, resulted in *chortle.*
10. Such blending is not limited to Carroll's work *Through the Looking-Glass;* indeed, several words in English—such as *smog, motel,* and *brunch*—were formed in this way.

B. Application in Literature
Using Commas
1. it,
2. Biography,
   game,
3. you,
   mother,
   Mother,
4. wit,
   course,

5. Art,
   me,
   That,
   indeed,
6. pleasure,
   dear,
7. writings,
8. Money,
   it,
9. secret,
   Eliza,
10. ignorance,

CHECK POINT
PAGES 763–772

You may wish to use the following check-point exercise as an informal evaluation of student mastery of the concepts covered in this handbook.

WRITING THEME Ireland

1. Ireland, also called Eire, has been an independent member of the British Commonwealth since Dec. 1921.
2. For all the charms of its island life, it has the highest rate of emigration of any European country.
3. Who could leave the idyllic, emerald-green beauty of Ireland?
4. The population, as a matter of fact, is declining.
5. The major cities of Dublin, Cork, Limerick, and Galway have long captured the imagination of visitors.
6. Not all visitors have been welcome: first, the Celts invaded about 300 B.C.; second, the Vikings, about A.D. 795; and third, the Angles and Normans, around A.D. 1169.
7. Overall, the population is homogeneous.
8. More than 94 percent are of Irish nationality, and 93.1 (ninety-three and one-tenth) percent are Roman Catholics.
9. Tourist guides often ask whether visitors have heard how St. Patrick banished the snakes from Ireland.
10. What a rich artistic and literary history Ireland offers!
11. Although anecdotes of Irish wit abound, some of the choicest involve playwright George Bernard Shaw.
12. Yes, Shaw was a crusty and idealistic and eccentric writer.
13. Inquiring solicitously, a hostess once asked him, "Are you enjoying yourself, Mr. Shaw?"
14. "Certainly! There is nothing else here to enjoy," he replied.
15. This exchange is attributed to Shaw; however, some claim it was the Irish-born author Oscar Wilde who said it.

Writing Theme
Ireland

6. And it is such a pleasure my dear such a very great pleasure when now and again I open the door and see someone standing there who is just *exactly* right.   **Roald Dahl**
7. In every man's writings the character of the writer must lie recorded.   **Johann Wolfgang von Goethe**
8. Money much as I enjoy it will never provide the drive to my life.   **Rita Mae Brown**
9. The secret Eliza is not having bad manners or good manners or any particular manners, but having the same manner for all human souls.   **George Bernard Shaw**
10. Until you understand a writer's ignorance presume yourself ignorant of his understandings.   **Samuel Taylor Coleridge**

CHECK POINT
PAGES 763–771

Rewrite the following sentences, adding periods, question marks, exclamation points, and commas as needed.

1. Ireland also called Eire has been an independent member of the British Commonwealth since Dec 1921
2. For all the charms of its island life it has the highest rate of emigration of any European country
3. Who could leave the idyllic emerald-green beauty of Ireland
4. The population as a matter of fact is declining
5. The major cities of Dublin Cork Limerick and Galway have long captured the imagination of visitors
6. Not all visitors have been welcome: first the Celts invaded about 300 BC; second the Vikings, about AD 795; and third the Angles and Normans, around AD 1169.
7. Overall the population is homogeneous
8. More than 94 percent are of Irish nationality, and 931 (ninety-three and one-tenth) percent are Roman Catholics
9. Tourist guides often ask whether visitors have heard how St Patrick banished the snakes from Ireland
10. What a rich artistic and literary history Ireland offers
11. Although anecdotes of Irish wit abound some of the choicest involve playwright George Bernard Shaw.
12. Yes Shaw was a crusty and idealistic and eccentric writer.
13. Inquiring solicitously a hostess once asked him, "Are you enjoying yourself Mr Shaw"
14. "Certainly There is nothing else here to enjoy," he replied.
15. This exchange is attributed to Shaw; however some claim it was the Irish-born author Oscar Wilde who said it

COMMAS: QUOTATIONS, COMPOUND SENTENCES, CLAUSES, AND PHRASES

Use commas to set off a direct quotation from the rest of the sentence.

The clause that identifies the source of a quotation may appear at the beginning, in the middle, or at the end of the sentence. When it follows the quotation, the comma goes inside the quotation marks.

> Francis said, "The Atomic Energy Commission recently sold some californium-252 for $1,000 per microgram."
> "But," said Midori, "that's about $350 billion a pound!"
> "I guess we won't be using that element in our chemistry experiment," Akesha said with a laugh.

Do not use commas with indirect quotations.

> Francis said that the Atomic Energy Commission had recently sold some californium-252 for $1,000 per microgram.

Commas in Compound Sentences

Use a comma before the conjunction that joins the two independent clauses of a compound sentence.

> The famous Hope diamond is said to be cursed, and many of its owners have died suddenly or mysteriously.
>
> Vincent van Gogh threw away his masterpieces, but his brother Theo saved them for posterity.

A sentence with a compound predicate needs no comma.

> The pilot *radioed* the control tower and *received* instructions to change runways.

Do not use a comma if the independent clauses of a compound sentence are very short and are joined by the conjunction *and, but, so, or,* or *nor.*

> The snake hissed and I stood still.

However, a comma should separate clauses joined by *yet* or *for.*

> The snake slithered away, yet I remained motionless.

Writing TIP

Three or more independent clauses in a series are usually separated by semicolons. If the clauses are short, they may be separated by commas.

Commas: Quotations, Compound Sentences, Clauses, and Phrases

Objective

- To identify rules for using commas in quotations, compound sentences, clauses, and phrases

Teaching Strategies

Cooperative Learning

Put separate groups of students in charge of explaining the four uses of commas covered on pages 773 to 775. Students within each group should brainstorm ideas for presenting the material to the class in an interesting, informative manner. Teaching strategies might include the use of audio-visual aids, such as posters or hand-outs. Some students may want to devise computer programs that teach the concepts in this lesson. Encourage creativity as well as attention to details regarding comma usage.

When students are ready, have each group present its teaching strategy to the class. Following each presentation, have other students summarize the rules for comma usage they have learned.

WRITING THEME   The Age of Reason

You may wish to encourage students to learn more about the Age of Reason and use it as the subject of a writing assignment.

A. Concept Check
Comma Usage
  1. "I think, therefore I am," wrote the French philosopher René Descartes in the year 1637.
  2. Correct
  3. Enlightenment philosophers held that each person has a rational will, and they believed that nature obeys universal, orderly laws.
  4. Correct
  5. "Nature," wrote the English poet Alexander Pope, "is a mighty maze, but not without plan."
  6. Newton's discoveries were controversial, but the leaders of the Enlightenment used them to support their theories.
  7. Writers emulated the classics, so prose was orderly and clear.
  8. Correct
  9. As a result of the publication of his dictionary, some pronunciations were fixed, and many spellings were standardized. *or* Correct
  10. "The material world," said the French philosopher Montesquieu, "has it laws, the beasts, their laws, and Man, his laws."

B. Application in Literature
Comma Usage
  Errors are underlined on page.

Practice Your Skills

A. CONCEPT CHECK

Using Commas   Rewrite the following sentences, adding commas where needed. If no additional commas are needed, write *Correct*.

  1. "I think; therefore I am" wrote the French philosopher René Descartes in the year 1637.
  2. These famous words announced the beginning of the Enlightenment and ushered in the Age of Reason in Europe.
  3. Enlightenment philosophers held that each person has a rational will and they believed that nature obeys universal, orderly laws.
  4. Reason, balance, and order permeated and shaped politics, science, and literature.
  5. "Nature" wrote the English poet Alexander Pope "is a mighty maze, but not without plan."
  6. Newton's discoveries were controversial but the leaders of the Enlightenment used them to support their theories.
  7. Writers emulated the classics so prose was orderly and clear.
  8. Samuel Johnson thought that order should prevail in the English language.
  9. As a result of the publication of his dictionary, some pronunciations were fixed and many spellings were standardized.
  10. "The material world" said the French philosopher Montesquieu "has its laws the beasts, their laws, and Man, his laws."

B. APPLICATION IN LITERATURE

Comma Usage   Rewrite the passage, adding eighteen missing commas. You will use several of the comma rules you have learned so far. Notice how the use of commas adds clarity and organization.

(1) During the Age of Reason in England Joseph Addison and Richard Steele attracted and amused a large reading public with their witty polished essays. (2) Addison and Steele had quite different personalities yet the two writers were friends from childhood. (3) Addison was quiet and reserved but Steele was warm open, and charming. (4) In the early years of the eighteenth century each author wrote and edited essays for London periodicals devoted to news poetry and town gossip. (5) The essays of Addison and Steele ranged along quite a broad spectrum of everyday life; consequently they became popular authors. (6) In the pages of Addison's paper *The Spectator* for example a reader of the time could recognize ordinary realistic situations in the lives of a cross-section of social types. (7) Addison wrote "I shall endeavor to enliven

---

morality with wit and to temper wit with morality. (8) There are none to whom this paper will be more useful" he continued "than to the female world." (9) One secret of Addison's popularity in fact was that *The Spectator* attracted a large readership of women. (10) Writing about his ambitious project to produce *The Spectator* on a daily basis Addison promised his readers to quit if he should ever be convicted of the sin of literary dullness.

C. Moulton, *Teaching English Literature*

Commas with Nonessential Clauses and Phrases

Use commas to set off nonessential clauses.

A **nonessential clause** adds additional information to a sentence and can be omitted without changing the meaning of the sentence. An **essential clause** adds information necessary to the meaning of the sentence and is not set off by commas.

Nonessential Clause	Vatican City, which is an independent state, encompasses 109 acres within Rome.
Essential Clause	The city that serves as the seat of the Roman Catholic Church is Vatican City.
Nonessential Clause	The painter Thomas Moran, who came from England, helped Americans see the beauty of their own country.
Essential Clause	The painter who helped Americans recognize the need for national parks was Thomas Moran.

Use commas to set off nonessential participial phrases.

A **nonessential participial phrase** adds detail to a sentence but does not change its meaning. An **essential participial phrase** is necessary to complete the meaning of a sentence. It is not set off by commas.

Nonessential Participial Phrase	The tourists, wishing to see a variety of European dwellings, visited both thatched cottages and castles. (The participial phrase can be dropped.)
Essential Participial Phrase	Tourists wishing to see a variety of European dwellings can visit thatched cottages and castles. (The phrase cannot be dropped.)

Writing
═TIP═

In formal writing, *which* introduces nonessential clauses, and *that* introduces essential clauses.

End Marks and Commas **775**

Critical Thinking

Drawing Conclusions Have students point out examples of appositives, clauses, and participial phrases. Lead them to conclude that although these elements differ grammatically, they are set off by commas when they are used as nonessential elements within a sentence.

Additional Resources
• Grammar and Usage Practice
  Book, p. 89

WRITING THEME   Italian Opera

Concept Check

Commas
   1. Correct
   2. Verdi, who came from a poor family, was born in 1813.
   3. At that time, students desiring a musical education generally applied to the Milan Conservatory.
   4. Verdi, who failed his entrance exams, had to study privately.
   5. Correct
   6. The young composer, grieving for the sudden deaths of his wife and two children, almost gave up opera altogether.
   7. In the 1840's, Italy, which was then ruled by Austria, experienced a wave of nationalism.
   8. Hoping to inspire Verdi, the manager of La Scala urged him to compose an opera about the Biblical King Nebuchadnezzar.
   9. The opera's theme, which centered on the king's oppression of captive Israelites, furnished a political parallel to Italy's situation.
   10. This work, which Verdi entitled *Nabucco,* was a huge success.
   11. Loving both music and freedom, Italians made Verdi their hero.
   12. Verdi's career, lasting over half a century, yielded twenty-six operas.
   13. Correct
   14. Correct
   15. At his funeral in 1901, the crowd saluted the composer, whom they loved, by spontaneously singing a chorus from *Nabucco. or* Correct

Commas: Other Uses

Objectives

• To apply rules for comma usage with dates, place names, letters, titles, and numbers
• To apply rules for the use of commas to avoid confusion and to indicate omitted words
• **Writing** To use commas correctly in writing

Writing Theme
Italian Opera

Interior of the Teatro Regio, one of Italy's many beautiful opera houses, by Domenico Oliviero

Practice Your Skills

CONCEPT CHECK

Commas   Rewrite the following sentences, adding commas where needed. If no additional commas are needed, write *Correct.*

1. The name that many music lovers consider the greatest in the annals of Italian opera is Giuseppe Verdi.
2. Verdi who came from a poor family was born in 1813.
3. At that time students desiring a musical education generally applied to the Milan Conservatory.
4. Verdi who failed his entrance exams had to study privately.
5. The first opera that he produced at La Scala in Milan enjoyed a moderate success.
6. The young composer grieving for the sudden deaths of his wife and two children almost gave up opera altogether.
7. In the 1840's Italy which was then ruled by Austria experienced a wave of nationalism.
8. Hoping to inspire Verdi the manager of La Scala urged him to compose an opera about the Biblical King Nebuchadnezzar.
9. The opera's theme which centered on the king's oppression of captive Israelites furnished a political parallel to Italy's situation.
10. This work which Verdi entitled *Nabucco* was a huge success.
11. Loving both music and freedom Italians made Verdi their hero.
12. Verdi's career lasting over half a century yielded twenty-six operas.
13. Three Verdi operas that were based on works of Shakespeare are *Macbeth, Otello,* and *Falstaff.*
14. Verdi's supreme ambition was to involve the emotions of his audiences in the drama that was played out onstage.
15. At his funeral in 1901 the crowd saluted the composer whom they loved by spontaneously singing a chorus from *Nabucco.*

C OMMAS: OTHER USES

Below are other common situations in which commas are used.

Commas in Dates, Place Names, and Letters

In dates, use a comma between the day of the month and the year. When only the month and year are given, no comma is used.

   June 5, 1932   September 1992

When a date falls within a sentence, use a comma after the year.

   July 20, 1969, was the date of the first moon landing.

776 Grammar Handbook

Use a comma between the name of a city or town and the name of its state or country.

San Antonio, Texas   Madrid, Spain   Sofia, Bulgaria

Use a comma after each item in an address or place name within a sentence. No comma separates the state and the ZIP code.

Mail sent to 210 Geneva Road, Enid, Oklahoma 12339, will reach me.

Managua, Nicaragua, has been the site of much suffering.

Use a comma after the salutation of a friendly letter. Use a comma after the closing of a friendly letter or a business letter.

Dear Janet,   Your friend,   Sincerely,

Commas with Titles and Numbers

A title following a personal name is set off with commas; business abbreviations such as *Inc.* or *Ltd.* following a company name are also set off with commas.

Rader, Inc., has promoted Olympia Stavros, CPA, to vice-president.

In numbers of more than three digits, use commas between groups of three digits counting from the right, with the exception of ZIP codes, phone numbers, years, and house numbers.

The diameter of the earth is 7,926 miles.

Commas to Avoid Confusion

Use a comma to separate words or phrases that might otherwise be misread.

One source of confusion occurs when the conjunctions *but* and *for* are mistaken for prepositions.

Confusing   Every council representative approved the resolution for the city's historic buildings were being destroyed.

Clear   Every council representative approved the resolution, for the city's historic buildings were being destroyed.

A noun following a verb or verbal can cause confusion.

Confusing   While cooking Derrick burned his hand.

Clear   While cooking, Derrick burned his hand.

Writing
—TIP—

Commas are used to add clarity to sentences. However, overuse of commas can make sentences less clear.

End Marks
and Commas   **777**

WRITING THEME   Track and Field

Students interested in track and field may wish to add this theme to a list of possible topics in their journals.

A. Concept Check
Comma Usage
1. Jim Thorpe was born on May 28, 1888, near Prague, Oklahoma.
2. Thorpe's background was well known, for his great-grandfather was Black Hawk, a famous chief of the Sauk tribe.
3. Charles, Jim's twin brother, was described as sweet and gentle; Jim, as boisterous and restless.
4. After his brother's death, Thorpe attended the Indian Industrial School in Carlisle, Pennsylvania.
5. While studying, Jim led the school to national fame in football.
6. Then a letter came:
Dear Mr. Peairs,
    Please send Jimmy home. His father is badly hurt. Hunting accident.
        Sincerely,
        Charlotte Thorpe
7. When Thorpe returned home, he found his father was healing; his mother, dying.
8. Despite this tragedy, Thorpe achieved success, for his athletic ability led him to the 1912 Olympic games in Stockholm, Sweden.
9. Until the 1912 Olympics, one athlete had always been champion of the pentathlon; another, of the decathlon.
10. Before, no single athlete had ever won both strenuous events.
11. Though they were demanding, Big Jim Thorpe won both events with ease.
12. He scored 8,412 out of a possible 10,000 points in the decathlon!

Writing Theme
Track and Field

An adverb at the beginning of a sentence may be mistaken for a preposition.

Confusing   Below the girl searched the ship's hold.

Clear   Below, the girl searched the ship's hold.

Use a comma to indicate the words left out of parallel word groups.

Sometimes a writer prefers not to repeat the same verb or the same subject and verb in a compound sentence; in such a sentence a comma indicates the missing element or elements.

The corn was tall; the wheat, golden.

Maria's culinary specialty is dessert; Daniel's, soup.

Practice Your Skills

A. CONCEPT CHECK

Commas   Rewrite the sentences, adding commas where needed.

1. Jim Thorpe was born on May 28 1888 near Prague Oklahoma.
2. Thorpe's background was well known for his great-grandfather was Black Hawk, a famous chief of the Sauk tribe.
3. Charles, Jim's twin brother, was described as sweet and gentle; Jim as boisterous and restless.
4. After his brother's death, Thorpe attended the Indian Industrial School in Carlisle Pennsylvania.
5. While studying Jim led the school to national fame in football.
6. Then a letter came:

   Dear Mr. Peairs
       Please send Jimmy home. His father is badly hurt. Hunting accident.
           Sincerely
           Charlotte Thorpe
7. When Thorpe returned home, he found his father was healing; his mother dying.
8. Despite this tragedy, Thorpe achieved success for his athletic ability led him to the 1912 Olympic games in Stockholm Sweden.
9. Until the 1912 Olympics, one athlete had always been champion of the pentathlon; another of the decathlon.
10. Before no single athlete had ever won both strenuous events.
11. Though they were demanding Big Jim Thorpe won both events with ease.
12. He scored 8412 out of a possible 10000 points in the decathlon!

13. In January 1913 the Amateur Athletic Union revoked his amateur status because he had earned a small salary playing baseball.
14. However, in 1973—twenty years after his death—the AAU restored his amateur standing; in 1982 his medals.
15. In 1949 before Thorpe was exonerated Warner Brothers Inc. produced the movie *Jim Thorpe, All American.*

B. REVISION SKILL

Comma Usage Rewrite the following friendly letter, adding commas where needed.

August 10 19--

Dear Juanita

I'm writing now to remind you about our goal: to see each other at the starting line on November 29 at the Park Forest Annual Community 10K Race. I've been training hard all summer in the area surrounding Boulder Colorado but now I'm back home in Irvine California putting the finishing touches on my training.

My new coach this season Diana T. Riggio Ph.D. really seems to know her stuff. In addition to our weekly mileage she makes us log at least one hour a day in the weight room. I'll probably have lifted over 20000 pounds by Thanksgiving!

I'll be at a special training camp for the next two weeks, before my first road race on August 25. You can address letters to me at Camp High Mileage RFD 12 Upland California 47647.

I hope your training is going well. Here's your tip for the month: By mentally rehearsing your race beforehand you can really improve your performance. Keep working on your 10000-meter pace!

On the run
Mary Beth

C. APPLICATION IN WRITING

A Sports Story Attend a sporting event at school or watch one on television. Then write a newspaper report on the event. Read several sports columns first, to get an idea of the style you should use. Use commas correctly in dates, for place names, and for titles.

13. In January 1913, the Amateur Athletic Union revoked his amateur status, because he had earned a small salary playing baseball.
14. However, in 1973—twenty years after his death—the AAU restored his amateur standing; in 1982, his medals.
15. in 1949, before Thorpe was exonerated, Warner Brothers, Inc., produced the movie *Jim Thorpe, All American.*

B. Revision Skill
Comma Usage
Errors are underlined on page.

August 10, 19—

Dear Juanita,

I'm writing now to remind you about our goal: to see each other at the starting line on November 29 at the state cross-country championships. I've been training hard all summer in the mountains near Boulder, Colorado, but now I'm back home in Irvine, California, putting the finishing touches on my training.

My new coach this season, Diana T. Riggio, Ph.D., really seems to know her stuff. In addition to our weekly mileage, she makes us log at least five hours in the weight room. I'll probably have lifted over 20,000 pounds by Thanksgiving!

I'll be at a special training camp for the next two weeks, before my first road race on August 25. You can address letters to me at Camp High Mileage, RFD 12, Upland, California 47647.

I hope your training is going well. Here's your tip for the month: By mentally rehearsing your race beforehand, you can really improve your performance. Keep working on your 10,000-meter pace!

On the run,
Mary Beth

C. Application in Writing
A Sports Story
Answers will vary.

You may want to use the following checkpoint exercises as an informal evaluation of student mastery of the concepts covered in this handbook.

Additional Resources
- Grammar and Usage Practice Book, p. 91

WRITING THEME   The Nightly News

1. Correct
2. On June 24, 1990, *The New York Times* published an interesting article about television news in various countries.
3. The writer of the article, who analyzed the similarities and differences of these programs, was a journalist named James Brooke.
4. Brooke asserted that news aired in such capital cities as Tel Aviv, Israel, and Paris, France, assumes the same format as our programs.
5. He wrote, "Studio sets may not be the sleek extravaganzas they often are here, but electronic paraphernalia is roughly equivalent."
6. According to Brooke, the anchor who delivers the news abroad is frequently well known; sometimes, revered as a celebrity.
7. "But beyond the trappings," Brooke noted, "lie deep differences."
8. "To begin with, much of the coverage abroad comes from state-owned networks and stations," he wrote.
9. In such places as Beijing, China, and Pretoria, South Africa, the result has been outright control of the news.
10. On such broadcasts, the news is commonly a reflection of government policy; the anchor, a mouthpiece for government leadership.
11. In America, of course, the Constitution protects news organizations, such as CBS, Inc., and Time, Inc., from governmental control.
12. Some countries, such as West Germany, have state-owned television stations, yet the newscasts seem to be balanced and fair.
13. Correct
14. In Rio de Janeiro, Brazil, for example, a candidate's ownership of a TV network was an influential factor in the election of a president.
15. In Israel, viewership of "Mabat," the nightly news program, can be as high as 90 percent, or 4,029,000 out of a population of 4,477,000.
16. American television networks, such as NBC, Inc., or ABC, Inc., would surely be pleased with ratings like that!

Writing Theme
The Nightly News

Rewrite the following sentences, adding commas where needed. If no additional commas are needed, write *Correct*.

1. Throughout the world, people wishing to be informed are turning increasingly to the television nightly news.
2. On June 24 1990 *The New York Times* published an interesting article about television news in various countries.
3. The writer of the article who analyzed the similarities and differences of these programs was a journalist named James Brooke.
4. Brooke asserted that news aired in such capital cities as Tel Aviv Israel and Paris France assumes the same format as our programs.
5. He wrote "Studio sets may not be the sleek extravaganzas they often are here but electronic paraphernalia is roughly equivalent."
6. According to Brooke, the anchor who delivers the news abroad is frequently well known; sometimes revered as a celebrity.
7. "But beyond the trappings" Brooke noted "lie deep differences."
8. "To begin with much of the coverage abroad comes from state-owned networks and stations" he wrote.
9. In such places as Beijing China and Pretoria South Africa the result has been outright control of the news.
10. On such broadcasts, the news is commonly a reflection of government policy; the anchor a mouthpiece for its leadership.
11. In America, of course, the Constitution protects news organizations, such as CBS Inc. and Time Inc. from governmental control.
12. Some countries such as West Germany have state-owned television stations yet the newscasts seem to be balanced and fair.
13. Brooke wrote that in the U. S., news organizations are basically spectators; overseas, news-gathering associations are political.
14. In Rio de Janeiro Brazil, for example, a candidate's ownership of a TV network was an influential factor in the election of a president.
15. In Israel viewership of "Mabat," the nightly news program, can be as high as 90 percent, or 4029000 out of a population of 4477000.
16. American television networks, such as NBC Inc. or ABC Inc. would surely be pleased with ratings like that!
17. "The Israelis are a nation of news hounds" Brooke wrote.
18. In Israel, according to Brooke, television news is serious and important; the broadcasts essentially neutral.
19. Elsewhere in Italy, for example, party bias is often evident on the part of state-owned stations.
20. Japanese television news tends to be respectful to authority yet some stations do air controversial issues—in the middle of the night!

17. "The Israelis are a nation of news hounds," Brooke wrote.
18. In Israel, according to Brooke, television news is serious and important; the broadcasts, essentially neutral.
19. Elsewhere, in Italy, for example, party bias is often evident on the part of state-owned stations.
20. Japanese television news tends to be respectful to authority, yet some stations do air controversial issues—in the middle of the night!

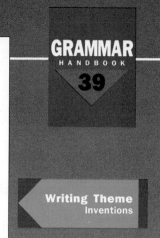

Writing Theme
Inventions

A. Using Punctuation Correctly Rewrite the following sentences, adding punctuation where necessary.

1. On Apr 15 1912 at 2:20 AM the British passenger ship *Titanic* sank to the floor of the Atlantic Ocean
2. The Titanic which experts considered unsinkable had collided with an iceberg about 2750 km northeast of New York City.
3. According to the US Senate Investigating Committee 1517 people lost their lives in the dark icy waters of the Atlantic.
4. Who could have predicted that oddly enough one of the most useful inventions of the twentieth century would be a product of this tragedy
5. The loss of the *Titanic* focused scientists' attention on how to detect underwater objects
6. L. F. Richardson a British meteorologist suggested using echoes as a means of iceberg detection.
7. A US radio pioneer Prof Reginald A Fessenden made the first successful experiments before World War I broke out in 1914.
8. Because they can determine the position size and depth of undersea objects echo-sounding devices offer many applications in both war and peace.
9. The US Navy for example uses hydrosearch systems to detect hostile submarines.
10. Oil companies use echoes to survey sea-level pipelines and commercial fishing companies use them for finding fish.

B. Finding Punctuation Errors For each item, identify where punctuation is missing. List any word that should be followed by an additional punctuation mark. Then place the mark correctly.

1. On May 12 1990 reporters in Ames Iowa interviewed a scientist for their *Iowa Today* program stressed science themes.
2. To discuss the transistor Dr Craig Jones Jr from Bell Telephone Laboratories Inc. was invited to the show.
3. "Tell us Dr. Jones about the transistor" said the moderator.
4. Jones asked what they would like to know
5. "Well tell us the basics: first who invented it; second what it is; and third how it is used" replied one interviewer.
6. Jones explained that John Bardeen Walter H Brattain and William B Shockley working together invented the transistor in 1947
7. "What is a transistor" asked a reporter on the panel
8. "A transistor you may recall is a device that amplifies controls and generates electrical signals" said Jones.
9. "For example transistors are used in radios television sets and hearing aids" he continued.

End Marks
and Commas   **781**

Application and Review

These activities are designed to allow your students to apply concepts presented in this handbook. In Exercises A, B, and C, students recognize and correct sentence punctuation by adding periods, commas, and end marks.

Additional Resources
- Tests and Assessment, Mastery Tests, pp. 66–67
- Elaboration, Revision, and Proofreading, p. 29

WRITING THEME   Inventions

A. Using Punctuation Correctly
1. On Apr. 15, 1912, at 2:20 A.M., the British passenger ship *Titanic* sank to the floor of the Atlantic Ocean.
2. The *Titanic*, which experts considered unsinkable, had collided with an iceberg about 2,750 km northeast of New York City.
3. According to the U.S. Senate Investigating Committee, 1,517 people lost their lives in the dark, icy waters of the Atlantic.
4. Who could have predicted that, oddly enough, one of the most useful inventions of the twentieth century would be a product of this tragedy?
5. The loss of the *Titanic* focused scientists' attention on how to detect underwater objects.
6. L. F. Richardson, a British meteorologist, suggested using echoes as a means of iceberg detection.
7. A U.S. radio pioneer, Prof. Reginald A. Fessenden, made the first successful experiments before World War I broke out in 1914.
8. Because they can determine the position, size, and depth of undersea objects, echo sounding devices offer many applications in both war and peace.
9. The U.S. Navy, for example, uses hydrosearch systems to detect hostile submarines.
10. Oil companies use echoes to survey sea-level pipelines, and commercial fishing companies use them for finding fish.

B. Finding Punctuation Errors

1. 12, 1990, Ames, Iowa, scientist,
2. transistor, Dr. Jones, Jr., Laboratories, Inc.,
3. us, Jones, transistor,
4. know.
5. Well, first, second, third, used,
6. Bardeen, H. Brattain, B. Shockley, together, 1947.
7. transistor? panel.
8. transistor, recall, amplifies, controls, signals,
9. example, radios, sets, aids,

10. reporter.
    twelve,
    99.9
    radio.
11. us,
    please,
    applications,
12. transistor,
    Jones,
13. transistor,
    afterward,
14. ft.
    long,
    ft.
    high,
    ft.
    100,000
15. Bardeen,
    Brattain,
    Shockley,
    physics,
    however,

C. Errors in Comma Usage

Errors are underlined on page.

Ethlie Ann Vare and Greg Ptacek, authors of *Mothers of Invention,* claim that in the case of Bette Nesmith Graham, "necessity was the mother of invention." Bette worked as a secretary at Texas Bank and Trust. Bette was a poor typist, but she had become adept at erasing her mistakes. In a new job as executive secretary, she was given an electric typewriter with a film ribbon, and she quickly learned that mistakes no longer erased easily. Alas, Bette was in trouble. She was, however, also creative.

Bette had noticed something when decorating the bank windows for the holidays. "When lettering, an artist never corrects by erasing but always paints over the error," she remembered. She decided to apply the technique to her typing errors. Bette explained, "I put some tempera waterbase paint in a bottle and took my watercolor brush to the office." Her solution worked, and she soon found herself mixing up batches of "Mistake Out" in her garage, developing what would become a commercial formula for a quick-drying, invisible correction fluid.

By the end of 1957, Bette had named her product Liquid Paper and was selling about a hundred bottles a month. The business continued to grow, and, by the time she died in 1980, Bette Nesmith Graham was a wealthy woman.

10. "Aha!" cried a reporter "When I was twelve I spent 999 (ninety-nine and nine-tenths) percent of my time listening to my transistor radio"
11. "Tell us please about its other applications" requested another reporter.
12. "The transistor" continued Jones "was critical in making computers smaller."
13. Before the transistor computers were enormous; afterward quite small indeed.
14. One early computer was 16 ft long 8 ft high and 4 ft deep; it contained 100000 soldered connections.
15. Bardeen Brattain and Shockley who shared the 1956 Nobel Prize for physics revolutionized the technology of electronics; however transistors were replaced by integrated circuits in the 1970's.

C. Errors in Comma Usage   Rewrite the following passage, correcting errors in the use of <u>end marks and commas.</u>

Ethlie Ann Vare and Greg Ptacek authors of *Mothers of Invention* claim that in the case of Bette Nesmith Graham "necessity was the mother of invention." Bette worked as a secretary at Texas Bank and Trust. Bette was a poor typist but she had become adept at erasing her mistakes In a new job as executive secretary she was given an electric typewriter with a film ribbon and she quickly learned that mistakes no longer erased easily. Alas Bette was in trouble She was however also creative.

Bette had noticed something when decorating the bank windows for the holidays. "When lettering an artist never corrects by erasing but always paints over the error" she remembered. She decided to apply the technique to her typing errors. Bette explained "I put some tempera waterbase paint in a bottle and took my watercolor brush to the office." Her solution worked and she soon found herself mixing up batches of "Mistake Out" in her garage developing what would become a commercial formula for a quick-drying invisible correction fluid

By the end of 1957 Bette had named her product Liquid Paper and was selling about a hundred bottles a month. The business continued to grow and by the time she died in 1980 Bette Nesmith Graham was a wealthy woman

On the Lightside

REPUNCTUATION

How important is punctuation? Read these entries from a New York *magazine contest. Entrants were asked to alter the meaning of a famous phrase by using punctuation, italics, or capitalization.*

What's that on the road? A head?

I can get it. For *you*, wholesale.

What's for dinner—Mother?

How do! I love thee! Let me count the ways.

R. Crusoe: "Thank God! It's *Friday*!"

Let *me* call YOU sweetheart.

What is this thing *called,* love?

Don't! Just stand there.

Look, before you leap . . .

Donald! *Duck!*

You're Rumple Stilt's kin.

A *Lice*? In *Wonder Land*?

Zip-a-dee-do-dah, zip-a-dee, Eh?

A horse? A *horse*? My kingdom for a HORSE?

"*I'm* a Yankee Doodle."
"Dandy."

Pop goes! The weasel.

Love is where? *You* find it!

Fly? ME? To the *moon*?

Take me out to the ball. Game?

I never promised *you* a rose garden.

Uncle, Sam wants you.

I remember you. Well?

First, *class* passengers only!

Half the world does not know how; the other half lives.

People who live in glass houses shouldn't. Throw stones!

Oh say, can *you* see by the dawn's early light?

Beware the fury of a patient, man.

What is so rare as a day in, June?

Do not *fold*: Spindle or Mutilate!

Rose's are red, *Violet's* are blue.

Rome, O Rome, O wherefore art thou?

"Simple," Simon says.

When I consider how, my life is spent.

What are you doing New Year's, Eve?

I love you for sentiment. AL REASONS.

"Jack Sprat could." "Eat?" "No!" "Fat, his wife, could." "Eat?" "No, lean!"

I *told* you. So?

Tom, Dick *and* Harry?

A. ROSEBY. Any other name would smell as sweet.

I love you. A. BUSHEL and A. PECK.

We have met. The enemy and the "Y" are ours.

The bear went over the mountain and what do you think? He saw!

Call me, Ishmael.

Mary Ann Madden, Ed.

On the Lightside

After students have read this feature, select some of the well-known phrases and write them on the chalkboard, punctuating them normally and leaving space underneath each. Then, in the blank space below each phrase, rewrite that phrase as punctuated in the feature. Ask volunteers to read each pair of phrases. Discuss how the punctuation in the second of the two phrases alters the original meaning.

Your students may be interested in writing their own pairs of famous phrases or sentences, altering their meanings by changing punctuation. Let students put on a comedy show using the repunctuated phrases in skits or in stand-up routines.

Grammar Handbook 40:
Semicolons, Colons, and Other Punctuation

The Semicolon

Objectives

- To use semicolons correctly in compound sentences
- To use semicolons between the parts of a series when the parts include commas
- **Writing** To use revision skills to place semicolons correctly

Teaching Strategies

Stumbling Block

Some students might hesitate to use semicolons for fear that these punctuation marks will make their writing appear too formal. Point out that semicolons are used less today than they once were, but they are useful for emphasizing the parallel nature of two ideas.

Teaching Tip: Items in Series

Tell students to use semicolons even if only one item in a series contains a comma. (The family shopped for turkey, fresh roasted; sweet potatoes; and fruit pies.) Here is an exception to the rule: if the item containing the comma is *last* in the series, commas can be used. (The family shopped for sweet potatoes, fruit pies, and turkey, freshly roasted.)

GRAMMAR
HANDBOOK
40

Semicolons, Colons, and Other Punctuation

THE SEMICOLON

Semicolons, like commas, separate sentence elements. A semicolon indicates a stronger break than a comma but not as strong a break as a period.

Semicolons Used with Commas

The independent clauses in a compound sentence are usually separated by a comma. However, if there are commas within the clauses, a semicolon is used to avoid confusion.

Use a semicolon between independent clauses joined by a conjunction if the first clause contains commas.

> Babe Didrikson Zaharias competed in swimming, tennis, and diving; but she won enduring fame as a result of her performance in golf and track.

> Kim, who had just learned to skate, had not yet learned how to stop; and she tumbled into the snowbank at the edge of the pond.

Use a semicolon between the parts of a series if there are commas within the parts.

> Three Connecticut patriots with the name Wolcott were Roger Wolcott, a colonial governor; Oliver Wolcott, a signer of the Declaration of Independence; and Oliver Wolcott, Jr., a secretary of the Treasury.

> New York's nickname is the Empire State; its motto, *Excelsior;* its flower, the rose; its bird, the bluebird.

Semicolons Between Main Clauses

The independent clauses in a compound sentence may be joined with a comma and a conjunction like *and* or *but,* or with just a semicolon.

> You may approve of the measure, *but* we do not.

> You may approve of the measure; we do not.

Use a semicolon to join the independent clauses of a compound sentence if no coordinating conjunction is used.

Mikhail Gorbachev took the reins of Soviet government in 1985; he promptly initiated a series of bold reforms.

Traveling medieval knights used a seal from their signet rings instead of cash; today travelers "pay" with credit cards.

In the sentences below, notice that the semicolon suggests a stronger relationship between the two ideas than a conjunction does.

Watergate was one of the biggest political scandals in the history of the United States, *and* it resulted in the resignation of Richard M. Nixon as President.

Watergate was one of the biggest political scandals in the history of the United States; it resulted in the resignation of Richard M. Nixon as President.

Do not use a semicolon to join unrelated clauses. A semicolon should be used only if the clauses are closely related.

Incorrect   Mary Cassatt was an American painter who became famous for her paintings of mothers and children; for many years she lived in France.

Correct   Mary Cassatt was an American painter who became famous for her paintings of mothers and children; she showed her subjects in everyday situations.

Semicolons and Conjunctive Adverbs

Use a semicolon before a conjunctive adverb or a parenthetical expression that joins the clauses of a compound sentence.

Getting children to sit still is not easy; however, most photographers are prepared for that.

All of us have special childhood memories; indeed, most family photo albums provide a record of such moments.

Note that conjunctive adverbs such as *however* and parenthetical expressions such as *indeed* are followed by a comma.

Writing
—TIP—

The method you choose to join clauses should reflect the relationship of ideas you wish to convey.

Mrs. Cassatt Reading to Her Grandchildren, 1880, Mary Cassatt

Semicolons, Colons, and Other Punctuation   **785**

A. Concept Check

Semicolons

1. In the fifth century A.D., the island of Britain was invaded by the Jutes and Angles from what is now known as Denmark; the Saxons, from what is now Germany; and the Frisians, from what is now Holland.

2. The native Celts were no match for the invaders; defeat was swift and complete.

3. These invasions from foreign lands continued for over a hundred years; the invaders who settled in Britain became collectively known as Anglo-Saxons.

4. Their culture became the basis for Angle-land, or English culture; their guttural Germanic language became what is known today as Old English.

5. At first glance, Old English looks quite foreign; however, a modern reader can recognize a number of words.

6. These words include *hwaet,* which means *what; cyning,* which means *king;* and *meado,* which means *mead* and later *meadow.*

7. To an Anglo-Saxon, life was a struggle to be endured; evil and death were inescapable; fame was the only true immortality.

8. The Anglo-Saxons were largely illiterate; however, they had a rich oral tradition.

9. As they celebrated in great mead halls, the Anglo-Saxons vividly described victories and battles; as a result, they created epic tales of legendary deeds.

10. The most famous surviving work in Old English is the poem *Beowulf;* it is the earliest known long literary work in English.

11. The main character, Beowulf, is King of the Geats; he comes to the aid of the King of the Danes.

12. The monsters in the poem are the man-eating Grendel, which Beowulf kills; Grendel's mother, which Beowulf also kills; sea serpents, which Beowulf wrestles underwater; and a fire-eating dragon, which kills Beowulf.

13. The epic *Beowulf* is captivating to read; on the other hand, it also serves as an invaluable source of historical information.

14. In 1939 archaeologists uncovered an ancient burial mound at Sutton Hoo; it contained more valuables dating from the Anglo-Saxon period than any other site yet unearthed.

15. A ship was discovered that dated from the seventh century A.D.; this would have been about a century before *Beowulf* was first recorded.

Practice Your Skills

A. CONCEPT CHECK

Semicolons   Rewrite the following sentences, substituting semicolons wherever necessary.

1. In the fifth century A.D., the island of Britain was invaded by the Jutes and Angles from what is now known as Denmark, the Saxons, from what is now Germany, and the Frisians, from what is now Holland.

2. The native Celts were no match for the invaders, defeat was swift and complete.

3. These invasions from foreign lands continued for over a hundred years, the invaders who settled in Britain became collectively known as Anglo-Saxons.

4. Their culture became the basis for Angle-land, or English culture, and their guttural Germanic language became what is known today as Old English.

5. At first glance, Old English looks quite foreign, however, a modern reader can recognize a number of words.

6. These words include *hwaet,* which means *what, cyning,* which means *king,* and *meado,* which means *mead* and later, *meadow.*

7. To an Anglo-Saxon, life was a struggle to be endured, and evil and death were inescapable, fame was the only true immortality.

8. The Anglo-Saxons were largely illiterate, however, they had a rich oral tradition.

9. As they celebrated in great mead halls, the Anglo-Saxons vividly described victories and battles, as a result, they created epic tales of legendary deeds.

10. The most famous surviving work in Old English is the poem *Beowulf,* it is the earliest known long literary work in English.

11. The main character, Beowulf, is King of the Geats, he comes to the aid of the King of the Danes.

12. The monsters in the poem are the man-eating Grendel, which Beowulf kills, Grendel's mother, which Beowulf also kills, sea serpents, which Beowulf wrestles underwater, and a fire-eating dragon, which kills Beowulf.

13. The epic *Beowulf* is captivating to read, on the other hand, it also serves as an invaluable source of historical information.

14. In 1939 archaeologists uncovered an ancient burial mound at Sutton Hoo, and it contained more valuables dating from the Anglo-Saxon period than any other site yet unearthed.

15. A ship was discovered that dated from the seventh century A.D., this would have been about a century before *Beowulf* was first recorded.

B. REVISION SKILL

Semicolons   Write the words before and after each missing semicolon in the following passage, and place the semicolon correctly.

(1) The history of English is usually divided into three periods: the Old English period, from A.D. 400 to A.D. 1100, the Middle English period, from A.D. 1100 to A.D. 1500, and the Modern English period, from A.D. 1500 to the present. (2) The cutoff dates for these periods are rough, arbitrary, and inexact, language changes continually. (3) In other words, one simply does not wake up one morning and find that the language has changed instead, such changes take place gradually.

(4) Sometimes, however, events occur that cause language to change more rapidly for example, the invasion and occupation of a country by people who speak a different language tends to result in rapid linguistic change as speakers of different languages borrow from one another. (5) The events that signal the cutoffs for major periods in the history of the English language are the Anglo-Saxon invasions of England, which started in the fifth century A.D., the conquest of England by the Norman French, which occurred in A.D. 1066, and the beginnings of English exploration and colonialism, which can be dated to roughly A.D. 1500.

THE COLON

The colon marks an important division in a sentence. It signals the reader that the material that follows is an explanation, an example, or a summation.

Use a colon to introduce a list of items.

Several parts of the sandal were leather: the upper sole, the strap, the vamp, and the midsole.

I had three chairs in my house: one for solitude, two for friendship, three for society.   **Henry David Thoreau**

In a sentence a colon often follows a word or phrase such as *these, the following,* or *as follows.*

Leading olive-growing countries include the following: Spain, Italy, Greece, Portugal, and Turkey.

Among the plays I have enjoyed are these: *Our Town, The Skin of Our Teeth, The Vegetable,* and *As You Like It.*

The Colon

Objectives

- To use colons to introduce lists, formal quotations, and explanations
- To use colons in conventional ways, such as after the salutation of a formal letter

Teaching Strategies

Teaching Tip: Sentence Fragments

The colon can be used to join a sentence fragment to the preceding sentence when the two have a "note that follows" relationship. For example:
    The day was ideal. Warm and mild.
    The day was ideal: warm and mild.
Point out that the word following the colon begins with a lowercase letter.

Linking Grammar and Literature

In the poem "The Colon," Richard Armour takes a humorous look at this mark of punctuation. Write the poem on the board, and give students the opportunity to discuss its unusual look at the colon.

    The colon resembles the eye of a beast:
    A tiger,
    A fox,
    Or a tomcat at least—
    Two eyes ever looking, two eyes open wide,
    That belong to a creature that lies on its side.

Cooperative Learning

In social studies texts and other content area books, have partners find examples of colons used for at least two different purposes. Students can then meet to share their findings and assess whether or not each usage is correct.

Stumbling Block

The main problem in the use of colons is the incorrect use of a colon immediately following a verb or preposition. You may want to write the following incorrect example on the board and have students correct it in two ways. (Three popular books by Charles Dickens are: *Oliver Twist, David Copperfield,* and *Great Expectations.* Three popular books by Charles Dickens are the following: *Oliver Twist, David Copperfield,* and *Great Expectations.* Three popular books by Charles Dickens are *Oliver Twist, David Copperfield,* and *Great Expectations.*)

Additional Resources
• Grammar and Usage Practice Book, p. 93

Writing ━TIP━

The expression *such as* functions as a preposition and should not be followed by a colon: *Lily was talented in many fields, such as drama and sports.*

Do not use a colon immediately after a preposition or a verb (unless the verb introduces a formal quotation).

Incorrect　Two of my favorite Katharine Hepburn movies are: *The African Queen* and *On Golden Pond.*

Correct　Two of my favorite Katharine Hepburn movies are *The African Queen* and *On Golden Pond.*

Correct　Two of my favorite Katharine Hepburn movies are the following: *The African Queen* and *On Golden Pond.*

Incorrect　The country of New Zealand consists of: the North Island and the South Island.

Correct　The country of New Zealand consists of the North Island and the South Island.

Correct　The country of New Zealand consists of two islands: North Island and South Island.

Use a colon to introduce a quotation that lacks explanatory words such as *he said* or *she said.*

Martha's answer was quiet but firm: "I'll stay here."

Use a colon to introduce a long or formal quotation.

Winston Churchill once said: "We shall defend our island, whatever the cost may be, we shall fight on the beaches . . . and in the streets, we shall fight in the hills; we shall never surrender."

Use a colon between two independent clauses when the second explains the first.

Mr. Jonas was in for a surprise: his car had a flat tire.

Other Uses of the Colon

A colon is conventionally used in the following ways: (1) after the salutation of a formal letter, (2) between the hour and minute figures of clock time, (3) between the chapter and verses in Biblical references, (4) between the title and subtitle of a book, (5) between the volume and number of a periodical or the volume and pages of periodicals, and (6) after labels that signal important ideas.

Dear Sir or Madam:	*Women's Labor History: In the Voices of the Women Who Lived It*
8:05 P.M.	*Time* 37:17–20 (volume and pages)
Job 3:2–4	Warning: High Voltage

Practice Your Skills

A. CONCEPT CHECK

Colons and Semicolons Copy the following items, adding colons and semicolons wherever necessary.

1. Hetty Robinson Green learned an important virtue early in life she learned the importance of thrift.
2. Green was raised in a prosperous New England family however, she failed to learn how to enjoy money.
3. At age thirty, in 1865, she received the following
4. Dear Miss Robinson

   We are writing to inform you that you are the beneficiary of two estates. The holdings include the balance of your father's estate, a sum of one million dollars one-half of your aunt's estate, another one million dollars and the interest that these funds have accrued. We have set an appointment for you at 900 Monday. Contact us if this is inconvenient.

   Sincerely,

   Barney and Brown Attorneys at Law
5. Later, in 1867, Hetty Robinson married Edward H. Green, who was also a millionaire yet she worked on to increase her wealth.
6. Green wisely put her funds into the following railroads, United States gold, bonds, and real estate.
7. The verse Ecclesiastes 11 1, about casting your bread upon the waters, certainly seemed true for her.
8. Her biographers noted an important aspect of her thrift "in the spending of money she might have been compared to an athlete who never broke training."
9. Green was afraid people would take advantage of her wealth therefore, she often pretended to be poor.
10. Her typical behavior included the following she dressed in rags, she denied herself a home by staying in cheap hotels, and she claimed she was a charity case.
11. On one memorable occasion, her son injured his knee Green refused to get him medical treatment.
12. Her stinginess certainly had dire consequences her son lost his leg from infection.
13. Green's excessive thrift brought results indeed, her family inherited over one hundred million dollars.
14. Green's son, who inherited a substantial portion of his mother's wealth, did not have his mother's problem he spent money readily.
15. His enjoyment of money was clear he bought yachts and diamonds, spending approximately three million dollars a year.

WRITING THEME Human Nature

You may want to encourage students to consider their own observations of human nature as a topic for a personal essay.

A. Concept Check
Colons and Semicolons
1. Hetty Robinson Green learned an important virtue early in life: she learned the importance of thrift.
2. Green was raised in a prosperous New England family; however, she failed to learn how to enjoy money.
3. At age thirty, in 1865, she received the following:
4. Dear Miss Robinson:
   We are writing to inform you that you are the beneficiary of two estates. The holdings include the balance of your father's estate, a sum of one million dollars; one-half of your aunt's estate, another one million dollars; and the interest that these funds have accrued. We have set an appointment for you at 9:00 Monday. Contact us if this is inconvenient.

   Sincerely,
   Barney and Brown Attorneys at Law
5. Later, in 1867, Hetty Robinson married Edward H. Green, who was also a millionaire; yet she worked on to increase her wealth.
6. Green wisely put her funds into the following: railroads, United States gold, bonds, and real estate.
7. The verse Ecclesiastes 11:1, about casting your bread upon the waters, certainly seemed true for her.
8. Her biographers noted an important aspect of her thrift: "in the spending of money she might have been compared to an athlete who never broke training."
9. Green was afraid people would take advantage of her wealth; therefore, she often pretended to be poor.
10. Her typical behavior included the following: she dressed in rags, she denied herself a home by staying in cheap hotels, and she claimed she was a charity case.
11. On one memorable occasion, her son injured his knee; Green refused to get him medical treatment.
12. Her stinginess certainly had dire consequences: her son lost his leg from infection.
13. Green's excessive thrift brought results; indeed, her family inherited over one hundred million dollars.
14. Green's son, who inherited a substantial portion of his mother's wealth, did not have his mother's problem; he spent money readily.
15. His enjoyment of money was clear: he bought yachts and diamonds, spending approximately three million dollars a year.

Writing Theme
Human Nature

B. **Application in Literature**
Semicolons and Colons
1. Eat not to dullness; drink not to elevation.   Benjamin Franklin
2. Things were as she suspected; she had been frank in her questions and Polly had been frank in her answers.   James Joyce
3. Jade Snow had chosen it [sociology] without thought, simply to meet a requirement; but that casual decision had completely revolutionized her thinking. . . .   Jade Snow Wong
4. Love must be learned, and learned again and again; there is no end to it. Hate needs no instruction, but waits only to be provoked.
            Katherine Ann Porter
5. Humanity has but three great enemies: fever, famine, and war.   Sir William Osler
6. Four be the things I am wiser to know: Idleness, sorrow, a friend, and a foe.
            Dorothy Parker
7. Nobody was smarter than anybody else; nobody was better looking than anybody else; nobody was stronger or quicker than anybody else.   Kurt Vonnegut, Jr.
8. After a little, the plumber emerged from the earth: first the light top of his head, then the burnt brow, and then the blue eyes fringed with whitest lash.   Kay Boyle
9. No matter what time I start the column, I finish it at 6:00. It's kind of spooky. I've tried starting it at 8:00 in the morning; I finish at 6:00. If I start at 5:00, I'll still finish at 6:00.
            Harry Stein
10. It was this way: Pamela knew her sister had left a will in Woodville's favor.
            Shirley Ann Grau
11. Advice is seldom welcome; those who want it the most always like it the least.
            Lord Chesterfield
12. It is a far, far better thing I do, than I have ever done; it is a far, far better rest that I go to than I have ever known.   Charles Dickens

The Dash

Objectives

- To use dashes to show abrupt breaks in thought
- To use dashes to set off long explanatory statements
- **Writing** To use dashes correctly in writing

B. **APPLICATION IN LITERATURE**

Semicolons and Colons Semicolons and colons have been omitted from the following passages. Write the sentences correctly, restoring the punctuation marks.

1. Eat not to dullness drink not to elevation.   **Benjamin Franklin**
2. Things were as she suspected she had been frank in her questions and Polly had been frank in her answers.   **James Joyce**
3. Jade Snow had chosen it [sociology] without thought, simply to meet a requirement but that casual decision had completely revolutionized her thinking . . .   **Jade Snow Wong**
4. Love must be learned, and learned again and again there is no end to it. Hate needs no instruction, but waits only to be provoked.
            Katherine Ann Porter
5. Humanity has but three great enemies fever, famine, and war.
            Sir William Osler
6. Four be the things I am wiser to know Idleness, sorrow, a friend, and a foe.   **Dorothy Parker**
7. Nobody was smarter than anybody else nobody was better looking than anybody else nobody was stronger or quicker than anybody else.   **Kurt Vonnegut, Jr.**
8. After a little, the plumber emerged from the earth first the light top of his head, then the burnt brow, and then the blue eyes fringed with whitest lash.   **Kay Boyle**
9. No matter what time I start the column, I finish it at 600. It's kind of spooky. I've tried starting it at 800 in the morning I finish at 600. If I start at 500, I'll still finish at 600.   **Harry Stein**
10. It was this way Pamela knew her sister had left a will in Woodville's favor.   **Shirley Ann Grau**
11. Advice is seldom welcome those who want it the most always like it the least.   **Lord Chesterfield**
12. It is a far, far better thing I do, than I have ever done it is a far, far better rest that I go to than I have ever known. **Charles Dickens**

James Joyce, Irish novelist, 1882-1941

THE DASH

Dashes are used to set off words that interrupt the main idea of a sentence. While commas set off material that is closely connected to the main idea, dashes indicate a looser connection. The words set off by dashes add extra information to an already complete thought. Dashes can also mean *in other words* or *that is* when they come before an explanation.

Use a dash to show an abrupt break in thought.

The Morrises plan to see *Hamlet*—it's their favorite play—at the Shakespeare Festival in Stratford, Ontario.

The trouble is—I suppose he knows it himself—he just can't get along with other people.

This use of the dash is especially appropriate in dialogue, where it adds a casual, conversational tone.

"Did you know that Annie Oakley—her nickname was 'Little Sure Shot'—stood just five feet tall?"

"Yes, and I know that the musical *Annie Get Your Gun*—have you seen it?—tells the story of her life."

"Her husband, Frank Butler, allowed her to shoot a dime out of his hand—can you imagine such trust?"

Use a dash to set off a long explanatory statement that interrupts the main thought of the sentence.

There was a feeling of curious anticipation—a feeling shared throughout the world—when Communist China first invited the President of the United States to visit Beijing.

Tammany Hall—a powerful political machine in New York City during the late 1800's—was often attacked by cartoonists.

When an explanatory statement contains a number of commas, setting it off with dashes serves to clarify meaning and reduce confusion for the readers.

Many prominent American poets—Elizabeth Bishop, Marianne Moore, and Robert Bly, to name just a few—have been published in that journal.

Punctuation Note Punctuation marks that belong to the material set off by dashes should be placed inside the dashes.

I saw Sue—do you remember her?—when I visited my old school last week.

Use a dash to set off a summarizing statement from the rest of a sentence.

Simplicity of operation, low cost, assembly-line production— these were the factors that Henry Ford introduced to revolutionize the manufacture of automobiles.

Writing
━TIP━

The overuse of dashes may confuse a reader or make your writing seem choppy.

Semicolons, Colons, and Other Punctuation **791**

Writing Theme
Literature

Practice Your Skills

A. CONCEPT CHECK

Dashes   Dashes have been omitted from the literary quotations below. Rewrite these passages and return them to their original form by using dashes where they should occur. Notice how dashes serve as guides for the reader, clarifying the writer's train of thought.

1. Suddenly one of them it must have been Chino reached out, grabbed Godfrey's beard, and pulled hard. With his other hand, he snatched off Godfrey's dark glasses. There was no reaction from Godfrey.   **Nat Hentoff**

2. The apartment was bright with big rooms and the funny smell was stronger inside. I found out what it was gefilte fish.   **Louise Meriwether**

3. Because of her creativity with flowers, even my memories of poverty are seen through a screen of blooms sunflowers, petunias, roses, dahlias, forsythia, spirea, delphiniums, verbena . . . and on and on.   **Alice Walker**

4. The Widow Wycherly if so fresh a damsel could be called a widow tripped up to the doctor's chair, with a mischievous merriment in her rosy face.   **Nathaniel Hawthorne**

5. One writes out of one thing only one's own experience.   **James Baldwin**

6. At last, after what seemed a long time it might have been five seconds, I dare say he [the elephant] sank flabbily to his knees.   **George Orwell**

7. From my fifteenth year save for a single interval I have lived about as solitary a life as a modern man can have.   **Thomas Wolfe**

8. The younger people, who grew up during the paper shortage, aren't used to filling the space. But that is journalism an ability to meet the challenge of filling the space.   **Rebecca West**

9. But today she passed the baker's by, climbed the stairs, went into the little dark room her room like a cupboard and sat down on the red eiderdown.   **Katherine Mansfield**

10. My well-fitted curriculum classes, homework, tennis, piano, editing was ordered with just one thought: to make room for the dance practice.   **Agnes De Mille**

B. APPLICATION IN WRITING

A Book Review   Think of a book that you read recently. What did you like about it? What were its weaknesses? Would you recommend it to a friend? Write a short book review, using semicolons, colons, and dashes correctly.

THE HYPHEN

Hyphens are sometimes used to combine words and word parts and sometimes used to separate them.

Use a hyphen in compound numbers from twenty-one through ninety-nine.

> thirty-one   fifty-six   eighty-eight

Use hyphens in fractions.

> She won the election by a two-thirds majority.

> Two-thirds of the members voted for the measure.

Use a hyphen in a compound adjective before a noun. Usually no hyphen is used when a compound adjective follows a linking verb.

Before a Noun   Eleanor is a well-informed voter.
After a Linking Verb   Eleanor is well informed.

Use a hyphen in certain compound nouns.

> sister-in-law   great-grandmother

Spelling Note   Since the rules for hyphenation of compound nouns and modifiers are very complex, it is wise to consult a dictionary.

Use a hyphen with the prefixes *all-*, *ex-*, and *self-*; with the suffix *-elect*; and with all prefixes before a proper noun or proper adjective.

> We invited the ex-senator to present a speech at the dedication of the new public library.

> President-elect Bush was prepared for the reporter's questions.

> The costume designer researched clothing worn in the post-Elizabethan period.

Use hyphens to prevent confusion and to avoid awkwardness.

For example, it is clearer to write *de-emphasis* rather than *deemphasis* in order to avoid a misreading of the word; similarly, it is clearer to write *co-chairperson* rather than *cochairperson*.

Use a hyphen if part of a word must be carried over from one line to the next.

> Ed felt strongly about the issue, so he wrote his representative a long letter explaining his views.

Writing
TIP

Don't use a hyphen when a modifier includes a word ending in *-ly*: *newly painted fence*.

The Hyphen

Objective

- To use hyphens in certain compound numbers, fractions, compound nouns and adjectives; after certain prefixes; and in spelling certain words

Teaching Strategies

Teaching Tip: Language

Explain that as the English language continues to develop, new compound nouns are formed and the hyphenation of existing compounds may change. A compound might appear first as two separate words, then as a hypenated word, and finally as a closed compound. However, this progression does not always take place. Some compound nouns, such as New Jersey and Hong Kong, will always be written as two separate words. When in doubt about the spelling of a compound, students should consult a dictionary.

Individualizing Instruction

LEP Students Pair these students with a partner who can help them follow this alternate procedure for the exercise.

  1. List the correctly hyphenated words.

  2. List the incorrectly hyphenated words.

  You may want to have LEP students look up each incorrectly hyphenated word in the dictionary and then write the word correctly.

Additional Resources
- Grammar and Usage Practice Book, p. 95

WRITING THEME Congressional Elections

  You may wish to encourage students to research Congressional elections as a topic for a social studies report.

Concept Check

Hyphens
1. well-informed, no-ticed
2. fa-vor
4. fifty-eight
5. first-term
9. representative-elect
10. Correct
14. better-funded
15. taxpayer-paid
16. self-defeating
18. ex-representatives

 Writing Theme
Congressional Elections

  Try to observe the following rules when hyphenating words at the end of a line.

1. Separate words only between syllables.
2. Hyphenate a word only if it has two or more syllables.
3. Leave at least two letters of the hyphenated word on each line.

Practice Your Skills

CONCEPT CHECK

Hyphens If a line in the following paragraph contains words that need to be hyphenated, write the line number and the correctly hyphenated words after the number. If a line contains words that are incorrectly hyphenated, write the line number and the correct hyphenation after the number. If a line contains correct hyphenation, write *Correct.* You may wish to consult a dictionary.

Example
1 In the 1986 congressional race, two thirds of the
2 winners received over sixty-five percent of the vote.
3 In other words, people elected to the U.S. Congr-
4 ess these days tend to win by substantial margins.

Line 1   two-thirds
Line 2   Correct
Line 3   Con-gress

1   Many well informed political commentators have notic-
2 ed that congressional races in the United States tend to f-
3 avor returning, or incumbent, candidates. Consider the
4 following statistics: in 1863 fifty eight percent of those
5 entering office after an election were first term
6 members. By contrast, in 1981 only sixteen percent of
7 entering representatives were first termers. What has
8 happened? Why is Congress now, more often than not, a
9 lifelong career? Why is your representative elect most
10 likely *not* a new face? The answer lies in the enor-
11 mous power that an incumbent has to get his or her
12 message out to the people. Incumbent representatives
13 receive more press coverage than their opponents. They
14 also have better funded campaigns. Finally, they can
15 make use of free, taxpayer paid mailings. Of course,
16 members of Congress generally feel that it would be self
17 defeating for them to pass legislation to make
18 congressional elections fairer. However, several ex
19 representatives have called for major reform in
20 congressional election practices.

PARENTHESES, BRACKETS, ELLIPSES

Parentheses and brackets are used to enclose information that is separate from the main idea of the sentence.

Parentheses

Use parentheses to set off the supplementary or explanatory material that is either nonessential or loosely connected to the sentence.

The Xhosa (kō′ sä) are a pastoral people who live in South Africa.

Edna St. Vincent Millay's poem "Renascence" (written in 1912) was composed when she was just nineteen years old.

Use parentheses to identify a source of information, such as author and page number of a reference.

"Things happened to young Walt Disney that he would recall with clarity in later years." **(Thomas 10)**

For more information on documenting sources of information, see Writer's Workshop 9, pages 283–284, and Writing Handbook 24, pages 486–487.

Use parentheses to enclose figures or letters that identify items in a series.

The years after the turn of the century were years of change for the people of England: (1) in social conditions, (2) in government, and (3) in the expansion of their empire.

Use parentheses to set off certain numerical information.

Call our toll-free number (800) 555–3211.

William Penn (1644–1718) founded the colony of Pennsylvania.

Place punctuation marks inside the parentheses when they belong to the parenthetical material. When punctuation marks belong to the main part of the sentence, place them outside the parentheses.

Walt Disney, American pioneer of animated cartoon films, 1901—1966

Objectives

- To use parentheses and brackets to enclose certain kinds of nonessential elements
- To use ellipses to show omissions in quoted material

Teaching Strategies

Teaching Tip: Research Papers

Point out that parentheses, brackets, and ellipses are especially useful for referring to and quoting sources in research papers. If the students' writing includes a research paper, have them point out specific ways to use these three marks in the report.

Stumbling Block

Some students may be confused by the fact that the uses of parentheses and dashes overlap. Explain that both dashes and parentheses are used to set off non-essential material that interrupts the sentence. However, parentheses have more conventional uses; for example, in research papers.

Linking Grammar and Literature

On the board, write the following lines from the writings of Henry David Thoreau:

Our life is frittered away by detail.
. . . Simplify, simplify.

Discuss how the use of ellipses helps to convey the meaning of these lines.

Additional Resources
• Grammar and Usage Practice Book, p. 96

WRITING THEME   Goethe

Concept Check
Parentheses and Brackets
1. Johann Wolfgang von Goethe (1749–1832) is believed by some to have been the most intelligent person who ever lived.
2. He made major contributions to many fields of endeavor: (1) to literature, (2) to the theory of optics, and (3) to botany and zoology.
3. One critic has written: "There is none to whom we can look more trustingly as the father of world literature than Goethe." (Spender 56)
4. Spender writes: "Poetry is not for him [Goethe] a refuge, a habitation, or a confessional; it is an occasion for a magnificent statement."
5. Literary scholar Jergen Kloss wrote: "Goethes' [Goethe's] most famous literary work is his *Faust,* an epic drama in verse."

CHECK POINT
PAGES 784–796

You may want to use the following Checkpoint exercises as an informal evaluation of student mastery of the concepts covered in this handbook.

◆ Individualizing Instruction

LD Students   For each sentence in the exercise, you may want to tell students which punctuation mark(s) to add. Before they make the corrections, have them refer to the lesson for guidance.

Writing Theme
Goethe

Writing Theme
Vincent van Gogh

Brackets

Use brackets to enclose corrections or to insert additional information into material quoted from a source.

"On the 4th [5th] of March, Hayes took office." (correction)

The letter read: "We have him [Jordahl] at our mercy." (an explanatory word inserted by the editor)

Ellipses

Use ellipses—three dots (. . .)—to indicate the omission of part of a quoted sentence. Use four dots—a period plus ellipses—when the omission is between sentences or after a sentence.

"Dear Madam: I have been shown in the files of the War Department . . . that you are the mother of five sons who have died gloriously on the field of battle. . . ."

Abraham Lincoln

Practice Your Skills

CONCEPT CHECK

Parentheses and Brackets   Revise each sentence, inserting parentheses and brackets as needed.

1. Johann Wolfgang von Goethe 1749–1832 is believed by some to have been the most intelligent person who ever lived.
2. He made major contributions to many fields of endeavor: 1 to literature, 2 to the theory of optics, and 3 to botany and zoology.
3. One critic has written: "There is none to whom we can look more trustingly as the father of world literature than Goethe." Spender 56
4. Spender writes: "Poetry is not for him Goethe a refuge, a habitation, or a confessional; it is an occasion for a magnificent statement."
5. Literary scholar Jergen Kloss wrote: "Goethes' Goethe's most famous literary work is his *Faust,* an epic drama in verse."

CHECK POINT
PAGES 784—796

Rewrite the sentences, adding or changing punctuation as necessary. Use semicolons, colons, dashes, hyphens, and parentheses.

1. Vincent van Gogh 1853–1890 sold only one painting in his lifetime nevertheless, he is considered a truly great artist.
2. The words of Proverbs 14,13 describe his personal life "Even in laughter the heart is sorrowful."

3. For roughly two thirds of his life, van Gogh his artistic career only lasted ten years tried several professions.
4. He worked for an art dealer in London, England, a bookseller in Dordrecht, Holland, and a church in Brussels, Belgium.
5. His work as a missionary with poverty stricken coal miners in Belgium certainly had an unfortunate end, he was fired.
6. In his letters to his brother Theo he explained how he channeled religious feeling into art "I want to paint . . . with that something of the eternal which the halo used to symbolize."
7. Van Gogh relied on his brother Theo was his lifeline for both moral and financial support.
8. In his letters to Theo, van Gogh also expressed his feelings on many subjects such as the following art, religion, and poetry.
9. Van Gogh's letters few can read them without being moved reveal a master of written as well as visual imagery.
10. Bold, brilliant, erratic, all describe the man and his art.
11. These artists influenced his work, giving him needed self confidence Jean-François Millet, Georges Seurat, Jean-Baptiste-Camille Corot.
12. He and artist Paul Gauguin were coworkers for two months however, their relationship was tempestuous.
13. Under great emotional strain, van Gogh cut off part of his left ear when he was thirty five years old.
14. He feared for his sanity from that point on, his mental anguish alternated with periods of artistic genius.
15. He produced works such as *Garden of the Asylum* and *Olive Trees,* and he experimented greatly with style and color.
16. Historian H.W. Janson wrote "Despairing of a cure, he committed suicide . . . art alone made his life worth living."
17. After his death the world acclaimed his genius thus, he is now one of the most well known artists of all time.
18. The book *Genius and Disaster The Ten Creative Years of Vincent van Gogh* gives us insight into a complex artist.
19. Impressively, van Gogh painted more than six hundred works of art how remarkable! in a ten year span.
20. Van Gogh did not become wealthy during his lifetime however, in the late 1980's, his painting *Irises* commanded one of the highest prices ever paid at auction for a piece of artwork $53.9 million.

The Garden of the Hospital at Arles, 1889, Vincent van Gogh

WRITING THEME Vincent van Gogh

1. Vincent van Gogh (1853–1890) sold only one painting in his lifetime; nevertheless, he is considered a truly great artist.
2. The words of Proverbs 14:13 describe his personal life: "Even in laughter the heart is sorrowful."
3. For roughly two-thirds of his life, van Gogh (his artistic career only lasted ten years) tried several professions.
4. He worked for an art dealer in London, England; a bookseller in Dordrecht, Holland; and a church in Brussels, Belgium.
5. His work as a missionary with poverty-stricken coal miners in Belgium certainly had an unfortunate end: he was fired.
6. In his letters to his brother Theo he explained how he channeled religious feeling into art: "I want to paint . . . with that something of the eternal which the halo used to symbolize."
7. Van Gogh relied on his brother—Theo was his lifeline—for both moral and financial support.
8. In his letters to Theo, van Gogh also expressed his feelings on many subjects such as the following: art, religion, and poetry.
9. Van Gogh's letters—few can read them without being moved—reveal a master of written as well as visual imagery.
10. Bold, brilliant, erratic—all describe the man and his art.
11. These artists influenced his work, giving him needed self-confidence: Jean-François Millet, Georges Seurat, Jean-Baptiste-Camille Corot.
12. He and artist Paul Gauguin were co-workers for two months; however, their relationship was tempestuous.
13. Under great emotional strain, van Gogh cut off part of his left ear when he was thirty-five years old.
14. He feared for his sanity from that point on; his mental anguish alternated with periods of artistic genius.
15. He produced works such as *Garden of the Asylum* and *Olive Trees;* and he experimented greatly with style and color.
16. Historian H.W. Janson wrote: "Despairing of a cure, he committed suicide . . . art alone made his life worth living."
17. After his death the world acclaimed his genius; thus, he is now one of the most well-known artists of all time.
18. The book *Genius and Disaster: The Ten Creative Years of Vincent van Gogh* gives us insight into a complex artist.
19. Impressively, van Gogh painted more than six hundred works of art—how remarkable!—in a ten-year span.
20. Van Gogh did not become wealthy during his lifetime; however, in the late 1980's, his painting *Irises* commanded one of the highest prices ever paid at auction for a piece of artwork ($53.9 million).

Humanities Connection

Art Note Vincent van Gogh painted *The Garden of the Hospital at Arles* in 1889, the year he was confined there for an emotional breakdown. He was inspired by the garden's colors, which, he told his brother, were even more brilliant at night. Van Gogh spent his two most creative and most tortured years in Arles before taking his own life in 1890.

Additional Resources
- Grammar and Usage Practice Book, p. 97

Application and Review

WRITING THEME Classification

A. Semicolons, Colons, and Other Punctuation

Slavic falls into three main subdivisions: East Slavic includes Great Russian (or just Russian), the common and literary language of Russia; Ruthenian (or Ukranian), spoken in the Ukraine; and White Russian (or Byelorussian), spoken to the north of the Ukraine. West Slavic includes Polish, Czech, the highly similar Slovak, and Serbian (or Wendish), a language spoken by a small group of people in East Germany; these languages have lost many of the early forms preserved in East Slavic. The South Slavic languages are Bulgarian, Serbo-Croatian, and Slovenian. The oldest Slavic writing . . . is in Old Bulgarian, sometimes called Old Church Slavic (or Old Church Slavonic), which remained a liturgical language long after it ceased to be generally spoken.

From *The Origins and Development of the English Language*

by Thomas Pyle

B. Punctuating Correctly

1. At 7:25 A.M. every Monday, Wednesday, and Friday, bleary-eyed students file into Biology 101.
2. For centuries, students have studied biology; thus *Linnaeus* should be a household word, but it's not.
3. Carolus Linnaeus (1707–1778) was a Swedish botanist.
4. Linnaeus—his family called him "the little botanist"—was the son of a clergyman in Rashult, Sweden.
5. Perhaps Ecclesiastes 3:1 inspired him: "To every thing there is a season, and a time to every purpose under heaven."
6. Linnaeus attended the university in Uppsala, northwest of Stockholm, Sweden; and he was appointed lecturer in botany there at the age of twenty-three.
7. There, the botanist Olof Celsius (not to be confused with Anders Celsius, who invented the temperature scale) helped Linnaeus's career.
8. In 1732, Linnaeus led an expedition to Lapland; as a result, he wrote *Flora Lapponica* (1737).
9. His contribution to science—not just the discovery of some little-known plant—is the system of classifying living things.

Additional Resources
- Tests and Assessment, Mastery Tests, pp. 68–69
- Elaboration, Revision, and Proofreading, p. 30

GRAMMAR HANDBOOK 40

Writing Theme Classification

A. Semicolons, Colons, and Other Punctuation Notice that the following paragraph has only four sentences. Much information is packed into these sentences through the use of punctuation: parentheses, semicolons, and a colon. Read the passage carefully and then restore any missing parentheses, semicolons, and colons.

Slavic falls into three main subdivisions East Slavic includes Great Russian (or just Russian), the common and literary language of Russia; Ruthenian or Ukrainian, spoken in the Ukraine and White Russian (or Byelorussian), spoken to the north of the Ukraine. West Slavic includes Polish, Czech, the highly similar Slovak, and Serbian or Wendish, a language spoken by a small group of people in East Germany these languages have lost many of the early forms preserved in East Slavic. The South Slavic languages are Bulgarian, Serbo-Croatian, and Slovenian. The oldest Slavic writing . . . is in Old Bulgarian, sometimes called Old Church Slavic or Old Church Slavonic, which remained a liturgical language long after it ceased to be generally spoken.

Thomas Pyle,
The Origins and Development of the English Language

B. Punctuating Correctly Rewrite the following sentences, punctuating them correctly.

1. At 725 A.M. every Monday, Wednesday, and Friday, bleary eyed students file into Biology 101.
2. For centuries, students have studied biology thus *Linnaeus* should be a household word, but it's not.
3. Carolus Linnaeus 1707–1778 was a Swedish botanist.
4. Linnaeus his family called him "the little botanist" was the son of a clergyman in Rashult, Sweden.
5. Perhaps Ecclesiastes 3 1 inspired him "To every thing there is a season, and a time to every purpose under heaven."
6. Linnaeus attended the university in Uppsala, northwest of Stockholm, Sweden, and he was appointed lecturer in botany there at the age of twenty three.
7. There, the botanist Olof Celsius not to be confused with Anders Celsius, who invented the temperature scale helped Linnaeus's career.
8. In 1732, Linnaeus led an expedition to Lapland as a result, he wrote *Flora Lapponica* 1737.
9. His contribution to science not just the discovery of some little known plant is the system of classifying living things.

10. The system, from highest to lowest rank, is as follows kingdom, phylum, class, order, family, genus, and species.
11. Professor Paul B. Weisz wrote "This . . . system of taxonomy has since become greatly elaborated and is now in universal use."
12. Consider the corn plant its phylum is *Tracheophyta,* class, *Angiospermae,* order, *Graminales,* and family, *Graminaceae.*
13. The system was useful in two ways 1 it gave scientists a method of classifying, or relating, flora and fauna; and 2 it set forth an order of taxonomies, or classifications.
14. One unappreciative student wrote this note "Thanks to you Lineus Linnaeus I'm playing with phyla and not the all star team!"
15. Linnaeus's manuscripts, herbarium, collections of insects and shells all are preserved by the Linnean Society in London.

C. More Correct Punctuation Rewrite the following passage, correcting errors in capitalization and spelling as well as errors in the use of punctuation.

A night person enjoys burning the midnight oil, watching the late movie, or trekking home at 600 A.M. from a party, but a morning person is up at the crack of dawn, ready to conquer the day. Are such concepts real or merely excuses for doing what we want when we want?

Sceintists have discovered that the body does function in accordence with rhythms moreover these all important rhythms vary from person to person. About one tenth of the population can be considered night people, and about one tenth morning people. The rest of us are in between. Body Temperture peaks later in night people and earlier in morning people. Did you know that our body temperature is not always 98.6 degrees Fahrenheit? Rather, it varies slightly over the course of the day in a predictible pattern, the rising and falling of body temperature is linked with cicles of activity and sleep.

Why is it important to understand our bodies rhythms? Over coming jet lag, adjusting to unusual work schedules, fighting diseases these are just a few possible applications of scientific research into biological rhythms.

10. The system, from highest to lowest rank, is as follows: kingdom, phylum, class, order, family, genus, and species.
11. Professor Paul B. Weisz wrote: "This . . . system of taxonomy has since become greatly elaborated and is now in universal use."
12. Consider the corn plant: its phylum is *Tracheophyta;* class, *Angiospermae;* order, *Graminales;* and family, *Graminaceae.*
13. The system was useful in two ways: (1) it gave scientists a method of classifying, or relating, flora and fauna; and (2) it set forth an order of taxonomies, or classifications.
14. One unappreciative student wrote this note: "Thanks to you Lineus [Linnaeus] I'm playing with phyla and not the all-star team!"
15. Linnaeus's manuscripts, herbarium, collections of insects and shells—all are preserved by the Linnean Society in London.

C. More Correct Punctuation

A night person enjoys burning the midnight oil, watching the late movie, or trekking home at 6:00 A.M. from a party; but a morning person is up at the crack of dawn, ready to conquer the day. Are such concepts real or merely excuses for doing what we want when we want?

Scientists have discovered that the body does function in accordance with rhythms; moreover, these all-important rhythms vary from person to person. About one-tenth of the population can be considered night people, and about one-tenth morning people. The rest of us are in between. Body temperature peaks later in night people and earlier in morning people. Did you know that our body temperature is not always 98.6 degrees Fahrenheit? Rather, it varies slightly over the course of the day in a predictable pattern; the rising and falling of body temperature is linked with cycles of activity and sleep.

Why is it important to understand our bodies' rhythms? Overcoming jet lag, adjusting to unusual work schedules, fighting diseases—these are just a few possible applications of scientific research into biological rhythms.

On the Lightside

Officially speaking, parentheses are used for material that is grammatically unnecessary to a sentence but too important to omit, or for explanatory material included within a text. You might point out that parentheses are often used for material—clauses, phrases, and sentences—that could have been punctuated in other ways. Dashes or commas are often used instead of parentheses. Sometimes no punctuation is needed at all, especially when the parentheses enclose a complete sentence. A few highly accomplished and idiosyncratic writers use parentheses as a habitual mannerism for information that is off the main point, or for flashbacks. (Faulkner is a chief example, as is Joseph Heller in *Something Happened.*) On the whole, the trend in modern writing is to eliminate unnecessary punctuation.

Invite students to re-punctuate the poem on this page using as few parentheses as possible. Advanced students may wish to create their own prose paragraphs or poetic stanzas, on any topic, using maximum parentheses.

On the Lightside

TALK ABOUT PARENTHESES

As you have learned, parentheses may be used to set off material that is nonessential or loosely connected to the sentence. The poem below is a humorous example of parentheses used to an extreme.

Of all the fleas that ever flew
(And flying fleas are rather few
((Because for proper flying you
(((Whether you are a flea or not)))
Need wings and things fleas have not got)))—

(I make the further point that fleas
Are thick as these parentheses
((An illustration (((you'll agree)))
Both apt and pleasing to a flea)))—

Now then where were we? Let me see—
Ah, yes—We said to fly you ought
(Whether you are a flea or not)
To have some wings (yes, at least two
((At least no less than two will do
(((And fleas have something less than one
((((One less, in fact (((((or, frankly, none,
Which ((((((as once more you will agree))))))
Limits the flying of a flea))))))))))))))).

And let me add that fleas that fly
are known as Flears. (You can see why.)
All I have said thus far is true.
(If it's not clear, that's up to you.
((You'll have to learn sometime, my dear,
That what is true may not be clear
(((While what is clear may not be true
((((And you'll be wiser when you do.))))))))))

Saturday Review

Sketchbook

To find creative writers, an advertising agency held a contest in which participants were asked to complete a series of writing assignments. Here are some of the assignments:

Write a "Dialogue in a Dark Alley." (Not more than 200 words).

You are a writer for Walletsize Books. Describe the history of the United States in one hundred words or less.

A delegation of Martians has just landed in a local park. They do not understand any Earth languages—only very basic symbols. Prepare a short speech comprised of pictures and symbols to welcome them and to tell them just what kind of place this is.

How would you complete one of these assignments? Be sure to capitalize and punctuate accurately as you write.

801

Objective

To use prompts from an advertising agency contest as springboards to informal writing

Using the Prompt

Remind students that the writing activities suggested in the Sketchbook are meant to be informal and will not be graded. They are intended to encourage creative thinking in a risk-free setting.

Ask students to recall advertisements that seem particularly unusual, either because of what they say or because of the graphics they use. Point out that advertising writers often attempt to be extremely creative in their ads and often reach for the unusual or even bizarre in order to draw attention to their products. After students read the directions and assignments, ask them what makes each assignment strange. Then encourage them to express their immediate responses to each assignment. You may wish to model your own first response to one of the assignments. Then have students select assignments to complete and encourage them to give themselves a stretch of time just to generate ideas and take notes before they actually begin writing. Be sure students recognize that their responses can be completely "off the wall."

You may want to use ideas in the Additional Sketches section with students who need a different starting point.

Have students keep their writing in their Writing Portfolios for possible use in other writing projects.

Apostrophes and Quotation Marks

Apostrophes

Objectives

- To use apostrophes to show possession; to indicate omitted letters; and to form the plural of letters, numbers, signs, and words used as words.
- **Writing** To use apostrophes correctly in personal and assigned writing

Teaching Strategies

Critical Thinking

Synthesizing Tell students that there are basically two ways to form possessives: (1) add apostrophe *s* or (2) add just apostrophe. Emphasize that the possessive of singular nouns and of irregular plural nouns are both formed by adding apostrophe *s*. (lecturer's podium, women's apparel) Only for plural nouns ending with -s do you add just an apostrophe. (nurses' station)

Personal Touch

Have some fun with the names in the Punctuation Note. Pronounce some of the words that would be formed if 's were added to these names (forming words like *Demosthenes's* and *Moses's*). Then invite students to do the same.

Teaching Tip: Compound Nouns

Draw a distinction between how to form the plural and the possessive of a compound noun. For a plural compound noun, add -s to the first word in the compound. (fathers-in-law) For a possessive compound noun, add 's to both the singular and plural forms. (father-in-law's and fathers-in-law's)

GRAMMAR HANDBOOK 41

Apostrophes and Quotation Marks

APOSTROPHES

The apostrophe is used to show possession, to indicate omitted letters, and to form certain plurals, such as those of numbers.

Using Apostrophes to Show Possession

Use the apostrophe to form the possessive of singular and plural nouns.

To form the possessive of a singular noun, add an apostrophe and an -s even if the noun ends in -s.

Emma's	writer's	city's
Tess's	duchess's	Joyce Carol Oates's

Punctuation Note The possessives of ancient classical names ending in -s and of names of more than one syllable with unaccented endings pronounced -eez are formed by adding just an apostrophe: *Demosthenes', R.S. Surtees', Ramses', Xerxes', Mars'*. The possessive of *Jesus* and *Moses* is formed the same way: *Jesus', Moses'*.

To form the possessive of a plural noun that ends in -s, add an apostrophe only.

senators'	churches'	Johnsons'	females'

To form the possessive of a plural noun that does not end in -s, add an apostrophe and -s.

women's	people's	mice's

To form the possessive of a compound noun, add an apostrophe or an apostrophe and -s, depending on the form of the noun.

mother-in-law's (singular)	mothers-in-law's (plural)
attorney general's (singular)	attorneys general's (plural) *or*
	attorney generals' (plural)

To form the possessive of nouns such as *Secretary of State* and *President of the United States*, add an apostrophe and an -s to the last word.

the Secretary of State's staff

Often it is preferable to use a prepositional phrase instead.

> the staff of the Secretary of State

In cases of joint possession, only the last name mentioned takes the possessive form. Add an apostrophe or an apostrophe and -s, depending on the form of the last noun.

> Gilbert and Sullivan's operettas
> Felipe and Inez's grandmother
> mothers and daughters' dinner

The rule for joint ownership also applies to the names of organizations and firms.

> Boswell, Banks, and Chubbs's recruiters
> Brown, Jackson, and Company's building

If possession is not joint, each name takes the possessive form.

> Stephanie's and Masumi's desks
> Van Dyke's and Rembrandt's use of light

If the possessive form is awkward, use a prepositional phrase instead.

> the desks belonging to Stephanie and Masumi
> the use of light by Van Dyke and Rembrandt

To form a possessive of an indefinite pronoun, add an apostrophe and an -s.

> anyone's   everyone's   another's   everybody's

To form the possessive of a compound indefinite pronoun, add an apostrophe as an -s to the last word.

> someone else's idea   no one else's grades

Do not use an apostrophe with a personal pronoun to show possession.

> hers   his   its   ours   theirs   yours

> That tennis racket is *hers*.
> The finish on that car has lost *its* shine.

When used as adjectives, nouns expressing time or amount take the possessive form.

> one day's pay   three days' pay
> one month's delay   two months' delay
> one dollar's worth   six dollars' worth

Writing ——TIP——

Careful writers check for correct apostrophe usage as they proofread.

Apostrophes and
Quotation Marks   **803**

Individualizing Instruction

ESL Students Most other languages do not use the apostrophe to show possession. For example, the French would say "the hat of George," not "George's hat." (le chapeau de Georges) Tell students about this feature of the French language and invite them to explain how their native language indicates possession.

Spot Check

To help students avoid confusing possessive pronouns with contractions, review these word pairs; *theirs, there's* and *its, it's.* Because these word pairs are homophones, they can be especially troublesome. Point out that the pronouns *theirs* and *its* show possession. (This book is theirs. The dog responded to its master.) Then write sentences using the contractions *there's* and *it's.* You may want to provide the following models:

   Where there's a will, there's a way.
   It's later than you think.

Discuss what two words each contraction stands for (there is, it is) and have students restate the sentences using these words.

Teaching Tip: Contractions With n't

In contractions, *not* is usually changed to *n't* and added to the verb, which retains its own spelling. (don't, shouldn't, isn't) The words *won't* and *can't* are the two contractions in which the verb changes its spelling. (will not and cannot) Remind students of these two exceptions.

Stumbling Block

Caution students to avoid unnecessary apostrophes in simple plurals. One error is occasionally made when signing greeting cards. For example, a correct way to sign a card for a family is with the plural, *the Johnsons* not *the Johnson's*.

Linking Grammar and Literature

On the board, write the following dialogue from Rudyard Kipling's *Captains Courageous:*
"Anchor's fouled. Penn's always losing 'em. Lost two this trip a'ready—on sandy bottom too—an' Dad says next one he loses, sure's fishin', he'll give him the kelleg. That 'u'd break Penn's heart."
First, have students find the contraction (he'll) and the possessive noun (Penn's in the last sentence). Then have students tell what letters have been left out in the other words containing an apostrophe.

Using Apostrophes to Show Omissions

Use an apostrophe in contractions to show where letters have been omitted.

hasn't = has not   he's = he is *or* he has

Use an apostrophe to indicate missing letters in dialect, poetry, or archaic speech.

"I *s'pose* you know Lila's *leavin'*." (dialect)
"Foul *whisp'rings* are abroad."   **William Shakespeare**

Use an apostrophe to show the omission of numbers

the Chicago Bulls' first loss of '88
the class of '92

Using Apostrophes to Form Certain Plurals

Use an apostrophe to show the plurals of letters, numerals, signs, and words referred to as words.

Allan forgot to dot the *i's* on the poster.
The 1970's saw the dawn of the microcomputer age.
His *7's* look like *9's*.
My writing has too many *and's* in it.

Usage Note   Letters and words used as words are italicized in print and underlined in handwritten and typewritten work.

Practice Your Skills

A. CONCEPT CHECK

Apostrophes For each of the following sentences, correctly rewrite each word containing an error in the use of apostrophes. If a sentence has no errors, write *Correct*.

1. There are no "ifs, and's, or buts" about it; human's throughout recorded history have been fascinated with achieving the goal of traveling at faster and faster speeds.
2. Perhaps the myth of the winged horse Pegasus' ascent to the skies inspired people to harness the horse's power and to dream of flight.
3. From the Roman's horse-drawn chariots to the American's sleek planes, technology has aided men and womens quest for moving at faster speeds.
4. As technology advanced, the three Rs of inventing—reading, writing, and rithmetic—changed rapidly.
5. Compared to the stagecoachs speed of nine miles' per hour, the inventors first cars seemed incredibly fast.
6. In the late 1800s, the twin brothers' Francis E. and Freelan O. Stanley built a steam-powered car that they called the Stanley Steamer.
7. Francis's and Freelan's car could travel at high speeds.
8. In 1906, the Stanley's car set a world's record at 127 miles per hour; no one elses' car at that time even came close to matching this amazing feat.
9. However, earthbound speeds did'nt satisfy humanitys thirst; it was flight that captured everyones' imagination.
10. Todays' high-technology airplanes are a far cry from Orville's and Wilbur's Wrights first inventions.
11. In airplane manufacturing companies, such as in Boeing and McDonnell Douglas's factories, every chief executive officers dream is attaining the fastest speeds in the safest ways' possible.
12. In the '50's, engineers' concerns focused on developing planes that traveled at the speed of sound (about 650 miles per hour at 35,000 feet).
13. Though planes soon filled people's cars with sonic booms, the quest for speedy travel did not end there.
14. In 69, Stafford's, Cernan's, and Young's flight set a record when *Apollo X*s speed reached 24,791 miles per hour at an altitude of 400,000 feet.
15. What would the ancient Romans with their chariots think of tomorrows quest to travel at the speed of light (186,181 miles per second)?

Apostrophes and Quotation Marks **805**

WRITING THEME Technology and Speed

You may want to have interested students research a related topic and use it as the subject of a report.

A. Concept Check

Apostrophes
1. if's; but's; humans
2. Correct
3. Romans'; Americans'; men and women's
4. R's; 'rithmetic
5. stagecoach's; miles; inventors'
6. 1800's; brothers
7. Francis
8. Stanleys'; no one else's
9. didn't; humanity's; everyone's
10. Today's; Orville; Wilbur; Wright's
11. Boeing's; officer's; ways
12. Correct
13. Correct
14. '69; Stafford; Cernan; *Apollo X*'s
15. tomorrow's

B. Proofreading Skill

Apostrophe Usage

Answers will vary. See suggested answers below.

No one's life has been unaffected by the quest for speed. Automatic teller machines dispense instant cash; eyeglasses are made in an hour's time; letters are transmitted across a continent without a second's delay. These are just a few of the innovations of the 1970's and 1980's that reflect America's demand for speed. Think of the time-saving devices finding their way into Americans' homes—for example, microwave ovens, remote controls, and food processors. Many of the world's time-saving services and products have originated in America. The credit for everything from fast-food restaurants to instantly developed photographs is ours.

Isn't our obsession with speed positive? Some people agree with the opinion expressed in Meyer Friedman and Ray Roseman's recent book that too much emphasis on hurrying leads to unhealthful stress. However, in many sociologists' opinions, fast consumer services have become a necessity in today's world.

C. Application in Writing

Personal Opinion Essay

Answers will vary.

B. PROOFREADING SKILL

Apostrophe Usage Rewrite the following paragraphs, correcting errors in spelling, capitalization, and punctuation. Pay close attention to the use of apostrophes.

No ones life has been unaffected by the quest for speed. Automatic teller machines dispense instant cash; Eyeglasses are made in an hours time; Letters are transmitted across a continent without a seconds delay. These are just a few of the inovations of the 1970s and 1980s that reflect Americas demand for speed. Think of the time-saving devices finding their way into Americans homes—for example, microwave ovens, remote controls, and food procesors. Many of the worlds time-saving services and products have originated in America, the credit for everything from fast-food restaurants to instantly-developed photographs is ours'.

Isnt our obsession with speed positive? Some people agree with the opinion expressed in Meyer Friedman's and Ray Roseman's recent book that to much emphasis on hurrying leads to unhealthful stress. However, in many sociologist's opinions, fast consumer services have become a necessity in todays world.

C. APPLICATION IN WRITING

Personal Opinion Essay What is your opinion about our culture's obsession with speed? Has technology done us a favor or not? Write a brief personal essay expressing and supporting your opinion. Use apostrophes correctly in your essay.

QUOTATION MARKS

Quotation marks are used to set off direct quotations, titles, and words used in special ways.

Direct and Indirect Quotations

Use quotation marks to set off a direct quotation.

"Is there an intermission during the performance?" asked Carolyn.

An indirect quotation is the repetition without direct quotation of something said. An indirect quotation is expressed as a subordinate clause.

Do not use quotation marks to set off an indirect quotation.

Carolyn asked whether there was an intermission during the performance.

Punctuation of Direct Quotations

The following rules govern the use of punctuation and capitalization for direct quotations.

Use quotation marks to enclose the exact words of a speaker or writer. Capitalize the first word of the quotation.

"Portable phones are changing the way businesses operate," said Mrs. Collins.
Mrs. Collins said, "Portable phones are changing the way businesses operate."

A comma at the end of quoted material is always placed inside the quotation marks. When the sentence ends with the quotation, the period falls inside the quotation marks.

If the quotation is a question or an exclamation, put the question mark or exclamation point inside the quotation marks. Do not use a comma.

"Shouldn't we cancel the *Times*?" asked Laverne.
"Don't touch that!" she shouted.

Put a question mark or an exclamation point outside the quotation marks if it is not part of the quoted material.

Why did she say, "I'll see you later"?
I was shocked to hear her say, "I'm thinking of resigning"!

Writing
═TIP═

In writing narratives, use quotation marks to set off the exact words of a character's thoughts.
Bob told himself, "Think fast."

Quotation Marks

Objectives

- To identify the correct use of punctuation and capitalization in direct quotations
- **Writing** To use quotation marks correctly in dialogue

Teaching Strategies

Linking Grammar and Writing

You might ask students to listen for interesting dialogues and try to reproduce one in their journals. Suggest that they try to catch the flavor of the dialogue, including contractions, slang words, and dialect. For example, ''He's playin' a neat guitar.'' Later, some students might want to expand their dialogue into a short story, asking peer editors to read the dialogue aloud and help them make it authentic.

Individualizing Instruction

ESL Students Quotations are marked in a variety of ways in other languages. Encourage ESL students to share conventions for indicating quotations in their native languages, and stress the difference in English.

Teaching Tip: Context

Remind students that newspapers and magazines often contain quoted material. Point out that conscientious newswriters guard against including quotes out of context. A partial quote can convey a meaning far different from the one originally intended. To illustrate this idea, help students compare the following quotes from Lincoln's *Gettysburg Address*. Students should decide which quote is more appropriate and why.

- But, in a larger sense, we cannot dedicate—we cannot consecrate—we cannot hallow—this ground.
- But, in a larger sense, we cannot dedicate—we cannot consecrate—we cannot hallow—this ground. The brave men, living and dead, who struggled here, have consecrated it far above our poor power to add or detract.

Linking Grammar and Literature

Display the following dialogue from Charles Dickens's *A Tale of Two Cities:*

"Eh well!" said Madame Defarge, raising her eyebrows with a cool business air. "It is necessary to register him. How do they call that man?"

"He is English."

"So much the better. His name?"

Point out that each change of speaker begins a new paragraph. Then have students use this dialogue to explain the conventions of using quotation marks.

Writing TIP

In writing reports, you can set off a long quoted passage, an excerpt, without quotation marks. Double-space and indent all lines from the left.

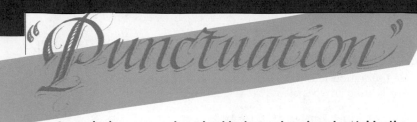

"Punctuation"

A semicolon or a colon should always be placed outside the quotation mark.

> These items were listed as "indispensable": laboratory tables, Bunsen burners, metal trays, and storage cabinets.
> My boss told me, "You have just one week of vacation this year"; I guess I'll stay close to home.

Enclose both parts of a divided quotation within quotation marks. Capitalize the first word of the second part of the quotation only if it begins a new sentence.

> "Take your time as you complete the test," said Mrs. Silva, "to avoid making errors due to haste."

In dialogue, a change in speaker is indicated by a new paragraph.

> "Scientific research today is well organized," Mrs. Yee said. "Scientists work in teams, with each scientist investigating one aspect of a problem."
> Gina asked politely, "Isn't it true that many inventions and discoveries are just a matter of luck?"
> "Yes, indeed," answered Mrs. Yee, with a laugh. "We call it *serendipity*. You need a little luck in science, just as you do in other fields."

Use single quotation marks to set off a quotation within a quotation.

> Diana reported, "When somebody told Churchill not to end sentences with prepositions, Sir Winston replied, 'That is the kind of nonsense up with which I will not put.'"
> Sheila asked, "Was it Roosevelt who said, 'The only thing we have to fear is fear itself'?"

In quoting passages of more than one paragraph, use a quotation mark at the beginning of each paragraph and at the end of only the last paragraph.

When a quotation is a fragment and does not begin the sentence, do not capitalize the first word of the quotation.

> In *Othello,* Shakespeare calls jealousy a "green-eyed monster."

Practice Your Skills

A. CONCEPT CHECK

Quotation Marks Rewrite each of the following sentences, correcting all errors in punctuation and capitalization. If a sentence contains no errors, write *Correct*.

1. Welcome to this edition of *Art and Artists* said the announcer today we will discuss surrealism and Salvador Dalí.
2. Our guest she continued is our local art expert, Nora Freemont.
3. Welcome, Nora she said to begin, can you tell us when the surrealist movement was at its height.
4. Freemont replied the movement was at its height in Paris in the 1920's and 1930's.
5. She pointed to a chart of the surrealist "greats:" Salvador Dalí, Joan Miró, André Masson, and Max Ernst.
6. Of these artists, the most flamboyant was Dalí she said.
7. Oh, dear thought the announcer I hope she doesn't talk about some of Dalí's wild exploits.
8. Freemont explained that Dalí was known for his outrageous attire, spiky waxed mustache, and actions.
9. Pointing to a photograph of *The Persistence of Memory,* Freemont exclaimed his dreamy landscapes are remarkable!
10. A woman once asked Dalí if it was hard to paint a picture said Freemont.
11. Smiling, Ms. Freemont continued Dalí replied no. It's either easy or impossible.
12. Freemont stated that Dalí found inspiration in the Spanish town of Cadaqués.
13. The poet Federico García Lorca once said that Cadaqués was 'counterpoised between sea and hill;' however, Dalí's mental landscapes never matched reality.
14. His landscapes said Freemont were filled with images that had no rational explanation.
15. What a surprise it was when Freemont said, Dalí died a recluse with only his mental images for comfort!

B. APPLICATION IN LITERATURE

Punctuation The following passage has been altered to include several errors in the use of punctuation, capitalization, and paragraphing. Rewrite the passage, returning it to its original form.

> I have visited a good deal of fine scenery before and since, but have found little that has pleased me more. . . . Far down the valley we could see Ravello and the sea, but that was the

Writing Theme
Artists' Perceptions

Woman at the Window at Figueras, Salvador Dali

Apostrophes and Quotation Marks   **809**

WRITING THEME   Artists' Perceptions

A. Concept Check
Quotation Marks
   1. "Welcome to this edition of *Art and Artists,*" said the announcer. "Today we will discuss surrealism and Salvador Dali."
   2. "Our guest," she continued, "Is our local art expert, Nora Freemont."
   3. "Welcome, Nora," she said. "To begin, can you tell us when the surrealist movement was at its height?"
   4. Freemont replied, "The movement was at its height in Paris in the 1920's and 1930's."
   5. She pointed to a chart of the surrealist "greats": Salvador Dali, Joan Miró, André Masson, and Max Ernst.
   6. "Of these artists, the most flamboyant was Dali," she said.
   7. "Oh, dear!" thought the announcer. "I hope she doesn't talk about some of Dali's wild exploits!"
   8. Correct
   9. Pointing to a photograph of *The Persistence of Memory,* Freemont exclaimed, "His dreamy landscapes are remarkable!"
   10. "A woman once asked Dali if it was hard to paint a picture," said Freemont.
   11. Smiling, Ms. Freemont continued, "Dali replied, 'No. It's either easy or impossible.'" *or* "Smiling," Ms. Freemont continued, "Dali replied, 'No. It's either easy or impossible.'"
   12. Correct
   13. The poet Federico García Lorca once said that Cadaqués was "counterpoised between sea and hill"; however, Dali's mental landscapes never matched reality.
   14. "His landscapes," said Freemont, "were filled with images that had no rational explanation."
   15. What a surprise it was when Freemont said, "Dali died a recluse with only his mental images for comfort"!

B. Application in Literature
Punctuation
   Answers may vary. You may wish to distribute a copy of the excerpt for students to make comparisons.
   I have visited a good deal of fine scenery before and since, but have found little that has pleased me more. . . . Far down the valley we could see Ravello and the sea, but that was the only sign of another world.

Humanities Connection

Art Note *Woman at a Window in Figueras,* by Salvador Dali (1904–1989), is a fairly tame example of the Spanish surrealist's work, which was later to absorb the influence of Freud's theory of the unconscious. Here already, though, Dali's legendary imagination shows through: the lip-like clouds and the "Ford" sign are jarring images in an otherwise placid scene.

"Oh, what a perfectly lovely place," said my daughter Rose. "What a picture it would make!"

"Yes," said Mr. Sandbach. "Many a famous European gallery would be proud to have a landscape . . . as beautiful as this upon its walls."

"On the contrary," said Leyland, "it would make a very poor picture. Indeed, it is not paintable at all."

"And why is that?" said Rose, with far more deference than he deserved.

"Look, in the first place," he replied, "how intolerably straight against the sky is the line of the hill. It would need breaking up and diversifying. And where we are standing, the whole thing is out of perspective. Besides, all the colouring is monotonous and crude."

"I do not know anything about pictures," I put in, "and I do not pretend to know; but I know what is beautiful when I see it, and I am thoroughly content with this."

"Indeed, who could help being contented!" said Miss Robinson.

E. M. Forster, "The Story of a Panic"

C. Application in Writing

Setting

Answers will vary.

Teaching Tip: Titles

Emphasize that rules for enclosing titles in quotation marks apply to works referred to by their title, not to titles the students may write at the top of their own story, poem, or report.

Many people have trouble remembering when to use quotation marks and when to use italics, or underlining, when writing titles. Explain that a good rule to follow is that works published separately (book and magazines) are printed in italics. Short works that are part of larger works (poems, stories, and articles) are enclosed in quotation marks.

Stumbling Block

Some writers overuse quotation marks for emphasis or irony, or to indicate slang words and phrases. Explain that such usage is appropriate in informal writing, such as in a friendly letter, but it should be kept to a minimum in formal writing. Emphasis and irony should be made clear by other means, such as word choice and phrasing. Slang should be omitted altogether or used, if at all, without quotation marks.

only sign of another world. Oh, what a perfectly lovely place said my daughter Rose. What a picture it would make! Yes, said Mr. Sandbach. Many a famous European gallery would be proud to have a landscape. . . . as beautiful as this upon its walls. On the contrary said Leyland, it would make a very poor picture. Indeed, it is not paintable at all. And why is that? said Rose, with far more deference than he deserved. Look, in the first place, he replied how intolerably straight against the sky is the line of the hill. It would need breaking up and diversifying. And where we are standing the whole thing is out of perspective. Besides all the colouring is monotonous and crude. I do not know anything about pictures I put in and I do not pretend to know: but I know what is beautiful when I see it, and I am thoroughly content with this. Indeed, who could help being contented! said Miss Robinson.

E. M. Forster, "The Story of a Panic"

C. APPLICATION IN WRITING

Setting Establish a setting for a science-fiction story or a Victorian Gothic mystery. Reveal the setting through the comments of two or three people. Combine narrative and dialogue to convey the details and mood of the setting.

Setting Off Titles

Use quotation marks to enclose chapter titles, part titles, and titles of short stories, poems, essays, articles, television episodes, songs, and short musical selections.

Chapter Title	Chapter 3: "Women in Colonial America"
Part Title	Part 3: "Europe in the Twentieth Century"
Short Story	Katherine Mansfield's "The Garden Party"
Poem	Emily Dickinson's "I'm Nobody"
Essay	Charles Lamb's "A Dissertation upon Roast Pig"
Article	"What's New about New Age Music?"
TV Episode	"Thanksgiving" on *The Cosby Show*
Song	"Auld Lang Syne"

The titles of books, magazines, newspapers, TV or radio series, plays, paintings, epic poems, or long musical compositions are underlined in writing or typing and italicized in print.

Setting Off Words Used in Special Ways

Use quotation marks to give special expression to words.

A writer may use quotation marks to show emphasis or irony or to set off words classified as slang.

> The "short paint job" my mother asked me to do took all day. (The phrase *short paint job* is being used ironically.)
> Mayor Richard J. Daley was known as the "Boss" of Chicago politics. (The word *Boss* is enclosed in quotation marks to show emphasis.)
> Two "far-out" fads of the 1970's were pet rocks and platform shoes. (The term *far-out* is enclosed in quotation marks because it is slang.)

Punctuation Note Foreign words and words referred to as words are italicized or underlined. Phrases, however, are usually put in quotation marks. Also underline or italicize letters or figures referred to as such.

> The word *pantophobia* refers to the fear of everything.
> Blanca ordered *rajas,* strips of roasted, peeled chiles.
> Sabrina asked what the phrase "purple prose" meant.

Practice Your Skills

A. CONCEPT CHECK

Quotation Marks and Underlining Rewrite the following sentences, adding quotation marks and underlining where necessary.

1. In the chapter The Home Fronts, C. L. Sulzberger describes civilian life during World War II.
2. In France, many civilians were part of la résistance, the resistance movement against the Nazis.
3. The British huddled together in bomb shelters, singing God Save the King and Roll out the Barrel as the Luftwaffe dropped bombs on their cities.
4. In the United States, the closest people came to the war was through movies such as Mrs. Miniver and Thirty Seconds over Tokyo.
5. During that time, girls wore huge sloppy Joe sweaters, saddle shoes, and short socks, dubbed bobbysox.
6. They swooned over Frank the Voice Sinatra and worked in munitions factories as W.O.W.'s, the acronym for Women Ordnance Workers.
7. People bought war bonds and planted small gardens, called victory gardens, to supplement their food rations.

Writing Theme
The 1940's

Apostrophes and Quotation Marks **811**

Linking Grammar and Literature

Display the following lines from Shakespeare's *Macbeth*:

> I had most need of blessing, and "Amen"
> Stuck in my throat.
> (II, 2, 33)

Ask students to explain how the quotation marks help to clarify the meaning.

> **Additional Resources**
> • Grammar and Usage Practice Book, p. 100

WRITING THEME   The 1940's

Interested students might enjoy interviewing people with memories of the 1940's and using their findings as the basis for a writing assignment.

A. Concept Check

Quotation Marks and Underlining

1. In the chapter "The Home Fronts," C. L. Sulzberger describes civilian life during World War II.
2. In France, many civilians were part of la résistance, the resistance movement against the Nazis.
3. The British huddled together in bomb shelters, singing "God Save the King" and "Roll out the Barrel" as the Luftwaffe dropped bombs on their cities.
4. In the United States, the closest people came to the war was through movies such as Mrs. Miniver and Thirty Seconds over Tokyo.
5. During that time, girls wore huge "sloppy Joe" sweaters, saddle shoes, and short socks, dubbed "bobbysox."
6. They swooned over Frank "the Voice" Sinatra and worked in munitions factories as W.O.W.'s, the acronym for "Women Ordnance Workers."
7. People bought war bonds and planted small gardens, called "victory gardens," to supplement their food rations.

8. The "V for victory" sign, made with the first two fingers to form the letter V, became a familiar gesture.

9. The war became real for everyone through Edward R. Murrow's many installments of his London after Dark radio program.

10. Likewise, songs such as "This Is the Army, Mr. Jones" let the people know what life was like for the soldiers—or "boys in fatigues."

B. Proofreading Skill

Quotation Marks and Underlining
Errors are underlined on page.

Many writers blossomed in the 1940's. Among them was Elizabeth Bowen, whose novel The Heat of the Day was set in wartime London. America's First Lady, Eleanor Roosevelt, wrote the essay "Must We Hate to Fight?" It was published in Saturday Review magazine. Poets also expressed their feelings about war and reflected on the fact that World War I was the so-called "war to end all wars." Charles Causley's poem "At the British War Cemetery, Bayeux" is a work on this theme. Many poets' works may be found in the anthology Poems of This War, a collection of poetry written during and about World War II.

Of course, not all creative people were focusing on the war. Walt Disney, for example, produced the movies Fantasia and Pinocchio, which let moviegoers enjoy the technology of animation. Noel Coward's play Blithe Spirit (1941) amused people in the theaters and, later, in the movie houses. J. B. Priestley, who was honored as one of the "living greats" in England when he received the Order of Merit, wrote the play An Inspector Calls. Also, his humorous essays, such as "The Marx Brothers," "Women and Clothes," and "No School Report," were published in his collection titled Delight (1949).

 Individualizing Instruction

Basic Students For Exercise A, you may want students to concentrate on one error at a time. Have them do the set of sentences three times, each time correcting just one of the errors mentioned in the instructions.

C H E C K P O I N T
PAGES 802–812

Additional Resources
• Grammar and Usage Practice Book, p. 101

WRITING THEME   O. Henry

A.

1. William Sydney Porter, who's better known as O. Henry, was, in his own words, "born and raised in 'No'th Ca'lina.'"

2. He learned the three R's in his aunt Evelina's school.

3. Tom Tate, a schoolmate in the 1860's, wrote that, even as a boy, Porter had a "quaint dry humor."

---

8. The V for victory sign, made with the first two fingers to form the letter V, became a familiar gesture.

9. The war became real for everyone through Edward R. Murrow's many installments of his London After Dark radio program.

10. Likewise, songs such as This Is the Army, Mr. Jones let people know what life was like for the soldiers—or boys in fatigues.

B. PROOFREADING SKILL

Quotation Marks and Underlining Rewrite the following paragraphs, adding quotation marks and underlining as necessary. Also, correct errors in spelling, capitalization, and punctuation.

Many writers blossomed in the 1940s. Among them was Elizabeth Bowen, who's novel The Heat of the Day was set in wartime london. Americas first lady, Eleanor Roosevelt, wrote the essay Must We Hate to Fight? It was published in the Saturday Review magazine. Poets also expressed their feelings about war and reflected on the fact that World War I was the so-called 'war to end all wars.' Charles Causley's poem At the British War Cemetery, Bayeux is a work on this theme. Many poets' works may be found in the anthology Poems of This War, a collection of poetry about World War II.

Of course, not all Creative People were focusing on the war. Walt Disney, for example, produced the movies Fantasia and Pinocchio, which let moviegoers enjoy the technology of annimation. Noel Coward's play Blithe Spirit (1941) amused people in the theaters and, later, in the movie houses. J. B. Priestley, who was honored as one of the *living greats* in England when he received the Order of Merit, wrote the play An Inspector Calls. Also, his humorous essays, such as The Marx Brothers, Women and Clothes, and No School Report, were published in his collection titled Delight (1949.)

C H E C K P O I N T
PAGES 802–812

A. Rewrite the following sentences, correcting errors in the use of apostrophes, quotation marks, and underlining.

1. William Sydney Porter, whos better known as O. Henry, was, in his own words, born and raised in 'No th Ca lina.'

2. He learned the three Rs in his aunt Evelinas school.

3. Tom Tate, a schoolmate in the 1860s, wrote that, even as a boy, Porter had a 'Quaint dry humor.'

Writing Theme
O. Henry

4. In Porters first comedy satire, his "dramatis personae" were characterized by the townfolks quirks and foibles.

5. It was some time before the young playwright was on speaking terms with some of his old friends said Tate.

6. Porter fondly recalled joining friends at Miss Ethels' or Miss Sallies' house and singing Swanee River.

7. An easygoing manner and joie de vivre were his', in spite of frequent 'bouts of ill health.

8. Porter once wrote that he was 'in the hands of a fine tyrant of a doctor;' nevertheless, he would complete a manuscript in two weeks time.

9. Later, in Texas, he served as the editor of a humor magazine "The Rolling Stone."

10. Porter even wrote poems for it, such as Nothing to Say.

11. The National Bank's of Austin accusation of embezzlement resulted in his serving what fellow inmates called a stint in the slammer.

12. Anyones assumption of his guilt, however, may be in error.

13. Many peoples opinion is that poor bookkeeping, not theft, was to blame.

14. Later, when Porter wrote as O. Henry, he lived in New York, which he nicknamed Bagdad-on-the-Subway.

15. No ones prose has stirred the heart so much as O. Henrys short story *The Gift of the Magi*.

B. APPLICATION IN LITERATURE

Punctuation   In the following passage, correct punctuation and paragraphing have been omitted. Rewrite the passage to return it to its original, correct form.

Dont lie to me she [Hetty] said, calmly. What were you going to do with that onion? The young man suppressed a cough and faced her resolutely. . . . I was going to eat it said he with emphatic slowness just as I told you before. And you have nothing else to eat at home? Not a thing. What kind of work do you do? I am not working at anything just now. Then why said Hetty, with her voice set on its sharpest edge do you lean out of a window and give orders to chauffeurs in green automobiles in the street below? Because madam said he in *accelerando* tones I pay the chauffeurs wages and I own the automobile—and also this onion—this onion, madam. He flourished the onion within an inch of Hettys nose. . . . Then why pursued Hetty, inflexibly were you going to eat a raw onion? My mother said the young man always made me eat one for a cold.

O. Henry, "The Third Ingredient"

4. In Porter's first comedy satire, his dramatis personae were characterized by the townfolks' quirks and foibles.

5. "It was some time before the young playwright was on speaking terms with some of his old friends," said Tate.

6. Porter fondly recalled joining friends at Miss Ethel's or Miss Sallie's house and singing "Swanee River."

7. An easygoing manner and joie de vivre were his, in spite of frequent bouts of ill health.

8. Porter once wrote that he was "in the hands of a fine tyrant of a doctor"; nevertheless, he would complete a manuscript in two weeks' time.

9. Later, in Texas, he served as the editor of a humor magazine, The Rolling Stone.

10. Porter even wrote poems for it, such as "Nothing to Say."

11. The National Bank of Austin's accusation of embezzlement resulted in his serving what his fellow inmates called "a stint in the slammer."

12. Anyone's assumption of his guilt, however, may be in error.

13. Many people's opinion is that poor bookkeeping, not theft, was to blame.

14. Later, when Porter wrote as O. Henry, he lived in New York, which he nicknamed "Bagdad-on-the-Subway."

15. No one's prose has stirred the heart so much as O. Henry's short story "The Gift of the Magi."

B. Application in Literature

Punctuation

"Don't lie to me," she [Hetty] said, calmly. "What were you going to do with that onion?"

The young man suppressed a cough and faced her resolutely. . . . "I was going to eat it," said he with emphatic slowness, "just as I told you before."

"And you have nothing else to eat at home?"

"Not a thing."

"What kind of work do you do?"

"I am not working at anything just now."

"Then why," said Hetty, with her voice set on its sharpest edge, "do you lean out of a window and give orders to chauffeurs in green automobiles in the street below?"

"Because, madam," said he in *accelerando* tones, "I pay the chauffeur's wages and I own the automobile—and also this onion—this onion, madam." He flourished the onion within an inch of Hetty's nose. . . .

"Then why," pursued Hetty, inflexibly, "were you going to eat a raw onion?"

"My mother," said the young man, "always made me eat one for a cold."

O. Henry, "The Third Ingredient"

Apostrophes and Quotation Marks   **813**

Application and Review

These activities are designed to allow your students to apply concepts presented in this handbook. In Exercises A and B, students use apostrophes, quotation marks, and underlining to correct the punctuation of sentences. In Exercise C, they correct punctuation errors in writing paragraphs of dialogue.

Additional Resources
- Tests and Assessment, Mastery Tests, pp. 70–71
- Elaboration, Revision, and Proofreading, p. 31

WRITING THEME   American Humorists

A. Apostrophes and Quotation Marks

1. Dotting the i's and crossing the t's didn't interest Samuel Clemens, better known as Mark Twain.
2. In fact, the colloquial phrase "to tickle their funny bones" might describe what Twain wished to do for his readers.
3. In his short story, "Extracts from Adam's Diary," Twain has Adam write, "The new creature says its name is Eve."
4. One critic said, "Twain's version of the folk tale 'Jim Smiley and His Jumping Frog' has established his reputation as a humorist."
5. With this story, "Washoe Giant, the wild humorist of the Sage Brush Hills," as Twain had been known in California, was now known in the East.
6. According to biographer Justin Kaplan, Twain's "variety of interests mirrored his country and his times": drama, storytelling, billiard playing, and inventing.
7. In 1906, A. B. Paine, a children's book author, said that he was honored to work on Samuel Clemens's biography.
8. Ernest Hemingway once said, "All modern American literature comes from one book by Mark Twain called *Huckleberry Finn*."
9. Kurt Vonnegut compared Hemingway's and Twain's writing.
10. He concluded that Hemingway has no ear for dialect and "he can't tell jokes"; thus, Twain remains the master.

B. Using Punctuation Correctly

Answers may vary. See suggested answers below.

1. One of America's foremost humorists in the 1940's was James Thurber.
2. No one else's witty sophistication matches that of Thurber.
3. The results of a lifetime's study of human nature can be found in Thurber's works.
4. "Most writers," said E. B. White, "would be glad to settle for any one of . . . Thurber's accomplishments."
5. Yet in '38, Thurber wrote the essay "E. B. W." that poked fun at E. B. White's exaggerated avoidance of people.

6. His story "The Catbird Seat" is a further example of his wit.
7. It was first published in The New Yorker in '42.
8. In this story the protagonist, Mr. Martin, decides to "rub out" his co-worker, Mrs. Ulgine Barrows.

GRAMMAR
HANDBOOK
41

Writing Theme
American Humorists

A. Apostrophes and Quotation Marks   Rewrite the following sentences, correcting any errors in the use of apostrophes, quotation marks, and underlining.

1. Dotting the is and crossing the ts didnt interest Samuel Clemens, better known as Mark Twain.
2. In fact, the colloquial phrase to tickle their funny bones might describe what Twain wished to do for his readers.
3. In his short story, Extracts from Adam's Diary, Twain has Adam write, 'The new creature says it's name is Eve'.
4. One critic said "Twains 'version of the folk tale "Jim Smiley and His Jumping Frog", has established his reputation as a humorist."
5. With this story 'Washoe Giant, the wild humorist of the Sage Brush Hills' as Twain had been known in California was now known in the East.
6. According to biographer Justin Kaplan, Twains "variety of interests mirrored his country and his times:" drama, storytelling, billiard playing, and inventing.
7. In 1906, A. B. Paine, a childrens' book author, said that he was honored to work on Samuel Clemens biography.
8. Ernest Hemingway once said, "all modern American literature comes from one book by Mark Twain called 'Huckleberry Finn.'"
9. Kurt Vonnegut compared Hemingway and Twain's writing.
10. He concluded that Hemingway has no ear for dialect and "he cant tell jokes;" thus, Twain remains the master.

B. Using Punctuation Correctly   Rewrite the following sentences, correcting any errors in the use of apostrophes, quotation marks, and underlining.

1. One of Americas foremost humorists in the 1940s was James Thurber.
2. No one elses witty sophistication matches that of Thurber.
3. The results of a lifetimes study of human nature can be found in Thurbers works.
4. Most writers, said E. B. White would be glad to settle for any one of. . . . Thurbers accomplishments.
5. Yet in 38, Thurber wrote the essay E. B. W. that poked fun at E. B. Whites exaggerated avoidance of people.
6. His story The Catbird Seat is a further example of his wit.
7. It was first published in The New Yorker in 42.
8. In this story the protagonist, Mr. Martin, decides to rub out his co-worker, Mrs. Ulgine Barrows.
9. The term rub out, in the words of the story, suggests nothing more than a correction of an error.

10. X. J. Kennedy's and Dorothy M. Kennedy's analysis of this work makes an interesting point.
11. One of the storys most delectable ironies they say occurs when Martin tells Barrows "Im sitting in the catbird seat'.
12. The complete story can be found in The Thurber Carnival.
13. The Catbird Seat should be recommended for everyones daily humor requirement.
14. Marc Connelly, author of the book Green Pastures, praised the work of Thurber.
15. He said, Thurber had a sense of laughter that was a cleansing thing.

C. Application in Literature The following passage includes errors in the use of apostrophes and quotation marks. Rewrite the passage using the correct punctuation. Also, although Thurber wrote the dialogue in two continuous paragraphs, follow the rules for paragraphing in rewriting it.

Mr. Martin got to the office at eight-thirty the next morning as usual. At a quarter to nine, Ulgine Barrows, who had never arrived at work before ten, swept into his office. Im reporting to Mr. Fitweiler now! she shouted. If he turns you over to the police, its no more than you deserve. Mr. Martin gave her a look of shocked surprise. I beg your pardon? he said. Mrs. Barrows snorted and bounced out of the room. . . .

Forty-five minutes later, Mrs. Barrows left the presidents office and. . . . Mr. Fitweiler sent for Mr. Martin. The head of the filing department, neat, quiet, attentive, stood in front of the old mans desk. Mr. Fitweiler was pale and nervous. . . . Martin, he said, you have been with us more than twenty years'. Twenty-two, sir, said Mr. Martin. In that time, pursued the president, your work and your—uh—manner have been exemplary. I trust so, sir, said Mr. Martin. I have understood, Martin, said Mr. Fitweiler, that you have never taken a drink or smoked. That is correct, sir, said Mr. Martin. Ah, yes. Mr. Fitweiler polished his glasses. . . . Mrs. Barrows, he said finally, Mrs. Barrows has worked hard, Martin, very hard. It grieves me to report that she has suffered a severe breakdown.

James Thurber, "The Catbird Seat"

Test 4

These exercises allow your students to practice skills acquired in Handbooks 38–41. You may wish to use the exercises to provide a thorough review of the material in these chapters or to evaluate student mastery of the concepts.

Additional Resources
- Grammar and Usage Practice Book, pp. 102–104
- Standardized Test Practice

Skills Assessment Test 4
1. A—Three Tales
   B—style:
2. A—Declaration of Independence
3. C—Ob and the Lena
4. C—thinners, or
5. A—Jerry Siegel and Joe Schuster's
   C—appearance
6. E
7. B—said,

Skills
ASSESSMENT

Directions One or more of the underlined sections in the following sentences may contain errors of grammar, usage, punctuation, spelling, or capitalization. Write the letters of each incorrect section. Then rewrite the item correctly. If there is no error in an item, write E.

> **Example** Novels <u>such as</u> "Heidi" and "Little Women" have long
>   A   B
> been considered <u>to be</u> classics of <u>childrens'</u> literature. <u>No error</u>
>   C   D   E
> **Answer** B—*Heidi* and *Little Women*, D—children's

1. Gustave Flaubert's book <u>"Three Tales"</u> consists of three stories, each illustrating a
                              A
   different <u>style</u> "The Legend of St. Julian the Hospitaller," a medieval <u>style;</u> "A
           B   C
   Simple Heart," a realistic <u>style; and "Herodias,"</u> a Biblical style. <u>No error</u>
                             D   E

2. The original <u>declaration of independence</u> <u>is preserved</u> in the
                     A   B
   <u>National Archives Building</u> in <u>Washington, D.C.</u> <u>No error</u>
       C   D   E

3. In the <u>U.S.S.R.</u> most <u>rivers, such as</u> the <u>ob and the lena,</u> flow <u>north.</u> <u>No error</u>
          A   B   C   D   E

4. Aspirin <u>should not be taken</u> by people <u>who must use</u> anticoagulants, blood
                 A   B
   <u>thinners or</u> certain drugs <u>that treat</u> diabetes. <u>No error</u>
       C   D   E

5. <u>Jerry Siegel's and Joe Schuster's</u> cartoon character <u>Superman</u> made his first
                  A   B
   <u>apearance</u> in the <u>1930's.</u> <u>No error</u>
       C   D   E

6. Of all the <u>creatures</u> on the <u>earth,</u> the clam <u>has</u> the <u>slowest</u> heart rate. <u>No error</u>
               A   B   C   D   E

7. Almost <u>two thousand</u> years ago Epictetus <u>said</u> "If you <u>wish to be</u> a <u>good</u> writer,
          A   B   C   D
   write." <u>No error</u>
        E

8. Thoreau <u>wrote, "the youth</u> gets together his materials to build a bridge to the
                A
<u>moon</u> or perchance a palace or temple on the <u>earth,</u> and at length the
 B   **C**
<u>middle-aged man</u> concludes to build a wood-shed with them." <u>No error</u>
     D   **E**

9. At the age of seventy one, actress <u>Sarah Bernhardt</u> had her leg amputated, but
            A   **B**
despite this operation and her advanced <u>age,</u> she continued <u>to preform.</u> <u>No error</u>
                             C   **D**   **E**

10. The work of <u>political cartoonist</u> Thomas Nast <u>1840-1902</u> helped to send the
                 A   **B**
<u>infamous</u> Boss Tweed to <u>prison.</u> <u>No error</u>
   C   **D**   **E**

11. Andy Warhol <u>was best known</u> for his paintings of commercial <u>products,</u> however,
             A   **B**
he <u>also</u> used silk-screen printing to reproduce pictures <u>from newspaper photographs.</u>
   C   **D**
<u>No error</u>
 E

12. Mercury and <u>Venus,</u> because they are between <u>earth</u> and the <u>Sun,</u> show phases very
            A   **B**   **C**
much <u>like</u> those of the moon. <u>No error</u>
     D   **E**

13. "A little <u>learning, wrote</u> Alexander Pope in one of <u>his</u> long <u>poems,</u> "is a dangerous
          A   **B**   **C**
<u>thing."</u> <u>No error</u>
 D   **E**

14. <u>N.A.S.A.</u> is the <u>Federal Agency</u> charged with the <u>responsibility</u> for managing the
   A   **B**   **C**
<u>nation's</u> space program. <u>No error</u>
  D   **E**

15. <u>El Dorado,</u> the legendary city of <u>gold,</u> was avidly sought by a multitude of <u>Spanish</u>
    A   **B**   **C**
conquistadors during the <u>eighteenth</u> century. <u>No error</u>
                  D   **E**

16. On <u>August 2, 1943,</u> the <u>"Amigiri,"</u> <u>a Japanese ship,</u> rammed and sank PT-109, a
      A   **B**   **C**
boat <u>commanded</u> by Lieutenant John F. Kennedy. <u>No error</u>
     D   **E**

17. A—"Help!
    B—here,"
18. B—tigers, which are extinct,
19. B—1800's
    C—Compromiser";
20. B—Morrisons
    C—their
21. E
22. E
23. C—its
24. B—Citizen Kane
25. E

17. "Help. I'm trapped under hear," yelled the motorist from beneath the collapsed
         A   B   C   D
    freeway. No error
    D   E

18. Saber-toothed tigers which are extinct open their jaws at a ninety-degree angle.
         A   B   C   D
    No error
    E

19. Henry Clay, a Whig politician of the early 1800s, was called "the Great
                   A   B
    Compromiser;" somehow that doesn't sound complimentary. No error
    C   D   E

20. For three weeks the Morrison's sailed there small boat around the Caribbean,
               A   B   C
    stopping at a different port every evening. No error
    D   E

21. "Is it true that three-fourths of the human body is made up of water?" Inez asked
     A   B   C
    the health teacher. No error
        D   E

22. The English word *reptile* comes from the Latin *repere,* meaning "to creep."
        A   C   D
    No error
    E

23. The *Washington Post* is one of the two most influential newspapers in the United
        A
    States; it's editorials help shape public opinion. No error
    B   C   D   E

24. Orson Welles is known for his film "Citizen Kane" and for his radio adaptation of
                 A   B
    H. G. Wells's novel *The War of the Worlds.* No error
    C   D   E

25. The poet William Butler Yeats married late in life and then moved
                 A   B
    into an old Norman castle called Thor Ballylee. No error
    C   D   E

Sketchbook

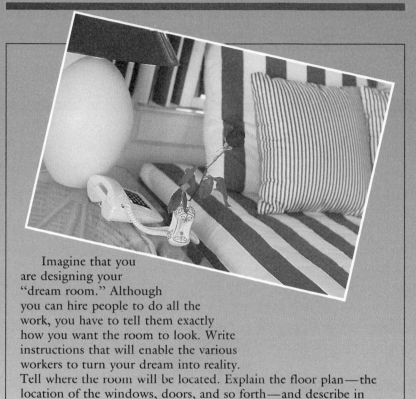

Imagine that you are designing your "dream room." Although you can hire people to do all the work, you have to tell them exactly how you want the room to look. Write instructions that will enable the various workers to turn your dream into reality. Tell where the room will be located. Explain the floor plan—the location of the windows, doors, and so forth—and describe in detail how the room should be decorated and furnished. Use correct punctuation in your instructions.

Additional Sketches

Write a fantasy dialogue between two living things or two inanimate objects in which each "character" tries to convince the other of its superiority. Make sure that you correctly capitalize and punctuate your dialogue.

A magazine publisher has asked you to create a new magazine for readers your own age. Write a proposal in which you suggest several different names for the magazine and titles for five or more possible articles for the premiere issue. Use quotation marks, apostrophes, and underlining properly.

819

Sketchbook

Objective

To use the theme of designing a "dream room" as a springboard to informal writing

Using the Prompt

Remind students that the writing activities suggested in the Sketchbook were designed to be informal in order to allow risk taking and discovery. They will not be graded.

Help students recognize the process involved in creating a "dream room." They will be giving directions not only to builders but also, once the room has been built, to interior decorators.

Students might work alone or in small collaborative learning groups, making large sketches of their "dream rooms" before writing their instructions. Encourage them to make sketches of familiar rooms as a starting point. Then have students modify their sketches, changing the shapes of the rooms and the positions of such elements as windows, doors, fireplaces, bookcases, and closets. Once the basic room has been finalized, students might draw or cut out of magazines furnishings for the room. Students might place these in their sketches, moving them around, or replacing them, or using both approaches until they finally have their perfect rooms. Students might also look through wallpaper sample books or paint samples for the perfect wall "treatments."

Once students have settled on their building and decorating ideas, have them write separate instructions for their builders and interior decorators.

The Additional Sketches section provides alternative topics for students who prefer a different starting point. Encourage students to keep their writing in their Writing Portfolios. They may wish to use ideas developed here when they work on other writing projects.

Post-Test

These exercises allow your students to practice skills acquired in the Grammar and Usage Handbook. You may wish to use the exercises as a thorough review of the material or as summative testing for the grammar and usage section of this text.

Additional Resources
• Standardized Test Practice

Skills Assessment Post Test
1. C—All." It
2. C—took
   D—effective
3. A—Many professional naturalists are sure that the so-called "wild man" of China, known only from hairs found in its leafy "bed" and from isolated sightings, actually exists.
4. C—fled from
5. C—higher
   D—China or Japan?
6. A—me
7. C—medieval
   D—instrument related to the guitar.

Skills
A S S E S S M E N T

Directions   One or more of the underlined sections in the following sentences may contain errors of grammar, usage, punctuation, spelling, or capitalization. Write the letters of each incorrect section. Then rewrite the item correctly. If there is no error in an item, write E.

> **Example**   The <u>leading roles</u> in the film <u>*Driving Miss Daisy*</u>
>   A   B
> <u>were played</u> by Jessica Tandy and <u>he.</u> <u>No error</u>
>   C   D   E
> **Answer**   D—him

1. The <u>Latin</u> expression <u>"Labor Omnia Vincit"</u> means "Labor Conquers <u>All" it</u> is
        A   B   C
   <u>Oklahoma's</u> state motto. <u>No error</u>
     D   E

2. Many species of animals became <u>extinct</u> before <u>conservationists</u> <u>had taken</u> <u>efective</u>
                                     A   B   C   D
   action. <u>No error</u>
         E

3. <u>Known only from hairs found in its leafy "bed" and from isolated sightings,</u> many
                                                A
   professional naturalists <u>are sure</u> that the so-called "wild man" of <u>China</u> actually
                              B   C
   <u>exists.</u> <u>No error</u>
     D   E

4. At the sight of <u>Patroclus</u> in the armor of <u>Achilles,</u> the fearful Trojans <u>fleed from</u>
                  A   B   C
   the <u>battlefield.</u> <u>No error</u>
        D   E

5. <u>Who</u> <u>exports</u> the <u>highest</u> volume of goods, <u>china or japan?</u> <u>No error</u>
    A   B   C   D   E

6. Just between you and <u>I,</u> I think that <u>T. S. Eliot's</u> *The Waste Land* <u>is</u> too obscure
                      A   B   C
   and fragmentary <u>to be considered</u> a finished work of art. <u>No error</u>
                  D   E

7. <u>The lute</u> <u>is</u> a <u>Medieval</u> stringed <u>instrument. Related to the guitar.</u> <u>No error</u>
     A   B   C   D   E

8. By the third chapter in the mystery <u>novel,</u> Marilyn had figured out <u>whom</u> the
    A   B
    murderer was and was no longer <u>anxious</u> to finish reading <u>it.</u> <u>No error</u>
                                    C   D   E

9. Everyone <u>should wear</u> <u>their</u> <u>most comfortable</u> pair of shoes for the hunger
              A   B   C
    Walkathon. <u>No error</u>
    D   E

10. The <u>Bostonians</u> claimed <u>that</u> they <u>didn't know nothing</u> about the <u>dumping</u> of the
        A   B   C   D
    tea into the harbor. <u>No error</u>
                         E

11. By the time this summer <u>ends;</u> the temperature <u>soars</u> above 100 degrees Fahrenheit
                            A   B
    many times, but <u>no one</u> really <u>knows</u> whether the high temperatures are due to the
                     C   D
    greenhouse effect. <u>No error</u>
                       E

12. The biologist felt <u>badly</u> about the cancelled trip to <u>Horicon Marsh</u> in Wisconsin
                       A   B
    because she had hoped to observe the <u>waterfoul</u> during their <u>fall</u> migration.
                                          C   D
    <u>No error</u>
    E

13. <u>One</u> of the <u>most enjoyable</u> parts of a vacation in the <u>greek</u> isles <u>are</u> the delicious
    A   B   C   D
    food. <u>No error</u>
          E

14. Tom Thumb, of the <u>Ringling Brothers and Barnum and Bailey Circus,</u> <u>was</u> tinier
                      A   B
    <u>than any</u> performer in the history <u>of show business.</u> <u>No error</u>
    C   D   E

15. "Nothing endures but <u>change,</u>" wrote <u>the philosopher Heraclitus,</u> and students of
                         A   B
    geology <u>attest to</u> the truth of <u>this</u> statement. <u>No error</u>
            C   D   E

16. While in prison, <u>O. Henry</u> <u>wrote</u> *The Gift of the Magi* and <u>many other short stories.</u>
                     A   B   C   D
    <u>No error</u>
    E

17. B—too
    C—weird
18. E
19. C—advertising
    D—Walking through the school, we saw many posters and signs advertising the concert.
20. A—taught
    C—Mozart
21. A—We
    B—today's
22. B—most barren
    D—there
23. A—Vietnam War Memorial
24. E
25. C—Sorbonne, was

17. The producer of the talk show decided that the segment <u>about the dancing snakes</u>
    A
    was just <u>to</u> <u>wierd</u> <u>to be shown</u> on the air. <u>No error</u>
         B **C**   **D**   **E**

18. When John Steinbeck lived <u>in Monterey, California,</u> there was a great sardine fish-
                              A
    ery in <u>Monterey Bay,</u> but now all the sardines have been killed by <u>overfishing, and</u>
           B   **C**
    the great canneries have <u>disappeared.</u> <u>No error</u>
                             D   **E**

19. We <u>saw</u> many <u>posters</u> and signs <u>advertizing</u> the concert, <u>walking through the school.</u>
         A   **B**   **C**   **D**
    <u>No error</u>
    E

20. Hayden <u>learned</u> Mozart <u>much</u> of what <u>he</u> knew <u>about writing symphonic music.</u>
            A   **B**   **C**   **D**
    <u>No error</u>
    E

21. <u>Us</u> science fiction buffs know that <u>todays</u> science fiction is <u>tomorrow's</u>
    A   **B**   **C**
    <u>ordinary daily reality.</u> <u>No error</u>
    D   **E**

22. <u>Deserts</u> are among the <u>most barrenest</u> places on the <u>earth, yet</u> even <u>their</u> life exists.
    A   **B**   **C**   **D**
    <u>No error</u>
    E

23. The designer of the <u>vietnam war memorial</u> originally planned that <u>it</u>
                         A   **B**
    <u>would represent</u> <u>all who fought</u> in the war. <u>No error</u>
    C   **D**   **E**

24. <u>Each</u> <u>of these</u> <u>elements</u>—nobelium, iodine, radium, and europium—<u>appears</u> in the
    A   **B**   **C**   **D**
    table. <u>No error</u>
           E

25. One of the <u>world's</u> <u>most famous universities,</u> the <u>Sorbonne was</u> founded in the
               A   **B**   **C**
    <u>1200's.</u> <u>No error</u>
    D   **E**

This appendix provides some of the material most commonly needed by student writers.

Appendix

© Eugene Mihaesco, 1991

IDEAS FOR WRITING

Writing ideas can come from just about any situation or experience. To stimulate your thinking, study the following lists. Then use your own discovery techniques to narrow your topic and organize it effectively.

Narrative
a bike race
a surprise ending
mending a relationship
leaving
no way out
the lesser of two evils
sudden good fortune
something from nothing
an unsolved mystery
a comic experience
a piano lesson
an unexpected encounter
making the news
a protest march

Descriptive
a December morning
sounds of a warm summer
    night
the circus
a favorite relative
an eccentric friend
a nonstop talker
a snowstorm
an airport at midnight
the coach's office
a famous place
electronic music
a snake
a courtroom
mosquitoes in paradise
an ocean beach
a science experiment
an empty stadium

Literary
an encounter with an
    intelligent being from
    another planet
a poem about someone you
    care for
a frightening experience
the Salem witches
gold mining in Alaska
a mysterious package
grappling with technology
    in everyday life
a medical discovery
a tall tale

Informative Exposition
What are "natural
    ingredients"?
Define selfishness.
What is jealousy?
Define one's "turf."
What does "cultural
    pluralism" mean?
What makes a good
    neighbor?
What is a stereotype?
What is the effect on society
    of good public schools?
What are the effects of
    television violence on
    children?
What causes a recession?
How have television news
    reports changed in the
    last 10 years?

How would you solve a
    currently important social
    issue?
What is the best way to raise
    money for a good cause?
Explain how to win a
    political campaign.
How can prime-time
    television be improved?

Persuasive
Should the government
    provide housing for
    homeless people?
What is a fair tax rate?
Should the United States
    convert to the metric
    system?
Should extremist groups be
    tolerated under the First
    Amendment?
Should drug tests be
    required of student
    athletes?
Should college admission be
    based solely on academic
    achievement?
Should anyone be allowed to
    censor art?
Should advertisers be
    allowed to use subliminal
    messages?
Should the federal
    government pay for all
    medical care?

Ideas for Writing in Subject Areas

The Arts
multimedia events and
  installations
realism in literature
How did jazz originate?
earth sculpture
Pennsylvania folk art
living museums
rock concerts in the 90's
Samuel Beckett
Shakespeare's plays with
  modern settings
the music of Duke Ellington
classical piano competitions
jazz dance
art censorship
Mozart's genius
John Huston's films

Science
acupuncture
songs of whales
causes/effects of ozone-
  layer thinning
how a CD player works
breaking an addiction
calculating the orbits of
  planets
magnetic resonance
  imaging
cancer research
laser technology
chemical warfare
predicting tornadoes
how radar works
space exploration
genome mapping

Social Science
the conference at Yalta
What motivated the early
  explorers?
the Children's Crusade
the worldwide economic
  depression of the 1930's
compare and contrast
  Europe after WWI and
  WWII.
the Industrial Revolution in
  Europe
the civil rights movement
laying the first trans-Atlantic
  cable
the statues at Easter Island
the beginnings of radio
the Magna Carta

Term Paper Topics

The Arts
cartoons that reflect society
Jane Austen's world
yellow journalism
Theater of the Absurd
protest songs
Indian pottery of the
  Southwest
the rise of female detectives
great landscape painters
music videos
how computer technology
  can alter photographs
history of science fiction
outdoor sculpture gardens
the life of Beethoven
designs of Helmut Jahn
Impressionism

Science
controlling viruses
carcinogens in food
  preservatives
insect communication
  systems
the Bermuda triangle
toxic waste control
aerospace medicine
What causes smog?
Why do people acquire
  habits?
What are the effects on
  people of continuous
  noise?
How is weather predicted?
What is a radio telescope?
industrial uses of lasers

Social Science
inside the Supreme Court
techniques of behavior
  modification
the Battle of Waterloo
the settlement of Alaska
ancient Japanese culture
Roman ruins in England
the Oregon Trail
the purpose of Stonehenge
the New Deal
the rise of Mao Zedong in
  China
demographic changes in the
  U.S.
the fall of the Berlin Wall
political importance of
  natural resources

OUTLINE FORM

Outlining helps you organize information and ideas in a concise and logical way. Outlining can also be an effective note-taking technique. Working from an outline as you write enables you to concentrate more on giving clarity and interest to the way in which you express ideas.

Methods of Outlining

Outlines can be both informal and formal. An **informal outline** is usually little more than a list of ideas or details arranged in the order in which the author wishes to present them. A **formal outline** is much more detailed. It shows the main points of a topic, subtopics that will also be covered, the order in which these main topics and subtopics are to be presented, and the relationships among them.

There are two types of formal outlines: sentence outlines and topic outlines. In a **sentence outline,** the thesis statement, the main topics, and the subtopics are all presented as complete sentences. In a **topic outline,** these same elements are presented as phrases.

A sentence ouline, shown below, is the most effective type to use for an essay.

The Colorado River: Lifeblood of the Southwest

Thesis Statement: The American Southwest depends on the resources of the Colorado River.

I. The Colorado River irrigates three million acres.
  A. The river is 1,450 miles long.
  B. It irrigates farmland in seven states and Mexico.
II. The Colorado River Compact regulates use of the water.
  A. In 1922, the seven basin states signed an agreement to regulate the use of the river's water.
  B. The compact covers new uses of the water.
    1. Hydroelectric power is supplied to southern Nevada and southern California for industries and homes.
    2. Drinking water is supplied to southern California and Arizona.

A topic outline, a portion of which is shown below, is less wordy.

How Streets Are Named

Purpose: to explain how various sources are used for naming streets.

 I. Geographical Features
  A. Terrain
   1. Prairie Street
   2. Cliff Drive
  B. Bodies of Water
   1. Ocean Parkway
   2. Riverside Drive
 II. Destinations
  A. Michigan Avenue
  B. Plymouth Road
 III. Famous People
  A. Presidents
   1. Washington
   2. Adams
  B. People Important to a City
   1. M. L. King Drive
   2. Rosa Parks Boulevard

Standard Outline Form   Following is a brief explanation of the form used in the sample outlines above.

1. Write the title at the top of the page. Below it, write a brief statement of your purpose.
2. Use the arrangement of numerals and letters that you see in the two models.
3. Indent each subheading, placing it directly under the first letter in the first word of the preceding heading.
4. Either use two or more subheadings or details under a heading or subheading, or don't use any at all. In other words, for every *A* there should be a *B*, and for every *1*, a *2*.
5. Items of the same rank in a topic outline should be parallel. That is, if *A* is a verb, then *B* also should be a verb. Subtopics and main topics, however, do not need to be parallel.
6. Capitalize the first word in each item. Do not use end punctuation in topic outlines.

B USINESS LETTERS

When you use the correct form for your business letter, you make a positive impression on your reader. Following are explanations of the parts of a business letter and examples of two correct business letter forms.

Block Form and Modified Block Form

Use plain, white, 8½″ x 11″ paper for all business letters, whether you handwrite or type them. In **block form,** all parts begin at the left margin. Use this form only when you type the letter. In **modified block form,** the heading, closing, and signature are aligned near the right margin; the other parts begin at the left margin.

Block Form

```
_____ Heading
_____
_____ Date

_____ Inside
_____ Address
_____

_____: Salutation

_____
_____
_____ Body
_____
_____

_____, Closing
           Signature
```

Modified Block Form

```
           Heading _____
                   _____
           Date    _____

_____ Inside
_____ Address
_____

_____: Salutation

_____
_____
_____ Body
_____
_____

           Closing _____,
           Signature
```

Heading The heading is written at the top of the page. The first line contains your street address; the second line contains your town or city, state, and ZIP code. Separate the city and state with a comma and write out the name of the state. The third line gives the date of the letter. Place the heading at the left or the right margin, depending on whether you use the block form or the modified block form.

Inside Address The inside address tells to whom the letter is being sent. Place the inside address at the left margin at least four lines below the heading. On the first line you should place the name of the receiver. If there is room, place the person's title on the same line, separated from the name by a comma. Otherwise, place the title on the next line. If you do not know the name of the person who will receive your letter, use the person's title or the name of the department. On the succeeding lines, place the company name and address, including the city, state, and ZIP code.

The inside address is important because occasionally a letter is opened by someone other than the addressee, and the envelope is discarded. If this happens, the name and address of the receiver can still be found in the inside address. Following are two typical inside addresses.

Ms. Deborah Aktar	Water Department
Gaia Computers, Inc.	City of Austin
1132 Falls Road	206 East Ninth Street
Coloma, Michigan 49038	Austin, Texas 78701

Salutation Position the salutation two lines below the inside address. Begin with the word *Dear*, follow it by the name of the person to whom you are writing, and end with a colon. Use only the person's last name, preceded by a title such as *Mr., Mrs., Ms., Dr.,* or *Professor.* If you do not know the person's name, use a general salutation such as *Ladies and Gentlemen.* Another alternative is to write to a department or to a position within a company. The following forms are acceptable:

Dear Mr. Sanders:	Dear Sir or Madam:
Dear Ms. Joyce:	Dear Product Information Department:
Dear Mrs. Alegria:	Dear Executive Director:

Body The body, the main part of the letter in which you write your message, begins two spaces below the salutation. The body may contain a single paragraph or several paragraphs. Leave a space between each paragraph.

Closing The closing is placed two lines below the body, in line with the heading. Closings commonly used for business letters include *Sincerely, Sincerely yours,* and *Very truly yours.* Note that only the first word is capitalized and that the closing ends with a comma.

Signature Type or print your name four spaces below the closing, and sign your name in the space between.

USING A WORD PROCESSOR

Because word processors are widely used in business, knowing word processing may increase your employment opportunities. Following are some techniques to help you use a word processor effectively.

Goal	Technique	Comment
Create a record of observations, ideas, and experiences that especially interest you.	Create a file that functions like an expandable notebook.	Your electronic notebook can become an efficient way to retrieve ideas quickly and expand on them freely.
Exchange ideas with other students.	Use a disk of class ideas, available to anyone in the class.	Each class member might have a file on this disk. By opening your own file, you can add an idea or read others' responses to your ideas.
Experiment with language and style.	Express the same idea in a number of different ways. Separate alternatives using slashes (/).	Later, use the search command to find the slashes. Choose the best alternative and delete the others.
Add, replace, or reorder text.	Use the insert, delete, replace, move, cut, and paste commands.	A word processor encourages revision and experimentation because changes are simple and easy to make.

Goal	Technique	Comment
Quickly input revisions you've marked on a printout.	Use the search command to locate each word or phrase you wish to change.	Using search enables you to move quickly through your paper as you make changes and corrections.
Check your spelling.	Activate the "spelling" command if your program has one. In addition, always proofread carefully.	The program will highlight misspellings, many typing errors, and most proper nouns. Proofread for errors the program cannot catch, such as incorrect words.
Simplify business communications.	Set up attractive formats for different types of business communications, such as letters and memos. Save time by using a small number of basic formats.	A word processor can help you send copies of a similar letter to many people or organizations. For each copy, keep the heading, body, and closing the same; change the date, inside address, and salutation.
Create the right format for your document.	Experiment with type sizes and styles. You may even want to try a page layout program and a high quality printer.	Using a desktop publishing program even allows you to integrate text and graphics. Perhaps you will decide to publish a newsletter for your organization.

TECHNIQUES FOR PEER RESPONSE

The following response techniques can help you give and receive useful responses as you share your writing with others. These techniques can also help you as the writer to be in charge of the feedback process and to find out what kinds of responses are most useful to you.

How to Use	When to Use
Sharing	
Read your words out loud to a peer. Your purpose is simply to share and to hear how your words sound. Your listeners may ask you to slow down or to read your piece again, but they offer no feedback or criticism of any kind.	Do this when you are just exploring and you don't want criticism. Reading to a peer is also useful when your writing is finished and you want to celebrate by sharing it with another person.
Saying Back or Restating	
Ask readers, "What do you hear me saying?" As readers say back what they hear, they are inviting you to figure out better what you really want to say.	Use this type of feedback when you are still exploring and when you want to find ways to change and develop your ideas.
Pointing	
Ask readers to tell you what they like best in your writing. Tell them to pick specific parts of the writing and to avoid simply saying, "I liked it."	Use this technique when you want to know what is getting through to readers or when you want some encouragement and support.

How to Use	When to Use
Summarizing	
Ask readers to tell you what they hear as the main meaning or message in your writing. Make clear that you don't want evaluation of the writing at this time.	Use this technique when you want to know what is getting through to readers.
Responding to Specific Features	
Ask for feedback on specific features of the writing such as the organization, or the persuasive power, or the spelling and punctuation. Ask readers to respond to specific questions, such as, "Are the ideas supported with enough examples?" "Did I persuade you?" "Is the organization clear enough so you could follow the ideas easily?"	Use when you want a quick overview of the strengths and weaknesses of your piece.
Replying	
Discuss the ideas in your writing with your readers. Ask readers to give you their ideas on the topic. Be sure to talk with your peer readers about *what* you have said, not *how* you have said it.	Use this strategy when you want to make your writing richer by using new ideas.
Playing Movies of the Reader's Mind	
Invite readers to tell you what happens inside their heads as they read your writing. Interrupt the reading and ask readers to tell you what they are thinking at the moment of interruption.	This technique is useful at any stage of the writing. Because it can lead to blunt criticism, use this peer response method only when you have a relationship of trust and support with your reader.

Adapted from *Sharing and Responding* by Peter Elbow and Pat Belanoff.

Techniques for
Peer Response   **833**

SENTENCE DIAGRAMING

A sentence diagram is a drawing that helps you understand how the parts of a sentence are related. In addition, diagraming sharpens your critical thinking skills by requiring you to analyze sentences, classify their parts, and determine relationships among those parts.

The base for a sentence diagram is made up of a horizontal main line crossed by a short vertical line.

Subjects and Verbs

Place the simple subject on the horizontal main line to the left of the vertical line. Place the simple predicate, or verb, to the right. Capitalize only those words that are capitalized in the sentence. Do not use punctuation except for abbreviations.

Stars twinkle.   Construction has begun.

| Stars | twinkle | | Construction | has begun |

Interrogative Sentences

In an interrogative sentence, the subject often comes after the verb or after part of the verb phrase. In diagraming, remember to place the subject before the verb to the left of the vertical line.

Is anyone studying?   Do animals dream?

| anyone | Is studying | | animals | Do dream |

Imperative Sentences

In an imperative sentence, the subject is usually not stated. Since commands are given to the person spoken to, the subject is understood to be *you*. To diagram an imperative sentence, place the understood subject *you* to the left of the vertical line. Then enclose *you* in parentheses. Place the verb to the right of the vertical line.

Go!   Rush!

| (you) | Go | | (you) | Rush |

Modifiers

Diagram adjectives and adverbs on slanted lines below the words they modify. If an adverb modifies an adjective or another adverb, write the adverb on an L–shaped line connected to the adjective or adverb that it modifies. Keep in mind that words like *not* and *never* are adverbs.

The old car would not start quickly enough.

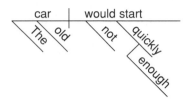

When two or more modifiers are connected by a conjunction, place the modifiers on slanted lines below the words they modify. Connect the slanted lines with a broken line and write the conjunction on it.

The untrained but eager staff worked quite competently.

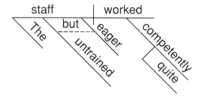

Direct and Indirect Objects

In a diagram, place the direct object on the main line after the verb. Separate the direct object from the verb with a vertical line that does not extend below the main line. Place indirect objects below the verb on lines parallel to the main line and connected to the main line by slanted lines, as you see here.

Bret was telling Sarah a long and implausible story.

Subject Complements

Place a predicate nominative or a predicate adjective on the main line after the verb. Separate the subject complement from the verb with a slanted line that extends in the direction of the subject.

Rosa is the nominee.
(*Predicate nominative*)

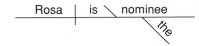

The foreman looked extremely proud.
(*Predicate adjective*)

Sentences with Compound Parts

To diagram compound parts, place the parts on parallel horizontal lines as shown below. Then connect the parallel lines with a broken line. On the broken line, write the conjunction that connects the compound parts. Attach the compound parts to the main line with solid diagonal lines. The sentence below has a compound subject and a compound verb.

James Joyce and Elizabeth Bowen left Ireland and wrote important novels.

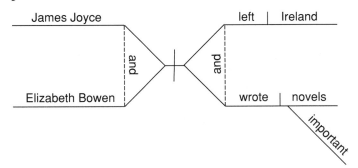

Compound Direct Objects and Indirect Objects To diagram compound direct objects or indirect objects, place the objects on parallel horizontal lines connected with a broken line. Write the conjunction on the broken line. Attach the compound parts to the main line as shown below.

The director gave Susan and me our scripts and costumes.

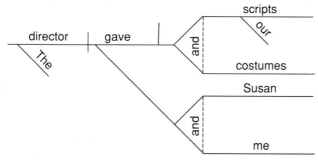

Prepositional Phrases

Draw a slanted line below the word the phrase modifies. From the slanted line, draw a line parallel to the main line. Place the preposition on the slanted line and the object of the preposition on the parallel line. Words that modify the object of the preposition are placed on slanted lines below the object.

Dom ordered a copy of the book.

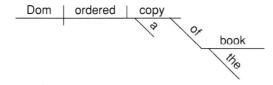

Under the house lived a fat raccoon.

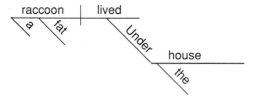

Gerunds and Gerund Phrases

To diagram a gerund, place it on a line drawn as a step (⌐L). Put the step on a forked line (∧) that stands on the main line. The placement of the forked line varies and is determined by how the gerund or gerund phrase is used.

We like trying foods from different countries. (*Gerund phrase used as direct object*)

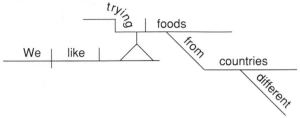

After arriving, the team gave a cheer. (*Gerund phrase used as the object of a preposition.*)

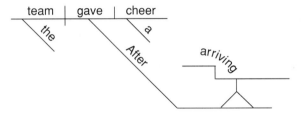

Participles and Participial Phrases

To diagram a participle, place the participle on an angled line below the word it modifies. If the participial phrase includes a direct object, separate the object and the participle with a vertical line. Place modifiers on slanted lines below words they modify.

Quickly calculating the risk, she scaled the wall.

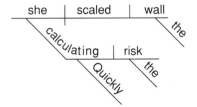

Infinitives and Infinitive Phrases

To diagram an infinitive, place the infinitive on an angled line. Write the word *to* on the slanted part and write the verb on the horizontal part of the angled line. Put the angled line on a forked line that stands on the main line. The placement shows how the infinitive or infinitive phrase is used in the sentence. In the sentences below, the infinitive is used first as a direct object and then as a subject.

Millie hoped to see a good play soon.

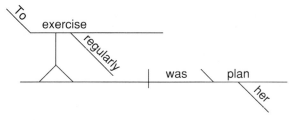

To exercise regularly was her plan.

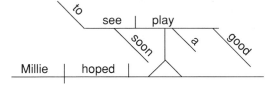

Appositives and Appositive Phrases

To diagram an appositive, place the appositive in parentheses after the word it identifies or explains. Place modifiers on slanted lines below the appositive.

The author, a dynamic speaker, lectured about UFO's.

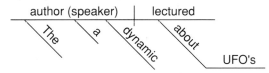

Adjective Clauses

To diagram an adjective clause, place the clause on its own horizontal line below the main line and diagram it as if it were a sentence. Use a broken line to connect the relative pronoun in the adjective clause to the word that the clause modifies.

The car that I borrowed belongs to Tammy.

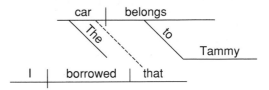

Adverb Clauses

To diagram an adverb clause, place the clause on its own horizontal line below the main line, and diagram the clause as if it were a sentence. Use a broken line to connect the adverb clause to the word it modifies. Write the subordinating conjunction on the broken line.

When his friend whistled, we dashed outside.

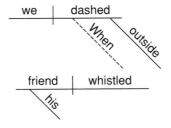

Noun Clauses

To diagram a noun clause, place the clause on a separate line that is attached to the main line with a forked line. The placement of the forked line in the diagram shows how the noun clause is used in the sentence. Diagram the word introducing the noun clause according to its function in the clause.

Whoever requested it got help. (*Noun clause used as subject*)

Compound Sentences

To diagram a compound sentence, place the independent clauses on parallel horizontal lines. Use a broken line with a step to connect the verb in one clause to the verb in the other clause. Write the conjunction on the step. If the clauses are joined by a semicolon, leave the step blank.

They accepted my story, but the editor delayed publication.

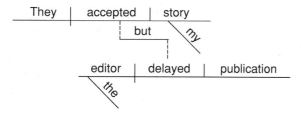

Complex Sentences

To diagram a complex sentence, decide whether the subordinate clause is an adjective clause, an adverb clause, or a noun clause. Then follow the rule for diagraming that kind of clause.

Compound-Complex Sentences

To diagram a compound-complex sentence, diagram the independent clauses first. Then attach the subordinate clause or clauses to the words they modify. Leave enough room to attach a subordinate clause where it belongs. For noun clauses, decide how the clause is used in the independent clause and place it accordingly.

The baseball bats were packed, but the helmets that the team needed were missing.

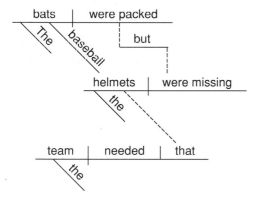

GLOSSARY FOR WRITERS

ALLEGORY a story in which the major events and characters have hidden or symbolic meanings; a quarrel between friends, for example, might represent a conflict between their native cultures.

ALLITERATION repetition of beginning sounds of words in poetry or prose; for example, the "c" sound in "creeping cat."

ALLUSION a reference to a historical or literary person, place, event, or aspect of culture.

ANALOGY a comparison used to explain an idea or support an argument. An analogy for strengthening a person's own values might be created by comparing that process with tending a garden.

ANALYSIS a way of thinking that involves taking apart, examining, and explaining a subject or idea.

ANECDOTE a brief story, told as an example to illustrate a point.

ARGUMENT speaking or writing that takes a position or states an opinion and provides the evidence or reasons to support it—often in a context of opposing points of view.

AUDIENCE the readers or listeners to whom any discourse is directed.

AUTOBIOGRAPHY a biography (life story) told by the person whose life it is.

BIAS to have a bias or be biased is to lean toward one side in an argument or contest; to be *unbiased* is to be neutral.

BRAINSTORMING a way of gathering many ideas by quickly listing them as they occur, without judging their usefulness.

CAUSE AND EFFECT a strategy for analyzing a subject by examining the reasons for specific actions or events or the consequences or results of certain causes.

CHARACTERIZATION the way people (the *characters*) are portrayed in a narrative work.

CLASSIFICATION a type of writing that involves systematically grouping items by some system or principle; frequently involves defining or comparing and contrasting items or groups of items.

CLICHÉ a phrase, figure of speech, or idea used so often that it is predictable, showing little imagination or thought, as in "Rain came down in buckets."

CLUSTERING a brainstorming technique that shows how ideas are connected to one another; gives a quick map of thoughts about a topic.

COHERENCE connectedness, a sense that parts hold together; an essay is coherent when its parts fit together logically and are linked by connecting words and phrases.

COLLABORATION working with other people; giving others support and advice; helping others solve problems.

COLLOQUIAL conversational, linguistically informal; the way people ordinarily speak in conversation.

COMPARISON AND CONTRAST a strategy for thinking or writing that involves explaining, defining, or evaluating subjects by showing how they resemble and differ from each other or from some standard for evaluation.

CONNOTATION the attitudes and feelings associated with a word or idea as opposed to its dictionary definition. The word "cheap" differs from "inexpensive" in its connotations.

CONTEXT the setting or situation in which something happens, particularly in which words or sentences are uttered or written.

CONTROVERSY a disagreement, often one that has attracted public interest.

COUNTERARGUMENT a refutation, an argument made to oppose (counter) another argument.

CRITICISM discourse (usually an essay) that analyzes something (usually a literary or artistic work) in order to evaluate how it does or does not succeed in communicating its meaning or achieving its purposes.

CUBING a method for discovering ideas about a topic by using six strategies (in any order) to investigate it: describe it, compare it, associate it, analyze it, apply it, argue for or against it.

DEDUCTIVE REASONING deriving a specific conclusion by reasoning from a general premise.

DENOTATION the literal meaning of a word, without its *connotations*.

DESCRIPTION an account, usually giving a dominant impression and emphasizing sensory detail, of what it is like to experience some object, scene, or person.

DIALECT a form of language (usually regional) differing from the standard language in pronunciation, word choice, and syntax. Southern American English or New England English or Australian English are dialects of English.

DIALOGUE the spoken conversation of fictional characters or actual persons as it is presented in a novel, story, poem, play, or essay.

DOCUMENTATION naming the documents or other sources used to provide the information reported in an essay or other discourse: usually cited in footnotes or in parentheses.

ELABORATION the development of an argument, description, narration, or explanation with details, evidence, and other support.

EXPOSITION writing whose purpose is to explain an idea or teach a process rather than to tell a story, describe something, or argue for a point of view.

FICTION made-up or imaginary happenings, as opposed to statements of fact or nonfiction. Short stories and novels are fiction, even though they may be based on real events. Essays, scientific articles, biographies, news stories are nonfiction.

FIGURATIVE LANGUAGE language that uses such figures of speech as similes, metaphors, and personification to show one thing as if it were something else.

FREEWRITING a way of discovering what you know or think or feel by writing rapidly, without stopping, without editing, and without looking back (until you finish) at what you've written.

GENERALIZATION a statement expressing a principle or drawing a conclusion based on examples or instances.

GLEANING a method of picking up ideas by observing events and by scanning through newspapers, magazines, and books and talking to others in order to find material to write about or to use in writing.

GRAPHIC ORGANIZER a method for visually organizing a complex body of information; includes charts, graphs, outlines, clusters, and tree diagrams.

IMAGERY figurative language and descriptions as the means of vividly rendering experience in language.

INDUCTIVE REASONING a method of thinking or organizing a discourse so that a series of instances or pieces of evidence lead to a conclusion or generalization.

INFERENCE a conclusion derived by reasoning from facts.

INTERPRETATION to explain the meaning of any text, set of facts, object, gesture, or event.

INVISIBLE WRITING typing with a dimmed computer screen or writing with an empty ball point pen on a paper that covers a piece of carbon paper and a clean bottom sheet.

IRONY a figure of speech in which the intended meaning is the opposite of the stated meaning—saying one thing and meaning another.

JARGON the special language and terminology used by people in the same profession or who share specialized interests.

KNOWLEDGE INVENTORY a list of statements or phrases representing what a writer knows about a topic, including questions to direct further research.

LEARNING LOG a journal or notebook used in connection with the study of a particular subject where a student records questions, problems, and state of understanding about the subject as it is studied and learned.

LOOPING a process for discovering ideas by freewriting on a topic, stopping to find promising ideas, then producing another freewrite on that subject, repeating the loop several times.

MEMOIR an account of true events told by a narrator who witnessed or participated in the events; usually focusing on the personalities and actions of persons other than the writer.

METAPHOR a figure of speech describing something by speaking of it as if it were something else, without using such terms as "like" or "as" to signal the relationship. To say "the dinner was a symphony of flavors" is to speak *metaphorically*.

MONOLOGUE a speech by one person without interruption by other voices. A *dramatic monologue* reveals the personality and experience of a person through a long speech.

MOOD feeling about a scene or subject created for a reader by a writer's selection of words and details; the mood of a piece of writing may be suspenseful, mysterious, peaceful, fearful, and so on.

NARRATION discourse that tells a story—either made up or true. Some common types of narrative are biographies, short stories, and novels.

NONSEXIST LANGUAGE language free from gender bias, representing the equality of men and women and showing them in both traditional and nontraditional roles.

ONOMATOPOEIA the use of words (usually in poetry) to suggest sounds; the *clinking* of knives and forks, the *trilling* of a flute.

PARENTHETICAL DOCUMENTATION the placement of citations or other documentation within the text and in parentheses.

PEER RESPONSE response to one's writing provided by writers who are peers or classmates rather than teachers or other editors.

PERSONIFICATION a figure of speech in which objects, events, abstract ideas, or animals are given human characteristics. "The crying of the wind" and "the trees danced" are examples of personification.

PERSUASION discourse focused on influencing a listener or reader to support a point of view or take an action. Examples of persuasive discourse would include political speeches, advertisements, position papers, editorials, and courtroom speeches by lawyers.

PLAGIARISM presenting the ideas or words of another as if they were one's own. Writers who use the ideas of others can avoid plagiarism by acknowledging their sources.

POINT OF VIEW the viewpoint or perspective through which the reader views the events in a story; defines what a narrator can know and tell about.

PORTFOLIO a place (usually a large folder) where writing is stored for future reference and review or to present for evaluation.

PRECIS a short summary of an essay, story, or speech, capturing only the essential elements.

PROOFREADING usually the last stage of the revising or editing process, when a writer checks work to discover typographical and other errors.

PROPAGANDA discourse aimed entirely at persuading an audience, often suggests distortions of truth; usually refers to manipulative political discourse.

SATIRE a literary form which ridicules or mocks the social practices or values of a society or group or important individual. To *satirize* something is to portray it in a way that shows it to be foolish.

SIMILE a figure of speech comparing two things that are essentially unlike, signaling the comparison with such words as "like" or "as."

SPATIAL ORDER a pattern of organization based on space used in descriptive writing; for example, a scene may be described from foreground to background, from left to right, from top to bottom.

STYLE refers to those features in a discourse or work of art that identify it as the work of a particular individual, type, period, or artistic philosophy.

SYMBOL a word, object, or action that suggests something other than itself, as a sword can stand for war, or in a story the desert might represent loneliness or solitude.

SYNTHESIS refers in writing or thinking to the putting together of ideas or information to reach a conclusion or achieve some insight or find a solution to a problem.

TONE the writer's attitude toward a subject—detached, ironic, serious, angry, and so on.

TOPIC SENTENCE a statement expressing the main point of a paragraph; the idea (stated or unstated) around which a paragraph is organized.

TREE DIAGRAM a visualized plan for an essay, also known as a "branching tree diagram" for the way it shows main and subordinate points as the trunk and main and minor branches of a tree.

TRITE PHRASE a phrase used so commonly that it lacks precise meaning and suggests a lack of imagination, thought, or originality.

UNITY oneness; the concept that in a written work all the parts must form a single whole, held together by a central theme or idea.

VENN DIAGRAM a way of representing the relationship between two items that are distinct but have common or overlapping elements.

VOICE the personality and distinct way of talking of a writer that allows a reader to "hear" a human personality in a piece of writing.

with titles and groups of words, 679
words between subject and verb, 669
with words of amount and time, 680
Airplanes, capitalizing names of, 749
Allegory, 842
Alliteration, 438, 647
Allusion, 842
Almanacs, 497
Ambiguous reference, 714
Amount, words of, and subject-verb
agreement, 680
an, 556
Analogy, 842
drawing, 366–67
false, 477
in standardized tests, 524–26
Analysis, 123, 842. *See also* Argument
analysis; Literary analysis; Subject
analysis
cause and effect in, 461
of character, 343–44
drafting, 171–72
flowcharts in, 345
news, 536, 537
process, 154
Analysis frames, 343
and, 606, 616, 766–67
Anecdotes, 842
in introductions, 366
Antecedent, 549
agreement with pronoun, 710–11
Antonyms, in standardized tests, 523–24
any, 674
anyone, 694
Apostrophes, 802–4
to form plurals, 804
to show omissions, 804
to show possession, 802–3
Appendix, 495
Application and Review, 566, 588, 626, 666,
686, 717, 738, 761, 781, 798, 814
Application letter, 510
Appositive phrases, 593
in sentence composing, 144
as sentence fragments, 621–22
Appositives, 593
commas with, 593, 770
diagraming, 839
essential, 593, 770
nonessential, 187, 593, 770
pronouns used with and as, 704
Argument analysis, 208–22
drafting, 214–16

prewriting, 210–13
publishing and presenting, 218
reviewing, 216
revising, 217–18
Argumentation, 183
Argumentative tasks, 316
Arguments
building, in debate, 504
types of, 475–76
Aristotelian invention, 377–78
Art works, capitalization of titles of, 757
Articles, (*a, an, the*), 556
capitalization in titles, 757
Assessment, writing for, 313–20, 328. *See
also* Evaluation standards; Peer
response; Skill assessment
Assonance, 438
Assumptions, looking for underlying, 213
Astronomical terms, capitalization of, 749
Atlases, 497
Audience, 842
for argument analysis, 213
for concepts and ideas, 119
identifying, 9, 59
in limiting topic, 337
for oral presentation, 201
for proposal, 181
for research report, 275
in responding to readings, 318
for subject analysis, 153
Author cards, 491
Autobiographical incident, 38–42
drafting, 41
prewriting, 40–41
publishing and presenting, 42
reviewing, 42
Autobiography, 842
Automobiles, capitalizing names of, 749
Auxiliary verbs, 553, 595
Awards, capitalization of, 752

B

B.C., 752
Bad, badly, 733
Bartlett's Familiar Quotations, 498
Base words, 465, 468
be, forms of, 668
Bias, 842
Biblical references, colon in, 788
Bibliography, 495. *See also* Works cited
working, 278
Bibliography cards. See source cards

in compound sentences, 440, 616
in complex sentences, 440, 618–19
diagraming, 840
as direct object, 574
as distinguished from phrase, 605
elliptical, 612
essential/nonessential, 609, 775
as fragments, 623
independent, 606
nonessential adjective, 609
noun, 613–14
as object of preposition, 561
punctuation for, 609
relative, 608
in sentence composing, 109–11
subordinate, 606–13
who and *whom*, 701–2
Clichés, 431, 843
Clip files, 332
Cluster maps, 339
Clustering, 843
Coherence, 843
    in longer writing, 388–91
    within paragraphs, 384–88
Collaboration, 117, 180, 843
Collaborative planning, 28, 85, 118–19,
    181–82, 212, 246, 358–64
Collaborative writing, 2, 140–43
Collective nouns, 547
    and pronoun-antecedent agreement, 711
    and verb agreement, 678
College admission tests
    preparing for and taking standardized,
        522–23
    questions and strategies for, 523–34
    types of, 521–22
College application, completing, 513
Colleges, investigating, 511–15
Colloquial English, 429, 843
Colon, 787–88
    in biblical reference, 788
    in business letters, 788
    to introduce formal quotation, 788
    to introduce list, 787
    in notations of time, 788
    in periodical citation, 788
    with quotation marks, 808
Comma fault, 583–84
Commas, 766–782
    to avoid confusion, 777–78
    in compound-complex sentences, 620
    in compound sentences, 616, 773

with conjunctive adverbs, 563
in dates, 776
with interrupters, 770–71
with introductory elements, 769
in letters, 777
with numbers, 777
with nonessential clauses and phrases,
    187, 593, 770, 775
with parenthetical definitions, 158
with personal titles, 744
in place names, 777
with quotation marks, 33, 157, 773
in quotations, 773
with semicolons, 766, 784
in series, 766–67
to set off parenthetical expressions, 158,
    770
to set off words or phrases, 286
with titles, 777
Comma splice, 583–84
Common nouns, 547, 744
Comparative degree, 723, 729–30
Comparison, 154, 214
    of adjectives, 723–25, 729–30
    of adverbs, 723–25, 729–30
Comparison and contrast, 122, 352, 682,
    843. *See also* Comparisons; Contrast
Comparison-and-contrast charts, 344
Comparisons
    analogies in, 30
    avoiding double, 729
    avoiding illogical, 729–30
    in extracting meaning from context, 461
    pronouns in, 706–7
    subordinate conjunctions showing, 563,
        611
Complements, 573–578
    diagraming, 836
    direct objects as, 574
    indirect objects as, 574–75
    objective, 576
    predicate adjective as, 553
    predicate noun as, 553
    predicate pronoun as, 553
    subject, 576
Complete predicate, 569
Complete subject, 569
Complex sentence, 440, 618–19
    diagraming, 841
Compound adjective, 793
Compound antecedent, 711
Compound-complex sentence, 440, 620

research and planning speeches, 230–31
reviewing, 232
preparation for, 503–4, 505–7
proposition in, 501–2
rebuttals in, 505–7
rehearsal and presentation, 506
researching proposition, 503
Decimals, periods with, 763
Declarative sentences, 571, 763
punctuation of, 763, 764
subject-verb order in, 571
Deductive arguments, 356–57, 475, 843
Definite article, 556
Definition
in argument analysis, 214
in extracting meaning from context, 460–61
in proposal, 183
in subject analysis, 154
in writing, 127
Degree
organization by, 353–54
transitional devices that show, 387
Demonstrative pronouns, 550
Denotation, 197, 844
Dependent clauses. *See* Subordinate clauses
Description, 60, 154, 844
presenting, 366
unity in, 383–84
See also Observation and description
Details
checking for significant, 69
incorporating, 379–81
in stories, 102
supporting, 349, 462
unrelated, 404
Dewey Decimal System, 491
Diagraming sentences, 834–41
Diagrams, 164
Dialectic organization, 356
Dialects, 432, 844
apostrophe to show omission in, 804
Dialogue, 60, 82
acting out conflict in, 227
dashes in, 791
in dramatic writing, 86, 453
in fiction, 452–53
holding, in generating ideas, 378
indicating change of speakers in, 808
internal, 335
in narrative, 807
in nonfiction, 455

nonstandard English in, 668
in poetry, 454
punctuation with, 808
in reflective essay, 32
in stories, 41, 102
writing realistic, 453
Diction, and style, 417, 426
Dictionaries, 119
abridged, 495
specialized, 496
Direct address, commas to set off, 770
Directions, capitalization of, 748–49
Directive adverbs, 559
Direct objects, 574
diagraming, 835, 837
distinguishing from adverb, 574
pronouns as, 696
subordinate clause as, 619
Direct quotations, 250, 482
capitalization of first word, 756
commas to set off, 773
punctuation of, 807–8
Divide-and-conquer method of problem solving, 473
Division, organization by, 352–53
Documentation, 214, 844
parenthetical, 486–88
of sources, 486–88
doesn't, subject-verb agreement with, 676
don't, subject-verb agreement with, 676
Double comparisons, 729
Double-entry journal, 242
Double negative, 734
Doublespeak, 223
Drafting, 6, 12–13, 361–64
argument analysis, 214–16
autobiographical incident, 41–42
computer in, 284
collaborative writing, 142
concepts and ideas, 121–24
critical review, 263–64
debate speeches, 230
dramatic writing, 86–88
journalistic narratives, 59–61
literary analysis, 246–48
monologue, 47–48
organizing, 59
personality profile, 69
project evaluation, 171–72
rebuttal, 195–96
reflective essay, 29–31
research report, 282–85

Acknowledgments for Teacher's Edition

37: Cartoon by Lee Canter. **157**: Chronicle Features: For THE FAR SIDE cartoon by Gary Larson. Reprinted by permission of Chronicle Features. **185**: Jane Yolen: For comments from *How to Enjoy Writing* by Jane and Isaac Asimov. Copyright © by Nightfall, Inc. Reprinted by permission of Jane Yolen. **281**: Scholastic, Inc.: For an excerpt from "Eternal, Infernal Teaching Truths" by Eileen Mella Hession. Copyright © 1981 by *Instructor* Magazine. Reprinted by permission of Scholastic, Inc. **434**: Henry Holt & Company, Inc.: Four lines from "Stopping By Woods On a Snowy Evening" from *The Poetry of Robert Frost,* edited by Edward Connery Latham. Copyright 1944, 1951 by Robert Frost. Reprinted by permission of Henry Holt & Company, Inc. **451**: Scholastic, Inc.: Cartoon by Randy Hall, from *Instructor* Magazine. Copyright © 1981. Reprinted by permission of Scholastic, Inc. **631**: Warner/Chappell Music, Inc.: For song lyrics from "Angels from Montgomery" by John Prine. Copyright ©1971 Walden Music, Inc. & Sour Grapes Music. All rights on behalf of Walden Music, Inc.

Sources of Quoted Materials

22: David R. Godine, Publisher, Inc.: For an excerpt from *Hunger of Memory* by Richard Rodriguez. Copyright © 1982 by Richard Rodriguez. Reprinted by permission of David R. Godine, Publisher, Inc. **54**: HarperCollins Publishers, Inc.: For an excerpt from *Small Victories* by Samuel G. Freedman. Copyright © 1990 by Samuel G. Freedman. Reprinted by permission of HarperCollins Publishers, Inc. **66**: Time Inc. Magazine Company: For excerpts from "Great Leapin' Lizards!" by Sally B. Donnelly, from *Time,* January 9, 1989. Copyright © 1989 The Time Inc. Magazine Company. Reprinted by permission. **80**: Grove Press, Inc.: For an excerpt from *The Elephant Man* by Bernard Pomerance. Copyright © 1979 by Bernard Pomerance. Reprinted by permission of Grove Weidenfeld. **104**: Houghton Mifflin Company: "The End of the World," from *New and Collected Poems: 1917-1982* by Archibald MacLeish. Copyright © 1985 by the Estate of Archibald MacLeish. Reprinted by permission of Houghton Mifflin Co. **132**: Discover Publications: For an excerpt from "The Ultimate Medicine" by Geoffrey Montgomery, from *Discover,* March 1990 issue. Copyright © 1990 Discover Publications. **148**: The Wigwag Magazine Company, Inc.: For excerpts from "Stuttering" by Denise Grady, which originally appeared in *Wigwag* magazine's February 1990 issue. **168**: Newsweek: For excerpts from "Kids with Causes" by Katrine Ames, from *Newsweek* Special Edition, Summer/Fall 1990. Copyright © 1990 Newsweek, Inc. All rights reserved. Reprinted by permission. **192**: Harper's Magazine: "Seeing Blindness" by Joanne Lucas, from *Harper's* May 1989 issue. Copyright © 1989 Harper's Magazine. All rights reserved. Reprinted from May 1989 issue with special permission. **197**: Field Publications: "Playing the Game of Denotations and Connotations" by Richard Lederer, from *Writing!,* April 1987 issue. Copyright © 1987 by Field Publications. Special reprint permission granted by *Writing!* Magazine. *Writing!* is a federally registered trademark of Field Publications. **208**: Time Inc. Magazine Company: For excerpts from "Owl vs. Man" by Ted Gup, from *Time,* June 25, 1990. Copyright © 1990 The Time Inc. Magazine Company. Reprinted by permission. **228**: People Weekly: For excerpts from "In Bike-Happy Hollywood, Gary Busey's Crash Revs Up the Helmet Controversy Again" by Jacob Young and Jack Kelley, from *People Weekly*'s December 19, 1988 issue. Copyright © 1988 Time, Inc. **494**: H. W. Wilson Company: Entry from *Readers' Guide to Periodical Literature.* Copyright © 1987 by the H. W. Wilson Company. **568**: Charles W. Marsh, Jr.: For excerpts from "When Nouns Go Bad" by Charles Marsh, from *American Way* magazine. Copyright 1988 by Charles Marsh. **783**: Mary Ann Madden: For excerpts from *Son of Giant Sea Tortoise* by Mary Ann Madden. Copyright © 1969-1975 (inclusive) by Mary Ann Madden. Reprinted by permission of the author. **800**: Omni Publications International Ltd.: "Talk About Embedding," from *Saturday Review.* The authors and editors have made every effort to trace the ownership of all copyrighted selections in this book and to make full acknowledgment for their use.

Illustration and Photography Credits:

Commissioned Illustrations: Sharon K. Broutzas: tr **207, 224-225**; Mark Chickinelli: **269, 271**; Leslie Cober: l **53, 54-55**, br **237, 260-261**; Ralph Creasman: b **52**; Ruta Daugavietis: border **44-45**; Meighan Depke: **355, 364,** l, r **393, 408 SPIDER-MAN: TM &** © 1990 Marvel Entertainment Group, Inc. All rights reserved; John S. Dykes: **22-23**; David Frampton: tr **79, 98-99**; Scott Harris: **135**; Nenad Jakesevic/Sonja Lamut: l **147, 148-149**; Vita Jay: **58**; Barbara Maslen: **469**; Marvin Mattelson: l **113, 115**; William McComb: **396**; Susan Nees: **7,** l **8, 9, 10,** bl, c **11,** bl, t **12, 65, 78, 108, 456, 545, 556, 626, 627, 638, 689, 743, 801**; Maria Thomas, Pendragon: **671, 808**; Holly Pribble: **657**; Deborah Sims: **223, 490, 783, 800**; Troy Thomas: **4,** tr **21, 38-39, 377, 596, 598, 631**; Robert Voigts: **165, 343, 381, 590**; Philippe Weisbecker: **183**; Suzan Wexler: tr **147, 162-163,** b **795, 812**; Leslie Wolf: **528**; **Assignment Photography:** Ryan Roessler: xii, br **147, 168-169, 171, 176** courtesy of WXRT 93 FM Chicago, l, tr **177 178-179, 192-193,** br **207, 228-229, 278, 361, 373,** l **421, 433, 498, 592, 671, 733, 748; Photos and Illustrations:** vi: James McMullan; **vii:** David Shannon; **viii:** © Marc Romanelli, The Image Bank, Chicago; **ix:** © 1984 Nancy Pendelton; **x:** Courtesy of Amoco Chemical Company; **xi:** Scot Stewart; **xiii:** Illustration © 1989 Farallon Computing, Inc. All rights reserved; **xiv:** © Hervy, Robert Harding Picture Library; **xv:** Mark Chickinelli; **xvi:** The Pierpont Morgan Library; **xvii: 1:** David Lui; **3:** © 1986 Curtis Parker; **8:** r George Y. Abe; **11:** r Paul Davis; **12:** r James McMullan; **16:** © Photofest; **18:** © ARS N.Y./SPADEM, Tate Gallery, London, Art Resource; **20:** © Robert Atwan. This map originally appeared in the April 1990 issue of "Wigwag Magazine"; **21:** br UPI/Bettmann; **25:** © T.S. Satyan, Black Star; **26:** David Shannon; **33:** Charles B. Slackman; **34:** © Dennis Murphy, Photographer; **41:** © John Madere, The Image Bank, Chicago; **43:** Giraudon/Art Resource; **44-45:** c © UPI/Bettmann; **47:** Spadem/Art Resource; **48:** The Far Side Cartoons by Gary Larson are reprinted by permission of Chronicle Features, San Francisco, CA; **53:** tr Carl Sissac, br H. Armstrong Roberts; **52:** t © Bank Langmore/

Photographer; **57**: © Marc Romanelli, The Image Bank, Chicago; **63**: © Kerry T. Givens, Bruce Coleman, Inc.; **66-67**: © Carl Sissac; **70-71**: *center* © H. Armstrong Roberts; **71**: *r* William Burlingham; **73**: Mick Wiggins; **79**: *l* The Bridgeman Art Library, *br* Wendell Minor; **80-81**: The Bridgeman Art Library; **84**: © 1984 Nancy Pendelton; **89**: Mary Lynn Blasutta; **93**: Stanislaw Fernandes; **96**: David Schleinkofer; **101**: Kurt Ritta; **102**: Guy Billout; **104-105**: © SuperStock; **105**: *r* Wendell Minor; **113**: *tr* Copyright Boeringer Ingelheim International GmbH, photo Lennart Nilsson;, *br* Rafal Olbinski; **117**: COPYRIGHT 1991 ARS NY/ADAGP; **118**: William Teason; **121**: Jeff Seaver; **123**: © Comstock, Inc.; **125**: Courtesy of Amoco Chemical Company; **126, 128, 129, 130**: © Comstock, Inc.; **132-133**: Copyright Boeringer Ingelheim International GmbH, photo Lennart Nilsson; **134**: © Lou Jones, The Image Bank, Chicago; **135**: Scott Harris; **137**: *t* © Comstock, Inc., *b* © Don Klumpt, The Image Bank, Chicago; **138-139**: Rafal Olbinski; **141**: David Wilcox; **146**: © Kobal Collection/SuperStock; **152**: Scot Stewart; **155**: John Rush; **159**: Scot Stewart; **167**: Steven Guarnaccia; **177**: *br* © Gary Irving, Tony Stone Worldwide; **185**: Drawing by Roland B. Wilson, © 1964 The New Yorker Magazine, Inc.; **189**: Evanston Township High School; **195**: Henrik Drescher; **198-199**: © Gary Irving, Tony Stone Worldwide; **202**: BASS & GOLDMAN, INC.; **206**: CALVIN AND HOBBES COPYRIGHT 1990 UNIVERSAL PRESS SYNDICATE. Reprinted with permission. All rights reserved; **207**: *l* © 1988 Doug Plummer, AllStock; **208**: *l* © 1988 Doug Plummer, AllStock; **208-209**: © Tony Stone Worldwide; **211**: Illustration © 1989 Farallon Computing, Inc. All rights reserved; **215**: Mark Frueh; **218**: Mark Chickinelli; **220**: Robert Neubecker; **236**: © 1980 Al Hirschfeld. Drawing reproduced by special arrangement with HirschfeldŪs exclusive representative, The Margo Feiden Galleries, Ltd., New York; **237**: *l* © Wendy Stone, Bruce Coleman, Inc., *tr* Penguin USA; **238-239**: © Wendy Stone, Bruce Coleman, Inc.; **239**: *br* © Robert P. Carr, Bruce Coleman, Inc.; **240**: © Wendy Stone, Bruce Coleman, Inc.; **240**: *b* © Robert P. Carr, Bruce Coleman, Inc.; **242**: ''Born Free'', by Edwin Salomon (Publisher: Jacques Soussana Graphics, Jerusalem); **247**: © Hervy, Robert Harding Picture Library; **253**: © UPI/Bettmann; **254-255**: *Because of Lozo Brown* by Larry L. King, illustrated by Amy Schwartz. Illustrations copyright © 1988 by Amy Schwartz. Reprinted by permission of the publisher, Viking Penguin, a division of Penguin Books USA, Inc.; **258**: CALVIN AND HOBBES COPYRIGHT UNIVERSAL PRESS SYNDICATE. Reprinted with permission. All rights reserved; **259**: Alabama Shakespeare Festival, photo by Overton; **263**: Charles White III; **268**: Bill Everitt, © Tom Stack and Associates; **271**: Mark Chickinelli; **274**: © Kobal Collection/SuperStock; **281**: © Robert Harding Picture Library; **282-283**: The Bridgeman Art Library; **287**: credit unknown; **298**: The Bridgeman Art Library; **302**: © H. Armstrong Roberts; **308**: Spadem/Art Resource; **309, 310**: The Pierpont Morgan Library; **311**: *b* © Eric Meola, The Image Bank, Chicago; **312**: *b* © Michael Melford, The Image Bank, Chicago; **314**: Anthony Russo; **319**: Giraudon/Art Resource; **321**: Mark Stearney; **324**: Alan Nils Adler; **326**: The Bridgeman Art Library; **328**: Jeff Jackson; **330**: THE FAR SIDE COPYRIGHT 1987 & 1988 UNIVERSAL PRESS SYNDICATE. Reprinted with permission. All rights reserved; **334**: Sandy Skoglund; **351**: *l, r* © Photofest; **355**: *l* © Jeff Foott, Bruce Coleman, Inc., *r* © John E. Swedberg, Bruce Coleman, Inc., *b* © UPI/Bettmann; **369**: © Byron Gin, Stockworks; **383**: © Michael Fogden, Bruce Coleman, Inc.; **389**: Ed Lindlof; **390**: National Gallery of Art, Washington D.C.; **393**: *c* William Jordan; **396**: William McComb; **399**: Steven Pietzsch; **401**: The Far Side Cartoons by Gary Larson are reprinted by permission of Chronicle Features, San Francisco, CA; **402**: Henrik Drescher; **410**: Tim Lewis; **415**: Jeff Jackson; **416**: The Far Side Cartoons by Gary Larson are reprinted by permission of Chronicle Features, San Francisco, CA.; **418, 419**: Mirko Ilic; **421**: *r* © Stephen Marks, The Image Bank, Chicago/Stockphotos, Inc.; **426**: Reproduced from ''A Study in Scarlet - The Hound of the Baskervilles'' (1986), *World's Best Reading Series,* The Reader's Digest Association, Inc. Used by permission; **428**: © Comstock, Inc.; **431**: Warren Gebert; **437**: Katherine Mahoney; **440**: Jeff Seaver; **445**: Ralph J. Brunke; **451**: C.F. Payne; **455**: © BURK UZZLE/Lee Gross Associates; **466, 467**: © H. Armstrong Roberts; **469**: Barbara Maslen; **472**: John S. Dykes; **477**: The Far Side Cartoons by Gary Larson are reprinted by permission of Chronicle Features, San Francisco, CA.; **484**: © H. Armstrong Roberts; **485**: © W. Metzen, H. Armstrong Roberts; **492**: *l* © The Granger Collection; **501**: © Liberty Collection/The Image Bank, Chicago; **505**: Steven Guarnaccia; **511**: Bob Radigan; **524**: *t* © Dennis Hallinan 1990, FPG International, Corp., *b* Christopher Rory; **531**: Bill Bruning; **535**: *t* © Dennis Brack, Black Star, *b* © Jeff Smith, The Image Bank, Chicago; **537**: Elwood H. Smith; **540**: Tate Gallery, London/Art Resource; **548**: Courtesy of the Chicago Maritime Museum after a painting by Charles Vickery; **552**: Chris Moore; **557**: Edward W. Acuna; **558**: Scala/Art Resource; **560**: THE FAR SIDE COPYRIGHT 1986 UNIVERSAL PRESS SYNDICATE. Reprinted with permission. All rights reserved; **564**: David McCall Johnston; **568**: Deb Linc; **570**: © The Kobal Collection/SuperStock; **573**: © Kerry T. Givens, Bruce Coleman, Inc.; **577**: Bob Ziering; **578**: Giraudon/Art Resource; **585**: David Tamura; **587**: © Adobe Systems Incorporated. All rights reserved; **591**: Photographic Collection, Museum of Modern Art, New York; **597**: David Wilcox; **600**: Library of Congress; **604**: *l* Don Doll, S.J., *r* © John Shaw, Bruce Coleman, Inc.; **605**: Mark English; **607**: David Montiel; **610**: *b* © Wardene Weisser, Bruce Coleman, Inc., *t* © William Amos, Bruce Coleman, Inc.; **613**: The Bridgeman Art Library; **617**: Karen Barbour; **618**: Steve Johnson; **619**: *t* © SuperStock, *b* © Photofest; **623**: © Design Photographers International, Inc.; **636**: John Rush; **638**: *bl* © Edwin Santos, Bruce Coleman, Inc., *br* © Frink Waterhouse, H. Armstrong Roberts; **643**: Ed Lindlof; **647**:

Administered by WB Music Corp. All rights reserved, used by permission. **756**: Faber & Faber, Ltd.: For an excerpt from "Prayer Before Birth" from *The Collected Poems of Louis MacNeice.* Reprinted by permission of Faber & Faber, Ltd. **785**: Marian Reiner: For "Markings: The Semicolon" by Eve Merriam, from *A Sky Full of Poems.* Copyright © 1964, 1970, 1973, by Eve Merriam. Reprinted by permission of Marian Reiner. **787**: Kathleen S. Armour: For "The Colon" by Richard Armour, from *On Your Marks: A Package of Punctuation.* Reprinted by permission of Kathleen S. Armour. The authors and editors have made every effort to trace the ownership of all copyrighted materials found in this book and to make full acknowledgment for their use.

Sally Wern Comport; **653:** Guy Billout; **662:** © B. Taylor, H. Armstrong Roberts; **672:** © O. Rebbot, Stock Boston; **677:** Barron Storey; **679:** Robert Crawford; **681:** Doug Johnson; **688:** c The Far Side Cartoons by Gary Larson are reprinted by permission of Chronicle Features, San Francisco, CA; **694:** t *left* Kurt Hansen, b © UPI/Bettmann; **698:** Greg Spalenka; **703:** Courtesy of Graceland; **705:** Giraudon/Art Resource; **707:** © Ellen Schuster, The Image Bank, Chicago; **708:** Gary Kurtz, © 1983 Lucas Film, Ltd.; **712:** Produced with permission of the U.S.P.S., illustration by Bob Peak; **716:** Thyssen-Bornemisza Collection/Art Resource. Courtesy of the Georgia O'Keeffe Foundation; **718:** James Endicott; **721:** Bartolomeo Bettera, Harmony; **722:** Liz Kathman-Grubow; **723:** Bridgeman Art Library; **727:** Dickran Palulian; **731:** Peter Stackpole, Life Magazine © Time Warner, Inc.; **736:** Scala/Art Resource; **747:** © H. Armstrong Roberts, Inc.; **751:** National Museum of American Art/Art Resource; **753:** © Al Gardner, Tony Stone Worldwide; **758:** Alan James Robinson; **760:** Gary Larson, Universal Press Syndicate; **765:** © Anthony Suau, Black Star; **768:** Musee d'Orsay/Art Resource; **776:** Scala/Art Resource; **779:** © Spencer Jones, Bruce Coleman, Inc.; **780:** Bob Conge; **785:** Bridgeman Art Library; **790:** Christine Bunn; **795:** t © Wide World Photos, Inc.; **797:** The Bridgeman Art Library; **804:** Jozef Sumichrast; **806:** l © The Granger Collection, r © The Image Bank, Chicago; **809:** Giraudon/Art Resource; **811:** © The Granger Collection; **819:** © Kaz Mori, The Image Bank, Chicago; **823:** Eugene Mihaesco. **Cover Photography :** Ryan Roessler